Kaplan Publishing are constantly finding ne
difference to your studies and our exciting
offer something different to students look

CW00494880

This book comes with free MyKaplan onlir
study anytime, anywhere. **This free online resource is**
separately and is included in the price of the book.

Having purchased this book, you have access to the following online study materials:

CONTENT	ACCA (including FBT, FMA, FFA)		FIA (excluding FBT, FMA, FFA)	
	Text	Kit	Text	Kit
Electronic version of the book	✓	✓	✓	✓
Knowledge checks with instant answers	✓		✓	
Material updates	✓	✓	✓	✓
Latest official ACCA exam questions*		✓		
Pocket Notes (digital copy)	✓		✓	
Study Planner	✓			
Progress Test including questions and answers	✓		✓	
Syllabus recap Videos		✓		✓
Revision Planner		✓		✓
Question Debrief and Walkthrough Videos		✓		
Mock Exam including questions and answers		✓		

* Excludes BT, MA, FA, FBT, FMA, FFA; for all other papers includes a selection of questions, as released by ACCA

How to access your online resources

Received this book as part of your Kaplan course?
If you have a MyKaplan account, your full online resources will be added automatically, in line with the information in your course confirmation email. If you've not used MyKaplan before, you'll be sent an activation email once your resources are ready.

Bought your book from Kaplan?
We'll automatically add your online resources to your MyKaplan account. If you've not used MyKaplan before, you'll be sent an activation email.

Bought your book from elsewhere?
Go to **www.mykaplan.co.uk/add-online-resources**
Enter the ISBN number found on the title page and back cover of this book.
Add the unique pass key number contained in the scratch panel below.
You may be required to enter additional information during this process to set up or confirm your account details.

This code can only be used once for the registration of this book online. This registration and your online content will expire when the examinations covered by this book have taken place. Please allow one hour from the time you submit your book details for us to process your request.

Please scratch the film to access your unique code.

Please be aware that this code is case-sensitive and you will need to include the dashes within the passcode, but not when entering the ISBN.

KAPLAN
PUBLISHING

ACCA

Strategic Professional – Options

Advanced Audit and Assurance (INT & UK) (AAA)

EXAM KIT

KAPLAN PUBLISHING

British Library Cataloguing-in-Publication Data

A catalogue record for this book is available from the British Library.

Published by:

Kaplan Publishing UK
Unit 2 The Business Centre
Molly Millar's Lane
Wokingham
Berkshire
RG41 2QZ

ISBN: 978-1-83996-397-1

Acknowledgements

These materials are reviewed by the ACCA examining team. The objective of the review is to ensure that the material properly covers the syllabus and study guide outcomes, used by the examining team in setting the exams, in the appropriate breadth and depth. The review does not ensure that every eventuality, combination or application of examinable topics is addressed by the ACCA Approved Content. Nor does the review comprise a detailed technical check of the content as the Approved Content Provider has its own quality assurance processes in place in this respect.

We are grateful to the Association of Chartered Certified Accountants and the Chartered Institute of Management Accountants for permission to reproduce past examination questions. The answers have been prepared by Kaplan Publishing.

CONTENTS

Section

Versions of some questions in this Exam Kit may also be available on the ACCA Practice Platform on the ACCA Website. They are a very useful reference, in particular to attempt using ACCA's exam software. However, you should be aware that ACCA will decide when those questions will be amended for syllabus changes or replaced, so they may differ slightly from the versions in this Exam Kit.

This document references IFRS® Standards and IAS® Standards, which are authored by the International Accounting Standards Board (the Board), and published in the 2022 IFRS Standards Red Book.

Key features in this edition

In addition to providing a wide ranging bank of real past exam questions, we have also included in this edition:

- An analysis of the recent new syllabus examinations.

- Exam specific information and advice on exam technique.

- Our recommended approach to make your revision for this particular subject as effective as possible.

  This includes step by step guidance on how best to use our Kaplan material (Study Text, pocket notes and exam kit) at this stage in your studies.

- Enhanced tutorial answers packed with specific key answer tips, technical tutorial notes and exam technique tips from our experienced tutors.

- Complementary online resources including full tutor debriefs and question assistance to point you in the right direction when you get stuck.

You will find a wealth of other resources to help you with your studies on the following sites:

www.MyKaplan.co.uk

www.accaglobal.com/student

Quality and accuracy are of the utmost importance to us so if you spot an error in any of our products, please send an email to mykaplanreporting@kaplan.com with full details.

Our Quality Co-ordinator will work with our technical team to verify the error and take action to ensure it is corrected in future editions.

INDEX TO QUESTIONS AND ANSWERS

INTRODUCTION

The exam format of Advanced Audit and Assurance changed in September 2018. Accordingly any older ACCA questions within this kit have been adapted to reflect the new style of exam and the new guidance. Where questions have been adapted from the original version, this is indicated in the end column of the index below with the mark *(A)*. The marking schemes included are indicative schemes which have been approved by ACCA as being representative of the real exam except where indicated. One question in the kit is not adapted from a past exam question and is not exam standard but has been included to provide greater syllabus coverage.

The specimen exam is included at the end of the kit.

KEY TO THE INDEX

ANSWER ENHANCEMENTS

We have added the following enhancements to the answers in this exam kit:

Key answer tips

All answers include key answer tips to help your understanding of each question.

Tutorial note

All answers include more tutorial notes to explain some of the technical points in more detail.

Top tutor tips

For all questions, we 'walk through the answer' giving guidance on how to approach the questions with helpful 'tips from a top tutor', together with technical tutor notes.

These answers are indicated with the 'footsteps' icon in the index.

ONLINE ENHANCEMENTS

 *Answer debrief*

For selected questions, we recommend that they are to be completed in full exam conditions (i.e. properly timed in a closed book environment).

In addition to the examining team's technical answer, enhanced with key answer tips and tutorial notes in this exam kit, online you can find an answer debrief by a top tutor that:

- works through the question in full

- explains key elements of the answer

- ensures that the easy marks are obtained as quickly as possible.

These questions are indicated with the 'video' icon in the index.

Answer debriefs will be available on MyKaplan at:

www.mykaplan.co.uk

28	Coram & Co		91	468	Sept 18 (A)
29	Brearley & Co		93	475	M18/J18 (A)
30	Basking		95	480	S17/D17(A)
31	Magnolia Group		97	486	M17/J17 (A)
32	Osier		100	494	M17/J17 (A)
33	Rope		101	499	S16/D16 (A)
34	Boston		103	506	M16/J16 (A)
35	Macau & Co		105	512	M16/J16 (A)
36	Darren		107	518	Jun 15 (A)
37	Thurman		108	523	S16/D16 (A)
38	Adder Group		110	528	Jun 15 (A)
39	Francis Group		112	535	Dec 14 (A)
40	Bradley		113	542	Jun 14 (A)
41	Snipe		115	550	Jun 12 (A)

Other assignments

42	Kobold		117	535	D22
43	Flynn		118	561	S21/D21 (A)
44	Moritz & Co		121	572	M20 (A)
45	Jansen & Co		123	581	Sept 18 (A)
46	Vizsla		126	588	M18/J18 (A)
47	Waters		128	593	Jun 14 (A)
48	Marr & Co		130	599	M22/J22 (A)
49	Cheetah		132	609	S17/D17 (A)
50	Sanzio		134	616	S15/D15 (A)
51	Baltimore		135	621	Dec 13 (A)
52	Jacob		137	630	Jun 11 (A)
53	Moosewood Hospital		139	636	M17/J17 (A)
54	Newman & Co		140	643	Dec 10 (A)
55	Beyer		142	649	S19/D19 (A)
56	Retriever		143	656	Jun 13 (A)
57	Lark & Co		145	661	Dec 11 (A)
58	Gannet & Co		147	667	Dec 12 (A)

Professional and ethical considerations, Quality management and Practice management

UK Syllabus only

INT Syllabus only

ANALYSIS OF PAST EXAMS

The table below summarises the key topics that have been tested in the new syllabus examinations to date.

	Specimen exam	Mar 20	Mar/ Jun 21	Sept/ Dec 21	Mar/ Jun 22	Sept 22	Dec 22
Regulatory Environment							
Regulatory framework including corporate governance							
Money laundering					✓		
Laws and regulations						✓	
Professional & ethical considerations							
Code of ethics	✓	✓	✓	✓	✓		
Fraud and error							
Professional liability							
Quality management & practice management							
Quality management	✓	✓	✓		✓	✓	
Advertising							
Tendering							
Acceptance of professional appointments	✓	✓		✓	✓		✓
Planning & conducting an audit of historical financial information							
Risk evaluation:							
Audit risk	✓	✓	✓	✓			
Business risk			✓			✓	✓
Risk of material misstatement					✓	✓	✓
Group audit situation	✓	✓					
Planning and materiality				✓		✓	✓
Professional scepticism				✓		✓	✓
Audit evidence:							
Sufficient/appropriate		✓					
Specific procedures	✓	✓	✓	✓	✓	✓	✓
Analytical procedures/Data analytics	✓	✓	✓	✓	✓		
Related parties							
Work of experts				✓			
Work of internal audit							

	Specimen exam	Mar 20	Mar/ Jun 21	Sept/ Dec 21	Mar/ Jun 22	Sept 22	Dec 22
Outsourcing							✓
Initial engagements				✓			
Comparatives							
Joint audits		✓					
Transnational audits							
Completion, review and reporting							
Evaluating misstatements and resolving outstanding issues	✓	✓	✓	✓	✓		✓
Subsequent events				✓			
Going concern						✓	
Reporting implications	✓		✓		✓	✓	✓
Critical appraisal of a draft report		✓					
Reporting in relation to other information published with FS	✓						
Reporting to those charged with governance				✓			
Other assignments							
Interim review							
Due diligence					✓		
Prospective financial information		✓		✓		✓	✓
Integrated reporting including social and environmental information	✓						
Forensic audit							
Insolvency (UK only)							
Performance information (INT only)							
Levels of assurance							
Advantages and disadvantages of audit							
Current Issues							

EXAM TECHNIQUE

- **Divide the time** you spend on questions in proportion to the marks on offer:

  The **time allowed** for this exam is 3 hours and 15 minutes/195 minutes.

  Read each question carefully, reviewing the format and content of the requirements so that you understand what you need to do.

  There are 80 technical marks and 20 professional skills marks. Professional skills marks should be achieved as you work through the technical marks.

  If 15 minutes are spent reading the examination requirements, your time allocation should be 2.25 minutes per mark (180/80). This gives 90 minutes for section A and 45 minutes for each section B question.

  If you do not allow a specific amount of time for reading and planning your time allocation will be 2.4 minutes per mark (195/80). This gives 97 minutes for section A and 49 minutes for each section B question.

  If you plan to spend more or less time on reading and planning, your time allocation per mark will be different.

  Whatever happens, **do not overrun on any part of any question!** Always keep your eye on the clock.

- **Skim through the whole exam**, assessing the level of difficulty of each question.

- **Decide the order** in which you think you will attempt each question. Options include:

  - Tackle the question you think is the easiest and you are most comfortable with first.

  - Tackle the Section A question first as this has the most marks attributable.

  - Alternatively, attempt Section B questions first as these are less likely to cause you to overrun on time meaning you are more likely to have time to attempt all questions.

  - It is usual, however, that students tackle their least favourite topic and/or the most difficult question last.

  - Whatever your approach, you must make sure that you leave enough time to attempt all questions fully and be very strict with yourself in timing each question.

- At the **beginning of the exam** take time to:

  - **Read the questions and examination requirements carefully** so that you understand them, and

  - **Plan** your answers.

- Stick to the question and **tailor your answer** to what you are asked.

  - Pay particular attention to the verbs in the question.

  - Pay attention to the signposts in the question.

  - State your assumptions if you do not understand what a question is asking. Even if you do not answer in precisely the way the examiner hoped, you may be given some credit, if your assumptions are reasonable.

- If you **get completely stuck** with a question **leave it** and **return to it later**.

KAPLAN PUBLISHING

- Spend the **last five minutes** of the examination:

  - Reading through your answers, and

  - Making any additions or corrections.

- You should do everything you can to make things easy for the marker.

  The marker will find it easier to identify the points you have made if your **answers are well spaced out** and **clearly referenced to the requirement** being answered.

- **Written questions**:

  Marks are normally awarded for depth of explanation and discussion. For this reason, lists and bullet points should be avoided unless specifically requested. Your answer should:

  - Have a clear structure using subheadings to improve the quality and clarity of your response.

  - Be concise.

- **Briefing note format**:

  Question one will ask you to present your answer in the form of briefing notes. Professional marks are awarded for this format.

  Make sure that you use the correct format – there are easy marks to gain here.

EXAM SPECIFIC INFORMATION

THE EXAM

FORMAT OF THE ADVANCED AUDIT AND ASSURANCE EXAM

	Total marks	Technical marks	Professional skills marks
Section A: One compulsory question	50	40	10
Section B: Two compulsory questions	50 (25 per question)	40 (20 per question)	10 (5 per question)
Overall	**100**	**80**	**20**

Total time allowed: 3 hours and 15 minutes.

The 'current' date in all AAA exam questions will be set at 1 July 20X5. Year-end dates will then be flexed around this depending on the nature of the question. For example, a question set at the planning stage of the audit may have a year-end of 30 June 20X5 or 31 July 20X5. A question set at the completion stage of the audit may have a year-end of 31 January 20X5 or 31 March 20X5.

Note that:

- Question 1

    This question will comprise a case study, worth 50 marks and will be set at the planning stage of the audit, for a single company, a group of companies, or potentially several audit clients.

    You will be provided with detailed information which may include extracts of financial information, strategic, operational and other relevant information for a client business, as well as extracts from audit working papers, including results of analytical procedures.

    The requirements will predominantly focus on syllabus areas A, B, C and D which cover the regulatory environment, professional and ethical considerations, quality management and practice management, and planning and conducting an audit of historical information. Other syllabus areas such as other assignments and current issues may also be included in this question.

    Unless specified otherwise, all exhibits should be considered when carrying out risk evaluations and candidates should ensure that they carefully read the partner's email for any specific guidance in relation to how the information should be used.

    It is recommended that candidates review all the exhibits while planning their answers to the question but as mentioned should ensure they take note of any guidance given by the examining team in terms of which exhibits are relevant to each requirement. Thus, allowing for more detailed analysis and focus on specific information where relevant.

    It is often the case that there will be interactions between the exhibits which will impact on the analysis performed by candidates. Candidates are encouraged to spend adequate time planning and aim to obtain a holistic view and understanding of the issues present in the question.

In a Section A question, the partner's email will always set out the detailed requirements which are to be answered and the mark allocation. It is recommended that candidates refer to the partner's email first to ensure that they understand what they are being asked to do and the best way to allocate their time to each requirement.

Candidates should consider the requirements whilst working through the exhibits to enable a tailored response to be made which utilises the specific information given in the question. Candidates should note that any relevant client specific information will be provided, and speculative answers will not obtain credit.

- **Questions 2 and 3**

  One question will focus exclusively on completion, review and reporting. There are a number of formats this question could adopt, including, but not limited to, assessing going concern, considering the impact of subsequent events, evaluating identified misstatements and the corresponding effect on the auditor's report. You may also be asked to critique an auditor's report or evaluate the matters to be included in a report to management or those charged with governance.

  The other question could cover any syllabus area except completion, review and reporting. Therefore the question may focus on a different aspect of the audit process such as reliance on the work of others or ethical issues arising with an audit client.

  Alternatively the question may focus on non-audit engagements such as due diligence, examination of a forecast, forensic audits, etc. Current issues and developments may be examined in this question.

- All questions will be broken down into several sub-requirements that test a range of topics.

- The majority of marks are given for applying your knowledge to specific case studies. There is little scope for 'knowledge dumping'. Some questions, such as those which require detailed understanding of the auditing standards or safeguards set out in the ethical code, will award some marks for knowledge but you should restrict the amount of information you present here and should still ensure that the comments you make are relevant to the scenario presented.

- Current issues and developments within the profession are examinable. For this type of question it is likely that a technical article on the relevant topic will be issued during the syllabus period. Students are advised to check for any recent technical articles published by the ACCA Examining Team. Examiner's reports emphasise the need for students to read up on current issues and recommend that students do not solely depend on the text book for this exam.

- Discussion questions are generally disliked by students, possibly because there is no right or wrong answer. The way to approach this type of question is to provide a balanced argument. Where a statement is given that you are required to discuss, give reasons why you agree with the statement and reasons why you disagree with the statement.

- 20 professional marks are available throughout the exam and will be awarded for:
  - Communication (question 1 only)
  - Analysis and evaluation
  - Professional scepticism and judgement
  - Commercial acumen.

UK VARIANT SPECIFIC INFORMATION

The following are the key differences between the UK and INT variant exams:

- Insolvency is a syllabus area which is only relevant for UK variant exams. This will not necessarily be examined every sitting. If it is examined it is likely to be one requirement that is changed from the INT variant.

- Questions on ethics and auditor's reports will require knowledge of UK guidance e.g. the FRC Ethical Standard and UK versions of the ISAs. The basic knowledge is the same for UK and INT but there are some variations in ethical safeguards and the elements of a UK auditor's report.

- Practice the UK specific questions in the Study Text and this exam kit to help prepare you for any UK specific questions.

PASS MARK

The pass mark for all ACCA Qualification examinations is 50%.

DETAILED SYLLABUS

The detailed syllabus and study guide written by the ACCA can be found at:

https://www.accaglobal.com/gb/en/student/exam-support-resources/professional-exams-study-resources/p7/syllabus-study-guide.html

KAPLAN'S RECOMMENDED REVISION APPROACH

QUESTION PRACTICE IS THE KEY TO SUCCESS

Success in professional examinations relies upon you acquiring a firm grasp of the required knowledge at the tuition phase. In order to be able to do the questions, knowledge is essential.

However, the difference between success and failure often hinges on your exam technique on the day and making the most of the revision phase of your studies.

The **Kaplan Study Text** is the starting point, designed to provide the underpinning knowledge to tackle all questions. However, in the revision phase, pouring over text books is not the answer.

Kaplan online progress tests help you consolidate your knowledge and understanding and are a useful tool to check whether you can remember key topic areas.

Kaplan pocket notes are designed to help you quickly revise a topic area, however you then need to practice questions. There is a need to progress to full exam standard questions as soon as possible, and to tie your exam technique and technical knowledge together.

The importance of question practice cannot be over-emphasised.

The recommended approach below is designed by expert tutors in the field, in conjunction with their knowledge of the examiner and their recent real exams.

The approach taken for the applied skills level exams is to revise by topic area. However, with the professional stage exams, a multi topic approach is required to answer the scenario based questions.

You need to practice as many questions as possible in the time you have left.

OUR AIM

Our aim is to get you to the stage where you can attempt exam standard questions confidently, to time, in a closed book environment, with no supplementary help (i.e. to simulate the real examination experience).

Practising your exam technique on real past examination questions, in timed conditions, is also vitally important for you to assess your progress and identify areas of weakness that may need more attention in the final run up to the examination.

In order to achieve this we recognise that initially you may feel the need to practice some questions with open book help and exceed the required time.

The approach below shows you which questions you should use to build up to coping with exam standard question practice, and references to the sources of information available should you need to revisit a topic area in more detail.

Remember that in the real examination, all you have to do is:

- Attempt all questions in the exam

- Only spend the allotted time on each question, and

- Get at least 50% of the marks allocated!

Try and practice this approach on every question you attempt from now to the real exam.

EXAMINER COMMENTS

We have included the examiners comments to the specific new syllabus examination questions in this kit for you to see the main pitfalls that students fall into with regard to technical content.

However, too many times in the general section of the report, the examiner comments that students had failed due to:

- 'Misallocation of time'

- 'Running out of time' and

- Showing signs of 'spending too much time on an earlier question and clearly rushing **the** answer to a subsequent question'.

Good exam technique is vital.

STRATEGIC PROFESSIONAL COMPUTER BASED EXAMINATIONS

We advise consulting the ACCA Global website for additional CBE revision resources. On the ACCA website there is a CBE demonstration. It is **ESSENTIAL** that you attempt this before your real CBE. You will become familiar with how to move around the CBE screens and the way that questions are formatted, increasing your confidence and speed in the actual exam.

Be sure you understand how to use the **software** before you start the exam. If in doubt, ask the assessment centre staff to explain it to you.

Questions are **displayed on the screen** and answers are entered using keyboard and mouse.

For additional support with your studies please also refer to the ACCA Global website.

THE KAPLAN AAA REVISION PLAN

Stage 1: Assess areas of strengths and weaknesses

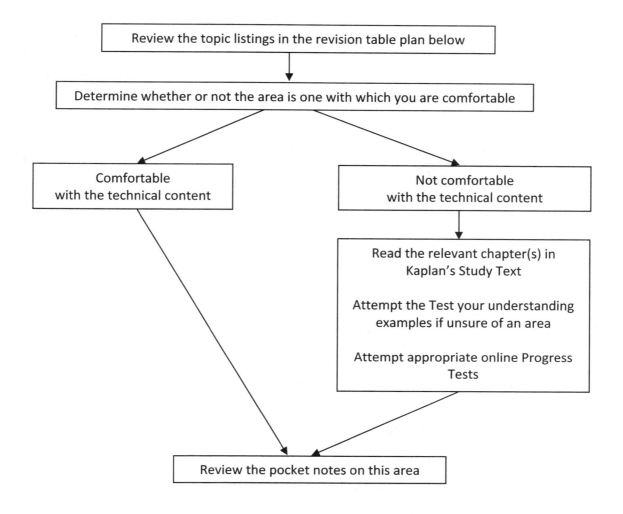

Stage 2: Practice questions

Follow the order of revision of topics as recommended in the revision table plan below and attempt the questions in the order suggested.

Try to avoid referring to text books and notes and the model answer until you have completed your attempt.

Try to answer the question in the allotted time.

Review your attempt with the model answer and assess how much of the answer you achieved in the allocated exam time.

Fill in the self-assessment box below and decide on your best course of action.

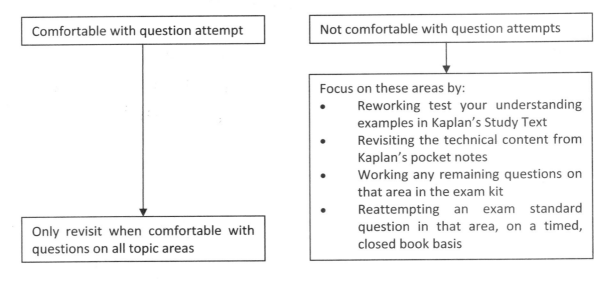

Note that:

The 'footsteps questions' give guidance on exam techniques and how you should have approached the question.

Stage 3: Final pre-exam revision

We recommend that you **attempt at least one three hour and 15 minute mock examination** containing a set of previously unseen exam standard questions.

It is important that you get a feel for the breadth of coverage of a real exam without advanced knowledge of the topic areas covered – just as you will expect to see on the real exam day.

Ideally this mock should be sat in timed, closed book, real exam conditions and could be:

- A mock examination offered by your tuition provider, and/or
- The last real examination.

KAPLAN'S DETAILED REVISION PLAN

	Topics	Study Text (and Pocket Note) Chapter	Questions to attempt	Tutor guidance	Date attempted	Self-assessment
1	Planning and conducting an audit including group audits.		1 2 3 4 5	Evaluation of audit risk, business and risk of material misstatement is fundamental to AAA. However, rather than discussing definitions you need to be able to perform a risk assessment for specific information given in a scenario. It is imperative to understand the difference between the three types of risk in order to answer the question correctly. The ability to generate audit procedures to address specific risks is essential.		
2	Completion, review and reporting		19 20 22 24 26	At the completion stage of an audit you need to consider a number of issues: whether there is sufficient appropriate evidence on file; if the audit plan has been followed; whether there are any material errors in the information under review; and the impact of these issues on the reports you will have to issue. One of the fundamental weaknesses identified by the examiner is a lack of understanding regarding auditor's reports. It is therefore important that you are able to assess a scenario and identify how it might impact upon your audit opinion and auditor's report. You also need to be able to discuss the content and purpose of reports to those charged with governance.		

KAPLAN PUBLISHING

AAA: ADVANCED AUDIT AND ASSURANCE (INT & UK)

3	Other assignments		42 48 54 55 57	There are many non-audit engagements that you could be asked to plan and perform. These include: • Review of interim financial information • Examination of prospective financial information • Due diligence • Forensic audits You also need to be able to discuss the ethical or professional considerations of an auditor accepting these engagements.	
4	Professional and ethical considerations		59 60 62 64	You need to be able to discuss and apply the code of ethics to given scenarios. In addition you also need to consider a wide range of practice management issues, such as: quality management within the firm; legal requirements; commercial strategy; and professional liability.	
5	UK Syllabus: Auditing aspects of insolvency		65 66 67 68 69	Students studying for the UK variant of AAA need to understand the procedures for placing a company into liquidation or administration.	
6	INT syllabus: Performance information in the public sector		70 71	Students studying for the INT variant exam need to be able to comment on the relevance and measurability of performance information as well as describe procedures that can be used to audit such information.	

Note that not all of the questions are referred to in the programme above. We have recommended an approach to build up from the basic to exam standard questions. The remaining questions are available in the kit for extra practice for those who require more question practise on some areas.

Section 1

PRACTICE QUESTIONS – SECTION A

PLANNING AND CONDUCTING AN AUDIT

1   **MERCURIO** *Walk in the footsteps of a top tutor*

It is 1 July 20X5. You are an audit manager in Arnott & Co, responsible for the audit of Mercurio Co, a listed company with a financial year ending 30 September 20X5. Mercurio Co is the country's leading specialist retailer of small domestic pets, pet food and pet accessories, operating 264 stores across the country.

The following exhibits, available below, provide information relevant to the question:

1   Partner's email – an email which you have received from Ted Hastings, the audit engagement partner.

2   Background information – information and matters relevant to audit planning.

3   Selected financial information – extracts from Mercurio Co's management accounts, including the results of preliminary analytical procedures, which have been performed by a member of the audit team.

4   Meeting notes – extracts from meeting notes taken at a recent meeting with the finance director of Mercurio Co.

This information should be used to answer the question requirement within your chosen response option(s).

Required:

Respond to the instructions in the email from the audit engagement partner. (40 marks)

Note: The split of the mark allocation is shown in the partner's email (Exhibit 1).

Professional marks will be awarded for the demonstration of skill in communication, analysis and evaluation, professional scepticism and judgement and commercial acumen in your answer. (10 marks)

(Total: 50 marks)

Exhibit 1 – Partner's email

To:	Audit manager
From:	Ted Hastings, Audit engagement partner
Subject:	audit planning Mercurio Co
Date:	1 July 20X5

Hello

With the year end approaching, I need you to start planning the audit of Mercurio Co. I met with the company's finance director, Kate Fleming, last week to discuss recent developments for the business. I have provided you with a summary of the matters discussed at the meeting along with some projected financial information. Based on the analysis I have done on this industry, it is appropriate for overall materiality to be based on the company's profit before tax as this is a key measure for investors and providers of finance.

I require you to prepare briefing notes for my use in which you:

(a)   Evaluate the significant business risks faced by Mercurio Co.   **(8 marks)**

(b)   Evaluate and prioritise the significant risks of material misstatement which need to be considered in our audit planning.   **(18 marks)**

Please note that you should NOT evaluate risks relating to the audit of animal inventory as these will be addressed separately at a later stage by an auditor's expert as in prior years.

Note: You should use ALL exhibits when carrying out the requested risk evaluations.

(c)   Discuss and conclude on the impact which outsourcing the credit control function will have on our audit planning.   **(7 marks)**

(d)   Design the principal audit procedures to be performed in respect of the holiday pay obligation.   **(7 marks)**

Thank you.

Exhibit 2 – Background information

Mercurio Co is a large listed company, established 15 years ago when the founders observed a growth in demand for pet-related products. The company has grown steadily and is now the largest retailer of pet-related products in the country, with over 7,000 employees, who are mainly staff working in the stores.

As well as selling pet-related products for a wide variety of animals, the stores also sell small animals such as rabbits and fish. Staff members are fully trained to give advice to customers on matters including nutrition and general animal health, and staff members are also trained in handling all types of animals which are sold. Some stores sell more unusual pets such as spiders, snakes and other reptiles and require compliance with specific import restrictions and welfare standards.

Mercurio Co also operates veterinary clinics within most of its stores. The veterinary clinics are staffed by fully qualified vets who offer a full range of veterinary services. Customers can pay as they go for appointments and treatment of their animals, or they can take out an annual pet healthcare plan which covers the cost of essential vaccinations and quarterly health checks. The pet healthcare plans are extremely popular as they offer good value for money to the customer, and the annual income from sales of these plans historically accounts for 10% of the company's revenue.

The costs associated with the vaccinations and health checks have risen over recent years, however, Mercurio Co has not been able to increase the prices due to customer price sensitivity over annual pet healthcare plans. The company's accounting policy is to recognise the revenue from the sale of a healthcare plan on the date when the healthcare plan commences.

Exhibit 3 – Selected financial information

Extracts from the management accounts of Mercurio Co for the year ending 30 September 20X5

	Note	Projected 20X5 $ million	Actual 20X4 $ million
Extract from Statement of profit or loss			
Revenue		803	745
Operating profit		172	110
Profit before tax		60	56
Extract from Statement of financial position			
Total assets		1,078	957
Included in total assets:			
Assets relating to stores purchased from Lakewell	1	171	–
Trade receivables	2	42	22
Goods in transit (part of inventory)	3	12	–
Cash and cash equivalents		36	81
Included in total liabilities:			
Holiday pay obligation		21.1	11.6
Employee numbers	4	7,000	6,200
Bank loans		251	75
Current ratio		2.6	1.4
Gearing ratio		31%	11%

Notes:

1   **Assets relating to stores purchased from Lakewell Co**

To expand into new locations, 20 stores were purchased from Lakewell Co, a clothing retailer, on 1 May 20X5, at a cost of $171 million. Mercurio Co purchased the stores using their cash reserves. Lakewell Co was facing going concern problems and offered the stores for sale as part of a restructuring programme.

The stores need to be completely refitted at an estimated cost of $9 million each. Mercurio Co's management has not yet decided how many of the stores will be retained for use in the business; any which are not retained will be sold. The stores will be refitted during the period November 20X5 to January 20X6.

2 **Trade receivables**

While the majority of sales are for cash, an increasing number of customers have credit accounts with Mercurio Co. The company offers credit customers 60 days' credit to pay for goods. The forecast trade receivables balance at 30 September 20X5 is $42 million (20X4 – $22 million). Due to the growth in sales to customers on account, in December 20X4, Mercurio Co engaged Fairbank Co, a service organisation, to provide the credit control function.

3 **Goods in transit**

In June 20X5, Mercurio Co purchased $12 million of pet food supplies from an international supplier, with the sales contract stating that ownership of the goods passed to Mercurio Co at the date of shipping. During transit, the ship carrying the goods was involved in an accident which destroyed the entire supply of goods. Mercurio Co's directors had arranged insurance on the shipment of goods, and the policy states that 80% of the goods destroyed are covered by the insurance. The latest correspondence from the insurance company was an informal email that the claim had been received and was due to be processed. These purchases are made in Mercurio Co's operating currency.

4 **Holiday pay obligation**

Mercurio Co has an internal audit department, who have been testing the controls in the company's payroll system. Internal audit procedures have revealed that some employees are duplicated on the payroll system; this seems to have happened when two different systems used for recording full-time and part-time staff were merged in October 20X4. Additionally, the internal audit team's procedures have found that while the systems have the capability of recording holidays taken by staff, this is not always used, and manual records are also maintained in relation to holiday entitlement. Employees are entitled to carry forward a maximum of 3 days of unused holiday entitlement to the next year. Management estimates a holiday pay obligation relating to unused holiday entitlement at the year end using the previous year's obligation and adjusting it for pay rises and changes in staff levels. The holiday pay obligation forecast for 30 September 20X5 is $21.1 million (20X4 – $11.6 million).

Exhibit 4 – Meeting notes

Notes from meeting with Kate Fleming, Mercurio Co finance director

This year has seen a significant business development for the company. The company has started to sell products under its own brand, introducing the 'Mercurio Range' of premium pet food and accessories. The products are manufactured in another country and imported, and purchases of Mercurio brand goods from foreign suppliers are predicted to be $7 million for the year to 30 September 20X5. The range was introduced for sale in June 20X5, and was heavily promoted. Having been only recently introduced, sales of products from the Mercurio Range will be insignificant in this year's financial statements. However, projections in the management accounts indicate that the Mercurio Range is expected to account for 30% of revenue in the financial year to 30 September 20X6.

During the year, Mercurio Co took out an additional bank loan to aid with cash flows for the new Mercurio brand promotion and the forthcoming refitting of the stores purchased from Lakewell Co.

END OF QUESTION

2   WINBERRY *Walk in the footsteps of a top tutor*

It is 1 July 20X5. You are a manager in the audit department of Quince & Co, a firm of Chartered Certified Accountants, and you are responsible for the audit of Winberry Co, a listed entity and an existing client of your firm. The company has a financial year ending 30 September 20X5, and you are about to start planning this year's audit.

The following exhibits, available below, provide information relevant to the question:

1   Partner's email – an email which you have received from Olivia Fig, the audit engagement partner.

2   Meeting notes – notes of a meeting which Olivia Fig recently attended with the audit committee of Winberry Co focusing on understanding the current operation and future strategy of the business.

3   Financial information – selected financial information from Winberry Co's management accounts.

4   Internet search – the headline results from an internet search performed by the audit team about the business and industry.

This information should be used to answer the question requirement within your chosen response option(s).

Required:

Respond to the instructions in the email from the audit engagement partner.   (40 marks)

Note: The split of the mark allocation is shown in the partner's email (Exhibit 1).

Professional marks will be awarded for the demonstration of skill in communication, analysis and evaluation, professional scepticism and judgement and commercial acumen in your answer.   (10 marks)

(Total: 50 marks)

Exhibit 1 – Partner's email

To: Audit manager

From: Olivia Fig, Audit engagement partner

Subject: Winberry Co audit planning

Date: 1 July 20X5

Hello

I attended a planning meeting last week with the finance director and a representative of the audit committee of Winberry Co, at which we discussed business developments during the year and plans for the future. I have provided you with my notes from this meeting, as well as some background information about the company from the permanent audit file. Based on the analysis I have done on this industry, it is appropriate for overall materiality to be based on profit before tax as this is a key focus for investors and providers of finance.

Using the information provided in all the exhibits, I require you to prepare briefing notes for my own use, in which you:

(a)   Evaluate the significant business risks facing the company.   **(10 marks)**

(b)   Evaluate and prioritise the significant risks of material misstatement to be considered in planning the audit for the financial year ending 30 September 20X5.   **(16 marks)**

Note: You should refer to ALL exhibits when carrying out the requested risk evaluations.

(c)   Design the principal audit procedures to be performed in respect of the classification of the investment in Luxury Pet Supplies (LPS) Co.   **(7 marks)**

(d)   With reference to the data protection issue referred to in Exhibit 2, discuss Quince & Co's responsibilities in relation to Winberry Co's compliance with laws and regulations.   **(7 marks)**

Thank you

Exhibit 2 – Meeting notes

Winberry Co is a listed company operating as a retailer in the online grocery market with coverage of 75% of the country. The company has a loyal and growing customer base who place orders via either the company's website or an application (app) which can be installed on a customer's mobile phone. Winberry Co fulfils grocery orders, delivering to customers' homes via a fleet of company-owned refrigerated delivery vehicles. Winberry Co prides itself on having a market-leading inventory system which ensures that customers can only order groceries which are currently available. This helps Winberry Co's customers avoid the inconvenience of ordering unavailable items.

A significant proportion of the groceries supplied by Winberry Co are perishable products, the sale and storage of which is highly regulated through food safety regulations. Winberry Co employs experienced food and product technology professionals to ensure that the company complies with all food safety legislation.

The directors of Winberry Co are pursuing ambitious expansion plans in order to establish a strong position in the home delivery grocery market and to explore business partnerships in associated markets.

International expansion

Winberry Co is planning to expand into the foreign country of Farland by setting up operations similar to its existing business. Farland uses the same currency as Winberry Co's existing operations. The investment is expected to cost $125 million. Winberry Co does not currently have the funds for this expansion itself but is in advanced negotiations with its current bankers, who are keen to provide loan financing on the same basis and covenant as the existing loan finance. The expansion is expected to occur in 20X6.

Data protection issue

Two months ago, Winberry Co suffered a cyber-security attack in which the personal information of 2,500 customers, including their credit card details, was stolen. According to a representative of the audit committee, the company's internal audit team had not properly assessed the cyber-security risks, which is a requirement of data protection legislation in the jurisdiction in which Winberry Co operates. The issue which led to the cyber-security attack has now been resolved. Winberry Co did not make any reports of the breach to regulators.

Exhibit 3 – Financial information

	Note	Projected to 30 September 20X5	Actual to 30 September 20X4
		$ million	$ million
Revenue			
Groceries	1	587	358
Pet goods (from LPS Co)	2	10	–
Total revenue		597	358
Operating profit		172	110
Profit before tax		**53**	**31**
Total assets		**957**	**884**
Included in total assets:			
Net assets as consolidated relating to the subsidiary, LPS Co	2	60	–
Property, plant and equipment – relating to fire damaged warehouse	3	67	70
Long-term borrowing	4	33	5
Number of subscription customers		**146,250**	–

Notes:

1   Groceries revenue includes revenue earned for a new initiative launched during the year by Winberry Co. This guarantees a weekly delivery slot for customers who sign up for a premium delivery pass. The premium delivery pass is an annual membership with a fee of $60. This fee is invoiced in advance and the revenue is recognised in full at the time of invoicing.

2   Winberry Co has entered into a joint venture agreement with Durian Co and is investing $30 million in a newly formed company, Luxury Pet Supplies Co (LPS Co), representing 50% of the share capital of the company. The remaining 50% shareholding is owned by Durian Co, a leading national chain of vets and pet goods suppliers. The contract behind this investment states that Winberry Co and Durian Co will work together to develop the supply of a range of pet supplies, food, toys and accessories. This joint venture agreement utilises the established online presence of Winberry Co and their distribution network, and Durian Co's existing knowledge of the pet goods supplies market. Both parties will have equal voting rights and equal rights to the net assets of LPS Co with profits to be shared equally. The investment is expected to take place in August 20X5. The finance director of Winberry Co plans to consolidate the results of LPS Co as a subsidiary; the share of the results attributable to Durian Co is shown as a non-controlling interest. 100% of LPS Co's revenue from incorporation is shown separately in the financial information above owing to Winberry Co's full compliance with IFRS 8 *Operating Segments*.

The finance director believes that despite Winberry Co and Durian Co each owning 50% of LPS Co and having equal representation on the board of directors, Winberry Co's contribution of knowledge to the joint venture is greater and therefore Winberry Co should consolidate the investment.

3   In January 20X5, there was a fire in one of Winberry Co's five warehouses which completely destroyed the premises, but fortunately no staff were injured. The warehouse serviced the northern region of Winberry Co's customer base. The finance director has not written down the carrying amount of the warehouse in property, plant and equipment as he is confident that the company's insurance policy will cover all costs. The insurance company has confirmed that they will repay Winberry Co for the inventory lost during the fire, however, the claim for the warehouse building and machinery is still ongoing. Winberry Co was able to utilise their remaining four warehouses to provide coverage to the northern region customers.

4   Long-term borrowing comprises a bank loan taken out by Winberry Co to fund the joint venture of LPS Co with Durian Co and the purchase of electric delivery vehicles. The bank issued the loan on the same terms as their existing loan which has a covenant that interest cover is maintained at 3.

Exhibit 4 – Internet search

Search results for Winberry Co

3 November 20X4 – Keeping up with demand, Winberry Co ahead in-home delivery grocery revolution

The groceries trade journal, 'Perishables Planet', reports that demand for online groceries delivery has reached an all-time high and shows no sign of slowing down. Traditional supermarkets cannot keep up with the demand, leaving opportunities for gains in market share for online operators.

15 January 20X5 – Local residents to bring legal action against Winberry Co

A group of 30 local residents who claim their health was affected by toxic fumes from the huge fire at Winberry Co's northern warehouse are bringing action to claim for compensation. The local residents' legal representative confirmed that they had served a claim against Winberry Co as they believe there were health and safety breaches due to failings in the sprinkler systems in bringing the fire under control quickly.

Winberry Co's health and safety department has launched an investigation which concluded warehouse staff had manually overridden the automatic sprinkler system to prevent water damage to goods.

18 February 20X5 – Eco-friendly vans cause delivery disruption for Winberry Co

A new fleet of 80 electric vehicles, costing $50,000 each, has caused delivery chaos to Winberry Co's loyal customers. The vehicles can only travel for 100 miles without requiring recharging, which has left customers experiencing delays of up to four hours for their groceries. The eco-friendly vans were initially selected for purchase by management based on a suitable delivery range, however, at the request of Winberry Co, the manufacturer of the vans added refrigeration units to each vehicle which has significantly reduced the distance the vans can travel on a single battery charge.

END OF QUESTION

3   PASCAL & CO *Walk in the footsteps of a top tutor*

It is 1 July 20X5. You are a manager in Pascal & Co, a firm of Chartered Certified Accountants, and you are responsible for the audit of The Infinite Co, a new audit client with a financial year ending 30 September 20X5. The Infinite Co is an owner managed family business. The company owns and operates a theme park, The Infinite Park, which includes theme park rides, arcade style games and food and drink outlets. Brian Fox, the audit engagement partner, met with the company's finance director yesterday to discuss recent developments and financial performance.

In addition, Brian has also requested that you review the client acceptance procedures, which were carried out on another new client, Meadow Co, which operates a similar business to The Infinite Co.

The following exhibits, available below, provide information relevant to the question:

1   Partner's email – an email which you have received from Brian Fox, the audit engagement partner in relation to The Infinite Co and Meadow Co.

2   Background information – information from The Infinite Co website giving background information about the company and its operations.

3   Meeting notes – notes from a meeting between Brian Fox and the finance director of The Infinite Co.

4   Preliminary analytical procedures – summary of key issues arising from preliminary analytical procedures, performed by the audit team, on The Infinite Co projected financial statements.

5   Meadow Co – a copy of the client acceptance assessment performed on Meadow Co prior to audit acceptance.

This information should be used to answer the question requirement within your chosen response option(s).

Required:

Respond to the instructions in the email from the audit engagement partner.   (40 marks)

Note: The split of the mark allocation is shown in the partner's email (Exhibit 1).

Professional marks will be awarded for the demonstration of skill in communication, analysis and evaluation, professional scepticism and judgement and commercial acumen in your answer.   (10 marks)

(Total: 50 marks)

Exhibit 1 – Partner's email

To:	Audit manager
From:	Brian Fox, Audit engagement partner
Subject:	Audit planning for The Infinite Co, and acceptance procedures for Meadow Co
Date:	1 July 20X5

Hello

You need to start planning The Infinite Co audit, and to help with this I have provided you with some relevant information. I met with the finance director yesterday to discuss a number of matters including some recent business developments. The finance director has been with the company since it was founded but is not a member of the family who own the company. Based on the analysis I have done on this industry, it is appropriate for overall materiality to be based on the profitability of the company.

Using the information provided in Exhibits 2, 3 and 4, I require you to prepare briefing notes for my own use, in which you:

(a) Evaluate and prioritise the significant risks of material misstatement to be considered in planning the audit for The Infinite Co for the financial year ending 30 September 20X5. **(20 marks)**

(b) Design the principal audit procedures to be performed on the impairment of the theme park rides. **(5 marks)**

As you are probably aware, the theme park industry has recently experienced some bad publicity relating to another one of our new audit clients, Meadow Co, whereby newspapers alleged the company was under investigation for money laundering. Meadow Co operates a similar business to The Infinite Co. As a result of this, in your briefing notes you should also:

(c) Discuss the responsibility of auditors with respect to money laundering and evaluate whether there are any indicators of money laundering activities by either The Infinite Co or its staff. **(7 marks)**

(d) Using Exhibit 5, conduct a review of the information contained in the Meadow Co client acceptance assessment to evaluate weaknesses in Pascal & Co's acceptance procedures and recommend improvements which should be implemented. **(8 marks)**

Thank you.

Exhibit 2 – Background information

The Infinite Park opened for business more than 40 years ago and today is one of the most popular theme parks in the country. The Infinite Park started out with a handful of simple theme park rides and has expanded to a 50-acre theme park with many different attractions. The theme park is split into two zones, each with its own unique attractions and each providing high-quality food, drink and shopping experiences.

The '**Speed Zone**' offers some of the biggest and best rides for those who like adventure.

The '**Family Zone**' offers smaller rides for children.

Recent business developments relating to both zones are described in Exhibit 3.

The Infinite Park accepts cash, all major credit cards and electronic payments. Tickets for large theme park rides are sold separately at the ticket station in the Speed Zone.

Exhibit 3 – Meeting notes

Operating licences

The company operates the theme park under two licences issued by the relevant government authority. One of these covers the operation and maintenance of the theme park rides, and the other is the licence to sell food and drinks. The theme park is subject to an annual visit by a government inspector.

Theme park rides

The latest external safety inspection was carried out in June 20X5 and, while the report has not been officially received, the inspector has raised several specific action points. It was noted that the maintenance schedules for the rides were not carried out in accordance with regulations. The inspector also expressed concern at the ageing of the rides and the lack of upgrades for modern safety features. The official report from the inspector is expected to be received by 31 July 20X5. There will then be a second inspection in October 20X5 to confirm that all issues have been addressed, after which the inspector will either approve or withhold the renewal of the operating licence in respect of the theme park rides. The finance director is confident that the licence will be renewed.

In April 20X5, the ticket station in the Speed Zone was upgraded to enable it to take electronic payments only. Prior to this, only cash payments could be accepted. As the amounts of cash handled there were often high, the managing director's sons were the only people allowed to sell tickets to reduce the risk of theft by employees. Now that payments are only electronic, staff are assigned to the ticket station through the normal park rota system. The finance director noted that unexpectedly this has resulted in a fall in ticket sales compared to the equivalent months last year.

Employees

The theme park staff comprise a small number of permanent staff supplemented with a large number of temporary seasonal staff in the summer months when the theme park is busy. Some of these staff are paid in cash. The company does not make deductions for payroll taxes for these temporary staff members as they are deemed to earn under the thresholds for paying tax. It is required practice in the tax jurisdiction in which The Infinite Co operates that employers deduct and pay income taxes on behalf of its employees. The company is 100% owned by the managing director and both his sons are employed as permanent members of staff at the park.

Food and drink

The sales of food and drink are generally equally split between cash and electronic payments. Sales in all the food outlets has been growing this year, however, the main restaurant has seen a fall in sales and margins over the last two months. This may be as a result of two cases of food poisoning which occurred in January and March and led to some negative publicity in a local newspaper. Several of the food poisoning victims are suing the company. The Infinite Co's legal adviser, who is a friend of the managing director, has suggested that the customers are unlikely to win the case, as they may have contracted the food poisoning elsewhere.

Gift shop sales

Recently, the theme park started employing staff to dress as famous children's animation characters and walk around the Family Zone to pose for photographs with children. Since the introduction of this practice, gift shop revenue has doubled. The gift shops sell merchandise created specifically for the theme park. However, there have been complaints about the quality of the products with customers complaining that they break easily.

The finance director mentioned that all the shops in the Family Zone have seen an increase in sales but he is particularly impressed with the performance of one of the gift shops where sales and margins are far higher than any other outlet in the theme park. In addition, as most of the sales are in cash, there are no fees to pay to the credit card company. The finance director also mentioned that one of the managing director's sons was recently transferred to this shop.

Sale and leaseback

The managing director wishes to release some funds from the business and, as such, has been negotiating a sale and leaseback arrangement with a national bank. The arrangement is expected to be in place before the financial year end. Under the terms of the arrangement, the company would sell the theme park buildings to the bank in exchange for a payment of $1 million, which is their current market value. The buildings would be leased back over 20 years at an annual rental of $75,000. This would incorporate an interest rate of 5%, which is the current market rate and the resulting net present value of the lease rental payments would be $934,666. The finance director intends to account for the sale as a disposal and the lease payments as rental expenses. The audit engagement partner, Brian Fox, has already reviewed the draft agreement and has concluded that the arrangement meets the criteria to be recognised as a sale.

Previous auditors

The finance director expressed his desire for a good auditor–client relationship and is hoping that we do not impose too many 'pointless rules' on the company like the previous auditors. He says that the managing director likes to be left uninterrupted to run his business without being bothered. The only two people with access to the accounting system are the finance director and the managing director, who sometimes makes money transfers to an international bank account which is held in his name.

Exhibit 4 – Preliminary analytical procedures

A summary of the key financial information and findings from the preliminary analytical procedures on The Infinite Co projected financial statements are detailed below:

Revenue $13.2 million (20X4: $11.9 million)

Profit before tax $2.3 million (20X4: $2.5 million)

Total assets $9.5 million (20X4: $9.6 million)

Property, plant and equipment

	$000	$000
Land	6,000	6,000
Buildings	854	821
Theme park rides	1,431	1,530
Other	75	76
	8,360	8,427

Land is held without depreciation under a revaluation model. The last valuation was performed seven years ago.

All other assets are held with a useful life of 30 years.

Provisions

Current liabilities include a general provision of $0.25 million (20X4: $0.13 million) which represent amounts set aside to cover unexpected costs.

Director's loan

Long-term liabilities include a $3 million (20X4: $3 million) loan from the managing director to the company.

Exhibit 5 – Meadow Co

Details of the audit acceptance assessment performed on Meadow Co prior to audit acceptance is detailed below:

Pascal & Co	
Client acceptance checklist	
Company name:	Meadow Co
Financial documents obtained:	Financial statements for last four years
References:	To be obtained
Previous auditor:	Doomsday & Co
Professional clearance obtained and reviewed:	Verbal – no issues
Intended users of financial statements:	Owner managers only
High/unusual risks – do any of the following apply? – **Public held shares** – **High risk industry** – **Developing business** – **Significant recent changes in management** – **Poor financial condition** – **Other**	None
Firm independence confirmed?	Yes
Firm competence confirmed?	Yes
Firm resources confirmed?	Yes
Fees agreed?	Yes
Money laundering procedures: – **Client identity confirmed** – **Company identity confirmed** – **Politically exposed persons at company** – **Money laundering risk assessment**	 Passport of owner and his wife Certificate of incorporation obtained None Low risk
Proposed partner:	To be confirmed
Signature of partner and date:	

No other paperwork appears to be filed with this document.

END OF QUESTION

4   GRUBER *Walk in the footsteps of a top tutor*

It is 1 July 20X5. You are a manager in the audit department of McClane & Co, a firm of Chartered Certified Accountants. You are assigned to the audit of Gruber Co which has a financial year ending 30 September 20X5.

Gruber Co is a new audit client of McClane & Co, the audit firm having been appointed in January 20X5. The audit was previously performed by Ellis Associates.

Gruber Co is owned and managed by the Gruber family, its principal operations being the design and construction of bespoke machinery used in the oil industry.

The following exhibits, available below, provide information relevant to the question:

1   Partner's email – an email which you have received from Al Powell, the audit engagement partner.

2   Business and governance – information and matters relevant to audit planning.

3   Financial information – extracts from Gruber Co's most recent management accounts.

4   Business developments – information relating to an investment property and customer contracts.

5   Meeting notes – extracts from meeting notes taken at a recent meeting with the board of directors of Gruber Co.

This information should be used to answer the question requirement within your chosen response option(s).

Required:

Respond to the instructions in the email from the audit engagement partner.   (40 marks)

Note: The split of the mark allocation is shown in the partner's email (Exhibit 1).

Professional marks will be awarded for the demonstration of skill in communication, analysis and evaluation, professional scepticism and judgement and commercial acumen in your answer.   (10 marks)

(Total: 50 marks)

Exhibit 1 – Partner's email

To: Audit manager

From: Al Powell, Audit engagement partner

Subject: Audit planning for Gruber Co

Date: 1 July 20X5

Hello

I have provided you with some information which you should use to help you with planning the audit of Gruber Co for the financial year ending 30 September 20X5. As you know, Gruber Co is a new audit client and the firm's client due diligence (know your client) and acceptance procedures were all successfully completed. Based on the analysis I have done on this industry, it is appropriate for overall materiality to be based on the profitability of the company.

Using the information provided, I require you to prepare briefing notes for my own use in which you:

(a) Discuss the matters specific to the planning of an initial audit engagement which should be considered in developing the audit strategy for Gruber Co.

Note: As above, you do NOT need to discuss matters relating to whether it was appropriate for McClane & Co to accept Gruber Co as an audit client, as the acceptance is confirmed. **(5 marks)**

(b) Evaluate and prioritise the significant audit risks to be considered in planning the company audit. **(21 marks)**

(c) Design the principal audit procedures to be performed in respect of the Nakatomi building, including those relating to the use of an expert to provide the fair value.

(6 marks)

(d) Using the information in Exhibit 5, discuss the ethical issues raised and recommend actions to be taken by our firm. **(8 marks)**

Thank you

Exhibit 2 – Business and governance

The company was established 15 years ago by Martin Gruber, an engineer who had patented a new type of machine used in the oil industry. Martin, who is the company's chief executive officer, owns 60% of the shares in the company, with the remainder split equally between his brother and sister, Craig and Iris Gruber.

The company's board of directors includes Craig Gruber as chief finance officer (CFO), Iris Gruber as marketing director, and a non-family member, Kali Hayes, who is director of operations. Gruber Co has 300 employees, most of whom are mechanical engineers.

Martin is planning to sell his shares and retire from the business. Craig and Iris, who are younger than Martin, will retain their shares and their board positions. Initial discussion with a potential acquirer for Martin's shares began last month.

The company owns a head office and leases a production facility where machines are designed and assembled under contract with individual customers. Typically, an order takes 14 months to complete, from the initial design through to installation at the customer's premises. This is due to the large size of the machinery being produced to customer order and the very specific requirements of customers.

Exhibit 3 – Financial information

Key information extracted from the management accounts

	Notes	Projected 30 September 20X5	Actual 30 September 20X4
		$ million	$ million
Revenue	1	75	65
Operating profit	2	18	10
Profit before tax	3	14	9
Total assets		120	88
Included in total assets:			
Intangible assets	4	19	10

Note 1   Revenue is derived from contracts involving the design, manufacture and installation of machinery to customer order. Currently, the company establishes all of its customer contracts to contain only one performance obligation – the successful installation of the machine at the customer's premises. However, around a quarter of the contracts also include a three-year support service for the machinery installed.

Note 2   Operating profit includes a profit of $2.2 million relating to the Argyle contract, details of which are given in Exhibit 4. This is the full amount of profit estimated to be made on the contract. The company's CFO suggests that while the company's accounting policy is to use the output method to determine the completion stage of a contract at the year end, it is appropriate to recognise the full amount of profit on this contract because the customer has paid in advance.

Note 3   Profit before tax includes an estimated increase in the fair value of the Nakatomi building investment property of $2 million. Details are provided about this investment in Exhibit 4.

Note 4   The change in value of intangible assets represents a transaction which took place in March 20X5, whereby Gruber Co purchased some designs from Martin Gruber for $9 million. The value of this transaction was determined by Martin Gruber. The audit engagement partner has asked for information to support this value, but nothing has yet been received from Martin.

Exhibit 4 – Business developments

Argyle contract

In October 20X4, Gruber Co entered into a significant contract to design, construct and install a large piece of machinery for a new customer, Argyle Co. In October 20X4, it was estimated that the design and construction of the machine would take 15 months, with installation estimated to take place in January 20X6. The agreed price of the machine is $6 million and Gruber Co will have incurred costs of $2.6 million in relation to this contract by 30 September 20X5. Based on the project plans, the estimated value of the work certified at 30 September 20X5 is $4 million and the estimated cost to complete is $1.2 million. As noted in Exhibit 3, operating profit includes a profit of $2.2 million relating to the Argyle contract.

Investment property

In October 20X4, following the completion of a significant contract, the company purchased an investment property, the Nakatomi building, for $15 million. The property is a retail development in the country's capital city. The company is going to appoint an expert to provide a valuation of the property and an initial estimate of the increase in fair value of $2 million has been included in the company's financial projections to 30 September 20X5.

Exhibit 5 – Meeting notes

A meeting took place yesterday in which the audit engagement partner discussed the potential sale of Martin Gruber's shares with the company directors.

The company directors revealed that Willis Co is the company with whom negotiations have started in relation to the sale of Martin Gruber's shares. Willis Co is an existing audit client of McClane & Co.

The directors have requested that McClane & Co assist them with the sale by performing a vendor's due diligence service, in which they would conduct an independent review of Gruber Co's financial position and future prospects and produce a report on their findings to be provided to Willis Co.

END OF QUESTION

5   PALE   *Walk in the footsteps of a top tutor*

It is 1 July 20X5. You are a manager in the audit department of Chief & Co, a firm of Chartered Certified Accountants. You are assigned to the audit of Pale Co which has a financial year ending 30 September 20X5.

Pale Co manages timber plantations, its core business being the management of timber plantations and the production and sale of a range of timber products. It is not currently a listed entity.

The following exhibits, available below, provide information relevant to the question:

1   Partner's email – an email which you have received from Harvey Rebus, the audit engagement partner.

2   Background information – information relevant to audit planning.

3   Notes from meeting – summary of business developments discussed at a recent meeting between the chief finance officer (CFO) and the audit engagement partner.

4   Key performance indicators – a summary of financial and non-financial information.

5   Notes from phone call – a summary of issues raised by the CFO during a discussion with the audit engagement partner.

This information should be used to answer the question requirement within your chosen response option(s).

Required:

Respond to the instructions in the email from the audit engagement partner. **(40 marks)**

Note: The split of the mark allocation is shown in the partner's email (Exhibit 1).

Professional marks will be awarded for the demonstration of skill in communication, analysis and evaluation, professional scepticism and judgement and commercial acumen in your answer. **(10 marks)**

(Total: 50 marks)

Exhibit 1 – Partner's email

To: Audit manager

From: Harvey Rebus, Audit engagement partner

Subject: Audit planning for Pale Co

Date: 1 July 20X5

Hello

I have provided you with some information which you should use to help you in planning the audit of Pale Co for the financial year ending 30 September 20X5. As you know, Pale Co is a new audit client of our firm. I hope you are looking forward to working on this interesting new client which is the first timber company we have secured as an audit client. You should also be aware that the management team is planning for Pale Co to achieve a stock market listing within the next two years. Based on the analysis I have done on this industry, it is appropriate for overall materiality to be based on the profitability of the company.

Using the information provided, I require you to prepare briefing notes for my own use in which you:

(a)   Evaluate the significant business risks to be considered in planning the audit of Pale Co. **(8 marks)**

(b)   Evaluate and prioritise the significant audit risks to be considered in planning the audit of Pale Co. **(20 marks)**

Note: In relation to the company's timber plantation asset (referred to in Exhibit 4) **you are only required to consider audit risks relating to changes in fair value.** Any other relevant audit risks relating to the timber plantation asset will be dealt with separately, later in the planning stage of the audit.

(c)   Design the audit procedures to be performed in relation to the change in fair value of the timber plantation asset caused by the recent storms. Your procedures should include those relating to the evaluation of the expert appointed by management and the work they have performed. **(6 marks)**

(d)   Using Exhibit 5, explain the ethical issues and other audit planning implications which arise in relation to the phone call from the company's chief finance officer, Mark York. **(6 marks)**

Thank you

Exhibit 2 – Background information

Pale Co owns and manages several large timber plantations. Approximately 5% of the trees are harvested each year. The company immediately processes the timber which is harvested from felled trees in its own sawmills (a facility where trees are processed into logs and other timber products). The processed timber, which is mainly logs and planks of wood, is then sold to a range of customers including construction companies and furniture manufacturers. Approximately 30% of the timber is exported. Your firm was appointed as auditor to Pale Co in March 20X5 following the resignation of the previous auditor, Hare Associates. As part of your firm's client acceptance procedures, communication was received from Hare Associates indicating that their reason for resignation was due to the retirement of the partner responsible for the audit and that they had no issues to bring to your attention regarding the audit. Pale Co has a small internal audit department with two staff who report to the company's CFO, as the company does not have an audit committee.

Exhibit 3 – Notes from meeting

Meeting date: 10 June 20X5

Attendees:　　Harvey Rebus, audit engagement partner

　　　　　　　　Mark York, chief finance officer (CFO)

Accounting policies

Mark York confirms that Pale Co applies the requirements of IAS 41 *Agriculture* as follows:

– 　Standing timber, which means trees which are growing in the timber plantation prior to being felled, are biological assets, measured at fair value less costs to sell. The change in the fair value less costs to sell is included in profit or loss for the period in which it arises.

– 　Felled trees are agricultural produce which are measured at fair value less costs to sell at the point of harvest. Immediately after felling, trees are processed, so that the value of felled trees awaiting processing is minimal at any point in time.

– 　Processed timber such as logs are measured in accordance with IAS 2 *Inventories*.

A technical expert from the audit firm has confirmed that the accounting policies outlined above appear appropriate in the context of Pale Co's activities.

International expansion

Pale Co's operations are currently all based in its home jurisdiction. However, the board has recently approved the acquisition of several large areas of tropical rainforest in Farland, a remote developing country. The expansion will allow the company to process new types of timber for which there is significant demand from luxury furniture manufacturers. The acquisition of the areas of the rainforest will cost $25 million and the purchase is due to take place in August 20X5. The cost of $25 million is equivalent to the fair value of the rainforest. Farland uses the same currency as Pale Co so the expansion is not creating any foreign exchange risk exposure to the company.

The purchase is being funded through a share issue to existing and new shareholders, who are mainly family members of the Pale family, who established the company 20 years ago. A share issue was the only option for funding the international expansion as the company is at the limit of its bank borrowing agreement.

An international development agency has agreed to provide a grant of $20 million to assist Pale Co in its Farland expansion, on condition that the expansion represents sustainable and ethical business practice. The grant is provided specifically for training the local workforce and building accommodation for the workforce in a town near to the rainforest.

The grant is due to be received in September 20X5 and relevant expenditure will commence in November 20X5. Mark York is planning to recognise half of the amount received as income in this year's financial statements, on the basis that it "will cover some of management's expenses in planning the international expansion".

Gold Standard

The company is proud to have recently been awarded an industry 'Gold Standard' accreditation for its sustainable timber management. To achieve the Gold Standard, which denotes the highest possible level of sustainable timber management and ethical business practice, the company must adhere to a number of strict standards. This includes maintaining the biodiversity of the timber plantation, ensuring that rare species of tree are not harvested, and that animal habitats within the timber plantation are preserved. To maintain the Gold Standard accreditation, one condition is that at least 80% of timber sold must be harvested according to the strict standards set by industry regulators. The Gold Standard applies to all of the company's activities, including the Farland expansion.

Contract with Royal Co

The company's revenue has increased this year, largely due to it signing a significant contract with a new customer, Royal Co. The contract was signed on the basis of Pale Co receiving the Gold Standard accreditation for its timber.

Legal case

A group of employees has recently commenced legal action against the company, claiming that breaches of health and safety guidelines regularly take place. The company has made some redundancies this year, which has put pressure on the remaining staff to work harder in order to maintain productivity; the employees are alleging that this has caused an increase in the number of accidents at work, some of which have resulted in fatalities. The company's management and legal advisors believe that the legal claim, which amounts to $19 million, is unjustified and will not be successful. Mark York does not intend to recognise a provision for the claim or make any disclosure in the financial statements in relation to this issue as it is at such an early stage in the legal proceedings.

Use of expert – change in fair value due to recent storms

In the last month, several storms caused damage to some areas of timber plantation. An independent expert has been appointment by management to determine the extent of damage caused and to quantify any financial implications, including determination of the change in fair value of the standing trees which have been damaged by the storm. The expert's report indicates a large number of trees have been completely destroyed, and many have been badly damaged. Based on the expert's report, management has determined that a reduction in fair value of $70.5 million should be recognised in respect of the timber plantation asset recognised in the statement of financial position.

Exhibit 4 – Key performance indicators

The information in the table below will be published as part of the Annual Report, in a section titled 'Key results for the year', which forms part of management's commentary on the company's performance. The financial information is before recognising the change in fair value of the timber plantation caused by the recent storm, and also before accounting for the government grant.

	Projected	Actual	% change
	30 September 20X5	**30 September 20X4**	
Financial key performance indicators:	$ million	$ million	
Revenue	42.5	40.3	+5.5%
Operating profit	22.0	21.0	+4.8%
Profit before tax	6.5	5.0	+30%
Social and environmental key performance indicators:			
% timber harvested in line with 'Gold Standard'	82%	85%	
Number of employees	1,300	1,420	
Total staff days lost due to accidents at work	78	65	

You are also provided with the following information relating to balances which are extracted from management accounts as at 30 June 20X5:

Total assets – $550 million (20X4 – $545 million)

Timber plantation – $500 million (20X4 – $490 million) – this amount, relating to standing timber, is before accounting for any change in value caused by the recent storms referred to in Exhibit 3.

Inventory – $15.4 million (20X4 – $9.2 million) – the increased level of inventory is explained by management as follows: "In the last two months, industrial action at the country's ports meant no containers of processed timber could be shipped to our export customers. The missed export sales so far amount to about $2.1 million. We continued to harvest and process timber during this time, leading to an increased level of inventory. The industrial action is ongoing."

Cash – $4.5 million (20X4 – $6.8 million) – cash levels are depleted this year due to inflationary pressures and demands for higher wages from our employees, which we have met.

Exhibit 5 – Notes from phone call

Notes from a phone call yesterday between Harvey Rebus, audit engagement partner and Mark York.

Request from Mark York

Pale Co publishes a wide range of non-financial social and environmental Key Performance Indicators (KPIs) as part of the Annual Report, including the three shown as part of Exhibit 4. Mark has asked if our firm can provide assurance on these KPIs as part of performing the annual audit. Mark has suggested that in order to pay for this extra work, the agreed audit fee will be increased by 20%, assuming that the assurance provided on the KPIs is favourable.

END OF QUESTION

6   RICK GROUP *Walk in the footsteps of a top tutor*

It is 1 July 20X5. You are a manager in the audit department of Atlanta & Co, a firm of Chartered Certified Accountants. You are working on the audit of the Rick Group (the Group), which has a financial year ending 30 September 20X5. The Group, a listed entity, offers an internet television network, with over 10 million subscription members in eight countries.

The following exhibits, available below, provide information relevant to the question:

1   Partner's email – an email which you have received from Carol Morgan, the Group audit engagement partner.

2   Background information – information and matters relevant to audit planning.

3   Selected financial information – extracts from Rick Group's management accounts and accompanying explanatory notes.

4   Extract from component auditor strategy document – an extract from the audit strategy document prepared by Neegan Associates, the component auditor which audits one of the Group's subsidiaries.

5   Potential new subsidiary – details of the planned acquisition of a new foreign subsidiary, Michonne Co, and a possible joint audit arrangement.

This information should be used to answer the question requirement within your chosen response option(s).

Required:

Respond to the instructions in the email from the audit engagement partner.   (40 marks)

Note: The split of the mark allocation is shown in the partner's email (Exhibit 1).

Professional marks will be awarded for the demonstration of skill in communication, analysis and evaluation, professional scepticism and judgement and commercial acumen in your answer.   (10 marks)

(Total: 50 marks)

Exhibit 1 – Partner's email

To: Audit manager

From: Carol Morgan, Audit engagement partner

Subject: Audit planning for the Rick Group

Date: 1 July 20X5

Hello

I have provided you with some information in the form of a number of exhibits which you should use to help you with planning the audit of the Rick Group (the Group) for the financial year ending 30 September 20X5.

Based on the analysis I have done on this industry, it is appropriate for overall materiality to be based on the profitability of the Group as this is a key focus for investors.

Using the information provided, I require you to prepare briefing notes for my own use in which you:

(a) Evaluate and prioritise the significant audit risks to be considered in planning the Group audit. **(21 marks)**

(b) Using the information provided in Exhibit 4:

   (i) Evaluate the extract from the component auditor's strategy, commenting on the audit strategy responses and ethical matters relating to the issues identified; and **(7 marks)**

   (ii) Design the principal audit procedures which you will instruct the component auditor to perform on the sale of property to the Group chief executive officer. **(6 marks)**

(c) Using Exhibit 5, discuss whether it is appropriate for a joint audit to be performed on Michonne Co, commenting on the advantages and disadvantages of a joint audit arrangement. **(6 marks)**

Thank you

Exhibit 2 – Background information

The Group started to offer an internet streaming service for films and TV programmes ten years ago. The Group's business model is to acquire licences for films and TV programmes and customers pay a monthly subscription fee to access them and watch online.

The Group has a subsidiary in each country in which it offers its subscription service. Atlanta & Co audits all of the subsidiaries with the exception of Daryl Co, one of the Group's foreign subsidiaries, which is audited by a local firm called Neegan Associates. All companies within the Group have the same financial year end, and with the exception of Daryl Co, which reports under local accounting standards, the Group companies all use IFRS® Accounting Standards as their financial reporting framework.

Matters relevant to audit planning

Following a discussion between the Group audit engagement partner and a representative of the Group audit committee, several matters were noted as being relevant to the audit planning:

Legal case

In January 20X5, a legal case was initiated against the Group by Glenn Co, a film production company. Glenn Co claims that the Group has infringed copyright by streaming a film in specific countries for which a licence has not been acquired. The Group insists that the film is covered by a general licence which was acquired several years ago. The Group finance director is not willing to recognise the legal claim within the financial statements as he is confident that the claim against the Group will not be successful, and he does not want to discuss it further with the audit team, emphasising that there is no relevant documentation available for evaluation at this time.

Daryl Co

Neegan Associates provides the audit service to Daryl Co, one of the Group's foreign subsidiaries. Daryl Co is one of the Group's larger subsidiaries, it is a listed company in its home jurisdiction, with total assets of $140 million. Due to internet service issues where Daryl Co is based, a significant number of customers have cancelled their subscriptions, and the company is projected to make a loss this year.

Daryl Co is the only subsidiary which does not follow IFRS Accounting Standards, as in its local jurisdiction companies must follow local accounting rules. It uses the same currency as the rest of the Group.

Daryl Co was acquired several years ago, and goodwill of $38 million is recognised in the Group financial statements in respect of the company.

Exhibit 3 – Selected financial information

	Note	Projected to 30 September 20X5	Actual to 30 September 20X4
		$ million	$ million
Group revenue	1	980	780
Operating profit		78.4	70.2
Profit before tax		**60.1**	**58.7**
Total assets		**780**	**600**
Included in total assets:			
Intangible assets – licences	2	580	420
Intangible assets – goodwill	3	135	135
Number of subscription customers		**10,500,000**	**8,070,000**

Notes:

1   The Group's main source of revenue is from monthly membership fees. Members are billed in advance of the start of their monthly membership and revenue is recognised when the bill is sent to the customer, all of whom pay by credit card. The price of a regular subscription has remained at $8.20 per month throughout 20X4 and 20X5. Occasionally, the Group offers a free trial period to new customers. This year, the Group also introduced a new premium subscription package, which allows customers to add two family members to their subscription for an additional fee of $5 per month.

2   The Group acquires content licences per title in order to stream film and TV content to its subscribers. The content licences are each for a fixed time period, varying between three and five years. The Group capitalises the cost per title as an intangible asset. Group policy is to amortise licences over a five-year period, the finance director justifies this as being 'the most prudent' accounting treatment.

3   Goodwill arising on business combinations is tested annually for impairment in accordance with IAS® 36 *Impairment of Assets*. Due to the strong performance of the Group, no impairment of goodwill has been recognised in recent years.

Exhibit 4 – Extract from component auditor strategy document

The points below are an extract from the audit strategy prepared by Neegan Associates in relation to their audit of Daryl Co. Other sections of the audit strategy, including the audit risk assessment, have been reviewed by the Group audit team and are considered satisfactory so you do not need to consider them. Materiality has been set by Neegan Associates, in agreement with Atlanta & Co, at $1.4 million.

Issue identified by Neegan Associates	Audit strategy response by Neegan Associates
Payroll From 1 October 20X4, payroll accounting services are provided to Daryl Co by Neegan Associates as an additional non-audit engagement.	**Planned audit procedures:** – Agree the total payroll figure, estimated to be $6 million, from the statement of profit or loss to the payroll reports generated by Neegan Associates. – No further audit procedures are considered necessary.
Sale of property Daryl Co sold a small, unused building located on the coast to the Group's chief executive officer (CEO) in February 20X5, for $50, 000. The amount is still outstanding for payment. The Group CEO is planning to use the property as a holiday home.	**Planned audit procedures:** – Confirm $50,000 is included in receivables within current assets. – No further audit procedures are considered necessary because the transaction is not material to the financial statements, and local accounting rules do not require disclosure of the transaction.

Exhibit 5 – Potential new subsidiary

The Group is planning the acquisition of a new foreign subsidiary, Michonne Co, which is located in Farland. The negotiations are at an advanced stage, and it is likely that the acquisition will take place in October 20X5.

The Group's audit committee has suggested that if the acquisition goes ahead, due to the distant location of the company and the fact that Atlanta & Co has no offices in Farland, a joint audit could be performed with Michonne Co's current auditors, Lucille Associates, a small local firm of Chartered Certified Accountants.

END OF QUESTION

7 **RYDER GROUP** *Walk in the footsteps of a top tutor*

 Answer debrief

It is 1 July 20X5. You are a manager in the audit department of Squire & Co, a firm of Chartered Certified Accountants, responsible for the audit of the Ryder Group (the Group), which has a financial year ending 30 September 20X5. The Group, a listed entity, operates in the hospitality sector, running restaurants, coffee shops and hotels.

Squire & Co audits the Group consolidated financial statements, and the individual financial statements of each Group company. All companies in the Group use IFRS Accounting Standards as their financial reporting framework.

The following exhibits, available below, provide information relevant to the question:

1   Partner's email – an email which you have received from Mo Iqbal, the Group audit engagement partner.

2   Background information – information about the Group's current structure and business activities.

3   Meeting notes – extracts from meeting notes taken at a recent meeting between Mo Iqbal and the Group finance director.

4   Selected financial projections – selected financial projections to 30 September 20X5 and comparative financial information.

5   Notes from audit committee call – notes taken by Mo Iqbal during a phone call with a representative of the audit committee.

This information should be used to answer the question requirement within your chosen response option(s).

Required:

Respond to the instructions in the email from the audit engagement partner.   (40 marks)

Note: The split of the mark allocation is shown in the partner's email (Exhibit 1).

Professional marks will be awarded for the demonstration of skill in communication, analysis and evaluation, professional scepticism and judgement and commercial acumen in your answer.   (10 marks)

(Total: 50 marks)

Exhibit 1 – Partner's email

To: Audit manager

From: Mo Iqbal, Group audit engagement partner

Subject: Ryder Group audit planning

Date: 1 July 20X5

Hello

You need to start planning the Ryder Group (the Group) audit, and to help with this I have provided you with some relevant information. I met with the Group finance director yesterday to discuss a number of matters including some recent business developments. I also spoke with a representative from the Group audit committee regarding several issues.

Based on the analysis I have done on this industry, it is appropriate for overall materiality to be based on the profitability of the Group as this is a key focus for investors.

Using the information provided, I require you to prepare briefing notes for my own use in which you:

(a)   Evaluate and prioritise the significant audit risks to be considered in planning the Group audit for the financial year ending 30 September 20X5. Given the planned Group restructuring, you should evaluate audit risks relating to disclosure issues at this stage in the audit planning.   **(21 marks)**

(b)   Identify the additional information which should be requested from management in order to effectively audit the disposal of Primal Burgers Co, and explain why this information is required.   **(4 marks)**

(c)   Design the principal audit procedures to be performed in respect of:

  (i)   The classification of the $48 million investment in Peppers Co, and

  (ii) The government grant of $20 million received in January 20X5.   **(8 marks)**

(d)   Using the notes from the audit committee phone call in Exhibit 5, discuss any ethical issues relevant to the Group audit, and recommend appropriate actions to be taken by our firm.   **(7 marks)**

Thank you.

Exhibit 2 – Background information

The Ryder Group is one of the country's leading hospitality providers. Over the last 15 years, the Group has grown steadily and has a range of successful hospitality brands, each brand being operated by a separate, wholly owned, subsidiary of the Group.

The Group is planning some restructuring, which is discussed in the notes from the client meeting (Exhibit 3). The Group structure shown below is the Group's existing structure, before any restructuring takes place.

Existing Group structure:

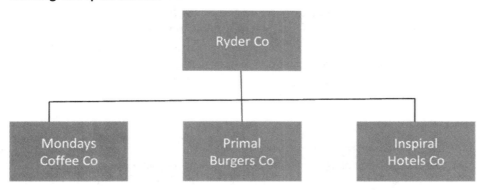

Information about each of the Group companies is given below:

Ryder Co is the parent company of the group, a listed company, which does not trade, and holds the shares in each subsidiary company.

Mondays Coffee Co operates one of the leading coffee shop chains in the country under the 'Mondays Coffee' brand. It enjoys a strong market share and operates more than 1,200 coffee shops across the country.

Primal Burgers Co operates over 150 fast food restaurants. In recent years, revenue from Primal Burgers Co has declined, but it still provides approximately 30% of Group revenue.

Inspiral Hotels Co is a successful hotel business, with over 75 hotels across the country. The Group acquired Inspiral Hotels Co three years ago, as part of a growth strategy based on diversification.

Exhibit 3 – Meeting notes

Group restructuring

The Group is restructuring, as part of a strategy for continued growth in revenue and profitability. As part of this strategy, the Group is investing $48 million in a newly formed company, Peppers Co, representing 50% of the share capital of the company. The remaining 50% shareholding is owned by Smiths Co, a property development company. The contract behind this investment states that the Group and Smiths Co will work together to develop six new hotels, all based at the country's major airports. The investment in Peppers Co is likely to take place in August 20X5.

Partly to provide some of the finance needed for the restructuring, and partly because of its declining revenue, the Group is planning to dispose of Primal Burgers Co. The board approved this disposal in March 20X5. Vendor's due diligence has been carried out by Usami & Co, a firm of Chartered Certified Accountants. Usami & Co conducted an independent review of the company's financial position and future prospects and produced a report on their findings, which is made available to potential buyers. At today's date, several potential buyers have expressed an interest and the Group expects that the disposal will take place just after the financial year end.

Due to the success of the Inspiral Hotels brand, the Group plans to expand its hotel offering, and a target company for acquisition has been identified. The Group aims to acquire Valentine Co, which operates the successful Valentine Hotel chain. Negotiations are underway, and it is likely that the acquisition will go ahead in the first quarter of the next financial year. The purchase price has yet to be agreed, but is likely to be around $100 million. Due diligence performed on Valentine Co indicates that the fair value of its identifiable net assets is $85 million.

Mondays Coffee drive-through

The Group has previously trialled 20 drive-through coffee shops situated on busy roads, which offer customers the convenience of purchasing coffee without leaving their cars. This year the Group opened 50 new drive-through coffee shops, open 24 hours a day, seven days a week, which have proven to be extremely popular with customers. The associated capital (asset) expenditure recognised in property, plant and equipment was $43 million, which, according to the Group finance director, includes the cost of constructing the coffee shops amounting to $28 million, and the cost of acquiring three-year licences to allow 24-hour trading, at a cost of $15 million. The Group's accounting policy is to depreciate property over 20 years, and a full year's worth of depreciation will be charged in the year to 30 September 20X5 in respect of the $43 million capitalised.

According to the Group finance director, the new drive-through coffee shops are projected to account for almost all of the increase in revenue generated from the Mondays Coffee brand in the year. His comment is based on data produced from the management information system which separately records revenue generated from the drive-through coffee shops so that management can assess its performance and determine the return on the $43 million of capital (asset) expenditure.

Government grant

The government provides grants to organisations which commit to investing in properties to reduce carbon emissions and energy consumption. Grants are also available to organisations to promote the benefits of recycling to their customers.

PRACTICE QUESTIONS – SECTION A : SECTION 1

In January 20X5, Ryder Co received a grant of $20 million. The only condition attached to the grant is that half of the amount must be used to upgrade existing assets to make them more environmentally friendly. None of the amount received has yet been spent, but it is planned that it will be used to finance capital (asset) expenditure across the Group's property portfolio. The other half of the grant will be used to fund an advertising campaign.

According to the Group finance director, the full $20 million is included within operating profit in the projected Group statement of profit or loss for the year (Exhibit 4).

Exhibit 4 – Selected financial projections

	Projected to 30 September 20X5	Projected to 30 September 20X5	Actual to 30 September 20X4	Actual to 30 September 20X4
	$ million	$ million	$ million	$ million
Subsidiary	Revenue	Assets	Revenue	Assets
Mondays Coffee Co	155	200	110	160
Primal Burgers Co	99	110	103	113
Inspiral Hotels Co	66	140	62	125
Total	**320**	**450**	**275**	**398**

The table above is based on management information which forms the basis of the segmental reporting disclosed in the notes to the financial statements.

Other financial information for the Group as a whole is given below:

	Projected to 30 September 20X5	Actual to 30 September 20X4
	$ million	$ million
Operating profit	76	72
Profit before tax	20	18
Total assets	475	450

Exhibit 5 – Notes from audit committee call

The Group audit committee is looking to appoint a firm of professional accountants to perform corporate finance work in relation to the planned Group restructuring. The audit committee understands that Squire & Co cannot provide this non-audit service as it would create a significant threat to auditor objectivity. However, the audit committee has asked if our firm can recommend another firm to perform the work. Following the call, the managing partner of Squire & Co has suggested that the firm recommend Ranger Associates, an unconnected firm, to carry out the work. If Ranger Associates is appointed, Squire & Co will charge Ranger Associates a referral fee equivalent to 10% of the fee for the corporate finance engagement.

In addition, the audit committee has asked Squire & Co to work with the Group internal audit team to design internal controls over the part of the accounting system which deals with revenue, and also evaluate the operating effectiveness of the internal controls.

END OF QUESTION

Calculate your allowed time, allocate the time to the separate parts..............

8 MARGOT *Walk in the footsteps of a top tutor*

It is 1 July 20X5. You are a manager in the audit department of Snow & Co, a firm of Chartered Certified Accountants, and you are responsible for the audit of Margot Co. The company has a financial year ending 30 September 20X5, and you are about to start planning the audit.

Margot Co produces fruit-based food products using agricultural produce grown on its farms. Ben Duval, the audit engagement partner, met with the company's finance director last week to discuss business developments in the year and recent financial performance.

The following exhibits, available below, provide information relevant to the question:

1 Partner's email – an email which you have received from Ben Duval, the audit engagement partner.

2 Meeting notes – extracts from meeting notes taken at a recent meeting with the finance director of Margot Co.

3 Reference document – document prepared by Snow & Co containing an overview of the accounting requirements applied in the agriculture sector.

4 Selected financial information – extracts from the latest management accounts of Margot Co and accompanying notes, including the results of preliminary analytical procedures, which have been performed by a member of the audit team.

5 Margot Co's business practices – an email which the audit engagement partner received from Len Larch, a production manager working at one of the company's olive farms.

This information should be used to answer the question requirement within your chosen response option(s).

Required:

Respond to the instructions in the email from the audit engagement partner. (40 marks)

Note: The split of the mark allocation is shown in the partner's email (Exhibit 1).

Professional marks will be awarded for the demonstration of skill in communication, analysis and evaluation, professional scepticism and judgement and commercial acumen in your answer. (10 marks)

(Total: 50 marks)

Exhibit 1 – Partner's email

To: Audit manager

From: Ben Duval, Audit engagement partner for Margot Co

Subject: Audit planning for Margot Co

Hello

I have provided you with some information in the form of a number of exhibits which you should use to help you with planning the audit of Margot Co for the financial year ending 30 September 20X5. Based on the analysis I have done on this industry, it is appropriate for overall materiality to be based on the profitability of the company as this is a key focus for the owners.

Using the information provided, I require you to prepare briefing notes for my own use in which you:

(a) Evaluate and prioritise the significant risks of material misstatement to be considered in planning the company's audit. You should not include risks of material misstatement relating to the valuation of the company's bearer plants or biological assets, which will be evaluated separately. **(21 marks)**

(b) Design the principal audit procedures to be used in the audit of the development cost capitalised in respect of the new packaging. **(5 marks)**

(c) Discuss the matters to be considered in planning to use an auditor's expert in the audit of the fruit, which are recognised as biological assets of the company. **(5 marks)**

In Exhibit 5, I have provided you with an email I received from Len Larch, one of the company's production managers. In respect of this, in your briefing notes you should also:

(d) Discuss the audit implications of the email from Len Larch, recommending any further action to be taken by our firm. **(9 marks)**

Thank you.

Exhibit 2 – Meeting notes

Meeting attendees:

Ben Duval, audit engagement partner, Snow & Co

Ayana Easton, finance director, Margot Co

Business background

Margot Co was established 30 years ago by Jim Margot, who began processing the fruit grown on his family farm to make a small range of food products including canned fruit and fruit juice. The business was relatively small until ten years ago, when the company began to expand by acquiring more farmland with different crops, and building new production facilities. This extended the range of food products which could be processed, which now includes olive oil, packaged nuts and frozen fruit. The company sells its products under the 'Fructus Gold' brand name, and the goods are sold in major supermarkets and online on the company's website.

The company is not listed, and the Margot family members are the company's majority shareholders. Jim Margot retired several years ago, his daughter, Mia Margot, is the company's chief executive officer, and other family members hold positions in senior management.

Business developments in the year

Online sales

In the last year, sales made through the company's website grew significantly. The finance director believes that this was in response to an advertising campaign costing $225,000, which promoted the 'Fructus Gold' brand and coincided with the launch of a new online sales portal on the company website designed to make online ordering easier. To encourage online sales, the company has regular special offers, with discounts periodically offered on a selection of product lines, and offers such as 'Buy One Get One Free' for a limited time on some products.

Research and development

Recently, concern over the level of plastic used in packaging has encouraged food producers to investigate the use of plastic-free packaging for their products. In October 20X4, the board approved a budget of $400,000 to be spent on research and development into new packaging for its products. By 31 May 20X5, $220,000 has been spent, with this amount being paid to ProPack, a firm of packaging specialists, to design and develop a range of plastic-free bottles, bags and containers. It is anticipated that the packaging will be ready for use in two years' time at which point the company will introduce it for use across its product range. ProPack is currently testing prototypes of items which have been developed, with encouraging results.

Use of an auditor's expert

The fruit growing on trees and the harvested agricultural produce are biological assets which were recognised at fair value of $3.1 million in the 20X4 audited financial statements. Due to the specialised nature of these assets, an auditor's expert will be used to provide evidence relating to their valuation. A resource document containing an overview of the accounting requirements in relation to the company's activities is provided in Exhibit 3.

Exhibit 3 – Reference document – Extract from Snow & Co's internal technical guidance for audit staff working with clients in the agriculture sector

IAS 16 *Property, Plant and Equipment* **– Bearer plants**

Definition: A bearer plant is defined under IAS 16 as 'a living plant that:

–   is used in the production or supply of agricultural produce

–   is expected to bear produce for more than one period; and

–   has a remote likelihood of being sold as agricultural produce, except for incidental scrap sales.'

In line with the requirements of IAS 16, bearer plants are recorded at accumulated cost until they reach maturity and then they are depreciated over their useful life.

IAS 41 *Agriculture* **– Biological assets**

Produce growing on bearer plants, and harvested agricultural produce are biological assets and should be accounted for under IAS 41. Biological assets are measured on initial recognition and at subsequent reporting dates at fair value less estimated costs to sell, unless fair value cannot be reliably measured. A gain or loss arising on initial recognition of agricultural produce at fair value less costs to sell shall be included in the statement of profit or loss for the period in which it arises.

IAS 2 *Inventories* **– Agricultural produce**

When agricultural produce enters the production process, it should be accounted for under IAS 2.

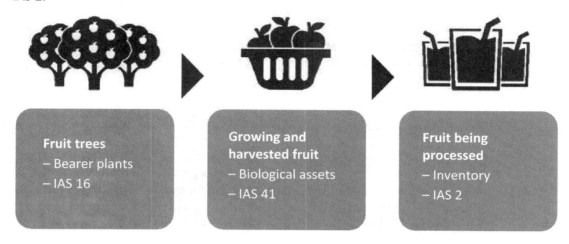

Exhibit 4 – Selected financial information

Extract from management accounts and results of preliminary analytical procedures

	Note	As at 30 September 20X5 Projected	As at 30 September 20X4 Actual
		$000	$000
Extract from statement of financial position:			
Total assets		**12,500**	**11,900**
Included in total assets:			
Intangible assets	1	525	50
Property, plant and equipment	2	6,150	6,470
Total current assets		3,350	2,190
Cash included in current assets		760	750
Current ratio		2.6	1.4
Extract from statement of profit or loss:			
Total revenue		**35,600**	**32,750**
Online sales included in total revenue		2,495	1,310
Operating margin		28%	26%
Return on capital employed		5%	4.5%
Profit before tax		**2,100**	**1,900**
Extract from statement of changes in equity:			
Dividend payments		1,200	1,000

Notes:

1   Intangible assets includes the following items:

	20X5	20X4
	$000	$000
Software development costs	80	50
Advertising costs relating to 'Fructus Gold' brand	225	0
Development costs in respect of new packaging	220	0
Total	525	50

Software development costs of $30,000 were capitalised during the year, which relate to development of the online sales portal. The finance director suggests that both the software development costs and the advertising costs should be capitalised because the increased sales in the year are a direct result of the advertising campaign and improvements in the online sales portal.

The 'Fructus Gold' brand name is not recognised in the statement of financial position, as it is an internally generated asset. This accounting treatment has been confirmed as correct and in accordance with IAS 38 *Intangible Assets*. The notes to the 20X4 financial statements disclosed that the estimated fair value of the brand name is $18 million.

2   Property, plant and equipment

One of the company's several factories, used to process fruit and produce fruit juice, was damaged in November 20X4 when a severe storm occurred. High winds destroyed part of the factory roof, and heavy rain led to flooding and damage to machinery and processing equipment. The factory has not operated since the storm, and the finance director has performed an impairment review on the building and plant and equipment. The carrying amount of $6.15 million includes $880,250 relating to the storm-damaged factory and its fixtures and fittings. The factory is a cash-generating unit for the purpose of impairment testing. The fair value less costs to sell has been estimated based on the sales proceeds which could be generated from selling the damaged machinery. The value in use is estimated based on the future sales which could be generated if the damage to the building is repaired and new machinery is put into the factory.

Exhibit 5 – Margot Co's business practices

To: Ben Duval

From: Len Larch

Subject: Business practices

Hello Ben

I obtained your contact details from your firm's website, I hope you don't mind me approaching you directly. I am emailing to voice some concerns over recent business practices at Margot Co.

In my role as production manager in one of the company's factories, I inspect samples of the fruit which comes into the factory from the company's farms, and speak to the farmers on a regular basis. Recently, several farmers told me that they have been instructed to use certain chemicals to spray the fruit trees, which should increase the fruit yield. However, some of these chemicals are prohibited for use in this country because they can be toxic to humans.

While talking to one of my friends who is a production manager from another factory, it transpired that he had also become suspicious that banned chemicals are being used in the farms. He raised the issue with one of the company directors, who allegedly gave him $10,000 and asked him not to discuss it with anyone. My friend said that I should ask for the same sum of money, but I felt uncomfortable and thought I should tell someone from outside the company about what is going on.

Please do not mention my name if you decide to investigate this further.

Thank you, Len.

END OF QUESTION

9   REDBACK SPORTS   *Walk in the footsteps of a top tutor*

It is 1 July 20X5. You are a manager in the audit department of Huntsman & Co, a firm of Chartered Certified Accountants, responsible for the audit of several companies and for evaluating the acceptance decisions in respect of potential new audit clients.

One of your audit clients is Redback Sports Co, which operates a chain of sport and leisure centres across the country. The company has a financial year ending 30 September 20X5, and you are about to start planning the audit. Stella Cross, the audit engagement partner, met with the company's finance director last week to discuss business developments in the year and recent financial performance.

In addition, Stella has been approached by Mick Emu, the managing director of Emu Gyms Co. Mick has enquired regarding whether Huntsman & Co can provide the company with an audit or limited assurance review, and Stella would like you to evaluate this request. Huntsman & Co already provides a payroll service to Emu Gyms Co and has assisted Mick with his personal tax planning in the past. Mick also has a suspicion that several employees are carrying out a fraud at the company, and he has asked whether an audit or limited assurance review would have alerted him earlier to the situation.

The following exhibits, available below, provide information relevant to the question:

1   Partner's email – an email which you have received from Stella Cross, the audit engagement partner, in respect of both Redback Sports Co and Emu Gyms Co.

2   Meeting notes – extracts from meeting notes taken at a recent meeting between Stella and the finance director of Redback Sports Co.

3   Selected financial information – extracts from the latest management accounts of Redback Sports Co.

4   Notes from phone call – notes of a telephone conversation which Stella had yesterday with Mick Emu, managing director of Emu Gyms Co.

This information should be used to answer the question requirement within your chosen response option(s).

Required:

Respond to the instructions in the email from the audit engagement partner.   **(40 marks)**

Note: The split of the mark allocation is shown in the partner's email (Exhibit 1).

Professional marks will be awarded for the demonstration of skill in communication, analysis and evaluation, professional scepticism and judgement and commercial acumen in your answer.   **(10 marks)**

(Total: 50 marks)

Exhibit 1 – Partner's email

To: Audit manager

From: Stella Cross, Audit engagement partner for Redback Sports Co

Subject: Audit planning for Redback Sports Co, and evaluation of accepting Emu Gyms Co as a potential audit client

Hello

I have provided you with some information in the form of a number of exhibits which you should use to help you with planning the audit of Redback Sports Co for the financial year ending 30 September 20X5. Based on the analysis I have done on this industry, and consideration of the company's strategic direction, it is appropriate for overall materiality to be based on the profitability of the company.

Using the information provided in Exhibits 2 and 3, I require you to prepare briefing notes for my own use in which you:

(a)   Evaluate the significant business risks to be considered in planning the company's audit.   **(10 marks)**

(b)   Evaluate and prioritise the significant risks of material misstatement to be considered in developing the audit strategy and audit plan.   **(18 marks)**

In Exhibit 4, I have also provided you with some information relating to Emu Gyms Co. In respect of this, in your briefing notes you should also:

(c)   (i)   Discuss the ethical and professional implications, recommending any further actions which should be taken by our firm, in respect of the request to accept an engagement to provide Emu Gyms Co with an audit or limited assurance review; and

      (ii)   Discuss whether an audit or limited assurance review of financial statements in previous years could have uncovered the suspected fraud being carried out at Emu Gyms Co.   **(12 marks)**

Thank you.

Exhibit 2 – Meeting notes

Meeting attendees:

Stella Cross, audit engagement partner, Huntsman & Co

Aneta Bay, finance director, Redback Sports Co

Date: 30 June 20X5

Business background

Redback Sports Co operates 20 sport and leisure centres around the country. Each centre has a large gym and a swimming pool, and many also have tennis and badminton courts. Given the nature of the company's operations, it has to comply with health and safety regulations set by the national regulatory body, and its facilities are inspected regularly to ensure that all regulations are being followed, and for the company to retain its operating licence.

The company is not listed and therefore does not need to comply with local corporate governance regulations. However, the company's chief operating officer and chairman consider it good practice to have independent input to the board, and there are two non-executive directors. One of the non-executive directors is a leisure industry expert who was chairman of a rival company, Lyre Leisure Co, for ten years.

The second non-executive director is an academic who specialises in organisational behaviour and who has written several books on performance management in the sport and leisure industry.

The company's board has approved a plan to expand through acquiring other leisure and sport facility providers. The strategy is not likely to be implemented for another two years, when the board would like the first acquisition to take place. However, potential target companies will be identified in the next 12 to 18 months. Ultimately, the board would like to seek a flotation of the company within five years, and they consider that expanding the company would improve profits and make a stock exchange listing more feasible.

Redback Sports Co has a small internal audit department with two staff who report to the finance director, as the board does not have an audit committee.

The company offers a membership scheme whereby, for an annual subscription, members can use the facilities at any of the centres. Customers who are not members can pay to access a centre for a day under the company's 'pay as you go' plan. The membership scheme accounts for approximately 85% of the company's revenue, with the remaining revenue resulting from 'pay as you go' sales.

Business developments in the year

The industry is competitive and the company's strategy is to encourage customers to renew their membership and to attract new members by offering a range of new activities. According to the finance director, a successful initiative which started in October 20X4 is the 'Healthy Kids' campaign; this offers children two hours coaching per week in a range of sports including swimming and tennis. This coaching is provided free as part of their parents' membership, and it has proved to be very successful – the finance director estimates that it has led to 3,000 new members since it was launched.

In January 20X5, the company opened a new coastal sport and leisure centre which, as well as offering the usual facilities, also has a scuba diving centre and offers other water sports facilities. An investment of $12 million was also made in new gym equipment across all centres, to ensure that the company offers the most modern facilities to its customers.

An advertising campaign has been launched, to promote the company brand generally, and to make customers aware of the investments in the facilities which have been made. As part of this campaign, the company paid $1 million to a famous athlete to endorse the company for a period of two years. The athlete will appear at the opening of the new coastal sports centre and has agreed to feature in poster advertisements for the next two years.

Redback Sports Co is also involved with a government initiative to help unemployed people have access to sport facilities. The company received a grant of $2 million in April 20X5, under the terms of which it allows unemployed people three hours of free access to its facilities per month. By the end of June, 33,900 free hours of facility use have been provided under this scheme. The government intends the initiative to run for three years, to promote long-term health of participants.

A new data management system has been introduced, which integrates membership information with accounting software. This allows more efficient management of the customer database which is used extensively for marketing purposes, as well as providing more timely information on financial performance to management. Data from the previous system was transferred to the new system in February 20X5, and the two systems ran in parallel for two months while training was given to staff and the new system was monitored.

One feature of the new system is that it records and reports on the free hours of access provided to unemployed people, which the company has to report on a monthly basis to the government.

Exhibit 3 – Selected financial information

Extracts from management accounts of Redback Sports Co

	Note	Based on projected figures to 30 September 20X5	Based on audited figures to 30 September 20X4
Revenue	1	$53 million	$45 million
Income from government grant	2	$2 million	–
Operating margin	3	15%	10.7%
Profit before tax		$6.9 million	$4.6 million
Capital (asset) expenditure and associated borrowings	4	$32 million	$20 million
Cash		$1.4 million	$5.6 million
Total assets		$130 million	$110 million
Number of sport and leisure centres	5	20	18
Number of members	6	38,000	33,800
Number of 'pay as you go' entry tickets sold		108,000	102,600

Notes

1   Revenue is forecast to increase significantly this year. This is largely due to the success of the advertising campaign featuring the celebrity athlete and the 'Healthy Kids' programme (referred to in Exhibit 2).

2   The grant received of $2 million, the details of which are explained in Exhibit 2, has been recognised in full as income for the year.

3   The company's operating expenses includes the following items:

	20X5	20X4
	$000	$000
Staff costs	15,300	14,300
Marketing	8,500	8,500
Maintenance and repairs of facilities	5,500	5,300

4   Capital (asset) expenditure was mostly financed through borrowings. On 1 October 20X4, a ten-year $30 million loan was received from the company's bank. The loan does not bear interest and is repayable at par value of $34 million. As well as the bank loan, a loan of $1 million was advanced to the company from its managing director, Bob Glider, on 1 February 20X5. The terms of this loan include 3% interest paid to Bob annually in arrears, and the capital will be repaid in seven years' time.

5   Two new sport and leisure centres were opened this year. As well as the coastal sport and leisure centre (referred to in Exhibit 2), a new centre was opened in an affluent urban area in the capital city.

6   The management information system shows that members visit a sport and leisure centre on average three times per week.

Exhibit 4 – Notes of a telephone conversation between Stella Cross and Mick Emu, managing director of Emu Gyms Co

Notes taken by Stella Cross:

Mick Emu phoned me this morning to discuss developments at Emu Gyms Co and to enquire whether our firm could carry out either an audit of the company's financial statements, or a limited assurance review of them. This would be the first time that the financial statements have been subject to audit or limited assurance review.

Business background

The company was founded by Mick four years ago, and since that time our firm has provided a payroll service for the company's staff, which now number 35 employees working in the company's four gyms, all located in urban areas. We have also provided Mick with advice on his personal tax position and financial planning in respect of his retirement, as he wants to sell the company in a few years' time. Mick runs the company with his son, Steve, who is a qualified personal trainer, and with his daughter, Siobhan, who is the marketing director. The company employs one accountant who prepares the management and financial accounts and who deals with customer memberships.

The company has grown quite rapidly in the last year, with revenue of $8 million for the financial year to 30 April 20X5, and with total assets of approximately $5.5 million. The comparative figures for 20X4 were revenue of $6.5 million and total assets of $4.8 million.

Suspected fraud

Mick mentioned that one of the reasons he would like an audit or limited assurance review of the financial statements is because he has noticed some unusual trends in the company's financial information. This has led him to suspect that several employees are carrying out a fraud. Each gym has a small shop selling gym wear and a café, where customers can buy light meals, drinks and snacks.

Mick has noticed that the cash receipts from sales in the shops and cafés have reduced significantly in the last year, however, there has been no reduction in purchases from suppliers. As a consequence, the gross margin for these sales as reported in the management accounts has fallen from 32% to 26%. This indicated to him that staff members could be giving away items for free to customers, or they could be taking inventories from the shops and cafés for their personal use or to sell.

The shops and cafés keep a relatively small amount of inventory which is replenished on a regular basis. Until this year, sales in the shops represented approximately 5%, and café sales represented approximately 8% of the company's revenue. The figures for this year are 3% and 6% respectively.

Mick wonders whether the potential fraud would have been uncovered earlier, had the financial statements been subject to audit or limited assurance review in previous years.

END OF QUESTION

10   EAGLE GROUP *Walk in the footsteps of a top tutor*

It is 1 July 20X5. You are a manager in the audit department of Bison & Co, a firm of Chartered Certified Accountants, responsible for the audit of the Eagle Group (the Group), which has a financial year ending 30 September 20X5. Your firm is appointed to audit the parent company, Eagle Co, and all of its subsidiaries, with the exception of Lynx Co, a newly acquired subsidiary located in a foreign country which is audited by a local firm of auditors, Vulture Associates. Lynx Co is projected to be loss making this year.

All companies in the Group report using IFRS Accounting Standards as the applicable financial reporting framework and have the same financial year end.

The following exhibits, available below, provide information relevant to the question:

1   Partner's email – An email which you have received from Maya Crag, the audit engagement partner.

2   Background information – information about the Group including a request from the Group finance director in respect of a non-audit engagement.

3   Selected financial information – extracts from the Group financial statements projected to 30 September 20X5 and comparatives, extracted from the management accounts, and accompanying explanatory notes.

4   Lynx Co goodwill calculation – management's determination of the goodwill arising on the acquisition of Lynx Co.

5   Extract from component auditor strategy document – an extract from the audit strategy document prepared by Vulture Associates relating to Lynx Co.

This information should be used to answer the question requirement within your chosen response option(s).

Required:

Respond to the instructions in the email from the audit engagement partner. **(40 marks)**

Note: The split of the mark allocation is shown in the partner's email (Exhibit 1).

Professional marks will be awarded for the demonstration of skill in communication, analysis and evaluation, professional scepticism and judgement and commercial acumen in your answer. **(10 marks)**

(Total: 50 marks)

Exhibit 1 – Partner's email

To: Audit manager

From: Maya Crag, Audit engagement partner

Subject: Audit planning for the Eagle Group

Hello

I have provided you with some information in the form of a number of exhibits which you should use in planning the audit of the Eagle Group (the Group). I held a meeting yesterday with the Group finance director and representatives from the Group audit committee, and we discussed a number of issues which will impact on the audit planning. Based on the analysis I have done on this industry, it is appropriate for overall materiality to be based on the profitability of the Group as this is a key focus for investors.

Using the information provided, I require you to prepare briefing notes for my own use in which you:

(a) Evaluate and prioritise the significant audit risks to be considered in planning the Group audit. You should use analytical procedures to assist in identifying audit risks. You are not required to consider audit risks relating to disclosure, as these will be planned for later in the audit process. **(23 marks)**

(b) Design the principal audit procedures to be used in the audit of the goodwill arising on the acquisition of Lynx Co. Management's calculation of the goodwill is shown in Exhibit 4. You do not need to consider the procedures relating to impairment testing, or to foreign currency retranslation, as these will be planned later in the audit. **(6 marks)**

(c) Using the information provided in Exhibit 5, evaluate the extract of the audit strategy prepared by Vulture Associates in respect of their audit of Lynx Co and discuss any implications for the Group audit. **(5 marks)**

(d) After considering the request in Exhibit 2 from the Group finance director in respect of our firm providing advice on the Group's integrated report, discuss the ethical and professional implications of this request, recommending any further actions which should be taken by our firm. **(6 marks)**

Thank you.

Exhibit 2 – Background information

The Group, which is a listed entity, operates in distribution, supply chain and logistics management. Its operations are worldwide, spanning more than 200 countries. The Group's strategy is to strengthen its market share and grow revenue in a sustainable manner by expansion into emerging markets. There are over 50 subsidiaries in the Group, many of which are international. There are three main business divisions: post and parcel delivery, commercial freight and supply chain management, each of which historically has provided approximately one-third of the Group's revenue.

A fourth business division which focuses purely on providing distribution channels for the oil and coal sector was established two years ago, and in 20X5 began to grow quite rapidly. It is forecast to provide 12% of the Group's revenue this year, growing to 15% in 20X6. This division is performing particularly well in developing economies.

In recent years, revenue has grown steadily, based mainly on growth in some locations where e-commerce is rapidly developing. This year, revenue is projected to decline slightly, which the Group attributes to increased competition, as a new distribution company has taken some of the Group's market share in a number of countries. However, the Group management team is confident that this is a short-term drop in revenue, and forecasts a return to growth in 20X6.

Innovation

The Group has invested in automating its warehousing facilities, and while it still employs more than 250,000 staff, many manual warehouse jobs are now performed by robots. Approximately 5,000 staff were made redundant early in this financial year due to automation of their work. Other innovations include increased use of automated loading and unloading of vehicles, and improvements in the technology used to monitor and manage inventory levels.

Integrated reporting

The Group is proud of this innovation and is keen to highlight these technological developments in its integrated report. The Group finance director has been asked to lead a project tasked with producing the Group's first integrated report. The finance director has sent the following request to the audit engagement partner:

'We would like your firm to assist us in developing our integrated report, and to provide assurance on it, as we believe this will enhance the credibility of the information it contains. Specifically, we would like your input into the choice of key performance indicators which should be presented, how to present them, and how they should be reconciled, where relevant, to financial information from the audited financial statements.'

The publication of an integrated report is not a requirement in the jurisdiction in which the Group is headquartered, but there is a growing pressure from stakeholders for an integrated report to be produced by listed reporting entities.

If Bison & Co accepts the engagement in relation to the Group's integrated report, the work would be performed by a team separate from the audit team.

Exhibit 3 – Selected financial information

Statement of financial position

	Note	As at 30 September 20X5 Projected $ million	As at 30 September 20X4 Actual $ million
Non-current assets			
Goodwill	1	1,100	970
Other intangible assets	2	200	170
Property, plant and equipment		657	600
Other investments		85	100
Total non-current assets		2,042	1,840
Current assets		1,450	1,420
Total assets		3,492	3,260
Equity and liabilities			
Equity			
Share capital	3	1,250	1,150
Retained earnings		840	780
Other components of equity		130	140
Non-controlling interest		25	23
		2,245	2,093
Non-current liabilities	4	650	620
Current liabilities		597	547
Total equity and liabilities		3,492	3,260

Statement of profit or loss

	Note	Year to 30 September 20X5 Projected $ million	Year to 30 September 20X4 Actual $ million
Revenue	5	5,770	5,990
Other operating income	6	120	80
Operating expenses	7	(5,540)	(5,800)
		———	———
Operating profit		350	270
Finance charges		(28)	(30)
		———	———
Profit before tax		322	240
Income tax expense		(64)	(60)
		———	———
Profit for the year		258	180
		———	———

Notes to the extracts from financial statements

Goodwill

1   Goodwill relates to the Group's subsidiaries, and is tested for impairment on an annual basis. Management will conduct the annual impairment review in September 20X5, but it is anticipated that no impairment will need to be recognised this year due to anticipated growth in revenue which is forecast for the next two years.

In December 20X4, the Group acquired an 80% controlling shareholding in Lynx Co, a listed company located in a foreign country, for consideration of $351 million. Management's determination of the goodwill arising on this acquisition is shown in Exhibit 4. Lynx Co is projected to be loss making this year.

Other intangible assets

2   Other intangible assets relate mostly to software and other technological development costs. During the year $35 million was spent on developing a new IT system for dealing with customer enquiries and processing customer orders. A further $20 million was spent on research and development into robots being used in warehouses, and $5 million on developing new accounting software. These costs have been capitalised as intangible assets and are all being amortised over a 15-year useful life.

Equity and non-current liabilities

3   A share issue in April 20X5 raised cash of $100 million, which was used to fund capital (asset) expenditure.

4   Non-current liabilities include borrowings of $550 million (20X4 – $500 million) and provisions of $100 million (20X4 – $120 million). Changes in financing during the year have impacted on the Group's weighted average cost of capital. Information from the Group's treasury management team suggests that the weighted average cost of capital is currently 10%.

Financial performance

5 Revenue has decreased by 3.7% over the year, due to a new competitor in the market taking some of the Group's market share.

6 Other operating income comprises the following items:

	20X5	**20X4**
	$ million	$ million
Reversal of provisions	60	40
Reversal of impairment losses on receivables and other assets	30	20
Foreign currency gains	28	23
Profit/(loss) on disposal of non-current assets	2	(3)
Total	120	80

7 Operating expenses includes the following items:

	20X5	**20X4**
	$ million	$ million
Staff costs	3,650	3,610
Cost of raw materials, consumables and supplies	1,725	1,780
Depreciation, amortisation and impairment	145	140
Other operating expenses	20	270
Total	5,540	5,800

Exhibit 4 – Lynx Co goodwill calculation

	Note	$ million
Cash consideration – paid 1 December 20X4		80
Contingent consideration	1	271
Total consideration		351
Fair value of non-controlling interest	2	49
		400
Less: Fair value of identifiable net assets	3	(300)
Goodwill		100

Notes:

1   The contingent consideration will be payable four years after the acquisition date and is calculated based on a payment of $525 million, only payable if Lynx Co reaches revenue and profit targets outlined in the purchase documentation. The amount included in the goodwill calculation has been discounted to present value using a discount factor based on an 18% interest rate.

2   The non-controlling interest is measured at fair value based on Lynx Co's share price on 1 December 20X4.

3   The assets and liabilities acquired and their fair values were determined by an independent firm of Chartered Certified Accountants, Sidewinder & Co, who was engaged by the Group to perform due diligence on Lynx Co prior to the acquisition taking place. A fair value uplift of $12 million was made in relation to property, plant and equipment.

Exhibit 5 – Extract from audit strategy – prepared by Vulture Associates in respect of the audit of Lynx Co

The point below is an extract from the audit strategy. Other sections of the audit strategy, including the audit risk assessment, have been reviewed by the Group audit team and are considered to be satisfactory.

Controls effectiveness

We will place reliance on internal controls, which will reduce the amount of substantive testing which needs to be performed. This is justified on the grounds that in the previous year's audit, controls were tested and found to be highly effective. We do not plan to re-test the controls, as according to management there have been no changes in systems or the control environment during the year.

END OF QUESTION

11   SUNSHINE HOTEL GROUP *Walk in the footsteps of a top tutor*

 Answer debrief

It is 1 July 20X5. You are a manager in the audit department of Dove & Co, responsible for the audit of the Sunshine Hotel Group (the Group), which has a financial year ending 30 September 20X5. You are about to start planning the Group audit for forthcoming year end and this is the first time that you are managing the audit.

The following exhibits, available below, provide information relevant to the question:

1   Partner's email – an email which you have received from John Starling, the audit engagement partner.

2   Background information – information about the Group's activities.

3   Meeting notes – extracts from meeting notes taken at a recent meeting with the finance director of the Sunshine Hotel Group.

4   Email from the Group finance director – extract from email from the Group finance director to John Starling, audit engagement partner.

5   Request from audit committee – request regarding the use of data analytics in future audits.

This information should be used to answer the question requirement within your chosen response option(s).

Required:

Respond to the instructions in the email from the audit engagement partner.   (40 marks)

Note: The split of the mark allocation is shown in the partner's email (Exhibit 1).

Professional marks will be awarded for the demonstration of skill in communication, analysis and evaluation, professional scepticism and judgement and commercial acumen in your answer.   **(10 marks)**

(Total: 50 marks)

Exhibit 1 – Partner's email

To: Audit manager

From: John Starling, audit engagement partner

Subject: Audit planning, the Sunshine Hotel Group

Hello

I have provided you with some information in the form of a number of exhibits which you should use in planning the audit of the Sunshine Hotel Group (the Group). I held a meeting yesterday with the Group finance director and a representative from the Group audit committee, and we discussed a number of business developments during the year and plans for the future. Based on the analysis I have done on this industry, it is appropriate for overall materiality to be based on the profitability of the Group.

Using the information provided in Exhibits 2, 3 and 4, I require you to prepare briefing notes for my use in which you:

(a) Evaluate the significant business risks facing the Group. **(8 marks)**

(b) Evaluate and prioritise the significant risks of material misstatement which should be considered when planning the audit. **(18 marks)**

(c) Using the information provided in Exhibit 4:

    (i) Discuss the additional implications for planning the Group audit and explain any relevant actions to be taken by the firm, and

    (ii) Design the audit procedures to be performed on the claim of $10 million, assuming that the audit team is given access to all relevant sources of audit evidence. **(8 marks)**

(d) In relation to the audit committee's request for information about the use of data analytics in Exhibit 5:

    (i) Explain the term data analytics and discuss how their use can improve audit quality.

    (ii) Explain how they could be used during the audit of the Sunshine Hotel Group. **(6 marks)**

Thank you.

Exhibit 2 – Background information

The Group owns and operates a chain of 20 luxury hotels, all located in popular beachside holiday resorts. The hotels operate on an 'all-inclusive' basis, whereby guests can consume unlimited food and drink, and take part in a variety of water sports including scuba diving as part of the price of their holiday. Each hotel has at least four restaurants and a number of bars. The 'Sunshine Hotel' brand is a market leader, with significant amounts spent each year on marketing to support the brand. The hotels are luxurious and maintained to a very high standard and are marketed as exclusive adult-only luxury holiday destinations.

When customers book to stay in the hotel, they are charged a deposit equivalent to 20% of the total cost of their stay, and a further 20% is payable eight weeks before arrival. The remaining 60% is settled on departure. If a booking is cancelled prior to a week before a guest's stay commences, then a full refund is given, but no refunds are given for cancellations within the week leading up to a guest's stay.

Exhibit 3 – Meeting notes

Financial performance

The Group has seen continued growth, with revenue for the year to 30 September 20X5 projected to be $125 million (20X4 – $110 million), and profit before tax projected to be $10 million (20X4 – $9 million).

According to the latest management accounts, the Group's total assets are currently $350 million. The 'Sunshine Hotel' brand is not recognised as an asset in the financial statements because it has been internally generated. The Group has cash of $20 million at today's date. Most of this cash is held on short-term deposit in a number of different currencies. Based on the latest management accounts, the Group's gearing ratio is 25%.

Moulin Blanche restaurants

In October 20X4, the Group entered into an agreement with an internationally acclaimed restaurant chain, Moulin Blanche, to open new restaurants in its five most popular hotels. The agreement cost $5 million, lasts for 10 years, and allows the Group to use the restaurant name, adopt the menus and decorate the restaurants in the style of Moulin Blanche. The cost of $5 million has been recognised within marketing expenses for the year. After a period of refurbishment, the new restaurants opened in all five hotels on 1 April 20X5.

International expansion

The Group is planning to expand its operations over the next three years by opening hotels in countries with increasingly popular tourist destinations.

As part of this strategy, in April 20X5 the Group purchased land in three new locations in Farland at a cost of $75 million. There are currently no specific plans for the development of these locations due to political instability in the country. In addition to the Farland acquisitions, an existing hotel complex was purchased from a competitor for $23 million. The hotel complex is located in a country where local legislation prohibits private ownership and use of beaches, so the Group's hotel guests cannot enjoy the private and exclusive use of a beach which is one of the Group's key selling points. For this reason, the Group has not yet developed the hotel complex and it is currently being used as a location for staff training.

All of these assets are recognised at cost as property, plant and equipment in the Group statement of financial position. Due to the problems with these recent acquisitions, the Group is planning to invest in alternative locations, with capital (asset) expenditure on sites in new locations of $45 million budgeted for 20X6. This will be funded entirely from an undrawn borrowing facility with the Group's bank which has a fixed interest rate of 3.5% per annum.

Hurricanes

Two of the Group's hotels are located in an area prone to hurricanes, and unfortunately only last week, a hurricane caused severe damage to both of these hotels. Under the Group's 'hurricane guarantee scheme', customers who were staying at the hotels at the time of the hurricane were transferred to other Group hotels, at no cost to the customer. Customers with bookings to stay at the closed hotels have been offered a refund of their deposits, or to transfer their reservation to a different Group hotel, under the terms of the scheme. The hotels are closed while the necessary repair work, which will take two months, is carried out at an estimated cost of $25 million. The repair work will be covered by the Group's insurance policy, which typically pays half of the estimated cost of repair work in advance, with the balance paid when the repair work is completed. No accounting entries have been made as yet in relation to the hurricane.

Exhibit 4 – Email from the Group finance director to John Starling, audit engagement partner

> **John**
>
> The Group's lawyer has received a letter from Ocean Protection, a multi-national pressure group which aims to safeguard marine environments. Ocean Protection is claiming that our hotel guests are causing environmental damage to delicate coral reefs when scuba diving under the supervision of the Group's scuba diving instructors.
>
> Ocean Protection is pressing charges against the Group, and alleges that our activities are in breach of international environmental protection legislation which is ratified by all of the countries in which the Group operates. Damages of $10 million are being sought, Ocean Protection suggesting that this amount would be used to protect the coral reefs from further damage.
>
> The Group is keen to avoid any media attention, so I am hoping to negotiate a lower level of payment and an agreement from Ocean Protection that they will not make the issue public knowledge.
>
> From an accounting point of view, we do not want to recognise a liability, as the disclosures will draw attention to the matter. We will account for any necessary payment when it is made, which is likely to be next year.
>
> I understand that your audit team will need to look at this issue, but I ask that you only speak to me about it, and do not speak to any other employees. Also, I do not want you to contact Ocean Protection as this could impact on our negotiation.

Exhibit 5 – Request from audit committee

The audit committee has heard that some audit firms are now using data analytics and have asked for further information. They are keen for data analytics to be used for the audit of the Sunshine Hotel Group as soon as possible and have indicated that this will be a key deciding factor when the audit is next put out to tender. They would like Dove & Co to explain what data analytics are and how they could be used during the audit to improve efficiency and quality.

END OF QUESTION

 Calculate your allowed time, allocate the time to the separate parts..............

12 LAUREL GROUP *Walk in the footsteps of a top tutor*

It is 1 July 20X5. You are a manager in Holly & Co, a firm of Chartered Certified Accountants, and you are responsible for the audit of the Laurel Group (the Group), a listed entity, with a financial year ending 30 September 20X5.

Holly & Co was appointed as Group auditor three years ago when the audit was put out for tender. Holly & Co audits all components of the Group.

The following exhibits, available below, provide information relevant to the question:

1   Partner's email – an email which you have received from Brigitte Sanders, the audit engagement partner.

2   Background information – a summary of relevant points from the permanent audit file.

3   Meeting notes – notes taken at a recent meeting between Brigitte Sanders and the Group finance director.

4   Selected financial information – extracts from the latest forecast financial statements with comparative figures and accompanying notes.

5   Request from the Group audit committee – request to perform a valuation of the shares of Oleander Co.

This information should be used to answer the question requirement within your chosen response option(s).

Required:

Respond to the instructions in the email from the audit engagement partner.   (40 marks)

Note: The split of the mark allocation is shown in the partner's email (Exhibit 1).

Professional marks will be awarded for the demonstration of skill in communication, analysis and evaluation, professional scepticism and judgement and commercial acumen in your answer.   **(10 marks)**

(Total: 50 marks)

Exhibit 1 – Partner's email

To: Audit manager

From: Brigitte Sanders, audit engagement partner

Subject: Audit planning – the Laurel Group

Hello

You need to start planning the Laurel Group audit, and to help you with this I have provided you with some relevant information. I met with the Group finance director and a representative of the audit committee yesterday to discuss recent business developments. Based on the analysis I have done on this industry, it is appropriate for overall materiality to be based on the profitability of the Group as this is a key focus for investors.

Using the information provided in Exhibits 2, 3 and 4, I require you to prepare briefing notes for my use in which you:

(a)   Evaluate and prioritise the significant risks of material misstatement to be considered in planning the Group audit. Your evaluation should utilise analytical procedures as a method for identifying relevant risks. **(24 marks)**

(b)   Design the principal audit procedures to be used in the audit of:

        (i)   The impairment of the Chico brand, and

        (ii)   The planned acquisition of Azalea Co. **(10 marks)**

(c)   Using the information provided in Exhibit 5, discuss the ethical issues raised by the request to perform the valuation of the shares of Oleander Co. **(6 marks)**

Thank you.

Exhibit 2 – Background information

Points from the permanent audit file

The Group is highly acquisitive, and there are more than 40 subsidiaries and 15 associates within the Group.

The Group produces cosmetics and beauty products which are sold under various brand names in more than 100 countries. Most of the brand names have been acquired with subsidiary companies.

Products include cosmetics, hair care products and perfumes for men and women. Research into new products is a significant activity, and the Group aims to bring new products to market on a regular basis.

Exhibit 3 – Meeting notes

During the year the Group has incurred significant expenditure in non-current assets with $20 million being spent on the acquisition of property, plant and equipment, and $20 million investment in new product development. Half of this expenditure has been funded by a loan and half has been funded from reserves.

In April 20X5, allegations were made in the press and by customers that some ingredients used in the Chico perfume range can cause skin irritations and more serious health problems. As a result, the Chico products have been withdrawn from sale and a $30 million impairment charge has been recognised in respect of the Chico brand name. Despite this issue, Group revenues have increased by 13% and Group management is confident that no other brands are affected.

Group management is currently negotiating the acquisition of Azalea Co, a large company which develops and sells a range of fine fragrances. It is planned that the acquisition will take place in early October 20X5, and the Group is hopeful that Azalea Co's products will replace the revenue stream lost from the withdrawal of its Chico perfume range. Due diligence is taking place currently, and Group management is hopeful that this will support the consideration of $130 million offered for 100% of Azalea Co's share capital. The Group's bank has agreed to provide a loan for this amount.

Exhibit 4 – Selected financial information

Consolidated statement of financial position as at 30 September

	Note	20X5 $m Projected	20X4 $m Actual
Non-current assets			
Property, plant and equipment	1	92	78
Intangible asset – goodwill	2	18	18
Intangible asset – acquired brand names	3	80	115
Intangible asset – development costs	4	25	10
		215	221
Current assets		143	107
Total assets		358	328
Equity and liabilities			
Equity			
Equity share capital		100	100
Retained earnings		106	98
Non-controlling interest		23	23
		229	221
Non-current liabilities			
Debenture loans	5	100	80
Deferred tax	6	10	2
Total non-current liabilities		110	82
Current liabilities		19	25
Total liabilities		129	107
Total equity and liabilities		358	328

Consolidated statement of profit or loss for the year to 30 September

	Projected 20X5 $m	Actual 20X4 $m
Revenue	220	195
Operating expenses	(185)	(158)
Operating profit	35	37
Finance costs	(7)	(7)
Profit before tax	28	30
Income tax expense	(3)	(3)
Profit for the year	25	27

Notes:

1   Capital (asset) expenditure of $20 million has been recorded so far during the year. The Group's accounting policy is to recognise assets at cost less depreciation. During the year, the directors performed a review of the estimated useful lives of the company's assets. It was concluded that many were too short and as a result, asset lives were extended and the projected depreciation charge for the year is $5 million less than the comparative figure.

2   Group management has performed an impairment review at the year end and concluded that goodwill is not impaired.

3   Acquired brand names are held at cost with no amortisation being charged on the grounds that the assets have an indefinite life. An annual impairment review is conducted on all brand names. A $30 million impairment has been recognised in respect of the Chico brand name as discussed above.

4   Development costs relate to expenditure incurred to develop new beauty products. Costs incurred in the research phase are expensed until the product is determined to be technologically feasible. Costs incurred after this stage are capitalised in accordance with IAS 38 *Intangible Assets*.

5   A $20 million loan was taken out in April 20X5, the cash being used to finance a specific new product development project.

6   The deferred tax liability relates to timing differences in respect of accelerated tax depreciation (capital allowances) on the Group's property, plant and equipment. The liability has increased following changes to the estimated useful lives of assets discussed in note 1.

Exhibit 5 – Request from the Group audit committee

In addition to the planned acquisition of Azalea Co, Group management is considering purchasing the entire shareholding of Oleander Co. The Group audit committee would like Holly & Co to perform a valuation of the shares of Oleander Co to determine whether the company is a viable investment. Oleander Co is an audit client of Holly & Co.

END OF QUESTION

13 ZED COMMUNICATIONS GROUP *Walk in the footsteps of a top tutor*

It is 1 July 20X5. The Zed Communications Group (ZCG) is an audit client of your firm, Tarantino & Co, with a financial year ending 30 September 20X5. You are the manager assigned to the forthcoming audit. ZCG is one of Tarantino & Co's largest audit clients.

The following exhibits, available below, provide information relevant to the question:

1	Partner's email – an email which you have received from Vincent Vega, the audit engagement partner.
2	Meeting notes – extracts from meeting notes taken at a recent meeting with the finance director of ZCG.
3	Internal audit report – extracts from the latest report of the internal audit department.
4	Selected financial information – extracts from latest management accounts.

This information should be used to answer the question requirement within your chosen response option(s).

Required:

Respond to the instructions in the email from the audit engagement partner.   (40 marks)

Note: The split of the mark allocation is shown in the partner's email (Exhibit 1).

Professional marks will be awarded for the demonstration of skill in communication, analysis and evaluation, professional scepticism and judgement and commercial acumen in your answer.   (10 marks)

(Total: 50 marks)

Exhibit 1 – Partner's email

To: Audit engagement manager

From: Vincent Vega, audit engagement partner

Subject: ZCG audit planning

Hello

I have provided you with some information in the form of a number of exhibits which you should use in planning the audit of Zed Communications Group (ZCG). I held a meeting yesterday with the Group finance director regarding the forthcoming audit. We also discussed the possibility of using the Group's internal audit team to improve audit efficiency. Based on the analysis I have done on this industry, it is appropriate for overall materiality to be based on the revenue of the group.

Using the information provided, I require you to prepare briefing notes for my use in which you:

(a)   Evaluate and prioritise the significant audit risks relevant to planning the final audit of ZCG.   **(18 marks)**

(b)   Discuss the matters to be considered in determining the assistance which could be provided by, and the amount of reliance, if any, which can be placed on the work of ZCG's internal audit department.   **(6 marks)**

(c)   Design the principal audit procedures to be performed in the audit of:

     (i)   The classification of the 50% equity shareholding in WTC as a joint venture, and

     (ii)   The measurement of the intangible asset recognised in respect of the licence to operate in Farland.   **(10 marks)**

(d)   Discuss the implication of a joint audit if the acquisition of the company in Neverland goes ahead.   **(6 marks)**

Thank you.

Exhibit 2 – Meeting notes

ZCG is a listed entity, one of the largest telecommunications providers in the country and is seeking to expand internationally. ZCG also provides broadband and fixed telephone line services. One of ZCG's strategic aims is to expand internationally, either by acquiring existing telecommunications providers in other countries, or by purchasing licences to operate in foreign countries. ZCG has identified a telecommunications company located overseas in Neverland. The Group's audit committee has suggested that once the acquisition is complete, due to the distant location of the company, a joint audit could be performed with the target company's current auditors.

In December 20X4, ZCG purchased a 50% equity shareholding in Wallace Telecoms Co (WTC), a company operating in several countries where ZCG previously had no interests. The other 50% is held by Wolf Communications Co. The cost of the 50% equity shareholding was $45 million. ZCG is planning to account for its investment in WTC as a joint venture in the Group financial statements.

On 1 October 20X3, ZCG purchased a licence to operate in Farland, a rapidly expanding economy, at a cost of $65 million. The licence lasts for 10 years from the date that it was purchased. Since purchasing the licence, ZCG has established its network coverage in Farland and the network became operational on 1 April 20X5. The licence was recognised as an intangible asset at cost in the Group statement of financial position at 30 September 20X4. Since the network became operational, customer demand has been less than anticipated due to a competitor offering a special deal to its existing customers to encourage them not to change providers.

Most of ZCG's mobile phone customers sign a contract under which they pay a fixed amount each month to use ZCG's mobile network, paying extra if they exceed the agreed data usage and airtime limits. The contract also allows connection to a fixed landline and internet access using broadband connection and most contracts run for two or three years.

In order to extend its broadband services, ZCG has started to purchase network capacity from third-party companies. ZCG enters a fixed-term contract to use a specified amount of the seller's network capacity, with the seller determining which of its network assets are used by ZCG in supplying network services to its customers. In the first six months of 20X5 financial year, ZCG purchased $17.8 million of network capacity from a range of suppliers, with the contract periods varying from twelve months to three years. The cost has been capitalised as an intangible asset.

Exhibit 3 – Internal audit report extracts

ZCG has a well-established internal audit department which is tasked with a range of activities including providing assurance to management over internal controls and assisting the Group's risk management team. The internal audit department is managed by Jules Winfield, a qualified accountant with many years' experience. An extract from the executive summary of the latest internal audit report to the Group finance director is shown below:

'We are pleased to report that ZCG's internal controls are working well and there have been no significant changes to systems and controls during the year. As a result of our testing of controls we uncovered only two financial irregularities which related to:

- Failure to obtain appropriate authorisation and approval of senior management expense claims, such as travel and other reimbursements. The unsubstantiated expense claims amounted to $575,000.

- Inadequate access controls over the Group's IT systems which resulted in a payroll fraud amounting to $750,000.'

Exhibit 4 – Selected financial information

Extracts from latest management accounts

	8 months to 31 May 20X5	Audited financial statements to 30 September 20X4
	$ million	$ million
Revenue:		
Europe	106	102
Americas	30	68
South East Asia	33	30
India	29	20
Total	198	220

	At 31 May 20X5	At 30 September 20X4
	$ million	$ million
Total assets	598	565

END OF QUESTION

14   DALI *Walk in the footsteps of a top tutor*

It is 1 July 20X5. You are a manager in the audit department of Mondrian & Co, a firm of Chartered Certified Accountants. This is the first year you will be responsible for the audit of Dali Co, a listed company. You are planning the audit of the financial statements for the year ending 30 September 20X5.

The following exhibits, available below, provide information relevant to the question:

1   Partner's email – an email which you have received from Sam Hockney, the audit engagement partner.

2   Background information – information and matters relevant to audit planning.

3   Meeting notes – extracts from meeting notes taken at a recent meeting with the finance director of Dali Co.

4   Request from the audit committee – request to perform a review of Dali Co's system of internal control.

5   Preliminary analytical procedures – results of preliminary analytical procedures performed by the audit team and other selected financial information.

This information should be used to answer the question requirement within your chosen response option(s).

Required:

Respond to the instructions in the email from the audit engagement partner.   (40 marks)

Note: The split of the mark allocation is shown in the partner's email (Exhibit 1).

Professional marks will be awarded for the demonstration of skill in communication, analysis and evaluation, professional scepticism and judgement and commercial acumen in your answer.   (10 marks)

(Total: 50 marks)

Exhibit 1 – Partner's email

To: Audit manager

From: Audit engagement partner, Sam Hockney

Regarding: Audit planning – Dali Co

Hello

I have provided you with some information in the form of a number of exhibits which you should use in planning the audit of the Dali Co. I held a meeting yesterday with the finance director and we discussed a number of issues which will impact on the audit planning. Based on the analysis I have done on this industry, it is appropriate for overall materiality to be based on the profitability of the company as this is a key focus for investors.

Using the information provided, I require you to prepare briefing notes for my use in which you:

(a)   Evaluate and prioritise the significant audit risks to be considered in planning the audit of Dali Co.   **(20 marks)**

(b)   Design the principal audit procedures to be used in respect of:

    (i)   The valuation of work in progress.

    (ii)   The recognition and measurement of the government grant.   **(10 marks)**

Using the information provided in Exhibit 4:

(c)   Briefly explain how the outsourcing of payroll will affect next year's audit.   **(4 marks)**

(d)   Identify and discuss the relevant ethical and professional issues raised, and recommend any actions necessary.   **(6 marks)**

Thank you.

Exhibit 2 – Background information

Dali Co was established 20 years ago and specialises in the design and manufacture of equipment and machinery used in the quarrying industry. Dali Co has become known as a leading supplier of machinery to customers operating quarries which extract stone used mainly for construction. Its customer base is located solely in its country of incorporation but most of the components used in Dali Co's manufacturing process are imported from foreign suppliers.

The machines and equipment made by Dali Co are mostly made to order in the company's three manufacturing sites. Customers approach Dali Co to design and develop a machine or piece of equipment specific to their needs. Where management considers that the design work will be significant, the customer is required to pay a 30% payment in advance, which is used to fund the design work. The remaining 70% is paid on delivery of the machine to the customer.

Typically, a machine takes three months to build, and a smaller piece of equipment takes on average six weeks. The design and manufacture of bespoke machinery involving payments in advance has increased during the year. Dali Co also manufactures a range of generic products which are offered for sale to all customers, including drills, conveyors and crushing equipment.

The projected financial statements for 20X5 recognise revenue of $138 million (20X4 – $135 million), profit before tax of $9.8 million (20X4 – $9.2 million) and total assets of $90 million (20X4 – $85 million). Dali Co became listed in its home jurisdiction in January 20X5, and is hoping to achieve a listing on a foreign stock exchange in June 20X6.

Exhibit 3 – Meeting notes

This year has been successful from a strategic point of view in that Dali Co achieved its stock exchange listing in January 20X5, and in doing so raised a significant amount of equity finance. The company's corporate governance was reviewed as part of the flotation process, resulting in the recruitment of three new non-executive directors and a new finance director.

In March 20X5, a cash-settled share-based payment plan was introduced for senior executives, who will receive a bonus on 30 September 20X7. The amount of the bonus will be based on the increase in Dali Co's share price from that at the date of the flotation, when it was $2.90, to the share price at 30 September 20X7. On the advice of the newly appointed finance director, no accounting entries have been made in respect of the plan, but the details relating to the cash-settled share-based payment plan will be disclosed in the notes to the financial statements.

The finance director recommended that the company's manufacturing sites should be revalued. An external valuation was performed in March 20X5, resulting in a revaluation surplus of $3.5 million being recognised in equity. The finance director has informed the audit committee that no deferred tax needs to be provided in respect of the valuation because the property is part of continuing operations and there is no plan for disposal.

In April 20X5, a government grant of $10 million was received as part of a government scheme to subsidise companies which operate in deprived areas. Specifically, $2 million of the grant compensates the company for wages and salaries incurred in the year to 30 September 20X5. The remaining grant relates to the continued operations in the deprived area, with a condition of the grant being that the manufacturing site in that area will remain operational until April 20Y0.

All of the company's manufacturing sites will be closed at the year end to allow the inventory counts to take place. According to the most recent management accounts which are available, work in progress is valued at $12 million (20X4 – $9.5 million) and the majority of these orders will not be complete until after the year end. In recent weeks several customers have returned equipment due to faults, and Dali Co offers a warranty to guarantee that defective items will be replaced free of charge.

Exhibit 4 – Request from the audit committee

The audit committee has asked whether it would be possible for the audit team to perform a review of the company's system of internal control. The new non-executive directors have raised concerns that controls are not as robust as they would expect for a listed company and are concerned about the increased risk of fraud, as well as inefficient commercial practices.

Due to the poor internal controls and the significance of the payroll cost for the company, the management team are considering outsourcing the payroll function. They have asked for a brief explanation of how this would impact next year's audit if they decide to go ahead with the suggestion.

Exhibit 5 – Preliminary analytical procedures

	Based on projected figures to 30 September 20X5	Based on audited figures to 30 September 20X4
Operating profit margin	15%	13%
Inventory holding period	175 days	150 days
Receivables collection period	90 days	70 days
Trade payables payment period	60 days	55 days
Earnings per share	75 cents per share	–
Share price	$3.50	–

END OF QUESTION

15 CONNOLLY *Walk in the footsteps of a top tutor*

It is 1 July 20X5. You are an audit manager in Davies & Co, responsible for the audit of Connolly Co, a listed company operating in the pharmaceutical industry. You are planning the audit of the financial statements for the year ending 30 September 20X5.

The following exhibits, available below, provide information relevant to the question:

1   Partner's email – an email which you have received from Ali Stone, the audit engagement partner.

2   Background information – information about the company's activities.

3   Meeting notes – minutes of meeting between Ali Stone and the finance director, Maggie Ram.

4   Selected financial information – extracts from the latest projected financial statements with comparative figures.

5   Request from the audit committee – request to provide additional services.

This information should be used to answer the question requirement within your chosen response option(s).

Required:

Respond to the instructions in the email from the audit engagement partner.   (40 marks)

Note: The split of the mark allocation is shown in the partner's email (Exhibit 1).

Professional marks will be awarded for the demonstration of skill in communication, analysis and evaluation, professional scepticism and judgement and commercial acumen in your answer.   (10 marks)

(Total: 50 marks)

Exhibit 1 – Partner's email

To: Audit manager

From: Ali Stone, Audit engagement partner

Subject: Audit planning – Connolly Co

Hello

You need to start planning the audit of Connolly Co, and to help with this I have provided you with some relevant information. I held a meeting yesterday with the company's finance director and we discussed a number of issues which will impact on the audit planning. I also spoke with a representative from the audit committee regarding a request for additional services Connolly Co would like our firm to provide. Based on the analysis I have done on this industry, it is appropriate for overall materiality to be based on the profitability of the company as this is a key focus for investors.

Using the information provided, I require you to prepare briefing notes for my use in which you:

(a)   Evaluate the significant business risks faced by Connolly Co.   **(10 marks)**

(b)   Evaluate and prioritise the significant risks of material misstatement to be considered when planning the audit.   **(18 marks)**

(c)   Design the principal audit procedures to be used in the audit of the acquired 'Cold Comforts' brand name.   **(6 marks)**

(d)   Using the information in Exhibit 5, discuss the ethical issues relevant to the audit firm, and recommend appropriate actions to be taken.   **(6 marks)**

Thank you.

Exhibit 2 – Background information

Connolly Co is a pharmaceutical company, developing drugs to be licensed for use around the world. Products include medicines such as tablets and medical gels and creams. Some drugs are sold over the counter at pharmacy stores, while others can only be prescribed for use by a doctor. The market is very competitive, encouraging rapid product innovation. New products are continually in development and improvements are made to existing formulations.

Four new drugs are in the research and development phase. Drugs have to meet very stringent regulatory requirements prior to being licensed for production and sale. Research and development involves human clinical trials, the results of which are scrutinised by the licensing authorities. It is common in the industry for patents to be acquired for new drugs and patent rights are rigorously defended, sometimes resulting in legal action against potential infringement.

The success of Connolly Co relies on the retention of highly skilled scientists to develop new medicines. Most scientific personnel have worked for Connolly Co for a number of years and staff turnover has traditionally been low. However, as competition within the industry has increased, staff retention has become more difficult with people leaving to join rival companies offering larger salaries and enhanced benefits.

Exhibit 3 – Meeting notes

In October 20X4, Connolly Co began to sell into a new market – that of animal health. This has been very successful, and the sales of veterinary pharmaceuticals and grooming products for livestock and pets amount to approximately 15% of total revenue for 20X5.

Another success in 20X5 was the acquisition of the 'Cold Comforts' brand from a rival company. Products to alleviate the symptoms of coughs and colds are sold under this brand. The brand cost $5 million and is being amortised over an estimated useful life of 15 years.

In February 20X5, a contract with a new overseas supplier was signed. All of the company's packaging is now supplied under this contract. Purchases are denominated in a foreign currency. Forward exchange contracts are not used.

In April 20X5, a legal claim was filed against the company by an individual who suffered severe and debilitating side effects when participating in a clinical trial. This appears to be an isolated case and no other claims have been received to date. The company's in-house legal team believe the claim will not be successful but it could take several years to settle which could cause significant reputational damage in the meantime. As a result, the company is considering offering the individual an out of court settlement. The company has asked the bank to make cash of $3 million available for this.

Connolly Co has also asked the bank for an extension of $10 million to its existing loan to support the ongoing development of new drugs.

Exhibit 4 – Selected financial information

	20X5 Projected	20X4 Actual audited
	$000	$000
Revenue	40,000	38,000
Operating profit	8,100	9,085
Operating profit margin	20%	24%
Earnings per share	25c	29c
Net cash flow	(1,200)	6,000
Research and development cash outflow in the year	(3,000)	(2,800)
Total development intangible asset recognised at the year end	50,000	48,000
Total assets	200,000	195,000
Gearing ratio (debt/equity)	0.8	0.9

Exhibit 5 – Request from the audit committee

As mentioned in Exhibit 3, Connolly Co has approached its bank to extend its borrowing facilities. Davies & Co has been asked by the audit committee to provide a guarantee to the bank in respect of this loan extension.

In addition, Connolly Co's management has asked Davies & Co to provide advice on how the company's accounting and management information systems may be improved. While the systems are not considered to create any significant control deficiencies at present, management would like to develop and implement new systems over the next twelve months before they become unreliable and cause errors. Management has asked for our firm's help with this as they have little specialist in-house knowledge in this area.

END OF QUESTION

16   ADAMS GROUP *Walk in the footsteps of a top tutor*

It is 1 July 20X5. You are a manager in Dando & Co, a firm of Chartered Certified Accountants responsible for the audit of the Adams Group, a listed entity for the year ended 31 May 20X5. The Group operates in the textile industry, buying cotton, silk and other raw materials to manufacture a range of goods including clothing, linen and soft furnishings. Goods are sold under the Adams brand name, which was acquired by the Group many years ago. Your firm was appointed as auditor in January 20X5.

The following exhibits, available below, provide information relevant to the question:

1   Partner's email – an email which you have received from Joss Dylan, the audit engagement partner.

2   Background information – information about the Group's current structure and business activities.

3   Selected financial information – extracts from the draft Group financial statements for the year ending 31 May 20X5.

4 Meeting notes – extracts from meeting notes taken at a recent meeting held between Joss Dylan and the Group's finance director and representatives from its audit committee.

This information should be used to answer the question requirement within your chosen response option(s).

Required:

Respond to the instructions in the email from the audit engagement partner. **(40 marks)**

Note: The split of the mark allocation is shown in the partner's email (Exhibit 1).

Professional marks will be awarded for the demonstration of skill in communication, analysis and evaluation, professional scepticism and judgement and commercial acumen in your answer. **(10 marks)**

(Total: 50 marks)

Exhibit 1 – Partner's email

To: Audit manager

From: Joss Dylan

Subject: Adams Group audit planning

Date: 1 July 20X5

Hello

I need you to begin planning the audit of the Adams Group (the Group) for the year ended 31 May 20X5. As you know, we have been appointed to audit the Group financial statements, and we have also been appointed to audit the financial statements of the parent company and of all subsidiaries of the Group except for a foreign subsidiary, Lynott Co, which is audited by a local firm, Clapton & Co. All components of the Group have the same year end of 31 May, report under IFRS Accounting Standards and in the same currency.

Based on the analysis I have done on this industry, it is appropriate for overall materiality to be based on the profitability of the Group.

Using the information provided, I require you to prepare briefing notes for my use in which you:

(a) Evaluate and prioritise the significant audit risks to be considered in planning the audit of the Group. Your evaluation should utilise analytical procedures for identifying relevant audit risks. **(20 marks)**

(b) Explain the matters to be considered, and the procedures to be performed, in respect of planning to use the work of Clapton & Co. **(8 marks)**

(c) Design the principal audit procedures to be performed in respect of the $12 million recognised as investment in associate. **(5 marks)**

(d) Using the information provided in Exhibit 4, identify and evaluate any ethical threats and other professional issues which arise from the requests made by the Group audit committee. **(7 marks)**

Thank you.

Exhibit 2 – Background information

The Group structure and information about each of the components of the Group is shown below:

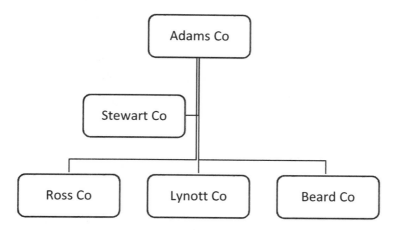

Ross Co, Lynott Co and Beard Co are all wholly owned, acquired subsidiaries which manufacture different textiles. Adams Co also owns 25% of Stewart Co, a company which is classified as an associate in the Group statement of financial position at a value of $12 million at 31 May 20X5. The shares in Stewart Co were acquired in January 20X5 for consideration of $11.5 million. Other than this recent investment in Stewart Co, the Group structure has remained unchanged for many years.

Information relevant to each of the subsidiaries

Adams Co is the parent company in the group and its main activities relate to holding the investments in its subsidiaries and also the brand name which was purchased many years ago. Adams Co imposes an annual management charge of $800,000 on each of its subsidiaries, with the charge for each financial year payable in the subsequent August.

Ross Co manufactures luxury silk clothing, with almost all of its output sold through approximately 200 department stores. Ross Co's draft statement of financial position recognises assets of $21.5 million at 31 May 20X5. Any silk clothing which has not been sold within 12 months is transferred to Lynott Co, where the silk material is recycled in its manufacturing process.

Lynott Co is located in Farland, where it can benefit from low cost labour in its factories. It produces low price fashion clothing for the mass market. A new inventory system was introduced in March 20X5 in order to introduce stronger controls over the movement of inventory between factories and stores. Lynott Co is audited by Clapton & Co, and its auditor's reports in all previous years have been unmodified. Clapton & Co is a small accounting and audit firm, but is a member of an international network of firms. Lynott Co's draft statement of financial position recognises assets of $24 million at 31 May 20X5.

Beard Co manufactures soft furnishings which it sells through an extensive network of retailers. The company is cash rich, and surplus cash is invested in a large portfolio of investment properties, which generate rental income. The Group's accounting policy is to measure investment properties at fair value. Beard Co's draft statement of financial position recognises assets of $28 million at 31 May 20X5, of which investment properties represent $10 million.

Exhibit 3 – Selected financial information

Draft consolidated statement of profit or loss and other comprehensive income

	Year ended 31 May 20X5 $000 Draft	Year ended 31 May 20X4 $000 Actual
Revenue	725,000	650,000
Cost of sales	(463,000)	(417,500)
Gross profit	262,000	232,500
Other income – rental income	200	150
Operating expenses	(250,000)	(225,000)
Operating profit	12,200	7,650
Net finance cost	(1,000)	(1,000)
Profit before tax	11,200	6,650
Income tax expense	(1,500)	(1,000)
Profit for the year	9,700	5,650
Other comprehensive income:		
Gain on investment property revaluation	1,000	3,000
Total comprehensive income	10,700	8,650

Draft consolidated statement of financial position

	31 May 20X5 $000 Draft	31 May 20X4 $000 Actual
Non-current assets		
Property, plant and equipment	45,000	45,000
Investment property (recognised at fair value)	10,000	7,500
Intangible asset – brand name (recognised at cost)	8,000	8,000
Investment in associate	12,000	–
	75,000	60,500
Current assets		
Inventories	12,000	6,000
Receivables	10,500	6,600
Cash	10,000	22,000
	32,500	34,600
Total assets	107,500	95,100
Equity and liabilities		
Share capital	35,000	35,000
Retained earnings	34,000	24,600
	69,000	59,600
Non-current liabilities		
Bank loan	20,000	20,000
Current liabilities		
Trade payables	16,000	13,500
Tax payable	2,500	2,000
	18,500	15,500
Total equity and liabilities	107,500	95,100

Exhibit 4 – Meeting notes

Recent publicity

During the year, the Group attracted negative publicity when an investigation by a well-known journalist alleged that child-labour was being used by several suppliers of raw materials to Lynott Co. The Group refuted the allegations, claiming that the suppliers in question had no contract to supply Lynott Co, and that the Group always uses raw materials from ethically responsible suppliers. The media coverage of the issue has now ended. The Group finance director is confident that the negative publicity has not affected sales of the Group's products, saying that in fact sales are buoyant, as indicated by the increase in Group revenue in the year.

Systems and accounting policies

The Group has a policy of non-amortisation of the Adams brand name. The brand name was acquired many years ago and is recognised at its original cost. The previous audit firm accepted the policy due to the strength of the brand name and the fact that the Group spends a significant amount each year on product development and marketing aimed at supporting the brand. The Group has maintained a good market share in the last few years and management is confident that this will continue to be the case.

As part of management's strategy to increase market share, a bonus scheme has been put in place across the Group under which senior managers will receive a bonus based on an increase in revenue.

Request for additional services

The Group's accounting and management information systems are out of date, and the Group would like to develop and implement new systems next year. The audit committee would like to obtain advice from Dando & Co on the new systems as they have little specialist in-house knowledge in this area.

In addition, the audit committee requests that the Group audit engagement partner attends a meeting with the Group's bank, which is planned to be held the week after the auditor's report is issued. The purpose of the meeting is for the Group to renegotiate its existing lending facility and to extend its loan, and will be attended by the Group finance director, a representative of the audit committee, as well as the bank manager. The Group is hoping that the audit partner will be able to confirm the Group's strong financial position at the meeting, and also confirm that the audit included procedures on going concern, specifically the audit of the Group's cash flow forecast for the next two years, which the bank has requested as part of their lending decision.

END OF QUESTION

Section 2

PRACTICE QUESTIONS – SECTION B

PLANNING AND CONDUCTING AN AUDIT OF HISTORICAL FINANCIAL INFORMATION

17   AWDRY *Walk in the footsteps of a top tutor*

(a)   ISA 540 *Auditing Accounting Estimates and Related Disclosures* (ISA 540) states that the auditor must obtain sufficient appropriate audit evidence to evaluate whether accounting estimates and related disclosures are reasonable in the context of the applicable financial reporting framework, or are misstated. ISA 540 includes enhanced requirements for risk assessment procedures and the auditor's work effort in responding to the assessed risks of material misstatement to support this evaluation.

Required:

Explain why accounting estimates are considered to be a source of high audit risk and discuss the reasons for an enhanced risk assessment to be carried out in relation to the audit of accounting estimates.   (8 marks)

(b)   It is 1 July 20X5. You are the manager responsible for the audit of Awdry Co, a listed entity whose principal activity is the operation of a regional railway network. The audit for the year ended 30 April 20X5 is the first year your firm has audited Awdry Co. The financial statements recognise total assets of $58 million and profit before tax of $7.4 million. The detailed audit fieldwork has started and the audit supervisor has brought the following matters to your attention in relation to the testing of key accounting estimates:

(i)   **Cash-settled share-based payment scheme**

On 1 May 20X4, Awdry Co granted 550,000 share appreciation rights to 55 executives and senior employees of the company with each eligible member of staff receiving 10,000 of the rights. The fair value of the rights was estimated on 30 April 20X5 by an external expert using an options pricing model at $4.50 each. Awdry Co prides itself on good employee relations and the senior management team has estimated that all 55 staff will qualify for the rights when they vest three years after the granting of the rights on 1 May 20X4. The company has recognised a straight-line expense in this year's draft accounts of $825,000.   **(6 marks)**

(ii)   Regulatory penalties

Awdry Co has been subject to a review by the national railways regulator following a complaint from a member of staff with safety concerns. The regulator identified breaches in safety regulations and issued a penalty notice on 30 November 20X4. Awdry Co has appealed against the initial penalty payable. Negotiations with the regulator are still ongoing and the amount payable has not yet been finalised. Awdry Co currently estimates that the total penalty payable as a result of the breach will be $1.3 million which it expects to repay in equal annual instalments over the next ten years with the first payment falling due on 1 May 20X5. The company's draft statement of profit or loss for the current year recognises an expense of $1.3 million and the draft statement of financial position includes a liability for the same amount.   **(6 marks)**

Required:

(i)   **Evaluate the client's accounting treatments and the difficulties which you might encounter when auditing each of the accounting estimates described above, and**

(ii)   **Design the audit procedures which should now be performed to gather sufficient and appropriate audit evidence.**

Note: The split of the mark allocation is shown against each of the issues above.

Professional marks will be awarded for the demonstration of skill in analysis and evaluation, professional scepticism and judgement and commercial acumen in your answer.   **(5 marks)**

(Total: 25 marks)

18   **TONY GROUP**   *Walk in the footsteps of a top tutor*

It is 1 July 20X5. You are an audit manager in Soprano & Co, working on the audit of the Tony Group (the Group), whose financial year ended on 31 March 20X5. This is the first time you have worked on the Group audit. The draft consolidated financial statements recognise profit before tax of $6 million (20X4 – $9 million) and total assets of $90 million (20X4 – $82 million). The Group manufactures equipment used in the oil extraction industry.

Goodwill of $10 million is recognised in the Group statement of financial position, having arisen on several business combinations over the last few years. An impairment review was conducted in March 20X5 by Silvio Dante, the Group finance director, and this year an impairment of $50,000 is to be recognised in respect of the goodwill.

Silvio has prepared a file of documentation to support the results of the impairment review, including notes on the assumptions used, his calculations, and conclusions. When he gave you this file, Silvio made the following comment:

'I don't think you should need any evidence other than that contained in my file. The assumptions used are straightforward, so you shouldn't need to look into them in detail. The assumptions are consistent with how we conducted impairment reviews in previous years and your firm has always agreed with the assumptions used, so you can check that back to last year's audit file. All of the calculations have been checked by the head of the Group's internal audit department.'

Required:

(a)   Explain the meaning of the term professional scepticism, and discuss its importance in planning and performing an audit.

(6 marks)

(b)   (i)   Discuss how professional scepticism should be applied to the statement made by Silvio.

(7 marks)

(ii) Design the principal audit procedures to be performed on the impairment of goodwill.

(7 marks)

Professional marks will be awarded for the demonstration of skill in analysis and evaluation and professional scepticism and judgement in your answer.

(5 marks)

(Total: 25 marks)

COMPLETION, REVIEW AND REPORTING

19   MARLOS *Walk in the footsteps of a top tutor*

It is 1 July 20X5. You are the manager responsible for the audit of Marlos Co and you are completing the audit of the financial statements for the year ended 31 March 20X5. Marlos Co is a listed company operating in the retail industry.

The following exhibit, available below, provides information relevant to the question:

1   Audit matters – summary of the key matters the audit supervisor has flagged for your attention.

This information should be used to answer the question requirements within the response option provided.

Exhibit 1 – Audit matters

The draft financial statements recognise total assets of $118 million and profit before tax of $11·5 million.

Materiality has been set for the audit at $1·1 million.

New property lease

Marlos Co expanded operations during the year and as part of this process arranged on 1 April 20X4 a new property lease. The lease contract is for seven years with a rent-free period of 12 months followed by six annual rental payments. The contract meets the IFRS® 16 *Leases* criteria to be classified as a lease. The financial statements recognise a right-of-use asset of $28·9 million and a corresponding liability of the same amount which has been correctly calculated at the effective interest rate implicit in the lease agreement.

Management has not charged any depreciation on the right-of-use asset, stating that the rent-free period should not result in an expense being included in the statement of profit or loss. Management proposes to begin depreciating the right-of-use asset in the next financial period and will depreciate the asset over the six years for which they make payments.

The finance cost in relation to the lease liability has been correctly accounted for in the financial statements.

Inventory

Marlos Co has recently negotiated arrangements with a new supplier. Included in the contract is a clause which allows the supplier to require return of the products at any time. Marlos Co can also return the products within a set period of time if they remain unsold. Inventory purchased from the new supplier with a value of $8·1 million is included in the company's financial statements as inventory at 31 March 20X5. These amounts are recognised at cost which is lower than the net realisable value of the products.

Required:

Using the information in Exhibits 1 and 2:

(a)   **Evaluate the matters to be considered on the completion of the audit and the audit evidence you should expect to find during your review of the relevant audit working papers.**

   Note: The following mark allocation is provided as guidance for this question:

   (i)   **Lease (9 marks)**

   (ii)   **Inventory (7 marks)**   **(16 marks)**

(b)   **Evaluate the implications for the auditor's report of Marlos Co, assuming that the inventory matter has been satisfactorily resolved but that no further adjustments or disclosures are made to the financial statements with respect to the new property lease.**   **(4 marks)**

Professional marks will be awarded for the demonstration of skill in analysis and evaluation and professional scepticism and judgement in your answer.   **(5 marks)**

(Total: 25 marks)

20   GELLER & CO *Walk in the footsteps of a top tutor*

It is 1 July 20X5. You are an audit manager in Bing & Co, working on the audit of Geller Co, a book and magazine publisher.

Geller Co has a financial year ended 31 March 20X5 and you are reviewing the work performed on going concern.

The following exhibits, available below, provide information relevant to the question:

1   Audit file notes – a summary of audit working papers relevant to going concern.

2   Cash flow forecast – a cash flow forecast covering the period to 31 March 20X7 prepared by management.

This information should be used to answer the question requirements within your chosen response option(s).

Exhibit 1 – Audit file notes

Audit working paper

Prepared by: An Auditor

Subject: Going concern issues highlighted for audit manager and proposal for auditor's report

Date: 29 June 20X5

Our audit work indicates that there are significant operating and financial problems facing the company. Management has prepared a cash flow forecast which they believe should provide evidence that Geller Co is a going concern.

Operating problems noted during the audit of going concern

Geller Co's business is significantly impacted by an industry-wide deterioration in demand for printed books and magazines. The company has recently acquired a digital publishing business at a cost of $25 million, and management is confident that Geller Co will soon be able to offer a broad range of digital books and magazines. However, authors of printed books will need to give consent for their books to be converted to a digital format. This consent must be obtained prior to the books being made available for sale on digital platforms.

Authors are paid royalties based on sales of their books, typically around 5% of the revenue generated from their titles. There is concern that due to the company's cash position, there may be delays in making royalty payments to some authors.

In addition, the rapid growth of online retailers has impacted negatively on the company's sales, as Geller Co has not, until recently, devoted marketing resources to engagement with online retailers. Analytical procedures show that revenue has declined by 20% this year, accelerating the trend seen in previous years. In the financial years ended 31 March 20X3 and 31 March 20X4, revenue fell by 10% and 12% respectively.

The company has recently contracted a very popular author to write a series of three children's books. The author, Chandler Muriel, who has sold millions of books worldwide, has delivered the first book in the series, which was published in January 20X5. Sales of the book since its publication have been disappointing, at only $135,000. Management explains that this is due to a rival company publishing a similar book in December 20X4. Chandler Muriel's second book is due to be published in August 20X5, and the third in January 20X6.

Financial issues

Geller Co faces a liquidity problem, having only $78,000 of cash at 31 March 20X5. The company has an overdraft facility of $250,000 and in addition, agreed undrawn borrowing facilities of $1 million. There is also an existing $5 million unsecured bank loan which is due for repayment on 30 September 20X5.

Disclosure relating to going concern

Management has confirmed that they will provide full details of the going concern issues facing Geller Co in the notes to the financial statements.

Happy Travels publishing range

Geller Co has made the decision to sell its popular Happy Travels range. This is a range of books aimed at the student traveller and include maps as well as suggested hostels and activities. Geller Co anticipates significant interest in the range, with a sale expected in January 20X6.

Exhibit 2 – Cash flow forecast for the two years ended 31 March 20X7

		Six-month periods to:			
		30 Sept	31 March	30 Sept	31 March
		20X5	20X6	20X6	20X7
	Note	$'000	$'000	$'000	$'000
Cash receipts from customers	1	10,000.00	10,200.00	10,404.00	10,924.20
Cash receipt from sale of Happy Travels range	2		6,000.00		
Cash outflows relating to operating expenses	3	(10,400.00)	(10,504.00)	(10,609.04)	(10,715.13)
Interest payments and other finance costs		(125.00)	(125.00)	(125.00)	0.00
Loan repayment	4			(5,000.00)	
Net cash flow		**(525.00)**	**5,571.00**	**(5,330.04)**	**209.07**
Opening cash		78.00	(447.00)	5,124.00	(206.04)
Closing cash		**(447.00)**	**5,124.00**	**(206.04)**	**3.03**

Notes and key assumptions:

1   Monthly sales are based on management's forecasts which predict sales growth of 2% in each six-month period. The sales growth is anticipated based on several assumptions, including that a full range of digital book and magazine titles will be available from 1 August 20X5 and that closer connections with online retailers will drive an increase in sales. In addition, management assumes that sales from Chandler Muriel's books will generate income of approximately $250,000 per six-month period.

2   Management has recently decided to sell the Happy Travels range of books. The estimated sales value of the range is based on a multiple of the annual sales generated by the range. This is the company's standard basis of calculating expected sale prices, which Geller Co has used in recent years when they have sold other ranges of books. Management is confident that a buyer will be found and that the sale will go ahead in January 20X6.

3   Operating expenses, including royalties, are forecast to increase by 1% per six-month period, in line with general costs of inflation.

4   Geller Co has a $5 million loan which is due for repayment on 30 September 20X5. Management has started the process of renegotiating the repayment terms of this loan, and is confident that the bank will agree to extend the repayment date to 30 September 20X6.

Required:

Using the information in Exhibits 1 and 2:

(a)   Evaluate the assumptions used by management and the completeness of the cash flow forecast prepared, explaining why particular assumptions should be challenged and approached with professional scepticism.   **(10 marks)**

(b)   Explain the audit evidence in respect of the CASH RECEIPTS included in the cash flow which you would expect to find in your review of the audit working papers on going concern.   **(5 marks)**

It is now 1 August 20X5 and you have not been able to obtain sufficient, appropriate audit evidence to support the assumptions used to prepare the cash flow forecast. In particular, there is no arrangement in place to sell the Happy Travels publishing range in January 20X6. The audit assistant proposes to issue an unmodified audit opinion but to include a Material Uncertainty Related to Going Concern section within the auditor's report to highlight the problems facing the company.

(c)   Discuss the appropriateness of the audit assistant's proposal for the auditor's report.   **(5 marks)**

Professional marks will be awarded for the demonstration of skill in analysis and evaluation, professional scepticism and judgement, and commercial acumen in your answer.   **(5 marks)**

(Total: 25 marks)

21   **WHEELER & CO** *Walk in the footsteps of a top tutor*

It is 1 July 20X5. You are an audit manager in Wheeler & Co, a firm of Chartered Certified Accountants. The audit fieldwork of one of your clients, Byres Co, for the year ended 31 March 20X5 is nearly complete. Byres Co is an unlisted, family-owned business which produces innovative cleaning equipment.

The following exhibits, available below, provide information relevant to the question:

1   Audit matters – Summary of the key issues the audit supervisor has flagged for your attention.

This information should be used to answer the question requirements within the response option provided.

Exhibit 1 – Audit matters

The draft financial statements recognise revenue of $55.5 million (20X4: $50 million), profit before tax for the year of $6.3 million (20X4: $5.4 million) and total assets of $31.6 million (20X4: $30.2 million).

New product

Byres Co has started development of a new smart vacuum cleaner which is operated by an application on a user's mobile phone. A working prototype of this product has been developed which generated significant interest at trade exhibitions. However, the current cost of production is $2,000 per unit after problems in product development caused the project costs to go over budget.

The audit team held discussions with the product design director, who informed them that he is sceptical as to whether there will be a sufficient market for this new product at a profitable selling price. The audit team has been provided with market research reports which suggest a maximum selling price of $1,000 is achievable. The owner and chief executive officer (CEO), William Byres, has assured the audit team that the total costs which have been incurred on the new product, totalling $250,000, meet the relevant recognition criteria and as such have been capitalised as an intangible asset in the financial statements. Commercial production of the new product has not yet commenced.

Warranty provision

Byres Co has an established standard warranty scheme in place for its retail customers where the company will refund retail customers for any reason within a 12-month period of the date of sale. This is a standard warranty, offered to all customers of Byres Co at no extra cost. Byres Co does not operate an extended warranty scheme. At any point in time, there is a significant amount of uncertainty in relation to the measurement of the warranty provision, but the finance director and finance department has previously estimated the provision at the year end based on a percentage of total sales. In previous years, the audit team has concluded that this has been a reasonable basis for the provision.

However, this year the CEO has also been involved in estimating the value of the year-end warranty provision. For the year ended 31 March 20X5, the warranty provision is $2.1 million, based on the CEO's estimate (20X4: $4.3 million). During discussions with the sales director, the audit team noted that neither the range of customers nor the nature of the warranties had changed significantly compared to the prior year. Discussions with the customer services manager have not indicated any unusual levels of complaints or faults with the products during the year which would justify a change in how the warranty provision should be estimated.

Required:

(a)   **Using the information in Exhibit 1, comment on the matters to be considered, and explain the audit evidence you should expect to find during your review of the audit working papers.** **(15 marks)**

  Note: The following mark allocation is provided as guidance for this question:

  (i)   New product (7 marks)

  (ii)   Warranty provision (8 marks)

It is now 1 September 20X5 and the auditor's report on Byres Co's financial statements for the year ended 31 March 20X5 is due to be issued in the next few days. The audit team has gathered sufficient and appropriate audit evidence in relation to the new product costs and appropriate adjustments have been made in respect of the associated research and development costs. However, management has indicated that they are not willing to make any further adjustments in relation to the warranty provision. Following further testing, the audit team has concluded that the warranty provision should have been determined using the same estimation method as in previous years, based on a percentage of sales.

(b)   **Discuss the implications for the auditor's report on the basis that no further adjustments have been made to the financial statements in relation to the warranty provision.** **(5 marks)**

Professional marks will be awarded for the demonstration of skill in analysis and evaluation and professional scepticism and judgement in your answer. **(5 marks)**

(Total: 25 marks)

22 SOL & CO *Walk in the footsteps of a top tutor*

It is 1 July 20X5. You are an audit manager in Sol & Co, a firm of Chartered Certified Accountants. You are currently working on two existing clients.

Arjan Co and Barnaby Co are both manufacturing companies with a financial year end of 31 March 20X5. Both audits are in the completion phase and you are in the process of reviewing the audit files.

The following exhibits, available below, provide information relevant to the question:

1   Arjan Co – selected results of the subsequent events and final analytical procedures which have been performed by the audit team.

2   Barnaby Co – details of an uncorrected misstatement which has been recorded during the audit.

This information should be used to answer the question requirements within the response option provided.

Exhibit 1 – Arjan Co

Arjan Co's draft financial statements show revenue of $120 million (20X4: $114 million), profit before tax of $11 million (20X4: $10.4 million) and total assets of $56 million (20X4: $74 million).

As part of your review of the audit file, you are considering the following results of the subsequent events procedures and final analytical procedures.

Subsequent events procedures

Newspaper reports in June 20X5 revealed that Cami Co, a significant customer of Arjan Co, entered liquidation and creditors are unlikely to receive more than 20% of amounts outstanding. The amount outstanding from Cami Co at 31 March 20X5 was $0.8 million. None of the amount outstanding has been received to date. No further work has been performed as a result of these procedures.

An extract of the final analytical procedures prepared by the audit assistant

---

(1) Inventory value

20X5: $4 million   **20X4:** $25 million

Auditor expectation

Inventory has fallen by 84% in the year.

This is in line with expectations as in November 20X4 management moved to a just-in-time (JIT) system for managing inventory.

Comment

The significant fall in inventory levels is consistent with a reduction in holding period.

Corroborating evidence

Auditor attendance at year-end inventory count, sample counts performed and count controls observed.

No inaccuracies were identified.

No further work over the completeness, accuracy and existence of inventory required.

Movement to JIT will reduce inventory holdings, so movement is in line with expectations. Per management lead times with suppliers average 20 days, hence inventory holding period is expected to be 20 days.

(2) Inventory holding period

20X5: 15 days   **20X4:** 94 days

Auditor expectation

Movement to JIT will reduce inventory holdings, so movement is in line with expectations. Per management lead times with suppliers average 20 days, hence inventory holding period is expected to be 20 days.

Comment

Inventory holding of 15 days appears to be shorter than expected. Management states that holdings are less than 20 days as customer orders are manufactured one week after an order is placed.

Corroborating evidence

A sample of customer contract terms was reviewed and confirmed that they state that orders are expected to be manufactured within five working days with fulfilment within 10 working days of order. This is consistent with the company's advertised terms and therefore supports the reduction in inventory holding period.

(3) Write down for obsolete inventory as % of inventory held

20X5: 10%   **20X4:** 5%

Auditor expectation

The move to a JIT system should eliminate obsolete inventory and the need for a write down, so the expectation would be that write downs would be lower or close to 0.

Comment

Management has advised that they do not currently have sufficient experience with the new system to ensure only required inventory has been ordered. As a result, they have taken a cautious approach to the write down.

Corroborating evidence

Total write down for obsolete inventory of $0.4 million in 20X5 is lower than the 20X4 amount of $1.25 million. This is less than 5% of profit before tax and therefore immaterial, so no further work performed.

(4) Receivables collection period

20X5: 53 days   **20X4:** 49 days

Auditor expectation

No changes in credit period have been enacted in the year, hence the collection period is expected to remain in line with prior years.

Comment

The increase in the receivables collection period relates to the slow payment of invoices by Cami Co, a major customer. The financial controller is confident that payment will be made.

Corroborating evidence

Outstanding invoice agreed to the list of individual customer balances and a sample of customer confirmations of the balance owed were obtained in writing.

(5) Allowance for irrecoverable receivables as % of total receivables

20X5: 3%   **20X4:** 5%

Auditor expectation

No changes have been made to controls over receivables during the year, so the allowance is expected to be in line with prior years.

Comment

The financial controller reviewed all trade receivables at the year end and concluded that fewer defaults were expected than in the prior year, hence the reduction in the allowance.

Corroborating evidence

Total fall in allowance of $0.5 million is below 5% of profit before tax and is therefore immaterial. No further work was performed.

Exhibit 2 – Barnaby Co

You are preparing for a discussion with the management of Barnaby Co about misstatements identified in the financial statements during the audit for the year ended 31 March 20X5. The audit working papers contain details of an uncorrected misstatement prepared by the audit team.

Machine sale

On 31 March 20X5, Barnaby Co sold a machine which was no longer in use. Under the terms of the sale agreement, the total sales price of the machine of $15 million would be paid on 31 March 20X6. The company has recognised the full sales value of $15 million when calculating profit on disposal for the asset and for the value of the receivable in the current year financial statements. The audit team has calculated that the net present value of the receivable at the reporting date of 31 March 20X5 is $13 million and therefore the profit on disposal and the receivable are overstated at the reporting date by $2 million. This is based on the company's cost of capital of 10% which has been calculated by the client. Sufficient and appropriate evidence has been obtained in relation to this calculation to conclude that 10% is an appropriate cost of capital. The schedule of uncorrected misstatements includes the following adjustment:

DR Statement of profit or loss $2 million

CR Statement of financial position $2 million

Barnaby Co's financial statements, prior to any adjustment for the items below, show profit before tax of $43 million (20X4: $45 million) and total assets of $105 million (20X4: $120 million).

Required:

(a)   Using the information in Exhibit 1:

    (i)   Evaluate the results of the subsequent events and final analytical procedures, commenting on any inconsistencies in relation to the audit evidence gathered.

    (ii)   Recommend the further actions to be taken which will enable the auditor to reach a conclusion on each matter.   (15 marks)

(b)   Using the information in Exhibit 2, recommend and explain the matters which should be discussed with management in relation to the uncorrected misstatement, including an assessment of the impact on the auditor's opinion if management does not make any changes.   (5 marks)

Professional marks will be awarded for the demonstration of skill in analysis and evaluation and professional scepticism and judgement in your answer.   (5 marks)

(Total: 25 marks)

23   MATTY   *Walk in the footsteps of a top tutor*

It is 1 July 20X5. You are a manager in Beth & Co, a firm of Chartered Certified Accountants, responsible for the audit of Matty Co for the year ended 31 March 20X5.

The following exhibits, available below, provide information relevant to the question:

1   Audit completion review – provides details of matters which have been brought to your attention by the audit supervisor.

2   Update and draft auditor's report – provides an update on the outcome of initial discussions with the client and details of the auditor's report which has now been drafted by the audit supervisor.

This information should be used to answer the question requirements within the response option provided.

Exhibit 1 – Audit completion review

Matty Co is a listed transport company which provides train and bus services for the public on a national basis. The audit of Matty Co for the year ended 31 March 20X5 is nearly complete and you are reviewing the audit working papers. Matty Co is a new audit client for Beth & Co this year. The previous auditors issued an unmodified opinion on the financial statements for the year ended 31 March 20X4.Matty Co's draft financial statements recognise revenue of $60.1 million (20X4 – $94.3 million), profit before tax of $10.5 million (20X4 – $22.1 million) and total assets of $28.4 million (20X4 – $31.1 million).

The audit supervisor has brought the following matters to your attention:

Railway operating licence and going concern

Matty Co has operated a national railway service for the last 19 years. Matty Co's national railway operations have been the subject of adverse publicity over the last 12 months in relation to the unreliability of its services including the late running of its trains. The licence to operate the national railway is put out to tender by the national government every five years. Matty Co's existing licence is due for renewal on 28 February 20X6.

The current tendering process is approaching completion and despite the recent operational problems, Matty Co was informed on 30 June 20X5 that the company was the government's preferred option. This was on the understanding that the company would address the recent criticisms of its poor service levels. The company was also informed that the tender would still be subject to a detailed review in one month's time prior to its being awarded. The national railway generated $40.2 million of revenue in 20X5 ($47.2 million in 20X4) and contributed pre-tax profit of $11.2 million this year ($13.3 million in 20X4).

Purchased customer list

On 1 April 20X4, Matty Co paid $6.9 million to acquire the customer list of Jess Coaches, a business which was terminating its operations. Jess Coaches hires out coaches and drivers to private and public sector customers. Its customer list includes many highly reputable listed companies and government bodies with a customer relationship and trading history going back more than 30 years.

On the basis of this trading history and the associated customer loyalty, the management of Matty Co assessed the useful life of the customer list as indefinite. The draft statement of financial position as at 31 March 20X5 recognises the customer list as an intangible asset at a total carrying amount of $6.9 million.

In the second half of the reporting period, however, two of Jess Coaches' largest clients moved to a new competitor. The management of Matty Co believe that while it would be difficult to identify a sales value for the customer list at the reporting date, they estimate the value in use of the customer list to be $7.2 million.

Exhibit 2 – Update and draft auditor's report

It is now 22 July 20X5 and all matters in relation to the purchased customer list have now been satisfactorily resolved.

Following the submission of a customer petition to the government complaining about the company's poor service levels, on 19 July 20X5 the government released a statement announcing that it had withdrawn Matty Co's preferred bidder status and was reopening the tender process for the national railway licence.

The company's finance director has provided details of a short disclosure note he plans to include in the financial statements which refers to the uncertainties in relation to the current status of the tender and possible going concern issues which might arise for the company as a result. The disclosure note concludes with a statement that the management of Matty Co is very confident that the company will be successful in the tender process and that it will retain the national railway licence for at least a further five years.

The draft auditor's report includes an unmodified audit opinion and a key audit matters section which refers to the disclosure note described above and to related uncertainties in relation to Matty Co's going concern status.

Required:

(a) Using the information in Exhibit 1, comment on the matters to be considered and explain the audit evidence you would expect to find during your review of the audit working papers on 1 July 20X5, in relation to the issues identified.

Note: The following mark allocation is provided as guidance for this question:

(i) Railway operating licence and going concern (7 marks)

(ii) Purchased customer list (8 marks)   (15 marks)

(b) With reference to Exhibit 2, and assuming that no further adjustments will be made to the financial statements in relation to the railway operating licence, evaluate the appropriateness of the draft auditor's report produced by the audit supervisor.
(5 marks)

Professional marks will be awarded for the demonstration of skill in analysis and evaluation and professional scepticism and judgement in your answer.   (5 marks)

(Total: 25 marks)

24   GOODMAN GROUP *Walk in the footsteps of a top tutor*

It is 1 July 20X5. You work in the audit department of Saul & Co. The Goodman Group (the Group) is an audit client of your firm and the audit for the financial year ended 31 December 20X4 is in the completion stage. The Group, which is not listed, installs and maintains security systems for businesses and residential customers.

Materiality for the audit of the Group financial statements has been determined to be $400,000.

The following exhibits, available below, provide information relevant to the question:

1   Completion matters – details regarding issues you have discovered during your review of the audit working papers.

2   Draft auditor's report and supplementary information.

This information should be used to answer the question requirements within the response option provided.

Exhibit 1 – Completion matters

Fraud

The Group finance director has informed the audit team that during the year, a fraud was carried out by a manager, Mike Trout, in one of the Group's procurement departments. The manager had raised fictitious supplier invoices and paid the invoiced amounts into his personal bank account. When questioned by the Group's finance director, Mike Trout confessed that he had stolen $40,000 from the Group. The finance director asked the audit team not to perform any procedures in relation to the fraud, as the amount is immaterial. He also stated that the financial statements would not be adjusted in relation to the fraud.

The only audit evidence on file is a written representation from management acknowledging the existence of the fraud, and a list of the fictitious invoices which had been raised by the manager, provided by the finance director.

The audit working papers conclude that the fraud is immaterial and no further work is needed.

Development costs

In August 20X4, the Group commenced development of a new security system, and incurred expenditure of $600,000 up to the financial year end, which has been capitalised as an intangible non-current asset. The only audit evidence obtained in relation to this balance is as follows:

–   Agreement of a sample of the costs included in the $600,000 capitalised to supporting documentation such as supplier invoices.

–   Cash flow projection for the project, which indicates that a positive cash flow will be generated by 20X8. The projection has been arithmetically checked.

–   A written representation from management stating that 'management considers that the development of this new product will be successful'.

You are aware that when the Group finance director was asked about the cash flow projection which he had prepared, he was reluctant to answer questions, simply saying that 'the assumptions underlying the projection have been agreed to assumptions contained in the Group's business plan'.

He provided a spreadsheet showing the projection but the underlying information could not be accessed as the file was password protected and the Group finance director would not provide the password to the audit team.

Trade receivables

Trade receivables recognised in the Group's current assets includes a balance of $500,000 relating to a specific customer, Hamlyn Co. As at 31 December 20X4, the balance was more than six months overdue for payment. The Group credit controller states that they are confident that the debt will be recovered in full, however as of 1 July 20X5, the debt had not been paid.

Exhibit 2 – Draft auditor's report and supplementary information

The audit work is now complete and the Group auditor's report is due to be issued in the next few days. Materiality for the audit of the Group financial statements has continued to be determined to be $400,000. You have been tasked with reviewing the draft auditor's report and the following supplementary information which has been prepared at the end of the audit:

–   The audit partner has concluded that the fraud is immaterial and that all necessary work has been performed by the audit team.

–   Further audit procedures were successfully performed on the development costs, and a conclusion was reached by the audit team that the recognition of the $600,000 as an intangible asset is appropriate.

–   A letter was received from Hamlyn Co's administrators on 29 July 20X5, stating that Hamlyn Co is in liquidation, and that its creditors will receive a payment of 10% of outstanding balances. The audit team has concluded that $50,000 can remain recognised as a trade receivable, and that $450,000 should be written off as irrecoverable. However, the Group refuses to make any adjustment, and the full $500,000 remains recognised as a trade receivable in the final Group financial statements.

Draft auditor's report

Based on the above conclusions, the audit supervisor has drafted the auditor's report which includes the following extract:

Basis for opinion and opinion

Audit procedures indicate that trade receivables are overstated by $500,000. For this reason, we consider that the Group financial statements are likely to be materially misstated and do not fairly present the financial position and performance of the Group for the year ended 31 December 20X4.

Emphasis of matter

There are two matters to which we draw your attention:

1   A fraud was discovered, as a result of which we have determined that $40,000 was stolen from the Group. This does not impact the financial statements but we wish to highlight the illegal activity which took place during the year.

2   The Group finance director obstructed our audit by refusing to allow access to audit evidence. He has also refused to adjust the financial statements in relation to the material misstatement of trade receivables, which led to the qualified audit opinion being issued. For this reason, we wish to resign as auditor with immediate effect.

Required:

(a) Using the information contained in Exhibit 1:

    (i) Discuss the implications of the fraud for the completion of the audit, and the actions to be taken by the auditor. **(6 marks)**

    (ii) In respect of the development costs ONLY:

        – Comment on the sufficiency and appropriateness of the audit evidence obtained, and

        – Recommend the actions to be taken by the auditor, including the further evidence which should be obtained. **(6 marks)**

(b) Using the information contained in Exhibit 2, critically appraise the extract from the proposed auditor's report of the Goodman Group for the year ended 31 December 20X4.

    Note: You are NOT required to re-draft the extracts from the auditor's report.

    (8 marks)

Professional marks will be awarded for the demonstration of skill in analysis and evaluation, professional scepticism and judgement and commercial acumen in your answer. **(5 marks)**

(Total: 25 marks)

25 LIFESON *Walk in the footsteps of a top tutor*

It is 1 July 20X5. You are a manager in the audit department of Peart & Co, a firm of Chartered Certified Accountants, responsible for the audit of Lifeson Co for the year ended 31 March 20X5. Lifeson Co is an unlisted retail company which is a new audit client of your firm this year. The company's draft financial statements recognise profit before tax of $2.15 million (20X4 – $1.95 million) and total assets of $13.8 million (20X4 – $12.7million).

The following exhibits, available below, provide information relevant to the question:

1   Completion matters – details regarding issues you have discovered during your review of the audit working papers.

2   Update on completion matters – provides an update on the outcome of initial discussions with the client.

This information should be used to answer the question requirements within the response option provided.

Exhibit 1 – Completion matters

The audit is nearly complete and you are reviewing the audit working papers. The audit supervisor has brought the following matters to your attention:

(i) Sale and leaseback transaction

On 31 March 20X5, Lifeson Co sold a property to a leasing company, Clive Co, for its fair value at this date. The property is situated in a sought after area with a high demand for rental properties for retail purposes. Clive Co has assessed the remaining life of the property to be in excess of 50 years, and under the terms of the sales agreement, Lifeson Co will lease the property back from Clive Co for a period of ten years.

Lifeson Co has treated the transaction as a sale and leaseback transaction in accordance with IFRS 16 *Leases*, and derecognised the property in its financial statements and recorded a sale in accordance with IFRS 15 *Revenue from Contracts with Customers*.

(ii)   Shopping mall

Lifeson Co purchased a shopping mall on 1 April 20X3 for $9.5 million. At the date of purchase, the mall was estimated to have a remaining useful life of 20 years and a nil residual value. On 31 March 20X4 following an impairment review, the property was written down to its recoverable amount based on value in use of $8.25 million and an impairment loss of $775,000 was recognised in the statement of profit or loss for the year ended 31 March 20X4.

Lifeson Co conducted a further impairment review as at 31 March 20X5 which indicated that the property's recoverable amount, based on value in use, was now $8.85 million. As a result, Lifeson Co has recognised an impairment reversal of $1.034 million in its profit before tax for the current year. The impairment reversal of $1.034 million has been calculated as its new recoverable amount of $8.85 million less its carrying amount of $7.816 million. The audit supervisor has prepared the following working paper which summarises the accounting transactions in relation to the shopping mall:

Summary of transactions

Date		$ million	Accounting treatment by management
1 April 20X3	Cost of asset	9.500	
	Depreciation (9.5m/20 years)	(0.475)	Depreciation charge for the year to 31 March 20X4
	Impairment	(0.775)	Impairment loss charged to profit for the year to 31 March 20X4
31 March 20X4	Carrying amount	8.250	
	Depreciation (8.25m/19 years)	(0.434)	Depreciation charge for the year to 31 March 20X5
		7.816	Carrying amount prior to impairment review
	Reversal of impairment	1.034	Reversal of impairment credited to profit for the year to 31 March 20X5
31 March 20X5	Carrying amount	8.850	

Exhibit 2 – Update on completion matters following discussions with management

It is now 1 September 20X5 and the auditor's report on Lifeson Co's financial statements for the year ended 31 March 20X5 is due to be issued in the next few days.

Following discussions with management, you are satisfied that the sale and leaseback transaction has been treated correctly and that you have gathered sufficient and appropriate audit evidence to support this treatment.

However, management has indicated that they are not willing to make any further adjustments to the financial statements in relation to the shopping mall and you are now considering the form and content of the auditor's report in relation to these matters.

Required:

(a)   **Using the information contained in Exhibit 1, comment on the matters to be considered and explain the audit evidence you would expect to find during your review of the audit working papers in respect of the issues described.**

   Note: The following mark allocation is provided as guidance for this question:

   (i)   **(10 marks)**

   (ii)   **(6 marks)**   **(16 marks)**

(b)   **Using the information contained in Exhibit 2, discuss the implications for the auditor's report on the basis that no further adjustments have been made to the financial statements in relation to the shopping mall.**   **(4 marks)**

Professional marks will be awarded for the demonstration of skill in analysis and evaluation and professional scepticism and judgement in your answer.   **(5 marks)**

                                                                                          (Total: 25 marks)

26   KILMISTER   *Walk in the footsteps of a top tutor*

It is 1 July 20X5. You are a manager in the audit department of Eddie & Co, a firm of Chartered Certified Accountants, responsible for the audit of several listed clients.

The following exhibits, available below, provide information relevant to the question:

1   Kilmister Co – Draft auditor's report.

2   Taylor Co completion matters – details regarding issues you have discovered during your review of the audit working papers.

This information should be used to answer the question requirements within the response option provided.

Exhibit 1 – Kilmister Co draft auditor's report

You are currently reviewing the draft auditor's report of Kilmister Co, a listed company specialising in the manufacture and installation of sound-proof partitions for domestic and industrial buildings for the year ended 31 March 20X5. Extracts from the draft auditor's report are shown below:

Independent auditor's report to the shareholders and directors of Kilmister Co

Basis for opinion

We conducted our audit of Kilmister Co (the Company) in accordance with International Standards on Auditing (ISAs). Our responsibilities under those standards are further described in the auditor's responsibilities for the audit of the financial statements section of our report. We are independent of the Company in accordance with the ethical requirements which are relevant to our audit of the financial statements in the jurisdiction in which the Company operates, and we have fulfilled our other ethical responsibilities in accordance with these requirements.

We believe that the audit evidence we have obtained is sufficient and appropriate to provide a basis for our opinion.

Opinion

We have audited the financial statements of Kilmister Co (the Company), which comprise the statement of financial position as at 31 March 20X5, and the statement of comprehensive income, statement of changes in equity and statement of cash flows for the year then ended, and notes to the financial statements, including a summary of significant accounting policies. In our opinion, the accompanying financial statements present fairly, in all material respects, the financial position of the Company as at 31 March 20X5, and of its financial performance and its cash flows for the year then ended in accordance with IFRS Accounting Standards.

Material uncertainty regarding going concern

The Company is financed by a long-term loan from its bankers which is due for redemption in August 20X5. At the date of this auditor's report, the Company is in the process of renegotiating the loan but has not yet reached a final agreement with its bankers. It is our view that the loan finance is essential to the continued survival of the Company and that at the time of reporting, therefore, the absence of a finalised agreement represents a material uncertainty regarding going concern. The financial statements have been prepared on a going concern basis but do not make any reference to the loan redemption or the ongoing negotiations with the bank. As the external auditor therefore, we are fulfilling our duty by bringing the matter to the attention of users of the financial statements.

Other information

The Company's principal activity is the manufacture and installation of sound-proof partitions for domestic and industrial buildings. The Company therefore engages in long-term contracts which are incomplete at the reporting date and which are material to its revenue figure. The installation process is complex and significant judgement is applied in assessing the percentage of completeness which is applied to calculate the revenue for the year. The significance of this judgement requires us to disclose the issue as other information which is relevant to the users of the financial statements.

Exhibit 2 – Taylor Co completion matters

Your firm, has asked you to perform an independent review of the working papers of Taylor Co which is a listed entity and has been an audit client of your firm for the last ten years. The audit fieldwork is almost complete and as part of your review, you have been asked to advise the audit team on the drafting of their report to those charged with governance. Taylor Co is a discount food retailer which operates 85 stores nationally. The financial statements for the year ended 30 April 20X5 recognise revenue of $247 million (20X4 – $242 million), profit before tax of $14.6 million (20X4 – $14.1 million) and total assets of $535 million (20X4 – $321 million).

After a period of rapid expansion, 20X5 has been a year in which Taylor Co has strengthened its existing position within the market and has not acquired any additional stores or businesses. The company's draft statement of financial position for 20X5 includes a property portfolio of $315 million all of which are legally owned by the entity. In the current year, the company has chosen to adopt a policy of revaluing its property portfolio for the first time and this is reflected in the draft figures for 20X5. The audit work on property, plant and equipment included testing a sample of the revaluations. Eddie & Co requested at the planning stage that independent, external valuation reports should be made available to the audit team at the start of the final audit visit. A number of these documents were not available when requested and it took three weeks for them to be received by the audit team.

The audit working papers also identify that on review of the non-current asset register, there were four properties with a total carrying amount of $11.1 million which had not yet been revalued and were still recorded at depreciated historic cost.

The audit supervisor's review of Taylor Co's board minutes identified that the company has renovated car parking facilities at 17 of its stores which has resulted in a significant increase in customer numbers and revenue at each of these locations. The total cost of the renovation work was $13.2 million and has been included in operating expenses for the current year. The audit file includes a working paper recording discussions with management which confirms that asset expenditure authorisation forms had not been completed for this expenditure.

Required:

(a)   **Using the information contained in Exhibit 1, critically appraise the extract from the draft auditor's report of Kilmister Co for the year ended 31 March 20X5.**

   Note: You are NOT required to re-draft the extracts from the auditor's report.
                                                                        (10 marks)

(b)   **Using the information contained in Exhibit 2, recommend the matters which should be included in Eddie & Co's report to those charged with governance of Taylor Co, and explain the reason for their inclusion.**   **(10 marks)**

Professional marks will be awarded for the demonstration of skill in analysis and evaluation, professional scepticism and judgement and commercial acumen in your answer.   **(5 marks)**

                                                                    (Total: 25 marks)

27   DALEY   *Walk in the footsteps of a top tutor*

It is 1 July 20X5. Daley Co has been a client of your firm for the last three years and you are the newly appointed audit manager on the audit for the year ended 31 March 20X5. Daley Co is a family owned, unlisted company which imports motor cars. The company buys cars from a variety of car manufacturers for sale to car dealerships and vehicle leasing companies within its own domestic market. The audit for the current reporting period is nearing completion and you are reviewing the working papers of the going concern section of the audit file.

The following exhibits, available below, provide information relevant to the question:

1   Extracts from the draft financial statements.

2   Supplementary information.

3   Notes of discussion with Daley Co's directors.

This information should be used to answer the question requirements within your chosen response option(s).

Exhibit 1 – Extracts from the draft financial statements

Statement of financial position	31 March 20X5 Draft $million	31 March 20X4 Actual $million
Assets		
Non-current assets		
Property, plant and equipment	13.5	14.6
	13.5	14.6
Current assets		
Inventory	5.8	3.7
Trade receivables	3.7	2.6
Cash at bank and in hand	–	0.6
	9.5	6.9
Total assets	23.0	21.5
Equity and liabilities		
Equity		
Share capital	1.0	1.0
Retained earnings	1.3	4.7
	2.3	5.7
Non-current liabilities		
Long-term borrowings	11.2	12.4
Provisions	3.5	0.5
	14.7	12.9
Current liabilities		
Trade payables	4.2	2.9
Bank overdraft	1.8	–
	6.0	2.9
Total equity and liabilities	23.0	21.5

Statement of profit or loss for the year	31 March 20X5 Draft $million	31 March 20X4 Actual $million
Revenue	11.3	8.8
Cost of sales	(4.4)	(2.9)
Gross profit	6.9	5.9
Other operating expenses	(9.1)	(1.3)
Operating profit	(2.2)	4.6
Finance costs	(1.5)	(0.7)
Profit before tax	(3.7)	3.9
Taxation	0.3	(1.3)
Net (loss)/profit for year	(3.4)	2.6

Exhibit 2 – Supplementary information

1   Daley Co has undergone a period of rapid expansion in recent years and is intending to buy new warehousing facilities in August 20X5 at a cost of $4.3 million.

2   In order to finance the new warehousing facilities, the company is in the process of negotiating new finance from its bankers. The loan application is for an amount of $5 million and is to be repaid over a period of four years.

3   The provision of $3.5 million in this year's statement of financial position relates to legal actions from five of Daley Co's largest customers. The actions relate to the claim that the company has sold cars which did not comply with domestic regulations.

4   The going concern working papers include a cash flow forecast for the 12 months ending 31 March 20X6. The cash flow forecast assumes that Daley Co's revenue will increase by 25% next year and that following the reorganisation of its credit control facility, its customers will pay on average after 60 days. The forecast also assumes that the bank will provide the new finance in August 20X5 and that the company will have a positive cash balance of $1.7 million by 31 March 20X6.

5   The financial statements have been prepared on a going concern basis and make no reference to any significant uncertainties in relation to going concern.

Exhibit 3 – Notes of discussion with Daley Co's directors

You have established through discussions with Daley Co's directors that they do not wish to disclose uncertainties over the going concern status of the company in the notes to the financial statements.

Required:

Using the information contained in Exhibits 1 and 2:

(a)   **Evaluate the matters which may cast doubt on Daley Co's ability to continue as a going concern. You should use analytical review where appropriate to help with your evaluation.**   **(8 marks)**

(b)   **Explain the audit evidence in respect of the cash flow forecast which you would expect to find during your review of the audit working papers on going concern.**
                                                                                            (7 marks)

Using the information contained in Exhibit 3:

(c)   Explain the possible reasons why the directors may wish to exclude these disclosures and evaluate the possible implications for the auditor's report.   (5 marks)

Professional marks will be awarded for the demonstration of skill in analysis and evaluation, professional scepticism and judgement and commercial acumen in your answer.   (5 marks)

(Total: 25 marks)

28   CORAM & CO *Walk in the footsteps of a top tutor*

It is 1 July 20X5. You are an audit manager in Coram & Co, a firm of Chartered Certified Accountants, responsible for the audit of several clients.

The following exhibits, available below, provide information relevant to the question:

1   Clark Co – completion matters to be discussed with the finance director.

2   Turner Co – points raised for your attention by the audit supervisor.

This information should be used to answer the question requirements within the response option provided.

Exhibit 1 – Clark Co

The audit of one of your clients, Clark Co, for the year ended 31 March 20X5 is nearly complete and the auditor's report is due to be issued next week. Clark Co is an unlisted, family owned business which specialises in the service and repair of both commercial and privately owned motor vehicles. The company operates from seven geographically distinct sites, each of which is considered a separate cash generating unit for impairment review purposes. The draft financial statements recognise profit before tax for the year of $2.3 million and total assets of $22 million.

The schedule of uncorrected misstatements included in Clark Co's audit working papers and prepared by the audit supervisor is shown below. You are due to attend a meeting with the finance director of Clark Co tomorrow, at which the uncorrected misstatements will be discussed.

	Statement of financial position	
	Debit	Credit
Schedule of uncorrected misstatements:	$	$
(i) Lease of testing equipment		
– lease assets	475,000	
– lease liabilities		475,000
(ii) Legal claim		
– contingent assets	1,200,000	
– provision for liabilities		1,200,000
Totals	1,675,000	1,675,000

(i) **Lease of testing equipment**

In the jurisdiction in which Clark Co operates, all motor vehicles over three years old are required to undergo an annual test of vehicle safety and roadworthiness. The annual test requires specialist testing equipment which is inspected by government officials on a regular basis. Following inspection visits in March 20X5, the government inspection report required Clark Co to replace the testing equipment at three of its sites. In order to comply with this requirement, Clark Co has agreed to lease new testing equipment from a leasing company on six-month leases. Under the terms of the leases, the company has no option to purchase the equipment.

The testing equipment was made available for use by Clark Co at each of the three sites on 31 March 20X5. The client has capitalised leases with a total carrying amount of $625,000 at two of the sites but has elected to take advantage of the IFRS 16 *Leases* exemption not to capitalise short-term leases at the largest of the three sites. As a result, the present value of the lease payments of $475,000 relating to this site has not been recognised on the company's statement of financial position.

(ii) **Legal claim**

A customer of Clark Co successfully sued the company for negligence in February 20X5 after suffering a personal injury at one of its sites. The court awarded the customer $1.2 million in damages and this had not yet been paid as at 31 March 20X5. The audit working papers include a copy of a verified letter dated 25 March 20X5 from an insurance company confirming that the claim is fully covered under Clark Co's public liability insurance policy. On the basis that the company has no net liability as a result of the claim, the finance director has not recognised any amounts in the financial statements and has not made any disclosures in relation to the matter.

Exhibit 2 – Turner Co

Turner Co is a listed financial institution offering loans and credit facilities to both commercial and retail customers. You have received an email from the audit supervisor who is currently supervising interim testing on systems and controls in relation to the audit for the year ending 31 August 20X5. The email gives the following details for your consideration:

One of the audit team members, Janette Stott, has provisionally agreed to take out a loan with Turner Co to finance the purchase of a domestic residence. The loan will be secured on the property and the client's business manager has promised Janette that he will ensure that she gets 'the very best deal which the bank can offer.'

The payroll manager at Turner Co has asked the audit supervisor if it would be possible for Coram & Co to provide a member of staff on secondment to work in the payroll department. The payroll manager has struggled to recruit a new supervisor for the organisation's main payroll system and wants to assign a qualified member of the audit firm's staff for an initial period of six months.

Required:

(a) **Using the information contained in Exhibit 1, recommend and explain the matters which should be discussed with management in relation to each of the proposed adjustments, including an assessment of their individual impact on the financial statements and on the auditor's opinion if management does not make the proposed adjustments.**

Note: The following mark allocation is provided as guidance for this question:

(i)   (7 marks)

(ii)   (5 marks)   (12 marks)

(b)   Using the information contained in Exhibit 2, comment on the ethical and professional issues raised in respect of the audit of Turner Co and recommend any actions to be taken by the audit firm.   (8 marks)

Professional marks will be awarded for the demonstration of skill in analysis and evaluation, professional scepticism and judgement and commercial acumen in your answer.   (5 marks)

(Total: 25 marks)

29   BREARLEY & CO   *Walk in the footsteps of a top tutor*

 Answer debrief

It is 1 July 20X5. You are an audit manager in Brearley & Co, responsible for the audits of Hughes Group and Blackmore Group.

The following exhibits, available below, provide information relevant to the question:

1   Hughes Group – completion matters brought to your attention by the audit senior.

2   Blackmore Group – draft auditor's report extracts prepared by the audit senior.

This information should be used to answer the question requirements within the response option provided.

Exhibit 1 – Hughes Group

You are responsible for the audit of the Hughes Group (the Group). You are reviewing the audit working papers for the consolidated financial statements relating to the year ended 31 March 20X5. The Group specialises in the wholesale supply of steel plate and sheet metals. The draft consolidated financial statements recognise revenue of $7,670 million (20X4 – $7,235 million), profit before tax of $55 million (20X4 – $80 million) and total assets of $1,560 million (20X4 – $1,275 million). Brearley & Co audits all of the individual company financial statements as well as the Group consolidated financial statements.

The audit senior has brought the following matters, regarding a number of the Group's companies, to your attention:

(i)   **Dilley Co**

The Group purchased 40% of the share capital and voting rights in Dilley Co on 1 May 20X4. Dilley Co is listed on an alternative stock exchange. The Group has also acquired options to purchase the remaining 60% of the issued shares at a 10% discount on the market value of the shares at the time of exercise. The options are exercisable for 18 months from 1 May 20X5. Dilley Co's draft financial statements for the year ended 31 March 20X5 recognise revenue of $90 million and a loss before tax of $12 million. The Group's finance director has equity accounted for Dilley Co as an associate in this year's group accounts and has included a loss before tax of $4.4 million in the consolidated statement of profit or loss.

(ii)   **Willis Co**

Willis Co is a foreign subsidiary whose functional and presentational currency is the same as Hughes Co and the remainder of the Group. The subsidiary specialises in the production of stainless steel and holds a significant portfolio of forward commodity options to hedge against fluctuations in raw material prices. The local jurisdiction does not mandate the use of IFRS Accounting Standards and the audit senior has noted that Willis Co follows local GAAP, whereby derivatives are disclosed in the notes to the financial statements but are not recognised as assets or liabilities in the statement of financial position. The disclosure note includes details of the maturity and exercise terms of the options and a directors' valuation stating that they have a total fair value of $6.1 million as at 31 March 20X5. The disclosure note states that all of the derivative contracts were entered into in the last three months of the reporting period and that they required no initial net investment.

Exhibit 2 – Blackmore Group

You are also responsible for the audit of the Blackmore Group (the Group), a listed manufacturer of high quality musical instruments, for the year ended 31 March 20X5. The draft financial statements of the Group recognise a loss before tax of $2.2 million (20X4 – loss of $1.5 million) and total assets of $14.1 million (20X4 – $18.3 million). The audit is nearing completion and the audit senior has drafted the auditor's report which contains the following extract:

Key audit matters

1   Valuation of financial instruments

The Group enters into structured forward contracts to purchase materials used in its manufacturing process. The valuation of these unquoted instruments involves guesswork and is based on internal models developed by the Group's finance director, Thomas Bolin. Mr Bolin joined the Group in January 20X5 and there is significant measurement uncertainty involved in his valuations as a result of his inexperience. As a result, the valuation of these contracts was significant to our audit.

2   Customer liquidation

Included in receivables shown on the consolidated statement of financial position is an amount of $287,253 from a customer which has ceased trading. On the basis that the Group has no security for this debt, we believe that the Group should make a full provision for impairment of $287,253 thereby reducing profit before tax for the year and total assets as at 31 March 20X5 by that amount.

Qualified opinion arising from disagreement about accounting treatment

In our opinion, except for the effect on the financial statements of the matter described above, the financial statements have been properly prepared in all material respects in accordance with IFRS Accounting Standards.

Required:

(a)   **Using the information contained in Exhibit 1, comment on the matters to be considered and explain the audit evidence you should expect to find during your review of the Hughes Group audit working papers in respect of each of the issues described.**

   Note: The following mark allocation is provided as guidance for this question:

   (i)   **(6 marks)**

   (ii)   **(5 marks)**   **(11 marks)**

(b)   Using the information contained in Exhibit 2, critically appraise the extract from the auditor's report on the consolidated financial statements of the Blackmore Group for the year ended 31 March 20X5.

Note: You are NOT required to re-draft the extract from the auditor's report.

(9 marks)

Professional marks will be awarded for the demonstration of skill in analysis and evaluation and professional scepticism and judgement in your answer.   (5 marks)

(Total: 25 marks)

 Calculate your allowed time, allocate the time to the separate parts...............

30   BASKING *Walk in the footsteps of a top tutor*

It is 1 July 20X5. You are responsible for the audit of Basking Co, a large, listed package delivery company. The audit of the financial statements for the year ended 31 March 20X5 is nearly complete and you are reviewing the audit working papers. The financial statements recognise revenue of $56,360 million (20X4 – $56,245 million), profit for the year of $2,550 million (20X4 – $2,630 million) and total assets of $37,546 million (20X4 – $38,765 million).

The following exhibits, available below, provide information relevant to the question:

1   Audit completion review – provides uncorrected misstatements to be discussed with the management team of Basking Co.

2   New computer system – details of Basking Co's new computer system and results of audit testing.

3   Audit reform proposals – details of proposals to improve quality and restore public confidence in the audit profession.

This information should be used to answer the question requirements within the response option provided.

Exhibit 1 – Audit completion review

The uncorrected misstatements identified during the audit of Basking Co are described below. The audit engagement partner is holding a meeting with the management team of Basking Co next week, at which the uncorrected misstatements will be discussed.

1   In September 20X4, the board of Basking Co approved a loan to, Mrs C Angel, who is a key member of the senior management team of the company. The total amount of the loan was $75,000. Following a review of the board minutes, it was discovered that the directors agreed that the amount was clearly trivial and have, therefore, not disclosed the loan in the notes to the financial statements.

2   During the year Basking Co reduced the value of their provision for customer refunds which is recognised in the financial statements. For the past five years the value of the provision has been calculated based on 7% of one month's sales, using an average monthly sales value. Management argued that due to improved internal processing systems, such a high rate of provision was no longer necessary and reduced it to 4%. Audit procedures found that refund levels were similar to previous years and there was insufficient evidence at this early stage to confirm whether the new system was more effective or not.

Exhibit 2 – New computer system

At the start of the year Basking Co replaced its computer system with an integrated system. The new system allows for real time tracking of packages once received by Basking Co from their customer. As soon as a package is delivered to its final destination the finance system is automatically updated for the revenue and an invoice generated. The audit team have extensively tested the new system and found no deficiencies in relation to the recording of revenue.

Exhibit 3 – Audit reform proposals

Audit reform on a global basis is an ongoing topic of discussion following multiple audit failures where public interest entities (PIEs) have discovered major fraud, gone bankrupt or needed government support despite the auditor having issued an unmodified opinion. Audit regulators around the world are considering significant reforms to improve audit quality and restore public confidence in the audit process.

Required:

(a)   Using the information contained in Exhibit 1, for each of the two issues described:

     (i)   Explain the matters which should be discussed with management in relation to each of the uncorrected misstatements.

     (ii)   Assuming that management does not adjust the misstatements identified, evaluate the effect of each on the audit opinion.

     Note: The following mark allocation is provided as guidance for this question:

     (1)   (4 marks)

     (2)   (5 marks)   (9 marks)

(b)   Using the information contained in Exhibit 2, describe the impact of the issue, if any, on the auditor's report in accordance with ISA 701 *Communicating Key Audit Matters in the Independent Auditor's Report*.   (5 marks)

(c)   Using Exhibit 3, discuss the main audit reform proposals being suggested by regulators to improve confidence in audits.   (6 marks)

Professional marks will be awarded for the demonstration of skill in analysis and evaluation, professional scepticism and judgement and commercial acumen in your answer.   (5 marks)

(Total: 25 marks)

31   MAGNOLIA GROUP *Walk in the footsteps of a top tutor*

It is 1 July 20X5. You are responsible for performing engagement quality reviews on selected audit clients of Crocus & Co, and you are currently performing a review on the audit of the Magnolia Group (the Group). The Group manufactures chemicals which are used in a range of industries, with one of the subsidiaries, Daisy Co, specialising in chemical engineering and developing products to be sold by the other Group companies. The Group's products sell in over 50 countries.

A group structure is shown below, each of the subsidiaries is wholly owned by Magnolia Co, the parent company of the Group:

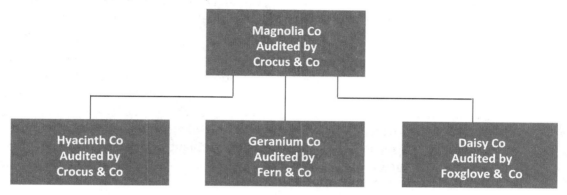

Crocus & Co is engaged to provide the audit of the Group financial statements and also the audit of Hyacinth Co and Magnolia Co. Geranium Co, a new subsidiary, is audited by a local firm of auditors based near the company's head office. Daisy Co is audited by an unconnected audit firm which specialises in the audit of companies involved with chemical engineering.

The Group's financial year ended on 31 March 20X5 and the audit is in the completion stage, with the auditor's report due to be issued in three weeks' time. The Group's draft consolidated financial statements recognise profit before tax of $7.5 million and total assets of $130 million.

The following exhibits, available below, provide information relevant to the question:

1   Notes from review of audit working papers – summary of issues identified in the audits of the three subsidiaries.

2   Daisy Co update – provides an update of the work performed to assess the going concern status of Daisy Co and intentions of the directors with regard to disclosures.

This information should be used to answer the question requirements within the response option provided.

Exhibit 1 – Notes from review of audit working papers

The notes from your review of the audit working papers are shown below, summarising the issues relevant to each subsidiary.

(i)   Hyacinth Co – internal controls and results of controls testing

The Group companies supply each other with various chemical products to be used in the manufacture of chemicals. Audit work performed at the interim stage at Hyacinth Co, including walk through procedures and internal control evaluations, concluded that internal controls over intra-group transactions were not effective, and this was documented in the audit file. At the final audit, tests of controls were performed to confirm this to be the case. The tests of controls confirmed that intra-group transactions are not being separately identified in the Group's accounting system and reconciliations of amounts owed between the subsidiaries are not performed.

The group audit manager has concluded on the audit working papers that 'as intra-group balances are cancelled on consolidation, this issue has no impact on the Group audit and no further work is necessary'. As part of the audit approach it was determined that extensive testing would be performed over the internal controls for capital (asset) expenditure at Hyacinth Co as it was identified during planning that the company had made significant acquisitions of plant and equipment during the year. Following controls testing the internal controls over asset expenditure were evaluated to be effective in Hyacinth Co.

The working papers conclude that 'based on the results of controls testing at Hyacinth Co, it is reasonable to assume that controls are effective across the Group' and substantive procedures on property, plant and equipment in each Group company have been planned and performed in response to this assessment.

(ii)   Geranium Co – new subsidiary

This subsidiary was acquired on 31 December 20X4 and is audited by Fern & Co. The Group audit strategy contains the following statement in relation to the audit of Geranium Co: 'Geranium Co will only be consolidated for three months and the post-acquisition profit for that period to be included in the Group financial statements is $150,000. On that basis, Geranium Co is immaterial to the Group financial statements and therefore our audit procedures are based on analytical procedures only.'

Other than the analytical procedures performed, there is no documentation in respect of Geranium Co or its audit firm Fern & Co included in the Group audit working papers.

The draft statement of financial position of Geranium Co recognises total assets of $30 million.

(iii)   Daisy Co – restriction on international trade

As well as being involved in chemical engineering and supplying chemicals for use by the other Group companies, Daisy Co specialises in producing chemicals which are used in the agricultural sector, and around half of its sales are made internationally.

Daisy Co is audited by Foxglove & Co, and the Group audit working papers contain the necessary evaluations to conclude that an appropriate level of understanding has been obtained in respect of the audit firm.

Foxglove & Co has provided your firm with a summary of key audit findings which includes the following statement: 'During the year new government environmental regulations have imposed restrictions on international trade in chemicals, with sales to many countries now prohibited.

Our audit work concludes that this does not create a significant going concern risk to Daisy Co, and we have confirmed that all inventories are measured at the lower of cost and net realisable value.'

The Group audit manager has concluded that 'I am happy that no further work is needed in this area – we can rely on the unmodified audit opinion to be issued by Foxglove & Co. This issue was not identified until it was raised by Foxglove & Co, it has not been mentioned to me by the Group board members, and it has no implications for the consolidated financial statements.'

The draft statement of financial position of Daisy Co recognises total assets of $8 million and the statement of profit or loss recognises profit before tax of $50,000.

The draft consolidated financial statements recognises goodwill in respect of Daisy Co of $3 million (20X4 – $3 million).

Exhibit 2 – Daisy Co update

Additional procedures have now been performed to assess the going concern status of Daisy Co and the group auditor has concluded that there is sufficient doubt to require disclosure of the uncertainty in the financial statements of Daisy Co. The directors of Daisy Co have stated that they do not intend to include any disclosure as they do not want to draw attention to going concern issues in case it causes further problems.

Required:

(a)   **Using the information contained in Exhibit 1, in respect of each of the matters described above, comment on the quality of the planning and performance of the Group audit, recommending any further actions to be taken by your firm, prior to finalising the Group auditor's report.**

   Note: The following mark allocation is provided as guidance for this question:

   (i)   **Hyacinth Co (6 marks)**

   (ii)   **Geranium Co (4 marks)**

   (iii)   **Daisy Co (5 marks)**   **(15 marks)**

(b)   **Using the information contained in Exhibit 2, discuss the effect of this issue on the auditor's reports of Daisy Co and the Magnolia Group.**   **(5 marks)**

Professional marks will be awarded for the demonstration of skill in analysis and evaluation, professional scepticism and judgement and commercial acumen in your answer.   **(5 marks)**

                                                                        (Total: 25 marks)

32 OSIER *Walk in the footsteps of a top tutor*

It is 1 July 20X5. You are the manager responsible for the audit of Osier Co, a jewellery manufacturer and retailer. The final audit for the year ended 31 March 20X5 is nearing completion and you are reviewing the audit working papers. The draft financial statements recognise total assets of $1,919 million (20X4 – $1,889 million), revenue of $1,052 million (20X4 – $997 million) and profit before tax of $107 million (20X4 – $110 million).

The following exhibits, available below, provide information relevant to the question:

1   Audit completion review – details of matters which have been brought to your attention by the audit supervisor.

2   Update on completion matters – provides an update on the impairment following discussion with the management team.

This information should be used to answer the question requirements within the response option provided.

Exhibit 1 – Audit completion review

Cost of inventory

Inventory costs include all purchase costs and the costs of conversion of raw materials into finished goods. Conversion costs include direct labour costs and an allocation of production overheads. Direct labour costs are calculated based on the average production time per unit of inventory, which is estimated by the production manager, multiplied by the estimated labour cost per hour, which is calculated using the forecast annual wages of production staff divided by the annual scheduled hours of production. Production overheads are all fixed and are allocated based upon the forecast annual units of production. At the year-end inventory was valued at $21 million (20X4 – $20 million).

Impairment

At the year end management performed an impairment review on its retail outlets, which are a cash generating unit for the purpose of conducting an impairment review. While internet sales grew rapidly during the year, sales from retail outlets declined, prompting the review. At 31 March 20X5 the carrying amount of the assets directly attributable to the retail outlets totalled $137 million, this includes both tangible assets and goodwill.

During the year management received a number of offers from parties interested in purchasing the retail outlets for an average of $125 million. They also estimated the disposal costs to be $1.5 million, based upon their experience of corporate acquisitions and disposals. Management estimated the value in use to be $128 million. This was based on the historic cash flows attributable to retail outlets inflated at a general rate of 1% per annum.

Consequently, the retail outlets were impaired by $9 million to restate them to their estimated recoverable amount of $128 million. The impairment was allocated against the tangible assets of the outlets on a pro rata basis, based upon the original carrying amount of each asset in the unit.

Exhibit 2 – Update following discussion with the management team

As a result of your review you have concluded that the retail outlets are overvalued by a further $9 million due to the assumptions used in management's assessment of value in use being too optimistic. The audit engagement partner has discussed the misstatement with the management team who have refused to make the necessary adjustment to the financial statements.

Required:

(a)   **Using the information in Exhibit 1, comment on the matters to be considered and explain the audit evidence you would expect to find during your review of the audit working papers on 1 July 20X5, in relation to the issues identified.**

       Note: The following mark allocation is provided as guidance for this question:

       (i)   Cost of inventory (7 marks)

       (ii)   Impairment (9 marks)   **(16 marks)**

(b)   **Using the information in Exhibit 2, and assuming that no further adjustments will be made to the financial statements, discuss the effect the uncorrected misstatement will have on the audit opinion and auditor's report.**   **(4 marks)**

Professional marks will be awarded for the demonstration of skill in analysis and evaluation and professional scepticism and judgement in your answer.   **(5 marks)**

                                                 (Total: 25 marks)

33   ROPE *Walk in the footsteps of a top tutor*

It is 1 July 20X5. You are an audit manager in Hitchcock & Co, a firm of Chartered Certified Accountants responsible for the audit of Rope Co for the year ended 30 April 20X5. The audit is nearing completion and the audit senior is working on the going concern section of the audit file.

The following exhibits, available below, provide information relevant to the question:

1   Cash flow forecast – forecast cash flows for three years to assess management's use of the going concern assumption.

2   Request from the chief executive – a request for the audit engagement partner to attend a meeting with the bank.

This information should be used to answer the question requirements within the response option provided.

Exhibit 1 – Going concern assessment

During a visit to the team performing the audit fieldwork, the audit senior shows you a cash flow forecast for the two years to 30 April 20X7 as prepared by management as part of their assessment of the going concern status of the company. The audit senior asks whether any of the forecast cash flows require any further investigation during the audit fieldwork.

The actual and forecast six-monthly cash flows for Rope Co for the periods ended:

	Actual			Forecast		
	31 Oct 20X4	30 April 20X5	31 Oct 20X5	30 April 20X6	31 Oct 20X6	30 April 20X7
	$000	$000	$000	$000	$000	$000
Operating cash flows						
Receipts from customers	13,935	14,050	14,300	14,700	14,950	15,400
Payments to suppliers	(10,725)	(10,850)	(11,050)	(11,400)	(11,600)	(12,000)
Salaries	(1,250)	(1,300)	(1,275)	(1,326)	(1,301)	(1,353)
Other operating cash payments	(1,875)	(1,850)	(1,913)	(1,887)	(1,951)	(1,925)
Other cash flows						
Sale of investments	–	–	–	–	–	500
Repayment of J Stewart loan	–	–	–	–	–	(500)
Repayment of bank loan	–	–	–	–	(1,500)	–
Receipt of bank loan	–	–	–	–	1,500	–
Cash flow for the period	85	50	62	87	98	122
Opening cash	(275)	(190)	(140)	(78)	9	107
Closing cash	(190)	(140)	(78)	9	107	229

The following additional information has been provided in support of the forecasts:

- Receipts from customers and payments to suppliers have been estimated based on detailed sales forecasts prepared by the sales director.

- Salaries and overheads have been estimated as the prior year cost plus general inflation of 2%.

- The bank loan expires on 5 August 20X6. The finance director expects to take out a matching facility with the current lender to pay off the existing debt.

- On 1 May 20X4, the chief executive, Mr J Stewart, gave the company a three-year, interest free loan secured by a fixed charge over the operational assets of Rope Co. The audit team was unaware of this loan prior to obtaining the cash flow forecast.

- The directors plan to sell some investments in listed shares to fund the repayment of the chief executive's loan. At 30 April 20X5, the investments were carried in the statement of financial position at their fair value of $350,000.

Exhibit 2 – Request from the chief executive

Rope Co's chief executive, Mr Stewart, has requested that the audit engagement partner accompanies him to the meeting with the bank where the matching loan will be discussed. Mr Stewart has hinted that if the partner does not accompany him to the meeting, he will put the audit out to tender.

Required:

(a)   Using the information contained in Exhibit 1:

    (i)   Evaluate the appropriateness of the cash flow forecast prepared by Rope Co and recommend the further audit procedures which should be performed.

(10 marks)

    (ii)   Comment on the matters to be considered in respect of the loan from Mr J Stewart and recommend the further audit procedures to be performed.

(5 marks)

(b)   Using the information contained in Exhibit 2, identify and discuss the ethical and other professional issues raised by the chief executive's request, and recommend any actions that should be taken by the audit firm.   **(5 marks)**

Professional marks will be awarded for the demonstration of skill in analysis and evaluation, professional scepticism and judgement and commercial acumen in your answer.   **(5 marks)**

(Total: 25 marks)

34   BOSTON   *Walk in the footsteps of a top tutor*

It is 1 July 20X5. You are the manager responsible for the audit of Boston Co, a producer of chocolate and confectionery. The audit of the financial statements for the year ended 31 March 20X5 is nearly complete and you are reviewing the audit working papers. The financial statements recognise revenue of $76 million, profit before tax for the year of $6.4 million and total assets of $104 million.

The following exhibits, available below, provide information relevant to the question:

1   Summary of uncorrected misstatements and notes – provides details of the summary of uncorrected misstatements to be discussed with management.

2   Details of an IAASB publication on climate-related risks.

This information should be used to answer the question requirements within the response option provided.

Exhibit 1 – Summary of uncorrected misstatements and notes

The summary of uncorrected misstatements included in Boston Co's audit working papers, including notes, is shown below. The audit engagement partner is holding a meeting with the management team of Boston Co next week, at which the uncorrected misstatements will be discussed.

| | Statement of profit or loss | | Statement of financial position | |
	Debit	Credit	Debit	Credit
Summary of uncorrected misstatements:	$	$	$	$
1. Impairment	500,000			500,000
2. Borrowing costs		75,000	75,000	
3. Investment		43,500	43,500	
Totals	500,000	118,500	118,500	500,000

Notes

1   Impairment

During the year Boston Co impaired one of its factories. The carrying amount of the assets attributable to the factory as a single, cash-generating unit totalled $3.6 million at the year end. The fair value less costs of disposal and the value in use were estimated to be $3 million and $3.5 million respectively and accordingly the asset was written down by $100,000 to reflect the impairment. Audit procedures revealed that management used growth rates attributable to the company as a whole to estimate value in use. Using growth rates attributable to the factory specifically, the audit team estimated the value in use to be $2.9 million.

2   Borrowing costs

Interest charges of $75,000 relating to a loan taken out during the year to finance the construction of a new manufacturing plant were included in finance charges recognised in profit for the year. The manufacturing plant is due for completion in February 20X6.

3   Investment

During the year Boston Co purchased 150,000 shares in Nebraska Co for $4.00 per share. Boston Co classified the investment as a financial asset held at fair value through profit or loss. On 31 March 20X5, the shares of Nebraska Co were trading for $4.29. At the year end the carrying amount of the investment in Boston Co's financial statements was $600,000.

Exhibit 2 – Climate-related risks

The IAASB has issued an audit practice alert relating to the auditor's consideration of climate-related risks. The alert provides guidance to auditors on how to apply existing ISAs to the specific issue of climate-related risks. The alert explains the responsibilities of management and auditors with respect to climate-related risks and covers the main auditing standards relevant to climate-related risks.

Required:

(a)   **Using the information contained in Exhibit 1:**

(i)   **Explain the matters which should be discussed with management in relation to each of the uncorrected misstatements, including an assessment of their individual impact on the financial statements.   (9 marks)**

(ii)   **Assuming that management does not adjust any of the misstatements, discuss the effect on the audit opinion and auditor's report.   (5 marks)**

(b)   **Using the information contained in Exhibit 2, discuss the main ways that climate-related risks will impact the planning and performance of an audit.   (6 marks)**

Professional marks will be awarded for the demonstration of skill in analysis and evaluation, professional scepticism and judgement, and commercial acumen in your answer.   (5 marks)

(Total: 25 marks)

35   MACAU & CO   *Walk in the footsteps of a top tutor*

It is 1 July 20X5. You are a senior manager in Macau & Co, a firm of Chartered Certified Accountants. In your capacity as engagement quality reviewer, you have been asked to review the audit files of Stanley Co and Kowloon Co, both of which have a financial year ended 31 March 20X5, and the audits of both companies are nearing completion.

The following exhibits, available below, provide information relevant to the question:

1   Stanley Co – provides a summary of issues identified during the review of the audit working papers.

2   Kowloon Co – points raised for your attention by the audit senior.

This information should be used to answer the question requirements within the response option provided.

Exhibit 1 – Stanley Co

Stanley Co is a frozen food processor, selling its products to wholesalers and supermarkets. From your review of the audit working papers, you have noted that the level of materiality was determined to be $1.5 million at the planning stage, and this materiality threshold has been used throughout the audit. There is no evidence on the audit file that this threshold has been reviewed during the course of the audit.

From your review of the audit planning, you know that a new packing machine with a cost of $1.6 million was acquired by Stanley Co in June 20X4, and is recognised in the draft statement of financial position at a carrying amount of $1.4 million at 31 March 20X5. The packing machine is located at the premises of Aberdeen Co, a distribution company which is used to pack and distribute a significant proportion of Stanley Co's products. The machine has not been physically verified by a member of the audit team.

The audit working papers conclude that 'we have obtained the purchase invoice and order in relation to the machine, and therefore can conclude that the asset is appropriately valued and that it exists. In addition, the managing director of Aberdeen Co has confirmed in writing that the machine is located at their premises and is in working order. No further work is needed in respect of this item.'

Inventory is recognised at $2 million in the draft statement of financial position. You have reviewed the results of audit procedures performed at the inventory count, where the test counts performed by the audit team indicated that the count of some items performed by the company's staff was not correct. The working papers state that 'the inventory count was not well organised' and conclude that 'however, the discrepancies were immaterial, so no further action is required'.

The audit senior spoke to you yesterday, voicing some concerns about the performance of the audit. A summary of his comments is shown below.

'The audit manager and audit engagement partner came to review the audit working papers on the same day towards the completion of the audit fieldwork. The audit partner asked me if there had been any issues on the sections of the audit which I had worked on, and when I said there had been no problems, he signed off the working papers after a quick look through them.

When reading the company's board minutes, I found several references to the audit engagement partner, Joe Lantau, who recommended that the company use the services of his brother, Mick Lantau, for advice on business development.

Based on Joe's recommendation, Mick, a management consultant has provided a consultancy service to Stanley Co since December 20X4. I mentioned this to Joe, and he told me not to record it in the audit working papers or to discuss it with anyone.'

Exhibit 2 – Kowloon Co

Kowloon Co works on contracts to design and manufacture large items of medical equipment such as radiotherapy and X-ray machines. The company specialises in the design, production and installation of bespoke machines under contract with individual customers, which are usually private medical companies. The draft financial statements recognise profit before tax of $950,000 and total assets of $7.5 million.

The audit senior has left the following note for your attention:

'One of Kowloon Co's major customers is the Bay Medical Centre (BMC), a private hospital. In September 20X4 a contract was entered into, under the terms of which Kowloon Co would design a new radiotherapy machine for BMC. The machine is based on a new innovation, and is being developed for the specific requirements of BMC.

It was estimated that the design and production of the machine would take 18 months with estimated installation in March 20X6. As at 31 March 20X5, Kowloon Co had invested heavily in the contract, and design costs totalling $350,000 have been recognised as work in progress in the draft statement of financial position. Deferred income of $200,000 is also recognised as a current liability, representing a payment made by BMC to finance part of the design costs. No other accounting entries have been made in respect of the contract with BMC.

As part of our subsequent events review, inspection of correspondence between Kowloon Co and BMC indicates that the contract has been cancelled by BMC as it is unable to pay for its completion. It appears that BMC lost a significant amount of funding towards in the first quarter of 20X5, impacting significantly on the financial position of the company. The manager responsible for the BMC contract confirms that BMC contacted him about the company's financial difficulties in March 20X5.

The matter has been discussed with Kowloon Co's finance director, who has stated that he is satisfied with the current accounting treatment and is not proposing to make any adjustments in light of the cancellation of the contract by BMC. The finance director has also advised that the loss of BMC as a customer will not be mentioned in the company's integrated report, as the finance director does not consider it significant enough to warrant discussion.

Kowloon Co is currently working on six contracts for customers other than BMC. Our audit evidence concludes that Kowloon Co does not face a threat to its going concern status due to the loss of BMC as a customer.'

Your review of the audit work performed on going concern supports this conclusion.

Required:

(a) **Using the information contained in Exhibit 1, comment on the quality of the audit performed discussing the quality management, ethical and other professional issues raised.** **(13 marks)**

(b) **Using the information contained in Exhibit 2, comment on the matters to be considered, and recommend the actions to be taken by the auditor.** **(7 marks)**

Professional marks will be awarded for the demonstration of skill in analysis and evaluation, professional scepticism and judgement, and commercial acumen in your answer. **(5 marks)**

(Total: 25 marks)

36 DARREN *Walk in the footsteps of a top tutor*

You are a manager in the audit department of Nidge & Co, a firm of Chartered Certified Accountants, responsible for the audit of Darren Co, a new audit client operating in the construction industry. Darren Co's financial year ended on 31 March 20X5, and the draft financial statements recognise profit before tax of $22.5 million (20X4 – $20 million) and total assets of $370 million, including cash of $3 million. The company typically works on three construction contracts at a time. The audit is nearly complete and you are reviewing the audit working papers. The audit senior has brought several matters to your attention in respect of the construction contracts in progress at the year end.

The following exhibits, available below, provide information relevant to the question:

1   Flyover Co – provides a summary of issues identified during the review of the audit working papers.

2   Newbuild Co – points raised for your attention by the audit senior.

3   Government contract – details of difficulties obtaining audit evidence in respect of a government contract.

This information should be used to answer the question requirements within the response option provided.

Exhibit 1 – Flyover Co

Darren Co is working on a major contract relating to the construction of a bridge for Flyover Co. Work started in September 20X4, and it is estimated that the contract will be completed in November 20X5. The contract price is $20 million, and it is estimated that a profit of $5 million will be made on completion of the contract. The full amount of this profit has been included in the statement of profit or loss for the year ended 31 March 20X5. Darren Co's management believes that this accounting treatment is appropriate given that the contract was signed during the financial year, and no problems have arisen in the work carried out so far.

Exhibit 2 – Newbuild Co

A significant contract was completed in November 20X4 for Newbuild Co. This contract related to the construction of a 20-mile highway in a remote area. In January 20X5, several large cracks appeared in the road surface after a period of unusually heavy rain, and the road had to be shut for ten weeks while repair work was carried out.

Newbuild Co paid for these repairs, but has taken legal action against Darren Co to recover the costs incurred of $40 million. Disclosure of this matter has been made in the notes to the financial statements. Audit evidence, including a written statement from Darren Co's lawyers, concludes that there is a possibility, but not a probability, of Darren Co having to settle the amount claimed.

Exhibit 3 – Government contract

During the year Darren Co successfully tendered for a government contract to construct a military building. $7 million of expenses relating to this construction were recorded in the statement of profit or loss. The audit team was given brief summaries of the costs incurred but when asked for further corroborating evidence, management stated that they had signed a confidentiality agreement with the military and were unable to provide any further details. The construction is expected to take a further 15 months to complete.

Required:

Discuss the implications of the matters described above on the completion of the audit and on the auditor's report, recommending any further actions which should be taken by the auditor in respect of:

(a)	Flyover Co, using Exhibit 1.	(8 marks)
(b)	Newbuild Co, using Exhibit 2.	(6 marks)
(c)	Government contract, using Exhibit 3.	(6 marks)

Professional marks will be awarded for the demonstration of skill in analysis and evaluation and professional scepticism and judgement in your answer. **(5 marks)**

(Total: 25 marks)

37 THURMAN *Walk in the footsteps of a top tutor*

It is 1 July 20X5. You are the manager responsible for the audit of Thurman Co, a manufacturing company which supplies stainless steel components to a wide range of industries. The company's financial year ended on 31 March 20X5 and you are reviewing the audit work which has been completed on a number of material balances and transactions: assets held for sale, asset expenditure and payroll expenses. A summary of the work which has been performed is given below and in each case the description of the audit work indicates the full extent of the audit procedures carried out by the audit team.

The following exhibits, available below, provide information relevant to the question:

1   Assets held for sale

2   Capital (asset) expenditure

3   Payroll expenses

This information should be used to answer the question requirements within the response option provided.

Exhibit 1 – Assets held for sale

Due to the planned disposal of one of Thurman Co's factory sites, the property and associated assets have been classified as held for sale in the financial statements. A manual journal has been posted by the finance director to reclassify the assets as current assets and to adjust the value of the assets for impairment and reversal of depreciation charged from the date at which the assets met the criteria to be classified as held for sale. The planned disposal was discussed with management. A brief note has been put into the audit working papers stating that in management's opinion the accounting treatment to classify the factory as held for sale is correct. The manual journal has been arithmetically checked by a different member of the audit team, and the amounts agreed back to the non-current asset register.

Exhibit 2 – Capital (asset) expenditure

When auditing the company's capital (asset) expenditure, the audit team selected a material transaction to test and found that key internal controls were not operating effectively. Authorisation had not been obtained for an order placed for several vehicles, and appropriate segregation of duties over initiating and processing the transaction was not maintained.

The audit team noted details of the internal control deficiencies and updated the systems notes on the permanent audit file to reflect the deficiencies. The audit work completed on this order was to agree the purchase of the vehicles to purchase invoices and to the bank ledger account/cash book and bank statement. The rest of the audit work in this area was completed in accordance with the audit programme.

Exhibit 3 – Payroll expenses

The payroll function is outsourced to Jackson Co, a service organisation which processes all of Thurman Co's salary expenses. The payroll expenses recognised in the financial statements have been traced back to year-end reports issued by Jackson Co. The audit team has had no direct contact with Jackson Co as the year-end reports were sent to Thurman Co's finance director who then passed them to the audit team.

Thurman Co employs a few casual workers who are paid in cash at the end of each month and are not entered into the payroll system. The audit team has agreed the cash payment made back to the petty cash records and the amounts involved are considered immaterial.

Required:

(a)   Using the information contained in Exhibit 1, comment on the sufficiency and appropriateness of the audit evidence obtained and recommend further audit procedures to be performed by the audit team in respect of the assets held for sale.

(7 marks)

(b)   Using the information contained in Exhibit 2:

(i)   Comment on the sufficiency and appropriateness of the audit evidence obtained.

(ii)   Recommend further audit procedures to be performed by the audit team.

(iii)   Explain the matters which should be included in a report in accordance with ISA 265 *Communicating Deficiencies in Internal Controls to Those Charged with Governance and Management.*

(9 marks)

(c)   Using the information contained in Exhibit 3, comment on the sufficiency and appropriateness of the audit evidence obtained and explain the control deficiencies which should be included in the report to Those Charged with Governance and Management in respect of payroll expenses.

(4 marks)

Professional marks will be awarded for the demonstration of skill in analysis and evaluation, professional scepticism and judgement and commercial acumen in your answer.

(5 marks)

(Total: 25 marks)

38   ADDER GROUP *Walk in the footsteps of a top tutor*

It is 1 July 20X5. You are a senior manager in Macau & Co, a firm of Chartered Certified Accountants. You are currently working on the audits of Adder Group and Marr Co, both of which are nearing completion.

The following exhibits, available below, provide information relevant to the question:

1   Adder Group – provides a summary of issues identified during the review of the audit working papers.

2   Marr Co – draft auditor's report and supplementary information.

This information should be used to answer the question requirements within the response option provided.

Exhibit 1 – Adder Group

The Adder Group (the Group) has been an audit client of your firm for several years. You have recently been assigned to act as audit manager, replacing a manager who has fallen ill, and the audit of the Group financial statements for the year ended 31 March 20X5 is underway. The Group's activities include property management and the provision of large storage facilities in warehouses owned by the Group. The draft consolidated financial statements recognise total assets of $150 million, and profit before tax of $20 million.

The audit engagement partner, Edmund Black, has asked you to review the audit working papers in relation to two audit issues which have been highlighted by the audit senior. Information on each of these issues is given below:

(i)   Sale and leaseback

In December 20X4, a leisure centre complex was sold for proceeds equivalent to its fair value of $35 million, the related assets have been derecognised from the Group statement of financial position, and a profit on disposal of $8 million is included in the Group statement of profit or loss for the year. The remaining useful life of the leisure centre complex was 21 years at the date of disposal.

The Group is leasing back the leisure centre complex to use in its ongoing operations, paying rentals annually in arrears. At the end of the 20-year lease arrangement, the Group has the option to repurchase the leisure centre complex for its market value at that time.

(ii)   Baldrick Co

In January 20X5, the Group acquired 52% of the equity shares of Baldrick Co. This company has not been consolidated into the Group as a subsidiary, and is instead accounted for as an associate. The Group finance director's reason for this accounting treatment is that Baldrick Co's operations have not yet been integrated with those of the rest of the Group. Baldrick Co's financial statements recognise total assets of $18 million and a loss for the year to 31 March 20X5 of $5 million.

Exhibit 2 – Marr Co

You are also responsible for the audit of Marr Co, with a year ended 28 February 20X5. The draft financial statements recognise profit for the year of $11 million. The materiality level used for performing the audit was $1.5 million. The audit is nearing completion, and several matters have been highlighted for your attention by the audit senior, Xi Smith. The matters have been discussed with management and will not be adjusted in the financial statements:

1   In January 20X5 a major customer went into administration. There was a balance of $2.5 million owing to Marr Co from this customer at 28 February 20X5 which is still included in trade receivables.

2   A court case began in December 20X4 involving an ex-employee who is suing Marr Co for unfair dismissal. Lawyers estimate that damages of $50,000 are probable to be paid. The financial statements include a note describing the court case and quantifying the potential damages but no adjustment has been made to include it in the statement of financial position or the statement of profit or loss.

Xi Smith has produced a draft auditor's report for your review, an extract of which is shown below:

Extract 1

Basis for opinion and disclaimer of opinion

Our audit procedures have proven conclusively that trade receivables are materially misstated. The finance director of Marr Co, Rita Gilmour, has refused to make an adjustment to write off a significant trade receivables balance. Therefore, in our opinion, the financial statements of Marr Co are materially misstated and we therefore express a disclaimer of opinion because we do not think they are fairly presented.

Extract 2

Emphasis of Matter paragraph

Marr Co is facing a legal claim for an amount of $50,000 from an ex-employee. In our opinion this amount should be recognised as a provision but it is not included in the statement of financial position. We draw your attention to this breach of the relevant International Financial Reporting Standard.

Required:

(a)   **Using the information contained in Exhibit 1, comment on the matters to be considered, and explain the audit evidence you should expect to find during your review of the audit working papers.**

       Note: The following mark allocation is provided as guidance for this question:

       (i)   Sale and leaseback (7 marks)

       (ii)   Baldrick Co (6 marks)   **(13 marks)**

(b)   **Using the information contained in Exhibit 2, critically appraise the proposed auditor's report of Marr Co for the year ended 28 February 20X5.**

       Note: You are NOT required to re-draft the extracts from the auditor's report.

                     (7 marks)

Professional marks will be awarded for the demonstration of skill in analysis and evaluation and professional scepticism and judgement in your answer.   **(5 marks)**

                                        (Total: 25 marks)

39   FRANCIS GROUP *Walk in the footsteps of a top tutor*

It is 1 July 20X5. You are a manager in the audit department of Williams & Co and you are reviewing the audit working papers in relation to the Francis Group (the Group), whose financial year ended on 31 March 20X5. Your firm audits all components of the Group, which consists of a parent company and three subsidiaries – Marks Co, Roberts Co and Teapot Co.

The Group manufactures engines which are then supplied to the car industry. The draft consolidated financial statements recognise profit for the year to 31 March 20X5 of $23 million (20X4 – $33 million) and total assets of $450 million (20X4 – $455 million).

The following exhibits, available below, provide information relevant to the question:

1   Audit completion review – provides details of matters which have been brought to your attention by the audit supervisor.

2   Insurance claim update – provides an update on the insurance claim relating to the natural disaster affecting the property complex.

This information should be used to answer the question requirements within the response option provided.

Exhibit 1 – Audit completion review

(i)   Goodwill

An 80% equity shareholding in Teapot Co was acquired on 1 April 20X4. Goodwill on the acquisition of $27 million was calculated at that date and remains recognised as an intangible asset at that value at the year end.

The goodwill calculation performed by the Group's management is shown below:

	$000
Purchase consideration	75,000
Fair value of 20% non-controlling interest	13,000
	88,000
Less:	
Fair value of Teapot Co's identifiable net assets at acquisition	(61,000)
Goodwill	27,000

In determining the fair value of identifiable net assets at acquisition, an upwards fair value adjustment of $300,000 was made to the book value of a property recognised in Teapot Co's financial statements at a carrying amount of $600,000.

(ii)   Property complex

In May 20X5, a natural disaster caused severe damage to the property complex housing the Group's head office and main manufacturing site. For health and safety reasons, a decision was made to demolish the property complex. The demolition took place three weeks after the damage was caused. The property had a carrying amount of $16 million at 31 March 20X5.

A contingent asset of $18 million has been recognised as a current asset and as deferred income in the Group statement of financial position at 31 March 20X5, representing the amount claimed under the Group's insurance policy in respect of the disaster.

Exhibit 2 – Insurance claim update

The insurance company has recently informed the Francis Group that the insurance claim has been rejected as the insurance policy had expired and not been renewed at the date the disaster occurred. The going concern status is not considered to be affected as the Group has sufficient assets to acquire a new head office and continue trading. The directors have refused to remove the contingent asset.

Required:

(a)   Using the information contained in Exhibit 1, comment on the matters to be considered, and explain the audit evidence you should expect to find during your review of the audit working papers in respect of each of the issues described above.

Note: The following mark allocation is provided as guidance for this question:

(i)   Goodwill (9 marks)

(ii)   Property complex (6 marks)   (15 marks)

(b)   Using the information contained in Exhibit 2, discuss the implications of the matter described above on the auditor's report, recommending any further actions which should be taken by the auditor.   (5 marks)

Professional marks will be awarded for the demonstration of skill in analysis and evaluation and professional scepticism and judgement in your answer.   (5 marks)

(Total: 25 marks)

40   BRADLEY   *Walk in the footsteps of a top tutor*

It is 1 July 20X5. The audit of Bradley Co's financial statements for the year ended 30 April 20X5 is nearly complete, and the auditor's report is due to be issued next week. Bradley Co operates steel processing plants at 20 locations and sells its output to manufacturers and engineering companies. You are performing an engagement quality review on the audit of Bradley Co, as it is a significant new client of your firm.

The following exhibits, available below, provide information relevant to the question:

1   Quality management issues – points raised for your attention by one of the audit assistants working on the audit of Bradley Co.

2   Schedule of uncorrected misstatements – provides details of the summary of uncorrected misstatements to be discussed with management.

This information should be used to answer the question requirements within the response option provided.

Exhibit 1 – Quality management issues

One of the audit assistants who has been working on the audit of Bradley Co made the following comments when discussing the completion of the audit with you:

'I was assigned to the audit of provisions. One of the provisions, amounting to $10,000, relates to a legal claim made against the company after an employee was injured in an accident at one of the steel processing plants. I read all of the correspondence relating to this, and tried to speak to Bradley Co's legal advisers, but was told by the finance director that I must not approach them and should only speak to him about the matter. He said that he is confident that only $10,000 needs to be recognised and that the legal advisers had confirmed this amount to him in a discussion of the matter. I noted in the audit working papers that I could not perform all of the planned audit procedures because I could not speak to the legal advisers. The audit manager told me to conclude that provisions are correctly recognised in the financial statements based on the evidence obtained, and to move on to my next piece of work. He said it didn't matter that I hadn't spoken to the legal advisers because the matter is immaterial to the financial statements.

'We received the final version of the financial statements and the chair's statement to be published with the financial statements yesterday. I have quickly looked at the financial statements but the audit manager said we need not perform a detailed analytical review on the financial statements as the audit was relatively low risk. The manager also said that he had discussed the chair's statement with the finance director so no further work on it is needed. The audit has been quite time pressured and I know that the client wants the auditor's report to be issued as soon as possible.'

Exhibit 2 – Schedule of uncorrected misstatements

The schedule of uncorrected misstatement included in Bradley Co's audit working papers is shown below, including notes to explain each matter included in the schedule. The financial statements recognise revenue of $2.5 million, and total assets of $35 million. The audit engagement partner is holding a meeting with management tomorrow, at which the uncorrected misstatements will be discussed.

		Statement of profit or loss		Statement of financial position	
		Debit	Credit	Debit	Credit
		$	$	$	$
1	Share-based payment scheme	300,000			300,000
2	Restructuring provision		50,000	50,000	
Totals		300,000	50,000	50,000	300,000

1   A share-based payment scheme was established in September 20X4. Management has not recognised any amount in the financial statements in relation to the scheme, arguing that due to the decline in Bradley Co's share price, the share options granted are unlikely to be exercised. The audit conclusion is that an expense and related equity figure should be included in the financial statements.

2   A provision has been recognised in respect of a restructuring involving the closure of one of the steel processing plants. Management approved the closure at a board meeting in April 20X5, but only announced the closure to employees in May 20X5. The audit conclusion is that the provision should not be recognised.

Required:

(a)   Using the information in Exhibit 1, explain the quality management and other professional issues raised by the audit assistant's comments, discussing any implications for the completion of the audit.   **(8 marks)**

(b)   Using the information in Exhibit 2:

    (i)   Explain the matters which should be discussed with management in relation to each of the uncorrected misstatements.   **(7 marks)**

    (ii)   Assuming that management does not adjust the misstatements, justify an appropriate audit opinion and explain the impact on the auditor's report.
    (5 marks)

Professional marks will be awarded for the demonstration of skill in analysis and evaluation, professional scepticism and judgement and commercial acumen in your answer.   **(5 marks)**

(Total: 25 marks)

41   **SNIPE**   *Walk in the footsteps of a top tutor*

It is 1 July 20X5. You are the partner responsible for performing an engagement quality review on the audit of Snipe Co. You are currently reviewing the audit working papers and draft auditor's report on the financial statements of Snipe Co for the year ended 31 March 20X5. The draft financial statements recognise revenue of $8.5 million, profit before tax of $1 million, and total assets of $175 million.

The following exhibits, available below, provide information relevant to the question:

1   Audit completion review – provides details of matters which have been brought to your attention during the review of the audit working papers.

2   Update and draft auditor's report – provides an update on the matters covered in Exhibit 1 as well as details of a recently discovered issue which has only just been brought to your attention and extracts of the auditor's report which have been drafted by the audit supervisor.

This information should be used to answer the question requirements within the response option provided.

Exhibit 1 – Audit completion review

(i)   New processing area

    During the year Snipe Co's factory was extended by the self-construction of a new processing area, at a total cost of $5 million. A loan of $4 million carrying an interest rate of 5% was taken out in respect of the construction on 1 May 20X4, when construction started with interest of $183,333 relating to the loan being recognised as a finance cost. The new processing area was ready for use on 1 November 20X4, and began to be used on 1 February 20X5. Its estimated useful life is 15 years and depreciation has been charged from 1 February.

(ii) Assets held for sale

Snipe Co owns a number of properties which have been classified as assets held for sale in the statement of financial position. The notes to the financial statements state that the properties are all due to be sold within one year. On classification as held for sale, in December 20X4, the properties were re-measured from carrying amount of $26 million to fair value less cost to sell of $24 million, which is the amount recognised in the statement of financial position at the year end.

(iii) Defined benefit pension plan

Snipe Co has in place a defined benefit pension plan for its employees. An actuarial valuation on 31 March 20X5 indicated that the plan is in deficit by $10.5 million. The deficit is not recognised in the statement of financial position.

Exhibit 2 – Update and draft auditor's report

It is now 22 July 20X5 and all matters in relation to the new processing area and assets held for sale have now been satisfactorily resolved, however, management have refused to recognise any amounts relating to the defined benefit pension plan. Based on the above conclusions, the audit supervisor has drafted the auditor's report which includes the following extract:

Explanation of adverse opinion in relation to pension

The financial statements do not include the company's pension plan. This deliberate omission contravenes accepted accounting practice and means that the accounts are not properly prepared.

Auditor's opinion

In our opinion, because of the significance of the matter discussed above, the financial statements do not give a true and fair view of the financial position of Snipe Co as at 31 March 20X5, and of its financial performance and cash flows for the year then ended in accordance with International Financial Reporting Standards.

Required:

(a) **Using the information contained in Exhibit 1, explain the matters that should be discussed with management in respect of each of the issues described above.**

Note: The following mark allocation is provided as guidance for this question:

(i)   New processing area (6 marks)

(ii)   Assets held for sale (5 marks)

(iii)   Defined benefit pension plan (4 marks)   (15 marks)

(b) **With reference to Exhibit 2, and assuming that no further adjustments will be made to the financial statements in relation to the defined benefit pension plan, evaluate the appropriateness of the draft auditor's report produced by the audit supervisor.**

Note: you are NOT required to re-draft the extract of the auditor's report. (5 marks)

Professional marks will be awarded for the demonstration of skill in analysis and evaluation, professional scepticism and judgement and commercial acumen in your answer.   **(5 marks)**

(Total: 25 marks)

OTHER ASSIGNMENTS

42   KOBOLD *Walk in the footsteps of a top tutor*

It is 1 July 20X5. You are a manager in Gnome & Co, a firm of Chartered Certified Accountants which offers a range of services to audit and non-audit clients.

Your firm has been asked to consider a potential engagement which is to review and provide an assurance report on a capital expenditure forecast for Kobold Co. The company does not wish to engage its audit provider to perform this engagement and Kobold Co is not currently a client of your firm.

The following exhibit, available below, provides information relevant to the question:

1   Capital (asset) expenditure forecast – a capital expenditure forecast for the 24 months beginning 1 September 20X5, prepared by Kobold Co's financial controller.

This information should be used to answer the question requirements within your chosen response option(s).

Exhibit 1 – Capital (asset) expenditure forecast

The forecast and associated assurance report are being prepared at the request of the company's bankers in support of an application for a loan to finance the construction of a new distribution centre on land currently owned by the company. The forecast has been prepared by the financial controller of Kobold Co who has recently been promoted into the role. This is the first capital expenditure forecast the new financial controller has prepared, however, he has previously been involved in preparing annual budgets and cash flow projections for Kobold Co. The forecast has been reviewed by the finance director and approved.

The assurance report needs to be completed as soon as possible because Kobold Co has entered into a contract to commence building work in October 20X5 and is reliant on the bank finance to make the agreed payments. It is possible to make the first payment to the builders from the company's existing overdraft facility, however, this facility is due for renewal in December 20X5.

Capital expenditure forecast for 24 months beginning 1 September 20X5

	12 months to August 20X6 $000	12 months to August 20X7 $000	Total $000
Legal fees	7		7
Architect and surveyor fees	15		15
Site preparation and tree removal	28		28
Structural building work	84	48	132
Interior fittings and refurbishment		35	35
Total	134	83	217

Additional information:

- The relevant regulatory authority has issued preliminary approval for the construction of the planned distribution centre subject to receiving updated structural calculations relating to the building materials meeting required regulations.

- Figures are based upon quotations from local contractors with agreed upon start dates assuming that the building work will commence in October 20X5. Payments to the contractors will be made at agreed completion stages of the project.

Required:

(a) **Evaluate the matters to be considered by Gnome & Co before accepting Kobold Co as a client and the engagement to review and report on the capital (asset) expenditure forecast.** **(10 marks)**

(b) **Assuming Gnome & Co accepts the engagement, recommend the examination procedures to be performed in respect of Kobold Co's capital (asset) expenditure forecast.** **(10 marks)**

Professional marks will be awarded for the demonstration of skill in analysis and evaluation, professional scepticism and judgement and commercial acumen in your answer. **(5 marks)**

(Total: 25 marks)

43 FLYNN *Walk in the footsteps of a top tutor*

It is 1 July 20X5. You are a manager in Kelly & Co, a firm of Chartered Certified Accountants which offers a range of assurance services.

The managing director of Flynn Co, which is not currently a client of Kelly & Co, has contacted you regarding a review engagement which he would like your firm to provide. Kelly& Co has already conducted specific client identification procedures in line with money laundering regulations with satisfactory results.

Flynn Co operates in the food processing industry, and the company is planning to build a new food processing facility in a foreign country. This will cost approximately $15 million to build, and Flynn Co has approached its lenders to provide the necessary finance.

The following exhibits, available below, provide information relevant to the question:

1   Flynn Co – information regarding Flynn Co and the review engagement your firm is invited to provide.

2   Cash flow forecast – a cash flow forecast and supporting notes and assumptions to be used in support of a loan application.

This information should be used to answer the question requirements within your chosen response option(s).

Exhibit 1 – Flynn Co

Flynn Co is an unlisted company whose main activity involves processing frozen food. The company has several processing plants in its home country and one located in a foreign country, Nearland. In order to expand its product range, the company is planning to build a new facility and begin processing in another foreign country, Farland.

Flynn Co has approached its provider of finance, Mortons Bank, to provide a $15 million loan which will cover the necessary asset expenditure. Nearland and Farland both have a different currency than that used by Flynn Co.

Mortons Bank has asked Flynn Co to provide a business plan for the next three years in support of the loan application. The business plan includes forecast statements of profit or loss and cash flow. The bank has requested that the forecasts be subject to an independent review and that a review report should be included with the loan application. Flynn Co is expecting to submit the business plan and review report to the bank on 5 August 20X5.

Flynn Co is audited by Roxie Associates. A new audit manager, Mary Sunshine, has recently been recruited to your firm from Flynn Co where she worked in the internal audit department, and she told you the following:

'I know that Flynn Co's auditor, Roxie Associates, has performed review engagements for the company in the past. I am aware that the latest external auditor's report, for the year ended 31 March 20X5, included a Material Uncertainty Related to Going Concern section due to the company's liquidity problems.'

In his communication with Kelly & Co, the managing director of Flynn Co has suggested that should Kelly & Co provide the report to the bank, and assuming that the finance is provided to the company, he will be willing to remove Roxie Associates as the company's auditor and appoint Kelly & Co to provide the audit service. The managing director has also requested that Mary Sunshine is part of the review team and the audit team, given her past experience with the company.

Exhibit 2 – Cash flow forecast

	Note	31 Dec 20X5 $000	30 June 20X6 $000	31 Dec 20X6 $000	30 June 20X7 $000	31 Dec 20X7 $000	30 June 20X8 $000
Average monthly sales	1	200	234	265	288	308	318
Revenue		1,200.00	1,404.00	1,589.33	1,727.60	1,846.80	1,909.60
Cash inflow from customers	2	1,050	1,201	1,399.5	1,578	1,723.5	1,836
Operating expenses	3	(920)	(940)	(1,080)	(1,150)	(1,280)	(1,340)
Marketing for new product ranges		–	(100)	–	–		–
Interest payments and other finance costs		(30)	(30)	(30)	(30)	(30)	(30)
Dividends		(100)	–	(100)	–	(100)	–
Loan receipt		15,000	–	–	–	–	–
Capital (asset) expenditure	4	(7,500)	(7,500)	–	–	–	–
Net cash flow		7,500	(7,369)	189.50	398	313.5	466
Opening cash		50	7,550	181	370.5	768.5	1,082
Closing cash		7,550	181	370.5	768.5	1,082	1,548

Notes and key assumptions:

1   Monthly sales are based on management's forecasts with predicted sales growth as follows:

Six months to 31 December 20X5	0%
Six months to 30 June 20X6	17%
Six months to 31 December 20X6	13.2%
Six months to 30 June 20X7	8.7%
Six months to 31 December 20X7	6.9%
Six months to 30 June 20X8	3.4%

Sales are expected to increase in 20X6 when the new processing facility opens in Farland. The new product ranges are expected to be very popular and the product launch will be supported by an advertising campaign. In addition to output from the new processing facility, production levels at existing facilities are planned to increase by at least 10%.

2   On average, cash is received from customers in the following pattern:

25% in month of sale

50% following month of sale

25% two months after sale

3   Operating expenses are forecast to increase over the three-year period as production increases. The company is expecting to benefit from economies of scale as production increases at each processing facility.

4   The new processing facility is planned to commence production on 31 March 20X6.

Required:

(a)   Using the information contained in Exhibit 1, evaluate the matters to be considered by Kelly & Co in deciding whether to accept Flynn Co as a client of the firm and whether to perform the review engagement to report on the business plan.

(8 marks)

Note: You do NOT need to include matters relating specifically to client due diligence (Know Your Client) procedures.

(b)   Using the information contained in Exhibits 1 and 2, and assuming Kelly & Co accepts the engagement to review Flynn Co's cash flow forecast:

(i)   Evaluate the assumptions used by management and the completeness of the cash flow forecast prepared, explaining why particular assumptions should be challenged and approached with professional scepticism, and   (5 marks)

(ii)   Design the examination procedures which should be performed in the review of Flynn Co's cash flow forecast.   (7 marks)

Professional marks will be awarded for the demonstration of skill in analysis and evaluation, professional scepticism and judgement and commercial acumen in your answer.   (5 marks)

(Total: 25 marks)

44   MORITZ & CO *Walk in the footsteps of a top tutor*

 Answer debrief

It is 1 July 20X5. You are a manager in Moritz & Co, a firm of Chartered Certified Accountants which offers a range of services to audit and non-audit clients.

The following exhibits, available below, provide information relevant to the question:

1   Lavenza Co – request to provide an assurance report on prospective financial information.

2   Beaufort Co – request for assistance in preparing the share prospectus document to support the company's flotation.

This information should be used to answer the question requirements within the response option provided.

Exhibit 1 – Lavenza Co

Your firm has been asked to consider a potential engagement to review and provide an assurance report on prospective financial information (PFI) for Lavenza Co, which is not an audit client of your firm. Moritz & Co has already conducted specific client identification procedures in line with money laundering regulations with satisfactory results.

Lavenza Co has approached your firm in order to obtain an independent assurance opinion on a cash flow forecast which is being prepared for its bankers in support of an application for an increase in its existing overdraft facility. The following cash flow forecast has been prepared by the finance director of Lavenza Co for the 12 months to 30 June 20X6:

Lavenza Co cash flow forecast for the 12 months ending 30 June 20X6

	3 months to 30 Sept 20X5	3 months to 31 Dec 20X5	3 months to 31 March 20X6	3 months to 30 June 20X6
	$000	$000	$000	$000
Operating cash receipts				
Cash sales – high street shops	4,343	4,690	5,065	5,471
Cash sales – online	6,782	7,053	7,335	7,628
Receipts from credit sales – online	11,987	12,346	12,717	13,099
	23,112	24,089	25,117	26,198
Operating cash payments				
Purchases of inventory	(10,846)	(11,388)	(11,730)	(12,316)
Salaries	(7,254)	(7,109)	(7,180)	(7,384)
Overheads	(6,459)	(6,265)	(6,391)	(6,659)
	(24,559)	(24,762)	(25,301)	(26,359)

Other cash flows

Initial costs of new high street shops	(2,143)	(1,128)		
Online marketing campaign	(624)	(431)	(386)	(278)
	(2,767)	(1,559)	(386)	(278)
Cash flow for the period	(4,214)	(2,232)	(570)	(439)
Opening cash	(9,193)	(13,407)	(15,639)	(16,209)
Closing cash	(13,407)	(15,639)	(16,209)	(16,648)

The following information is also relevant:

1   Lavenza Co is a retailer of academic text books which it sells through its own network of book shops and online through its website. The revenue from the website includes both cash sales and sales on credit to educational institutions. The company has provided historical analysis of its trade receivables indicating that for sales made on credit, 10% pay in the month of the sale, 62% after 30 days, 16% after 60 days, 8% after 90 days and the remainder are irrecoverable debts.

2   The company already has an established presence in large cities with universities but has seen a decline in its core operations in recent years which has led to a decrease in revenue and a fall in liquidity. In order to reverse these trends, the company is planning to extend its operations by opening new shops in small cities with universities and large colleges.

3   Lavenza Co's management is planning an online marketing campaign targeted at the university sector which they believe will increase the company's market share by approximately 3%.

4   The company has an existing overdraft facility of $12 million with its bankers and has requested an increase in the facility to $17 million.

Exhibit 2 – Beaufort Co

You have also been asked to provide an accountant's report for an audit client, Beaufort Co, which intends to list on the stock market in September 20X5.

Beaufort Co has been an audit client of Moritz & Co for the last eight years, preparing financial statements to 31 March each year. Throughout this period, the managing partner at your firm, Frances Stein, has taken personal responsibility for the audit and has increased the total fee income from the client to the level where it represented 16.2% of Moritz & Co's total fee income in 20X5 (15.4%: 20X4). In addition to performing the annual audit, Moritz & Co also provides accounting and bookkeeping services for Beaufort Co. The accounting and bookkeeping services include the preparation of the monthly payroll for the client and maintaining all of the financial records of a small, immaterial division of the company.

The managing director of Beaufort Co, Margaret Shelley, has asked your firm for assistance in the preparation of the share prospectus document which will be used to support the company's flotation.

The contents of the prospectus document will include the following elements:

– Key historical financial information prepared to 31 August 20X5

– Profit forecasts

– A summary of the key risks relating to the client's business

– A business plan outlining the future prospects of the company and recommending the shares to investors.

Margaret Shelley has asked if Mortiz & Co can also provide an accountant's report which will be included in the prospectus and which will cover each of these elements.

Required:

(a) **Using the information contained in Exhibit 1:**

(i) **Explain the matters to be considered by Moritz & Co before accepting the engagement to review and report on Lavenza Co's prospective financial information, and** (6 marks)

(ii) **Assuming Moritz & Co accepts the engagement, design the examination procedures which should be performed in respect of Lavenza Co's cash flow forecast.** (7 marks)

(b) **Using the information contained in Exhibit 2, comment on the ethical and professional issues arising as a result of Beaufort Co's planned listing and the services which it has requested from Moritz & Co.** (7 marks)

Professional marks will be awarded for the demonstration of skill in analysis and evaluation, professional scepticism and judgement and commercial acumen in your answer. (5 marks)

(Total: 25 marks)

 Calculate your allowed time, allocate the time to the separate parts...............

---

45 **JANSEN & CO** *Walk in the footsteps of a top tutor*

You are an audit manager in Jansen & Co which offers a range of audit and other assurance services to its clients.

The following exhibits, available below, provide information relevant to the question:

1 Narley Co – request to provide an assurance report on prospective financial information.

2 Watson Co – provides details of matters which have been brought to your attention by the audit supervisor.

This information should be used to answer the question requirements within the response option provided.

Exhibit 1 – Narley Co

One of your audit clients is Narley Co which operates a commercial haulage company. Narley Co has been an audit client for the last five years and is currently planning a significant expansion of its operations into a new geographical area and jurisdiction. In order to finance the planned expansion, Narley Co needs funds to purchase additional heavy goods vehicles, expand its warehousing facilities and recruit more drivers.

The company is also planning a major advertising and marketing campaign targeted at potential customers in the new jurisdiction.

Narley Co's finance director, Suzanne Seddon, has approached you to ask if your firm will provide a report on the prospective financial information which has been prepared in support of a loan application. The application is for a new long-term loan of $22 million from the company's current lender which it intends to use exclusively to finance the planned expansion. The company currently has an existing long-term loan of $31 million from the same bank which is redeemable in five years' time.

Suzanne Seddon has provided you with the following extract from the prospective financial information which will form part of the company's loan application:

Forecast statements of profit or loss

	Note	Year ended 30 June 20X5 Unaudited $000	Year ending 30 June 20X6 Forecast $000	Year ending 30 June 20X7 Forecast $000
Revenue	1	138,861	174,965	225,705
Cost of sales	2	(104,862)	(124,786)	(157,230)
Administrative expenses	3	(22,936)	(21,984)	(20,743)
Operating profit		11,063	28,195	47,732
Finance costs	4	(1,450)	(1,638)	(1,597)
Profit before tax		9,613	26,557	46,135

Notes:

1   Revenue represents the amounts derived from the provision of haulage services to commercial customers operating principally in the retail sector. Narley Co's board of directors believes that trade in both its existing and new markets will experience significant growth over the next two years.

2   Cost of sales comprises the costs of warehousing and distribution including relevant staff costs, maintenance and repair of vehicles and depreciation of property, equipment and vehicles.

3   Administrative expenses are mainly the costs of running Narley Co's central head office facility.

4   Finance costs represent the cost of servicing long-term finance from Narley Co's bankers.

Exhibit 2 – Watson Co

One of your colleagues at Jansen & Co, Rodney Evans, has been taken ill at short notice and you have been temporarily assigned as audit manager on Watson Co, an IT consultancy company which is listed on a second tier investment market. The final audit of Watson Co for the year ended 31 March 20X5 is approaching completion and you are in the process of reviewing the audit working papers. The draft financial statements for the year recognise profit before tax for the year of $54.2 million and total assets of $23.1 million.

The audit supervisor, who is a part-qualified chartered certified accountant, has sent you an email from which the following extract is taken:

'It's great to have you on board as I was beginning to worry that there would be no manager review of our working papers prior to the final audit clearance meeting next week.

One issue which I wanted to check with you is that Watson Co has introduced a cash-settled share-based payment scheme by granting its directors share appreciation rights (SARs) for the first time this year. This was not identified at planning as a high risk area.

The SARs were granted on 1 April 20X4 at which date the client obtained a valuation of the rights which was performed by an external firm of valuers. I have filed a copy of the valuation report and I have looked up the valuers online and have found a very professional looking website which confirms that they know what they are doing.

The cost of the SARs scheme based on this valuation is being appropriately recognised over the three-year vesting period and a straight-line expense of $195,000 has been recognised in the statement of profit or loss on this basis. A corresponding equity reserve has also been correctly recognised on the statement of financial position. The amount also seems immaterial and I can't see any need to propose any amendments to the financial statements in relation to either the amounts recognised or the disclosures made in the notes to the financial statements.'

Required:

(a)   Using the information contained in Exhibit 1:

(i)   Explain the matters which should be considered by Jansen & Co before accepting the engagement to review and report on Narley Co's prospective financial information.   (6 marks)

(ii)   Assuming Jansen & Co accepts the engagement, design the examination procedures which should be performed in respect of Narley Co's forecast statements of profit or loss.   (7 marks)

(b)   Using the information contained in Exhibit 2, comment on the quality of the planning and performance of the audit of Watson Co discussing the quality management and other professional issues raised.   (7 marks)

Professional marks will be awarded for the demonstration of skill in analysis and evaluation, professional scepticism and judgement and commercial acumen in your answer.   (5 marks)

(Total: 25 marks)

46 VIZSLA *Walk in the footsteps of a top tutor*

It is 1 July 20X5. You are an audit manager in Pointer & Co, a firm of Chartered Certified Accountants which offers a range of assurance services.

The following exhibits, available below, provide information relevant to the question:

1 Potential new client, Setter Co.

2 Review of prospective financial information for Vizsla Co.

This information should be used to answer the question requirements within your chosen response option(s).

Exhibit 1 – Potential new client, Setter Co

The managing director of Setter Co, Gordon Potts, has recently contacted you as the company is looking to appoint a provider of assurance services including providing a limited assurance review on the company's financial statements, tax planning advice and preparation of both the company's and his personal tax computations for submission to the tax authorities.

Setter Co is a small company looking to expand in the next few years. You have done some research on both Setter Co and Gordon Potts and have confirmed that the company is small enough to be exempt from audit. The company is owner-managed, with the Potts family owning 90% of the share capital. Gordon Potts is a director and majority shareholder of three other companies. An article in a newspaper from several years ago about Gordon Potts indicated that one of his companies was once fined for breach of employment law and that he had used money from one of the company's pension plans to set up a business abroad, appointing his son as the managing director of that business.

Exhibit 2 – Review of prospective financial information for Vizsla Co

Pointer & Co has agreed to perform an assurance engagement for Vizsla Co. The engagement will be a review of prospective financial information which is needed to support the company's overdraft facilities. Vizsla Co had a financial year ended 31 December 20X4, and an unmodified opinion was issued on these financial statements last month. Pointer & Co's partner responsible for ethics has agreed that any threats to objectivity will be reduced to an acceptable level through the use of a team separate from the audit team to perform the work.

The operating profit forecast for the two years to 30 June 20X7 prepared by a member of the accounting team of Vizsla Co is shown below, along with some accompanying notes.

	Note	Six months to 31 December 20X5	Six months to 30 June 20X6	Six months to 31 December 20X6	Six months to 30 June 20X7
		$000	$000	$000	$000
Revenue	1	12,800	16,900	13,700	18,900
Gross profit %		34%	45%	36%	46%
Operating costs:					
Staff costs		(2,800)	(2,900)	(2,800)	(2,900)
Design costs	2	(1,200)	(1,200)	(1,250)	(1,250)
Marketing		(900)	(1,000)	(1,100)	(1,100)
Interest on overdraft	3	(25)	(10)	–	–
Other expenses	4	(3,840)	(5,070)	(4,110)	(5,670)
Operating profit		4,035	6,720	4,440	7,980

Notes:

1   Vizsla Co is a producer of greetings cards and giftware, the demand for which is seasonal in nature.

2   Design costs are mostly payroll costs of the staff working in the company's design team, and the costs relate to the design and development of new product ranges.

3   Vizsla Co has agreed with its bank to clear its overdraft by 1 December 20X6, and the management team is confident that after that point the company will not need an overdraft facility.

4   The total 'Other expenses' is calculated based on 30% of the projected revenue for the six-month period.

Required:

(a)   **Using the information contained in Exhibit 1, explain the importance of performing customer due diligence (know your client procedures) and recommend the information which should be obtained.**   **(11 marks)**

(b)   **Using the information contained in Exhibit 2, design the examination procedures which should be performed in the review of Vizsla Co's profit forecast.**   **(9 marks)**

Professional marks will be awarded for the demonstration of skill in analysis and evaluation, professional scepticism and judgement and commercial acumen in your answer.   **(5 marks)**

(Total: 25 marks)

47   WATERS *Walk in the footsteps of a top tutor*

It is 1 July 20X5. You are a manager in Hunt & Co, a firm which offers a range of services to audit and non-audit clients. You have been asked to consider a potential engagement to review and provide a report on the prospective financial information of Waters Co, a company which has been an audit client of Hunt & Co for six years. The audit of the financial statements for the year ended 31 May 20X5 has just commenced.

The following exhibits, available below, provide information relevant to the question:

1   Waters Co – information regarding Waters Co and the review engagement your firm is invited to provide.

2   Cash flow forecast – a cash flow forecast and supporting notes and assumptions to be used in support of a loan application.

This information should be used to answer the question requirements within your chosen response option(s).

Exhibit 1 – Waters Co

Waters Co operates a chain of cinemas across the country. Currently its cinemas are out of date and use projectors which cannot show films made using new technology, which are becoming more popular. Management is planning to invest in all of its cinemas in order to attract more customers. The company has sufficient cash to fund half of the necessary asset expenditure, but has approached its bank with a loan application of $8 million for the remainder of the funds required. Most of the cash will be used to invest in equipment and fittings, such as new projectors and larger screens, enabling new technology films to be shown in all cinemas. The remaining cash will be used for refurbishment of the cinemas. Prior to finalising the application for the funding from the bank, the finance director has also asked if the audit engagement partner will assist him in presenting the final version of the strategic plan, in relation to the refurbishment, to the board as he knows that Hunt & Co has several clients in the industry and the partner will be able to confirm that the plan is consistent with what others in the industry are doing.

The draft forecast statements of profit or loss for the years ending 31 May 20X6 and 20X7 are shown below, along with the key assumptions which have been used in their preparation. The unaudited statement of profit or loss for the year ended 31 May 20X5 is also shown below. The forecast has been prepared for use by the bank in making its lending decision, and will be accompanied by other prospective financial information including a forecast statement of cash flows.

Exhibit 2 – Cash flow forecast

Forecast statement of profit or loss

	Year ended 31 May 20X5 Unaudited $000	Note to forecast information	Year ending 31 May 20X6 Forecast $000	Year ending 31 May 20X7 Forecast $000
Revenue	35,000	1	43,000	46,000
Operating expenses	(28,250)	2	(31,500)	(32,100)
	———		———	———
Operating profit	6,750		11,500	13,900
Finance costs	(1,700)		(2,000)	(1,900)
	———		———	———
Profit before tax	5,050		9,500	12,000
	———		———	———

Note 1: The forecast increase in revenue is based on the following assumptions:

(i) All cinemas will be fitted with new projectors and larger screens to show new technology films by September 20X5.

(ii) Ticket prices will increase from $7.50 to $10 from 1 September 20X5.

Note 2: Operating expenses include mainly staff costs, depreciation of property and equipment, and repairs and maintenance to the cinemas.

Required:

(a) Using the information contained in Exhibit 1, evaluate the matters to be considered by Hunt & Co before accepting the engagement to review and report on Waters Co's prospective financial information. **(6 marks)**

(b) Using the information contained in Exhibits 1 and 2, and assuming Hunt & Co accepts the engagement to review Waters Co's cash flow forecast, design the examination procedures which should be performed in the review of Waters Co's forecast statement of profit or loss. **(10 marks)**

(c) Discuss the content of the report which would be issued on the prospective financial information, explaining the level of assurance which is provided. **(4 marks)**

Professional marks will be awarded for the demonstration of skill in analysis and evaluation, professional scepticism and judgement and commercial acumen in your answer. **(5 marks)**

(Total: 25 marks)

48 MARR & CO *Walk in the footsteps of a top tutor*

It is 1 July 20X5. You are a manager in Marr & Co, a firm of Chartered Certified Accountants and you are currently carrying out work for Morrissey Co.

Marr & Co is a relatively small firm, with annual practice income of $15 million, of which approximately half is generated from providing tax, corporate finance and accounting services to its clients. Marr & Co also has a number of audit clients, all of which are manufacturing companies, and a dedicated team of staff work on these audit clients.

The following exhibits, available below, provide information relevant to the question:

1   Background information – details about Morrissey Co and a due diligence assignment relating to Brodie Co.

2   Brodie Co – information on Brodie Co's intangible assets and financing arrangements.

3   Email from finance director – an email you received from Morrissey Co's finance director.

This information should be used to answer the question requirements within the response option provided.

Exhibit 1 – Background information

Marr & Co has been appointed by Morrissey Co, a textile manufacturer and not currently an audit client of Marr & Co, to carry out a due diligence assignment. Marr & Co conducted all necessary client acceptance procedures prior to agreeing to perform the due diligence assignment, which you will assist the partner in planning.

Morrissey Co has identified Brodie Co for potential acquisition. Brodie Co is also a textile manufacturer, and the company has grown rapidly in the last five years, its growth based on the success of its organic textiles, which it sells to clothing manufacturers.

The terms of the due diligence assignment include that Marr & Co should focus part of its investigation on the intangible assets of Brodie Co, in particular the valuation of these assets and their operational significance, and also on the company's financing arrangements.

Exhibit 2 – Brodie Co

From a discussion with the finance director of Morrissey Co, you have the following information about the intangible assets of the target company, Brodie Co:

Brodie Co imports some of the dyes used in its manufacturing process, for which an import licence is necessary. The three-year import licence costs $1.5 million and is recognised as an intangible asset in the financial statements, amortised over three years.

The company's textiles are manufactured using the unique 'PureFab' manufacturing process, which was developed to increase the durability of its organic textiles. The 'PureFab' manufacturing process is protected by a patent, which was secured seven years ago and which prevents other manufacturers from using the same process or describing products as 'PureFab' textiles. The cost of the patent was $1 million and this is recognised as an intangible asset in the company's financial statements, amortised over 10 years, which is the life of the patent.

You have also gathered the following information about Brodie Co's current financing arrangements:

Source of finance	$'000	Further comments
Equity shares	6,800	This is the value of the company's issued equity shares
Bank loan	2,400	Secured on the company's property, plant and equipment
Venture capital	3,600	Loaned to the company three years ago, to fund construction of manufacturing plant

Exhibit 3 – Email from finance director

To: Audit engagement partner

From: Paul Hook, Finance director, Morrissey Co

Subject: Appointment as auditor

Date: 1 December 20X5

Hello

Following the successful acquisition of Brodie Co, we would like to appoint your firm as auditor. The appointment would include the audit of Morrissey Co, Brodie Co, and the consolidated financial statements of the new Group, for the financial year ending 31 December 20X5.

With this being the first acquisition made by Morrissey Co, our accountants have little experience with Group accounting, and I qualified a long time ago, so we are also expecting your firm to prepare the consolidated financial statements from the individual financial statements of Morrissey Co and Brodie Co, which I will provide to you. We don't think the consolidated financial statements will really be used, so to save time we will not publish notes to the Group financial statements – the individual accounts provide all of the information which users might need.

We have notified our existing audit provider, Butler Associates, that we wish to remove them from office. We are in a dispute with Butler Associates regarding fees – having negotiated a reduction in audit fee compared to the previous year, an invoice they sent to us in respect of last year's audit contains an unexpected additional amount. When we queried this with Butler Associates, they justified the amount as relating to additional work performed on payroll, which they felt was necessary due to a number of errors they had found in payroll processing. We have also informed the management of Brodie Co that we intend to replace their audit provider with Marr & Co.

Assuming that your firm accepts appointment as auditor, we will invite the partner and manager assigned to the audit to attend a textile industry conference. I think this will help you to obtain a better understanding of the industry, as well as giving you the opportunity to meet some other textile manufacturers. You could do some networking and perhaps meet new potential clients. We will pay for all of your conference expenses and for the flights; the conference is being held in a top hotel in Hawaii.

I look forward to hearing from you.

Paul

Required:

(a) Using the information in Exhibits 1 and 2:

  (i) Explain the specific enquiries you should make of Brodie Co's management relevant to the company's intangible assets.

  (ii) Recommend, with reasons, the principal additional information which should be made available by Brodie Co's management in relation to the company's financing arrangements. **(12 marks)**

It is now 1 December 20X5. Prior to the acquisition of Brodie Co, Marr & Co was appointed to provide corporate finance advice to Morrissey Co in relation to raising finance of approximately $35 million to fund the acquisition. You have now received an email from the finance director of Morrissey Co.

Using the information in Exhibit 3:

(b) Comment on the ethical and professional issues to be considered by Marr & Co in relation to the request from the finance director. **(8 marks)**

Professional marks will be awarded for the demonstration of skill in analysis and evaluation, professional scepticism and judgement and commercial acumen in your answer. **(5 marks)**

(Total: 25 marks)

49 **CHEETAH** *Walk in the footsteps of a top tutor*

It is 1 July 20X5. You are a manager in Leopard & Co, a firm of Chartered Certified Accountants which offers a range of assurance services. You are currently assigned to a due diligence engagement for one of your firm's audit clients, Cheetah Co, a manufacturer of bespoke furniture. The audit of Cheetah Co is conducted by a team from a different department. You have never been involved in the audit of this client.

The following exhibits, available below, provide information relevant to the question:

1   Zebra Co – details of Zebra Co, potential acquisition target by Cheetah Co.

2   Request from Cheetah Co management – request to attend meeting with Cheetah Co's bank.

This information should be used to answer the question requirements within the response option provided.

Exhibit 1 – Zebra Co

Leopard & Co has been engaged to conduct a financial and operational due diligence review of Zebra Co, a company which has been identified as a potential acquisition target by Cheetah Co, due to the synergies offered and the potential to expand the existing production facilities. As part of the due diligence review, you have been asked to provide a valuation of Zebra Co's assets and liabilities and an analysis of the company's operating profit forecasts. This will assist Cheetah Co in determining an appropriate purchase price for Zebra Co.

During the engagement fieldwork your team identified two matters, which require your further consideration, as follows:

1 While reviewing correspondence with customers in relation to outstanding receivables, one of the team found a letter from a large retailer, for which Zebra Co produces a number of unique products, providing advanced notice that they are not renewing their purchasing agreement when the current one expires. The customer advised that they are switching to a new entrant to the market who is substantially cheaper than Zebra Co. A brief analysis identified that the customer provides, on average, almost 5% of Zebra Co's annual revenues.

2 Zebra Co owns a piece of land which was given to it as a gift by the local authorities ten years ago. The land surrounds the entrance to the main production premises and is designated as a nature reserve. Restrictions were imposed on the usage of the land which also limit who the owner is able to sell the land to in the future. The land has zero carrying amount in the financial statements.

No additional matters have arisen for your consideration. You are also aware that the financial statements for the last ten years have been audited and no modifications have been made to the auditor's opinion during this period.

Exhibit 2 – Request from Cheetah Co management

The management team of Cheetah Co has also approached Leopard & Co to ask whether representatives of the firm would be available to attend a meeting with the company's bankers, who they are hoping will finance the acquisition of Zebra Co, to support the management team in conveying the suitability of the acquisition of Zebra Co.

For the meeting the bank requires the most up-to-date interim accounts of Cheetah Co with the accompanying auditor's independent interim review report. Your firm is due to complete the interim review shortly and the management team of Cheetah Co has requested that the interim review is completed quickly so that it does not hold up negotiations with the bank, stating that if it does, it may affect the outcome of the next audit tender, which is due to take place after the completion of this year's audit.

Required:

(a) **Using the information contained in Exhibit 1:**

    (i) **Explain why each matter requires further investigation as part of the due diligence review, and** **(6 marks)**

    (ii) **Recommend the investigation procedures to be performed.** **(6 marks)**

(b) **Using the information contained in Exhibit 2, comment on the ethical and professional issues raised, and recommend any actions which should be taken in respect of the request from the management team of Cheetah Co.** **(8 marks)**

Professional marks will be awarded for the demonstration of skill in analysis and evaluation, professional scepticism and judgement and commercial acumen in your answer. **(5 marks)**

(Total: 25 marks)

50   SANZIO   *Walk in the footsteps of a top tutor*

It is 1 July 20X5. You are a manager in Raphael & Co, a firm of Chartered Certified Accountants which offers a range of assurance services. Raphael & Co has 12 offices and 30 partners, 10 of whom are members of ACCA.

The following exhibits, available below, provide information relevant to the question:

1   Draft advertisement – draft advertisement to be placed in newspapers.

2   Sanzio Co – request to provide due diligence engagement for Sanzio Co.

This information should be used to answer the question requirements within the response option provided.

Exhibit 1 – Draft advertisement

An advertisement has been drafted as part of the firm's drive to increase the number of clients. It is suggested that it should be placed in a number of quality national as well as local newspapers:

> Have you had enough of your accountant charging you too much for poor quality services?
>
> Does your business need a kick-start?
>
> Look no further. Raphael & Co provides the most comprehensive range of finance and accountancy services in the country as well as having the leading tax team in the country who are just waiting to save you money.
>
> Still not sure? We guarantee to be cheaper than your existing service provider and for the month of January we are offering free business advice to all new audit clients.
>
> Drop in and see us at your local office for a free consultation.
>
> Raphael & Co, Chartered Certified Accountants.

Exhibit 2 – Sanzio Co

As a result of advertising, Raphael & Co has been appointed by Sanzio Co to perform a due diligence review of a potential acquisition target, Titian Tyres Co. As part of the due diligence review and to allow for consideration of an appropriate offer price, Sanzio Co has requested that you identify and value all the assets and liabilities of Titian Tyres Co, including items which may not currently be reported in the statement of financial position.

Sanzio Co is a large, privately owned company operating only in this country, which sells spare parts and accessories for cars, vans and bicycles. Titian Tyres Co is a national chain of vehicle service centres, specialising in the repair and replacement of tyres, although the company also offers a complete range of engine and bodywork services as well. If the acquisition is successful, the management of Sanzio Co intends to open a Titian Tyres service centre in each of its stores.

One of the reasons for Titian Tyres Co's success is their internally generated customer database, which records all customer service details. Using the information contained on the database software, the company's operating system automatically informs previous customers when their vehicle is due for its next service via email, mobile phone text or automated letter. It also informs a customer service team to telephone the customer if they fail to book a service within two weeks of receiving the notification.

According to the management of Titian Tyres Co, repeat business makes up over 60% of annual sales and management believes that this is a distinct competitive advantage over other service centres.

Titian Tyres Co also recently purchased a licence to distribute a new, innovative tyre which was designed and patented in the United States. The tyre is made of 100% recycled materials and, due to a new manufacturing process, is more hardwearing and therefore needs replacing less often. Titian Tyres Co paid $5 million for the licence and the company is currently the sole, licenced distributor in this country.

During a brief review of Titian Tyres Co's most recent financial statements for the year ended 31 March 20X5, you notice a contingent liability disclosure in the notes relating to compensation claims made after the fitting of faulty engine parts during 20X4. The management of Titian Tyres Co has stated that the fault lies with the manufacturer of the part and that they have made a claim against the manufacturer for the total amount sought by the affected customers.

Required:

(a) **Using the information contained in Exhibit 1, comment on the suitability of the advertisement discussing any ethical and professional issues raised.** **(7 marks)**

Using the information contained in Exhibit 2:

(b) (i) **Recommend, with reasons, the principal additional information which should be made available to assist with your valuation of Titian Tyres Co's intangible assets.** **(8 marks)**

    (ii) **Explain the specific enquiries you should make of Titian Tyres Co's management relevant to the contingent liability disclosed in the financial statements.** **(5 marks)**

Professional marks will be awarded for the demonstration of skill in analysis and evaluation, professional scepticism and judgement and commercial acumen in your answer. **(5 marks)**

(Total: 25 marks)

51 BALTIMORE *Walk in the footsteps of a top tutor*

It is 1 July 20X5. You are a manager in the business advisory department of Goleen & Co. Your firm has been approached by Mark Clear, Baltimore Co's managing director, to provide assurance to Baltimore Co, a company which is not an audit client of your firm, on a potential acquisition.

The following exhibits, available below, provide information relevant to the question:

1   Baltimore Co – background information on Baltimore Co and the due diligence engagement your firm is invited to provide.

2   Mizzen Co – information on potential acquisition target, Mizzen Co.

3   Financial information – extracts from Mizzen Co's audited financial statements for the last four years.

This information should be used to answer the question requirements within the response option provided.

Exhibit 1 – Baltimore Co

Baltimore Co is a book publisher specialising in publishing textbooks and academic journals. In the last few years the market has changed significantly, with the majority of customers purchasing books from online sellers. This has led to a reduction in profits, and we recognise that we need to diversify our product range in order to survive. As a result of this, we decided to offer a subscription-based website to customers, which would provide the customer with access to our full range of textbooks and journals online.

On investigating how to set up this website, we found that we lack sufficient knowledge and resources to develop it ourselves and began to look for another company which has the necessary skills, with a view to acquiring the company. We have identified Mizzen Co as a potential acquisition, and we have approached the bank for a loan which will be used to finance the acquisition if it goes ahead.

Baltimore Co has not previously acquired another company. We would like to engage your firm to provide guidance regarding the acquisition. We understand that a due diligence review would be advisable prior to deciding on whether to go ahead with the acquisition but are unsure about the type of conclusion that would be issued and whether it would be similar to the opinion in an auditor's report.

Exhibit 2 – Mizzen Co

Mizzen Co was established four years ago by two university graduates, Vic Sandhu and Lou Lien, who secured funds from a venture capitalist company, BizGrow, to set up the company. Vic and Lou created a new type of website interface which has proven extremely popular, and which led to the company growing rapidly and building a good reputation. They continue to innovate and have won awards for website design. Vic and Lou have a minority shareholding in Mizzen Co.

Mizzen Co employs 50 people and operates from premises owned by BizGrow, for which a nominal rent of $1,000 is paid annually. The company uses few assets other than computer equipment and fixtures and fittings. The biggest expense is wages and salaries and due to increased demand for website development, freelance specialists have been used in the financial year ended 31 March 20X5. According to the most recent audited financial statements, Mizzen Co has a bank balance of $500,000.

The company has three revenue streams:

1   Developing and maintaining websites for corporate customers. Mizzen Co charges a one-off fee to its customers for the initial development of a website and for maintaining the website for two years. The amount of this fee depends on the size and complexity of the website and averages at $10,000 per website. The customer can then choose to pay another one-off fee, averaging $2,000, for Mizzen Co to provide maintenance for a further five years.

2   Mizzen Co has also developed a subscription-based website on which it provides access to technical material for computer specialists. Customers pay an annual fee of $250 which gives them unlimited access to the website. This accounts for approximately 30% of Mizzen Co's total revenue.

3   The company has built up several customer databases which are made available, for a fee, to other companies for marketing purposes. This is the smallest revenue stream, accounting for approximately 20% of Mizzen Co's total revenue.

Exhibit 3 – Financial information

Statement of profit or loss

	Year ended 31 March 20X5 $000	Year ended 31 March 20X4 $000	Year ended 31 March 20X3 $000	Year ended 31 March 20X2 $000
Revenue	4,268	3,450	2,150	500
Operating expenses	(2,118)	(2,010)	(1,290)	(1,000)
Operating profit/(loss)	2,150	1,440	860	(500)
Finance costs	(250)	(250)	(250)	–
Profit/(loss) before tax	1,900	1,190	610	(500)
Income tax expense	(475)	(300)	(140)	–
Profit/(loss) for the year	1,425	890	470	(500)

There were no items of other comprehensive income recognised in any year.

Required:

(a) Using the information in Exhibits 1 and 2, discuss the benefits to Baltimore Co of a due diligence review being performed on Mizzen Co and comment on the type of conclusion which would be issued compared to an auditor's report. **(8 marks)**

(b) Using the information in all exhibits, identify and explain the matters which you would focus on in your due diligence review and recommend the additional information which you will need to perform your work. **(12 marks)**

Professional marks will be awarded for the demonstration of skill in analysis and evaluation, professional scepticism and judgement and commercial acumen in your answer. **(5 marks)**

(Total: 25 marks)

52 JACOB *Walk in the footsteps of a top tutor*

It is 1 July 20X5. You are a manager in the business advisory department of Austen & Co. Your firm has been approached by the directors of Jacob Co, an audit client of your firm, to provide a due diligence review in respect of a potential acquisition, Locke Co.

The following exhibits, available below, provide information relevant to the question:

1 Jacob Co – background information on Jacob Co and the due diligence engagement your firm is invited to provide.

2 Locke Co – information on potential acquisition target, Locke Co.

3 Request to provide advice – request from Jacob Co's management to provide advice on a tender for subcontracting services to Burke Co.

This information should be used to answer the question requirements within the response option provided.

Exhibit 1 – Jacob Co

Jacob Co, an audit client of your firm, is a large privately owned company whose operations involve a repair and maintenance service for domestic customers. The company offers a range of services, such as plumbing and electrical repairs and maintenance, and the repair of domestic appliances such as washing machines and cookers, as well as dealing with emergencies such as damage caused by flooding. All work is covered by a two-year warranty.

The directors of Jacob Co have been seeking to acquire expertise in the repair and maintenance of swimming pools and hot tubs as this is a service increasingly requested, but not offered by the company. They have recently identified Locke Co as a potential acquisition. Preliminary discussions have been held between the directors of the two companies with a view to the acquisition of Locke Co by Jacob Co. This will be the first acquisition performed by the current management team of Jacob Co.

Exhibit 2 – Locke Co

Locke Co is owner-managed, with three of the five board members being the original founders of the company, which was incorporated thirty years ago. The head office is located in a prestigious building, which is owned by the founders' family estate. The company recently acquired a separate piece of land on which a new head office is to be built.

The company has grown rapidly in the last three years as more affluent customers can afford the cost of installing and maintaining swimming pools and hot tubs. The expansion was funded by a significant bank loan. The company relies on an overdraft facility in the winter months when less operating cash inflows arise from maintenance work.

Locke Co enjoys a good reputation, though this was tarnished last year by a complaint by a famous actor who claimed that, following maintenance of his swimming pool by Locke Co's employees, the water contained a chemical which damaged his skin. A court case is ongoing and is attracting media attention.

The company's financial year end is 31 March. Its accounting function is outsourced to Austin Co, a local provider of accounting and tax services.

Exhibit 3 – Request to provide advice on a tender

Jacob Co is tendering for an important contract to provide subcontracting services to Burke Co. Burke Co is also an audit client of your firm and Jacob Co's management has asked your firm to provide advice on the tender it is preparing.

Required:

(a)   Using the information in Exhibits 1 and 2:

(i)   Discuss the potential benefits to Jacob Co of having an externally provided due diligence review. **(6 marks)**

(ii)   Recommend additional information which should be made available for your firm's due diligence review, and explain the need for the information. **(9 marks)**

(b)   Using the information in Exhibit 3, explain the ethical and professional matters your firm should consider in deciding whether to provide advice to Jacob Co on the tender. **(5 marks)**

Professional marks will be awarded for the demonstration of skill in analysis and evaluation, professional scepticism and judgement and commercial acumen in your answer. (5 marks)

(Total: 25 marks)

53   MOOSEWOOD HOSPITAL *Walk in the footsteps of a top tutor*

It is 1 July 20X5. You are the manager responsible for the audit of Moosewood Hospital Co, for the year ended 31 March 20X5, working in the audit department of Fern & Co. Moosewood Hospital Co is a private sector medical facility, where patients undergo minor surgical procedures and receive treatments such as physiotherapy.

The following exhibits, available below, provide information relevant to the question:

1   Valuation of medical inventories – provides details of an issue identified during the audit of inventory.

2   Key performance indicators – details of the key performance indicators to be included in Moosewood Co's integrated report.

This information should be used to answer the question requirements within your chosen response option(s).

Exhibit 1 – Valuation of medical inventories

You have recently visited the audit team, who are currently on site performing the fieldwork, to review the work performed to date and to discuss their progress. During your visit the audit senior informed you of the following matter.

During a review of the valuation of medical inventories, including medicines used in a variety of treatments at the hospital, it was noted that a number of items had passed their recommended use by dates. These were recorded on an inventory spreadsheet maintained by the financial controller and were easy to spot because they were highlighted in red. One of the audit team inspected a sample of the inventories in question and confirmed that their use by dates had expired. When asked about this, the financial controller stated that the audit team must be mistaken. The audit team requested to look at the spreadsheet again but he refused. The next day the finance director confronted the audit team accusing them of extending their investigations 'beyond their remit'. He also threatened to remove them from the premises if they continued to ask questions which were not relevant to the audit of the hospital's financial statements. Since then, the audit team has been unable to complete the audit of medical inventories. They have also noted that the room where the inventories were previously kept has been emptied.

Exhibit 2 – Key performance indicators

Fern & Co is also engaged to produce an assurance report on the performance information of Moosewood Hospital Co which is included in the company's integrated report. The integrated report will be published on the company's website later in the year, and is not part of the information published with the financial statements.

Fern & Co has a specialist team, independent from the audit department, which provides assurance on key performance indicators. Under the terms of the engagement, this team is required to provide assurance with regard to both the accuracy and completeness of the key performance indicators which are used to monitor the hospital's efficiency and effectiveness. Several of the key performance indicators included in the draft integrated report, all of which the Hospital claims to have met, are shown below:

1   To maintain an average patient to nurse ratio of no more than 6:1.

2   To achieve a minimum 75% annual usage of surgical rooms.

3   To ensure that the rate of admissions within 28 days for previously treated conditions does not exceed 3%.

Required:

(a) Using the information in Exhibit 1, identify and explain the ethical and professional issues raised and recommend any actions which should be taken in respect of the matter described by the audit senior. **(8 marks)**

Using the information in Exhibit 2:

(b) (i) Discuss the benefits of independent assurance being provided on the key performance indicators included in the integrated report of Moosewood Hospital Co to the company's management and to external users of the report. **(4 marks)**

(ii) Recommend the examination procedures which should be used in obtaining assurance relating to the key performance indicators of Moosewood Hospital Co. **(8 marks)**

Professional marks will be awarded for the demonstration of skill in analysis and evaluation, professional scepticism and judgement and commercial acumen in your answer. **(5 marks)**

(Total: 25 marks)

54 NEWMAN & CO *Walk in the footsteps of a top tutor*

It is 1 July 20X5. You are a manager in Newman & Co, a global firm of Chartered Certified Accountants. You are responsible for evaluating proposed engagements and for recommending to the partners whether or not an engagement should be accepted by your firm.

The following exhibits, available below, provide information relevant to the question:

1 Eastwood Co – request to perform assurance over Eastwood Co's sustainability report.

2 Faster Jets Co – request to perform an assurance engagement on Faster Jets Co's corporate social responsibility report.

This information should be used to answer the question requirements within the response option provided.

Exhibit 1 – Eastwood Co

Eastwood Co, a listed company, is an existing audit client and is an international mail services operator, with a global network including 220 countries and 300,000 employees. The company offers mail and freight services to individual and corporate customers, as well as storage and logistical services.

Eastwood Co takes its corporate social responsibility seriously, and publishes sustainability key performance indicators (KPIs) in a Sustainability Report, which is published with the financial statements in the annual report. The KPIs include CO_2 emissions, energy usage, and charitable donations. Partly in response to requests from shareholders and pressure groups, Eastwood Co's management has decided that in the forthcoming annual report, the KPIs should be accompanied by an independent assurance report. An approach has been made to your firm to provide this report in addition to the audit. Your firm has recently established a specialist social, environmental and sustainability assurance department based in Oldtown, and if the engagement to report on the Sustainability Report is accepted, it would be performed by members of that team, who would not be involved with the audit.

You have also had a meeting with Ali Monroe, the manager responsible for the audit of Eastwood Co, and notes of the meeting are given below:

Notes from meeting with audit manager, Ali Monroe

Newman & Co has audited Eastwood Co for three years, and it is a major audit client of our firm, due to its global presence and recent listing on two major stock exchanges. The audit is managed from our office in Oldtown, which is also the location of the global headquarters of Eastwood Co.

We have not done any work on the KPIs, other than review them for consistency, as we would with any 'other information' issued with the financial statements. The KPIs are produced by Eastwood Co's Sustainability Department, located in Fartown.

We have performed audit procedures on the charitable donations, as this is disclosed in a note to the financial statements, and our evidence indicates that there have been donations of $9 million this year, which is the amount disclosed in the note. However, the draft KPI is a different figure – $10.5 million, and this is the figure highlighted in the draft Chair's Statement as well as the draft Sustainability Report. $9 million is material to the financial statements.

The audit work is nearly complete, and the annual report is to be published in about four weeks, in time for the company meeting, scheduled for August 20X5.

Exhibit 2 – Faster Jets Co

Newman & Co has also been engaged to perform an assurance engagement on Faster Jets Co's corporate social responsibility (CSR) report. Faster Jets Co is an airline company and is a new audit client of Newman & Co. This engagement will be performed by the specialist social, environmental and sustainability assurance department and there are no ethical threats created by the provision of this service in addition to the audit. An extract from the draft CSR report is shown below.

CSR objective	CSR target	Performance in 20X5
Invest in local communities and contribute to charitable causes	Develop our Local Learning Initiative and offer free one day education programmes to schools	$750,000 was spent on the Local Learning Initiative and 2,250 children attended education days
	Build relationships with global charities and offer free flights to charitable organisations	800 free flights with a value of $560,000 were provided to charities
Reduce environmental impact of operations	Reduce the amount of vehicle fuel used on business travel by our employees	The number of miles travelled in vehicles reduced by 5%, and the amount spent on vehicle fuel reduced by 7%

Required:

(a) Using the information in Exhibit 1, evaluate the matters which should be considered before your firm accepts the invitation to perform an assurance engagement on the Sustainability Report of Eastwood Co. **(10 marks)**

(b) Using the information in Exhibit 2, design the procedures to be used to gain assurance on the validity of the performance information in Faster Jets Co's CSR report. **(6 marks)**

(c) Discuss the difficulties in measuring and reporting on social, environmental and sustainability performance. **(4 marks)**

Professional marks will be awarded for the demonstration of skill in analysis and evaluation, professional scepticism and judgement and commercial acumen in your answer. **(5 marks)**

(Total: 25 marks)

55   BEYER   *Walk in the footsteps of a top tutor*

It is 1 July 20X5. You are a manager in the forensic department of your firm, Kaffe & Co. You have received a request from Beyer Co about an inventory fraud. Beyer Co is not currently a client of your firm.

Beyer Co manufactures and sells parts used in the automotive industry to both car manufacturers and to garages specialising in the repair and servicing of cars.

The following exhibits, available below, provide information relevant to the question:

1   Beyer Co – request to perform a forensic investigation.

2   Inventory fraud – details of the fraud allegations of the whistleblower.

This information should be used to answer the question requirements within the response option provided.

Exhibit 1 – Beyer Co

The audit committee would like Kaffe & Co to perform a forensic investigation to quantify the loss suffered as a result of the inventory fraud which was brought to the attention of the company's audit committee by a whistleblower, and to recommend improvements in the company's internal controls to avoid similar issues in the future. In addition, the audit committee has mentioned that although the quantification of the loss is to form the basis of an insurance claim, the matter has been reported to the police who will be investigating the matter further.

Exhibit 2 – Inventory fraud

Having accepted the engagement, the operations director provides you with the following summary of the allegations of the whistleblower:

'The warehouse manager has been working with one of the sales representatives to despatch goods to a fictitious customer which the warehouse manager has created on the despatch system. The sales orders are input by the sales representative into the despatch system which is not directly linked to the invoicing and accounting system. After the goods despatch note is issued by the warehouse manager and the goods leave the warehouse for delivery to the fictitious customer, the sales representative cancels the original order. The warehouse manager reverses the despatch immediately so that the daily report on inventory movement used to generate invoices in the sales system does not reflect movement of the goods. The sales representative takes delivery of the goods at the address of the fictitious customer and then sells the parts on the internet, splitting the proceeds with the warehouse manager. The warehouse manager supervises and participates in all inventory counts and this way ensures he is able to adjust the records of inventory to disguise the missing items.'

The operations director has informed you that no authorisation is required for either the cancellation of orders or the reversal of despatch notes.

Required:

(a)   Using the information in Exhibit 1, evaluate the matters which should be considered before your firm accepts the invitation to perform a forensic investigation for Beyer Co.   (8 marks)

Using the information in Exhibit 2:

(b)   (i)   Recommend the procedures which should be performed in order to quantify the inventory loss, and   (6 marks)

      (ii) Evaluate the deficiencies in Beyer Co's internal control system, and explain how they contributed to the fraud, together with recommendations to prevent such a fraud reoccurring.   (6 marks)

Professional marks will be awarded for the demonstration of skill in analysis and evaluation, professional scepticism and judgement and commercial acumen in your answer.   (5 marks)

(Total: 25 marks)

56   RETRIEVER *Walk in the footsteps of a top tutor*

 Answer debrief

It is 1 July 20X5. Kennel & Co, a firm of Chartered Certified Accountants, is the external audit provider for the Retriever Group (the Group), a manufacturer of mobile phones and laptop computers. The Group obtained a stock exchange listing in July 20X4. The audit of the consolidated financial statements for the year ended 28 February 20X5 is nearing completion. You are a manager in the audit department of Kennel & Co, responsible for conducting engagement quality reviews on listed audit clients.

The following exhibits, available below, provide information relevant to the question:

1   Quality management issues – comments from team members of how the audit was planned and carried out.

2   Request to perform a forensic accounting service – details of a burglary at the Group's warehouse and a request to determine the amount to be claimed.

This information should be used to answer the question requirements within the response option provided.

Exhibit 1 – Quality management issues

You have discussed the Group audit with some of the junior members of the audit team, one of whom made the following comments about how it was planned and carried out.

Audit junior's comments

The audit has been quite time pressured. The audit manager told the juniors not to perform some of the planned audit procedures on items such as directors' emoluments and share capital as they are considered to be low risk. He also instructed us not to use the firm's statistical sampling methods in selecting trade receivables balances for testing, as it would be quicker to pick the sample based on our own judgement.

Two of the juniors were given the tasks of auditing trade payables and going concern. The audit manager asked us to review each other's work as it would be good training for us, and he didn't have time to review everything.

I was discussing the Group's tax position with the financial controller, when she said that she was struggling to calculate the deferred tax asset that should be recognised. The deferred tax asset has arisen because several of the Group's subsidiaries have been loss making this year, creating unutilised tax losses. As I had just studied deferred tax at college I did the calculation of the Group's deferred tax position for her. The audit manager said this saved time as we now would not have to audit the deferred tax figure.

The financial controller also asked for my advice as to how the tax losses could be utilised by the Group in the future. I provided her with some tax planning recommendations, for which she was very grateful.

Exhibit 2 – Request to perform a forensic accounting service

The audit committee of the Group has contacted Kennel & Co to discuss an incident that took place on 1 June 20X5. On that date, there was a burglary at the Group's warehouse where inventory is stored prior to despatch to customers. CCTV filmed the thieves loading a lorry belonging to the Group with boxes containing finished goods. The last inventory count took place on 30 April 20X5.

The Group has insurance cover in place and Kennel & Co's forensic accounting department has been asked to provide a forensic accounting service to determine the amount to be claimed in respect of the burglary. The insurance covers the cost of assets lost as a result of thefts.

It is thought that the amount of the claim will be immaterial to the Group's financial statements, and there is no ethical threat in Kennel & Co's forensic accounting department providing the forensic accounting service.

Required:

(a) Using the information in Exhibit 1, evaluate the quality management, ethical and other professional matters arising in respect of the planning and performance of the audit of the Retriever Group. **(14 marks)**

(b) Using the information in Exhibit 2, recommend the procedures to be performed in determining the amount of the insurance claim. **(6 marks)**

Professional marks will be awarded for the demonstration of skill in analysis and evaluation, professional scepticism and judgement and commercial acumen in your answer. **(5 marks)**

(Total: 25 marks)

 Calculate your allowed time, allocate the time to the separate parts..............

57 LARK & CO *Walk in the footsteps of a top tutor*

It is 1 July 20X5. You are an audit manager working for Lark & Co, a firm of Chartered Certified Accountants. You are currently working on several clients. Issues have recently arisen in relation to three different clients which require your attention.

The following exhibits, available below, provide information relevant to the question:

1   Chestnut Co – request to perform a forensic investigation in relation to a fraud.

2   Heron Co – details of unusual transactions identified during the audit of revenue.

3   Coot Co – audit completion matters in relation to payroll raised by the audit junior.

This information should be used to answer the question requirements within the response option provided.

Exhibit 1 – Chestnut Co

Chestnut Co is a large company which provides information technology services to business customers. The finance director of Chestnut Co, Jack Privet, contacted you this morning, saying:

'I was alerted yesterday to a fraud being conducted by members of our sales team. It appears that several sales representatives have been claiming reimbursement for fictitious travel and client entertaining expenses and inflating actual expenses incurred. Specifically, it has been alleged that the sales representatives have claimed on expenses for items such as gifts for clients and office supplies which were never actually purchased, claimed for business-class airline tickets but in reality had purchased economy tickets, claimed for non-existent business mileage and used the company credit card to purchase items for personal use. I am very worried about the scale of this fraud, as travel and client entertainment is one of our biggest expenses.

All of the alleged fraudsters have been suspended pending an investigation, which I would like your firm to conduct. We will prosecute these employees to attempt to recoup our losses if evidence shows that a fraud has indeed occurred, so your firm would need to provide an expert witness in the event of a court case. Can we meet tomorrow to discuss this potential assignment?'

Chestnut Co has a small internal audit department and in previous years the evidence obtained by Lark & Co as part of the external audit has indicated that the control environment of the company is generally good. The audit opinion on the financial statements for the year ended 31 January 20X5 was unmodified.

Exhibit 2 – Heron Co

Heron Co is an owner-managed business which operates a chain of bars and restaurants. This is your firm's first year auditing the client and the audit for the year ended 30 April 20X5 is underway. The audit senior has sent a note for your attention:

'When I was auditing revenue I noticed something strange. Heron Co's revenue, which is almost entirely cash based, is recognised at $5.5 million in the draft financial statements. However, the accounting system shows that till receipts for cash paid by customers amount to only $3.5 million. This seemed odd, so I questioned Ava Gull, the financial controller about this. She said that Jack Heron, the company's owner, deals with cash receipts and posts through journals dealing with cash and revenue. Ava asked Jack the reason for these journals but he refused to give an explanation.

While auditing cash, I noticed a payment of $2 million made by electronic transfer from the company's bank account to an overseas financial institution. The bank statement showed that the transfer was authorised by Jack Heron, but no other documentation regarding the transfer was available.

Alarmed by the size of this transaction, and the lack of evidence to support it, I questioned Jack Heron, asking him about the source of cash receipts and the reason for electronic transfer. He would not give any answers and became quite aggressive.'

Exhibit 3 – Coot Co

You are currently reviewing the working papers of the audit of Coot Co for the year ended 31 March 20X5. In the working papers dealing with payroll, the audit junior has commented as follows:

'Several new employees have been added to the company's payroll during the year, with combined payments of $125,000 being made to them. There does not appear to be any authorisation for these additions. When I questioned the payroll supervisor who made the amendments, she said that no authorisation was needed because the new employees are only working for the company on a temporary basis.

However, when discussing staffing levels with management, it was stated that no new employees have been taken on this year. Other than the tests of controls planned, no other audit work has been performed.'

Required:

(a) Using the information in Exhibit 1, explain the matters that should be discussed in the meeting with Jack Privet in respect of planning the investigation into the alleged fraudulent activity at Chestnut Co. **(6 marks)**

(b) Using the information in Exhibit 2, discuss the implications of the circumstances described in the audit senior's notes and the nature of any reporting which should take place in respect of Heron Co. **(9 marks)**

(c) Using the information in Exhibit 3, discuss how professional scepticism should be applied to the audit of Coot Co's payroll and recommend any further actions that should be taken by the auditor. **(5 marks)**

Professional marks will be awarded for the demonstration of skill in analysis and evaluation and professional scepticism and judgement in your answer. **(5 marks)**

(Total: 25 marks)

58 GANNET & CO *Walk in the footsteps of a top tutor*

It is 1 July 20X5. You are a senior manager in Gannet & Co, a firm of Chartered Certified Accountants. You are currently working on the engagements of Guillemot Co and Gull Co.

The following exhibits, available below, provide information relevant to the question:

1   Guillemot Co – completion matters relating to a review of interim financial statements.

2   Gull Co – planned stock exchange listing and governance matters.

This information should be used to answer the question requirements within the response option provided.

Exhibit 1 – Guillemot Co

You are responsible for the audit of Guillemot Co, a listed company, and you are completing the review of its interim financial statements for the six months ended 31 May 20X5. Guillemot Co is a car manufacturer, and historically has offered a three-year warranty on cars sold. The financial statements for the year ended 30 November 20X4 included a warranty provision of $1.5 million and recognised total assets of $27.5 million. You are aware that on 1 February 20X5, due to cost cutting measures, Guillemot Co stopped offering warranties on cars sold. The interim financial statements for the six months ended 31 May 20X5 do not recognise any warranty provision. Total assets are $30 million at 31 May 20X5.

Exhibit 2 – Gull Co

You are also responsible for the audit of Gull Co, a large, private company which is currently owned by the Brenner family, who own the majority of the company's shares.

Following the completion of the audit this year, the finance director, Jim Brenner, contacted you and told you that the family is considering listing the company on the stock exchange. They would like to recruit one of your audit partners for a six-month period to help prepare for the listing.

Currently, most of the executive director roles are performed by family members, except for the directors of operations and human resources, who are both long-serving employees. The board operates no audit committee and there is only one non-executive director, who works elsewhere as an IT consultant. The board is concerned that the necessary skills and personnel to support the listing are not currently present within the company and is planning to recruit new members to the board. Other than the recruitment of new board members, Gull Co is not planning on making any changes to its governance structure prior to or subsequent to listing.

Gull Co has a financial year ending 31 October 20X5, and audit planning is scheduled to take place in August 20X5.

Required:

(a)   **Using the information in Exhibit 1:**

(i)   **Explain the principal analytical procedures that should be used to gather evidence in a review of interim financial information.** (7 marks)

(ii)   **Assess the matters that should be considered in forming a conclusion on Guillemot Co's interim financial statements, and the implications for the review report.** (4 marks)

(b) Using the information in Exhibit 2:

(i) Comment on the ethical and professional issues arising in relation to the temporary recruitment of the audit partner for Gull Co. **(4 marks)**

(ii) Comment on the implications the governance structure and proposed listing may have on the audit process. **(5 marks)**

Professional marks will be awarded for the demonstration of skill in analysis and evaluation and professional scepticism and judgement in your answer. **(5 marks)**

(Total: 25 marks)

PROFESSIONAL AND ETHICAL CONSIDERATIONS, QUALITY MANAGEMENT AND PRACTICE MANAGEMENT

59   FORSYTHIA GROUP *Walk in the footsteps of a top tutor*

It is 1 July 20X5. You are an audit manager in Magnolia & Co, and you are currently conducting an Engagement Quality Review on the audit of the Forsythia Group (the Group), which is a listed entity. Your firm is appointed to audit the consolidated financial statements and the individual financial statements of all Group companies.

The following exhibit, available below, provides information relevant to the question:

1   Forsythia Group – summary of comments made by the audit team regarding the performance of the audit.

This information should be used to answer the question requirement within the response option provided.

Exhibit 1 – Forsythia Group

The audit of the Forsythia Group (the Group) for the year ended 31 March 20X5 is in the completion stage and the auditor's report is due to be issued next week.

The Group has diverse operations, focusing on manufacturing, but is also involved with activities in some other areas, such as agriculture. The draft consolidated financial statements include revenue of $129 million (20X4: $113 million), profit before tax of $18.6 million (20X4: $23.2 million) and total assets of $465 million (20X4: $460 million).

You have discussed the Group audit with a junior member of the audit team, who made the following comments about how it was planned and carried out:

'On 10 June 20X5, the Group acquired another subsidiary, Robin Co, which is forecast to increase the Group's total revenue by around 20%. This meant that the Group chief finance officer (CFO) had little time to discuss matters with the audit team. The acquisition has taken place quickly, and so did not form part of the audit planning, which took place in January 20X5. The audit engagement partner said that we did not need to perform audit work on any aspect of the acquisition as, according to the CFO, it will all be accounted for in next year's financial statements.

Due to pressure to reduce the costs of the audit, the audit manager arranged for the audit procedures on revenue recognised by several significant subsidiaries, including a subsidiary in the agricultural industry, to be delegated to Camelia Associates, an unconnected firm. The audit manager said that we can rely on the evidence obtained by Camelia Associates as they are a firm of qualified accountants.

I also audited the Group's intangible assets, which involved evaluating the assumptions relating to the appropriateness of capitalisation of $1.2 million of development costs in the year. I could not discuss this with the CFO and no one else was available, so I agreed the assumptions, for example, relating to technical feasibility and commercial viability, to the Group's business plan and concluded that they were consistent. This is the first year that development costs have been recognised as an intangible asset in the Group financial statements.

Yew Co, which operates in the agricultural industry, is a subsidiary of the Group. At the audit planning stage, in line with the previous year's audit, it was not identified as a component which needs to be visited for audit work to be performed. However, due to the specialist nature of the operations of the company, a consultant should have been used to provide input on some technical matters, as stated in the audit strategy and audit plan. Due to cost implications, the consultant was not engaged, and the section of the audit strategy and audit plan containing instructions relating to the consultant was deleted from the audit files.'

Following your conversation with the audit assistant, you reviewed the audit working papers and found the following:

– The audit evidence obtained by Camelia Associates has not been reviewed by the audit manager or partner.

– No further evidence has been obtained relating to the development expenditure.

– Yew Co has total assets of $60.5 million (20X4: $83 million) and revenue of $6.5 million (20X4: $6.4 million).

Required:

Evaluate the quality management and other professional matters identified during your review in respect of the planning and performance of the Forsythia Group audit, and recommend appropriate actions to be taken. **(20 marks)**

Professional marks will be awarded for the demonstration of skill in analysis and evaluation, professional scepticism and judgement, and commercial acumen in your answer. **(5 marks)**

(Total: 25 marks)

60 **JAMES & CO** *Walk in the footsteps of a top tutor*

It is 1 July 20X5. You are an audit manager in James & Co, a firm of Chartered Certified Accountants. Your role includes performing post-issuance audit quality reviews, and you are currently reviewing the audit of the Bond Group (the Group), which had a financial year ended 31 January 20X5, and in respect of which an unmodified audit opinion was issued last month. The Group supplies computer components, specialising in graphics cards.

You are reviewing the Group audit file as well as the audit files for three of the Group's subsidiaries. All of these subsidiaries are significant components of the Group and have a financial year end of 31 January 20X5. Each subsidiary's audit opinion was also unmodified.

You have been provided with the following exhibits, which provide information about the Bond Group and the points you have identified for each subsidiary in the group:

1   Cameron Co – points you have identified from your review of the information provided by the component auditor.

2   Dean Co – points you have identified during your audit quality review.

3   Horner Co – points you have identified during your audit quality review.

This information should be used to answer the question requirements within the response option provided.

Exhibit 1 – Cameron Co

Your firm audits all Group companies with the exception of Cameron Co, a subsidiary which was acquired during the last financial year.

Cameron Co was acquired by the Group in April 20X4, and is audited by Carrey Associates, a small local firm. Cameron Co also outsources its internal audit function to Carrey Associates. The section of the external audit working papers provided by Carrey Associates and relevant to internal controls contains very little documentation other than a cross reference to the files maintained by the internal audit team, and a statement that 'we can rely on the internal controls as they were tested by our firm in May 20X4'. In respect of Carrey Associates, the Group audit working papers contain the following statement: 'our firm can rely on the work of Carrey Associates, as one of James & Co's audit partners left the firm to become an audit partner at Carrey Associates, and he was involved with the audit of Cameron Co'. Other than some background about Carrey Associates which had been printed off from the firm's website to provide background information, there is nothing else on file in relation to the firm.

The Group audit working papers also include a note relating to the consolidation of Cameron Co into the Group financial statements. Cameron Co prepares its individual financial statements using local accounting rules, which is allowed under national regulation, it does not use IFRS Accounting Standards which are applied by the rest of the Group. The Group audit partner commented in the working papers that 'local accounting rules are very similar to IFRS Accounting Standards so there is no need to perform any additional audit work in relation to the consolidation of Cameron Co due to it using different accounting policies to the rest of the Group'.

Exhibit 2 – Dean Co

Dean Co owns a small number of shares in Corden Co, amounting to a 2% shareholding. The investment is accounted for as a financial asset at fair value through profit or loss, as required by IFRS 9 *Financial Instruments*. Corden Co's shares are not traded in an active market, and the value of $68,000 which is recognised in Dean Co's financial statements is management's estimate of fair value, based on an offer received for the shareholding in April 20X4.

The audit team checked the arithmetic of management's computation but did not obtain further audit evidence, because according to the audit conclusion 'the value of the shareholding is below the Group materiality level'. The latest financial statements of Corden Co, prepared to 31 January 20X5, are included in the audit file to provide 'background information', and show that the company has net assets of $550,000. Materiality for the Group consolidated financial statements was determined to be $350,000.

Exhibit 3 – Horner Co

During the audit of Horner Co, the audit team became aware of a breach of data protection regulation, whereby an employee of the company had made its customer database available to a third party. This disclosure is in contravention of the regulation.

The audit working papers refer briefly to this situation, and conclude that 'it has little to do with the audit, as no one outside of the company is aware'. No further investigations were made by the audit team, and the audit manager noted in the working papers that 'the matter does not need to be discussed any further with Horner Co's or the Group's management teams as I have received assurance that the person responsible for the breach of regulation has been dismissed'.

Required:

In relation to the matters described in Exhibits 1 to 3, comment on the quality of the planning and performance of the Group audit and the audit of the components of the Group, discussing the quality management and other professional issues raised in respect of:

(a)	**Cameron Co, using Exhibit 1**	**(8 marks)**
(b)	**Dean Co, using Exhibit 2**	**(5 marks)**
(c)	**Horner Co, using Exhibit 3**	**(7 marks)**

Professional marks will be awarded for the demonstration of skill in analysis and evaluation, professional scepticism and judgement and commercial acumen in your answer.

(5 marks)

(Total: 25 marks)

61   THOMASSON & CO *Walk in the footsteps of a top tutor*

It is 1 July 20X5. You are an audit manager in Thomasson & Co, a firm of Chartered Certified Accountants. You have recently been assigned to the audit of Clean Co for the year ended 31 March 20X5. Clean Co is an unlisted company and has been an audit client of your firm for a number of years.

The following exhibits, available below, provide information relevant to the question:

1   Clean Co – information regarding Clean Co.

2   Audit working paper review – issues identified from a review of the audit working papers and an initial meeting with Simon Blackers.

This information should be used to answer the question requirements within the response option provided.

Exhibit 1 – Clean Co

Clean Co is a national distributor of cleaning products. The company buys the cleaning products from wholesalers and employs a team of approximately 750 sales staff around the country who sell the company's products to both domestic households and small to medium-sized businesses. Around 75% of Clean Co's sales transactions are cash based and each of the company's sales staff prepares a cash sales report on a monthly basis. According to Clean Co's chief executive, Simon Blackers, and in order to foster 'an entrepreneurial spirit' amongst the staff, each staff member (including the senior management team) is encouraged to make cash sales and is paid on a commission basis to sell the company's products to friends and family. Simon Blackers leads the way with this scheme and recently sold cleaning products with a value of $33,000 to a business associate. The funds have been transferred directly into an off-shore bank account in the company's name on which Simon is the sole signatory.

Exhibit 2 – Review of audit working papers

Your review of the audit working papers and an initial meeting with Simon Blackers have identified the following potential issues:

Following your review of the audit engagement letter and the working papers of the taxation section of the audit file, you have established that Thomasson & Co performed the taxation computation for Clean Co and completed the tax returns for both the company and Simon Blackers personally. All of the taxation services have been invoiced to Clean Co as part of the total fee for the audit and professional services. Simon Blackers' personal tax return includes a significant number of transactions involving the purchase and sale of properties in various international locations. The taxation working papers include a detailed review of a number of off-shore bank accounts in Simon Blackers' name which identified the property transactions.

During your initial meeting, Simon Blackers informed you that Clean Co is planning to develop a new website in order to offer online sales to its customers. Thomasson & Co has been asked to provide assistance with the design and implementation of the website and online sales system.

Required:

(a)   Using the information in Exhibits 1 and 2:

   (i)   Discuss the policies and procedures which Thomasson & Co should have in place in relation to an anti-money laundering programme, and   **(4 marks)**

   (ii)   Evaluate whether there are any indicators of money laundering activities by either Clean Co or its staff.   **(6 marks)**

(b)   Using the information in Exhibit 2, comment on the ethical and professional issues arising from your review of the audit working papers and recommend any actions which should now be taken by Thomasson & Co.   **(10 marks)**

Professional marks will be awarded for the demonstration of skill in analysis and evaluation, professional scepticism and judgement and commercial acumen in your answer.   **(5 marks)**

(Total: 25 marks)

62   WESTON & CO *Walk in the footsteps of a top tutor*

It is 1 July 20X5. You are an audit manager in Weston & Co which is an international firm of Chartered Certified Accountants with branches in many countries and which offers a range of audit and assurance services to its clients. Your responsibilities include reviewing ethical matters which arise with audit clients, and dealing with approaches from prospective audit clients.

The following exhibits, available below, provide information relevant to the question:

1   Jones Co – invitation to tender for the audit of Jones Co.

2   Ordway Co – rotation of audit engagement partner for the audit of Ordway Co.

This information should be used to answer the question requirements within the response option provided.

Exhibit 1 – Jones Co

The management of Jones Co has invited Weston & Co to submit an audit proposal (tender document) for their consideration. Jones Co was established only two years ago, but has grown rapidly, and this will be the first year that an audit is required. In previous years a limited assurance review was performed on its financial statements by an unrelated audit firm. The company specialises in the recruitment of medical personnel and some of its start-up funding was raised from a venture capital company. There are plans for the company to open branches overseas to help recruit personnel from foreign countries.

Jones Co has one full-time accountant who uses an off-the-shelf accounting package to record transactions and to prepare financial information. The company has a financial year ending 30 September 20X5.

The following comment was made by Bentley Jones, the company's founder and owner manager, in relation to the audit proposal and potential audit fee:

'I am looking for a firm of auditors who will give me a competitive audit fee. I am hoping that the fee will be quite low, as I am willing to pay more for services that I consider more beneficial to the business, such as strategic advice. I would like the audit fee to be linked to Jones Co's success in expanding overseas as a result of the audit firm's advice. Hopefully the audit will not be too disruptive and I would like it completed within four months of the year end.'

Exhibit 2 – Ordway Co

Ordway Co is a long-standing audit client of your firm and is a listed company. Bobby Wellington has acted as audit engagement partner for INT: seven years/UK: five years and understands that a new audit partner needs to be appointed to take his place. Bobby is hoping to stay in contact with the client and act as the engagement quality reviewer in forthcoming audits of Ordway Co.

Required:

(a)   Using the information in Exhibit 1:

(i)   Explain the specific matters to be included in the audit proposal (tender document), other than those relating to the audit fee.   **(8 marks)**

(ii)   Assuming Weston & Co is appointed to provide the audit service to Jones Co, discuss the issues to be considered by the audit firm in determining a fee for the audit including any ethical matters raised.   **(6 marks)**

(b)   Using the information in Exhibit 2, explain the ethical threats raised by the long association of senior audit personnel with an audit client and the relevant safeguards to be applied, and discuss whether Bobby Wellington can act as engagement quality reviewer in the future audits of Ordway Co.   **(6 marks)**

Professional marks will be awarded for the demonstration of skill in analysis and evaluation, professional scepticism and judgement and commercial acumen in your answer.   **(5 marks)**

(Total: 25 marks)

63   DRAGON GROUP *Walk in the footsteps of a top tutor*

It is 1 July 20X5. You are a senior manager in Unicorn & Co, a global firm of Chartered Certified Accountants, with offices in over 150 countries across the world. Unicorn & Co has been invited to tender for the Dragon Group audit (including the audit of all subsidiaries). You manage a department within the firm which specialises in the audit of retail companies, and you have been assigned the task of drafting the tender document. You recently held a meeting with Edmund Jalousie, the group finance director, in which you discussed the current group structure, recent acquisitions, and the group's plans for future expansion.

The following exhibit, available below, provides information relevant to the question:

1   Dragon Group – background information.

This information should be used to answer the question requirement within the response option provided.

Exhibit 1 – Dragon Group

The Dragon Group is a large group of companies operating in the furniture retail trade. The group has expanded rapidly in the last three years, by acquiring several subsidiaries each year. The management of the parent company, Dragon Co, a listed company, has decided to put the audit of the group and all subsidiaries out to tender, as the current audit firm is not seeking re-election. The financial year end of the Dragon Group is 30 September 20X5.

Meeting notes – Dragon Group

Group structure

The parent company owns 20 subsidiaries, all of which are wholly owned. Half of the subsidiaries are located in the same country as the parent, and half overseas. Most of the foreign subsidiaries report under the same financial reporting framework as Dragon Co, but several prepare financial statements using local accounting rules.

Acquisitions during the year

Two companies were purchased in March 20X5, both located in this country:

(i) Mermaid Co, a company which operates 20 furniture retail outlets. The audit opinion expressed by the incumbent auditors on the financial statements for the year ended 30 September 20X4 was modified due to material misstatement as a result of non-disclosure of a contingent liability. The contingent liability relates to a court case which is still ongoing.

(ii) Minotaur Co, a large company, whose operations are distribution and warehousing. This represents a diversification away from retail, and it is hoped that the Dragon Group will benefit from significant economies of scale as a result of the acquisition.

Other matters

The acquisitive strategy of the group over the last few years has led to significant growth. Group revenue has increased by 25% in the last three years, and is predicted to increase by a further 35% in the next four years as the acquisition of more subsidiaries is planned. The Dragon Group has raised finance for the acquisitions in the past by becoming listed on the stock exchanges of three different countries. A new listing on a foreign stock exchange is planned for January 20X6. For this reason, management would like the group audit completed by 31 December 20X5.

Required:

(a) **Recommend and describe the principal matters to be included in your firm's tender document to provide the audit service to the Dragon Group.** **(8 marks)**

(b) **Using the specific information provided, evaluate the matters that should be considered before accepting the audit engagement, in the event of your firm being successful in the tender.** **(6 marks)**

(c) **Discuss how transnational audits may differ from other audits of historical information and how this may contribute to a higher level of audit risk in relation to the audit of Dragon Group.** **(6 marks)**

Professional marks will be awarded for the demonstration of skill in analysis and evaluation, professional scepticism and judgement and commercial acumen in your answer. **(5 marks)**

(Total: 25 marks)

64 SPANIEL *Walk in the footsteps of a top tutor*

It is 1 July 20X5. You are a manager in Groom & Co, a firm of Chartered Certified Accountants. You have just attended a monthly meeting of audit partners and managers at which client-related matters were discussed.

The following exhibits, available below, provide information relevant to the question:

1 Spaniel Co – information regarding a fraud discovered at Spaniel Co after the auditor's report was issued.

2 Bulldog Co – details of Bulldog Co's treasury management function.

3 Fraud and revenue recognition – extract from ISA 240 *The Auditor's Responsibilities Relating to Fraud in an Audit of Financial Statements*.

This information should be used to answer the question requirements within the response option provided.

Exhibit 1 – Spaniel Co

The auditor's report on the financial statements of Spaniel Co, a long-standing audit client, for the year ended 31 December 20X4 was issued in April 20X5, and was unmodified. In June 20X5, Spaniel Co's audit committee contacted the audit engagement partner to discuss a fraud that had been discovered. The company's internal auditors estimate that $4.5 million has been stolen in a payroll fraud, which has been operating since June 20X4. The audit engagement partner commented that neither tests of controls nor substantive audit procedures were conducted on payroll in the audit of the latest financial statements as in previous years' audits there were no deficiencies found in controls over payroll. The total assets recognised in Spaniel Co's financial statements at 31 December 20X4 were $80 million. Spaniel Co is considering suing Groom & Co for the total amount of cash stolen from the company, claiming that the audit firm was negligent in conducting the audit.

Exhibit 2 – Bulldog Co

Bulldog Co is a clothing manufacturer, which has recently expanded its operations overseas. To manage exposure to cash flows denominated in foreign currencies, the company has set up a treasury management function, which is responsible for entering into hedge transactions such as forward exchange contracts. These transactions are likely to be material to the financial statements. The audit partner is about to commence planning the audit for the year ending 31 July 20X5.

Exhibit 3 – Fraud and revenue recognition

According to ISA 240 *The Auditor's Responsibilities Relating to Fraud in an Audit of Financial Statements*:

'When identifying and assessing the risks of material misstatement due to fraud, the auditor shall, based on a presumption that there are risks of fraud in revenue recognition, evaluate which types of revenue, revenue transactions or assertions give rise to such risks.'

Required:

(a) Using the information in Exhibit 1, explain the matters that should be considered in determining whether Groom & Co is liable to Spaniel Co in respect of the fraud.

(5 marks)

(b) Using the information in Exhibit 2, discuss why the audit of financial instruments is particularly challenging, and explain the matters to be considered in planning the audit of Bulldog Co's forward exchange contracts. (10 marks)

(c) Using the information in Exhibit 3, discuss why the auditor should presume that there are risks of fraud in revenue recognition and why ISA 240 requires specific auditor responses in relation to the risks identified. (5 marks)

Professional marks will be awarded for the demonstration of skill in analysis and evaluation and professional scepticism and judgement in your answer. (5 marks)

(Total: 25 marks)

UK SYLLABUS ONLY

65 ALUCARD *Walk in the footsteps of a top tutor*

You have also been asked to advise the directors of a different audit client, Alucard Ltd, in relation to potential insolvency procedures and their implications for the directors.

You have been the manager responsible for the audit of Alucard Ltd for the last three years. Alucard Ltd manufactures pet foods which it sells to wholesale and retail customers both in the UK and internationally. The company has experienced a decrease in profitability in recent years as a result of increased trading tariffs making its products more expensive for its international customers. Alucard Ltd has experienced a significant fall in demand for its products and five months ago, the company's largest international customer, Holden Co, cancelled its contract with Alucard Ltd. Historically, Holden Co has represented approximately 45% of Alucard Ltd's total sales revenue.

The company's managing director, Bella Lugosi, remains confident that the company will be able to replace the lost sales and has insisted on maintaining existing operating levels. As a result, Alucard Ltd's payables payment period has increased from 45 days to 73 days over the last five months and the company's cash position has deteriorated to the point where it is unable to pay its creditors as they fall due. A review of the client's records has also identified that the company has three months of arrears of unpaid taxes including PAYE and NIC and has received penalty notices in relation to its failure to file its last audited financial statements with Companies House. The company's management accounts have shown a negative cash balance in excess of its overdraft facility and a net liabilities position for the last three months.

The directors of Alucard Ltd have approached you in relation to their concerns about the company's current financial difficulties and potential insolvency. They have also heard that if directors are found to have conducted fraudulent or wrongful trading, there can be significant consequences including personal liability to the company's creditors.

They have asked you to prepare information to be presented at next week's board meeting in order to advise them on:

(i)   the key features of the administration process, and

(ii)   whether based on the information provided, they might be personally liable to Alucard Ltd's creditors.

Required:

Respond to the request made by the directors of Alucard Ltd.   **(10 marks)**

66   KRUPT *Walk in the footsteps of a top tutor*

Krupt Ltd is a family owned business which has been an audit client of Jansen & Co for many years and on which you have been the audit manager for the last two years. The audit for the year ended 30 June 20X8 is approaching completion and the audit supervisor has asked for your advice in relation to recent developments at the client.

Krupt Ltd is a wholesaler of electronic goods and is owned by Mr and Mrs Krupt who are both 50% shareholders and directors of the company. The company's principal source of finance is a loan from Hongclays Bank of £1.2 million which is secured by a floating charge over the company's inventory. The bank has also taken out personal guarantees on the domestic residence owned jointly by Mr and Mrs Krupt under the terms of which the bank has the right to take possession of the property in the event that it cannot recover its debts from the company.

As part of the going concern review, the audit supervisor, Jemma Jones, has scrutinised the management accounts for the first four months of the current reporting period and has identified that the company is making significant losses which she believes to be unsustainable. She has also inspected correspondence between the company and Hongclays Bank which indicates that the company has already breached key loan covenants.

Jemma has been informed by the company's procurement manager that Krupt Ltd has recently taken delivery of a large quantity of a new inventory line with a value of £0.75 million which it has purchased on credit from one of its suppliers. At present the company also has other inventory with a total value of approximately £0.5 million. Based on a review of the company's bank statements and cash flow forecasts, Jemma does not believe that there is any realistic prospect that the company will be able to pay this supplier for the foreseeable future and is concerned about the possible implications of this transaction for the directors of the company. Jemma has not come across these issues before. She has a clear sense that something is wrong and she has asked you to:

Required:

(i)   **Explain the concepts of fraudulent and wrongful trading and**

(ii)   **Evaluate the possible implications of the circumstances and transactions noted during the going concern review for the directors of Krupt Ltd.**   **(10 marks)**

67 KANDINSKY *Walk in the footsteps of a top tutor*

Malevich & Co is a firm of Chartered Certified Accountants offering audit and assurance services to a large portfolio of clients. You are a manager in the audit department responsible for the audit of two clients, Kandinsky Ltd and Viola Ltd.

(a) Kandinsky Ltd is a manufacturer of luxury food items including chocolate and other confectionery which are often sold as gift items individually or in hampers containing a selection of expensive items from the range of products. The company has a financial year ended 31 July 20X5, much of the planned audit work has been completed, and you are reviewing issues which have been raised by the audit senior. Due to an economic recession sales of products have fallen sharply this year and measures have been implemented to support the company's cash flow. You are aware that the company only has £150,000 in cash at the year end.

Extracts from the draft financial statements and other relevant information are given below.

	Note	July 20X5 (Draft) £000	July 20X4 (Actual) £000
Revenue		2,440	3,950
Operating expenses		(2,100)	(2,800)
Finance charge		(520)	(500)
(Loss)/profit before tax		(180)	650
Total assets		10,400	13,500
Long-term liabilities – bank loan	1	3,500	3,000
Short-term liabilities – trade payables	2	900	650
Disclosed in notes to financial statements:			
Undrawn borrowing facilities	3	500	1,000
Contingent liability	4	120	–

Notes:

1   The bank loan was extended in March 20X5 by drawing on the borrowing facilities offered by the bank. The loan carries a fixed interest rate and is secured on the company's property including the head office and manufacturing site. The first repayment of loan capital is due on 30 June 20X6 when £350,000 is due to be paid.

2   Kandinsky Ltd renegotiated its terms of trade with its main supplier of cocoa beans, and extended payment terms from 50 days to 80 days in order to improve working capital.

3   The borrowing facilities are due to be reviewed by the bank in April 20X6 and contain covenants including that interest cover is maintained at 2, and the ratio of bank loan to operating profit does not exceed 4:1.

4   The contingent liability relates to a letter of support which Kandinsky Ltd has provided to its main supplier of cane sugar which is facing difficult trading conditions.

Required:

In respect of the audit of Kandinsky Ltd:

Identify and explain the matters which may cast significant doubt on the Kandinsky Ltd's ability to continue as a going concern, and recommend the audit procedures to be performed in relation to the going concern matters identified.

(13 marks)

(b) You are also responsible for the audit of Viola Ltd, a small engineering company located in the Midlands with a financial year ended 31 March 20X5. The auditor's report for the financial year then ended, which was issued in September 20X5, contained an Emphasis of Matter paragraph outlining the going concern issues facing the company, but was otherwise unmodified.

The finance director of Viola Ltd phoned you yesterday to discuss some recent developments at the company. His comments are shown in the note below:

'I am getting in touch to update you on our situation and to ask for your firm's advice.

As you know, in the last financial year the company lost several contracts and we had to make a number of staff redundant. In recent months further contracts have been lost and Viola Ltd has faced severe working capital problems, resulting in the sale of some of our plant in order to meet liabilities as they fall due. We are restricted on the assets which can be sold as the company's bank loan is secured by a floating charge over non-current assets. In November 20X5 the accounts recognised net liabilities of £500,000 and without securing further finance, the future of the company does not look good.

We are tendering for three new contracts to supply components to local car manufacturers. However, our bank is reluctant to extend our borrowing facilities until the contracts are secured, which may not be for another few months.

My fellow directors are becoming concerned about the possibility of our creditors applying for compulsory liquidation of the company, which we want to avoid if possible. We also wish to avoid a creditor's voluntary liquidation. Can you please advise me on the alternatives which are available given the company's precarious financial situation? I need you to explain the procedures involved with any alternatives which you can recommend, and describe the impact on the employees and directors of the company.'

Required:

Respond to the instructions in the note from the finance director. **(12 marks)**

(Total: 25 marks)

68   HUNT & CO *Walk in the footsteps of a top tutor*

(a)   Coxon Ltd is a chain of high street stores selling books, CDs and computer games. Unfortunately, it has not been able to compete with internet sites selling the same goods at a much cheaper price, and for the last two years the company has been loss making. The company was placed into compulsory liquidation last week due to being unable to pay its debts as they fall due.

The finance director, James Corgan, has contacted your firm, Hunt & Co, seeking advice on several issues to do with the liquidation. His comments are shown in the note below:

'We had thought for some time that the company was in financial difficulties, having lost market share to competitors, but we hoped to turn the company around. Things came to a head in January 20X4 when the accounts showed a net liabilities position for the first time, and several loan covenants had been breached. However, we decided to continue to trade in order to maximise cash inflows, keep staff employed for a few months longer, and try to negotiate finance from new providers. During this period, we continued to order goods from several suppliers. However, the cash position deteriorated and in May 20X4 creditors applied to the court for the compulsory winding up of the company. The court has appointed liquidators who are about to commence the winding up.

As you can imagine, myself and the other directors are very worried about the situation. We have heard that we may be personally liable for some of the company's debts. Is this correct, and what are the potential consequences for us? Also, can you explain the impact of the compulsory liquidation process for our employees and for creditors?'

Required:

Respond to the instructions in the note from the finance director.   (12 marks)

(b)   Hunt & Co also audits Jay Ltd, a company with a year ended 30 September. The auditor's report for the year ended 30 September 20X3 was issued in December 20X3 and was unmodified. Jay Ltd operates two separate divisions both of which manufacture food supplements – 'Jay Sport' manufactures food supplements targeted at athletes, and 'Jay Plus' is targeted at the general public.

One of the key ingredients used in the 'Jay Sport' range has been found to have harmful side effects, so very few sales from that range have been made in the current financial year. The company is struggling to manage its working capital and meet interest payments on loans.

The directors are anxious about the future of the company and the audit engagement partner, Bill Kingfisher, has been asked to attend a meeting with them tomorrow to discuss their concerns over the financial performance and position of Jay Ltd.

Extract from Jay Ltd's management accounts at 31 May 20X4 (unaudited)

Statement of financial position

	£000
Property, plant and equipment	12,800
Inventory	500
Trade receivables	400
Cash	0
Total assets	13,700
Share capital	100
Retained earnings	(1,050)
Long-term borrowings (secured with a fixed charge over property, plant and equipment)	12,000
Trade payables (including employees' wages of £300,000)	1,250
Bank overdraft	1,400
Total equity and liabilities	13,700

Statement of profit or loss (extract)

	Jay Sport £000	Jay Plus £000	Total £000
Revenue	50	1,450	1,500
Operating costs	(800)	(1,200)	(2,000)
Operating loss/profit	(750)	250	(500)
Finance costs			(800)
Loss before tax			(1,300)

Required:

(i)   Examine the financial position of Jay Ltd and determine whether the company is insolvent. **(4 marks)**

(ii)   Evaluate, reaching a recommendation, the options available to the directors in terms of the future of the company. **(9 marks)**

(Total: 25 marks)

69 BUTLER (A) *Walk in the footsteps of a top tutor*

Butler Ltd is a new audit client of your firm. You are the manager responsible for the audit of the financial statements for the year ended 31 May 20X1. Audit work is due to commence this week. Butler Ltd designs and manufactures aircraft engines and spare parts, and is a subsidiary of a multi-national group. The future of the company is uncertain, as against a background of economic recession, sales have been declining, several significant customer contracts have been cancelled unexpectedly, and competition from overseas has damaged the market share previously enjoyed by Butler Ltd. The management of Butler Ltd is concerned that given the company's poor liquidity position, the company could be placed into compulsory liquidation. Management have prepared a cash flow forecast for the first three months of the next financial year, and are currently preparing the forecasts for the whole 12-month period.

Extracts from the draft financial statements are shown below:

Statement of financial position	31 May 20X1 Draft	31 May 20X0 Actual
Assets	£ million	£ million
Non-current assets		
Intangible assets (note 1)	200	180
Property, plant and equipment (note 2)	1,300	1,200
Deferred tax asset (note 3)	235	20
Financial assets	25	35
	1,760	1,435
Current assets		
Inventories	1,300	800
Trade receivables	2,100	1,860
	3,400	2,660
Total assets	5,160	4,095
Equity and liabilities		
Equity		
Share capital	300	300
Retained earnings	(525)	95
	(225)	395
Non-current liabilities		
Long-term borrowings (note 4)	1,900	1,350
Provisions (note 5)	185	150
	2,085	1,500

Current liabilities		
Short-term borrowings (note 6)	800	400
Trade payables	2,500	1,800
	3,300	2,200
Total equity and liabilities	5,160	4,095

Notes to the statement of financial position:

Note 1   Intangible assets comprise goodwill on the acquisition of subsidiaries (£80 million), and development costs capitalised on engine development projects (£120 million).

Note 2   Property, plant and equipment includes land and buildings valued at £25 million, over which a fixed charge exists.

Note 3   The deferred tax asset has arisen following several loss-making years suffered by the company. The asset represents the tax benefit of unutilised tax losses carried forward.

Note 4   Long-term borrowings include a debenture due for repayment in July 20X2, and a loan from Butler Ltd's parent company due for repayment in December 20X2.

Note 5   Provisions relate to warranties provided to customers.

Note 6   Short-term borrowings comprise an overdraft (£25 million), a short-term loan (£60 million) due for repayment in August 20X1, and a bank loan (£715 million) repayable in September 20X1.

Cash flow forecast for the three months to 31 August 20X1

	June 20X1 £ million	July 20X1 £ million	August 20X1 £ million
Cash inflows			
Cash receipts from customers (note 1)	175	195	220
Loan receipt (note 2)		150	
Government subsidy (note 3)			50
Sales of financial assets	50		
Total cash inflows	225	345	270
Cash outflows			
Operating cash outflows	200	200	290
Interest payments	40	40	40
Loan repayment			60
Total cash outflows	240	240	390
Net cash flow for the month	(15)	105	(120)
Opening cash	(25)	(40)	65
Closing cash	(40)	65	(55)

Notes to the cash flow forecast:

This cash flow forecast has been prepared by the management of Butler Ltd, and is based on the following assumptions:

1   Cash receipts from customers should accelerate given the anticipated improvement in economic conditions. In addition, the company has committed extra resources to the credit control function, in order to speed up collection of overdue debts.

2   The loan expected to be received in July 20X1 is currently being negotiated with our parent company, Rubery Ltd.

3   The government subsidy will be received once our application has been approved. The subsidy is awarded to companies which operate in areas of high unemployment and it subsidises the wages and salaries paid to staff.

Required:

(a)   Identify and explain any matters arising from your review of the draft statement of financial position, and the cash flow forecast, which may cast significant doubt on the company's ability to continue as a going concern.   **(10 marks)**

(b)   Recommend the principal audit procedures to be carried out on the cash flow forecast.   **(8 marks)**

(c)   (i)   Explain the procedures involved in placing a company into compulsory liquidation.   **(4 marks)**

        (ii)   Explain the consequences of a compulsory liquidation for Butler Ltd's payables (creditors), employees and shareholders.   **(3 marks)**

(Total: 25 marks)

INT SYLLABUS ONLY

70 KANDINSKY *Walk in the footsteps of a top tutor*

Malevich & Co is a firm of Chartered Certified Accountants offering audit and assurance services to a large portfolio of clients. You are a manager in the audit department responsible for the audit of two clients, Kandinsky Co and the Rothko University, both of which have a financial year ended 31 July 20X5. The audits of both clients are being completed and you are reviewing issues which have been raised by the audit seniors.

(a) Kandinsky Co is a manufacturer of luxury food items including chocolate and other confectionery which are often sold as gift items individually or in hampers containing a selection of expensive items from the range of products. Due to an economic recession sales of products have fallen sharply this year and measures have been implemented to support the company's cash flow. You are aware that the company only has $150,000 in cash at the year end.

Extracts from the draft financial statements and other relevant information are given below.

	Note	July 20X5 (Draft) $000	July 20X4 (Actual) $000
Revenue		2,440	3,950
Operating expenses		(2,100)	(2,800)
Finance charge		(520)	(500)
(Loss)/profit before tax		(180)	650
Total assets		10,400	13,500
Long-term liabilities – bank loan	1	3,500	3,000
Short-term liabilities – trade payables	2	900	650
Disclosed in notes to financial statements:			
Undrawn borrowing facilities	3	500	1,000
Contingent liability	4	120	–

Notes:

1 The bank loan was extended in March 20X5 by drawing on the borrowing facilities offered by the bank. The loan carries a fixed interest rate and is secured on the company's property including the head office and manufacturing site. The first repayment of loan capital is due on 30 June 20X6 when $350,000 is due to be paid.

2 Kandinsky Co renegotiated its terms of trade with its main supplier of cocoa beans, and extended payment terms from 50 days to 80 days in order to improve working capital.

3 The borrowing facilities are due to be reviewed by the bank in April 20X6 and contain covenants including that interest cover is maintained at 2, and the ratio of bank loan to operating profit does not exceed 4:1.

4 The contingent liability relates to a letter of support which Kandinsky Co has provided to its main supplier of cane sugar which is facing difficult trading conditions.

Required:

In respect of the audit of Kandinsky Co:

(i)　Identify and explain the matters which may cast significant doubt on the company's ability to continue as a going concern.　**(9 marks)**

(ii)　Recommend the audit procedures to be performed in relation to the going concern matters identified.　**(6 marks)**

(b)　The Rothko University, a public sector entity, is a small university with approximately 2,000 students, which was established 10 years ago and specialises in vocational study programmes leading to the award of degrees in business, accountancy, finance, law and marketing. The highest performing students achieve a distinction on completing their degree programme, indicating excellence in the knowledge and understanding of their subject. Students pay tuition fees of $10,000 per year, and the degree programme is typically three years long.

The audit work in respect of the year ended 31 July 20X5 is almost complete, but the audit senior has not yet completed the audit work in respect of performance information which is being published with the annual financial statements for the first time this year. It is a requirement in the jurisdiction in which the Rothko University is located that the performance information is audited as part of the external audit.

Details on the performance information are given below:

Performance area	Performance measure	20X5 result
Graduation rate	% of students who complete their degree programme	85%
Academic performance	% of students achieving a distinction	20%
Employability	% of students who on graduation obtain graduate level employment	65%
Course satisfaction	% of students who rate their university experience as excellent or very good	70%

Required:

(i)　Discuss the relevance and measurability of the reported performance information.

(ii)　Recommend the examination procedures to be used in auditing the performance information.

Note: The total marks will be split equally between each part.　**(10 marks)**

(Total: 25 marks)

THE FOLLOWING QUESTION IS NOT EXAM STANDARD BUT HAS BEEN INCLUDED TO PROVIDE VALUABLE QUESTION PRACTICE.

71   PUBLIC SECTOR ORGANISATIONS *Walk in the footsteps of a top tutor*

(a)   Define the terms 'performance audit' and 'performance information'.   (2 marks)

(b)   Suggest performance targets that could be measured for each of the following public sector organisations:

   (i)   Local police department   (3 marks)

   (ii)   Local hospital   (3 marks)

   (iii)   Local council.   (3 marks)

(c)   Identify the stakeholder groups which might rely on the performance information produced by the public sector organisations in part (b) and explain how they could use such information.   (9 marks)

(d)   Explain the difficulties encountered by auditors when auditing performance information.   (5 marks)

(Total: 25 marks)

Section 3

ANSWERS TO PRACTICE QUESTIONS – SECTION A

1 MERCURIO *Walk in the footsteps of a top tutor*

Top tutor tips

Determination of materiality: *The email from the partner states that materiality should be based on profit, therefore at the start of your answer you should calculate the range for materiality using that benchmark and justify a figure within that range. If it is a new audit client or a client where there are apparent control risks, materiality should be set at the lower end of the range. If it is an existing client, materiality may be able to be set at the higher end of the range depending on the other risks mentioned in the scenario. The examining team will give credit for any reasonable explanation of the chosen materiality threshold, as the mark is to recognise that there is the application of professional judgement and that a candidate can justify their response. It is not required that candidates select the identical percentage or figure, or that they provide a justification identical to that shown in the model answer. The examiner's comments for this question state that materiality could be justified at any figure within the materiality range. See the full examiner's comments with examples at the end of the answer.*

Part (a) *requires evaluation of business risks. When describing business risks remember to explain the impact it will have on the company i.e. impact on profit or cash flow. The business risks should be relatable to the financial statements as the auditor will only consider business risks which will also give rise to a risk of material misstatement.*

Part (b) *asks for risks of material misstatement. Risk of material misstatement is usually due to non-compliance with an accounting standard, although it also includes control risk. Think about the requirements of the relevant accounting standards and what the client might be doing incorrectly.*

Prioritisation of risks: *One mark is awarded for the prioritisation of the risks of material misstatement. The mark is for the act of justifying the reason, not for the actual justification used (i.e. a range of completely different answers could be awarded the mark), therefore if a reasonable explanation is given, the mark will be awarded. Prioritisation can be achieved by either ordering your answer in priority order and stating this is the case, or by summarising in a brief conclusion which risk, or risks, are most significant.*

Part (c) covers the impact of outsourcing on the audit. The client has outsourced the credit control function during the year and therefore the auditor will need to obtain some of the audit evidence in respect of receivables differently from how they have in the past. Knowledge of the applicable auditing standard is required here.

Part (d) asks for audit procedures over the holiday pay obligation. The procedures should enable the auditor to obtain evidence to determine whether the liability is complete and accurate. Make sure your procedures are clear and provide enough detail that they can be easily followed by the audit team.

Professional skills

Professional skills will be awarded for:

Communication – responding to the instructions in the partner's email such as preparing your answers in the form of briefing notes and using the stated benchmark for materiality.

Analysis and evaluation – applying the information from the scenario to answer the question and explaining the issues in sufficient depth.

Professional scepticism and judgement – justifying an appropriate materiality level, demonstrating critical thinking and being alert to possible manipulation and management bias.

Where relevant, professional marks will be awarded for commercial acumen which requires making practical and plausible recommendations and considering the wider implications of issues to the audit firm.

Briefing notes

To: Ted Hastings, audit engagement partner

From: Audit manager

Subject: Mercurio Co audit planning

Date: 1 July 20X5

Introduction

These notes are prepared to assist in planning the audit of Mercurio Co for the year ending 30 September 20X5. Using information provided by the company's finance director, the business risks facing the company are evaluated, and the significant risks of material misstatement are identified, prioritised and explained. In addition, the notes discuss the impact which the company's outsourced credit control function will have on our audit planning, and finally recommend the principal audit procedures in relation to the holiday pay obligation.

Materiality

For the purposes of these briefing notes, the overall materiality level used to assess the significance of identified risks is $3 million based on the profitability of the company, as requested.

Justification

Using profit before tax of $60 million as a suggested benchmark results in a suggested range of $3 million (5% × $60 million) to $6 million (10% × $60 million).

Although Mercurio Co is an existing client, the company is listed and has taken out new loans during the year, significantly increasing the level of scrutiny from outside investors. There has also been a significant amount of change in the business operations with the purchase of properties from Lakewell Co since the last financial statements. Due to the increased detection risk, materiality should be set at the lower end of the range.

This benchmark is only a starting point for determining materiality and professional judgement will need to be applied in determining a final level to be used during the course of the audit.

(a)   Business risk evaluation

Animal welfare

The company sells animals and pet-related products and there is a risk that animal welfare standards are not maintained. The animals which are for sale must be kept in a safe and clean environment, and any breaches of any relevant regulations bring risk to the reputation of the company. Any bad publicity or scandal created by ill-treatment of animals is likely to attract media attention. This risk extends into the supply chain, and the suppliers of animals should also have a high regard for animal welfare. Further, the company should ensure that it is only buying animals from reputable suppliers to ensure Mercurio Co avoids buying animals which do not have appropriate documentation or have unknown or illegal origin.

Veterinary services

A further regulatory risk arises in relation to the veterinary services offered. There is a risk of employing vets who are not appropriately qualified and experienced, exposing pets to a poor quality of health care. There is a risk that pets are injured or die while under the care of the vets which leads again to a reputational risk, as well as having possible legal consequences.

There is also a financial risk that a proportion of the pet healthcare plans do not generate a profit or positive cash flow for the company. The costs of providing the veterinary care in some cases may be greater than the income generated from the sale of the plan to the customer. The fact that the plans are good value for money for the customer indicates that the company may generate a very small return, even on the plans which are profitable. Mercurio Co may consider the pet healthcare plans to be a loss leader whereby customers are retained by the affordable annual plans and will make more profitable purchases on other treatments, pet food and pet accessories. The business risk remains, however, that potentially loss-making pet healthcare plans can have a significant profit and cash flow impacts on Mercurio Co if the more lucrative additional revenue does not occur.

Training of staff

Staff must be appropriately trained, and there is a risk that training is not sufficient or not appropriate. Staff are required to handle animals and they may injure themselves or an animal if it is not handled correctly. This risk would be particularly applicable to the more unusual animals such as spiders and snakes. Inadequate training or a breach of health and safety regulations in the staff handling of animals could result in legal and/or reputational consequences for Mercurio Co. There could also be a risk of poorly trained staff mishandling an animal and as a result causing injury to a customer.

The training in respect of offering nutritional and other advice to customers must also be robust, as there is a risk that the wrong advice could be given which could result in a significant reputational damage, loss of customer goodwill and potential claims for damages if customers do not have faith in or are harmed by the advice provided.

Store expansion

The acquisition of 20 stores from Lakewell Co caused a significant cash outflow, and this may put pressure on the company's liquidity, especially given the projected reduction in cash of $45 million in the year to 30 September 20X5. The stores which are retained need to be refitted, and the estimated $180 million (20 × $9 million) cost of this will put further pressure on cash flow.

The company is projecting to only have cash available of $36 million at 30 September 20X5, which would not even cover the cost to refit five of the stores. It is unlikely that the company would want to use all of its cash for this purpose, and additional long-term finance may need to be taken out. If the company is unable to raise the finance necessary to complete the refurbishment, it may need to halt all or part of the project which would impact on revenues and cash inflows. It is notable that Mercurio Co took out a loan during the year, but despite this there was still a significant cash outflow.

In addition, the refurbishment project appears to be running on a very tight timescale; it may be over optimistic to consider that all of the refurbishment can take place in a three-month period from November 20X5 to January 20X6. Any delays in opening stores will have a negative effect on revenues and cash inflows.

For the stores which are not retained, there may be problems in selling them on if they are not in good locations or are in a poor state of repair, so Mercurio Co may be left with assets which it does not want to use and are difficult to sell. The fact that Lakewell Co was facing going concern problems could indicate that the stores were not a good investment.

Mercurio brand

Importing the new Mercurio Range products from foreign countries exposes the company to the risks associated with international trade, such as currency exposure, inflation and changing regulatory frameworks. With sales of goods from the range expected to become significant next year, the supply chain with these suppliers will become increasingly important, so issues such as dealing with exchange gains and losses will become more significant for the company. There is also a risk associated with the quality of goods produced in foreign countries, if regulations are not so stringent in the country of production.

There is also a risk that the amount invested in the Mercurio Range does not yield a satisfactory return on investment. The projected sales figures may be over optimistic and it may take longer for the new brand to become established, especially if there are already well-established brands on the market. The company may not have the resources to compete effectively with other brands.

Poor quality financial reporting and management information produced by company systems

There seems to be a risk that business systems are not operating effectively, indicated by the problems experienced with the payroll system. Issues of this type could be replicated in other systems resulting in inaccurate financial reporting and management information. It will be difficult for management to make sound strategic and operational decisions if the information they are using is not fit for purpose.

Controls over payroll do not appear to be effective and the problems in the payroll system indicate a risk of fraud. Employee records could have been duplicated on purpose with the objective of paying an employee twice. Other fraudulent activity such as the creation of fictitious employees could also have happened.

There is also a risk of tax implications if the payroll system and controls surrounding it are not sufficiently robust. Employee taxes could be incorrectly calculated and underpaid. This is a compliance risk, and the company could face fines or penalties if tax regulations have not been complied with.

Tutorial note

Credit will be awarded for other relevant business risks evaluated, for example, the cash-based nature of operations, the impact on working capital management of customers being allowed credit, difficulties in managing and controlling a large number of stores, and risks associated with the outsourcing of the credit control function.

(b) **Risks of material misstatement**

Classification and measurement of acquired properties

The properties acquired from Lakewell Co are material, as they are clearly above the determined materiality threshold.

There is a risk that the properties are not classified appropriately according to management's intention. The properties which will be refitted should be classified as property, plant and equipment. Any properties which are going to be sold should be classified either as assets held for sale or as investment property, depending on whether the criteria of IFRS® 5 *Non-current Assets Held for Sale and Discontinued Operations* or IAS® 40 *Investment Property* have been met. For example, if management is committed to a plan for disposal which is likely to occur within 12 months and the assets are being actively marketed by the year end, then the properties are likely to meet the IFRS 5 criteria, but if they are going to be held for the longer term and not for future use by Mercurio Co, then they are more likely to meet the IAS 40 criteria. Mercurio Co's plans to refit the stores may mean that they do not meet the definition of investment property or assets held for sale.

There are measurement and disclosure implications of inappropriate classification, for example, investment properties may be measured at fair value, while assets held for sale are measured at the lower of carrying amount and fair value less costs to sell. The properties could therefore be over or understated in value if their classification is not appropriate.

Total assets are forecast to increase by 12.6% which is consistent with the new retail shops purchased during the year as well as an increase in trade receivables. The gearing ratio is shown to have decreased by 20 percentage points, consistent with the new bank loan which has been taken out to aid with cash flow for the refitting of the retail units and expenditure to support the new Mercurio Range. Trade receivables have increased by 91% which is an unusual movement and not explained by the information received from the client. The current ratio has increased by 86% during the year which has not been explained by discussions with the client to date.

The extract from the company statement of financial position does not give sufficient detail on the total current assets and current liabilities to explain the movements which must have occurred. Owing to the fact that Mercurio Co is seeking new finance for the store refurbishments, professional scepticism should be maintained as there is a motivation for the directors to overstate the current ratio in order to make more favourable loan applications.

Revenue recognition

The pet healthcare plans create a risk of misstatement in respect of the timing of revenue recognition. With payment being made in advance for an annual plan, there is a risk that revenue is not recognised at the correct time. According to IFRS 15 *Revenue from Contracts with Customers*, revenue should be recognised when the entity satisfies a performance obligation.

In the case of the pet healthcare plans, there is a risk that Mercurio Co has recognised the revenue too early, as the company has a performance obligation up until the end of the healthcare contract. Revenue should be recognised when a performance obligation under the contract has been performed, for example, when each quarterly health check has been carried out.

There is a risk of overstatement of revenue and understatement of the contract obligation (deferred revenue) if revenue is recognised before a performance obligation has been satisfied.

This is clearly a material issue because the income from sales of these plans historically represents 10% of revenue and above the materiality threshold which has been determined.

There will be pressure for the company to show good financial performance; this is compounded by the company's ambitious expansion plans in terms of the increased number of stores and new brand. Pressure to return a better performance creates an incentive for management bias which means that management may use earnings management techniques, or other methods of creative accounting, to create a healthier picture of financial performance than is actually the case. This creates an inherent risk of material misstatement, at the financial statement level.

Operating profit is projected to increase by 56.4%, which is in contrast to increases of 7.8% and 7.1% for revenue and profit before tax respectively. The anomaly is unexplained by the information received to date from the client, however, there is a risk that operating profits are being overstated in order to provide an overly optimistic perception of Mercurio Co, particularly if operating profit is a key metric in loan applications. Arnott & Co should exercise caution with classifications between profit and loss entries affecting items reported below operating profit as this may seek to overstate operating profit.

Holiday pay obligation

The holiday pay obligation forecast for 30 September 20X5 is a material balance. The amount of the obligation has increased by 81.9% from the previous year, which is a significant movement indicating that the estimate for 20X5 may be overstated. In addition, given that the company has 7,000 employees, on the basis of the holiday pay obligation being estimated at $21.1 million, this gives an average obligation per employee of $3,014, which seems high. Employee numbers have increased by 13% from the previous year, meaning that the average obligation per employee has risen by 61% from $1,871 in 20X4.

The obligation is based on a management estimate, which relies on management's judgement and therefore also contains an inherent risk of management bias. The obligation is calculated on the basis of the previous year's provision adjusted for changes in staffing levels and rates of pay. As previously mentioned, the employee numbers have increased by 13% from the prior year and there is no indication that rates of pay have changed considerably.

In addition, the lack of controls over the payroll system and the fact that manual records are being used and sometimes holidays not recorded means that management's estimate may not be based on robust information. This risk also extends back into the corresponding figure for 30 September 20X4.

There is a further risk that the accrual has not been determined in accordance with IAS 19 *Employee Benefits*, which requires an obligation to be recognised in respect of accumulating paid absences only. Management may not have considered whether the employees' holiday pay is accumulating or non-accumulating when measuring the obligation, resulting in an incorrect determination of the amount to be recognised. The employees are permitted to carry forward a maximum of three days of holiday pay and therefore accumulated holiday pay from prior years is not likely to fully explain the large increase in the holiday pay obligation.

Lost shipment

According to the contract with the international supplier, ownership of the goods which were destroyed in transit had passed to Mercurio Co and therefore any loss should be recognised in the financial statements. Mercurio Co is recognising the goods at the purchase price of $12 million in the statement of financial position and this is incorrect as the inventory has been destroyed. The destroyed inventory is clearly above the materiality threshold which has been determined.

There is a risk of material misstatement that profit and inventory have been overstated. Management bias could have led to the accounting treatments suggested by the finance director, which work to improve the company's profit and total assets for the year.

The insurance policy gives rise to a possible contingent asset. The inflow of economic benefits is probable as Mercurio Co has received informal confirmation from the insurance company that they are processing the claim. Contingent assets are possible assets whose existence will be confirmed by the occurrence or non-occurrence of uncertain future events which are not wholly within the control of the entity.

In line with IAS 37 *Provisions, Contingent Liabilities and Contingent Assets*, such assets should not be recognised, but they are disclosed when it is more likely than not that an inflow of economic benefits will occur. However, when the inflow of benefits is virtually certain, an asset is recognised in the statement of financial position, because that asset is no longer considered to be contingent.

It is therefore appropriate that Mercurio Co discloses the contingent assets of $9.6 million for the insurance claim receivable, however, it should not be recognised as an asset as the successful payout of the claim is not virtually certain.

There is a risk of inadequate disclosure or inappropriate treatment of the insurance claim.

Conclusion

The risks of material misstatement have been ordered with regard for the estimated magnitude of any misstatement and the likelihood of such a misstatement occurring. For example, the purchase of the stores for refurbishment is the highest quantitative area which is deemed to be at risk of material statement, as it is newly occurring in the year and there is a significant risk of management bias in the classification. Similarly, revenue recognition of the annual pet healthcare plans is estimated to affect up to 10% of revenue and could also impact prior year figures, resulting in a high-risk prioritisation.

In contrast, foreign exchange movements are carried out as standard by many companies and should be at lower risk of material misstatement than the other risks as outlined above.

Tutorial note

Credit will be awarded for other relevant risks of material misstatement identified and explained, for example, the control risk and associated potential misstatements in relation to payroll expenses, misstatement in respect of the credit control function impacting on trade receivables, the valuation of own-brand inventories which have yet to demonstrate their saleability, and any impairment which may need to be recognised in respect of stores which are not going to be retained for future use.

(a) **Impact of outsourcing the credit control function on audit planning**

ISA 402 *Audit Considerations Relating to an Entity Using a Service Organisation* is the source of guidance for auditors when an audited entity chooses to outsource one or more business activities. The objective of ISA 402, which is relevant to the planning stage of the audit, is that the auditor should obtain an understanding of the nature and significance of the services provided by the service organisation and their effect on the user entity's internal control relevant to the audit, sufficient to identify and assess the risks of material misstatement.

According to ISA 402, when obtaining this understanding, the following matters should be considered:

- The nature of the services provided by the service organisation and the significance of those services to the user entity, including the effect thereof on the user entity's internal control.

- The nature and materiality of the transactions processed or accounts or financial reporting processes affected by the service organisation.

- The degree of interaction between the activities of the service organisation and those of the user entity.

- The nature of the relationship between the user entity and the service organisation, including the relevant contractual terms for the activities undertaken by the service organisation.

The auditor therefore needs to understand the nature of the service which is performed by Fairbank Co. A key consideration is whether Fairbank Co's services are limited to recording and processing transactions, or whether they execute transactions, therefore taking on accountability for those transactions.

Given that Fairbank Co is providing a credit control function, the audit firm must understand whether Fairbank Co is, for example, making decisions about adjustments which may be needed to adjust for irrecoverable debt or the level of allowance for receivables, and the materiality of the amounts involved.

The audit firm should conduct procedures at the planning stage to develop this understanding, including:

– Review the contract between Mercurio Co and Fairbank Co to understand the terms of the engagement.

– Review reports issued by Fairbank Co, for example, to determine the effectiveness of the credit control function performed.

– Document how the systems of Fairbank Co and Mercurio Co interface to understand how the credit control function impacts on Mercurio Co's accounting records.

If the audit firm needs to develop a further understanding in order to assess the risk of material misstatement in relation to the service organisation's activities, then further activities should be planned for, including:

– Obtaining a type 1 or type 2 report, if available.

– Contacting the service organisation, through the user entity, to obtain specific information.

– Visiting the service organisation and performing procedures which will provide the necessary information about the relevant controls at the service organisation.

– Using another auditor to perform procedures which will provide the necessary information about the relevant controls at the service organisation.

Tutorial note

Credit will be awarded where candidates briefly explain type 1 and type 2 reports.

In conclusion, the audit firm must ensure that they use appropriately skilled and experienced staff to adequately assess the service organisation. Additionally, Arnott & Co should plan for additional time to ensure that the service organisation is contacted with sufficient time so that the required information and any visits are conducted in advance of the final audit work.

(d) Procedures in respect of the holiday pay obligation

– Discuss with management the method used to estimate the obligation to understand the assumptions used.

– Confirm that management's estimation techniques are in accordance with the requirements of IAS 19.

– Discuss with management and assess the controls around who has responsibility for calculating the accrual and how this is reviewed and approved.

– Discuss with management the source of information which has been used to develop the estimate, confirming whether this is the manual records which have been maintained.

- Agree the pay rise and changes in staffing levels to human resources records.

- Agree staff numbers from payroll records to the holiday accrual schedule and confirming to the numbers included in the management accounts.

- Develop a point estimate or a range to evaluate management's point estimate using information sources based on:

  - Discussions with a representative of the human resources department regarding the company's policy on holiday pay, particularly to determine whether it is accumulating or non-accumulating.

  - Reviews of a sample of employee contracts to confirm their holiday entitlement and whether it is accumulating or non-accumulating.

  - The manual records recording holiday leave taken before the year end.

  - An estimate of the holiday leave which has not been taken at the year end.

- Obtain written representations from management on whether they believe the significant assumptions used in making accounting estimates are reasonable.

- Review the outcome of the prior year accrual to verify how effective management has been in prior periods at estimating this obligation.

Tutorial note

Performing tests of controls is unlikely to be effective given the deficiencies in the system described in the scenario.

Examiner's comments

General comments

Well prepared candidates scored good marks on this question, particularly when focusing on the specific scenario. Where a candidate prepared an answer tailored to the scenario and focused on the requirement, high technical and professional skills marks were obtained.

Some candidates continued to produce very vague answers which were not tailored to the specific scenario and, therefore, did not achieve high technical or professional skills marks. This exam requires candidates to demonstrate both technical knowledge but also, they need to be able to apply this knowledge to a specific scenario. Generic responses with speculative risks not evident from the detail provided in the scenario will gain little credit. Candidates should use the specific information provided within the scenario demonstrating both knowledge and application of skills to pass each requirement.

Requirement (a)

In this section of the question, candidates were required to use the specific information provided in the scenario to identify and evaluate the significant business risks in relation to Mercurio Co. In the AAA exam, significant risks are considered to be those which would have a significant impact on the client business and where there is a significant probability of these risks occurring, after any mitigations stated in the information provided. Risks that are of a remote likelihood of occurring, already mitigated against or will have an insignificant impact are not considered to be 'significant risks'.

Candidates are required to identify what is significant in the context of the specific scenario, demonstrating good professional judgement and an ability to disseminate the important information whilst assessing the risks which may affect the audit.

It is pleasing to see many candidates were able to focus on the risks arising, describing the impact on the business of Mercurio Co, however a much smaller proportion of candidates evaluated the significance of these risks by assimilation of the information from the different exhibits. For example, many candidates were able to identify the risk that the pet healthcare plans were a financial risk for the company (Exhibit 2) owing to the company's inability to raise prices due to customer price sensitivity and amid rising costs. Stronger candidates then went on to assess that this risk in the context of both the likelihood of losses occurring and the magnitude of the revenue stream, being a core service that consisted of 10% revenue and would be likely to bring in further sales of food and accessories in the pet stores. An alternative evaluation that was credited was the consideration of the financial risk of the pet healthcare plans against continually rising costs and whether it was strategically beneficial to increase prices at the present time or in the future. These candidates not only provided a well thought out evaluation for the purpose of scoring technical marks, but many went on to demonstrate the skill of commercial acumen in recognising the service as a loss leader.

Weaker candidates often discussed the implication of the risk without attempting to evaluate the scale of the risk. Typical responses by candidates who did not score sufficient credit to pass the exam would simply state that something which had occurred in the scenario, such as "there might be difficulties in paying back loans" whilst failing to relate the threat to any of the specific information in the scenario, such as the lack of current financing required to renovate the stores purchased from Lakewell and the implications of this on the business. Professional scepticism could be demonstrated in this area when candidates questioned management's decision to purchase the 20 stores whilst not having a proper business plan in place and the risks to the business as a result of this lack of planning.

Some candidates remarked that going concern was a risk because the company would fail to pay back the loans that were due, however this was not indicated in the scenario and although cash balances had decreased it is normal for profitable businesses to fund expansion with loan financing.

Overall, in this section many candidates were able to identify sufficient risks to pass the requirement. Fewer candidates identified the business risks of the company's poor internal controls and the impact on business decisions. In summary, candidates did not seem to have difficulty in identifying business risks and the implication on the company; however, the differentiator between stronger and weaker candidates was their ability to evaluate the risks and demonstrate their professional skills of commercial acumen and professional scepticism.

Requirement (b)

This requirement is typical in volume and nature to many planning questions and examines a major area of the syllabus – risk. It is important to recognise that the requirement asked for an evaluation, not simply a list of risks, nor a strategy or procedures to address those risks. The examining team are testing whether candidates understand how and why a risk arises and the implications this has on the financial statements or the audit itself. Candidates are expected to perform relevant analysis to support an evaluation of risks of material misstatement (RoMMs). There were 18 technical marks available in this part of the question in addition to a significant number of professional skills marks for the analysis. It was disappointing to see that candidates often achieved strong marks in this section for the identification of the RoMMs but fewer obtained the marks for the evaluation of those risks. Many candidates are continuing to rely on basic or generic explanations, which fail to refer to the information in the scenario.

Candidates who refer to the specific information provide more in-depth answers and are also able to assess the scale of the risk in the context of the specific audit client.

Materiality

Specific marks were available in this requirement for the calculation and application of materiality in line with the new syllabus guidance and for the prioritisation of the risks identified. Whilst a significant number of candidates appeared prepared for the new syllabus and followed the new materiality guidance, there remained few who attempted to prioritise risks and were unable to access the professional skills marks for this skill.

Candidates are expected to initially determine a materiality threshold for the audit, as would be used in practice. Three technical marks are available for the materiality determination. Candidates are expected to demonstrate a knowledge of the appropriate percentage range for the benchmark instructed by the audit partner (in this question, profit before tax was to be utilised with candidates expected to use 5 - 10% as their range), calculate the monetary amount in respect of the range. Candidates must then use their professional judgement to select an appropriate materiality threshold given the risk levels which exist in the audit and provide a brief justification for their choice. Each of these steps examines a different aspect of the understanding and skills required of an auditor. It was disappointing to note that some candidates initially calculated a range appropriately, then failed to justify a materiality threshold for the audit. The examining team will give credit for any reasonable explanation of the chosen materiality threshold, as the mark is to recognise that there is the application of professional judgement and that a candidate can justify their response. It is not required that candidates select the identical percentage or figure, or that they provide a justification identical to that shown in the model answer. For example, in this question, some candidates stated the higher end of the range was justified because this was an existing client, some stated the lower end was more appropriate due to the accounting errors that the finance director was making. Alternative answers which were awarded credit included those which suggested that an amount in the middle of the range was appropriate, because whilst this was an existing client, the rapid expansion and increased loan finance would bring the financial statements under increasing scrutiny. All of these obtained the mark for justifying the chosen materiality threshold.

Evaluation of the risks

Candidates were then required to evaluate the significant risks. In determining which risks are the most significant, candidates are demonstrating an understanding of risk, how it arises and how the audit will focus on those issues most likely to cause a material misstatement. Candidates that demonstrated a depth of evaluation were awarded more credit than those more generic responses. An issue that arises repeatedly is candidates attempting to find 9 risks for an 18-mark question and conducting little or no in-depth analysis of any of them. This will not be sufficient to attain a pass mark. This means some of the risks stated in these answers will be speculative or not significant and, therefore, will not obtain credit. This also increases the time pressure for candidates as they are trying to cover too many risks and these risks which are identified are often not developed in sufficient depth to obtain a pass mark. Once again, examples seen by the examining team that do not attain credit included risks that don't arise at all in the scenario such as a provision for the refit of stores, or the split of loans between current and non-current which is neither a significant ROMM nor business risk. These speculative risks are not given credit. The scenario contained information which gave rise to five significant risks, of which the majority of candidates were able to identify at least four. These were the classification and measurement of properties, revenue recognition related to the pet healthcare plans, trade receivables, lack of controls relating to holiday pay and the missing shipment.

Each of these could be evaluated in the context of the scenario using the information provided, ensuring that the underlying accounting treatment was correct. In this exam, financial reporting knowledge from the SBR syllabus and previous FR and FA exams is deemed knowledge. The majority of marks available in AAA will be for the application of the financial reporting knowledge to the specific audit scenario, not simply for the knowledge itself. In Exhibit 3, candidates were provided with the trade receivables figure with comparatives and many correctly calculated the percentage increase. In addition, a narrative on trade receivables was provided stating (i) an increasing number of customers have credit accounts, and (ii) a service organisation is now engaged to provide the credit control function. For this Strategic Professional level exam, candidates are expected to provide further analysis in order to obtain credit, rather than simply relating the increase in trade receivables directly to a ROMM. Candidates need to explain the changes to the organisation which can help to explain the increase year on year. Stronger candidates were able to understand the numerical and narrative explanations and determine that a ROMM existed in relation to trade receivables owing to the outsourcing of the credit control function and lack of visibility of the recovery of debts. Candidates who further develop this ROMM such as by questioning management's motive for overstating trade receivables, could achieve credit for professional skills marks by displaying scepticism and judgement. It was pleasing to see that candidates could link the issues of trade receivables and loan financing proposing that management may wish to present more positive financial statements in order to increase the likelihood of gaining further loan financing in the future. Weaker candidates who discussed generic management bias which is not linked to a specific risk, such as "the company is listed therefore management want to perform earnings management" did not obtain credit. Consistent with the September examination, it was disappointing to see that few candidates attempted any prioritisation of the risks as specifically stated in the requirement. Professional skill marks were available to the candidates who attempted this requirement. Candidates were expected to identify the most significant risks, and then provide a brief justification for their choice. Again, credit was awarded for candidates who offered a reasonable explanation, and therefore, a range of possible explanations are valid. Candidates should be aware this mark is for the act of justifying the reason not for the actual justification used. Candidates can obtain these marks by either ordering their answer in priority order and stating this is the case or by summarising in a brief conclusion which risk, or risks, are most significant. Where candidates use this latter method, if a candidate does not state which one or two risks are the most significant but simply lists some or all their identified risks, this will not be sufficient for credit.

Requirement (c)

Part (c) required candidates to discuss and conclude on the impact of outsourcing the credit control function – this topic could attract credit in parts (a), (b) and (c) of the question and was unfortunately often poorly understood throughout. A significant proportion of students attempted to answer as if it was an acceptance question and rote learnt answers in this context naturally scored very poorly. Despite the requirement requesting a conclusion and the marking guide allowing a generous interpretation of this, few candidates attempted to provide a conclusion. In addition, a professional mark was available under the communication category to recognise those candidates who applied their answer to the scenario and the service organisation being related to credit control. This could be awarded where candidates had, for example, suggested procedures relating to the outsourcing of credit control to a service organisation, however, it was often lacking in candidates' responses.

Requirement (d)

This requirement is typical of a section A question and requires candidates to design audit procedures to address a specific risk arising in the question. In this question, the procedures were to determine the holiday pay obligation, which had been described in Exhibit 3.

Exhibit 3 explains that the holiday obligation was a management estimate in this scenario as Mercurio Co's systems had failed due to duplication issues and could not be relied upon. A sizeable proportion of students failed to appreciate that the procedures would need to be directed to the estimate and instead focussed on the failed systems which caused low marks in an area where students normally score well. Credit was awarded where candidates described valid procedures for the development of an auditor's estimate. The strongest candidates gained a professional mark under analysis and evaluation for designing procedures which addressed the areas of judgement i.e. how to audit the assumptions that were made by management in their estimate. Candidates were generally able to pass this requirement, however with fewer marks than is typical of a procedures question.

Overall professional skills marks

In additional to the professional skill marks described within the different sections of the question, marks were available for communication overall. These marks were awarded for the use of a report header and introduction, presentation and relevance of answer and clarity of explanations. The majority of candidates achieved maximum marks in this area.

	ACCA Marking guide	
		Marks
(a)	**Business risk evaluation** Up to 2 marks for each business risk (unless indicated otherwise). Marks may be awarded for other, relevant business risks not included in the marking guide. • Animal welfare regulations • Compliance risk in respect of veterinary services provided • Staff competence (inappropriately qualified vets, risk of inadequately trained staff (up to 4 marks) • Financial risk that pet healthcare plans do not generate profit/cash inflow • Property acquisition and future refitting costs • Mercurio brand products • Poor quality financial reporting and management information being produced from systems	
	Maximum	**8**
(b)	**Evaluation and prioritisation of risks of material misstatement** Up to 3 marks for each risk of material misstatement (unless indicated otherwise). Marks may be awarded for other, relevant risks not included in the marking guide. In addition, ½ mark for relevant trends or calculations which form part of the evaluation of risk (max 3 marks). Appropriate materiality calculations up to 2 marks and justification of materiality should be awarded to 1 mark. • Pressure on results • Classification and measurement of properties • Revenue recognition • Lack of controls regarding holiday pay (4 marks) • Missing shipment	
	Maximum	**18**

(c) **Impact of outsourcing the credit control function**
Generally, 1 mark for each valid point discussed
- Need to obtain understanding of nature and significance of services provided including (½ mark each):
  - Nature of services provided
  - Nature and materiality of transactions processed
  - Degree of interaction
  - Contractual terms
- Examples of procedures to be performed (1 mark each)
  - Review the contract between Mercurio Co and Fairbank Co
  - Review reports issued by Fairbank Co
  - Document how the systems of Fairbank Co and Mercurio Co interface
- Further procedures if necessary to determine the risk of material misstatement (1 mark each)
  - Obtaining a type 1 or type 2 report, if available
  - Contacting the service organisation to obtain specific information
  - Visiting the service organisation and performing procedures
  - Using another auditor to perform procedures

Maximum 7

(d) **Procedures in relation to holiday pay obligation**
Generally, 1 mark for each well-explained procedure:
- Discuss with management the method used to estimate the obligation to understand the assumptions used
- Confirm that management's estimation techniques are in accordance with IAS 19
- Discuss with management who prepares the calculation and how it is approved
- Discuss with management the source of information which has been used to develop the estimate
- Agree staff numbers from payroll records to the holiday accrual schedule
- Agree the pay rise and changes in staffing levels to HR records to verify accuracy of the estimations used
- Develop a point estimate or range to evaluate management's estimate using information sources based on:
  - Discussion with human resources representative regarding the company's policy on holiday pay, particularly to determine whether it is accumulating or non-accumulating
  - Employee contracts to confirm their holiday entitlement and whether it is accumulating or non-accumulating
  - Manual records of holiday leave taken before the year end
  - Estimate of the holiday leave not yet taken at the year end
- Review the outcome of the previous period's estimates
- Obtain a written representation from management on whether they believe significant assumptions used in making accounting estimates are reasonable

Maximum 7

Professional marks

Communication

- Briefing note format and structure – use of headings/subheadings and an introduction
- Style, language and clarity – appropriate layout and tone of briefing notes, presentation of materiality and relevant calculations, appropriate use of the CBE tools, easy to follow and understand
- Effectiveness and clarity of communication – answer is relevant and tailored to the scenario
- Adherence to the specific requests made by the audit engagement partner

Analysis and evaluation

- Appropriate use of the information to determine and apply suitable specific calculations which are relevant to the scenario
- Risk evaluation is effectively prioritised, focusing on significance and only taking account of risks which would result in material misstatements
- Identification of procedures or actions which address the areas of judgement in the impairment calculation

Professional scepticism and professional judgement

- Effective challenge of information supplied and techniques carried out to support key facts and/or decisions
- Determination and justification of suitable materiality level appropriately and consistently applied
- Appropriate application of professional judgement to draw conclusions and make informed decisions about the courses of action which are appropriate in the context of the audit engagement
- Identification of possible management bias or error

Commercial acumen

- Demonstration of wider commercial awareness applied to the scenario to evaluate business risks

Maximum	10
Total	50

2 WINBERRY *Walk in the footsteps of a top tutor*

Top tutor tips

Determination of materiality: *The email from the partner states that materiality should be based on profit, therefore at the start of your answer you should calculate the range for materiality using that benchmark and justify a figure within that range. If it is a new audit client or a client where there are apparent control risks, materiality should be set at the lower end of the range. If it is an existing client, materiality may be able to be set at the higher end of the range depending on the other risks mentioned in the scenario. The examining team will give credit for any reasonable explanation of the chosen materiality threshold, as the mark is to recognise that there is the application of professional judgement and that a candidate can justify their response. It is not required that candidates select the identical percentage or figure, or that they provide a justification identical to that shown in the model answer. The examiner's comments for this question state that materiality could be justified at any figure within the materiality range. See the full examiner's comments with examples at the end of the answer.*

Part (a) requires evaluation of business risks. When describing business risks remember to explain the impact it will have on the company i.e. impact on profit or cash flow. The business risks should be relatable to the financial statements as the auditor will only consider business risks which will also give rise to a risk of material misstatement.

Part (b) asks risks of material misstatement. Risk of material misstatement is usually due to non-compliance with an accounting standard, although it also includes control risk. Think about the requirements of the relevant accounting standards and what the client might be doing incorrectly.

Prioritisation of risks: One mark is awarded for the prioritisation of the risks of material misstatement. The mark is for the act of justifying the reason, not for the actual justification used (i.e. a range of completely different answers could be awarded the mark), therefore if a reasonable explanation is given, the mark will be awarded. Prioritisation can be achieved by either ordering your answer in priority order and stating this is the case, or by summarising in a brief conclusion which risk, or risks, are most significant.

Part (c) asks for audit procedures over the classification of the investment in LPS Co. The procedures should enable the auditor to obtain evidence to determine whether the relevant financial reporting standard has been complied with. Make sure your procedures are clear and provide enough detail that they can be easily followed by the audit team.

Part (d) asks for a discussion of auditor's responsibilities in relation to compliance with laws and regulations. This requires knowledge of the relevant auditing standard. State the requirements of the ISA and apply them to the scenario.

Professional skills

Professional skills will be awarded for:

Communication – responding to the instructions in the partner's email such as preparing your answers in the form of briefing notes and using the stated benchmark for materiality.

Analysis and evaluation – applying the information from the scenario to answer the question and explaining the issues in sufficient depth.

Professional scepticism and judgement – justifying an appropriate materiality level, demonstrating critical thinking and being alert to possible manipulation and management bias.

Where relevant, professional marks will be awarded for commercial acumen which requires making practical and plausible recommendations and considering the wider implications of issues to the audit firm.

Briefing notes

To: Olivia Fig, audit engagement partner

From: Audit manager

Subject: Audit planning in relation to Winberry Co

Date: 1 July 20X5

Introduction

These briefing notes have been prepared to assist in planning the audit of Winberry Co. The notes begin with an evaluation of the significant business risks facing the company and continue with an evaluation and prioritisation of the significant risks of material misstatement which should be considered in planning the audit. The significant risks of material misstatement have been structured to prioritise the risks in terms of the likelihood and magnitude of misstatement in relation to each risk.

The notes also include the recommended principal audit procedures which have been designed in respect of the investment in Luxury Pet Supplies Co (LPS Co) and the warehouse assets following a recent fire. Finally, the notes consider the audit implications of a cyber-attack which took place during the year.

Materiality

For the purposes of these briefing notes, the overall materiality level used to assess the significance of identified risks is $4 million based on the profitability of the company, as requested.

Justification

Using profit before tax of $53 million as a suggested benchmark results in a suggested range of $2.65 million (5% × $53 million) to $5.3 million (10% × $53 million).

This is an existing client and we have cumulative knowledge and experience of Winberry Co, however, the changes to the company's operations in the year increase the level of risk in the current year. Materiality should be set at the midpoint of the range.

This benchmark is only a starting point for determining materiality and professional judgement will need to be applied in determining a final level to be used during the course of the audit.

(a)   Evaluation of significant business risks

Damage to operations caused by the warehouse fire

The fire has caused the destruction of the warehouse servicing Winberry Co's northern customer base. Winberry Co will certainly incur higher costs to increase capacity at the existing warehouses and, more significantly, incur greater transport costs by using alternative warehouses to supply this region.

If there is disruption to services due to an interruption of grocery service, then this will cause a detrimental effect to Winberry Co's reputation which is likely to result in a fall in sales and profit.

The damage to Winberry Co's business could be amplified by the fact that online grocery delivery is a growing market and a failure to adequately service new customers to the sector could restrict this growth opportunity.

International expansion

The expansion into Farland introduces a business risk in that the company will be managing operations in a foreign country for the first time. Farland may have different laws and regulations compared to the company's home jurisdiction, so there is a heightened risk of non-compliance.

The types of groceries typically bought by consumers in Farland may be different from Winberry Co's home jurisdiction and management may not have experience in their procurement, distribution and sale.

There are also risks associated with Winberry Co's ability to set up an overseas distribution network, including the warehouses, delivery vehicles and suitably qualified staff and to comply with foreign legislation.

All of these issues create a risk that the international expansion may not be successful, and at the same time will represent a drain on management's time and resources. Operations in the home country of Winberry Co may suffer as a result.

Investment in LPS Co

The joint venture represents a new method of expansion for Winberry Co and introduces a possible reputational risk if they are unable to replicate their own high standards in the joint venture. Any quality issues with products or delivery problems with LPS Co could have repercussions for Winberry Co's reputation and this may, consequently, lead to a reduction in sales.

There is also the possibility of a clash in management styles and techniques of the two different partners in the joint venture leading to conflict, which may affect the business strategy, management focus and consequently impact financial performance.

Management may struggle to deal with the increased number of operations which they need to monitor and control, or they may focus so much on ensuring the success of the new joint venture that existing activities are neglected.

These issues heighten the risk of the joint venture failing to be successful and produce a satisfactory return on the $30 million initial investment.

Loan finance

The $125 million expansion into Farland is to be funded by loan finance. The additional debt financing will increase Winberry Co's gearing and result in a higher business risk to ensure that the international expansion is successful and that the interest-bearing loan is covered without detriment to the cash flow of the existing business.

Winberry Co's existing bank loans have the covenant that interest cover must remain above 3. The expansion and additional proposed loan will therefore make it more difficult to maintain the required interest cover level and if the international expansion fails, Winberry Co is at risk of defaulting on the bank covenant and the bank recalling the loan.

Due to the recent joint venture, rapid growth in sales and the planned expansion into Farland, Winberry Co is at risk from overtrading. The current management team may not be able to adequately control the high level of growth and may neglect Winberry Co's core business, causing loss of market share. This is particularly heightened as the home delivery grocery market is noted as experiencing high levels of growth and will attract strong competition.

Eco-friendly delivery vans

The eco-friendly delivery vans have been noted as causing delays of up to four hours, which will cause inconvenience to Winberry Co's customers and reputational damage. Winberry Co's customers value the convenience of grocery delivery and a four-hour delay would severely negate this perceived benefit. Winberry Co would be likely to lose customers if the delivery delays continue and therefore sales and profits would suffer, as well as the company having to bear the cost of any compensation or refunds which could be claimed by customers for the delays to their deliveries.

Legal case

The legal case being brought against Winberry Co by local residents regarding the warehouse which was destroyed by fire will first cause reputational damage when the media report on the case and Winberry Co is associated with toxic fumes and damage to public health. The result of the internet search demonstrates that the case is already reported in the public domain and therefore some reputational damage is likely, thereby reducing sales and profits.

There is also the business risk that the legal case will require defending or settlement and therefore legal fees or compensation payments will be incurred, with a further risk of having to pay damages and fines if Winberry Co is found liable of damaging public health through toxic fumes from the warehouse fire.

The information provided regarding Winberry Co's staff circumventing safety controls increases the likelihood that Winberry Co will be found negligent and possibly lose the legal case.

Cyber-security attack

The internet search, if accurate, states that the company has not fulfilled the requirements of the data protection legislation and corporate governance principles. This may result in reputational damage to the firm as well as the possible requirement to pay fines or penalties which both could result in cash outflows from Winberry Co, whether it is by cash payments or reduced sales. The risk of a fine or penalty is increased due to the fact that the directors of Winberry Co have not reported the breach to the regulator.

The apparent concealment of the data breach, by management not reporting the issue to regulators, may also indicate a lack of integrity or a lack of understanding by management, of law and regulations. The audit team should also consider the impact on the reliance on corporate governance matters concerning the business.

Tutorial note

Credit will be given to candidates who refer to the potential corporate governance issues due to Winberry Co being a listed company.

Perishable products

The nature of Winberry Co's grocery delivery is that a large proportion of inventory is perishable and therefore has a limited shelf life. The perishable nature of the goods means that any delays to delivery, such as those caused by the breakdown of the eco-friendly delivery vans, will have a greater impact to the profits of Winberry Co than if the goods were not perishable. This means that there is a significant risk of wastage and any inefficiency in storage or distribution will increase spoilage of inventory and result in a loss of profit for Winberry Co.

In addition, the joint venture of LPS Co will introduce a new range of perishable products which will have different storage requirements.

(b) **Evaluation of risk of material misstatement**

Financial analysis

Revenue is projected to increase by 66.8%, operating profit by 56.4% and profit before tax by 71%, all of which are broadly consistent with each other. During the year, Winberry Co has a new premium delivery pass revenue stream; however, this is not sufficient to explain the projected increase in revenue.

Total assets are forecast to increase by 8.3% which may seem overly optimistic given that a large warehouse has been destroyed by fire during the year without being written down, and Winberry Co is accounting for the assets of the new joint venture in LPS Co in their entirety by incorrectly consolidating LPS Co as a subsidiary. There is a risk that assets are overstated.

Warehouse fire

The most significant identified risk would be the assessment of the carrying amount of the fire damaged warehouse which is clearly above the materiality threshold of $4 million.

The damage to the warehouse should have triggered an impairment review, as required by IAS 36 *Impairment of Assets*. However, the finance director has wrongly assumed that the insurance cover on the warehouse relieves Winberry Co of the requirement to properly assess the impairment of the warehouse and perform the calculations in accordance with IAS 36.

Impairment is measured by comparing the carrying amount of an asset with its recoverable amount. The recoverable amount is the higher of value in use and fair value less costs to sell the asset.

The significance of the warehouse fire is not simply a quantitative one, but also an indicator of potential management bias and the impact of their judgement on the financial statements. The risks of material misstatement regarding this issue are, therefore, of high significance to the audit team.

As the warehouse has been destroyed by the fire, it is likely that the value in use is nil and the fair value less costs to sell would also have to consider the warehouse in its current condition as the warehouse is badly damaged and the machinery needs to be completely replaced.

According to IAS 36, the cash flow projections which are used to determine the value in use of the impaired asset should relate to the asset in its current condition – expenditures to improve or enhance the asset's performance should not be anticipated, however, the finance director has not carried out an impairment review as he is confident the company's insurance policy will cover the cost of reinstating it to its previous condition.

This is against the criteria of IAS 36 and there is a risk that property plant and equipment (PPE) is overstated and the impairment cost is understated.

In addition, it is important that any amount claimed through the insurance policy is recognised separately from the warehouse PPE. It is important that the current status of the insurance claim is verified during the audit process and, if necessary, prior to the completion of the audit. This will determine to what extent the warehouse should be impaired in the financial statements.

Investment in LPS Co

The financial information shows that LPS Co revenue is projected to reach $10 million this year. The investment is expected to occur in August 20X5, so based on these projections the $10 million revenue is for a maximum of two months, which is clearly above the determined materiality threshold. Winberry Co is also recognising the total assets of the joint venture of $60 million which is also in excess of the materiality threshold.

From the information provided in the extract from the management accounts, it seems that the investment is a joint venture, with control of LPS Co shared between Winberry Co and Durian Co. IFRS 11 *Joint Arrangements* defines a joint venture as a joint arrangement whereby the parties who have joint control of the arrangement have rights to the net assets of the arrangement.

IFRS 11 requires that a joint venturer recognises its interest in a joint venture as an investment and shall account for that investment using the equity method in accordance with IAS 28 *Investments in Associates and Joint Ventures.*

The finance director has stated that he intends to consolidate the results of LPS Co; the share of the results attributable to Durian Co is shown as a non-controlling interest. The finance director believes that despite Winberry Co and Durian Co each owning 50% of LPS Co and having equal representation on the board of directors, Winberry Co's contribution of knowledge to the joint venture is greater and therefore Winberry should consolidate the investment as a subsidiary. This treatment is contrary to IFRS 11, whereby the control is considered to be joint if the investors in the venture have equal shareholdings and equal representation on the board of directors.

There is no evidence that Winberry Co holds a right to veto decisions, which is a possible way the finance director could justify that Winberry Co holds overall control and would be entitled to consolidate LPS Co.

The impact of the full consolidation of LPS Co by Winberry Co as a subsidiary would not have a net effect of overstating Winberry Co's retained profit or net assets. This is because the non-controlling interest of Durian Co would be represented on the statement of profit or loss and statement of financial position. The attributable profit and equity of non-controlling interests belonging to Durian Co would be shown in the proportion agreed of 50%, however, the gross totals of all areas in Winberry Co's statement of financial position and profit or loss would be inflated by LPS Co being incorrectly consolidated as a subsidiary undertaking.

The consolidation of the full results of LPS Co would, however, increase Winberry Co's revenue, operating profit and total assets which may be the motivation for the finance director to claim that Winberry Co controls LPS Co and is entitled to fully consolidate the results.

Revenue recognition – premium delivery pass

There is a risk arising from Winberry Co recognising revenue for customers in advance of the satisfaction of the performance obligation for the annual premium delivery pass, with revenue recognised when the invoice is sent to the customer. This is leading to early recognition of revenue, i.e. recognising prior to the company providing a service to its customers.

IFRS 15 *Revenue from Contracts with Customers* requires that revenue is recognised when a performance obligation is satisfied by transferring a promised good or service to a customer. As the premium delivery pass covers 12 months and the company is providing the service over time, it can be difficult to determine how much service has been provided and therefore the amount of revenue which can be recognised at a particular point in time.

It does not appear that the requirements of IFRS 15 are being adhered to and there is a risk that revenue is being overstated and deferred income is understated.

Winberry Co also has a further revenue recognition risk that revenue from orders is recognised at the point of order rather than at the time of delivery. As previously stated, IFRS 15 states that revenue is recognised when a performance obligation is satisfied and in Winberry Co's case, this would be when the goods are delivered to the customer. There is a risk that revenue is being overstated and deferred income is understated.

Tutorial note

Credit can be awarded where the candidate assumes that the delivery pass revenue does not accrue evenly.

Corporate governance

The recent cyber-security attack could highlight that internal controls are deficient within the company. Even though this particular problem has now been rectified, if Winberry Co had not properly identified or responded to these cyber-security risks, there remains the possibility that there could be other areas which are deficient, leading to control risk.

The issue also indicates that the audit committee is not appropriately fulfilling its responsibilities with regards to internal audit which could indicate wider weaknesses in the company's corporate governance arrangements and resulting in increasing risk of material misstatement.

Legal provision

The internet search results show that a legal case was brought against Winberry Co in January 20X5. From the information provided, it is not possible to determine if the amount involved is material, however, there should be appropriate consideration as to whether the court case gives rise to an obligation at the reporting date.

According to IAS 37 *Provisions, Contingent Liabilities and Contingent Assets*, a provision should be recognised as a liability if there is a present obligation as a result of past events which gives rise to a probable outflow of economic benefit which can be reliably measured. The warehouse fire is a known event, so if there has been harm brought about to people in the local area as result of this, then it is feasible that there is a liability as a result of a past event.

A risk of material misstatement therefore arises that if any necessary provision is not recognised, liabilities and expenses will be understated. If there is a possible obligation at the reporting date, then disclosure of the contingent liability should be made in the notes to the financial statements.

There is a risk of inadequate disclosure. This is a risk whether the situation gives rise to a provision or a contingent liability, as provisions also have disclosure requirements which may not be complied with.

A further risk is that any legal fees associated with the claim have not been accrued within the financial statements. As the claim has arisen during the year, the expense must be included in this year's profit or loss account, even if the claim is still ongoing at the year end.

The fact that the legal claim was not discussed at the meeting with the audit partner may cast doubt on the overall integrity of senior management, and on the credibility of the financial statements. Management representations should be approached with a degree of professional scepticism during the audit.

Pressure on results

The company is a listed entity and the shareholders will be looking for a return on their investment in the form of a dividend payment and there will be pressure for the company to show good financial performance; this is compounded by the company's ambitious international expansion plans and the requirement to maintain adequate interest cover to continue to meet the bank's covenant. Pressure to return a better performance creates an incentive for management bias which means that management may use earnings management techniques, or other methods of creative accounting, to create a healthier picture of financial performance than is actually the case.

This creates an inherent risk of material misstatement, at the financial statement level. Management bias could also have led to some of the accounting treatments suggested by the finance director, such as the early recognition of revenue from the premium delivery pass, which works to improve the company's profit and total assets for the year.

Eco-friendly delivery vans

The eco-friendly delivery vans noted in the internet search total $4million (80 × $50,000) and this meets the threshold of materiality. There is a risk, however, that the eco-friendly delivery vans are impaired as the ability of the vans to make deliveries in line with Winberry Co's delivery schedules appears to be reduced.

Impairment is measured by comparing the carrying amount of an asset with its recoverable amount. The recoverable amount is the higher of value in use and fair value less costs to sell the asset.

There is a risk that the value in use is lowered due to the reduced ability of the eco-friendly vans to deliver goods efficiently and effectively. The fair value less costs to sell of the assets may also be impacted by the delivery range of the vans. There is a risk that the carrying amount PPE value of the eco-friendly vans is overstated and the impairment expense is understated.

Conclusion

The risks of material misstatement have been ordered with regard to the estimated magnitude of any misstatement and the likelihood of such a misstatement occurring. For example, the warehouse fire is the highest quantitative area which is deemed to be at risk of material misstatement, is newly occurring in the year and there is a significant risk of management bias in the measurement of the impairment. Similarly, the joint venture with Durian Co is quantitatively material and a fundamental change in both operation and accounting for Winberry Co, so deemed high risk. In contrast, the eco-friendly delivery vans are borderline to the stated threshold of materiality and therefore at lower risk of material misstatement than the other risks as outlined above.

In conclusion, Winberry Co has a significant number of audit and business risks which could result in material misstatement in the financial statements. Quince & Co should reassess their assessed level of planning materiality to ensure that the risk profile of the company is adequately reflected in the level of testing planned. The audit should be planned to assign highly competent staff for the high risk, judgemental areas of the audit such as the impairment of the fire damaged warehouse.

(c) **Audit procedures**

Principal audit procedures in respect of the classification of the investment in LPS Co

- Obtain the legal documentation supporting the investment and agree the details of the investment including:

    – The rights and obligations of the investing parties to understand the implications for the reporting by Winberry Co in the financial statements

    – The date of the investment

    – Number of shares purchased and the voting rights attached to the shares to assist in the understanding of the control of the venture

    – The nature of the profit-sharing arrangement between Winberry Co and Durian Co

    – The nature of access to LPS Co's assets under the terms of the agreement

    – Contact and communication with the auditors of the joint venture if not Quince & Co

    – Confirmation that there is no restriction of the company's shared control of LPS Co.

- Review board minutes to understand the business rationale for the investment and to assess the amount of control/existence of joint control of the venture.

- Review minutes of relevant meetings between the company and Durian Co to confirm that control is shared between the two investors and to understand the nature of the relationship and the decision-making process, particularly if any party holds the right to veto decisions.

- Obtain documentation such as LPS Co's organisational structure to confirm that the company has successfully appointed members to the board of the company and that those members have equal power to the members appointed by Durian Co.

(d) **Auditor's responsibilities in relation to an audit client's compliance with laws and regulations**

Winberry Co appears to be in breach of relevant law and regulations regarding the protection of customer data. ISA 250/ISA (UK) 250A *Consideration of Laws and Regulations in an Audit of Financial Statements* states that while it is management's responsibility to ensure the entity's operations are conducted in accordance with the provisions of laws and regulations, the auditor is responsible for obtaining sufficient and appropriate audit evidence regarding compliance with laws and regulations. Auditors need to assess the evidence especially where non-compliance has an impact on the financial statements or where any non-compliance will affect the entity's ability to continue its operations.

The auditor is required by ISA 315 (Revised) *Identifying and Assessing the Risks of Material Misstatement* to gain an understanding of the legal and regulatory framework in which the audited entity operates. This will help the auditor to identify non-compliance and to assess the implications of non-compliance. Therefore, the auditor should ensure they have a full knowledge and understanding of the data protection regulations in order to evaluate the implications of non-compliance by Winberry Co.

ISA 250/ISA (UK) 250A requires when non-compliance is identified or suspected, the auditor shall obtain an understanding of the nature of the act and the circumstances in which it has occurred, and further information to evaluate the possible effect on the financial statements.

Procedures must be performed to obtain evidence about the instances of non-compliance in relation to the data protection breach, for example, discussions with management to understand how the data breach occurred.

In addition, the audit team should perform further procedures, for example, discussion with Winberry Co's legal advisers to understand the legal and operational consequences of the breach including likely fines and exposure to litigation and assess the materiality of such exposure.

ISA 250/ISA (UK) 250A requires the auditor to determine whether they have a responsibility to report the identified or suspected non-compliance to parties outside the entity. In the event that management or those charged with governance of Winberry Co fail to make the necessary disclosures to the regulatory authorities, Quince & Co should consider whether they should make the disclosure. This will depend on matters including whether there is a legal duty to disclose or whether it is considered to be in the public interest to do so.

As Winberry Co has not yet notified the regulator or the affected users, Quince & Co should initially encourage the directors to report the issue themselves before making disclosures they deem are required under the auditor's obligations described above.

Auditors should comply with the fundamental principle of confidentiality, and if disclosure were to be made by the auditor, it would be advisable to seek legal advice on the matter.

In exceptional circumstances where the auditor believes there may be an imminent breach of a law or regulation, they may need to disclose the matter immediately to an appropriate authority. The decision to disclose will always be a matter for the auditor's judgement and where the disclosure is made in good faith, it will not constitute a breach of the duty of confidentiality.

Examiner's comments

General comments

Many candidates scored well on this question, particularly when focusing on the specific scenario. Where a candidate prepared an answer tailored to the scenario and focused on the requirement, high technical and professional skills marks were obtained.

Some candidates continued to produce very vague answers which were not tailored to the specific scenario and, therefore, did not achieve high technical or professional skills marks. This exam requires candidates to demonstrate both technical knowledge but also, they need to be able to apply this knowledge to a specific scenario. Generic responses with speculative risks not evident from the detail provided in the scenario will gain little credit. Candidates should use the specific information provided within the scenario demonstrating both knowledge and application of skills to pass each requirement.

A minority of candidates continued to use answers which appear to be taken from past questions and discuss issues which are not present in the question being attempted. This will not obtain credit.

Requirement (a)

In this section of the question, candidates were required to use the specific information provided in the scenario to identify and evaluate the significant business risks in relation to Winberry Co. In the AAA exam, significant risks are considered to be those which would have a significant impact on the client business and where there is a significant probability of these risks occurring, after any mitigations stated in the information provided. Risks that are of a remote likelihood of occurring, already mitigated against or will have an insignificant impact are not considered to be 'significant risks'.

Candidates are required to identify what is significant in the context of the specific scenario, demonstrating good professional judgement and an ability to disseminate the important information whilst assessing the risks which may affect the audit.

It is pleasing to see many candidates were able to focus on the risks arising, describing the impact on the business of Winberry Co, and evaluating the significance by assimilation of the information from the different exhibits. For example, many candidates were able to identify the risk that the insurance claim for damaged property (Exhibit 3) might not be successful and were able to describe the impact on the company cashflows for the initial credit. Stronger candidates then went on to assess that this risk in the light of the deliberate deactivation of the sprinkler system, may mean that the insurance claim is unsuccessful. These candidates not only provided a well thought out evaluation for the purpose of scoring technical marks, but were also demonstrating the skill of professional scepticism in recognising the insurance claim might not be successful. Credit was also available for the demonstration of commercial acumen in appreciating the claim was less likely to be successful given that the fire safety systems had been overridden as this contributed to the levels of damage incurred at the warehouse.

Weaker candidates often discussed the implication of the risk without attempting to evaluate the scale of the risk. Typical responses by candidates who did not score sufficient credit to pass the exam would simply state that something which had occurred in the scenario, such as "there might be a fire in the warehouse" whilst failing to assess the implication on the business.

A well evaluated risk has in depth analysis. Candidates writing only a sentence or two are unlikely to attain many of the marks available for each risk.

Some candidates described risks which were not considered significant for credit. The most common ones seen by the examining team were currency risks arising in a proposed expansion overseas, despite being told that the two countries use the same currency. Other weaker responses suggested that food safety breaches may occur, even though candidates were told that this risk was mitigated using food safety specialists. Other candidates remarked that going concern was a risk because the company might lose its licence to operate, even though no information was provided in the scenario to suggest a licence was required to operate. Candidates are not expected to know which industries are subject to specific licencing arrangements and as such will be told in a question if the specific industry requires a licence.

Overall, in this section many candidates were able to identify sufficient risks to pass the requirement. Fewer candidates identified the risks of the company' decision to diversify into a new industry through a joint venture, or the cost implications relating to the poor performance of the electric vehicles. These were topics less frequently seen in past questions and served as a differentiator between stronger candidates who were able to identify the risks from the scenario and demonstrate their professional skills of analysis and evaluation of the evidence provided.

Requirement (b)

This requirement is typical in volume and nature to many planning questions and examines a major area of the syllabus – risk. It is important to notice that the requirement asked for an evaluation, not simply a list of risks, nor a strategy or procedures to address those risks. The examining team are testing whether candidates understand how and why a risk arises and the implications this has on the financial statements or the audit itself.

Candidates are expected to perform relevant analysis to support an evaluation of risks of material misstatement (RoMMs). There were 16 technical marks available in this part of the question in addition to a significant number of professional skills marks for the analysis. It was disappointing to see that candidates often achieved strong marks in this section for the identification of the RoMMs but fewer obtained the marks for the evaluation of those risks.

Many candidates are continuing to rely on basic or generic explanations, which fail to refer to the information in the scenario. Candidates who refer to the specific information provide more in-depth answers and are also able to assess the scale of the risk in the context of the specific audit client.

Materiality

Specific marks were available in this requirement for the calculation and application of materiality in line with the new syllabus guidance and for the prioritisation of the risks identified. Whilst a significant number of candidates appeared prepared for the new syllabus and followed the new materiality guidance, very few attempted to prioritise risks and were unable to access the professional skills marks for this skill.

Candidates are expected to initially determine a materiality threshold for the audit, as would be used in practice. Three technical marks are available for the materiality determination. Candidates are expected to demonstrate a knowledge of the appropriate percentage range for the benchmark instructed by the audit partner (in this question, profit before tax was to be utilised with candidates expected to use 5 - 10% as their range), calculate the monetary amount in respect of the range. Candidates must then use their professional judgement to select an appropriate materiality threshold given the risk levels which exist in the audit and provide a brief justification for their choice. Each of these steps examines a different aspect of understanding or skills required of an auditor.

It was disappointing to note that some candidates calculated a range appropriately, then failed to justify a materiality threshold for the audit. The examining team will give credit for any reasonable explanation of the chosen materiality threshold, as the mark is to recognise that there is the application of professional judgement and that a candidate can justify their response. It is not required that candidates select the identical percentage or figure, or that they provide a justification identical to that shown in the model answer. For example, in this question, some candidates stated the higher end of the range was justified because this was an existing client, some stated the lower end was more appropriate due to the accounting errors that the finance director was making. Alternative answers which were awarded credit included those who suggested that an amount in the middle of the range was appropriate, because whilst this was an existing client, the expansion into a new market increased the risk. All of these obtained the mark for justifying the chosen materiality threshold.

Evaluation of the risks

Candidates were then required to evaluate the significant risks. In determining which risks are the most significant, candidates are demonstrating an understanding of risk, how it arises and how the audit will focus on those most likely to cause a material misstatement. Candidates that demonstrated a depth of evaluation were awarded more credit than those more generic responses.

An issue that arises repeatedly is candidates attempting to find 8 risks for a 16-mark question and conducting little or no in-depth analysis of any of them. This will not be sufficient to attain a pass mark. This means some of the risks stated in these answers will be speculative or not significant and, therefore, will not obtain credit.

This also increases the time pressure for candidates as they are trying to cover too many risks and these risks which are identified are often not developed in sufficient depth to obtain a pass mark.

Once again, examples seen by the examining team that do not attain credit included risks that don't arise at all in the scenario such as currency risk and the risk interest on loans was not capitalised into assets in the course of construction. Weaker students were identifying issues in error due to a failure to apply their financial reporting knowledge correctly. Examples included a suggestion that a contingent asset should be recognised for the insurance claim, even though this would not meet the recognition criteria under IAS 37 *Provisions, Contingent Liabilities and Contingent Assets*. Other risks which were not deemed significant included inventory write downs, however, this risk has been mitigated in the scenario as the information states that inventory was well controlled and likely to be immaterial given the perishable nature of food.

The scenario contained information which gave rise to six significant risks, of which most candidates were able to identify at least four. These were asset impairments of warehouse, misclassification of an investment, provisions, revenue recognition, impairment of electric vehicles and control risks over data. Each of these could be evaluated in the context of the scenario using the information provided, ensuring that the underlying accounting treatment was correct. In this exam, financial reporting knowledge from the SBR syllabus and previous FR and FA exams is deemed assumed knowledge. The majority of marks available in AAA will be for the application of the financial reporting knowledge to the specific audit scenario, not simply for the knowledge itself.

In Exhibit 4, candidates were told of legal action by local residents affected by toxic fumes from the fire at one of the company's warehouses. Most candidates were able to identify that this would potentially give rise to a provision. Credit was available for determining whether a provision would be required and applying the appropriate criteria under IAS 37. In this question, the obligating event was emission of toxic fumes, the past event was the fire during the year, the probability of the company having to settle the claim was unknown, however, given that the company employees had deactivated the sprinklers, it was more likely than not that the company would be held responsible for the fire. No reliable estimate was available from the information provided but legal advisors would be able to determine a reasonable expected amount. It was pleasing to note that many candidates were able to perform this evaluation.

Candidates who identified missing information that would be needed by the auditors in assessing the requirement for a provision, for example, the estimate from legal advisors, gained credit for professional skill marks by demonstrating professional scepticism and judgement. Candidates who demonstrated strong evaluation and professional scepticism skills then went on to question the integrity of management, as this information about the fire only came to the attention of the audit team following an internet search rather than directly from management. Stronger candidates assessed the impact of this omission on the inherent risk in the audit and reliability of representations from management. These candidates were able to attain full marks for the evaluation along with professional skills marks for the skills demonstrated. Weaker candidates tended to state the criteria for a provision and the risk that provision would be understated. This does not demonstrate skills expected of an auditor and does not constitute an evaluation. This is a statement of accounting knowledge.

Candidates should incorporate trend analysis supporting their risks and any links to management bias into their evaluation points on specific risks. For example, with the risk described above, candidates can link the management failure to recognise a provision as a possible indicator of management bias, as this would avoid breaching the loan covenants. Many candidates calculate a large number of ratios and trends which were never discussed in the context of a significant risk and cannot be awarded credit as a result. Professional skills marks are available for the use of appropriate calculations in the evaluation of a risk. Irrelevant calculations or those not used in the discussion of significant risks will not be awarded credit.

Candidates were awarded professional scepticism marks for possible indicators of management bias, such as the need to raise funds for expansion and the requirement to maintain interest cover at 3 or higher. Weaker candidates who discuss generic bias which is not linked to a specific risk, such as "the company is listed therefore management want to perform earnings management" do not obtain credit. It is expected that candidates will identify specific bias risk for a specific scenario to obtain credit. Appropriate professional scepticism is a key skill required of auditors.

It was disappointing to see that very few candidates attempted any prioritisation of the risks as specifically stated in the requirement. Professional skill marks were available to the candidates who attempted this requirement. Candidates were expected to identify the most significant risks, and then provide a brief justification for their choice. Again, credit was awarded for candidates who offered a reasonable explanation, and therefore, a range of possible explanations are valid. Candidates should be aware this mark is for the act of justifying the reason not for the actual justification used. Candidates can obtain these marks by either ordering their answer in priority order **and stating this is the case** or by summarising in a conclusion which risk, or risks are the most significant. Where candidates use this latter method, if a candidate does not state which one or two risks are the most significant but simply lists some or all their identified risks, this will not be sufficient for credit.

Requirement (c)

This requirement is typical of a section A question and requires candidates to design audit procedures to address a specific risk arising in the question. In this question, the procedures were to determine the correct classification of an investment which has been treated as a subsidiary by the client, but which is more likely to be a joint venture.

Candidates were generally able to pass this requirement with stronger candidates attaining maximum marks. These supplied procedures which identified sources of information available to the auditor who can then determine whether the company has control over LPS Co, or whether it meets the criteria of a joint venture. The published model answer to this question contains a list of appropriate procedures.

Weaker candidates who did not pay attention to the wording of the requirement and focus on the significant risk of classification instead gave procedures covering lower risk assertions such as cost and acquisition date or asked for a management representation stating this was a subsidiary, which would not be an appropriate form of evidence to justify the incorrect classification.

A surprising number of candidates suggested proportionate consolidation should be used to account for the new joint venture despite this method being removed from IFRS Accounting Standards in 2013.

Professional skills marks available for this requirement focused on communication skills demonstrated through the ability of candidates to follow the specific instructions provided by the audit partner to focus on classification.

Requirement (d)

Candidates needed to have sufficient knowledge of auditing standards ISA250 *Consideration of Laws and Regulations in an Audit of Financial Statements* and ISA315 (Revised) *Identifying and Assessing the Risks of Material Misstatement.* These standards require the auditor to understand the risks of non-compliance of management with laws and regulations, and describe how auditors should respond to non-compliance by management. This technical auditing knowledge is required to be applied to the specific scenario to achieve a pass mark for this requirement. Candidates were provided with specific information on the relevant legal requirements and how the client had breached those requirements.

In general, candidates who applied their knowledge to the scenario scored high or full marks and those who simply stated the auditor responsibilities in more general terms scored poorly.

Stronger candidates who discussed the lack of integrity displayed through management's reluctance to self-report, and who then evaluated the impact of this behaviour in the context of the wider audit were awarded additional professional scepticism and judgement marks. It was pleasing to see some candidates linking the requirements of assessing client continuation procedures with the introduction of ISQM 1.

Overall professional skills marks

In addition to the professional skill marks described within the different sections of the question, three marks were available for communication overall. These were awarded for the use of a report header and introduction, presentation and relevance of answer and clarity of explanations.

	ACCA Marking guide		Marks
(a)	**Business risk evaluation**		
	Up to 2 marks for each business risk (unless indicated otherwise). Marks may be awarded for other, relevant business risks not included in the marking guide.		
	In addition, ½ mark for relevant trends or calculations which form part of the evaluation of business risk (max 3 marks across the whole question).		
	• Damage to operations – warehouse fire		
	• International expansion		
	• Investment in Luxury Pet Supplies Co		
	• Loan finance		
	• Eco-friendly delivery vans		
	• Legal case		
	• Cyber-attack		
	• Perishable products		
		Maximum	10
(b)	**Risk of material misstatement evaluation**		
	Up to 3 marks for each risk of material misstatement (unless indicated otherwise). Marks may be awarded for other, relevant risks not included in the marking guide.		
	Appropriate materiality calculations and justified materiality level should be awarded to a maximum of 3 marks.		
	• Warehouse fire		
	• Revenue recognition – annual membership		
	• Investment in LPS Co		
	• Corporate governance (max 2 marks)		
	• Eco-friendly delivery vans		
	• Legal provision		
	• Pressure on results (max 2 marks)		
		Maximum	16

(c) **Principal audit procedures in respect of the classification of the investment in Luxury Pet Supplies ('LPS') Co**

Generally, 1 mark for each well explained audit procedure. Examples are provided below. Marks will be awarded for other relevant points.

- Obtain the legal documentation supporting the investment and agree the details of the investment including:
  - The rights and obligations of the investing parties
  - The date of the investment and the voting rights attached to the shares to assist in the understanding of the control of the venture
  - Number of shares purchased and the voting rights attached to the shares
  - The nature of the profit-sharing arrangement between Winberry Co and Durian Co
  - The nature of access to LPS Co's assets under the terms of the agreement
  - Confirmation that there is no restriction of the company's shared control of LPS Co
- Review board minutes to understand the business rationale for the investment
- Review minutes of relevant meetings between the company and Durian Co to confirm that control is shared between the two investors and to understand the nature of the relationship and the decision-making process, particularly if any party holds the right to veto decisions
- Obtain documentation such as LPS Co's organisational structure to confirm that the company has successfully appointed members to the board of the company and that those members have equal power to the members appointed by Durian Co

Maximum	**7**

(d) **Auditor's responsibilities in relation to an audit client's compliance with laws and regulations**

Generally, 1 mark for each explained or applied point:

- Management responsibility for laws and regulations
- Auditor responsibility re non-compliance with law and regulations, specifically data protection
- Auditor required to understand legal framework as part of understanding the business
- Evidence required to understand and evaluate the impact on FS
- Must perform procedures in this regard
- Reporting requirements (up to 3 marks)
- Confidentiality

Maximum	**7**

Professional marks

Communication

- Briefing note format and structure – use of headings/subheadings and an introduction
- Style, language and clarity – appropriate layout and tone of briefing notes, presentation of materiality and relevant calculations, appropriate use of the CBE tools, easy to follow and understand
- Effectiveness and clarity of communication – answer is relevant and tailored to the scenario
- Adherence to the specific requests made by the audit engagement partner

Analysis and evaluation
- Appropriate use of the information to determine and apply suitable specific calculations which are relevant to the scenario
- Risk evaluation (ROMMs) is effectively prioritised, focusing on significance and only taking account of risks which would result in material misstatements
- Balanced discussion of the issues connected to the auditor's responsibilities in relation to laws and regulations, resulting in a justified conclusion

Professional scepticism and professional judgement
- Displays scepticism by questioning and challenging management's treatment of specific accounting issues or the identification of unusual or unexpected movements, missing/incomplete information or challenging presented information
- Determination and justification of suitable materiality level appropriately and consistently applied
- Identification and recognition of a possible and valid management bias indicator, with the consideration of the impact on the financial statements and the possible reasons for management's preference for certain accounting treatments e.g. impairment of assets, revenue recognition, provisions
- Recognition of need to establish the audit status of the joint venture and make professional contact with the auditors of the joint venture
- Effective application of technical and ethical guidance to effectively challenge and critically assess how management has responded to the data breach in the question

Commercial acumen
- Use of effective examples and/or calculations from the scenario to illustrate points or recommendations
- Appropriate use of the industry information to evaluate business risks

Maximum	10
Total	50

3   **PASCAL & CO** *Walk in the footsteps of a top tutor*

Top tutor tips

Determination of materiality: *The email from the partner states that materiality should be based on profit, therefore at the start of your answer you should calculate the range for materiality using that benchmark and justify a figure within that range. If it is a new audit client or a client where there are apparent control risks, materiality should be set at the lower end of the range. If it is an existing client, materiality may be able to be set at the higher end of the range depending on the other risks mentioned in the scenario. The examining team will give credit for any reasonable explanation of the chosen materiality threshold, as the mark is to recognise that there is the application of professional judgement and that a candidate can justify their response. It is not required that candidates select the identical percentage or figure, or that they provide a justification identical to that shown in the model answer.*

Part (a) asks risks of material misstatement. Risk of material misstatement is usually due to non-compliance with an accounting standard, although it also includes control risk. Think about the requirements of the relevant accounting standards and what the client might be doing incorrectly.

Prioritisation of risks: One mark is awarded for the prioritisation of the risks of material misstatement. The mark is for the act of justifying the reason, not for the actual justification used (i.e. a range of completely different answers could be awarded the mark), therefore if a reasonable explanation is given, the mark will be awarded. Prioritisation can be achieved by either ordering your answer in priority order and stating this is the case, or by summarising in a brief conclusion which risk, or risks, are most significant.

Part (b) asks for audit procedures over the valuation of the theme park rides. The procedures should enable the auditor to obtain evidence to determine whether the relevant financial reporting standard has been complied with. Make sure your procedures are clear and provide enough detail that they can be easily followed by the audit team.

Part (c) requires knowledge of money laundering regulations that accountancy firms must follow. This is a knowledge-based requirement. The requirement goes on to ask for indicators of money laundering in the scenario. Look for evidence of unusual or complex cash transactions.

Part (d) is a quality management requirement centred around acceptance procedures. Clients should only be accepted if they are an acceptable level of risk. Work through the client acceptance checklist in the exhibit and critique the responses/evidence obtained.

Professional skills

Professional skills will be awarded for:

Communication – responding to the instructions in the partner's email such as preparing your answers in the form of briefing notes and using the stated benchmark for materiality.

Analysis and evaluation – applying the information from the scenario to answer the question and explaining the issues in sufficient depth.

Professional scepticism and judgement – justifying an appropriate materiality level, demonstrating critical thinking and being alert to possible manipulation and management bias.

Where relevant, professional marks will be awarded for commercial acumen which requires making practical and plausible recommendations and considering the wider implications of issues to the audit firm.

Briefing notes

To: Brian Fox, Audit engagement partner

From: Audit manager

Subject: Audit planning in relation to The Infinite Co and assessment of client acceptance performed on Meadow Co

Date: 1 July 20X5

Introduction

These briefing notes have been prepared to assist in planning the audit of The Infinite Co for the year ending 30 September 20X5. The notes begin with an evaluation of the significant risks of material misstatement which should be considered in planning the audit. The significant risks of material misstatement have been structured to prioritise the risks in terms of the likelihood and magnitude of misstatement in relation to each risk. The notes include the recommended principal audit procedures which have been designed in respect of the valuation of the theme park rides. A discussion of the matters to be considered and the implication for the audit of the issues surrounding the renewal of the operating licence for the rides is provided along with recommended actions to be taken by the firm. The notes then discuss risk factors relating to money laundering arising from The Infinite Co's operations and our responsibility as auditors with respect to money laundering. Finally, the notes evaluate the weaknesses in Pascal & Co's client acceptance of the client Meadow Co and recommend improvements to the firm's client acceptance procedures.

Materiality

For the purposes of these briefing notes, the overall materiality level used to assess the significance of identified risks is $115,000 based on the profitability of the company, as requested.

Justification

Using profit before tax of $2.3 million as a suggested benchmark results in a suggested range of $115,000 (5% × $2.3 million) to $230,000 (10% × $2.3 million).

The risk level is high based on this being a new audit client with a significant control deficiency related to management override. Materiality should be set at the lower end of the range.

This benchmark is only a starting point for determining materiality and professional judgement will need to be applied in determining a final level to be used during the course of the audit.

(a)   Evaluation of risks of material misstatement

Licence/going concern

The company is dependent on licences for its ability to operate.

There is a risk that these licences are revoked if breaches in regulations occur. The company will then not be allowed to offer the products and services covered by the licence, affecting the company's ability to operate as a going concern. In particular, the licence to operate the theme park rides may be revoked due to health and safety breaches. Although this is not the sole activity at the park, it does form a major part of the offering on which other areas rely to attract customers. The potential loss of the operating licence may require disclosures to be made in the notes to the accounts describing the uncertainty arising.

Disclosures are material to the users' understanding of the financial statements and there is a risk that these disclosures are not included within the financial statements.

Valuation of land

The company holds land of $6 million which is highly material by reference to the benchmark calculated above.

The company is correct not to depreciate the land held. The use of a revaluation model is permitted by IAS 16 *Property, Plant and Equipment*, however, where this is used, the valuation must be kept up to date. The most recent valuation was carried out seven years ago and this is likely to require updating for 20X5. Any gain or loss on revaluation, which is not a result of impairment, should be shown within other comprehensive income and recognised in equity. As such values require specialist knowledge to calculate, it is likely that an expert will be required to value the land.

There is a risk of inaccurate valuation of land if the valuation is not up to date or if the valuer is not appropriately independent and qualified. This is likely to result in either an over or understatement of the land and equity.

Valuation of rides

The rides of $1.4 million are material to the financial statements by reference to the threshold calculated above.

According to IAS 36 *Impairment of Assets*, an entity should assess at the end of each reporting period whether there is any indication that an asset or a cash generating unit may be impaired. If any such indication exists, the entity shall estimate the recoverable amount of the asset.

The standard states that potential impairment indicators include obsolescence and physical damage. The findings of the government inspector suggesting that the assets are aging, lack modern safety features and are not properly maintained are all indicators of impairment and as such management should prepare an impairment review of the park's rides.

IAS 36 states that an asset or cash generating unit is impaired when the carrying amount exceeds the recoverable amount and it defines recoverable amount as the higher of the fair value less costs of disposal and the value in use.

There is a risk that management does not conduct an impairment review or that the review does not take into account the inspector's findings resulting in the overvaluation of property, plant and equipment and understatement of costs.

Revenue

The Infinite Co operates a business where a large amount of revenue is received in cash. In a company where a substantial proportion of revenue is generated through cash sales, there is a high risk of unrecorded sales arising from the theft of cash received from customers. This risk is increased through the use of so many casual workers.

Management appears to try to reduce this risk via the use of management's family in areas where cash accepted is unusually high. However, it is not possible for family members to accept all cash sales. If this is the case, then revenues and cash may be understated.

There is also a risk of revenue overstatement within the park. As The Infinite Co's business is cash based, it provides an ideal environment for cash acquired through illegal activities to be legitimised by adding it to the cash paid genuinely by customers and posting it through the accounts. This is discussed further later in these notes.

Sale and leaseback

The company is entering into a sale and leaseback with regard to the park buildings. The value of the buildings in the projected statement of financial position is $854,000 which is material based on the threshold calculated above.

Under IFRS 16 *Leases*, where a sale has occurred, The Infinite Co should recognise a right of use asset for the buildings replacing the previously held building asset. This would be measured at the proportion of the previous carrying amount which is retained for use by The Infinite Co.

The present value of the lease in this case is $934,666. This represents 93.5% $934,666/$1,000,000) of the market value of the buildings. The proportion of the previous carrying amount which is retained for use by the company is therefore 93.5% of the carrying amount of $854,000, which equates to $798,205.

The Infinite Co should therefore recognise a right of use asset of $798,205 and a lease liability at present value of the future cash payments of $934,666. It will recognise a cash receipt of $1,000,000 and derecognise property, plant and equipment of $854,000. The remaining difference is the gain on disposal of the buildings which is recognised in the statement of profit or loss.

	Debit	Credit
Cash	$1,000,000	
Right of use asset	$798,205	
Property, plant and equipment		$854,000
Lease liability		$934,666
Gain on disposal		$9,539

The finance director intends to account for the sale as a simple disposal and then recognise a rental expense each year. This would result in a gain of $146,000 being recognised on the disposal, overstating profit on disposal. In addition, both assets and liabilities would be understated as the right of use asset and the present value of lease payments would not be included in the statement of financial position. Failure to unwind the discount on the lease liability would result in an understatement of finance costs and the rentals charged against profit would overstate expenses.

Legal cases – food poisoning

There is currently outstanding litigation against the company. The amounts of the claims are not yet known. Management is not planning on making disclosures in the financial statements regarding the case as this may prejudice the outcome of the case.

IAS 37 *Provisions, Contingent Liabilities and Contingent Assets* requires that contingent liabilities are disclosed in the notes to the financial statements, hence there is a risk of insufficient disclosure which could be material by nature.

General provisions

The projected statement of financial position shows a general provision of $250,000 which is material to the statement of financial position based on the threshold calculated above.

IAS 37 states that an entity must recognise a provision if, and only if:

– a present obligation (legal or constructive) has arisen as a result of a past event (the obligating event),

– payment is probable ('more likely than not'), and

– the amount can be estimated reliably.

The general provision does not appear to relate to a present obligation and, as such, is not permitted. This could be a means by which the company reduces profits in order to reduce the tax payable or a means of profit smoothing. As a result, it is likely that if this provision remains, then liabilities are overstated and expenses overstated.

Related party disclosures

The managing director appears to move funds from the company with the description 'drawings'. It is unclear if this represents salary, dividends or a loan.

IAS 24 *Related Party Disclosures* defines a related party transaction as a transfer of resources, services, or obligations between related parties, regardless of whether a price is charged. Related party transactions are material by nature. As the managing director is a related party, this means that transactions between himself and the company will need to be disclosed in the notes to the financial statements.

There is a risk that appropriate disclosures are not made for all related party transactions.

Payroll

The payment of wages in cash creates a risk that not all wages payments are recorded in the financial statements and therefore wages paid out of cash sales are unrecorded as well as the associated cash sales; there is therefore a risk both revenue and expenses are understated.

In addition, there is a risk with employees paid in cash that incomplete deductions have been made for employee taxes. This may give rise to further compliance risks and liabilities for unpaid employee tax.

Management override

The owner manager and his family appear to take a very active role in the business and to fail to make a distinction between the business as a separate entity and themselves. There is evidence that management bypasses controls within the business through direct access to the company funds and accounts. There is a lack of segregation of duties and given that the management appears to have a disregard for certain laws and regulations, this is likely to mean that the control environment is weak and there is a resulting higher risk of fraud and error in the financial statements.

(b)   Audit procedures in relation to the impairment of rides

-    Obtain the report from the safety inspector and review the outcome of the inspection to identify specific rides of concern and to understand maintenance failings which could be an indicator of impairment.

-    Obtain and review the regulations regarding the maintenance and upgrades of rides to understand the company's obligations in this respect in order to assist in assessment of value in use.

-    Obtain The Infinite Co's maintenance reports and review the schedule in comparison to the regulations to identify any rides which may not be appropriately maintained or defective and hence provide indicators of impairment of specific rides.

-    Obtain and cast management's impairment review of the rides and assess whether the assumptions are in line with the auditor's understanding.

-    Calculate an auditor's estimation of impairment or engage an expert to value the rides and compare with management's impairment review to corroborate their calculations.

-    If an auditor's expert is used to value the rides, consider the reasonableness of assumptions used and completeness of the information assessed.

-    Assess the competence, scope and independence of the auditor's expert.

-    Physically inspect the rides on the park to ensure they are operational and that there is customer demand for the rides to support value in use calculations.

-    Obtain any ride usage and closure statistics held by management to ensure the rides are operational and hence a value in use valuation would be appropriate.

(c)   Money laundering

Money laundering is defined as the process by which criminals attempt to conceal the origin and ownership of the proceeds of their criminal activity, allowing them to maintain control over the proceeds and, ultimately, providing a legitimate cover for the sources of their income.

Auditors responsibilities in relation to money laundering:

-    Perform customer due diligence, i.e. procedures designed to acquire knowledge about the firm's clients and prospective clients and to verify their identity as well as monitor business relationships and transactions.

-    Create channels for internal reporting within the audit firm including appointment of a money laundering reporting officer (MLRO) to receive the money laundering reports to which personnel report suspicions or knowledge of money laundering activities.

-    Keep records, including details of customer due diligence and supporting evidence for business relationships, which need to be kept for five years after the end of a relationship and records of transactions, which also need to be kept for five years.

-    Take measures to make relevant employees aware of the law relating to money laundering and terrorist finance, and to train those employees in how to recognise and deal with transactions which may be related to money laundering or terrorist financing.

-    Put in place ongoing monitoring procedures to ensure that policies are up to date and being followed.

The MLRO will be responsible for reporting incidents to the relevant authorities. Auditors must be careful to avoid tipping off any party suspected of money laundering.

The Infinite Co's business is cash based, making it an ideal environment for cash acquired through illegal activities to be legitimised by adding it to the cash paid genuinely by customers and posting it through the financial statements. This is known as placement.

There are a lot of cash transactions and it would be possible to incorporate funds to be laundered with the funds from customers. The ticket sales for rides would be an ideal place for this to occur as there is no monitoring of the number of people actually taking part in the ride, so actual sales would be hard to prove.

The fact that ride sales have fallen since the introduction of electronic payments and at the same time the gift shop run by the owner's son has seen increased volumes of cash sales and higher margins suggests that this may have been the case previously and that the shop may now be used for money laundering.

The use of family members for areas of high cash transactions and the managing director making transfers to his international account outside of the normal accounting for the business further increases the risk that money laundering may be occurring.

It may be that the staffing choice is for the valid business purpose of reducing risk of theft from staff and that the transactions are properly accounted for and valid, however, it is not clear in this case.

The fact that the managing director likes to be left in peace and the finance director does not query transactions could also represent a red flag.

(d)   Acceptance procedures

Auditors are required, prior to establishing a client relationship or accepting an engagement, to have controls in place to address the risks arising from it. The risk profile of the business should show where particular risks are likely to arise, and so where certain procedures will be needed to tackle them. These procedures should be easy to understand and easy to use for all relevant employees who will need them. Sufficient flexibility should be built in to allow the procedures to identify, and adapt to, unusual situations.

Different clients will have different levels of risk and the level of risk should dictate the level of client due diligence performed.

Criticisms of the content of the client acceptance documentation

Overall, the acceptance document appears too brief and there is a lack of information to support the conclusions within the document. Where a conclusion is given in the acceptance form, the evidence to support that conclusion should be filed with it.

There is no section evidencing and justifying the type of customer due diligence required. Depending on the nature of the client and the risks, either standard, simplified or enhanced due diligence will be required. The form of due diligence to be used and the basis for that decision should be included within the acceptance documentation. Part of this would include an assessment of client integrity, which does not appear to be considered anywhere on the form, even though it is a requirement of ISQM 1 *Quality Management For Firms That Perform Audits or Reviews of Financial Statements, or Other Assurance or Related Services Engagements.*

ISQM 1 also requires the firm to consider whether it is competent to perform the engagement and has the capabilities, including time and resources, to do so and whether it can comply with relevant ethical requirements. None of these issues appear to have been considered.

There is no reference to the beneficial owners and the control structure of the company. The auditor should seek to prove the identity of the company and key individuals including all directors and shareholders with more than 25% of the shares or voting rights of the company. There should also be a section for the source of wealth and funds of the business.

The money laundering risk assessment is too brief. This should identify whether there are any potential areas of high risk for money laundering. Such things include: unusual or unexplained transactions, a cash intensive business, and unusual or complicated corporate structures.

Specific criticisms of the information gathered for Meadow Co

The first thing to note is that the documentation does not state what its objective is, so that the person completing it is obtaining the information with its objective in mind, for example, the following could be included at the beginning of the assessment:

Objective

To obtain appropriate evidence regarding the organisation and the identity of its owners in order to comply with the money laundering regulations.

The assessment should also document:

–   Whether full understanding has been gained regarding the ownership structure of the organisation.

–   Evidence which has been obtained regarding the organisation's activity and how it has been established and agreed as bona fide.

No references have been received prior to acceptance of the client which means that the firm's client due diligence procedures have not been properly adhered to.

The professional clearance from the predecessor auditor should be received in writing prior to acceptance and this should be reviewed for potential issues and filed with the form on the permanent file. Where this is not received, the firm should document the reasons why and whether they have reported this to their regulatory body.

Client risk assessment states that the company has no high/unusual risk. A cash-based business is likely to give rise to risks and the fact that Meadow Co is being investigated with respect to money laundering suggests that risks existed which were not considered on the acceptance form.

The money laundering section appears too brief. Client identity would involve more people than just the owner and his wife. This should be extended to shareholders who ultimately own or control more than 25% of the shares along with other directors of the company. If the business is deemed to be sufficiently high risk that enhanced due diligence is required, then a second document such as a driving licence would also be required.

For confirming the company identity, a certificate of incorporation alone is not sufficient to confirm the principal trading address, current directors and major shareholders.

The checklist does not state whether it has been confirmed that the person the firm is dealing with is properly authorised to do so by the client. It should document the appropriate steps taken to be satisfied that the person the firm dealing with is properly authorised by the client.

There has been no partner assigned to the client prior to acceptance and no signature of a partner to approve the client acceptance. This is a failure in the firm's control procedures as it should not be possible to accept new clients without partner level approval and evidence that the risk assessment has been reviewed.

Conclusion

These briefing notes have evaluated the risks of material misstatement relating to the audit of The Infinite Co. The risks of material misstatement have been ordered with regard to the estimated magnitude of any misstatement and the likelihood of such a misstatement occurring. The most significant risk relates to the health and safety breaches which could result in licences to operate being revoked impacting on going concern

The notes go on to recommend audit procedures in relation to the impairment of the theme park rides and discuss the indicators of money laundering within the company. Finally, the notes look at the weaknesses in the firm's acceptance procedures in relation to Meadow Co. These weaknesses will need to be addressed in future decisions to avoid the firm taking on clients or work when it is not appropriate to do so.

> **Examiner's comments**
>
> **Introduction to the question**
>
> - The current date is the 1 July 20X5 and the client has a year end of 30 September 20X5. The scenario is set three months prior to the year end with the audit taking place sometime after the client year end. This indicates the planning stage of an assignment with the audit taking place in October or later. Note, this is normal and does not indicate there is a lack of time to plan the audit.
> - Infinite Co is family owned and managed – this means the company is not listed and is not required to follow corporate governance best practice
> - Infinite Co operates a theme park and has suffered an impairment of some rides due to lack of maintenance. The company also hold land on a revaluation model. A number of candidates demonstrated a lack of general understanding of IAS16 *Property, Plant and Equipment*, either stating it was incorrect not to depreciate land or that it must be considered for impairment under IAS 38 *Intangible Assets* every year. This was a straightforward risk that land value had not been considered for several years and under IAS 16 the valuation must be kept up to date.
> - Infinite Co had included a general provision for unexpected costs which had increased during the year. A significant number of candidates failed to identify that the general provision did not meet the criteria of IAS 37 *Provisions, Contingent Liabilities and Contingent Assets* and, therefore, demonstrated a lack of understanding of basic financial reporting knowledge, with a number stating the provision was likely understated.
> - It is important to note that whilst Infinite Co is an initial audit engagement, the requirement for part (a) is to evaluate risk of material misstatement and not audit risk, therefore comments relating to an increase in detection risk due to lack of understanding of the client would not be relevant. Marks were available for discussion of the risk of errors in the opening balances or adopting consistent accounting policies in consecutive years.

- It is important to note that there are specific instructions where attention is drawn in the audit partner's email. The information details that Exhibits 2,3 and 4 are required in order to address the risk of material misstatement in part (a) and for the evaluation of the indicators of impairment in part (c). The partners email clearly defines that Exhibit 5 is required to formulate an answer for part (d) relating to a different audit client, Meadow Co.

Requirement (a)

This requirement is typical in volume and nature to many planning questions and examines a major area of the syllabus - risk. It is important to notice that the requirement asked for an evaluation, not simply a list of risks, nor a strategy or procedures to address those risks. The examining team are testing whether candidates can understand how and why a risk arises and the implications that this has on the financial statements or the audit itself. They are looking for an assessment of materiality, a demonstration of knowledge of the underlying accounting rules and the application of that to the scenario to identify the potential impact on the financial statements. A well evaluated risk has in depth analysis. Candidates writing only a sentence or two are unlikely to attain many of the marks available for each risk. Candidates are reminded that there are useful technical and exam guidance articles on the ACCA website which will provide additional support in approaching and answering questions on risk.

An issue that arises repeatedly is that candidates are attempting to find 10 risks for a 20-mark question and conducting little or no in-depth analysis of any of them. This will not be able to attain a pass mark. This means some of the risks stated in these candidate answers will be speculative or not significant and, therefore, will not obtain credit.

Candidates should be aware of the published marking guides for risk questions and understand how marks are credited. Each risk generally has a minimum of three marks attached to it. More complex risks carry additional credit. Some of the areas of risk in the marking guide are deemed more basic financial accounting issues and therefore carry lower marks and therefore should be more easily obtained by candidates. Materiality and calculation marks are over and above the marks available for the discussion of a risk.

The requirement asks only for significant risks of material misstatements, which mean risks that are specific to the scenario, non-routine or require management to make estimates or are subject to judgemental assumptions have the potential to give rise to a material misstatement. Speculative risks, arising from routine transactions generally will not obtain credit. Candidates demonstrating strong professional skills will be able to differentiate between speculative and specific risks, and not spend time discussing topics which will not obtain credit.

Candidates are told general information that the company was opened more than 40 years ago and is a family-owned business operating a theme park with various attractions and revenue obtained in cash, credit cards and electronic payments.

Candidates must remember when discussing risks, that it is important to relate them to the scenario rather than discuss abstract or generic risks. This is particularly an issue when discussing management bias risk.

This is a key concept to understand for auditors as it can impact on judgements made by management in deriving their figures for the financial statements. Candidates must be able to demonstrate that they understand the concept of management bias and can identify it in practice.

The examining team are often faced with two standard candidate responses to management bias risk in Section A questions: "the client is listed so management will be biased to keep shareholders happy" or "the client is not listed so the owners will be biased to keep profits low and save tax". The first statement doesn't include scenario specific reasons for this conclusion and is therefore too vague and generic. The second implies that all non-listed clients are concerned with aiming for lower payments in respect of tax. Again, this is a generic statement, and unless there is information in the scenario that specifically alludes to this, then candidates will not receive credit for making this point. In both cases, neither will be credited as an evaluation of management bias for a specific scenario.

Candidates are told the company is a family-owned business and that family members are actively involved in the day to day running of the business. The specific management bias point in this scenario is the ability of management to override controls.

To score more than a ½ mark for the identification of the specific bias risk, this will have to be evaluated by candidates. Suggested explanations may include:

- Lack of segregation of duties

- Disregard of laws and regulations – scenario states the rides have not been maintained on a regular basis, are aged and lack safety features

- Evidence of bypass of controls as the scenario states there is evidence of access to company funds.

The beginning of the evaluation will score the initial mark. It should then be linked to the scenario to illustrate areas where this could potentially happen or appears to be happening. In this question, this is reinforced by the specific examples in the scenario. There are examples of the risks stated above to enable an evaluation to be made with specific reference to this question and scenario. Candidates might find it sensible to address management bias after they have analysed the other risks in the question.

Candidates were generally able to identify the key risks and, were able to apply correct accounting rules to support their analysis. There were areas of more general accounting principles, that were not well attempted and disappointing to note. Commentary on how each of those areas was tackled is below.

- Impairment of assets arose around the theme park rides that showed a lack of upgrades for modern safety features. Candidates need to identify the indicator of impairment from the scenario, which in this instance is the aging of the rides and lack of safety features. Many of the candidates correctly identified the relevant accounting rule, yet a number failed to fully state the rule and therefore failed to gain the full marks available.

- Following from the impairment risk of the theme park rides, the scenario then details the risk regarding the revocation of the licence to operate the theme park rides. This should, therefore, be deemed a potential indicator of going concern. There was a mixed response here, with many identifying the uncertainty regarding going concern, yet evaluating that there was a risk of the financial statements being prepared on the incorrect basis (which is unlikely), rather than identifying the potential lack of disclosure in the notes to the financial statements for the uncertainty. This failed to earn additional marks for the evaluation of the risk. Whilst the licence is important for the company to operate the theme park rides, it is not the sole activity of the client that would render the operations to cease.

- Land was held by the company under a revaluation model and is not depreciated. The company is correct not to depreciate land. It is disappointing to note a significant number of candidates stated that it was incorrect not to depreciate land and therefore stated that the risk was that the carrying amount of land was overstated.

  A number of candidates stated that the land needs to be revalued every year and tested for impairment, whereas under IAS 16 *Property, Plant & Equipment,* land under a revaluation model requires the valuation to be kept up to date. This demonstrates a lack of knowledge of straightforward accounting principles for property, plant and equipment, and a misunderstanding of accounting for property, plant and equipment. A number of candidates also stated any gain/loss from revaluation should be shown in the statement of profit or loss, whereas it should be shown in the statement of other comprehensive income.

- Revenue recognition was split into two main areas. The scenario detailed that it was a cash-based business and there was a risk of the overstatement of revenue due to money laundering. There was a risk that proceeds from illegal activities could be added to the cash balance potentially overstating both cash and revenue. The majority of candidates correctly identified this risk and scored well. The second consideration of revenue recognition related to revenue being understated due to the risk from theft of cash sales, which was particularly linked to the high volume of casual seasonal staff.

  It was surprising that the marks available for this angle of revenue recognition were missed, with several candidates incorrectly discussing risks for errors arising due to the company moving to electronic payments and staff being untrained on how to operate the system. A minority of candidates incorrectly identified and described how revenue can only be recognised when a customer has physically ridden the theme park rides.

- The sale and leaseback transaction was a new issue which arose during the year, with the company entering into the arrangement in respect of the park buildings. Candidates struggled with the calculations here and the trend marks available were generally not obtained. Generally, this risk was poorly answered with candidates failing to score anywhere near the maximum marks available for the risk of misstatement.

  Management recognising the transaction as a sale is incorrect, instead, a right of use asset, at the proportion of the retained carrying amount, should be recognised along with a corresponding liability at the present value of the future cash payments. The accounting treatment is deemed as more complex and therefore the risk is worth more than the general three marks per risk. The majority of candidates correctly identified the treatment was incorrect, yet they scored poorly regarding the accounting rules and failed to score relevant trend marks that were available, such as the calculation of the amount to recognise as a right to use asset and the correct calculation of the gain on disposal.

- A significant number of candidates demonstrated a lack of financial reporting knowledge by stating a risk of material misstatement linked to IFRS 8 *Segmental Reporting* as the company has a number of streams of income. The company is a privately-owned company and therefore segmental reporting under IFRS 8 is not applicable. IFRS 8 is applicable to companies whose debt or equity securities are publicly traded. Candidates were not awarded credit where risks surrounding a lack of segmental disclosure was discussed.

- The legal case (contingent liability) and general provision were identified in the scenario and several candidates failed to deal with them correctly.

  Many candidates failed to link the detail in the scenario and merely stated that liabilities may be understated, even though the detail stated that the level of claims was unknown and therefore unlikely to meet the criteria of IAS 37. No marks were awarded as the issue here would have been a lack of disclosure regarding the legal case in the financial statements.

  The general provision was poorly answered with a number of candidates failing to identify that a general provision for unexpected costs cannot be recognised under IAS 37 as it does not meet the criteria of the accounting standard. Many candidates linked the general provision to the legal case and stated the provision was understated, rather than overstated as should not have been recognised at all.

  If the lack of provision was linked to the detail of the lawyer being an acquaintance of the director, and that they may not be objective in their advice, credit was given for the development and evaluation of a risk regarding potential understatement of the liability.

- Exhibit 4 gave the candidates details of analytical procedures. Candidates should remember that calculations are only credited when the resulting figures are discussed in their answer in the context of a risk. Simply calculating a ratio will not obtain credit. The skill examined is the ability to calculate a relevant ratio or trend to identify a risk or support an evaluation of a risk. It is at that point that the calculation mark is awarded.

  Overall, this requirement was answered reasonably well by many candidates yet more than expected numbers of candidates failed to identify the easier risks in the scenario and demonstrated a weaker than expected level of more basic accounting treatment. This resulted in many candidates failing to obtain what should have been easier marks.

Requirement (b)

This requirement was well answered by a majority of candidates with practical, well described procedures given. The model answer provides a list of procedures which are indicative of the areas the examining team credited. Where a candidate suggests a procedure not on the list in the model answer, they will still obtain credit providing it is relevant and practicable.

Requirement (c)

The requirement was focused on the responsibility that auditors have regarding money laundering and to evaluate the indicators detailed in the scenario with respect to money laundering. Additional credit was awarded if a candidate successfully linked the scenario specific indicator to the stage of money laundering.

Generally, the requirement was well answered in response to candidates evaluating the indicators within the question suggesting there was a risk of money laundering. Examples included:

- Infinite Co is a cash-based business and it is therefore easy to mix the cash obtained from potentially illegal activities with the cash obtained from the sale of tickets for the theme park, linked to placement.

- Due to the owners' sons operating both the rides and gift shop, where margins have increased significantly, implying that this may be another indicator of money laundering.

- International transfers to foreign banks accounts may be an indicator of money laundering, more specifically, the layering stage.

The most alarming issue highlighted in a significant number of candidate responses is where candidates stated that a suspicion of money laundering should be disclosed to those charged with governance, the audit committee (even though in the present scenario the company didn't have one) and a minority of candidates stated it should be disclosed in the notes to the financial statements or the audit report in the public interest.

This action would amount to the auditor committing a criminal offence of tipping off the client, and it is disappointing to see the number of candidates who fail to understand the difference money laundering and fraud.

Requirement (d)

The final requirement was focused on reviewing the acceptance assessment procedures performed by the auditors on a different company, Meadow Co. Candidates were required to discuss the weaknesses in the procedures performed and recommend improvements the firm should implement.

There was a mixed response here, which candidates either answered well and were able to evaluate the weaknesses, or stated general acceptance procedures to be performed and failed to respond specifically to the requirement.

It was noted that a number of candidates discussed the need to communicate with the previous auditor, which is correct for a requirement for general consideration at acceptance.

In the context of this scenario, however, the extract of the acceptance assessment stated that verbal clearance had been obtained, hence the previous auditor had been contacted. A number of candidates failed to recognise that the issue in this weakness was that only a verbal confirmation had been received and that this should have been obtained in writing. Where candidates discussed the weaknesses specific to the scenario, marks were awarded, however, generic comments regarding communication with the previous auditors did not meet the requirement and demonstrated candidates failed to successfully understand the requirement.

A further point of weak development was in reference to the money laundering section. Many candidates correctly identified that money laundering assessment was inadequate, and provided weak evaluations as to why it was too brief. There were several responses that stated the details obtained from the owner and his wife were insufficient, yet they failed to identify that the auditors should have performed client identification procedures to involve additional individuals and this should have been extended to any shareholders holding more than 25% shareholding along with other directors of the company. A number of candidates failed to identify this issue.

ACCA Marking guide		
		Marks

(a) **Evaluation of risk of material misstatement**

Up to 3 marks for each risk of material misstatement evaluated unless otherwise indicated. Marks may be awarded for other, relevant risks not included in the marking guide.

Appropriate materiality calculations (max 2 marks) and justified materiality level should be awarded to a maximum of 1 mark.

In addition, ½ mark for each relevant trend or ratio calculation which form part of the risk evaluation (max 3 marks).

- Going concern – potential operating licence withdrawal
- Valuation of land – lack of recent valuation
- Valuation of theme park rides – impairment
- Revenue, risk of overstatement (2 marks)
- Revenue, risk of understatement
- Sale and leaseback (up to a max of 5 marks)
- Legal case – contingent liability (2 marks)
- General provisions
- Related party transactions (2 marks)
- Payroll costs – cash based
- Management override/lack of segregation of duties (up to 2 marks)

Maximum **20**

(b) **Audit procedures in relation to the theme park rides**

Generally, 1 mark for each well explained audit procedure. Examples are provided below. Marks will be awarded for other relevant points.

- Obtain the report from the safety inspector and review the outcome of the inspection to identify specific rides of concern and to understand maintenance failings
- Obtain and review the regulations regarding the maintenance and upgrades of rides to understand the company's obligations in this respect
- Obtain The Infinite Co's maintenance reports and review the schedule in comparison to the regulations to identify any rides which may not be appropriately maintained or defective
- Obtain a list of rides and their depreciation rates and assess whether the rates are realistic given the age of rides by comparing with industry averages and the safety report findings
- Obtain management's impairment review of the rides and assess whether the assumptions are in line with the auditor's understanding
- Cast management's impairment review
- Calculate an auditor's estimation of impairment or engage an expert to value the rides and compare with management's impairment review to corroborate their calculations
- Physically inspect the rides on the park to ensure they are operational and that there is customer demand for the rides
- Obtain any ride usage and closure statistics held by management to ensure the rides are operational

Maximum **5**

(c)   **Money laundering**

Generally, 1 mark for each relevant point of discussion/explanation:

- Definition of money laundering
- Customer due diligence
- Reporting channels
- Record keeping
- Training
- Cash-based business/placement
- Unexpected trends in ride sales/shop sales and margins
- Use of family
- Money transfers

| | Maximum | 7 |

(d)   **Acceptance procedures**

Generally, 1 mark for each relevant point of discussion/explanation:

- General requirement for customer due diligence (CDD) before acceptance
- Level of CDD depends on the level of risk at client
- Form too brief
- Form lacks supporting evidence
- No justification of CDD level required
- Insufficient identification of beneficial owners and directors
- Money laundering flags not all considered
- References outstanding
- Professional clearance should be in writing and reviewed
- Risk assessment appears incorrect/insufficient
- Company identity does not prove current directors and address
- No partner assigned/approval

| | Maximum | 8 |

Professional marks

Communication

- Briefing note format and structure – use of headings/subheadings and an introduction
- Style, language and clarity – appropriate layout and tone of briefing notes, presentation of materiality and relevant calculations, appropriate use of the CBE tools, easy to follow and understand
- Effectiveness and clarity of communication – answer is relevant and tailored to the scenario
- Adherence to the specific requests made by the audit engagement partner

Analysis and evaluation

- Appropriate use of the information to determine and apply suitable calculations
- Appropriate use of the information to design appropriate audit procedures relating to the valuation of the theme park rides
- Effective prioritisation of the results of the evaluation of risks to demonstrate the likelihood and magnitude of risks and to facilitate the allocation of appropriate responses

Professional scepticism and professional judgement

– Appropriate application of professional judgement to draw conclusions and make informed decisions following recognition of unusual or unexpected movements, missing/incomplete information or challenging presented information as part of the risk evaluation

– Determination and justification of a suitable materiality level, appropriately and consistently applied

– Identification of possible management bias and consideration of the impact on the financial statements and the possible reasons for management's preference for certain accounting treatments e.g. out of date valuations, recognition of a general provision

– Effective application of technical and ethical guidance to effectively challenge and critically assess areas of significant management judgement

Commercial acumen

– Use of effective examples and/or calculations from the scenario to illustrate points or recommendations

– Audit procedures are practical and plausible in the context of the scenario

– Appropriate recognition of the wider implications when assessing the client acceptance assessment for Meadow Co

Maximum	10
Total	50

4 GRUBER *Walk in the footsteps of a top tutor*

Top tutor tips

Determination of materiality: The email from the partner states that materiality should be based on profit, therefore at the start of your answer you should calculate the range for materiality using that benchmark and justify a figure within that range. If it is a new audit client or a client where there are apparent control risks, materiality should be set at the lower end of the range. If it is an existing client, materiality may be able to be set at the higher end of the range depending on the other risks mentioned in the scenario. The examining team will give credit for any reasonable explanation of the chosen materiality threshold, as the mark is to recognise that there is the application of professional judgement and that a candidate can justify their response. It is not required that candidates select the identical percentage or figure, or that they provide a justification identical to that shown in the model answer.

Part (a) asks for the matters which should be considered when developing the audit strategy for a new audit client. This requires knowledge of ISA 510 and ISA 300. Think about the additional risks when auditing a client for the first time that will need to be appropriately covered in the audit strategy.

Part (b): Audit risk comprises the risk that the financial statements contain material misstatement and detection risk. Risk of material misstatement is usually due to non-compliance with an accounting standard, although it also includes control risk. Think about the requirements of the relevant accounting standards and what the client might be doing incorrectly. Detection risks are the risks the auditor fails to detect the material misstatements within the financial statements and include auditing a client for the first time or where there is a tight reporting deadline.

Prioritisation of risks: One mark is awarded for the prioritisation of the audit risks. The mark is for the act of justifying the reason, not for the actual justification used (i.e. a range of completely different answers could be awarded the mark), therefore if a reasonable explanation is given, the mark will be awarded. Prioritisation can be achieved by either ordering your answer in priority order and stating this is the case, or by summarising in a brief conclusion which risk, or risks, are most significant.

Part (c) asks for audit procedures over the building including the use of an expert. The procedures should enable the auditor to obtain evidence to determine whether the relevant financial reporting standard has been complied with. Make sure your procedures are clear and provide enough detail that they can be easily followed by the audit team.

Part (d) covers ethical considerations of providing an audit client with a vendor's due diligence engagement involving the purchase of shares of another audit client, thereby creating a conflict of interest. In addition, there are ethical threats which arise regardless of the potential buyer being an audit client.

Professional skills

Professional skills will be awarded for:

Communication – responding to the instructions in the partner's email such as preparing your answers in the form of briefing notes and using the stated benchmark for materiality.

Analysis and evaluation – applying the information from the scenario to answer the question and explaining the issues in sufficient depth.

Professional scepticism and judgement – justifying an appropriate materiality level, demonstrating critical thinking and being alert to possible manipulation and management bias.

Where relevant, professional marks will be awarded for commercial acumen which requires making practical and plausible recommendations and considering the wider implications of issues to the audit firm.

Briefing notes

To: Al Powell, Audit engagement partner

From: Audit manager

Subject: Gruber Co – Audit planning

Date: 1 July 20X5

Introduction

These briefing notes are prepared to assist with planning the audit of Gruber Co for the financial year ending 30 September 20X5. The notes begin by discussing the implications of this being an initial audit engagement and then move onto evaluate the significant audit risks which should be considered in planning the audit. The significant audit risks have been structured to prioritise the risks in terms of the likelihood and magnitude of misstatement in relation to each risk or the significance to the audit. The notes also recommend the audit procedures to be performed in relation to an investment property. Finally, the notes address the ethical issues arising from a meeting with the company's management team.

Materiality

For the purposes of these briefing notes, the overall materiality level used to assess the significance of identified risks is $0.7 million based on the profitability of the company, as requested.

Justification

Using profit before tax or operating profit as a suggested benchmark results in a suggested range of $0.7 million (5% × $14 million) to $1.8 million (10% × $18 million).

As this is a new client and therefore an initial audit engagement, due to the increased detection risk, materiality should be set at the lower level of the range.

This benchmark is only a starting point for determining materiality and professional judgement will need to be applied in determining a final level to be used during the course of the audit.

(a) **Initial audit engagement**

In an initial audit engagement, there are several factors which should be considered in addition to the planning procedures which are carried out for every audit. ISA 300/ISA (UK) 300 *Planning an Audit of Financial Statements* provides guidance in this area.

ISA 300 suggests that unless prohibited by laws or regulation, arrangements should be made with the predecessor auditor, for example, to review their working papers. Therefore, communication should be made with Ellis Associates to request access to their working papers for the financial year ended 30 September 20X4.

The review of the previous year's working papers would help McClane & Co in planning the audit, for example, as it may highlight matters pertinent to the audit of opening balances or an assessment of the appropriateness of Gruber Co's accounting policies.

For example, Ellis Associates may have information on file regarding previous transactions between Martin Gruber and the company, or other related party transactions.

It will also be important to consider whether any previous years' auditor's reports were modified, and if so, the reason for the modification.

As part of the client acceptance process, professional clearance should have been sought from Ellis Associates. Any matters which were brought to the attention of McClane & Co when professional clearance was obtained should be considered for their potential impact on the audit strategy.

In addition, any ethical issues raised during client acceptance should be considered in terms of their potential impact on the audit strategy, for example the need for an independent partner review of the audit, especially given the recent meeting with the company's management and their request for a non-audit service to be performed.

There should also be consideration of the matters which were discussed with Gruber Co's management in connection with the appointment of McClane & Co as auditors. The audit team should also consider any major issues which have been discussed with management at initial meetings and how these matters impact on the overall audit strategy and audit plan. For example, the accounting treatment applied to construction contracts may have been discussed given that this is a significant accounting policy applied in the company's financial statements.

Particular care should be taken in planning the audit procedures necessary to obtain sufficient appropriate audit evidence regarding opening balances, and procedures should be planned in accordance with ISA 510/ISA (UK) 510 *Initial Audit Engagements – Opening Balances*. Procedures should be performed to determine whether the opening balances reflect the application of appropriate accounting policies and determining whether the prior period's closing balances have been correctly brought forward into the current period.

With an initial audit engagement, it is particularly important to develop an understanding of the business, including the legal and regulatory framework applicable to the company. This understanding must be fully documented and will help the audit team to perform effective analytical procedures and to develop an appropriate audit strategy. Obtaining knowledge of the business will also help to identify whether it will be necessary to plan for the use of auditor's experts, for example in relation to accounting for customer contracts.

McClane & Co may have quality management procedures in place for use in the case of initial engagements, for example, the involvement of another partner or senior individual to review the overall audit strategy prior to commencing significant audit procedures. Compliance with any such procedures should be fully documented.

Given that this is a new audit client, and because of other risk factors to be discussed in the next part of these briefing notes, when developing the audit strategy consideration should be given to using an experienced audit team in order to reduce detection risk.

(b) **Audit risk**

New audit client

This is the first year that McClane & Co has audited the company which increases detection risk as our firm does not have experience with the client, making it more difficult to detect material misstatements. However, this risk can be mitigated through rigorous audit planning, including obtaining a thorough understanding of the business of the company.

In addition, as discussed in part (a), there is a risk that opening balances and comparative information may not be correct as the prior year figures were not audited by McClane & Co and therefore, we should plan to audit the opening balances carefully, in accordance with ISA 510 to ensure that opening balances and comparative information are both free from material misstatement.

McClane & Co will need to communicate with Ellis Associates to arrange to review their files to identify any potential issues with prior audits.

Management bias

The company's major shareholder, Martin Gruber, is planning to sell his shares in the company and initial discussions have already taken place with a potential purchaser. This situation means that there is a risk of management bias in that Martin will want to maximise the sale price and for this reason there is a risk that assets will be overstated and revenue and profitability maximised, as he will want the company's financial statements to reflect as good a financial position and performance as possible.

Given the owner-managed status of the company it could be easy for Martin to override controls relating to financial reporting, and/or to put pressure on the chief finance officer (CFO), who is his brother, to manipulate the financial statements. Several of the risks discussed below indicate that management bias could have been applied in a number of accounting treatments, in particular the valuation of investment property and recognition and measurement of intangible assets.

Analytical procedures – overstatement of revenue/profit

Analytical procedures of the financial information provided shows that:

- Revenue is projected to increase by 15.4%

- Operating profit is projected to increase by 80%

- Profit before tax is projected to increase by 55.6%

While there may be relevant and appropriate explanations for these trends, the auditor should be alert to the possibility that revenue and profit could be deliberately overstated. The trend in operating profit is particularly concerning, and management will need to provide explanations and corroboratory evidence in support of these projections. Martin Gruber has incentive for the financial statements to show growth in revenue and profit given the potential sale of his shares, so there is a risk of aggressive earnings management.

Recognition of revenue – support service

The company sells around one quarter if its machines under a contract which includes a support service, but all contracts are currently being established with only one performance obligation. There is a risk that the revenue related to these contracts is not being separated into component parts as required by IFRS 15 *Revenue from Contracts with Customers*.

IFRS 15 requires that when accounting for revenue, the performance obligations in the contract are identified and where a contract has multiple performance obligations, revenue should be allocated to the performance obligations in the contract by reference to their relative standalone selling prices.

There is an audit risk that Gruber Co is not disaggregating the contract revenue between the obligation relating to the supply and installation of the machine and the provision of the support service. This could result in revenue being overstated if the revenue relating to the support service is recognised at the same time as the rest of the revenue.

Recognition of revenue/profit – Argyle contract

The CFO's suggestion that the full amount of profit can be recognised this year in respect of this contract is incorrect. When performing long-term contracts, IFRS 15 states that appropriate methods of measuring progress towards the satisfaction of a performance obligation i.e. the completion of the contract, include output methods and input methods which are based on determining the stage of completion of the performance obligation by reference to the value to the customer of the goods or services transferred to date relative to the remaining goods or services promised under the contract (output method) or on the basis of the entity's efforts or inputs to the satisfaction of a performance obligation (input method).

Based on the company's stated accounting policy, which is to use the output method, the stage of completion should be based on work certified, which is projected to be $4 million compared with the contract price of $6 million, giving a percentage completion of 66.7%. The company should therefore recognise 66.7% of the estimated $2.2 million profit on the contract, which is $1.47 million. Profit is therefore overstated by $730,000. This is material based on the threshold of $0.7 million. The accounting treatment could be an indication of management bias, and the desire of Martin Gruber to overstate profit for the year.

The audit team should also consider whether the accounting treatment applied to other contracts deviates from the company's stated accounting policy and whether there are further material misstatements in this regard.

Investment property

The $15 million invested in the Nakatomi building is material. The change in fair value of $2 million which is recognised within profit is also material.

It is appropriate that the property is measured at fair value and that the gain is recognised within profit. This is in accordance with IAS 40 *Investment Properties* which permits entities to choose between a fair value model, and a cost model for the measurement of investment properties. When the fair value model is used, gains or losses arising from changes in the fair value of investment property must be included in net profit or loss for the period in which it arises.

An audit risk arises from the size of the fair value gain which has been recognised. The property was only purchased at the start of financial year, and an increase in fair value of 13.3% in a twelve-month period is significant. The valuation of the property by the expert has yet to be performed, so the fair value currently included in the financial statements could be an attempt by management to boost profit for the year, for the reasons discussed above.

The level of subjectivity which may be involved in determining the fair value increases the risk of material misstatement. Risk is heightened as Gruber Co may hire an expert who is known to them in order to achieve a higher fair value which will manipulate the profits for the year and therefore the objectivity of the expert used is also a risk.

Tutorial note

Credit will also be awarded for discussion of whether the use of an auditor's expert is appropriate.

Intangible asset

The intangible asset recognised in the year at cost to the company of $9 million, is material to the financial statements. It is also material by nature as it is a transaction between the company and the majority shareholder and chief executive officer, making it a related party transaction, which will be discussed in more detail below.

There is a risk of management bias relating to this transaction. Given that Martin is planning to sell his shares, there is a significant risk that the transaction is an attempt to window-dress the financial statements in order to maximise the asset value, influence the business valuation and ultimately increase the amount which Martin receives on selling his shares. Martin may also have engineered the transaction as a way to remove funds from the company without having to pay a dividend.

It is questionable whether Martin has sold anything at all to the company. Robust audit procedures will need to be performed to determine the existence of an asset in relation to the 'designs' which have been sold to the company. They could possibly relate to assets such as patents or some kind of intellectual property, but both the existence and valuation of such assets needs to be supported by documentation from Martin, which has not been provided to the audit team.

The lack of corroboratory evidence increases the risk of this being a 'fake' transaction which needs to be approached with a very high degree of professional scepticism. For these reasons, there is a significant risk that intangible assets are overstated by a material amount.

There is also a risk that the $10 million opening balance of intangible assets is overstated, especially given that this is a new audit client. Martin may have set up similar transactions in the past, resulting in the recognition of intangible assets which may not be appropriate.

Tutorial note

Credit will also be awarded for discussion regarding the specific accounting treatment of intangible assets, e.g. whether IAS 38 criteria for recognition have been met and whether non-amortisation of assets is appropriate as trends indicate that the recognised assets are not amortised.

Related party transaction

The sale of the designs by Martin to Gruber Co is a related party transaction according to the definition of IAS 24 *Related Party Disclosures*. A related party is a person who has control or joint control over the reporting entity, therefore Martin is a related party of Gruber Co and the sale of his designs is a related party transaction which is defined in IAS 24 as a transfer of resources, services, or obligations between related parties, regardless of whether a price is charged.

There is a risk that disclosure of the transaction is not made in accordance with IAS 24 which requires that if there have been transactions between related parties, there should be disclosure regarding the nature of the related party relationship as well as information about the transactions and outstanding balances where necessary.

(c) **Audit procedures in respect of The Nakatomi Building**

–   Review board minutes for details of the reason for the purchase, to understand the business rationale, and confirm board approval of the transaction.

–   Agree the $15 million paid to the company's bank ledger account/cash book and bank statements.

–   Agree the carrying amount of the property to Gruber Co's non-current asset register to confirm the initial value of the property has been recorded appropriately.

–   Obtain proof of ownership e.g. title deeds, legal documentation to confirm that the company owns the building.

–   Visit the building to obtain evidence of existence and occupancy of the building by retail establishments to confirm that the property has been appropriately classified as an investment property.

–   Obtain and inspect rental agreements for the retailers who occupy the Nakatomi Building, to confirm that the property is not owner-occupied and that it generates a rental income to verify classification.

- Enquire as to whether the company holds any other investment property, and if so, confirm it is also held at fair value to confirm that the accounting treatment is consistent for all investment property.

- Discuss with management the rationale for the accounting policy choice to measure the property at fair value and confirm that the notes to the financial statements state that this is the company's accounting policy.

- With regard to the expert appointed by management to provide the valuation for the building:

    • Obtain information to confirm the experience and qualifications held by the expert, e.g. certificate of registration with a recognised professional body.

    • Obtain confirmation of the expert's independence from Gruber Co and its management team.

    • Review the instructions provided to the expert by management and agree that the valuation method is in accordance with IFRS requirements and can be relied upon as appropriate audit evidence.

    • Obtain the final report issued by the expert and assess that the assumptions and methods used and conclusions reached by the expert are in line with the auditor's understanding of the business, confirm that the expert's valuation has been used as the valuation recognised in the financial statements, and investigate any discrepancies.

    • Confirm that the valuation has been carried out at the reporting date and in accordance with the company's accounting policy.

    • If the valuation is at a different date to the reporting date assess the reasonableness of the valuation reflected in the financial statements.

    • Reperform any calculations contained in the expert's working papers.

(d) **Ethical issues**

Potential sale of shares

The request for McClane & Co to perform a vendor due diligence service creates a conflict of interest. A conflict of interest arises when an audit firm provides a service in relation to two or more clients whose interests in respect of the matter are in conflict.

Conflict of interest is related to objectivity. The IESBA *International Code of Ethics for Accountants* (the Code)/FRC Ethical Standard states that objectivity requires the professional accountant not to compromise professional judgement because of bias, conflict of interest or the undue influence of others. It is a requirement of the Code that a professional accountant shall not allow a conflict of interest to compromise professional judgement.

In this case, the interests of Gruber Co and Willis Co will be conflicting; Willis Co will want to purchase the shares for the lowest possible amount and Martin Gruber will want to sell them for the highest possible amount. This creates, therefore, a significant threat to the objectivity of McClane & Co, who may be seen to be acting in the interest of one party at the expense of the other.

The problem is exacerbated by the nature of the engagement. The audit firm may be privy to confidential information gained during their time as auditor of Gruber Co. If the audit firm were to divulge this to Willis Co, it would give them a potentially unfair advantage over the other client and would be a breach of confidentiality.

In all cases of conflict of interest, the audit firm should make full disclosure to both parties and ask them both to confirm that they give permission for the service to be provided. It is likely that one of the parties will refuse permission in which case the service should not be provided.

If consent by both parties were to be provided, McClane & Co could safeguard the threats created by the situation by:

- having separate engagement teams who are provided with clear policies and procedures on maintaining confidentiality

- having an appropriate reviewer who is not involved in providing either service to the two clients, to review the work performed to assess whether key judgements and conclusions are appropriate

- using confidentiality agreements signed by the relevant personnel

- establishing separation of confidential information physically and electronically.

The Code states that providing a valuation service can give rise to an advocacy threat, which means that McClane & Co would be promoting the interests of their client in relation to the sales price, thus impacting objectivity.

Safeguards such as the following could reduce the threat to an acceptable level:

- Use of separate teams to perform the valuation service and the audit of Gruber Co, and

- Having an independent second partner review the audit of Gruber Co.

There is also a risk that performing such a service would result in the firm assuming a management responsibility because if the audit firm performs the valuation service they could be perceived to be performing a role of management, therefore not appearing to be objective from the audit client. Assuming a management responsibility for an audit client is prohibited in the Code.

If McClane & Co were to value the shares, there is also a threat in relation to subsequent audits of Willis Co and the new group which will be formed, as in performing the valuation of Martin Gruber's shares they would subsequently be auditing their own valuation work when they audit the new Group's consolidated financial statements. The self-review threat leads to an objectivity threat as the audit team may lack professional scepticism in their audit of the investment in Willis Co's financial statements, and over-rely on the valuation performed by colleagues from McClane & Co.

The self-review threat can be reduced to an acceptable level by the use of appropriate safeguards including:

- Use of separate teams to perform the valuation service and the audit of Willis Co, and

- Having an independent second partner review the audit of Willis Co.

The Code suggests that if the valuation would involve both a significant degree of subjective judgement and have a material effect on the financial statements, then it is likely the valuation service should not be performed. McClane & Co should therefore carefully consider whether it is appropriate to perform the service, evaluating the potential materiality of the shares and the level of subjective judgement involved.

Conclusion

These briefing notes have evaluated the audit risks relating to the audit of Gruber Co and highlight the issues caused by this being an initial audit engagement. The audit risks have been ordered with regard to the estimated impact on the audit, magnitude of any misstatement, and the likelihood of such a misstatement occurring. The most significant risk relates to this being a new audit client as the firm has no cumulative knowledge and experience. This will make recognising management bias more difficult. The incentives for management to manipulate the accounts affects multiple areas of the financial statements such as revenue recognition and valuation of investment property and intangibles.

The notes also recommend audit procedures in relation to a new investment property, and conclude that due to a significant conflict of interest and possible restrictions in line with the ethical code, it is unlikely that McClane & Co can provide a vendor due diligence service to Gruber Co.

Examiner's comments

This question was a typical Section A question set at the planning stage, with requirements focusing on matters specific to the planning stage of an initial audit engagement, an evaluation of the significant audit risks, recommending specific audit procedures in relation to an investment property and ethical issues. The Section A question is where candidates perform best and there have been more focused answers in recent sessions. It is pleasing to see that candidates appear to have taken note of the guidance provided by the examining team in this area.

The entity in this scenario was a new client to the audit firm, with the core business being the design and construction of bespoke machinery within the oil industry. Candidates should note that they are not expected to have detailed industry specific knowledge when answering questions in this examination and the scenario will always have enough information to enable sufficient specific risks to be identified and evaluated to achieve full marks.

Several exhibits were provided to candidates to enable them to develop an understanding of the specific issues relevant to the audit.

Unless specified otherwise, all exhibits should be considered when carrying out risk evaluations and candidates should ensure that they carefully read the partner's email for any specific guidance in relation to how the information should be used.

It is recommended that candidates review all the exhibits while planning their answers to the question but as mentioned should ensure they take note of any guidance given by the examining team in terms of which exhibits are relevant to each requirement. Thus, allowing for more detailed analysis and focus on specific information where relevant.

It is often the case that there will be interactions between the exhibits which will impact on the analysis performed by candidates. Candidates are encouraged to spend adequate time planning and aim to obtain a holistic view and understanding of the issues present in the question.

Introduction to the question

- The current date is the 1 July 20X5 and the client has a year end of 30 September 20X5. The scenario is set three months prior to the year end with the audit taking place sometime after the client year end. This indicates the planning stage of an assignment with the audit taking place in October or later. *Note – this is normal and does not indicate there is a lack of time to plan the audit.*

- The scenario states that the appropriate client acceptance and due diligence procedures were successfully completed prior to the acceptance of the client in January 20X5. Therefore, candidates will not obtain credit for repeating these acceptance procedures, including obtaining professional clearance from the previous auditor, as well as assessing whether the firm has the relevant skills and resources to undertake this audit. The candidates are not required to assess whether it was suitable to accept this client and will not gain credit in doing so.

- Gruber Co is family owned and managed – this means the company is not listed and is not required to follow corporate governance best practice

- Gruber Co designs and produces bespoke machines for their customers. (*We are later told these are under contract. This is important for revenue recognition and the ability to recognise revenue over time for the performance obligation to supply and install the machines. There appears to be a gap in the technical knowledge of a significant number of candidates.*)

Exhibit 1 – Partner's email

In a Section A question, the partner's email will always set out the detailed requirements which are to be answered and the mark allocation. It is recommended that candidates refer to the partner's email first to ensure that they understand what they are being asked to do and the best way to allocate their time to each requirement.

It is important to note that there are two specific instructions which attention is drawn to in the audit partner's email. Firstly, that the acceptance procedures have already been undertaken on Gruber Co (and therefore, no credit will be given) and secondly, that Exhibit 5 is to be disregarded for the evaluation of risks (only relevant for requirement d).

With this context in mind, candidates should then consider the requirements while working through the remaining exhibits to enable a tailored response to be made which utilises the specific information given in the question. Candidates should note that any relevant client specific information will be provided, and speculative answers will not obtain credit.

Requirement (a)

This requirement required candidates to consider matters which are relevant to the initial audit of a new client. Disappointingly, many candidates struggled to attempt the question or omitted it entirely.

Stronger candidates were able to discuss planning issues specific to first time audits such as the interaction with previous auditors with regard to working papers; for example, in assessing the appropriateness of the accounting policies used by the client, details of related parties and transactions etc. They were also able to take more general planning matters and describe them in the context of a new client, for example allowing additional time for understanding of systems and controls due to the lack of knowledge from previous audits, as well as the requirement to audit the opening balances.

Weaker candidates tended to either focus on acceptance, for example, requesting clearance from previous auditors, which has already been obtained, or discussed generic planning matters relevant to all audits such as assigning a team, understanding the business and agreeing deadlines. As the requirement asks for specific matters to be "considered in developing the audit strategy for Gruber Co", the examining team are asking for matters which are relevant to Gruber Co rather than generic or non-specific ones.

Overall, this requirement appeared to distinguish those who approach audit from a practical stance from those who demonstrated knowledge of generic planning matters but were unable to apply them to a specific situation. In this examination, it was crucial for candidates to apply their knowledge of the planning and early stages of the audit process in order to gain credit in this exam.

Requirement (b)

This requirement is typical in volume and nature to many planning questions and examines a major area of the syllabus – risk. It is important to notice that the requirement asked for an evaluation, not simply a list of risks, nor a strategy or procedures to address those risks. The examining team are testing whether candidates understand how and why a risk arises and the implications this has on the financial statements or the audit itself. They are looking for an assessment of materiality, a demonstration of knowledge of the underlying accounting rules and the application of that to the scenario to identify the potential impact on the financial statements. A well evaluated risk has in depth analysis. Candidates writing only a sentence or two are unlikely to attain many of the marks available for each risk.

An issue that arises repeatedly is candidates attempting to find 12 risks for a 24-mark question and conducting little or no in-depth analysis of any of them. This will not be able to attain a pass mark. This means some of the risks stated in these answers will be speculative or not significant and, therefore, will not obtain credit.

Candidates should be aware of the published marking guides for risk questions and understand how marks are credited. Each risk generally has a minimum of three marks attached to it. More complex risks carry additional credit. Materiality and calculation marks are over and above the marks available for the discussion of a risk. The marking guide for this question has eight areas of risks, two of which centre around revenue recognition and one arises from an analytical review.

The requirement asks only for significant audit risks, which mean risks that are either specific to the scenario, non-routine or judgemental and have the potential to give rise to a material misstatement or give rise to a specific detection risk. Speculative risks, arising from routine transactions generally will not obtain credit. Candidates demonstrating strong professional skills will be able to differentiate between speculative and specific risks, and not spend time discussing topics which will not obtain credit. As a demonstration of this skill, consider the various properties that the client has in this scenario.

Exhibit 2 – Business and governance

Candidates are told that the client owns a head office property and leases a production facility. The client has purchased a new investment property in a retail development. If we consider the risks in these different areas:

- Head office building owned outright – this is routine Property, Plant and Equipment (PPE). Under a historical-cost method the only risk to this as an ongoing transaction is the estimate of useful life. Candidates are not given a value for this property, nor told that the client is depreciating over an unreasonable life. As depreciation of PPE is generally a low-risk area and there is nothing new or unusual about the property given, it does not give rise to a significant audit risk.

- Leased production facility – leases are not a judgemental area of financial statements in most cases. In the absence of further information, it would be speculative to think that this lease might be under a year and covered by the exemption to general lease rules requiring the recognition of a right of use asset. This is not a new lease where the client may not understand lease accounting nor is judgement involved in accounting for it.

  No financial information has been included to enable the calculation of materiality, so there is no basis to assume this is a significant risk. If following lease accounting rules had been a significant risk, this would have been identified during acceptance and information given about inappropriate treatment being utilised.

- New investment property – this is an area of risk as it is a new transaction for the client, and there are requirements for classification which must be met. The client also has the choice between two different acceptable accounting policies and the method the client has chosen involves judgement and estimates of fair value. In addition, the values are given to allow a materiality calculation to be performed and the client has estimated the fair value gain themselves which is out of their expertise range. These judgements and choices may reflect management bias. This is the significant risk that candidates need to address.

Candidates must remember when discussing risks, that it is important to relate them to the scenario rather than discuss abstract or generic risks.

This is particularly an issue when discussing management bias risk. This is a key concept to understand for auditors as it can impact on judgements made by management in deriving their figures for the financial statements. Candidates must be able to demonstrate they understand the concept of management bias and can identify it in practice. The examining team are often faced with two standard candidate responses to management bias risk in section A questions: "the client is listed so management will be biased to keep shareholders happy" or "the client is not listed so the owners will be biased to keep profits low and save tax". The first statement doesn't include scenario specific reasons for this conclusion and is therefore too vague and generic. The second implies that all non-listed clients are concerned with aiming for lower payments in respect of tax. Again, this is a generic statement, and unless there is information in the scenario that specifically alludes to this, then candidates will not receive credit for making this point. In both cases, neither will be credited as an evaluation of management bias for a specific scenario.

Candidates are told that the business is owner managed, and that the main shareholder is in the process of selling his shares in the company. The specific management bias point in this scenario is the desire to make the company look as attractive as possible for a potential buyer. That is the specific identification of the management bias threat. To score more than a ½ mark for the identification of the specific bias risk, this will have to be evaluated by candidates. Suggested explanations may include:

- The company's aim to show strong profitability could lead to early or inappropriate recognition of revenue or the understatement of costs.

- Management may wish to make the statement of financial position look strong, such as by the overstatement of assets.

This is the beginning of the evaluation and will score the initial mark. It should then be tied into the scenario to illustrate areas where this could potentially happen or appears to be happening. In this question this is all reinforced by the scenario. There are specific examples of each of those given to enable an evaluation to be made with reference to this question and scenario. Candidates might find it sensible to address management bias holistically after they have analysed the other risks in the question.

The analytical procedures a candidate could calculate and comment on include movements in key ratios to support the empiric bias risks detailed above. Candidates should remember that calculations are only credited when the resulting figures are discussed in their answer in the context of a risk. Simply calculating a ratio will not obtain credit.

The skill examined is the ability to calculate a relevant ratio or trend to identify a risk or support an evaluation of a risk. It is at that point that the calculation mark is awarded.

Exhibit 3 – Financial information/Exhibit 4- Business developments

Candidates were generally able to identify the key risks and, in most cases, were able to apply correct accounting rules to support their analysis. The technical financial reporting topics in this question were generally well attempted and many candidates demonstrated a strong knowledge of the underlying financial reporting required to be able to analyse the risks. Commentary on how each of those areas was tackled is below.

- Revenue recognition of separate performance obligations in a single contract where a three-year service contract was bundled with installation of the machine – this was well handled by many candidates with most appreciating that deferral of an element of the price over the three years was necessary. A significant minority however, suggested a provision for the costs should be made for the three-year service contract which is not the case.

- Revenue recognition of a long-term contract paid in advance (Argyle contract), was the area where most candidates struggled with the calculations. The client was using the output method as a policy for determining the appropriate profits to be recognised at the year end however had treated one contract on a cash basis to bring forward profit recognition. Candidates almost always identified this was not appropriate with around half correctly saying that the output method policy should be applied. The application of the output method to costs to recognise, was most frequently miscalculated, however this minor error did not prevent many candidates achieving strong marks for the evaluation. The remaining candidates did not appear to have knowledge of the methods permitted for this type of contract and suggested no revenue or profit could be recognised until installation.

- Investment property – this was also very well answered. A minority of candidates believed gains on investment property should be taken through other comprehensive income rather than profit, but most candidates were able to identify both the correct accounting treatment and the risks arising from the valuation provided by management.

- Sale of designs – Most candidates here recognised that intangible assets require a reliable value to be estimated as part of the recognition criteria and questioned the legitimacy of the transaction. Additional credit was allowed in this section with respect to the patent value in the brought forward figures given that this has apparently not been amortised and the duration of the patent may not be indefinite.

- Related party transaction – most candidates recognised and appropriately evaluated this risk.

Overall, this requirement was answered well by many candidates.

Requirement (c)

This requirement was well answered by a majority of candidates with practical, well described procedures given. The model answer provides a list of procedures which are indicative of the areas the examining team credited. Where a candidate suggests a procedure not on the list in the model answer they will still obtain credit providing it is relevant and practicable.

Exhibit 5 – Meeting notes

This final requirement was focused on the ethical issues surrounding a conflict of interest between two clients and the provision of non-audit services to a non-listed company.

Requirement (d)

The conflict of interest risks were generally well identified by candidates, although not always well described. Candidates generally appreciated the safeguards available and the requirement for consent from both parties.

The self-review threat arising with respect to the vendors due diligence and the safeguards available were again well performed. Some candidates lost time discussing rules for listed clients which Gruber Co is not, so the answers were irrelevant. It should be noted that candidates sitting a location specific version of this exam such as UK or SGP, would have a slightly different answer here and should refer to the model answer published for their specific version of the examination.

Candidates are reminded that in the INT version of the exam the examiners are unable to credit ethical standards specific to an individual country and can only credit answers which are consistent with the examinable documents for the syllabus. Candidates should therefore not use the UK/IRL/SGP specific versions of the ethical standards in the INT examination.

The advocacy threat arising from the due diligence work was the most often missed threat in candidates' discussions.

Overall, the responses from candidates on this question were stronger than in previous sessions and some good specific responses were seen.

	ACCA Marking guide	
		Marks
(a)	**Initial audit**	
	Generally, up to 1 mark for each relevant point discussed, including:	
	– Communicate with the previous auditor, review their working papers for significant planning issues	
	– Consider whether any previous auditor's reports were modified	
	– Consider any matters which were raised when professional clearance was obtained	
	– Consider impact of any ethical issues, e.g. the need for independent partner review	
	– Consider matters discussed with management during our firm's appointment, e.g. accounting treatment of construction contracts	
	– Need to develop thorough business understanding including in relation to significant accounting policies	
	– Risk of misstatement in opening balances/previously applied accounting policies	
	– Firm's quality control procedures for new audit clients	
	– Need to use experienced audit team to reduce detection risk	
	Maximum	**5**
(b)	**Evaluation of audit risks**	
	Up to 3 marks for each audit risk evaluated unless otherwise indicated. Marks may be awarded for other, relevant risks not included in the marking guide.	
	Appropriate materiality calculations (max 2 marks) and justified materiality level should be awarded to a maximum of 1 mark.	
	In addition, ½ mark for each relevant trend or calculation which form part of the evaluation of audit risk (max 3 marks).	
	– New client (up to 2 marks)	
	– Management bias due to sale of shares (up to 2 marks)	
	– Overstatement of revenue/profit – from analytical review (max 2 marks)	
	– Recognition of revenue – support service	
	– Recognition of revenue/profit – Argyle contract	
	– Investment property (max 4 marks)	
	– Sale of designs (max 4 marks)	
	– Related party transaction	
	Maximum	**21**
(c)	**Audit procedures**	
	Up to 1 mark for each relevant audit procedure. Examples are provided below. Marks will be awarded for other relevant points.	
	– Review board minutes for details of the reason for the purchase, to understand the business rationale, and confirm board approval of the transaction	
	– Agree the amount paid to the company's bank ledger account/cash book and bank statements	
	– Agree the carrying amount of the property to Gruber Co's non-current asset register to confirm the initial value of the property has been recorded appropriately	
	– Obtain proof of ownership, e.g. title deeds, legal documentation to confirm that the company owns the building	
	– Visit the building to obtain evidence of existence and occupancy of the building by retail establishments to confirm that the property has been appropriately classified as an investment property	
	– Obtain and inspect rental agreements for the retailers who occupy the Nakatomi building, to confirm that the property is not owner-occupied and that it generates a rental income	

- Enquire as to whether the company holds any other investment property, and if so, confirm it is also held at fair value to confirm that the accounting treatment is consistent for all investment property
- Discuss with management the rationale for the accounting policy choice to measure the property at fair value and confirm that the notes to the financial statements state that this is the company's accounting policy
- With regard to the expert appointed by management to provide the valuation for the building (up to 4 marks):
  - Obtain information to confirm the experience and qualifications held by the expert, e.g. certificate of registration with a recognised professional body
  - Obtain confirmation of the expert's independence from Gruber Co and its management team
  - Review the instructions provided to the expert by management, and agree that the valuation method is in accordance with IFRS requirements
  - Obtain the final report issued by the expert and assess that the assumptions and methods used and conclusions reached by the expert are in line with the auditor's understanding of the business
  - Confirm that the valuation has been carried out at the reporting date and in accordance with the company's accounting policy
  - If the valuation is at a different date to the reporting date, assess the reasonableness of the valuation reflected in the financial statements
  - Reperform any calculations contained in the expert's working papers

Maximum	**6**

(d) **Ethical issues**

Up to 1 mark for each relevant, explained point:

- Conflict of interest between Gruber Co and Willis Co
- Conflict of interest impact on auditor's objectivity
- Requirement that a professional accountant shall not allow a conflict of interest to compromise professional judgement
- Risk relates to the valuation of the Gruber shares
- Risk of breach of confidentiality
- Full disclosure to be made to both parties and consent obtained
- Safeguards may be used to reduce the threat to objectivity (max 2 marks)
- Advocacy threat in relation to Gruber Co
- Safeguards to reduce advocacy threat (max 2 marks)
- Management responsibilities in relation to Gruber Co
- Self-review threat re audit of investment in Willis Co
- Safeguards to reduce self-review threat (max 2 marks)
- Valuation should not be provided if material impact on financial statements and involves significant degree of subjective judgement

Maximum	**8**

Professional marks

Communication

- Briefing note format and structure – use of headings/subheadings and an introduction
- Style, language and clarity – appropriate layout and tone of briefing notes, presentation of materiality and relevant calculations, appropriate use of the CBE tools, easy to follow and understand
- Effectiveness and clarity of communication – answer is relevant and tailored to the scenario
- Adherence to the specific requests made by the audit engagement partner

Analysis and evaluation

- Appropriate use of the information to determine and apply suitable calculations
- Appropriate use of the information to design appropriate audit procedures relating to the Nakatomi building
- Effective prioritisation of the results of the evaluation of audit risks to demonstrate the likelihood and magnitude of risks and to facilitate the allocation of appropriate responses

Professional scepticism and professional judgement

- Appropriate application of professional judgement to draw conclusions and make informed decisions following recognition of unusual or unexpected movements, missing/incomplete information or challenging presented information as part of the risk evaluation
- Determination and justification of a suitable materiality level, appropriately and consistently applied
- Identification of possible management bias and consideration of the impact on the financial statements and the possible reasons for management's preference for certain accounting treatments
- Effective application of technical and ethical guidance to effectively challenge and critically assess areas of significant management judgement

Commercial acumen

- Use of effective examples and/or calculations from the scenario to illustrate points or recommendations
- Audit procedures are practical and plausible in the context of the scenario
- Appropriate recognition of the wider implications when considering the request to provide a vendor's due diligence service

Maximum	10
Total	50

5   PALE *Walk in the footsteps of a top tutor*

Top tutor tips

Determination of materiality: *The email from the partner states that materiality should be based on profit, therefore at the start of your answer you should calculate the range for materiality using that benchmark and justify a figure within that range. If it is a new audit client or a client where there are apparent control risks, materiality should be set at the lower end of the range. If it is an existing client, materiality may be able to be set at the higher end of the range depending on the other risks mentioned in the scenario. The examining team will give credit for any reasonable explanation of the chosen materiality threshold, as the mark is to recognise that there is the application of professional judgement and that a candidate can justify their response. It is not required that candidates select the identical percentage or figure, or that they provide a justification identical to that shown in the model answer.*

Part (a) *requires evaluation of business risks. When describing business risks remember to explain the impact it will have on the company i.e. impact on profit or cash flow. The business risks should be relatable to the financial statements as the auditor will only consider business risks which will also give rise to a risk of material misstatement.*

Part (b) *asks you to evaluate the audit risks to be considered when planning the audit. Audit risk comprises the risk that the financial statements contain material misstatement and detection risk. Risk of material misstatement is usually due to non-compliance with an accounting standard, although it also includes control risk. Think about the requirements of the relevant accounting standards and what the client might be doing incorrectly. Detection risks are the risks the auditor fails to detect the material misstatements within the financial statements and include auditing a client for the first time or where there is a tight reporting deadline. The requirement specifically instructs you to only consider risks relating to changes in fair value in relation to the timber plantation, therefore there will be no marks available for discussion of any other risks.*

Prioritisation of risks: *One mark is awarded for the prioritisation of the audit risks. The mark is for the act of justifying the reason, not for the actual justification used (i.e. a range of completely different answers could be awarded the mark), therefore if a reasonable explanation is given, the mark will be awarded. Prioritisation can be achieved by either ordering your answer in priority order and stating this is the case, or by summarising in a brief conclusion which risk, or risks, are most significant.*

Part (c) *asks for audit procedures in respect of the change in fair value of the timber plantation asset. The procedures should enable the auditor to obtain evidence to determine whether the relevant financial reporting standard has been complied with. Make sure your procedures are clear and provide enough detail that they can be easily followed by the audit team. Again, there is a specific instruction within the requirement to help you answer appropriately. Here you are told to include procedures to assess the work of the management expert.*

Part (d) *covers ethical issues relating to a request for an assurance service over KPIs. Identify and explain the threats arising. Discuss whether the threats are significant and state any actions the firm should take to mitigate the threats.*

> *Professional skills*
>
> *Professional skills will be awarded for:*
>
> *Communication – responding to the instructions in the partner's email such as preparing your answers in the form of briefing notes and using the stated benchmark for materiality.*
>
> *Analysis and evaluation – applying the information from the scenario to answer the question and explaining the issues in sufficient depth.*
>
> *Professional scepticism and judgement – justifying an appropriate materiality level, demonstrating critical thinking and being alert to possible manipulation and management bias.*
>
> *Where relevant, professional marks will be awarded for commercial acumen which requires making practical and plausible recommendations and considering the wider implications of issues to the audit firm.*

Briefing notes

To: Harvey Rebus, Audit engagement partner

From: Audit manager

Subject: Audit planning in relation to Pale Co

Date: 1 July 20X5

Introduction

These briefing notes have been prepared to assist in planning the audit of Pale Co. The notes begin with an evaluation of the business risks facing the company and continue by evaluating the significant audit risks which should be considered in planning the audit. The significant audit risks have been structured to prioritise the risks in terms of the likelihood and magnitude of misstatement in relation to each risk or the significance to the audit.

The notes also include the recommended principal audit procedures which have been designed in respect of a change in fair value to the company's timber plantation following a recent storm. Finally, the notes discuss the ethical issues arising from a recent phone call with the company's chief finance officer (CFO).

Materiality

For the purposes of these briefing notes, the overall materiality level used to assess the significance of identified risks is $325,000 based on the profitability of the company, as requested.

Justification

Using profit before tax of $6.5 million as a suggested benchmark results in a suggested range of $325,000 to $650,000 (5% and 10% respectively).

Given the increased inherent risk of management bias (discussed below) and the fact that this is a new client, materiality should be set at the lower end of the range.

This benchmark is only a starting point for determining materiality and professional judgement will need to be applied in determining a final level to be used during the course of the audit.

(a) **Business risks**

International expansion

The expansion into Farland introduces a business risk in that the company will be managing operations in a foreign country for the first time. Farland is remote, so it may be difficult for Pale Co's management team to plan regular visits to the new operations, so establishing robust management oversight and controls could be difficult.

In addition, Farland may have different laws and regulations compared to the company's home jurisdiction, so there is a heightened risk of non-compliance. Even the type of trees growing in the rainforest will be different, and management may not have experience in their harvesting, processing and the sale of timber products.

All of these issues create a risk that the international expansion may not be successful, and at the same time will represent a drain on management's time and resources. Operations in the home country of Pale Co may suffer as a result.

Gold Standard accreditation

There is a risk that the Gold Standard accreditation may not be renewed, with implications for reputation, and more specifically for the new contract with Royal Co, which largely accounts for an increase of 5.5% in the company's revenue this year.

Several of the key performance indicators (KPIs) which need to be met to retain the Gold Standard seem to be in jeopardy, for example, there has been a decline in the percentage of timber which is harvested in line with Gold Standard requirements, and the projected metric of 82% is only just above the required level of 80%.

In addition, the Gold Standard is linked to ethical business practice, and there are some indications that the company's business ethics are questionable, for example, the legal case being brought by employees. If the Gold Standard accreditation is lost, Royal Co and other customers may cancel contracts, resulting in a loss of revenue and cash flow.

Legal case

The legal action against the company by its own employees is a significant risk. If the issue becomes public knowledge, there will be reputational problems, and the amount which is being claimed, $19 million, exceeds the company's cash balance.

If the legal claim were to go against the company, it would struggle to find the funds to pay the damages given that it is already at the limit of its borrowing arrangements.

The situation could also indicate poor governance of the company, if decisions are being made which put the lives of employees at risk and result in days lost due to accidents at work, and the matter seems to be dismissed as unimportant by the management team and legal advisers.

Damage to assets caused by storms

The recent storms have caused significant damage to the company's timber plantation asset. Unpredictable weather patterns could cause further harm or even totally destroy the company's timber plantations.

Assuming that trees will be replanted to replace the damage caused by the storm, it can take many years for trees to grow to a harvestable size, so the company faces a significant depletion of its future cash inflows for years to come.

This risk is very difficult to mitigate, perhaps the diversification into tropical rainforest is a way to reduce the risk exposure of the company's operations being concentrated in one geographical area.

Liquidity

The financial information provided indicates that the company's liquidity position has deteriorated over the year. The company has only $4.5 million of cash – a reduction of 33.8% compared to the end of the last financial year. While this has been explained as due to inflationary pressures, management should be doing more to maintain a reasonable level of cash in order to properly manage its working capital. Inventory levels have increased significantly by 67.4% and while again the reason for the increase has been explained by management, if the inventory of processed timber cannot be shipped to customers in the near future, working capital will continue to deteriorate.

The company may become unable to meet obligations as they fall due, especially if the industrial action continues to restrict the possibility of export sales which account for 30% of the company's revenue.

Industrial action

The industrial action at the country's ports has already meant lost sales, and, as explained above, there is a risk that revenue and cash inflows will continue to be negatively impacted.

Export sales account for 30% of total revenue, approximately $12.75 million, making this a potentially very significant issue should the industrial action continue. Customers may begin to look elsewhere for their supply of timber, leading to cancelled future orders and contracts.

There is also an issue that the increased storage of timber which is awaiting export to foreign customers will incur additional storage costs.

Tutorial note

Credit will be awarded for discussion of other relevant business risks, for example, the solvency issue raised by the company being at the limit of its borrowing agreement, the lack of cash other than relating to the government grant available for establishing operations in Farland, the lack of an audit committee and independent internal audit team, the reputational damage which may be caused by the legal case, and the inflationary pressures which will make costs hard to control.

(b) **Evaluation of audit risks**

New client

This is the first year in which Chief & Co has audited the company, which increases detection risk, as our firm does not have experience with the client, making it more difficult to detect material misstatements.

In addition, there is a risk that opening balances and comparative information may not be correct. The prior year figures were not audited by Chief & Co, therefore we should plan to audit the opening balances carefully, in accordance with ISA 510 *Initial Audit Engagements – Opening Balances*, to ensure that opening balances and comparative information are both free from material misstatement.

Tutorial note

Credit will also be awarded for discussion of Pale Co operating in a specialised industry, which could create a detection risk given the audit firm's lack of experience in auditing clients in this industry.

Corporate governance

The company does not have to comply with corporate governance requirements as it is not a listed entity. However, it is good practice to have an established audit committee, especially for a large company like Pale Co which is seeking a stock market flotation in the relatively near future.

The internal audit team is small and lacking in independence as they report directly to the CFO. This means that the scope of their work is likely to be quite limited due to insufficient resources, and any recommendations made could potentially be ignored by Mark York. This has implications for controls over financial reporting, which could be deficient, and increases control risk.

There is a high scope for errors in financial reporting processes and for deliberate manipulation of balances and transactions, as the internal audit team does not have sufficient resources for thorough monitoring and reporting.

Pressure on results

The company is not a listed entity, but the existing and new shareholders will be looking for a return on their investment in the form of a dividend payment. In addition, in the run up to a potential stock market flotation, there will be pressure for the company to show good financial performance. The company also has ambitious international expansion plans.

Pressure to return a better performance creates an incentive for management bias which means that management may use earnings management techniques, or other methods of creative accounting, to create a healthier picture of financial performance than is actually the case. This creates an inherent risk of material misstatement at the financial statement level.

The fact that the projected profit before tax is 30% higher than the previous year's figure could indicate that operating expenses are understated. Management bias could also have led to some of the accounting treatments suggested by Mark York, which work to improve the company's profit for the year.

Going concern

There are several indicators that despite its projected increase in revenue and profit, the company faces going concern problems. These indicators include, but are not limited to, operational problems including the destroyed timber plantation and industrial action, reputational damage caused by the legal claim, financial problems caused by lack of cash and the fact that its results are likely to be much worse than that projected by management when the decrease in fair value of the destroyed timber plantation is taken into account. These matters are discussed in detail below.

Management should provide a note to the financial statements which discusses any material uncertainty over the company's ability to continue as a going concern. If management fails to disclose this note, or provides the note but with inadequate detail, a significant audit risk will be created.

Government grant

A government grant of $20 million has been awarded to Pale Co which is material to the projected statement of financial position. Mark York has suggested that he will recognise $10 million of the amount received in profit for the year – projected profit before tax is only $6.5 million, so increasing the profit by this amount would be highly material to the statement of profit or loss.

The audit risk relates to whether this should be recognised as income in the current accounting period. IAS 20 *Accounting for Government Grants and Disclosure of Government Assistance* requires that government grants are recognised in profit or loss on a systematic basis over the periods in which the entity recognises expenses for the related costs for which the grants are intended to compensate.

Mark York is planning to recognise half of the grant as income this year, however, this is not appropriately justified. The grant has not been awarded to compensate for management time in planning the international expansion, so the appropriate accounting treatment would seem to be that the entire amount of the grant should be recognised as deferred income in this financial year, as the expenditure for which the grant is specifically provided has not yet been incurred.

Therefore, there is a risk that the company will recognise the income too early, leading to overstated profit and understated liabilities.

Tutorial note

Credit will also be awarded for discussion relating to the company's use of the grant for building accommodation for employees, and relevant audit risks, e.g. the recognition of the accommodation as property, plant and equipment and treatment of the part of the grant relating to the construction of assets.

There could be a further issue in that the terms of the grant may require complete or partial repayment if the conditions of the grant are not satisfied, for example, if Pale Co does not retain its Gold Standard accreditation or if the circumstances of the employees' legal case are considered to be indicative of unethical business practice by the company.

The company should evaluate whether the terms are likely to be met, and if not, should consider whether it would be appropriate to recognise a provision or disclose a contingent liability in the notes to the financial statements. According to IAS 37 *Provisions, Contingent Liabilities and Contingent Assets*, a provision should be recognised where a present obligation exists as a result of a past event which can be reliably measured and is probable to result in an outflow of economic benefit.

The risk is therefore that this has not been considered by management, leading possibly to understated liabilities or inadequate disclosure as required by IAS 37.

Legal case

The legal case could also give rise to a risk of understated liabilities or inadequate disclosure if the company fails to provide for the $19 million claimed by employees or to disclose the matter as a contingent liability.

It will be a matter of significant judgement to decide whether the legal claim is likely to go against Pale Co or not at this early stage, however, the matter is material, and being close to three times projected profit for the year therefore warrants careful consideration. Due to its sensitive nature, the auditor may also consider the issue to be material by nature.

Reduction in fair value of timber plantation

The company's timber plantation asset, prior to recognising any change in fair value, is projected to amount to 90.9% of the company's total assets and is therefore highly material.

The company has correctly obtained an expert's opinion on the change in fair value of the destroyed and damaged trees caused by the storm. The expert's valuation has helped management to determine that a reduction in fair value of $70.5 million should be recognised in the financial statements within profit. This amount is material in its own right. When the loss in value is recognised, it will turn the projected profit into a significant loss.

There is a risk that management will not recognise the loss in full due to the impact it will have on profit. This is therefore a very significant issue for the audit planning.

There is a risk that the expert's valuation is not appropriate, for example, if the expert does not have appropriate expertise to perform this specialist valuation, which would lead to issues in whether the valuation can be relied upon.

In addition, the expert has considered only the value of the destroyed and damaged trees and not considered any other impact of the storm, for example, if other assets such as roads and buildings have been affected by the storm and should be tested for impairment.

Therefore, based on the issues discussed above, there is a risk that the loss is not fully recognised in profit for the year, and the carrying amount of non-current assets is overstated.

Inventory

The level of inventory has increased significantly, by 67.4%, and the value of inventory at 30 June 20X5 of $15.4 million is material.

There is a risk that if the industrial action continues, and the company cannot fulfil its export sale contracts, the customers will cancel their orders. The inventory then may not be saleable to other customers, perhaps if the timber has been cut to customer specification or requires modification to secure a sale to a different customer. According to IAS 2 *Inventories*, inventory should be recognised at the lower of cost and net realisable value.

There is an audit risk that inventory is overstated if any necessary write down to net realisable value is not recognised. This would result in overstated current assets and overstated profit.

(c)   Change in fair value of the timber plantation asset

- Obtain the expert's report on the value of the destroyed and damaged timber plantation to:

  - Gain understanding and allow evaluation of the methodology and assumptions used, e.g. the basis of determining the amount of any income which may be generated from the timber to be salvaged from damaged trees.

  - Confirm the geographical extent of damage by the storm.

  - Confirm the basis of determining whether trees have been completely destroyed or damaged.

- Discuss the expert's methodology and assumptions with management to confirm their rationale and compliance with the measurement requirements of IAS 41 *Agriculture*.

- Obtain confirmation of the expert's qualifications and experience in assessing storm damage to timber plantation assets and quantifying financial losses.

- Obtain confirmation that the expert is independent from Pale Co and its management team.

- If possible, visit the site of the storm damage to form a view on the scale of the destruction and to evaluate whether any assets other than the trees have been destroyed or damaged.

- Discuss with management the actions which have been taken in response to the storm, e.g. the extent of progress made to clear the destroyed trees and harvest the damaged trees.

- Obtain any documentation relating to any potential sale of damaged trees, e.g. customer orders, to confirm any realisable value of damaged trees.

- From the non-current asset register, confirm the carrying amount of the standing trees prior to any change in fair value being recognised.

- Consider whether the use of an auditor's expert is necessary to provide sufficient and appropriate evidence given the materiality of the figures.

- Develop an auditor's estimate of the fair value of the timber plantation, in accordance with the IAS 41 requirements, and compare to management's estimate of the change in fair value.

- Obtain a copy of the company's insurance policy and review the terms and conditions to confirm whether the storm damage is covered by insurance.

(d)   Assurance on key performance indicators (KPIs)

Self-review threat

There are several issues to consider with regard to providing this service. A significant issue relates to auditor objectivity. The KPIs include financial and non-financial metrics. The financial metrics, including revenue, operating profit and profit before tax, will be extracted from, or reconciled to, the figures as shown in the audited financial statements.

While the KPIs will not form part of the audited financial statements, they will be published in the annual report and therefore form part of the 'other information' in relation to which the auditor has responsibilities under ISA 720 *The Auditor's Responsibilities Relating to Other Information*. ISA 720 requires that auditors read the other information in order to identify any material inconsistencies between the financial statements and the other information.

There is therefore a potential self-review threat to objectivity in that the audit firm has been asked to provide assurance on these KPIs which would be read by the audit team as part of their review of other information. The team performing the assurance work would be reluctant to raise queries or highlight errors which may have been made during the external audit when reading the other information.

Tutorial note

Credit will be awarded for discussion of other relevant threats to objectivity created by providing an assurance service on the KPIs, including the advocacy threat and self-interest threats.

The IESBA *International Code of Ethics for Professional Accountants* (the *Code*)/FRC Ethical Standard provides guidance when auditors provide additional services to an audit client. Chief & Co needs to evaluate the significance of the threat and consider whether any safeguards can reduce the threat to an acceptable level. For example, a partner who is independent should be involved in reviewing the audit work performed.

Contingent fee

There is also an ethical issue in respect to the fee proposed by Pale Co for the assurance engagement. If the firm decides to take on the engagement, it should be treated as an engagement separate from the audit and with a separate fee charged for the work and confirmed in a separate engagement letter. The suggestion to simply amend and increase the audit fee and to determine it on a contingent basis, as in the fee is only payable if the assurance is favourable, is not appropriate.

Contingent fees can give rise to a self-interest threat, as it is in the financial interest of the audit firm to give a favourable assurance opinion in order to secure the income.

The *Code* prohibits the use of contingent fees for audit services, but they are allowed for other types of work, depending on factors such as the nature of the engagement and the range of possible fee outcomes. The most prudent course of action, should Chief & Co take on the engagement, would be to charge the fee on a non-contingent basis, separate from the audit fee, to remove any ethical issues relating to the fee.

Competence

Aside from ethical issues, Chief & Co must also consider whether they have the competence to perform the work. Providing assurance on non-financial KPIs is quite a specialist area, and it could be that the audit firm does not have the appropriate levels of expertise and experience to provide a quality service. In particular, the firm would need to ensure that it fully understands the Gold Standard accreditation.

Given that this is a specialised industry, and this is the first client which Chief & Co has in the industry, it is questionable whether the firm has the competence to carry out the work.

Resources

Aside from competence, the firm should also consider whether it has resources in terms of staff availability to complete the work to the desired deadline and to perform appropriate reviews of the work which has been completed.

Conclusion

These briefing notes highlight that the company faces significant business risk, in particular, in relation to its financial position and the recent storm damage. There are a number of significant audit risks which will need to be carefully considered during the planning of the audit, to ensure that an appropriate audit strategy is devised. The most significant audit risk relates to this being a new audit client means the firm has no cumulative knowledge and experience increasing detection risk. This will make it more difficult to identify areas of management bias due to the pressure on results which could then impact going concern. We need to perform detailed work on the highly material change in fair value of the timber plantation due to the recent storm, as detailed in the notes. Finally, there are ethical matters to be discussed with management and incorporated into our audit planning. The assurance engagement on the company's KPIs should only go ahead once all ethical implications have been carefully evaluated and appropriate safeguards put in place.

Examiner's comments

This question was a typical Section A question set at the planning stage, with requirements covering business risk, audit risk, audit procedures and ethics, for 50 marks. Typically, each session the Section A question is where candidates perform best and there have been progressively better and more focused answers in recent sessions. It is pleasing to see that candidates appear to have taken note of the guidance provided by the examining team in this area.

The entity in this scenario was a new client to the audit firm, with the core business being the management of timber plantations and the production and sale of a range of timber products. The company was not listed but was aiming to achieve a listing in the next two years.

Several exhibits were provided to candidates to enable them to develop an understanding of the specific issues relevant to the audit. These were as follows:

- Partner's email – this exhibit typically provides the detailed requirements for the question.

- Background information on the company – includes information the audit engagement partner deems relevant to audit planning.

- Notes from meeting – summary of business developments discussed at a recent meeting between the chief finance officer (CFO) and the audit engagement partner.

- Key performance indicators – a summary of financial and non-financial information.

- Notes from phone call – summary of issues raised by the CFO during a discussion with the audit engagement partner.

Unless specified otherwise, all exhibits should be considered when identifying business risks and audit risks and candidates should ensure that they carefully read the partner's email for any specific guidance in relation to how the information should be used.

It is recommended that candidates review all the exhibits while planning their answers to the question but as mentioned should ensure they take note of any guidance given by the examining team in terms of which exhibits are relevant to each requirement. Thus, allowing for more detailed analysis and focus on specific information where relevant.

It is often the case that there will be interactions between the exhibits which will impact on the analysis performed by candidates. Candidates are encouraged to spend adequate time planning and aim to obtain a holistic view and understanding of the issues present in the question.

An important thing to note for all questions in the AAA examination is the stage of the audit process the scenario relates to. Often candidates do not remain focused on the audit stage and produce answers which are nonsensical in the context. For example, it is common for candidates in planning questions, which are set prior to the financial year end, to state that the audit will be performed under significant time pressure because there is only three months left before the year end. Candidates should note that the final audit happens after the year end. Planning before the year end is not leaving it too late and is an appropriate response to avoid such time pressure; ensuring that the audit is well planned prior to its commencement.

In this scenario, the company is not listed but is aiming for a listing in the next two years, and they operate in the management of timber plantations and the production and sales of a range of timber products.

Candidates are not expected to have detailed industry specific knowledge when answering questions in this examination and the scenario will always have enough information to enable sufficient specific risks to be identified and evaluated to achieve full marks.

When attempting the Section A question, candidates will find it useful to break down the information given in the scenario. It is also helpful to consider why specific information has been provided and how it impacts the evaluation of risk in this scenario.

Introduction to the question

The current date is 1 July 20X5 and the company's year end is September 20X5 – hence the scenario is set three months prior to the year end in this question so year-end financials are not currently available but will be available when the audit is performed after the year end.

The firm was appointed auditor in March 20X5 – therefore this is a new client. It is important to remember in reaching this position, the firm has already performed relevant client acceptance procedures, obtained professional clearance from the previous auditor, and determined that the firm has the competence and resources to provide this audit.

The audit risks arising from a new client relate to opening balances, as these were audited by a different firm in the prior year, and heightened detection risk, because the firm has less experience with and knowledge of a new client.

Discussions surrounding whether the firm is competent or assigning more experienced staff to the audit will not obtain credit as the requirement is to evaluate the audit risks not to question whether the firm should have accepted the client or to provide an audit approach to those risks.

It is important in reducing time pressure that candidates do not spend time addressing points outside the scope of the requirement.

Candidates should be alert to the risk of potential management manipulation as even though the client is not listed, existing and new shareholders will look for a return on their investment, and in the run up to the potential stock market listing, there is pressure to show strong financial performance. It is important that candidates link the risk of management bias to the specifics of the question to achieve credit. This is relevant to audit risks in part (b), yet a number of candidates make the mistake of discussing it as a business risk under part (a).

Exhibit 1 – Partner's email

In a Section A question, the partner's email will always set out the detailed requirements which are to be answered and the mark allocation. It is recommended that candidates refer to the partner's email first to ensure that they understand what they are being asked to do and the best way to allocate their time to each requirement. By reading the requirements first it is easier for candidates to then read through the rest of the information, building that holistic and relevant understanding of the issues pertinent to the question as they go.

There is a further note for candidates drawing attention to a specific instruction linked to Exhibit 4, which candidates must pay attention to. In this instance the note instructs candidates that in part (b) audit risk, they are to only discuss risk relating to the change in fair value of the timber plantation, therefore candidates that discussed other risks would not receive credit as they have been specifically excluded from the question.

Requirement (a)

This requirement indicated for candidates to evaluate the business risks to be considered in planning the audit of Pale Co.

Details relating to the business risks are given below within the details provided in relation to the exhibits.

Requirement (b)

Part (b) required candidates to evaluate the audit risks to be considered in planning the audit of Pale Co.

Details relating to audit risk are given below in the details provided in relation to the exhibits.

Exhibit 2 – Background information

In Exhibit 2 candidates are provided with an overview of the company. The relevance of each piece of information is described below:

Company operations

Background information detailing timber is processed and sold to customers with approximately 30% of timber exported – this signals a business risk that the company may be exposed to exchange rate fluctuations/volatility.

The audit firm was appointed in March 20X5 – this signals a potential audit risk due to lack of knowledge of the client and also combined with the information in the partner's email about this being the firm's first client in this specialised industry further increases the detection risk and hence audit risk.

A small internal audit team which reports to the CFO as the company does not have an audit committee – this information signals there is a lack of independence due to the lack of an audit committee which may increase control risk, therefore increases the audit risk due to increased risk of errors in the financial statements.

Exhibit 3 – Notes from meeting

In Exhibit 3 candidates are provided with a summary of business developments discussed at a recent meeting between the chief finance officer (CFO) and the audit engagement partner.

Accounting policies

This gives details of the accounting policy applied relating to the timber products. Standing timber prior to being felled are biological assets, felled trees are agricultural produce measured at fair value less costs to sell and processed timber is measured in accordance with IAS 2 *Inventories*.

The question states a technical expert has confirmed the policies are appropriate, therefore candidates that discussed these as risks did not receive credit. This was provided to give candidates guidance and support in relation to the relevant accounting treatment specified in IAS 41 *Agriculture*.

International expansion

International expansion – this signals a business risk that operations are being managed in a foreign country for the first time, therefore management oversight and controls may be difficult. Also, laws and regulations may differ therefore there is a risk of non-compliance. The question states that Farland uses the same currency therefore there is no business risk relating to foreign exchange on the purchase of the new plantation, and no credit is available.

The purchase funded through a share issue was not a related party transaction, this signalled a potential liquidity issue as the company had reached the limit of the bank borrowing and therefore a potential solvency issue.

A grant of $20 million had been issued with conditions attached. This signals a business risk of conditions being breached resulting in repayment of the grant and therefore potential liquidity issues, such as a lack of cash flow to repay the grant.

Candidates who linked the withdrawal of the grant due to legal proceedings for unethical business practice and described the risk would equally achieve credit.

This also signals an audit risk in that the grant has been incorrectly accounted for as per IAS 20 *Accounting for Government Grants and Disclosure of Governance Assistance*, as the grant should be recognised in profit or loss on a systematic basis over the periods in which the company recognises expenses for the related costs the grant is intended to compensate. The grant received has been incorrectly accounted for and should have been recognised as deferred income and therefore income is overstated, and liabilities are understated. There is also the identification of a provision for any repayment due for breaching the conditions. Several candidates made the mistake of stating assets were overstated.

Gold standard accreditation

The company had been awarded an industry gold standard accreditation. The accreditation had strict conditions attached relating to all operations including the new expansion in Farland. The company had also signed a significant contract with a new customer on the basis of the accreditation – this signals a business risk of non-compliance with the strict conditions resulting in withdrawal of the gold standard and potential loss of the new customer. A number of candidates correctly identified the risk yet went on to incorrectly identify that if the customer were lost then revenue would be incorrectly recognised, which was not relevant. Any sales made with the customer would be valid sales and would not need to be derecognised due to loss of the standard. If the customer cancelled the contract future sales would cease which would link to a business risk of revenue falling affecting overall profitability and liquidity.

Legal Case

Action was brought against the company by employees – this signals a business risk due to reputational damage and liquidity issues with the claim exceeding the current cash balance (which can be found in Exhibit 4). This also highlights poor governance within the company as management deemed it as unimportant.

An audit risk is linked to inadequate disclosure of the issue or whether a provision is required. The scenario states that the claim is in the early stages and therefore it is difficult to decide the likelihood of the outcome, yet candidates should explain the accounting rule applicable and the potential impact on the financial statements if a provision is not recognised.

For example, liabilities are understated and profit is overstated or if disclosure is not presented. Marks were also available in part (b) for materiality linked to the audit risk of the $19 million claim.

Change in valuation of the timber plantation

Storm damage resulted in a reduction in fair value of the timber plantation. A number of candidates responded in part (b) under audit risk, with details of accounting rules for impairment, yet the question stated an expert had been appointed to assess the damage and that management had determined a reduction in fair value of $70.5 million.

The issue arising is whether the $70.5 million is deemed appropriate, as to whether the expert has sufficient experience to perform a specialist valuation, and a risk that management may fail to recognise the loss in full as this would have the impact of turning the company's profit to a loss.

Candidates who proceeded to discuss procedures under part (a) or part (b) to test the independence or competence of the expert would not receive credit here, as this is failing to answer the requirement to assess the risk associated with the issue.

There was also an audit risk that other assets may have been affected by the storm and should be tested for impairment, which would result in other assets potentially being overstated if an impairment review had not been undertaken, and profit being overstated, which a significant number of candidates failed to recognise.

Generally, the responses to risk, being business risk for part (a) and audit risk for part (b) were answered well. Candidates fail to score well where there is regurgitation from the question with little development, yet candidates who identify the risk and develop the impact of the risk to either the business for part (a) or as an audit risk under part (b) can easily achieve full marks.

Exhibit 4 – Key performance information

This exhibit provides financial information which provides the source for analytical procedures to be performed. Candidates should be aware that unless a ratio, trend or calculation is discussed in the context of a risk then that calculation will not be awarded marks as it is only through this discussion that the calculation becomes relevant. Hence candidates should not spend time calculating lots of ratios and trends they will not use.

Key points to take from the financial information are as follows:

- The percentage changes for revenue, operating profit and profit before tax were all given in the question, therefore trend calculations would not be awarded for simply repeating these numbers. Some candidates identified that while profit had increased by 5.5%, profit before tax had increased by 30% which did not look consistent. This issue could indicate a risk of expenses being understated, particularly linked to the reduction in fair value not being fully recognised. Where candidates adopted this approach credit would be awarded for the discussion surrounding the potential risk.

- By performing a few simple calculations, it is apparent that the company's working capital position has deteriorated. Cash has fallen by 33.8% along with an increase in inventory of 67.4%, which is explained due to inventory held at ports as a result of industrial action leads to liquidity issues.

  There is an audit risk in that if industrial action continues, inventory which cannot be sold to customers or sold to a different customer due to any specific specifications, would require to be written down to the lower of cost and net realisable value and therefore if any necessary write down has not taken place the inventory and profit will be overstated.

Exhibit 5 – Notes from phone call

This exhibit provided candidates with notes of a discussion between the audit engagement partner and the CFO regarding a request to provide assurance on KPI's which are published as part of the annual report. Candidates were clearly directed to use this exhibit to answer requirement (d).

Requirement (c)

Generally, answers to procedure-based requirements are handled well by candidates. Detailed guidance on how to describe audit procedures can be found on the ACCA website.

The requirement was to design procedures in relation to the change in fair value of the timber plantation caused by the recent storms. The requirement stated that answers should include those relating to evaluating the expert appointed and the work they have performed in calculating the reduction in the fair value.

Generally, this requirement was well answered.

The suggested solution provides examples of typical procedures which are valid, and candidates are encouraged to review these procedures carefully to ensure they understand the source, purpose, and relevance of each procedure.

Candidates should also remember that each procedure is only worth 1 mark hence producing a list of 20 procedures for 6 marks is likely to add unnecessary time pressure in the exam.

Requirement (d)

This required candidates to explain the ethical issues arising from the phone call detailed in Exhibit 5, from the CFO.

The company publishes non-financial and environmental KPIs as part of the annual report and requested the audit firm to provide assurance on the KPIs as part of performing the audit and offered a 20% increase in the audit fee if the assurance provided was favourable.

Firstly, several candidates incorrectly discussed fee thresholds for a listed client when determining if the fee could be undertaken yet failed to recognise this was a contingent fee and is prohibited by the IESBA International Code of Ethics for Professional Accountants (the Code) and unfortunately received no marks. There were few candidates that identified the fee for assurance work could be on a contingent basis, yet it is more prudent to not undertake the basis.

Pale Co is not a listed company, as the question states it is looking to achieve listing in the next two years, therefore the work can be undertaken so long as safeguards are put in place and the fee is separate from the audit.

The ethical threats were generally well recognised, but candidates continue to score relatively low marks for ethics due to not sufficiently explaining the ethical threat linked to the scenario and the implication of the threat to the auditor and therefore lose what are potentially easy marks, especially as a large proportion of knowledge of ethics is assumed knowledge from other ACCA examinations.

Marks were available for considering other planning implications, such as competence of the auditor to perform the assurance on the KPIs due to their specialist nature and whether the firm has sufficient resources to undertake the work. It was disappointing to see candidates not consider these implications and therefore not achieve what are relatively easy marks.

Overall responses were mixed and candidates who answered the ethical issues sufficiently scored highly, yet candidates who merely identify the ethical threat with no linkage to the scenario and explanation tended to score low marks.

ACCA Marking guide		
		Marks
(a)	**Business risks** Up to 2 marks for each business risk evaluated. In addition, ½ mark for each relevant trend or calculation which form part of a relevant explanation of the risk (max 2 marks). – International expansion – Gold Standard accreditation – Legal case – Damage to assets caused by storm – Liquidity – Industrial action	
	Maximum	**8**
(b)	**Evaluation of audit risks** Up to 3 marks for each significant audit risk evaluated unless otherwise indicated. Marks may be awarded for other, relevant risks not included in the marking guide. Appropriate materiality calculations (max 2 marks) and justified materiality level should be awarded to a maximum of 1 mark. In addition, ½ mark for each relevant trend or calculation which form part of a relevant explanation of the risk (max 2 marks). – New client (up to 2 marks) – Corporate governance (up to 2 marks) – Pressure on results – Government grant (up to 4 marks) – Legal case – Change in fair value of standing trees – Inventory (up to 2 marks) – Going concern	
	Maximum	**20**
(c)	**Audit procedures** 1 mark for each well explained audit procedure, examples of which include: – Obtain the expert's report on the value of the storm-damaged timber plantation to understand methodology and overall results – Discuss the expert's methodology and assumptions with management to confirm their rationale and compliance with accounting requirements – Obtain confirmation of the expert's qualifications and experience – Obtain confirmation that the expert is independent – Visit the site of the storm damage to form a view on the scale of the destruction – Discuss with management the actions which have been taken in response to the storm – Obtain any documentation relating to the potential sale of damaged trees – From the non-current asset register, confirm the carrying amount of the standing trees prior to any change in fair value being recognised – Consider whether the use of an auditor's expert is necessary to provide sufficient and appropriate evidence given the materiality of the figures – Develop an auditor's estimate of the change in fair value and compare to management's estimate – Obtain a copy of the company's insurance policy and review the terms and conditions to confirm whether the storm damage is covered by insurance	
	Maximum	**6**

(d)	**Ethical issues**	
	1 mark for each point discussed:	
	– KPIs are 'other information' which the auditor must review for material inconsistencies	
	– Self-review threat to objectivity (additional credit to be awarded for other relevant threats to objectivity explained)	
	– Assurance can be provided on the KPIs if safeguards can reduce threat to an acceptable level	
	– Example of safeguard, e.g. separate team to perform the work, separate partner review	
	– Fee for the assurance work must be separate from the audit fee	
	– Fee for audit cannot be on a contingent basis	
	– Fee for assurance work can be on a contingent basis but more prudent if not on that basis	
	– Competence issues due to specialist nature of the work	
	– Resource issues, i.e. staff availability to perform the work	
	Maximum	**6**
	Professional marks	
	Communication	
	– Briefing note format and structure – use of headings/subheadings and an introduction	
	– Style, language and clarity – appropriate layout and tone of briefing notes, presentation of materiality and relevant calculations, appropriate use of the CBE tools, easy to follow and understand	
	– Effectiveness and clarity of communication – answer is relevant and tailored to the scenario	
	– Adherence to the specific requests made by the audit engagement partner	
	Analysis and evaluation	
	– Appropriate use of the information to determine and apply suitable calculations	
	– Appropriate use of the information to design appropriate audit procedures relating to the timber plantation	
	– Effective prioritisation of the results of the evaluation of audit risks to demonstrate the likelihood and magnitude of risks and to facilitate the allocation of appropriate responses	
	Professional scepticism and professional judgement	
	– Appropriate application of professional judgement to draw conclusions and make informed decisions following recognition of unusual or unexpected movements, missing/incomplete information or challenging presented information as part of the risk evaluation	
	– Determination and justification of a suitable materiality level, appropriately and consistently applied	
	– Identification of possible management bias and consideration of the impact on the financial statements and the possible reasons for management's preference for certain accounting treatments	
	– Effective application of technical and ethical guidance to effectively challenge and critically assess areas of significant management judgement	
	Commercial acumen	
	– Use of effective examples and/or calculations from the scenario to illustrate points or recommendations	
	– Audit procedures are practical and plausible in the context of the scenario	
	– Appropriate recognition of the wider implications when considering the request to provide assurance over the KPIs	
	Maximum	**10**
Total		**50**

6 **RICK GROUP** *Walk in the footsteps of a top tutor*

Top tutor tips

Determination of materiality: *The email from the partner states that materiality should be based on profit, therefore at the start of your answer you should calculate the range for materiality using that benchmark and justify a figure within that range. If it is a new audit client or a client where there are apparent control risks, materiality should be set at the lower end of the range. If it is an existing client, materiality may be able to be set at the higher end of the range depending on the other risks mentioned in the scenario. The examining team will give credit for any reasonable explanation of the chosen materiality threshold, as the mark is to recognise that there is the application of professional judgement and that a candidate can justify their response. It is not required that candidates select the identical percentage or figure, or that they provide a justification identical to that shown in the model answer.*

Part (a) *asks you to evaluate the audit risks to be considered when planning the audit. Audit risk comprises the risk that the financial statements contain material misstatement and detection risk. Risk of material misstatement is usually due to non-compliance with an accounting standard, although it also includes control risk. Think about the requirements of the relevant accounting standards and what the client might be doing incorrectly. Detection risks are the risks the auditor fails to detect the material misstatements within the financial statements and include auditing a client for the first time or where there is a tight reporting deadline.*

Prioritisation of risks: *One mark is awarded for the prioritisation of the audit risks. The mark is for the act of justifying the reason, not for the actual justification used (i.e. a range of completely different answers could be awarded the mark), therefore if a reasonable explanation is given, the mark will be awarded. Prioritisation can be achieved by either ordering your answer in priority order and stating this is the case, or by summarising in a brief conclusion which risk, or risks, are most significant.*

Part (b) (i) *asks for an evaluation of the component auditor's audit strategy. This is similar in approach to a requirement asking for an evaluation of the quality of the planning. Consider whether the component auditor has complied with auditing and ethical standards. Provide suggestions of additional work that will be required. Eagle part (c) contains a similar requirement.*

Part (b) (ii) *asks for audit procedures that the component auditor should perform in respect of the sale of property to the Group CEO. This is no different to a requirement asking for procedures your own audit firm should perform. The procedures should enable the auditor to obtain evidence to determine whether the relevant financial reporting standard has been complied with. Make sure your procedures are clear and provide enough detail that they can be easily followed by the audit team.*

Part (c) *requires advantages and disadvantages of joint audits. This is rote-learned knowledge from the study text and should therefore be quite straightforward. Sunshine Hotel Group requirement (e) contains a similar requirement.*

Professional skills

Professional skills will be awarded for:

Communication – responding to the instructions in the partner's email such as preparing your answers in the form of briefing notes and using the stated benchmark for materiality.

Analysis and evaluation – applying the information from the scenario to answer the question and explaining the issues in sufficient depth.

Professional scepticism and judgement – justifying an appropriate materiality level, demonstrating critical thinking and being alert to possible manipulation and management bias.

Where relevant, professional marks will be awarded for commercial acumen which requires making practical and plausible recommendations and considering the wider implications of issues to the audit firm.

Briefing notes

To: Audit engagement partner

From: Audit manager

Subject: Rick Group – Audit planning

Date: 1 July 20X5

Introduction

These briefing notes are prepared to assist with planning the audit of the Rick Group (the Group) for the financial year ending 30 September 20X5. The notes contain an evaluation of the significant audit risks, which should be considered in planning the Group audit. The notes also evaluate the audit strategy, which has been prepared by Neegan Associates for the audit of Daryl Co and recommend further audit procedures to be performed by the component auditors. Finally, the briefing notes address the issue of a potential joint audit, should a new subsidiary be acquired in Farland next year.

Materiality

For the purposes of these briefing notes, the overall materiality level used to assess the significance of identified risks is $6 million based on the profitability of the Group, as requested.

Justification

Using profit before tax of $60.1 million as a suggested benchmark results in a suggested range of $3,005,000 (5% × $60.1 million) to $6,010,000 (10% × $60.1 million).

This is an existing client, and no significant control issues have been noted at the planning stage or in previous audits. Therefore, the overall risk assessment is deemed to be low. Materiality should be set at the higher end of the range.

This benchmark is only a starting point for determining materiality and professional judgement will need to be applied in determining a final level to be used during the course of the audit.

(a) **Audit risk evaluation**

Financial analysis

Balances which are subject to judgement should be considered carefully when assessing audit risks of the Group. Licences are significant as they are intangible assets representing 74.4% of total Group assets. The audit work will need to ensure that the valuation and that of the goodwill of Daryl Co, which has seen significant trading issues during the year.

The financial information shows that total revenue is projected to increase by 25.6% this financial year. This is a significant increase and it could indicate that revenue is overstated. However, the number of subscription members is projected to increase by 30.1%, so possibly the increase in revenue is simply as a result of the Group attracting more customers – but this is a very significant increase and will need to be substantiated.

The audit risks for these areas are considered further in these briefing notes.

Reliance on component auditors

Daryl Co's assets represent 17.9% of the Group's total projected assets. Given the materiality of Daryl Co, the Group audit team needs to consider the extent of reliance which can be placed on the audit of the company conducted by Neegan Associates.

The independence and competence of Neegan Associates will need to be evaluated by the Group audit team, though presumably as the audit firm already has experience of Neegan Associates from previous years' audits, this evaluation will already have been performed. However, independence is threatened by the fact that Neegan Associates has been engaged in providing a non-audit service to Daryl Co since 1 October 20X4. This matter is discussed further in the section of the briefing notes dealing with the component auditor's strategy. Any material misstatements which may remain uncorrected in Daryl Co will impact on the consolidated financial statements, leading to audit risk at the Group level.

Daryl Co – possible impairment

The goodwill in relation to Daryl Co is material to the Group financial statements based on the threshold of $6 million.

According to IAS 36 *Impairment of Assets*, goodwill should be tested for impairment annually, which is the Group's accounting policy. The audit strategy prepared by Neegan Associates indicates that Daryl Co is loss making this year, which is an indication of impairment. Therefore, management will need to factor this into their impairment review.

As the Group's performance in the past has been strong, no goodwill impairment has been recognised, and management may lack experience in dealing with a loss-making subsidiary as part of their impairment testing.

For these reasons, there is an audit risk that goodwill could be overstated, and expenses understated, if any necessary impairment loss is not correctly determined and recognised.

Trend in revenue

The financial information shows that total revenue is projected to increase by 25.6% this financial year.

However, when looking at revenue per customer per year, this is projected to fall from $96.65 in 20X4 to $93.33 in 20X5. Revenue per customer per month is therefore projected to fall from $8.05 in 20X4 to $7.78 in 20X5. These trends seem to contradict the introduction of the new premium subscription package, which should bring in additional revenue per customer.

Possibly the premium subscription has not been taken up by many customers. It is, however, unusual to see a downwards trend in revenue per customer per month, given that the price of a regular subscription has remained the same as in the previous year, at $8.20 per month. Possibly the figures are impacted by the free trial period offered to new customers. These trends will need to be investigated to ensure that revenue is being measured appropriately and recognised at the correct point in time.

There is also a risk arising from the Group invoicing customers in advance, with revenue recognised when the bill is sent to the customer. Possibly this could lead to early recognition of revenue, i.e. recognising prior to the Group providing a service to its customers.

IFRS 15 *Revenue from Contracts with Customers* requires that revenue is recognised when a performance obligation is satisfied by transferring a promised good or service to a customer, and when providing a service over time, it can be difficult to determine how much service has been provided and therefore the amount of revenue which can be recognised at a particular point in time. There is therefore a risk of overstatement of revenue if the requirements of IFRS 15 are not adhered to.

Amortisation of licences

The licences recognised as intangible assets are highly material to the Group. Given that each licence is for a fixed period, it is appropriate to amortise the cost of each licence over that fixed period in accordance with IAS 38 *Intangible Assets*, which requires that the cost of an intangible asset with a finite useful life should be amortised on a systematic basis over its life.

Therefore, the Group's accounting policy to amortise all licences over a five-year period may be too simplistic, especially given the significance of the balance to the Group financial statements. Some of the licences have a shorter life, and some may be longer, indicating that the determination of amortisation for the class of assets as a whole may not be accurate, leading to over or undervaluation of intangible assets and over or understatement of profit.

The finance director's assertion that the accounting policy is 'the most prudent' is not appropriate. The accounting policy should be based on the specific, relevant IAS 38 requirements. It could be a means of earnings management, i.e. to minimise the amortisation charge and maximise profits.

The auditor should also consider whether this issue has arisen in previous years' audits. The Group may have changed its estimation technique with regard to amortisation of intangible assets. If this is the case, the rationale for the change must be understood.

Legal case

In January 20X5, a legal case was brought against the Group. From the information provided, it is not possible to determine if it is material, however, there should be appropriate consideration as to whether the court case gives rise to an obligation at the reporting date.

According to IAS 37 *Provisions, Contingent Liabilities and Contingent Assets*, a provision should be recognised as a liability if there is a present obligation as a result of past events which gives rise to a probable outflow of economic benefit which can be reliably measured. There is therefore an audit risk that if any necessary provision is not recognised, liabilities and expenses will be understated.

If there is a possible obligation at the reporting date, then disclosure of the contingent liability should be made in the notes to the financial statements. There is a risk of inadequate disclosure if the Group finance director refuses to make appropriate disclosure in the notes – this is an audit risk whether the situation gives rise to a provision or a contingent liability, as provisions also have disclosure requirements which may not be complied with.

Group finance director's attitude

There may be a further issue related to the legal case regarding the attitude of the Group finance director, who appears to have dismissed the accounting implications of the legal case and is reluctant to discuss the matter with the audit team. This could indicate that the Group finance director is deliberately obstructing the work of the audit team, and perhaps has something to hide. This indicates a potential wider issue, that the Group finance director is imposing a limitation on the scope of the audit. The Group audit strategy should consider this issue, and the audit engagement partner may wish to discuss the issue with the Group audit committee as a matter of urgency.

This increases the risk that the legal claim will not be recognised appropriately in the financial statements, and the audit team must approach this issue with a heightened degree of professional scepticism.

There may be other areas in which professional scepticism should be applied, for instance, in respect of the amortisation of intangible assets, which will be discussed later in the briefing notes, and where the Group finance director appears to be using inappropriate justifications for the Group's accounting treatment of licence fees.

Daryl Co – local accounting rules

This company is the only component of the Group which does not use IFRS Accounting Standards as its financial reporting framework. Daryl Co's financial statements will be prepared under local accounting rules and audited by Neegan Associates on that basis. In accordance with IFRS 3 *Business Combinations*, for the purpose of consolidation the Group's accounting policies must be applied to all balances and transactions which form part of the consolidated financial statements. There is an audit risk that the Group's policies are not applied correctly, meaning that the amounts consolidated in respect of Daryl Co are not recognised, measured or disclosed appropriately.

Post-year-end acquisition of Michonne Co

The acquisition of Michonne Co is planned to take place within a month of the reporting date. It is therefore a significant event which is taking place after the year end and as such, it falls under the scope of IAS 10 *Events After the Reporting Period*.

According to IAS 10, a non-adjusting event is an event which is indicative of a condition which arose after the end of the reporting period, and which should be disclosed if they are of such importance that non-disclosure would affect the ability of users to make proper evaluations and decisions. The required disclosure includes the nature of the event and an estimate of its financial effect or a statement that a reasonable estimate of the effect cannot be made.

In addition, IFRS 3 requires disclosure of information about a business combination whose acquisition date is after the end of the reporting period but before the financial statements are authorised for issue.

There is therefore an audit risk that the disclosure in relation to the acquisition of Michonne Co is not complete or accurate.

(b)   (i)   Evaluation of component auditor's audit strategy

Audit of payroll

The audit work planned on payroll appears to be limited due to the audit firm, Neegan Associates, having performed a payroll service for Daryl Co since 1 October 20X4. This is not appropriate and will not provide sufficient and appropriate audit evidence regarding the $6 million payroll expense. Given that payroll is material to the company's financial statements, based on Neegan Associates' own materiality threshold of $1.4 million, further testing will be required.

An ethical threat to auditor's independence is raised by the provision of the payroll service to the client. There is a significant self-review threat which means that Neegan Associates is over-relying on the work they have performed on payroll as a non-audit engagement and are not planning to audit the $6 million at all.

Providing this type of non-audit service might be allowed in the jurisdiction where Neegan Associates operates. However, according to ISA 600/ISA (UK) 600 *Special Considerations – Audits of Group Financial Statements (Including the Work of Component Auditors)*, when performing work on the financial information of a component for a group audit, the component auditor is subject to ethical requirements which are relevant to the group audit. Such requirements may be different or in addition to those applying to the component auditor when performing a statutory audit in the component auditor's jurisdiction.

Therefore, the IESBA International Code of Ethics for Professional Accountants (the Code)/FRC Ethical Standard should be applied. This states that for a listed company, a firm shall not provide accounting or bookkeeping services, including payroll services, which results in financial information which forms the basis of financial statements on which the firm will provide an opinion. Therefore, as Daryl Co is listed, the service should not have been provided.

There also needs to be discussion of the situation with Neegan Associates and the management of Daryl Co and the Group, with the objective of ensuring that an alternative provider is found for the payroll accounting services.

Sale of property

In the individual financial statements of Daryl Co, under local accounting rules the sale of property to the Group chief executive officer (CEO) does not need to be disclosed. However, from the Group perspective, it meets the definition of a related party transaction under IAS 24 *Related Party Disclosures*, and will need to be disclosed in the consolidated financial statements.

As the transaction would also be considered to be material by nature, the Group audit team must therefore provide instructions to Neegan Associates on the additional audit work to be performed which will enable sufficient and appropriate evidence to be obtained in respect of the transaction and disclosure. These procedures will be outlined in the next section of these briefing notes.

The cash proceeds arising on the sale of the property are well below the materiality level determined by Neegan Associates, so this might justify the minimal audit procedures which have been planned in relation to the individual financial statements. However, the procedures do not consider how the profit or loss being made on the disposal is determined or whether the asset has been properly removed from the accounting records. The carrying amount of the asset itself may be material to the financial statements of the company.

There may be an incentive to recognise a higher profit than is appropriate on this transaction due to trading difficulties encountered by the company during the year, so the transaction may be at risk of material misstatement with the objective of maximising the profit recognised.

There is no evidence that the transaction is bona fide – the CEO has not yet paid for the property and the whole transaction could be an attempt to window dress the financial statements. Overall, this evaluation has indicated that there are problems in how Neegan Associates has planned the audit of Daryl Co. The audit work which is planned will not provide sufficient, appropriate audit evidence in relation to the issues identified.

Therefore, the Group audit team will need to consider the overall planning of the audit of Daryl Co and the level of testing they subsequently request that Neegan Associates carries out to satisfy themselves of the accuracy of the figures presented in Daryl Co's financial statements for inclusion in the consolidated financial statements.

(ii)   **Audit procedures on sale of property**

–   Review board minutes to see if the property sale has been deliberated, i.e. has the rationale for the transaction been discussed, and formally approved by the company's board.

–   Agree the $50,000 sale price to the legal documentation relating to the sale of the property to the Group CEO.

–   Confirm the carrying amount of the property at the date of disposal to underlying accounting records and the non-current asset register.

–   Confirm that the asset has been removed from the company accounts at the date of disposal.

–   Obtain management's determination of profit or loss on disposal, reperform the calculation based on supporting evidence, and agree the profit or loss is recognised appropriately in the company statement of profit or loss.

–   Obtain an estimate of the fair value of the property, for example, by comparison to the current market price of similar properties and consider the reasonableness of the transaction and sale price.

–   Obtain written representations from company management that all matters related to this related party transaction have been disclosed to the Group management and to the Group audit team.

–   Obtain written representation from the Group CEO regarding the transaction, to confirm the amount which is outstanding, and the likely timescale for payment.

–   Review cash receipts after the reporting date to confirm whether or not the $50,000 has been received from the Group CEO.

(c)   Discussion and justification for a joint audit of Michonne Co

In a joint audit, two or more audit firms are responsible for conducting the audit and for issuing the audit opinion. The main advantage of a joint audit of Michonne Co is that the local audit firm's understanding and experience will be retained, and that will be a valuable input to the audit. At the same time, Atlanta & Co can provide additional skills and resources if necessary.

Farland may have different regulations to the rest of the Group, for example, there may be a different financial reporting framework. It therefore makes sense for Lucille Associates, the local auditors, to retain some input to the audit as they will have detailed knowledge of such regulations.

The fact that the company is located in a distant location means that from a practical point of view it may be difficult for Atlanta & Co to provide staff to perform the majority of the audit work. It will be more cost effective for this to be carried out by local auditors.

Two audit firms can also stand together against aggressive accounting treatments. In this way, a joint audit can enhance the quality of the audit. The benchmarking which takes place between the two firms raises the level of service quality.

Disadvantages of a joint audit of Michonne Co

The main disadvantage is that for the Group, having a joint audit is likely to be more expensive than appointing just one audit firm. However, the costs are likely to be less than if Atlanta & Co took sole responsibility, as having the current auditors retain an involvement will at least cut down on travel expenses. Due to the size of the respective firms, Lucille Associates will probably offer a cheaper audit service than Atlanta & Co.

For the audit firms, there may be problems in deciding on responsibilities, allocating work, and they will need to work very closely together to ensure that no duties go underperformed, and that the quality of the audit is maintained. There is a risk that the two firms will not agree on a range of matters, for example, audit methodology, resources needed and review procedures, which would make the working relationship difficult to manage.

Problems could arise in terms of liability because both firms have provided the audit opinion; in the event of litigation, both firms would be jointly liable. While both of the firms would be insured, they could blame each other for any negligence which was discovered, making the litigation process more complex than if a single audit firm had provided the audit opinion.

Recommendation

On balance, the merits of performing a joint audit outweigh the possible disadvantages, especially if the two audit firms can agree on the division of work and pool their expertise and resources to provide a high-quality audit.

Conclusion

The briefing notes indicate that there are several significant audit risks to be addressed. The most significant risks relate to the subsidiary of Daryl Co as this represents a significant proportion of the group financial statements and there is doubt over the quality of the audit work performed by the component auditor. In addition, the accounting treatment in respect of the legal claim is another significant risk due to the reluctance by the finance director to provide details about the nature or size of the claim. In respect of the component audit firm, there are some concerns over the adequacy of their audit planning, which will need further consideration in developing the Group audit strategy. Finally, performing a joint audit on Michonne Co appears to be a good way to perform a high-quality audit on this new subsidiary.

Examiner's comments

This question was a compulsory 50-mark case study consisting of four parts and focused on the planning phase of the group audit of an existing client. The group was a listed entity and offered a subscription-based internet streaming service for films and TV programmes.

It should be noted that only a brief introduction is required, and time should not be spent writing a half-page introduction or a lengthy conclusion. For a structured, well presented answer, simple headed paragraphs are enough. Candidates need not be concerned with spending time underlining or numbering headings, so long as it is clear which question is being attempted.

Requirement (a) asked candidates to evaluate the audit risks arising from the scenario in the question. The group was a listed entity and a subscription-based internet provider of films and TV programmes. Candidates generally performed well on this section of the question, yet it was disappointing to see candidates focus on what appeared to be rote learnt risks and points which were not relevant to the question.

A number of candidates discussed the risk of the foreign subsidiaries having different year ends to the group, yet the question clearly stated all companies within the group had the same year end, and no marks were awarded. General consolidation risks, intra-group eliminations, disclosures required for listed entities were all deemed speculative risks and did not receive credit. There was no evidence within the question that the group companies traded with each other or that the group was recently listed and therefore may not adhere to stock market listing requirements or corporate governance requirements, for example. Candidates are advised to use the detail of the specific scenario given and discuss the risks accordingly to demonstrate application of audit knowledge to a given scenario.

A further area that demonstrated a lack of application to the scenario surrounded the impairment of goodwill performed by the group on an annual basis. A number of candidates discussed the general treatment of goodwill, that it is to be tested for impairment on an annual basis and that management had not tested impairment and therefore concluding on the financial statement impact that goodwill would be overstated. The question clearly referred to the group correctly performing the annual impairment review but had not recognised impairment due to strong performance. The key issue here was the indicator of impairment within the foreign subsidiary and the impact this would have on the impairment review performed.

Some other common issues noted in candidate answers for Audit Risk included:

- Discussing audit procedures to be performed which did not meet the question requirement and therefore no credit was awarded. If required, this will normally form a separate requirement within the question and should be answered where applicable.

- Several candidates appear to only possess a brief overview of the accounting standards without sufficient knowledge of the underlying principles. It is disappointing to see, for example, the accounting rule for IAS 37 *Provisions, Contingent Liabilities and Contingent Assets* not described sufficiently considering it is one of the easier accounting standards for candidates to apply.

Overall, candidates would be advised to read the requirement carefully to ensure the answer given is relevant and not too generic to avoid losing marks that would be easily achievable.

Candidates that demonstrated good technique in calculating materiality, identifying the audit risk in the scenario, discussing the relevant accounting treatment and finally the impact the error will have on the financial statements scored well.

Requirement (b) (i) asked candidates to evaluate an extract from the component auditor's strategy for three issues and to also comment on the ethical issues arising from the issues identified.

Generally, the responses to the evaluation of the component auditor's strategy were disappointing. The question stated that **only** the points within the extract were to be reviewed and that other sections of the strategy, including risk assessment had been reviewed already by the group audit team and considered satisfactory. A number of candidates continued to comment that due to the lack of other detail, the component auditors were not competent and should not be relied upon.

The question was testing the candidates' knowledge of understanding the difference between the component audit for the individual subsidiary financial statements compared to that of the group. There is a significant gap in candidates' learning relating to this.

A number of candidates showed a lack of understanding regarding materiality, and stated that materiality thresholds are stated within the ISA (International Standards of Auditing), when this is not correct as there are no set rules as to how the level of materiality should be arrived at, rather a percentage is applied to a chosen benchmark as a starting point. Many candidates did not mention the importance of auditor judgement in relation to materiality. Where candidates referred to the auditor being in breach of the auditing standard in the calculation of materiality, marks could not be awarded without further development.

A number of candidates were unable to appreciate the difference between the component financial statements and the group financial statements. A number of candidates referred to the related party transaction to the group CEO requiring disclosure in the notes to the financial statements. The key issue here is that the related party transaction is required to be disclosed in the consolidated financial statements from the group perspective and therefore needed to be specifically addressed as part of the group audit.

Requirement (b) (ii) asked candidates to design the principal audit procedures which would be instructed to the component auditor to perform on the sale of the property to the Group CEO. Overall candidates scored well here, yet there were instances that were disappointing to note such as significant numbers suggesting procedures to check physical existence of the property (that had been sold before the year end), or to verify the asset was remaining in the asset register, again despite the asset being sold to the CEO prior to the year end.

Candidates that applied good technique to procedures questions, such as stating what procedure they would perform along with the purpose of the procedures will score well.

Requirement (c) asked candidates to discuss the appropriateness of a joint audit in relation to a planned acquisition of a new foreign subsidiary and to state advantages and disadvantages of a joint audit. This requirement should have scored well, as it was an easier requirement and was answered well by students who had learnt the topic area. However, a number of students appeared to confuse a joint audit with a group and component audit situations and therefore marks would not be awarded for discussions of discussing competence of the component auditor and ethical requirements as these were not relevant to the requirement.

	ACCA Marking guide	Marks
(a)	**Audit risk evaluation**	
	Up to 3 marks for each significant audit risk evaluated (unless indicated otherwise). Marks may be awarded for other, relevant audit risks not included in the marking guide.	
	In addition, ½ mark for relevant trends or calculations which form part of the evaluation of audit risk (max 3 marks).	
	Appropriate materiality calculations (max 2 marks) and justified materiality level should be awarded to a maximum of 1 mark.	
	– Analytical review	
	– Reliance on component auditor (2 marks)	
	– Daryl Co – possible impairment	
	– Trends in revenue and revenue recognition (2 marks)	
	– Amortisation of licences	
	– Legal case	
	– Group finance director's attitude (2 marks)	
	– Daryl Co – local accounting rules (2 marks)	
	– Post-year-end acquisition of Michonne Co	
	Maximum	21
(b) (i)	**Evaluation of Neegan Associates' audit strategy**	
	Up to 1 mark for each issue evaluated:	
	Payroll	
	– Further procedures necessary given the materiality of the payroll	
	– Requirement of ISA 600 that same ethical guidelines should be applied	
	– Self-review threat from Neegan Associates providing the service – explained	
	– The service should not have been provided due to Daryl Co's listed status	

Sale of property

– Transaction should be disclosed in Group accounts and is material by nature
– No consideration of whether the profit on disposal has been properly determined
– Risk that the transaction is subject to bias given that company is loss making
– Property might not even have been sold, could be window dressing
– No procedures to confirm asset has been removed from the financial statements or on the recoverability of the amount outstanding
– Conclusion on audit quality

Maximum	7

(ii) **Audit procedures on sale of property**

– Review board minutes to see if the property sale has been discussed and formally approved by the company's board
– Agree the $50,000 sale price to the legal documentation relating to the sale of the property to the Group CEO
– Confirm the book value of the property at the date of disposal to underlying accounting records and non-current asset register
– Confirm that the asset has been removed from the company accounts at the date of disposal
– Obtain management's determination of profit or loss on disposal, reperform the calculation based on supporting evidence, and agree the profit or loss is recognised appropriately in the company statement of profit or loss
– Obtain an estimate of the fair value of the property, for example, by comparison to the current market price of similar properties
– Obtain written representations from company management that all matters related to this related party transaction have been disclosed to the Group management and to the Group audit team
– Obtain written representation from the Group CEO regarding the transaction, to confirm the amount which is outstanding, and the likely timescale for payment
– Review cash receipts after the reporting date to confirm whether or not the $50,000 has been received from the Group CEO

Maximum	6

(c) **Joint audit**

Up to 1 mark for each relevant point discussed:

Justification in favour of joint audit

– Retain local auditors' knowledge of company
– Local auditors' knowledge of local regulations
– Atlanta & Co can provide additional skills and resources
– Cost effective – reduce travel expenses, local firm likely to be cheaper
– Enhanced audit quality

Possible disadvantages of joint audit

– Employing two audit firms could be more expensive
– Problems in allocating work and determining responsibilities
– Auditor liability issues
– Recommendation

Maximum	6

Professional marks

Communication

- Briefing note format and structure – use of headings/subheadings and an introduction
- Style, language and clarity – appropriate layout and tone of briefing notes, presentation of materiality and relevant calculations, appropriate use of the CBE tools, easy to follow and understand
- Effectiveness and clarity of communication – answer is relevant and tailored to the scenario
- Adherence to the specific requests made by the audit engagement partner

Analysis and evaluation

- Appropriate use of the information to determine and apply suitable calculations
- Appropriate use of the information relating to the sale of the property to design appropriate audit procedures
- Effective prioritisation of the results of the audit risk evaluation to demonstrate the likelihood and magnitude of risks and to facilitate the allocation of appropriate responses
- Balanced discussion of the professional and practical issues when evaluating working with component auditors in a Group engagement

Professional scepticism and professional judgement

- Appropriate application of professional judgement to draw conclusions and make informed decisions following recognition of unusual or unexpected movements, missing/incomplete information or challenging presented information as part of the risk evaluation
- Determination and justification of a suitable materiality level, appropriately and consistently applied
- Identification of possible management bias and consideration of the impact on the financial statements and the possible reasons for management's preference for certain accounting treatments
- Effective application of technical and ethical guidance to effectively challenge and critically assess how management has responded to the legal claim and the adequacy of any provision or disclosure requirements

Commercial acumen

- Use of effective examples and/or calculations from the scenario to illustrate points or recommendations
- Audit procedures are practical and plausible in the context of the scenario
- Appropriate recognition of the wider implications when considering entering into a joint audit engagement

Maximum	10
Total	50

7   RYDER GROUP *Walk in the footsteps of a top tutor*

Top tutor tips

Determination of materiality: The email from the partner states that materiality should be based on profit, therefore at the start of your answer you should calculate the range for materiality using that benchmark and justify a figure within that range. If it is a new audit client or a client where there are apparent control risks, materiality should be set at the lower end of the range. If it is an existing client, materiality may be able to be set at the higher end of the range depending on the other risks mentioned in the scenario. The examining team will give credit for any reasonable explanation of the chosen materiality threshold, as the mark is to recognise that there is the application of professional judgement and that a candidate can justify their response. It is not required that candidates select the identical percentage or figure, or that they provide a justification identical to that shown in the model answer.

Part (a) asks you to evaluate the audit risks to be considered when planning the audit. Audit risk comprises the risk that the financial statements contain material misstatement and detection risk. Risk of material misstatement is usually due to non-compliance with an accounting standard, although it also includes control risk. Think about the requirements of the relevant accounting standards and what the client might be doing incorrectly. Detection risks are the risks the auditor fails to detect the material misstatements within the financial statements and include auditing a client for the first time or where there is a tight reporting deadline. The requirement specifically instructs you to consider risks relating to disclosure, therefore make sure you include these.

Prioritisation of risks: One mark is awarded for the prioritisation of the audit risks. The mark is for the act of justifying the reason, not for the actual justification used (i.e. a range of completely different answers could be awarded the mark), therefore if a reasonable explanation is given, the mark will be awarded. Prioritisation can be achieved by either ordering your answer in priority order and stating this is the case, or by summarising in a brief conclusion which risk, or risks, are most significant.

Part (b) asks for additional information to effectively audit the disposal of a subsidiary. Think about how the disposal should be accounted for and therefore what information you will need to confirm the client has accounted for it in accordance with the applicable financial reporting framework.

Part (c) asks for audit procedures in respect of the investment in Peppers Co and the government grant. The procedures should enable the auditor to obtain evidence to determine whether the relevant financial reporting standard has been complied with. Make sure your procedures are clear and provide enough detail that they can be easily followed by the audit team.

Part (d) covers ethical considerations of providing a listed audit client with an additional service to design internal controls over a revenue system. In addition, the ethical considerations of referring a client to another firm in return for a referral fee need to be discussed. For each issue, explain the ethical threat arising and state the actions the firm should take to manage or eliminate the threats. Where possible, discuss the significance of the threat.

KAPLAN PUBLISHING

Professional skills

Professional skills will be awarded for:

Communication – responding to the instructions in the partner's email such as preparing your answers in the form of briefing notes and using the stated benchmark for materiality.

Analysis and evaluation – applying the information from the scenario to answer the question and explaining the issues in sufficient depth.

Professional scepticism and judgement – justifying an appropriate materiality level, demonstrating critical thinking and being alert to possible manipulation and management bias.

Where relevant, professional marks will be awarded for commercial acumen which requires making practical and plausible recommendations and considering the wider implications of issues to the audit firm.

Briefing notes

To: Mo Iqbal, audit engagement partner

From: Audit manager

Subject: Audit planning in relation to the Ryder Group

Date: 1 July 20X5

Introduction

These briefing notes have been prepared to assist in planning the audit of the Ryder Group (the Group). The notes begin with an evaluation of the significant audit risks which should be considered in planning the audit. The notes then identify and explain the additional information required to plan the audit of a significant disposal which is expected to take place shortly after the financial year end. The notes also include the recommended principal audit procedures which have been designed in respect of an investment made in a joint arrangement and a government grant received in the year. Finally, the notes discuss ethical matters arising from requests made by the Group audit committee.

Materiality

For the purposes of these briefing notes, the overall materiality level used to assess the significance of identified risks is $1.5 million based on the profitability of the Group, as requested.

Justification

Using profit before tax of $20 million as a suggested benchmark results in a suggested range of $1 million (5% × $20 million) to $2 million (10% × $20 million).

This is an existing client, and no significant control issues have been noted at the planning stage or in previous audits, however, the group restructuring increases audit risk compared with previous years giving a medium level of risk overall. Materiality should be set at the midpoint of the range.

This benchmark is only a starting point for determining materiality and professional judgement will need to be applied in determining a final level to be used during the course of the audit.

(a)   **Evaluation of significant audit risks**

Planned disposal of Primal Burgers Co and acquisition of Valentine Co – events after the reporting date

The Group is planning a significant restructuring. The disposal of Primal Burgers Co is planned to take place shortly after the year end, and the disposal will have a material impact on the Group financial statements given that Primal Burgers Co accounts for 23.2% of projected Group total assets and 30.9% of projected Group revenue.

The acquisition of Valentine Co, which is planned to take place in the first quarter of the next financial year, will be material to the Group, with the anticipated cost of investment and the fair value of identifiable net assets of Valentine Co representing 21.1% and 17.9% of projected Group assets respectively.

Both events will fall under the scope of IAS 10 *Events After the Reporting Period*, meeting the definition of a non-adjusting event. IAS 10 requires that non-adjusting events should be disclosed if they are of such importance that non-disclosure would affect the ability of users to make proper evaluations and decisions.

The required disclosure is the nature of the event and an estimate of its financial effect or a statement that a reasonable estimate of the effect cannot be made. The audit risk is that incomplete or inaccurate disclosure relating to the acquisition and disposal is provided in the notes to the financial statements.

Disposal of Primal Burgers Co – assets held for sale and discontinued operations

The planned disposal should be accounted for under IFRS 5 *Non-current Assets Held for Sale and Discontinued Operations*, which requires that once certain conditions are met, a disposal group of assets should be classified as held for sale. The conditions include:

- management is committed to a plan to sell

- the asset is available for immediate sale

- an active programme to locate a buyer is initiated

- the sale is highly probable, within 12 months of classification as held for sale

- the asset is being actively marketed for sale at a sales price reasonable in relation to its fair value

- actions required to complete the plan indicate that it is unlikely that plan will be significantly changed or withdrawn.

Assuming that the conditions are met, which seems likely given that the board approved the sale in March 20X5 and that potential purchasers have already expressed an interest, the assets held in the disposal group should be reclassified as assets held for sale and measured at the lower of carrying amount and fair value less costs to sell. The assets should not be depreciated after reclassification.

IFRS 5 also requires that immediately prior to classifying an asset or disposal group as held for sale, impairment is measured and recognised in accordance with the applicable IFRS Accounting Standards, which in this case would be IAS 16 *Property, Plant and Equipment* and IAS 36 *Impairment of Assets.*

Several audit risks arise as a result of the disposal. First there is a risk that the assets are not treated as a disposal group for the purpose of IFRS 5 and have continued to be depreciated. Assets are possibly overvalued if an impairment review has not been performed or assets not measured at the lower of carrying amount and fair value less costs to sell. The fact that Primal Burgers Co's revenue is projected to fall by 3.9% indicates that impairment of assets could be an issue, increasing the risk of misstatement.

There is also a risk relating to disclosure, as assets and liabilities held for sale should be recognised separately from other assets and liabilities in the statement of financial position, and if they have not been appropriately reclassified, then non-current assets and liabilities will be overstated.

There is also an audit risk that Primal Burgers Co is not treated as a discontinued operation in accordance with IFRS 5. A discontinued operation is defined as a component of an entity which either has been disposed of or is classified as held for sale, and represents a separate major line of business or a geographical area of operations and is part of a single co-ordinated plan to dispose of a separate major line of business or geographical area of operations.

Given the materiality of Primal Burgers Co and its products being a separate line of business for the Group, it meets the definition of a discontinued operation. In accordance with IFRS 5, the post-tax profit or loss of the discontinued operation and the post-tax gain or loss recognised on the measurement to fair value less cost to sell or on the disposal of the disposal group should be presented as a single amount on the face of the statement of comprehensive income.

In addition, detailed disclosure of revenue, expenses, pre-tax profit or loss and related income taxes is required either in the notes or in the statement of comprehensive income in a section distinct from continuing operations. The risk is that the necessary disclosures are not made, leading to incorrect presentation of Group profit or loss and incomplete information in the notes to the Group financial statements.

Disposal of Primal Burgers Co – potential for manipulation

A further audit risk relating to the disposal of Primal Burgers Co is that the results of the subsidiary could be manipulated to make it look more favourable to any potential purchaser. The financial information indicates that this subsidiary's revenue has declined and therefore it could be that management attempts to manipulate the financial statements to present a healthier financial performance to potential buyers. For example, costs could be suppressed or shifted to other Group companies to maintain the profit of Primal Burgers Co and make it more attractive to purchasers.

Tutorial note

Credit will be awarded for the evaluation of other relevant audit risks relating to the disposal, for example, in relation to the presentation of information in the Group statement of cash flows.

Investment in Peppers Co

The Group will be investing $48 million in Peppers Co which is material to the Group financial statements based on the threshold of $1.5 million.

From the information provided, it seems that the investment is a joint venture, with control of Peppers Co shared between the Group and Smiths Co. IFRS 11 *Joint Arrangements* defines a joint venture as a joint arrangement whereby the parties who have joint control of the arrangement have rights to the net assets of the arrangement.

IFRS 11 requires that a joint venturer recognises its interest in a joint venture as an investment and shall account for that investment using the equity method in accordance with IAS 28 *Investments in Associates and Joint Ventures*. Audit risk arises if the Group fails to apply equity accounting to the investment, which may lead to an under or overstated value of investment and incorrect presentation of income and expenses relating to the joint venture in the Group statement of profit or loss.

Mondays Coffee drive-through –asset (capital) expenditure

During the year, there has been significant expenditure relating to 50 new drive-through coffee shops. The total amount capitalised is $43 million, of which $15 million relates to acquiring operating licences. The audit risk relates to the classification of the licences within property, plant and equipment, they should instead be recognised as intangible assets.

This error is material based on the threshold of $1.5 million. If the error is uncorrected, property, plant and equipment is overstated and intangible assets are understated.

A consequence of the misclassification is that the $15 million should be amortised over its specific useful life of three years, so assuming that a full year's worth of amortisation should have been expensed, this amounts to $5 million. Currently, the amount has been treated as property, plant and equipment and depreciated over a 20-year life, so $0.75 million has been expensed. Therefore, expenses are understated by $4.25 million which is material. There is therefore an audit risk that Group profit is significantly overstated.

Tutorial note

Credit will be awarded for the evaluation of other relevant audit risks, for example, including expenditure incurred in establishing the coffee shops is not appropriately classified between assets and expenses, and that a 20-year estimated life appears long given the nature and usage of the assets involved.

Mondays Coffee drive-through – reportable operating segment

According to the Group finance director, revenue from the new drive-through coffee shops accounts for almost all of the increase in revenue from Mondays Coffee Co. The financial information shows that Mondays Coffee Co revenue is projected to increase by $45 million this year. Total Group revenue is projected to be $320 million; $45 million is 14.1% of this total.

The revenue from the drive-through coffee shops could be a reportable operating segment under IFRS 8 *Operating Segments*.

An operating segment is a component of an entity:

- which engages in business activities from which it may earn revenues and incur expenses

- whose operating results are reviewed regularly by the entity's chief operating decision maker to make decisions about resources to be allocated to the segment and assess its performance, and

- for which discrete financial information is available.

IFRS 8 requires an entity to report financial and descriptive information about its reportable segments. Reportable segments are operating segments or aggregations of operating segments which meet specified criteria, including that its reported revenue is 10% or more of the combined revenue of all operating segments.

It seems that the drive-through coffee shops should be treated as a reportable segment given that discrete information is available through the Group's management information system, the results are reviewed, and it generates more than 10% of Group revenue. The audit risk is that disclosure is not provided at all in relation to this reportable segment, or that disclosure is incomplete in the final version of the financial statements.

Tutorial note

Credit will also be awarded for evaluation of the significance of the increase in revenue from the new drive-through coffee shops, and whether this could indicate overstatement of revenue. Other relevant audit risks will be credited, for example, relating to possible system changes introduced to incorporate the drive-through coffee shops in the financial reporting system.

Government grant

The Group received a government grant of $20 million which is material to the Group statement of financial position based on the threshold of $1.5 million. In addition, if the $20 million grant receipt had not been recognised in full as income this financial year, the projected Group profit before tax would be $0. The recognition as income is therefore extremely significant to the Group financial statements.

The grant should be accounted for in accordance with IAS 20 *Accounting for Government Grants and Disclosure of Government Assistance* which requires government grants to be recognised in profit or loss on a systematic basis over the periods in which the entity recognises as expenses the related costs for which the grants are intended to compensate.

The two parts of the grant should be accounted for separately. The amount relating to asset (capital) expenditure should be deferred on the statement of financial position and assuming that the grant will be used to upgrade items of property, plant and equipment, the grant should then be recognised in profit or loss over the periods in which depreciation expense on the assets to which it relates is recognised.

The part of the grant relating to promotional activity should be recognised in profit or loss in the same period as the relevant expenses – which may be this year, or could be the next financial year, depending on when the expenses relating to the advertising campaign are incurred.

It is likely that if funds are not used in the manner intended by the government, i.e. that half of it is used to make the assets more environmentally friendly, then some or all of the grant would be repayable. This would mean that a provision or contingent liability should be recognised/disclosed, and there is an audit risk that liabilities are understated if any amount probable to be repaid is not accounted for as a provision, or that insufficient disclosure is made in the note to the financial statements if a contingent liability arises.

Therefore, the audit risk is that Group profit is overstated by a maximum amount of $20 million, and liabilities understated by the same amount. The accounting treatment could be a deliberate attempt to enhance the appearance of the Group profit for the year, and this issue should be approached with a high degree of professional scepticism during the audit.

(b) **Additional information required to plan the audit of the disposal of Primal Burgers Co**

- The individual financial statements of Primal Burgers Co, to ascertain the detail of the amounts recognised – this will assist the audit team in planning to audit the compliance with measurement and disclosure requirements of IFRS 5 and to confirm materiality of the balances involved.

- A copy of the vendor's due diligence report produced by Usami & Co, to ascertain key findings, e.g. valuations of assets and liabilities; this will help in planning to audit the measurement of the disposal group and whether any impairment should be recognised.

- Further information surrounding the reasons for disposal, from the Group board minutes at which approval was given for the disposal, to enable the auditor to develop an understanding of management's rationale and how the disposal fits in with the Group restructuring as a whole.

- Information regarding the potential acquirers of Primal Burgers Co and the stage of negotiations, this will help the audit team develop an expectation as to whether the disposal is likely to take place after the year end and the potential sales price.

- Any preliminary determination by management of the anticipated profit or loss on disposal and expectation of any impairment to the value of assets held in the disposal group.

- Obtain a copy of management's assessment/workings of the impact on the Group's financial position on the sale of Primal Burgers Co and the overall impact of the restructure of the Group.

(c) **(i)** **Principal audit procedures in respect of the classification of the investment in Peppers Co**

- Obtain the legal documentation supporting the investment and agree the details of the investment including:

    – The date of the investment

    – Amount paid

    –   Number of shares purchased

    –   The voting rights attached to the shares

    –   The nature of the profit-sharing arrangement between the Group and Smiths Co

    –   The nature of access to Peppers Co's assets under the terms of the agreement

    –   Confirmation that there is no restriction of the Group's shared control of Peppers Co.

- Review board minutes to confirm the approval of the investment and to understand the business rationale for the investment.

- Review minutes of relevant meetings between the Group and Smiths Co to confirm that control is shared between the two investors and to understand the nature of the relationship and the decision-making process.

- Obtain documentation such as Peppers Co's organisational structure to confirm that the Group has successfully appointed members to the board of the company and that those members have equal power to the members appointed by Smiths Co.

(ii)   **Principal audit procedures in respect of the government grant received**

- Obtain the documentation relating to the grant and review to obtain an understanding of:

    –   The terms of the grant including the amount received, and in particular requirements relating to the specific use of the funds

    –   The date by which the funds must be used

    –   Any clauses relating to repayment of some or all of the grant should certain conditions arise.

- Agree the amount received to bank statements and Ryder Co's bank ledger account/cash book.

- Obtain and review the Group's asset (capital) expenditure forecast to confirm the amount planned to be spent on assets relating to environmental matters.

- Discuss the use of the grant to fund an advertising campaign with an appropriate person, e.g. Group marketing director, and review any plans to use the funds for promotional purposes to confirm that recycling features in the campaign, as intended by the government.

- Confirm, through agreement to marketing plans, whether any funds will be spent during this financial year.

- Obtain a written representation from management that the grant received will be used for the specific purposes required by the government.

(d) **Ethical issues**

Referral fee

The Group audit committee understands that Squire & Co cannot provide a corporate finance service, but could recommend another firm, Ranger Associates, for this work, for which the firm would earn a referral fee. The Code states that this creates a self-interest threat to objectivity and to professional competence and due care.

The self-interest threat arises from the income generated from the referral, and this may result in the audit firm recommending another firm for the work without proper consideration of their competence to perform the engagement.

The *Code* does not prohibit referral fees but the significance of the threats should be evaluated and safeguards applied to reduce the threats to an acceptable level. Safeguards may include:

- Disclosing to the Group in writing the arrangement for a referral fee to be received from Ranger Associates, and

- Obtaining advance agreement from the Group that the arrangement is acceptable.

Therefore, the matter should be discussed again with the Group audit committee, and if the committee confirms agreement with the proposed referral fee, Squire & Co can recommend Ranger Associates to perform the corporate finance work for the Group.

Internal audit

A further threat arises from the audit committee's request for Squire & Co to work with the Group internal audit team to design and evaluate internal controls relating to revenue. The Code suggests that providing an audit client with an internal audit service might create a self-review threat to objectivity. This is because in subsequent audits the audit team may use the internal audit work performed in their audit of revenue. They may over-rely on the internal controls designed and evaluated by the audit firm or will not apply an appropriate level of scepticism when assessing the work.

In addition, a threat of management responsibility arises, whereby the audit firm is making decisions and using judgement which is properly the responsibility of management. The Code states that taking responsibility for designing, implementing, monitoring and maintaining internal control is assuming management responsibility.

According to the Code, an audit firm must not assume management responsibility for an audit client because the threat to independence created is so significant that no safeguards could reduce it to an acceptable level.

Specifically, in relation to public interest entities, the Code further states that an audit firm shall not provide internal audit services which relate to a significant part of controls over financial reporting, financial accounting systems which are significant to the financial statements or amounts or disclosures which are material to the financial statements.

Therefore, Squire & Co should politely decline the request made by the audit committee and ensure that the committee is fully aware of the ethical issues raised by their requests.

Conclusion

These briefing notes indicate that there is a range of audit risks to be considered in planning the forthcoming Group audit, many of the more significant risks relate to the Group's plans to restructure and the disposal of Primal Burgers Co as this affects classification of assets held for sale and provides incentive for manipulation. The government grant is another significant audit risk given the impact on profit for the year. The notes contain recommended audit procedures which have been designed in relation to two material audit issues. In respect of the ethical issues identified, our firm should not provide internal audit assistance to the Group, however, a referral fee from Ranger Associates is acceptable, provided the Group agrees to the arrangement.

Examiner's comments

This question was set at the planning stage of the audit for an existing client. The scenario revolved around a long-established group of companies audited by the same audit firm. The group was undergoing restructuring with several proposed changes to group structure some of which would not occur until after the year end.

Part (a) required candidates to describe audit risks arising in relation to the group audit and was similar to the requirements seen in many past questions. Candidates generally appeared well prepared for this question and were able to identify several audit risks and evaluate them in such a way as to obtain a pass mark. When evaluating risks, candidates are advised to always bring in specific references to the scenario, give the details of the accounting treatment required where possible and the financial statement implications arising as a result of the audit risk. Candidates should ensure they provide an appropriate calculation of materiality and a conclusion as to whether an item is material or not material. Both of these are required for credit to be awarded.

Common issues arising on this requirement were as follows:

- Candidates giving rote-learnt risks with no application to the scenario, for example stating that this was a new client (it was an existing client) or that a significant risk to a listed company is management bias without referring to any specific bias drivers from the scenario (e.g. to prove the success of a restructuring strategy, to maximise the sales price for a subsidiary being disposed of) or demonstrating where the bias might impact on the financial statements (e.g. the incorrect recognition of the grant received in profit or the under amortisation of a three-year licence). Candidates must relate the audit risks to the information provided which will be different in every examination.

- Candidates describing audit risks that were highly unlikely to be a genuine risk – for example many candidates thought there was an audit risk that an acquisition planned for next year might be included in this year's consolidation in error or that a disposal the group were hoping to make post year end required the company to entirely remove the assets and liabilities from the consolidated financial statements and replace it with the profit on disposal.

- Candidates not fully understanding the basic concepts of control or influence in the context of group accounts, for example stating that a 50% shareholding means a company must be a subsidiary. While a shareholding over 50% might be indicative that control exists or a shareholding in the region 20-50% may indicate influence exists, the principles underlying financial reporting are based on substance not just strict percentage rules.

Part (b) required additional information to plan the audit of a disposal. This was well answered by candidates who appreciated that this did not relate to the final audit procedures but information that could be requested in advance.

Part (c) required audit procedures regarding a government grant and the classification of an investment in a joint venture. Generally, this requirement was well answered although common errors with the requirement regarding the joint venture were to cover a wider scope than classification or instead to give procedures for a totally different transaction from the scenario (e.g. a common incorrect answer was to list procedures relating to the audit of the PPE investment in a different group company). These errors arose from a lack of attention to the specific requirement.

Part (d) was an ethics requirement and candidates' answers tended to be weak here. Many candidates simply listed the names of ethical threats without any application to the specific scenario. This is disappointing given the specific guidance published on the ACCA website as to what is required in terms of description for credit to be awarded in this area. Here candidates demonstrated that they had learned a list of threats but failed to demonstrate that they understood them or knew how they applied to a question. Candidates also demonstrated insufficient detailed knowledge of the IESBA International Code of Ethics for Professional Accountants. Candidates often incorrectly stated that referral fees are not permitted, but recommended the use of a separate team to devise and test controls over revenue as an internal audit assignment which, for a listed company, is prohibited.

ACCA Marking guide		
		Marks
(a)	**Evaluation of audit risks** Up to 3 marks for each audit risk evaluated unless otherwise indicated. Marks may be awarded for other, relevant risks not included in the marking guide. In addition, ½ mark for each relevant trend or calculation which forms part of the audit risk evaluation (max 3 marks). Appropriate materiality calculations (max 2 marks) and justified materiality level should be awarded to a maximum of 1 mark. – Disclosure of events after the reporting period in respect of Group restructuring – risk of inadequate disclosure – Assets held for sale in respect of planned disposal of Primal Burgers Co – risk assets not measured or recognised appropriately as assets held for sale (up to 4 marks) – Discontinued operation – risk that Group statement of profit or loss does not reflect results of Primal Burgers Co as a discontinued operation – Disposal of Primal Burgers Co – incentive for manipulation (2 marks) – Joint arrangement in Peppers Co – risk that the investment is not equity accounted – Misclassification of operating licence in respect of Mondays Coffee Co drive-throughs as PPE, impact on measurement of PPE and intangible assets and associated expenses – Mondays Coffee Co drive-throughs likely to be a reportable segment – risk of incomplete disclosure of operating segments – Government grant – risk that conditions will not be met and a liability should be recognised for repayment of the grant		
	Maximum	21

(b)   **Additional information required to plan the audit of the planned disposal of Primal Burgers Co**

Up to 1 mark for each piece of additional information recommended:

- The financial statements of Primal Burgers Co, to ascertain the detail of the amounts recognised
- A copy of the vendor's due diligence report to ascertain key findings, e.g. valuations of assets and liabilities
- Information surrounding the reasons for disposal, from the Group board minutes at which approval was given for the disposal
- Information regarding the potential acquirers of Primal Burgers Co and the stage of negotiations
- Any preliminary determination by management of the anticipated profit or loss on disposal and expectation of any impairment to the value of assets held in the disposal group
- Obtain a copy of management's assessment/workings of the impact on the Group's financial position on the sale of Primal Burgers Co and the overall impact of the restructure of the Group

Maximum	4

(c)   **Principal audit procedures**

Up to 1 mark for each well-designed audit procedure.

(i)   The 50% investment in Peppers Co

- Obtain the legal documentation supporting the investment and agree the details of the investment including (max 2 marks):
  - The date of the investment
  - Amount paid
  - Number of shares purchased
  - The voting rights attached to the shares
  - The nature of the profit-sharing arrangement between the Group and Smiths Co
  - The nature of access to Peppers Co's assets under the terms of the agreement
  - Confirmation that there is no restriction of the Group's shared control of Peppers Co
- Review board minutes to confirm the approval of the investment and to understand the business rationale for the investment
- Review minutes of relevant meetings between the Group and Smiths Co to confirm that control is shared between the two investors and to understand the nature of the relationship and the decision-making process
- Obtain documentation such as Peppers Co's organisational structure to confirm that the Group has successfully appointed members to the board of the company and that those members have equal power to the members appointed by Smiths Co

(ii)   The government grant

- Obtain the documentation relating to the grant and review to obtain understanding of:
  - The terms of the grant, in particular requirements relating to the specific use of the funds
  - The date by which the funds must be used
  - Any clauses relating to repayment of some or all of the grant should certain conditions arise
- Agree the amount received to bank statement and bank ledger account/cash book of Ryder Co

– Obtain and review the Group's asset (capital) expenditure forecast to confirm the amount planned to be spent on assets relating to environmental matters	
– Discuss the use of the grant to fund an advertising campaign with an appropriate person, e.g. Group marketing director, and review any plans to use the funds for promotional purposes to confirm that recycling features in the campaign, as intended by the government	
– Confirm, through agreement to marketing plans, whether any funds will be spent during this financial year	
– Obtain a written representation from management that the grant received will be used for the specific purposes required by the government	

Maximum 8

(d) **Ethical issues**

Up to 1 mark for each point explained:

– Referral fee – self-interest threat to objectivity and professional competence explained

– Can earn referral fee as long as safeguards used – disclose to client and obtain agreement (up to 2 marks)

– Internal audit assistance – self-review threat explained

– Internal audit assistance – management responsibility threat explained

– No safeguards can reduce threat relating to management responsibility

– For PIE client cannot provide internal audit assistance

– Audit firm therefore cannot provide internal audit assistance

Maximum 7

Professional marks

Communication

– Briefing note format and structure – use of headings/subheadings and an introduction

– Style, language and clarity – appropriate layout and tone of briefing notes, presentation of materiality and relevant calculations, appropriate use of the CBE tools, easy to follow and understand

– Effectiveness and clarity of communication – answer is relevant and tailored to the scenario

– Adherence to the specific requests made by the audit engagement partner

Analysis and evaluation

– Appropriate use of the information to determine and apply suitable calculations

– Appropriate use of the information to design appropriate audit procedures relating to the investment in Peppers Co and the government grant

– Effective prioritisation of the results of the evaluation of audit risks to demonstrate the likelihood and magnitude of risks and to facilitate the allocation of appropriate responses

Professional scepticism and professional judgement

– Appropriate application of professional judgement to draw conclusions and make informed decisions following recognition of unusual or unexpected movements, missing/incomplete information or challenging presented information as part of the risk evaluation

– Determination and justification of a suitable materiality level, appropriately and consistently applied		
– Identification of possible management bias and consideration of the impact on the financial statements and the possible reasons for management's preference for certain accounting treatments		
– Effective application of technical and ethical guidance to effectively challenge and critically assess the accounting treatment of the group restructuring		
Commercial acumen		
– Use of effective examples and/or calculations from the scenario to illustrate points or recommendations		
– Audit procedures are practical and plausible in the context of the scenario		
– Appropriate recognition of the wider implications when considering the referral of Ranger Associates and the request to work with internal audit to design internal controls for the revenue system		
Maximum		10
Total		50

8 **MARGOT** *Walk in the footsteps of a top tutor*

Top tutor tips

Determination of materiality: The email from the partner states that materiality should be based on profit, therefore at the start of your answer you should calculate the range for materiality using that benchmark and justify a figure within that range. If it is a new audit client or a client where there are apparent control risks, materiality should be set at the lower end of the range. If it is an existing client, materiality may be able to be set at the higher end of the range depending on the other risks mentioned in the scenario. The examining team will give credit for any reasonable explanation of the chosen materiality threshold, as the mark is to recognise that there is the application of professional judgement and that a candidate can justify their response. It is not required that candidates select the identical percentage or figure, or that they provide a justification identical to that shown in the model answer.

*Part (a) requires evaluation of risks of material misstatement. Here you need to explain how the financial statements might not have been prepared in accordance with the applicable financial reporting standard. Refer to the requirements of the relevant standards in your answer. Explain which balances or classes of transactions are at risk of over or understatement and why. Note that the requirement explicitly instructs you not to include risks relating to the **valuation** of bearer plants or biological assets. Other risks of material misstatement such as classification will be acceptable.*

Prioritisation of risks: One mark is awarded for the prioritisation of the risks of material misstatement. The mark is for the act of justifying the reason, not for the actual justification used (i.e. a range of completely different answers could be awarded the mark), therefore if a reasonable explanation is given, the mark will be awarded. Prioritisation can be achieved by either ordering your answer in priority order and stating this is the case, or by summarising in a brief conclusion which risk, or risks, are most significant.

Part (b) asks audit procedures in respect of the development costs. The procedures should enable the auditor to obtain evidence to determine whether the relevant financial reporting standard has been complied with. Make sure your procedures are clear and provide enough detail that they can be easily followed by the audit team.

Part (c) requires the matters to consider when using the work of an expert. This requires knowledge of the relevant auditing standard.

Part (d) deals with the auditor's responsibilities in relation to laws and regulations and the actions that should be taken when non-compliance is brought to the attention of the auditor. This requires knowledge of the relevant auditing standard.

Professional skills

Professional skills will be awarded for:

Communication – responding to the instructions in the partner's email such as preparing your answers in the form of briefing notes and using the stated benchmark for materiality.

Analysis and evaluation – applying the information from the scenario to answer the question and explaining the issues in sufficient depth.

Professional scepticism and judgement – justifying an appropriate materiality level, demonstrating critical thinking and being alert to possible manipulation and management bias.

Where relevant, professional marks will be awarded for commercial acumen which requires making practical and plausible recommendations and considering the wider implications of issues to the audit firm.

Briefing notes

To: Ben Duval, Audit engagement partner

From: Audit manager

Subject: Audit planning for Margot Co

Date: 1 July 20X5

Introduction

These briefing notes are prepared in respect of audit planning for our client Margot Co. The notes begin with an evaluation of the significant risks of material misstatement which should be considered in planning the audit. The notes then contain the audit procedures which have been designed in relation to the capitalised development costs. A discussion is provided on the use of an auditor's expert in the audit of the company's biological assets. Finally, a member of the client's staff has alerted us to some suspicious behaviour, which could indicate a breach of law and regulations. The notes discuss this issue and recommend actions to be taken by our firm.

Materiality

For the purposes of these briefing notes, the overall materiality level used to assess the significance of identified risks is $150,000 based on the profitability of the company, as requested.

Justification

Using profit before tax of $2.1 million as a suggested benchmark results in a suggested range of $105,000 (5% × $2.1 million) to $210,000 (10% × $2.1 million).

This is an existing client, and no significant control issues have been noted at the planning stage or in previous audits. However, due to the risk of management bias discussed below, audit risk is deemed higher than in previous years giving a medium level of risk overall. Materiality should be set at the midpoint of the range.

This benchmark is only a starting point for determining materiality and professional judgement will need to be applied in determining a final level to be used during the course of the audit.

(a)   **Evaluation of significant risks of material misstatement**

Results from preliminary analytical procedures

The limited analytical procedures which have been performed indicate several potential risks of material misstatement. First, the current ratio has increased significantly, from 1.4 in 20X4, to a projected figure of 2.6 in 20X5. Using the information provided, the current liabilities in 20X4 were $1.564 million ($2.19 million/1.4) and are projected to be $1.288 million in 20X5 ($3.35 million/2.6).

Current ratio

Current assets are projected to increase by 53% and current liabilities projected to reduce by 17.6%. Given that the management accounts show that the cash balance is relatively static, there is a risk that other current assets, presumably inventory and receivables, could be overstated.

Profitability

Looking at the operating profit margin and return on capital employed, both ratios have improved by a small amount. This trend is worthy of scrutiny during the audit as the offers and discounts offered to customers by the company should act negatively on margins and profitability, so the improvements in ratios could indicate a potential overstatement of operating profit.

Revenue

Another trend which is worth further investigation relates to online sales, which are projected to increase by 90.5% in the year. This is a significant increase, and while the finance director has asserted that the increase in sales is due to the success of the advertising campaign, this needs to be corroborated further. There is a risk of overstatement of revenue in relation to online sales which is explored in more detail below.

There is also a risk that revenue from other sources is overstated. Excluding online sales, revenue from other sources is projected to increase by 5.3%, a significant increase, which could also indicate overstatement of revenue.

Management bias

This is a private company where a majority of shares are owned by the Margot family. This brings a risk of management bias, especially as one of the family members is the company's chief executive officer, who is in a position to influence the financial statements. The extract from the management accounts shows that a significant dividend payment is made each year, so there is an expectation from the family members that the company will make sufficient profit to be able to pay these dividends each year.

There is therefore a significant inherent risk at the financial statement level that profit will be overstated. The risk that the financial statements are being deliberately manipulated is indicated by the accounting treatment applied to impairment which is discussed in more detail below.

Online sales

The online sales make up an increasing proportion of the company's revenue – according to the management accounts online sales are projected to represent 7% of total revenue in 20X5 (4% – 20X4).

Online sales can bring several risks of material misstatement, for instance, cut off and timing of revenue recognition can be problematic. In the case of Margot Co, risks attach to the discounts which are offered on online sales as the discounts offered to customers appear to change frequently. This brings some complexity into the accounting, and the company should ensure that internal controls are operating effectively so that the accounting system is updated whenever the level and range of discounts and offers to customers are changed. Revenue could be over or understated if discounts are not accounted for appropriately, either because a discount is not recorded at all by the accounting system or is applied to the wrong products.

Tutorial note

Credit will be awarded for other risks relating to online sales, where relevant to the question scenario, for example, related to the launch of the new online sales portal, which implies a change to the system used to record revenue, with related control risks.

Research and development

In this financial year, $220,000 of research and development costs have been capitalised as an intangible asset. This is considered material to the financial statements based on the threshold of $150,000.

This relates to research and development into new plastic-free packaging. According to IAS 38 *Intangible Assets*, a distinction has to be made between research costs, which must be expensed, and development costs, which should only be capitalised if certain criteria are met including that the technical and commercial feasibility of the asset has been established.

It appears that the full amount paid to ProPack has been capitalised, which indicates that no distinction has been made between research costs and development costs. Only development costs can be capitalised, so there is a potential overstatement of the intangible asset if it includes research costs, which should be expensed. This means that the entity must intend and be able to complete the intangible asset and either use it or sell it and be able to demonstrate how the asset will generate future economic benefits.

There is a further risk of material misstatement because costs which are development costs may have been capitalised but the necessary criteria demonstrating that an asset has been created have not been met. Given that ProPack is only at the stage of testing prototypes, it appears that there is not yet demonstrable evidence that the new packaging is technically feasible or that Margot Co will be able to use the packaging.

In addition, there may problems in demonstrating that Margot Co has control of the development of new packaging, given that the development has been outsourced to another company. In this case, the IAS 38 criteria for capitalisation do not appear to have been met. This will result in overstatement of intangible assets and understatement of operating expenses.

Impaired factory

The carrying amount of the impaired factory of $880,250 is material by reference to the threshold calculated above. The damage to the factory has triggered an impairment review, as required by IAS 36 *Impairment of Assets*. However, the finance director has not prepared the impairment calculations in accordance with IAS 36, specifically the recoverable amount has not been correctly determined. The recoverable amount is the higher of value in use and fair value less costs to sell the asset.

According to IAS 36, the cash flow projections which are used to determine the value in use of the impaired asset should relate to the asset in its current condition – expenditures to improve or enhance the asset's performance should not be anticipated. The finance director's estimate of value in use is based on the assumption that the building is repaired and new machinery purchased – neither of these assumptions should be included in the determination of value in use.

It is likely that the value in use, when properly determined, is much lower than the finance director's estimate, meaning that the impairment loss to be recognised is greater than finance director's calculations. There is also a risk that the fair value less cost to sell is overestimated. Therefore, there is a risk that the impairment loss is understated, and the carrying amount of the asset is overstated.

Tutorial note

Credit will be awarded for further development of the impairment issue, for example, whether the impairment loss has been appropriately allocated over the assets of the cash generating unit.

Software and advertising costs capitalised

During the year, software development costs of $30,000 and advertising costs of $225,000 are capitalised as intangible assets. The advertising costs are material as they exceed the threshold of $150,000.

The advertising costs have been incurred to support the 'Fructus Gold' brand name, and the finance director justifies the capitalisation on the grounds that the advertising expenditure has led to an increase in sales. However, IAS 38 specifically states that advertising and promotional costs must not be recognised as intangible assets and must be expensed. Therefore, intangible assets are overstated and operating expenses understated by a material amount.

The software development costs are not considered to be material to the financial statements, and therefore in isolation do not represent a significant risk of material misstatement in monetary terms, especially given that according to IAS 38, it is appropriate to capitalise internally developed software costs assuming that the costs incurred give rise to an asset.

However, this matter is being highlighted because the finance director has used a similar justification for capitalising the advertising costs, which are likely to be materially misstated, as discussed above, and therefore this gives rise to a general concern over whether all costs relating to intangible assets are being treated appropriately.

Identification and potential misclassification of assets

There is a risk that the agricultural assets are not identified and/or classified appropriately, which will have an implication for the valuation of the assets. For example, it may be difficult to distinguish between bearer plants and fruit growing on the trees, and it might be hard to identify the stage of development of fruit on the trees.

This potentially impacts on the valuation of the assets, because bearer plants are measured at cost and depreciated in accordance with IAS 16 *Property, Plant and Equipment*, whereas the fruit should be measured at fair value in accordance with IAS 41 *Agriculture*.

Tutorial note

Credit will be awarded for other, relevant risks of material misstatement, for example, the risk that the storm may have damaged assets other than the factory, in particular the bearer plants, which may have suffered impairment, and the risk that inventory may be overstated due to perishable nature of the goods.

(b) **Audit procedures**

Research and development costs

- Discuss the project to develop new packaging with management, to develop an understanding of matters such as how the company intends to use the new packaging, the stage of development reached by the year end and whether the project may need additional funding.

- Obtain and review progress reports and correspondence from ProPack which will indicate the progress made so far.

- Obtain and review the contract with ProPack to determine contractual terms and if the asset will be owned and controlled by Margot Co and that ProPack does not have any continuing interest in the development once it is complete.

- After receiving client's permission, arrange to discuss the project with ProPack, to obtain further understanding on a range of matters including technical feasibility and the results of the testing on the prototype.

- Discuss with the company's production and marketing directors to obtain understanding of how the company will use the new packaging.

- Obtain any financial budgets prepared in relation to the project, to confirm the amount of expenditure which has been approved, and that the costs are clearly distinguishable.

- By reference to the company's cash position and available finance, evaluate whether Margot Co has sufficient funds to complete the development.

- Obtain samples of the prototype packaging from ProPack, to confirm existence.

- Agree the amount spent to date to invoices submitted by ProPack, and to the company's cash records.

Tutorial note

Credit will be awarded for other relevant audit procedures, for example, in relation to assessing whether there are any reasons to doubt whether ProPack can continue the development.

(c) **Matters to consider before placing reliance on the work of the auditor's expert**

ISA 620 *Using the Work of an Auditor's Expert* contains requirements relating to the objectivity, competence and capabilities of the auditor's expert, the scope and objectives of their work, and assessing their work.

Objectivity

According to ISA 620, the auditor shall evaluate whether the auditor's expert has the necessary objectivity and this should include inquiry regarding interests and relationships which may create a threat to the expert's objectivity. The audit firm will need to ensure that the expert has no connection to Margot Co, for example, that they are not a related party of the company or any person in a position of influence over the financial statements.

If the expert's objectivity is threatened, little or no reliance can be placed on their work, and the audit firm should not treat it as a reliable source of audit evidence.

Competence

ISA 620 also requires the competence of the expert to be considered; this should include considering the expert's membership of appropriate professional bodies. Any doubts over the competence of the expert will reduce the reliability of audit evidence obtained.

The expert should in this case have experience in valuing the fruit which are the agricultural assets recognised in the statement of financial position, and be familiar with the framework for measuring fair value of these assets in accordance with IAS 41 *Agriculture* and IFRS 13 *Fair Value Measurement*.

Scope of work

ISA 620 requires the auditor to agree the scope of work with the expert. This may include agreement of the objectives of the work, how the expert's work will be used by the auditor and the methodology and key assumptions to be used.

In assessing the work performed by the expert, the auditor should confirm that the scope of the work is as agreed at the start of the engagement. If the expert has deviated from the agreed scope of work, it is likely to be less relevant and reliable.

Relevance of conclusions

ISA 620 states that the auditor shall evaluate the relevance and adequacy of the expert's findings or conclusions. This will involve consideration of the source data which was used, the appropriateness of assumptions and the reasons for any changes in methodology or assumptions. The conclusion should be consistent with other relevant audit findings and with the auditor's general understanding of the business.

If the work involves using source data which is significant to their workings, the audit team should plan to assess the relevance, completeness and accuracy of that data. Any inconsistencies should be investigated as they may indicate evidence which is not reliable.

Tutorial note

Credit will be awarded for more specific comments in relation to evaluating the expert's work, for example, reperformance of calculations, and establishing that assumptions are in line with the auditor's understanding of the entity.

(d) Audit implications of email from Len Larch

The alleged use of prohibited chemicals raises concerns that the company may not be complying with relevant law and regulations. The auditor needs to consider the requirements of ISA 250 *Consideration of Laws and Regulations in an Audit of Financial Statements*. ISA 250 states that while it is management's responsibility to ensure that the entity's operations are conducted in accordance with the provisions of laws and regulation, the auditor does have some responsibility in relation to compliance with laws and regulations, especially where a non-compliance has an impact on the financial statements.

There is also an ethical issue in that one of the production managers may have been bribed by one of the company directors. Clearly, if this is true, it indicates a lack of integrity and would seem to confirm that the chemicals which are being used are prohibited.

Tutorial note

UK syllabus: There is a risk that the Bribery Act (2010) has been breached by the inducement offered by the production manager.

The auditor is required by ISA 315 (Revised 2019) *Identifying and Assessing the Risks of Material Misstatement* to gain an understanding of the legal and regulatory framework in which the audited entity operates. This will help the auditor to identify non-compliance and to assess the implications of non-compliance.

The auditor should ensure a full knowledge and understanding of the laws and regulations relevant to the use of chemicals in the company's farms, and the implications of non-compliance.

ISA 250 requires that when non-compliance is identified or suspected, the auditor shall obtain an understanding of the nature of the act and the circumstances in which it has occurred, and further information to evaluate the possible effect on the financial statements.

Procedures should be performed to obtain evidence about the suspected non-compliance, for example, to speak to the company's farm managers to understand whether the allegations are founded in fact. In addition, the audit team could perform further procedures, for example, reviewing purchase invoices to establish if these chemicals are actually being purchased and used in the business, and if so, on whose authority.

ISA 250 requires the matter to be discussed with management and where appropriate with those charged with governance. Given the potential severity of the situation, and that the chemicals may be toxic, there is the risk of poisoning the company's employees or customers, and the matter should be communicated as soon as possible.

The auditor should attempt to find out whether any member of management had issued instructions for these chemicals to be used, i.e. that there is a deliberate breach of law and regulations. ISA 250 suggests that when the auditor suspects management or those charged with governance of being involved with the non-compliance, the matter should be communicated to the next level of 'higher authority' such as an audit committee or supervisory board.

Given the family-managed nature of Margot Co, it may be that no higher authority exists, in which case the audit firm should take appropriate legal advice if it thinks that the matter may not be communicated by the entity.

The auditor needs to consider the potential implications for the financial statements. The non-compliance, if proven to have taken place, could lead to regulatory authorities imposing fines or penalties on Margot Co, which may need to be provided for in the financial statements. Audit procedures should be performed to determine the amount, materiality and probability of payment of any such fine or penalty imposed.

In addition, there is a risk that the use of chemicals means that inventory of harvested fruit and the fruit trees are contaminated with poisonous chemicals and possibly will need to be destroyed. The assets could therefore need to be written down in value. If any necessary impairment of the assets is not recognised, then non-current assets and current assets could be misstated. The audit team should therefore plan procedures to determine the value of the contaminated assets.

There may be a going concern issue once the non-compliance and its implications has been established and the facts get out into the media. There could be considerable impact on the reputation of the company and its brand if customers stop purchasing the products for fear of a health risk and this could affect the going concern of the business.

In terms of reporting non-compliance to the relevant regulatory authorities, ISA 250 requires the auditor to determine whether they have a responsibility to report the identified or suspected non-compliance to parties outside the entity.

In the event that management or those charged with governance of the company fails to make the necessary disclosures to the regulatory authorities, the auditor should consider whether they should make the disclosure. This will depend on matters including whether there is a legal duty to disclose or whether it is considered to be in the public interest to do so.

Confidentiality is also an issue, and if disclosure were to be made by the auditor, it would be advisable to seek legal advice on the matter. Further advice on disclosure in the public interest is given by the IESBA's pronouncement on *Responding to Non-Compliance with Laws and Regulations* (NOCLAR). The guidance gives examples of situations where disclosure might be appropriate such as an entity being involved in bribery and breaches of regulation which might impact adversely on public health and safety.

The standard also clarifies that in exceptional circumstances where the auditor believes there may be an imminent breach of a law or regulation, they may need to disclose the matter immediately.

The decision to disclose will always be a matter for the auditor's judgement and where the disclosure is made in good faith, it will not constitute a breach of the duty of confidentiality.

Tutorial note

UK syllabus: ISA (UK) 250 A states that the auditor should discuss this with those charged with governance and if the entity does not voluntarily report the matter itself or is unable to provide evidence that the matter has been reported, the auditor reports it.

According to ISA (UK) 250 A, determination of where the balance of public interest lies requires careful consideration. An auditor whose suspicions have been aroused uses professional judgement to determine whether the auditor's misgivings justify the auditor in carrying the matter further or are too insubstantial to deserve reporting. The auditor is protected from the risk of liability for breach of confidence or defamation provided that the disclosure is made in the public interest, and such disclosure is made to an appropriate body or person, and there is no malice motivating the disclosure.

Conclusion

These briefing notes have indicated that there are several significant risks of material misstatement to consider while planning the audit of Margot Co. The most significant risk relates to the significant increase in revenue which is due to almost double from last year. More information is needed to perform a detailed analytical review, which may highlight further potential risks. The briefing notes also recommend relevant audit procedures for the research and development costs. We will plan to use the work of an expert, following the requirements of ISA 620. Finally, we need to consider carefully the issues raised by Len Larch, as it seems that the company is operating in breach of relevant laws and regulations, and that this is a deliberate act involving bribery of company employees. There are implications for our audit planning in that we must plan to obtain detailed information about the situation, and consider our reporting responsibilities in light of the severity of the situation and its implications for public health.

Examiner's comments

Requirement (a) asked candidates to evaluate the risks of material misstatement arising from the scenario. This was generally well answered with the majority of candidates able to follow a structured approach of calculating materiality, stating the relevant accounting rule applied to the specifics of the scenario, describing the risk that arose and the resulting impact on the financial statements. It was pleasing to see that fewer candidates diverted to answering from a business risk perspective, but where this did occur, no marks could be awarded.

Candidates are reminded to read the question requirements carefully and ensure they are answering the question set. As in previous sittings, the examining team highlighted within the scenario that there was an internally generated brand which had been accounted for correctly and should not be recognised within the statement of financial position. A significant number of candidates still described this as a risk of material misstatement, clearly wasting time on an area that was not a risk. Several candidates who did identify that the brand was correctly accounted for, continued to describe how the internally generated brand, while not recognised should be tested for impairment. This demonstrates an area of weakness regarding basic financial reporting knowledge. Candidates would benefit from refreshing their knowledge on reporting standards for intangible assets and taking note of the guidance provided in the scenario by the examining team. A further area of weakness was noted with regards to the family-owned business having a lack of corporate governance, audit committee and lack of controls leading to a risk of material misstatement. A significant number of candidates discussed the risk in very general terms, not linking any risk of management bias to the specifics of the question and therefore failed to score what would be regarded as standard risk marks that are easily achievable.

Some other common issues noted in candidate answers for RoMM included:

– Discussing audit procedures to be performed which did not meet the question requirement and therefore no credit awarded. If required, this will normally form a separate requirement within the question and should be answered where applicable.

– Including detailed definitions of audit risk or risks of material misstatement. The briefing notes are prepared for the audit engagement partner and this type of information is not required.

– Lack of basic knowledge of double entry and assumption that every double entry has one under and one overstatement e.g. if liabilities are understated, then expenses must be overstated.

– Lack of correct direction of risk or not being precise in terms of the financial statement impact, e.g. "liabilities will be under/overstated ".

Requirement (b) required candidates to design principal audit procedures for specific area of risk identified within requirement (a). Candidate answers were weaker than the previous sitting, with many candidates providing procedures which referred to a weak information source or poorly explained purpose and were often not detailed enough to score full marks.

Some common issues noted in candidate answers for this requirement included:

– Focusing on board meeting minutes where this was not an appropriate source for a procedure based on the requirement.

– Procedures which simply stated "obtain relevant documents" which is not specific or detailed enough to score full marks.

– Requests to obtain written representations from management without being specific regarding what should be confirmed, or were not relevant to the area for which procedures were being performed.

The final requirements required candidates to discuss considerations for the use of an auditor's expert and for candidates to discuss the audit implications and actions to be taken, regarding professional and ethical issues present in the scenario. There were many strong answers in response to considerations regarding the use of the auditor's expert, but some candidates failed to address the level of detail required in line with ISA 620 *Using the Work of an Auditor's Expert*.

Weaker answers focussed on practical considerations, such as whether the expert had the time and resources to perform the work rather than the key areas of the standard such as objectivity, competence, scope of work and relevance of conclusions.

It is disappointing to note that answers to ethics requirements continue to be weak, with many candidates not sufficiently justifying how the threat has arisen in line with the specifics of the scenario or the implication that arises for the auditor. Both considerations are needed in order score marks. Candidates undoubtedly know the name of the ethical threats and have an assumed knowledge from previous studies at AA yet continue to score poorly at AAA level. Candidates would benefit from reading the exam technique article published on ACCA's website for detailed guidance on how to discuss ethical threats.

ACCA Marking guide		
		Marks
(a)	**Risk of material misstatement**	
	Up to 3 marks for each significant risk of material misstatement evaluated unless otherwise indicated. Marks may be awarded for other, relevant risks not included in the marking guide.	
	In addition, ½ mark for each relevant trend or calculation which form part of analytical review (max 2 marks).	
	Appropriate materiality calculations (max 2 marks) and justified materiality level should be awarded to a maximum of 1 mark.	
	– Current ratio – related audit risks, e.g. overstatement of inventory/receivables	
	– Improvements in margin and ROCE – possible overstatement of profit given the discounts offered to customers	
	– Online sales – trend indicates possible overstatement of revenue	
	– Management bias	
	– Discounts offered on online sales	
	– Research and development – risk that expenditure should not have been capitalised and that research and development costs have not been distinguished	
	– Impairment – risk that the value in use and therefore impairment loss is not correct	
	– Intangible assets – whether amounts should have been capitalised	
	– Bearer plants/biological assets/inventory – potentially difficult to distinguish the assets, with implications for their valuation	
	Maximum	21
(b)	**Audit procedures research and development costs**	
	Up to 1 mark for each well described procedure:	
	Research and development costs	
	– Discuss the project to develop new packaging with management, to develop an understanding of matters such as how the company intends to use the new packaging, the stage of development reached by the year end and whether the project may need additional funding	
	– Obtain and review reports and correspondence from ProPack which will indicate the progress made so far	
	– Obtain and review the contract with ProPack to determine contractual terms and if the asset will be owned and controlled by Margot Co and that ProPack does not have any continuing interest in the development once it is complete	
	– Discuss the project with ProPack, to obtain further understanding on a range of matters including technical feasibility and the results of testing of the prototype	

– Discuss with the company's production and marketing directors to obtain understanding of how the company will use the new packaging	
– Obtain any financial budgets prepared in relation to the project, to confirm the amount of expenditure which has been approved, and that the costs are clearly distinguishable	
– By reference to the company's cash position and available finance, evaluate whether Margot Co has sufficient funds to complete the development	
– Obtain samples of the prototype packaging from Propack, to confirm existence	
– Agree the amount spent to date to invoices submitted by ProPack, and to the company's cash records	

Maximum **5**

(c) **Use of an auditor's expert**

Up to 2 marks for each well explained point:
– Objectivity
– Competence
– Scope of work
– Relevance of conclusions

Maximum **5**

(d) **Impact of email on audit**

Up to 2 marks for each well explained point:
– Use of chemicals likely to be a breach of laws and regulations
– Bribe indicates lack of integrity and that the activity is a non-compliance
– Auditor needs to understand laws and regulations applicable to the Group
– Further evidence should be obtained and the matter discussed with management
– Issue of lack of 'higher authority' as Margot Co is family owned and need to take legal advice
– Provisions for fines and penalties
– Valuation of inventory and biological assets
– Potential going concern issue due to bad publicity and impact on reputation
– Auditor may have a legal duty to disclose, or consider disclosing in the public interest
– Discussion of how requirements of NOCLAR relate to the scenario
– The audit firm may wish to seek legal advice regarding the situation (1 mark)

Maximum **9**

Professional marks
Communication
– Briefing note format and structure – use of headings/subheadings and an introduction
– Style, language and clarity – appropriate layout and tone of briefing notes, presentation of materiality and relevant calculations, appropriate use of the CBE tools, easy to follow and understand
– Effectiveness and clarity of communication – answer is relevant and tailored to the scenario
– Adherence to the specific requests made by the audit engagement partner

Analysis and evaluation

– Appropriate use of the information to determine and apply suitable calculations

– Appropriate use of the information to design appropriate audit procedures relating to the impairment of the factory and development costs

– Effective prioritisation of the results of the evaluation of risks of material misstatement to demonstrate the likelihood and magnitude of risks and to facilitate the allocation of appropriate responses

Professional scepticism and professional judgement

– Appropriate application of professional judgement to draw conclusions and make informed decisions following recognition of unusual or unexpected movements, missing/incomplete information or challenging presented information as part of the risk evaluation

– Determination and justification of a suitable materiality level, appropriately and consistently applied

– Identification of possible management bias and consideration of the impact on the financial statements and the possible reasons for management's preference for certain accounting treatments

– Effective application of technical and ethical guidance to effectively challenge and critically assess the work of the auditor's expert in respect of biological assets

Commercial acumen

– Use of effective examples and/or calculations from the scenario to illustrate points or recommendations

– Audit procedures are practical and plausible in the context of the scenario

– Appropriate recognition of the wider implications when considering the email from Len Larch

Maximum	10
Total	50

9 REDBACK SPORTS *Walk in the footsteps of a top tutor*

Top tutor tips

Determination of materiality: *The email from the partner states that materiality should be based on profit, therefore at the start of your answer you should calculate the range for materiality using that benchmark and justify a figure within that range. If it is a new audit client or a client where there are apparent control risks, materiality should be set at the lower end of the range. If it is an existing client, materiality may be able to be set at the higher end of the range depending on the other risks mentioned in the scenario. The examining team will give credit for any reasonable explanation of the chosen materiality threshold, as the mark is to recognise that there is the application of professional judgement and that a candidate can justify their response. It is not required that candidates select the identical percentage or figure, or that they provide a justification identical to that shown in the model answer.*

Part (a) *requires evaluation of business risks. When describing business risks remember to explain the impact it will have on the company i.e. impact on profit or cash flow. The business risks should be relatable to the financial statements as the auditor will only consider business risks which will also give rise to a risk of material misstatement.*

Part (b) asks for risks of material misstatement. Here you need to explain how the financial statements might not have been prepared in accordance with the applicable financial reporting standard. Refer to the requirements of the relevant standards in your answer. Explain which balances or classes of transactions are at risk of over or understatement and why.

Prioritisation of risks: One mark is awarded for the prioritisation of the risks of material misstatement. The mark is for the act of justifying the reason, not for the actual justification used (i.e. a range of completely different answers could be awarded the mark), therefore if a reasonable explanation is given, the mark will be awarded. Prioritisation can be achieved by either ordering your answer in priority order and stating this is the case, or by summarising in a brief conclusion which risk, or risks, are most significant.

Part (c) focuses on ethical and professional issues that would be created if the firm accepts appointment to perform an audit or review for Emu Gyms Co. The relevant threats should be explained and appropriate safeguards suggested. The requirement also asks for a discussion of whether an audit or limited assurance review could have uncovered a fraud. Discuss the limitations of each type of engagement including the types of procedures that are performed for each. Remember that fraud is an intentional act of deception which means it may be difficult to identify due to concealment.

Professional skills

Professional skills will be awarded for:

Communication – responding to the instructions in the partner's email such as preparing your answers in the form of briefing notes and using the stated benchmark for materiality.

Analysis and evaluation – applying the information from the scenario to answer the question and explaining the issues in sufficient depth.

Professional scepticism and judgement – justifying an appropriate materiality level, demonstrating critical thinking and being alert to possible manipulation and management bias.

Where relevant, professional marks will be awarded for commercial acumen which requires making practical and plausible recommendations and considering the wider implications of issues to the audit firm.

Briefing notes

To: Stella Cross, audit engagement partner

From: Audit manager

Subject: Audit of Redback Sports Co and potential provision of an audit or limited assurance review to Emu Gyms Co

Date: 1 July 20X5

Introduction

The first part of these briefing notes has been prepared in relation to the audit of Redback Sports Co. The audit planning will commence shortly, and these notes evaluate the business risks and the significant risks of material misstatement to be considered in planning the audit.

The second part of the briefing notes focuses on Emu Gyms Co, and the ethical and professional issues that would be created if our firm provides an audit or a limited assurance review of the company's financial statements.

The notes finish by discussing a question which has been raised by the company's managing director, in relation to a suspected fraud at the company.

Materiality

For the purposes of these briefing notes, the overall materiality level used to assess the significance of identified risks is $345,000 based on the profitability of the company, as requested.

Justification

Using profit before tax of $6.9 million as a suggested benchmark results in a suggested range of $345,000 (5% × $6.9 million) to $690,000 (10% × $6.9 million).

There is indication of management bias within the financial statements, and therefore inherent risk is increased. In addition, control risk is increased due to the governance issues discussed below. Materiality should be set at the lower end of the range.

This benchmark is only a starting point for determining materiality and professional judgement will need to be applied in determining a final level to be used during the course of the audit.

(a)   **Evaluation of business risks to be considered in planning the audit of Redback Sports Co**

Corporate governance

The company does not have to comply with corporate governance requirements as it is not a listed entity, and it is good to note that the board includes two non-executive directors who seem able to offer independent views on strategy and management. However, the company lacks an audit committee and the internal audit team is small and lacking in independence as they report directly to the finance director. This means that the scope of their work is likely to be quite limited due to insufficient resources, and any recommendations made could potentially be ignored by the finance director.

Overall, this could lead to deficiencies in controls and inefficiencies in business operations. In addition, given that the company is looking to achieve a stock market listing in the next few years, it would be good practice to implement stronger governance procedures sooner rather than later. For example, having two non-executive directors may not be enough to meet the corporate governance requirements in the company's jurisdiction.

Health and safety regulations

The company operates in a highly regulated industry, and the risk of non-compliance with various laws and regulations is high. The sport and leisure industry has strict health and safety regulations which must be complied with, and there are regular health and safety inspections to ensure that regulations are being adhered to.

If the company is found not to be in compliance with the relevant regulations, its operating licence could be revoked, which would have reputational consequences, and ultimately could impact on the company's going concern status.

In addition to the risk of non-compliance, it will be costly to reduce this risk to an acceptable level, for example, through regular staff training on health and safety, leading to cash flow and profit implications. This is particularly relevant to the more adventurous sporting activities such as scuba diving, which the company has recently started to offer.

Asset (capital) expenditure and maintenance requirements

The company's success relies on gyms being equipped with modern equipment, and the other facilities such as tennis courts being maintained to a high standard. This requires a high annual expenditure, for example, this year alone $5.5 million has been incurred on maintenance and repairs.

Such high annual expenditure is a big drain on cash, and the company could face liquidity problems if cash inflows from customers are not maintained.

Liquidity and overtrading

The company's cash position is projected to deteriorate significantly, with the level of cash falling from $5.6 million to $1.4 million in the year. At the same time, revenue and profit before tax are both projected to increase, by 17.8% and 50% respectively.

While there is some doubt over the integrity of the figures reported by management, which will be discussed in the next section of the briefing notes, the trends could indicate that the company is expanding too quickly and overtrading, focusing on generating revenue rather than on managing cash flows appropriately. This is particularly concerning given the company's plans for further expansion in the next few years.

Capacity

There could be problems facing the company in terms of the capacity of its facilities. Membership has increased significantly during the year, by 12.4%, and the number of pay as you go visits has increased by 5.3%. Although two new sport and leisure centres have opened this year, this may not be sufficient expansion, and there may be times when the facilities are overcrowded.

This may deter members from renewing their membership, and pay as you go customers might prefer to use other sport and leisure providers if overcrowding becomes problematical. The 'Healthy Kids' programme, and the government initiative to provide free access to the unemployed will exacerbate this problem.

Competition and marketing expenses

The industry is competitive, which itself is a business risk, meaning there is pressure on the company to maintain its market share and customer base. There may be pressure to cut membership or pay as you go prices, which will impact on profit margins and cash flow.

The company appears to spend a lot on marketing to support its brand. This year, $8.5 million has been spent on marketing, which equates to 16% of revenue. This is a huge drain on cash and will impact significantly on the company's liquidity position.

Government initiative

While the company's involvement with the government initiative to promote a healthy lifestyle to unemployed people is commendable, it may not prove popular with the existing sport and leisure centre members and pay as you go customers.

The initiative will put pressure on the capacity of the gyms, and could lead to the facilities becoming crowded, especially at peak time. This could lead to memberships not being renewed, and pay as you go customers moving to other providers. There is also an opportunity cost issue for the company, as the $2 million grant receipt does not appear to be particularly profitable in terms of the number of hours of free access to the gyms which have to be provided for the next three years.

There is an associated risk in that the company's systems need to be capable of accurately recording the number of free hours which are provided under this initiative, as this has to be reported on a monthly basis. The risk is that the systems do not capture the necessary information accurately, which could lead to reporting false information to the government.

There is evidence that this system of recording could be overstating the hours of free access, as according to the finance director, 33,900 free hours have already been provided, which in the three-month period since the start of the initiative in April 20X5 equates to 11,300 hours per month, which seems high as this implies that approximately 3,800 people have responded to the initiative.

Expansion plans

The expansion plans could take management's attention away from running the business, especially if identification of potential target companies becomes a time-consuming process over the next year. Management controls over existing operations could deteriorate while attention is focused on the planned expansion and possible future flotation.

If there is pressure from existing shareholders for the expansion to be successful and flotation to take place, management could be pressured into making unwise decisions to increase the pace of development of the company's activities.

New data management system

Introducing a new data management system can create a business risk in that insufficient training may have been provided and/or appropriate internal controls may not have been designed or implemented in relation to the new system, increasing the risk of inaccurate recording, processing and reporting of information.

This would have a negative impact on management's ability to monitor the company's performance. Given that the new system is linked to the company's accounting software, there is a related audit risk, which will be discussed in the next section of these briefing notes.

(b)   Risk of material misstatement evaluation

Management bias

The company has ambitious expansion plans, and is aiming to achieve a stock market listing within five years. This can create significant pressure on management to report strong financial performance, and the risk of earnings management is high. This can lead to a range of inappropriate accounting treatments including early recognition of revenue and other income and deferral of expenses.

There is some indication that earnings management may have taken place this year, for example, revenue is projected to increase by 17.8%, whereas the number of members, who provide the majority of the company's revenue, has increased by only 12.4%. Profit before tax is projected to increase by 50%. These trends indicate that income could be overstated and expenses understated, the specific reasons for which are evaluated below.

Corporate governance and internal controls

As discussed in the previous section, the company lacks an audit committee and only has a small internal audit team which is not operating independently. This has implications for controls over financial reporting, which could be deficient, and increases control risk.

There is a high scope for errors in financial reporting processes and for deliberate manipulation of balances and transactions, as the internal audit team does not have sufficient resources for thorough monitoring and reporting.

Revenue recognition

With 85% of revenue being from members' subscriptions, there is a risk that revenue is recognised incorrectly. There is a risk that the timing of revenue recognition is not appropriate, for example, if an annual membership is recognised in full when it is received by the company, rather than being recognised over the period of membership, thereby overstating revenue.

There are multiple revenue streams which complicates the financial reporting process and increases the risk. As well as members paying an annual subscription, customers can pay for access under the pay as you go scheme. In addition, the free access to the unemployed should not result in revenue recognition, but must be properly recorded as it has to be reported to the government on a monthly basis.

As discussed above, it is possible that the system is not recording the free access provided to the unemployed accurately, and that figures may be overstated.

Government grant

The company has received a $2 million grant this year, which has been recognised as other operating income. The amount is material as it exceeds the threshold of $345,000.

The risk of material misstatement relates to whether this should all have been recognised as income in the current accounting period. IAS 20 *Accounting for Government Grants and Disclosure of Government Assistance* requires that government grants are recognised in profit or loss on a systematic basis over the periods in which the entity recognises expenses for the related costs for which the grants are intended to compensate.

Redback Sports Co has recognised all the income this year, however, the scheme is intended to run for three years. Therefore, there is a risk that the company has recognised the income too early, and a proportion of it should be deferred. This leads to overstated profit and understated liabilities.

There could be a further issue in that the terms of the grant may require complete or partial repayment if the required number of hours of free access to sport facilities is not met. If any such terms exist, the company should evaluate whether the terms are likely to be met, and if not, should consider whether it would be appropriate to recognise a provision or disclose a contingent liability in the notes to the financial statements.

The risk is therefore that this has not been considered by management, leading possibly to understated liabilities or inadequate disclosure as required by IAS 37 *Provisions, Contingent Liabilities and Contingent Assets.*

Bank loan

During the year, the company took out a significant loan of $30 million. This is material as it exceeds the threshold set above.

The loan has been issued at a deep discount and there is a risk of material misstatement in that the finance costs associated with this loan may not be accounted for in accordance with IFRS 9 *Financial Instruments.*

IFRS 9 requires that the finance cost associated with a deep discount – in this case the $4 million difference between the amount received by Redback Sports Co of $30 million, and the amount repayable on maturity of the debt of $34 million – should be amortised over the term of the loan.

The risk is that finance costs and non-current liabilities will be understated if the appropriate finance cost is not accrued in this financial year.

Asset (capital) expenditure and maintenance costs

The company has high levels of both asset expenditure and maintenance costs. There is a risk of material misstatement that asset expenditure and operating expenditure have not been appropriately separated for accounting purposes.

For example, maintenance costs could be incorrectly capitalised into non-current assets, overstating assets and understating operating expenses. This could be indicated by maintenance costs representing 10.4% of revenue this year, compared to 11.7% in the previous year.

Asset expenditure is recorded at $32 million this year compared to $20 million in the previous year; this significant increase can be at least partly explained by two new centres being opened in the year, but audit work will need to focus on the possible overstatement of non-current assets.

Related party transaction

The managing director of Redback Sports Co, Bob Glider, has made a loan to the company of $1 million. This is material by nature as it is a related party transaction according to IAS 24 *Related Party Disclosures* given that the loan to the company is from a member of key management personnel.

The relevant disclosures as required by IAS 24 must be made in the notes to the financial statements, and there is a risk that the disclosures are incomplete. The necessary disclosures include information on the nature of the related party transaction, its amount, and the relevant terms and conditions of the loan.

There is also a risk that interest will not be accrued on the loan. The loan was made on 1 February 20X5, so by the year end interest of $20,000 ($1m × 3% × 8/12) should be accrued. This is not material in monetary terms to the financial statements, however, audit judgement may conclude that it is material given the related party nature of the transaction.

Data management system

The introduction of new systems, especially those which interface with the accounting system, creates a risk of material misstatement. Errors could have been made in the transfer of data from the old to the new system, and as this system deals with membership information, it is likely to impact on how revenue is recorded and processed.

Not all staff may yet have been trained in operating the system, leading to a higher risk of error, and controls may not yet have been fully implemented. This all means that transactions and balances relating to members are at risk of misstatement.

Fee paid to celebrity athlete

The $1 million paid to the celebrity athlete is material as it exceeds the threshold of $345,000.

Given that the athlete is providing a service to the company for two years, the cost should be recognised over that two-year period, with an element of the cost deferred.

If all of the expense has been recognised this year, profit is understated and assets are understated.

Operating expenses

Operating expenses includes staff costs, which are projected to increase by 7%, marketing costs, which are projected to stay at the same amount compared to 20X4, and maintenance and repair costs which have increased by 3.8%.

Given the increase in revenue of 17.8%, and the scale of operations increasing by the opening of two new centres, these categories of expenses would be expected to increase by a larger amount this year.

It could be that expenses have been omitted in error, or have been deliberately excluded, thereby understating expenses and overstating profit. These trends should be discussed with management, especially the staff costs of $15.3 million, as this alone is highly material.

(c) (i) **Ethical and professional issues**

Payroll service

Huntsman & Co provides the payroll service to Emu Gyms Co. This would give rise to a self-review threat because our firm has determined the payroll figures which form part of the financial statements which would then be subject to audit or limited assurance review and may result in over reliance on the payroll figures included in the financial statements.

Huntsman & Co should consider whether the payroll figure is material to the financial statements, and whether safeguards can be used to reduce any ethical threats to an acceptable level, for example, through the use of separate teams to provide the audit or limited assurance review and the payroll services and by having an independent second partner to review the work performed. If safeguards do not reduce the threats to an acceptable level, then the payroll service should not be carried out in addition to the audit or limited assurance review.

Providing the payroll service could also be seen as acting on behalf of management, further impairing the objectivity of the audit or limited assurance review provided on the financial statements. However, if the payroll service is purely routine transaction processing in its nature, this is less of a threat.

According to the IESBA *International Code of Ethics for Professional Accountants*, in order to avoid the risk of assuming a management responsibility, prior to accepting the non-audit service the firm should satisfy itself that company management:

- has designated an individual who possesses suitable skill, knowledge and experience to be responsible for client decisions and oversee the services

- will provide oversight of the services and evaluate the adequacy of the results of the services performed; and

- accept responsibility for the actions, if any, to be taken arising from the results of the services.

Conflict of interest

A further potential ethical issue arises in that our firm audits Redback Sports Co, which could be a competitor of Emu Gyms Co despite their difference in size. This situation can create a conflict of interest.

According to the IESBA *International Code of Ethics for Professional Accountants*, before accepting a new client relationship or engagement, the audit firm should identify circumstances which could give rise to a conflict of interest and evaluate the significance of any ethical threats raised.

In this case, Huntsman & Co should disclose to both Emu Gyms Co and Redback Sports Co that the firm acts for both companies and obtain consent from both companies. The firm should also use separate teams to carry out work for the two companies and establish appropriate review procedures by an independent member of the firm.

Huntsman & Co should also remain alert for changes in circumstances which may make the conflict of interest more of an issue, for example, if Redback Sports Co identified that Emu Gyms Co could be a potential target company to acquire as part of its planned growth strategy.

(ii) **Suspected fraud**

An audit and a limited assurance review differ in their scope and in the nature of procedures which are performed. It is not the purpose of either an audit or a limited assurance review to detect or prevent fraud, this is the responsibility of management, but arguably the indicators of fraud may have been noticed earlier if either had been performed.

In an audit, there is a wide scope in the work performed. Audit procedures are comprehensive, including tests of detail and tests of control, and will cover all material aspects of the financial statements. Given that historically the revenue from shop and café sales represented 5% and 8% of the company's revenue, these would represent a material source of revenue, and there would have been audit testing of the revenue transactions, including tests of detail performed on a sample basis. Additionally, the change in gross profit margin from 32% to 26% would have alerted the auditor to an unusual trend, leading to additional audit procedures being performed.

Part of the audit process is documenting and evaluating internal controls, and this would have involved an assessment of the controls over sales in the shops and cafés and over inventory. It is likely that deficiencies in internal controls, which may be allowing fraud to be carried out unnoticed, would be detected by the audit process and then communicated to management.

However, it is possible that even with an audit being conducted, the fraud might not have been detected. This is because frauds are usually concealed, and particularly if the employees involved have been colluding to carry out the fraud, it would be difficult to detect, especially if there has been deliberate falsification of accounting records.

In addition, the amounts involved are not highly material, the amount of inventory held by the company is small, meaning that this may not have been classified as an area with a high risk of material misstatement if an audit had been conducted. The inventory held at the shops is not likely to be material, and the inventory count might not have been attended by the audit team.

Also, the detailed testing of sales transactions may not have uncovered the fraud given that the fraud appears to be based on theft of inventory. It is possible that the fraud would only have been uncovered through detailed testing of the controls over movement of inventory.

If a limited assurance review had been carried out, again it may have uncovered the fraud, but it is less likely compared to an audit. This is because a limited assurance review has a narrower scope than an audit, and investigation procedures are usually limited to only enquiry and analytical review. Tests of controls and detailed tests of detail are not carried out and therefore control deficiencies would not be picked up or reported to management, and it is not likely that inventory in the shop and café would have been a priority for review.

In conclusion, Mick is correct in thinking that if the company's financial statements had been subject to audit or limited assurance review before now, the suspected fraud is likely to have been uncovered by the audit, and may have been uncovered by a limited assurance review. However, if the fraud was well concealed, it is possible that even an audit would not have uncovered the activities of the fraudsters.

Conclusion

The evaluation in relation to Redback Sports Co indicates that the company faces a range of business risks, for instance, possible overtrading and problems with liquidity. There are also a number of significant audit risks which will impact on our audit planning, for example, the accounting treatment which has been applied to a government grant, and possible understatement of expenses. There is a significant risk of management bias given the company's plans for expansion. In relation to Emu Gyms Co, our firm should be able to provide a limited assurance review or audit of the company, provided that safeguards are put in place to reduce ethical threats, in particular self-review in relation to payroll costs, to an acceptable level. Finally, a discussion has been provided which considers whether an audit or limited assurance review would have uncovered the fraud which Mick suspects is taking place.

Examiner's comments

Requirements (a) and (b) focused on audit planning for an existing audit client and requirement (c) related to a non-audit client.

Requirement (a) asked candidates to evaluate the business risks arising from the scenario in the question which focused on an existing audit client which operated a number of sports and leisure centres. This requirement is historically one where candidates achieve a strong pass and this trend continued in this exam. It was pleasing to see that most candidates focused on the risks arising from the scenario and avoided speculative or generic risks. There were two marks available for each business risk and it should be noted that factors from the scenario could be described in a number of different ways in order to attract credit for that risk. The key here is that candidates look for a variety of indicators within the scenario on which to base their evaluation. Some candidates could improve their time management and marks here by avoiding repeating the same risk from lots of different angles – failure of the expansion strategy for example could be discussed in terms of a stock exchange listing, new gyms opened, diversification of services offered or acquisition plans however there are only two marks available for a risk connected to this indicator so discussing all of those in depth meant candidates didn't' have the time to describe sufficient risks. Candidates that remained focused here often achieved full marks.

Those that focused on solely expansion and health and safety compliance from several different angles tended to only score four of the available marks.

Although this requirement provided candidates with a strong start to the examination, there were a significant number of candidates who demonstrated a lack of understanding over the role of non-executive directors in relation to the scenario. Non-executive directors (NEDs) are typically brought onto a board for their knowledge and skill in a particular field. One such director in the question had previously been the chairman of a rival company. This director brought industry specific business experience to the board and this practice is typical in the business world, however many candidates appeared to think that he would leak information back to the company where he had previously held a non-executive position, out of loyalty. Very few candidates identified the real weaknesses in the board, such as a lack of financial expertise amongst the NEDs and a lack of an audit committee. It is often the case in exam answers that candidates do not appear to understand the difference between executive directors/management and NEDs/those charged with governance (TCWG) and as a result use the terms management and TCWG interchangeably.

Part (b) required candidates to evaluate the risks of material misstatements (RoMM) arising from the scenario. This was generally well attempted by the majority of candidates and covered financial reporting issues such as revenue recognition, the treatment of government grants, related party transactions and loan finance, alongside control risks such as the lack of independence of the internal audit department and systems changes. Where RoMMs covered financial reporting issues, candidates who followed the process of calculating materiality, stating the relevant accounting rule and applying that to the scenario to show where the risk arose and the impact on the financial statements were able to score full marks on risks covered. Some common issues in candidate answers included:

- Interpreting the question as all audit risks rather than RoMM which meant time was lost discussing detection risks which could not attain marks.

- Lack of knowledge of basic double entry and the subsequent impact on the financial statements.

- Discussing speculative risks not present in the scenario such as brands and intangible assets.

- Giving audit procedures for each risk which is not required and therefore attains no credit.

It should be noted that when the question asks for RoMM, it does not require the definition of risks, theory behind audit or the audit approach to address the risks. Candidates who have studied past exams will have noted that in planning questions where audit procedures are required this has been asked for as a separate requirement and only cover specific areas of the scenario.

Part (c) introduced another client into the scenario. Candidates needed to evaluate ethical and professional issues with respect to an engagement to provide either an audit or a limited assurance review for an existing non-audit client. It was disappointing that while most candidates know the names of ethical threats the majority of candidates still do not sufficiently justify how they arise or the implication, both of which are needed to score the marks at this level. In this case, a self-review threat arose with respect to payroll work done at the client. The firm also provided tax advice to the owner but not the company. Typical answers that candidates wrote which would not attain any credit included:

- Providing other services gives rise to a self-review threat – this statement shows no appreciation of which services give rise to this threat nor any implication.

- Providing personal tax services to the owner is a self-review threat – this is incorrect, there is generally no financial statement/audit impact arising from the owner's personal tax (if there were it would be given in the scenario).

- Providing payroll services gives rise to self-review – this answer is better but still does not demonstrate that candidates know that the threat arises because the payroll figure is a material figure in the financial statements and would therefore be subject to audit by the firm.

Often candidates who were able to link the self-review threat to the audit of the payroll figure would not describe the implication of the threat to enable them to score a full mark. Simply saying that self-review means the auditor is not objective does not demonstrate understanding of the concept – how that lack of objectivity manifests is also required. Detailed guidance on how to discuss ethical threats for the AAA examination is provided in a recent technical article which can be found on the ACCA website. Candidates often missed the conflict of interest between the first client in the question and the second client.

The final requirement asked candidates to discuss whether an audit or limited assurance engagement would have identified a fraud in a minor revenue stream at the second client in previous years. Candidates who discussed materiality, sampling and the different level of testing that the two alternatives would provide tended to score well. A common mistake from candidates was to discuss forensic audits to investigate fraud which was not something asked for in the requirement. Many candidates appeared to incorrectly think that a limited review of financial statements as an alternative to an audit is the same as a review of prospective financial information.

	ACCA Marking guide	Marks
(a)	**Business risk evaluation** Up to 2 marks for each business risk identified and explained. Marks may be awarded for other, relevant business risks not included in the marking guide. In addition, allow ½ mark for relevant trends which form part of the business risk evaluation, e.g. % increase in revenue and profit before tax. – Deficiencies in corporate governance/internal audit arrangements – Health and safety regulations – risk of non-compliance – Asset expenditure and maintenance – drain on cash flow – Liquidity problems and possible overtrading – Capacity restraints – due to big increase in members and government initiative – Marketing expenses – drain on cash – Government initiative – may impact negatively on existing memberships and risk that reporting to the government is not accurate – Expansion plans – could distract management – New management information system – risk inaccurate recording	
	Maximum	10
(b)	**Risk of material misstatement evaluation** Up to 3 marks for each significant risk of material misstatement evaluated (unless indicated otherwise). Marks may be awarded for other, relevant audit risks not included in the marking guide. In addition, ½ mark for relevant trends which form part of the audit risk evaluation (max 3 marks). Appropriate materiality calculations (max 2 marks) and justified materiality level should be awarded to a maximum of 1 mark. – Management bias – risk revenue/profit overstated, expenses understated – Deficiencies in internal controls – possibly ineffective audit committee (max 2 marks)	

- Revenue recognition – members' subscriptions and multiple streams of revenue
- Government grant – risk income recognised too early and provisions not recognised
- Bank loan – risk that deep discount not treated as finance cost
- Asset expenditure and maintenance costs – risk of misclassification
- Related party transaction – risk of inadequate disclosure and that finance costs not accrued
- Data management system – risk in transfer of data and lack of controls
- Amount paid to celebrity athlete – risk cost not spread over two-year period (max 2 marks)
- Staff costs and maintenance costs – risk of understatement (max 2 marks)

	Maximum	18

(c)   (i)   Ethical and professional issues
Up to 2 marks for each issue evaluated:
- Self-review threat due to providing payroll service
- Assessing management responsibility
- Conflict of interest as act for Redback Sports Co
- Safeguards/actions re potential conflict of interest (1 mark each)

(ii)   Suspected fraud
Up to 2 marks for each point of discussion:
- Audit has wider scope with tests of detail and tests of control being likely to have uncovered the fraud
- Limited assurance review only includes enquiry and analytical review
- Limited assurance review less likely to have uncovered the fraud
- Even with audit, fraud could have been concealed and may not have been detected

	Maximum	12

Professional marks
Communication
- Briefing note format and structure – use of headings/subheadings and an introduction
- Style, language and clarity – appropriate layout and tone of briefing notes, presentation of materiality and relevant calculations, appropriate use of the CBE tools, easy to follow and understand
- Effectiveness and clarity of communication – answer is relevant and tailored to the scenario
- Adherence to the specific requests made by the audit engagement partner

Analysis and evaluation
- Appropriate use of the information to determine and apply suitable calculations
- Effective prioritisation of the results of the evaluation of risks of material misstatement to demonstrate the likelihood and magnitude of risks and to facilitate the allocation of appropriate responses

Professional scepticism and professional judgement
- Appropriate application of professional judgement to draw conclusions and make informed decisions following recognition of unusual or unexpected movements, missing/incomplete information or challenging presented information as part of the risk evaluation
- Determination and justification of a suitable materiality level, appropriately and consistently applied
- Identification of possible management bias and consideration of the impact on the financial statements and the possible reasons for management's preference for certain accounting treatments

– Effective application of technical and ethical guidance to effectively challenge and critically assess how management has accounted for areas of significant judgement		
Commercial acumen		
– Use of effective examples and/or calculations from the scenario to illustrate points or recommendations		
– Appropriate recognition of the wider implications when considering the request by Emu Gyms Co		
Maximum		**10**
Total		**50**

10 EAGLE GROUP *Walk in the footsteps of a top tutor*

Top tutor tips

Determination of materiality: The email from the partner states that materiality should be based on profit, therefore at the start of your answer you should calculate the range for materiality using that benchmark and justify a figure within that range. If it is a new audit client or a client where there are apparent control risks, materiality should be set at the lower end of the range. If it is an existing client, materiality may be able to be set at the higher end of the range depending on the other risks mentioned in the scenario. The examining team will give credit for any reasonable explanation of the chosen materiality threshold, as the mark is to recognise that there is the application of professional judgement and that a candidate can justify their response. It is not required that candidates select the identical percentage or figure, or that they provide a justification identical to that shown in the model answer.

Part (a) asks you to evaluate the audit risks to be considered when planning the audit. Audit risk comprises the risk that the financial statements contain material misstatement and detection risk. Risk of material misstatement is usually due to non-compliance with an accounting standard, although it also includes control risk. Think about the requirements of the relevant accounting standards and what the client might be doing incorrectly. Detection risks are the risks the auditor fails to detect the material misstatements within the financial statements and include auditing a client for the first time or where there is a tight reporting deadline.

Prioritisation of risks: One mark is awarded for the prioritisation of the audit risks. The mark is for the act of justifying the reason, not for the actual justification used (i.e. a range of completely different answers could be awarded the mark), therefore if a reasonable explanation is given, the mark will be awarded. Prioritisation can be achieved by either ordering your answer in priority order and stating this is the case, or by summarising in a brief conclusion which risk, or risks, are most significant.

Part (b) asks for audit procedures in respect of goodwill. Make sure your procedures are clear and provide enough detail that they can be followed. Pay attention to the note which instructs you NOT to consider impairment testing or foreign currency retranslation. There will be no marks awarded for these points so do not waste time considering them.

Part (c) requires you to evaluate the planning and comment on any issues arising from the proposed audit strategy of the component auditor. This is essentially a quality management question but focused on the planning of the audit rather than the audit work that has been performed during the audit.

Part (d) covers a common ethical issue relating to provision of a non-audit service to an audit client. Your answer should explain the ethical threats that would arise, evaluate the significance of the threats and state the actions the firm should take to manage the threats.

Professional skills

Professional skills will be awarded for:

Communication – responding to the instructions in the partner's email such as preparing your answers in the form of briefing notes and using the stated benchmark for materiality.

Analysis and evaluation – applying the information from the scenario to answer the question and explaining the issues in sufficient depth.

Professional scepticism and judgement – justifying an appropriate materiality level, demonstrating critical thinking and being alert to possible manipulation and management bias.

Where relevant, professional marks will be awarded for commercial acumen which requires making practical and plausible recommendations and considering the wider implications of issues to the audit firm.

Briefing notes

To: Maya Crag, audit engagement partner

From: Audit manager

Subject: Eagle Group – audit planning

Date: 1 July 20X5

Introduction

These briefing notes are prepared to assist with planning the audit of the Eagle Group (the Group). The notes contain an evaluation of the significant audit risks which should be considered in planning the Group audit. The notes also recommend the principal audit procedures to be used in the audit of the goodwill which has arisen in respect of a newly acquired subsidiary. The notes then go on to evaluate an extract from the audit strategy which has been prepared by a component auditor. Finally, the Group finance director has requested our firm to provide a non-audit service in relation to the Group's integrated report, and the notes discuss the professional and ethical implications of this request.

Materiality

For the purposes of these briefing notes, the overall materiality level used to assess the significance of identified risks is $30 million based on the profitability of the Group, as requested.

Justification

Using profit before tax of $322 million as a suggested benchmark results in a suggested range of $16.1 million (5% × $322 million) to $32.2 million (10% × $322 million).

The overall risk level is low as this is an existing client, and no significant control issues have been noted at the planning stage or in previous audits. Materiality should be set at the higher end of the range.

This benchmark is only a starting point for determining materiality and professional judgement will need to be applied in determining a final level to be used during the course of the audit.

(a) **Evaluation of audit risk**

Selected analytical procedures and associated audit risk evaluation

	20X5	**20X4**
Operating profit margin	350/5,770 × 100 = 6.1%	270/5,990 × 100 = 4.5%
Return on capital employed	(350/2,245 + 650) × 100 = 12.1%	(270/2,093 + 620) × 100 = 10%
Current ratio	1,450/597 = 2.4	1,420/547 = 2.6
Debt/equity	550/2,245 × 100 = 24.5%	500/2,093 × 100 = 23.9%
Interest cover	350/28 = 12.5	270/30 = 9
Effective tax rate	64/322 × 100 = 19.9%	60/240 × 100 = 25%

Operating profit margin and operating expenses

The Group's operating profit margin has increased from 4.5% to 6.1% despite a fall in revenue of 3.7%. This is due to a reduction in operating expenses of 4.5% and increase in other operating income of 50%. Return on capital employed shows a similar positive trend, despite the fall in revenue. There is an audit risk that expenses are understated, with the reduction in expenses being proportionately more than the reduction in revenue.

Within operating expenses, the trends for each component are different – cost of raw materials consumables and supplies has decreased by 3.1%, which appears reasonable given the decline in revenue of 3.7%. However, staff costs have increased slightly by 1.1% which seems inconsistent with the revenue trend and with the increased automation of operations which has led to 5,000 staff being made redundant, which presumably means lower payroll costs this year. Expenses could have been misclassified into staff costs in error.

Depreciation, amortisation and impairment have increased by 3.6%, which is not a significant change, but will need to be investigated to consider how each element of the category has changed in the year. The most noticeable trend within operating expenses is that the other operating expenses category has reduced very significantly. The amount recognised this financial year is only 7.4% of the amount recognised the previous year which appears totally inconsistent with the other trends noted. It could be that some costs, for example, accrued expenses, have not yet been accounted for, or that the 20X4 figure was unusually high.

Other operating income

There is an audit risk that other operating income is overstated. According to the information in note 6, during the year a credit of $60 million has been recognised in profit for reversals of provisions, this is 50% greater than the amount recognised in the previous year. In addition, a credit of $30 million has been recognised for reversals of impairment losses which is material based on the threshold stated above. There is a risk that these figures have been manipulated in order to boost profits, as an earnings management technique, in reaction to the fall in revenue in the year.

The risk of management bias is high given the listed status of the Group, hence expectations from shareholders for a positive growth trend. The profit recognised on asset disposal and the increase in foreign currency gains could also be an indication of attempts to boost operating profit this year.

Current ratio and gearing

Looking at the other ratios, the current ratio and gearing ratio do not indicate audit risks, however, more detail is needed to fully conclude on the liquidity and solvency position of the Group, and whether there are any hidden trends which are obscured by the high-level analysis which has been performed with the information provided.

The interest cover has increased, due to both an increase in operating profit and a reduction in finance charges. This seems contradictory to the increase in borrowings of $50 million, as a result of this an increase in finance charges would be expected. There is an audit risk that finance charges are understated.

Effective tax rate

The effective tax rate has fallen from 25% to 19.9%. An audit risk arises in that the tax expense and associated liability could be understated. This could indicate management bias as the financial statements suggest that accounting profit has increased, but the profit chargeable to tax used to determine the tax expense for the year appears to have decreased. There could be alternative explanations, for instance a fall in the rate of tax levied by the authorities, which will need to be investigated by the audit team.

Consolidation of foreign subsidiaries

Given that the Group has many foreign subsidiaries, including the recent investment in Lynx Co, audit risks relating to their consolidation are potentially significant. Lynx Co has net assets with a fair value of $300 million according to the goodwill calculation provided by management, representing 8.6% of the Group's total assets and 13.4% of Group net assets. This makes Lynx Co material to the Group. Audit risks relevant to Lynx Co's status as a foreign subsidiary also attach to the Group's other foreign subsidiaries.

According to IAS 21 *The Effects of Changes in Foreign Exchange Rates*, the assets and liabilities of Lynx Co and other foreign subsidiaries should be retranslated using the closing exchange rate. Its income and expenses should be retranslated at the exchange rates at the dates of the transactions. The risk is that incorrect exchange rates are used for the retranslations. This could result in over/understatement of the assets, liabilities, income and expenses which are consolidated, including goodwill. It would also mean that the exchange gains and losses arising on retranslation and to be included in Group other comprehensive income are incorrectly determined.

In addition, Lynx Co was acquired on 1 December 20X4 and its income and expenses should have been consolidated from that date. There is a risk that the full year's income and expenses have been consolidated, leading to a risk of understatement of Group profit given that Lynx Co is forecast to be loss making this year, according to the audit strategy prepared by Vulture Associates.

Measurement and recognition of exchange gains and losses

The calculation of exchange gains and losses can be complex, and there is a risk that it is not calculated correctly, or that some elements are omitted, for example, the exchange gain or loss on goodwill may be missed out of the calculation.

IAS 21 states that exchange gains and losses arising as a result of the retranslation of the subsidiary's balances are recognised in other comprehensive income. The risk is incorrect classification, for example, the gain or loss could be recognised incorrectly as part of profit for the year, for example, included in the $28 million foreign currency gains which form part of other operating income, which would be incorrect. The amount recognised within other operating income has increased, as only $23 million foreign currency gains were recognised the previous year, indicating a potential risk of overstatement.

Goodwill

The total goodwill recognised in the Group statement of financial position is $1,100 million, making it highly material.

Analytical review shows that the goodwill figure has increased by $130 million during the year. The goodwill relating to the acquisition of Lynx Co is $100 million according to management's calculations. Therefore, there appears to be an unexplained increase in value of goodwill of $30 million during the year which is material. There is an audit risk that the goodwill figure is overstated, unless justified by additional acquisitions or possibly by changes in value on the retranslation of goodwill relating to foreign subsidiaries, though this latter point would seem unlikely given the large size of the unexplained increase in value.

According to IFRS 3 *Business Combinations*, goodwill should be subject to an impairment review on an annual basis. Management has asserted that while they will test goodwill for impairment prior to the financial year end, they do not think that any impairment will be recognised. This view is based on what could be optimistic assumptions about further growth in revenue, and it is likely that the assumptions used in management's impairment review are similarly overoptimistic. Therefore, there is a risk that goodwill will be overstated and Group operating expenses understated if impairment losses have not been correctly determined and recognised.

Initial measurement of goodwill arising on acquisition of Lynx Co

In order for goodwill to be calculated, the assets and liabilities of Lynx Co must have been identified and measured at fair value at the date of acquisition. Risks of material misstatement arise because the various components of goodwill each have specific risks attached. The goodwill of $100 million is material to the Group by reference to the threshold calculated above.

A specific risk arises in relation to the fair value of net assets acquired. Not all assets and liabilities may have been identified, for example, contingent liabilities and contingent assets may be omitted.

A further risk relates to measurement at fair value, which is subjective and based on assumptions which may not be valid. The fair value of Lynx Co's net assets according to the goodwill calculation is $300 million, having been subject to a fair value uplift of $12 million. This was provided by an independent firm of accountants, which provides some comfort on the validity of the figure.

There is also a risk that the cost of investment is not stated correctly, for example, that the contingent consideration has not been determined on an appropriate basis.

First, the interest rate used to determine the discount factor is 18% which seems high given that the Group's weighted average cost of capital is stated to be 10%.

Second, the contingent consideration is only payable if Lynx Co reaches certain profit targets. Given that the company, according to Vulture Associate's audit strategy, is projected to be loss making, it could be that the contingent consideration need not be recognised at all, or determined to be a lower figure than that currently recognised, based on a lower probability of it having to be paid.

The results of the analytical review have indicated that the other side of the journal entry for the contingent consideration is not described as a component of the non-current liabilities and the accounting for this will need to be clarified as there is a risk that it has been recorded incorrectly, perhaps as a component of equity.

Intangible assets

In relation to expenditure on intangible assets during the year, which totals $60 million, there are several audit risks. First, there is a question over whether all of this amount should have been capitalised as an intangible asset. Capitalisation is only appropriate where an asset has been created, and specifically in relation to development costs, the criteria from IAS 38 *Intangible Assets* must all be met. There is a risk that if any criteria have not been met, for example, if there is no probable future economic benefit from research into the new technology, then the amount should be expensed. There is a risk that intangible assets are overstated and operating expenses understated.

There is also an unexplained trend, in that intangible assets has only increased by $30 million, yet expenditure on intangible assets, according to management information, is $60 million. More information is needed to reconcile the expenditure as stated by management to the movement in intangible assets recognised in the Group statement of financial position.

Second, there is a risk that the amortisation period is not appropriate. It seems that the same useful life of 15 years has been applied to all of the different categories of intangible assets; this is not likely to be specific enough, for example, the useful life of an accounting system will not be the same as for development of robots. Fifteen years also seems to be a long period – usually technology-related assets are written off over a relatively short period to take account of rapid developments in technology. In respect of amortisation periods being too long, there is a risk that intangible assets are overstated and operating expenses understated.

Detection risk in relation to Lynx Co

Lynx Co is the only subsidiary which is not audited by Bison & Co. This gives rise to a risk that the quality of the audit of Lynx Co may not be to the same standard as Bison & Co, as Vulture Associates may not be used to auditing companies which form part of a listed group and results in increased detection risk at the Group level. The risk is increased by the problems with the audit strategy prepared by Vulture Associates, which will be discussed in part (c) to these briefing notes, which indicate that the audit of Lynx Co has not been appropriately planned in accordance with ISA requirements. Since our firm has not worked with Vulture Associates previously, we are not familiar with their methods and we may have issues with the quality of their work. The detection risk is high in relation to Lynx Co's balances which will form part of the consolidated financial statements.

(b)   Principal audit procedures on the goodwill arising on the acquisition of Lynx Co

- Obtain the legal documentation pertaining to the acquisition, and review to confirm that the figures included in the goodwill calculation relating to consideration paid and payable are accurate and complete. In particular, confirm the targets to be used as the basis for payment of the contingent consideration in four years' time.

- Also confirm from the purchase documentation that the Group has obtained an 80% shareholding and that this conveys control, i.e. the shares carry voting rights and there is no restriction on the Group exercising their control over Lynx Co.

- Agree the $80 million cash paid to the bank statement and bank ledger account/cash book of the acquiring company (presumably the parent company of the Group).

- Review the board minutes for discussions relating to the acquisition, and for the relevant minute of board approval.

- For the contingent consideration, obtain management's calculation of the present value of $271 million, and evaluate assumptions used in the calculation, in particular to consider the probability of payment by obtaining revenue and profit forecasts for Lynx Co for the next four years.

- Discuss with management the reason for using an 18% interest rate in the calculation, asking them to justify the use of this interest rate when the Group's weighted average cost of capital is stated at 10%.

- Evaluate management's rationale for using the 18% interest rate, concluding as to whether it is appropriate.

- Confirm that the fair value of the non-controlling interest has been calculated based on an externally available share price at the date of acquisition. Agree the share price used in management's calculation to stock market records showing the share price of Lynx Co at the date of acquisition.

- Obtain a copy of the due diligence report issued by Sidewinder & Co, review for confirmation of acquired assets and liabilities and their fair values.

- Evaluate the methods used to determine the fair value of acquired assets, including the property, and liabilities to confirm compliance with IFRS 3 and IFRS 13 *Fair Value Measurement*.

- Review the calculation of net assets acquired to confirm that Group accounting policies have been applied.

(c) **Evaluation of the extract of the audit strategy prepared by Vulture Associates in respect of their audit of Lynx Co**

It appears that ISA requirements have not been followed, meaning that the quality of the audit planned by Vulture Associates is in doubt.

In relation to reliance on internal controls, ISA 330/ISA (UK) 330 *The Auditor's Responses to Assessed Risks* contains requirements in relation to relying on work performed during previous audits on internal controls. ISA 330 states that if the auditor plans to use audit evidence from a previous audit about the operating effectiveness of specific controls, the auditor shall establish the continuing relevance of that evidence by obtaining audit evidence about whether significant changes in those controls have occurred subsequent to the previous audit.

The auditor shall obtain this evidence by performing inquiry combined with observation or inspection, to confirm the understanding of those specific controls, and if there have been changes which affect the continuing relevance of the audit evidence from the previous audit, the auditor shall test the controls in the current audit.

If there have not been such changes, the auditor shall test the controls at least once in every third audit, and shall test some controls each audit to avoid the possibility of testing all the controls on which the auditor intends to rely on a single audit period with no testing of controls in the subsequent two audit periods.

Therefore, in order to comply with ISA 330, Vulture Associates needs to do more than simply accept management's assertion that there have been no changes to controls. There needs to be some observation or inspection of controls, to confirm that there have been no changes, and this work and an appropriate conclusion need to be documented in the audit working papers.

In addition, there should be some testing of internal controls each year, so Vulture Associates should plan to perform some test of controls each year, so that over a three-year cycle, all controls are tested to confirm that controls are still operating effectively and therefore can continue to be relied upon.

The Group audit team should discuss this issue with Vulture Associates to ensure that adequate controls testing is performed. If, for some reason, Vulture Associates does not amend its audit strategy, then the Group audit team may decide to perform additional testing, given that Lynx Co is material to the Group.

(d) **Ethical and professional implications of the request to provide a non-audit service on the Group's integrated report**

There are several issues to consider with regard to providing this service.

A significant issue relates to auditor objectivity. The IESBA *International Code of Ethics for Professional Accountants* (the *Code*) and the FRC Ethical Standard provide guidance on situations where the auditor is asked by the client to provide non-assurance services. Bison & Co needs to evaluate the significance of the threat and consider whether any safeguards can reduce the threat to an acceptable level.

While the integrated report is not part of the audited financial statements, the report will contain financial key performance indicators (KPIs), and the Group has asked for input specifically relating to the reconciliations between these KPIs and financial information contained in the financial statements. There is therefore a potential self-review threat to objectivity in that the audit firm has been asked to provide assurance on these KPIs which are related to figures which have been subject to external audit by the firm. The team performing the work will be reluctant to raise queries or highlight errors which have been made during the external audit when assessing the reconciliations of KPIs to audited financial information.

It could also be perceived that Bison & Co is taking on management responsibility by helping to determine content to be included in the integrated report, which is a threat to objectivity. The *Code* states that the audit firm shall not assume management responsibility for an audit client and that the threats created are so significant that safeguards cannot reduce them to an acceptable level.

While the *Code* does not specifically state that helping the client to determine the content of its integrated report is taking on management responsibility, certainly there could be that perception as the auditor will be involved in setting measurements which the company will benchmark itself against.

Additionally, working with management on the integrated report could create a familiarity threat to objectivity whereby close working relationships are formed, and the auditor becomes closely aligned with the views of management and is unable to approach the work with an appropriate degree of professional scepticism.

There is a potential problem in terms of compliance with ISA 720/ISA (UK) 720 *The Auditor's Responsibilities Relating to Other Information*, should Bison & Co accept the engagement. ISA 720 requires that auditors read other information in order to identify any material inconsistencies between the financial statements and information in the other information.

ISA 720 applies only to other information in the annual report, and it is not stated whether the Group's integrated report will be included in the annual report, or as a standalone document. Based on the above, it would seem unlikely that Bison & Co can provide this service to the Group, due to the threats to objectivity created.

Should the firm decide to take on the engagement, safeguards should be used to minimise the threats. For example, a partner who is independent should be involved in reviewing the audit work performed.

Aside from ethical issues, Bison & Co must also consider whether they have the competence to perform the work. Advising on the production of an integrated report is quite a specialist area, and it could be that the audit firm does not have the appropriate levels of expertise and experience to provide a quality service to the Group.

The fact that the Group wants to highlight its technological achievements, and presumably will select a range of non-financial KPIs and technological issues to discuss in the integrated report, makes the issue of competence more significant, as the audit firm may not have the necessary technical knowledge to provide advice in this area.

Aside from competence, the firm should also consider whether it has resources in terms of staff availability to complete the work to the desired deadline and to perform appropriate reviews of the work which has been completed.

Finally, given that the Group is a listed entity, it should comply with relevant corporate governance requirements. This means that the audit firm may be prohibited from providing services in addition to providing the external audit to the Group. The audit committee should apply the Group's policy on the engagement of the external auditor to supply non-audit services, the objective of which should be to ensure that the provision of such services does not impair the external auditor's independence or objectivity.

The Group's audit committee will need to approve the provision of the service before it can be taken on, and in making this decision they should consider a number of matters, for instance, the audit committee should consider whether the skills and experience of the audit firm make it the most suitable supplier of the non-audit service, whether there are safeguards in place to eliminate or reduce to an acceptable level any threat to objectivity and the level of fees to be incurred relative to the audit fee.

Conclusion

These briefing notes indicate that there are a number of audit risks to be considered in planning the audit, and that management needs to supply the audit team with a range of additional information for more thorough audit planning to be carried out. The audit of goodwill is an area of significant audit risk due to the subjectivity involved and the fact that there is a significant unexplained increase.

The goodwill arising on acquisition of Lynx Co is a particular risk due to the discount factor used in the calculation of the contingent consideration which appears to be unreasonable. The notes recommend the principal audit procedures which should be conducted. An evaluation of the audit strategy prepared by Vulture Associates indicates that their audit of Lynx Co might not be a high-quality audit. Finally, our firm needs to discuss the request to assist in preparing the Group's integrated report with the Group audit committee, and it seems unlikely given the threat of management involvement that we would be able to carry out this work for the Group.

Examiner's comments

Question one was a 50-mark case study style question set at the planning stage for an audit. The client was a large international listed distribution company which had a new foreign subsidiary acquisition in the year.

The first requirement was to produce an analysis of audit risks using analytical review of financials and other information provided on specific issues arising during the year. The majority of marks were available for the evaluation of significant audit risks, which is consistent with past requirements of this type. This requirement was generally well attempted by the majority of candidates who calculated relevant ratios, discussed the risks arising from unexpected trends and relationships, and then analysed the risks arising from the specific issues described in the question. Using this approach and providing an evaluation containing the required level of detail, well prepared candidates were able to identify the specific risks from the information provided and score a clear pass on this part of the question.

The model answers provided to recent past audit risk questions will illustrate how to structure answers to achieve maximum credit on this sort of requirement. It was pleasing to note that very few candidates spent time describing the theory of audit risk which is not required and should not be included in an answer unless the examiner has asked for it.

Despite the good attempt made on this part of the examination there were some common exam technique issues which resulted in difficulties for candidates in terms of attaining marks and managing their time. The first of these was the approach taken by some candidates to the analytical review.

Common issues arising from the analytical review were:

- Calculating too many ratios and trends which were not then mentioned in the main body of the candidate's answer and were a waste of effort – candidates are expected to demonstrate the auditing skill of knowing which items are unlikely to give rise to an audit risk – for example an immaterial area of the statement of financial position that hasn't moved much since the previous year and is not referred to in the question scenario is less likely to contain an audit risk. Candidates should consider how many risks and calculations are likely to be needed to score full marks rather than calculate 30+ ratio/trends which they then do not have time to discuss. A few key ratios along the lines of those seen in the answers to past questions are most likely to direct candidates on where to focus.

- Calculating ratios and then not referring to them – an analytical review is not simply calculating ratios. The ability to calculate ratios is examined within earlier parts of the qualification. It is what the results show that is the applied skill in this area and candidates who do not use the results of their calculations to draw conclusions and identify risks will not be able to attain credit.

- Not calculating any ratios – ignoring the requirement to perform an analytical review will restrict the risks identified from the scenario and hence make scoring maximum credit very difficult. This was most apparent in scripts from candidates sitting the UK version of the examination where many scored very few marks on this section of the question.

Another common mistake candidates made on this requirement was to spend a lot of time discussing speculative risks which generally do not obtain credit. The fact that a company is multinational with many subsidiaries does not automatically result in a key audit risk regarding the inability of the company to know how to perform a consolidation, or to account for foreign currency. The fact that this is not a new client and the audit engagement partner did not raise any concerns in this regard in the past should be taken as a sign that these are not key issues. Candidates should instead focus on the details given in the scenario that the engagement partner thought relevant to highlight. In this case, the acquisition of a new subsidiary and the risks arising from what is a significant non-routine transaction, the significant spend during the year on research and development which has been capitalised, and the fact that management does not believe there is any impairment of assets despite falling revenues. Recent past question answers illustrate the sort of risks which are considered relevant to the accompanying scenarios. Speculative risks do not attract credit in the examination and it is surprising that candidates chose to evaluate such risks when there were so many specific risks contained within the scenario. This session it was disappointing how many candidates opened with speculative risks such as failure to cancel intra-group balances, failure to account for day-to-day foreign currency transactions, and the control risk arising from international subsidiaries.

Candidates would score better if they were to prioritise risks in their planning and to focus on the ones described in detail by the examiner in the scenario rather than reproducing a rote learnt list of general points which do not demonstrate any application of knowledge to the scenario itself. A related mistake made by candidates was to discuss operating segments and EPS disclosures despite the requirement stating that these should not be considered. This has been the case in several sessions where the examiner has requested candidates do not consider presentation risks.

Other commonly seen technical errors arose in relation to provisions where candidates would assume that redundancies early in the financial year would give rise to a year-end redundancy provision. Post-year-end redundancies are those which may give rise to a provision. Similarly, candidates often thought that, because automation was introduced during the year, it was likely that a similar strategy would exist in the future therefore provisions should be made for more redundancies "just in case". Such reasoning demonstrates a lack of comprehension of the fundamental concept of a liability and the requirement for a constructive obligation to exist before a provision can be made. For up–to-date examples of how audit risk is examined and the sort of points the examiner expects to be raised from a given scenario, candidates should refer to the recent published exams available on the ACCA website. Candidates should note however that these are illustrative and that not every risk covered in those examples will be relevant to future questions on audit risk. A helpful exercise might be to map back the areas covered in the model answers to the indicators in the specific scenario to better understand how the examiner's answers reflect the specific areas of the information provided. In particular the September 2018 exam should provide an illustration of the type and volume of calculations that the examiner considered appropriate based on the marks available and the information provided. In addition to these issues, otherwise capable candidates failed to attain a strong mark on this section of the examination by failing to address the requirement.

Particularly common in the UK and Irish versions of the examination was candidates discussing issues in terms of business risk or audit procedures, which were not asked for, and not actually evaluating the audit risk. Often candidates referred to accounting standards by number but made no attempt to describe the accounting treatment or to apply it to the scenario to determine the risks of material misstatement or would simply say that areas might be misstated without reference to the balance or direction of misstatement.

The second requirement asked candidates to provide audit procedures on the goodwill figure at acquisition for the subsidiary purchased in the year. Where candidates focused on the specific requirement and addressed the acquisition figure they generally scored full marks or close to full marks. Some candidates limited their marks here by discussing impairment reviews and disclosures instead.

The third requirement asked candidates to review and evaluate the component auditor's strategy. This was the area of Question one which caused candidates the most difficulty. The requirement asked candidates to specifically focus only on the issue mentioned and that all other considerations were satisfactory. Despite this a majority of candidates wrote answers describing the assessment of independence and competence of the component auditor. The strategy stated the intention to audit using a controls-based strategy but without testing controls this year as prior year results were good. Those that did go so far as to appraise the component strategy often thought that a controls-based approach was not permitted, and substantive testing should be performed in all places. Very few candidates appeared to appreciate that controls may be tested on a three-year cycle rather than every year.

The final requirement related to the client's request for the auditor to be involved in choosing KPIs for inclusion in the client's integrated report and to provide assurance on the report. Many candidates realised that there were ethical issues arising from this but did not explain specifically how they would arise or what the implication would be. Candidates should be prepared to give such detail in order to demonstrate understanding rather than simply list without explanation every possible threat to independence.

	ACCA Marking guide	
		Marks

(a) **Audit risk evaluation**

Up to 3 marks for each audit risk identified and explained. Marks may be awarded for other relevant audit risks not included in the marking guide.

In addition, 1 mark for relevant ratios and ½ mark for relevant trends which form part of analytical review to a max of 5 marks.

Appropriate materiality calculations (max 2 marks) and justified materiality level should be awarded to a maximum of 1 mark.

- Operating profit margin and ROCE changes – risk understated expenses/ overstated revenue
- Trends within operating expenses and related audit risks, e.g. misclassification of expenses
- Other operating income – risk of overstatement
- Risk of management bias due to listed status (max 2 marks)
- Current ratio & gearing and related audit risks – understated finance costs
- Effective tax rate – understatement of tax expense (max 2 marks)
- Consolidation of foreign subsidiaries
- Recognition and measurement of foreign exchange gains and losses
- Goodwill –measurement risk – lack of impairment review
- Goodwill on acquisition of Lynx Co (max 4 for detailed discussion)
- Intangible assets – audit risks in relation to unexplained movement in the year, whether amounts should have been capitalised and amortisation period (max 5 marks)
- Increased detection risk regarding Lynx Co due to be audited by a component auditor

	Maximum	23

(b) **Audit procedures on the goodwill recognised on acquisition of Lynx Co**

Up to 1 mark for each well described procedure

- Obtain and review legal documentation, in particular confirm the targets used as the basis for payment of contingent consideration
- Confirm that the Group has obtained an 80% shareholding and that this conveys control
- Agree the $80 million cash paid to the bank statement and bank ledger account/cash book of the acquiring company
- Review the board minutes for relevant discussions including the minute of board approval
- Obtain management's calculation of contingent consideration, and evaluate assumptions used
- Discuss the 18% interest rate used in determining the discount factor and evaluate the justification given by management
- Confirm that the fair value of the non-controlling interest has been calculated based on an externally available share price at the date of acquisition by agreeing to stock market records
- Obtain a copy of the due diligence report issued by Sidewinder & Co, review for confirmation of acquired assets and liabilities and their fair values
- Evaluation of the methods used to determine the fair value of acquired assets, including the property, and liabilities to confirm compliance with IFRS 3 and IFRS 13 *Fair Value Measurement*
- Review the calculation of net assets acquired to confirm that Group accounting policies have been applied

	Maximum	6

(c) **Evaluation of Vulture Co's audit strategy**
Up to 2 marks for each issue evaluated
Controls effectiveness
- Evidence needs to be obtained to confirm that controls have not changed
- Controls should be tested in a three-year cycle in order to place continued reliance on them
- Group audit team may decide to perform additional tests of control of Vulture Associates do not amend their strategy
- Conclusion on audit quality (1 mark)

Maximum	5

(d) **Ethical issues relating to request to assist management in preparing an integrated report**
Up to 2 marks for each relevant point explained, and 1 mark for relevant safeguard or action
- Explain the threats to objectivity created – self-review, familiarity and management involvement (1 mark each if fully explained)
- Conclusion as to whether service can be provided, following on from justification
- Suggest appropriate safeguards if engagement accepted, e.g. independent review (1 mark each)
- Explain that audit committee would need to approve the engagement
- Bison & Co to consider competence and resource availability
- Discuss with audit committee (1 mark)

Maximum	6

Professional marks
Communication
- Briefing note format and structure – use of headings/subheadings and an introduction
- Style, language and clarity – appropriate layout and tone of briefing notes, presentation of materiality and relevant calculations, appropriate use of the CBE tools, easy to follow and understand
- Effectiveness and clarity of communication – answer is relevant and tailored to the scenario
- Adherence to the specific requests made by the audit engagement partner

Analysis and evaluation
- Appropriate use of the information to determine and apply suitable calculations
- Appropriate use of the information to design appropriate audit procedures relating to goodwill arising on acquisition of Lynx Co
- Effective prioritisation of the results of the audit risk evaluation to demonstrate the likelihood and magnitude of risks and to facilitate the allocation of appropriate responses
- Balanced discussion of the professional and practical issues when evaluating working with component auditors in a Group engagement

Professional scepticism and professional judgement
- Appropriate application of professional judgement to draw conclusions and make informed decisions following recognition of unusual or unexpected movements, missing/incomplete information or challenging presented information as part of the risk evaluation
- Determination and justification of a suitable materiality level, appropriately and consistently applied
- Identification of possible management bias and consideration of the impact on the financial statements and the possible reasons for management's preference for certain accounting treatments
- Effective application of technical and ethical guidance to effectively challenge and critically assess how management has accounted for areas of significant judgement

Commercial acumen		
– Use of effective examples and/or calculations from the scenario to illustrate points or recommendations		
– Audit procedures are practical and plausible in the context of the scenario		
– Appropriate recognition of the wider implications when considering the request to select KPIs for inclusion in, and provide assurance, on the integrated report		
Maximum		10
Total		50

11 SUNSHINE HOTEL GROUP *Walk in the footsteps of a top tutor*

Top tutor tips

Determination of materiality: The email from the partner states that materiality should be based on profit, therefore at the start of your answer you should calculate the range for materiality using that benchmark and justify a figure within that range. If it is a new audit client or a client where there are apparent control risks, materiality should be set at the lower end of the range. If it is an existing client, materiality may be able to be set at the higher end of the range depending on the other risks mentioned in the scenario. The examining team will give credit for any reasonable explanation of the chosen materiality threshold, as the mark is to recognise that there is the application of professional judgement and that a candidate can justify their response. It is not required that candidates select the identical percentage or figure, or that they provide a justification identical to that shown in the model answer.

Part (a): When describing business risks, remember to explain the impact it will have on the company i.e. impact on profit or cash flow. The business risks must be ones which could impact the financial statements in order for the auditor to consider them.

Part (b): For risks of material misstatement, you need to explain how the financial statements may not have been prepared in accordance with the applicable financial reporting standard.

Prioritisation of risks: One mark is awarded for the prioritisation of the risks of material misstatement. The mark is for the act of justifying the reason, not for the actual justification used (i.e. a range of completely different answers could be awarded the mark), therefore if a reasonable explanation is given, the mark will be awarded. Prioritisation can be achieved by either ordering your answer in priority order and stating this is the case, or by summarising in a brief conclusion which risk, or risks, are most significant.

Part (c)(i): Consider how the auditor should deal with the issue of being asked to only speak with the Group FD regarding the claim from Ocean Protection.

Part (c)(ii) asks for audit procedures in respect of the claim for environmental damage caused by hotel guests. Make sure your procedures are clear and provide enough detail that they can be followed by the audit team.

Part (d) covers data analytics. You should read the relevant sections of the study text in this area and look out for any articles published on the topic.

> **Professional skills**
>
> Professional skills will be awarded for:
>
> Communication – responding to the instructions in the partner's email such as preparing your answers in the form of briefing notes and using the stated benchmark for materiality.
>
> Analysis and evaluation – applying the information from the scenario to answer the question and explaining the issues in sufficient depth.
>
> Professional scepticism and judgement – justifying an appropriate materiality level, demonstrating critical thinking and being alert to possible manipulation and management bias.
>
> Where relevant, professional marks will be awarded for commercial acumen which requires making practical and plausible recommendations and considering the wider implications of issues to the audit firm.

Briefing notes

To: John Starling, audit engagement partner

From: Audit manager

Subject: Sunshine Hotel Group – audit planning

Date: 1 July 20X5

Introduction

These briefing notes relate to the initial audit planning for the Sunshine Hotel Group (the Group). As requested, the notes contain an evaluation of the business risks facing our client, and the significant risks of material misstatement to be considered in our audit planning. The notes contain a discussion of the impact which an email received from the Group finance director relating to a claim for damages will have on our audit planning, as well as the recommended actions to be taken by Dove & Co and principal procedures which should be carried out in relation to this claim. Finally, the notes discuss how data analytics could be used in future audits of the Sunshine Hotel Group.

Materiality

For the purposes of these briefing notes, the overall materiality level used to assess the significance of identified risks is $1 million based on the profitability of the Group, as requested.

Justification

Using profit before tax of $10 million as a suggested benchmark results in a suggested range of $0.5 million (5% × $10 million) to $1 million (10% × $10 million).

This is an existing client, and no significant control issues have been noted at the planning stage or in previous audits. Therefore, the overall risk assessment is deemed to be low. Materiality should be set at the higher end of the range.

This benchmark is only a starting point for determining materiality and professional judgement will need to be applied in determining a final level to be used during the course of the audit.

(a)   **Evaluation of business risks**

Luxury product

The Group offers a luxury product aimed at an exclusive market. This in itself creates a business risk, as the Group's activities are not diversified, and any decline in demand will immediately impact on profitability and cash flows.

The demand for luxury holidays will be sensitive to economic problems such as recession and travel to international destinations will be affected by events in the transportation industry, for example, if oil prices increase, there will be a knock-on effect on air fares, meaning less demand for the Group's hotels.

Business expansion – inappropriate strategy

It is questionable whether the Group has a sound policy on expansion, given the problems encountered with recent acquisitions which have involved expanding into locations with political instability and local regulations which seem incompatible with the Group's operations and strategic goals.

The Group would appear to have invested $98 million in these unsuitable locations, and it is doubtful whether an appropriate return on these investments will be possible. There is a risk that further unsuitable investments will be made as a result of poor strategic decisions on where to locate new hotels.

The Group appears to have a strategy of fairly rapid expansion, acquiring new sites and a hotel complex without properly investigating their appropriateness and fit with the Group's business model.

Business expansion – finance

The Group is planning further expansion with asset (capital) expenditure of $45 million planned for new sites in 20X6 which will be financed by a bank loan. While the Group's gearing is currently low at 25%, the additional finance being taken out from the Group's lending facility will increase gearing and incur additional interest charges of $1.6 million per annum, which is 16% of the projected profit before tax for the year. The increased debt and finance charges could impact on existing loan covenants and the additional interest payments will have cash flow as well as profit implications.

A further $25 million is needed for renovating the hotels which were damaged following a hurricane. Despite the fact that the repair work following the hurricane will ultimately be covered by insurance, the Group's asset (capital) expenditure at this time appears very high, and needs to be underpinned by sound financial planning in order to maintain solvency, especially given that only half of the insurance claim in relation to repair work will be paid in advance and it may take some time to recover the full amount given the significant sums involved.

Moulin Blanche agreement

$5 million has been spent on an agreement which allows the company to use the Moulin Blanche name. This represents a significant outflow of cash where the benefits may take time to materialise or may not materialise to the extent of the level of investment.

If there is any damage to the reputation of the Moulin Blanche chain, this may have an effect on the Moulin Blanche restaurants at the Sunshine Hotel Group resulting in a much lower return on investment than anticipated.

Profit margins and cash management

The nature of the business means that overheads will be high and profit margins likely to be low. Based on the projected profit before tax, the projected margin for 20X5 is 8%, and for 20X4 was 8.2%.

Annual expenses on marketing and advertising are high, and given the focus on luxury, a lot will need to be spent on maintenance of the hotels, purchasing quality food and drink, and training staff to provide high levels of customer service.

Offering all-inclusive holidays will also have implications for profit margins and for managing working capital as services, as well as food and drink, will have to be available whether guests use or consume them or not. The Group will need to maintain a high rate of room occupancy in order to maintain cash flows and profit margins.

Cash management might be particularly problematic given that the majority of cash is received on departure, rather than when the guests book their stay.

Refunds to customers following the recent hurricane will also impact on cash flows, as will the repairs needed to the damaged hotels.

International operations

The Group's international operations expose it to a number of risks. One which has already been mentioned relates to local regulations. With any international operation there is risk of non-compliance with local laws and regulations which could affect business operations.

Additionally, political and economic instability introduces possible unpredictability into operations, making it difficult to plan and budget for the Group's activities, as seen with the recent investment in a politically unstable area which is not yet generating a return for the Group.

There are also foreign exchange issues, which unless properly managed, for example, by using currency derivatives, can introduce volatility to profit and cash flows.

Hurricanes

The hurricane guarantee scheme exposes the Group to unforeseeable costs in the event of a hurricane disrupting operations. The costs of moving guests to another hotel could be high, as could the costs of refunding customer deposits if they choose to cancel their booking rather than transfer to a different hotel.

The cost of renovation in the case of hotels being damaged by hurricanes is also high and while this is covered by insurance, the Group will still need to fund the repair work before the full amount claimed on insurance is received which as discussed above will put significant pressure on the Group's cash flow.

In addition, having two hotels which have been damaged by hurricanes closed for several months while repair work is carried out will result in lost revenue and cash inflows.

Claim relating to environmental damage

This is potentially a very serious matter, should it become public knowledge. The reputational damage could be significant, especially given that the Group markets itself as a luxury brand. Consumers are likely to react unfavourably to the allegations that the Group's activities are harming the environment. This could result in cancellation of existing bookings and lower demand in the future, impacting on revenue and cash flows.

The email relating to the claim from Ocean Protection refers to international legislation and therefore this issue could impact in all of the countries in which the Group operates. The Group is hoping to negotiate with Ocean Protection to reduce the amount which is potentially payable and minimise media attention, but this may not be successful, Ocean Protection may not be willing to keep the issue out of the public eye or to settle for a smaller monetary amount.

(b)   Significant risks of material misstatement

Revenue recognition

The Group's revenue could be over or understated due to timing issues relating to the recognition of revenue. Customers pay 40% of the cost of their holiday in advance, and the Group has to refund any bookings which are cancelled a week or more before a guest is due to stay at a hotel.

There is a risk that revenue is recognised when deposits are received, which would be against the requirements of IFRS 15 *Revenue from Contracts with Customers*, which states that revenue should be recognised when, or as, an entity satisfies a performance obligation.

Therefore, the deposits should be recognised within current liabilities as a contract liability (deferred revenue) until the guest's stay.

There is the risk that revenue is overstated and contract liabilities within current liabilities are understated if revenue is recognised on payment.

Tutorial note

Credit will be awarded for discussion of further risk of misstatement relating to revenue recognition, for example, when the Group satisfies its performance obligations and whether the goods and services provided to hotel guests are separate revenue streams.

Foreign exchange

The Group holds $20 million in cash at the year end, most of which is held in foreign currencies. This is material to the financial statements based on the threshold calculated above.

According to IAS 21 *The Effects of Changes in Foreign Exchange Rates*, at the reporting date foreign currency monetary amounts should be reported using the closing exchange rate, and the exchange difference should be reported as part of profit or loss.

There is a risk that the cash holdings are not retranslated using an appropriate year-end exchange rate, causing assets and profit to be over or understated.

Licence agreement

The cost of the agreement with Moulin Blanche of $5 million is material to profit based on the threshold of $1 million.

The agreement appears to be a licensing arrangement, and as such it should be recognised in accordance with IAS 38 *Intangible Assets*, which requires initial recognition at cost and subsequent amortisation over the life of the asset, if the life is finite.

The current accounting treatment appears to be incorrect, because the cost has been treated as a marketing expense, leading to understatement of non-current assets and understatement of profit for the year by a significant amount. If the financial statements are not adjusted, they will contain a material misstatement, with implications for the auditor's report.

As the restaurants were opened on 1 April 20X5, six months after the licence was agreed, it would seem appropriate to amortise the asset over the remaining term of the agreement of 9½ years as this is the timeframe over which the licence will generate economic benefit. The annual amortisation expense would be $526,316, so if six months is recognised in this financial year, $263,158 should be charged to operating expenses, resulting in profit being closer to $14.74 million for the year.

Impairment of non-current assets due to political instability and regulatory issues

The sites acquired at a cost of $75 million, and the hotel complex acquired at a cost of $23 million are material to the Group financial statements based on the threshold above.

There are risks associated with the measurement of the assets, which are recognised as property, plant and equipment, as the assets could be impaired. None of these assets is currently being used by the Group in line with their principal activities, and there are indications that their recoverable value may be less than their cost. Due to the political instability and the regulatory issues, it seems that the assets may never generate the value in use which was anticipated, and their fair value may also have fallen below cost.

Therefore, in accordance with IAS 36 *Impairment of Assets*, management should conduct an impairment review, to determine the recoverable amount of the assets and whether any impairment loss should be recognised.

The risk is that assets are overstated, and profit overstated, if any necessary impairment of assets is not recognised at the reporting date.

Effect of the hurricane

Two of the Group's hotels are closed due to extensive damage caused by a recent hurricane. It is anticipated that the Group's insurance policy will cover the damage of $25 million and the terms of the policy are that half will be paid in advance and the remainder on completion of the repairs, although this will need confirming during our audit testing. The accounting for these events will need to be carefully considered as there is a risk that assets and profit are overstated if the damage and subsequent claim have not been accounted for correctly.

The damage caused to the hotels and resultant loss of revenue is likely to represent an indicator of impairment which should be recorded in line with IAS 36. IAS 16 *Property, Plant and Equipment* requires the impairment and derecognition of PPE and any subsequent compensation claims to be treated as separate economic events and accounted for separately in the period they occur. The standard specifically states that it is not appropriate to net the events off and not record an impairment loss because there is an insurance claim in relation to the same assets.

As such, this may mean that the Group has to account for the impairment loss in the current year but cannot recognise the compensation claim until the next financial period as this can only be recognised when the compensation becomes receivable. If it is indeed the case that the insurance company will pay half of the claim in advance, then it is likely that $12.5m could be included in profit or loss in the current year.

Provision/contingent liability

The letter received from Ocean Protection indicates that it may be necessary to recognise a provision or disclose a contingent liability, in respect of the $10 million damages which have been claimed. The amount is material based on the threshold of $1 million.

According to IAS 37 *Provisions, Contingent Liabilities and Contingent Assets*, a provision should be recognised if there is a present obligation as a result of a past event, and that there is a probable outflow of future economic benefits for which a reliable estimate can be made.

It remains to be seen as to whether the Group can be held liable for the damage to the coral reefs. However, the finance director seems to be implying that the Group would like to reach a settlement, in which case a provision should be recognised.

A provision could therefore be necessary, but this depends on the negotiations between the Group and Ocean Protection, the outcome of which can only be confirmed following further investigation by the audit team during the final audit.

A contingent liability arises where there is either a possible obligation depending on whether some uncertain future event occurs, or a present obligation but payment is not probable or the amount cannot be measured reliably.

There is a risk that adequate disclosure is not provided in the notes to the financial statements, especially given the finance director's reluctance to draw attention to the matter.

Tutorial note

Credit would also be awarded for discussion of other relevant risks of material misstatements.

(c)   (i)   Implications for audit planning

The finance director's requests which restrict the audit team's ability to obtain audit evidence in relation to the environmental damage claim are inappropriate. In particular, the finance director should not dictate to the audit engagement partner that the audit team may not speak to Group employees.

According to ISA 210/ISA (UK) 210 *Agreeing the Terms of Audit Engagements*, the management of a client should acknowledge their responsibility to provide the auditor with access to all information which is relevant to the preparation of the financial statements which includes unrestricted access to persons within the entity from whom the auditor determines it necessary to obtain audit evidence.

This would appear to be an imposed limitation on scope, and the audit engagement partner should raise this issue with the Group's audit committee. The audit committee should be involved at the planning stage to obtain comfort that a quality audit will be performed, in accordance with corporate governance best practice, and therefore the audit committee should be able to intervene with the finance director's demands and allow the audit team full access to the relevant information, including the ability to contact Ocean Protection and the Group's lawyers.

The finance director would appear to lack integrity as he is trying to keep the issue a secret, possibly from others within the Group as well as the public. The audit engagement partner should consider whether other representations made by the finance director should be treated with an added emphasis on professional scepticism, and the risk of management bias leading to a risk of material misstatement could be high. This should be discussed during the audit team briefing meeting.

There is also an issue arising in relation to ISA 250/ISA (UK) 250 *Consideration of Laws and Regulations in an Audit of Financial Statements*, which requires that if the auditor becomes aware of information concerning an instance of non-compliance or suspected non-compliance with laws and regulations, the auditor shall obtain an understanding of the act and the circumstances in which it has occurred, and further information to evaluate the possible effect on the financial statements.

Therefore, the audit plan should contain planned audit procedures which are sufficient for the audit team to conclude on the accounting treatment and on whether the auditor has any reporting responsibilities outside the Group, for example, to communicate a breach of international environmental protection legislation to the appropriate authorities.

(ii) **Planned audit procedures**

– Obtain the letter received from Ocean Protection and review to understand the basis of the claim, for example, to confirm if it refers to a specific incident when damage was caused to the coral reefs.

– Discuss the issue with the Group's legal adviser, to understand whether in their opinion, the Group could be liable for the damages, for example, to ascertain if there is any evidence that the damage to the coral reef was caused by activities of the Group or its customers.

– Discuss with the Group's legal adviser the remit and scope of the legislation in relation to environmental protection to ensure an appropriate level of understanding in relation to the regulatory framework within which the Group operates.

– Discuss with management and those charged with governance the procedures which the Group utilises to ensure that it is identifying and ensuring compliance with relevant legislation.

– Obtain an understanding, through enquiry with relevant employees, such as those responsible for scuba diving and other water sports, as to the nature of activities which take place, the locations and frequency of scuba diving trips, and the level of supervision which the Group provides to its guests involved in these activities.

– Obtain and read all correspondence between the Group and Ocean Protection, to track the progress of the legal claim up to the date that the auditor's report is issued, and to form an opinion on its treatment in the financial statements.

– Obtain a written representation from management, as required by ISA 250, that all known instances of non-compliance, whether suspected or otherwise, have been made known to the auditor.

–   Discuss the issue with those charged with governance, including discussion of whether the Group has taken any necessary steps to inform the relevant external authorities, if the Group has not complied with the international environmental protection legislation.

–   Review the disclosures, if any, provided in the notes to the financial statements, to conclude as to whether the disclosure is sufficient for compliance with IAS 37.

–   Read the other information published with the financial statements, including chairman's statement and directors' report, to assess whether any disclosure relating to the issue has been made, and if so, whether it is consistent with the financial statements.

(d)   (i)   Data analytics

Data analytics is the science and art of discovering and analysing patterns, deviations and inconsistencies, and extracting other useful information in the data of underlying or related subject matter of an audit through analysis, modelling, visualisation for the purpose of planning and performing the audit.

Data analytics can allow the interrogation of 100% of the transactions in a population where the data set is complete and can be provided to the auditor.

Essentially data analytics is a progression from using computer assisted audit techniques to perform analytical procedures.

How data analytics can improve audit quality

As there is potential to audit 100% of the transactions, detection risk is significantly reduced.

Audit procedures can be performed more quickly resulting in more time being available to analyse the information and exercise professional scepticism.

There is likely to be greater interaction between the audit firm and the audit committee throughout the year which is likely to result in the firm's knowledge of the business being updated on a regular basis as compared with a traditional year-end audit where the understanding is updated during the planning stage.

Specifically, in relation to the Sunshine Hotel Group, audit quality can be improved by improving the consistency of the audits of the subsidiaries within the group, irrespective of which office of the firm performs the audit.

This means the auditor is more likely to issue an appropriate audit opinion.

(ii)   How they can be used in the audit of Sunshine Hotel Group

•   Testing journals as required by ISA 240/ISA (UK) 240 *The Auditor's Responsibilities Relating to Fraud in an Audit of Financial Statements.*

•   Analysing the performance of hotels against other hotels in the group to identify inconsistencies and potential misstatements (fraud or error) for further investigation.

•   Analysing the performance of hotels against competitors to identify inconsistencies.

•   Analysing occupancy rates of hotels to assist with analytics over revenue.

•   Analysing the level of inventory write-offs for food, drink and toiletries which may indicate theft.

Conclusion

These briefing notes highlight that the Group faces significant and varied business risks, in particular in relation to its expansion strategy which is possibly unsound. This creates a significant risk of material misstatement relating to the valuation of non-current assets in areas where land has been purchased but potentially will not provide any future economic benefits. The risks relating to the hurricane in terms of impairment of assets and treatment of the insurance claim are also significant. This is due to the fact they are influenced by management judgement and the magnitude of their impact on the financial statements. These risks will need to be carefully considered during the planning of the Group audit to ensure that an appropriate audit strategy is devised. Several issues are raised by the claim from Ocean Protection, and our audit programme should contain detailed and specific procedures to enable the audit team to form a conclusion on an appropriate accounting treatment.

Examiner's comments

This question was set at the planning stage of the audit cycle and was set pre year end. The question asked candidates to evaluate the business risks and risks of material misstatement from a scenario given on a luxury hotel company. Generally, candidates did well in these sections and were capable of producing explained answers that often scored close to maximum marks. When preparing for future exams candidates are advised to try and remain focused on the risks which arise from the scenario given for while there are additional risks which may be relevant and obtain credit outside of those there are adequate marks available for explaining the risks arising from the information given. In particular, when addressing risks of material misstatements candidates are more likely to attract credit for the material issues described by the examiner than from those they hypothesise might be present and which may be considered immaterial. It should also be noted that when the examiner states that company brand is not capitalised because it was internally generated this means that it does not give rises to a risk of material misstatement that it should have been on the statement on financial position. Where brands are examined in planning questions the examiner will generally flag whether they are internally generated or purchased. One important piece of information candidates need to take note of is the year-end date. Planning questions are generally set prior to the year end. None of the events within the scenario were subsequent events as they had already taken place prior to the year end.

In part (c) candidates were asked to respond to an email from the finance director of the client. The first connected requirement asked for the implication of the director restricting access of the auditor to information regarding a legal claim and thus giving rise to a potential limitation of scope and some additional points on confidentiality and compliance with laws and regulations. Disappointingly the majority of candidates did not appear to identify that the requirement was specifically referenced to the finance director's email and discussed how to audit the risks identified in part b or made general points on auditing subsidiaries. Attention to the wording of requirements is vital to perform well in examinations in general. In the requirement where candidates were asked for audit procedures in relation to a legal case, this was well answered.

		ACCA Marking guide	
			Marks

(a) **Business risk evaluation**

Generally, up to 2 marks for each business risk evaluated, in addition.

Allow ½ mark for each relevant calculation, e.g. profit margin.

- Luxury product – sensitive to changes in consumer's disposable income
- Inappropriate business strategy
- Finance
- Financial implications of business expansion including impact on gearing, interest cover and cash flows
- Moulin Blanche agreement
- Profit margins and cash flows
- International operations
- Hurricanes
- Claim relating to environmental damage – reputational issue, loss of customers

                                                 Maximum   **8**

(b) **Significant risks of material misstatement**

Up to 3 marks for each risk evaluated which requires discussion of the accounting treatment and identification of the associated risk of misstatement. Appropriate materiality calculations (max 2 marks) and justified materiality level should be awarded to a maximum of 1 mark.

- Revenue recognition
- Cash/foreign exchange
- Licence agreement
- Impairment of property, plant and equipment – political instability and regulatory issues
- Impairment of assets – effect of hurricane
- Provision/contingent liability regarding legal claim
- Repairs to properties damaged by hurricane

                                                 Maximum   **18**

(c) **(i)** **Implications for audit planning**

Up to 1½ marks for each point of discussion/appropriate action.

- Limitation in scope imposed by finance director, not in accordance with agreeing the terms of an audit engagement
- Discuss with audit committee, who should intervene to remove the limitation
- Finance director lacks integrity, increase application of professional scepticism and increased audit risk
- Consider required response when an instance of non-compliance is suspected and the reporting responsibilities of the auditor

(ii) **Audit procedures**

Up to 1 mark for each well described audit procedure.

- Obtain the letter received from Ocean Protection, review to understand the basis of the claim
- Discuss the issue with the Group's legal adviser, to understand whether in their opinion, the Group could be liable for the damages
- Discuss with legal advisers to obtain understanding of the remit and scope of the legislation in relation to environmental protection
- Discuss with management the procedures which the Group utilises to ensure that it is identifying and ensuring compliance with relevant legislation
- Obtain an understanding, through enquiry with relevant employees, such as those responsible for scuba diving and other water sports, as to the nature of activities which take place

- Obtain and read all correspondence between the Group and Ocean Protection up to the date that the auditor's report is issued
- Obtain a written representation from management
- Discuss the issue with those charged with governance
- Review the disclosures, if any, provided in the notes to the financial statements
- Read the other information published with the financial statements for consistency with the financial statements

Maximum for part c   **8**

(d)   **Data analytics**

1 mark per point.

(i)   Explanation
- Analysing patterns, deviations and inconsistencies
- 100% interrogation of transactions
- Progression of CAATs

Improve quality
- 100% testing possible
- More time to apply professional scepticism
- More likely to issue appropriate opinion

(ii)   How they can be used during the audit
- Journal testing
- Sensitivity analysis
- Analysis of performance of hotels
- Analysis of performance against competitors
- Analysis of inventory write-offs

Maximum for part d   **6**

Professional marks

Communication
- Briefing notes format and structure – use of headings/sub-headings and an introduction
- Style, language and clarity – appropriate layout and tone of briefing notes, presentation of materiality and relevant calculations, appropriate use of the CBE tools, easy to follow and understand
- Effectiveness and clarity of communication – answer is relevant and tailored to the scenario
- Adherence to the specific requests made by the audit engagement partner

Analysis and evaluation
- Appropriate use of the information to determine suitable calculations
- Appropriate use of the information to support discussions and draw appropriate conclusions
- Assimilation of all relevant information to ensure that the risk evaluation performed considers the impact of contradictory or unusual movements
- Effective prioritisation of the results of the risk evaluation to demonstrate the likelihood and magnitude of risks and to facilitate the allocation of appropriate responses
- Balanced discussion of the information to objectively make a recommendation or decision

Professional scepticism and judgement
- Effective challenge of information supplied, and techniques carried out to support key facts and/or decisions
- Determination and justification of a suitable materiality level, appropriately and consistently applied
- Appropriate application of professional judgement to draw conclusions and make informed decisions about the courses of action which are appropriate in the context of the audit engagement

Commercial acumen

- Audit procedures are practical and plausible in the context of the scenario
- Use of effective examples and/or calculations from the scenario to illustrate points or recommendations
- Recognition of the appropriate commercial considerations of the audit firm

Maximum	10
Total	50

12 LAUREL GROUP *Walk in the footsteps of a top tutor*

Top tutor tips

Determination of materiality: *The email from the partner states that materiality should be based on profit, therefore at the start of your answer you should calculate the range for materiality using that benchmark and justify a figure within that range. If it is a new audit client or a client where there are apparent control risks, materiality should be set at the lower end of the range. If it is an existing client, materiality may be able to be set at the higher end of the range depending on the other risks mentioned in the scenario. The examining team will give credit for any reasonable explanation of the chosen materiality threshold, as the mark is to recognise that there is the application of professional judgement and that a candidate can justify their response. It is not required that candidates select the identical percentage or figure, or that they provide a justification identical to that shown in the model answer.*

Part (a). *When evaluating the risks of material misstatement include the relevant accounting treatment required for the balance being discussed and why the client might not be using the appropriate treatment. State the risk to the balance i.e. whether it is likely to be understated or overstated. Where numbers are provided you can calculate whether the balance is material as this helps assess the significance of the risk.*

Prioritisation of risks: *One mark is awarded for the prioritisation of the risks of material misstatement. The mark is for the act of justifying the reason, not for the actual justification used (i.e. a range of completely different answers could be awarded the mark), therefore if a reasonable explanation is given, the mark will be awarded. Prioritisation can be achieved by either ordering your answer in priority order and stating this is the case, or by summarising in a brief conclusion which risk, or risks, are most significant.*

Part (b) *requires audit procedures to be performed in respect of the brand and acquisition of a subsidiary. Procedures should provide sufficient description of the evidence to be obtained and how the auditor should obtain it.*

Part (c) *requires discussion of the ethical issues arising from performing a valuation of a company that the client is looking to acquire. Make sure you explain the issues properly. Marks will be limited if only a brief explanation is given. At this level you should be able to discuss whether the threat is a significant threat. Make sure you give a conclusion on the actions that need to be taken by the audit firm.*

> *Professional skills*
>
> *Professional skills will be awarded for:*
>
> *Communication – responding to the instructions in the partner's email such as preparing your answers in the form of briefing notes and using the stated benchmark for materiality.*
>
> *Analysis and evaluation – applying the information from the scenario to answer the question and explaining the issues in sufficient depth.*
>
> *Professional scepticism and judgement – justifying an appropriate materiality level, demonstrating critical thinking and being alert to possible manipulation and management bias.*
>
> *Where relevant, professional marks will be awarded for commercial acumen which requires making practical and plausible recommendations and considering the wider implications of issues to the audit firm.*

Briefing notes

To: Brigitte Sanders, audit engagement partner

From: Audit manager

Subject: Audit planning – Laurel Group

Date: 1 July 20X5

Introduction

These briefing notes are intended for use in planning the audit of the Laurel Group (the Group). The notes contain an evaluation of significant risks of material misstatement, which have been identified using information provided by the client following a meeting with the Group finance director and performing selected analytical procedures. The notes then recommend the principal audit procedures to be performed in respect of an impaired brand and a planned acquisition which will take place after the reporting date. Finally, the notes discuss the ethical issues that could arise if the firm performs a valuation service for the Laurel Group.

Materiality

For the purposes of these briefing notes, the overall materiality level used to assess the significance of identified risks is $2.5 million based on the profitability of the Group, as requested.

Justification

Using profit before tax of $28 million as a suggested benchmark results in a suggested range of $1.4 million (5% × $28 million) to $2.8 million (10% × $28 million).

This is an existing client, and no significant control issues have been noted at the planning stage or in previous audits. Therefore, the overall risk assessment is deemed to be low. Materiality should be set at the higher end of the range.

This benchmark is only a starting point for determining materiality and professional judgement will need to be applied in determining a final level to be used during the course of the audit.

(a)   **Evaluation of risk of material misstatement**

Selected analytical procedures and associated evaluation of risk of material misstatement

	20X5	20X4
Operating profit margin	35/220 × 100 = 15.9%	37/195 × 100 = 19%
Return on capital employed	(35/229 + 110) × 100 = 10.3%	(37/221 + 82) × 100 = 12.2%
Interest cover	35/7 = 5	37/7 = 5.3
Effective tax rate	3/28 × 100 = 10.7%	3/30 × 100 = 10%
Current ratio	143/19 = 7.5	107/25 = 4.3
Gearing ratio	(100/100 + 229) × 100 = 30.4%	(80/80 + 221) × 100 = 26.6%

Chico brand name and associated issues

The Group finance director states that the Chico brand name has been impaired by $30 million. However, the brand name intangible asset has fallen by $35 million in the year, so there is an unexplained reduction of $5 million. This may have been caused by the impairment or sale of another brand, and additional information should be sought to explain the movement in the year as this unexplained difference is material.

The audit team will need to verify whether the $30 million impairment recognised in relation to the Chico brand name is a full impairment of the amount recognised in relation to that specific brand within intangible assets. Given that the branded products have been withdrawn from sale, it should be fully written off. If any amount remains recognised, then intangible assets and operating profit will be overstated.

The impairment charge of $30 million is highly material by reference to the threshold and may warrant separate disclosure. There is a risk that the necessary disclosures are not made in relation to the discontinuance and/or the impairment of assets.

There is also a risk that other brands could be impaired, for example, if the harmful ingredients used in the Chico brand are used in other perfume ranges. Management has stated that it believes there is no effect on other brands, however, the audit team must be sceptical of this as it is unlikely that management would want to recognise an additional impairment charge given the loan application and the reduction in profit during the year. The impairment recognised in the financial statements could therefore be understated.

There is also a risk that inventories are overstated if there are any Chico items included in the amount recognised within current assets. Any Chico products should be written down to the lower of cost and net realisable value in accordance with IAS 2 *Inventories*, and presumably the net realisable value would be zero.

There is a possibility that some non-current assets used in the production of the Chico fragrance may need to be measured and disclosed in accordance with IAS 36 *Impairment of Assets* and/or IFRS 5 *Assets Held for Sale and Discontinued Operations*. This would depend on whether the assets are impaired or meet the criteria to be classified as held for sale, for example, whether they constitute a separate major line of business.

There may also be an issue relating to the health issues caused by use of the Chico products. It is likely that customers may have already brought legal claims against the Group if they have suffered skin problems after using the products. If claims have not yet arisen, they may occur in the future.

There is a risk that necessary provisions have not been made, or that contingent liabilities have not been disclosed in the notes to the financial statements in accordance with IAS 37 *Provisions, Contingent Liabilities and Contingent Assets*. This would mean that potentially liabilities are understated and operating profit is overstated, or that disclosures are incomplete.

Loans and related finance costs

Gearing has increased due to the $20 million loan taken out. The interest cover is stable and indeed the finance cost recognised is constant at $7 million each year. It would be expected that finance charges should increase to take account of interest accruing on the new element of the loan. There is therefore a risk that finance charges and the associated accrual are understated.

It is noted that the Group is going to take out another significant loan of $130 million should the acquisition of Azalea Co go ahead as planned in early October. Recognition of this loan as a liability will result in the gearing ratio increasing significantly to 50.1%.

Several risks arise in respect of this additional loan of $130 million. First, the timing of its receipt is important. If the deal is to take place in early October, the finance would need to be in place in advance, and therefore it is likely that the loan is taken out just prior to the year end. In this case it would need to be recognised and disclosed in accordance with IFRS 9 *Financial Instruments* and IFRS 7 *Financial Instruments: Disclosures*, and there is a risk that the liability is not measured appropriately or that disclosure is incomplete. Given the materiality of the loan, this is a significant risk.

Goodwill

Goodwill of $18 million is recognised in the statement of financial position and is material.

An impairment review of goodwill must be carried out annually for each cash-generating unit in accordance with IAS 36 *Impairment of Assets*.

Goodwill has not been impaired this year; we shall need to carry out a review of management's annual impairment test to assess its appropriateness and whether any of the goodwill has been impaired by the media coverage of the Chico product allegations. This means that goodwill and operating profit could be overstated if any necessary impairment has not been recognised.

Development costs

According to note 5 to the forecast financial statements, the $20 million loan was used to finance a specific new product development project. However, development costs within intangible assets have increased by only $15 million. The difference of $5 million is not explained by analytical review on the draft financial statements, and there is a risk that not all the amount spent on development costs has been capitalised, meaning that the intangible asset could be understated.

Conversely, it could be the case that that $5 million of the amount spent was not eligible for capitalisation under the recognition rules of IAS 38 *Intangible Assets*. However, as discussed above, the movement in operating expenses does not suggest that $5 million of research costs has been expensed. It may also be that the company continues to hold the $5 million in cash and this may be supported by the significant increase in current assets in the year.

Revenue and operating expenses

Revenue is projected to increase by 12.8% in the year, whereas operating expenses increased by 17.1%, explaining the reduction in operating profit margin from 19% in 20X4 to 15.9% in 20X5. The trend in return on capital employed is consistent, with the return falling from 12.2% to 10.3%.

Assuming the impairment loss of $30 million has been included in operating expenses, it would be expected that operating expenses should increase by at least $30 million. However, operating expenses have increased by only $27 million during the year. If the $30 million impairment loss is excluded, it would seem that operating expenses have actually decreased by $3 million, which is not in line with expectations given the substantial increase in revenue.

There is therefore a risk that operating expenses are understated and consequently profit is overstated. Detailed audit procedures will need to be performed to investigate the possible omission of expenses from the statement of profit or loss.

Conversely, there is also the risk that revenue is overstated given the withdrawal of the Chico branded products, implying that revenue should decrease due to lost sales from this revenue stream.

Property, plant and equipment

The change to the estimated useful lives of property, plant and equipment has increased profit by $5 million, which is material based on the threshold of $2.5 million.

This change in accounting estimate is permitted, but the audit team should be sceptical and carefully consider whether the change is justified. If the change was found to be inappropriate it would need to be corrected, increasing operating expenses by $5 million, reducing operating profit to $30 million and the operating profit margin would fall to only 13.6%.

This would be a significant reduction in profit and it could be that management bias is a risk factor, especially given the sizeable loan which is about to be agreed meaning that the projected financial statements may have already been scrutinised by the Group's bank.

Tax expense and deferred tax liability

The Group's effective tax rate appears stable, increasing from 10% to 10.7% in the year. However, given the significant movement in the deferred tax liability there should be a corresponding change in the tax expense, assuming that the additional deferred tax should be charged to profit or loss. Currently, it is unclear how this increase in the deferred tax liability has been recorded.

The finance director states that the change in the deferred tax liability relates to the changes in estimated useful lives of assets and associated accelerated tax depreciation (capital allowances). However, the impact on profit of the change to estimated useful lives amounts to $5 million, so the $8 million increase in deferred tax seems inappropriate and it is likely that the liability is overstated.

The deferred tax liability has increased by five times, and the $10 million recognised in the year-end projection is material based on the threshold above. The changes in deferred tax and the related property, plant and equipment therefore does not appear to be proportionate and the amount recognised could be misstated.

Acquisition of Azalea Co

The acquisition is planned to take place in early October and assuming it takes place, it will be a significant event to be disclosed in accordance with IAS 10 *Events After the Reporting Period*. Details of the acquisition will also need to be disclosed to comply with IFRS 3 *Business Combinations* which requires disclosure of information about a business combination whose acquisition date is after the end of the reporting period but before the financial statements are authorised for issue. There is a risk that the necessary disclosures are not made which would be a significant risk of material misstatement given the materiality of the acquisition.

Current assets

The current ratio has increased sharply in the year from 4.3 to 7.5. This could indicate that current assets are overstated or current liabilities understated and the reasons for the significant change must be discussed with the client as part of audit planning, in order to identify any specific risks such as potential overstatement of inventory included in current assets, for example, if any Chico inventory is not yet written down in value.

Retained earnings

Retained earnings have increased by $8 million. Projected profit for the year is $25 million, therefore there is an unexplained reconciling item between retained earnings brought forward and carried forward (98 + 25 − 106 = 17). The difference of $17 million could be due to a dividend paid in the financial year, but additional information including a statement of changes in equity is required in order to plan an appropriate audit response.

Tutorial note

Credit will be awarded for evaluation of other relevant risks of material misstatement including management bias due to the loan of $130 million being provided, and the complex and acquisitive nature of the Group, which leads to inherent risk of misstatement in relation to business combinations.

(b) **Audit procedures**

(i) **Impairment of Chico brand**

- Obtain management's calculations relevant to the impairment and review to understand methodology, for example, whether the brand has been entirely or partly written off.

- Evaluate the assumptions used by management in their impairment review and consider their reasonableness.

- Confirm the carrying amount of the Chico brand pre-impairment to prior year financial statements or management accounts.

- From management accounts, obtain a breakdown of total revenue by brand, to evaluate the significance of the Chico brand to financial performance and whether it constitutes a separate line of business for disclosure as a discontinued operation.

- If the brand is not fully written off, discuss with management the reasons for this treatment given that the brand is now discontinued.

- Obtain a breakdown of operating expenses to confirm that the impairment is included.

- Review the presentation of the income statement, considering whether separate disclosure of the impairment is necessary given its materiality.

(ii) Acquisition of Azalea Co

- Read board minutes to understand the rationale for the acquisition, and to see that the acquisition is approved.

- Discuss with Group management the way that control will be exercised over Azalea Co, enquiring as to whether the Group can determine the board members of Azalea Co.

- Review the minutes of relevant meetings held between management of the Group and Azalea Co to confirm matters such as:

  - That the deal is likely to go ahead

  - The likely timescale

  - The amount and nature of consideration to be paid

  - The shareholding to be acquired and whether equity or non-equity shares

  - The planned operational integration (if any) of Azalea Co into the Group.

- Obtain any due diligence reports which have been obtained by the Group and review for matters which may need to be disclosed in accordance with IAS 10 or IFRS 3.

- Obtain copies of the finance agreement for the funds used to purchase Azalea Co.

- After the reporting date, agree the cash consideration paid to bank records.

(c) Oleander Co

Conflict of interest

A conflict of interest arises when a firm provides a service in relation to two or more clients whose interests in respect of the matter are in conflict.

In this case, the interests of Laurel Group and Oleander Co will be conflicting. Laurel Group will want to purchase the shares for the lowest possible amount and the owner of Oleander Co will want to sell them for the highest possible amount. This creates a significant threat to the objectivity of Holly & Co, who may be seen to be acting in the interest of one party at the expense of the other.

The problem is exacerbated by the nature of the engagement; Laurel Group will use information about the company, including operational information, to bargain over the price. Holly & Co may be privy to private information gained during their time as auditor of Oleander Co which Laurel Group might not have become aware of during normal due diligence procedures. If Holly & Co were to divulge this to Laurel Group, it would give them a potentially unfair advantage over the other client and would be a breach of confidentiality.

Self-review threat

Performing the valuation service for Laurel Group would also create a self-review threat because Holly & Co would have a significant influence over the valuation of Oleander Co, which would consequently be used to consolidate their accounts into the new, enlarged group which Holly & Co would be responsible for auditing in the future.

Actions

It is possible to reduce both the conflict of interest and self-review threats by using different teams to conduct the various services provided.

The IESBA *International Code of Ethics for Professional Accountants* and the FRC Ethical Standard both stipulate that a firm should not provide valuation services for a listed client if the valuation has a material effect on the financial statements which are consequently audited.

Therefore, before accepting the assignment, Holly & Co should consider the potential impact of the transaction and, if they believe it will be material, they should politely decline the engagement.

Conclusion

These briefing notes indicate that there are many potentially significant risks of material misstatement to be considered in planning the Group audit. The most significant risk relates to the Chico brand name which has been written down by a material amount. The subjectivity involved with the valuation of such assets makes this a significant risk. There are also less significant associated risks relating to the valuation of Chico branded inventory and potential impact to other brands. A range of audit procedures have been designed, which should reduce our detection risk in relation to the impaired brand and the planned acquisition of Azalea Co after the year end. In respect of the request to perform a valuation service, we should decline this offer due to the significant threats arising.

Examiner's comments

This question presented the scenario of a large cosmetics group and candidates were presented with three requirements.

Part (a) required risks of material misstatement in the audit to be considered, including using analytical procedures, and a full statement of financial position and statement of profit or loss were provided. This was generally well-answered as there were lots of potential risks to discuss. Candidates that did not score well often concentrated on explaining audit procedures rather than evaluating risks. Disappointingly many candidates only calculated one or two ratios or trends even though the question asked for analytical procedures and contained a full page of numerical data to analyse. Candidates' inability to utilise all the information provided when evaluating risks continues to be an area of concern and continues to demonstrate that candidates must improve their exam technique in this regard.

Part (b) was split into two sections, firstly the audit procedures related to the impairment of a brand. This was reasonably answered with some good procedures highlighted but many candidates erroneously digressed into seeking the original cost of the brand and discussing whether any claims were being made against the company which would have been better-included in part (a).

The audit procedures related to the planned acquisition were generally well-answered with sensible procedures such as reviewing the due diligence report, board minutes and discussions with management about the likelihood of success. Theorising about whether the acquisition would be a subsidiary or associate, or suggesting audit procedures for the enlarged group did not answer the requirement.

In part (c) candidates often missed either the conflict of interest or the listed status of the company.

	ACCA Marking guide	
		Marks
(a)	**Risk of material misstatement evaluation**	
	Up to 3 marks for each significant risk evaluated unless otherwise indicated. Marks may be awarded for other, relevant risks not included in the marking guide.	
	Generally 1 mark for each ratio (including comparative) calculated, and ½ mark for relevant trends calculated, up to a maximum of 5 marks.	
	Appropriate materiality calculations (max 2 marks) and justified materiality level should be awarded to a maximum of 1 mark.	
	– Impairment to Chico brand may be understated if full carrying amount of brand not written off	
	– Impairment may affect other brands	
	– Chico inventories and NCA may need to be written off – risk of overstated assets	
	– A provision may be needed for customer claims – risk of understated liabilities	
	– Significant new loan liability to be taken on around the reporting date – recognition, measurement and disclosure risks	
	– Management bias risk due to new loan being taken out	
	– Understatement of finance costs	
	– Risk that goodwill has not been tested for impairment	
	– Unexplained/inconsistent movement in intangible assets/loan raised to finance development	
	– Understatement of operating expenses excluding the impairment loss	
	– Change to PPE useful lives may not be appropriate – overstated assets and profit	
	– Tax expense and deferred tax liability	
	– Acquisition of Azalea Co	
	– Overstatement of current assets/understatement of current liabilities	
	– Unreconciled movement in retained earnings	
	Maximum	24
(b)	**Audit procedures**	
	Up to 1 mark for each well described procedure.	
	(i) Impairment of brand name	
	– Obtain management's calculations relevant to the impairment and review to understand methodology	
	– Evaluate the assumptions used by management in their impairment review and consider their reasonableness	
	– Confirm the carrying amount of the Chico brand pre-impairment to prior year financial statements or management accounts	

- From management accounts, obtain a breakdown of total revenue by brand, to evaluate the significance of the Chico brand
- If the brand is not fully written off, discuss with management the reasons for this treatment given that the brand is now discontinued
- Obtain a breakdown of operating expenses to confirm that the impairment is included
- Review the presentation of the income statement, considering whether separate disclosure of the impairment is necessary given its materiality

(ii) **Acquisition of Azalea Co**
- Read board minutes to understand the rationale for the acquisition, and to see that the acquisition is approved
- Discuss with Group management the way that control will be exercised over Azalea Co, enquiring as to whether the Group can determine the board members of Azalea Co
- Review the minutes of relevant meetings held between management of the Group and Azalea Co to confirm matters such as:
  - That the deal is likely to go ahead
  - The likely timescale
  - The amount and nature of consideration to be paid
  - The shareholding to be acquired and whether equity or non-equity shares
  - The planned operational integration (if any) of Azalea Co into the Group
- Obtain any due diligence reports which have been obtained by the Group and review for matters which may need to be disclosed in accordance with IAS 10 or IFRS 3
- After the reporting date, agree the cash consideration paid to bank records

Maximum 10

(c) **Ethical issues**
Generally up to 1½ marks for each well explained matter and 1 mark for each well explained and relevant response to the matters identified.
Note: Only ½ mark will be awarded for brief identification of a matter. Further marks will be awarded for explaining why the threat/matter is relevant in this specific context. Likewise, only ½ mark will be awarded for brief response. Only well explained responses should score a full mark.
- Conflict of interest with competing audit clients
- Potentially private information held by Holly & Co in relation to Oleander Co
- Self-review threat caused by valuation service
- Possible use of separate teams (max 1 mark)
- Not permitted to conduct valuation service for audit client (max 1 mark)

Maximum 6

Professional skills
Communication
- Briefing note format and structure – use of headings/sub-headings and an introduction
- Style, language and clarity – appropriate layout and tone of briefing notes, presentation of materiality and relevant calculations, appropriate use of the CBE tools, easy to follow and understand
- Effectiveness and clarity of communication – answer is relevant and tailored to the scenario
- Adherence to the specific requests made by the audit engagement partner

Analysis and evaluation
- Appropriate use of the information to determine and apply suitable calculations
- Appropriate use of the information relating to the impairment of the Chico brand and the planned acquisition of Azalea Co to design appropriate audit procedures
- Effective prioritisation of the results of the evaluation of risks of material misstatement to demonstrate the likelihood and magnitude of risks and to facilitate the allocation of appropriate responses

Professional scepticism and professional judgement
- Appropriate application of professional judgement to draw conclusions and make informed decisions following recognition of unusual or unexpected movements, missing/incomplete information or challenging presented information as part of the risk evaluation
- Determination and justification of a suitable materiality level, appropriately and consistently applied
- Identification of possible management bias and consideration of the impact on the financial statements and the possible reasons for management's preference for certain accounting treatments
- Effective application of technical and ethical guidance to effectively challenge and critically assess how management has responded to the Chico brand issue including the need for a provision or disclosure and the reasonableness of management's impairment review

Commercial acumen
- Use of effective examples and/or calculations from the scenario to illustrate points or recommendations
- Audit procedures are practical and plausible in the context of the scenario
- Appropriate recognition of the wider implications when considering the request to perform a valuation of the shares of Oleander Co

Maximum	10
Total	50

13 ZED COMMUNICATIONS GROUP *Walk in the footsteps of a top tutor*

> *Top tutor tips*
>
> ***Determination of materiality:*** *The email from the partner states that materiality should be based on profit, therefore at the start of your answer you should calculate the range for materiality using that benchmark and justify a figure within that range. If it is a new audit client or a client where there are apparent control risks, materiality should be set at the lower end of the range. If it is an existing client, materiality may be able to be set at the higher end of the range depending on the other risks mentioned in the scenario. The examining team will give credit for any reasonable explanation of the chosen materiality threshold, as the mark is to recognise that there is the application of professional judgement and that a candidate can justify their response. It is not required that candidates select the identical percentage or figure, or that they provide a justification identical to that shown in the model answer.*

Part (a) *asks for audit risks. Audit risk comprises the risk that the financial statements contain material misstatement and detection risk. Risk of material misstatement is usually due to non-compliance with an accounting standard, although it also includes control risk. Think about the requirements of the relevant accounting standards and what the client might be doing incorrectly. Detection risks are the risks the auditor fails to detect the material misstatements within the financial statements and include auditing a client for the first time or where there is a tight reporting deadline.*

Prioritisation of risks: *One mark is awarded for the prioritisation of the audit risks. The mark is for the act of justifying the reason, not for the actual justification used (i.e. a range of completely different answers could be awarded the mark), therefore if a reasonable explanation is given, the mark will be awarded. Prioritisation can be achieved by either ordering your answer in priority order and stating this is the case, or by summarising in a brief conclusion which risk, or risks, are most significant.*

Part (b) *requires matters to be considered before relying on the work of the client's internal audit department. This requires text book knowledge to be applied to the details of the scenario. Look out for information that indicates the internal audit department is experienced and qualified as this will indicate evidence of competence. The requirement also refers to assistance from the internal audit department. This is different to relying on the work of the internal auditor as direct assistance is where the internal audit helps with the external audit procedures. There are many restrictions given in ISA 610 and your answer should cover the most important ones.*

Part (c) *asks for procedures in respect of the shareholding in the joint venture and the licence acquired during the year. Procedures are very regularly examined as a follow on from audit risks. Make sure the procedures are adequately described so that the person performing the procedure will know what to do.*

Part (d) *requires the implications of a joint audit. Explain how this can help the audit process and how it may cause difficulties.*

Professional skills

Professional skills will be awarded for:

Communication – responding to the instructions in the partner's email such as preparing your answers in the form of briefing notes and using the stated benchmark for materiality.

Analysis and evaluation – applying the information from the scenario to answer the question and explaining the issues in sufficient depth.

Professional scepticism and judgement – justifying an appropriate materiality level, demonstrating critical thinking and being alert to possible manipulation and management bias.

Where relevant, professional marks will be awarded for commercial acumen which requires making practical and plausible recommendations and considering the wider implications of issues to the audit firm.

Briefing notes

To: Vincent Vega, audit engagement partner

From: Audit engagement manager

Subject: Audit planning – ZCG

Introduction

These briefing notes have been prepared to assist in the audit planning of ZCG, and contain an evaluation of the significant audit risks to be considered in our audit planning, and a discussion of the matters to be considered in determining whether to place reliance on the Group's internal audit department. The notes provide audit procedures to be performed on the classification of the investment in WTC and on the measurement of a licence. The notes also discuss the implications of a joint audit arrangement if ZCG acquires the company in Neverland.

Materiality

For the purposes of these briefing notes, the overall materiality level used to assess the significance of identified risks is $1.25 million based on the revenue of the Group, as requested.

Justification

Using revenue of $198 million as a suggested benchmark results in a suggested range of $1 million (0.5% × $198 million) to $2 million (1% × $198 million).

This is an existing client but control issues have been noted at the planning stage which increases the risk of material misstatement. Therefore, the overall risk assessment is deemed to be medium/high. Materiality should be towards the lower end of the range.

This benchmark is only a starting point for determining materiality and professional judgement will need to be applied in determining a final level to be used during the course of the audit.

(a)   Evaluation of audit risks

Recognition of 50% equity shareholding in WTC

The 50% equity shareholding is likely to give rise to a joint venture under which control of WTC is shared between ZCG and Wolf Communications Co.

IFRS 11 *Joint Arrangements* requires that an investor which has joint control over a joint venture should recognise its investment using the equity method of accounting in accordance with IAS 28 *Investments in Associates and Joint Ventures*.

Audit risk arises in that despite owning 50% of the equity shares of WTC, ZCG may not actually share control with Wolf Communications, for example, if Wolf Communications retains a right to veto decisions or if ZCG cannot appoint an equal number of board members in order to make joint decisions with board members appointed by Wolf Communications. If ZCG does not have joint control, then WTC should not be treated as a joint venture.

Assuming that there is shared control, an audit risk arises in that ZCG may not have correctly applied equity accounting, thereby potentially over or understating ZCG's investment and resulting in incorrect presentation in the consolidated statement of financial position and statement of profit or loss. The cost of the investment in WTC of $45 million is material to the Group.

Revenue recognition

Given the significance of revenue recognition to the Group's financial statements, the potential misapplication of IFRS 15 *Revenue from Contracts with Customers*.

ZCG is supplying customers with a multiple-element contract and is providing access to a mobile phone network, a fixed landline and a broadband service, so there are multiple performance obligations. ZCG must allocate the revenue from each contract to each of these obligations, in line with IFRS 15, and therefore there is a significant audit risk that this is not done correctly.

ZCG should have robust systems in place to ensure that contracts can be 'unbundled', enabling the revenue relating to each obligation to be separately determined, otherwise there is a significant risk that the revenue element attributable to each component will be over or understated.

There is also a risk that the revenue will not be recognised in the correct period. Revenue should be recognised when a performance obligation is satisfied, which in this case is over a period of time. Contracts vary in length, lasting two or three years, so there is an audit risk that the timing of revenue recognition is not appropriate.

The fact that total revenue, when extrapolated for the 12-month period, is expected to increase by 35% could indicate that revenue is being recognised too early. This could indicate a misapplication of IFRS 15, possibly changes to accounting policies which have been made on adoption of IFRS 15 are not appropriate.

IFRS 15 contains significant disclosure requirements and there is a risk that ZCG fails to provide sufficient disclosure on a range of matters relevant to its contracts with customers, including the significant judgements made in applying IFRS 15 to those contracts and sufficient disaggregation of the necessary disclosures.

Given the significant volume of individual customer contracts and the complexity of the accounting treatment, revenue recognition is a significant audit risk.

Right to use network capacity

The payment of $17.8 million to acquire access to network capacity is material based on the threshold.

It seems that risk and reward does not pass to ZCG in respect of the assets being used and the seller retains control over the use of its network assets. The network capacity should not be recognised as an intangible asset of ZCG and the Group is currently adopting an inappropriate accounting treatment which has resulted in intangible assets being overstated.

The accounting treatment for these rights should be discussed with ZCG as soon as possible. The most appropriate accounting treatment would seem to be for ZCG to record the cost of the right to use the network capacity as a prepayment and recognise the cost in profit or loss on a straight-line basis over the term of the agreements and this accounting treatment should be reflected in the financial statements as soon as possible.

The audit team will need to be made aware of the risk that prepayments and operating expenses are over or understated if the cost has not been treated as a prepayment and/or is not released to profit or loss over an appropriate period.

A further risk is the payment to the network provider is for a specified amount of access to the network provider's network. There is a risk is that ZCG has exceeded the allocated allowance and that any necessary additional payment due for excess usage is not recognised in the financial statements.

Internal controls and fraud risk

The internal audit department has reported that internal controls are 'working well'. This statement will need to be substantiated but gives the impression that control risk is likely to be low. The work of the internal control department will be discussed in more detail in the next section of the briefing notes.

However, it is worth noting that two irregularities have been found to be operating during the year, giving rise to audit risk. Although the total monetary amount of each is immaterial, the fact that they have occurred indicates that there are significant internal control deficiencies which could mean that other irregularities are occurring. We will need to carefully plan our audit approach to expenses and payroll in light of the increased fraud risk.

The lack of approval and authorisation of expenses discovered by internal audit is concerning as this appears to involve higher level management and may call into question management integrity.

We should review the work of internal audit to establish if this is an area where controls have been overridden or if there are current gaps within the control framework. We should review and update our systems notes to identify where reliance can potentially be placed on controls and where there are deficiencies.

The issue uncovered by internal audit in relation to payroll suggests that there is inadequate control over the Group's IT system. Access controls, which form part of the Group's general IT controls, are weak which means that other areas of the system may be vulnerable.

This significantly increases control risk and as a result presents a significant area of audit risk. We will need to ensure that we carefully plan our approach as this may mean that there are areas of the system where no reliance can be placed on internal controls and appropriate alternative procedures will need to be applied.

Amortisation of licence to operate in Farland

The licence acquired on 1 October 20X3 should be recognised as an intangible asset and amortised on a systematic basis over its useful life.

According to IAS 38 *Intangible Assets,* the amortisation method should reflect the pattern of benefits, or if the pattern cannot be determined reliably, the straight-line method of amortisation should be used.

Amortisation should begin when the asset is available for use, meaning when it is in the location and condition necessary for it to be capable of operating in the manner which management intends. ZCG therefore should begin to amortise the licence on 1 April 20X5 and amortise over the remaining licence period of eight and a half years.

The audit risk is that amortisation did not commence at the right point in time or that it has been determined using an inappropriate useful life, leading to over or understatement of the amortisation charge to profit as well as the carrying amount of the intangible asset.

Assuming that it is appropriate to use the straight-line method, amortisation for the year to 30 September 20X5 should be $3.8 million ($65/8.5 \times 6/12$). This represents 1.3% of extrapolated revenue for the year of $297 million ($198 \times 12/8$) and is therefore material, and the amortisation will be more material next year when a full year's charge to profit is made.

Impairment of the Farland licence

IAS 38 does not require an annual impairment review to be conducted for all intangible assets. However, management should consider whether there are indicators of impairment and if necessary perform an impairment review on the licence.

The competitor's actions which appear to have reduced customer demand to a level below that anticipated is an indicator of potential impairment, so management must calculate the recoverable amount of the licence and compare to its carrying amount in order to determine if the asset is impaired.

There is a risk that the licence is overstated in value, and operating profit also overstated if any necessary impairment has not been recognised.

Segmental reporting

Being a listed entity, ZCG should provide segmental information in the notes to the financial statements in accordance with IFRS 8 *Operating Segments*.

The audit risk is that the segmental information provided is not sufficiently detailed and/or not based on the information reported internally to the Group's chief operating decision maker.

There are some unusual trends in the segmental revenue figures from the management accounts. For example, revenue from south east Asia appears to have increased significantly – if the 20X5 revenue figure is extrapolated to a 12-month period, the projected revenue from that segment is $49.5 million, an increase of 65% compared to 20X4.

There is a risk that revenues have been misallocated between segments and that the disclosure is inaccurate.

(b) **Matters which should be considered in determining the amount of reliance, if any, which can be placed on the work of ZCG's internal audit department**

According to ISA 610 *Using the Work of Internal Auditors*, the external auditor may decide to use the work of the audit client's internal audit function to modify the nature or timing, or reduce the extent, of audit procedures to be performed directly by the external auditor.

Note that in some jurisdictions the external auditor may be prohibited, or restricted to some extent, by law or regulation from using the work of the internal audit function. Tarantino & Co should consider whether it is prohibited by the law or regulations which it must adhere to from relying on the work of ZCG's internal audit department or using the internal auditors to provide direct assistance.

Evaluate the internal audit function

Tarantino & Co must evaluate the internal audit department to determine whether its work is suitable by evaluating:

- The extent to which the internal audit function's organisational status and relevant policies and procedures support the objectivity of the internal auditors

- The level of competence of the internal audit function, and

- Whether the internal audit function applies a systematic and disciplined approach, including quality management.

Objectivity

One of the key issues to be evaluated is objectivity – the internal audit department should be unbiased in their work and be able to report their findings without being subject to the influence of others. The fact that the latest internal audit report is addressed to ZCG's finance director could indicate that there is a conflict of interest, as the internal audit department should report directly to the audit committee or to those charged with governance in order to maintain their independence.

Competence

The internal audit team is managed by a qualified accountant who is presumably technically competent, though the nature and status of his qualification should be determined. Tarantino & Co should consider whether the rest of the internal audit department is staffed by professional accountants, whether ZCG has a training programme in place for the internal auditors, for example, to ensure that they are up to date with IFRS requirements such as IFRS 15, and whether there are sufficient resources for the internal auditors to carry out their duties in a large multi-national organisation.

When assessing competency, consideration must also be given to the overall findings which were reported regarding the deficiencies in the current internal control system. The internal audit department has concluded that controls are working well despite there being two instances of fraud in the year which may have more serious ramifications than first suggested.

Scope of work

The scope of work carried out in this area and the resultant recommendations will need to be reviewed. This may further suggest that the internal audit department is not free to investigate or report their findings due to the current reporting chains.

If there are doubts over either the objectivity or the competence of the internal audit department, then Tarantino & Co should not rely on their work.

Systematic and disciplined approach

In order to determine whether the internal audit department works in a systematic and disciplined way, Tarantino & Co should consider matters including the nature of documentation which is produced by the department and whether effective quality procedures are in place such as direction, supervision and review of work carried out.

Direct assistance

If Tarantino & Co wants to use the internal audit function to provide direct assistance, then the firm should:

- obtain written agreement from an authorised representative of the entity that the internal auditors will be allowed to follow the external auditor's instructions, and that the entity will not intervene in the work the internal auditor performs for the external auditor, and

- obtain written agreement from the internal auditors that they will keep confidential specific matters as instructed by the external auditor and inform the external auditor of any threat to their objectivity.

If these confirmations cannot be obtained, then the internal auditors should not be used to provide direct assistance.

UK syllabus: In the UK, ISA (UK) 610 prohibits the use of internal auditors in providing direct assistance to the external auditor. Direct assistance is the use of internal auditors to perform audit procedures under the direction, supervision and review of the external auditor. However, the internal auditors can be used to provide non-direct assistance, for example, we may review their reports on risk management as a way of obtaining business understanding and identifying business risks and risks of material misstatement.

(c) (i) **Audit procedures on the classification of the 50% shareholding in WTC**

- Obtain the legal documentation supporting the investment and agree the details of the investment including:

    - The date of the investment

    - Amount paid

    - Number of shares purchased

    - The voting rights attached to the shares

    - The nature of the profit sharing arrangement between ZCG and Wolf Communications

    - The nature of access to WTC's assets under the terms of the agreement

    - Confirmation that there is no restriction of ZCG's shared control of WTC.

- Read board minutes to confirm the approval of the investment and to understand the business rationale for the investment.

- Read minutes of relevant meetings between ZCG and Wolf Communications to confirm that control is shared between the two companies and to understand the nature of the relationship and the decision-making process.

- Obtain documentation such as WTC's organisational structure to confirm that ZCG has successfully appointed members to the board of WTC and that those members have equal power to the members appointed by Wolf Communications.

(ii) **Audit procedures on the measurement of the operating licence to operate in Farland**

- Obtain the licence agreement and confirm the length of the licence period to be 10 years from the date it was granted.

- Confirm whether the licence can be renewed at the end of the 10-year period, as this may impact on the estimated useful life and amortisation.

- Reperform management's calculation of the amortisation charged as an expense in 20X5.

- Discuss with management the process for identifying an appropriate amortisation method and where relevant, how the pattern of future economic benefits associated with the licence have been determined.

- Confirm with management that the Farland network became operational on 1 April 20X5.

- Review a sample of contracts with customers in Farland to verify that contracts commenced from the operational date.

- Enquire with management on the existence of any factors indicating that a shorter useful life is appropriate, for example, the stability of market demand in Farland or possible restrictions on the network capacity in Farland.

- Review management accounts and cash flow forecasts to confirm that Farland is generating an income stream and is predicted to continue to generate cash.

- Obtain a written representation from management confirming that there are no indications of impairment of the licence of which management is aware.

(d)   Joint audit

In a joint audit, two or more audit firms are responsible for conducting the audit and for issuing the audit opinion. This enables the local audit firm's understanding and experience to be retained which will be a valuable input to the audit. At the same time, Tarantino & Co can provide additional skills and resources if necessary.

Neverland may have different regulations to the rest of the Group, for example, there may be a different financial reporting framework. It makes sense for the local auditors, therefore, to retain some input to the audit as they will have detailed knowledge of such regulations.

The fact that the company is located in a distant location means that from a practical point of view it may be difficult for Tarantino & Co to provide staff for performing the bulk of the audit work. It will be more cost effective for this to be carried out by local auditors.

Two audit firms can also stand together against aggressive accounting treatments. In this way, a joint audit can enhance the quality of the audit. The benchmarking that takes place between the two firms raises the level of service quality.

The main disadvantage is that for the Group, having a joint audit is likely to be more expensive than appointing just one audit firm. However, the costs are likely to be less than if Tarantino & Co took sole responsibility, as having the current auditors retain an involvement will at least cut down on travel expenses. The small local firm will probably offer a cheaper audit service than Tarantino & Co.

For the audit firms, there may be problems in deciding on responsibilities, allocating work, and they will need to work very closely together to ensure that no duties go underperformed, and that the quality of the audit is maintained.

Conclusion

These briefing notes highlight that there are a number of audit risks to be addressed, in particular revenue recognition, and fraud risks appear to be significant issues requiring a robust response from the audit team. Revenue recognition within ZCG is particularly complex given the nature of the services provided. We will need to carefully consider whether it is appropriate to receive direct assistance from the internal audit department. It appears the conclusions of the internal audit department are not appropriate and indicate a lack of competence. If this is the case, the work of internal audit should not be relied on and we will need to plan to perform our own procedures in this area.

Examiner's comments

This question followed the pattern of previous examinations and was set at the planning stage of the audit/assurance cycle. The context of the question was a large company looking to expand its international presence through different means.

Part (a) was a standard audit risk requirement and should have been an area where candidates were able to score strong marks for identifying audit risks from the scenario and describing the effects on the financial statements and elements of audit risk. This part of the question was disappointingly answered by many candidates. There is a tendency for weaker candidates to produce long but irrelevant answers. There is no place in this requirement for describing the audit risk model or discussing ethical issues. If ethical issues were required, this would be flagged as a separate requirement. In this scenario the client was not a new client and had pre-existing international revenue streams, demonstrated by the prior year segmental revenue comparatives, therefore discussing detection risk due to a lack of auditor knowledge of the client or inability to audit international revenue was not relevant. The risks in this type of question are flagged up in the scenario and should be addressed using up to date knowledge of financial reporting standards to describe appropriate accounting treatment and highlighting the potential impact of errors on the financial statements. Generally, the direction of the error will be required to score well, simply stating that intangibles may be over or understated will not gain full credit as this does not demonstrate the level of knowledge which is required.

Audit risk continues to be an area that candidates find difficult and particularly it continues to be noted that many candidates fail to engage with the information provided in enough depth, specifically when provided with extracts from financial statements. Candidates are again reminded that in order to provide a full answer in relation to audit risk they should utilise and analyse all the information that is provided.

Candidates were also required to discuss the considerations to be taken into account when assessing whether and how to use internal audit to assist the external auditor. The majority of candidates were able to list the criteria as per ISA 610 *Using the Work of Internal Auditors*, to assess against and relate that back to the scenario, which was an improvement on the last time this standard was examined.

Candidates were required to provide the principal audit procedures to obtain audit evidence in relation to the classification of a joint venture and the measurement of an intangible asset. The majority of candidates performed satisfactorily in this requirement but again many had not read the requirement carefully enough and described tests covering other financial statement assertions than those required – for example assessing the cost of the joint venture which was not relevant to the classification risk, or failing to take into account that the intangible had been purchased in the prior year so the cost would have been audited at that point so audit procedures should have focused on confirming the brought forward figure and any adjustments for amortisation or impairment.

The final requirement asked for a discussion of a joint audit being performed on a soon to be acquired subsidiary. Most candidates could identify points, though often they were not discussed at all and the answer amounted to little more than a list of bullet points, which would not have attracted many marks. Some answers seemed to confuse a joint audit with an audit involving component auditors, and some used the fact that the foreign audit firm was a small firm to argue that it could not possibly be competent enough to perform an audit or have a good ethical standing.

	ACCA Marking guide	
		Marks

(a) **Evaluation of audit risk**

Generally, up to 3 marks for each significant risk evaluated unless otherwise indicated. Marks may be awarded for other, relevant risks not included in the marking guide.

Appropriate materiality calculations (max 2 marks) and justified materiality level should be awarded to a maximum of 1 mark.

In addition, ½ mark for each relevant trend or calculation which form part of the evaluation of audit risk (max 3 marks).

– Recognition of 50% equity shareholding in WTC
– Revenue recognition – max 5 marks if discuss a range of issues specific to IFRS 15 including multiple element contracts, timing of recognition, disclosure requirements, volume of transactions
– Right to use network capacity
– Internal controls and fraud risk – up to 4 marks for a detailed discussion of fraud risk
– Amortisation of licence to operate in Farland
– Possible impairment of licence
– Segmental reporting

| | Maximum | **18** |

(b) **Internal audit**

Generally up to 2 marks for discussion of each relevant matter:

– General introduction, comment on prohibition in some jurisdictions
– Objectivity
– Competence
– Disciplined and systematic approach
– Using the internal auditors to provide direct assistance

| | Maximum | **6** |

(c) **Audit procedures**

Generally 1 mark for each well explained audit procedure:

(i) **Investment in WTC**

– Obtain the legal documentation supporting the investment and agree the details of the investment (max 2 marks for details of items to be verified)
– Read board minutes for approval of the investment understanding of the business rationale for the investment
– Read minutes of relevant meetings between ZCG and Wolf Communications to confirm shared control and shared decision-making process
– Confirm that ZCG has successfully appointed members to the board of WTC and that board decisions are made equally

(ii) **Amortisation of licence**

– Obtain the licence agreement and confirm the length of the licence period
– Confirm whether the licence can be renewed at the end of the 10-year period
– Reperform management's calculation of the amortisation charged as an expense in 20X5
– Discuss with management the process for determining the method of amortisation
– Review management accounts to confirm that the Farland network became operational on 1 April 20X5 and that Farland is generating a revenue stream from that date
– Review customer contracts to confirm network operational from 1 April 20X5

– Enquire with management on the existence of factors indicating that a shorter useful life is appropriate		
– Review management accounts and cash flow forecasts to confirm that Farland is generating an income stream and is predicted to continue to generate cash		
– Obtain a management representation to confirm that there are no indications of impairment of the licence of which management is aware		
Maximum	10	

(d) **Joint audit**

Up to 1 mark for each point discussed:
– Retain local auditors' knowledge of company
– Local auditors' knowledge of local regulations
– Tarantino & Co can provide additional skills and resources
– Cost effective – reduce travel expenses, local firm likely to be cheaper
– Enhanced audit quality
– But employing two audit firms could be more expensive
– Problems in allocating work – could increase audit risk

Maximum	6

Professional marks
Communication
– Briefing note format and structure – use of headings/sub-headings and an introduction
– Style, language and clarity – appropriate layout and tone of briefing notes, presentation of materiality and relevant calculations, appropriate use of the CBE tools, easy to follow and understand
– Effectiveness and clarity of communication – answer is relevant and tailored to the scenario
– Adherence to the specific requests made by the audit engagement partner

Analysis and evaluation
– Appropriate use of the information to determine and apply suitable calculations
– Appropriate use of the information to design appropriate audit procedures relating to the investment in WTC and amortisation of the licence
– Effective prioritisation of the results of the audit risk evaluation to demonstrate the likelihood and magnitude of risks and to facilitate the allocation of appropriate responses
– Balanced discussion of the professional and practical issues when evaluating whether reliance can be placed on the work of the internal audit department

Professional scepticism and professional judgement
– Appropriate application of professional judgement to draw conclusions and make informed decisions following recognition of unusual or unexpected movements, missing/incomplete information or challenging presented information as part of the risk evaluation
– Determination and justification of a suitable materiality level, appropriately and consistently applied
– Identification of possible management bias and consideration of the impact on the financial statements and the possible reasons for management's preference for certain accounting treatments
– Effective application of technical and ethical guidance to effectively challenge and critically assess how management has accounted for areas of significant judgement

Commercial acumen

- Use of effective examples and/or calculations from the scenario to illustrate points or recommendations
- Audit procedures are practical and plausible in the context of the scenario
- Appropriate recognition of the wider implications when considering entering into a joint audit engagement

	–––
	10
	–––
Total	50
	–––

14 DALI *Walk in the footsteps of a top tutor*

Top tutor tips

Determination of materiality: The email from the partner states that materiality should be based on profit, therefore at the start of your answer you should calculate the range for materiality using that benchmark and justify a figure within that range. If it is a new audit client or a client where there are apparent control risks, materiality should be set at the lower end of the range. If it is an existing client, materiality may be able to be set at the higher end of the range depending on the other risks mentioned in the scenario. The examining team will give credit for any reasonable explanation of the chosen materiality threshold, as the mark is to recognise that there is the application of professional judgement and that a candidate can justify their response. It is not required that candidates select the identical percentage or figure, or that they provide a justification identical to that shown in the model answer.

Part (a) asks for evaluation of audit risks. Audit risk comprises the risk that the financial statements contain material misstatement and detection risk. Risk of material misstatement is usually due to non-compliance with an accounting standard. Think about the requirements of the relevant accounting standards and what the client might be doing incorrectly. Detection risks are the risks the auditor fails to detect the material misstatements within the financial statements and include auditing a client for the first time or where there is a tight reporting deadline. Where there is a subsequent requirement for audit procedures as in part (b), these are areas of audit risk that should be included in your answer to part (a).

Prioritisation of risks: One mark is awarded for the prioritisation of the audit risks. The mark is for the act of justifying the reason, not for the actual justification used (i.e. a range of completely different answers could be awarded the mark), therefore if a reasonable explanation is given, the mark will be awarded. Prioritisation can be achieved by either ordering your answer in priority order and stating this is the case, or by summarising in a brief conclusion which risk, or risks, are most significant.

Part (b) asks for procedures in respect of work in progress and the government grant. Procedures should be specific in terms of what the auditor needs to do to obtain the evidence they need.

Part (c) asks for the impact outsourcing of payroll will have on the audit. You need to suggest how the auditor will obtain sufficient appropriate evidence from the service provider performing the payroll service.

Part (d) asks for the ethical issues arising if the audit firm performs a review of the internal control systems. It is important here to recognise that Dali is a listed company and therefore greater restrictions apply.

Professional skills

Professional skills will be awarded for:

Communication – responding to the instructions in the partner's email such as preparing your answers in the form of briefing notes and using the stated benchmark for materiality.

Analysis and evaluation – applying the information from the scenario to answer the question and explaining the issues in sufficient depth.

Professional scepticism and judgement – justifying an appropriate materiality level, demonstrating critical thinking and being alert to possible manipulation and management bias.

Where relevant, professional marks will be awarded for commercial acumen which requires making practical and plausible recommendations and considering the wider implications of issues to the audit firm.

Briefing notes

To: Sam Hockney, audit engagement partner

From: Audit manager

Subject: Audit planning – Dali Co

Date: 1 July 20X5

Introduction

These briefing notes evaluate the significant audit risks in relation to Dali Co, our manufacturing client supplying machinery and equipment to the quarrying industry. The notes then explain the principal audit procedures to be performed in respect of the valuation of work in progress, and the government grant received during the year. The impact on next year's audit due to the outsourcing of payroll is also discussed. Finally, the notes discuss the ethical and professional issues which need to be addressed as a result of the comments made by the audit committee.

Materiality

For the purposes of these briefing notes, the overall materiality level used to assess the significance of identified risks is $500,000 based on the profitability of the company, as requested.

Justification

Using profit before tax of $9.8 million as a suggested benchmark results in a suggested range of $490,000 (5% × $9.8 million) to $980,000 (10% × $9.8 million).

This existing client is newly listed, creating a risk of manipulation. Control issues have also been identified at the planning stage. Therefore, the overall risk assessment is deemed to be high. Materiality should be set at the lower end of the range.

This benchmark is only a starting point for determining materiality and professional judgement will need to be applied in determining a final level to be used during the course of the audit.

(a)   **Audit risk evaluation**

Stock exchange listing and pressure on results

The listing obtained during the year can create inherent risk at the financial statement level because management may feel under pressure to achieve good results in this financial year.

The flotation raised equity capital, so there will be new shareholders who will want to see strong performance in the expectation of a dividend pay-out.

In addition, the introduction of the cash-settled share-based payment plan motivates management to produce financial statements which show a favourable performance and position which is likely to lead to an increase in the company's share price.

There is a risk that revenue and profits may be overstated. Revenue has increased by 2.2% and profit before tax by 6.5%, which may indicate overstatement.

Payment in advance and revenue recognition under contract with customers

For items where significant design work is needed, Dali Co receives a payment in advance. This gives rise to risk in terms of when that part of the revenue generated from a sale of goods is recognised.

According to IFRS 15 *Revenue from Contracts with Customers*, revenue should only be recognised as or when the entity has fulfilled its performance obligations within the contract. The performance obligations will be satisfied either over time or at a point in time.

Bespoke machinery

If the machines are so bespoke that they cannot be sold to an alternative customer, the revenue should be recognised over time. This would mean that some or all of the advance payment could be recognised before the machine is completed and the asset is transferred to the customer.

There is a risk that an inappropriate amount of revenue has been recognised at the reporting date.

There is additional audit risk created if a customer were to cancel a contract part way through its completion, the bespoke work in progress may be worthless and would need to be written off according to IAS 2 *Inventories*. There is therefore a risk of overstated work in progress.

Generic machinery

For generic machines which are likely to be able to be sold to an alternative customer for minimal additional cost, revenue should be recognised at a point in time. In this case the advance payment is more than likely in respect of the performance obligation of providing the customer with the manufactured product. Therefore, at the point when the payment is received, it should be treated as a contract liability as the conditions for recognition of revenue are unlikely to have been met at this point in time. The revenue should be deferred and recognised when the customer obtains control of the asset.

There is a risk that revenue is recognised too early, especially given the risk of management bias and the incentive to overstate revenue and profit as discussed above.

Cash-settled share-based payment scheme

This falls under the scope of IFRS 2 *Share-based Payment* which states that the liability in respect of the plan should be measured at fair value at the year end.

The increase in the share price from $2.90 at flotation to $3.50 (projected) at the year end indicates that a liability should be recognised at 30 September 20X5 based on the fair value of the liability which has accrued up to that date, with the expense recognised in the statement of profit or loss.

This accounting treatment has not been followed leading to understated liabilities and overstated profit, and the disclosure in respect of the plan may not be sufficient to meet the requirements of IFRS 2 which requires extensive disclosures including the effect of share-based payment transactions on the entity's profit or loss for the period and on its financial position.

Government grant recognition

The government grant of $10 million is material to the financial statements based on the threshold above.

A risk arises in relation to the recognition of the grant. IAS 20 *Accounting for Government Grants and Disclosure of Government Assistance* requires that a grant is recognised as income over the period necessary to match the grant received with the related costs for which they are intended to compensate.

Therefore, the $2 million relating to costs incurred this year should be recognised as income, but the remainder should be released to profit on a systematic basis; in this case it would seem appropriate to release on a straight-line basis until April 20Y0.

The risk is that the grant has been recognised on an inappropriate basis leading to over or understated profit for the year. The part of the grant not recognised in profit should be recognised in the statement of financial position.

IAS 20 allows classification as deferred income, or alternatively the amount can be netted against the assets to which the grant relates. There is therefore also a risk that the amount is recognised elsewhere in the statement of financial position, leading to incorrect presentation and disclosure.

If the terms of the grant have been breached, the grant or an element of it may need to be repaid. There is therefore a risk that if there is any breach, the associated provision for repayment is not recognised, understating liabilities.

Inventory valuation

Work in progress has increased by 26.3% in the current year and is material at $12 million which exceeds the threshold calculated above.

The valuation of work in progress is likely to be complex as many different jobs for different customers are ongoing at the year end, and each will have a different stage of completion and cost base at the year end.

There are also issues more generally with the valuation of inventory, due to the customer returns of items which have recently occurred showing that there are problems with the quality of the goods supplied.

For items which have been returned, the net realisable value is likely to be less than the cost of the item indicating that a write-off may be necessary to reduce the value of the inventory according to IAS 2.

The increase in the inventory holding period shows that there is an increase in slow-moving inventory this year, which also indicates that inventory may be overstated.

Provision in respect of returned goods

A provision should be recognised where a reliable estimate can be made in relation to a probable outflow of economic resources and an obligating event has taken place.

The fact that Dali Co replaces faulty products free of charge indicates that a provision should be recognised based on the best estimate of the future economic outflow.

The risk is that no provision or an insufficient provision in relation to the warranty has been recognised, leading to understated liabilities and operating expenses.

Revaluation of property

The decision to revalue the company's manufacturing sites creates several risks. First, revaluation involves establishing a current market price or fair value for each property included in the revaluation, which can be a subjective exercise, leading to inherent risk that the valuations may not be appropriate.

A risk also arises in that IAS 16 *Property, Plant and Equipment* requires all assets in the same class to be revalued, so if any properties which are manufacturing sites have not been included in the revaluation exercise, the amounts recognised will not be correct.

There is also a risk that depreciation has not been recalculated on the new, higher value of the properties, leading to overstatement of non-current assets and understatement of operating expenses.

IAS 16 also requires a significant level of disclosure in relation to a policy of revaluation, so there is a risk that the necessary disclosures are incomplete. The revaluation surplus of $3.5 million recognised in equity represents is material based on the threshold above.

Deferred tax recognition

IAS 12 *Income Taxes* requires deferred tax to be recognised in respect of taxable temporary differences which arise between the carrying amount and tax base of assets and liabilities, including the differences which arise on the revaluation of non-current assets, regardless of whether the assets are likely to be disposed of in the foreseeable future.

The finance director's suggestion that deferred tax should not be provided for is therefore incorrect, and at present liabilities are understated, representing an error in the statement of financial position. There is no profit impact, however, as the deferred tax would be recognised in equity.

Depending on the rate of tax which would be used to determine the necessary provision, it may not be material to the financial statements.

Control risk

The new non-executive directors have expressed concern over the effectiveness of internal controls and the increased risk of fraud. Expenses may be processed which do not relate to the company, fictitious suppliers or employees could be set up on the systems in the absence of any related controls. The financial statements may be materially misstated due to either fraud or error which has not been prevented or detected by the internal control system.

Payroll costs in particular may be materially misstated as the management team are considering outsourcing the payroll function as a result of the control deficiencies.

New directors

During the year several new non-executive directors were appointed, as well as a new finance director.

While this may serve to strengthen the corporate governance structure including the control environment, equally the introduction of new personnel could mean inexperience and a control risk, particularly if the finance director is lacking in experience.

Some of the suggestions and accounting treatments made by the finance director indicate that their knowledge of the applicable financial reporting framework is weak, signalling that errors may occur in the preparation of the financial statements.

Foreign exchange transactions

Dali Co purchases many components from foreign suppliers and is therefore likely to be transacting and making payments in foreign currencies.

According to IAS 21 *The Effects of Changes in Foreign Exchange Rates*, transactions should be initially recorded using the spot rate, and monetary items such as trade payables should be retranslated at the year end using the closing rate. Exchange gains and losses should be recognised within profit for the year.

The risk is that the incorrect exchange rate is used for the translation and retranslation, or that the retranslation does not happen at the year end, in which case trade payables and profit could be over or understated, depending on the movement in the exchange rate. The company may have entered into hedging arrangements as a way to reduce exposure to foreign exchange fluctuations.

There is a risk that hedging arrangements are not identified and accounted for as such in line with IFRS 9 *Financial Instruments* which could mean incomplete recognition of derivative financial assets or liabilities and the inappropriate treatment of associated gains or losses.

Working capital

The preliminary analytical review reveals that Dali Co is struggling to manage its working capital. The liquidity ratios provided show that the operating cycle has increased from 165 days in 20X4 to 205 days in 20X5.

The company may be finding it difficult to collect cash from customers, as the receivables period has increased by 20 days, and in turn the payment period to suppliers has increased by five days.

If there is doubt over the collectability of receivables, then certain balances may need to be written off, and there is a risk of overstatement of receivables and understatement of operating expenses if bad debts are not recognised.

Disclosure for listed companies

This is the first set of financial statements produced since Dali Co became listed.

There is a risk that the new finance director will not be familiar with the requirements specific to listed companies, for example, the company now falls under the scope of IAS 33 *Earnings per Share* and IFRS 8 *Operating Segments* for the first time. There is a risk of incomplete or inaccurate disclosures in respect of these standards and also in respect of any listing rules in the jurisdiction in which the company is listed.

Tutorial note

Credit will be awarded for other relevant audit risks.

(b) **(i)** **Audit procedures in respect of the valuation of work in progress**

- Obtain a schedule itemising the jobs included in work in progress at the year end, cast it and agree the total to the general ledger and draft financial statements.

- Agree a sample of items from the schedule to the inventory count records.

- For a sample of jobs included on the schedule:

  - Agree costs to supporting documentation such as supplier's invoice and payroll records.

  - For any overheads absorbed into the work in progress valuation, review the basis of the absorption and assess its reasonableness.

  - Assess how the degree of completion of the job has been determined at the year end and agree the stage of completion of the job to records taken at the inventory count.

  - Agree the details of the job specification to customer order.

  - Confirm that net realisable value is greater than cost by agreeing the contract price and cash received from the customer post year end.

- To assess the completeness of work in progress, select a sample of customer orders and trace through to the list of jobs included in work in progress.

(ii) **Audit procedures in respect of the recognition and measurement of the government grant**

- Obtain the documentation relating to the grant to confirm the amount, the date the cash was received, and the terms on which the grant was awarded.

- Review the documentation for any conditions attached to the grant, for example, is there a requirement that a certain number of people are employed at the manufacturing plant?

- Discuss with management the method of recognition of the amount received, in particular how much of the grant has been recognised in profit and the treatment of the amount deferred in the statement of financial position.

- For the part of the grant relating to wages and salaries, confirm that the grant criteria have been complied with by examining payroll records and timesheets to verify that $2 million has been spent on wages in the deprived area.

- For the part of the grant relating to continued operation of the manufacturing site, determine the basis on which this is being released into profit and recalculate to confirm accuracy of management's calculations.

- Review forecasts and budgets in relation to the manufacturing site to assess the likelihood of its continued operations until 20Y0.

- Using the draft financial statements, confirm the accounting treatment outlined by discussion with management has been applied and recalculate the amounts recognised.

- Confirm the cash received to bank statement and bank ledger account/cash book.

(c)   Impact of outsourcing on the audit

Outsourcing is when certain functions within a business are contracted out to third parties known as service organisations. It is common for companies to outsource one or more of it functions, with payroll, IT and human resources being examples of functions which are typically outsourced.

Outsourcing does have an impact on audit planning. ISA 402 *Audit Considerations Relating to an Entity Using a Service Organisation* requires the auditor to obtain an understanding of how the audited entity (also known as the user entity) uses the services of a service organisation in the user entity's operations, including the following matters:

- The nature of the services provided by the service organisation and the significance of those services to the audited entity, including the effect on internal control

- The nature and materiality of the transactions processed or accounts or financial reporting processes affected by the service organisation

- The degree of interaction between the activities of the service organisation and those of the audited entity

- The nature of the relationship between the audited entity and the service organisation, including the relevant contractual terms.

The reasons for the auditor being required to understand these matters is so that any risk of material misstatement created by the use of the service organisation can be identified and an appropriate response planned.

The auditor is also required under ISA 402 to evaluate the design and implementation of relevant controls at the audited entity which relate to the services provided by the service organisation, including those which are applied to the transactions processed by the service organisation. This is to obtain understanding of the control risk associated with the outsourced function, for example, whether the transactions and information provided by the service organisation is monitored and whether checks are performed prior to inclusion in the financial statements.

Information should be available from the audited entity to enable the understanding outlined above to be obtained, for example, through reports received from the service organisation, technical manuals and the contract between the audited entity and the service organisation.

The auditor may decide that further work is necessary in order to evaluate the risk of material misstatement associated with the outsourcing arrangement's impact on the financial statements. It is common for a report on the description and design of controls at a service organisation to be obtained.

A type 1 report focuses on the description and design of controls, whereas a type 2 report also covers the operating effectiveness of the controls. This type of report can provide some assurance over the controls which should have operated at the service organisation.

Alternatively, the auditor may decide to contact the service organisation to request specific information, to visit the service organisation and perform procedures, probably tests on controls, or to use another auditor to perform such procedures. All of these methods of evaluating the service organisation's controls require permission from the client and can be time consuming to perform.

The purpose of obtaining the understanding above is to help the auditor to determine the level of competence of the service organisation, and whether it is independent of the audited entity. This will then impact on the risk of material misstatement assessed for the outsourced function.

(d) **Review of internal controls**

Reviewing the internal controls of an audit client which are relevant to the financial reporting system would create a self-review threat as the auditor would consequently assess the effectiveness of the control system during the external audit.

The design, implementation and maintenance of internal controls are also management responsibilities. If the auditor were to assist in this process, it may be considered that they were assuming these management responsibilities. This creates potential self-review, self-interest and familiarity threat. The latter arises because the audit firm could be considered to be aligning their views and interests to those of management.

Threats caused by adopting management responsibilities are so significant that there are no safeguards which could reduce the threats to an acceptable level.

The only effective measures which could be adopted would be those which ensured the audit firm did not adopt a management responsibility, such as ensuring that the client has assigned competent personnel to be responsible at all times for reviewing internal control review reports and for determining which of the recommendations from the report are to be implemented.

As Dali Co is listed and also an audit client, then the audit firm should not provide internal audit services which relate to a significant part of the internal controls relevant to financial reporting. Given that this is the main expertise of the audit firm, it is likely that they will be required to perform some work in this area and this service would therefore not be appropriate.

If Dali Co would like the firm to perform a review of internal controls not related to the financial reporting system, Mondrian & Co would need to consider whether they have the professional competencies to complete the engagement to the necessary standard of quality.

Tutorial note

UK syllabus: *Internal audit services must not be provided to listed audit clients, therefore the request must be declined.*

Concerns regarding deterioration in controls

One of the responsibilities of the auditor is to evaluate the design and implementation of the client's controls relevant to the audit in order to assist with the identification of risks of material misstatement. This includes the specific requirement to consider the risk of material misstatement due to fraud.

If deficiencies in internal controls are identified, the auditor has to assess the potential impact on the financial statements and design a suitable response in order to reduce audit risk to an acceptable level. The auditor is also responsible for communicating significant deficiencies in internal control to those charged with governance on a timely basis.

The audit committee has suggested that a number of internal control deficiencies have recently been identified which they were not previously aware of. This suggests that these were not issues identified or reported to those charged with governance by the auditor.

If these internal control deficiencies relate to systems relevant to the audit, it may suggest that the audit firm's consideration of the internal control system failed to detect these potential problems, which may indicate ineffective audit planning. If so, this increases the risk that the audit procedures designed were inappropriate and that there is a heightened risk that the audit team failed to detect material misstatements during the audit. In the worst case scenario this could mean that Mondrian & Co issued an inappropriate audit opinion.

The audit committee of Dali Co has not specified which controls appear to have deteriorated and whether these are related to the audit or not. There is also no indication of the potential scale of any fraud or inefficient commercial practice. It is possible that the risks resulting from the deficiencies are so small that they did not lead to a risk of material misstatement. In these circumstances, the audit team may have identified the deficiencies as not being significant and reported them to an appropriate level of operating management.

In order to assess this further, the manager should examine the audit file and review the documentation in relation to the evaluation of the internal controls of Dali Co and assess any subsequent communications to management and those charged with governance. The concerns raised by the audit committee should be noted as points to take forward into next year's audit, when they should be reviewed and evaluated as part of planning the audit.

Additionally, Mondrian & Co should contact the audit committee of Dali Co to seek further clarification on the nature and extent of the deficiencies identified and whether this has resulted in any actual or suspected acts of fraud.

Conclusion

These briefing notes indicate that there are many areas of potential audit risk to be considered when developing the audit strategy for Dali Co. The government grant is the most significant risk as it is clear that the accounting treatment is not in compliance with the relevant accounting standard and this has a material effect on profit for the year. The audit procedures designed in respect of work in progress and the government grant received will provide assurance on these significant issues. The audit file should include a point forward in respect of the outsourcing of payroll to ensure the planning of next year's audit incorporates the need to obtain information from the service organisation. In respect of the request to review the internal control systems, the firm should decline given the self-review threat. We should also consider whether our audit should have identified these control issues during our work and review the work performed over controls again to ensure there are no quality issues.

Examiner's comments

Candidates were required to provide an analysis of audit risks for a manufacturer of bespoke and generic machines. Performance on this requirement was good with the majority of candidates correctly describing audit risks rather than business risks. This is an area that most candidates are well prepared on, however stronger answers were able to develop and apply the relevant accounting treatment. Those able to identify specific areas of the financial statements which would be affected and to correctly identify whether the risk was over or understatement tended to score the strongest marks. A significant minority of candidates thought that the client was new to the firm as opposed to simply having a change in manager and spent time addressing opening balances and new client procedures which were not relevant to the question. Candidates are again reminded to read the question carefully and consider the context of the scenario both in terms of client history and timeframe before answering the question.

Candidates were further required to provide audit procedures for the valuation of work in progress (WIP) and a government grant. With respect to the former, candidates often cited the need for an expert to value WIP rather than focusing on the components of cost and NRV in the machines. Similarly, there were a number of candidates who requested written representations from management on WIP despite the figure not being an issue where the knowledge was confined to management or one of management's intentions. Candidates are once again reminded that a written representation is not a suitable substitute for sufficient appropriate evidence.

The audit procedures relevant to the grant were generally well described.

The next requirement focused on outsourcing, and asked candidates to consider how the outsourcing would affect audit planning. There were some good attempts, with most answers identifying issues in relation to access to information, assessment of the internal controls at the service organisation, and the competence of the service organisation. Disappointingly, few answers mentioned type 1 and type 2 reports that are typically obtained in this situation, and many tried to focus on ethical matters such as independence, and therefore didn't specifically address the requirement.

Candidates were also asked to advise the listed audit client asking for a review of their control systems due to concerns about weaknesses in controls. Few candidates recognised the potential implications on the accuracy of the previous auditor's report and that these potential weaknesses could undermine the opinion. Clearly further details were needed to establish if the deficiencies in control would have had any significant impact on those financial statements.

Many candidates simply provided a discussion of the advantages to the client of having a review of the internal control system but failed to appreciate that undertaking such a review for a listed client would be prohibited by the Code, and this again demonstrated that many candidates did not have a good enough understanding of the requirement of the ethical guidelines. In such circumstances opting for a separate team is not an effective safeguard and the review should not be done.

	ACCA Marking guide	Marks
(a)	**Evaluation of audit risks**	
	Up to 3 marks for each significant risk evaluated unless otherwise indicated. Marks may be awarded for other, relevant risks not included in the marking guide.	
	Appropriate materiality calculations (max 2 marks) and justified materiality level should be awarded to a maximum of 1 mark.	
	In addition, ½ mark for each relevant trend or calculation which form part of the evaluation of audit risk (max 3 marks).	
	– Stock exchange listing and pressure on results	
	– Payment in advance and revenue recognition	
	– Potential for cancelled contracts and implication for valuation of WIP	
	– Cash-settled share-based payment scheme	
	– Government grant recognition and potential for repayment if terms are breached	
	– Inventory valuation	
	– Provision in respect of returned goods	
	– Revaluation of property	
	– Deferred tax recognition	
	– Control risk	
	– New directors	
	– Foreign exchange transactions and potential derivatives	
	– Working capital	
	– Disclosure for listed companies	
	Maximum	**20**
(b)	**Audit procedures**	
	1 mark for each well explained audit procedure:	
(i)	**Valuation of work in progress**	
	– Obtain a schedule itemising the jobs included in work in progress at the year end, cast it and agree the total to the general ledger and draft financial statements	
	– Agree a sample of items from the schedule to the inventory count records	
	– For a sample of jobs included on the schedule:	
	• Agree costs to supporting documentation such as supplier's invoice and payroll records	
	• For any overheads absorbed into the work in progress valuation, review the basis of the absorption and assess its reasonableness	
	• Assess how the degree of completion of the job has been determined at the year end and agree the stage of completion of the job to records taken at the inventory count	
	• Agree the details of the job specification to customer order	
	• Confirm that net realisable value is greater than cost by agreeing the contract price and cash received from the customer post year end	
	– To assess the completeness of work in progress, select a sample of customer orders and trace through to the list of jobs included in work in progress	

(ii) **Government grant**
- Obtain the documentation relating to the grant to confirm the amount, the date the cash was received, and the terms on which the grant was awarded
- Review the documentation for any conditions attached to the grant, for example, is there a requirement that a certain number of people are employed at the manufacturing plant?
- Discuss with management the method of recognition of the amount received, in particular how much of the grant has been recognised in profit and the treatment of the amount deferred in the statement of financial position
- For the part of the grant relating to continued operation of the manufacturing plant, determine the basis on which this is being released into profit, assess its reasonableness and recalculate to confirm accuracy of management's calculations
- Review forecasts and budgets in relation to the manufacturing plant to assess the likelihood of its continued operations until 20Y0
- Using the draft financial statements, confirm the accounting treatment outlined by discussion with management has been applied and recalculate the amounts recognised
- Confirm the cash received to bank statement and bank ledger account/cash book

Maximum	10

(c) **Impact of outsourcing on audit**
Up to 1½ marks for each comment/explanation/definition:
- Need to assess significance of outsourced function on financial statements
- Need to understand relationship and interaction between audited entity and service organisation
- Obtain understanding of the service organisation including internal controls
- Means of obtaining understanding – type 1 and type 2 reports
- Other means of obtaining understanding – requesting information, performing tests on controls at the service organisation

Maximum	4

(d) **Review of internal controls**
Generally 1 mark for each well explained ethical and professional threat; ½ mark available for each recommended safeguard:
- Self-review threat
- Management responsibility: self-interest and familiarity threat
- No safeguards which can reduce management threat
- Possible safeguards to avoid management threat
- Restriction on internal audit services for listed clients
- Competence if review is not related to financial controls
- Responsibilities of auditor in relation to internal controls
- Possible deficiency in external audit procedures
- Nature/severity of deficiencies not clear

Maximum	6

Professional marks
Communication
- Briefing note format and structure – use of headings/sub-headings and an introduction
- Style, language and clarity – appropriate layout and tone of briefing notes, presentation of materiality and relevant calculations, appropriate use of the CBE tools, easy to follow and understand
- Effectiveness and clarity of communication – answer is relevant and tailored to the scenario
- Adherence to the specific requests made by the audit engagement partner

Analysis and evaluation

- Appropriate use of the information to determine and apply suitable calculations
- Appropriate use of the information to design appropriate audit procedures relating to work in progress and the government grant
- Effective prioritisation of the results of the audit risk evaluation to demonstrate the likelihood and magnitude of risks and to facilitate the allocation of appropriate responses

Professional scepticism and professional judgement

- Appropriate application of professional judgement to draw conclusions and make informed decisions following recognition of unusual or unexpected movements, missing/incomplete information or challenging presented information as part of the risk evaluation
- Determination and justification of a suitable materiality level, appropriately and consistently applied
- Identification of possible management bias and consideration of the impact on the financial statements and the possible reasons for management's preference for certain accounting treatments
- Effective application of technical and ethical guidance to effectively challenge and critically assess areas of significant judgement

Commercial acumen

- Use of effective examples and/or calculations from the scenario to illustrate points or recommendations
- Audit procedures are practical and plausible in the context of the scenario
- Appropriate recognition of the wider implications when considering the use of a service organisation in subsequent audits and the request to review the company's internal control system

	10
Total	50

15 CONNOLLY   *Walk in the footsteps of a top tutor*

Top tutor tips

Determination of materiality: *The email from the partner states that materiality should be based on profit, therefore at the start of your answer you should calculate the range for materiality using that benchmark and justify a figure within that range. If it is a new audit client or a client where there are apparent control risks, materiality should be set at the lower end of the range. If it is an existing client, materiality may be able to be set at the higher end of the range depending on the other risks mentioned in the scenario. The examining team will give credit for any reasonable explanation of the chosen materiality threshold, as the mark is to recognise that there is the application of professional judgement and that a candidate can justify their response. It is not required that candidates select the identical percentage or figure, or that they provide a justification identical to that shown in the model answer.*

Part (a). *Business risks are the risk the company does not meet its strategic objectives i.e. the issues management are concerned about. Explain the impact of the issue to the company's profits or cash flows.*

Part (b). You are then asked for risks of material misstatement, i.e. the risk that the financial statements contain material misstatement. This is usually due to non-compliance with an accounting standard. Think about the requirements of the relevant accounting standard and what the client might be doing incorrectly.

Prioritisation of risks: One mark is awarded for the prioritisation of the risks of material misstatement. The mark is for the act of justifying the reason, not for the actual justification used (i.e. a range of completely different answers could be awarded the mark), therefore if a reasonable explanation is given, the mark will be awarded. Prioritisation can be achieved by either ordering your answer in priority order and stating this is the case, or by summarising in a brief conclusion which risk, or risks, are most significant.

Part (c) asks for procedures in respect of the newly acquired brand name. Procedures should be specific in terms of what the auditor needs to do to obtain the evidence they need.

Part (d) requires discussion of ethical issues arising as a result of the loan guarantee and the request for advice. To earn the marks, make sure you identify and explain the threats, discuss whether the threats are significant and finally suggest how to safeguard against them.

Professional skills

Professional skills will be awarded for:

Communication – responding to the instructions in the partner's email such as preparing your answers in the form of briefing notes and using the stated benchmark for materiality.

Analysis and evaluation – applying the information from the scenario to answer the question and explaining the issues in sufficient depth.

Professional scepticism and judgement – justifying an appropriate materiality level, demonstrating critical thinking and being alert to possible manipulation and management bias.

Where relevant, professional marks will be awarded for commercial acumen which requires making practical and plausible recommendations and considering the wider implications of issues to the audit firm.

Briefing notes

To: Ali Stone, audit engagement partner

From: Audit manager

Subject: Audit planning – Connolly Co

Date: 1 July 20X5

Introduction

These briefing notes are prepared to assist in planning the audit of Connolly Co. Specifically, the briefing notes will evaluate the business risks and significant risks of material misstatement to be considered when planning the audit of Connolly Co, recommend audit procedures in relation to a new brand acquired during the year, and finally explain the ethical threats to our firm.

Materiality

For the purposes of these briefing notes, the overall materiality level used to assess the significance of identified risks is $750,000 based on the profitability of the company, as requested.

Justification

Using operating profit of $8.1 million as a suggested benchmark results in a suggested range of $405,000 (5% × $8.1 million) to $810,000 (10% × $8.1 million).

This is an existing client, and no significant control issues have been noted at the planning stage or in previous audits. However, due to the risk of management bias discussed below, audit risk is deemed higher than in previous years.

This benchmark is only a starting point for determining materiality and professional judgement will need to be applied in determining a final level to be used during the course of the audit.

(a) **Business risks**

Regulatory risks – licencing and patents

A significant regulatory risk relates to the highly regulated nature of the industry in which the company operates.

If any of Connolly Co's products fail to be licensed for development and sale, it would mean that costs already incurred are wasted. Research and development costs are significant. For example, in 20X5 the cash outflow in relation to research and development amounts to 7.5% of revenue, and the failure to obtain the necessary licences is a major threat to the company's business objectives.

In developing new products and improving existing products, Connolly Co must be careful not to breach any competitor's existing patent. In the event of this occurring, significant legal costs could be incurred in defending the company's legal position. Time and effort must be spent monitoring product developments to ensure legal compliance with existing patents. Similarly, while patents serve to protect Connolly Co's products, if a competitor were found to be in breach of one of the company's patents, costs of bringing legal action against that company could be substantial.

Skilled personnel

The nature of Connolly Co's operations demands a skilled workforce with the necessary scientific knowledge to be able to develop new drugs. Loss of personnel, especially to competitors in the industry, would be a drain on the remaining resources and in the worst case scenario it could delay the development and launch of new products. It may be difficult to attract and retain skilled staff given the pending court case and potential reputational damage to the company.

Rapid growth/overtrading

During the year Connolly Co has acquired a new brand name and range of products, and has also diversified into a new market, that of animal health products. While diversification has commercial and strategic advantages, it can bring risks. Management may struggle to deal with the increased number of operations which they need to monitor and control, or they may focus so much on ensuring the success of the new business segments that existing activities are neglected. There may also be additional costs associated with the diversification which puts pressure on cash and on the margins of the enlarged business.

The fall in operating profit margin from 24% to 20%, and earnings per share, is a worrying sign for shareholders, though for the reasons explained above this may not be the start of a long-term trend as several events in this year have put one-off pressure on margins. However, there could be a risk of overtrading as the company's revenue has increased by 5.2%.

Cash flow and liquidity issues

Connolly Co seems to be struggling to maintain its cash position, as this year its cash flow is negative by $1.2 million. Contributing factors to this will include the costs of acquiring the 'Cold Comforts' brand name, expenditure to launch the new animal-related product line, and the cash outflow in relation to ongoing research and development, which has increased by 7.1% in the year. The first two of these are one-off issues and may not create a cause for concern over long-term cash management issues, but the company must be careful to maintain a positive cash inflow from its operating activities to provide a sound foundation for future activities.

Companies operating in this industry must be careful to manage cash flows due to the nature of the product lifecycle, meaning that large amounts have to be expended long before any revenue is generated, in some cases the time lag may be many years before any cash inflow is derived from expenditure on research activities.

Request for finance

The fact that the company has approached its bank to make cash available in the event of damages of $3 million having to be paid out indicates that the company is not very liquid, and is relying to some degree on external finance.

If the bank refuses to extend existing borrowing facilities, the company may have to find finance from other sources, for example, from an alternative external provider of funds or from an issue of equity shares, which may be difficult to achieve and expensive. The company has relatively high gearing, which may deter potential providers of finance or discourage potential equity investors.

If finance is refused, the company may not be able to pay liabilities as they fall due, and other operational problems may arise, for example, an inability to continue to fund in-progress research and development projects. Ultimately this would result in a going concern problem, though much more information is needed to assess if this is a risk at this year end.

Court case and bad publicity

The court case against the company will create reputational damage. Publicity over people suffering side effects while participating in clinical trials will undoubtedly lead to bad publicity, affecting market share especially if competitors take advantage of the situation. It is also likely that the bad publicity will lead to increased scrutiny of the company's activities making it more vulnerable should further problems arise.

Imported goods

Connolly Co imports all of its packaging from overseas. This exposes the company to exchange rate volatility and consequentially cash flow fluctuations. The company chooses not to mitigate this risk by using forward exchange contracts. Exchange gains and losses can also cause volatility in profits.

Heavy reliance on imports means that transportation costs will be high and this will put pressure on Connolly Co's margins. It is not just the cost that is an issue – reliance on imports is risky as supply could be disrupted due to aviation problems, such as the grounding of aircraft after volcanic eruptions or terrorist activities.

Reliance on imported goods increases the likelihood of a stock out. Unless Connolly Co keeps a reasonable level of packaging in inventory, production would have to be halted if supply were interrupted, creating idle time and inefficiencies, and causing loss of customer goodwill.

Reliance on single supplier

All of Connolly Co's packaging is supplied by one overseas supplier. This level of reliance is extremely risky, as any disruption to the supplier's operations, for example, due to financial difficulties or political interference, could result in the curtailment of supply, leading to similar problems of stock outs and halted production as discussed above.

(b)   Risks of material misstatement

Inherent risk of management bias

Connolly Co's management is attempting to raise finance, and the bank will use its financial statements as part of their lending decision. There is therefore pressure on management to present a favourable position. This may lead to bias in how balances and transactions are measured and presented.

For example, there is a risk that earnings management techniques are used to overstate revenue and understate expenses in order to maximise the profit recognised. Estimates included in the financial statements are also subject to higher risk. ISA 540 (Revised) *Auditing Accounting Estimates and Related Disclosures* states that auditors shall review the judgements and decisions made by management in the making of accounting estimates to identify whether there are indicators of management bias.

Court case – provisions and contingent liabilities

The court case which has been brought against Connolly Co may give rise to a present obligation as a result of a past event, and if there is a probable outflow of economic benefit which can be measured reliably, then a provision should be recognised. The clinical trial took place before year end, so the obligating event has occurred. If the company agrees an out of court settlement with the individual before the year end, or it is expected that the individual will agree to a settlement, there will be a probable outflow of economic benefits and a provision should be recognised.

If the company decides not to try for an out of court settlement, an assessment of probability of the case going against Connolly Co will need to be made. If it is considered that there is a possible rather than probable outflow of economic benefit, a contingent liability will need to be disclosed.

The risk is that either a necessary provision is not recognised, understating liabilities and expenses, or that a contingent liability is not appropriately disclosed in the notes to the financial statements, in accordance with IAS 37 *Provisions, Contingent Liabilities and Contingent Assets*.

Legal fees relating to the court case should also be accrued if they have been incurred before the year end, and failure to do so will understate current liabilities and understate expenses.

Development costs

There is a significant risk that the requirements of IAS 38 *Intangible Assets* have not been followed. Research costs must be expensed and strict criteria must be applied to development expenditure to determine whether it should be capitalised and recognised as an intangible asset.

Development costs are capitalised only after technical and commercial feasibility of the asset for sale or use have been established, and Connolly Co must demonstrate an intention and ability to complete the development and that it will generate future economic benefits.

The risk is that research costs have been inappropriately classified as development costs and then capitalised, overstating assets and understating expenses.

When an intangible asset has a finite useful life, it should be amortised systematically over that life. For a development asset, the amortisation should correspond with the pattern of economic benefits generated from the sale of associated goods. The risk is that the amortisation period has not been appropriately assessed resulting in over or understatement of capitalised development costs and expenses.

A specific risk relates to the drug which was being developed but in relation to which there have been side effects during the clinical trials. It is unlikely that the costs in relation to this product development continue to meet the criteria for capitalisation, so there is a risk that they have not been written off, overstating assets and profit.

Brand name

The company acquired the 'Cold Comforts' brand from a rival company during the year for $5 million. This is material to the financial statements.

Connolly Co must be confident that the Cold Comforts brand will generate economic benefits equivalent to or greater than the carrying amount included in the financial statements either through sales of products carrying the Cold Comforts name or through sale of the brand name itself.

The risk is that the asset is overvalued if $5 million was not an appropriate fair value for the brand or if the amortisation period of 15 years is not appropriate.

Patents – recognition and amortisation

The cost of acquiring patents for products should be capitalised and recognised as an intangible asset as the patent provides protection over the economic benefit to be derived. Once recognised, patents should be amortised over the period of their duration.

If patent costs have been expensed rather than capitalised, this would understate assets and overstate expenses. If amortisation has not been charged, this will overstate assets and understate expenses.

Segmental reporting

The diversification into the new product area relating to animal health may warrant separate disclosure according to IFRS 8 *Operating Segments*. This requires listed companies to disclose in a note to the financial statements the performance of the company disaggregated over its operating or geographical segments, as the information is viewed by management.

As the new product area has been successful and contributes 15% to revenue, it could be seen as a significant operating segment, and disclosure of its revenue, profit and other figures may be required. The risk is non-disclosure or incomplete disclosure of the necessary information.

Foreign currency transactions

The majority of Connolly Co's packaging is imported, leading to risk in the accounting treatment of foreign currency transactions. According to IAS 21 *The Effects of Changes in Foreign Exchange Rates,* foreign currency transactions should be initially recognised having been translated using the spot rate, or an average rate may be used if exchange rates do not fluctuate significantly.

The risk on initial recognition is that an inappropriate exchange rate has been used in the translation of the amount, causing an inaccurate expense, current liability and inventory valuation to be recorded, which may be over or understated in value.

Further risk arises in the accounting treatment of balances relating to foreign currency at the year end. Payables denominated in a foreign currency must be retranslated using the closing rate, with exchange gains or losses recognised in profit or loss for the year.

The risk is that the year-end retranslation does not take place, or that an inappropriate exchange rate is used for the retranslation, leading to over or understated current liabilities and operating expenses.

Risk also exists relating to transactions that are settled within the year, if the correct exchange gain or loss has not been included in profit. Inventory should not be retranslated at the year end as it is a non-monetary item, so any retranslation of inventory would result in over or undervaluation of inventory and profit.

Tutorial note

More than the required number of risks of material misstatement have been included in this answer for illustrative purposes. Credit will be awarded for the identification and explanation of other relevant risks.

(c) **Audit procedures in relation to the purchased brand name**

- Review board minutes for evidence of discussion of the purchase of the acquired brand, and for its approval.

- Agree the cost of $5 million to the company's bank ledger account/cash book and bank statement.

- Obtain the purchase agreement and confirm the rights of Connolly Co in respect of the brand.

- Discuss with management the estimated useful life of the brand of 15 years and obtain an understanding of how 15 years has been determined as appropriate.

- If the 15-year useful life is a period stipulated in the purchase document, confirm to the terms of the agreement.

- If the 15-year useful life is based on the life expectancy of the product, obtain an understanding of the basis for this, for example, by reviewing a cash flow forecast of sales of the product.

- Obtain any market research or customer satisfaction surveys to confirm the existence of a revenue stream.

- Consider whether there are any indicators of potential impairment at the year end by obtaining pre-year-end sales information and reviewing terms of contracts to supply the products to pharmacies.

- Recalculate the amortisation expense for the year and agree the charge to the financial statements, and confirm adequacy of disclosure in the notes to the financial statements.

(d) **Ethical threats**

There are two ethical threats relevant to the audit firm.

Guarantee in respect of bank loan

The provision of such a guarantee represents a financial interest in an audit client, and creates a self-interest threat because the audit firm has an interest in the financial position of the client. The audit firm may be reluctant to request adjustments to the financial statements that would result in the firm having to honour the guarantee.

If an audit firm guarantees a loan to an audit client, the self-interest threat created would be so significant that no safeguards could reduce the threat to an acceptable level unless the loan or guarantee is immaterial to both the audit firm and the client.

In this case the loan would be material as it represents 5% of Connolly Co's total assets, and would also be considered material in nature because of the company's need for the additional finance.

UK syllabus: FRC Ethical Standard section 2 states that audit firms, persons in a position to influence the conduct and outcome of the audit and immediate family members of such persons shall not make a loan to, or guarantee the borrowings of, an audited entity or its affiliates unless this represents a deposit made with a bank or similar deposit-taking institution in the ordinary course of business and on normal business terms. An intimidation as well as a self-interest threat arises when an audit firm makes a loan to, or guarantees a loan in respect of, an audited entity.

Advice on accounting and management information systems

If advice is given, it would constitute the provision of a non-assurance service to an audit client. Services related to IT systems including the design or implementation of hardware or software systems may create a self-review threat. This is because when auditing the financial statements, the auditor would assess the systems which they had recommended and may be reluctant to criticise them if they are ineffective.

There is also a risk of assuming the responsibility of management, especially as Connolly Co has little experience in this area, so would rely on the auditor's suggestions and be less inclined to make their own decision.

In the case of an audit client which is a public interest entity, an audit firm shall not provide services involving the design or implementation of IT systems which form a significant part of the internal control over financial reporting or which generate information which is significant to the client's accounting records or financial statements on which the firm will express an opinion.

The audit firm should not provide a service to give advice on the accounting systems. With further clarification on the nature of the management information systems and the update required to them, it may be possible for the audit firm to provide a service to Connolly Co, as long as those systems are outside of the financial reporting system. However, it may be prudent for the audit firm to decline offering any advice on systems to the client.

These ethical issues should be discussed with those charged with governance of Connolly Co, with an explanation provided as to why the audit firm cannot guarantee the loan or provide the non-audit service to the company.

UK syllabus: FRC Ethical Standard section 5 states that the audit firm shall not undertake an engagement to design, provide or implement information technology systems for an audited entity where the systems concerned would be important to any significant part of the accounting system or to the production of the financial statements and the auditor would place significant reliance upon them as part of the audit of the financial statements; or for the purposes of the information technology services, the audit firm would undertake part of the role of management.

Conclusion

Connolly Co faces a variety of business risks, some of which are generic to the industry in which it operates, while others are more entity-specific. A number of risks of material misstatement are significant, in particular, risks relating to the treatment of development costs, and the court case due to the incentive management has to improve the picture of the company's performance and financial position in order to obtain the loan extension. Audit planning must ensure that appropriate responses are designed for each of them. Two ethical issues have been raised by requests from the client for our firm to provide a loan guarantee and to provide advice on systems, both of which create significant threats to independence and objectivity, and the matters must be discussed with the client before advising that we are unable to provide the guarantee or to provide the systems advice.

Examiner's comments

This question centred on planning the audit of a listed company operating in the pharmaceutical industry. Candidates were provided with background information about the company's products and the environment in which the company, Connolly Co, operated. In addition, information was provided in the form of minutes from a meeting with Connolly's finance director, covering several issues relevant to the audit. These included details of requests made to the company's bank for further finance, a successful diversification into a new market, the acquisition of a new brand during the year, an ongoing court case against the company following problems during a medical trial of its products, and an out of date management information system. Key financial information in the form of extracts from projected financial statements along with comparative information was also provided in the scenario.

The business risk requirement was generally well attempted, and in fact for many candidates this was the best attempted out of all of the question requirements. Most candidates proved able to identify and discuss many of the relevant business risks within their briefing notes and the risks surrounding non-compliance with stringent regulations, the risk of losing the licenses necessary to produce pharmaceutical products, the lack of cash to support ongoing product development, the risks attached to diversifying into a new market, and reputational risks associated with the court case against the company were generally well discussed. The best answers made full use of the information provided and performed analysis of the financial information, allowing for identification of the less obvious but often pertinent risks, such as that without the revenue derived from the new market entered into during the year the company's total revenue would have fallen by a significant amount. The key weakness present in many answers continues to be the poor quality of explanations. Weaker answers tended to just repeat facts given in the scenario with little attempt to discuss or evaluate them. Some answers began with a lengthy discussion of the definition of business risk which was not necessary and demonstrates a lack of judgement when the briefing notes are being requested by an audit partner. Further many answers were very repetitive and did not consider the number of distinct business risks that would be required for the marks available. Many candidates discussed at length risks over going concern that were tenuous or lacked appropriate explanation.

Many candidates also confused business risk and audit risk and therefore provided responses that were not relevant to the question.

The next requirement asked candidates to evaluate risks of material misstatement to be considered in planning the audit. Performance in this area was very mixed. There were some excellent answers to this requirement, with many candidates achieving close to full marks. Most candidates were able to identify the risks surrounding inappropriate accounting treatment which could lead to material misstatements, and were also able to quantify the materiality of the matters discussed. The risks that were most commonly discussed related to provisions, recognition of research and development costs, the valuation of potentially obsolete inventory, and the segmental reporting that would be likely required in relation to the new market entered into during the year. The best answers were well structured in how they explained the potential misstatement and included in their evaluation of each risk an identification of the risk factor from the scenario (e.g. the court case ongoing against the company), a determination of materiality where possible given the information in the question, a clear comment on the appropriateness of the accounting treatment where relevant, and the impact on the financial statements (e.g. non-recognition of a provision in relation to the court case could lead to an understatement of liabilities and an overstatement of operating profit). Only the better candidates identified that requesting additional finance from the bank to cover the damages from the court case implied that the outcome was probable rather than possible and should be provided for. Weaker answers failed to observe the number of risks of material misstatement that had been asked for, with a significant minority wasting valuable time by providing more risks than required.

Many candidates discussed a risk of material misstatement relating to accounting for the loan that had been applied for, but given that this had not yet been received it would not give rise to a risk of this nature in this reporting period. Other candidates discussed at length the issue of going concern and that the company's financial statements should be prepared on a break-up basis but there was certainly not enough evidence in the scenario to justify this as a risk of material misstatement. Other weaknesses in relation to this requirement included:

- Incorrect materiality calculations or stating that a balance was material with no justification.

- Lack of understanding of some accounting treatments, e.g. saying that intangible assets must be measured at fair value.

- Vague attempts to explain the risk of material misstatement along the lines of 'there is a risk it is not accounted for properly' or 'there is a risk the relevant accounting standard is not followed' – these points are too vague to score marks.

The next requirement asked candidates to design the principal audit procedures to be performed in respect of a brand name that had been acquired during the year. Answers to this requirement were very mixed, as is typical for requirements relating to audit procedures. The best answers provided well explained procedures that clearly set out how the test would be performed and where appropriate the documentation that would be used. Weaker answers contained vague or very brief lists that were not specific enough to constitute an audit procedure and therefore did not earn marks. Examples of weaker answer points include 'assess value of the brand' (this is not an audit procedure – how should the assessment take place?), 'discuss accounting treatment with management' (what specifically should be discussed?), 'look at the purchase contract' (what information should the auditor be looking for within the contract?).

Candidates should ensure that procedures contain an actual instruction describing an action to be performed to satisfy a specific objective. A minority of candidates thought that rather than acquiring a specific asset i.e. the brand, as stated in the question, a company had been purchased. This led to candidates providing irrelevant audit procedures and wrongly discussing the accounting treatment for goodwill. Candidates are reminded to read the question extremely carefully.

The final requirement asked candidates to discuss the ethical issues arising from the engagement and to recommend appropriate actions. There were two matters present in the scenario that were appropriate to discuss – the fact that Connolly Co's bank had asked the audit firm to guarantee the loan extension that had been requested, and that the audit firm had been asked to give advice on the new management information system planned to be introduced the following year. This requirement was generally well attempted with the majority of candidates correctly identifying the two issues and providing some relevant discussion for each. Most candidates were able to explain the ethical threats associated with the issues and recognised that the significance of the threats would need to be determined. Many candidates appreciated that due to Connolly Co's listed status it qualified as a public interest entity, and therefore the threats to objectivity were heightened. Many candidates demonstrated sound judgement by concluding that the services should not be provided to the audit client as it would be unlikely that safeguards could reduce the threats to an acceptable level. However, credit was awarded where candidates mentioned the types of safeguards that could be considered. Weaker answers for this requirement identified the wrong ethical threats or failed to identify the significance of the company's listed status, concluding that it would be acceptable to provide the services. Other answers digressed into discussions on the general ethical issues surrounding the testing of medicines on animals or humans, which was not relevant to the question requirement.

ACCA Marking guide		*Marks*
(a)	**Evaluation of business risks** Generally, up to 2 marks for each business risk evaluated. In addition, ½ mark for each relevant trend or calculation and used as part of the risk evaluation. – Regulatory risk – licensing of products, patent infringement – Skilled workforce – Rapid growth/overtrading – Cash flow and liquidity – Request for finance – Court case – bad publicity and further scrutiny – Imported goods – Reliance on single supplier	
	Maximum	**10**
(b)	**Risks of material misstatement** Up to 3 marks for each significant ROMM evaluated unless otherwise indicated. Marks may be awarded for other, relevant risks not included in the marking guide. Appropriate materiality calculations (max 2 marks) and justified materiality level should be awarded to a maximum of 1 mark. – Management bias – Court case – provision or contingent liability – Development costs – recognition, amortisation (4 marks) – Brand name – Patent costs – Segmental reporting – Foreign exchange transactions (4 marks)	
	Maximum	**18**

(c) **Procedures in relation to purchased brand name**

Generally 1 mark for each relevant, well described audit procedure:

– Review board minutes for approval
– Agree the cost of $5 million to the bank ledger account/cash book and bank statement
– Obtain the purchase agreement and confirm the rights of Connolly Co
– Discuss with management the estimated useful life of the brand of 15 years and obtain an understanding of how 15 years has been determined as appropriate
– If the 15-year useful life is a period stipulated in the purchase document, confirm to the terms of the agreement
– If the 15-year useful life is based on the life expectancy of the product, review a cash flow forecast of sales of the product
– Obtain any market research or customer satisfaction surveys
– Consider whether there are any indicators of potential impairment
– Recalculate the amortisation expense for the year and confirm adequacy of disclosure in notes to the financial statements

Maximum	6

(d) **Ethical matters**

Generally up to 1 mark for each point discussed:

– Loan guarantee is a financial self-interest threat
– The loan is material and guarantee should not be given
– The advice on systems would be a non-audit service
– Self-review threat created
– Threat of assuming management responsibility
– Can only be provided if systems unrelated to financial reporting
– In this case the advice relating to accounting systems must not be given
– Advisable not to provide the advice on MIS
– Discuss both matters with management/TCWG

Maximum	6

Professional marks

Communication

– Briefing note format and structure – use of headings/sub-headings and an introduction
– Style, language and clarity – appropriate layout and tone of briefing notes, presentation of materiality and relevant calculations, appropriate use of the CBE tools, easy to follow and understand
– Effectiveness and clarity of communication – answer is relevant and tailored to the scenario
– Adherence to the specific requests made by the audit engagement partner

Analysis and evaluation

– Appropriate use of the information to determine and apply suitable calculations
– Appropriate use of the information to design appropriate audit procedures relating to the brand name
– Effective prioritisation of the results of the evaluation of risks of material misstatement to demonstrate the likelihood and magnitude of risks and to facilitate the allocation of appropriate responses

Professional scepticism and professional judgement		
– Appropriate application of professional judgement to draw conclusions and make informed decisions following recognition of unusual or unexpected movements, missing/incomplete information or challenging presented information as part of the risk evaluation		
– Determination and justification of a suitable materiality level, appropriately and consistently applied		
– Identification of possible management bias and consideration of the impact on the financial statements and the possible reasons for management's preference for certain accounting treatments		
– Effective application of technical and ethical guidance to effectively challenge and critically assess how management has accounted for areas of significant judgement		
Commercial acumen		
– Use of effective examples and/or calculations from the scenario to illustrate points or recommendations		
– Audit procedures are practical and plausible in the context of the scenario		
– Appropriate recognition of the wider implications when considering the request by the audit committee to perform additional services		
Maximum		10
Total		50

16 ADAMS GROUP *Walk in the footsteps of a top tutor*

Top tutor tips

Determination of materiality: *The email from the partner states that materiality should be based on profit, therefore at the start of your answer you should calculate the range for materiality using that benchmark and justify a figure within that range. If it is a new audit client or a client where there are apparent control risks, materiality should be set at the lower end of the range. If it is an existing client, materiality may be able to be set at the higher end of the range depending on the other risks mentioned in the scenario. The examining team will give credit for any reasonable explanation of the chosen materiality threshold, as the mark is to recognise that there is the application of professional judgement and that a candidate can justify their response. It is not required that candidates select the identical percentage or figure, or that they provide a justification identical to that shown in the model answer.*

Part (a) *asks for audit risks, i.e. the risks of material misstatement and any detection risks. Knowledge of the examinable accounting standards is essential to answer this question. For the areas of the financial statements, explain how the client might have incorrectly accounted for the balances. Detection risk is the risk the auditor does not detect the misstatements in the financial statements. Look out for information in the scenario that indicates it is a new audit client or a client which operates from multiple locations which may make it difficult for the auditor to visit the locations required to obtain sufficient appropriate evidence.*

Prioritisation of risks: One mark is awarded for the prioritisation of the audit risks. The mark is for the act of justifying the reason, not for the actual justification used (i.e. a range of completely different answers could be awarded the mark), therefore if a reasonable explanation is given, the mark will be awarded. Prioritisation can be achieved by either ordering your answer in priority order and stating this is the case, or by summarising in a brief conclusion which risk, or risks, are most significant.

Part (b) asks for matters to be considered before using the work of a component auditor. This should be straightforward rote learned knowledge of the ISA requirements applied to the scenario.

Part (c) asks for procedures in respect of the investment in associate. Procedures are very regularly examined as a follow on from audit risks. Make sure the procedures are adequately described so that the person performing the procedure will know what to do.

Part (d) asks for ethical threats and other professional issues arising. When discussing ethical threats try to evaluate the significance of the threat as this will affect how the auditor should manage the threat.

Professional skills

Professional skills will be awarded for:

Communication – responding to the instructions in the partner's email such as preparing your answers in the form of briefing notes and using the stated benchmark for materiality.

Analysis and evaluation – applying the information from the scenario to answer the question and explaining the issues in sufficient depth.

Professional scepticism and judgement – justifying an appropriate materiality level, demonstrating critical thinking and being alert to possible manipulation and management bias.

Where relevant, professional marks will be awarded for commercial acumen which requires making practical and plausible recommendations and considering the wider implications of issues to the audit firm.

Briefing notes

To: Joss Dylan, Audit engagement partner

From: Audit manager

Subject: Audit planning for the Adams Group

Date: 1 July 20X5

Introduction

These briefing notes are prepared for use by the audit engagement partner of the Adams Group, and relate to the planning of the audit of the Group for the year ended 31 May 20X5. The notes contain an evaluation of the significant audit risks to be considered when planning the audit, and the matters to be considered in respect of using the work of Clapton & Co, and the relevant procedures to be performed. The notes also detail the procedures to be conducted in relation to the investment in Stewart Co, an associate of the group. Finally, the notes discuss the ethical and professional issues which need to be addressed as a result of the requests made by the audit committee of the Adams Group.

Materiality

For the purposes of these briefing notes, the overall materiality level used to assess the significance of identified risks is $560,000 based on the profitability of the Group, as requested.

Justification

Using profit before tax of $11.2 million as a suggested benchmark results in a suggested range of $560,000 (5% × $11.2 million) to $1,120,000 (10% × $11.2 million).

As this is a new client and therefore an initial audit engagement, there is increased detection risk. Therefore, the overall risk assessment is deemed to be high. Materiality should be set at the lower end of the range.

This benchmark is only a starting point for determining materiality and professional judgement will need to be applied in determining a final level to be used during the course of the audit.

(a)   **Evaluation of audit risk**

New audit client

The Group is a new client of our firm which may create detection risk as we have no previous experience with the client. However, thorough planning procedures which focus on obtaining a detailed knowledge and understanding of the Group and its activities will minimise this risk. We need to obtain a thorough understanding of each of the subsidiaries as they are all material to the Group, with Ross Co, Lynott Co and Beard Co's assets representing respectively 20%, 22.3% and 26% of Group assets. There is also a significant risk that comparative information and opening balances are not correct.

Analytical review

Relevant trends and ratio calculations:

—   Revenue increased by 11.5%

—   Gross profit increased by 12.7%

—   Operating profit increased by 59.5%

—   Cash fallen by 54.5%

—   Inventories increased by 100%

—   Receivables increased by 59.1%

	20X5	20X4
Gross profit margin	36.1%	35.8%
Operating profit margin	1.7%	1.2%
Interest cover	12.2	7.7
Current ratio	1.8	2.2
Gearing	22.5%	25.1%

Revenue

The analytical review indicates that the Group's revenue generation and profitability has improved during the year. There could be valid business reasons to explain the trends, however, the audit team should be alert for possible overstatement of revenue and understatement of expenses.

The risk is increased due to the bonus scheme which gives rise to a risk of material misstatement at the financial statement level. Management will be biased towards accounting treatments which lead to overstatement of revenue, for example, the early recognition of revenue.

There is also a risk of management manipulation of the financial statements due to the renegotiation of the Group's lending facilities, for example, it would be favourable to present a good interest cover to the bank as an analysis of interest cover is likely to feature in their lending decision.

Current assets

The current ratio has fallen, largely due to the significant reduction in cash of 54.5%. Other changes within current assets could indicate audit risk, as both inventories and trade receivables have increased significantly, by 100% and 59.1% respectively. Given that revenue has increased by only 11.5% in the year, these increases appear very large and could indicate potential overstatement.

Property, plant and equipment

The analytical review also reveals that the amount recognised in respect of property, plant and equipment has not changed over the year. This seems unlikely to be reasonable, as the Group would presumably have incurred some asset (capital) expenditure in the year, disposed of some assets and charged depreciation. There are implications for operating profit, which, for example, is overstated if any necessary depreciation has not been charged.

Brand name – lack of amortisation

The brand of $8 million is material based on the threshold above. It is recognised in the statement of financial position as an intangible asset which is appropriate given that the brand is a purchased intangible asset. However, the asset is recognised at its original cost and there is risk attached to the policy of non-amortisation of the brand.

IAS 38 *Intangible Assets* states that an intangible asset with a finite useful life is amortised, and an intangible asset with an indefinite useful life is not. The risk is that the assumption that the brand has an indefinite life is not correct, and that the asset is overstated and operating expenses understated through the lack of an annual amortisation charge against the asset.

Brand name – potential impairment

There is also a risk that the brand could be impaired given the bad publicity and allegations made by the journalist against the Group. IAS 36 *Impairment of Assets* requires an impairment review to be carried out when indicators of potential impairment exist.

The allegations may have damaged the Group's reputation, with consequential impact on revenue and cash flows, though the increase of 11.5% in the Group's revenue could indicate that this is not the case, as claimed by the Group finance director. However, sales of certain products could be in decline, and the fact that inventories have doubled in value could indicate problems in selling some of the Group's products.

The risk is that if any necessary impairment has not been recognised, the asset is overstated and operating expenses understated by the amount of the impairment loss.

Associate – lack of Group knowledge of accounting treatment

A new associate, which is material to the Group, has been acquired during the year, which gives rise to several risks.

Because this is the first addition to the Group for many years, there is an inherent risk that the Group lacks accounting knowledge on the appropriate accounting treatment. Associates are accounted for under IAS 28 *Investments in Associates and Joint Ventures*, which states that an entity with joint control of, or significant influence over, an investee shall account for its investment in an associate or a joint venture using the equity method.

There is a risk that the equity method has not been properly applied. The investment in the associate recognised in the statement of financial position has increased in value since acquisition by $0.5 million, presumably due to the inclusion of the Group's share of profit arising since investment. There is a risk that this has not been calculated correctly, for example, it is not based on the correct share of profit, and the investment may therefore be over- or understated.

Associate – possible impairment

Risk also arises in relation to any possible impairment of the investment, which may cause it to be overstated in both the individual financial statements of Adams Co, and the Group financial statements.

Associate – disclosure of income

There is a disclosure issue, as the Group's share of post-investment profit of Stewart Co should be included as a line item in the statement of profit or loss using the equity method.

The draft statement of profit or loss and other comprehensive income does not show income from the associate as a separate line item. It may have been omitted or netted against operating expenses, and the risk is inappropriate presentation of the income from investment.

Associate – classification

There is a risk that the investment should not have been classified as an associate. According to IAS 28, if an entity holds, directly or indirectly, 20% or more of the voting power of the investee, it is presumed that the entity has significant influence, unless it can be clearly demonstrated that this is not the case.

If the 25% holding does not give rise to significant influence, for example, if the shares do not convey voting rights, it should be classified as an investment rather than an associate. There is a risk of inappropriate classification, recognition and measurement of the investment in Stewart Co.

Ross Co's inventory in multiple locations

A risk arises in relation to inventory, which is held in each of the department stores. There is a risk that controls are not sufficiently strong in respect of the movement of inventory and counting procedures at the year end, as it will be hard for Ross Co to ensure that all locations are subject to robust inventory counting procedures. This control risk leads to potential over or understatement of inventory and cost of sales.

Beard Co's investment properties

The investment properties are material to both Beard Co's individual financial statements, and also to the Group's financial statements.

According to IAS 40 *Investment Property*, an entity can use either the fair value model or the cost model to measure investment property. When the fair value model is used the gain is recognised in profit or loss. The draft consolidated statement of profit or loss and other comprehensive income includes the investment property revaluation gain as other comprehensive income rather than as profit or loss, and therefore the gain is not presented in accordance with IAS 40.

An accounting error may have been made in the adjustment made to increase the value of the investment property. The statement of financial position shows an increase in value of investment properties of $2.5 million, however, the gain in the statement of profit or loss and other comprehensive income is stated at $1 million which is material based on the threshold. There is a risk that the gain is understated and part of the gain may have been classified elsewhere in profit or loss.

It would be important to obtain information on the type of properties which have been invested in, and whether there have been any additions to the portfolio during the year, as part of the movement in the investment property balance during the year could be explained by acquisitions and disposals. Information should also be obtained on any disposals of investment properties during the year, and whether a profit or loss was made on such disposals.

The possible error discussed above in relation to the presentation of the investment property gain is also relevant to the comparative information, which may also be materially misstated. This increases the risk that other balances and transactions in prior years have been incorrectly accounted for. The use of professional scepticism should be stressed during the audit, and further procedures planned on opening balances and comparative information.

Further information should be sought from the previous auditor of the Group in relation to the accounting treatment for the investment properties, and whether it had been identified as an error, in which case the auditor's reports of both Beard Co and the Group should have been modified. A review of prior year auditor's reports is necessary, as well as a review of the previous audit firm's working papers, assuming permission is given for this to take place.

Bonus scheme

It is noticeable from the draft statement of financial position that there is no accrual recognised in respect of the bonus scheme, unless it has been included inappropriately in trade or tax payables. This indicates a potential understatement of liabilities and overstatement of profit if any necessary accrual has not been made for any bonus which is payable.

Systems and controls

The audit committee states that the Group's systems are out of date. This may give rise to control risk across the Group as a whole. In addition, Lynott Co has implemented a new inventory control system. A new system introduced during the year can create control risk.

With any new system, there are risks that controls may take time to develop or be properly understood, and the risk of error in relation to inventories is relatively high.

Management charges

The management charges imposed by the parent company on the subsidiaries represent intra-group transactions. In the individual financial statements of each subsidiary, there should be an accrual of $800,000 for the management charge payable in August 20X5, and Adams Co's individual financial statements should include $2.4 million as a receivable. There is a risk that these payables and the corresponding receivable have not been accrued in the individual financial statements.

At Group level, the intra-group balances should be eliminated on consolidation. If this has not happened, the liabilities and receivables in the Group financial statements will be overstated, though there would be no net effect on Group profit if the balances were not eliminated.

Tutorial note

Credit will also be awarded for comments on relevant issues to do with transfer pricing and relevant tax implications which have not been considered and recognised appropriately in the financial statements.

Inventory

Inventory is material to the Group and the draft consolidated statement of financial position shows that inventory has doubled in the year. Given that the Group is involved in retail, there could be issues to do with obsolescence of inventory, leading to potentially overstated inventory and overstatement of profit if any necessary write down is not recognised. This may be especially the case for the mass market fashion clothing made by Lynott Co.

Intra-group transfers

Ross Co transfers goods to Lynott Co for recycling when its goods are considered obsolete. There is a risk that at Group level the intra-group trading is not eliminated on consolidation, which would lead to overstated receivables and payables. In addition, if the inventory is transferred at a profit or loss, which is then not realised by the Group at the year end, the Group inventory figure and operating profit could be over- or understated if any necessary provision for unrealised profit or loss is not recognised.

Goodwill

The draft consolidated statement of financial position does not recognise goodwill, which is unusual for a Group with three subsidiaries. It may be that no goodwill arose on the acquisitions, or that the goodwill has been fully written off by impairment. However, there is a risk of understatement of intangible assets at the Group level.

Component auditor

Lynott Co is audited by an overseas firm of auditors. This may introduce audit risk in that Dando & Co will be relying to some extent on their work. Careful planning will be needed to reduce this risk to a minimum, and this is discussed in the next section of the briefing notes.

Tutorial note

Credit will be awarded for relevant calculations which form part of relevant analytical review performed, such as calculations relating to profit margins, liquidity and gearing, and for discussion which is relevant to the evaluation of audit risk. Credit will also be awarded for discussion of other relevant audit risks, for example, risks associated with the lack of a deferred tax figure in the statement of financial position, and the change in effective tax rate.

(b) **Matters to be considered and procedures to be performed in respect of using the work of Clapton & Co**

The requirements in respect of using the work of component auditors are given in ISA 600 (Revised) *Special Considerations – Audits of Group Financial Statements (Including the Work of Component Auditors)*. ISA 600 (Revised) requires that if the Group engagement team plans to use a component auditor to perform work on the financial information of a component, the Group audit partner must consider whether:

– the Group audit team will be able to be involved in the work of the component auditor.

– the component auditor is competent and capable of performing the work assigned to them. This includes consideration of whether the component auditor has the relevant industry specific skills and technical knowledge to adequately obtain evidence on the component. As Lynott Co reports under IFRS Accounting Standards, there is less likelihood of Clapton & Co having a knowledge gap in terms of the Group's applicable financial reporting framework than if the company used local accounting rules. The fact that Clapton & Co is a member of an international network means it is likely to have access to regular training programmes and technical updates which adds to the credibility of their audit work.

– the component auditor understands and will comply with the ethical requirements which are relevant to the group audit and, in particular, is independent. When performing work on the financial information of a component for a group audit, the component auditor is subject to ethical requirements which are relevant to the group audit. Given that Clapton & Co is based in Farland, the ethical requirements in that location may be different, possibly less stringent, to those followed by the Group.

– the component auditor operates in a regulatory environment which actively oversees auditors should be understood. The Group audit team should ascertain whether independent oversight bodies have been established in the jurisdiction in which Clapton & Co operates, to oversee the auditing profession and monitor the quality of audit. This allows greater reliance to be placed on their work.

In addition to the matters discussed above, the risk of material misstatement in the subsidiary being audited by the component auditor must be fully assessed, as areas of high risk may require input from the Group audit team. For areas of high risk, such as Lynott Co's inventories, the Group audit team may consider providing instructions to the component auditor on the audit procedures to be performed.

The group auditor will set the performance materiality level for the component to apply.

The group auditor must communicate matters relevant to risk assessment, related party transactions and going concern which impact the component auditor's procedures.

Procedures

– Review the local ethical code (if any) followed by Clapton & Co, and compare with the IESBA *International Code of Ethics for Professional Accountants* for any significant difference in requirements and principles.

– Obtain confirmation from Clapton & Co of adherence to any local ethical code and the IESBA *Code*. Establish through discussion or questionnaire whether Clapton & Co is a member of an auditing regulatory body, and the professional qualifications issued by that body.

– Obtain confirmations of membership from the professional body to which Clapton & Co belongs, or the authorities by which it is licensed.

– Discuss the audit methodology used by Clapton & Co in the audit of Lynott Co, and compare it to those used under ISAs.

– Ascertain the quality management policies and procedures used by Clapton & Co, both firm-wide and those applied to individual audit engagements.

– Request any results of monitoring or inspection visits conducted by the regulatory authority under which Clapton & Co operates.

(c)   Audit procedures over the investment in associate

– Obtain the legal documents relating to the share acquisition, and review to confirm the terms and conditions including the number of shares purchased and the voting rights attached to each share.

– Agree the cost of investment of $11.5 million to the legal documentation and to Adams Co's bank statement and bank ledger account/cash book.

– Review the minutes of Group management meetings to understand the business rationale for the investment, and to confirm that the Group intends to exercise significant influence over Stewart Co, for example, through appointment of board members.

– Obtain management's calculation to determine the $12 million recognised in the Group financial statements, review the method of the calculation for compliance with IAS 28.

– Obtain the financial statements of Stewart Co to confirm the amount of profit made in the year and confirm that the Group's share of that profit is included in the Group financial statements.

– Enquire with management as to whether any impairment review of the investment in Stewart Co has taken place, and if so, obtain management's workings and review the assumptions used and the method of calculation.

(d)   Ethical matters

Advice on accounting and management information systems

The first threat relates to the audit committee's request for our firm to provide advice on the new accounting and management information systems to be implemented next year. If the advice were given, it would constitute the provision of a non-assurance service to an audit client. The IESBA's *International Code of Ethics for Professional Accountants* has detailed guidance in this area and specific requirements in the case of a public interest entity such as the Group which is a listed entity.

The *Code* states that services related to IT systems including the design or implementation of hardware or software systems may create a self-review threat. This is because when auditing the financial statements, the auditor would assess the systems which they had recommended, and an objective assessment would be difficult to achieve as the auditor would be reluctant to find errors or shortcomings in the recommendations and work performed by their firm. There is also a risk of assuming the responsibility of management, especially as the Group apparently has little experience in this area, so would rely on the auditor's suggestions and be less inclined to make their own decision.

In the case of an audit client which is a public interest entity, the Code states that an audit firm shall not provide services involving the design or implementation of IT systems which form a significant part of the internal control over financial reporting or which generate information which is significant to the client's accounting records or financial statements on which the firm will express an opinion.

The audit firm should not provide a service to give advice on the accounting systems. With further clarification on the nature of the management information systems and the update required to them, it may be possible for the audit firm to provide a service to the Group, as long as those systems are outside the financial reporting system. However, it may be prudent for the audit firm to decline offering any advice on systems to the client especially as Adams Group is a listed entity.

Meeting with the bank

Second, the audit committee has asked the audit engagement partner to attend a meeting with the bank, the objective of the meeting being the renegotiation of the Group's lending facilities. This is an advocacy threat to objectivity, as the audit partner will be supporting the client in its renegotiation and may be perceived as supporting or confirming the Group's financial position.

If the partner were to attend the meeting and confirm the strength of the Group's financial position, or confirm any work performed on the cash flow forecast, there could be legal implications. These actions would potentially expose Dando & Co to liability, it could be perceived that the audit firm is in some way guaranteeing the loan or guaranteeing that the Group is in a position to service the debt. The partner should not attend the meeting or be seen to be supporting the Group in its attempt to raise further finance.

These ethical issues should be discussed with those charged with governance of the Group, with an explanation provided as to why the audit firm cannot attend the meeting with the bank.

Conclusion

These briefing notes have shown that there are several significant audit risks. The most significant relates to this being a new audit client which makes it more difficult for us to recognise management bias as we do not have any cumulative knowledge and experience of the client. Therefore, the movements identified by the preliminary analytical review may be more challenging to understand and interpret, particularly as they may be due to management bias.

Examiner's comments

This question was based on planning the audit of a new client – the Adams Group. The Group comprised a parent company, three subsidiaries, one of which was located overseas, and an associate which had been acquired during the year. Information relevant to each of the components of the Group was detailed in the form of narrative notes and draft consolidated financial statements were also provided. The notes contained information on the Group's activities, details of intra-group transactions, a portfolio of investment properties held by one of the subsidiaries, a new system introduced in relation to inventory, and a bonus for management based on revenue. Details were also provided in respect of the auditors of the overseas subsidiary, which had retained the services of a small local firm.

The first requirement asked candidates to evaluate the audit risks to be considered in planning the audit of the Group. This is a very typical requirement for the first question in the exam, and while it was encouraging to see that many candidates had clearly revised this part of the syllabus, there were many whose answers were extremely disappointing. The best answers worked through the information provided in the question to identify the various audit risks, and evaluated them by, including an assessment of materiality and a discussion of the significance of the risks identified. Most candidates proved able to include a discussion of the most obvious of the risks in their briefing notes, including the management bonus, the classification of the associate, the valuation of investment properties and the potential control risk caused by implementing a new system during the year. Only the better candidates identified the risks arising from the opening balances and comparative information (due to this being a new audit client for the firm), the lack of presentation of income from the associate in the Group statement of profit or loss, the incorrect treatment of the investment property revaluation gains (which should be recognised as part of profit for the year) and the change in the effective tax rate. The best answers included in their evaluation of each audit risk an identification of the risk factor from the scenario (e.g. the measurement of the investment properties), a determination of materiality where possible given the information in the question, a clear comment on the appropriateness of the accounting treatment where relevant, and the impact on the financial statements (e.g. not cancelling intra-group transactions would lead to overstated revenue, cost of sales, receivables and payables).

The key weakness present in many answers was the poor quality of explanations. Most candidates could identify a reasonable range of risks but could not develop their answer to demonstrate a clear evaluation of that risk, in a suitable structure, like the one discussed above. For example, having identified that the portfolio of investment properties would give rise to some kind of audit risk, many candidates would then attempt to expand their answer with vague comments such as 'there is risk this is not accounted for properly', 'there is risk in the accounting treatment' or 'there is risk that IAS 40 will not be followed'. This type of comment does not represent a detailed evaluation of audit risk and does not earn credit.

Other weaknesses seen in many answers included:

- Incorrect materiality calculations or stating that a balance is material without justification

- Incorrect analysis of the financial statements provided or incorrect trend calculations, the most common of which was stating that inventory had increased by 50% when it had doubled

- Too much emphasis on business risk with no development or discussion of the audit implications

- Not using the draft financial statements at all to identify audit risks

- Not identifying from the scenario that all Group members use the same financial reporting framework and report in the same currency, leading to sometimes lengthy discussion of irrelevant matters

- Long introductions including definitions of audit risk, showing a lack of appreciation of the fact that the notes are for an audit partner, and general discussions about audit planning

- Lack of understanding of certain accounting treatments such as equity accounting for associates and the correct treatment of investment properties

- Focusing on goodwill – despite the fact that no goodwill was recognised in the Group financial statements many answers discussed at length that it must be tested for impairment annually

- Suggesting that the bonus scheme would lead to manipulation of expenses, when the bonus was based on revenue.

Requirement (b) asked candidates to explain the matters to be considered, and the procedures to be performed, in respect of planning to use the work of the component auditor. This requirement was relatively well attempted, with the majority of answers covering a range of relevant matters and associated procedures. It was clear that many candidates had studied this part of the syllabus, and could apply their knowledge to the question scenario. Most candidates identified that the component audit firm was a small firm, so resourcing the audit could be an issue, and that due to its overseas location there may be differences in the ethical code and auditing standards used by the firm. Weaker answers incorrectly discussed the problem of the overseas subsidiary not reporting under IFRS Accounting Standards (the question clearly stated that it did) and tended to focus on accounting issues rather than answering the question requirement. Some answers were also very brief for the marks available, amounting to little more than a few sentences or a short list of bullet points.

ACCA Marking guide		
		Marks

(a)	**Audit risk evaluation**
	Up to 3 marks for each audit risk evaluated unless otherwise indicated.
	Marks may be awarded for other, relevant risks not included in the marking guide.
	Appropriate materiality calculations (max 2 marks) and justified materiality level should be awarded to a maximum of 1 mark.
	In addition, ½ mark for each relevant trend or calculation which form part of the evaluation of audit risk (max 3 marks).
	– New audit client (max 2 marks)
	– Analytical review:
	    • Increased revenue and profitability, risk of overstatement
	    • Increased current ratio, risk of overstatement of current assets
	    • Unusual trend in PPE, risk of over- or understatement
	– Brand name – indefinite useful life and lack of amortisation
	– Brand name – potential impairment and overstatement if not recognised
	– Equity accounting – measurement of associate and possible impairment
	– Disclosure of income from associate
	– Classification as an associate
	– Ross Co's inventory – control issues relating to multi-location of inventory
	– Beard Co's investment property – measurement of the gain
	– Beard Co's investment property – incorrect classification of gain
	– Possible error in comparative information and need for scepticism
	– Bonus scheme – inherent risk of overstating revenue (max 2 marks)
	– Lynott Co's new inventory control system
	– Elimination of management charges
	– Inventories – movement in the year and potential overstatement (max 2 marks)
	– Intra-group trading (inventories)
	– Goodwill – none recognised (max 2 marks)
	– Reliance on component auditor (max 2 marks)	

	Maximum	**20**
(b)	**Using the work of a component auditor** Up to 2 marks for each matter explained: – Involvement in component auditor's work – Professional competence and capability of component auditor – Compliance with ethical requirements – Existence of a regulated environment – Assess level of risk in the subsidiary audited by the component auditor – Set component auditor performance materiality – Communicate matters relating to risk assessment, related party transactions and going concern	

1 mark for each relevant procedure:
- Review the local ethical code (if any) and compare with the IESBA *Code*
- Obtain confirmation from Clapton & Co of adherence to any local ethical code and the IESBA *Code*
- Establish whether Clapton & Co is a member of an auditing regulatory body, and the professional qualifications
- Obtain confirmations from the professional body to which Clapton & Co belong, or the authorities by which it is licensed
- Discuss the audit methodology used by Clapton & Co in the audit of Lynott Co, and compare it to those used under ISAs
- Ascertain the quality management policies and procedures used by Clapton & Co, both firm-wide and those applied to individual audit engagements
- Request any results of monitoring or inspection visits conducted by the regulatory authority under which Clapton & Co operates

	Maximum	8

(c) **Procedures to be performed in respect of investment in associate**
Generally 1 mark for each well explained audit procedure:
- Obtain and review the legal documents for key information
- Agree the cost of investment of $11.5 million to the legal documentation and bank statement and bank ledger account/cash book
- Review the minutes of Group management meetings for understanding of the rationale behind the investment and means of exercising significant influence
- Obtain and review management's calculation to determine the $12 million
- Obtain the financial statements of Stewart Co to confirm the amount of profit made in the year and confirm that the Group's share of that profit is included in the Group financial statements
- Enquire with management as to whether any impairment review of the investment in Stewart Co has taken place, and if so, obtain management's workings and review the assumptions used and the method of calculation

	Maximum	5

(d) **Ethical issues**
Generally up to 1 mark for each relevant point of discussion/explanation:
- Advice on new systems is a non-assurance service to an audit client
- Gives rise to a self-review threat and risk of taking on management responsibility (1 mark for each threat explained)
- Advice on new systems should not be given where systems form significant part of internal control over financial reporting
- Risk increased because Group is listed entity, service should not be provided
- Attending meeting with bank is an advocacy threat
- Legal implication for the firm if partner 'confirms' work performed
- Partner should not attend meeting with bank
- Matters and reasons for declining services should be discussed with Group audit committee

	Maximum	7

Professional marks

Communication

– Briefing note format and structure – use of headings/sub-headings and an introduction

– Style, language and clarity – appropriate layout and tone of briefing notes, presentation of materiality and relevant calculations, appropriate use of the CBE tools, easy to follow and understand

– Effectiveness and clarity of communication – answer is relevant and tailored to the scenario

– Adherence to the specific requests made by the audit engagement partner

Analysis and evaluation

– Appropriate use of the information to determine and apply suitable calculations

– Appropriate use of the information to design appropriate audit procedures relating to the investment in associate

– Effective prioritisation of the results of the audit risk evaluation to demonstrate the likelihood and magnitude of risks and to facilitate the allocation of appropriate responses

– Balanced discussion of the professional and practical issues when evaluating working with component auditors in a Group engagement

Professional scepticism and professional judgement

– Appropriate application of professional judgement to draw conclusions and make informed decisions following recognition of unusual or unexpected movements, missing/incomplete information or challenging presented information as part of the risk evaluation

– Determination and justification of a suitable materiality level, appropriately and consistently applied

– Identification of possible management bias and consideration of the impact on the financial statements and the possible reasons for management's preference for certain accounting treatments

– Effective application of technical and ethical guidance to effectively challenge and critically assess areas of significant management judgement

Commercial acumen

– Use of effective examples and/or calculations from the scenario to illustrate points or recommendations

– Appropriate recognition of the wider implications when evaluating ethical threats

– Audit procedures are practical and plausible in the context of the scenario

Maximum	**10**
Total	**50**

Section 4

ANSWERS TO PRACTICE QUESTIONS – SECTION B

PLANNING AND CONDUCTING AN AUDIT OF HISTORICAL FINANCIAL INFORMATION

17   AWDRY *WALK IN THE FOOTSTEPS OF A TOP TUTOR*

Top tutor tips

Part (a) requires knowledge of a specific auditing standard in relation to an area which if difficult to audit, accounting estimates. These are areas of higher risk of material misstatement and require more audit attention. Technical articles are often issued by the examining team covering areas such as these and you should take time to read and understand them.

Part (b) asks for an evaluation of the client's accounting treatment, including the difficulties that might be encountered when auditing accounting estimates. This requires a discussion of the subjectivity of the estimate and the extent to which the client will need to use their own judgement to determine the estimate. The question then asks for audit procedures in respect of the estimates. Audit procedures should be written in such a way that a member of the audit team can carry them out, therefore make sure they are sufficiently detailed. Audit procedures are used to obtain sufficient and appropriate evidence regarding the client's accounting treatment. Be clear about the source of the evidence and how the procedure should be carried out as vague procedures will not earn marks.

(a)   ISA 540 *Auditing Accounting Estimates and Related Disclosures*

ISA 540 applies to all accounting estimates from the simplest depreciation calculation through to the most complex of derivative financial instruments and expected credit losses.

While the simpler accounting estimates will not generally give rise to high audit risk, many measurements based on estimates, including fair value measurements and impairments in relation to financial instruments, are imprecise and subjective in nature and will give rise to high inherent risk.

ISA 540 emphasises that the risk of material misstatement in relation to the audit of accounting estimates is impacted by three key factors: complexity, the application of management judgement and estimation uncertainty.

Fair value measurements and impairments in relation to financial instruments are likely to involve significant, complex judgements, for example, regarding market conditions, the timing of cash flows and the future intentions of the entity. The valuations will often involve complex models built on significant assumptions such as the predicted timing of cash flows, the most appropriate discount factor to use and judgements about probability weighted averages.

Management may not always have sufficient knowledge and experience in making these judgements. Moreover, there may even be a deliberate attempt by management to manipulate the value of an estimate in order to window dress the financial statements.

Professional scepticism is key to the audit of accounting estimates and ISA 540 contains provisions which are designed to enhance the auditor's application of professional scepticism and a consideration of the potential for management bias.

The increased emphasis on the use of fair value measurement and extensive disclosure requirements in IFRS Accounting Standards, such as IFRS 9 *Financial Instruments* and IFRS 13 *Fair Value Measurement*, reflect the increasing complexity of the business environment. Given the increased emphasis on the use of external sources in IFRS 13 and in making accounting estimates such as fair values, ISA 540 clarifies the requirements on the use of such information as it is in the public interest to do so.

The risk that an entity's internal systems and controls fail to prevent and detect valuation errors also needs to be assessed as part of the overall assessment of audit risk. In relation to complex fair value and impairment estimates, a particular problem is that the measurement is likely to be performed infrequently for external reporting purposes and outside the normal accounting and management systems. This is especially true where the valuation is performed by an external specialist. As a non-routine event, therefore, the assessment of fair value is likely not to have the same level of monitoring or controls as a day-to-day business transaction and may give rise to high control risk.

The auditor should always seek to manage detection risk at an acceptable level through effective planning and execution of audit procedures. However, the audit team may lack knowledge and experience in dealing with the estimation technique in question and therefore may be unlikely to detect errors in the valuation and modelling techniques applied by the client. Any resulting over-reliance on an external specialist could also lead to errors not being identified.

(b) **Difficulties in auditing accounting estimates and procedures**

(i) **Cash-settled share-based payment scheme**

The expense recognised this year of $825,000 in respect of the cash-settled share-based payment scheme represents 11.1% of profit before tax and is therefore material to Awdry Co's statement of profit or loss for the year. The related liability of $825,000 which would be recognised on the statement of financial position is on the borderline of materiality to assets at 1.4%.

IFRS 2 *Share-Based Payment* requires that for cash-settled share-based payment transactions, the entity should measure the services acquired and the liability incurred at the fair value of the liability. Moreover, it states that until the liability is settled, the entity should remeasure the fair value of the liability at the end of each reporting period and at the date of settlement, with any changes in fair value recognised in profit or loss for the period.

In the case of Awdry Co, the expense and the associated liability has been calculated based on the fair value of the rights as at the reporting date and the treatment therefore complies with the requirements of IFRS 2 ($4.50 × 550,000 × 1/3 = $825,000).

IFRS 2 also requires that the amount recognised as an expense for cash-settled share-based payments should be based on the best available estimate of the number of awards which are expected to vest. The entity must therefore estimate the number of awards which are expected to vest.

In this case, management's estimate that all 55 staff will qualify for the rights appears to be based on a perception of good historic staff relations which may be inaccurate and the expectation that none of the eligible staff will leave over the three-year vesting period may prove to be unrealistic. The predictive nature of management's estimate in this regard represents a challenge to the auditor as it is difficult to obtain reliable evidence.

The fair value estimate of $4.50 is based on an options pricing models which is an example of a complex valuation model which, according to ISA 540 (Revised), is built on significant estimates and assumptions and is therefore challenging to audit. The initial choice of which option-pricing model to use is also a matter of judgement and whichever model is selected, it will incorporate judgemental inputs such as the current risk-free interest rate and measures of share price volatility.

Procedures:

- Obtain a copy of the contractual documentation for the share-based payment scheme and supporting file notes detailing principal terms and confirm:

    - grant date and vesting date

    - number of executives and senior employees awarded share appreciation rights

    - number of share appreciation rights awarded to each individual member of staff

    - conditions attaching to the share appreciation rights.

- Perform an assessment of the appropriateness of the model used to value the share appreciation rights and confirm that it is in line with the requirements of IFRS 2.

- Obtain details of the external expert used and assess the appropriateness of their appointment by considering their professional certification, experience, reputation and objectivity.

- Perform a review of the expert's valuation including an assessment of the assumptions used in order to determine the fair value of the share appreciation rights.

- Obtain details of historic staff turnover rates obtained from the human resources department including actual data for the first year of the vesting period and consider this in conjunction with the assumptions made by management.

- Perform a review of the forecast staffing levels through to the end of the vesting period including an assessment of the reasonableness of the assumptions used and their consistency with other budgets and forecasts.

- Discuss the basis of staff retention assumptions with management and challenge their appropriateness.

- Perform sensitivity analyses on both the valuation model and the staffing forecasts.

(ii) Regulatory penalties

The expense recognised in this year's statement of profit or loss for the year of $1.3 million is material to both profit (17.6%) and assets (2.2%).

According to IAS 37 *Provisions, Contingent Liabilities and Contingent Assets*, the fine should be measured at its present value at the reporting date. IAS 37 states that where the effect of the time value of money is material, the amount of a provision should be the present value of the expenditures expected to be required to settle the obligation and that the discount rate used in the calculation should be a pre-tax rate which reflects current market assessments of the time value of money and the risks specific to the liability.

The cash flows for the repayment of the fine over the ten years should therefore be discounted at an appropriate rate to present value as at 30 April 20X5.

The audit of the provision represents a challenge for the auditor in a number of respects. First, it is difficult to estimate the amount payable as it has not yet been finalised and the amount currently recognised is an estimate based on management's judgement. These difficulties are compounded by IAS 37 requirements to measure the provision at present value.

The measurement process therefore also requires management to predict the payment dates and to identify an appropriate pre-tax rate to be applied as the discount factor. Both of these will require a significant level of management judgement which will be a challenge for the auditor to obtain sufficient relevant and reliable evidence on.

Moreover, there is also the possibility of other provisions being needed in relation to the costs of remedying the safety issues which the regulator has identified and in relation to other potentially unidentified safety problems. Here, addressing the completeness assertion will represent a key challenge to the auditor as it is inherently difficult to predict all of the costs to be incurred in the future especially when they have not yet been determined.

Procedures:

- Obtain a copy of the regulator's notice detailing the date of the issue and any indication of the amount of the penalty to be paid by Awdry Co.

- Obtain a copy of any draft instalment agreement detailing the timing and amount of each repayment.

- Review Awdry Co's correspondence with the regulator for evidence of the amount payable and details of the repayment schedule.

- Confirm to post-year-end bank ledger account/cash book and bank statements if any amounts have been paid after the year end.

- Inspect Awdry Co's correspondence with its lawyers in order to ascertain current status of negotiations and the views of its legal advisers.

- Review Awdry Co's cash flow statements and forecasts in order to assess the company's ability to pay the instalments.

- Enquire of management in relation to the current status of the negotiations; the need to measure the provision at present value and their non-compliance with IAS 37 (i.e. their failure to measure the provision at present value).

- Review the board minutes for evidence of management's discussion of the penalty, any planned remedial action to address safety issues and any other possible safety issues.

- Discuss with management the need for the company to perform a calculation of the present value of the provision (including identification of an appropriate discount rate).

Examiner's comments

Requirement (a) required candidates to discuss accounting estimates as being an area of high risk. Overall candidates had a good attempt at this requirement, and candidates that had read the article written by the examining team had the potential to score highly.

Requirement (b) required candidates to evaluate the accounting treatment of two estimates given in the scenario. A large number of candidates demonstrated a weak understanding of the SBR syllabus and scored very poor marks. It was disappointing to note a lack of understanding of provisions. Only a limited number of candidates correctly stated the rule under IAS 37 *Provisions, Contingent Liabilities and Contingent Assets,* in relation to where the effect of the time value of money is material the provision should be recognised at present value. There was a clear indication in the question that this was relevant and it was disappointing that more candidates did not identify this.

The quality of answers for this question was generally of a weaker standard and candidates were not able to demonstrate application of their knowledge of SBR in an audit context to the scenario.

ACCA Marking guide		
		Marks
(a)	**ISA 540 Auditing Accounting Estimates and Related Disclosures**	
	Generally 1 mark per point.	
	Accounting estimates are source of high audit risk:	
	– Inherent risk:	
	• Subjectivity/uncertainty	
	• Deliberate manipulation	
	• Complexity	
	– Control risk:	
	• Non-routine transactions	

- Detection risk:
  - Audit team may lack knowledge/experience; and
  - May over rely on auditor's or expert

Reasons for enhanced risk assessment

- Increasingly complex business environment and increased complexity in IFRS Accounting Standards
- Increased emphasis on use of fair value in IFRS Accounting Standards (IFRS 9 and IFRS 13)
- Professional scepticism is key in the audit of accounting estimates; ISA 540 contains provisions designed to enhance auditor's application of professional scepticism and consideration of potential for management bias
- Given increased use of external sources in making accounting estimates, ISA 540 clarifies requirements on use of such information as it is in public interest to do so

Maximum marks	8

(b) **Difficulties and procedures**

Generally up to 1 mark for each difficulty evaluated and each relevant procedure designed.

(i) Cash-settled share-based payments

- Material expense to profit and borderline material to assets (with calculation(s))
- Treatment complies with IFRS 2 rules for accounting for cash settled share-based payments

Difficulties when performing audit:

- Management assumption of 100% staff retention may be unrealistic
- Predicted staff retention is estimation based on historic trends and future expectations; actual outcomes unlikely to correspond exactly
- Options pricing models are complex and challenging to audit
- Judgement involved in which option pricing model to use
- Option pricing models include judgemental inputs such as current risk-free interest rate and measures of share price volatility

Procedures:

- Obtain copy of share-based payments agreement and supporting file notes detailing principal terms (½ mark per term agreed)
- Perform assessment of appropriateness of model used to value rights/options
- Obtain details of external expert used including assessment of professional certification, experience, reputation and objectivity
- Critically review expert's valuation including assessment of assumptions used to determine fair value of the SARs
- Obtain details of historic staff turnover rates obtained from human resources/payroll department
- Review of forecast staffing levels through to end of vesting period including assessment of reasonableness of assumptions based on auditor's knowledge and understanding of client
- Discuss basis of staff retention assumptions with management and challenge their appropriateness
- Perform sensitivity analyses on valuation model and staffing forecasts

Maximum marks	6

(ii) **Regulatory penalties**
- Material expense to profit and assets (with calculation)
- Expense and provision should have been recognised at present value per IAS 37

Difficulties when performing audit:
- Difficult to estimate final amount payable as not yet finalised; amount currently recognised is based on management's judgement
- Difficulties are compounded by need to measure at PV and therefore also predict payment dates and identify appropriate pre-tax rate; both require significant level of management judgement
- Also possibility of other provisions needed, e.g. for costs of correcting current issues and/or for other unidentified safety problems
- Addressing completeness assertion here is challenging and also difficult to predict as costs to be incurred in future and have not yet been determined

Procedures:
- Obtain copy of regulator's notice detailing date of issue and any quantification of amount of penalty payable by Awdry Co
- Obtain copy of any draft instalment agreement detailing the timing and amount of each repayment
- Review correspondence with regulator for evidence of amount payable and details of repayment schedule
- Confirm payment to bank statement
- Review correspondence with Awdry Co's lawyers to ascertain current status of negotiations and views of legal advisors
- Review of cash flow statements and forecasts to assess company's ability to pay instalments
- Discuss with management the current status of negotiations; accounting treatment and non-compliance with IAS 37 (failure to measure at PV)
- Review board minutes for evidence of discussion of penalty, remedial action to address safety issues and any other possible safety issues
- Request client calculation of present value (including identification of appropriate discount rate)

Maximum	6

Professional marks
Analysis and evaluation
- Appropriate use of the information to support discussion, draw appropriate conclusions and design appropriate responses
- Identification of omissions from the analysis or further analysis which could be carried out
- Appropriate application of professional judgement to draw conclusions and make informed decisions about the actions which are appropriate in the context and stage of the engagement
- Appropriate use of the information to determine and apply suitable calculations

Professional scepticism and judgement
- Effective challenge and critical assessment of the conduct and extent of the audit work and evidence obtained with appropriate conclusions
- Appropriate application of professional judgement to draw conclusions and make informed decisions about the actions which are appropriate in the context and stage of the engagement
- Demonstration of the ability to probe for further information

Commercial acumen		
– Use of effective examples and/or calculations from the scenario to illustrate points or recommendations		
– Audit procedures are practical and plausible in the context of the scenario		
	Maximum	5
Total		25

18 TONY GROUP *Walk in the footsteps of a top tutor*

Top tutor tips

This past exam question focuses on professional scepticism which is now more likely to be examined through professional skills rather than as a full question. This question is still very useful for exam preparation as professional scepticism is a professional skill that will appear in every exam question, and therefore this can be used to develop your technique in this area.

Part (a) deals with professional scepticism. This question followed the publication of a relevant technical article prior to the exam. Students are reminded to pay attention to technical articles published by the examining team in the run up to the exam. Professional scepticism is an essential characteristic all auditors and assurance providers must demonstrate and you must understand what it means and be able to explain how it can be applied during an engagement.

Part (b) looks at how to apply professional scepticism to a situation. Think about whether there is any incentive for management to mislead the auditor and whether they appear to be trying to influence the audit by withholding information. The audit procedures designed over goodwill should demonstrate the application of professional scepticism.

(a) Professional scepticism is defined in ISA 200 *Overall Objectives of the Independent Auditor and the Conduct of an Audit in Accordance with International Standards on Auditing* as an attitude that includes a questioning mind, being alert to conditions which may indicate possible misstatement due to error or fraud and a critical assessment of audit evidence.

ISA 200 requires the auditor to plan and perform an audit with professional scepticism, recognising that circumstances may exist which cause the financial statements to be materially misstated. It is important to use professional scepticism at all stages of the audit. Professional scepticism can reduce the risk of material misstatements caused by fraud going undetected.

Professional scepticism includes being alert to the existence of contradictory audit evidence and being able to assess assumptions and judgements critically and without bias, and being ready to challenge management where necessary. It is also important that the auditor considers the reliability of information provided by management during the audit.

Recently, regulatory bodies such as the IAASB have stressed the importance of the auditor's use of professional scepticism. The increased use of principles-based financial reporting frameworks such as IFRS Accounting Standards, and the prevalence of fair value accounting which introduces subjectivity and judgement into financial reporting are examples of the reasons why the use of professional scepticism by auditors is increasingly important. It is imperative that professional scepticism is applied to areas of financial reporting which are complex or highly judgemental.

Going concern assessments and related party transactions are also examples of areas where management must exercise judgement in determining the appropriate accounting treatment, and where the potential for management bias is high. Therefore, these areas need to be approached with professional scepticism.

The application of professional scepticism is closely aligned with maintaining objectivity, and it is difficult to remain sufficiently sceptical when certain threats to objectivity are present. Ultimately, the exercise of professional scepticism should work to reduce audit risk by ensuring that the auditor has sufficient and appropriate evidence to support the audit opinion, and that all evidence obtained, especially in relation to areas of high risk of material misstatement, has been critically evaluated and is based on reliable information.

(b)　**(i)**　The finance director seems to be dictating the audit work to be performed. The audit manager should decide the extent of audit procedures in response to the risk of material misstatement identified. The manager should consider why the finance director seems so insistent that his file is used as the main source of audit evidence. He may be hiding something relevant to the impairment which would be revealed if the auditor looked at other sources of evidence.

The Group's profit before tax has fallen by 33.3%, indicating that a significant impairment loss amounting to more than the $50,000 calculated by the finance director may need to be recognised. There is a risk of material misstatement in that the impairment loss is understated, and there is a risk that management bias has resulted in an inappropriate determination of the loss.

The auditor therefore needs to be sceptical and alert for factors indicating that the loss is greater than that calculated by the finance director. Impairment testing is a complex and subjective area, and could be easily manipulated by management wishing to reduce the size of the loss recognised.

The audit manager should obtain corroborative evidence regarding the assumptions used and not just confirm that the assumptions are in line with management's risk assessment or the prior year audit file. The reliability of this source of evidence is not strong as it is prepared by management. An important part of professional scepticism is challenging management's assumptions, especially in an area of high judgement such as impairment testing.

The internal auditor checking the figures is also not a reliable source of evidence, as it is client generated. The internal auditor may have been pressured to confirm the finance director's calculations.

Professional scepticism should also be applied to the comment that the assumptions are the same as in previous years. New factors impacting on impairment may have arisen during this year, affecting the determination of the impairment loss and up-to-date evidence on the assumptions used in this year's calculation should be sought.

The audit team should also remain alert when auditing balances and transactions other than goodwill in case there are other areas where Silvio does not appear to be providing all evidence required or where he is suggesting the audit approach to be taken.

While his comment does not seem to be intimidating in nature, the audit team should recognise that if Silvio does have something to hide in relation to the goodwill impairment, he may become more aggressive, in which case the matter should be brought to the attention of the firm's ethics partner and discussed with those charged with governance of the Group.

(ii) Audit procedures – impairment of goodwill

- Confirm the assumptions used in the impairment test agree with the auditor's understanding of the business based on the current year's risk assessment procedures, e.g. assess the reasonableness of assumptions on cash flow projections.

- Confirm that the impairment review includes the goodwill relating to all business combinations.

- Consider the impact of the auditor's assessment of going concern on the impairment review, e.g. the impact on the assumption relating to growth rates which have been used as part of the impairment calculations.

- Obtain an understanding of the controls over the management's process of performing the impairment test including tests of the operating effectiveness of any controls in place, for example, over the review and approval of assumptions or inputs by appropriate levels of management and, where appropriate, those charged with governance.

- Confirm whether management has performed the impairment test or has used an expert.

- Agree the figures in the impairment review calculation e.g. discount rates, to auditor-obtained supporting documentation.

- Develop an independent estimate of the impairment loss and compare it to that prepared by management.

- Confirm that the impairment calculations exclude cash flows relating to tax and finance items.

- Perform sensitivity analysis to consider whether, and if so how, management has considered alternative assumptions and the impact of any alternative assumptions on the impairment calculations.

- Check the arithmetic accuracy of the calculations used in the impairment calculations.

Tutorial note

Credit will be awarded for other relevant audit procedures recommended.

Examiner's comments

This question focused on professional scepticism, the audit of goodwill impairment, and a forensic investigation into alleged bribery payments made by several of the audit client's employees.

Requirement (a) was a discussion, asking candidates to explain the meaning of the term professional scepticism and to discuss its importance in planning and performing an audit. It was clear that many candidates had read and understood the contents of a recent article on the topic of professional scepticism. Most answers provided an appropriate definition of professional scepticism and went on to discuss how it links to audit quality. Stronger candidates also discussed how the auditor should apply professional scepticism when considering the risk of material misstatement associated with fraud and areas of the financial statements that rely on the application of judgement. Few candidates however, discussed the recent activities of the regulatory bodies in respect of professional scepticism.

The second part of the question involved a scenario which described how the finance director of the Tony Group was insisting that the audit firm should rely on a file prepared by him in their audit of goodwill impairment. The file contained workings and assumptions and had been checked by the Group's head of internal audit. The requirement asked candidates to discuss how professional scepticism should be applied to the scenario, and to explain the principal audit procedures to be performed on the impairment of goodwill. Many candidates were able to explain that the Group finance director was intimidating the audit firm, that his workings were not sufficient as a source of evidence, and that he may have something to hide. It was disappointing that few candidates appreciated that the Group's profit before tax had fallen significantly, and therefore the small impairment to goodwill suggested by the finance director was unlikely to be sufficient in the circumstances, and probably influenced by management bias. Most candidates did however realise that the audit firm should perform their own workings and not place complete reliance on the procedures that had been performed by the head of internal audit.

The requirement relating to procedures on goodwill impairment was poorly attempted. The evidence points provided by candidates for this requirement tended to revolve around recalculation or a discussion with management. Very few suggested specific procedures that would allow the auditor to develop their own expectation in terms of the impairment necessary, which could then be compared with the finance director's workings. This was disappointing, as impairment has featured in several exams as an audit issue and is a topic that candidates should be better prepared to tackle. Many candidates did not answer the question, and simply described the accounting treatment for goodwill, or suggested procedures that were relevant to the calculation of goodwill at acquisition but not relevant to a review of its impairment.

		ACCA Marking guide	
			Marks

(a) **Professional scepticism discussion**

Generally, up to 1½ marks for each point discussed, including:
- Definition of professional scepticism (1 mark for definition)
- Explaining professional scepticism
- Link between professional scepticism and ethics/objectivity
- Importance in relation to complex and subjective areas of the audit
- Importance in relation to the audit of going concern
- Discussion of regulatory bodies actions in relation to professional scepticism

                                  Maximum 6

(b) (i) **Applying professional scepticism**

Generally, up to 1½ marks for each point discussed, and 1 mark for calculation of materiality.
- Risk that impairment loss understated due to Group's fall in profit
- The determination of the impairment loss is judgemental and subject to management bias
- Auditor should question the reasons for finance director's insistence that no other audit work is needed
- Evidence provided by the finance director is not reliable (client generated)
- Assumptions are unlikely to have stayed the same since last year
- Audit team should remain alert for other instances where professional scepticism is needed
- Possible threat of intimidation by the finance director

         Maximum 7

(ii) **Procedures on impairment**

Generally, 1 mark for each procedure explained:
- Review all assumptions used in preparing projected cash flows
- Confirm that the impairment review includes the goodwill relating to all business combinations
- Consider impact of auditor's assessment of the Group's going concern status
- Consider operating effectiveness of any controls in place
- Confirm whether management has performed the impairment test or used an expert
- Recalculate amounts based on auditor-generated inputs
- Develop an independent estimate of the impairment loss and compare to that prepared by management
- Confirm that the impairment calculations exclude cash flows relating to tax and finance items
- Perform sensitivity analysis
- Check the arithmetic accuracy of the calculations

         Maximum 7

Professional marks
Analysis and evaluation
- Appropriate use of the information to support discussions and draw appropriate conclusions and design appropriate responses
- Appropriate assessment of the ethical and professional issues raised, using examples where relevant, to support overall comments
- Identification of omissions from the analysis or further analysis which could be carried out

Professional scepticism and professional judgement	
– Effective application of technical and ethical guidance to effectively challenge and critically assess the audit evidence	
– Demonstration of the ability to question contradictory information and probe for further information	
– Demonstration of the ability to apply appropriate professional judgement to draw conclusions and make informed decisions about the courses of action appropriate	
– Effective challenge and critical assessment of the conduct and extent of the audit work and evidence obtained with appropriate conclusions	
– . Appropriate application of professional judgement to draw conclusions and make informed decisions about the actions which are appropriate in the context and stage of the engagement	
Maximum	5
Total	25

COMPLETION, REVIEW AND REPORTING

19   **MARLOS** *Walk in the footsteps of a top tutor*

Top tutor tips

Part (a) asks for the matters to be considered and the audit evidence that should be on file during your review of the audit file. Use the 'MARE' approach. First, consider the materiality of the issue. Next discuss the appropriate accounting treatment and give the risks of material misstatement that would arise if the appropriate treatment is not followed. Finally, the evidence is what you would expect to be recorded on the audit file when you come to review it.

For part (b) you need to state the impact to the auditor's report if the client does not amend the financial statements in respect of one of the issues presented in the scenario. State the impact to both the report and opinion as a result of the issue. Don't waste time stating the reporting implications if the issue is corrected as this is not part of the requirement.

(a)   **Matters and evidence**

New property lease

The right-of-use asset value exceeds the materiality threshold of $1.1 million and as such is material. IFRS 16 *Leases* requires that on inception of a lease, a lease liability is initially measured at the present value of the lease payments not paid at the commencement date, discounted at the rate implicit in the lease if that can be readily determined. Here, this appears to have been correctly created.

A right-of-use asset should initially be measured at the initial lease liability, plus any lease payments made at or before the commencement date (less any lease incentives) plus the initial estimate of any restoration costs and any direct costs incurred. This right-of-use asset should be depreciated over the term of the lease. This asset will be accounted for under a cost model where the right-of-use asset is measured at cost less accumulated depreciation and any accumulated impairment.

The rent-free period alters the timing of the cash flows relating to the lease but it does not alter the measurement of the right-of-use asset or lease liability calculated. Therefore, depreciation should be charged as the entity has the use of the asset, even if no lease payments have been yet been made.

The depreciation which should have been charged on the asset in the first year is $4.1 million ($28.9 million/7 years). This amount is significantly over the materiality threshold for the audit. This means that non-current assets are overstated and expenses are understated by a material amount. As such, it represents a material misstatement unless management adjusts the amount.

Evidence

- Copy of the lease contract to agree the period, the payments required, the implicit interest rate and whether there is any requirement to restore the condition of the building to support the amounts to be included in the financial statements.

- Evidence that a physical inspection was performed to confirm the existence of the building and its condition to determine if there are any indicators of impairment.

- A copy of management's calculation of the present value of the lease obligation and right-of-use asset agreed back to the underlying lease amount.

- A recalculation of management's figures with respect to the lease asset.

- A copy of the extract of the non-current asset register to confirm the amounts capitalised and a breakdown of liabilities to confirm the year-end value of the lease liability.

- Copy of the company policy to review the accounting treatment regarding depreciation of non-current assets is consistent.

- Notes of a discussion with management regarding the use of the asset and cash flows arising from the new store to determine whether there are indicators that the asset may be impaired.

- A copy of the proposed financial statement disclosures in relation to the lease, for example, the finance costs of leases and the maturity of the liability.

Inventory

The inventory held by Marlos Co purchased from the new supplier is held on consignment. Marlos Co has no control over the inventory as the supplier can require unsold inventory to be returned and Marlos Co has the right to return the inventory. In accordance with IFRS 15 *Revenue from Contracts with Customers*, the inventory remains the property of the supplier until Marlos Co has sold the inventory to a third party. This means that the inventory should only be recognised as a purchase and corresponding inventory amount where Marlos Co no longer has a right to return the assets, i.e. when they are sold to a customer.

As such, $8.1 million of inventory should not be recognised in the financial statements of Marlos Co. Instead, Marlos Co will show a receivable due from the new supplier to the inventory purchase price as they potentially have the right to receive a refund for this amount. Ownership and control of the inventory is still with the supplier until it has been sold by Marlos Co.

Currently, Marlos Co is recognising the asset of the inventory ($8.1 million) but as it can be returned for a refund, this misclassification results in inventory being overstated and trade receivables understated. This amount is significantly higher than the materiality level for the company audit and is a material misstatement in classification. The net impact on net current assets, however, is nil.

Tutorial note

Credit will be given if the candidate states that payment is not required until Marlos Co has sold the inventory to a third party. It is not determined from the scenario that this inventory has been paid for, and some consignment inventory only falls due for payment once the goods have passed to the third party (i.e. the supplier no longer controls the inventory).

Evidence

- Copy of the contract with the new supplier to understand and confirm the terms and conditions of the sale or return arrangement and the amounts involved.

- Copy of the inventory records to confirm the total value of inventory received from the new supplier which was unsold at the year end.

- Obtain confirmation from the supplier of the amounts outstanding in respect of these goods.

- Agree amounts refunded to Marlos Co post year end to the supplier information, such as a credit note, received post year end and the bank statement if a refund was received.

- A copy of the calculation of how much of the inventory held was eligible for return, cast for accuracy and agreed to contract terms.

- Discussion with management about the misclassification of the inventory which can be returned and their reasoning for classifying this as inventory.

(b) **Evaluation of the impact on the auditor's report**

In respect of the depreciation charge for the leased property, it appears that the profit for the year is overstated by $4.1 million. This is a material misstatement in the financial statements, but as this represents a single item only, the misstatement could be considered material but not pervasive.

As such, the audit opinion should be modified and a qualified opinion should be given on the basis of a material misstatement. This will be presented in the qualified opinion paragraph at the start of the auditor's report.

This will be followed by a basis of qualified opinion paragraph which will explain the reason for the qualification and quantify the impact of the misstatement.

Examiner's comments

This 25-mark question was set at the completion and reporting stage of an audit. As is typical of reporting questions, the examining team saw some of the strongest and some of the weakest demonstrations of auditing competence from candidates in Marlos Co. This was a matters and evidence question with two accounting issues; incorrect depreciation of a right-of-use asset and consignment inventory that had been incorrectly accounted for in the client's financial statements. Candidates appeared comfortable with the familiar format of the question and the answers provided were appropriately structured however the majority of candidates failed to make any attempt at the professional skills that were also examined in the question of professional scepticism and judgement and analysis and evaluation.

Requirement (a)

The accounting error in the depreciation of the right-of-use asset was correctly identified and explained by the majority of candidates. A large number of candidates calculated the error and compared this error to the materiality threshold in the question in order to conclude that this constituted a material misstatement. Some candidates continued to use the entire asset value to assess materiality or failed to compare the error to the materiality threshold provided in the question and therefore missed out on valuable marks. Evidence areas were well addressed by most candidates for this issue; however, many candidates failed to develop their answer sufficiently to gain professional skills marks on this issue. The lack of professional skills marks awarded was disappointing as it was reasonable to suggest that there may be management bias on the incorrect accounting treatment due to a desire to manipulate profits. The inventory matter was less well addressed by candidates as a significant number failed to appreciate that the accounting issue was that consignment inventory was being accounted for as if it was owned and controlled by Marlos Co. Some students strayed into discussing the business risk aspects of this arrangement which was outside of the scope of this question. The failure to identify the accounting error affected the follow-on marks for evidence, however sensible descriptions of evidence were awarded credit, such as consideration of whether the inventory had been paid for and obtaining the supplier's confirmation of goods that remained unsold at the year end. As previously mentioned, there was a disappointing lack of understanding of the accounting issue and this also had an impact on the professional skills marks. Firstly, there was a lack of any attempt to critique management's treatment of the inventory and furthermore candidates did not appear comfortable with the double entry here and failed to appreciate that the error had no effect on net assets. This meant that the error which could be judged as an area of management incompetence rather than bias and therefore suggested the possibility of further errors to the financial statements as a result was often not identified.

Requirement (b)

This part of the question was either answered very well or very poorly. As with elsewhere in the exam, candidates could only score sufficient credit to pass this requirement by following the instructions and applying their answers to the scenario. Some candidates continued to produce answers that failed to decide on an appropriate audit report by offering a range of different audit opinions which does not address the requirement and therefore cannot attract credit. Follow on marks for the title and content of the basis of opinion paragraphs were awarded where appropriate, however few candidates made their description of the content of the basis of opinion paragraphs sufficiently detailed and applied to be awarded maximum credit. This was disappointing as many candidates had demonstrated sufficient understanding of the accounting issue in part (a), and so these marks should have been achievable.

Professional skills marks associated with this part of question were awarded for analysis and evaluation in the context of the scenario and the use of judgement to determine an appropriate audit opinion. Strong candidates could confidently achieve maximum technical and professional skills marks in this area.

	ACCA Marking guide	
		Marks
(a)	**Matters and evidence**	
	Generally, up to 1 mark for each matter explained and each well described piece of evidence.	
	New property lease	
	Matters	
	– Correct accounting treatment of leases	
	– Requirement to depreciate/calculation of the missing depreciation	
	– Financial statement implications re depreciation	
	– Materiality assessed	
	Evidence	
	– Copy of the lease contract to agree terms and conditions	
	– Evidence that a physical inspection was performed to confirm the existence and conditions of the building	
	– A copy of management's calculation of the present value of the lease obligation and right-of-use asset agreed back to the underlying lease amount	
	– Recalculation of management's figures	
	– Copy of the non-current asset register extract to confirm the amounts capitalised and a breakdown of liabilities to confirm the year-end value of the lease liability	
	– Copy of the company policy to review the accounting treatment	
	– Notes of a discussion with management regarding the use of the asset and cash flows arising from the new store	
	– Copy of the proposed financial statement disclosures	
	Maximum	9
	Inventory	
	Matters	
	– Accounting treatment for inventory held on a consignment basis	
	– Financial statement implication	
	– Classification error	
	– Accounting treatment	
	– Assessment of the materiality of the misstatement	
	Evidence	
	– Copy of the contract with the new supplier to understand and confirm the terms and conditions of the arrangement	
	– Copy of the inventory records to confirm the total value of inventory received and unsold at the year end, identified as being returned	
	– Confirmation from the supplier of the amounts outstanding in respect of these goods	
	– Credit note received post year end and bank statement if a refund was received to confirm amounts refunded post year end	
	– Copy of the calculation of how much of the inventory held was eligible for return	
	– Notes of discussion with management about the misclassification of the inventory which can be returned	
	Maximum	7

(b)	**Auditor's report** Generally, 1 mark for each relevant and well explained point. – Material not pervasive with justification – Qualified on the basis of material misstatement – Positioning of opinion/basis of opinion – Explanation of the specific content of the basis of opinion paragraph in relation to the specific scenario – Titles of paragraphs impacted		
		Maximum	**4**
	Professional marks **Analysis and evaluation** • Appropriate use of the information to support discussion, draw appropriate conclusions and design appropriate responses • Appropriate recognition of the implications for the auditor's report • Balanced assessment of the information to determine the appropriate audit opinion in the circumstances **Professional scepticism and judgement** • Effective challenge of information, evidence and assumptions supplied and demonstration of judgement in relation to the risks in the question • Evaluation of the pervasiveness of the misstatements, providing a justified conclusion which is appropriate in the context of the scenario		
		Maximum	**5**
Total			**25**

20   GELLER   *Walk in the footsteps of a top tutor*

Top tutor tips

Part (a) requires an evaluation of the assumptions used in a cash flow forecast which is being assessed as part of the auditor's going concern procedures. Even though this is an audit engagement, take the same approach as you would for a non-audit engagement to examine a cash flow forecast. Professional scepticism needs to be exercised for both. When the forecast is used to support the going concern basis, the client will want to make the forecast to look positive as they will not want to draw attention to uncertainties that require disclosure in the financial statements.

In part (b), you need to give the evidence you would expect the audit team to have obtained in respect of the cash receipts only. There will be no marks for evidence over payments. Evidence is the information documented in the audit file that has been obtained from performing an audit procedure. It should be as detailed as an audit procedure in that it needs to explain why the evidence has been obtained. A list of pieces of evidence with no explanation will not be sufficient to score full marks.

In part (c) you need to consider which audit opinion is appropriate in the circumstances, compare that with the audit assistant's proposal and if you disagree with the proposal, explain why.

(a) **Evaluation of the assumptions used by management in preparing the cash flow forecast**

Cash receipts from customers

Management has assumed growth of 2% in each six-month period, which appears optimistic given that this year revenue has decreased by 20%, which is a continuation and worsening of a longer-term trend.

The assumptions underpinning management's expectation of a reversal in this downward trend in revenue both appear to be flawed for a number of reasons:

- First, the assumption that a full range of digital book and magazine titles will be available in August 20X5 seems extremely optimistic. The digital publishing acquisition is a recent event, and there is no indication from the information provided by management as to how a full digital offering will be created by August 20X5, which is only one month away.

- The cash flow forecast contains no specific expenditure relating to the creation of this digital portfolio, so it is unclear how this business development is supported given the apparent lack of resources being devoted to it.

- There are also no specific cash flows included in the forecast relating to forging closer connections with online retailers, so it is difficult to see how this assumption is supported.

- In addition, not all authors may give permission for their books to be converted into digital format, so the company may not be able to offer a full range, as is suggested.

- If the sale of the Happy Travels range goes ahead, the company will lose the cash receipts from sales of those titles.

Second, the assumption that Chandler Muriel's books will generate $250,000 each six-month period should be challenged, for the following reasons:

- The first book has apparently not sold well, so there is a question over whether this book, and the others in the series which are due to be published in the next two years, will generate this level of income.

- It may also be overly optimistic to assume that Chandler Muriel will be able to deliver the books for publication in quick succession, in time to meet the publication deadlines set by Geller Co.

- In addition, it seems odd that the income assumed to be generated is $250,000 per six months – this round sum figure should be challenged.

- With the publication of additional books in the series, it would be expected that the income stream would increase rather than remain static.

The final point in relation to the cash receipts from customers included in the forecast is that the 2% sales growth has not been applied consistently. The final six-month period, to 31 March 20X7, is based on a 5% increase in cash receipts. The reason for this should be challenged – it could be a genuine mistake, or it could be a deliberate manipulation. Without a 5% increase in the final six-month period, the cash position is negative, a motive for management bias in the calculations.

Cash receipt from sale of Happy Travels range

The decision to sell this range of books has only recently been made, and it may be optimistic to assume that the sale will actually go ahead, especially given the industry-wide deterioration in demand for printed books. Even if a buyer is found, the sale may not go ahead in January 20X6, which is only six months away.

In addition, the estimated cash receipt on sale should be challenged. Just because other ranges of books have successfully sold in the past, with a sale price based on a multiple of annual sales, it does not mean that the same model can be used for this particular range of books.

Management has an incentive to include an estimated sales receipt which will cover the bank loan repayment which is due to be paid, according to the forecast and presuming the repayment date is successfully extended, in September 20X6. This is a significant motivation for overestimating the amount to be raised on the sale of Happy Travels.

Operating expenses

It is overly simplistic to assume an increase in operating expenses of 1% per six-month period based on inflation. This may be an attempt to understate operating expenses and improve the appearance of the cash flow forecast. Some operating expenses may be missing, e.g. as mentioned above, any specific operating expenses required to create the digital range of books and magazines, and marketing expenses related to promoting sales using online retailers.

Operating expenses are likely to include advances paid to authors and royalty payments relating to the volume of sales of their books. If sales are expected to increase by 2% per six-month period, then royalty payments would be also expected to increase, but this does not appear to have been factored into the operating cash outflows.

In addition, there are no specific cash outflows in relation to the recently acquired digital publishing division, yet it is likely that significant costs and cash outflows are likely to be incurred in merging this into the existing business and preparing the digital books and magazines which are due to be launched next month.

Interest payments and other finance costs

This cash outflow is static at $125,000 until the point at which the forecast assumes that the loan will be repaid. This should be challenged, because the company is clearly using an overdraft for many months and will also need to utilise the undrawn borrowing facilities once the overdraft limit of $250,000 is breached – this is forecast to happen in the six-month period to 30 September 20X5. The finance costs should therefore increase and fluctuate, depending on the utilisation of the overdraft and borrowing facility which takes place.

In addition, assuming no finance costs in the final six-month period should be challenged – the company has a negative cash position forecast at 30 September 20X6, so there presumably will be some overdraft interest payments which will need to be made.

Loan repayment

It is not certain that the bank will agree to renegotiate the loan repayment date to 30 September 20X6, which is the date assumed in the cash flow forecast. This assumption may be over-optimistic and an attempt to move the timing of the significant cash outflow on the loan repayment to after the company has received the cash on disposal of Happy Travels (which itself is uncertain).

If the bank does not agree to change the repayment date, or if the sale of Happy Travels is delayed or does not take place, or does not raise at least $5 million, then it will not be possible for Geller Co to repay the bank loan. This would cause serious going concern problems, and therefore creates significant pressure on the company's management to manipulate the timing and the amount of the cash flows.

Tax expenses

There does not appear to be any cash flows relating to tax payments included in the forecast. If management is claiming that there will be no tax payments during the period covered by the forecast, this assertion needs to be approached with professional scepticism as it is unlikely that no tax payments at all will occur during this time. These payments may be deliberately omitted to improve the cash flow position as shown in the forecast.

Dividends

No dividend payments are included in the cash flow forecast, which could be a genuine situation if shareholders are not expecting to receive any dividend payment in the next few years. However, the omission of dividend payments could be a way for management to improve the cash flow forecast.

Conclusion

There is a significant risk that the assumptions used in preparation of the cash flow forecast are not realistic and have been applied to make the cash flow forecast look positive in an attempt to present a much more favourable impression of the company's going concern position to the audit team.

(b) **Evidence expected on cash receipts**

- Notes of a discussion with appropriate personnel, e.g. sales director and commissioning editors, to obtain understanding of how management justify a 2% growth rate per six-month period given the company's recent declining revenues, including specific evidence relating to the company's plans to develop closer relations with online retailers.

- Copies of any signed customer contracts, e.g. from physical or online retailers, and copies of market research performed on the company's product ranges to corroborate the forecast sales figures. This evidence should be both general in nature and also specific to the range of books to be published by Chandler Muriel, to justify the specific sales forecast in respect of this book series.

- A copy of the signed contract between Geller Co and Chandler Muriel to confirm the expected publication dates of the books and the amounts of any advances and royalty payments due.

- Relating to the plans to launch a full range of digital books and magazines:

  - Notes of a discussion with management regarding the process which has been made and confirmation that the author agreements have been obtained and the readiness of the digital platform.

  - For a sample of authors, a copy of their agreement to allow Geller Co to create and publish digital versions of their books.

- Notes of a discussion with management regarding the plans to sell the Happy Travels range, specifically to confirm:

  - whether any buyers have yet expressed an interest, and if so, the stage of any negotiations

  - understanding of the rationale used by management in using the multiple of annual sales model to estimate the potential sales value of Happy Travels.

- Confirmation, from a review of board minutes, that the sale of the Happy Travels range has been discussed and approved by management.

- Confirmation that the assumptions in relation to cash receipts underpinning the cash flow forecast are consistent with the audit team's knowledge of the business and the environment in which Geller Co is operating.

- Sensitivity analysis performed on cash receipts by varying the key assumptions and an assessment of the impact of these variations on the company's forecast cash position.

- Written representations from management confirming the reasonableness of their assumptions relating to cash receipts and that all relevant information has been provided to Bing & Co.

- A review of the bank ledger account/cash book from 1 April 20X5 to the date of the auditor's report, identifying any significant cash receipts which do not appear to have been included in the forecasts.

(c)   Auditor's report

The audit assistant is correct to identify that there is a significant going concern issue facing Geller Co due to the uncertainty over the sale of the Happy Travels publishing range, and as a consequence, the company may be unable to repay its borrowings. If sufficient evidence were available to support the use of the going concern basis of accounting in the financial statements and to confirm the adequacy of relevant notes to the financial statements, an unmodified opinion could be issued, and the auditor's report would include a Material Uncertainty Related to Going Concern section to highlight the issue for users of the auditor's report.

However, the lack of evidence over the assumptions used in the cash flow forecast and in particular in relation to the sale of the Happy Travels range means that the auditor should consider modifying the audit opinion in accordance with ISA 705/ISA (UK) 705 *Modifications to the Opinion in the Independent Auditor's Report*. ISA 705 requires that the auditor shall disclaim an opinion when the auditor is unable to obtain sufficient, appropriate audit evidence on which to base the opinion, and the auditor concludes that the possible effects on the financial statements of undetected misstatements, if any, could be both material and pervasive.

The seriousness of the going concern problems facing Geller Co, particularly whether the company will be able to use the sales proceeds from the sale of the Happy Travels range to repay its borrowings, should be considered both material and pervasive as it impacts on the survival of the company.

When the auditor disclaims an opinion due to an inability to obtain sufficient, appropriate audit evidence, ISA 705/ISA (UK) 705 requires that the auditor shall:

- State that the auditor does not express an opinion on the financial statements.

- State that, because of the significance of the matter(s) described in the Basis for Disclaimer of Opinion section, the auditor has not been able to obtain sufficient, appropriate audit evidence to provide a basis for an audit opinion on the financial statements.

- Instead of stating the financial statements have been audited, state that the auditor was engaged to audit the financial statements.

A Basis for Disclaimer of Opinion section should be included in the auditor's report to explain the reasons for the inability to obtain sufficient, appropriate evidence.

Tutorial note

*Credit is awarded where candidates assess and **justify** that the impact on the financial statements is not pervasive. Credit is awarded for concluding, based on this justification, that a qualified audit opinion is appropriate, as the issue of the inability to obtain sufficient, appropriate evidence is material but not pervasive.*

Examiner's comments

This question was set at the completion and reporting stage of an audit. As is typical of reporting questions, this is where the examining team see some of the strongest and some of the weakest demonstrations of auditing competence from candidates. This was a completion question centred around the going concern assessment of an audit client in a declining market.

Going concern and audit reporting are two areas most crucial for an auditor to understand but are two of the areas where overall candidate performance is disappointing. Candidates often do not demonstrate professional scepticism when auditing client information involving the future and often are unable to devise ways to assess the prospective financial information rather than the more historical information which is examined at AA. This is compounded by a reluctance to evaluate opinion options rather than replicating a knowledge of the types of audit opinion that is examined already at AA.

Requirement (a)

Candidates were expected to demonstrate professional scepticism to challenge the assumptions supporting the cash flow forecast which management had used to justify the going concern basis for the financial statements. Candidates were expected to evaluate these assumptions, as given in the cash flow forecast (Exhibit 2) against the specific business environment (Exhibit 1). There were also items omitted from the cash flow forecast and candidates should use their professional judgement to determine any missing information such as capital (asset) expenditure, tax, or dividends.

Candidates who performed well on this requirement were able to link the assumptions to the specific business environment, demonstrating professional scepticism when questioning the basis of the judgements made by management. These stronger candidates gained credit for both technical marks for the specific evaluation points as well as professional skills marks for the demonstration of professional scepticism by challenging managements' assumptions with specific explanations. Marks were also available for the demonstration of commercial acumen when making this challenge. Examples of commercial acumen seen in candidates answers included questioning whether the bank would agree to extend a repayment date given the current performance of the company, whether a higher interest rate might be charged by the bank on any extension of repayment due to the higher default risk the loan would carry or questioning management's assertion that books two and three in a series would sell more than book one, given that people generally would read book one in a series before moving onto a sequel.

Weaker candidates tended to simply state an assumption should be challenged without justifying why or made comments relating to similar past questions which were not relevant to this specific scenario and forecast.

Requirement (b)

This part of the question was either answered very well or very poorly. Those candidates who appreciated they needed to support the assumptions in the forecast with regard to future cash receipts did very well, with any valid procedure being awarded credit. Areas which attracted credit included verifying typical payment patterns for existing customers, quantifying the progress on obtaining digital publication rights from authors, identifying whether any potential buyers had expressed an interest in purchasing the Happy Travels range of books, and obtaining any contracts signed with digital outlets. Candidates were also credited for assessing the reliability of the first period of the forecast with the actual results to date during the forecast period. A particularly useful approach by candidates was to take each of the assumptions in the cash flow being assessed and describing a procedure to assess whether it was reasonable.

Weaker candidates who provided generic procedures not tailored to the scenario obtained little credit, for example, reference to a written management representation supporting the information or generic reviews of board minutes. These are weak forms of evidence, and the content of such sources must be specifically described and appropriate to obtain credit. The model answer published alongside this examiner's report contains examples of specific content which would attract credit. It is also important to note that some superficially similar procedures have very different levels of validity in this situation. For example, comparing customer payment patterns to historical payment trends and credit terms to help assess whether the pattern of receipts from customers settling sales invoices, is valid. Comparing forecast sales receipts to historical sales levels is not appropriate as we are told that the market and sales levels have been declining year on year, yet management are predicting growth this year. This means last year's sales are not indicative of the forecast sales, so the comparison is not appropriate.

Professional skills marks attached to this requirement overlapped with requirement (a) where professional scepticism was displayed in relation to the assumptions being tested. A further professional skills mark was available for analysis and evaluation where candidate's procedures were relevant to supporting the assumptions. This did not require the procedures to be correct as that was deemed a technical skill, but it was given for the appropriate focus of the procedures.

Candidates are reminded that reading the requirement carefully is vital and ensuring that they are responding to the specific area being tested or the correct assumption to be verified.

Requirement (c)

The requirement then moved the candidates forward in time to the next stage of the audit process. Candidates should read this additional information carefully to ensure that they are answering the requirement completely. It was disappointing to note that candidates performed poorly on this requirement. Candidates were told that sufficient audit evidence had not been obtained to allow the auditor to conclude on the appropriateness of preparing the financial statements on a going concern basis. The audit assistant had proposed using a material uncertainty relating to going concern paragraph (MURGC) as the client management had agreed full disclosure of the going concern uncertainties in the financial statements (Exhibit 1). Candidates should have explained that the MURGC paragraph is used when the **audit opinion is unmodified,** and the client has made adequate disclosure of the uncertainty. Candidates were expected to assess whether it was appropriate to propose the unmodified opinion, using the information in the scenario to make the determination: The information stated that the auditor could not obtain **sufficient appropriate audit evidence** to support the assumptions in the cash flow. When the auditor has not been able to obtain sufficient appropriate audit evidence over a material aspect of the financial statements there are two options for the opinion:

1) a qualified opinion on the basis of the inability to obtain sufficient appropriate audit evidence where the issue is **material and not pervasive,** or

2) the auditor may provide a disclaimer where no opinion is issued if the matter is **material and pervasive**.

Stronger candidates received credit for assessing and justifying whether this matter is pervasive to the financial statements. As it related to the going concern of the company, this would generally be considered pervasive, however this is a matter of judgement. Candidates obtained credit for the act of making that judgement and the explanations given, and this was followed through to the audit opinion marks. Candidates who did not make that judgement obtained credit for demonstrating that this was an inability to obtain sufficient appropriate evidence, rather than a material misstatement but would not gain the credit available for the assessment of pervasiveness and the conclusion reached because of that assessment.

Some candidates appeared to believe the financial statement should not have been prepared on the basis of going concern, concluding instead that a pervasive misstatement existed. If the auditor had disagreed with the basis of preparation, rather than concluded that they had been unable to obtain sufficient appropriate evidence, this would have been stated in the question.

These weaker candidates would be recommended to revise their understanding of the going concern basis of accounting. The Conceptual Framework states that *"financial statements are normally prepared on the assumption that the reporting entity is a going concern and will continue in operation for the foreseeable future. Hence, it is assumed that the entity has neither the intention nor the need to enter liquidation or to cease trading. If such an intention or need exists, the financial statements may have to be prepared on a different basis"*.

As with the rest of the exam, candidates could only pass this requirement when the answer was applied to the specific scenario in the question. A knowledge of different types of auditor's reports alone would not gain sufficient credit to pass this requirement.

Professional skills marks associated with this part of question were awarded for analysis and evaluation in the context of the scenario and the use of judgement to determine an appropriate audit opinion.

		ACCA marking guide		
				Marks

(a) **Evaluation of assumptions**

Generally, up to 1 mark for each relevant point of evaluation:

- Cash receipts from customers:
  - Creation of digital publishing division
  - Relationships with online retailers
  - Authors' permission for online versions of products
  - Sales from Chandler Muriel's books
- Sale of Happy Travels
- Operating expenses including advances to authors, royalties, marketing expenses for new Chandler Muriel books, digital book costs (licences, administration, software)
- Interest payments
- Loan repayment
- Missing tax expense
- Dividends
- Conclusion

Maximum	**10**

(b) **Evidence expected on cash receipts**

- Notes of a discussion with appropriate personnel, e.g. sales director and commissioning editors, to obtain understanding of how management justify a 2% growth rate per six-month period given the company's recent declining revenues, including specific evidence relating to the company's plans to develop closer relations with online retailers
- Copies of any signed customer contracts, e.g. from physical or online retailers, and copies of market research performed on the company's product ranges to corroborate the forecast sales figures. This evidence should be both general in nature and also specific to the range of books to be published by Chandler Muriel, to justify the specific sales forecast in respect of this book series
- A copy of the signed contract between Geller Co and Chandler Muriel to confirm the expected publication dates of the books and the amounts of any advances and royalty payments due
- Relating to the plans to launch a full range of digital books and magazines:
  - Notes of a discussion with management regarding the process which has been made and confirmation that the author agreements have been obtained and the readiness of the digital platform
  - For a sample of authors, a copy of their agreement to allow Geller Co to create and publish digital versions of their books
- Notes of a discussion with management regarding the plans to sell the Happy Travels range, specifically to confirm:
  - whether any buyers have yet expressed an interest, and if so, the stage of any negotiations
  - understanding of the rationale used by management in using the multiple of annual sales model to estimate the potential sales value of Happy Travels
- Confirmation, from a review of board minutes, that the sale of the Happy Travels range has been discussed and approved by management
- Confirmation that the assumptions in relation to cash receipts underpinning the cash flow forecast are consistent with the audit team's knowledge of the business and the environment in which Geller Co is operating
- Sensitivity analysis performed on cash receipts by varying the key assumptions and an assessment of the impact of these variations on the company's forecast cash position

- Written representations from management confirming the reasonableness of their assumptions relating to cash receipts and that all relevant information has been provided to Bing & Co
- A review of the bank ledger account/cash book from 1 April 20X5 to the date of the auditor's report, identifying any significant cash receipts which do not appear to have been included in the forecasts

| | Maximum | 5 |

(c) **Auditor's report**

Up to 1 mark for each relevant point explained:

- If sufficient and appropriate evidence obtained, the assistant's suggestion would be appropriate
- But lack of evidence means that the opinion should be modified
- Likely to be both material and pervasive, so a disclaimer of opinion is appropriate OR Justification of a qualified opinion where the issue is deemed to be material and not pervasive
- Basis for Disclaimer of Opinion section to be provided (if deemed to be pervasive); OR Basis for Qualified Opinion section to be provided
- Other impacts on auditor's report (max 2 marks)

Tutorial note: Candidates must explain their rationale regarding the pervasiveness of the issue to gain the credit. A conclusion is required and credit is awarded for justification and the correct impact on the auditor's report using that judgement.

| | Maximum | 5 |

Professional marks

Analysis and evaluation

- Appropriate assessment of the issues raised in relation to Geller Co's going concern situation, using examples where relevant to support overall comments
- Identification of omissions from the analysis with an effective appraisal of the information to make suitable recommendations for appropriate courses of action

Professional scepticism and professional judgement

- Effective challenge and critical assessment of how management has prepared the cash flow forecast, with appropriate conclusions
- Balanced assessment and use of professional judgement of the information to conclude upon the appropriate audit opinion in the circumstances

Commercial acumen

- Appropriate recognition of the wider implications on the engagement, the audit firm and the company

| | Maximum | 5 |

| **Total** | | **25** |

21   WHEELER & CO   *Walk in the footsteps of a top tutor*

Top tutor tips

Part (a) asks for the matters to be considered and the audit evidence that should be on file during your review of the audit file. Use the 'MARE' approach. First, consider the materiality of the issue. Next discuss the appropriate accounting treatment and give the risks of material misstatement that would arise if the appropriate treatment is not followed. Finally, the evidence is what you would expect to be recorded on the audit file when you come to review it.

For part (b) you need to state the impact to the auditor's report if the client does not amend the financial statements. State the impact to both the report and opinion as a result of the issue. Don't waste time stating the reporting implications if the issue is corrected as this is not part of the requirement.

Matters and audit evidence in relation to Byres Co

(a)   (i)   **Matters and evidence in relation to the new product**

Matters

The carrying amount of the capitalised development costs in relation to the new product are immaterial as they amount to 0.8% of assets and immaterial to profit before tax at 4.0%.

There is a significant risk that the requirements of IAS 38 Intangible Assets have not been followed. Research costs must be expensed and strict criteria must be applied to development expenditure to determine whether it should be capitalised and recognised as an intangible asset. Development costs are capitalised only after technical and commercial feasibility of the asset for sale or use have been established. Byres Co must also demonstrate an intention and ability to complete the development and that it will generate future economic benefits. Additionally, Byres Co must demonstrate the existence of a market, which given the product design director's comments appears uncertain.

There is a risk that research costs have been inappropriately classified as development costs and then capitalised, overstating assets and understating expenses. The product design director is uncertain as to whether the new product will generate sufficient economic benefits due to the sale price being unlikely to exceed the production costs per unit. It is therefore unlikely that the costs in relation to this product development continue to meet the criteria for capitalisation, so there is a risk that they have not been written off, overstating assets and profit.

Evidence expected to be on file:

–   Review of board minutes for discussions relating to the commercial feasibility of the smart vacuum cleaners.

–   Notes of a discussion with management regarding the accounting treatment of the research costs and confirmation that they were written off.

- A schedule itemising the individual costs capitalised to date in the production of the smart vacuum cleaner prototype to ensure there are no research elements.

- Review of the results of tests performed on the products to demonstrate that the prototype is fully operational.

- Analysis of Byres Co's budgets for the development of the prototype against actual expenditure to determine if the product costs have deviated significantly from original budgets.

- Alternative market research of any similar existing products to determine if a price point over $2,000 per unit would be commercially viable.

- Details of discussions with the product design director of any difficulties in the development of this product which have caused it to run over budget.

- Written representation from management detailing their intention to complete the project, including a commitment of resources and the ability to fund the future cash requirements to bring the product to market.

(i) **Matters and evidence in relation to the warranty provision**

Matters

The warranty provision is material as it amounts to 6·6% of total assets and 33.3% of profit before tax respectively. The provision has changed in value over the year, declining by $2.2 million which is a significant reduction of 51.2%. This is despite revenue increasing during the year by $5.5 million which is a significant increase of 11.0% and the provision has historically and effectively been based on a percentage of total sales in prior years.

Based on the information provided, in 20X4, the warranty provision was 8·6% of revenue (4.3/50m). In 20X5, the warranty provision is only 3.8% (2.1/55.5m) of revenue. Therefore, since the chief executive officer's (CEO) involvement with estimating the warranty provision, the value of the provision has reduced significantly compared to the value which would normally be expected.

According to ISA 540 *Auditing Accounting Estimates and Related Disclosures*, the audit team should have tested how management made the accounting estimate, and the data on which it is based. The audit team should also have tested the operating effectiveness of any relevant controls and developed their own point estimate or range in order to evaluate management's estimate.

The value of the warranty provision would normally be expected to increase in line with revenue, particularly as the sales director has indicated neither the range of customers nor the nature of the warranty have changed significantly compared to the prior year. There has also not been any change in the level of customer complaints or faulty items which, if present, may indicate problems with the quality of the company's products. The audit team must fully understand the reasons for the reduction in the warranty provision. There could be valid reasons, for example, the sales mix between products could be different which failed to trigger a similar level of warranty provision, but the change in value should be fully investigated by the team.

Consideration should also be given to the accounting entries which have been made to effect the change in the value of the provision. The validity of any credit entry to profit as a result of the reduction in value of the provision should have been scrutinised as this could indicate creative accountancy and earnings management. In the event that the provision has been underestimated in the current year, then future accounting periods would require higher expenses charged to the statement of profit or loss.

In previous years, the finance director and finance department had dealt with the judgement when estimating the warranty provision, however, this year the CEO has had significant input. There is therefore an increased risk of management bias in the estimation techniques. The audit team should approach this issue with professional scepticism and consider the motivation of the CEO in involving himself in accounting issues which had previously been left to the finance director.

Evidence expected to be on file

- A copy of management's calculation of the $2.1 million warranty provision, with all components agreed to underlying documentation, and arithmetically checked.

- Notes of a meeting with management, at which the reasons for the reduction in the warranty provision were discussed, including the key assumptions used by management.

- Analysis of total sales in terms of product mix against prior years with investigation into differences and a quantification of the effect this might have on the warranty provision.

- A copy of any quality control reports, disaggregated by product, reviewed for any indications that certain product lines have fewer warranty claims than in previous years.

- Notes of the meeting with the customer services manager where the levels of customer complaints and product faults were discussed.

- A comparison of the prior year's calculation with actual warranties claimed post year end to determine the accuracy.

- An evaluation of all key assumptions, considering consistency with the auditor's knowledge of the business, and a conclusion on their validity.

- An independent estimate prepared by the audit team, compared to management's estimate, and with significant variances discussed with management.

- A schedule obtained from management showing the movement in the provision in the accounting period, checked for arithmetic accuracy, and with opening and closing figures agreed to the draft financial statements and general ledger.

- Evaluation by the audit team, and a conclusion on the appropriateness of the accounting entries used, especially in relation to the profit impact of the entries.

- A file note documenting that the auditor has requested an adjustment requiring the warranty provision to be increased in line with the prior year estimation method.

(b)   Implications for the auditor's report

Warranty provision

Accounting estimates are always difficult to determine with any degree of certainty, however, the work carried out by the audit team suggests that the value of the warranty provision has been suppressed. Assuming that the provision should have increased consistently with the increase in revenue of 11%, it would be expected that the year-end warranty provision should be around $4.8 million. The actual provision recorded in Byres Co's financial statements is only $2.1 million; therefore, the liability appears to be understated by $2.7 million. At 8.5% of total assets, the likely error in the provision is highly material to the statement of financial position.

Overall impact on the auditor's report

The misstatement in relation to the warranty provision is individually material and if management fails to amend the financial statements, the auditor's opinion should be modified due to the material, but not pervasive, misstatement. The misstatement of the warranty provision is confined to specific accounts in the financial statements and does not represent a substantial proportion of the financial statements. A qualified opinion should therefore be given.

The auditor's report should include a qualified opinion paragraph at the start of the report. This paragraph should be followed immediately by a basis for qualified opinion paragraph which should explain the reasons for the qualified auditor's opinion and which should quantify the impact of the matters identified on the financial statements.

Examiner's comments

This question was set at the completion and reporting stage of an audit. As is typical of reporting questions, this is where the examining team see some of the strongest and some of the weakest demonstrations of auditing competence from candidates.

Stronger candidates often display strong practical skills, incorporating a good understanding of materiality and risk, a strong knowledge of the financial reporting which is needed to perform an audit, an ability to distinguish between auditor and client information and an understanding of the difference between the financial statements, an auditor's report and an audit opinion.

Weaker candidates tend to lack the underlying knowledge of double entry accounting and are unable to distinguish between the client and the audit firm, between the financial statements and the auditor's report or demonstrate a good understanding of the concept of materiality.

Requirement (a)

This question covered the treatment of a new product capitalised as an intangible asset and a warranty provision. Candidates were required to consider the matters that would be discussed with management regarding to the treatment of the issue highlighted in the scenario and to discuss the evidence the auditor would expect to see on the audit file.

Successful candidates identified the new product capitalised as development costs was unlikely to meet the criteria in IAS 38 *Intangible Assets*, as the selling price is noted to be less than the cost incurred and therefore would be loss making.

To answer the requirement successfully the candidate should take an approach of:

- Calculate materiality of the issue

- Identify the incorrect accounting treatment by the client – linked to the scenario

- State the relevant accounting rule – how it should be dealt with

- The impact on the financial statements

The new product is recognised as development costs under IAS 38 and it was disappointing to note candidates who made reference to 'PIRATE' criteria. Whilst this is used as an acronym for candidates to assist them in retaining the knowledge of the criteria of IAS 38, marks will not be awarded unless a candidate demonstrates they have the knowledge of the criteria by listing them out specifically.

A number of candidates incorrectly stated that 4% of profit before tax was material, whereas it is below the benchmark of 5% and, therefore, not material. Calculating materiality incorrectly in a Section B question will ultimately affect how candidates answer the impact on the audit opinion. This latter requirement is normally examined separately, resulting in marks lost due to suggesting an incorrect impact on the audit opinion.

The warranty provision had declined in comparison with prior year by over 50%. Materiality was generally successfully calculated correctly for this matter, and most candidates were awarded the additional trend marks available. The main issue here was that there was a reduction in the warranty provision, yet revenue had increased, this appears inconsistent as there is an expectation the warranty provision would increase in line with increasing revenue. Candidates were required to identify this as being a potential management manipulation of the figures and that the auditors should adopt an increased level of professional scepticism.

Successful candidates scored well regarding the evidence expected to be on file in response to both matters in the scenario. The evidence is required to be specific to the issue and examples of evidence for the new product that related to more general capitalisation criteria, rather than assessing that the development cost has been potentially incorrectly capitalised. Therefore, where candidates document general evidence for the creation of a provision or general capitalisation of intangible assets, they would fail to score marks.

Overall, the majority of candidates performed well in this requirement.

Requirement (b)

Candidates were asked to assess the implication on the auditor's report if the adjustment to the warranty provision is not corrected.

Stronger candidates correctly calculated the materiality of the understated liability and fully evaluated the misstatement was not material. For candidates to score maximum marks, the term 'not pervasive' must be explained, for example, it is isolated to one issue and the financial statements as a whole are not impacted. Where candidates merely say the impact is pervasive with no explanation, credit will be restricted.

Candidates should then indicate the correct opinion to be given, in this instance a qualified opinion due to a material misstatement.

Candidates should evaluate the impact on the report, in that the basis of opinion paragraph, which is situated below the opinion paragraph is used to explain the reason for the modification.

It is disappointing to note the number of candidates who continue to discuss the use of an Emphasis of Matter paragraph in response to this issue, which is wholly irrelevant, along with a number of candidates referring to the need for a Key Audit Matter paragraph, yet the scenario clearly stated the client is not listed.

It is concerning that there are still candidates who use outdated terminology when discussing the implications of misstatements on the auditor's opinion. Candidates are continuing to show a lack of knowledge regarding the content of auditor's reports and audit opinions issued.

	ACCA Marking guide	Marks
(a)	**Matters and evidence in relation to Byres Co** Generally, up to 1 mark for each matter explained and each piece of evidence recommended (unless otherwise stated). **(i) Matters and evidence in relation to the new product** **Matters** – Materiality – Discussion of whether meets classification requirements – Risk – Accounting treatment **Evidence** – Review of board minutes for discussions relating to the commercial feasibility of the smart vacuum cleaners – A schedule itemising the individual costs capitalised to date in the production of the smart vacuum cleaner prototype to ensure there are no research elements – Notes of a discussion with management regarding the accounting treatment of the research costs and confirmation that they were written off – Review of the results of tests performed on the products to demonstrate that the prototype is fully working – Analysis of Byres Co's budgets for the development of the prototype against actual expenditure to determine if the product costs have deviated significantly from original budgets – Market research of any similar existing products to determine if a price point over $2,000 per unit would be commercially viable – Details of discussions with the product design director of any difficulties in the development of this product which have caused it to run over budget – Written representation from management detailing their intention to complete the project, including a commitment of resources and the ability to fund the future cash requirements to bring the product to market	
	Maximum	7
	(ii) Matters and evidence in relation to the warranty provision **Matters** – Materiality – Discussion of estimates – Risk – Accounting treatment – Influence of CEO **Evidence** – A copy of management's calculation of the $2.1 million warranty provision, with all components agreed to underlying documentation, and arithmetically checked – Notes of a meeting with management, at which the reasons for the reduction in the warranty provision were discussed, including the key assumptions used by management	

- Analysis of total sales in terms of product mix against prior years with investigation into differences and a quantification of the effect this might have on the warranty provision
- A copy of any quality control reports, disaggregated by product, reviewed for any indications that certain product lines have fewer warranty claims than in previous years
- Notes of the meeting with the customer services manager where the levels of customer complaints and product faults were discussed
- A comparison of the prior year's calculation with actual warranties claimed post year end to determine the accuracy
- An evaluation of all key assumptions, considering consistency with the auditor's knowledge of the business, and a conclusion on their validity
- An independent estimate prepared by the audit team, compared to management's estimate, and with significant variances discussed with management
- A schedule obtained from management showing the movement in the provision in the accounting period, checked for arithmetic accuracy, and with opening and closing figures agreed to the draft financial statements and general ledger
- Evaluation by the audit team, and a conclusion on the appropriateness of the accounting entries used, especially in relation to the profit impact of the entries
- A file note documenting that the auditor has requested an adjustment requiring the warranty provision to be increased in line with prior year estimation method

Maximum	**8**

(b) **Auditor's report**
Generally, 1 mark for each relevant and well explained point.
- Material misstatement due to inappropriate accounting estimates
- Calculation of possible misstatement
- Matter is not pervasive
- Qualified audit opinion
- Basis of qualified audit opinion

Maximum	**5**

Professional marks
Analysis and evaluation
- Appropriate use of the information to support discussion, draw appropriate conclusions and design appropriate responses
- Identification of omissions from the analysis or further analysis which could be carried out
- Balanced assessment of the information to determine the appropriate audit opinion in the circumstances
- Effective appraisal of the information to make suitable recommendations for appropriate courses of action

Professional scepticism and judgement
- Effective challenge of information, evidence and assumptions supplied and, techniques carried out to support key facts and/or decisions
- Appropriate application of professional judgement to draw conclusions and make informed decisions about the actions which are appropriate in the context and stage of the engagement

Maximum	**5**
Total	**25**

22   SOL & CO *Walk in the footsteps of a top tutor*

Top tutor tips

Part (a) requires evaluation of the result of subsequent events final analytical review procedures. You are required to review the audit work to ascertain whether the conclusions made by the audit team member are supported by the work done. If more evidence is needed or where the conclusions are not valid, further actions need to be recommended. This style of question hasn't been asked in this way before, but takes a practical approach which you should be familiar with if you work in an audit environment.

Part (b) is a more common requirement that has been examined many times. Matters to discuss with management require an assessment of materiality, a discussion of the accounting treatment required and the misstatement arising if the correct accounting treatment is not followed. To finish, you need to then consider the impact on the audit opinion e.g. unmodified, qualified or adverse. Note that the requirement only asks for the impact on the opinion, not the report, therefore there is no need to discuss the basis for opinion paragraph.

(a)   Arjan Co – evaluation of subsequent events and final analytical procedures

Analytical procedures are performed as an overall review of the financial statements at the end of the audit to assess whether they are consistent with the auditor's understanding of the entity. Subsequent events procedures ensure that the sufficient and appropriate evidence in relation to events occurring up to the date of the auditor's report are appropriately reflected in the financial statements. Part of the final review process will include a review of the results of audit procedures to ensure that they support the findings and overall conclusions which have been drawn by the audit team.

Inventory

The move to a just-in-time (JIT) inventory system is consistent with a fall in the inventory levels and inventory holding period. Evidence to corroborate the year-end inventory balance has been primarily provided in the form of inventory count attendance for which no issues were identified. The extent of work performed at the inventory count is unclear from the documentation provided and it would be unusual that no further work was required on the existence and completeness of year-end inventory beyond inventory count attendance.

It would be expected that the auditors perform a reconciliation of the inventory count data to the detailed analysis of the year-end inventory report during the audit to ensure that the report is accurately reflecting the inventory count data. It would also be expected that the accuracy of the cost of the inventory is tested with reference to purchase invoices and overhead absorption calculations for work in progress and finished goods on hand. As such the evidence referred to in the final analytical procedures is insufficient to be able to conclude on the existence, completeness and accuracy of the inventory amounts held.

The increase in the write off for obsolete inventory as a percentage of inventory held is more unexpected. Even though this would still mean a smaller total amount of obsolete inventory held than in the previous year, it would not be expected that a higher obsolescence rate would be seen under a JIT system as theoretically, inventory is only ordered to satisfy specific demand.

As such more evidence needs to be obtained in this regard, particularly as estimates such as these are susceptible to management manipulation and may be used to manipulate the profit of the company.

Further discussions with management and production staff are needed to identify how this figure has been derived. It may be the case that the amount relates to specific items which should have been written off already, for example if those goods are for a specific cancelled order.

It could also be the case that this figure is based on a general percentage amount of inventory held at the year end. As inventory should be assessed on a line by line basis rather than as a general adjustment, the auditor would need to determine whether this would result in a material misstatement.

The comment that the current allowance for obsolete inventory is immaterial and therefore no further work has been performed is inappropriate. A misstatement in this allowance could be material in conjunction with other misstatements and at present there is no evidence as to whether this value is under or overstated.

The auditor should obtain the details of how the allowance has been calculated and assess the appropriateness of the assumptions and methods used by Arjan Co.

The auditor should review slow-moving items and perform further net realisable value testing to ensure that any slow-moving lines of inventory have a sales value in excess of their cost or are written down if appropriate.

Trade receivables

The increase in the receivables collection period compared with the prior year appears to suggest trade receivables may be overstated due to an understatement of the allowance for irrecoverable trade receivables. The audit team has relied on direct confirmations from trade receivables as evidence of recoverability and this is inappropriate. While direct confirmation of balances can provide evidence over the existence and accuracy of balances it does not provide sufficient evidence of recoverability and therefore the valuation of trade receivables. The auditor should have performed after-date cash testing to ensure that year-end balances have in fact been settled post year end.

In addition, the results of the subsequent events procedures contradict the assertion of the credit controller that Cami Co will settle their outstanding balance. The subsequent event identified for Arjan Co has been identified after the date of the financial statements but prior to the issue of the auditor's report.

Procedures must therefore be performed to corroborate the accuracy of the newspaper story and to establish whether there is an impact on the financial statements requiring adjustment or disclosure. Given the late payments made by Cami Co to Arjan Co during the year ended 31 March 20X5 and the fact that Cami Co has entered liquidation so soon after the financial year end, it is likely this would be classed as an adjusting event under IAS 10 *Events after the Reporting Period*, providing evidence of conditions existing at the end of the reporting period.

Management should be asked to write off any amounts which will be irrecoverable as a result of Cami Co entering liquidation. Any inventory ordered specifically for Cami Co should also be assessed to ensure it can be sold to other customers.

As with inventory, it is inappropriate to conclude that no further work is required because the reduction in the allowance is not material. It is possible that the allowance could be materially understated and further procedures should have been performed to confirm this is not the case.

(b)   Barnaby Co – uncorrected misstatement and impact on audit opinion

During the completion stage of the audit, the effect of uncorrected misstatements must be evaluated by the auditor, as required by ISA 450 *Evaluation of Misstatements Identified During the Audit*. This requires that the auditor obtains an understanding of management's reasons for not making recommended adjustments to the financial statements and that they take this into account when evaluating whether the financial statements as a whole are free from material misstatement.

In order to maintain accurate accounting records, management should be encouraged to adjust for all misstatements to ensure the risk of material misstatements in future periods is reduced due to the cumulative effect of immaterial uncorrected misstatements.

ISA 450 also requires that the auditor communicates with those charged with governance about uncorrected misstatements and the effect which they, individually or in aggregate, may have on the opinion in the auditor's report. Both matters included in the schedule of uncorrected misstatements will be discussed below and the impact on the auditor's opinion considered individually.

Machine sale

IFRS 9 *Financial Instruments*, requires receivables such as that arising on sale of the machine, to be recognised initially at fair value and held on an amortised cost basis.

The fair value of the receivable in this case is the amount due in one year, discounted back to the reporting date. Management recording the transaction at cash settlement value will result in an overstatement of receivables and an overstatement of profit on the disposal of the machine.

The amount of the overstatement is $2 million. This represents 1.9% of assets and 4.7% of profit before tax and therefore is material to the statement of financial position but not to the statement of profit or loss.

Management should be requested to make an adjustment for the misstatement.

If management do not amend the financial statements with respect to the machine sale, then the auditor will issue a qualified opinion on the basis of a material misstatement.

As the misstatement does not represent a substantial portion of the financial statements, this would not be considered pervasive.

Tutorial note

Candidates will also be awarded credit for materiality assed in a qualitative nature in respect of misapplication of an accounting policy.

Examiner's comments

This question was set at the completion and reporting stage of an audit. As is typical of reporting questions, this is where the examining team see some of the strongest and some of the weakest demonstrations of auditing competence from candidates.

Stronger candidates often display strong practical skills, incorporating a good understanding of materiality and risk, a strong knowledge of the financial reporting which is needed to perform an audit, an ability to distinguish between auditor and client information and an understanding of the difference between financial statements, an auditor's report and an audit opinion.

Weaker candidates tend to lack the underlying knowledge of double entry accounting and are unable to distinguish between the client and the audit firm, between the financial statements and the auditor's report or demonstrate a good understanding of the concept of materiality.

This question demonstrated all of these strengths and weaknesses and differentiated candidates who understood the nature of audit compared to those who had learnt knowledge but who struggled to apply it in a professional context.

Requirement (a)

Candidates were provided with:

1   The result of the subsequent events procedures which are performed at the end of the audit process as close to signing the auditor's report as possible; and

2   Results of the final analytical procedures performed by the audit team which would be reviewed by the audit manager and partner after completion of the main fieldwork stage of the audit. This would enable them to assess whether the evidence supports the transactions and balances presented in the financial statements.

The key things to note about this are:

*   Information is auditor prepared not a client document.

*   The year end was three months ago, and the main fieldwork stage of the audit is complete.

Candidates were expected to evaluate the information provided and to identify inconsistencies between the results of testing and the auditor expectation. Candidates were then asked for suitable procedures, relevant to the scenario, to enable the auditor to reach a conclusion i.e., what else is needed to determine if the information in the financial statements is not materially misstated and suggest actions where appropriate.

Candidates generally handled the evaluation of the subsequent events procedures well. Most candidates were able identify the adjusting subsequent event where a major customer of the company had gone into liquidation. They were able to tie this back into the receivables analysis in the analytical procedures and recommend the action of requesting the write off of the irrecoverable amounts and the procedure of obtaining confirmation from the liquidator. Common errors made in this section were:

*   Assuming a post-year-end liquidation was a non-adjusting event (this is highly unlikely given the timescales.

*   Confusing the write off of irrecoverable debt with the allowance for trade receivables.

- Looking for post-year-end amounts received from the customer in liquidation despite being told there had not been any, or requesting the customer confirm the year-end balance a second time which does not address recoverability of the balance.

This requirement tested the candidates' appreciation of the purpose of analytical procedures at the completion stage of an audit (rather than at planning or during field work stages) and the concept of materiality. Candidates here generally either did very well or poorly with no middle ground.

Candidates that understood that this was generated by the auditor, rather than the client, and that the ratios were calculated by the auditor in order to identify risks or a deviation from expectation, were able to highlight the issues. They were then able to identify gaps in the testing of balances where certain assertions had not been addressed.

For example, for trade receivables, candidates needed to identify the inconsistency between the reduction in the receivables allowance despite the increase in the receivables collection period. The work performed had been focused on the existence and accuracy of the year-end balances via confirmations, but recoverability of the balances had not been assessed. Pleasingly, many candidates were able to suggest recalculating the ratios after the adjustment for the liquidation bad debt identified in the subsequent events testing and analysing the recoverability of other balances by analysing post-year-end cash receipts from other customers. Weaker candidates suggested requesting confirmations of the year-end balance from a bigger sample than already tested. This was inappropriate as the scope of this test only addressed existence and accuracy, and also by three months after the year end many outstanding balances would have been settled, which is a key method for assessing the recoverability of the debts.

Inventory was similarly handled by candidates. Stronger candidates appreciated that the ratios and trends calculated were auditor generated to help identify risk, such as the risk of inventory obsolescence and were able to suggest procedures to help address this issue. They were also able to demonstrate an understanding that inventory count procedures performed in the scenario could assist with existence and accuracy of inventory, but that the lack of follow up to the year-end inventory listings used during the audit meant the test was incomplete and testing also had not addressed cut-off or valuation.

Weaker candidates here appeared to think the client had calculated the ratios and the auditor needed to prove they were correct. Many wasted time trying to prove the inventory holding period calculations, rather than appreciating that the shorter than expected holding length combined with the increase in management's provision rate could suggest that obsolete inventory was a low risk, or an indicator inventory may be understated. Candidates often failed to distinguish between the management process of using a 'just in time' approach to inventory purchases and the accounting systems that feed into the financial statements. Many candidates still fail to distinguish between what is pre and post year end and many suggested the auditor go back to the inventory count and look for obsolete inventory despite it being three months in the past.

Very few candidates identified the weakness in the evidence regarding materiality conclusions. In the scenario, the allowance for obsolete inventory and the fall in the allowance for irrecoverable inventory were immaterial and the worksheet contained the conclusions that this meant no further work needed to be performed. When looking for an overstatement of assets through inappropriately low allowances for write offs, it is the difference between the carrying amount of the assets and the actual recoverable value of the assets which should be assessed for materiality and that an immaterial write off which should have been a material write off could result in a material misstatement.

Requirement (b)

Candidates were presented with an uncorrected misstatement compiled by the audit team. This is a relatively common format for completion questions, yet candidates often treat the points in the exhibit as a "matters and evidence" type question, giving the accounting rules and all the procedures which would have been expected to be on file. Candidates need to ensure that they read the requirement to the question carefully to gain credit and not waste time.

These errors are presented in an auditor's schedule of uncorrected misstatements stating the correct accounting treatment and the correct double entries in terms of the impact on the financial statements. Candidates who give an answer saying the adjustments are incorrect and explain how to incorrectly account for the issues will not obtain credit. This question covered the omitted discounting of a long-term receivable. Candidates were given the explanation of the correct accounting treatment in the scenario, so they could access the audit skill points without being overly reliant on the underlying financial reporting.

Candidates were first asked to recommend and explain matters which should be discussed with the management in relation to the uncorrected misstatement. They were expected to explain to management the reasons for correcting the error. For matters, candidates can discuss the materiality of the issue, the correct accounting treatment and the impact on the financial statements if the error is not corrected.

Candidates were then asked to assess the impact of the uncorrected misstatement on the auditor's opinion. Auditors would need to explain to management and then if not corrected, further explanation would be necessary to those charged with governance. Stronger candidates were able to identify the matters to be explained, giving an appropriate discussion of materiality, as well as describing the treatment.

It is concerning that there are still candidates who use outdated terminology when discussing the implications of misstatements on the auditor's opinion. Stating a 'modified except for' opinion will not be given credit. Candidates are continuing to show a lack of knowledge regarding the content of auditor's reports, and incorrectly stating that a material misstatement gives rise to an adverse opinion and that an immaterial misstatement gives rise to a qualified opinion. This demonstrates a lack of understanding of the concept of materiality or the understanding of what those additional paragraphs would potentially contain.

	ACCA Marking guide		Marks
(a)	**Arjan Co – evaluation of subsequent events and final analytical procedures** Generally up to 1 mark for each valid comment of evaluation and 1 mark for each relevant further action or procedure in relation to: – Inventory value – Inventory holding period – Inventory allowance – Receivables collection period – Receivables allowance		
		Maximum	15

(b)   **Barnaby Co – uncorrected misstatement and impact on audit opinion**

Generally 1 mark per point explained.

–   Encourage management to amend all misstatements
–   Communicate the effect of the misstatement to those charged with governance
–   Machine sale inappropriate accounting treatment
–   Impact of error – overstatement of receivables and profit on disposal
–   Materiality
–   Qualified opinion due to material misstatement
–   Not pervasive as not a substantial proportion of the financial statements

Maximum	**5**

Professional marks

Analysis and evaluation

•   Appropriate use of the information to support discussion, draw appropriate conclusions and design appropriate responses
•   Identification of omissions from the analysis or further analysis which could be carried out
•   Balanced assessment of the information to determine the appropriate audit opinion in the circumstances
•   Effective appraisal of the information to make suitable recommendations for appropriate courses of action

Professional scepticism and judgement

•   Effective challenge of information, evidence and assumptions supplied and, techniques carried out to support key facts and/or decisions
•   Appropriate application of professional judgement to draw conclusions and make informed decisions about the actions which are appropriate in the context and stage of the engagement

Maximum	**5**
Total	**25**

23   MATTY   *Walk in the footsteps of a top tutor*

Top tutor tips

Part (a) asks for the matters to be considered and the audit evidence that should be on file during your review of the audit file. Use the 'MARE' approach. First, consider the materiality of the issue. Next discuss the appropriate accounting treatment and give the risks of material misstatement that would arise if the appropriate treatment is not followed. Finally, the evidence is what you would expect to be recorded on the audit file when you come to review it.

Part (b) asks for a critical appraisal of the draft auditor's report. You should think about whether the suggestions are appropriate, including the type of opinion and paragraphs to be included.

(a) **Matters and evidence**

(i) **Railway operating licence**

Matters

Uncertainties in relation to going concern

Uncertainties in relation to going concern must be disclosed by management and ISA 570 (Revised) *Going Concern* requires the auditor to assess the adequacy of this disclosure. The principal matter raised by the unresolved status of the licence tender is the potential impact on Matty Co's financial performance and financial position if the company is unsuccessful in the tender process. This in turn creates uncertainties in relation to the going concern status of the company.

The licence is due for renewal on 28 February 20X6 which is 11 months from the reporting date and therefore within the foreseeable future for the purpose of the going concern review. Although the company has been informed that it is the preferred bidder, there are still significant doubts as to whether the licence will be renewed given the government's requirement that the company addresses the recent criticisms and the pending review in one month's time.

The revenue generated from the national railway licence represents 66.9% of Matty Co's revenue for year and is highly material to the company's statement of profit or loss for the year and critical to its operations.

It is also significant that the national railway licence contributed profit before tax of $11.2 million which is 106.7% of this year's profit; without this contribution to the company's profit this year, the company would be loss-making.

In addition to these considerations, even with the inclusion of the national railway licence in this year's results, Matty Co's performance is deteriorating as evidenced by its declining revenue (down by 36.3%) and profit before tax (down by 52.5%). The company's assets are also down by 8.7% on the prior year which may be indicative of a business which is struggling to renew its capital (asset) expenditure and maintains its liquidity.

Evidence

– A review of the press reports in relation to the late running of Matty Co's trains and the quality of its service to assess the seriousness and significance of the issue.

– A review of any correspondence files between Matty Co and the government transport department in order to identify any developments in the licence renewal process and consider their impact on the likely renewal of the licence.

– Notes of discussions held between the auditor and the management of Matty Co in relation to any contingency plans if the company fails to secure the national railway licence; for example, any other licences or opportunities which may exist in the market and any emergency sources of finance which might be available to the company.

– A review of the company's board minutes for evidence of management discussion of the status of the tender process and of any contingency plans.

- A review and analysis of budgets and cash flow forecasts by the auditor in order to assess the ability of the company to survive as a going concern for the foreseeable future.

- Copies of the company's bank facilities reviewed to assess the feasibility of the company's ability to operate within them should they be unsuccessful in winning the contract.

- Written representations from management in relation to the status of the tender process and management's expectations of its expected outcome.

(ii)   Purchased customer list

Matters

Assessment of useful life

The carrying amount of the customer list purchased from Jess Coaches is highly material to Matty Co's draft statement of financial position at 24.3% of total assets.

According to IAS 38 *Intangible Assets*, a reporting entity should recognise intangible assets initially at cost and should assess whether an intangible asset's useful life is finite or indefinite. An assessment of a useful life as indefinite is only appropriate if on an analysis of all of the relevant factors, there is no foreseeable limit to the period over which the intangible is expected to generate net cash inflows for the entity. This assessment requires a significant level of judgement to be exercised and the subjectivity of the carrying amount creates a high level of risk for the auditor.

In this case, the trading history of Jess Coaches prior to its acquisition by Matty Co may provide some evidence that there is no foreseeable limit to the period over which the purchased customer list can be expected to generate cash flows. However, this assumption needs to be assessed carefully by the auditor. Intangible assets with an indefinite life should not be amortised according to IAS 38.

Impairment review

IAS 38 also requires a reporting entity to test intangible assets with an indefinite useful life annually for impairment. This impairment review would involve a comparison of the carrying amount of the customer list to its recoverable amount which, given the difficulty in identifying a sales value for the customer list, is likely to be based on an assessment of its value in use.

The assessment of value in use is a highly subjective exercise which involves an estimate of the future cash flows the entity expects to derive from the customer list, expectations about possible variations in the amount or timing of these future cash flows and the time value of money represented by the current market risk-free rate of interest.

Management's assessment of value in use as $7.2 million appears to be very close to the asset's carrying amount of $6.9 million and it is possible that management may have manipulated its assumption to avoid the recognition of an impairment loss. The auditor will therefore need to carefully review and consider management's assessment of value in use and the assumptions implicit in its calculation.

In addition to these considerations, the emergence of a new competitor which is capable of taking major customers away from Jess Coaches and the loss of two key customers already are indicators that the intangible asset may indeed be impaired. If the recoverable amounts of the intangible assets are therefore less than their total carrying amount of $6.9 million at the reporting date, an impairment loss should be recognised in the statement of profit or loss for the year and the intangible assets should be written down accordingly.

Evidence

– A copy of the purchase agreement to identify the details of the acquisition including the purchase consideration, the assets acquired and the date of the acquisition agreed to the detail included in the accounting records.

– Agreement of the purchase consideration of $6.9 million to the company's bank ledger account/cash book and bank statement to confirm purchase price.

– A review of Jess Coaches' trading history and any market research which has been performed on the ability of the purchased customer list for evidence of how it will generate future revenue for Matty Co.

– A copy of the client's schedule calculating the value in use of the purchased customer list as $7.2 million and a confirmation of the schedule's mathematical accuracy.

– A review and assessment of the company's cash flow forecast which has been used to support the value in use of $7.2 million agreed to the value in use calculation.

– A discussion with management in relation to the basis of the calculation of value in use and an assessment by the auditor of the reasonableness of management's key assumptions.

– A sensitivity analysis performed by the auditor varying these key assumptions and an assessment of the materiality of the potential impact of varying the assumptions on the calculation of the value in use of the customer list.

– A review of Matty Co's management accounts for the reporting period and for the post reporting date period to date in order to identify and quantify the cash flows generated by Jess Coaches' customer list and any significant variances investigated.

– A comparison of the discount rate used in the value in use calculation to published market rates and notes of discussions with management in relation to the basis of any adjustments made by management, in order to ensure that an appropriate rate has been used.

– Written representations from management confirming that to the best of its knowledge, the assumptions used in the calculation of value in use are reasonable and appropriate and that in its opinion, the purchased customer list is not impaired and its carrying amount is fairly stated.

(b)   Appropriateness of the draft auditor's report

The finance director has agreed to include a short note to the financial statements to disclose information relating to the material uncertainty relating to going concern. The note must be reviewed for completeness and if the auditor assesses that the client's disclosure is not adequate, a modified audit opinion would be appropriate in relation to a material misstatement as a result of the inadequate disclosure.

The form of the opinion would be qualified 'except for' or adverse depending on the auditor's judgement of the matter's pervasiveness to the financial statements. In this case, adverse may be the appropriate form of audit opinion given that the disclosure note is described as 'short' and that management may appear to negate the significance of the uncertainties by stating that they are 'very confident' that they will be successful in the tender process. A full description of the status of the tender negotiations as at the date of the auditor's report and their potential impact on the financial statements should then be detailed in the 'Basis for qualified or adverse opinion' paragraph.

However, if on the other hand, the outcome of the auditor's assessment is that the client's financial statement disclosures are considered by the auditor to be appropriate, the material uncertainty in relation to going concern should be disclosed in a separate section entitled 'Material uncertainties related to going concern' which should appear immediately below the 'Basis for opinion' paragraph and not in the key audit matters (KAM) section of the auditor's report. According to ISA 570, the material uncertainty related to going concern section should:

- Draw attention to the note in the financial statements which discloses the going concern issue; and

- State that these events or conditions indicate that a material uncertainty exists which may cast significant doubt on the entity's ability to continue as a going concern and that the auditor's opinion is not modified in respect of the matter.

Matty Co is a listed entity and according to ISA 701 *Communicating Key Audit Matters in the Independent Auditor's Report*, KAM disclosures are required in the auditor's report for high risk areas, significant judgements and the effect of significant events or transactions which occurred during period. The assessment of the useful life of the customer list as indefinite and management's conclusion that the intangible assets are not impaired are areas of both significant judgement and high risk given their materiality. The auditor should consider disclosing these matters in the KAM section of the auditor's report.

Examiner's comments

This was a two-part question set at the completion and reporting stage of the audit.

The first part focused on matters to consider and audit evidence you would expect to find on the audit file as part of your review of the audit working papers in relation to issues identified. The second part moved candidates forward in time and gave them an update on the outcome of some of the issues and details of the proposed auditor's report. Candidates were asked to evaluate the appropriateness of the draft auditor's report if no further adjustments were made for the issues.

Matty Co is a listed transport company providing train and bus services, and they are also a new client for the audit firm. The company's year end was 31 March 20X5. The candidates were given some issues which had been identified by the auditor during the audit fieldwork and had been brought to the attention of the audit manager as part of the review of the audit work prior to signing the auditor's report.

(a) (i) Railway operating licence and going concern

Matty Co had received adverse publicity due to poor service on its national railway service and the licence to operate the railway is put out to tender by the national government every five years, with the renewal of the licence to run the service due in February 20X6.

The company received notification that they are the preferred choice for the licence at renewal, on the understanding that the company would resolve the recent poor performance.

A number of candidates incorrectly discussed accounting rules surrounding intangible assets and deemed the licence to be a purchased intangible and therefore that an impairment review was required.

The main issue in the scenario is the going concern status of Matty Co, due to the potential loss of the licence awarded by the national government to run the railway service. This service contributed 66.9% of revenue for the company during the year and some simple analysis suggested that the loss of the railway revenue would result in the company becoming loss making.

A significant number of candidates failed to recognise the indicator of going concern and the requirement for management to disclose this material uncertainty in the notes to the financial statements.

Responses by candidates for the matters to consider were generally poorly answered due to failing to recognise the issue in the scenario and generally seeing the reference to a licence which led them off on a tangent of discussing intangible assets and impairment along with the impact on the financial statements. The issue of going concern was clearly flagged in the scenario and requirement.

The evidence to consider was generally well answered, yet candidates should note that this licence is due for renewal every five years, therefore general comments to review the licence agreement were not the most relevant in the context of the question.

It was also disappointing to see candidates referring to visiting the train station to review the train timetable and to verify if the trains were in fact late. This is a review of the working files prior to issuing the audit opinion and therefore procedures have already been performed. It is also an unlikely procedure for the auditor to perform.

(a) (ii) Purchased customer list

The issue raised to the audit manager was in relation to a customer list acquired during the year to hire out coaches and drivers to the private and public sector.

Management of the company had assessed the useful life of the customer list as indefinite and recognised it within the financial statements at a carrying amount of $6.9 million. Management had stated that it was difficult to measure the customer list and had estimated the value in use at $7.2 million.

A number of candidates misread the information and deemed the company had recognised the customer list at $7.2 million and therefore stated it was incorrectly recognised, which was not the case as the company had recorded the intangible asset at the lower amount of $6.9 million. The issue here is whether management's assessment of the value in use of $7.2 million is reasonable, particularly as two of the largest customers moved to a new competitor, which is an indicator of impairment. There is a risk that management had overestimated the value in use to avoid the recognition of an impairment loss.

Regarding the evidence to consider on the audit file, responses were well answered. A list of evidence expected is given within the model answer published alongside the question.

Requirement (b)

This required candidates to evaluate the appropriateness of the draft auditor's report if no further adjustments were made regarding the railway operating licence. It was made clear to candidates in the exhibit that the matters in relation to the customer list had been resolved.

Overall, the responses were poor, with candidates demonstrating a general lack of knowledge of reporting, in particular the contents of an auditor's report.

There were very few candidates that linked the details for part (a) (i) and the loss of the railway operating licence as to the effect on the auditor's report based on whether the disclosure note for the material uncertainty regarding going concern was appropriate or not.

Many candidates followed on from part (a) (i) where they assumed the uncertainty meant the financial statements should be prepared on a breakup basis and therefore received no marks.

Candidates demonstrated limited understanding of the use of the Material Uncertainty Related to Going Concern section and when it was appropriate, with many stating it would be used when the opinion is modified, showing a fundamental lack of understanding of the relevant ISAs. It was also concerning to see candidates responding that an Emphasis of Matter paragraph should be used for listed clients, which was again fundamentally incorrect.

ACCA Marking guide	
	Marks

(a)   **Matters to consider and evidence on file**
Generally up to 1 mark for each matter explained and each piece of evidence recommended.
   (i)   **Railway licence**
     Matters
     –   Management should disclose material uncertainties and auditor should assess adequacy of this disclosure
     –   Significant uncertainty exists over renewal of licence
     –   Materiality of national railway contribution to revenue/profit
     –   Without national railway licence, company would be loss-making
     –   Company has deteriorating performance, declining revenue, profit and assets
     –   Company may be unable to renew assets and maintain liquidity
     Evidence
     –   A review of the press reports in relation to the late running of Matty Co's trains and the quality of its service to assess the seriousness and significance of the issue
     – A review of any correspondence files between Matty Co and the government transport department in order to identify any developments in the licence renewal process and consider their impact on the likely renewal of the licence	

- Notes of discussions held between the auditor and the management of Matty Co in relation to any contingency plans if the company fails to secure the national railway licence; for example, any other licences or opportunities which may exist in the market and any emergency sources of finance which might be available to the company
- A review of the company's board minutes for evidence of management discussion of the status of the tender process and of any contingency plans
- A review and analysis of budgets and cash flow forecasts by the auditor in order to assess the ability of the company to survive as a going concern for the foreseeable future
- Copies of the company's bank facilities reviewed to assess the feasibility of the company's ability to operate within them should they be unsuccessful in winning the contract
- Written representations from management in relation to the status of the tender process and management's expectations of its expected outcome

Maximum	7

(ii) **Purchase of customer list**

Matters

- Materiality of customer list
- Accounting rules for intangible assets with indefinite life
- Assessment is matter of significant judgement and high audit risk
- Indefinite useful life must be substantiated
- Must test intangible assets with indefinite useful lives annually for impairment
- Accounting rules for impairment review
- Possible manipulation by management to avoid impairment loss
- Loss of two major customers/new competitor – possible impairment indicators
- If recoverable amount is less than carrying amount, impairment loss should be recognised in P/L for year

Evidence

- A copy of the purchase agreement to identify the details of the acquisition including the purchase consideration, the assets acquired and the date of the acquisition agreed to the detail included in the accounting records
- Agreement of the purchase consideration of $6.9 million to the company's bank ledger account/cash book and bank statement to confirm purchase price
- A review of Jess Coaches' trading history and any market research which has been performed on the ability of the purchased customer list for evidence of how it will generate future revenue for Matty Co
- A copy of the client's schedule calculating the value in use of the purchased customer list as $7.2 million and a confirmation of the schedule's mathematical accuracy
- A review and assessment of the company's cash flow forecast which has been used to support the value in use of $7.2 million agreed to the value in use calculation
- A discussion with management in relation to the basis of the calculation of value in use and an assessment by the auditor of the reasonableness of management's key assumptions
- A sensitivity analysis performed by the auditor varying these key assumptions and an assessment of the materiality of the potential impact of varying the assumptions on the calculation of the value in use of the customer list

–	A review of Matty Co's management accounts for the reporting period and for the post reporting date period to date in order to identify and quantify the cash flows generated by Jess Coaches' customer list and any significant variances investigated	
–	A comparison of the discount rate used in the value in use calculation to published market rates and notes of discussions with management in relation to the basis of any adjustments made by management, in order to ensure that an appropriate rate has been used	
–	Written representations from management confirming that to the best of its knowledge, the assumptions used in the calculation of value in use are reasonable and appropriate and that in its opinion, the purchased customer list is not impaired and its carrying amount is fairly stated	
	Maximum	**8**

(b) **Appropriateness of the draft auditor's report**

Generally 1 mark for each reporting implication explained.

- Inappropriate disclosure – modified opinion due to material misstatement
- Opinion would be qualified or adverse based on auditor's judgement of pervasiveness
- Discussion of pervasiveness – disclosure paragraph may lack detail/be contradictory
- If disclosures not adequate, matter should be detailed in 'Basis for qualified/adverse opinion' paragraph
- Disclosure adequate, uncertainties should be disclosed in separate section/'Material uncertainties related to going concern'/not KAM
- KAM disclosures required for high risk areas, significant judgements and the effect of significant events or transactions which occurred during period
- Inclusion as KAM carrying amount of customer list/management's conclusion that intangibles not impaired

Maximum	**5**

Professional marks

Analysis and evaluation

- Appropriate use of the information to support discussion, draw appropriate conclusions and design appropriate responses
- Identification of omissions from the analysis or further analysis which could be carried out
- Balanced assessment of the information to determine the appropriate audit opinion in the circumstances

Professional scepticism and judgement

- Effective challenge of information, evidence and assumptions supplied and, techniques carried out to support key facts and/or decisions
- Appropriate application of professional judgement to draw conclusions and make informed decisions about the actions which are appropriate in the context and stage of the engagement

Maximum	**5**
Total	**25**

24   GOODMAN GROUP   *Walk in the footsteps of a top tutor*

Top tutor tips

Part (a) (i) requires discussion of the implications of the fraud on the audit. Draw on your knowledge of ISA 240.

Part (a) (ii) asks for comment on whether the evidence obtained is sufficient and appropriate. Has enough work been done? Has the most reliable form of evidence been obtained? Think about what evidence you would expect to be on file. Compare this with the evidence that has been obtained. Any difference between what you would do and what has been done indicates that sufficient appropriate evidence has not been obtained. This should then form your answer to the final part which asks for further evidence which should be obtained.

Part (b) asks for a critical appraisal of the draft auditor's report extracts. Don't just focus on whether the opinion is appropriate. You should also think about the titles of the paragraphs included and whether the names are correct, the order in which they appear, whether the required information that should be included has been included and whether the wording used is professional and appropriate and whether any additional communications are appropriate.

(a)   (i)   Fraud

If the full extent of the fraud is $40,000, then the audit team is correct to determine that the fraud is immaterial to the financial statements. However, without performing further procedures it is not possible to reach that conclusion. There is no auditor-generated evidence to support the assertion that $40,000 is the total amount of stolen funds.

Relying solely on a conversation between the Group finance director and the manager who carried out the fraud and a list of invoices provided by the Group finance director is not acceptable as this evidence is not sufficiently reliable.

Indeed, the Group finance director could be involved with the fraud, and is attempting to deceive the auditor and minimise the suspected scale of the fraud in order to deter further procedures being carried out, or investigation or actions being taken. The auditor should approach the comments made by the Group finance director with an attitude of professional scepticism, especially given that he has asked the audit team not to investigate further, which raises suspicion that he may be covering up the fact that the fraud was on a larger scale than has been made known to the auditor.

There are two courses of action for the auditor. First, further independent investigations should be carried out in order for the auditor to obtain sufficient and appropriate evidence relating to the amount of the fraud. This is particularly important given that the Group finance director seems unwilling to make any adjustment to the financial statements. If the fraud is actually more financially significant, the financial statements could be materially misstated, but without further audit evidence, the auditor cannot determine whether this is the case.

Second, the auditor should consider whether reporting is necessary. ISA 240/ ISA (UK) 240 *The Auditor's Responsibilities Relating to Fraud in an Audit of Financial Statements* requires that when fraud has taken place, auditors shall communicate these matters on a timely basis to the appropriate level of management in order to inform those with primary responsibility for the prevention and detection of fraud of matters relevant to their responsibilities. Given that the Group finance director alerted the auditor to the fraud, it seems likely that management and those charged with governance are already aware of the fraud. However, the auditor should consider whether a formal, written communication is needed.

In addition to reporting to management and those charged with governance, ISA 240 requires that the auditor shall determine whether there is a responsibility to report the occurrence or suspicion to a party outside the entity. The auditor's duty to maintain the confidentiality of client information makes such reporting potentially difficult, and the auditor may wish to take legal advice before reporting externally.

Tutorial note

Anti-money laundering legislation is likely to impose a duty on auditors to report suspected money laundering activity. Suspicions relating to fraud are likely to be required to be reported under this legislation. Credit will be awarded for relevant consideration of whether Saul & Co should report the fraud on this basis.

(ii) **Development costs**

Given that the development costs are material to the Group financial statements, more audit work should have been carried out to determine whether it is acceptable that all, or some, of the $600,000 should have been capitalised. There is a risk that research costs, which must be expensed, have not been distinguished from development costs, which can only be capitalised when certain criteria have been met. Currently, there is not sufficient, appropriate audit evidence to conclude that the accounting treatment is appropriate, and intangible assets could be materially misstated.

Agreement of amounts to invoice provides evidence of the value of expenditure, but does not provide sufficient, appropriate evidence as to the nature of the expenditure, i.e. the procedure is not necessarily an evaluation of whether it is an asset or an expense.

Performing an arithmetic check on a spreadsheet does provide some evidence over the accuracy of the calculations but does not provide sufficient, appropriate evidence on the validity of the projections, and in particular, there is no evidence that the assumptions are sound. Given that the Group finance director has not allowed the audit team access to information supporting the spreadsheet and has refused to answer questions, he may have something to hide, and the audit of the projection should be approached with a high degree of professional scepticism. The assumptions may not be sound and may contradict other audit evidence.

The attitude and actions of the Group finance director, which indicate a lack of integrity, should be discussed with the audit committee, as the committee should be in a position to discuss the situation with him, with the objective of making all necessary information available to the audit team.

Finally, there appears to be over-reliance on a written representation from management. ISA 580 *Written Representations* states that written representations should be used to support other audit evidence and are not sufficient evidence on their own. In this situation, it appears that the representation is the only evidence which has been sought in regard to the likely success of the new product development which is inappropriate.

Further evidence should be obtained to distinguish between research costs and development costs, and to support whether the development costs meet the recognition criteria in IAS 38 *Intangible Assets,* and to confirm whether all of the $600,000 should be capitalised. Further evidence should be obtained, including:

– A discussion with the project manager to obtain their view on the likely launch date for the new product, anticipated level of demand, any problems foreseen with completion of the project.

– A further review of a sample of the costs included in the $600,000, including evaluation of whether the costs are capital or revenue in nature.

– For the sample of costs, review purchase invoices and ensure they are in the name of the company to confirm the rights and obligations assertion of the capitalised costs.

– Results of any market research to support the assertion that the new product will generate future economic benefit.

– A discussion with management to identify how they have incurred development costs without carrying out any research first.

– Assuming that the Group finance director makes the supporting documentation, including assumptions, available to the audit team, the assumptions should be reviewed for reasonableness, with the auditor considering whether they are in line with business understanding and with other audit evidence obtained.

(b)   Critique of auditor's report

Headings and structure

The report should not have the opinion and basis for opinion combined in one paragraph. The report should start with the opinion paragraph, which is then followed by the basis for opinion.

In addition to separating out the paragraphs, they should be given appropriate headings. According to ISA 705 *Modifications to the Opinion in the Independent Auditor's Report*, when the opinion is modified, the heading should be used to denote the type of modification which is being made to the opinion.

In this case the title 'Qualified opinion' seems most appropriate. The basis for opinion paragraph should be headed 'Basis for qualified opinion'.

Qualified opinion

The qualified opinion paragraph should be worded differently. According to ISA 705, when the opinion is modified the following wording should be used 'except for the effects of the matter(s) described in the Basis for Qualified Opinion section, the accompanying financial statements present fairly, in all material respects (or give a true and fair view of)...'.

The draft opinion paragraph uses different wording – in particular, using the phrase 'the financial statements are likely to be materially misstated' does not indicate that a firm conclusion has been reached, and could give users of the report some doubt as to the credibility of the auditor's opinion.

Basis for qualified opinion

This paragraph should contain further information on the reasons for the modification including a description and quantification of the financial effects of the material misstatement. In this case, the paragraph should refer to the overstatement of trade receivables of $450,000, and the overstatement of profit by the same amount. Currently, the paragraph refers to an overstatement of $500,000, which contradicts the conclusion based on audit evidence.

Emphasis of matter paragraph

According to ISA 706 *Emphasis of Matter Paragraphs and Other Matter Paragraphs in the Independent Auditor's Report*, an emphasis of matter (EOM) paragraph is used when the auditor considers it necessary to draw users' attention to a matter which is of such importance that it is fundamental to users' understanding of the financial statements. The matter discussed in the EOM paragraph must be properly presented and disclosed in the financial statements.

The draft auditor's report includes an EOM which is being used to discuss two matters, neither of which are appropriate for inclusion in an EOM. First, the EOM describes the fraud which has taken place during the year. This matter is immaterial in monetary terms and therefore is not likely to be considered to be fundamental to users' understanding of the financial statements.

In addition, it is not professional to highlight illegal activity in this way, and it could increase the risk of litigation from the Group, as this amounts to a breach of confidentiality.

Second, the EOM refers to the difficulties encountered in the audit of trade receivables due to the Group finance director refusing to allow full access to necessary sources of evidence. This matter should not be reported to shareholders in the auditor's report. The appropriate method of reporting is to those charged with governance of the Group, as required by ISA 260/ISA (UK) 260 *Communication With Those Charged With Governance*. ISA 260 requires the auditor to communicate to those charged with governance regarding a range of matters, including significant difficulties, if any, encountered during the audit.

Related to this, stating that it is the Group finance director personally who is responsible for the material misstatement and hence the modification of the auditor's opinion is not professional and could raise further legal problems, for example, the Group finance director could accuse the audit firm of making false statements or defamation of character.

In addition, referring to the potential resignation of the audit firm anywhere in the auditor's report is not appropriate. This matter should be discussed with those charged with governance who will then take the matter up with the Group's shareholders.

Examiner's comments

This question was a 25-mark compulsory question which focused on completion and reporting and was in two sections.

Requirement (a)

Part (i) required candidates to discuss the implications of a fraud which had occurred during the year for the completion of the audit and any actions to be taken by the auditor.

Generally, candidates performed poorly on this requirement with a significant number of candidates believing that an immaterial fraud would result in the audit opinion being qualified, which is disappointing.

Several candidates discussed the fraud and inferred an internal control issue within the procurement department, but only a minority went on to consider an overall internal control issue and that internal controls should be reassessed, or substantive testing should be performed.

A number of candidates suggested a list of controls that should be recommended for the procurement department, which did not meet the question requirement and therefore scored no marks.

Part (ii) asked candidates to comment on the sufficiency and appropriateness of audit evidence obtained in respect of development costs capitalised and to recommend actions to be taken by the auditor, including further evidence to be obtained. The requirement was generally poorly answered by candidates. A number of candidates' comments that a sample of invoices selected for testing was not appropriate and that 100% of invoices should be tested. A significant number of candidates correctly identified that the evidence on file for the development costs was not sufficient but missed the point that it could include research costs and went along the angle of approval of the costs to be capitalised in general. A significant number of candidates stated the accounting standard rules for capitalisation of development costs, yet the requirement was not a 'matters to consider and evidence expected to be on file' requirement and therefore was not relevant to the question and did not receive credit.

Requirement (b)

Candidates were asked to critically appraise an extract from the auditor's report, which had been incorrectly prepared and required amendment.

This requirement was a roll forward from the requirement in (a), and not a standalone critique style question. A number of candidates missed the narrative that two of the three issues had been resolved, being the audit partner concluding the fraud was immaterial and all necessary work had now been performed, and that further procedures surrounding the development costs had been performed and that is was deemed appropriate that the costs were capitalised correctly. Candidates that did not focus on the narrative did not realise these two issues should not have been included within the report and continued to appraise them incorrectly.

The majority of candidates were able to correctly identify the format issues within the report such as the incorrect structure. The wording of the extract suggested an adverse opinion was being given, and many candidates identified this was incorrect, it being more likely a qualified opinion was appropriate in the circumstances.

Candidates were not expected to discuss what would or would not be present in a full report. Where candidates discussed, for example, "the signature of the partner is missing" or "responsibilities of the auditor are missing", this was not relevant to the requirement, which asked candidates to specifically critique the extract as presented. Discussion of given extracts of auditor's reports, again, should follow a structured approach and practicing questions of this nature should allow candidates to score strong marks in these requirements.

Candidates would benefit from a more detailed knowledge of ISA 700 *Forming an Opinion and Reporting on Financial Statements*, in particular to review the appendices which show real examples of the auditor's report and typical wording which is appropriate.

ACCA Marking guide	Marks
Generally up to 1 mark for each relevant point of discussion/action or further evidence: **(a)** **(i)** **Fraud** – Cannot determine whether fraud is immaterial without obtaining further evidence – Insufficient to rely on a conversation between Group finance director and the alleged fraudster as a source of evidence – Group finance director could be involved and attempting to conceal the true extent of the fraud – Audit team needs to use professional scepticism in relation to assertions made about the fraud – Financial statements could be materially misstated/Group finance director refusing to adjust – Auditor should consider reporting responsibilities to management/those charged with governance (TCWG) – Potential to report externally after taking legal advice – Consideration of client confidentiality Maximum	6
(ii) **Development costs** – Development costs are material and the audit work performed is insufficient to determine whether research costs have been inappropriately capitalised – Intangible assets could be materially overstated and profit overstated – Agreeing amounts to invoices does not confirm the nature of the expenditure – Arithmetically checking the spreadsheet does not provide assurance on the assumptions which underpin the projections – The Group finance director refusing to allow full access to the spreadsheet increases risk and the audit team should apply professional scepticism – Attitude and actions of the Group finance director should be discussed with TCWG – Reliance on a written representation is not appropriate – Further evidence (1 mark for each evidence point explained) Maximum	6

(b)	**Critique of draft auditor's report**		

(b) **Critique of draft auditor's report**
Generally up to 1 mark for each point explained:
- Combination of opinion and basis for opinion paragraphs not appropriate
- Headings not correct – should be qualified opinion and basis for qualified opinion
- Qualified opinion paragraph wording is ambiguous and needs clarification
- Basis for qualified opinion paragraph should contain further details on the rationale for the auditor's opinion
- Explanation of proper use of emphasis of matter paragraph
- Fraud is immaterial and not fundamental to users' understanding
- Not professional to mention fraud in the auditor's report
- Difficulties in the audit should be reported to TCWG, not to the shareholders in the auditor's report
- Unprofessional and possible libellous wording used in relation to the Group finance director
- Not appropriate to mention resignation in the auditor's report – should be discussed with TCWG

Maximum | **8**

Professional marks
Analysis and evaluation
- Effective analysis and identification of issues and omissions in the draft auditor's report
- Appropriate use of the information to support discussion, draw appropriate conclusions and design appropriate responses
- Appropriate recommendations in relation to necessary actions which reflect the stage of engagement

Professional scepticism and judgement
- Effective challenge and critical assessment of the conduct and extent of the audit work and evidence obtained with appropriate conclusions
- Appropriate application of professional judgement to draw conclusions and make informed decisions about the actions which are appropriate in the context and stage of the engagement
- Demonstration of the ability to probe for further information

Commercial acumen
- Inclusion of appropriate recommendations regarding how Those Charged with Governance and the audit firm should respond to the situation

Maximum | **5**

Total | **25**

25   LIFESON *Walk in the footsteps of a top tutor*

Top tutor tips

Part (a) requires discussion of two accounting matters. First, consider the materiality of the issue. Next discuss the appropriate accounting treatment and give the risks of material misstatement that would arise if the appropriate treatment is not followed. Finally, the evidence is what you would expect to be recorded on the audit file when you come to review it. Be specific about the evidence in the same way as you would be specific when writing an audit procedure.

For part (b) you need to state the impact to the auditor's report if the client does not amend the financial statements. State the impact to both the report and opinion as a result of the issue. Don't waste time stating the reporting implications if the issue is corrected as this is not part of the requirement.

(a)   (i)   Sale and leaseback transaction

Matters

Transfer of control

The auditor needs to consider the correct treatment of the sale and leaseback transaction as required by IFRS 16 *Leases* which requires that an assessment should be performed based on the criteria specified in IFRS 15 *Revenue from Contracts with Customers* as to whether control of the asset has been retained by the seller or whether it has passed to the buyer.

Control of an asset is defined by IFRS 15 as the ability to direct the use of and obtain substantially all of the remaining benefits from the asset. This includes the ability to prevent others from directing the use of and obtaining the benefits from the asset. The benefits related to the asset are the potential cash flows which may be obtained directly or indirectly.

Right-of-use asset

In this case, the lease term of ten years appears short compared to the asset's remaining life which is expected to exceed 50 years and given the demand for retail properties for rent in the area, it seems likely that Clive Co will direct the use of and obtain substantially all of the remaining benefits from the asset including the potential cash flows in the future.

On the basis of the information available, the proposed derecognition of the property in Lifeson Co's financial statements and the recording of the transaction as a sale in accordance with IFRS 15 appears to be correct. Lifeson Co should therefore derecognise the property and recognise a right-of-use asset based on the proportion of the previous carrying amount of the asset effectively retained under the terms of the lease.

In addition, it should recognise a financial liability based on the present value of the lease payments and any gain or loss arising on the transaction should be recognised in profit or loss for the year.

In this case, the asset has been correctly derecognised but the auditor should investigate whether the company has recognised the right-of-use asset at the correct amount.

Evidence expected to be on file

- A copy of the sale and leaseback agreement reviewed to confirm the key details including in particular the rights of the lessee and the lessor to control the asset.

- A working paper detailing all key aspects of the agreement required to identify the detailed accounting treatment including the sale proceeds, rental amounts and timings, the lease term and the interest rate implicit in the lease.

- Agreement of the sale proceeds as per the sale agreement to the bank ledger account/cash book and bank statement to confirm the correct calculation of the gain or loss on disposal.

- Notes of discussions with management in relation to the transfer of control to confirm whether the correct treatment of the sale and leaseback arrangement has been determined.

- A copy of any client working papers in relation to the calculation of the right-of-use asset to identify whether the client has recognised the right-of-use asset at the correct amount.

- A review of the board minutes for evidence of management's discussion of the sale and leaseback transaction and any evidence in relation to the transfer of control.

- A review of the local property market including trade journals, press articles, official statistics to confirm high demand for retail leases.

- A review of surveyor reports on the property to confirm the expected remaining life of the property.

- A copy of the client's working papers for the calculation of the present value of the lease payments and a recalculation of the present value of the lease payments by the auditor in order to form a basis for confirming the detailed accounting treatment of the lease.

- Agreement of the carrying amount of the property to the non-current asset register to determine whether the correct amount has been derecognised and whether the gain or loss on disposal has been recorded correctly.

- A schedule calculating any gain or loss on the transaction, recalculated by the audit team and confirming that it only represents the gain or loss on rights transferred to Clive Co.

- Review of the draft financial statements to confirm that details of the sale and leaseback transaction, such as the gain or loss arising on the transaction, have been disclosed in line with the requirements of IFRS 16.

(ii)   **Asset impairment**

Matters

Materiality

The carrying amount of the shopping mall represents 64.1% ($8.85 million/ $13.8 million) of Lifeson Co's total assets at the reporting date and is therefore highly material to the company's financial statements.

Value in use

The auditor should consider whether the client's calculation of the shopping mall's recoverable amount based on value in use is in line with the requirements of IAS 36 *Impairment of Assets*. This should include an assessment of whether the client has used an appropriate discount factor for calculating value in use based on the rate which reflects current market assessments of the time value of money and the risks specific to the asset.

In line with IAS 36's definition of recoverable amount as the higher of its fair value less costs to sell and its value in use, the auditor should also consider whether the fair value less selling costs of the shopping mall exceeds its value in use.

Reversal of impairment loss

IAS 36 requires that the increased carrying amount of an asset, such as property, attributable to a reversal of an impairment loss should not exceed the carrying amount which would have been determined, net of depreciation, had no impairment loss been recognised for the asset in prior years.

In this case, therefore, recognition of the reversal of the impairment loss should be calculated as follows.

	$million	$million
Carrying amount as at 31 March 20X5 prior to recognition of impairment reversal ($8.25m × 18/19)		7.816
Recoverable amount based on impairment review as at 31 March 20X5	8.850	
Capped to $9.5m × 18/20 =	8.550	8.550
		———
Impairment reversal to be recognised		0.734
		———

As a result of Lifeson Co's failure to limit the impairment reversal to $0.734 million, profit and assets are overstated by $300,000 (1.034m – 0.734m).

Evidence expected to be on file

• Agreement of the opening balances for the property to the non-current asset register as at 1 April 20X4 to confirm the correct amount has been brought forward in the client's working papers.

• Physical inspection of the shopping mall property to confirm its condition, occupancy level and to assess the reasonableness of the depreciation policy and forecast cash flows for the value in use calculation.

- Copy of the client working papers for impairment review giving evidence of the client's basis for assessing the fair value less selling costs of the mall and detailed calculations of its value in use.

- Copy of the client's cash flow forecasts and budgets supporting the value in use calculations.

- Notes of discussions with management in relation to the bases for the calculation of recoverable amount including an assessment of the reasonableness of the assumptions used by management in its forecasts and calculations and the appropriateness of the discount factor used in the value in use calculations.

- Written representations attesting to the reasonableness of its assumptions and other related management judgements.

- A recalculation of the value in use of the shopping mall by the auditor in order to confirm the accuracy of the client's calculation.

- Sensitivity analyses on the forecasts and the value in use calculations in order to assess the impact of any changes in the key assumptions.

- External confirmation of the shopping mall's net realisable value by an appropriately qualified, independent expert in order to ensure the recoverable amount has been correctly determined.

- Notes of discussions with management in relation to the incorrect recording of the impairment reversal and the need to include the error in the auditor's schedule of uncorrected misstatements.

(b) **Implications for the auditor's report**

Based on the analysis and discussion above, there is a misstatement in the financial statements in relation to the shopping mall which may have implications for this year's auditor's report.

Lifeson Co has incorrectly recognised the full impairment reversal of $1.034 million in profit for the year. As per IAS 36, the reversal of an impairment loss should not exceed the carrying amount which would have been determined had no impairment loss been recognised. Based on depreciation over a 20-year useful life, the carrying amount of the asset should be capped at $8.550 million and the reversal of the impairment to be recognised at $0.734 million ($8.550 million – $7.816 million).

Assets and profit are currently overstated by $300,000 representing 2.2% of total assets and 14% of profit before tax which is material to both the statement of financial position and statement of profit or loss.

The misstatement is individually material and if management fails to amend the financial statements, the auditor's opinion should be modified due to the material, but not pervasive, misstatement of the shopping mall in relation to both the statement of financial position and the statement of profit or loss for the year.

The auditor's report should include a qualified 'except for' opinion paragraph at the start of report.

This paragraph should be followed immediately by a basis for qualified opinion paragraph which should explain the reasons for the qualified auditor's opinion and which should quantify the impact of the matters identified on the financial statements.

Examiner's comments

This question was set at the completion stage of an audit and proved difficult for many candidates. In part (a) two property-related issues were described for an audit client of the firm and candidates were required to analyse the matters to be considered (e.g. materiality, accounting treatments permitted, how that applied to the client in question, potential errors) and the evidence that would be expected on file in order to be able to conclude on the issues. Topics covered were a sale and leaseback, where control had passed to the lessor and the reversal of an impairment relating to a property being used by the company.

Very few candidates appeared to understand the concept of control underpinning the sale and lease back – often candidates performed the appropriate test of considering the proportion of the life of the property that would be leased back but then incorrectly concluded that renting the property for one fifth of its life was effectively still owning the property. What was more concerning was that a significant minority of candidates were still discussing the concept of operating and finance leases and applying outdated accounting standards to a topic that has been examinable under IFRS16 *Leases* for several sessions.

With regards to the impairment reversal, candidate performance was mixed. Many candidates realised that the reversal would be restricted and were able to obtain credit even if they didn't appreciate that the reversal was not restricted to the previous impairment charge but should be restricted to the written down value the asset would have had, had it not been impaired in the first place. Beyond that however many candidates suggested that the excess value of that amount could be recognised within Other Comprehensive Income which is not the case unless the company is using a revaluation model rather than a cost model for properties.

Many candidates were able to identify relevant audit procedures for the above accounting issues. In some instances, this was the case even where they did not appear to fully understand the accounting issues themselves.

Part (b) required candidates to consider the effect of the misstatement in relation to the reversal of the impairment on the auditor's report. Here candidates often assessed the significance of the misstatement by reference to the entire asset value rather than the error amount, resulting in the conclusion that an immaterial misstatement would result in an adverse opinion. It is vital that candidates appreciate the concept of materiality and are able to correctly apply it at this level.

		Marks
ACCA Marking guide		

(a)   **Matters and evidence**

Generally up to 1 mark for each matter explained and each piece of evidence recommended (unless otherwise stated).

(i)   **Sale and leaseback transaction**

Matters

- Consider treatment of sale and leaseback transaction as required by IFRS 16
- Assess whether control of asset has transferred to buyer
- Whether asset transfer is sale in line with IFRS 15
- IFRS 15 criteria based on transfer of control; ability to direct, use and obtain substantially all remaining benefits of asset
- Derecognise property and recognise right-of-use asset based on proportion of asset retained
- Recognise financial liability based on PV of lease payments
- Recognise gain/loss on transaction in P/L for year
- Reasoned conclusion that treatment appears to be correct on basis of information available

Evidence

- Copy of sale and leaseback agreement to confirm key details, e.g. rights of lessee and lessor to control asset; also: proceeds, rental amounts and timings, lease term, interest rate
- Discussions with management about transfer of control and correct treatment of sale and leaseback arrangement
- Board minutes for evidence of discussion of sale and leaseback transaction
- Review of local property market including trade journals, press articles, official statistics to confirm high demand for retail leases
- Review of surveyor reports on building to confirm expected life
- Agreement of carrying amount of property to non-current asset register
- Agreement of sale proceeds to bank ledger account/cash book and bank statement
- Copy of client working papers for present value of lease payments
- Recalculation of PV of lease payments by auditor
- Review of financial statements to confirm that details of sale and leaseback transaction disclosed in line with IFRS 16 requirements

	Maximum	10

(ii)   Shopping mall – asset impairment

Matters

- Materiality
- Whether client's calculation of recoverable amount based on value in use is in line with requirements of IAS 36
- Discussion of whether client has used appropriate discount factor for calculating value in use
- Whether NRV of shopping mall exceeds its value in use (at both dates)
- Reversal of impairment loss should be capped to depreciated historic cost had no impairment loss been recognised
- Resulting error: overstatement of profit and assets by $300,000

Evidence

- Agreement of opening balances for property to non-current asset register
- Physical inspection of shopping mall to confirm condition, occupancy level and reasonableness of depreciation policy and of management's cash flow forecasts
- Copy of client working papers for impairment review giving details of NRV of mall and value in use calculations
- Copy of client cash flow forecasts and budgets supporting value in use calculations
- Notes of discussions with management and assessment of reasonableness of assumptions used in forecasts and appropriateness of discount factor used in value in use calculations
- Management representations attesting to the reasonableness of assumptions and other related management judgements
- Recalculation of value in use by auditor
- Sensitivity analyses on forecasts and value in use calculations
- External confirmation of the shopping mall's net realisable value by an appropriately qualified, independent expert
- Notes of discussions with management in relation to incorrect recording of impairment reversal and need to include error in auditor's schedule of uncorrected misstatements

	Maximum	6

(b)	**Auditor's report** – Material misstatement due to inappropriate application of IAS 36 – Matter is not pervasive – Qualified audit opinion – Basis of qualified opinion paragraph		
		Maximum	**4**
	Professional marks **Analysis and evaluation** – Appropriate use of the information to support discussion, draw appropriate conclusions and design appropriate responses – Identification of omissions from the analysis or further analysis which could be carried out – Balanced assessment of the information to determine the appropriate audit opinion in the circumstances **Professional scepticism and judgement** – Effective challenge of information, evidence and assumptions supplied and, techniques carried out to support key facts and/or decisions – Appropriate application of professional judgement to draw conclusions and make informed decisions about the actions which are appropriate in the context and stage of the engagement		
		Maximum	**5**
Total			**25**

26 KILMISTER *Walk in the footsteps of a top tutor*

Top tutor tips

Part (a) asks for a critical appraisal of the draft auditor's report extracts. Don't just focus on whether the opinion is appropriate. You should also think about the titles of the paragraphs included and whether the names are correct, the order they appear in, whether the required information that should be included has been included and whether the wording used is professional and appropriate.

Part (b) asks for the matters which should be reported to those charged with governance at the end of the audit. In accordance with ISA 260, the auditor must report matters relating to significant control deficiencies, uncorrected misstatements which may impact the auditor's report and matters affecting independence for listed clients. In your answer you should explain why any control deficiencies are significant and the implications for the company, explain why the financial statements are misstated as a result of the client's accounting treatment.

(a) **Kilmister Co – Critical appraisal of extract from draft auditor's report**

Presentation and structure of auditor's report extract

The structure and format of the auditor's report is prescribed by ISA 700/ISA (UK) 700 *Forming an Opinion and Reporting on Financial Statements.* The auditor's report should be addressed solely to the shareholders of the reporting entity and the title should not include any reference to the directors of Kilmister Co. In addition, the first two paragraphs are presented in the incorrect order, the Opinion paragraph should precede the Basis for Opinion paragraph.

Reference to ethical code

ISA 700 requires that in the Basis for Opinion paragraph, the auditor should identify the relevant ethical code, naming the IESBA *International Code of Ethics for Professional Accountants*/FRC Ethical Standard. The draft auditor's report does not specifically refer to the ethical code which has been applied during the audit and is therefore not in compliance with the requirements of ISA 700.

Material uncertainty regarding going concern

ISA 570/ISA (UK) 570 *Going Concern* provides guidance on how an auditor should report uncertainties regarding going concern in the auditor's report. According to ISA 570, if adequate disclosure about the material uncertainty is not made in the financial statements, the auditor should express a qualified opinion or adverse opinion as appropriate.

The use of a 'material uncertainty regarding going concern' paragraph in the draft auditor's report extract is therefore incorrect. This paragraph should only be used when adequate disclosure has been made by the directors in the financial statements and would include a cross reference to this disclosure. Given that this disclosure has not been made, this is therefore not appropriate in this case.

In this case, therefore, the absence of any disclosure in the financial statements in relation to the uncertainties regarding going concern is grounds for a modification of the auditor's opinion. The modification is due to a material misstatement in relation to the absence of this key disclosure.

If, in the auditor's professional judgement, the impact of this non-disclosure on the financial statements is material but not pervasive, a qualified 'except for' opinion should be issued. In this case, the opinion paragraph should be headed 'qualified opinion' and this should be followed immediately by a 'basis for qualified opinion' paragraph.

If, on the other hand, the auditor believes that the impact on the financial statements of the non-disclosure is both material and pervasive, an adverse opinion should be given. The opinion paragraph should then be headed 'adverse opinion' and should be followed immediately by a 'basis for adverse opinion' paragraph.

In addition, details of the uncertainty regarding going concern should be given in the basis for qualified or adverse opinion paragraph.

Long-term contracts

The use of the 'other information' section in this context is inappropriate. This section should be used to describe the auditor's responsibilities for 'other information' (e.g. the rest of the annual report, including the management report) and the outcome of fulfilling those responsibilities.

The disclosure regarding long-term contracts is more in line with the requirements of ISA 701/ISA (UK) 701 *Communicating Key Audit Matters in the Independent Auditor's Report*, where key audit matters are those which in the auditor's professional judgement were of most significance to the audit.

In determining which matters to report, the auditor should take into account areas of significant auditor attention in performing the audit, including:

–   Areas of higher assessed risk of material misstatement, or significant risks identified in accordance with ISA 315 (Revised 2019) *Identifying and Assessing the Risks of Material Misstatement.*

–   Significant auditor judgements relating to areas in the financial statements which involved significant management judgement, including accounting estimates which have been identified as having high estimation uncertainty.

–   The effect on the audit of significant events or transactions which occurred during the period.

The extract from the draft auditor's report states that significant judgement is applied in assessing the percentage of completeness of material long-term contracts and that this percentage is then applied in calculating the revenue for the year. This is a matter of high risk requiring significant auditor attention and given that Kilmister Co is a listed entity, it would be appropriate for this to be disclosed in the KAM section of the auditor's report.

The KAM section of the auditor's report should begin with an introductory paragraph explaining what a KAM is.

The KAM section should then explain why this matter is considered to be a KAM due to the significant judgement involved in assessing the percentage completeness of the long-term contracts and the high risk of material misstatement associated with this judgement process.

The KAM section should also include an explanation of how the KAM was addressed by the audit process. In this case, this might include, for example, an evaluation of the controls designed and implemented by Kilmister Co to monitor the progress of and the amounts owing on service and construction contracts; a review of the financial performance of key contracts against budgets and historical trends; and challenging management's estimates and judgements in respect of the progress to date on the contracts.

(b)   Taylor Co – Report to those charged with governance

A report to those charged with governance (TCWG) is produced to communicate matters relating to the external audit to those who are ultimately responsible for the financial statements. ISA 260/ISA (UK) 260 *Communication With Those Charged With Governance* requires the auditor to communicate many matters including independence and other ethical issues and the significant findings from the audit. In the case of Taylor Co, the matters to be communicated would include the following:

Revaluation of property portfolio

According to ISA 260/ISA (UK) 260, the significant findings from the audit include the auditor's views about significant qualitative aspects of the entity's accounting practices including accounting policies and any circumstances which affect the form and content of the auditor's report.

In the case of Taylor Co, the significant findings from the audit would relate to the changes in the accounting policy in relation to the revaluation of property and related material misstatements and the following matters should be communicated.

IAS 16 *Property, Plant and Equipment* states the revaluation policy should be consistent across a class of assets.

Four properties, which are material to the statement of financial position at 2.1% of total assets, are still carried at depreciated historic cost. This therefore represents a breach of IAS 16 and a material misstatement, which will impact on the form and content of the auditor's report.

According to ISA 260/ISA (UK) 260, the significant findings from the audit also include significant difficulties encountered during audit such as information delays.

The independent external valuation reports requested by Eddie & Co at the planning stage were not available when requested by the auditor and it took three weeks before they were received by the audit team.

The auditor should report this delay to those charged with governance, detailing its impact on the efficiency of the audit process together with any resulting increase in the audit fee.

Renovation of car parking facilities

The renovation expenditure on the car parking facilities at Taylor Co's properties should be recognised as an asset according to IAS 16 if it is probable that future economic benefits associated with the item will flow to the entity and the cost of the item can be measured reliably.

In Taylor Co's case, the cost has been quantified as $13.2 million and it has already derived economic benefits in the form of a significant increase in customer numbers and revenue at each of these locations. The expenditure should therefore be capitalised and its inclusion in operating expenses is not in compliance with IAS 16.

The amount of $13.2 million is also material to the statement of financial position at 2.5% of total assets.

The incorrect application of IAS 16 and the material misstatement should be included in a report to TCWG as a significant finding from the audit which will impact on the form and content of the auditor's report.

ISA 265/ISA (UK) 265 *Communicating Deficiencies in Internal Control to Those Charged With Governance and Management* requires the auditor to communicate appropriately to those charged with governance deficiencies in internal control which the auditor has identified during the audit and which, in the auditor's professional judgement, are of sufficient importance to merit their respective attentions.

The audit working papers include minutes of discussions with management which confirm that authorisation had not been gained for this expenditure. The lack of authorisation indicates a lack of management oversight and a serious weakness in control which could allow fraud to occur.

Furthermore, the lack of integrity shown by management in going ahead with the renovation works without the necessary permission is an example of management override and could be indicative of the tone set throughout the organisation.

This therefore represents a high risk matter and they may wish to implement controls and procedures to prevent further breaches.

The report to those charged with governance should include full details on this significant deficiency in internal control and should include recommendations to management in order to reduce the associated business risk.

Examiner's comments

This question was a 25-mark compulsory question which focused on completion and reporting and was in two sections.

Requirement (a) for 10 marks, asked candidates to critically appraise an extract from an auditor's report which had been incorrectly prepared and required amendment. The majority of responses were extremely disappointing and generally reflects weak knowledge of auditor reporting requirements. There remain a number of candidates who continue to show a lack of understanding of basic ISA requirements such as incorrectly suggesting that an unmodified opinion should have 'unmodified' in the title of the opinion or that a material uncertainty related to going concern should be included within an emphasis of matter paragraph. Many candidates suggested that the use of "we believe" in the auditor's report is not appropriate wording, or that the use of "in our opinion" suggests that the auditor is not independent from the client and therefore a familiarity threat is present. This demonstrates a significant lack of understanding of auditor's reports and ISA 700 *Forming an Opinion and Reporting on Financial Statements*. Candidates were not expected to discuss what would or would not be present in a full report. Where candidates discussed, for example, "the signature of the partner is missing" or "responsibilities of the auditor are missing", this was not relevant to the requirement, which asked candidates to specifically critique the extract as presented. Discussion of given extracts of auditor's reports, again, should follow a structured approach and practising questions of this nature should allow candidates to score strong marks in these requirements. Candidates would benefit from increased knowledge of ISA 700, and in particular should review the appendices which show real examples of auditor's report and typical wording which is appropriate.

Requirement (b) required candidates to discuss, along with reasons for discussion, specific matters raised in the scenario which should be reported to those charged with governance. Generally, candidates identified the "matters to be included" and used an approach of calculating the materiality of the issue, discussing the relevant accounting standard and how the matter had been dealt with incorrectly. However, candidates were vague on why matters should be included within a report to those charged with governance and continued to answer the question as if it were asking about the impact on the audit opinion. This demonstrates a lack of understanding of the question requirement by a number of candidates.

		Marks
	ACCA Marking guide	
(a)	**Kilmister Co**	
	Critical appraisal of extract from draft auditor's report	
	Up to 1 mark per issue explained	
	– Addressee should be shareholders (not directors)	
	– Incorrect order – opinion paragraph should be before basis for opinion	
	– Lack of specific reference to ethical code	
	Material uncertainty re going concern:	
	– Opinion paragraph should be headed 'qualified/adverse opinion' followed by 'basis for qualified/adverse opinion'	
	– Modification due to material misstatement re absence of disclosure – 'except for' or adverse depending on auditor's professional judgement re level of impact on financial statements	

- Incorrect use of 'material uncertainty regarding going concern' paragraph – this paragraph should be used when adequate disclosure has been made by directors in financial statements
- Details of uncertainty re going concerns should be given in basis for qualified/adverse opinion paragraph

Long term contracts:
- Incorrect use of 'other information' paragraph – should be used to describe auditor's responsibilities for 'other information' (e.g. rest of the annual report, including management report) and outcome of fulfilling those responsibilities
- Issue is area of significant auditor judgement which should be considered for inclusion as KAM which as a listed company, Kilmister Co should disclose in separate KAM section of auditor's report
- KAM section should include explanation of what is a KAM
- KAM section should explain why matter is considered to be KAM
- KAM section should also explain how KAM was addressed by audit process

Maximum	**10**

(b) **Taylor Co**
Report to those charged with governance
Generally up to 1 mark for each matter identified and explained
Revaluation of property portfolio
- Significant findings from audit should be reported to TCWG
- These include significant changes in accounting policy and material misstatements
- Revaluation of PPE should be consistent across a class of assets (IAS 16), four properties still carried at depreciated historic cost
- Four properties are material to SOFP (2.1% assets)
- Significant findings from audit also include significant difficulties encountered during audit such as information delays
- Delay makes audit less efficient and may result in increase in audit fee

Renovation of car parking facilities
- Taylor Co has derived economic benefits from expenditure, should be capitalised
- Material to SOFP (2.5% of assets)
- Incorrect application of IAS 16 and potential material misstatement should be included in report to TCWG as significant finding from audit
- Lack of authorisation indicates lack of management oversight and serious weakness in control which could allow fraud to occur
- Lack of integrity shown by management going ahead with renovation works without the necessary permission is an example of management override and could be the tone set throughout organisation
- Therefore this is a high risk matter and they may wish to implement controls and procedures to prevent further breaches
- Report to TCWG should include recommendations to management to reduce business risk

Maximum	**10**

Professional marks
Analysis and evaluation
- Effective analysis and identification of issues and omissions in the draft auditor's report
- Appropriate use of the information to support discussion, draw appropriate conclusions and design appropriate responses
- Appropriate recommendations in relation to necessary actions which reflect the stage of engagement

Professional scepticism and judgement
- Effective challenge and critical assessment of the conduct and extent of the audit work and evidence obtained with appropriate conclusions
- Appropriate application of professional judgement to draw conclusions and make informed decisions about the actions which are appropriate in the context and stage of the engagement
- Demonstration of the ability to probe for further information

Commercial acumen
- Inclusion of appropriate recommendations regarding how Those Charged with Governance and the audit firm should respond to the situation

Maximum	5
Total	25

27 DALEY *Walk in the footsteps of a top tutor*

Top tutor tips

Part (a) requires indicators of going concern issues. Going concern means the company is likely to be able to continue trading for the foreseeable future. The company will have difficulty continuing to trade if it does not have enough cash to pay its liabilities when they fall due. Look for the indicators in the scenario which could mean the cash inflows are not sufficient to cover the cash outflows.

Part (b) requires audit evidence on the cash flow forecast. Evidence needs to be obtained to assess the reasonableness of the assumptions used to prepare the forecast. The transactions have not yet occurred so limited supporting documentation will be available, for example, invoices will not exist at this point. However, some evidence will exist to support management's assumptions and this is what the auditor will need to obtain.

Part (c) asks for the reasons why the directors may not want to make disclosure of the going concern difficulties and the reporting implications if they do not make adequate disclosure. When suggesting an audit opinion, you must state the wording of that opinion and justify your choice as this will be where the majority of the marks will be awarded.

(a) Going concern indicators

There are a range of matters which cast doubt on Daley Co's ability to continue as a going concern. In particular, the company appears to be exhibiting many of the indicators of a business which is overtrading.

Revenue and profitability

Daley Co has experienced a significant increase in revenue of 28.4% which may not be sustainable in the short to medium term without additional external sources of finance.

The company is also experiencing a significant decline in its operating profit margin and net profit margin. It is notable that even after taking account of the provision, other operating expenses have increased by more than 4.3 times ((9.1 − 3.5)/1.3) resulting in an overall loss of $3.4 million in the current reporting period.

It is possible that the company has had to reduce its selling prices in order to achieve the high level of sales growth and that this has resulted in a negative net profit margin this year of (30.1%).

Liquidity and working capital

Daley Co has also suffered a decline in liquidity as evidenced by a fall in its current ratio from 2.4 to 1.6 and in its acid test ratio from 1.1 to 0.6.

A review of the company's working capital ratios indicates long and worsening inventory holding periods (481 days in 20X5 compared to 466 days in 20X4) and overall inventory has increased by 57% which may be indicative of problems in relation to the saleability of inventory which is in breach of domestic regulations.

The company is currently taking on average 120 days to collect its trade debts (108 days in 20X4) and requires an average of 348 days in 20X5 (365 days in 20X4) to pay its trade payables. Although this is a fall in the average payment period compared to the prior year, it still appears to be a long period which may be related to ongoing payment disputes in relation to the regulatory breaches noted previously.

Overall, trade payables have increased by 44.8% on the prior year and the company may struggle to settle this liability given its worsening cash position, which may in turn result in a loss of goodwill with its suppliers and a refusal to supply or to withdraw credit in the future which would severely restrict the company's operations.

The poor working capital management and declining liquidity have resulted in Daley Co's cash position deteriorating from a positive position of $0.6 million in 20X4 to an overdraft of $1.8 million in 20X5 which is significant at 7.8% of total assets.

Gearing and finance

In addition to problems with short-term finance and liquidity, Daley Co is also exhibiting a significant increase in gearing as evidenced by the increase in debt to equity from 2.3 in 20X4 to 6.4 in 20X5 and a fall in interest cover from 6.6 times to (1.5) times over the same period, indicating that the business is unable to service its current levels of finance.

The company's finance costs as a percentage of long-term borrowings have increased from 5.6% in 20X4 to 13.4% in 20X5. This may be due at least in part to the interest on the overdraft proving to be an expensive way of financing the entity's operations and if the overdraft has not been agreed with the bank, the company may be incurring additional penalties and charges thereby putting additional strain on the company's cash flows.

The increasing finance costs may also reflect lenders already perceiving Daley Co to be a high credit risk. It is also notable that non-current assets have decreased by 7.5% this year which suggests that the business is also struggling to replace and renew its existing capital (asset) expenditure levels. If this is the case, it may cast further doubt on the feasibility of the planned expansion of its operations.

Legal claim

Given Daley Co's current financial position, it seems unlikely that the business will be able to settle the legal claim of $3.5 million which threatens to place severe demands on the company's cash flow. Indeed, if there is a prospect of more claims arising in the future, the problems with the saleability of inventory and management of working capital as a result of the regulatory breaches discussed earlier may worsen further leading to a greater deterioration in the company's cash flow position.

Cash flow forecast

Overall, Daley Co's ability to continue to trade appears to be dependent on obtaining the new bank finance which it has assumed in its cash flow forecast. The bank financing is needed to meet existing liabilities and it is doubtful whether sufficient funding will be available in order to finance the proposed expansion.

Moreover, the forecast itself appears to be unrealistic in its other assumptions. In particular, the projected trade receivable collection period of 60 days may well be unachievable on the basis of the historic ratios identified above.

A return to a positive cash position is dependent on obtaining the new bank finance which may not be forthcoming based on the bank's assessment of the business's current financial position and performance.

(b) **Audit evidence on the cash flow forecast**

The audit working papers should include sufficient evidence that appropriate audit procedures have been conducted in relation to the assumption that Daley Co is a going concern at the reporting date, including the following:

- Evidence of agreement of the opening cash position to the bank ledger account/cash book and bank reconciliation.

- Reperformance by the audit team of the client's calculations in preparing the forecast in order to check its arithmetic accuracy.

- Notes from meetings with management detailing discussion of the key assumptions made by management in the preparation of the forecast (including the growth rate and receivables collection period) and an assessment of the consistency of the assumptions with the auditor's knowledge of the business and with management's intentions regarding the future of the company and corroborating evidence of assumptions.

- Evaluation by the audit team of previous profit and other financial forecasts and their outcome in order to assess the consistency of the cash flow forecast with other prospective information prepared by management.

- A comparison of the cash flow forecast for the period April to June 20X5 with management accounts for the same period in order to assess the accuracy of the forecast compared to actual data to date.

- Results of analytical review of the items included in the cash flow forecast including, for example, a detailed review of the breakdown of different categories of expenses in order to identify any items which may have been omitted.

- A review of correspondence with Daley Co's lawyers in relation to the legal claims in order to assess the likelihood of losing the actions, the likely cost and the possibility of further claims arising in the future.

- Based on the review of legal correspondence, confirmation that the settlement of the legal claims has been appropriately included in the cash flow forecast.

- A review of correspondence with Daley Co's bankers and supporting documentation for both the company's existing loan facilities and the proposed new loan.

- Minutes of discussions with management in relation to the likelihood of obtaining the new loan.

- Based on these reviews and discussions, a recalculation by the auditor of the finance cost and confirmation that the finance cost and the receipt of the loan have been accurately reflected in the cash flow forecast.

- Working paper detailing the review of the documentation in relation to the new warehousing agreeing the cost and checking that the cash outflow is included in the forecast at the correct amount and at the correct date.

- A review of board minutes in relation to the company's current trading position and the ongoing negotiations for the proposed new bank finance.

- A consideration of the impact on cash flows and liquidity when the company is incurring the additional costs of compliance with all laws and regulations.

(c) **Reasons for non-disclosure and implications for the auditor's report**

Motives for directors not wishing to make going concern disclosures

The directors' motives for non-disclosure of uncertainties in relation to going concern seem likely to reflect a desire to present the company in a positive light to investors and other third parties. This is a particularly sensitive issue at a time when the company is planning a major expansion and is seeking to raise significant new finance while struggling to manage its liquidity and working capital.

The disclosure of uncertainties in relation to going concern may deter the bank from lending the new finance and may lead to a loss of confidence and goodwill with key suppliers and customers.

Implications for the auditor's report

ISA 705/ISA (UK) 705 *Modifications to the Opinion in the Independent Auditor's Report* requires the auditor to modify the opinion in the auditor's report when they conclude that, based on the audit evidence obtained, the financial statements as a whole are not free from material misstatement.

The failure to include disclosures regarding material uncertainties in relation to going concern in Daley Co's financial statements represents a material omission which will therefore require a modification of the auditor's opinion. In this case, the auditor must exercise professional judgement and assess whether the absence of this disclosure is material but not pervasive to the financial statements or whether it is material and pervasive to the financial statements.

Material but not pervasive

If the auditor concludes that the omission of the required disclosures in relation to the going concern uncertainties is material but not pervasive to the financial statements, a qualified audit opinion on the grounds of material misstatement is appropriate, as the directors have failed to include required disclosures.

The auditor will include a 'Qualified Opinion' paragraph at the start of the auditor's report which will state that the financial statements are presented fairly in all material respects 'except for' the absence of this disclosure.

The qualified opinion paragraph will be followed immediately by a 'Basis for Qualified Opinion' paragraph which will give details of the going concern uncertainties in relation to Daley Co and explain that the financial statements do not adequately disclose these uncertainties.

Material and pervasive

If the auditor concludes that the omission of the required disclosures in relation to the going concern uncertainties is material and pervasive to the financial statements, an adverse audit opinion on the grounds of material misstatement is appropriate as in the auditor's opinion the lack of these disclosures will have a fundamental impact on the users' understanding of the financial statements.

The auditor will include an 'Adverse Opinion' paragraph at the start of the auditor's report which will state that the financial statements are not presented fairly in all material respects.

The adverse opinion paragraph will be followed immediately by a 'Basis for Adverse Opinion' paragraph which will give details of the going concern uncertainties in relation to Daley Co and explain that in the opinion of the auditor, the omission of key disclosures in this respect are fundamental and pervasive to the financial statements and therefore require an adverse opinion.

Tutorial note

Key audit matters (KAM) disclosures are not relevant for Daley Co as it is not listed.

Examiner's comments

This was a 25-mark question covering the going concern assessment for a non-listed client and was set at the completion stage of the audit.

Requirement (a) asked candidates to evaluate matters which cast doubt on a client's ability to continue as a going concern (GC). Candidates were directed to analytical review of a cash flow forecast to aid in their evaluation and those who used the quantitative and discursive parts of the scenario to describe the GC risk indicators with an explanation of how that impacted on the company's future tended to score high marks on this question. Candidates who merely calculated ratios and stated the direction of movement or simply stated that an increase in the receivables collection period showed going concern issues attained very few marks. It is important candidates demonstrate their knowledge of how each matter gives rise to an issue for trading as a going concern. For example, a fuller explanation would be that the increase in the receivables collection period may mean that there are irrecoverable debts which should be written off, increasing losses further, or that slow collection would decrease liquidity and therefore put pressure on the ability of the company to make payments as they fell due. A technique candidates could employ here would be to ask themselves why as they get to the end of a sentence, allowing them to add a second sentence demonstrating their understanding. A minority of candidates appeared to lack focus on the question requirement and answered this as a RoMM discussion, covering risks of material misstatements in the forecast rather than relating the scenario to the GC issues required.

Part (b) requested an explanation of the audit evidence which would be needed with respect to the forecast and candidates scored best when they remembered this was future/ prospective information, not historical, and where they related it specifically to the information given. For example, candidates who looked for specific assumptions in the information provided and devised sources of evidence to support each of those assumptions were able to attain far more marks than candidates who simply said evaluate the assumptions used by management in preparing the forecast. It is important that candidates appreciate that no two questions are the same and that the information given in the question should always be used to drive their answer.

Finally, part (c) required candidates to explain why the directors may wish to exclude disclosures relating to going concern uncertainties in the notes to the financial statements and the possible implications on the auditor's report. Candidates were generally able to identify the reasons for non-disclosure but performed very poorly on the auditor's report implications. Many candidates wrongly stated that the directors omitting a required disclosure would not constitute a material misstatement. Many therefore went on to conclude that the opinion would be unmodified but that going concern disclosures would be made in the auditor's report instead of in the notes to the financial statements. This is not the case and candidates should ensure they are familiar with the reporting requirements in ISA 570 *Going Concern*. Some candidates suggested including such disclosures in the Key Audit Matters section or to include an Emphasis of Matter paragraph both of which would be inappropriate.

ACCA Marking guide		
		Marks
(a)	**Going concern indicators**	
	Up to 1 mark for each well-explained going concern indicator discussed	
	Up to 3 marks for calculation of relevant ratios and trends.	
	Revenue and profitability	
	– Significant increase in revenue of 28.4% (potential overtrading indicator) – Declining profit margins	
	– Increase in effective interest rate on long-term debt (lenders perceive as higher risk)	
	– Loss-making	
	Liquidity and working capital	
	– Declining liquidity	
	– Cash position has moved from positive to negative (overdraft) during year – Poor working capital management	
	Gearing and finance	
	– Increased gearing	
	– Decline in interest cover	
	– Failure to replace non-current assets (7.5% decrease in year)	
	Legal claim	
	– Significant legal claim, company does not appear to have cash to settle it	
	Cash flow forecast	
	– Cash flow forecast indicates improving liquidity and working capital, however, this appears optimistic (e.g. growth rate, receivable collection period assumptions)	
	– Return to positive cash dependent on these assumptions and obtaining new bank finance which may not be forthcoming	
	– Company is dependent on obtaining new bank finance	
	Maximum	8

(b)   **Audit evidence on cash flow forecast**
Generally 1 mark for each well described source of audit evidence:
–   Agreement of the opening cash position to bank ledger account/cash book and bank reconciliation
–   Accuracy check – recalculation
–   Discuss key assumptions made by management in preparation of forecast (including growth rate and receivables collection period), assess consistency with auditor's knowledge of the business and with management's intentions regarding the future of the company
–   Agreement that the cash flow forecast is consistent with profit and other financial forecasts which have been prepared by management
–   Comparison of the cash flow forecast for the period April – June 20X5 with management accounts for the same period
–   Analytical review of the items included in the cash flow forecast, for example, categories of expenses, to look for items which may have been omitted
–   Review legal correspondence in relation to legal claims and assess likelihood of losing actions, likely cost and likelihood of further actions in future
–   If appropriate, ensure settlement of legal claims has been included in forecast
–   Review correspondence with bank and supporting documentation for existing and proposed loan facilities
–   Discuss with management likelihood of obtaining new finance
–   Check calculation of finance cost and inclusion in forecast
–   Ensure amount and timing of receipt of new finance is accurately reflected in forecast
–   Inspect documentation in relation to new warehousing agreeing cost and check that cash outflow is included in forecast at correct amount and timing
–   Review of board minutes re company's current trading position and ongoing negotiations with bankers
–   Consideration of impact on cash flows and liquidity when company is incurring additional costs of compliance with all laws and regulations

| | **Maximum** | **7** |

(c)   **Directors' reasons for non-disclosure and implications for auditor's report**
Generally up to 1 mark for each point discussed:
Possible reasons for non-disclosure
–   Desire to present company in positive light to investors and other third parties
–   Particularly significant given current position of company, e.g. seeking to raise new finance; struggling to manage liquidity and working capital; need to maintain confidence with suppliers and customers especially with arrival of new competitor
Implications for auditor's report
–   Auditor must assess whether absence of disclosure is material but not pervasive to financial statements or whether it is material and pervasive to financial statements
Material but not pervasive
–   Qualified opinion due to material misstatement ('except for' incomplete disclosure)
–   Basis for qualified opinion paragraph to be included giving details of going concern uncertainties and that financial statements do not adequately disclose these uncertainties
Material and pervasive
–   Adverse opinion due to material misstatement where the financial statements 'do not present fairly'
–   Basis for adverse opinion paragraph explaining grounds for adverse opinion
–   Position of opinion and basis for (qualified/adverse) opinion paragraphs
–   Well reasoned conclusion on whether issue is pervasive

| | **Maximum** | **5** |

Professional marks

Analysis and evaluation

- Appropriate use of the information to support discussion, draw appropriate conclusions and design appropriate responses
- Identification of omissions from the analysis or further analysis which could be carried out
- Balanced assessment of the information to determine the appropriate audit opinion in the circumstances

Professional scepticism and judgement

- Effective challenge of information, evidence and assumptions supplied and, techniques carried out to support key facts and/or decisions
- Appropriate application of professional judgement to draw conclusions and make informed decisions about the actions which are appropriate in the context and stage of the engagement

Commercial acumen

- Use of effective examples and/or calculations from the scenario to illustrate points or recommendations
- Appropriate recognition of the wider implications when considering why the directors may wish to exclude going concern disclosures

Maximum	5
Total	25

28 CORAM & CO *Walk in the footsteps of a top tutor*

Top tutor tips

Part (a) provides you with the schedule of uncorrected misstatements for an audit client and asks for the matters to be discussed with management. Calculate whether the proposed adjustment is material. If it is material the adjustment must be made in order to avoid a modified opinion. You also need to explain the accounting treatment that they should have applied. Finish off by explaining the impact on the auditor's opinion if management does not make the proposed adjustments. The requirement only asks for the impact on the opinion, not the report, so do not waste time expanding beyond the opinion section. This is a typical completion and reporting question seen on many recent past papers which emphasises the importance of practising past papers to prepare for the exam.

Part (b) is an ethical and professional issues question. There are two separate issues and you should deal with them in turn. Identify the type of threat, explain how the threat could influence the audit, discuss whether the threat is significant and finish off by explaining the safeguards the firm should take to reduce the threat to an acceptable level.

(a) Clark Co

Matters to be discussed with management in relation to the audit supervisor's proposed adjustments

(i) Lease of testing equipment

The lease at Clark Co's largest site is material to the statement of financial position at 2.2% of total assets. The leases at the other two sites are also material at 2.8% of total assets.

The general recognition and measurement requirements of IFRS 16 *Leases* require lessees to recognise a right-of-use asset and a lease liability at the commencement date of the lease at the present value of the lease payments. The standard defines the commencement date as the date the asset is available for use by the lessee. Given that the commencement date is 31 March 20X5 therefore, it is appropriate on this basis to recognise the lease on the statement of financial position as at this date.

It is significant, however, that IFRS 16 also contains an optional exemption for short-term leases of less than 12 months' duration with no purchase option. If Clark Co elects to apply this exemption, it does not recognise the leased assets or lease liabilities on the statement of financial position but rather, it recognises the lease payments associated with those leases as an expense in the statement of profit or loss for the year on either a straight-line basis over the lease term or another systematic basis.

However, IFRS 16 also requires that if this exemption is taken, it must be applied consistently by each class of underlying asset. Hence in this case, the client must either capitalise the leases across all three of the sites or apply the exemption consistently and not capitalise the leases across any of the sites. On either of these bases, as the commencement date of the lease coincides with the reporting date, there would not yet be any impact on Clark Co's statement of profit or loss for the year.

The audit manager should discuss the option of taking the short-term lease exemption with the finance director at tomorrow's meeting:

(i)   if the client elects not to take the exemption across the three sites, assets and liabilities will be materially understated. Hence the audit supervisor's proposed adjustment is correct and a right-of-use asset and lease liability of $475,000 should be recognised on the statement of financial position.

(ii)   Alternatively, if the client does elect to take the exemption across all three sites, then assets and liabilities are materially overstated and right-of-use assets and lease liabilities of $625,000 should be derecognised on the statement of financial position.

Impact on audit opinion

If the client does not make any adjustment to the financial statements, the statement of financial position is materially misstated on the basis of misapplication of an accounting standard and the audit opinion should be qualified on this basis with an 'except for' opinion.

(ii)   Legal claim

The legal claim is material to the statement of financial position being 5.5% of Clark Co's total assets.

Following the requirements of IAS 37 *Provisions, Contingent Liabilities and Contingent Assets*, a provision should be recognised when: an entity has a present obligation (legal or constructive) as a result of a past event; it is probable that an outflow of resources embodying economic benefits will be required to settle the obligation; and a reliable estimate can be made of the amount of the obligation.

In this case the customer has already won the action against the company, the amount of the claim has been agreed by the courts and settlement is still outstanding at the reporting date. Hence, a provision of $1.2 million should be recognised on the statement of financial position.

IAS 37 also states that contingent assets are not recognised in financial statements since this may result in the recognition of income which may never be realised. However, the standard continues by stating that when the realisation of income is virtually certain, then the related asset is not a contingent asset and its recognition is appropriate. With respect to Clark Co's insurance claim therefore and the verified letter dated 25 March 20X5, the settlement of the claim as at the reporting date is virtually certain and an asset should be recognised separately on the statement of financial position.

The audit supervisor's proposed adjustment is correct and the finance director should therefore be requested to adjust the financial statements to include the separate recognition of the asset and the provision. If the adjustment is not made, both assets and liabilities will be materially misstated. There is no net impact on the statement of profit or loss for the year.

The finance director should also be advised that the financial statements should include full disclosure of the facts and amounts surrounding the provision for the legal claim together with full details of the expected reimbursement from the insurance company recognised as an asset.

Impact on audit opinion

If the client does not make any adjustment to the financial statements, the statement of financial position is materially misstated and the audit opinion should be qualified on this basis with an 'except for' opinion.

(b)   Turner Co

Ethical and professional issues and actions to be taken by the audit firm

Loan to member of the audit team

According to the IESBA *International Code of Ethics for Professional Accountants* (the *Code*) and the FRC Ethical Standard, a loan to a member of the audit team may create a threat to the auditor's independence. If the loan is not made under normal lending procedures, and terms and conditions, a self-interest threat would be created as a result of Janette Stott's financial interest in the audit client. The self-interest threat arises because of the potential personal benefit derived which may motivate the audit team member to behave in a manner aimed at protecting that benefit.

Such a threat would be so significant that no safeguards could reduce the threat to an acceptable level. It follows therefore that the audit team member should not accept such a loan or guarantee. The *Code*, however, also states that a loan from an audit client which is a bank or similar institution to a member of the audit team which is made under normal lending procedures, is acceptable. Examples of such loans include home mortgages, car loans and credit card balances.

In addition, an intimidation threat to objectivity may arise where a loan is made from the audit client to a member of the audit team. The threat arises because of a fear that the audit client may, for example, change the terms of the loan or recall the loan, thus influencing the behaviour of the auditor.

It is possible therefore that the secured loan may be ethically acceptable and the key issue is whether 'the very best terms which the bank can offer' fall within Turner Co's normal lending procedures, and terms and conditions. The bank's standard lending terms and conditions should be obtained and reviewed alongside the documentation for Janette Stott's loan.

Ultimately, the audit engagement partner is responsible for ensuring that ethical principles are not breached, so the partner should be involved with the discussions.

The matter should be discussed with Janette and the client's business manager in order to establish whether the loan is to be made under the bank's normal lending procedures.

Janette should be advised of the outcome of the review and Turner Co's business manager should be advised of this decision, explaining the rationale and ethical rules behind it.

Temporary staff assignment

The *Code* states that the lending of staff to an audit client may create a self-review threat to auditor independence. The self-review threat arises when an auditor reviews work which they themselves have previously performed – for example, if the external auditor is involved in the process of preparing the payroll figures for inclusion in the financial statements and then audits them. As a result, there is a risk that the auditor would not be sufficiently objective in performing the audit and may fail to identify any shortcomings in their own work.

In addition, there is a risk of the staff member assuming management responsibilities if they are involved in making judgements and decisions which are the remit of management.

Such assistance can only therefore be given for a short period of time and the audit firm's staff must not assume management responsibilities and must not be involved in any activities specifically prohibited.

The individual must not be included on the audit team.

Tutorial note

According to the FRC Ethical Standard, a short period of time is generally expected to be no more than a small number of months. The client has requested staff for six months, which may be considered too long a period to avoid ethical threats from arising.

INT syllabus

According to the *Code*, an audit firm cannot provide accounting and bookkeeping services (including payroll) to listed clients which form the basis of financial statements on which the firm will express an opinion.

UK syllabus

According to the FRC Ethical Standard, payroll services must not be provided to a public interest entity. Therefore, the audit manager should decline the proposed staff assignment in relation to payroll services, explaining to the client the reasons why the Ethical Standard prohibits the provision of this service.

Examiner's comments

Part (a) was presented as a list of proposed audit adjustments. The requirement asked for the matters to discuss with management and the impact on the audit opinion should management fail to adjust the errors. Candidates often did not remain focused on the requirement and detailed effects elsewhere in the auditor's report and the other actions they would take if management did not agree to amend the errors. In this question, the correct accounting treatment was described for leases in addition to presenting the correctly calculated audit adjustments. Candidates often scored well in this requirement if they explained why the proposed treatments by the directors were not compliant with accounting standards (requirement for consistency in accounting policies and the requirement not to net off assets and liabilities). Common mistakes made in this question arose where candidates determined the directors were right and the auditors wrong.

Candidates should note that when presenting audit opinions, it is not sufficient to say the opinion would be modified as this could mean any of four possibilities. Candidates should state the type of modification proposed e.g. qualified on the basis of material misstatement to score the mark. Simply writing qualified will not attract full marks as this could refer to either a material misstatement or an inability to obtain sufficient evidence. Similarly, when justifying the severity of a modified opinion candidates should justify whether something is pervasive or simply material to obtain the full mark. Simply stating something is not pervasive will only receive ½ a mark. This is consistent with the way audit reporting is marked in the Audit and Assurance paper and candidates should be used to this approach. Candidates who struggle with the format of auditor's reports should refer to the exam technique article which describes the key components and how to make a decision as to whether an item is pervasive or not.

Another weakness in answers provided here was to use out-of-date accounting standards to produce an answer. The examinable documents for Strategic Business Reporting are also examinable for this examination. While the majority of answers correctly applied IFRS 16 *Leases* to the question (the relevant parts of the standard were described within the scenario) a significant portion of the UK and IRL candidates continued to reference outdated treatment based on the definitions of operating and finance leases. It is important to note that the examinable versions of standards are those listed in the examinable documents area of the ACCA website and often this is in advance of the implementation in some jurisdictions.

Part (b) was less well answered. Candidates were presented with two ethical issues for eight marks and often were unable to describe how the threats arose. In particular, other than the common mistake of not adequately explaining the threats to objectivity that were present specific to the scenario, candidates appeared unable to differentiate between a loan from any audit client and a loan on normal commercial terms from a client that happened to be a financial institution. Similarly, candidates did not appear to be able to differentiate between the safeguards appropriate for a non-listed client and one which was. This was particularly the case on the UK and IRL exams.

	ACCA Marking guide	
		Marks

(a) **Clarke Co**

Matters to be discussed and individual impact on financial statements

Generally up to 2 marks for full discussion of each matter and impact on opinion.

– Lease at largest site is material to SOFP at 2.2% of total assets; leases at other two sites are also material at 2.8% of total assets (max 1 mark)

– General requirement of IFRS 16 to capitalise all leases on SOFP as right-of-use assets at PV of lease payments from commencement date (i.e. date asset is available for use)

– IFRS 16 exemption (optional) for short-term leases of less than 12 months with no purchase option hence if client elects, no need to recognise lease on SOFP (n.b. no P/L effect yet as commencement date at year end)

– Short-term lease exemption must be made by class of underlying asset, hence treatment across three sites must be consistent

– To discuss exemption with FD at meeting: if elects not to take exemption across the three sites, assets and liabilities are materially understated; hence the proposed adjustment is correct and a right-of-use asset and lease liability of $475,000 should be recognised

– Alternatively, if client does elect to take exemption across all three sites, then assets and liabilities are materially overstated and right-of-use assets and lease liabilities of $625,000 should be derecognised

Impact on audit opinion:

If client makes no adjustment, the statement of financial position is materially misstated and the audit opinion should be qualified on this basis with an 'except for' opinion

| | **Maximum** | **7** |

Legal claim

– Claim is material to SOFP at 5.5% of total assets (max 1 mark)

– Provision should be recognised per IAS 37 as unpaid, probable liability at reporting date

– Asset should also be recognised as payment by insurance company is virtually certain

– The asset and liability should be shown separately on the SOFP and not offset; there is no net impact on P/L; as a result both assets and liabilities are materially understated

– Full details of both provision and contingent asset should be disclosed in notes to financial statements

Impact on audit opinion:

If client makes no adjustment, the statement of financial position is materially misstated and the audit opinion should be qualified on this basis with an 'except for' opinion

| | **Maximum** | **5** |

(b) **Turner Co**

Ethical and professional issues and actions to be taken by audit firm

Generally up to 1 mark for each issue and action.

Loan to member of the audit team

Issues:

– Potential self-interest threat to auditor independence

– Key issue is whether 'the very best deal which the bank can offer' is made under normal lending procedures, terms and conditions

– If not, self-interest threat created would be so significant that no safeguards could reduce it to acceptable level and Janette should be told not to take loan

– If it is made under bank's normal lending procedures, terms and conditions, the loan does not create a threat to auditor's independence and Janette may accept the loan	

Actions:
- Discuss terms and conditions of loan with Janette and business manager
- Obtain draft loan documents and review details in order to establish whether under normal lending procedures, terms and conditions
- Inform audit engagement partner, who is responsible for ethical compliance
- Advise Janette on outcome of review and whether she can accept loan and advise business manager of decision explaining rationale/ethical rules

Maximum	4

Temporary staff assignment

Issues:
- Potential self-review threat to auditor independence
- Must not assume management responsibilities or provide non-assurance services prohibited by the *Code*
- Cannot provide accounting and bookkeeping services (including payroll) to audit client which is a public interest entity
- Exception if services relate to matters which are collectively immaterial to financial statements

Actions:
- Discuss details of proposed role of seconded member of staff with payroll manager/other key client contacts in order to establish significance/materiality of role to financial statements
- Advise client of outcome of these enquiries/decision; seems likely that will have to decline assignment of staff member as payroll supervisor as role appears to be material/significant to financial statements – listed/public interest entity, supervisory/management role requiring qualified member of staff on main payroll system

Maximum	4
Maximum for part b	8

Professional marks

Analysis and evaluation
- Appropriate use of the information to support discussion, draw appropriate conclusions and design appropriate responses
- Effective appraisal of the information to make suitable recommendations for appropriate courses of action
- Balanced assessment of the information to determine the appropriate audit opinion in the circumstances

Professional scepticism and judgement
- Effective challenge and critical assessment of the evidence supplied with appropriate conclusions
- Appropriate application of professional judgement to draw conclusions and make informed decisions about the actions which are appropriate in the context and stage of the engagement

Commercial acumen
- Inclusion of appropriate recommendations regarding the ethical and professional issues facing the firm
- Appropriate recognition of the wider implications on the engagement, the audit firm and the company

Maximum	5
Total	25

29 BREARLEY & CO *Walk in the footsteps of a top tutor*

Top tutor tips

Part (a) asks for the matters to be considered and the audit evidence that should be on file during your review of the audit file. Use the 'MARE' approach. First, consider the materiality of the issue. Next discuss the appropriate accounting treatment and give the risks of material misstatement that would arise if the appropriate treatment is not followed. Finally, the evidence is what you would expect to be recorded on the audit file when you come to review it.

Part (b) asks for a critical appraisal of the draft auditor's report extracts. Don't just focus on whether the opinion is appropriate. You should also think about the titles of the paragraphs included and whether the names are correct, the order they appear in, whether the required information that should be included has been included and whether the wording used is professional and appropriate.

(a) (i) Dilley Co

Matters

The key matter to be considered is the status of the investment in Dilley Co in the consolidated financial statements of the Group. Although the 40% holding falls within the usual percentage presumption range for an associate following IAS 28 *Investments in Associates and Joint Ventures*, the existence of the share options over the remaining 60% is indicative of control following IFRS 10 *Consolidated Financial Statements*. IFRS 10 contains specific guidance on situations where control may exist when the investor does not hold a majority of the voting rights.

According to IFRS 10, control and therefore status as a subsidiary may be based on potential voting rights provided such rights are substantive. In the case of Dilley Co, the potential voting rights are exercisable in the near future (within one month of the reporting date) and the 10% discount on market price makes them commercially attractive to the Group. The options therefore represent substantive potential voting rights and Dilley Co's statement of profit or loss should be consolidated line by line from the date of acquisition.

The 40% holding in Dilley Co has been held for 11 months of the current reporting period. The time apportioned revenue of $82.5 million ($90 million × 11/12) is therefore material to the consolidated financial statements at 1.1%.

On the same basis, the time apportioned loss before tax is $11 million ($12 million × 11/12) which is $6.6 million greater than the loss recognised under the equity method of $4.4 million.

The difference is also material to the financial statements at 12% of the Group's profit before tax. Given the loss making status of Dilley Co, there is an incentive not to consolidate the entity. The auditor should exercise professional scepticism and consider whether there are any implications in relation to management integrity.

Evidence

- A copy of the legal documents supporting the acquisition of the shares and the options including the voting rights and the terms of exercise for the options.

- A review of the audit working papers for Dilley Co, including details of the issued share capital and the associated voting rights attached to shares.

- The group board minutes relating to the acquisition and the intentions of management in relation to Dilley Co.

- Written representations from management on the degree of influence exercised over Dilley Co and the future intentions of management in relation to the share options.

(ii) Willis Co

Matters

The fair value of the derivatives of $6.1 million is material to consolidated profit before tax at 11.1% but in isolation, it is immaterial to consolidated assets at 0.4%.

IFRS 9 *Financial Instruments* requires the recognition of derivatives on the statement of financial position at fair value with the associated gains and losses being recognised in profit or loss for the period.

The fair value of $6.1 million should therefore be included in current assets on the Group's consolidated statement of financial position and given that the options were entered into in the last three months of the period at no initial net investment, a fair value gain of $6.1 million should also be recorded in the Group's consolidated statement of profit or loss for the year.

The treatment of the derivatives under local GAAP is acceptable in Willis Co's individual entity financial statements. For group purposes, however, accounting policies must be consistent and the profit before tax in the draft consolidated financial statements is materially understated.

The auditor must also exercise professional scepticism with regard to whether the directors have the required expertise to value the derivatives and should consider the need for independent, external evidence of the fair value of the options at the reporting date.

Evidence

- Details of the fair value of the options based on prices derived from an active market or if this is not available, an independent expert valuation.

- Audit documentation of the review of derivative contracts and confirmation of the terms and maturity dates.

- Notes of a discussion with management in relation to the basis of their valuation and the accounting treatment required in the consolidated financial statements.

(b) Critical appraisal of the draft auditor's report

There are a number of issues to consider in critically appraising the auditor's report extract which has been drafted by the audit senior. These include the following:

Key audit matters (KAM)

The section should include an introductory paragraph explaining the concept of KAM in order for users of the auditor's report to understand its importance and significance. The introduction should also clearly state that the auditor is not forming a separate opinion on the items identified as KAM.

Valuation of financial instruments

This is an area of significant audit judgement with a high risk of material misstatement, hence inclusion as KAM is appropriate although the disclosure should explain the factors which led the auditor to determine the matter was a KAM. It would also aid user understanding further if the auditor's report quantified the size and significance of the issue and explained its impact on the nature and extent of the audit effort.

The auditor should describe how the KAM was addressed in the audit, and although this is a matter for auditor judgement, the auditor may describe aspects of the auditor's response or approach, provide a brief overview of the procedures performed and an indication of the outcome of the procedures. Based on the current wording, the users of the auditor's report would have no clear indication of how the auditor has gathered evidence over this key area.

There are also several issues in relation to the detailed drafting of the paragraph. The report should not refer to the Group's finance director by name and should not imply criticism of him as result of his inexperience. The use of the word 'guesswork' is inappropriate and undermines the credibility of the audit and financial reporting process.

Customer liquidation

The amount owed by the customer of $287,253 is material to the loss before tax at 13.1% and to assets at 2%. The 'except for' qualification on the grounds of material misstatement is therefore appropriate. However, the details of the material misstatement should not be included in the KAM section at all but should be given in the basis for qualified opinion paragraph.

This should also be clearly cross referenced within the opinion paragraph itself. Furthermore, the wording of the report currently references reducing the profit before tax when it should refer to increasing the loss before tax.

Opinion paragraph

This is incorrectly positioned and incorrectly titled. It should be at the start of the auditor's report and should simply be titled 'Qualified Opinion'. The opinion paragraph should be clearly cross referenced to the 'Basis for Qualified Opinion' paragraph which should be placed immediately below the opinion paragraph and should clearly describe the issue which has given rise to a qualified opinion. As above, the 'except for' qualification on the grounds of materiality is appropriate.

Examiner's comments

This question was centred on the review of a Group of companies and required candidates to consider the matters outlined and to explain what audit evidence would be required.

The first scenario described the accounting treatment of a new acquisition in which the client company had acquired 40% of the voting shares but with an option to acquire the remaining 60% at a discount to the market value. IFRS 10 *Consolidated Financial Statements* contains specific guidance on such situations when the investor may have control even when a majority of the shares are not held. In this case as the options were exercisable in the near future the acquisition should have been treated as a subsidiary rather than an associate. This question tended to produce poor answers as the majority of candidates proved to be unfamiliar with the relevant accounting standard and hence did not realise the accounting for the acquisition was incorrect.

The second scenario included a foreign subsidiary that used local GAAP rather than IFRS. The subsidiary had forward commodity options with a fair value of $6.1m that had been disclosed at the year end rather than included on the statement of financial position. Stronger candidates were able to recognise that on consolidation the subsidiary accounts should be aligned with IFRS and the derivatives recognised on the consolidated statement of financial position at fair value with the associated gains or losses being recognised in the consolidated statement of profit or loss. Further credit was then available for considering the evidence required to support the value of the derivatives. A number of weaker candidates disappointingly discussed the need to translate the year-end financial statements of the subsidiary although the question had specifically stated that the subsidiary had the same functional and presentational currency as the parent.

The second requirement was to critically appraise an extract from an auditor's report, which had been incorrectly prepared and needed amendment. It was clear that the candidates had read the relevant article and were able to identify that the sections were in the wrong order, contained inappropriate wording and that the key audit matters paragraph had been incorrectly used. Good candidates were able to explain when an issue should be included as a key audit matter or if the issue would result in a qualification and hence needed to be part of the basis of opinion paragraph.

ACCA Marking guide		Marks
(a) **Matters to consider and evidence on file** Generally up to 1 mark for each matter explained and each piece of evidence recommended. **(i)** **Dilley Co** **Matters** – Materiality – IFRS 10 definition of subsidiary is based on control and contains specific guidance on situations where control may exist when investor does NOT hold majority of voting rights – Control and subsidiary status may be based on potential voting rights; following IFRS 10 rights do not have to be currently exercisable but must be 'substantive' – Here potential voting rights are exercisable in near future and are 'in the money', hence likely to be subsidiary; consolidated SOCI should therefore include line by line consolidation for 11 months and a loss of $11 million in relation to Dilley Co – Difference of $6.6 million is material to group SOCI; management have incentive not to consolidate (especially in light of declining profitability) – Group revenue should include $82.5 million for Dilley Co and will therefore also be materially understated **Evidence** – Copy of legal documents supporting acquisition of shares and options including voting rights and terms of exercise for options – Audit working papers for Dilley Co confirming details of issued share capital and associated voting rights – Board minutes relating to acquisition and management intentions in relation to Dilley Co – Management representations on degree of influence and future intentions – Copy of the adjusting journal required to reflect the correct treatment in the financial statements		
Maximum		6

   (ii) **Willis Co**

     Matters

     –   Materiality

     –   Group accounting policies should be consistent

     –   Treatment is acceptable in individual entity financial statements but not for Group accounts

     –   IFRS 9 requires recognition of derivatives on SOFP at fair value with gains and losses in profit or loss for period

     –   Fair value of derivatives is material to group profit (with supporting calculation)

     –   Directors may not have expertise required for valuation of the options

     –   Need for external independent evidence of fair value at reporting date

     Evidence

     –   Fair value based on market prices or if not available, independent expert valuation

     –   Audit documentation of review of derivative contracts and confirmation of terms and maturity dates

     –   Notes of discussion with management in relation to the basis of their valuation and the accounting treatment

     –   Copy of the adjusting journal required to reflect the correct treatment in the financial statements

                     Maximum **5**

(b) **Critical appraisal of the draft auditor's report**

   In general up to 1 mark for each well explained point:

   KAM section

   –   KAM section should include introductory paragraph explaining what KAMs are

   –   Auditor not forming separate opinion on KAM

   Valuation of financial instruments

   –   Area of significant audit judgement with high risk of material misstatement, hence inclusion as KAM potentially appropriate

   –   Would aid user understanding if:

     •   quantified size/significance of issue

     •   explained impact on nature and extent of audit effort

   –   Inappropriate drafting of paragraph:

     •   should not refer to FD by name

     •   should not imply criticism of him as result of inexperience

     •   choice of language 'guesswork' undermines credibility of audit and financial reporting process

   Customer liquidation

   –   Material to profit and assets (with calculation)

   –   Details of material misstatement should not be included in KAM section at all but should be given in basis for qualified opinion paragraph and should be clearly cross referenced to opinion paragraph

   –   Wording refers to reducing profit before tax when it should refer to increasing the loss before tax

   Opinion paragraph

   –   Incorrectly positioned, should now be at start of auditor's report and should be clearly cross referenced to basis of opinion paragraph below which details the material misstatement

   –   Incorrect title, it should be headed simply 'Qualified Opinion'

   –   Except for qualification appropriate on grounds of material misstatement

                     Maximum **9**

Professional marks

Analysis and evaluation

– Effective analysis and identification of issues and omissions in the draft auditor's report

– Appropriate use of the information to support discussion, draw appropriate conclusions and design appropriate responses

– Appropriate recommendations in relation to necessary actions which reflect the stage of engagement

Professional scepticism and judgement

– Effective challenge and critical assessment of the conduct and extent of the audit work and evidence obtained with appropriate conclusions

– Appropriate application of professional judgement to draw conclusions and make informed decisions about the actions which are appropriate in the context and stage of the engagement

– Demonstration of the ability to probe for further information

Maximum	5
Total	25

30 BASKING *Walk in the footsteps of a top tutor*

Top tutor tips

Part (a) asks for matters to be discussed with management followed by the reporting implications. This is a typical question seen on many recent past papers which emphasises the importance of practising past papers to prepare for the exam.

Part (b) requires knowledge and application of the key audit matters section within an auditor's report for a listed company. You need to know the types of matters that would be referred to in a KAM and be able to describe the information that would be included in the KAM.

Part (c) covers current issues and developments within the audit profession. The study text provides several resources to help with this syllabus area. Spend some time reading the latest articles on developments in the profession to keep up to date with what is happening.

(a) (1) Loan

Matters

The loan represents a related party transaction as it is between the company and one of its key management personnel.

The value of the loan may be trivial; it certainly is not material to the financial statements by value. Regardless, related party transactions are material by nature.

In these circumstances, the directors of the company may be abusing their position and power for their own personal gain and it is likely that the loan is being provided to Mrs Angel on favourable or non-commercial terms.

For this reason, details relating to the loan must be disclosed in the financial statements, including the amount of the loan, who the loan has been made to and the amount outstanding at the end of the year.

The auditor in this circumstance will disagree with the judgement applied by management in their application of IAS 24 *Related Party Transactions* and the auditor should request that the additional disclosures are added to the financial statements.

Opinion

If management refuses to make the recommended adjustments to the financial statements, then the auditor will conclude that the financial statements are materially misstated due to a lack of appropriate disclosure. While the adjustment is material by nature, a lack of disclosure is unlikely to be considered to be pervasive to the financial statements as a whole.

In these circumstances the auditor should issue a qualified opinion, stating that 'except for' the matters identified the financial statements are fairly presented.

(2)   Provision

Matters

A provision for 7% of one month's sales would total $328 million ($56,360m/ 12 × 7%). Reducing it to 4% would create a provision of $188 million ($56,360m/ 12 × 4%). As a result of the change in calculation, the amount of the provision would be reduced by $140 million.

As well as reducing the provision recognised on the statement of financial position, the release of the provision would also increase the profit reported by $140 million. At 5.5% of profit and 0.37% of total assets, the adjustment is material to the statement of profit or loss but not to the statement of financial position.

This is clearly a matter of judgement. The change must, however, be reasonable and supported by evidence that it is more appropriate to the circumstances of the business. The audit team has found no evidence to support the change made by management.

The risk associated with this is heightened because the release of provisions is a known earnings management technique and Basking Co has suffered a reduction in profits this year. The auditor must apply professional scepticism in these circumstances and be aware that management may be using this as a device to restore profits to help achieve their annual targets.

In these circumstances, it would be appropriate to ask the management team of Basking Co for some form of evidence that the change to their system will lead to a lower rate of refunds. In the absence of any evidence the auditor should explain that the change is purely speculative and as it appears to be unjustified at the present time, that Basking Co should revert back to the original provision until there is evidence of improved effectiveness.

Opinion

If management refuses to amend the provision, it is likely that the auditor will conclude that the financial statements are materially misstated. In isolation it is unlikely that the auditor will conclude that this is a pervasive matter as it has limited impact on the financial statements as a whole.

In these circumstances, the auditor should issue a qualified opinion, stating that 'except for' the matters identified the financial statements are fairly presented.

(b)   **New computer system**

Basking Co is a listed entity therefore a Key Audit Matters (KAM) section will be required in the auditor's report.

These are matters that, in the auditor's professional judgement, were of most significance in the audit and required significant attention during the audit and are selected from matters communicated with those charged with governance.

Examples of matters to be included in a KAM are areas of significant audit risk and areas requiring significant auditor judgement relating to areas of the financial statements.

In the auditor's report of Basking Co, the KAM section should include a reference to the audit risk related to accuracy and completeness of revenue as a result of the new computer system.

The KAM should detail why this was considered to be an area of significance in the audit and therefore determined to be a KAM.

It should also explain how the matter was addressed in the audit and the auditor should provide a brief overview of the audit procedures adopted such as tests of controls over the new system and substantive tests over revenue.

(c)   **Global audit reform**

The main audit reform proposals centre on enhancing auditor independence and increasing competition.

Fees

Despite restrictions on the level of fees which can be earned from listed clients before safeguards need to be applied, the amount of fees earned continues to create a significant self-interest threat which provides incentive for auditors to allow inappropriate accounting treatments to go uncorrected and unreported.

The IESBA has revised the International Code of Ethics for Professional Accountants to require audit firms to cease to act as auditor for a public interest entity (PIE) if fee dependency continues for five consecutive years. This requirement has applied in some countries, such as the UK, for some time.

In addition, the revised IESBA Code introduced fee dependency limits for non-listed clients and now states that independence is threatened if fees exceed 30% of the firm's total fees for five consecutive years.

The Codes of Ethics also state that the provision of non-audit services should not influence the audit fee and the audit fee should be a standalone fee.

Provision of other services to audit clients

The Codes of Ethics which apply to auditors contain restrictions on the type of services which can be provided to PIEs, however services are still being provided and result in a significant self-review threat when auditors then have to audit transactions and balances they, or their firm, helped to create.

One proposal is to break up accountancy firms so that firms can only provide audit services or other accountancy services, but not both, to eliminate the self-review threat.

A less severe proposal is for firms to have an organisational split, rather than a structural split, whereby the audit division of an accountancy firm is separated from the rest of the organisation and has its own separate management team, chief executive and board.

Both of these proposals would potentially see more work being taken on by mid-tier firms which would reduce dependency on a client, reduce the level of familiarity between the firm and client, and provide increased competition for audit and accountancy services.

Mandatory firm rotation (MFR)

Familiarity due to long association with an audit client results in reduced professional scepticism and objectivity. The Codes of Ethics and corporate governance regulations require some element of rotation of senior audit personnel or the firm or both. These vary by country.

MFR would require the company to replace the audit firm periodically. In the UK this is every 20 years provided there has been a competitive tender after ten years. In South Africa, audit firms must be rotated after ten years.

Benefits of MFR include the new audit firm taking a fresh look at the company which may identify inappropriate accounting practices which the previous audit firm had either not identified or had been reluctant to raise with the client for fear of upsetting the relationship that had been established. It may also open the door for more mid-tier firms to audit PIEs as audit firms will have to wait a number of years before being able to be tender for the audit again.

However, many countries that once required MFR have since removed the restriction due to adverse effects. A higher probability of errors was found in first year audits due to a lack of knowledge of the client and this caused a reduction in audit quality rather than the desired increase. Another disadvantage of MFR is the additional costs involved for both the client and the audit firm. The client will need to provide additional assistance to the incoming audit firm in the first year or two in obtaining an understanding of the company and its environment. The audit firm may actually apply less professional scepticism in the first year or two when they should be increasing professional scepticism in order to save time and recoup the additional costs incurred in the early years.

Joint audits

To overcome the issue of a loss of knowledge about an entity which arises with MFR, joint audits have been proposed for PIEs. A joint audit is where two or more firms are responsible for the audit with one of the firms being a non-Big 4 firm. However, many big firms are reluctant for this change as they are concerned that the smaller firms do not have the competence or experience to be involved with such large audits.

State appointed auditor

Another suggestion is that instead of the company appointing its own auditor, the government should appoint an auditor for it to reduce any threats of familiarity or conflicts of interest in the process. This is not a common practice at present.

Increased disclosure by audit firms on how the audit has been performed

Investigations by regulators have identified that in many cases, audit work is performed by staff with little or insufficient experience, and the level of supervision and review required for such work is inadequate. In the case of one audit failure, the audit partner was found to have spent just two hours on the client and the manager in charge had only one year of post-qualification experience.

A proposal to address this issue is for auditors to report on audit team composition, time spent on the audit engagement by each grade of person, the profitability of the engagement to the firm and the level of audit partner remuneration.

Tutorial note

Audit failures have been a frequent occurrence since the 2008 global financial crisis. Some of the highest profile cases include Wirecard, Patisserie Valerie, Petrobras, Steinhoff and Carillion. Failures of large listed entities affect the company, the individual shareholders, pension funds of millions of people who invest in them, and the employees and their families. Stakeholders other than the company and its shareholders as a body have no legal right to compensation from the audit firm as there is no duty of care owed to them.

In Britain, only 75% of the sample of audits from the 350 largest-listed companies for the year ending December 2017 met quality standards. In the UK, the Big 4 firms have a target of 90% of audits to be assessed as 'Good' and in 2019, none of the firms achieved this target. Some firms have only achieved a 'Good' rating on half of the audits inspected. A report by the Public Company Accounting Oversight Board (PCAOB) in the USA found that 31% of audits conducted by Big 4 firms were inadequate. Despite this failure rate, the number of enforcement actions and the level of fines issued is insignificant in comparison. As such, auditors do not have sufficient incentive to improve the quality of their work.

The main reasons given for the failures is a lack of auditor independence, including a failure by the auditor to sufficiently challenge management, and a lack of competition in the audit market leading to a level of complacency auditors.

Examiner's comments

Candidates were required to cover what should be discussed with management and the effect on the audit opinion of two accounting issues. This was well answered by well-prepared candidates however a significant portion of candidates failed to calculate materiality correctly. There was also a lack of appreciation that related party transactions are material by nature. Candidates should note that the requirement specifically asked for the effect on the audit opinion not the full auditor's report so there was no credit available for describing the basis of opinion. There are still a number of candidates who show a lack of understanding of misstatements and propose emphasis of matter paragraphs as an alternative to qualifying the opinion for factual misstatements or to explain immaterial/trivial items.

		ACCA Marking guide	
			Marks

(a) In general, up to 1 mark for each relevant and adequate point of explanation. ½ mark should be awarded for relevant points which are either too brief or poorly explained.

(1)   Loan
- Related party transaction
- Material by nature
- Requires full disclosure in the financial statements
- Failure to adjust leads to a material but not pervasive misstatement
- Qualified opinion

Maximum   **4**

(2)   Provision
- Calculation of potential provision values and value of adjustment
- Adjustment is material to statement of profit or loss
- Matter of judgement – must be reasoned and supported with evidence
- Potential for earnings management
- Request management to reinstate full provision
- Failure to adjust leads to a material but not pervasive misstatement
- Qualified opinion

Maximum   **5**

(b)   New computer system
- Listed company therefore KAM required
- KAM – matters of significance during the audit requiring extra attention and selected from those charged with governance
- Examples of matters to be included in a KAM section
- KAM should detail audit risk related to revenue
- KAM should detail why it was an area of significance
- KAM should detail how the matter was addressed

Maximum   **5**

(c)   Global audit reform
In general, up to 1 mark for each relevant and adequate point of explanation unless otherwise indicated. ½ mark should be awarded for relevant points which are either too brief or poorly explained.
- General discussion of need for reforms
- Reducing fee dependency
- Structural split of accountancy firms to prevent provision of non-audit services to audit clients
- Organisational split of accountancy firms
- Restrictions of provision of other services will reduce dependency and familiarity and increase competition
- Mandatory firm rotation (up to 3 marks)
- Joint audits
- State appointed auditor
- Increased disclosure by audit firms of team composition, time spent on the audit, profitability, partner remuneration

Maximum   **6**

Professional marks

Analysis and evaluation

- Effective analysis and identification of issues and omissions in the draft auditor's report
- Appropriate use of the information to support discussion, draw appropriate conclusions and design appropriate responses
- Appropriate recommendations in relation to necessary actions which reflect the stage of engagement
- Balanced assessment of the information to determine the appropriate audit opinion in the circumstances

Professional scepticism and judgement

- Effective challenge and critical assessment of the conduct and extent of the audit work and evidence obtained with appropriate conclusions
- Appropriate application of professional judgement to draw conclusions and make informed decisions about the actions which are appropriate in the context and stage of the engagement

Commercial acumen

- Inclusion of appropriate recommendations regarding how Those Charged with Governance and the audit firm should respond to the situation
- Demonstrates awareness of wider external factors or implications, for the audit profession in relation to audit reform proposals

Maximum	5
Total	25

31 MAGNOLIA GROUP *Walk in the footsteps of a top tutor*

Top tutor tips

Part (a) of the requirement asks for quality and other professional issues raised in relation to three subsidiaries. Quality management is a common topic in the exam. Consider whether the audit has been performed in accordance with professional standards and whether the auditor has conducted the work with due professional care. Consider how you would have audited the matters described and whether the auditor has performed those procedures. If not, include them as further actions and procedures.

For part (b) you need to state the impact to the auditor's report if the client does not amend the financial statements. State the impact to both the report and opinion as a result of the issues. When considering the impact to the group auditor's report you must consider whether the issue affecting the subsidiary is material to the group as a whole.

(a) Quality of audit planning and performance

(i) Hyacinth Co – internal controls and results of control testing

Where assessment of internal controls at the initial stage of the audit concludes that controls are ineffective there is no necessity to perform tests of controls, which was an incorrect response in the Group audit. Tests of controls should not be performed in order to confirm that controls are not effective.

According to ISA 330/ISA (UK) 330 *The Auditor's Response to Assessed Risks*, the auditor should only use tests of control as a method of gathering evidence where there is an expectation that controls are operating effectively.

The correct response should have been to increase substantive audit procedures around the area of intra-group transactions. Given that the Group companies supply each other with chemical products to use in their manufacturing processes, the volume and monetary amount of the intra-group transactions could be significant. Related party transactions are often an area of significant risk and intra-group balances can be an easy way to manipulate the individual company accounts.

The comment made by the audit manager that 'no further work is necessary' on the intra-group transactions seems to be based on the concept that intra-group balances are cancelled in the Group financial statements at consolidation. This is true, but audit work should be performed on these transactions because they will still be recognised in the individual financial statements and audit evidence should be obtained to support the value of the transactions and balances. Further, if these balances have not been appropriately reconciled, this could create significant issues on consolidation.

In addition, if no audit work is performed on the intra-group transactions then no assurance can be obtained over the value of adjustments made during the consolidation process to eliminate them. Also audit work should be performed to determine the validity of any provision for unrealised profit recognised in the Group financial statements. There does not appear to be any audit evidence at all to support the necessary consolidation adjustments which is a significant deficiency in the quality of the group audit. It seems that the communications between Group and component auditors is not robust. The instructions given by Crocus & Co to the component auditors seem to lack detail, for example, Crocus & Co should be instructing the component auditors to carry out specific procedures on intra-group balances and transactions.

In relation to controls over capital (asset) expenditure, it is not appropriate to conclude that controls will be effective across the Group just because they are effective in one of the Group components. Testing the controls in one component cannot provide assurance that the control risk in the other components is at the same level. This is particularly the case for Geranium Co, which is a recent acquisition, and Crocus & Co has no previous knowledge of its control environment and processes.

It is possible that the audit of capital (asset) expenditure in the Group components other than Hyacinth Co is not of acceptable quality due to over-reliance on controls over which no assurance has been obtained. The instructions given to the component auditors may not have been based on an appropriate audit strategy in relation to the audit of capital (asset) expenditure.

Crocus & Co, in its evaluation of the work performed by the component auditors, should have assessed the level of testing which was performed on Daisy Co and Geranium Co's internal controls over capital (asset) expenditure, and the conclusions which were drawn. Sufficient and appropriate audit evidence may not have been obtained, leading to a risk of material misstatement of property, plant and equipment.

Further actions to be taken

The deficiencies in internal control over intra-group transactions should be brought to the attention of Group management. ISA 600 / ISA (UK) 600 *Special Considerations – Audits of Group Financial Statements (Including the Work of Component Auditors)* requires that the group engagement team shall determine which identified deficiencies in internal control to communicate to those charged with governance and group management. This should include group-wide controls and controls over the consolidation process.

The audit working papers for the component companies should be reviewed to establish if any audit procedures on intra-group balances and transactions have been performed at the company level.

In respect of the audit work on capital (asset) expenditure, the Group audit team should firstly determine the materiality of expenditure in each component and if material, ensure that further substantive audit procedures are performed either by the component auditor or by the Group audit team.

(ii) Geranium Co – new subsidiary

Audit planning and performance

The audit manager's conclusion that Geranium is immaterial to the Group financial statements is based on the profit to be consolidated, which amounts to 2% of Group profit before tax. However, the assets of Geranium Co amount to 23.1% of Group total assets and therefore the subsidiary is material to the Group on that basis.

The Group audit team should consider whether Geranium Co should be visited for audit work to be performed. According to ISA 600 (Revised), matters influencing whether a component should be visited include newly formed components or components in which significant changes have taken place. As Geranium Co was acquired during the year and represents a material amount of Group assets, it is likely that audit procedures should encompass more than just analytical procedures.

The audit evidence obtained by the group audit team in respect of Geranium Co therefore needs to be more robust in order for the Group audit manager to reach a conclusion on its balances which will be consolidated.

The lack of audit working papers indicates that there has been no communication with the component auditors. This is a significant quality problem and a breach of ISA 600 which requires that the group audit team obtains an understanding of the component, and communicates matters relevant to risk assessment, related party transactions and going concern, which will impact the component auditor's design of work.

This is especially the case given that Geranium Co is a new component of the group, and this is Crocus & Co's first experience of working with their auditors.

Further actions to be taken

The component auditor's independence and competence should be evaluated, and procedures should be performed to evaluate whether the component auditor operates in a regulatory environment which actively oversees auditors. These could be achieved through a discussion with the component auditor and requesting them to complete a questionnaire on these matters for evaluation by the group audit team.

The Group audit team should liaise with the component auditor as soon as possible in order to discuss their audit findings, obtain access to their working papers, and ultimately decide on the specific nature of the further procedures to be performed.

(iii) **Daisy Co – restriction on international trade**

Audit planning and performance

The new government environmental regulations which have imposed restrictions on international trade could create a significant risk of material misstatement at the group level.

A risk arises in relation to the goodwill balance, which is material at 2.3% of group assets. The government regulation is an indicator that goodwill could be impaired, but an assessment of goodwill is required regardless of the existence of such indicators.

The audit working papers will need to be carefully reviewed to ascertain the extent of work, if any, which has been performed on the goodwill of Daisy Co. The audit manager's comment that the issue has no impact on the consolidated accounts implies that this matter may not have been factored into any goodwill assessment which has taken place as part of audit procedures. Therefore, the quality of the audit evidence to support the goodwill balance of $3 million is in doubt.

It is not sufficient to rely solely on the audit opinion issued by Foxglove & Co. ISA 600 (Revised) requires the Group auditor to evaluate the appropriateness of the audit procedures performed by the component auditor.

There is a risk that not all of the implications of the government regulations have been addressed by Foxglove & Co during their audit. For example, they should have considered the overall going concern status of the company, and the impact on the valuation of property, plant and equipment as well as inventories.

There is also a risk that does not appear to have been considered by the Group audit manager in that the government regulation may affect other components of the group due to Daisy Co's role in the group of developing and providing products to the other group companies, and therefore any restrictions on Daisy Co's operations may affect all the other components of the group. This issue may also raise concerns over the work which has been conducted in relation to ISA 250/ISA (UK) 250 *Consideration of Laws and Regulations in an Audit of Financial Statements* and there is a risk that the Group auditor's assessment of the legal and regulatory framework that affects the Group has not been sufficiently understood or documented.

The fact that the Group's board members have not mentioned the regulation to the Group audit manager could indicate that the Group's management is trying to hide the situation from the auditor. The audit manager should exercise professional scepticism and enquire further into the matter, as discussed below. If the Group's management were genuinely unaware of the new regulations then corporate governance, especially in relation to risk monitoring and assessment would appear to be deficient. This impacts on the audit by increasing the risk of management bias and actions of management which may deliberately mislead the auditor.

In summary, this situation indicates a lack of quality in the group audit due to the over reliance on the audit findings of the component auditor. In addition, the group audit manager seems not to have considered the wider implications of the government regulation on the risk assessment for the group as a whole.

Further actions to be taken

Request the audit working papers from Foxglove & Co and review the work performed on the government regulation and its impact on the financial statements and going concern.

The group assessment of going concern will need to be re-evaluated, taking into account the impact of the government regulation on the other Group companies. Given that the Group sells products in over 50 countries, it is likely that it is not just Daisy Co which is affected by this new regulation, and additional audit work should be performed on evaluating the going concern status of each company and of the Group as a whole.

Conclusion

Overall, the problems noted in the Group audit indicate that the Group audit manager lacks competence, and that inappropriate judgements have been made. There are several instances of ISA requirements not being followed and the audit has not been performed with sufficient due care for professional standards. The Group audit manager should receive training on Group accounting and Group audit issues in order to resolve the deficiencies identified in the planning and performance of this audit, and to ensure that future audits are managed appropriately.

(b) **Auditor's opinion and report**

Daisy Co

The financial statements of Daisy Co will be materially misstated if the required disclosure is not made.

The auditor must use professional judgement to determine whether the effect is material but not pervasive or material and pervasive.

Assuming it is material but not pervasive, a qualified opinion should be expressed, with the auditor stating in the opinion that except for the effects of the matters described in the basis for qualified opinion paragraph, the financial statements show a true and fair view.

The basis for qualified opinion should contain a description of the matters giving rise to the qualification.

Magnolia Group

The impact to the group auditor's report will depend on whether the going concern status of the group as a whole is affected.

If there are no material uncertainties affecting the group's status, an unmodified opinion and report will be issued.

If the going concern issues affect the group, group management may make adequate disclosure which will result in an unmodified opinion. The auditor's report would need to include a Material Uncertainty Related to Going Concern section which would draw the user's attention to the client's disclosure note.

If management do not make the required disclosure in the consolidated financial statements, the auditor's opinion would be modified in the same way as for Daisy Co, with a qualified opinion.

Examiner's comments

This question focused on a group audit with component auditors and audit issues in each of the subsidiaries. This question was not well-answered overall with many candidates appearing not to understand the concept of the level of control required by the group auditor and the amount of instruction and interaction required with component auditors.

Part (a) considered a poorly-planned audit where the audit manager had concluded at the interim audit that intra-group balances which were not being properly accounted for did not matter "as they were eliminated on consolidation" yet he repeated the same tests and reliance on controls at the final audit. Candidates seemed unable to grasp that, because of the control failures, substantive work (such as reconciliations) was required and that this control failure should be highlighted to management at the interim stage so they could take steps to resolve these issues in advance of the final audit. Additionally, the manager tested capital (asset) expenditure controls in only one subsidiary and concluded that those results could be applied to the rest of the group without further testing. Many candidates discussed generically how to audit capital (asset) expenditure and did not consider the relevant issues raised in the scenario and that it would be necessary to evaluate the work of the component auditors and identify what additional procedures might be required.

The second subsidiary had been acquired during the year and had a different auditor. Candidates generally failed to recognise that the role of the component auditor is firstly to audit the subsidiary for its whole financial year, regardless of the change of ownership. Most did not appreciate that the group auditor needs to issue instructions to the component auditor, assess their competence and independence and review and document their work as part of the group audit. Incorrectly blaming the component auditor for a poorly-planned group audit showed a lack of knowledge of the fundamentals of how a group audit works.

The third subsidiary had a potential going concern issue but the component auditors had concluded that there was not a significant risk. Strong answers proposed a more detailed review of the component auditor's work and conclusions along with an assessment of their competence and then considered the impact on the group as a whole. It is evident that there is poor understanding that goodwill arising in the consolidated accounts is held in the consolidated statement of financial position and not in the financial statements of the subsidiary and that assessing any potential impairment is the role of the group auditor, not the component auditor. Candidates are advised to make sure that they are knowledgeable of the requirements of the ISAs in this area.

ACCA Marking guide	
	Marks
Generally, 1 mark for each relevant point identified and explained. Allow maximum 1 mark for comments on the competence of the Group audit manager and the need for additional training. These marks can be awarded in any section of the question.	
(a) **(i)** **Hyacinth Co** **Quality of audit work**	
– Performing tests of controls not an appropriate response where controls are deficient	
– Intra-group balances and transactions should be audited even if cancelled on consolidation	
– If not performed then the cancellation and determination of provisions for unrealised profit may not be correct	
– Inappropriate assumption on the strength of group-wide controls. The work of component auditors on capital (asset) expenditure controls should have been evaluated	
– Audit evidence may be lacking on capital (asset) expenditure and property, plant and equipment	
Further actions	
– Communicate with those charged with governance on the control deficiency	
– Review working papers on components for evidence on intra-group balances	
Maximum	6
(ii) **Geranium Co** **Quality of audit work**	
– Assessment of materiality in relation to the Group	
– Consider whether Geranium Co should be visited for audit work to be performed	
– Audit evidence from analytical review is insufficient to support group audit opinion	
– Understanding of the component should have been obtained and matters communicated relevant to the component auditor's procedures	
Further actions	
– Obtain understanding of independence, competence and regulatory framework of Fern & Co	
– Liaise with Fern & Co in order to obtain more information and decide on nature of further audit procedures	
Maximum	4
(iii) **Daisy Co** **Quality of audit work**	
– Goodwill relating to Daisy Co likely to be overstated – not identified by audit manager	
– Cannot rely solely on component auditor's opinion	
– Group auditor must evaluate the procedures performed by the component auditor	
– Further impacts may not have been identified e.g. impairment of other assets	
– Impact on other group components and group going concern should be evaluated	
– Lack of audit manager's professional scepticism and increased audit risk	

		Further actions		
		– Request working papers of Foxglove & Co for review		
		– Re-evaluate Group going concern assessment		
		Maximum	**5**	

(b)   **Auditor's opinion and report**
Generally up to 1 mark for each relevant point explained
Daisy Co
–   Lack of disclosure – material misstatement
–   Discussion of whether it is pervasive
–   Qualified opinion
–   Basis for qualified opinion paragraph
Magnolia Group
–   Depends on whether going concern of group is affected
–   Unmodified opinion if not affected
–   Unmodified opinion with additional communication (MURTGC) if disclosure made
–   Qualified opinion if disclosure not made

Maximum	**5**

Professional marks
Analysis and evaluation
–   Appropriate use of the information to support discussion, draw appropriate conclusions and design appropriate responses
–   Appropriate assessment of the quality and professional issues raised, using examples where relevant to support overall comments
–   Effective appraisal of the information to make suitable recommendations for appropriate courses of action
–   Balanced assessment of the information to determine the appropriate audit opinion in the circumstances
Professional scepticism and judgement
–   Effective challenge and critical assessment of the evidence supplied with appropriate conclusions
–   Demonstration of the ability to probe into the reasons for quality issues including the identification of missing information or additional information which would be required
–   Appropriate application of professional judgement to draw conclusions and make informed comments regarding the quality of the work carried out
Commercial acumen
–   Inclusion of appropriate recommendations regarding the additional actions required by the firm
–   Appropriate recognition of the wider implications on the engagement, the audit firm and the company

Maximum	**5**

Total		**25**

32 OSIER *Walk in the footsteps of a top tutor*

Top tutor tips

For 'Matters and evidence' questions, use the 'MARE' approach to make it easier to score the required number of marks. First, consider the materiality of the issue. Next discuss the appropriate accounting treatment and give the risks of material misstatement that would arise if the appropriate treatment is not followed. Finally, the evidence is what you would expect to be recorded on the audit file when you come to review it. Be specific about the evidence, don't just say 'supporting documentation', suggest what that documentation would be and what it would show. Assume that half of the marks will be for matters and half of the marks will be for evidence.

In part (b) you need to determine whether or not the audit opinion should be modified. Identify the type of opinion required considering whether the misstatement is not material; material but not pervasive; or material and pervasive. Then go on to discuss any other impact to the auditor's report such as an explanation as to why the opinion is modified or any additional communications required.

(a) (i) Cost of inventory

Matters

Materiality

Inventory costs represent 1.1% of total assets and 19.6% of profit. Inventory is therefore material to both the statement of financial position and the statement of profit or loss.

Risk of material misstatement

The calculation of the cost of inventory is complex. This complexity increases the risk of error in the calculation, which increases the risk of misstatement.

The calculation is also subject to a number of estimates; the average production time per unit, the forecast annual wage cost, the scheduled hours of production and the forecast units of production are all estimates. These estimates increase the risk of both error and manipulation of the calculation to suit management's bias.

Given both the complexity and subjectivity involved in the calculation there is a significant risk that the inventory cost may be misstated.

Evidence expected to be on file

– Documentation of the system for obtaining the data used in the costing exercise and calculating the final cost. This should identify the key controls that operate in this system and there should be evidence on file that these controls have been appropriately tested.

– A copy of the summary of inventory purchase costs. A sample of the purchase costs, including the additional costs of transport and handling, should have been confirmed through inspection of original purchase invoices, copies of which should also be on file.

- Documentation of the results of a discussion with the production manager to ascertain how they estimate the average production time per unit of inventory. Any calculations referred to by management should have been reperformed by the audit team to confirm their mathematical accuracy and agreed to corroborating documentation.

- A copy of the calculation of the forecast annual wage cost. The initial staffing levels should have been confirmed through inspection of current human resource records and for a sample of the staff their initial wages should have been confirmed through inspection of payroll records.

- Forecast wage increments should have been agreed to either post-year-end confirmation issued by human resources or minutes of board meetings approving pay rises.

- Documentation of the results of a discussion with management regarding how the forecast is made and who is ultimately responsible for reviewing and approving the forecast.

- A copy of the calculation of forecast units of production. This should have been analytically reviewed in comparison to the previous year's production levels. Where there are significant differences explanations should have been sought from management.

- A copy of the calculation of forecast production overheads. This should have been analytically reviewed by category of overhead in relation to the previous year to identify any significant variances. Corroborating evidence, such as rental and utilities agreements, should have been obtained where possible.

- Evidence on all management's schedules that the figures have been recalculated by the audit team to confirm the mathematical accuracy of management's calculations.

(ii)   Impairment

Matters

Materiality

The impairment of $9 million represents 0.47% of total assets and 8.41% of profit. While it is not material to the statement of financial position it is material to the statement of profit or loss.

Calculation of recoverable amount

The fair value of the retail outlets, the disposal costs and the value in use are all management estimates. This increases the risk of material misstatement through both error and management manipulation of the reported figures.

In particular, while the estimate for the fair value appears to have a reasonable basis, the estimate of value in use appears to be too basic. The assumption that the cash flows attributable to the whole of the retail division will grow at 1% per annum is too simplistic and appears to lack commercial justification. It is likely that each retail outlet will be subject to regional variations in growth and growth rates will also be subject to annual fluctuations based upon economic variables. There is also no justification as to why 1% growth has been selected to represent 'poor performance', at the very least this should be benchmarked to more widespread and reliable growth forecasts, e.g. national forecasts of economic growth.

Allocation of the impairment

The impairment has been allocated against all of the tangible assets in the cash generating unit. This is incorrect; as a cash generating unit the impairment should firstly be allocated against any goodwill relating to the cash generating unit in accordance with IAS 36 *Impairment of Assets*. It should then be allocated against the remaining assets on a pro-rata basis bearing in mind that an asset should not be impaired below the highest of either its fair value less costs of disposal or its value in use.

Evidence expected to be on file

– Copies of the offers received to purchase the retail outlets, confirming the amounts offered. These should have been used to recalculate the average used for the estimate of fair value.

– Documentation of enquiries with management with regard to how they estimated the disposal costs and what experience they have had with the sale of similar operations.

– A copy of the forecast cash flows attributable to the retail outlets. This should contain evidence of analytical review in comparison to the year ended 31 March 20X5 to confirm the accuracy of the base cash flows.

– Evidence of a recalculation of the future cash flows using management's estimates of 1% growth to confirm the mathematical accuracy of management's calculation.

– Evidence of a recalculation of the value in use using a range of growth rates to assess the sensitivity of management's calculations to economic variables. The differences between these valuations and management's valuation should have been reviewed to assess the likelihood of a material under or overvaluation.

– Evidence of an analytical review of performance by retail outlet or geographical area of operations, referenced to sales and cash flow records where available, to confirm whether growth rates are consistent across the brand or whether there are variances.

– Documentation of enquiries with management relating to their expectations for specific retail outlets or areas of operations and whether there are any specific matters which they are aware of which may affect regional performance, e.g. the opening of new out-of-town shopping facilities or competitors setting up in the same location.

– A schedule of any goodwill included in the statement of financial position with analysis of its various components to assess whether any part is attributable to the retail outlets as a cash generating unit. This is specifically relevant to any acquired brands which may be sold through the retail stores or any retail brands acquired by Osier Co.

– A recalculation of the allocation of the impairment by the auditor, firstly against any goodwill determined to be attributable to the cash generating unit, then against the remaining assets pro rata.

– Copies of previous forecasts. Where the retail outlets forecast performance exceeds the 1% currently predicted by management there should be evidence of discussion with management to ascertain the reasons for changing their outlook.

(b)   **Auditor's report and opinion**

The misstatement of $9 million represents 0.5% of total assets and 8.4% of profit before tax. It is not, therefore, material to the statement of financial position but it is material to the statement of profit or loss.

The opinion will therefore be modified as a result of material misstatement.

The matter is unlikely to be considered pervasive as the required adjustment would not lead to a reported profit being restated as a loss and only the retail assets will be affected.

In these circumstances the auditor would issue a qualified audit opinion stating that 'except for' this matter the financial statements are fairly presented.

The auditor should also include a 'Basis for Qualified Opinion' paragraph below the opinion paragraph. This should describe and quantify the financial effects of the misstatement.

Examiner's comments

There were two scenarios where candidates were asked to describe the matters and audit evidence that would be expected in each. Overall there appeared to be a poor understanding of the accounting issues raised by the scenarios.

Part (ai) concerned the audit of manufactured inventory and the appropriate inclusion of overhead and labour costs. Most identified the need to check the components back to source documentation and review the reasonableness of the process but many candidates concentrated on discussing auditing and accounting standards rather than detailing the evidence that should have been gathered. However, this was the best answered of the three sections.

Part (aii) related to an impairment review of a retailer's property portfolio caused by diminishing shop sales countered by growing internet sales. Many candidates simply discussed whether or not an impairment review should be carried out as there were indicators of impairment (falling retail sales) but this was a given from the question as the review had already been undertaken. Few questioned whether it was reasonable to base the value in use on the assumption that sales would grow by 1% a year when in reality they were falling. Candidates appeared unwilling to challenge this underlying assumption which actually lacked commercial justification.

ACCA Marking guide	
	Marks

Generally, up to 1 mark for each well explained matter and 1 mark for each well explained piece of evidence recommended.
Note: Marks will be awarded for explanations of why calculations and balances are complex or subjective and how this affects their accuracy. Simple statements that calculations and balances are complex or subjective will be awarded a maximum of ½ mark each, where relevant.
(a)   (i)   **Cost of inventory**
               Matters
               –   Materiality
               –   Complexity of calculation
               – Subjectivity in calculation	

Evidence
- Documentation of systems and controls
- Summary of purchase costs and matching to purchase invoices
- Calculation of forecast wages matched to underlying HR and payroll records
- Confirmations of wage increments/rises
- Calculation of forecast production units reviewed in comparison to prior year
- Calculation of forecast overheads corroborated to new agreements

Maximum	7

(ii) Impairment
Matters
- Materiality
- Uncertainty relating to estimates
- Growth rate assumption in relation to value in use
- Allocation of impairment does not seem to be correct

Evidence
- Copies of offers for retail outlets
- Copy of forecast cash flows relating to retail outlets
- Recalculation of forecasts using management's predictions
- Analytical review by unit/geographical region to assess appropriateness of general growth rate
- Notes re discussion about retail prospects by area
- Schedule of goodwill analysed by division
- Recalculation of allocation of impairment
- Copies of previous forecasts

Maximum	9

(b) Auditor's opinion and report
Generally up to 1 mark for each relevant point explained
- Materiality calculation of misstatement
- Discussion of whether it is pervasive
- Qualified opinion
- Basis for qualified opinion paragraph

Maximum	4

Professional marks
Analysis and evaluation
- Appropriate use of the information to support discussion, draw appropriate conclusions and design appropriate responses
- Identification of omissions from the analysis or further analysis which could be carried out
- Balanced assessment of the information to determine the appropriate audit opinion in the circumstances

Professional scepticism and judgement
- Effective challenge of information, evidence and assumptions supplied and, techniques carried out to support key facts and/or decisions
- Appropriate application of professional judgement to draw conclusions and make informed decisions about the actions which are appropriate in the context and stage of the engagement

Maximum	5
Total	25

33 ROPE *Walk in the footsteps of a top tutor*

Top tutor tips

Part (a) requires skills from PFI engagements to be applied to the going concern work performed in an audit. The auditor will assess the reasonableness of forecasts prepared by management to evaluate their use of the going concern basis of accounting. Use exactly the same approach as you would use for a PFI engagement. Professional scepticism is still required as there may be going concern issues that management do not want to disclose and therefore the forecast may be based on unrealistic assumptions.

When dealing with the ethical and professional issues in part (b) remember to consider the significance of the issues as well as identifying them and explaining them. Safeguards should also be included in your answer.

(a) (i) The cash flow forecast of Rope Co

When a company has prepared a cash flow forecast as part of their assessment of going concern, in accordance with ISA 570 *Going Concern* the auditor needs to evaluate the reliability of the underlying data used to prepare the forecast and to determine whether there is adequate support for the assumptions underlying the forecast. There are a number of issues relating to the forecast which raise concerns about the assessment of Rope's going concern status and therefore warrant further investigation.

Receipts from customers

There was little growth in cash receipts in the second half of the year ended 30 April 20X5 (0.8%), yet in each consequent six-month period management predicts a significant rise in receipts of between 1.7% and 3.0%.

This could be based on overly optimistic forecasts in relation to sales growth for the same period. If sales forecasts are too optimistic, this could eliminate the forecast small positive cash flows, which could leave the company in a net overdraft position for the entire two-year period.

The movement in relation to customer receipts is a key assumption underpinning the return to a positive cash position and needs to be scrutinised further.

Salaries and other payments

While **annual** receipts from customers and payments to suppliers are forecast to rise during the forecast period by 8.5% and 9.4%, respectively, the amounts attributable to salaries and other operating payments are only forecast to rise by 4.1%.

Workings

$000's	Annual receipts	Annual payments	Salaries and other payments
20X7	14,950 + 15,400 = 30,350	11,600 + 12,000 = 23,600	1,301 + 1,353 + 1,951 + 1,925 = 6,530
20X5	13,935 + 14,050 = 27,985	10,725 + 10,850 = 21,575	1,250 +1,300 + 1,875 + 1,850 = 6,275
Difference	2,365	2,025	255
% increase	8.5%	9.4%.	4.1%

This is based on management's simple assumption of a general 2% annual inflation in these costs. This seems to be overly simplistic and will require further investigation. Salary costs could be forecast using a more sophisticated methodology based on required employee numbers and average wages/salaries.

The significant forecast increase in sales suggests that operating activities will increase over the next two years and it might be expected that staff requirements may increase in line with this. For similar reasons, it is likely that a larger increase in other operating costs would be required to match the increased administrative burden of producing and selling more goods and/or services.

Sale of investments

Management is planning to sell some investments in listed shareholdings for $500,000 to repay a loan to the chief executive. At 30 April 20X5, however, the fair value of the investments was only $350,000. As the fair value of these investments is revalued at the end of each year based upon the current share price, this is assumed to reflect the amount at which the shares were trading at the end of April. Management is therefore expecting the shares to increase in value by $150,000 in the space of two years, which represents a 43% rise. This is an extremely optimistic assumption in comparison to average rates of growth across most stock markets.

It therefore appears likely that there will be a shortfall in the amount raised to repay Mr Stewart. Rope Co will therefore have to supplement the amount received from selling investments with cash from other sources, which will lead to a reduction in the cash position in comparison to the forecasts.

Repayment of the bank loan

The bank loan is due for repayment 15 months after the year end. Management is assuming that they will be able to fund the repayment with a new loan facility from the same finance provider. Without any agreement in place from the provider, this represents a significant assumption.

Without a new facility Rope Co will have no means with which to repay their obligation, which could lead to the lender taking action to recover the loan amount. This could include seizing assets which were provided as security over the loan or commencing insolvency proceedings.

In either case, this could have a significant impact on Rope's ability to trade into the foreseeable future and, therefore, the loan repayment event represents a material uncertainty which may need to be fully disclosed in the financial statements of Rope Co.

Missing cash flows

There seems to be a lack of consideration of a number of non-operating cash flows which one might expect to see in a two-year forecast. For example, most companies maintain a practice of regular replacement of old, inefficient tangible non-current assets as opposed to making larger, less regular replacements which may create a significant drain on cash resources in one particular year. The forecast currently has no allocation for capital investment. In a similar fashion, there are no cash flows related to tax and dividend payments. It is possible that such transactions have been overlooked in the preparation of the forecast.

Further audit procedures

- Obtain a copy of the latest interim financial statements and compare the actual post-year-end sales performance with the forecast sales upon which the cash flow forecast is based.

- Discuss with management the rationale for the expected increase in customer receipts and where possible confirm this to customer correspondence, orders or contracts.

- Inspect the documentation detailing the terms of the loan with Mr Stewart to confirm the amount outstanding and the agreed date of repayment.

- Inspect the terms of the bank loan to confirm the final amount due for repayment, the date of repayment and whether any assets have been accepted as security for the loan.

- Enquire of management whether they have entered into any negotiations with their bank, or any other financial institution, to provide a replacement loan in August 20X6. If so, request corroborating evidence such as signed agreements, agreements in principle or correspondence with the financial institutions.

- Enquire of management whether they have any contingency plans in place to repay both loans on time should they not be able to raise the required amount through selling investments and obtaining new loan agreements.

- Perform an analytical review of actual monthly payroll costs incurred obtained from the payroll department. Include any available payment periods after 30 April 20X5 to help ascertain whether management's assumptions regarding salaries are appropriate. Seek corroborating evidence for any fluctuations in cost such as HR records confirming pay awards and changes in staff.

- Perform an analytical review of actual other operational costs and consider the level of other costs as a percentage of sales. Compare this to the levels included in the forecast. Investigate any significant differences.

- Corroborate the lack of investment in new tangible non-current assets by performing an analytical review of the levels of additions and disposals over the last, say, five years to see if this supports the absence of any allocation for this in the short-term future and consider this in light of our understanding of the entity and its production process.

- Compare the cash flow forecasts to any capital (asset) expenditure forecasts prepared by Rope Co to ensure that the cash flow forecast is consistent with this. Ask management to explain any differences identified.

- Review the non-current asset register and identify any assets with a zero or negligible carrying amount which could indicate that the assets have fulfilled their useful lives and are due for replacement.

- Inspect the bank ledger account/cash book post year end to see if there are any significant cash transactions which do not appear to have been included in the forecasts, in particular cash transactions relating to purchases or disposals of assets and dividend payments.

- Review the outcome of previous forecasts prepared by management to assess how effective management has been in the past at preparing accurate forecasts.

- Obtain written representations from management confirming that they have no intention to either purchase or dispose of non-current assets or to pay dividends over the next two years.

(a) (ii) **Matters relating to the loan from Mr J Stewart**

Related party transaction

As a key member of staff at Rope Co, the loan from the chief executive represents a related party transaction. As such, the transaction and related outstanding balances must be fully disclosed in the financial statements in accordance with IAS 24 *Related Party Disclosures*.

This means that the nature of the related party relationship, the nature and the amount of the loan, the amounts outstanding at the year end and the terms and conditions of the loan, including a description of the fixed charge, must be disclosed in the notes to the financial statements.

Interest free loan measurement

The loan was received during the current year ended 30 April 20X5. The loan liability should have been initially recorded at its fair value, which would normally be the transaction price of $500,000. IFRS 9 *Financial Instruments*, however, states that in the case of an interest free loan, the fair value should be measured as the present value of all future cash flows discounted using the prevailing market rates for similar instruments.

While it will be difficult to identify a similar instrument due to the nature of the relationship between the lender and the company, a similar instrument should be identified based upon the currency used, the loan term and any other similar factors, for example, a three-year $ loan from a bank.

At the year end, the outstanding loan liability should have been measured using the amortised cost method and the effective interest calculated should be recognised as a finance charge in the statement of profit or loss.

Further audit procedures

- Inspect the loan agreement to confirm the amounts loaned to the company, and the other relevant terms including the rate of interest, the repayment date and the associated penalties for late payment.

- Inspect the related party disclosures in the financial statements to ensure that they provide sufficient information and accurately reflect the terms and amounts relating to the transaction.

- Additional procedures will need to be performed regarding the completeness of related party transactions as the loan with Mr Stewart was not identified through normal audit procedures.

- The market rate used in the calculation of the fair value of the loan should be compared to a range of suitable instruments, e.g. three-year bank loans, to ascertain its appropriateness. Following this, the calculation should be checked for arithmetical accuracy.

- The amount recorded for the initial loan value and the year-end value should be recalculated using the appropriate discount factor and market rate to confirm the arithmetical accuracy of management's calculations.

- Review the loan liability recognised in the financial statements to ensure that the appropriate, discounted figure has been used.

- Reconcile the effective interest rate for 20X5 from the amortised cost calculation to the finance charges in the statement of profit or loss to confirm that this is appropriately included in profits.

(b) Ethical and professional issues

The request to attend a meeting with the company's bank can give rise to an advocacy threat to objectivity. An advocacy threat is the threat that a professional accountant will promote a client's or employer's position to the point that the professional accountant's objectivity is compromised.

In this case, the chief executive may want the audit engagement partner to support a view that Rope Co will be able to continue as a going concern and that the loan ultimately will be repaid. This means that the audit partner is promoting the client which leads to the creation of an advocacy threat.

In addition, from a legal perspective, the audit firm must be careful not to create the impression that they are in any way guaranteeing the future existence of the company or providing assurance on the draft financial statements. In legal terms, attending the meeting and promoting the interests of the client could create legal 'proximity', which increases the risk of legal action against the auditor in the event of Rope Co defaulting on any loan provided by the bank.

It may be possible for a partner other than the audit engagement partner to attend the meeting with the bank, which would be a form of safeguard against the ethical threat.

The audit firm's partner responsible for ethics should consider the severity of the threat and whether this, or another safeguard, could reduce the threat to an acceptable level.

An audit firm being threatened with dismissal from a client engagement represents an intimidation threat. The chief executive's actions should also lead to questions over his integrity.

The audit firm may wish to consider resigning from the audit if the threat becomes too severe.

Examiner's comments

Part (a) required candidates to appraise the forecast and suggest further procedures in assessing the use of the report as part of the going concern review during the audit. This was generally well answered by the majority of candidates attempting the question.

In the next part, candidates were required to discuss a loan from the chief executive to the company. This had been provided during the year being audited and the audit was still ongoing. Stronger candidates appropriately recognised this as a related party transaction and commented on the materiality and disclosure requirements before going on to describe procedures to perform. There were a significant number of candidates who had failed to take in to account the date the loan was provided and assumed it was missed in the prior year audit so instead focused their answers on a perceived lack of integrity of the directors, inappropriate levels of disclosure in prior year financial statements and audit qualifications.

The final requirement outlined the situation where the audit engagement partner had been asked to accompany the chief executive to a meeting with the bank where additional finance would be sought, and there was an intimidation threat in that the client had threatened to put the audit out for tender. Again, candidates generally did well on this requirement, identifying and explaining the correct ethical threats, and on the whole recommending appropriate courses of action. The only problem in some scripts was a focus on the lack of integrity of the chief executive, rather than discussing specific ethical threats raised.

ACCA Marking guide	Marks
Generally up to 1½ marks for each well explained matter and 1 mark for each well explained procedure recommended: (a) (i) **Cash flow forecast** **Matters** – Potential overestimation of cash receipts from customers – Lower than forecast sales may lead to net overdraft – Potential underestimation of salary and other operating payments – Simplistic assumption of cost inflation – Investments do not match management's forecast disposal valuation – Assumption of growth in value of investments is very optimistic – Ability to repay loans dependent upon other assumptions – Lack of specific consideration of non-operating cash flows **Procedures** – Review latest interim financial statements – Discuss forecast sales and customer receipts with management – Inspect J Stewart loan agreement – Inspect terms of bank loan – Enquire of management whether they have begun renegotiations regarding bank loan facility – Enquire with management about contingency plans – Perform analytical review of payroll costs – Perform analytical review of other operating costs – Inspect non-current asset registers – Inspect post-year-end bank ledger account/cash book – Review outcomes of previous management forecasts – Obtain written representations from management (max ½ mark)	
Maximum	10

	(ii)	**J Stewart loan**	
		Matters	
		– Provision of the loan represents a related party transaction	
		– Disclosure requirements of RPT	
		– Calculation of fair value for an interest free loan	
		– Determination of market rates for a similar instrument	
		– Valuation of loan at end of year using amortised cost method	
		Procedures	
		– Inspect terms of loan agreement	
		– Inspect related party disclosures in the financial statements	
		– Additional procedures in relation to potential other RPTs	
		– Compare market rate used to range of suitable instruments	
		– Recalculate initial and year-end loan amounts	
		– Reconcile effective interest rate from amortised cost calculation to statement of P&L	
		Maximum	**5**
(b)		**Ethical and professional issues**	
		Generally 1 mark for each point identified and discussed:	
		– Advocacy threat created by attending meeting	
		– Chief executive may want the engagement partner to support the going concern status of the company	
		– Legal proximity may be created by attending meeting	
		– Different partner should attend the meeting	
		– Ethics partner should consider severity of threat	
		– Intimidation threat from threat of removal from office	
		– Integrity of the chief executive questionable	
		– Consider resignation	
		Maximum	**5**

Professional marks

Analysis and evaluation

– Appropriate use of the information to support discussion, draw appropriate conclusions and design appropriate responses

– Identification of omissions from the analysis or further analysis which could be carried out

– Appropriate assessment of the ethical and professional issues raised, using examples where relevant, to support overall comments

Professional scepticism and judgement

– Effective challenge and critical assessment of the assumptions used by management in preparing the cash flow forecast

– Appropriate application of professional judgement to draw conclusions and make informed decisions about the actions which are appropriate in the context and stage of the engagement

– Demonstration of the ability to probe for further information in order to make an assessment of the completeness of the cash flow forecast

– Appropriate recommendations and justification of the assurance procedures to be undertaken in respect of the cash flow forecast

Commercial acumen

– Use of effective examples and/or calculations from the scenario to illustrate points or recommendations

– Demonstration of commercial awareness by recognising wider issues which may affect the forecast and the assumptions by management

Maximum	**5**
Total	**25**

34   BOSTON *Walk in the footsteps of a top tutor*

Top tutor tips

Part (a) (i) asks for matters to be discussed with management in relation to three uncorrected misstatements. You can take the same approach as a 'matters' question i.e. state whether the issue is material, the accounting treatment required and the risk to the financial statements.

For part (a) (ii) you need to state the impact to the auditor's report if the client does not amend the financial statements. Consider the aggregate effect of the misstatements to assess whether there is a material misstatement. State the impact to both the report and opinion as a result of the issues. Don't waste time stating the reporting implications if the issues are corrected as this is not part of the requirement.

Part (b) is a current issues question relating to climate-related risks. The examiner will often publish an article on current issues which are due to be examined therefore students are advised to keep checking the ACCA website for any new published articles.

(a)   (i)   Matters to discuss at meeting

During the completion stage of the audit, the effect of uncorrected misstatements must be evaluated by the auditor, as required by ISA 450/ ISA (UK) 450 *Evaluation of Misstatements Identified during the Audit*. This requires that the auditor obtains an understanding of management's reasons for not making recommended adjustments to the financial statements and that they take this into account when evaluating whether the financial statements as a whole are free from material misstatement.

In order to maintain accurate accounting records, management should be encouraged to record all misstatements to ensure that the risk of material misstatements in future periods is reduced due to the cumulative effect of immaterial uncorrected misstatements.

ISA 450 also requires that the auditor communicates with those charged with governance about uncorrected misstatements and the effect that they, individually or in aggregate, may have on the opinion in the auditor's report. Each of the matters included in the summary of uncorrected misstatements will be discussed below and the impact on the auditor's report considered individually and in aggregate.

Impairment

When performing an impairment test, in accordance with IAS 36 *Impairment of Assets*, the carrying amount of the asset (or cash generating unit) in question is compared to the recoverable amount of the asset. If the recoverable amount is lower than the carrying amount an impairment loss should be recognised, reducing the asset down from its carrying amount to the recoverable amount.

The recoverable amount is calculated as the higher of the fair value less costs to sell and value in use. In relation to the cash generating unit, Boston Co estimated that the greater of these two figures was the value in use at $3.5 million. This was compared to the carrying amount of $3.6 million and the asset has been impaired by $100,000 accordingly.

The findings of audit procedures carried out suggest that an inappropriate estimate was used in the calculation of value in use. Boston Co applied the company's annual growth rates when estimating the cash flows attributable to the cash generating unit. A more relevant estimate for the growth rates, specific to the cash generating unit, was available and should have been used.

This would have generated a value in use of $2.9 million which is lower than fair value less cost to sell of $3 million, and therefore $3 million should be used as the recoverable amount. As management already impaired the asset to $3.5 million, a further impairment of $500,000 is required to value it appropriately at $3 million.

At the meeting management should be asked why they used the company's forecast growth rates, rather than the factory's growth rates and whether any matters have arisen since the audit to suggest that the growth rates used by the audit team are now inappropriate.

The adjustment represents 7.8% of profit and 0.5% of total assets. While not material to the statement of financial position, it is material to profit.

If management does not adjust for this or provide justifications as to why their valuation is more appropriate, this will lead to a material misstatement of the financial statements.

Borrowing costs

Interest charges are borrowing costs. The borrowing costs relating to the construction of qualifying assets, such as property and plant, should be capitalised during the construction period, in accordance with IAS 23 *Borrowing Costs*.

As the manufacturing plant is not due for completion until November 20X6, it is still a qualifying asset and the interest should have been capitalised. Boston Co has incorrectly expensed the interest as part of the finance charges for the year.

The correcting adjustment is therefore to reduce finance charges and to add the interest to the cost of the asset on the statement of financial position.

The charges of $75,000 represent 1.2% of profit and 0.07% of assets so are not material to either profit or the statement of financial position.

Investment in Nebraska

The investment in Nebraska has been designated as fair value through profit or loss. As per IFRS 9 *Financial Instruments*, the value at the year end must be adjusted to reflect the fair value of the investment, and any gain or loss recognised in the statement of profit or loss.

The fair value of the investment at the year end is $643,500 (150,000 shares × $4.29). This represents an increase in the fair value of $43,500, which should be taken to the statement of profit or loss as a gain. The carrying amount of the investment should also be increased by this amount.

$43,500 represents 0.7% of profit and 0.04% of total assets. It is therefore not material individually to either profit or the statement of financial position.

(ii) **Impact on the audit opinion and auditor's report**

When considering their opinion, the auditor must conclude whether the financial statements as a whole are free from material misstatement. In order to do this, they must consider whether any remaining uncorrected misstatements are material, either on an individual basis or in aggregate.

The aggregate effect of the misstatements would be to overstate Boston Co's profit by $381,500 ($500,000 – $118,500). Total assets on the statement of financial position would also be overstated by this amount.

This represents 6% of profit and 0.4% of total assets. The overstatement would therefore be material to the statement of profit or loss on an aggregate basis but not to the statement of financial position.

However, as the necessary adjustment regarding the impairment of the factory building is individually material, management should be informed that if the valuation calculated by the audit team is more appropriate then failure to incorporate this adjustment will result in the auditor concluding that the financial statements are materially misstated. Based upon this, a modification to the audit opinion in accordance with ISA 705 *Modifications to the Opinion in the Independent Auditor's Report* will be required.

The type of modification depends on the significance of the material misstatement. In this case, the misstatement regarding the impairment is material to the financial statements, but is unlikely to be considered pervasive. This is supported by the fact that the adjustment is not material to the statement of financial position and it is therefore unlikely that the auditor will conclude that the financial statements as a whole are misleading.

A qualified opinion should be expressed, with the auditor stating in the opinion that the financial statements show a true and fair view 'except for' the effects of the matters described in the basis for qualified opinion paragraph.

The basis for qualified opinion paragraph should include a description of the matter giving rise to the qualification, including quantification of the financial effects of the misstatement.

The remaining uncorrected misstatements are, individually and in aggregate, immaterial to the financial statements and it will be at the discretion of management to amend and will have no impact on the auditor's report.

(b) **Climate-related risks (CRR) – impact on planning and performing the audit**

During the planning stage, the auditor must obtain an understanding of the entity, the industry in which the entity operates and its system of internal control. This will help the auditor understand the level of exposure the client has to CRR which must be taken into consideration when identifying and assessing risks of material misstatement and designing appropriate audit procedures.

Industries directly exposed to CRR include energy, agriculture, transportation, construction and manufacturing. Other industries may be indirectly exposed due to supply chain issues.

Companies directly exposed to CRR may have risks of material misstatement related to impairment of assets, provisions, going concern, adequacy of disclosures, amongst others.

When the auditor obtains an understanding of the entity's system of internal control, they must understand the components of internal control such as the entity's risk assessment process for identifying climate-related business risks which are relevant to financial reporting.

Due to the inter-relationship between risk and materiality, the assessment of CRR will also impact the determination of materiality, with preliminary materiality likely to be set at a lower amount for entities which are more exposed to CRR. The auditor must also consider the information needs of users and assess whether certain balances and disclosures affected by CRR will influence users' decisions as these may be material by nature.

Some governments have brought in requirements for disclosures relating to CRR and therefore as part of their consideration of laws and regulations, auditors will need to ensure compliance with these new requirements.

The results of the auditor's risk assessment will influence the design of appropriate audit procedures responsive to those risks. Where CRR are significant, procedures which provide more persuasive evidence will need to be performed to ensure sufficient and appropriate evidence is obtained, particularly in respect of balances affected by estimation uncertainty such as valuation of assets which may be affected by impairment.

For some areas such as estimation of energy resources (e.g. gas, fossil fuels) an auditor's expert may need to be used to provide audit evidence. The requirements of ISA 620 will therefore apply.

The going concern status of some entities may be uncertain for example where extreme weather is becoming more common causing devastating effects year on year. CRR will need to be taken into account by management when assessing the ability to continue as a going concern, and then by the auditor when evaluating management's use of the going concern basis of accounting, and when assessing the adequacy of disclosures of material uncertainties relating to going concern.

If the auditor is not satisfied that the financial statements are free from material misstatements related to climate issues, the auditor must consider the impact on the auditor's report and opinion. Even if climate-related issues are appropriately accounted for, there may be a need for additional communication in the auditor's report such as inclusion in the key audit matters section for a listed company or the need for a material uncertainty related to going concern paragraph where the client has adequately disclosed the issues.

Finally, where climate-related matters are included in the other published information within the annual report, and such information is made available to the auditor before the audit is finalised, the auditor will need to read this other information and report any misstatements in accordance with ISA 720.

Examiner's comments

The question set out three potential audit adjustments and candidates were required to discuss each, considering the individual and aggregate impact on the auditor's report. The values of each potential adjustment were given in the question so there were materiality marks available and many candidates scored these but performed less well in discussing the associated issues. Most of the adjustments were relatively straightforward such as the capitalisation of loan interest, and revaluation of investments and the issues around these were reasonably answered. The issue of impairment was less well answered.

There was significant inconsistency in answers where candidates concluded that an issue was not material but concluded that the audit opinion required modification. Furthermore, candidates need to ensure that they understand what Emphasis of Matter and Other Matters paragraphs are. They are not a substitute for a modified opinion and should only be used where there are significant issues that the auditor wants to bring to the attention of the users of the accounts.

ACCA Marking guide				Marks
(a)	(i)	**Summary of uncorrected misstatements**		
		In general up to 1 mark for each point of explanation and up to ½ mark for each appropriate calculation:		
		General comments		
		– Obtaining an understanding of management's reasons		
		– Encourage management to amend all misstatements		
		– Communicate effect of misstatements to TCWG		
		Impairment		
		– Explanation of original calculation		
		– Inappropriate estimates used		
		– Revised impairments		
		– Justification of the proposed adjustment		
		– Request further clarification at meeting		
		– Matter is material individually		
		Borrowing costs		
		– Capitalisation rules		
		– Qualifying asset		
		– Identification of incorrect treatment of interest costs		
		– Explanation of adjustment		
		– Not material individually		
		Investment		
		– Need to revalue investment to fair value at year end		
		– Calculation of fair value (½ max) and adjustment (½ max)		
		– Gain taken to statement of profit and loss		
		– Not material individually		
		Maximum		**9**
	(ii)	**Auditor's report**		
		Generally up to 1 mark for each point discussed		
		– Aggregate impact on financial statements		
		– Material to profit		
		– Impairment individually material		
		– Modification of opinion due to a material misstatement		
		– Discussion of whether it is pervasive		
		– Qualified opinion		
		– Basis for qualified opinion paragraph		
		– Remaining misstatements immaterial – no impact on the opinion		
		Maximum		**5**

(b)	**Climate-related risks (CRR)**		

(b)   **Climate-related risks (CRR)**
Generally up to 1 mark for each point discussed
– Understanding the entity, the industry, controls, exposure to CRR
– Identification of ROMM related to climate factors
– Understanding the entity's system of internal control including the entity's risk assessment process relevant to financial reporting with respect to CRR
– Impact on materiality assessment
– Consideration of laws and regulations
– Designing appropriate audit procedures responsive to risks
– Audit procedures for balances affected by estimation uncertainty
– Reliance on auditor's expert
– Going concern impact
– Audit reporting implications e.g. modified opinion, KAM, MURTGC
– Need to read other information and report any misstatements in accordance with ISA 720

                                                                 Maximum | **6**

Professional marks
Analysis and evaluation
– Appropriate use of the information to support discussion, draw appropriate conclusions and design appropriate responses
– Effective appraisal of the information to make suitable recommendations for appropriate courses of action
– Balanced assessment of the information to determine the appropriate audit opinion in the circumstances
Professional scepticism and judgement
– Effective challenge and critical assessment of the evidence supplied with appropriate conclusions
– Appropriate application of professional judgement to draw conclusions and make informed decisions about the actions which are appropriate in the context and stage of the engagement
Commercial acumen
– Inclusion of appropriate recommendations regarding current issues facing the firm
– Appropriate recognition of the wider implications on the engagement, the audit firm and the company

                                                                 Maximum | **5**

Total | **25**

35 MACAU & CO *Walk in the footsteps of a top tutor*

Top tutor tips

Part (a) requires evaluation of quality management, ethical and other professional matters arising. This is a regularly examined topic. Typical issues to look out for in such a question are: whether the work has been assigned to the appropriate level of staff, whether sufficient time has been allocated for the audit, whether ISAs have been followed (e.g. has sufficient appropriate evidence been obtained), whether any ethical threats have been addressed appropriately and whether adequate quality procedures have been performed in respect of the engagement such as adequate levels of supervision and review.

Part (b) is a typical completion requirement asking for matters to be considered at the completion stage of the audit. This is examined very frequently and the 'MAR' approach can help to provide structure to answers. MAR stands for:

Materiality – calculate whether the issue is material.

Accounting treatment – state the required treatment and why the client's treatment is wrong.

Risk – to the financial statements and the impact on the audit opinion if not corrected.

(a)   Quality management, ethical and professional matters

The audit of Stanley Co does not seem to have been performed with a high regard for the quality of the audit and there appear to be several ways in which the ISA requirements have been breached.

Materiality

First, it is not appropriate that the materiality level was determined at the planning stage of the audit but has not been reviewed or adjusted since. ISA 320/ISA (UK) 320 *Materiality in Planning and Performing an Audit* requires the auditor to determine materiality for the financial statements as a whole at the planning stage of the audit, and to revise it as the audit progresses as necessary where new facts and information become available which impact on materiality. It may be the case that no revision to the materiality which was initially determined is necessary, but a review should have taken place and this should be clearly documented in the audit working papers.

Audit of property, plant and equipment

The audit of the packing machine has not been properly carried out, and there seems to be a lack of sufficient, appropriate audit evidence to support the audit conclusion. The cost of the asset is material, based on the initial materiality, therefore there is a risk of material misstatement if sufficient and appropriate evidence is not obtained. By the year end, the asset's carrying amount is less than materiality, presumably due to depreciation being charged, but this does not negate the need for obtaining robust audit evidence for the cost and subsequent measurement of the asset.

The packing machine should have been physically verified. Obtaining the order and invoice does not confirm the existence of the machine, or that it is in working order. In addition, without a physical verification, the audit team would be unaware of problems such as physical damage to the machine or obsolescence, which could indicate impairment of the asset.

Relying on the distribution company to provide evidence on the existence and use of the asset is not appropriate. ISA 500/ISA (UK) 500 *Audit Evidence* states that audit evidence obtained directly by the auditor is more reliable than audit evidence obtained indirectly or by inference. External confirmations can be used to provide audit evidence but in this case the external confirmation should corroborate evidence obtained directly by the auditor, rather than be the only source of evidence. The relationship between Stanley Co and Aberdeen Co should also be understood by the auditor, and evidence should be obtained to confirm whether or not the two companies are related parties, as this would impact on the extent to which the external confirmation can be relied upon as a source of evidence.

Inventory count

In respect of the inventory count attendance, the audit team should have discussed the discrepancies with management as they could indicate more widespread problems with the inventory count. Given the comment that the inventory count appeared unorganised, it is possible that count instructions were not being followed or that some items had not been included in the count.

One of the requirements of ISA 501/ISA (UK) 501 *Audit Evidence – Specific Considerations for Selected Items* is that while attending an inventory count, the auditor shall evaluate management's instructions and procedures for recording and controlling the results of the entity's physical inventory counting.

It is not clear from the conclusion of the audit work whether the problems noted at the inventory count have been discussed with management. The auditor attending the inventory count should have raised the issues at the time and assessed whether a recount of all of the inventory was required.

Training may need to be provided to audit staff to ensure that they understand the auditor's role at an inventory count and can deal with problems which may arise in the appropriate manner.

The discrepancies noted at the inventory count should be subject to further audit work. The results of the test counts should be extrapolated over the population in order to evaluate the potential misstatement of inventory as a whole. The results should then be evaluated in accordance with ISA 450/ISA (UK) 450 *Evaluation of Misstatements Identified during the Audit* which requires that the auditor shall accumulate misstatements identified during the audit, other than those which are clearly trivial, and that misstatements should be discussed with management.

The issues raised by the way in which the inventory count was performed could represent a significant control deficiency and should be raised with those charged with governance in accordance with ISA 265 *Communicating Deficiencies in Internal Control to Those Charged with Governance and Management.*

Working paper review

The audit senior's comments in relation to the review by the manager and partner indicate that elements of ISA 220/ISA (UK) 220 (Revised) *Quality Management for an Audit of Financial Statements* have been breached. ISA 220 requires that the engagement partner shall, through a review of the audit documentation and discussion with the engagement team, be satisfied that sufficient appropriate audit evidence has been obtained to support the conclusions reached and for the auditor's report to be issued.

It appears that in this case the partner has not properly reviewed the working papers, instead relying on the audit senior's comment that there were no problems in the audit work. ISA 220 does state that the audit partner need not review all audit documentation, but only a 'quick look' at the working papers could indicate that areas of risk or critical judgement have not been reviewed in sufficient detail.

There is also an issue in that the manager and partner reviews took place at the same time and near the completion of the audit fieldwork. Reviews should happen on a timely basis throughout the audit to enable problems to be resolved at an appropriate time. Reviews should also be hierarchical and it appears that the audit partner has not reviewed the work of the audit manager.

Ethical considerations

Finally, there appears to be a potential threat to objectivity due to the audit engagement partner's brother providing a management consultancy service to the audit client. This amounts to a self-interest threat in that the partner's brother receives income from the audit client. The audit partner's objectivity is therefore threatened, and this is a significant risk due to his position of influence over the audit. He may even receive an introducer's commission from his brother.

The matter should be investigated further, and a senior member of the audit firm or the firm's partner responsible for ethics should discuss the comments made in Stanley Co's board minutes with Joe Lantau in order to evaluate the ethical threat and determine any necessary actions. The amount which is being paid to Mick Lantau should be made known, as well as whether the amount is a market rate, and whether other providers of management advice were considered by the company.

The partner's comments to the audit junior indicate a lack of integrity, and indicate that the partner may have something to hide, which increases the threat to objectivity. The audit partner may need to be removed from the audit and his work reviewed.

(b) Matters to consider and actions to take

The work in progress represents 4.7% of total assets and is therefore material to the statement of financial position. The deferred income is also material at 2.7% of total assets.

Even though the correspondence with BMC is dated after the end of the reporting period, BMC was suffering from financial problems during the year ending 31 March 20X5 which was notified to Kowloon Co before the year end. Therefore, the cancellation of the contract appears to meet the definition of an adjusting event under IAS 10 *Events after the Reporting Period* because it confirms conditions which existed at the year end.

Management must consider whether it is still appropriate to recognise the work in progress as an asset. According to IFRS 15 *Revenue from Contracts with Customers*, costs incurred to fulfil a contract are recognised as an asset if and only if all of the following criteria are met:

- The costs relate directly to a contract (or a specific anticipated contract)

- The costs generate or enhance resources of the entity which will be used in satisfying performance obligations in the future

- The costs are expected to be recovered.

The cancellation of the contract indicates that the costs of the work in progress are not recoverable from BMC, in which case the balance should be written off. Management is not planning to amend the balances recognised at the year end, and the audit team should investigate the reasons for this. Possibly management is asserting that the machine design costs could be utilised for a different contract, despite the fact that the machine was developed specifically for BMC.

Audit work should focus on the contractual arrangements between Kowloon Co and BMC, particularly in relation to the ownership of the rights to the design work which has taken place. If the design work has been based on an innovation by BMC, then it needs to be determined if this information can still be used.

If the design work which has been undertaken to date can be used by Kowloon and results in an ability to develop a new type of product for other customers, there is the possibility that the costs (excluding any research costs) could be capitalised in line with IAS 38 *Intangible Assets*. This should be discussed with the project manager and finance director to assess if this has been considered and if the capitalisation criteria of IAS 38 can be satisfied.

The accounting treatment of the deferred income also needs to be considered. Depending on the terms of the contract with BMC, the amount could be repayable, though this may not be the case given that it is BMC which has cancelled the contract. If part or all of the amount is repayable, it can remain recognised as a current liability. If it is not repayable, it should be released to the statement of profit or loss.

If the costs cannot be capitalised, then there is a loss which needs to be recognised. Assuming that the advance payment is non-refundable, the net position of the development cost and the deferred income balances result in a loss of $150,000. This represents 15.8% of profit for the year and is material.

If any necessary adjustments are not made there will be implications for the auditor's report, which would contain a modified opinion due to material misstatement.

Due to the significance of the matter to the financial statements, the contract cancellation and loss of BMC as a customer should be discussed in the other information to be issued with the financial statements, in this case in the integrated report.

The audit firm must consider its responsibilities in respect of ISA 720 *The Auditor's Responsibilities Relating to Other Information in Documents Containing Audited Financial Statements*. ISA 720 requires the auditor to read the other information to identify material inconsistencies, if any, with the audited financial statements.

Depending on the wording used in the integrated report when referring to the company's activities during the year and its financial performance, omitting to mention the cancellation of the contract could constitute a material misstatement of fact or a material inconsistency.

The matter should be discussed with management, who should be encouraged not only to amend the financial statements but also to discuss the cancellation of the contract in the integrated report. If management refuses to make the necessary amendments and disclosures, the matter should be discussed with those charged with governance and/or the company's legal counsel.

Examiner's comments

This question combined two familiar formats by asking candidates to comment on the quality of the audit work performed and discuss the quality, ethical and professional issues raised in part (a) and to comment on the matters arising in relation to a number of financial reporting issues in part (b).

In part (a), there was tendency to re-write statements of fact from the question which scored no marks but stronger candidates discussed the issues and explained why the firm's actions were clearly inappropriate. Very few candidates were able to discuss the need for materiality to be constantly reviewed throughout the audit in light of changing circumstances. However, most candidates picked up that a significant addition to property, plant and equipment sited at a supplier's premises needed to be physically verified and that reliance on third-party evidence for existence was inappropriate in the circumstances.

The inventory count had been poorly performed but few candidates developed this to consider where the real audit risks may lie and the need to inform management of the weakness in internal controls and for the auditors to investigate the discrepancies and extend their testing. Improper manager/partner review was highlighted by the majority of candidates but the implications of the partner's cursory review were not always followed through to a logical conclusion.

Part (b). In relation to the matters to consider, candidates were faced with a situation where the client had encountered a cancelled manufacturing contract. Most candidates scored the materiality marks for both the value of WIP and deferred income. A significant number of candidates discussed how WIP should have been calculated and its composition without realising that this was irrelevant as it needed to be recognised at nil unless a further use for it could be validly identified. Stronger candidates identified that the client may be able to levy a compensation claim for breach of contract. A worrying number of candidates also believed that writing off a deferred income creditor was a cost rather than a credit to the statement of profit or loss which shows a more fundamental lack of accounting knowledge. Likewise, many candidates confused WIP with R&D contracts and raised irrelevancies such as depreciation. The question stated that going concern was not an issue yet many candidates discussed this in depth as part of their answer. Candidates must realise that if the question makes a statement of this nature then marks will not be awarded for discussion, regardless of the quality of their answer and are again reminded to read the question scenario carefully.

<table>
<tr><td colspan="3" align="center">**ACCA Marking guide**</td></tr>
<tr><td></td><td></td><td>*Marks*</td></tr>
<tr><td>(a)</td><td>**Quality, ethical and other professional issues**
Generally up to 1 mark for each point explained:
– Materiality should be reviewed as the audit progresses
– Insufficient audit evidence obtained in relation to packing machine:
1 mark for comment on materiality
1 mark for comment on physical verification
1 mark for comment on external confirmation
1 mark for comment on whether the distribution company is a related party
1 mark for comment on assertions/inappropriate audit conclusion
– Lack of organisation at inventory count should have been discussed with management
– Extrapolate test count discrepancies over the population
– Audit staff may need training on inventory count attendance
– Accumulate misstatements and discuss with management
– The inaccuracy of the client's test counts should be reported to management as a control deficiency
– Insufficient review performed by audit manager
– Review left too late and should be ongoing during the audit
– Potential self-interest threat regarding audit engagement partner's brother
– Matter should be investigated and notified to audit firm's ethical partner
– The audit partner lacks integrity, maybe has something to hide
– The partner may need to be removed from the audit and his work reviewed</td><td></td></tr>
<tr><td></td><td align="right">**Maximum**</td><td>13</td></tr>
<tr><td>(b)</td><td>**Matters and actions to take**
Generally 1 mark per comment/recommended action explained:
– Calculation and determination of materiality (1 mark for each of the work in progress and the deferred income)
– Contract cancellation is an adjusting event after the reporting period
– The work in progress should be written off and charged to profit unless it can be used on a different contract
– The deferred income may be repayable, if not it should be released to profit
– Reporting implications if necessary adjustments not made
– Integrated report may be inconsistent with financial statements or contain a misstatement of fact
– Auditor's responsibility to read the integrated report to identify inconsistencies/misstatements
– Matters to be discussed with management/those charged with governance</td><td></td></tr>
<tr><td></td><td align="right">**Maximum**</td><td>7</td></tr>
<tr><td></td><td>**Professional marks**
Analysis and evaluation
– Appropriate use of the information to support discussion, draw appropriate conclusions and design appropriate responses
– Appropriate assessment of the quality and professional issues raised, using examples where relevant to support overall comments
– Effective appraisal of the information to make suitable recommendations for appropriate courses of action</td><td></td></tr>
</table>

Professional scepticism and judgement – Effective challenge and critical assessment of the evidence supplied with appropriate conclusions – Demonstration of the ability to probe into the reasons for quality issues including the identification of missing information or additional information which would be required – Appropriate application of professional judgement to draw conclusions and make informed comments regarding the quality of the work carried out **Commercial acumen** – Inclusion of appropriate recommendations regarding the additional actions required by the firm – Appropriate recognition of the wider implications on the engagement, the audit firm and the company	
Maximum	5
Total	25

36 DARREN *Walk in the footsteps of a top tutor*

Top tutor tips

Requirements (a) and (b) requires discussion of the relevant accounting treatment in the same way as you would approach a 'Matters' question. Assess the materiality of the issue, discuss the accounting treatment and explain the impact on the financial statements. To finish off, you need to explain the impact on the auditor's report if the issues are not resolved.

Requirement (c) deals with a limitation of scope being imposed by management. Your answer should cover how the auditor should respond when they cannot obtain sufficient appropriate evidence.

(a) Flyover Co

The total estimated profit of $5 million which has been recognised in the statement of profit or loss represents 22.2% of profit for the year and is therefore material.

In accordance with IFRS 15 *Revenue from Contracts with Customers,* revenue is recognised when or as the performance obligations within the contract are satisfied.

Performance obligations fulfilled over time

In the case of the construction of a bridge, the performance obligations are likely to be fulfilled over time as the bridge is unlikely to have an alternative use, i.e. it is unlikely to be able to be sold to another customer if Flyover Co were to cancel the contract part way through.

Where revenue is recognised over time the revenue recognised should be based on progress towards the satisfaction of the performance obligation. Revenue can be measured according to inputs such as time elapsed or costs incurred, or output, such as surveys.

Darren Co has recognised 100% of the contract profit even though the contract is not yet complete. The contract period is 15 months, and by the year end the contract has been ongoing for seven months only. Therefore, the profit has been recognised too early and is overstated.

Based on the time period in months, it appears that the contract is 7/15 complete, and therefore profit in the region of $2.3 million ($5 million × 7/15) can be recognised, and that profit is overstated by $2.7 million. The overstatement is material at 12% of profit before tax.

Tutorial note

This calculation provides a rough guide only and is included for the purposes of assessing whether the possible misstatement might be material. Alternative progress measures can be used and the entity should select a method that best measures progress towards the performance obligations. Other methods may be more appropriate.

Performance obligations fulfilled at a point in time

If the revenue should be recognised at a point in time then the revenue should only be recognised when the control of the bridge asset is transferred to Flyover Co. The $5 million recognised at the reporting date should be reversed as profit is overstated.

The audit firm needs to clarify Darren Co's revenue recognition policy and confirm whether the revenue should be recognised over time or at a point in time.

Further evidence should be obtained to determine the amount of revenue which can be recognised, including:

- Discuss with management the methods available to measure progress towards performance obligations and assess the reasonableness of the method used.

- Scrutinise the contract terms to ensure all performance obligations within the contract have been identified.

- Review surveys of work performed by 31 March 20X5 to estimate progress towards the satisfaction of each performance obligation at the reporting date.

- Read correspondence with the customer to confirm that the contract is progressing in a satisfactory way.

If any necessary adjustment is not made, then profit is overstated by a material amount. This gives rise to a material misstatement, and the audit opinion should be modified.

A qualified 'except for' opinion should be given, and the Basis for Qualified Opinion paragraph should explain the reason for the qualification, including a quantification of the misstatement.

This is only one contract, and Darren Co typically works on three contracts at a time. Further audit work is likely to be needed in respect of any other contracts which are currently being carried out. If the same accounting treatment has been applied to other contracts, the misstatement may be even greater, and could potentially result in an adverse opinion if the accumulated misstatements were considered by the auditor to be both material and pervasive to the financial statements.

In addition, Darren Co may have been using an inappropriate accounting treatment in previous years, and therefore there may be misstatements in the opening balances. This should be discussed with management to determine how contracts have been accounted for historically. Any errors which may be discovered should be corrected retrospectively, leading to further adjustments to the financial statements.

(b)   Newbuild Co

The amount claimed by Newbuild Co is material to the financial statements, representing 10.8% of total assets and 178% of profit before tax. It is also likely to be considered material by nature, as the possible payment is much larger than the amount of cash recognised in the financial statements at the year end.

The implications for the going concern status of Darren Co should be considered. The matter should be discussed with management to obtain an understanding of how Darren Co could meet any necessary cash payment. Due to the potential for such a sizeable cash payment, management should confirm that should the amount become payable, the company has adequate resources to fund the cash outflow, for example, through the existence of lending facilities.

The correct accounting treatment seems to have been applied. According to IAS 37 *Provisions, Contingent Liabilities and Contingent Assets*, if an amount is possible, rather than probable to be paid, then it is treated as a contingent liability, and a note to the accounts should be provided to describe the nature of the situation, an estimate of the possible financial effect and an indication of any uncertainties.

To ensure that IAS 37 has been complied with, the auditor should review the contents of the note for completeness and accuracy. Events after the reporting date should also be considered, for example, legal correspondence should be reviewed, to confirm that the probability of payment has not changed by the time of the auditor's report being signed.

Due to the size of the potential cash outflow, the auditor should consider including a Material Uncertainty Related to Going Concern section in the auditor's report.

The going concern section should include a clear reference to the note to the financial statements where the matter is disclosed. The paragraph should also make it clear that the audit opinion is not modified in respect of this matter.

(c)   Government contract

The expenses represent 31.1% of profit for the year so they are material to the financial statements.

Nidge & Co is unable to obtain sufficient appropriate evidence relating to the expenses. Given the limitation imposed by management, the auditor will be unable to form a conclusion about the occurrence, completeness, accuracy or classification of the associated expenses.

ISA 705 *Modifications to the Opinion in the Independent Auditor's Report* requires that when management imposes a limitation on the scope of the audit, the auditor should request that they remove the limitation.

If management refuses, the auditor should communicate the matter to those charged with governance, explaining the implications of the matter and the impact on this year's audit opinion.

In addition, as this is a matter which is likely to arise again in future audits, the auditor should stress that the compound effect of this in the future may give rise to both a material and pervasive matter, which would give rise to a disclaimer of opinion.

As well as the implications on the auditor's report, those charged with governance should be informed that in accordance with ISA 210 *Agreeing the Terms of Audit Engagements,* the auditor may not be able to continue with the audit engagement in the future if management continues to impose the limitation on the scope of the auditor's work and the auditor believes that it may result in them disclaiming their opinion.

In the current year under these circumstances, it will be necessary to issue a modified opinion. Given the claimed value of the expenses, it is likely that the matter will be considered material but not pervasive to the financial statements and a qualified opinion will be issued.

The 'Basis for Qualified Opinion' paragraph should describe the matter giving rise to the modification.

Examiner's comments

This question was based on the audit of Darren Co, a company operating in the construction industry and a new client of Nidge & Co. Information was provided in respect of several issues at the completion stage of the audit, and for each issue candidates were required to discuss the implication for the completion of the audit and for the auditor's report, and to recommend further actions to be taken. Generally, the question was well attempted by many candidates who seemed well prepared for a question of this type.

Part (a) described how Darren's financial statements recognised all of the profit relating to a long-term construction contract even though it was only part completed at the year end. Candidates performed well on this requirement, providing answers which confidently discussed both the inappropriate accounting treatment and the implications for the audit opinion if the material misstatements identified were not corrected by management. Some candidates missed out on marks by not recommending any further actions or by only discussing the impact for the audit opinion itself and not the overall impact on the auditor's report, failing to mention the need for a Basis for Opinion paragraph within the auditor's report. Only the strongest candidates realised that this incorrect accounting treatment may have been applied to other contracts and that opening balances may be incorrect given that this was a new audit client.

Part (b) provided information on a completed contract in respect of which Darren Co was facing legal action due to problems that had arisen following completion. The scenario stated that disclosure on the matter had been made in the notes to the financial statements and that the audit evidence on file concluded there to be a possibility of Darren Co having to pay the damages claimed. Candidates again seemed confident of the accounting rules, yet many suggested that a provision should be made for the damages. This may be because candidates assumed that there should be some implication for the auditor's opinion given the facts of the scenario, but this was not the case. The other significant issue was that Darren Co could not afford to pay the damages given its small cash balance, and this could raise a threat to the going concern status of the company. Only the strongest candidates made this connection and were able to explain clearly the implications for the auditor's report. In this scenario the issue was that a disclosure would be sufficient, as long as there was only a possibility that the claim would need to be paid, but the crucial aspect was that audit firm would need to audit the disclosure carefully to obtain evidence as to its sufficiency especially given the potential impact on going concern. As in part (a), the further actions were generally not given, other than a generic suggestion to "discuss with management".

ACCA Marking guide		
		Marks
Generally up to 1 mark for each relevant point explained, with 1 mark for correct determination of materiality.		
(a) **Flyover Co**		
– Profit recognised is material		
– Profit should be recognised by reference to stage of completion		
– Profit appears to be overstated/recognised too early		
– Further actions (1 mark each):		
• Review company's stated accounting policy		
• Review contract terms for revenue recognition trigger points		
• Verify stage of completion using surveyor's reports		
• Correspondence with customer to confirm contract progress		
– Material misstatement leading to qualification of audit opinion		
– Basis for Qualified Opinion paragraph		
– Other contracts need to be reviewed		
– Opening balances could also be materially misstated		
Maximum		**8**
(b) **Newbuild Co**		
– Possible cash payment material by monetary amount and by nature		
– Going concern implication due to size of possible cash outflow		
– Treatment as a contingent liability appears correct		
– Further actions (1 mark each):		
• Review post-year-end legal correspondence		
• Confirm financing in place if amount becomes payable		
• Read note to accounts to ensure complete and accurate		
– Material uncertainty related to going concern paragraph to highlight the significant uncertainty		
– Content of the Material uncertainty related to going concern paragraph		
Maximum		**6**
(c) **Government contract**		
– Expenses are material (must include relevant calculation)		
– Management imposed limitation on scope		
– Auditor should request that management removes the limitation		
– Communication of potential impact to those charged with governance		
– Impact on future audits		
– If limitation is not removed, audit opinion will be modified		
– Matter is material but not pervasive – qualified opinion		
– Basis for qualified opinion paragraph		
Maximum		**6**
Professional marks		
Analysis and evaluation		
• Appropriate use of the information to support discussion, draw appropriate conclusions and design appropriate responses		
• Identification of omissions from the analysis or further analysis which could be carried out		
• Balanced assessment of the information to determine the appropriate audit opinion in the circumstances		

Professional scepticism and judgement

- Effective challenge of information, evidence and assumptions supplied and, techniques carried out to support key facts and/or decisions
- Appropriate application of professional judgement to draw conclusions and make informed decisions about the actions which are appropriate in the context and stage of the engagement

Maximum	5
Total	25

37 THURMAN *Walk in the footsteps of a top tutor*

Top tutor tips

This question examines the review stage of the audit but in a different way to the usual 'matters and evidence' questions seen in past exams. The question asks for comment on whether the evidence obtained is sufficient and appropriate. Has enough work been done? Has the most reliable form of evidence been obtained? Enquiries and written representations are the least reliable forms of evidence so ideally there will be better evidence than this on file. Think about what evidence you would expect to be on file. Compare this with the evidence that has been obtained. Any difference between what you would do and what has been done indicates that sufficient appropriate evidence has not been obtained.

If a requirement asks for further procedures, include the procedures that should have been performed by this stage in the audit that have not been performed.

For the requirements asking for the control deficiencies to be reported, draw on your prior learning for audit and assurance at the applied skills level where you had to explain the implications of a deficiency and provide recommendations to overcome the deficiency.

(a) Assets held for sale

Sufficiency and appropriateness of the audit evidence obtained

The evidence does not appear to be sufficient to draw a conclusion on the appropriateness of classifying the property and any other related assets and liabilities as held for sale.

A discussion with management regarding the accounting treatment is relevant, as the audit team will need to understand management's rationale. However, management's explanation should not be accepted at face value and should be corroborated through further audit procedures.

It is not sufficient to simply put management's justification for the accounting treatment on the audit file and conclude that it is correct. For example, the factory can only be classified as held for sale if it is available for immediate sale in its current condition, which may not be the case.

In terms of the manual journal, checking that it is arithmetically correct, while relevant, is not sufficient evidence. Further evidence should be obtained in order to conclude that the basis of the calculation is in accordance with IFRS 5 *Non-current Assets Held for Sale and Discontinued Operations* and there should be consideration as to whether other requirements of the standard other than those related to the reclassification and measurement of the asset have been complied with.

For example, the results specific to the factory may need to be disclosed as a discontinued operation in the statement of profit or loss and the statement of cash flows. No audit evidence appears to have been obtained in respect of these issues.

Further audit procedures

- Review board minutes to confirm that the sale of the factory has been approved and to agree the date of the approval to the board minutes and relevant staff announcements.

- Obtain correspondence with estate agents to confirm that the factory is being actively marketed.

- Obtain confirmation, for example, by a review of production schedules, inventory movement records and payroll records, that production at the factory has stopped and thus it is available for immediate sale.

- Use an auditor's expert to confirm the fair value of the property and agree that this figure has been used in the impairment calculation.

- Using management accounts, determine whether the factory is a separate major line of business in which case its results should be disclosed as a discontinued operation.

(b)   Capital (asset) expenditure

(i)   Sufficiency and appropriateness of the audit evidence obtained

The audit work has revealed that internal controls have not been operating and this should have led to more extensive testing of capital (asset) expenditure, rather than the audit programme being completed as planned. Generally, the audit team should extend audit testing on capital (asset) expenditure, for example, by extending sample testing and reducing the level of materiality applied in audit tests.

The audit team should also investigate why the controls are not operating, considering whether they are being deliberately ignored or overridden, whether time pressure or lack of resources is making the controls difficult to operate, or if there is a suspicion of collusion and possible fraud.

The procedures on the purchase of the vehicles do not appear to cover all relevant assertions, for example, there is nothing to confirm that Thurman Co has correctly depreciated the vehicles or that they are actually owned and being used by the company, or even that they exist.

(ii)   Further audit procedures

- Obtain the insurance documents to confirm that Thurman Co is paying the relevant insurance for the vehicles.

- Physically verify the vehicles and confirm that they are being used by employees on company business.

- Obtain the log book/vehicle registration document and other relevant ownership documents such as those issued by the vehicle licensing body, to confirm the right of Thurman Co to recognise the vehicles.

- Trace the vehicles to the company's non-current asset register.

- Recalculate the depreciation which should have been charged on the vehicles and agree to the statement of profit or loss for the year.

(iii) Report to those charged with governance

ISA 265/ISA (UK) 265 *Communicating Deficiencies in Internal Controls to Those Charged with Governance and Management* requires the auditor to communicate significant deficiencies in internal control to those charged with governance and management. In deciding whether a control deficiency is significant, one of the matters which should be considered is the importance of the control to the financial reporting process.

The auditor should report to those charged with governance that there appears to be a deficiency in internal controls. While the audit team's findings do not indicate that a fraud is taking place, the lack of segregation of duties and the failure to obtain appropriate authorisation makes it easy for assets to be misappropriated and creates a significant fraud risk.

The audit firm should explain the implications of the control deficiencies to management and recommend improvements. For example, authorisation should be a pre-requisite for any order over a certain monetary amount. Thurman Co should also be encouraged to improve the control environment, for example, by training staff on the importance of controls and setting an appropriate tone at the top so that there is no tolerance of controls being ignored or deliberately circumvented.

(c) Payroll

Sufficiency and appropriateness of the audit evidence obtained

The audit work in respect of the payroll needs to be much more thorough. Simply agreeing the amounts to the reports issued by Jackson Co provides no evidence on the completeness, accuracy or validity of the payroll figures recognised in the financial statements.

The audit team seems to have relied on Jackson's year-end reports as being accurate and the requirements of ISA 402/ISA (UK) 402 *Audit Considerations Relating to an Entity Using a Service Organisation* do not appear to have been followed.

The audit team needs to obtain assurance on the controls which Jackson Co has implemented in order to assess the risk of material misstatement in the payroll figures and to respond to the risk with appropriate audit procedures. The controls which Thurman Co uses to verify the information received from Jackson Co also need to be understood.

With the permission of Thurman Co, the audit team should contact Jackson Co with the objective of obtaining more information which can be used to assess how the payroll has been processed, and the controls which are in place. The controls in place at Thurman Co should be documented and tested.

It is recommended that further substantive procedures should be carried out to provide a wider range of evidence on the payroll expense recognised in the financial statements.

In relation to the casual employees, the fact that the amount involved is immaterial means that the audit team does not need to perform any further detailed audit procedures as there is no risk of material misstatement. However, as there is a risk over the completeness of these costs, the controls in place to ensure this process is effectively managed should be discussed with management and documented.

Report to those charged with governance

The fact that casual employees are being paid from petty cash without being put onto the company's payroll indicates that Thurman Co may not be complying with relevant regulations, for example, that appropriate payroll taxes are not being paid. Despite the amounts involved being immaterial, the potential non-compliance should be reported to those charged with governance, along with a recommendation that all employees, whether casual or not, should be processed through the company's payroll system. There may be implications for the financial statements if fines or penalties are imposed by the tax authorities in respect of the non-compliance.

Examiner's comments

This question was set in the completion stage of the audit and as is generally the case with completion questions, it was focused on the accounting treatment and audit evidence obtained on three issues. In this case, candidates were also required to discuss the impact of the issues found on the report to those charged with governance. Candidates generally demonstrated a good knowledge of the financial reporting implications of the areas and were often able to identify that the evidence obtained was insufficient and suggest further procedures. For many candidates the control deficiencies in the company and the implication of a deficiency in controls on further audit strategy and testing was not always identified. Candidates' responses to the matters to include in the report were variable with some candidates discussing auditor's report modifications (despite no errors being flagged) or giving general answers to the contents of the report with no reference to the scenario in the exam.

ACCA Marking guide	
	Marks
Generally 1 mark for each relevant point.	
(a) **Asset held for sale**	
Audit evidence	
– Discussion is relevant but management's assertions must be corroborated	
– Discussion alone is not sufficient to reach an audit conclusion	
– Evidence not obtained on whether IFRS 5 classification criteria have been met	
– Evidence not obtained on whether disclosure of discontinued operations is necessary	
Further procedures	
– Review board minutes to confirm the sale approval and date	
– Correspondence with estate agents to confirm that the factory is being actively marketed	
– Confirmation, for example, by a review of production schedules, inventory movement records and payroll records that production at the factory has stopped	
– Auditor's expert to confirm the fair value of the property	
– Determine whether the factory is a separate major line of business and should be disclosed as a discontinued operation	
Maximum	7

(b)   **Capital (asset) expenditure**

    (i)   **Audit evidence**

       –   Testing should have been extended after the control deficiency was identified

       –   Reason for the controls not operating effectively should be investigated

       –   Increases the fraud risk in relation to capital (asset) expenditure

       –   Not all assertions have been covered by audit testing in respect of the vehicles purchased

    (ii)   **Further audit procedures**

       –   Obtain the insurance documents to confirm that Thurman Co is paying the relevant insurance for the vehicles

       –   Physically verify the vehicles and confirm that they are being used by employees on company business

       –   Obtain the log book and other relevant ownership documents to confirm the right of Thurman Co to recognise the vehicles

       –   Trace the vehicles to the company's fixed asset register

       –   Recalculate the depreciation which should have been charged on the vehicles

    (iii)   **Report to those charged with governance**

       –   Explain the deficiencies and the implications, i.e. increased fraud risk

       –   Recommend improvements to specific controls and to the general control environment

Maximum	**9**

(c)   **Payroll**

Audit work

–   Agreeing payroll to the service organisation's report does not provide sufficient evidence on completeness, accuracy or validity of the amounts

–   The controls at the service organisation must be assessed for their adequacy

–   No further work needed on the petty cash payments to casual workers as the amount is not material

Report to those charged with governance

–   There is not a significant control deficiency as the amounts involved are immaterial

–   Potential non-compliance with regulations, e.g. tax regulation should be reported

–   Recommend that all workers are put through payroll to ensure compliance

Maximum	**4**

Professional marks

Analysis and evaluation

–   Appropriate use of the information to support discussion, draw appropriate conclusions and design appropriate responses

–   Appropriate assessment of the quality and professional issues raised, using examples where relevant to support overall comments

–   Effective appraisal of the information to make suitable recommendations for appropriate courses of action

Professional scepticism and judgement

–   Effective challenge and critical assessment of the evidence supplied with appropriate conclusions

–   Demonstration of the ability to probe into the reasons for quality issues including the identification of missing information or additional information which would be required

–   Appropriate application of professional judgement to draw conclusions and make informed comments regarding the quality of the work carried out

Commercial acumen			
– Inclusion of appropriate recommendations in the report to those charged with governance and management			
		Maximum	5
Total			25

38 ADDER GROUP *Walk in the footsteps of a top tutor*

Top tutor tips

For 'Matters and evidence' questions, use the 'MARE' approach to make it easier to score the required number of marks. First, consider the materiality of the issue. Next discuss the appropriate accounting treatment and give the risks of material misstatement that would arise if the appropriate treatment is not followed. Finally, the evidence is what you would expect to be recorded on the audit file when you come to review it. Be specific about the evidence, don't say 'supporting documentation', suggest what that documentation would be and what it would show. Assume that half of the marks will be for matters and half of the marks will be for evidence.

Part (b) asks for a critical appraisal of the draft report extracts. This is a common reporting question seen several times in previous exams and should not cause problems for students who are familiar with the format of an auditor's report and who have practised this style of question before. Work your way through the auditor's report and think about whether the wording is appropriate, the order of the paragraphs is correct, the names of the paragraphs are correct and ultimately, whether you agree with the opinion suggested.

(a) (i) Sale and leaseback

The sale and leaseback transaction is material to the Group statement of financial position. The proceeds received on the sale of the property, equivalent to the fair value of the assets, represents 23.3% of Group assets, and the carrying amount of the assets disposed of were $27 million ($35 million – $8 million), representing 18% of Group assets. In addition, the profit recognised on the disposal represents 40% of the Group's profit for the year, so it is highly material to the statement of profit or loss.

The accounting treatment does not appear to be in accordance with IFRS 16 *Leases*. IFRS 16 says the accounting treatment of a sale and leaseback depends on whether a performance obligation, as defined in IFRS 15 *Revenue from Contracts with Customers,* has been satisfied. Adder Group will be obtaining substantially all of the asset's remaining benefits, suggesting that control has not passed to the buyer.

Therefore, the transfer of the asset does not represent a 'sale'. As such, the asset should remain recognised in the statement of financial position, and the proceeds received from the sale should be recognised as a financial liability.

The Group's profit is materially overstated, and the total assets and liabilities are materially understated.

The following adjustments should be recommended to management:

DR	Property, plant and equipment	$27 million
DR	Profit or loss	$8 million
CR	Financial liability	$35 million

The complex should be depreciated over the final four months of the year, giving rise to depreciation of $0.5 million ($27 million/20 years × 4/12). The adjustment required is:

DR	Profit or loss	$0.5 million
CR	Property, plant and equipment	$0.5 million

The finance charge on the financial liability which has accrued since the transfer of the asset should be quantified, its materiality determined, and the appropriate adjustment communicated to management.

If the adjustments are not made, the Group financial statements will contain a material misstatement, with implications for the auditor's opinion, which would be modified due to a material misstatement following the misapplication of IFRS 16 to the sale and leaseback transaction.

Evidence:

• A copy of the lease, signed by the buyer-lessor, and a review of its major clauses to confirm that control of the asset remains with the Group.

• Review of forecasts and budgets to confirm that economic benefit is expected to be generated through the continued use of the property complex.

• Agreement of the $35 million cash proceeds to the bank statement and bank ledger account/cash book.

• Physical inspection of the property complex to confirm that it is being used by the Group.

• Confirmation of the fair value of the property complex, possibly using an auditor's expert, in which case the expert's report should be included in the audit working papers.

• Where fair value has been established using an auditor's or management expert, evaluation of the expert's work including confirmation that the fair value is determined according to the applicable financial reporting framework, and that all assumptions are reasonable.

• Minutes of a discussion with management regarding the accounting treatment and including an auditor's request to amend the financial statements.

• A copy of insurance documents stating that the Group is responsible for insuring the property complex.

• Recalculation of finance charge and depreciation expense in relation to the leased asset.

(ii) **Baldrick Co**

The Group's interest in Baldrick Co is material, as the company's assets are equivalent to 12% of total Group assets, and its loss is equivalent to 25% of the Group's profit.

It is questionable whether Baldrick Co should have been accounted for as an associate. An associate arises where there is significant influence over an investee, according to IAS 28 *Investments in Associates and Joint Ventures*. Significant influence is typified by an equity shareholding of 20 – 50%, so the Group's shareholding of 52% would seem to indicate that the Group exercises control, rather than significant influence.

However, it may be that even with a 52% shareholding, the Group cannot exercise control, for example, if it is prevented from doing so due to agreements between other shareholders, or because it cannot appoint members to the board of Baldrick Co. This would be unusual though, so audit evidence must be sought on the nature of the shareholding in Baldrick Co and whether the Group actually exercises control or significant influence over the company. Baldrick Co not having been integrated into the Group's activities is not a valid reason for its non-consolidation as a subsidiary.

If the Group does have a controlling interest, and Baldrick Co remains recognised as an associate, the Group financial statements will be materially misstated, with implications for the auditor's opinion, which would be modified due to the application of an inappropriate accounting treatment.

If Baldrick Co should be treated as a subsidiary rather than an associate, then the company's loss for the year should be consolidated from the date of acquisition which was 1 January 20X5. Therefore, a loss of $1.25 million ($5 million × 3/12) should be consolidated into Group profit. The loss which has already been recognised, assuming that equity accounting has been correctly applied, would be $650,000 ($5 million × 3/12 × 52%), therefore an additional loss of $600,000 needs to be recognised.

In addition, there are presentation issues to consider. Equity accounting requires the investment in the associate to be recognised on one line in the statement of financial position, and the income from the associate to be disclosed on one line of the statement of profit or loss.

Treating Baldrick Co as a subsidiary will require a line-by-line consolidation, which will have a significant impact on numerous balances within the financial statements.

The combination of adjustments in relation to the sale and leaseback transaction and the consolidation of Baldrick Co as a subsidiary may be considered pervasive to the Group financial statements, and if so, and the necessary adjustments are not made, then the audit opinion could be adverse.

Evidence:

- Agreement of the cash paid to acquire Baldrick Co to the bank ledger account/ cash book and bank statements.
- Review of board minutes for discussion of the change in Group structure and for authorisation of the acquisition.
- Review of legal documentation pertaining to the acquisition of Baldrick Co, to confirm the number of equity shares acquired, and the rights attached to the shareholding, e.g. the ability to appoint board members.

- Inspection of other supporting documentation relating to the acquisition such as due diligence reports.

- Notes of discussion with management regarding the exercise of control over Baldrick Co, e.g. the planned level of participation in its operating and financial decisions.

- Review of forecasts and budgets to assess the plans for integrating Baldrick Co into the Group.

- Ensure that correct time apportionment has been applied in calculating the amount of losses recognised in the consolidation of Baldrick Co.

- Evaluation and recalculation of amounts recognised in Group equity in respect of Baldrick Co, in particular the determination of pre and post-acquisition results.

(b)   Opinion and basis for opinion paragraphs not separate

In terms of structure, the basis for opinion and opinion paragraphs should not be combined together. When the auditor modifies the opinion on the financial statements, the auditor shall include a paragraph in the auditor's report which provides a description of the matter giving rise to the modification. Therefore, the auditor's report needs to be amended to include two separate paragraphs.

The auditor should use the heading 'Basis for Qualified Opinion', 'Basis for Adverse Opinion', or 'Basis for Disclaimer of Opinion', as appropriate.

'Proven conclusively'

The paragraph states that audit procedures have 'proven conclusively' in respect of trade receivables. This term is misleading, implying that every transaction has been tested. Audit procedures provide a reasonable, but not absolute, level of assurance on the financial statements, and conclusive proof is not an appropriate term to be used in the auditor's report.

Quantification of potential adjustment

The amount of the potential adjustment to trade receivables and its financial impact should be included in the paragraph. If there is a material misstatement of the financial statements which relates to specific amounts in the financial statements (including quantitative disclosures), the auditor shall include in the basis for modification paragraph a description and quantification of the financial effects of the misstatement, unless impracticable. The relevant financial reporting standard should also be referred to.

Unprofessional wording

The paragraph uses unprofessional wording by naming the finance director. The auditor's report should refer to management collectively and not single out one person as being responsible for the financial statements. In addition, it should not state that she 'refused' to make an adjustment.

Type of opinion

The incorrect type of modified audit opinion seems to have been given. The trade receivables balance is material at $2.5 million, which is in excess of the materiality threshold of $1.5 million used in the audit and so a qualification due to material misstatement seems necessary. The auditor's report uses a disclaimer of opinion, which is used when the auditor cannot form an opinion, usually due to lack of audit evidence, which does not appear to be the case here.

Level of modification

In addition, the level of modification seems incorrect. The matter is material at 22.7% of profit but is unlikely to be pervasive to the financial statements. Therefore, a qualified 'except for' opinion is sufficient.

Emphasis of matter paragraph

The use of an Emphasis of Matter paragraph in respect of the court case is not appropriate. An Emphasis of Matter paragraph is used to refer to a matter appropriately presented or disclosed in the financial statements which, in the auditor's judgement, is of such importance that it is fundamental to users' understanding of the financial statements.

The court case and its potential legal consequences are not material, being well below the materiality threshold of $1.5 million. The matter is certainly not fundamental to users' understanding of the financial statements. Due to the immaterial nature of the matter it need not be referred to in the auditor's report at all.

The auditor has reached the conclusion that the court case has not been accounted for correctly. The Emphasis of Matter paragraph should only be used to highlight matters which have been appropriately accounted for and disclosed within the financial statements, and its use to describe non-compliance with the relevant financial reporting standard is not appropriate.

Examiner's comments

The first requirement asked candidates to comment on the matters to be considered and explain the audit evidence they would expect to find in a review of the working papers relating to the audit of the Adder Group. Candidates who have practised past exam papers will be familiar with requirements of this type, and with scenarios set in the completion stage of the audit.

The first issue related to a sale and leaseback arrangement. The Adder Group had derecognised the asset and recognised a profit on disposal. Candidates had to discuss whether the accounting treatment appeared appropriate. Answers on the whole were good. Most candidates proved able to confidently discuss whether the lease had been appropriately classified and accounted for. In addition, almost all candidates correctly determined the materiality of the balances and could provide some specific and well explained points on audit evidence.

The second issue related to the acquisition of a 52% shareholding in Baldrick Co, which had been accounted for as an associate in the consolidated financial statements. Again, candidates were able to identify that the accounting treatment seemed incorrect, and could explain their reasoning. Fewer candidates appreciated that the loss-making status of Baldrick Co was the possible explanation for the Group's reluctance to consolidate it as a subsidiary and therefore that the Group's profits were overstated. Most candidates could provide some evidence points, with the most commonly cited being the board approval of the acquisition and agreeing the cash paid to bank statements. Fewer candidates could suggest how the audit firm should obtain evidence on the exercise of control by the parent company or on the mechanics of the consolidation that should have taken place.

Requirement (b) asked for a critical appraisal of a proposed auditor's report. The report contained many errors of fact and of judgement, and well prepared candidates scored highly here. There were some quite obvious matters that most candidates discussed, for example that the structure of the report was not correct, the wording was not professional, the basis for opinion paragraph lacked sufficient detail, and the nature of the modification was wrong in the circumstances described in the scenario. Most candidates also commented on the incorrect use of the Emphasis of Matter paragraph and correctly determined the materiality of the two issues described in the scenario. Overall however, answers to this requirement were often too short for the marks available, and while most issues had been identified, they were not always well explained.

ACCA Marking guide

			Marks
(a)	Generally up to 1 mark for each matter explained and each piece of evidence recommended.		
	(i)	**Sale and leaseback**	
		Matters:	
		– Correct determination of materiality	
		– IFRS 16 treatment	
		– Assets and liabilities understated, profit overstated	
		– Adjustment recommended	
		– Depreciation should be re-measured	
		– Finance charge accrual	
		– Implications for auditor's report if not adjusted	
		Evidence:	
		– A copy of the lease	
		– Forecasts and budgets	
		– Physical inspection of the property complex	
		– Confirmation of the fair value of the property	
		– Evaluation of the expert's work	
		– Bank statement and bank ledger account/cash book	
		– Minutes of a discussion with management	
		– A copy of insurance documents	
		– Recalculation of finance charge and depreciation	
		Maximum	7
	(ii)	**Baldrick Co**	
		Matters:	
		– Correct determination of materiality of Baldrick Co	
		– If Group exercises control, Baldrick Co is a subsidiary	
		– Need to determine nature of the Group's interest in Baldrick Co	
		– Impact on audit opinion is at least qualification due to material misstatement	
		– Discussion of impact on Group profit	
		– Presentation issues	
		– Impact could be pervasive in combination with the sale and leaseback	

Evidence:

- Bank ledger account/cash book and bank statements
- Board minutes for authorisation
- Legal documentation for the acquisition of Baldrick Co
- Due diligence reports
- Notes of discussion with management regarding control
- Plans for integrating Baldrick Co into the Group
- Ensure that losses from the date of acquisition only are consolidated
- Evaluation and recalculation of amounts recognised in Group equity in respect of Baldrick Co

Maximum	6

(b) **Evaluation of draft auditor's report**

Generally 1 mark for each reporting implication explained.

- Incorrect presentation and combining of Opinion and Basis for Opinion paragraphs
- Wording regarding 'proven conclusively' is inappropriate
- Description of material misstatement should include quantification and impact on financial statements
- The relevant financial reporting standard should be referred to
- Unprofessional wording regarding the finance director
- Inappropriate opinion given – should be modified due to material misstatement not due to disclaimer of opinion
- Level of modification incorrect – it is material but not pervasive
- Court case not fundamental so not appropriate to include in Emphasis of Matter paragraph
- Emphasis of Matter should only be used for matters appropriately accounted for which is not the case

Maximum	7

Professional marks

Analysis and evaluation

- Appropriate use of the information to support discussion, draw appropriate conclusions and design appropriate responses
- Identification of omissions from the analysis or further analysis which could be carried out
- Balanced assessment of the information to determine the appropriate audit opinion in the circumstances

Professional scepticism and judgement

- Effective challenge of information, evidence and assumptions supplied and, techniques carried out to support key facts and/or decisions
- Appropriate application of professional judgement to draw conclusions and make informed decisions about the actions which are appropriate in the context and stage of the engagement

Maximum	5
Total	25

39 FRANCIS GROUP *Walk in the footsteps of a top tutor*

Top tutor tips

This question is a typical 'matters and evidence' question. Use the 'MARE' approach. First, consider the materiality of the issue. Next discuss the appropriate accounting treatment and give the risks of material misstatement that would arise if the appropriate treatment is not followed. Finally, the evidence is what you would expect to be recorded on the audit file when you come to review it. Be specific about the evidence, don't say 'supporting documentation', and suggest what that documentation would be and what it would show. The mark allocation is given for each issue, therefore deal with both matters and evidence for the acquisition of Teapot, then matters and evidence in respect of the property complex.

For part (b) you need to state the impact to the auditor's report if the client does not amend the financial statements. State the impact to both the report and opinion as a result of the issue. Don't waste time stating the reporting implications if the issue is corrected as this is not part of the requirement. You are also asked for any further actions which should be taken by the auditor. This must be actions that would be taken at this late stage in the audit immediately before signing the auditor's report.

(a) (i) Measurement of goodwill on acquisition

The goodwill arising on the acquisition of Teapot Co is material to the Group financial statements, representing 6% of total assets.

The goodwill should be recognised as an intangible asset and measured according to IAS 38 *Intangible Assets* and IFRS 3 *Business Combinations*.

The purchase consideration should reflect the fair value of total consideration paid and payable, and there is a risk that the amount shown in the calculation is not complete, for example, if any deferred or contingent consideration has not been included.

The non-controlling interest has been measured at fair value. This is permitted by IFRS 3, and the decision to measure at fair value can be made on an investment by investment basis. The important issue is the basis for measurement of fair value.

If Teapot Co is a listed company, then the market value of its shares at the date of acquisition can be used and this is a reliable measurement.

If Teapot Co is not listed, then management should have used estimation techniques according to the fair value hierarchy of inputs contained in IFRS 13 *Fair Value Measurement*. This would introduce subjectivity into the measurement of non-controlling interest and goodwill and the method of determining fair value must be clearly understood by the auditor.

The net assets acquired should be all identifiable assets and liabilities at the date of acquisition. For such a significant acquisition some form of due diligence investigation should have been performed, and one of the objectives of this would be to determine the existence of assets and liabilities, even those not recognised in Teapot Co's individual financial statements.

There is a risk that not all acquired assets and liabilities have been identified, or that they have not been appropriately measured at fair value, which would lead to over or understatement of goodwill and incomplete recording of assets and liabilities in the consolidated financial statements.

The fair value adjustment of $300,000 made in relation to Teapot Co's property is not material to the Group accounts, representing less than 1% of total assets. However, the auditor should confirm that additional depreciation is being charged at Group level in respect of the fair value uplift. Though the value of the depreciation would not be material to the consolidated financial statements, for completeness and accuracy the adjustment should be made.

The auditor should also consider if any further adjustments need to be made to Teapot Co's net assets to ensure that Group accounting policies have been applied. IFRS 3 requires consistency in accounting policies across Group members, so if the necessary adjustments have not been made, the assets and liabilities will be over or understated on consolidation.

Evidence

- Agreement of the purchase consideration to the legal documentation pertaining to the acquisition, and a review of the documents to ensure that the figures included in the goodwill calculation are complete.

- Agreement of the $75 million to the bank statement and bank ledger account/cash book of the acquiring company (presumably the parent company of the Group).

- Review of board minutes for discussions relating to the acquisition, and for the relevant minute of board approval.

- A review of the purchase documentation and a register of significant shareholders of Teapot Co to confirm the 20% non-controlling interest.

- If Teapot Co's shares are not listed, a discussion with management as to how the fair value of the non-controlling interest has been determined and evaluation of the appropriateness of the method used.

- If Teapot Co's shares are listed, confirmation that the fair value of the non-controlling interest has been calculated based on an externally available share price at the date of acquisition.

- A copy of any due diligence report relevant to the acquisition, reviewed for confirmation of acquired assets and liabilities and their fair values.

- An evaluation of the methods used to determine the fair value of acquired assets, including the property, and liabilities to confirm compliance with IFRS 3 and IFRS 13.

- Review of depreciation calculations, and recalculation, to confirm that additional depreciation is being charged on the fair value uplift.

- A review of the calculation of net assets acquired to confirm that Group accounting policies have been applied.

Impairment of goodwill

IAS 38 requires that goodwill is tested annually for impairment regardless of whether indicators of potential impairment exist. The goodwill in relation to Teapot Co is recognised at the same amount at the year end as it was at acquisition, indicating that no impairment has been recognised. It could be that management has performed an impairment review and has concluded that there is no impairment, or that no impairment review has been performed at all.

However, Group profit has declined by 30.3% over the year, which in itself is an indicator of potential impairment of the Group's assets, so it is unlikely that no impairment exists unless the fall in revenue relates to parts of the Group's activities which are unrelated to Teapot Co.

There is a risk that Group assets are overstated and profit overstated if any necessary impairment has not been recognised.

Evidence

- Discussion with management regarding the potential impairment of Group assets and confirmation as to whether an impairment review has been performed.

- A copy of any impairment review performed by management, with scrutiny of the assumptions used, and reperformance of calculations.

- The auditor's impairment evaluation and calculation compared with that of management.

(ii)   Property complex

The carrying amount of the property complex is material to the Group financial statements, representing 3.6% of total assets.

The natural disaster is a subsequent event, and its accounting treatment should be in accordance with IAS 10 *Events After the Reporting Period*. IAS 10 distinguishes between adjusting and non-adjusting events, the classification being dependent on whether the event provides additional information about conditions already existing at the year-end. The natural disaster is a non-adjusting event as it indicates a condition which arose after the year end.

Disclosure is necessary in a note to the financial statements to describe the impact of the natural disaster, and quantify the effect which it will have on next year's financial statements.

The demolition of the property complex should be explained in the note to the financial statements and reference made to the monetary amounts involved. Consideration should be made of any other costs which will be incurred, e.g. if there is inventory to be written off, and the costs of the demolition itself.

The contingent asset of $18 million should not have been recognised as per IAS 37 *Provisions, Contingent Liabilities and Contingent Assets*. Even if the amount were virtually certain to be received, the fact that it relates to the non-adjusting event after the reporting period means that it cannot be recognised as an asset and deferred income at the year end.

The financial statements should be adjusted to remove the contingent asset and the deferred income. The amount is material at 4% of total assets. There would be no profit impact of this adjustment as the $18 million has not been recognised in the statement of profit or loss.

Evidence

- A copy of any press release made by the Group after the natural disaster, and relevant media reports of the natural disaster, in particular focusing on its impact on the property complex.

- Photographic evidence of the site after the natural disaster, and of the demolished site.

- A copy of the note to the financial statements describing the event, reviewed for completeness and accuracy.

- A schedule of the costs of the demolition, with a sample agreed to supporting documentation, e.g. invoices for work performed and confirmation that this is included in the costs described in the note to the financial statements.

- A schedule showing the value of inventories and items such as fixtures and fittings at the time of the disaster, and confirmation that this is included in the costs described in the note to the financial statements.

- A copy of the insurance claim and correspondence with the Group's insurers to confirm that the property is insured.

- Confirmation that an adjustment has been made to reverse out the contingent asset and deferred income which has been recognised.

(b)   Implications for the auditor's report

The contingent asset should not be recognised. The event is a non-adjusting event therefore disclosure is required but no accounting entries.

Even if the event had occurred before the year end, the correspondence received from the insurance company provides evidence that the insurance company will not pay the claim therefore there will be no future receipt of economic benefits.

The auditor should review the financial statements to identify whether any disclosure has been made of the issue. If no disclosure has been made the financial statements will be materially misstated due to lack of disclosure of the non-adjusting event and overstatement of contingent assets.

The issue is likely to be considered material but not pervasive as the misstatement only represents 4% of total assets. Going concern is not affected.

The audit opinion should be modified with a qualified opinion. The opinion will state 'except for' this matter the financial statements give a true and fair view.

Within the auditor's report the basis for opinion will be changed to a basis for qualified opinion. This will include an explanation of the reason for issuing a qualified opinion.

The basis for qualified opinion will also describe the financial impact the misstatement has on the financial statements in respect of the current year and accumulated reserves.

Examiner's comments

This question contained information relevant to the audit completion of the Francis Group. Candidates were asked in respect of each issue to comment on the matters to be considered and explain the audit evidence they should expect to find during a review of the audit working papers. This type of requirement is common in this paper, and it was encouraging to see that many candidates had obviously practised past exam questions containing similar requirements. Most candidates approached each of the issues in a sensible manner by firstly determining the materiality of the matters involved, considering the appropriate financial reporting treatment and risk of misstatement, and then providing some examples of appropriate audit evidence relevant to the matters discussed. However, the question was not well attempted by all, and it was usually a lack of knowledge of financial reporting requirements, and/or an inability to explain the relevant audit evidence that let some candidates down.

Requirement (a)(i) related to an acquisition of a subsidiary that had taken place during the year. A goodwill calculation had been provided, along with information regarding a fair value adjustment relevant to the net assets of the subsidiary at acquisition. Candidates were able to achieve a good mark here if they tackled each component of the information provided in turn and used that approach to deliver a structured answer.

In relation to the goodwill calculation, many candidates identified that no impairment had been recognised, and therefore that the goodwill balance may be overvalued. Only the strongest candidates mentioned that a significant drop in the Group's profit for the year meant that it would be very likely that an impairment loss should be recognised. It was worrying to see how many candidates referred to the need for goodwill to be amortised over a useful life – a practice that has not been allowed under IFRS 3 *Business Combinations* for many years. Fewer candidates touched on the measurement issues in relation to the non-controlling interest component of goodwill, which was usually ignored in answers.

Looking at the fair value adjustment to net assets, most candidates recognised that this would be a subjective issue and that ideally an independent valuer's report or due diligence report would be required as audit evidence to justify the adjustment. Weaker candidates thought that the accounting treatment of goodwill was incorrect and set about correcting the perceived errors.

Some incorrect accounting treatments frequently discussed included:

- Goodwill should be amortised over an estimated useful life (discussed above)

- Goodwill only needs to be tested for impairment when indicators of impairment exist

- Non-controlling interest should not be part of the goodwill calculation

- Fair value adjustments are not required and are an indication of fraudulent financial reporting.

The evidence points provided by candidates for this requirement tended to revolve around recalculations of the various balances, and confirming figures to supporting documentation such as the purchase documentation and due diligence reports. These were all valid evidence points but it would benefit candidates to consider a wider range of evidence that may be available especially in relation to the more subjective and therefore higher risk elements, for example a discussion with management regarding the need for an impairment review of goodwill or a review and assessment of the methods used to determine the fair value of the non- controlling interest.

Requirement (a)(ii) related to a natural disaster that had taken place two months after the year end, resulting in the demolition of the Group's head office and main manufacturing site. The Group had claimed under its insurance an amount in excess of the value of the demolished property, and the whole amount of the claim was recognised in the statement of financial position as a current asset and deferred income. This requirement was generally well answered, with almost all candidates correctly determining the materiality of the property complex and the contingent asset. Most candidates also appreciated that the auditor should consider the event to be a non-adjusting event after the reporting date, requiring disclosure in the notes to the financial statements, in line with the requirements of IAS 10 *Events After the Reporting Period*. The audit evidence suggested was usually relevant and sensible, tending to focus on the insurance claim, discussing the need for demolition with management, and evidence from documents such as health and safety reports on the necessity for the demolition. Many answers identified that a key part of the audit evidence would be in the form of a review of the sufficiency of the required notes to the financial statements describing and quantifying the financial implications of the non-adjusting event. In a minority of scripts candidates suggested that the event was actually an adjusting event and that impairment of the property complex should be recognised in this financial year. Weaker answers to this requirement suggested that the event should be recognised by impairing the property complex and recognising the contingent asset. However, encouragingly even where candidates had discussed the incorrect accounting treatment, the evidence points provided were generally appropriate to the scenario.

In summary the question was well attempted by many candidates, with the matters to consider element of the requirements usually better attempted than the audit evidence points. It was clear that many candidates had practised past questions of this type and were well prepared for the style of question requirement.

In the UK and IRL adapted papers it was much more common to see references to incorrect financial reporting requirements, specifically that goodwill must be amortised over an estimated useful life. Candidates are reminded that if they choose to attempt the UK or IRL adapted paper, the financial reporting requirements are still based on IFRS Accounting Standards, as in the INT paper, and therefore discussing financial reporting requirements of UK and Irish GAAP will not score credit.

ACCA Marking guide				
				Marks
Generally 1 mark for each matter considered/evidence point explained:				
(a)	(i)	**Teapot Co**		
		Matters		
		– Materiality of the goodwill		
		– Purchase price/consideration to be at fair value		
		– Risk of understatement if components of consideration not included		
		– Non-controlling interest at fair value – determination of fair value if Teapot Co is listed		
		– Non-controlling interest at fair value – determination of fair value if Teapot Co is not listed		
		– Use of fair value hierarchy to determine fair value		
		– Risk that not all acquired assets and liabilities have been separately identified		
		– Risk in the measurement of acquired assets and liabilities – judgemental		
		– Additional depreciation to be charged on fair value uplift		
		– Group accounting policies to be applied to net assets acquired on consolidation		
		– Impairment indicator exists – fall in revenue		
		– Impairment review required regardless for goodwill		
		– Risk goodwill and Group profit overstated if necessary impairment not recognised		

Evidence
- Agreement of the purchase consideration
- Agreement of the $75 million to the bank statement and bank ledger account/cash book
- Review of board minutes for discussions relating to the acquisition
- A review of the purchase documentation and a register of significant shareholders of Teapot Co to confirm the 20% NCI
- If Teapot Co's shares are not listed, a discussion with management as to how the fair value of the non-controlling interest has been determined
- If Teapot Co's shares are listed, confirmation that the fair value of the non-controlling interest has been calculated based on an externally available share price at the date of acquisition
- A copy of any due diligence report relevant to the acquisition
- An evaluation of the methods used to determine the fair value of acquired assets
- Review of depreciation calculations, and recalculation
- A review of the calculation of net assets acquired
- Discussion with management regarding the potential impairment of Group assets
- A copy of any impairment review performed by management

| | **Maximum** | 9 |

(ii) **Property complex**
Matters
- Materiality of the asset (calculation) and significance to profit
- Identify event as non-adjusting
- Describe content of note to financial statements
- Consider other costs, e.g. inventories to be written off
- Contingent asset/deferred income should not be recognised

Evidence
- A copy of any press release/media reports
- Photographic evidence of the site after the natural disaster and of the demolished site
- A copy of the note to the financial statements describing the event
- A schedule of the costs of the demolition, with a sample agreed to supporting documentation
- A schedule showing the value of inventories and items such as fixtures and fittings
- A copy of the insurance claim
- Confirmation of the removal of the contingent asset from the financial statements

| | **Maximum** | 6 |

(b) **Auditor's report**
Generally up to 1 mark for each point explained
- Contingent asset should not be recognised
- Insurance company refusing to pay out therefore no receipt
- Review financial statements for disclosure of event
- Material but not pervasive
- Qualified 'except for'
- Basis for qualified opinion explains the misstatement
- Basis for qualified quantifies the misstatement

| | **Maximum** | 5 |

Professional marks	
Analysis and evaluation	
– Appropriate use of the information to support discussion, draw appropriate conclusions and design appropriate responses	
– Identification of omissions from the analysis or further analysis which could be carried out	
– Balanced assessment of the information to determine the appropriate audit opinion in the circumstances	
Professional scepticism and judgement	
– Effective challenge of information, evidence and assumptions supplied and, techniques carried out to support key facts and/or decisions	
– Appropriate application of professional judgement to draw conclusions and make informed decisions about the actions which are appropriate in the context and stage of the engagement	
Maximum	5
Total	25

40 BRADLEY *Walk in the footsteps of a top tutor*

Top tutor tips

Part (a) asks for quality management and other professional issues raised in relation to the completion of the audit. Quality issues are increasingly common in the exam. Consider whether the audit has been performed in accordance with professional standards and whether the auditor has conducted the work with professional scepticism and due professional care.

Part (b) (i) asks for matters to be discussed with management in relation to three uncorrected misstatements. You can take the same approach as a 'matters' question i.e. state whether the issue is material, the accounting treatment required and the risk to the financial statements.

For part (b) (ii) you need to state the impact to the auditor's report if the client does not amend the financial statements. Consider the aggregate effect of the misstatements to assess whether there is a material misstatement. State the impact to both the report and opinion as a result of the issues. Don't waste time stating the reporting implications if the issues are corrected as this is not part of the requirement.

(a)   Quality, ethical and other issues

Provision

The first comment made by the audit assistant shows that the audit of the provision in relation to the legal claim has not been properly carried out, and it would seem that there is not sufficient, appropriate audit evidence to conclude that provisions are fairly stated.

First, the finance director telling the audit assistant not to approach the company's legal advisers would appear to be placing a limitation on the evidence which can be obtained. Also, the finance director could have used his seniority to intimidate the audit assistant.

The situation indicates that the finance director may be trying to hide something, and professional scepticism should be exercised. Possibly the finance director knows that the amount which should be provided is much larger than the $10,000, and he is reluctant to recognise a larger liability in the financial statements or that the legal advisers are aware of other provisions which should be included in the financial statements which are currently not being recognised.

As the key risk for provisions is understatement, the audit team should not so readily accept the finance director's assessment that the amount included is complete. The audit team should challenge his statement regarding the adequacy of the provision and ask for written evidence, for example, confirmation from the legal advisers.

It is also concerning that the audit manager told the audit assistant to conclude on the audit work when the planned procedures had not been performed. This does not provide good direction to the audit team and increases audit risk. There could be a material misstatement if the provision is significantly understated, and there is not sufficient evidence on the audit file to currently support the conclusions drawn.

Overall review

It is a requirement of ISA 520 *Analytical Procedures* that analytical procedures are performed at the overall review stage of the audit. An objective of ISA 520 is that the auditor should design and perform analytical procedures near the end of the audit which assist the auditor when forming their opinion as to whether the financial statements are consistent with the auditor's understanding of the entity.

It is unlikely that the audit senior's 'quick look' at Bradley Co's financial statements is adequate to meet the requirements of ISA 520 and audit documentation would seem to be inadequate. If the audit manager, or another auditor, does not perform a detailed analytical review on Bradley Co's financial statements as part of the completion of the audit, there is a breach of ISA 520. Failing to perform the final analytical review could mean that further errors are not found.

The auditor will not be able to check that the presentation of the financial statements conforms to the requirements of the applicable financial reporting framework. It is also doubtful whether a full check on the presentation and disclosure in the financial statements has been made. The firm should evidence this through the use of a disclosure checklist.

The lack of final analytical review increases audit risk. Because Bradley Co is a new audit client, it is particularly important that the analytical review is performed as detection risk is higher than for longer-standing audit engagements where the auditor has developed a cumulative knowledge of the audit client.

The fact that the audit manager suggested that a detailed review was not necessary shows a lack of knowledge and understanding of ISA requirements. An audit client being assessed as low risk does not negate the need for analytical review to be performed, which the audit manager should know. Alternatively, the audit manager may have known that analytical review should have been performed, but regardless of this still instructed the audit senior not to perform the review, maybe due to time pressure. The audit manager should be asked about the reason for his instruction and given further training if necessary.

The manager is not providing proper direction and supervision of the audit assistant, which goes against the principles of ISA 220 (Revised) *Quality Management for an Audit of Financial Statements*, and ISQM 1 *Quality Management for Firms that Perform Audits or Reviews of Financial Statements or Other Assurance or Related Services Engagements*. Both of these discuss the importance of the audit team having proper direction and supervision as part of ensuring a good quality of audit engagement performance.

Chair's statement

The final issue relates to the chair's statement. ISA 720 *The Auditor's Responsibilities Relating to Other Information* requires that the auditor shall read the other information to identify material inconsistencies, if any, with the audited financial statements.

The audit manager has discussed the chair's statement but this does not necessarily mean that the manager had read it for the purpose of identifying potential misstatements, and it might not have been read at all.

Even if the manager has read the chair's statement, there may not be any audit documentation to show that this has been done or the conclusion of the work. The manager needs to be asked exactly what work has been done, and what documentation exists. As the work performed does not comply with the ISA 720 requirements, then the necessary procedures must be performed before the auditor's report is issued. This is especially important as the necessary paragraphs will need to be included within the auditor's report setting out that the other information has been obtained, the responsibility that the auditor has for the other information explained and whether anything needs to be reported in relation to any inconsistencies.

Again, the situation could indicate the audit manager's lack of knowledge of ISA requirements, or that a short-cut is being taken, probably as a result of time pressure. In either case the quality of the audit is in jeopardy.

(b) (i) Evaluation of uncorrected misstatements

During the completion stage of the audit, the effect of uncorrected misstatements must be evaluated by the auditor, as required by ISA 450 *Evaluation of Misstatements Identified during the Audit*.

In the event that management refuses to correct some or all of the misstatements communicated by the auditor, ISA 450 requires that the auditor shall obtain an understanding of management's reasons for not making the corrections and shall take that understanding into account when evaluating whether the financial statements as a whole are free from material misstatement. Therefore, a discussion with management is essential in helping the auditor to form an audit opinion.

ISA 450 also requires that the auditor shall communicate with those charged with governance about uncorrected misstatements and the effect that they, individually or in aggregate, may have on the opinion in the auditor's report.

Each of the matters included in the schedule of uncorrected misstatements will be discussed below and the impact on the auditor's report considered individually and in aggregate.

Share-based payment scheme

The adjustment in relation to the share-based payment scheme is material individually to the statement of profit or loss, representing 12% of revenue. It represents less than 1% of total assets and is not material to the statement of financial position.

IFRS 2 *Share-based Payment* requires an expense and a corresponding entry to equity to be recognised over the vesting period of a share-based payment scheme, with the amount recognised based on the fair value of equity instruments granted. Management's argument that no expense should be recognised because the options are unlikely to be exercised is not correct.

IFRS 2 would classify the fall in Bradley Co's share price as a market condition, and these are not relevant to determining whether an expense is recognised or the amount of it.

Management should be requested to make the necessary adjustment to recognise the expense and entry to equity of $300,000. If this is not recognised, the financial statements will contain a material misstatement, with consequences for the auditor's opinion.

Restructuring provision

The adjustment in relation to the provision is material to the statement of profit or loss, representing 2% of revenue. It represents less than 1% of total assets so is not material to the statement of financial position.

The provision appears to have been recognised too early. IAS 37 *Provisions, Contingent Liabilities and Contingent Assets* requires that for a restructuring provision to be recognised, there must be a present obligation as a result of a past event, and that is only when a detailed formal plan is in place and the entity has started to implement the plan, or announced its main features to those affected.

A board decision is insufficient to create a present obligation as a result of a past event. The provision should be recognised in May 20X5 when the announcement to employees was made.

Management should be asked to explain why they have included the provision in the financial statements, for example, there may have been an earlier announcement before 30 April 20X5 of which the auditor is unaware.

In the absence of any such further information, management should be informed that the accounting treatment of the provision is a material misstatement, which if it remains unadjusted will have implications for the auditor's opinion.

(ii) **Impact on auditor's report**

The audit opinion must be modified when the auditor concludes that the financial statements as a whole are not free from material misstatement.

The auditor must consider whether any uncorrected misstatements are material, either on an individual basis, or in aggregate.

Aggregate materiality position

In aggregate, the misstatements have a net effect of $250,000 ($300,000 – $50,000), meaning that if left unadjusted, profit and the statement of financial position will be overstated by $250,000. This is material to profit, at 10% of revenue, but is not material to the statement of financial position at less than 1% of total assets.

Impact on auditor's report

The misstatements in relation to the share-based payment scheme and restructuring provision are individually material to the statement of profit or loss and therefore management should be requested to make these adjustments in order to avoid a modified opinion. The type of modification depends on the significance of the material misstatement.

In this case, the misstatements in aggregate are material to the financial statements, but are unlikely to be considered pervasive even though they relate to a number of balances in the financial statements as they do not represent a substantial proportion of the financial statements. This is supported by the fact that the adjustment is not material to the statement of financial position. It is therefore unlikely that the auditor will conclude that the financial statements as a whole are misleading.

A qualified opinion should be expressed, with the auditor stating in the opinion that except for the effects of the matters described in the basis for qualified opinion paragraph, the financial statements show a true and fair view.

The basis for qualified opinion paragraph which is positioned immediately after the opinion paragraph, should contain a description of the matters giving rise to the qualification. This should include a description and quantification of the financial effects of the misstatement.

Examiner's comments

This question scenario was set at the completion stage of the audit of Bradley Co, a significant new audit client, with the auditor's report due to be issued in the next week.

Requirement (a) provided some information in the form of a comment made by the audit senior, who indicated that there may have been some problems with the performance of the audit. The concerns raised included the lack of a detailed review of the final version of the financial statements and the chairman's statement had been discussed with the finance director but no further work had been conducted. The justification for not carrying out these tasks was the conclusion by the audit manager that the audit was relatively low risk. The requirement asked candidates to explain the quality and other professional issues raised by the audit senior's comments. Candidates did not perform well on this requirement, which was somewhat surprising as in the past questions on quality management issues have been well attempted. Only a minority of candidates were able to identify that the audit of a significant new client could not be classified as low risk, and that a final review would be needed on the financial statements at the completion stage of the audit. Very few candidates however mentioned that final analytical review is a requirement of ISA 520 *Analytical Procedures* and even fewer could explain why the final review is so important prior to the issuance of the auditor's report. In respect of the work performed on the chairman's statement, few candidates identified that there was a lack of documentation of the work performed, but most at least understood the auditor's responsibilities in relation to the chairman's statement.

Generally, the answers to this requirement were not made relevant to the information given in the scenario and instead mentioned general features of quality management such as the need for supervision and review. This will earn minimal credit, as marks are severely limited when answer points are not related to the scenario. Many answers discussed at length the reporting implications of uncorrected inconsistencies in the chairman's statement, but discussing this in a lot of detail was not answering the question requirement.

Requirements (b) dealt with the evaluation of misstatements and their potential implications for the auditor's opinion and report. The information was presented as a schedule of proposed adjustments to uncorrected misstatements in relation to a share-based payment scheme and a restructuring provision. In each case the auditor's proposed correcting journal was presented, along with an explanation of the audit findings and audit conclusion on the matter. Requirement (b)(i) asked for an explanation of the matters to be discussed with management in relation to each of the uncorrected misstatements, and requirement (b)(ii) asked candidates to justify an appropriate audit opinion assuming that management does not make the proposed adjustments. Both requirement (b)(i) and (b)(ii) were not well attempted. Answers were much too brief for the marks available and unfortunately many candidates could not competently demonstrate that they understand the topic of auditors' reports. Firstly, in relation to the share-based payment, the required financial reporting requirements were not well understood, with most candidates suggesting that a provision should be created rather than an adjustment made to equity, which was disappointing as this detail was actually given in the question. In relation to the restructuring provision, many candidates did not consider the specific requirements of IAS 37 *Provisions, Contingent Liabilities and Contingent Assets* in relation to restructuring provisions, and instead applied the general recognition criteria for provisions to the scenario.

On the whole, the only marks that many candidates were awarded in this requirement were for materiality calculations. There seems to be very little knowledge or understanding of ISA 450 *Evaluation of Misstatements Identified during the Audit* with almost no candidates differentiating between judgemental misstatements and misstatements caused by a breach of IFRS Accounting Standards.

The answers in relation to the impact on the auditor's report were also disappointing. Only the very best candidates considered the aggregate effect of the misstatements in discussing the audit opinion. Weaker candidates simply stated that each of the material misstatements would result in a qualified 'except for' opinion.

Candidates must appreciate that the process of justifying an audit opinion and explaining the implication for the auditor's report is a core area of the syllabus. It is regularly examined and it should not come as a surprise to see this topic in the exam. The presentation of information in this question should not have made the question more difficult, in fact having information presented in the form of journals with totals given should make understanding the question easier. Further, the structure of the requirement into two distinct sections should have helped candidates understand that they were being asked to consider the issues first and then to aggregate the effect of the misstatements before assessing the impact on the auditor's report.

ACCA Marking guide		
(a)	**Explanation of quality and other professional issues**	*Marks*
	Generally up to 1 mark for each point explained:	
	– Insufficient audit evidence obtained in relation to legal provision	
	– Possible limitation of scope imposed by management and intimidation threat	
	– Matter is immaterial but the issue is potential understatement of provisions	
	– Further procedures should be performed, necessary to exercise professional scepticism	
	– Audit manager's instructions are not appropriate and increase detection risk	
	– Analytical review mandatory at the final review stage	
	– Objective to ensure that financial statements consistent with auditor's understanding	
	– A quick look unlikely to be sufficient	
	– The fact that it is deemed low risk does not negate the need for analytical review	
	– Lack of analytical review increases audit risk	
	– Other information must be read with objective of identifying material inconsistencies	
	– Manager to be questioned to see what work has been done and what documentation exists	
	– Likely that chair's statement needs to be properly read and audit conclusion documented	
	– Audit manager lacks understanding of ISA requirements	
	– Audit manager may need further training	
	– Time pressure increases detection risk and impacts on the quality of the audit performed	
	Maximum	**8**
(b) **(i)**	**Explain matters to be considered in forming audit opinion**	
	Generally 1 mark for each point explained:	
	– ISAs require auditor to understand management's reason for not adjusting misstatements	
	– ISAs require auditor to communicate impact of unadjusted misstatement on opinion	
	Share-based payment	
	– Materiality assessment including appropriate calculation	
	– Fall in share price not valid reason for not recognising expense and credit to equity	
	– Material misstatement due to breach of financial reporting standards, encourage management to make necessary adjustment	
	Provision	
	– Materiality assessment including appropriate calculation	
	– Provision recognised too early, obligating event when closure announced	
	– Material misstatement due to breach of financial reporting standards	
	– Consider if any additional information to explain recognition of provision e.g. announcement before year end which auditor unaware of	
	– Encourage management to make necessary adjustment	
	Maximum	**7**

(ii)	**Impact on auditor's report**		

(ii) **Impact on auditor's report**

Generally up to 1 mark per point explained:

- Determination of aggregate impact of adjustments and combined materiality
- Individually material misstatements must be corrected to avoid a modified opinion
- Material misstatement and modified opinion necessary
- Discussion as to whether misstatement is material but not pervasive or material and pervasive
- Qualified opinion, except for wording
- Basis for qualified opinion paragraph to include a description and quantification of the financial effects of the misstatement

Maximum   5

Professional marks

Analysis and evaluation

- Appropriate use of the information to support discussion, draw appropriate conclusions and design appropriate responses
- Appropriate assessment of the quality and professional issues raised, using examples where relevant to support overall comments
- Effective appraisal of the information to make suitable recommendations for appropriate courses of action
- Balanced assessment of the information to determine the appropriate audit opinion in the circumstances

Professional scepticism and judgement

- Effective challenge and critical assessment of the evidence supplied with appropriate conclusions
- Demonstration of the ability to probe into the reasons for quality issues including the identification of missing information or additional information which would be required
- Appropriate application of professional judgement to draw conclusions and make informed comments regarding the quality of the work carried out

Commercial acumen

- Inclusion of appropriate recommendations regarding the additional actions required by the firm
- Appropriate recognition of the wider implications on the engagement, the audit firm and the company

Maximum   5

Total   25

41   SNIPE *Walk in the footsteps of a top tutor*

Top tutor tips

Part (a) is a typical 'audit matters' question. First, consider the materiality of the issue. Next discuss the appropriate accounting treatment and give the risks of material misstatement that would arise if the appropriate treatment is not followed.

Part (b) asks for a critical appraisal of the draft report extracts. Don't just focus on whether the opinion is appropriate. You should also think about the titles of the paragraphs included and whether the names are correct, the order they appear in, whether the required information that should be included has been included and whether the wording used is professional and appropriate.

(a)   (i)   New processing area

According to IAS 23 *Borrowing Costs,* borrowing costs that are directly attributable to the acquisition, construction or production of a qualifying asset should be capitalised as part of the cost of that asset. The directly attributable costs, including borrowing costs, relating to the new processing area should be capitalised as property, plant and equipment.

The borrowing costs should be capitalised only during the period of construction, with capitalisation ceasing when substantially all the activities necessary to prepare the qualifying asset for its intended use or sale are complete. In this case, the new processing area was ready for use on 1 November, so borrowing costs should have been capitalised from 1 May 20X4 to 1 November 20X4. From 1 November 20X4 interest should have been recognised within finance costs.

Borrowing costs of $100,000, which represents six months' interest on the loan ($4m × 5% × 6/12) should have been capitalised as part of the cost of the asset and $83,333 ($4m × 5% × 5/12) should have been included in finance costs. This is material being 10% of profit before tax.

Property, plant and equipment is understated by $100,000 and finance costs overstated by the same amount due to borrowing costs being treated as finance costs.

According to IAS 16 *Property, Plant and Equipment,* depreciation of an asset begins when it is in the location and condition necessary for it to be capable of operating in the manner intended by management. The new processing area should be depreciated from 1 November 20X4 rather than February 20X5.

Depreciation is currently misstated by two months' charge amounting to $55,555 ($5m/15 years × 2/12) understating both expenses and property, plant and equipment. This is material being 5.6% of profit before tax.

(ii) **Assets held for sale**

The properties classified as assets held for sale are material to the financial statements as the year-end carrying amount of $24 million represent 13.7% of total assets.

Assets can only be classified as held for sale if the conditions referred to in IFRS 5 *Non-current Assets Held for Sale and Discontinued Operations* are met. The conditions include the following:

- Management is committed to a plan to sell

- The assets are available for immediate sale

- An active programme to locate a buyer is initiated

- The sale is highly probable, within 12 months of classification as held for sale (subject to limited exceptions)

- The asset is being actively marketed for sale at a sales price reasonable in relation to its fair value

- Actions required to complete the plan indicate that it is unlikely that the plan will be significantly changed or withdrawn.

There is a risk that the assets have been inappropriately classified if the above conditions have not been met.

IFRS 5 requires that at classification as held for sale, assets are measured at the lower of carrying amount and fair value less costs to sell. This appears to have been correctly accounted for when classification occurred in December 20X4.

Though not specifically required by IFRS 5, an impairment review should take place at 31 March 20X5, to ensure that there is no further impairment of the properties to be recognised at the year end. If an impairment review has not taken place, the assets may be misstated in value.

The assets should not be depreciated after being classified as held for sale, therefore the auditor should confirm with management and through inspection of the asset register that depreciation has ceased from December 20X4.

Disclosure is needed in the notes to the financial statements to include a description of the non-current assets classified as held for sale, a description of the facts and circumstances of the sale and its expected timing, and a quantification of the impairment loss and where in the statement of profit or loss and other comprehensive income it is recognised. If full disclosure has not been made, the auditor must discuss with management the need for additional disclosure.

(iii) **Defined benefit pension plan**

The deficit of $10.5 million is material to the financial statements as it represents 6% of total assets.

IAS 19 *Employee Benefits* requires the deficit to be recognised in the statement of financial position. The current and past service costs and net interest should be recognised in the statement of profit or loss. Any actuarial gains or losses should be included within other comprehensive income.

Extensive disclosures are in relation to the characteristics of the plan and associated risks, the amounts included in the financial statements in relation the plan and a description of how the plan may affect the amount, timing and uncertainty of the future cash flows.

The requirements of IAS 19 must be discussed with management as currently liabilities and possibly expenses and other comprehensive income are materially misstated.

(b) The **description and explanation** provided for the adverse opinion is not sufficient, for a number of reasons. Firstly, the matter is not quantified. The paragraph should clearly state the amount of $10.5 million, and state that this is material to the financial statements.

There is **no description of the impact of this omission** on the financial statements. The paragraph does not say whether the pension plan is in surplus or deficit, i.e. whether it is an asset or a liability which is omitted from the financial statements. Wording such as 'if the deficit had been recognised, total liabilities would increase by $10.5 million, and shareholders' equity would reduce by the same amount' should be included.

It is **not clear whether any accounting for the pension plan has taken place** at all. As well as recognising the plan surplus or deficit in the statement of financial position, accounting entries are also required to deal with other items such as the current service cost of the plan, and any actuarial gains or losses which have arisen during the year. Whether these have been omitted as well, and their potential impact on profit or equity is not mentioned.

No reference is made to the relevant accounting standard IAS 19 *Employee Benefits*. Reference should be made in order to help users' understanding of the breach of accounting standards that has been made.

The **use of the word 'deliberate'** when describing the omission of the pension plan is not professional, sounds accusatory and may not be correct. The plan may have been omitted in error and an adjustment to the financial statements may have been suggested by the audit firm and is being considered by management.

It is **unlikely that this issue alone would be sufficient to give rise to an adverse opinion**. An adverse opinion should be given when misstatements are both material and pervasive to the financial statements. The amount of the deficit, and therefore the liability that should be recognised, is $10.5 million, which represents 6% of total assets. The amount is definitely material, but would not be considered pervasive to the financial statements.

The **titles and positioning of the two paragraphs** included in the extract are not appropriate. In this case, the titles are incorrect, and the paragraphs should be switched round, so that the basis for modification is provided **after** the opinion.

The opinion paragraph should be entitled 'Adverse Opinion'.

When the auditor modifies the opinion, the 'Basis for Adverse Opinion', should describe the matter giving rise to the modification.

Tutorial note

Where a misstatement is confined to specific elements of the financial statements, it would only be considered pervasive if it represents a substantial proportion of the financial statements.

Examiner's comments

Part (a) described the self-construction of new property, plant and equipment at a client. A loan had been taken out to help finance the construction, and financial information was provided in relation to the asset and the loan. Candidates should have been familiar with this type of question requirement, as it commonly features in the exam. Sound answers contained a calculation and explanation of the materiality of the asset and of the borrowing costs that had been capitalised, followed by a discussion of the appropriate accounting treatment, including whether the borrowing cost should be capitalised, and when depreciation in relation to the asset should commence. There were some sound answers here, with candidates demonstrating sound knowledge of the relevant financial reporting standard requirements, and going on to provide some very well described and relevant audit procedures. Weaker answers said that it was not possible to capitalise borrowing costs, or incorrectly thought that the construction should be accounted for as some kind of long-term construction contract.

The second issue described a number of properties that had been classified as held for sale. Information was given on the carrying amount and fair value less cost to sell of the properties. Most answers were satisfactory, largely because candidates were confident in explaining the relevant financial reporting requirements and applying them to the brief scenario.

Part (b) involved the critique of an extract from the auditor's report. The report contained an adverse opinion, which most candidates spotted, in relation to the non-recognition of a defined benefit pension deficit on the company's statement of financial position. There were some sound answers here, and candidates' performance in questions of this type has shown a definite improvement. Some answers not only identified but also provided an explanation of the problems with the auditor's report. The majority of answers suggested that an 'except for' qualification may be more suitable than an adverse opinion, and correctly calculated the materiality of the pension plan deficit to support their discussion. A significant proportion of answers picked up on the order of the paragraphs in the report and on the incorrect wording used in the headings, and on the lack of explanation that had been provided in the report regarding the material misstatement. Fewer answers discussed the inappropriate use of the phrase 'deliberate omission'. The weaker answers tended to just list out bullet points with no explanation, limiting the amount of marks that could be awarded. Other weaker answers attempted to discuss the appropriate accounting treatment for the pension, often incorrectly.

	ACCA Marking guide	Marks
(a)	Generally 1 mark for each point explained:	
	(i) **New processing area**	
	– IAS 23 definition of borrowing costs – directly attributable to the asset	
	– Borrowing costs should be capitalised during period of construction	
	– Calculation of borrowing costs and finance costs for the year	
	– Misstatement of borrowing costs is material (calculation)	
	– PPE understated and finance costs overstated	
	– Depreciate from date asset is ready to use	
	– Calculation of misstatement to depreciation	
	– Misstatement of depreciation is material (calculation)	
	Maximum	6

	(ii)	**Assets held for sale**	
		– Assets held for sale are material (calculation)	
		– Conditions required to classify assets as held for sale (up to 2 marks)	
		– Re-measurement at classification appears correct	
		– Further impairment review may be needed at year end	
		– Depreciation should not be charged after reclassification	
		– Disclosure in notes to financial statements	
		Maximum	**5**

	(iii)	**Defined benefit pension plan**	
		– Actuarial deficit is material (calculation)	
		– IAS 19 – amounts to be recognised (up to 2 marks)	
		– Extensive disclosure requirements (up to 2 marks)	
		– Discuss treatment with management	
		Maximum	**4**

(b) **Auditor's report**

Generally 1 mark per comment:
- Amounts not quantified
- Impact on financial statements not described
- Unclear from report if any accounting taken place
- No reference made to relevant accounting standard
- Use of word 'deliberate' not professional
- Discuss whether adverse opinion appropriate
- Inappropriate headings
- Paragraph order

Maximum	**5**

Professional marks

Analysis and evaluation
- Appropriate use of the information to support discussion, draw appropriate conclusions and design appropriate responses
- Identification of omissions from the analysis or further analysis which could be carried out
- Balanced assessment of the information to determine the appropriate audit opinion in the circumstances

Professional scepticism and judgement
- Effective challenge of information, evidence and assumptions supplied and, techniques carried out to support key facts and/or decisions
- Appropriate application of professional judgement to draw conclusions and make informed decisions about the actions which are appropriate in the context and stage of the engagement

Commercial acumen
- Demonstrate insight and perception in understanding the wider implications and acumen in arriving at suitable conclusions

Maximum	**5**
Total	**25**

OTHER ASSIGNMENTS

42   KOBOLD *Walk in the footsteps of a top tutor*

Top tutor tips

Part (a) requires matters to consider before accepting a PFI engagement. Use the scenario to identify specific matters for this question rather than giving rote-learned answers. At this level you must be able to apply knowledge to a given situation.

In part (b) the examination procedures need to focus on obtaining evidence to support the assumptions used to prepare the forecast. Remember that these transactions have not happened as of yet so you will not be able to inspect invoices, etc. Instead, consider the assumptions provided in the scenario and assess whether there is justification for them. There are clues in the scenario; for example, the notes to the forecast mention regulatory authority approval, calculations, and quotations.

(a)   Matters to consider before accepting the review engagement

When determining whether to enter into a professional relationship with a new client, an assurance firm is required to assess whether this would be possible under the criteria of ISQM1 *Quality Management for Firms that Perform Audits or Reviews of Financial Statements or Other Assurance or Related Service Engagements*.

Gnome & Co should also ensure that they are following the IESBA *International Code of Ethics for Professional Accountants* (the Code).

Integrity and ethical values of the client

Gnome & Co will be required to perform customer due diligence and in particular will be expected to consider the identity and business reputation of Kobold Co's principal owners, key management, and those charged with governance. This will also involve obtaining documents to prove the identity of such people using a passport or other legal documents and considering whether there are any indications that the client might be involved in money laundering or other criminal activities.

The firm will also need to consider management's reasons for appointing a different firm from its auditors and the potential for management bias in the preparation of the capital expenditure forecast in support of the application for finance. In order to provide an assurance report on forecasts such as this, a good understanding of the client and its business is required, and the current audit firm will usually have the requisite knowledge and understanding. Gnome & Co should therefore consider whether the use of a different firm creates a risk that the client may be hoping that the firm may not be in a position to effectively challenge the key assumptions underlying the preparation of the forecast. When a professional accountant is asked to perform work for a non-audit client, they should be given permission by the client to contact its auditors in order to obtain relevant information. If this permission is not given, the appointment should be declined.

In addition, Gnome & Co should consider the attitude of the client and the risk of bias given that Kobold Co has entered into a contract prior to obtaining finance. This could mean that the forecast might be manipulated to ensure the highest possibility of the bank providing finance or that management may pressure Gnome & Co to present a favourable opinion regarding the forecast due to the risk management has taken by committing to the building work before finance has been made available.

Performance of the engagement in accordance with professional, legal and regulatory standards

It would be expected that, as a firm providing audit and related services, Gnome & Co has staff within the firm who have appropriate competence and capabilities to perform the assurance on the capital expenditure forecast. However, the short deadline of October 20X5 may limit the resources, in respect of both the availability of staff and being able to obtain sufficient evidence, which may put pressure on the firm to perform the work in the time scale required. This might impact on the quality of the engagement which can be performed. Where this is the case, Gnome & Co should not accept the engagement.

Ethical issues

Given that Kobold Co is not currently a client of Gnome & Co, the firm's independence from Kobold Co will not have been previously considered. In this regard, it is important to ensure that there are no threats to the firm's objectivity which might prevent it from accepting the appointment. If the firm is not independent and its objectivity is compromised, the reliability of the assurance report will be undermined.

Gnome & Co should also consider whether there are any conflicts of interest between Kobold Co and any of the firm's existing clients. Where any such conflicts exist, Gnome & Co would be required to notify both Kobold Co and the existing client explaining the situation and proposed safeguards which will be implemented to mitigate the risk.

The intended use of the information

Gnome & Co must consider, for example, whether the capital expenditure forecast and assurance report will be used solely for the purpose of securing the loan. If Kobold Co is planning to use the assurance report for purposes other than raising the loan, such as renewal of its overdraft facility, this must be made clear to Gnome & Co.

Whether the information will be for general or limited distribution

Gnome & Co needs to consider who will receive the report and potentially rely upon it as this will impact on the firm's assessment of the risk associated with the engagement. If the capital expenditure forecast is intended for general distribution, this will increase the level of risk for Gnome & Co as a larger audience will rely on it. In this case, the information should be used solely in support of the application to the bank and should not be made available to other parties. It is important this is confirmed before accepting the engagement to limit the risk of the engagement.

The period covered by the capital expenditure forecast and the nature of the key assumptions used

Gnome & Co must also consider the period covered by the forecast and the nature of the key assumptions which have been used in its preparation. Short-term forecasts are likely to be easier to verify and provide assurance on than longer term projections. ISAE 3400 *The Examination of Prospective Financial Information* states that a prospective financial information (PFI) engagement should not be accepted when the assumptions used in its preparation are clearly unrealistic or when the practitioner believes that the PFI will be inappropriate for its intended use. In the case of Kobold Co, although the forecast is only for two years, some of the assumptions used in the forecast may be unreliable, particularly given the inexperience of the new financial controller, such as the basis for estimations, forecasting of future costs, timing of future payments.

The scope of the work

Gnome & Co will need to consider the specific terms of the engagement, the level of assurance being sought by Kobold Co and the form of the report required by the bank. Gnome & Co will need to identify clearly the elements which it is being asked to report on – for example, is it being asked to report on the capital expenditure forecast only or is the firm also being asked to report on accompanying narrative or other prospective financial information. Due to the uncertainty of forecasts and the inevitable subjectivity involved in their preparation, Gnome & Co will need to confirm that it is only being asked to provide negative assurance as to whether management's assumptions provide a reasonable basis for the capital expenditure forecast and to give an opinion as to whether it is properly prepared on the basis of these assumptions.

(b)   Examination procedures on the capital (asset) expenditure forecast

–   Obtain detailed analyses of each category of capital expenditure and cast to confirm their arithmetical accuracy.

–   Obtain a copy of the draft loan agreement to review for the terms of the repayment of the capital amount, the interest rate, as well as any guarantees or securities required on the loan amount.

–   Obtain a copy of the planning approval confirmation from the local planning authority and review it for any conditions attached to the approval and confirm the cost of such conditions have been included in the cash flow forecast.

–   Review Kobold Co's correspondence file with the company's legal advisers and the local planning authorities in order to identify all relevant costs and to confirm approval for the project to proceed.

–   Inspect the contracts with the architect and the surveyor and confirm the terms of engagement including their fees and agree inclusion in the forecast.

–   Obtain and review the architect's plans and the surveyor's reports in order to confirm management's intention to construct the distribution centre and in order to develop an understanding of its key features including its size and location.

–   Confirm the estimated costs of the site preparation and the building by reference to the quotations from the respective construction contractors.

–   Review the proposed interior designs for the facility and confirm proposed fittings to supplier price lists.

- Discuss the key assumptions underlying the preparation of the forecast with management, including:

  - The timings of any stage payments

  - Price changes over the two-year period

  - Variability of costs and whether building costs are fixed or variable should issues arise

  - Confirm that the assumptions appear reasonable and are consistent with the firm's knowledge and understanding of the client.

- Discuss with management whether any additional costs might have been omitted from its costing analyses including, for example, interest and capital repayments on the loan, the landscaping of grounds or upgrades to road access.

- Review the board minutes for evidence of any issues arising in relation to the project or in relation to any other recent loan applications.

- Analytically review the forecast trends in cash flows comparing with them with historical capital expenditure statements and other data which is available for the industry and local economy.

- Perform sensitivity analyses on the capital expenditure forecast by varying the key assumptions (in particular, in relation to payment periods) and assessing the impact of these variations on the company's capital expenditure forecast.

- Obtain written representations from management confirming the reasonableness of their assumptions and that all relevant information has been provided to Gnome & Co.

Examiner's comments

This 25-mark question was based on a capital (asset) expenditure forecast for a company with two requirements, firstly to evaluate acceptance matters for the review and report of the forecast, and secondly, to recommend the examination procedures to be performed. Professional skill marks were available for analysis and evaluation, professional scepticism and judgement and commercial acumen.

The question required candidates to appreciate that Gnome & Co, the firm looking to undertake the review, was not the current auditor of the prospective client.

Requirement (a)

Answers to this question were some of the best across the paper. The requirement appeared to be well understood by the majority of candidates and answers were of sufficient length that time pressure did not seem to have shortened responses.

Some candidates misunderstood the scenario whereby Gnome & Co are not the current auditor and therefore their answers were directed away from critically analysing the possible reason for the client not using their current auditor for the forecast. This limited the number of technical and professional skills marks that could be achieved due to attempting the question from the wrong perspective. Where candidates failed to score well, they had neglected to apply their answers to the specific details in the scenario and produced generic rote learned lists that would score limited technical credit and miss out on valuable professional skills marks. Although candidates scored well overall and there was a good grasp of the technical content, marks could have been improved for many candidates by giving reference to the wider implications of the engagement for the firm, and thereby demonstrating commercial acumen. This involved a slight alteration in the candidate's perspective when considering the acceptance criteria by considering it for the firm as a whole rather than for the engagement in isolation. Candidates who displayed commercial acumen considered issues such as resourcing limitations in the wider firm and fee issues that made reference to the scenario. A further professional mark was available for candidates who gave a reasoned conclusion of whether the engagement should be accepted or not, and it was important that this was borne out a balanced discussion of the points developed in the technical marks in order to display the appropriate level of professional judgement.

Requirement (b)

The second requirement requested examination procedures on the capex forecast and was generally well received by candidates. The lack of time pressure was apparent as there was no additional reading from the first part of the question and many students produced sufficiently detailed and high scoring answers. Weaker candidates requested the same documentation types for each of the elements of the forecast, e.g. repeated quotes and invoices, and marks here were restricted. Stronger candidates were able to identify possible omissions from the information provided in the scenario, such as interest on the loan that was being applied for. Candidates are encouraged to produce a carefully considered list of examination procedures, which are specific to the scenario, rather than long and unwieldy lists that are less accurate and repetitive as there is professional credit in concise and detailed information, which is reflected in the awarding of the analysis and evaluation professional mark.

ACCA Marking guide	Marks

(a) **Evaluate the matters to be considered by Gnome & Co before accepting Kobold Co as a client and the engagement to review and report on the capital (asset) expenditure forecast**
 Generally, 1 mark for each relevant point explained:
 – Client integrity – customer due diligence
 – Client integrity – decision not to use existing auditor
    • Need to understand the business
    • May not sufficiently question assumptions
    • Access to auditor
 – Capability – competence
 – Capability – resource availability
 – Ethical issues – independence
 – Ethical issues – conflict of interest
 – Ethical issues – conflict of interest
 – Professional issues – intended use/distribution
 – Professional issues – nature of assumptions/time period
 – Professional issues – scope of work	

Maximum	10

(b) **Examination procedures**

Generally, 1 mark for each well-described procedure. Examples include, but are not limited to:

- Obtain detailed analyses of each category of capital expenditure and cast to confirm their arithmetical accuracy
- Obtain a copy of the draft loan agreement to review for the terms of the repayment, interest rate, guarantees or securities
- Obtain a copy of the planning approval confirmation and review for any conditions attached to the approval and confirm the costs have been included in the cash flow forecast
- Review correspondence with the company's legal advisers and the local planning authorities to identify all relevant costs and to confirm approval for the project to proceed
- Inspect the contracts with the architect and the surveyor and confirm the terms of engagement including their fees
- Obtain and review the architect's plans and the surveyor's reports to confirm management's intention to construct the distribution centre and develop an understanding of key features
- Inspect construction contractors' quotations to confirm estimated site preparation costs and the building
- Review the proposed interior designs for the facility and confirm proposed fittings to supplier price lists
- Discuss the key assumptions underlying the preparation of the forecast with management, including:
  - The timings of any stage payments
  - Price changes over the two-year period
  - Variability of costs and whether building costs are fixed or variable should issues arise
  - Confirm that the assumptions appear reasonable and are consistent with the firm's knowledge and understanding
- Discuss any additional costs which might have been omitted from its costing analyses including, e.g., interest and capital repayments on the loan, the landscaping of grounds or upgrades to road access
- Review board minutes for evidence of issues arising in relation to the project or in relation to any other recent loan applications
- Analytically review the forecast trends in cash flows comparing with them with historical asset expenditure and other data which is available for the sector and local economy
- Perform sensitivity analyses on the forecast by varying the key assumptions (in particular, in relation to growth rates and payment periods) and assessing the impact of these variations on the company's forecast cash position
- Obtain written representations from management confirming the reasonableness of their assumptions and that all relevant information has been provided to Gnome & Co

		Maximum	**10**

Professional marks

Analysis and evaluation

- Appropriate assessment of the relevant ethical and professional issues relating to acceptance of the engagement, using examples where relevant to support overall comments
- Identification of omissions from the forecast and identifying further analysis which could be carried out, with an appraisal on the elements of the forecast
- Evaluation of the available evidence by the identification of further specific sources of information in order to validate and corroborate assumptions and estimations made in the forecast by the client

Professional scepticism and professional judgement – Effective challenge and critical assessment of the acceptance considerations supplied with appropriate conclusions – Effective challenge and critical assessment of the assumptions used by management in preparing the asset expenditure forecast – Demonstration of the ability to probe for further information in order to make an assessment of the completeness of the cash flow forecast – Demonstration of professional judgement in identifying where procedures should focus on the riskier areas of the forecast to recommend suitable procedures **Commercial acumen** – Demonstration of commercial awareness by recognising wider issues which may affect the forecast and the assumptions by management	
Maximum	5
Total	**25**

43 FLYNN *Walk in the footsteps of a top tutor*

Top tutor tips

Part (a) requires matters to consider before accepting a PFI engagement. Use the scenario to identify specific matters for this question rather than giving rote-learned answers. At this level you must be able to apply knowledge to a given situation.

In part (b) (i), you need to critically appraise the assumptions provided in the scenario. Use your professional scepticism to evaluate whether the assumptions are reasonable and complete.

In part (b) (ii) the examination procedures need to focus on obtaining evidence to support the assumptions used to prepare the forecast. Remember that these transactions have not happened as of yet so you will not be able to inspect invoices, etc. Instead, consider the assumptions provided in the scenario and assess whether there is justification for them.

(a)   Matters to be considered before accepting Flynn Co as a client of the firm and performing the review engagement

Requirements and guidance relevant to accepting and continuing client relationships is contained in ISQM 1 *Quality Management for Firms that Perform Audits or Reviews of Financial Statements or Other Assurance or Related Services Engagements*. The fundamental requirements are that a firm must consider:

– Whether the relevant ethical requirements can be complied with;

– The integrity of the client, and whether there is information which would lead it to conclude that the client lacks integrity; and

– Whether the firm has the appropriate competence and resources.

Ethical issues

In terms of ethics there are several matters to consider. First, it appears from the communication with the company's managing director that Flynn Co is encouraging Kelly & Co to accept the review engagement by offering the audit appointment as a 'reward' assuming that the outcome of the loan application is successful. This creates a self-interest threat in that Kelly & Co has a financial interest in accepting Flynn Co as a client and performing the review engagement in order to secure appointment as the company's auditor.

An advocacy threat is also created because Kelly & Co has an incentive to promote Flynn Co to the bank to ensure that the loan will be provided, and this may impact the quality and objectivity of the review engagement.

Kelly & Co should consider whether any safeguards can be implemented to reduce any ethical threats to an acceptable level, for example, using an independent second partner to review the work performed for the review engagement. If safeguards do not reduce the threats to an acceptable level, then the review engagement should not be performed.

Finally, the fact that Mary Sunshine, an audit manager of Kelly & Co has recently been recruited from Flynn Co raises ethical threats to objectivity. The IESBA *International Code of Ethics for Professional Accountants* states that self-interest, self-review and familiarity threats may arise where an audit team member has recently served as director, officer or employee of the client. These threats could arise should Mary Sunshine be part of the audit team, as suggested by Flynn Co's managing director. The provisions of the Code apply to review engagements as well as audit engagements and therefore are applicable to the review of the cash flow forecast.

Given that Mary Sunshine had previously worked in internal audit at Flynn Co, the self-review threat could arise, should she be included in the review engagement team, as she may lack the necessary professional scepticism to challenge the forecasts prepared by Flynn Co. However, given that Mary was part of internal audit at Flynn Co, she would not have been in a position to exert influence over the financial statements, so the risk is reduced. However, she may also have close personal relationships with the staff at Flynn Co making it likely that she would want to secure a favourable outcome for the loan application, impacting on her objectivity.

These threats to objectivity may appear significant but they can be reduced to an acceptable level by ensuring that Mary is not included in the review team and should Kelly & Co become audit provider to Flynn Co, ensuring that she is not involved with the audit this year.

Client integrity

One issue relating to client integrity is the incentive that has been offered for Kelly & Co to become audit provider should the loan application be successful. In relation to client integrity, ISQM 1 suggests that the firm should consider the reasons for the proposed appointment of the firm and non-reappointment of the previous firm as a matter relating to client integrity.

In this case, the fact that the latest auditor's report contained a Material Uncertainty Related to Going Concern section and the comments by Mary Sunshine indicates that Flynn Co has financial problems and in particular, it appears that liquidity issues are creating doubts over going concern. Therefore, management of Flynn Co may be reluctant to appoint their existing audit firm to provide the review service on the basis that the audit firm may not be likely to support the application.

Related to this, Kelly & Co should carefully consider the going concern issue, as it creates a higher risk for the review engagement. The firm could become exposed to liability issues, should the bank provide the loan, and Flynn Co not be able to repay the amount advanced. For this reason, it could be that the existing audit firm has been approached to provide the review engagement but has declined the assignment.

Competence and resources

There seems no reason why Kelly & Co would not have the competence to carry out the assignment to review the cash flow forecast. Being a firm of Chartered Certified Accountants and performing a range of assurance services means that the firm has the relevant knowledge and experience to perform a high quality review of a cash flow forecast for a business which does not appear to be a very complex organisation.

However, as discussed above, this is a high-risk engagement due to the going concern problems of Flynn Co. Should the work be performed, it is likely that Kelly & Co would want to include experienced and senior staff in the review engagement team, in order to reduce risk exposure. It may be that such staff are not available at this time.

Resourcing could be a problem given that Flynn Co expects the loan application to be submitted on 5 August 20X5, which is just over a month from now. Kelly & Co may not have capacity to provide staff to carry out the review engagement and the tight deadline could impact the quality of the work performed. Kelly & Co should discuss with Flynn Co whether there is any flexibility regarding the deadline, with the objective of having longer to plan and carry out the work required.

Matters specific to ISAE 3400 *The Examination of Prospective Financial Information*

Kelly & Co should also consider the matters outlined in ISAE 3400, which suggests that before accepting an engagement to examine prospective financial information, the auditor would consider, amongst other things:

– The intended use of the information

– Whether the information will be for general or limited distribution

– The nature of the assumptions, that is, whether they are best-estimate or hypothetical assumptions

– The elements to be included in the information

– The period covered by the information.

Review engagements can vary in terms of the level of work that is required, depending on the level of assurance that is required from the review. This level of assurance required will impact on the scale of the assignment. Kelly & Co should clarify the expected form and content and expected wording of the review report and who will be using the review report, so they understand the risk exposure for the firm.

ISAE 3400 also contains a requirement that the auditor should not accept, or should withdraw from, an engagement when the assumptions are clearly unrealistic or when the auditor believes that the prospective financial information will be inappropriate for its intended use.

The above matters should be discussed with Flynn Co as soon as possible, to help Kelly & Co to establish whether to proceed with the engagement.

(b) **(i)** **Evaluation of the assumptions used by management in preparing the cash flow forecast**

Monthly sales figures

The forecast of monthly sales figures appears overly optimistic, e.g. the expected revenue growth of 17% in the period to 30 June 20X6 appears optimistic given that the new production plant is only expected to open in March 20X6. Expectations of popularity of the new product range in particular may be overly optimistic, the successful launch of a new product is not guaranteed, even if it is supported by an advertising campaign.

Even if the processing plant is ready for use from 31 March 20X6, as stated in the forecast assumptions, it only leaves three months for a very significant increase in sales resulting from new product ranges produced at the plant to be achieved. Management may be manipulating the forecast to accelerate the cash inflows in order to reduce the payback period of the capital (asset) expenditure.

New processing plant – commencement of operations

Assuming that the loan is advanced in August 20X5, this allows only seven months for the construction and fitting of the new processing plant, which seems a short timeframe for this to take place. Management may be being over optimistic in their assessment of how quickly the plant can be constructed and brought into use.

In addition, there is no cash flow specific to factory start-up costs, e.g. staff recruitment and training, included in the cash flow forecast. There is a possibility that these costs have been omitted in error or deliberately in order to show the total cost of the new processing plant as $15 million i.e. the costs will all be covered by the loan which has been applied for, and that no further costs will be incurred.

Increase in production capacity

Management's assumption that production capacity can be increased without any need for capital (asset) expenditure at existing production facilities should be challenged by the audit team. This assumption relies on there being spare capacity in the existing facilities, which may not be the case.

Reduction in operating expenses

Management's claim that economies of scale are being achieved, therefore improving operating margins, may not be appropriate and is an attempt to overstate the cash position shown in the forecast. Opening a new production facility separately located from the company's other production plants in a foreign country is unlikely to achieve economies of scale, certainly not in the timescale suggested by management.

Foreign exchange transactions

The cash flow forecast does not indicate how foreign exchange transactions have been dealt with. Transactions relating to the existing processing plant in Nearland, and more significantly, the capital (asset) expenditure and other transactions for the new plant in Farland are in a foreign currency but the effect of exchange rates on cash flows are not shown in the forecast. Management could be ignoring these impacts relating to foreign exchange to reduce the volatility of cash flows as presented in the forecast.

Finance costs

It is unusual that interest costs and other finance costs are completely static, indicating that the amount has not been accurately calculated. The amount also appears very low – if the category includes interest costs only, these amount to only $60,000 per annum which equates to only 0.4% of the $15 million loan. It appears that management is underestimating the interest costs, especially if the company has existing debt on which interest is being paid. It could also be the case that the company has existing debt which needs to be repaid – there is no cash outflow relating to capital repayments within the forecast.

Tax expenses

There does not appear to be any cash flows relating to tax payments included in the forecast. If management is claiming that there will be no tax payments during the period covered by the forecast, this assertion needs to be approached with professional scepticism as it is unlikely that no tax payments at all will occur during this time. These payments may be deliberately omitted to improve the cash flow position as shown in the forecast.

Conclusion

Given the material uncertainty over going concern highlighted in the recent auditor's report there is a significant risk that the assumptions used in preparation of the cash flow forecast are not realistic and have been applied to make the cash flow forecast look more favourable in an attempt to secure the loan finance from the bank.

(ii) **Examination procedures on the cash flow forecast**

- Re-cast the forecast to ensure it is arithmetically correct.

- Agree the opening cash balance of $50,000 to bank statement and management accounts.

- Discuss with appropriate personnel, e.g. sales director and product development team, to obtain understanding of the new product ranges to be produced in Farland and the basis for management's assumption regarding the expected popularity of the new products leading to the forecast high levels of demand.

- Obtain supporting evidence for the projected increase in sales attributed to the new product range, e.g. correspondence with potential customers and any signed customer contracts, results of market research.

- Obtain and review the plans for marketing the new product ranges including analysis of the planned expenditure of $100,000 and confirm there are no additional planned expenses to confirm completeness.

- Obtain and review supporting documentation for management's assertion that production levels in existing processing facilities will increase by 10%, e.g. review production budgets, orders placed with suppliers for inputs to the processing, which should help to corroborate the assertion.

- Compare the monthly sales figures in the cash flow forecast to those in the profit forecast to ensure consistency.

- For the pattern of cash inflows from sales, confirm that the timing of cash receipts from customers used in the forecast agrees with those evidenced from past records e.g. management accounts, aged receivables listing. Discuss any discrepancy with management.

- Recalculate the patterns of cash flows based on management's historical analysis of credit sales to confirm that the forecast has been properly prepared on the basis of these assumptions.

- Obtain a breakdown showing the components of operating expenses; perform analytical procedures comparing the forecasts to the actual expenses included in the audited financial statements, in particular reviewing for completeness and classification, and discuss results with management.

- Analyse the trend in operating expenses, compare with the trend in sales e.g. over the whole period of the forecast, sales increase by 60% over the period of the forecast, whereas operating expenses increase by much less, only 45% over the same period.

- Discuss the timing of cash flows relating to operating expenses with the preparer of the forecast to obtain understanding of how these figures have been determined.

- Compare the level of operating expenses with historical financial information and with the profit forecast and discuss any significant variances with management.

- Assess whether there are any missing categories of cash flow, e.g. there does not appear to be any cash flows relating to tax payments. Discuss any potentially omitted expense categories with management to understand why they have not been included in the forecast.

- Enquire with management how foreign exchange transactions have been dealt with in the forecast.

- Agree interest costs to existing and potential loan documents or other relevant supporting documentation.

- For the planned capital (asset) expenditure, obtain a detailed breakdown of the costs included in the $15 million planned expenditure and agree a sample of costs to supporting documentation e.g. quotes for construction, cost of land acquisition, quotes from suppliers of plant and machinery to verify the completeness of the estimated cost of the construction of the new facility.

- Confirm the exchange rate which has been used to determine the $ value of the anticipated capital (asset) expenditure which has been included in the forecast.

- Confirm by agreeing to historical financial statements that the level of dividend of $100,000 each year appears in line with previous payments. Given the company's going concern problems it may be that dividends have not been paid in recent years, in which case the forecast level of dividend payable should be discussed with management.

- Review the planned capital (asset) expenditure for any missing expenses, e.g. does it include incidental costs such as installing health and safety equipment, testing of machinery prior to use.

- Enquire with management to understand whether or how start-up costs for the new processing facility which are not capital in nature have been included in the cash flow forecast e.g. recruitment and training of staff.

- Obtain supporting evidence that the new processing facility will be ready for use on 31 March 20X6, as claimed by management, e.g. a project plan provided by the construction firm.

- Obtain the published financial statements and auditor's report of Flynn Co for the year ended 31 March 20X5 and review the content of the auditor's report to confirm the opinion issued and the Material Uncertainty Related to Going Concern paragraph.

- Given the material uncertainty related to going concern highlighted in the auditor's report, request permission to communicate with the auditor to discuss the going concern issues, to obtain understanding and to assist in evaluating the assumptions underpinning the cash flow forecast.

- Assuming that permission is given to communicate with the auditor, discuss the specific nature of the liquidity issue as mentioned in their auditor's report, e.g. have previous applications for finance been rejected, are there any specific factors contributing to financial distress in this financial year.

- Confirm that the assumptions underpinning the cash flow forecast are consistent with those used in the rest of the business plan to be provided to Mortons Bank.

- Review the outcomes of previous management forecasts and assess their accuracy compared to actual data.

- Assess the competence and experience of the preparer of the forecast.

- Confirm the consistency of the accounting policies used in the preparation of the forecast financial statements with those used in the last audited financial statements.

- For a sample of operating expenses, review the supporting documentation such as invoices and utility bills and agree the amount paid each month to the bank ledger account/cash book.

- Agree the predicted collection and payment periods to the most recent receivables and payables records.

- Perform sensitivity analyses on the cash flow forecast by varying the key assumptions (in particular, in relation to growth rates and payment periods) and assessing the impact of these variations on the company's forecast cash position.

- Obtain written representations from management confirming the reasonableness of their assumptions and that all relevant information has been provided to Kelly & Co.

- Request confirmation from the bank of the potential terms of the additional finance being negotiated, to confirm the interest rate.

- Review board minutes for approval of the purchase, and approval that the finance will be raised from Morton's Bank.

- Enquire about any other potential sources of finance in case Mortons Bank fail to provide the full amount required, or in case the new premises cost more than the estimated amount.

- Inspect the bank ledger account/cash book from 1 July 20X5 to see if there are any significant cash transactions that do not appear to have been included in the forecasts.

Examiner's comments

This question covered the client acceptance and non-assurance services areas of the syllabus. Candidates generally produced a complete answer covering all requirements. Part b(ii) was the strongest part of candidates' answers with many good procedures being given. In part (a), many answers lacked the depth of discussion required for an evaluation rather than a list of criteria.

Requirement (a)

Candidates should note that there are two elements covered by this requirement – the decision to accept the client as a client of the firm in principle, and the second decision regarding whether it was appropriate to perform the review engagement. These considerations overlap and it is acceptable for a candidate to consider these two elements combined using a combination of ISQM 1 *Quality Management for Firms that Perform Audits or Reviews of Financial Statements or Other Assurance and Related Services Engagements* and ISAE 3400 *The Examination of Prospective Financial Information* to generate a list of points to address.

Candidates often produce an answer demonstrating that they know the areas to be considered when accepting a new client or a new engagement for an existing client. However, after demonstrating this knowledge, sometimes with an explanation of what they entail, candidates will then fail to apply that knowledge to the specific scenario. This is not an evaluation and is therefore not addressing the requirement. Unapplied points tend to carry a maximum amount of credit regardless of that mark cap, they will not be awarded more than ½ mark each, and as such, candidates will not be able to pass this requirement. In order to pass the requirement candidates will need to apply the ethical guidance to the scenario.

For example, when deciding whether to accept a client, many candidates will correctly state the key requirements of ISQM 1; Client integrity, compliance with ethical requirements and whether the firm has appropriate competence and resources, but then fail to show how the information in the scenario is assessed against these criteria. It is essential, in order to gain full credit, that the knowledge is applied to the information given in the scenario.

Consider the different responses seen by the examining team:

"Client integrity – the firm must assess the integrity of the potential client to determine whether they wish to be associated with the client." – this is unapplied, it can't obtain more than ½ mark credit and will be part of the cap of unapplied points.

"Client integrity – the firm must assess the integrity of the potential client. Mary has told us that the latest auditor's report is expected to be issued with a material uncertainty paragraph in relation to going concern. The fact that the potential client did not tell us this themselves suggests management may be hiding something. This would suggest that there is a high risk to the engagement as the client may not have integrity and we may be unable to place reliance on information provided to us by the client."

This answer is applied to the scenario – there would be a mark for the specific 'red flag' identified from the scenario for client integrity and a further mark for developing that point into how it would impact the risk for the firm.

This scenario had three different 'red flags' regarding client integrity and candidates would receive credit for each flag identified as well as the development into how this might impact the assignment and the risk to the firm.

The evaluation arises when the considerations required by the ethical guidance are applied to the scenario. Therefore, identifying specific criteria for this particular client, applying that information with other indicators from the scenario, in order to assess the risk and other implications for the firm.

Candidates are commonly producing a wide range of points, often which are not developed with any depth.

Similarly, when addressing the ethical requirements and competence/resources there were specific issues flagged in the scenario which would develop those criteria into an evaluation, and these can be seen in the model answer.

Some candidates were failing to answer the requirement relevant to the given scenario, instead they were answering a generic acceptance question. In this question, we are not the current or prospective auditor. The requirement is specific to the acceptance for this assurance engagement reviewing a cash flow forecast. Candidates who stated points around self-review when auditing the financial statements or the request for professional clearance for audit from the existing auditor did not attain credit. While there was a self-review threat (one of the firm's employees previously worked at the prospective client) and credit for communication with the existing auditors if permitted by the client (to follow up on the going concern issues), addressing these in the wrong context would not obtain credit. This is consistent with how issues such as ethical threats are marked, and candidates are encouraged to review the technical article on technique on the ACCA website.

Candidates could also obtain some credit for evaluation of the ISAE 3400 criteria where it was applied to the scenario, such as the forecast period of three years making it higher risk as more estimation is required. This credit was more limited as there is less depth of evaluation with respect to the decision with the information provided. While it is important to know the addressee of the report or the elements included, the overriding areas in determining the decision to accept or reject the client are those covered in ISQM1 in this specific scenario.

Candidates should use the evaluation process to derive a reasoned conclusion based on that analysis. Credit is given to such a conclusion however no marks are awarded for simply stating accept or decline where that is not a reasoned conclusion based on a valid evaluation. There is often no specific right or wrong conclusion in the examination, the mark is awarded for the process of reaching that decision. Failure to reach a conclusion means that credit cannot be obtained so candidates should ensure they make their decision clear on the acceptance of the engagement or declining the service.

A final point to note is that candidates were instructed not to consider matters related to client due diligence (know your client procedures), so no marks were available for proving identity etc.

Requirement (b)

The second part of the question assumed the assurance assignment has been accepted and was broken into two sub-requirements to assist candidates in the process of determining the procedures to be performed. Detailed information was provided for the forecast and the assumptions in Exhibit 2.

The first part enabled candidates to focus on the forecast given and evaluate the assumptions of management and the completeness of the forecast. This allowed candidates to demonstrate professional scepticism and at the same time generate ideas for areas to address with relevant procedures. Scepticism is a key skill for auditors and candidates were able to score a full mark for each assumption challenged appropriately. For example, the level of sales growth in the first period might be too high if there are building delays which reduce the months for which the new facility would be contributing to sales. Additionally, marks were awarded for the identification of each missing item from the cash flow.

The second part of the requirement was to design examination procedures for use when reviewing the cash flow forecast. This area was generally well covered and is typically well answered by candidates who have practised past questions of this nature. Candidates should note however that as far as possible, procedures should be applied to the specific information in the forecast and information provided, rather than a pre learnt list of general procedures that apply to all forecast reviews (e.g. casting the forecast, assessing the accuracy of past forecasts, assessing the competence of the preparer) as these available marks are limited. As such, a pass mark is not possible unless specific procedures are also covered. Candidates should note that giving an answer learnt for a past exam question will not demonstrate the application skills required for a pass in this examination.

Candidates looking for further specific detail on how to create depth in their answers should refer to the technical articles on the ACCA website.

ACCA Marking guide		Marks
(a)	**Ethical and other matters to be considered before accepting Flynn Co as a client and performing the review engagement** Up to 1 mark for each matter explained: – General requirement of ISQM 1 **Ethical matters:** – Self-interest threat from incentive to secure the audit appointment – Advocacy threat from promoting loan application – Mary Sunshine – potential self-review and familiarity threats explained (1 marks each) – Recommended safeguards to reduce threats to an acceptable level (1 mark each to max 2) **Integrity matters:** – Incentive offered to Kelly & Co could indicate a lack of integrity – Reason for not appointing existing audit firm for the review engagement – Risk exposure for Kelly & Co given Flynn Co's going concern problems **Competence and resources:** – Competence to perform the work – a review engagement should not be a problem – But due to higher risk, more experienced and senior staff should be assigned to the team – Short deadline could impact on quality of the work performed – The deadline should be negotiated and extended if possible **ISAE 3400 considerations** ½ mark each to max 2 marks: – The intended use of the information – Whether the information will be for general or limited distribution – The nature of the assumptions, that is, whether they are best estimate or hypothetical assumptions – The elements to be included in the information	

- The period covered by the information
- Engagement should not be performed if assumptions unrealistic or PFI not appropriate for use
- Level of assurance to be provided and expected users of the report – impacts on scale of work to be performed

| | Maximum | 8 |

(b) **(i)** **Evaluation of assumptions**

Generally, up to 1 mark for each relevant point of evaluation:
- Monthly sales figures – popularity of products
- Monthly sale figures – speed at which sales can be generated
- New processing facility – date of starting production
- New processing facility – lack of start-up costs
- Increase in production capacity
- Reduction in operating expenses and economies of scale
- Foreign exchange – not included to mask potential volatility
- Finance costs – unlikely to be static
- Tax expenses – missing expenses
- Conclusion

| | Maximum | 5 |

(ii) **Examination procedures and professional scepticism**

Up to 1 mark for each procedure explained. In addition, ½ mark for relevant calculations, e.g. trend analysis, up to a maximum of 2 marks.

See model answer for detail of examination procedures covering:
- General procedures (to a maximum of 2 marks)
- Revenue
- Operating expenses
- Inclusion of foreign exchange transactions
- Interest and finance costs
- Tax and dividend cash flows
- Planned capital (asset) expenditure
- Going concern issues highlighted by the auditor's report

| | Maximum | 7 |

Professional marks
Analysis and evaluation
- Appropriate use of the information to support discussions and draw appropriate conclusions
- Appropriate assessment of the ethical and professional issues raised, using examples where relevant, to support overall comments
- Balanced discussion of the issues connected to a non-assurance engagement, resulting in a justified conclusion and proposed course of action

Professional scepticism and professional judgement
- Effective challenge and critical assessment of the assumptions used by management in preparing the cash flow forecast
- Demonstration of the ability to probe for further information in order to make an assessment of the completeness of the cash flow forecast
- Appropriate recommendations and justification of the assurance procedures to be undertaken in respect of the cash flow forecast

Commercial acumen		
– Demonstration of commercial awareness by recognising wider issues which may affect the forecast and the assumptions by management		
	Maximum	5
Total		25

44   MORITZ & CO   *Walk in the footsteps of a top tutor*

Top tutor tips

Part (a)(i) requires matters to consider before accepting a PFI engagement. ISAE 3400 outlines specific acceptance considerations for this type of engagement therefore knowledge of the professional standards is needed to answer this requirement.

In part (a)(ii) the examination procedures need to focus on assessing the reasonableness of the assumptions used to prepare the forecast. Remember that these transactions have not happened as of yet so you will not be able to inspect invoices, etc. Instead, think about how the client determined the forecast figures and assess whether this is reasonable. Include some of the more general procedures that apply to every client for some easy marks.

Part (b) covers ethical issues. Identify the type of threat, explain how the threat could influence the audit, discuss whether the threat is significant and finish off by explaining the safeguards given in the relevant Code of Ethics the firm should take to reduce the threat to an acceptable level.

(a)   **Lavenza Co**

(i)   **Matters to consider before accepting the review engagement**

Before accepting the review engagement to review and provide an assurance report on Lavenza Co's cash flow forecast, ISAE 3400 *The Examination of Prospective Financial Information* identifies a number of matters which need to be considered:

The intended use of the information

Moritz & Co must consider, for example, whether the cash flow forecast and assurance report will be used solely for the purpose of the increase in Lavenza Co's overdraft facility. If Lavenza Co is planning to use the assurance report for purposes other than an extension to its current overdraft, for example, to arrange new loan finance from the company's bank, this must be made clear to Moritz & Co.

Whether the information will be for general or limited distribution

Moritz & Co needs to consider who will receive the report and potentially rely upon it as this will impact on the firm's assessment of the risk associated with the engagement. If the cash flow forecast is intended for general distribution, this will increase the level of risk for Moritz & Co as a larger audience will rely on it.

In this case, if the information will be used solely in support of the application to the bank and will not be made available to other parties, this should be confirmed before accepting the engagement and will reduce the risk of the assignment.

The period covered by the cash flow forecast and the key assumptions used

Moritz & Co must also consider the period covered by the cash flow forecast and the key assumptions which have been used in its preparation. Short-term forecasts are likely to be easier to verify and provide assurance on than longer term projections. ISAE 3400 states that a prospective financial information (PFI) engagement should not be accepted when the assumptions used in its preparation are clearly unrealistic or when the practitioner believes that the PFI will be inappropriate for its intended use. In the case of Lavenza Co, although the forecast is only for 12 months, the growth rates assumed in relation to its operating cash receipts may, for example, be judged to be unrealistic given recent trends in its business and the requested overdraft facility of $17 million for the next six months may prove to be insufficient.

The scope of the work

Moritz & Co will need to consider the specific terms of the engagement, the level of assurance being sought by Lavenza Co and the form of the report required by the bank. Moritz & Co will need to identify clearly the elements which it is being asked to report on – for example, is it being asked to report on the cash flow forecast only or is the firm also being asked to report on accompanying narrative or other PFI. Due to the uncertainty of forecasts and the inevitable subjectivity involved in their preparation, Moritz & Co will need to confirm that it is only being asked to provide negative assurance as to whether management's assumptions provide a reasonable basis for the cash flow forecast and to give an opinion as to whether it is properly prepared on the basis of these assumptions.

Resources and skills

The firm needs to consider whether it has sufficient staff available with the appropriate skills and experience needed to perform the PFI engagement for Lavenza Co. Moritz & Co should also consider whether it can meet the deadline for completing the work and whether it will have access to all relevant information and client staff. Given the company's predicted need for cash in the next six months, presumably the extended overdraft facility will need to be provided very soon and this may lead to Moritz & Co being under pressure to meet a tight reporting deadline.

Client integrity

ISQM 1 *Quality Management for Firms that Perform Audits or Reviews of Financial Statements, or Other Assurance or Related Services Engagements* requires Moritz & Co to consider the integrity of Lavenza Co's management in relation to the acceptance decision. In particular, the firm should consider management's reasons for appointing a different firm from its auditors and the potential for management bias in the preparation of a cash flow forecast in support of its required overdraft facility.

In addition to the matters identified by ISAE 3400 and ISQM 1, Moritz & Co should also consider the following ethical matters before accepting the review engagement:

Ethical matters

Given that Moritz & Co are not the auditors, the firm's independence from Lavenza Co will not have been previously considered. In this regard, it is important to ensure that there are no threats to the firm's objectivity which might prevent it from accepting the appointment. If the firm is not independent and its objectivity is compromised, the reliability of the assurance report will be undermined.

Moritz & Co should also consider why the auditors have not been asked to provide the assurance report on Lavenza Co's cash flow forecast. In order to provide an assurance report on PFI, a good understanding of the client and its business is required and the incumbent audit firm will usually have the requisite knowledge and understanding. Moritz & Co should therefore consider whether the use of a different firm creates a risk that the client may be hoping that the firm may not be in a position to effectively challenge the key assumptions underlying the preparation of the forecast. When a professional accountant is asked to perform work for a non-audit client, they should be given permission by the client to contact its auditors in order to obtain relevant information. If this permission is not given, the appointment should be declined.

Overall, Moritz & Co must assess the risks associated with the review engagement and should not accept an engagement when the assumptions are clearly unrealistic or when the firm believes that the prospective financial information will be inappropriate for its intended use.

(ii) **Examination procedures on cash flow forecast**

- Cast the cash flow forecast to confirm its mathematical accuracy.

- Confirm the consistency of the accounting policies used in the preparation of the forecast financial statements with those used in the last audited financial statements.

- Agree the opening cash position of $9,193,000 to the bank ledger account/cash book and the bank statement.

- Discuss the key assumptions underlying the preparation of the forecast with management, including:

  - the predicted growth rates in operating cash receipts of 13.4% over the year compared to an equivalent growth rate of only 7.3% in operating cash payments.

  - the stated collection period in relation to receivables.

  - confirm that the assumptions appear reasonable and are consistent with the firm's knowledge and understanding of the client.

- Analytically review the forecast trends in cash flows comparing with them with historical cash flow statements and other forecast data which is available for the sector and local economy and investigate any significant differences.

- Agree the predicted collection period to the most recent receivables ledger.

- Recalculate the patterns of cash flows based on management's historical analysis of credit sales to confirm that the forecast has been properly prepared on the basis of these assumptions.

- Perform sensitivity analyses on the cash flow forecast by varying the key assumptions (in particular, in relation to growth rates and collection period) and assessing the impact of these variations on the company's forecast cash position.

- Agree the salary payments to the latest payroll records and bank ledger account/cash book payments analyses to confirm accuracy and completeness.

- Obtain and review a breakdown of the forecast overhead payments and compare it to historical management accounts and current budgets. Review the schedule to ensure that non-cash items such as depreciation, amortisation and bad debts have not been included.

- For a sample of overhead costs, review the supporting documentation such as invoices and utility bills and agree the amount paid each month to the bank ledger account/cash book.

- Obtain and review budgets and analyses of costs to date for the new shops and the online marketing campaign ensuring that the forecast includes all of the budgeted costs and does not include any costs which have already been incurred. Agree a sample of costs to supporting documentation such as invoices, quotations and lease agreements.

- Review board minutes for discussion of the new shops and the marketing campaign.

- Review the outcomes of previous management forecasts and assess their accuracy compared to actual data.

- Discuss possible cost omissions with the preparer of the forecast, for example, Lavenza Co's cash flow forecast does not include finance costs, tax payments and does not include any capital (asset) expenditure other than the new shops.

- Obtain written representations from management confirming the reasonableness of their assumptions and that all relevant information has been provided to Moritz & Co.

- Request confirmation from the bank of the potential terms of the additional finance being negotiated, to confirm the interest rate.

- Consider whether the finance charge in the forecast cash flow appears reasonable.

Tutorial note

Credit will be awarded for relevant numerical analysis of the cash flow forecast applied appropriately within the answer.

(b)   Beaufort Co – ethical and professional issues arising

Long association of senior audit personnel

Frances Stein's eight-year tenure as audit engagement partner creates a familiarity threat for Moritz & Co. The threat arises because using the same senior audit personnel on an audit assignment over a long period of time may cause the auditor to become too familiar and too trusting with the client resulting in less professional scepticism being exercised and the possibility of material misstatements going undetected.

INT	UK
According to the IESBA International Code of Ethics for Professional Accountants (the Code), with listed audit clients key audit partners must be rotated after **seven years** unless exceptional circumstances arise. In this case, the Code permits the partner's tenure to be extended for **one further year** where deemed necessary in order to maintain audit quality.	According to the FRC Ethical Standard, key audit partners must be rotated after **five years** and should not return within five years unless exceptional circumstances arise. In this case, the Ethical Standard permits the partner's tenure to be extended for a **further two years** where deemed necessary in order to maintain audit quality.
The Code also clarifies that if an existing audit client becomes listed, the length of time which the partner has already served on the client is included in the period to be considered. In the case of Beaufort Co, therefore, Frances Stein has already served as a key audit partner for the maximum possible period of eight years and following the listing of the client next year, it would be appropriate for her to be replaced by another audit partner.	The Ethical Standard clarifies that if an existing audit client becomes listed, the length of time the engagement partner has served the entity in that capacity is taken into account in calculating the period before the engagement partner is rotated off the engagement team. If the audit engagement partner has already served four or more years they may continue for a maximum of two years.
The Code does allow an exception, which states that with the agreement of those charged with governance, she could serve for a maximum of an additional two years. After this, she may not serve as a key partner on the audit for a minimum of five further years.	Where the audit committee of a listed entity decide that a degree of flexibility over the timing of rotation is necessary to safeguard the quality of the engagement and the firm agrees, the engagement partner may continue in for an additional period of up to two years, so that no longer than seven years in total is spent in the position of engagement partner.

Fee dependence

Over dependence on an audit client for fee income leads to a self-interest and intimidation threat for the auditor. The self-interest threat arises as the firm will have a financial interest in the client due to its dependency on the client and its concern about the impact on its business if it were to lose the client.

INT	UK
In the case of a listed client, the Code states that an audit firm's independence is threatened and should be reviewed if the total fees from a single client exceed 15% of its total fee income for two consecutive years.	The FRC Ethical Standard states where it is expected that the total fees receivable from an audited entity will regularly exceed 15% of the annual fee income (10% if listed) of the audit firm, the firm shall not act as the auditor of that entity.
In this case, the 15% limit has been exceeded in both 20X4 and 20X5 and following the listing of the company's shares in September 20X5, Moritz & Co is required to review its dependence on the client.	In this case, the 15% limit has been exceeded in both 20X4 and 20X5 and fees are likely to increase once the entity is listed due to the additional work required for listed clients, therefore Moritz & Co should resign as the firm will be too dependent on the client.
If retained as a client, the level of fees should be disclosed to those charged with governance and it should be discussed whether prior to the audit opinion being issued, having an independent pre-issuance or post-issuance review performed on the engagement by an external party or by the firm's professional regulatory body is enough to mitigate the threat.	
If fees remain at this level for five consecutive years, the firm must resign as auditor after the audit opinion on the 5th year is issued	

Provision of bookkeeping and accounting services

The provision of bookkeeping and accounting services for Beaufort Co creates a self-review threat for Moritz & Co. The self-review threat arises because the auditor is generating figures for inclusion in the financial statements on which they will then give an opinion. As a result, the auditor may be less likely to highlight errors if they are aware that another member of the firm has calculated the figures.

For a listed client, the Code and the FRC Ethical Standard state that a firm is not permitted to provide accounting and bookkeeping services.

Tutorial note – INT syllabus

The Code does, however, make an exception for divisions of a company if the services are of a routine and mechanical nature, a separate team is used and the service which the firm provides relates to matters which are immaterial to the division and the company. Following Beaufort Co's listing in September 20X5, therefore, Moritz & Co will no longer be able to provide the payroll services for Beaufort Co although it may still be able to maintain the financial records for the small division if the conditions stated in the Code are satisfied.

Share prospectus

Moritz & Co has been asked to assist in the preparation of the share prospectus document and to provide an accountant's report on financial data, business risks and a business plan which recommends the shares to investors. Performance of these services for Beaufort Co would create an advocacy threat for the auditor. The advocacy threat arises because the auditor is effectively being asked to promote and represent their client's position to the point where the auditor's objectivity is compromised.

The Code and the FRC Ethical Standard prohibit an auditor from acting in this way for an audit client and Moritz & Co should politely decline to assist in the preparation of the document and to endorse the recommendation to investors to purchase the shares.

It may be possible, however, for the auditor to provide an accountant's report on some elements of the prospectus. Moritz & Co may be able to provide an opinion on the financial information if, for example, it limits the form of opinion to stating that it has been properly compiled on the basis stated within the document and that this basis is consistent with the accounting policies of the company.

Examiner's comments

This question was a 25-mark compulsory question which focused on acceptance of an engagement to review a report on prospective financial information (PFI) and procedures to be performed on the cash flow statement.

Requirement (a) (i) required candidates to explain the matters to be considered before accepting the PFI engagement. This was a requirement where candidates would be expected to score highly, and overall did achieve good marks. The only noticeable point from candidate answers related to considerations of client due diligence to be considered as the question clearly stated this had already been performed, therefore where discussed as a consideration credit would not be available.

Requirement (ii) required candidates to recommend procedures to be performed in respect of the cash flow statement. Overall, candidates made a good attempt at the requirement and scored well. It was disappointing to see a small number of candidates answer the requirement using only analytical procedures i.e. calculating trends and ratios as this alone did not answer the requirement and therefore scored minimal credit.

Requirement (b) required candidates to comment on ethical and professional issues arising from a planned listing of an existing client, and services which had been requested of the auditor.

Overall, candidates had a reasonable attempt at the ethical issues arising. However, it is extremely disappointing to see incorrect rules stated for partner rotation and fee levels relating to a listed entity. It is important for candidates to ensure they have sufficient knowledge of ethical guidelines and can apply these guidelines appropriately to a question scenario.

The quality of answers was generally of a good standard and candidates were able to demonstrate application of their knowledge to the scenario.

		ACCA Marking guide		
				Marks

(a) **Lavenza Co**

(i) **Matters to consider before accepting the review engagement**

Up to 2 marks for each matter explained:

– Intended use of the cash flow forecast

– Distribution of the information

– Period covered by the cash flow forecast and key assumptions used

– Scope of the work

– Resources and skills

– Client integrity

– Ethical matters

Maximum   **6**

(ii) **Examination procedures on cash flow forecast**

Generally 1 mark for each specific procedure described:

– Cast the forecast to confirm accuracy

– Confirm consistency of accounting policies with those used in last audited financial statements

– Agree opening cash position to bank ledger account/cash book and bank statement

– Discuss key assumptions underlying forecast with management

– Analytically review cash flow trends comparing with historical data

– Agree average collection and payment periods to recent receivables and payables records

– Recalculate patterns of cash flows based on management's assumptions

– Perform sensitivity analyses varying key assumptions

– Agree salaries to latest payroll records

– Obtain and review breakdown of overhead costs

– For sample of overhead costs, review supporting documentation

– Obtain and review budgets and analyses of costs to date for new shops and marketing campaign

– Review board minutes for discussion of new shops and marketing campaign

– Review outcomes of previous management forecasts

– Discuss possible cost omissions with preparer, e.g. finance costs, capital (asset) expenditure, tax payments

– Obtain written representations from management (with justification)

– Request confirmation from the bank of potential terms of additional finance to confirm the interest rate

– Consider whether finance charge in forecast cash flow appears reasonable

Maximum   **7**

(b)   **Beaufort Co – ethical issues arising as result of planned listing**

Generally up to 1 mark for each issue explained:

Long association of senior audit personnel

–   Familiarity threat – explained

–   Rotation with appropriate cooling-off period

Fee dependence

–   Self-interest and intimidation threats to auditor – explained

–   **INT:** Independent quality pre-issuance review should be performed and full disclosure made to TCWG

–   **UK:** Resign from the engagement

Provision of bookkeeping and accounting services

–   Self-review threat – explained

–   Which cannot be reduced to acceptable level following Beaufort Co's listing on stock market

Share prospectus

–   Advocacy threat – explained

–   Moritz & Co should decline to assist in preparation of document and to endorse recommendation to investors to purchase shares

–   Opinion on the financial information should be limited to confirming that it is properly compiled on basis stated in document and is consistent with company's accounting policies

Maximum	**7**

Professional marks

Analysis and evaluation

–   Appropriate use of the information to support discussions and draw appropriate conclusions

–   Appropriate assessment of the ethical and professional issues raised, using examples where relevant, to support overall comments

–   Balanced discussion of the issues connected to a non-assurance engagement, resulting in a justified conclusion and proposed course of action

Professional scepticism and professional judgement

–   Effective challenge and critical assessment of the assumptions used by management in preparing the cash flow forecast

–   Demonstration of the ability to probe for further information in order to make an assessment of the completeness of the cash flow forecast

–   Appropriate recommendations and justification of the assurance procedures to be undertaken in respect of the cash flow forecast

Commercial acumen

–   Demonstration of commercial awareness by recognising wider issues which may affect the forecast and the assumptions by management

Maximum	**5**
Total	**25**

45   JANSEN & CO *Walk in the footsteps of a top tutor*

Top tutor tips

Part (a)(i) requires matters to consider before accepting a PFI engagement. The firm should only take on work of an acceptable level of risk so think about the risks that could arise by providing the assurance requested. There are specific acceptance considerations given in ISAE 3400 and you should aim to include some of these in your answer.

In part (a)(ii) the examination procedures need to focus on assessing the reasonableness of the assumptions used to prepare the forecast. Remember that these transactions have not happened as of yet so you will not be able to inspect invoices, etc. Instead, think about how the client determined the forecast figures and assess whether this is reasonable. Include some of the more general procedures that apply to every client for some easy marks.

Part (b) requires evaluation of the quality of the planning and performance of the audit. Typical issues to look out for in such a question are: whether the work has been assigned to the appropriate level of staff, whether the audit team have demonstrated competence and professional judgement, whether the ISAs been followed, whether the timing and frequency of reviews is appropriate.

(a)   (i)   Matters to be considered before acceptance of engagement

When considering acceptance of the engagement to review Narley Co's prospective financial information (PFI), Jansen & Co must consider whether it is ethically acceptable to perform the review.

The review of the PFI represents a non-assurance service and the IESBA *International Code of Ethics for Professional Accountants* (the *Code*) states that providing this service in addition to the audit may create an advocacy threat. An advocacy threat arises when the auditor is asked to promote or represent their client in some way. In this situation there is a risk of the auditor being seen to promote the interests of the client with a third party such as a bank. As a result, there is a danger that the auditor will be biased in favour of the client and therefore cannot be fully objective.

Accepting the assignment may also create a self-interest threat as a result of the auditor being perceived to have an interest in the outcome of negotiations with a third party and which may motivate the auditor to behave in order to protect that interest.

A self-review threat may also arise because the negotiations may result in facts and amounts which will form part of the audited financial statements. As a result, the auditor will be auditing financial statements which in part at least represent work which they themselves have performed. It follows that there is a risk that the auditor will not be sufficiently objective in performing the audit and may fail to identify any shortcomings in their own work.

In the case of Narley Co, the advocacy threat appears to be particularly significant as the audit firm could be seen to be promoting the interests of the audit client to the bank. The auditor should therefore only accept the engagement if adequate safeguards can be put in place to manage the threat to independence to an acceptable level.

Potential safeguards might include the following:

- The use of separate teams of suitably experienced staff for the audit and the review of the PFI.

- Independent senior review of the PFI working papers.

- Discussion of the potential ethical issues and threats to auditor independence with those charged with governance at Narley Co.

It should be noted, however, that it would not be possible to manage a significant advocacy threat through such safeguards and in such a case the appointment should not be accepted.

ISAE 3400 *The Examination of Prospective Financial Information* provides further guidance on the issues which the auditor should consider before accepting an engagement to examine PFI. According to ISAE 3400, the auditor should consider amongst other things:

- The intended use of the information – for example, whether it will be used solely for the purpose of the proposed loan finance.

- Whether the information will be for general or limited distribution – the auditor needs to consider who will receive the report and potentially rely upon it.

- The nature of the assumptions, that is, whether they are best-estimate or hypothetical assumptions – in this case it seems likely that they will be best estimate assumptions as Narley Co expects to obtain finance in order to fund its planned expansion.

- The elements to be included in the information – Jansen & Co needs to clarify the exact content of the PFI which they are being asked to report on, for example, whether it only includes the forecast statements of profit or loss or whether it also includes forecast statements of financial position and forecast cash flow statements; and

- The period covered by the information – shorter term forecasts are likely to be more reliable than projections over a longer period.

Jansen & Co must also consider whether the firm has sufficient staff available with the appropriate skills and experience to perform the review engagement in line with the client's required reporting deadlines.

Overall, the auditor must assess the risks associated with the review engagement and should not accept an engagement when the assumptions are clearly unrealistic or when the auditor believes that the prospective financial information will be inappropriate for its intended use.

(ii) **Examination procedures to be performed**

The examination procedures which should be performed in respect of Narley Co's forecast statements of profit or loss include the following:

– Recalculation of the forecast statements of profit or loss to confirm arithmetic accuracy.

– Confirmation that the accounting policies used in the forecast statements are consistent with those used in the audited financial statements and that they comply with IFRS.

– Discuss the key assumptions which have been made by the client in the preparation of the forecast statements with management assessing their reasonableness and consistency with the audit firm's cumulative knowledge and understanding of the client.

– Review of market research documentation in Narley Co's existing markets and the new market and discuss it with management to assess whether the growth patterns being forecast in revenue represent reasonable and realistic expectations.

– Obtain copies of any new customer contracts for existing and new markets to confirm the reasonableness of the projected growth in revenue.

– Obtain a written representation from management confirming the reasonableness and completeness of the assumptions they have made in preparing the forecasts.

– The competence and experience of the client staff who have prepared the forecasts should be assessed; the assessment should include the accuracy of PFI which has been prepared in previous periods and the reasons for any significant variances compared to actual outcomes.

– Recalculation of depreciation to ensure the correct inclusion of depreciation on the new HGVs and warehousing facilities within the forecast statements.

– Obtain and review a breakdown of operating expenses in order to ensure that all items have been appropriately included, for example: advertising and marketing costs for the campaign in the new jurisdiction; additional staff costs for the new drivers including recruitment expenses; any trading tariffs relevant to operating in the new market and any foreign currency and exchange implications.

– Recent utility bills should be inspected and an assessment of the reasonableness of forecast utility overheads should be performed.

– Obtain and review the supporting documentation for Narley Co's existing loan agreements with the bank as well as the draft documentation for the new loan; the forecast finance costs should be recalculated and agreed to the forecast statements.

- Perform analytical review, followed by discussion with management to seek corroborating evidence of key trends and ratios including:

  - Growth in revenue (26% from 20X5 to 20X6; 29% from 20X6 to 20X7)

  - Cost of sales as a percentage of revenue (75.5% in 20X5; 71.3% in 20X6; 69.7% in 20X7)

  - The declining trend in administrative expenses (decrease of 4.2% from 20X5 to 20X6; 5.6% from 20X6 to 20X7)

  - The increase in the profit (PBT) margin (6.9% in 20X5; 15.2% in 20X6; 20.4% in 20X7).

(b)   Watson Co

Quality management issues raised by the audit supervisor's email

ISA 220 (Revised) *Quality Management for an Audit of Financial Statements* requires the auditor to implement quality management procedures at the engagement level which provide reasonable assurance that the audit complies with professional standards and applicable legal and regulatory requirements and that the auditor's report is appropriate in the circumstances.

The overall quality of each audit assignment is the responsibility of the audit engagement partner and effective engagement performance entails adequate direction, consultation, supervision and review.

In this case, the conduct of the audit raises a number of quality management issues in relation to the effective performance of the audit of Watson Co's financial statements, including the following:

Share-based payment scheme:

The failure to identify the new cash-settled share-based payment scheme as a potentially high risk area indicates inadequate planning and a lack of consultation with the client. The share-based payment scheme is a complex and judgemental area and given that the scheme was only introduced in the year, it should have been identified as a key area of audit risk.

The assignment of a part-qualified supervisor to the audit of a listed entity is also indicative of poor audit planning. The audit supervisor appears to have inadequate skills and expertise to audit this public interest entity. This is evidenced by the incorrect treatment of the share-based payment scheme and the audit supervisor's comment that basing the expense in the profit or loss account on the valuation at the date of grant is appropriate and that the recognition of an equity reserve on the statement of financial position is correct in the email to the audit manager.

According to IFRS 2 *Share-based Payments*, the valuation of the share appreciation rights for a cash-settled scheme should be updated at the reporting date and the standard requires recognition of the cumulative cost of the scheme as a liability, not as an equity reserve.

The audit supervisor also fails to recognise that a share-based payment scheme with the directors constitutes a related party transaction. While the cost of the scheme this year of $195,000 is immaterial on a quantitative basis (it represents only 0.36% of profit before taxation and 0.84% of total assets), as a related party transaction with directors, the scheme should be considered to be material by nature.

Therefore, it should be fully disclosed in the notes to the financial statements in accordance with IAS 24 *Related Party Disclosures*.

The related party disclosures are particularly important for a listed entity such as Watson Co. In line with ISA 450 *Evaluation of Misstatements Identified During the Audit*, all misstatements should be accumulated and therefore the error should also have been included in the audit working papers and adjustment should have been requested.

Other quality issues include:

–   It is clear that the audit manager should have been replaced earlier and that Jansen & Co has failed to provide adequate direction and supervision of the audit.

–   Jansen & Co has also failed to monitor the progress of the audit and therefore to update and change the audit plan as necessary during the course of the audit as required by ISA 300 *Planning an Audit of Financial Statements*. This is evidenced by the fact that the audit clearance meeting is scheduled for next week and the initial manager review is only just taking place.

    In addition, there appears to be no evidence of engagement partner oversight over the course of the audit fieldwork and it is the engagement partner's responsibility to ensure that they have reviewed the documentation to ensure that sufficient appropriate evidence has been obtained and that the auditor's report issued in the circumstances is appropriate.

–   There appears to be a lack of audit evidence in relation to the firm of external valuers which has been used to value the share options. ISA 500 *Audit Evidence* requires the auditor to obtain sufficient and appropriate audit evidence that the valuation work performed by the management expert is adequate for the purposes of the audit.

    The auditor must therefore evaluate whether management's expert possesses the necessary competence, capabilities and objectivity to perform the valuations and whether the scope of their work is satisfactory for audit purposes. The 'checking out' of the expert online with reference to a website is clearly inadequate for audit purposes and this again reflects the inexperience and lack of expertise of the audit supervisor and poor audit planning with respect to the staffing on the audit.

Examiner's comments

Part (a) asked for the considerations for an audit firm when deciding whether it could provide assurance on prospective financial information. Candidates could score well on this requirement if they had prepared by reviewing similar past requirements or if they were aware of the content of ISAE 3400 *The Examination of Prospective Financial Information*. The main weaknesses in answers on this requirement was where candidates did not tailor their answer to an existing client and hence lost time giving detail on customer due diligence, or where candidates did not give detail on the ethical threats arising.

This is a common area where candidates lose marks. Another area of this requirement where candidates limited their capacity to score well was by focusing on post-acceptance issues such as the production of an engagement letter rather than the pre-acceptance decision issues.

Candidates were then asked to describe procedures to be performed on the profit forecast. The majority of candidates scored well on this section and a large number of answers provided a much clearer description of audit procedures than that seen in previous sessions. A minority of candidates made bland comments about agreeing opening balances and loan covenants which were not relevant to the statement of profit or loss.

The final requirement was a quality management question which was similar to past exams where candidates are required to describe quality failings. While few candidates scored full marks here the answers provided were generally good if candidates had allocated sufficient time to this requirement.

ACCA Marking guide		
		Marks

(a) (i)   Matters to be considered before acceptance of engagement
Up to 2 marks for each matter explained
- Auditor independence including potentially significant advocacy threat and possible self-review and self-interest threats
- Intended use of report, e.g. solely for bank or wider distribution
- Nature of assumptions and time period covered (in this case two years)
- Availability of experienced, competent staff and time frame for assurance work
- Appropriate safeguards to reduce risks to acceptable level
- Details of PFI to be given to bank, e.g. forecast P/L only

                                            Maximum   **6**

(ii)   Examination procedures
Generally, up to 1 mark for each described procedure. Also allow 1 mark for each relevant analytical procedure used to max of 3 marks
General procedures
- Re-cast the forecast to ensure it is arithmetically correct
- Confirm the consistency of accounting policies applied
- Discuss key assumptions with management and assess reasonableness
- Obtain written representations from management on reasonableness and completeness of assumptions
- Assess competence and experience of client staff preparing forecasts including accuracy of PFI prepared in previous periods and reasons for any significant variances

Specific procedures
- Review market research documentation and discuss with management
- Obtain and review customer contracts for new customers to confirm projected growth in revenue
- Perform analytical review of key trends. Up to 3 marks for analysis of key trends by candidates including:
  - Growth in revenue
  - Cost of sales as % of revenue
  - Declining trend in admin expenses
  - Increase in net profit margin
- Review of asset expenditure forecasts and agreement to invoices/supplier quotations
- Recalculate depreciation and ensure correct inclusion of depreciation on new HGVs and warehousing facilities
- Obtain and review breakdown of operating expenses; ensure all items appropriately included, e.g. advertising/marketing costs; additional staff costs for new drivers including recruitment expenses; any trading tariffs with overseas market and any forex implications

–	Inspect recent utility bills and assess reasonableness of forecast utility overheads	
–	Obtain and review documentation for existing loan agreements with bank and draft documentation for new loan and recalculate finance costs	
	Maximum	**7**

(b) **Watson Co**

Generally up to 1 mark for each issue discussed

– Inadequate planning/consultation with client re SBP scheme (ISA 220)

– Complex judgemental area, should have been identified as high risk

– Part-qualified supervisor, inadequate skills and expertise for this listed client

– Treatment of SBP is incorrect, valuation should have been updated at year end for cash-based scheme

– Recognition as equity reserve is also incorrect, IFRS 2 requires recognition as liability for cash-based scheme

– SBP is immaterial quantitatively (extra 1 mark for relevant calculation and comment) but scheme is RPT with directors which is material by nature especially for listed entity

– Error should have been calculated and adjustment requested

– The matter should have been included in the related party disclosure notes in accordance with IAS 24

– Inadequate staffing – audit manager should have been replaced earlier

– Insufficient monitoring and supervision by audit manager and no evidence of partner oversight during course of audit work

– Failure to update and change audit plan as necessary during course of audit (ISA 300); clearance meeting is next week and manager review is only just taking place

– Lack of audit evidence re external valuer – competence, capabilities, objectivity, scope of work; reference to website is inadequate and reflects inexperience and lack of expertise of supervisor (up to 2 marks for development of discussion)

	Maximum	**7**

Professional marks

Analysis and evaluation

– Appropriate use of the information to support discussions and draw appropriate conclusions

– Appropriate assessment of the quality management and professional issues raised, using examples where relevant, to support overall comments

– Balanced discussion of the issues connected to a non-assurance engagement, resulting in a justified conclusion and proposed course of action

Professional scepticism and professional judgement

– Effective challenge and critical assessment of the assumptions used by management in preparing the forecast

– Demonstration of the ability to probe for further information in order to make an assessment of the completeness of the forecast

– Appropriate recommendations and justification of the assurance procedures to be undertaken in respect of the forecast

Commercial acumen

– Demonstration of commercial awareness by recognising wider issues which may affect the forecast and the assumptions by management

	Maximum	**5**
Total		**25**

46 VIZSLA *Walk in the footsteps of a top tutor*

Top tutor tips

Part (a) requires knowledge of money laundering responsibilities. This is straightforward knowledge from the study text.

In part (b) the examination procedures need to focus on assessing the reasonableness of the assumptions used to prepare the forecast. Remember that these transactions have not happened as of yet so you will not be able to inspect invoices, etc. Instead, think about how the client determined the forecast figures and assess whether this is reasonable. Include some of the more general procedures that apply to every client for some easy marks.

(a) **The importance of obtaining customer due diligence and the information which should be obtained**

Customer due diligence (CDD), also called know your client procedures, is needed as part of anti-money laundering regulations, which all audit firms should have in place when accepting new clients. It refers to the firm obtaining information to be able to identify who the prospective client is and verify identity by reference to independent and reliable source material. This is a crucial part of risk assessment when taking on a new client and allows the firm to understand not only the identity of the prospective client, but also the nature of the business and its source of funds.

Specifically, the firm should address the following as part of customer due diligence:

– Identify the customer and verify their identity using documents, data or information obtained from a reliable and independent source.

– Confirm the identities of all shareholders, including the specific family members who collectively own 90% of the company's share capital, and the other shareholder(s) who own the remaining 10%.

– Identify any beneficial owner who is not the client. This is the individual (or individuals) behind the client who ultimately own or control the client or on whose behalf a transaction or activity is being conducted.

– Where a business relationship is established, understand the purpose and intended nature of the relationship, for example, details of the customer's business or the source of the funds.

Businesses must also conduct ongoing monitoring to identify large, unusual or suspicious transactions as part of CDD. All of the documents obtained for the purpose of carrying out CDD checks must be retained for a minimum of five years from the end of the business relationship.

In this scenario, the information which should be obtained includes:

– To confirm the identity of Gordon Potts, photographic evidence, for example his passport, should be seen and a copy taken, along with other means of identification showing his address, for example, recent utility bills or bank statements.

- In relation to Setter Co, the company certificate of incorporation should be seen, to confirm its legal status and the date and place of incorporation.

- A Companies House search (or equivalent) on Setter Co should take place. This will confirm the existence of the company, the shareholders and directors and will provide some financial information. This will confirm that Gordon Potts is the 'beneficial owner' of the entity – i.e. that he is the person who owns or controls, directly or indirectly, more than 25% of the shares or voting rights or who otherwise exercises control over the directors.

- The identity of the other companies controlled by Gordon Potts should also be found, and searches on them conducted, to confirm their existence and the nature of the relationship with Setter Co.

- The latest financial statements of Setter Co, and the other companies in which Gordon Potts has an interest should be reviewed. This will help Pointer & Co to understand the businesses and their relationship with each other, identify the sources of income and whether there are significant transactions between the companies.

- Identify the source of funding for the company, whether there are bank loans or other providers of finance, and the nature of the finance provided in terms of when it is repayable, whether any company assets are provided as collateral for the debt, and whether Gordon Potts or other shareholders have made personal guarantees in respect of any sources of company finance.

- While not strictly part of confirming the identity of Gordon or his companies, Pointer & Co would clearly need to obtain further information about the breach of employment law, and confirm the facts surrounding the situation. Currently the only information available is from a newspaper article and this may not be a credible source.

(b)   Examination procedures on the operating profit forecast of Vizsla Co

General procedures:

- Enquire as to the identity of the preparer of the operating profit forecast, and assess their competence, especially given that interest costs have been included as part of operating profit which is incorrect.

- Obtain an understanding as to the procedures and controls which have been followed in the preparation of the forecast, for example, has the forecast been approved by a senior member of the company's accounting team.

- Confirm that the accounting policies applied in Vizsla Co's financial statements have been consistently applied in the preparation of the operating profit forecast, for example, that design costs are expensed rather than capitalised as a development cost.

- Confirm that the assumptions underpinning the forecast are in line with knowledge of the business obtained from performing the company's audit, for example, the seasonality of the sales can be confirmed by looking at the audit evidence obtained in the audit of revenue.

- Re-cast the forecast to ensure it is arithmetically correct.

Specific procedures:

- Enquire whether a more detailed profit forecast is available, or ask management to prepare one, for example, detailing out cost of sales and other expenses. In addition, request a forecast statement of financial position and statement of cash flows.

Tutorial note

There could be matters which make the profit forecast unachievable revealed through assessment of the statement of financial position and statement of cash flows, e.g. the timing of the working capital cycle may make achieving the profit forecast unachievable if funds are not available at certain points of time especially given the seasonal nature of the business.

- Request that management prepares a profit forecast in the same format as audited financial statements and in accordance with IFRS Accounting Standards, i.e. the interest cost should be shown below the operating profit line.

- Having obtained the cost of sales figure for each six-month period, recalculate the gross profit figures given in the forecast.

- Compare this to gross profit margins in the prior year audited financial statements and investigate any anomalies.

- Having obtained a breakdown showing the components of cost of sales and other expenses, for each significant category of expense, perform analytical review to confirm that the forecast costs appear to be in line with expectations, and discuss any unusually high or low forecast costs with management.

- Based on the above, assess whether there are any missing categories of expenditure which have not been included in the forecast, e.g. there is no depreciation included in the forecast.

- For revenue, which is forecast to increase by a significant amount (e.g. 11.8% increase comparing the six months ending 30 June 20X6 and 30 June 20X7), consider whether the forecast appears overly optimistic. For instance, there is not a corresponding increase in marketing costs to support the forecast increase in revenue.

- Compare revenue in the year forecast to 31 December 20X6 with revenue from prior years' audited financial statements.

- Investigate any unusual trends through discussion with management.

- Review any marketing plans and discuss with an appropriate senior member of staff, for example, the sales director, to establish the rationale for forecasting a significant increase in revenue, for example, there may be plans to introduce new product lines. Consider this in light of the fact that design costs and marketing are not forecast to increase by a significant amount.

- Review the design costs as they appear to be fairly static with just a small increase to achieve a much bigger % increase in revenue. Discuss with management and assess if such an increase in revenue can be achieved with such a small increase in design costs.

- Confirm costs to appropriate supporting documentation, e.g. staff costs to human resources projected costs, marketing costs to advertising budgets.

- Assess whether the overdraft is likely to be repaid in December 20X6, for example, by obtaining and reviewing the cash flow forecast prepared for the same period as the operating profit forecast.

- Discuss with management the rationale for using 30% of revenue as a basis for determining the amount of other expenses. In addition, compare this to the results of audit procedures performed on expenses to gauge whether 30% appears to be a reasonable basis.

Examiner's comments

Part (a) related to the matters which should be considered in respect of the acceptance of a potential new client. The potential new client had a questionable history and not enough candidates explored this in sufficient detail.

The importance of new customer due diligence was a requirement of this question and this was poorly answered as many confused this with a due diligence review. Many candidates talked about initial acceptance procedures such as reviewing accounts and contacting the previous auditor rather than concentrating on the main Customer Due Diligence (CDD) procedures such as money laundering, sources of client funds, the identity of the beneficial owner, any shadow directors and other companies owned by the prospective client. Other candidates incorrectly discussed procedures, which would be undertaken when performing audit planning. Most, however, did pick up on needing photographic identification, Companies House searches and Certificates of Incorporation as proof of identification as well as wanting to understand the previous issues of alleged pension fund misappropriation & breach of employment laws.

Part (b) required candidates to recommend examination procedures to be used when reviewing a profit forecast and was generally well answered with all of the main areas covered. Candidates were able to include the need to identify who prepared the forecast and their competence, unusual trends in revenue, revenues growing quicker than costs and the risk of management bias while the objective of the forecast was to procure a bank loan. Marks were also available for calculating relevant trends and good candidates were able to earn extra credit here.

	ACCA Marking guide		Marks

<table>
<tr><td>(a)</td><td colspan="2">Customer due diligence – reasons and recommended information</td></tr>
</table>

(a) **Customer due diligence – reasons and recommended information**
Up to 1½ marks for each point explained/recommended
- Part of anti-money laundering regulations (up to 3 marks for detailed explanation of regulations)
- Identity of Gordon Potts – passport, recent utility bills or bank statements
- Identity of other shareholders including the other family members and other 10% shareholders
- Setter Co – the company certificate of incorporation, to confirm legal status, date and place of incorporation
- A Companies House search (or equivalent) on Setter Co – confirm the existence of the company, the shareholders and directors, beneficial owners
- Other companies controlled by Gordon Potts – confirm their existence and the nature of the relationship with Setter Co
- Review of the latest financial statements of Setter Co, and the other companies in which Gordon Potts has an interest should be reviewed
- Identify the source of funding, when funding is repayable and the existence of any security provided by the company or by personal guarantee of owners
- Facts surrounding the breach of employment law as reported by the newspaper

Maximum | **11**

(b) **Examination procedures**
Up to 1 mark for each procedure explained. In addition, ½ mark for relevant calculations, e.g. trend analysis, up to a maximum of 2 marks
General procedures
- Identity of the preparer of the operating profit forecast, and assess their competence
- Understanding the procedures/controls which have been followed in the preparation of the forecast
- Confirm the consistency of accounting policies applied
- Confirm that the assumptions underpinning the forecast are in line with knowledge of the business obtained from performing the company's audit
- Re-cast the forecast to ensure it is arithmetically correct

Specific procedures
- Ask management to prepare a more detailed profit forecast in an appropriate format and to provide forecast statement of financial position and statement of cash flows
- Recalculate the gross profit margins and compare with gross profit margins from audited financial statements
- Obtain a breakdown showing the components of cost of sales and other expenses; perform analytical review and discuss results
- Assess whether there are any missing categories of expenditure
- For revenue, consider whether the forecast appears overly optimistic – allow credit for calculation of appropriate trends from the forecast
- Compare revenue forecast with revenue from prior years' audited financial statements. Investigate any unusual trends through discussion with management
- Review any marketing plans and discuss with an appropriate senior member of staff, for example, the sales director
- Review design costs, discuss with management and assess if such an increase in revenue can be achieved with such a small increase in design costs
- Confirm costs to appropriate supporting documentation, e.g. staff costs to human resources projected costs, marketing costs to advertising budgets

– Obtain and review the cash flow forecast prepared for the same period as the operating profit forecast		
– Discuss with management the rationale for using 30% of revenue as a basis for determining the amount of other expenses		
Maximum		**9**

Professional marks
Analysis and evaluation
– Appropriate use of the information to support discussions and draw appropriate conclusions
– Appropriate assessment of the ethical and professional issues raised, using examples where relevant, to support overall comments
– Balanced discussion of the issues connected to a non-assurance engagement, resulting in a justified conclusion and proposed course of action

Professional scepticism and professional judgement
– Effective challenge and critical assessment of the assumptions used by management in preparing the forecast
– Demonstration of the ability to probe for further information in order to make an assessment of the completeness of the forecast
– Appropriate recommendations and justification of the assurance procedures to be undertaken in respect of the forecast

Commercial acumen
– Demonstration of commercial awareness by recognising wider issues which may affect the firm is the services are provided to Setter Co and Vizsla Co

Maximum		**5**
Total		**25**

47 WATERS *Walk in the footsteps of a top tutor*

Top tutor tips

Matters to consider before accepting an engagement should be straightforward as this question has been asked on many previous exam papers. Think about what might cause the accountancy firm to decline the work e.g. level of risk, insufficient resources.

Examination procedures need to focus on assessing the reasonableness of the assumptions used to prepare the forecast. Remember that these transactions have not happened as of yet so you will not be able to inspect invoices, etc. Instead, think about how the client determined the forecast figures and assess whether that is reasonable. Analytical procedures and inquiries will be the main procedures to use. There may be some documents you can inspect such as quotations for new equipment.

In the final part of the question apply your knowledge of auditor's reports to the assurance report on the forecast to identify the contents of the report. Make sure you address the second element of the requirement which asks for an explanation of the level of assurance provided by the report.

(a) Before accepting the engagement to examine Waters Co's prospective financial information, there are several matters to be considered.

Ethical matters

A significant matter is whether it is ethically acceptable to perform the engagement. The engagement would constitute a non-assurance service provided to an audited entity which may create self-interest, self-review and advocacy threats to independence.

Advocacy threat

In this case, the advocacy threat may be deemed particularly significant as Hunt & Co could be perceived as promoting the client's position to the bank. The engagement should only be provided if safeguards can be used to reduce the threat to an acceptable level, which may include:

- Having a professional accountant who was not involved with the non-assurance service review the non-assurance work performed or otherwise advise as necessary.

- Discussing ethical issues with those charged with governance of the client.

- Using separate teams to work on the audit and on the PFI engagement.

Assuming management responsibilities

The request by the finance director to assist him in presenting the final version of the strategic plan to the board also needs to be considered. The request to be involved in confirming that the plan is consistent with competitors suggests that if the board is not satisfied the company may not move forward with the plan or apply for the bank funding. If the engagement partner is involved, this would likely result in the firm taking on a management responsibility as they are essentially supporting the strategic direction suggested by management.

Further, by attending the presentation the partner could be seen to be communicating with the board on behalf of management. Both of these activities are now referenced as management activities in the *Code* and therefore the firm should advise the finance director that Hunt & Co may be able to perform the review for the purposes of the bank but the firm will not be able to take part in the presentation.

Requirements of ISAE 3400 *The Examination of Prospective Information*

As well as ethical matters, ISAE 3400 *The Examination of Prospective Information* requires that certain matters are considered before the engagement is accepted.

Scope of the work

Hunt & Co must also consider the specific terms of the engagement. For example, the firm will need to clarify whether the bank has requested an assurance report to be issued, and what exact information will be included in the application to the bank. It is likely that more than just a forecast statement of profit or loss is required, for example, a forecast statement of cash flows and accompanying narrative, including key assumptions is likely to be required for a lending decision to be made.

Intended use of the information

ISAE 3400 also requires that consideration should be given to the intended use of the information, and whether it is for general or limited distribution. It seems in this case the assurance engagement and its report will be used solely in connection with raising bank finance, but this should be confirmed before accepting the engagement.

Period covered by the PFI

The period covered by the prospective financial information and the key assumptions should also be considered. ISAE 3400 states that the auditor should not accept an engagement when the assumptions used are clearly unrealistic or when the auditor believes that the prospective financial information will be inappropriate for its intended use. For example, the assumption that the necessary capital (asset) expenditure can take place by September 20X5 may be overly optimistic.

Resources and skills

The firm should also consider whether there are staff available with appropriate skills and experience to perform the PFI engagement, and the deadline by which the work needs to be completed. If the work on the cinemas is scheduled to be completed by September 20X5, presumably the cash will have to be provided very soon, meaning a tight deadline for the engagement to be performed.

(b) **Examination procedures**

- Agreement that the accounting policies used in preparing the forecast statement of profit or loss are consistent with those used in historical financial information and comply with IFRS Accounting Standards.

- The forecast should be cast to confirm accuracy.

- The time frame of the work to be carried out needs to be discussed with management, with enquiry being made to ascertain how the work can be carried out in such a short period of time, for example, will all cinemas be closed for the period of refurbishment? This will help to confirm the accuracy of the revenue and expenses recognised.

- Review of market research documents and review of prices charged by competitors showing new technology films to support the assumption regarding increase in price and consumer appetite for the films.

- Analytical review followed by discussion with management on the trend in revenue, which is forecast to increase by 22.9% and 7% in the years to 31 May 20X6 and 20X7 respectively.

- Consider the capacity of the cinemas and the number of screenings which can take place to assess the reasonableness of projected revenue.

- Analytical review of the composition of operating expenses to ensure that all expenses are included at a reasonable amount. In 20X5, operating expenses are 80.7% of revenue, but this is forecast to reduce to 73.4% in 20X6 and to 69.8% in 20X7, indicating understatement of forecast expenses.

- Review the list of operating expenses to ensure that any loss to be recognised on the disposal of old equipment has been included, or that profit on disposal has been netted off.

- Quotations received from potential suppliers of the new technology should be reviewed to verify the amount of the capital (asset) expenditure and therefore that depreciation included in the forecast statement of profit or loss appears reasonable.

- Recalculation of depreciation expense and confirmation that depreciation on the new technology has been included and correctly calculated and agrees to the forecast statement of financial position.

- Recalculation of finance cost to ensure that interest payable on the new bank loan has been included, with confirmation of the rate of interest to bank documentation.

- Review of capital (asset) expenditure budgets, cash flow forecasts and any other information to accompany the forecast statement of profit or loss for consistency, and confirmation that the amount planned to be spent on the cinemas can be met with the amount of finance applied for as well Waters Co's own cash balance.

(c) **Report on prospective financial information**

ISAE 3400 contains requirements on the content of a report on prospective financial information, stating that it should contain, in addition to a title, addressee and being appropriately signed and dated:

– Identification of the prospective financial information.

– A reference to the ISAE or relevant national standards or practices applicable to the examination of prospective financial information.

– A statement that management is responsible for the prospective financial information including the assumptions on which it is based.

– When applicable, a reference to the purpose and/or restricted distribution of the prospective financial information.

– An opinion as to whether the prospective financial information is properly prepared on the basis of the assumptions and is presented in accordance with the relevant financial reporting framework.

– Appropriate caveats concerning the achievability of the results indicated by the prospective financial information.

Level of assurance

In terms of the assurance level, the report will include a statement of negative assurance as to whether the assumptions provide a reasonable basis for the prospective financial information. This is a lower level of assurance than that given in an audit of historical financial information. The assurance provided is limited due to the future orientation of the information subject to review, and because the nature of the investigative procedures performed are less detailed and substantive in nature.

Examiner's comments

The scenario centred on Waters Co, an audit client, that had approached your firm to provide a report on prospective financial information which would be used by the company's bank in making a significant lending decision. The amount advanced would be used to upgrade the cinemas operated by Waters Co and a forecast statement of profit or loss was provided in the scenario, along with some of the assumptions used in its preparation by management.

The first requirement asked candidates to explain the matters to be considered by the audit firm before accepting the engagement to report on the prospective financial information. The quality of answers here was quite good, with almost all candidates making a reasonable attempt to discuss relevant matters including ethical issues, resource availability, the scope of the engagement and the nature of the assumptions used in the forecast. Where candidates scored less well on this requirement it was often due to lack of application to the scenario. A minority of answers amounted to little more than a bullet point list, often posed as questions (e.g. 'are there any ethical matters to consider', 'who is the report for', 'why is the report needed'), and while these are matters to consider the lack of any application to the scenario limits the amount of credit that can be awarded.

The next requirement asked for examination procedures to be used in respect of the forecast statement of profit or loss, assuming the engagement is accepted. This was also quite well attempted by many candidates, who used the information provided to generate specific and relevant enquiries and other procedures. Weaker answers tended to write very vague comments which were not tailored to the scenario or explained, or were just incorrect, such as. 'obtain representations', 'agree forecast to audited financial statements', 'check whether assumptions are realistic', 'perform analytical procedures'.

ACCA Marking guide		
		Marks
(a)	**Matters to consider before accepting the engagement** Up to 2 marks for each matter explained:	
	– Independence – types of threats raised	
	– Appropriate safeguards (max 2 marks)	
	– Request for assistance with presenting the strategic plan is a management responsibility	
	– No safeguards can reduce threat to an acceptable level and the assistance should not be provided	
	– Competence and time frame	
	– Elements to be included in the application and intended use	
	– Key assumptions and time period covered	
	Maximum	6
(b)	**Examination procedures** Generally, up to 1 mark for each described procedure. Also allow 1 mark for each relevant analytical procedure used to max of 3 marks	
	– Agreement that the accounting policies used in preparing the forecast information are consistent with those used in historical financial information and comply with IFRS Accounting Standards	
	– The forecast should be cast to confirm accuracy	
	– Review of capital (asset) expenditure forecasts	
	– Quotations received from potential suppliers of the new technology should be reviewed	
	– The time frame of the work to be carried out needs to be discussed with management	
	– Review of market research documents and review of prices charged by competitors	
	– Analytical review followed by discussion with management on the trend in revenue	

	–	Revenue is forecast to increase by 22.9% and 7% in the years to 31 May 20X6 and 20X7 respectively	
	–	Analytical review of the composition of operating expenses	
	–	In 20X5, operating expenses are 80.7% of revenue, but this is forecast to reduce to 73.4% in 20X6 and to 69.8% in 20X7	
	–	Recalculation of depreciation expense and agreement to forecast statement of financial position	
	–	Recalculation of finance cost to ensure that interest payable with confirmation of the rate of interest to bank documentation	

$$\text{Maximum} \qquad 10$$

(c) **Content of the report**

½ mark for each relevant content element identified (up to 2 marks) and up to 2 marks for discussion of the level of assurance provided.

–　Content elements:

- reference to relevant ISAE or national standards
- statement of management responsibility
- reference to purpose and distribution of report
- opinion on basis of assumptions and application of relevant financial reporting framework
- caveats on achievability of results

–　Assurance is based on negative assurance

–　Assurance limited by future orientation of the subject matter and nature of procedures used

$$\text{Maximum} \qquad 4$$

Professional marks
Analysis and evaluation

–　Appropriate use of the information to support discussions and draw appropriate conclusions

–　Appropriate assessment of the ethical and professional issues raised, using examples where relevant, to support overall comments

–　Balanced discussion of the issues connected to a non-assurance engagement, resulting in a justified conclusion and proposed course of action

Professional scepticism and professional judgement

–　Effective challenge and critical assessment of the assumptions used by management in preparing the forecast

–　Demonstration of the ability to probe for further information in order to make an assessment of the completeness of the forecast

–　Appropriate recommendations and justification of the assurance procedures to be undertaken in respect of the forecast

Commercial acumen

–　Demonstration of commercial awareness by recognising wider issues which may affect the forecast and the assumptions by management

$$\text{Maximum} \qquad 5$$

Total　　　　　　　　　　　　　　　　　　　　　　　25

48   MARR & CO *Walk in the footsteps of a top tutor*

Top tutor tips

Part (a) covers a due diligence engagement. The aim of the due diligence assignment is to gather information for the client to help them make an investment decision and minimise the risk of making a bad investment. The scenario states that the due diligence investigation should focus on the valuation of the intangible assets and their operational significance, therefore in part (i), generate enquiries that focus on this. In part (ii), think about the evidence that should exist to provide information about the company's financing arrangements. The sources of finance are given in the scenario so try and generate two or three points for each source.

Part (b) covers ethical and professional issues. For ethical issues, identify the type of threat, explain how the threat could influence the audit, discuss whether the threat is significant and finish off by explaining the safeguards the firm should take to reduce the threat to an acceptable level. Professional issues can be any other issues affecting the firm such as quality management or other practice management issues. A common sense approach can be used here.

(a)   (i)   Specific enquiries relating to Brodie Co's intangible assets

In relation to the import licence

– Enquire with management to ascertain the acquisition date of the import licence and confirm that the licence lasts for three years. This indicates to Morrissey Co when the next licence will need to be acquired.

– Obtain evidence (original invoice, contract, details of the terms and conditions regarding the import licence) regarding the initial cost and expected period which the licence will be valid for to assess whether the current amount in the financial statements (cost and amortisation) is accurate.

– To obtain understanding of the nature and scope of the licence, discuss and confirm the terms with management, including the specific goods covered by the licence and whether the licence applies to goods imported only from certain countries.

– Ask management to provide information to show the value of purchases of dye made during the financial year under the import licence – this will indicate how important the licence is to the operations of the company and whether it is essential that the licence is reacquired once it expires.

– Enquire with management whether they envisage any problem with the import licence being reacquired at the end of the three-year period, for example, if there were political sanctions against the country from which the dye is imported. Any potential problems with reacquiring the licence could disrupt the company's procurement and manufacturing process.

- Enquire with management whether there have been any breaches of the import licence, such as fines, which could affect the likelihood of Brodie Co obtaining a new import licence once the three years are complete.

- Discuss with management whether there are any plans to source the dye from an alternative supplier, perhaps a supplier for which an import licence would not be necessary, saving on the cost of reacquiring a licence.

In relation to the patent

- Obtain evidence (original invoice, contract, details of the terms and conditions regarding the patent) regarding the initial cost and expected period which the patent will be valid for to assess whether the current amount in the financial statements (cost and amortisation) is accurate.

- Discuss the terms of the patent, to obtain an understanding of matters including:

  • The specific manufacturing process to which it relates,

  • Whether the patent applies to all of the company's manufacturing, or just part of it,

  • If the patent applies just in the country in which it was issued, or does it apply in other countries.

- Discuss whether the patent can be renewed when it expires, and if so, whether an additional fee is payable to the patent authority. This will help Morrissey Co to understand the period over which the manufacturing process can be protected in the future.

- Enquire with management as to whether there have been any infringements of the patent by competitors, or whether management is aware of any competitors developing a similar manufacturing process. This could indicate that when the patent expires in three years, and if it cannot be renewed, the company will face increased competition should other manufacturers develop a similar production process.

- Assess whether there is any impairment of the patent, caused by a new process superceding the one attached to the patent.

- Discuss with management whether there are any factors which may affect the carrying amount of the patent in the financial statements.

- Ask management to provide information showing the value of sales made under the 'PureFab' label, to confirm that there is economic benefit being generated from the patented manufacturing process.

- Request permission that the Intellectual Property Office (or local equivalent) send Marr & Co a certified copy of the register entry. This will include details of the owner of the patent and the time period for the patent.

(ii)   **Additional information to be made available in relation to the company's financing arrangements**

–   In relation to the equity shares, the number of equity shares in issue, the value per share, and the voting rights attached to each share. This is essential information for Morrissey Co to consider how many shares to acquire in order to gain control of Brodie Co.

–   The company's authorised share capital, to ascertain the capacity of Brodie Co to issue further shares. This will help form an understanding as to whether Morrissey Co's shareholding will result from a fresh share issue or whether existing shareholders will need to be bought out of their shareholding.

–   The rate of interest payable on the bank loan and venture capitalist funds, whether interest is fixed or variable rate for forecasting the relevant cash flows.

–   The redemption dates of the bank loan and venture capitalist funds, and whether a premium is payable on the redemption of any debt, for forecasting the relevant cash flows.

–   Whether any loan covenants exist, in particular in relation to the bank loan, and the terms of such covenants. The acquisition itself could trigger a breach of covenant or lead to changes in payment terms.

–   Management should also be asked to confirm whether any covenants have been breached in the past, this indicates their capability of managing the company's finances.

–   In relation to the bank loan, details of the charge over company property, plant and equipment, in particular whether it is a fixed charge over certain assets, for example, does it apply specifically to the company's head office, or manufacturing plant.

–   The terms of the finance provided by the venture capitalists, in particular the repayment date and the terms of repayment, for example, whether some or all of the debt could be converted to equity shares. The existence of convertible debt would mean a potential future dilution of control in relation to Morrissey Co's shareholding in Brodie Co.

–   Details of any other sources of finance used by the company, for example, lease arrangements, debt factoring, directors' loans to the company. This is to ensure that all sources of finance have been identified and that Morrissey Co has complete understanding of Brodie Co's financing arrangements.

–   Enquire if management has any plans for alternative arrangements should current facilities not be extended, this will give an idea of how the company will overcome any difficulties encountered as a result of not being able to renegotiate current facilities.

(b) **Ethical and professional issues**

Ethical issues

On the acceptance of client relationships and audit engagements, ISA 220/ISA (UK) 220 *Quality Management for an Audit of Financial Statements* requires the audit firm to determine whether the firm and the engagement team can comply with relevant ethical requirements. This involves consideration of many factors, for example, whether there are any existing relationships between the audit firm and potential client, which could create threats to auditor objectivity.

In this case, a significant self-review threat arises should Marr & Co accept the appointment as auditor. The threat arises because Marr & Co, having performed the due diligence assignment on Brodie Co, and having helped Morrissey Co with the financial arrangements relating to the acquisition, will have been involved with many aspects of the individual and Group financial statements. This means that the audit firm may not approach elements of the audit of the financial statements with appropriate professional scepticism, not properly evaluating the results of previous judgements made, and over-relying on the work previously performed by the audit firm.

Marr & Co will need to evaluate the significance of this threat, based on matters such as the materiality of the balances and transactions involved, for example, the intangible assets of Brodie Co, and the level of subjectivity involved. It may be possible for Marr & Co to safeguard against the threat, for example, by using staff on the audit who had not previously worked on the due diligence or corporate finance engagements.

A related self-review threat relates to the finance director's request for Marr & Co to produce the Group financial statements. The IESBA *International Code of Ethics for Professional Accountants* (the Code)/FRC Ethical Standard state that providing an audit client with accounting and bookkeeping services, such as preparing accounting records or financial statements, might create a self-review threat (as explained above) and also a risk of assuming management responsibilities when the firm subsequently audits the financial statements. The risk of assuming a management responsibility arises where the auditor is taking on the decisions and responsibilities belonging to management, in this case, the preparation of the Group financial statements.

The significance of the self-review threat and risk of assuming a management responsibility depends on the nature and extent of the accounting services provided to the audit client and the level of public interest in the entity. The Code states that the audit firm shall not provide services related to the preparation of accounting records and financial statements to an audit client unless the services are of a routine and mechanical nature. Preparing the Group accounts would not be routine and mechanical – it would involve the auditor making judgements and taking responsibility for the whole of the consolidated financial statements. This would also be perceived as taking on significant management responsibility, and Marr & Co should decline the service on this basis.

There is also a possible self-interest threat arising from the range of services provided to Morrissey Co. This could give rise to fee dependency, meaning that the audit firm is reluctant to act in a way which could jeopardise the relationship between audit firm and client, for fear of losing the fee income. The potential level of fee income should be estimated and compared to Marr & Co's total practice income, to see if fee dependency could be an issue.

A further ethical issue arises from the invitation from Morrissey Co to attend the industry conference in Hawaii. The offer by the client to pay for the audit partner and manager to attend this event constitutes an offer of gifts and hospitality, which according to the Code can give rise to familiarity, self-interest and intimidation threats to objectivity.

The familiarity threat means that close relationships between the client and audit firm lead to the auditor being too sympathetic or accepting of the client's work, resulting in a loss of professional scepticism. The self-interest and intimidation threats arise due to the financial benefit of the gifts and hospitality, which could be seen as a bribe, and impact on the perceptions of the auditor's objectivity. The audit firm is likely to act in a way to keep the client happy, for example, overlooking accounting errors such as those indicated in the payroll system, in order to secure the trip to Hawaii.

The Code states that the existence and significance of any threat will depend on the nature, value, and intent of the offer, and should not be accepted unless clearly trivial or inconsequential. The offer of the trip to Hawaii should be declined as its value is likely to be more than trivial or inconsequential. The finance director may not realise that his offer puts the audit firm in a difficult position, and the problem raised by his offer should be explained, and the offer turned down.

ISA 220 contains a specific requirement that the auditor shall include in the audit documentation all significant threats to the firm's independence as well as the safeguards applied to mitigate those threats. The matters outlined above and the auditor's responses should be appropriately documented in accordance with ISA 220.

Other professional issues

Integrity

ISQM 1 *Quality Management for Firms that Perform Audits or Reviews of Financial Statements or Other Assurance or Related Services Engagements* suggests that the reasons for the proposed appointment of the firm and removal of the previous firm should be considered when evaluating client integrity. According to ISQM 1, one of the matters, which impacts on integrity, is whether the client is aggressively concerned with maintaining the audit fee as low as possible.

The comment made by the finance director regarding the reason for dismissal of Butler Associates could indicate that Morrissey Co has an expectation of low fees, which can impact on the quality of the audit and can increase detection risk if too few resources are allocated to the audit in an attempt to reduce the audit firm's costs.

The removal of the previous audit firm could also indicate that Morrissey Co may be difficult to deal with, possibly confrontational and aggressive in their attitude to the audit firm, though the invite to attend the industry event in Hawaii could indicate that management is keen to establish a good relationship with the audit firm. Their concerns regarding the previous audit firm's invoice may also be legitimate.

Audit preconditions

ISA 210 *Agreeing the Terms of Audit Engagements* requires an audit firm to establish whether the preconditions for an audit are present and if certain preconditions are not present, the audit engagement should not be accepted.

In this case, the finance director has stated that he does not want to provide notes to the consolidated financial statements, on the grounds that they are not useful. Failing to disclose notes to the consolidated financial statements would mean that they are not prepared in accordance with IFRS Accounting Standards.

IAS 1 *Presentation of Financial Statements* requires notes, comprising a summary of significant accounting policies and other explanatory notes, to be presented in order for the financial statements to be complete.

This matter will need to be discussed, and if the audit firm believes that management will not accept that they have a responsibility to prepare consolidated financial statements in accordance with IFRS Accounting Standards, then the appointment should not be accepted.

Internal control and quality of financial reporting

There is evidence that the internal control environment may not be strong due to the errors found by Butler Associates in payroll processing. In addition, the request by the finance director also raises an issue relating to the competence of the client. A finance director would be expected to have the necessary knowledge and skill to be able to prepare consolidated financial statements, and the fact that he has asked for assistance could indicate that there will be a high inherent risk of material misstatement in the financial statements. While these issues do not mean that the audit should be declined, they indicate that Marr & Co would need to approach the audit as high risk.

Competence and resources

Marr & Co should consider whether audit staff have experience in the textile industry and whether there will be enough staff available at the time when the audit needs to be performed. Manufacturing is not particularly unusual or challenging for an audit firm, so competence is unlikely to present a problem, especially as Marr & Co already has several audit clients who are manufacturers.

It is important to note that Marr & Co is a relatively small audit firm, and especially with the year end being less than a month away, there may be pressure on resources if the firm's other audit clients have the same year end, meaning that audit staff are already busy with other work. The firm should therefore confirm that it is able to complete the audit engagement within the timescale.

Examiner's comments

This was a question relating to a due diligence assignment for a non-audit client, whereby the firm was required to focus on two separate intangible assets, a licence and a patent. Candidates needed to consider the operational significance and valuation of the intangible assets. The assignment also required candidates to discuss additional information required by the practitioner and to evaluate why they would need information regarding the company's financing arrangements.

The requirement asked candidates to discuss specific enquiries that should be made with the management team regarding the intangible assets which consisted of the licence and the patent. The assignment is a due diligence assignment, not an audit, and therefore detailed substantive procedures would not be performed.

Weaker candidates listed detailed substantive procedures to test intangible assets, yet this did not meet the requirement. The requirement specifically stated that the procedures should be limited to enquiries. Candidates who merely discussed audit procedures to test intangible assets and did not focus on the attention to the enquiries would not be credited. Candidates needed to make enquiries concerning the valuation and the significance of the assets to the company from an operational point of view.

Strong candidates made a reasonable attempt at evaluating discussions to be made to the client concerning the assets, such as:

–   when the licence was acquired and the term of the licence to determine when the renewal of the licence is required

–   the terms and conditions of the licence to assist the practitioner in determining any restrictions on the licence

–   any likely issues associated with re acquiring the licence in the future

–   the terms of the patent and whether the patent can be renewed at the expiration date.

A well attempted answer tailored the response to consider why we would make specific enquiries as part of the due diligence assignment for the acquirer to have detailed information regarding the target company to assist in their decision-making process.

Generally, the depth of answers fell short of that expected from a professional level candidate. Candidates are advised to read the specific question requirement to develop a clear understanding of what is expected within their response. Due diligence is an area that should be answered well as there is no double entry accounting knowledge being evaluated.

The second requirement in part (a) required candidates to recommend the additional information which would be required and made available to them regarding the target companies' financial arrangements. The target company's sources of finance relate to equity shares, a bank loan and finance from a venture capitalist.

Generally, the requirement was poorly answered with the main issue noted being the lack of understanding by the candidates on the difference between performing audit procedures and discussing additional information required relating to specific items.

Additional information is required to gain a better understanding surrounding a certain issue/area and does not necessarily need to be in the form of documentary evidence. The information can also be obtained from making enquiries with management alongside reviewing documentation.

The additional information required for this requirement related purely to the equity share capital, the bank loan and the venture capitalist loan, for example:

–   the number of shares in issue and the value of the shares including if voting rights are attached

–   the interest rate on the loan and the venture capitalist loan

–   whether any covenants exist on the loan or security over the target company assets

–   do the target company have any other sources of finance

–   what are the target company plans to secure alternative funding should existing finance not be renewed.

These are all gaps in the knowledge of the practitioner which would require further investigation in order to perform the due diligence assignment and report the facts back to the acquiring company to enable them to make a decision regarding future acquisition.

Strong candidates evaluated the additional information required and also evaluated why we would need it, yet weaker candidates merely stated substantive procedures to address risk around the sources of finance which did not meet the question requirement.

Requirement (b) is a standard ethics and professional issues requirement. AAA candidates should expect ethics to be examinable, and this requirement should achieve high marks based on brought forward knowledge from previous ACCA examinations including detailed knowledge from AA.

Exhibit 3 related to an email received from the finance director requesting the audit firm to be appointed as auditors following the successful acquisition of the target company. The audit firm was involved in the due diligence assignment for the acquisition of this target company.

There were a number of ethical threats candidates could have evaluated and recommended safeguard for along with professional issues. Such threats included assessing the competence of the management team, the threat to audit quality, whether the audit firm has sufficient competence and resources as it is noted in the requirement this is a small audit firm and they may, potentially lack available resources with the level of experience required.

Strong candidates successfully identified the threats and linked the threat to the specific detail in the scenario along with an explanation of how the threat will impact the auditor and the fundamental principles that we are required to adhere to. Safeguards and actions were also considered in order to bring the threat down to an acceptable level.

Weaker candidates merely identified the threat with little or no explanation, for example, the offer of the trip to attend the conference paid for by the client. Where candidates merely say there is a self-interest threat, yet do not link it to the detail in the scenario, no credit will be awarded due to a lack of demonstrating knowledge of ethical threats which can be applied to the specific scenario.

A number of candidates did not read the scenario sufficiently and discussed the self-review threat linked to the corporate finance advice and stated an action that the corporate finance advice should be decline.

The question clearly stated the audit firm were appointed to provide corporate finance advice prior to the acquisition of the target company. At that point in the process the audit firm was not the auditor, the firm was appointed as auditor following the acquisition of the target company. Comments relating to the decline of the corporate finance advice were therefore not relevant as this had already taken place.

Candidates are advised to read the exhibits clearly and make note of the exhibits to be used for each requirement.

Overall, a mixed response, generally the level of detail in candidate responses show insufficient depth on how the threat arose and the impact it would have on the auditor and the fundamental principles it threatens, showing lack of explanation and application of knowledge to the scenario. Candidates demonstrate they understand which threat is being examined yet often do not explain this sufficiently and fail to spot the other professional issues in the question.

ACCA Marking guide			
			Marks

(a)   (i)   **Specific enquiries relating to Brodie Co's intangible asset**

Up to 1 mark for each enquiry recommended and adequately explained.

In relation to the import licence

– Acquisition date of the import licence, and confirm that the licence lasts for three years. This indicates to Morrissey Co when the next licence will need to be acquired

– Obtain evidence (original invoice, contract, details of the terms and conditions regarding the import licence) regarding the initial cost and expected period which the licence will be valid for to assess whether the current amount in the financial statements (cost and amortisation) is accurate

– The terms of the licence, including the specific goods covered by the licence and whether the licence applies to goods imported only from certain countries

– Value of purchases of dye made during the financial year under the import licence – this will indicate how important the licence is to the operations of the company

– Any problem foreseen with the import licence being reacquired at the end of the three-year period, any potential problems with reacquiring the licence could disrupt the company's procurement and manufacturing process

– Any plans to source the dye from an alternative supplier, perhaps a supplier for which an import licence would not be necessary, saving on the cost of reacquiring a licence

– Enquire with management whether there have been any breaches of the import licence, such as fines, which could affect the likelihood of Brodie Co obtaining a new import licence once the three years are complete

In relation to the patent:

– Obtain evidence (original invoice, contract, details of the terms and conditions regarding the patent) regarding the initial cost and expected period which the patent will be valid for to assess whether the current amount in the financial statements (cost and amortisation) is accurate

– The terms of the patent, to obtain an understanding of matters including: the specific manufacturing process to which it relates, whether the patent applies to all of the company's manufacturing, and if the patent applies just in the country in which it was issued, or does it apply in other countries

– Whether the patent can be renewed when it expires, and if so, whether an additional fee is payable to the patent authority

– Whether there have been any infringements or any competitors developing a similar manufacturing process, indicating increased competition

– Discuss with management whether there are any factors which may affect the carrying amount of the patent in the financial statements

– The value of sales made under the 'PureFab' label, to confirm that there is economic benefit being generated from the patented manufacturing process

– Request permission that the Intellectual Property Office (or local equivalent) send a certified copy of the register entry. This will include details of the owner of the patent and the time period for the patent

(ii) **Additional information relating to financing arrangements**
Up to 1 mark for each enquiry recommended and adequately explained.

– The number of equity shares in issue, the value per share, and the voting rights attached to each share, to consider how many shares to acquire in order to gain control

– The company's authorised share capital, to provide understanding as to whether Morrissey Co's shareholding will be a fresh share issue or whether existing shareholders will need to be bought out of their shareholding

– The rate of interest payable on the bank loan and venture capitalist funds, whether interest is fixed or variable rate for forecasting the relevant cash flows

– The redemption dates of the bank loan and venture capitalist funds, and whether a premium is payable on the redemption of any debt, for forecasting the relevant cash flows

– Whether any loan covenants exist, in particular in relation to the bank loan, and the terms of such covenants; the acquisition itself could trigger a breach of covenant

– Whether any covenants have been breached in the past, this indicates management's capability of managing the company's finance

– Bank loan details on the charge over company property, plant and equipment, whether it is a fixed charge over certain assets

– The terms of the finance provided by the venture capitalists, in particular the repayment date and the terms of repayment, whether some or all of the debt could be converted to equity shares indicating potential future dilution of control

– Details of any other sources of finance used by the company, to ensure that all sources of finance have been identified

– Enquire if management has any plans for alternative arrangements should current facilities not be extended, this will give an idea of how the company will overcome any difficulties encountered as a result of not being able to renegotiate current facilities

Maximum	**12**

(b) **Ethical and other professional matters**
Generally, 1 mark for each relevant and well explained point and 1 mark for each relevant and appropriate safeguard.

– Ethical issue – self-review threat regarding having previously performed due diligence and corporate finance work

– Safeguards: separate team for audit

– Ethical issue – self-review threat regarding preparation of consolidated financial statements (management threat)

– No safeguard appropriate – management to prepare the consolidated financial statements – not 'routine or mechanical in nature'

– Ethical issue – self-interest threat from providing range of services, fee dependency

– Ethical issue – self-interest and familiarity threats re gifts and hospitality

– Low fee and impact on audit quality

– Non-reappointment of previous audit firm – intimidation/dispute over fees

– Audit preconditions – ISA 210 requirements and management responsibility to prepare complete financial statements

– Competence of management and quality of financial reporting

– Competence and resources

Maximum	**8**

Professional marks

Analysis and evaluation

- Appropriate use of the information to support discussion, draw appropriate conclusions and design appropriate responses
- Appropriate assessment of the professional issues raised, using examples where relevant to support overall comments
- Effective appraisal of the information to make suitable recommendations for appropriate courses of action

Professional scepticism and judgement

- Effective challenge of information, evidence and assumptions supplied and, techniques carried out to support key facts and/or decisions
- Identification of missing information or additional information which would be required
- Appropriate application of professional judgement to draw conclusions and make informed decisions

Commercial acumen

- Inclusion of appropriate recommendations in respect of the ethical and professional issues raised
- Demonstrate awareness of any wider external factors or implications, in a given scenario
- Show insight and perception in understanding the wider implications of the due diligence engagement

Maximum	5
Total	25

49 CHEETAH *Walk in the footsteps of a top tutor*

Top tutor tips

Part (a) requires an explanation of why the issues require further attention. Here you need to look at how the issues could impact the value of the company and therefore the price to be paid for the company.

Part (b) looks at the ethical and professional issues of conducting a review of interim financial information in a short time frame with the report being relied on by the bank providing the finance for the acquisition. This is quite a straightforward ethical situation. Make sure you explain the issues. Stating the name of a threat is not an explanation. You must say how this could affect the behaviour of the auditor or the outcome of the audit.

(a) (i) Why the matters require further investigation

Termination of contract

Impact on forecasts

The loss of the customer may lead to a reduction in forecast revenue by as much as 5% per year. This may also lead to a reduction in costs specifically relevant to servicing the customer. For example, sales staff specifically allocated to servicing this client.

This is significant because the forecast future cash flows of Zebra Co will be critical in determining the value of the company and the price offered by Cheetah Co. It is therefore vital to establish all of the potential revenue and cost implications of the loss of the customer to ascertain the impact on the purchase price.

Wider implications of new competitor

The customer referred to has switched to a new, cheaper supplier. This may have wider implications if the new supplier is directly targeting the customers of Zebra Co. It is possible that other customers may switch to the new supplier in the future, which would have further implications on future revenue and cost forecasts.

It may not be possible to determine the potential impact of the new supplier at this point, which increases the level of uncertainty associated with the potential acquisition. Cheetah Co may be able to use this uncertainty as a tool for bargaining with the owners of Zebra Co over the final agreed price.

Possible impairment of other assets

The loss of a major customer may be an indication of impairment of the assets of Zebra Co. This will be particularly relevant if Zebra Co holds specific assets for manufacturing the unique furniture products made for this client.

As well as production assets, Zebra Co may also be holding inventories which are specifically relevant to the customer which cannot be re-used elsewhere or sold to other customers. If this is the case, these inventories will almost certainly be impaired.

If not performed at the year end, it may now be appropriate to conduct an impairment review to ensure that the valuation of the assets, as presented in the financial statements, is still appropriate in the circumstances.

Gifted land

Possible restriction on sale

The restriction on the sale of the land may mean that Zebra Co is prohibited from including the land as part of the acquisition by Cheetah Co. It is likely that following acquisition, Cheetah Co will not be able to initiate a sale of the land to an external company or develop or change its current use. This may act as a deal breaker if Cheetah Co is not able to obtain control over the land surrounding the entrance to the production facilities.

If Zebra Co is not permitted to include the land as part of the deal with Cheetah Co, then this may also have an impact on the purchase price as the owners of Zebra Co may have attributed some value to the land in their expectation of the price which they can achieve. If so, it will be important to ascertain the value attributed to the land by the owners to negotiate the reduction of the purchase price.

Possible limitation on future usage

If the land can be included as part of the acquisition deal, the restrictions may also mean that Cheetah Co is not able to use the land for their intended purpose, such as the future expansion of production facilities, resulting in the acquisition of Zebra Co not being an appropriate strategic fit for Cheetah Co if one of the key aims is future expansion. If this is the case, then this will severely limit the value of the land to the company.

If the land can be acquired but cannot be developed, it is likely that there will be ongoing maintenance costs and potentially other requirements and conditions regarding the upkeep of the nature reserve set out by the local authority, which need to be understood as part of the review. The cost of maintenance may result in a net annual cost to the business and this needs to be quantified as part of the due diligence work.

It will be vital to ascertain what restrictions are in place and whether the directors of Cheetah Co believe they can extract any value from the use of the land.

Based upon this, the directors of Cheetah Co may wish to try and negotiate the purchase of Zebra Co without the associated land or they may wish to negotiate a lower price based on the restricted usage.

Uncertainty regarding valuation

It may be difficult to accurately value the piece of land. The value attributed to it in the financial statements is zero, so this may not provide an appropriate basis for estimating the resale value. A land valuation expert may be able to provide an estimation of the current market value of the land without restriction on its use but they may find it difficult to accurately value how much it is worth with the local authority restrictions. It may also be difficult to value the land based on the future cash flows attributable to it if it is not currently in use and its future usage is uncertain.

As a result, the valuation of the land may become a point of significant negotiation between the directors of Cheetah Co and Zebra Co. This may also become a deal breaker if the two parties are unable to reach agreement on the matter.

(ii) **Procedures**

Termination of contract

- Analytically review the total historic value of revenue earned from the customer to help determine an appropriate estimate for the potential loss of future revenues and cash inflows.

- Enquire of management whether the loss of the customer will have any other repercussions, such as the sale of specific assets or the redundancy of staff and the costs associated with this if such action was required.

- Perform an analytical review to identify other major customers by value of revenue contributions to the business. For all major customers identified, review any supply agreements/contracts in place to determine when they expire.

- If any contracts with major customers are due to expire within the next few years, enquire of management whether any discussions have taken place with those customers in relation to renegotiating the terms.

- Obtain any correspondence available with the identified major customers to identify whether there is any indication that they may attempt to either renegotiate the terms of their agreements or switch them to a new supplier.

- Enquire of a relevant manager, such as a production manager or sales manager, whether there is any specific inventory which has been produced in relation to the customer who is not renewing their agreement. If this is the case, obtain a breakdown of the total inventories produced for this client and discuss with management whether they will be able to sell this inventory at full price given the notice to terminate the contract.

- Inspect the forecasts prepared by management to ensure that the changes to the revenue and cost streams identified above have been appropriately incorporated.

Gifted land

- Review the terms supplied when the land was originally gifted to Zebra Co. Identify the specific restrictions in relation to how the land may be used and who the land may be sold to in the future.

- Enquire of a legal adviser whether this will have any impact in relation to the sale of the land to Cheetah Co and their consequent usage of it.

- Engage a land valuation expert to provide a valuation of the land. Ask them to consider the implications of the restrictions imposed upon the land in the valuation.

- If Zebra Co is not permitted to sell the land, or the restrictions imposed on the usage of the land are too restrictive, seek legal advice in relation to the potential options, including whether the land can be gifted back to the local authority prior to the acquisition.

- Inspect the forecasts prepared by the management of Zebra Co to identify the specific forecast costs and revenues associated with the usage of the land. Prepare a revised version of the forecasts which excludes these revenues and costs to identify the potential implications on the forecasts if the deal is conducted excluding the gifted land.

(b)   Ethical and other professional issues

Advocacy threat

Accompanying the client to a meeting with their bankers will create an advocacy threat to objectivity as Leopard & Co may be perceived to be representatives of Cheetah Co.

This is particularly relevant as the bank may wish to establish a number of facts relating to the suitability of providing finance to Cheetah Co. For example, they may ask for representations that the company will continue as a going concern and that any forecast cash flows presented are accurate.

As Cheetah Co's auditor, these questions may be directed at the firm's representatives and the bank may take any response provided to their questions as assurance over these matters.

Management responsibility

Leopard & Co must also be careful that in providing services relating to the potential acquisition of Zebra Co and the associated financing arrangements that the firm is not assuming a management responsibility.

Although the terms of the engagement have not yet been confirmed, it is likely that by attending the meeting with the client, the audit firm will give the impression of supporting the acquisition of Zebra Co and therefore give credit to the decision.

The IESBA *International Code of Ethics for Professional Accountants* (the Code)/FRC Ethical Standard specifically states that the firm shall not assume a management responsibility for an audit client as the threats created would be so significant that no safeguards could reduce the threats to an acceptable level.

Self-review threat – loan transaction

Providing assistance in finance raising transactions for audit clients also creates a self-review threat to objectivity. A self-review threat arises where the outcome or consequences of a corporate finance service provided by the audit firm may be material to the financial statements under review.

This is a particular problem as the transaction will directly affect the financial statements, which the audit team will be responsible for auditing in consequent financial periods and therefore the audit team is likely to be more accepting of information provided or may not investigate issues as thoroughly, as the team may feel that much of this has been done via the due diligence.

Self-review threat – interim review

Reviewing the work of the team engaged in the interim financial statements review would also create a self-review threat to objectivity as the audit team would be reviewing the work of another team within the audit firm.

It may be perceived externally that the purpose of reviewing the progress of the interim review is to ensure that any output from this does not impact the attempt by Cheetah Co to secure the loan finance.

Intimidation threat

The request by Cheetah Co to ensure that the interim review does not impede the application for a loan may be perceived as intimidation by the client. It appears as though they are putting pressure on Leopard & Co to finish the work based on the deadlines imposed by the bank, rather than those originally agreed with the client.

This may force the auditor into changing their approach to any remaining procedures which would be considered to be undue influence of the client over the procedures performed.

This appears to be supported by a further threat relating to the upcoming tender for the audit. The management team of Cheetah Co appears to be suggesting that failing to ensure the interim review is completed on time for the loan decision may have an adverse impact on any consequent tender bid.

Purpose of meeting

It is not clear why representatives of Leopard & Co have been invited to attend the meeting with the bank. The purpose of both the due diligence service and the interim review is to report to the directors and owners of Cheetah Co, respectively. The firm has no responsibility to report to any third party, including potential lenders.

There may be an expectation for Leopard & Co to provide assurances to the bank in relation to the accuracy of forecasts presented or the financial position of Cheetah Co. If this is the case, it is outside the scope of any of the current engagements and Leopard & Co would not be in a position to provide this assurance.

Actions

The firm should ascertain the purpose of attending the meeting with the bank; if there is any expectation that it will provide assurances to the bank, then the request should be declined, explaining to Cheetah Co that the firm's responsibilities extend to reporting to the management and the owners of the company and not to any third parties.

If there is no expectation to provide any assurances and the firm is expected to attend the meeting solely in regard to the role of providing due diligence services to Cheetah Co and assisting them in determining a purchase price, then it may be possible for representatives of Leopard & Co to attend.

It must be made clear, however, that no members of the audit team/interim audit team will be able to attend and the firm will not be permitted to make any representations to the bank. A written representation should be obtained from management clarifying these points.

In order to reduce the risk of Leopard & Co assuming a management responsibility, the representation should also state that Cheetah Co has assigned responsibility for the final decisions relating to the acquisition and financing to a suitably experienced individual within the company.

Further, that Cheetah Co's management will provide oversight of the services performed, will evaluate the adequacy of the outcome of the services for the purposes of Cheetah Co, and accept responsibility for the actions to be taken as a result of the services performed by Leopard & Co.

On balance, Leopard & Co may consider that the threats, both real and perceived, are too great and it would be most prudent not to attend the meeting. If this is the case, Leopard & Co should politely decline the invitation, explaining the reasons why it is inappropriate.

Leopard & Co should communicate with the directors of Cheetah Co explaining that the firm is unable to be involved in the interim review or to review any of the working papers. Leopard & Co should explain the reasons to the client.

The firm should also explain that, if the client has any concerns, they should communicate with the interim review engagement partner to ascertain a reasonable timeframe for conclusion of this engagement.

Examiner's comments

This question focused on due diligence where a separate team from the firm were working on due diligence at an audit client. Here two issues had been identified and candidates had to explain why they warranted further investigation and what procedures they would perform. Stronger candidates here were able to see the future implication for the valuation of the target company from both the loss of a major customer and a new entrant into the market, and from the ownership of land with restricted use. Candidates should try to remain focused on the future value of the company in such questions and not dwell on the financial reporting aspects. Here there was a piece of land recorded in the accounts at its historical cost of zero as it had been gifted. A significant portion of candidates spent time on this fact and stated that it was in breach of accounting rules not to revalue PPE. This is not the case. A revaluation model may be adopted by companies but is not required. The market value of the land was important in valuing the company but its carrying amount was not for the purposes of this question.

Part (b) of this question addressed ethical issues which would arise if the firm was to attend a meeting with the bank regarding financing for this acquisition and this requirement was well answered with well-prepared candidates being able to recognise advocacy and intimidation threats. Candidates often missed the point that a separate team was already preparing the due diligence, as detailed in the scenario and incorrectly recognised the use of separate teams as a safeguard, which was not relevant. It should be noted that to attract credit for ethical threats candidates should not simply state the name of the threat, they should explain what it means and relate it to the scenario. Simply listing the name of ethical threats does not attract credit. An example of wording required to attract the full credit for advocacy is: 'The client's request for the auditor to attend the meeting with the bank would create an advocacy threat to objectivity, as the auditor would be perceived to be representing the client to the bank, and therefore the bank may take assurance from the auditors' response regarding the suitability of providing finance.'

ACCA Marking guide			
			Marks
(a)	**(i)**	**Due diligence investigation**	
		Up to 2 marks for each matter discussed.	
		Termination of contract	
		– Impact on forecast revenues, costs and cash flows	
		– Wider implications of a new, cheaper supplier entering the market	
		– Potential impairment of assets employed specifically for the client	
		Gifted land	
		– Possible restriction on sale to Cheetah Co	
		– Possible restriction on how land is used if purchased	
		– Uncertainty regarding how to value the land	
		Maximum	**6**
	(ii)	**Investigation procedures**	
		Up to 1 mark for each adequately explained procedure. Award ½ mark for relevant procedures which are poorly explained.	
		– Analytically review historic sales to customer	
		– Enquire of management about further repercussions	
		– Analytically review sales by customer to identify other major ones	
		– Review trade contracts/agreements with other major customers	
		– Inspect correspondence with major customers	
		– Identify inventories produced specifically for customer	
		– Inspect forecasts to ensure adequate adjustment made	
		– Inspect terms of gifted land	
		– Enquire of legal adviser re. impact of restrictions	
		– Seek a valuation from an expert	
		– Identify potential options for land	
		– Prepare revised forecast excluding land	
		Maximum	**6**

(b) **Ethical and professional issues**
Generally 1 mark per point:
–   Advocacy threat
–   Management responsibility
–   Self-review: loan transaction
–   Self-review: interim review
–   Intimidation threat
–   Purpose/scope of meeting
–   Ascertain purpose of attending meeting
–   Obtain written representation
–   Politely decline to attend
–   Explain that you are unable to review interim engagement progress

Maximum   8

Professional marks
Analysis and evaluation
–   Appropriate use of the information to support discussion, draw appropriate conclusions and design appropriate responses
–   Appropriate assessment of the ethical and professional issues raised, using examples where relevant to support overall comments
–   Effective appraisal of the information to make suitable recommendations for appropriate courses of action

Professional scepticism and judgement
–   Effective challenge and critical assessment of the evidence supplied with appropriate conclusions
–   Identification of missing information or additional information which would be required
–   Appropriate application of professional judgement to draw conclusions and make informed comments

Commercial acumen
–   Inclusion of appropriate recommendations in respect of the ethical and professional issues raised

Maximum   5

Total   25

50   SANZIO   *Walk in the footsteps of a top tutor*

Top tutor tips

Part (a) requires an assessment of the suitability of a proposed advertisement. Advertisements must not contain any content which would reflect adversely on the profession or other members. They must not contain misleading information which misrepresents the firm or the services the firm offers.

Part (b)(i) asks for the information you would require to assist in your valuation of the Titian Tyres' intangible assets, primarily the customer database and the licence. The customer database is an internally generated asset therefore won't be included in the financial statements of Titian Tyres. Remember that the value of an asset is dependent on the expected future cash flows so identify information that would help assess the level of future cash flows that could be generated from the assets.

Part (b)(ii) asks for enquiries to be made regarding the contingent liability included in the notes to the financial statements. Here you should be trying to assess the likelihood of payment and the potential amount of the payment.

(a) **Advertisement**

Accountant charging you too much for poor quality services

Accountants are permitted to advertise subject to the requirements in the ACCA Code of Ethics and Conduct that the advert should 'not reflect adversely on the professional accountant, ACCA or the accounting profession'. The advert does not appear to be in keeping with this principle as it suggests that other accountancy firms charge inappropriately high fees and that the quality of their services is questionable. This discredits the services offered by other professional accountants as well as implying that the services offered by Raphael & Co are far superior.

Most comprehensive range of services

The advert states that the firm offers 'the most comprehensive range of finance and accountancy services in the country'. This is misleading. With 12 offices and only 30 partners, Raphael & Co is unlikely to be one of the largest accountancy firms in the country and is therefore unlikely to offer the most comprehensive range of services. If it is misleading, this statement must be withdrawn from the advertisement.

Leading tax team

The advert also implies that they have the country's leading tax team. It is not possible to substantiate this claim as it is not possible to measure the effectiveness of tax teams and even if it were, no such measure currently exists. This is, therefore, also potentially misleading and should be withdrawn from the advert.

Tax team waiting to save you money

The suggestion that the tax experts are waiting to save the client money is inappropriate. No such guarantees can be made because tax professionals must apply relevant tax legislation in an objective manner. This may lead to a reduction in a client's current tax expense or it may not. Any failure to apply these regulations appropriately could raise questions about the professional behaviour of the practitioner.

Guarantee to be cheaper than your existing service provider

Guaranteeing to be cheaper than other service providers is often referred to as 'lowballing'. This could create a potential self-interest threat to objectivity and it could also threaten professional competence and due care if the practitioner is unable to apply the appropriate professional standards for that level of fee.

[**UK syllabus:** FRC Ethical Standard section 4 states that the audit engagement partner shall be satisfied and able to demonstrate that the audit engagement has assigned to it sufficient partners and staff with appropriate time and skill to perform the audit in accordance with all applicable auditing and ethical standards, irrespective of the audit fee to be charged.]

Business advice to audit clients

Offering business advice to audit clients creates a potential self-review threat to objectivity. It depends on the sort of advice offered but it is possible that the auditor in consequent years may have to audit aspects of the business affected by the advice given. This would be particularly relevant if the practitioner provided advice with regard to systems design. It would be possible to offer both services if Raphael & Co can use different teams to provide each service. Given that they have 12 offices, it may be possible to keep these services completely separate and they may be able to offer both.

[**UK syllabus**: According to FRC Ethical Standard section 5, offering a non-audit service such as business advice to audit clients potentially creates self-interest, self-review, management and advocacy threats to objectivity.]

Free advice

Offering services for free as part of a promotion is not prohibited but, similar to lowballing, this increases the threat to competence and due care if sufficient time and resources are not allocated to the task. This may also devalue the services offered by Raphael & Co as they may be perceived as being a promotional tool as opposed to a professional service.

Firms of accountants are permitted to offer free consultations, so this does not create any specific threats. The phrase 'drop in and see us' may cause a problem with potential clients though as it may not always be possible to expect to see senior staff members without an appointment. To avoid damaging the professional profile of the firm, Raphael & Co would need to make sure they had a dedicated member of staff available to meet potential customers who is available without prior notice.

Chartered Certified Accountants

Finally, Raphael & Co is not permitted to use the term 'Chartered Certified Accountants' because fewer than 50% of the partners of the firm are ACCA members. This reference should be removed.

(b) (i) **Intangible assets – further information**

Customer database

- A copy of the most recent financial statements to identify the current carrying amount of any purchased intangibles relating to the database, such as computer software.

- A copy of the original purchase agreement for the software to identify the age of the software and when any product licences expire.

- A copy of the original purchase/ongoing maintenance contracts for the software to identify the continuing costs of maintaining the system at its current level of efficiency.

- Historic records of sales by customer to verify management's statement that repeat customers make up over 60% of annual sales.

- Copies of a sample of recent automated customer communications traced to customer bookings/sales records to confirm the current efficacy of the system.

- Sales forecasts for the foreseeable future to assess the potential future cash flows attributable to the customer database system to assess its value when determining the potential purchase price.

Licence

- A copy of the original purchase agreement for the licence to confirm the $5 million cost and the exclusivity of the agreement.

- The original purchase agreement can also be used to identify whether any further incremental/contingent considerations or royalties are due in the future.

- A copy of the licence agreement to confirm whether the licence is for a fixed period of time or not and to confirm the exclusivity of the licence.

- A breakdown of the sales figures relating to the new tyres to enable comparison of the performance of the new tyres to existing brands.

- Forecasts showing the expected future sales attributable to the new tyres to confirm the continued inflow of economic benefit from the asset.

(ii) **Contingent liabilities – enquiries**

- Enquire of management and ascertain if any legal advice has been sought to determine who is liable to pay compensation in these cases, Titian Tyres Co or the supplier of the parts.

- Enquire whether or not management has sought any legal advice with regard to the likelihood of having to settle the claims.

- Enquire if management has records showing how many vehicles have been fitted with the faulty parts and whether these have been used in any estimates of the likely settlement costs.

- Discuss with management the level of claims which have been settled since the year end. Compare this with the original estimation to establish how effective management has been in making these estimates.

- Enquire of management for how long the company used the faulty parts and for what portion of this time period the known claims relate to.

- Discuss with management the details of any new claims which have been made since the year end which were not included in any estimations of the cost of settlement included in the contingent liability disclosure in the financial statements.

- Discuss with management their assessment of any risk that further claims will be made of which they are currently unaware.

- Enquire of management if other quality problems have been experienced with other parts from the same supplier.

Examiner's comments

Part (a) required students to critique the appropriateness of advertising being utilised by the firm. The majority of students were well prepared to answer this question with a format that has been used before, and were able to confidently identify and evaluate the ethical issues associated with the proposed advertisement.

In part (b) the question focused on the work that may be performed during a due diligence assignment and specifically around the valuation of specific assets and liabilities within a target company. The question here asked for further information that may be required and enquiries that would be made in order to provide assurance on such items. Candidates produced the strongest answers with respect to the valuation of a purchased licence albeit often focusing on initial recording rather than current values/impairment. The valuation of an internally generated database proved harder as many candidates quoted the financial reporting rules and concluded it should not be presented within the financial statements.

The final item related to a contingent liability that was presented in the target company's financial statements. Answers to this were of mixed quality but it was disappointing how many candidates again lost sight of the assignment being one of due diligence and made comments regarding the financial statements disclosure requirement. Candidates are reminded that more effective reading and planning would allow a clearer understanding of what is being asked for and that time should be spent ensuring that answers are tailored to the specifics of the question.

ACCA Marking guide	
	Marks
(a) Advertisement Up to 1½ marks for each point of evaluation and up to 1 mark for each response recommended. – Advert reflects adversely on other professional accountants – Misleading with regards to size of firm – Misleading comments regarding expertise of tax team – Threat to professional behaviour by guaranteeing to save tax – Lowballing – self-interest threat and threat to professional competence and due care – Potential self-review threat from business advice – Free consultations permitted – Remove misleading claims from advert – Separate teams for audit and other services advertised **Maximum**	 **7**
(b) (i) Additional Information Up to 1 mark for each piece of information recommended and adequately explained. **Database:** – Most recent financial statements (carrying amount) – Original software purchase agreement – Software maintenance contract – Historic records of sales by customer – Sample customer communications – Sales forecasts **Licence:** – Original purchase agreement (cost) – Original purchase agreement (incremental/contingent consideration) – Licence terms and conditions – Sales figures for new brand – Forecast sales for new brand **Maximum**	 **8**
(ii) Enquiries Up to 1 mark for enquiry recommended and adequately explained. – Legal advice regarding who bears the liability – Legal advice regarding likelihood of settlement – Basis of estimation of liability – Settlement of claims since year end – How long faulty parts used for – New claims since year end – Risk of further claims – Quality problems with other parts – Original purchase agreement (incremental/contingent consideration)	

– Licence terms and conditions		
– Sales figures for new brand		
– Forecast sales for new brand		
Maximum		5

Professional marks

Analysis and evaluation

– Appropriate use of the information to support discussion, draw appropriate conclusions and design appropriate responses

– Appropriate assessment of the professional issues raised, using examples where relevant to support overall comments

– Effective appraisal of the information to make suitable recommendations for appropriate courses of action

Professional scepticism and judgement

– Effective challenge and critical assessment of the evidence supplied with appropriate conclusions

– Identification of missing information or additional information which would be required

– Appropriate application of professional judgement to draw conclusions and make informed comments

Commercial acumen

– Show insight and perception in understanding the wider implications and impact of implementing relevant recommendations and demonstrate acumen in arriving at suitable conclusions

– Demonstrate awareness of any wider external factors or implications, in a given scenario

Maximum		5
Total		25

---

51 BALTIMORE *Walk in the footsteps of a top tutor*

Top tutor tips

Part (a) requires discussion of the benefits of a due diligence review being performed prior to the acquisition of a company. There were indications in the scenario that the client did not have the skill to do this and you are expected to identify these points and use them in your answer. The question then asks for the type of conclusion, i.e. level of assurance, to be issued on the due diligence review and to compare this to an audit which should be a straightforward requirement.

Part (b) asked for matters to focus on during the due diligence review. A due diligence review is performed to find information relevant to the client's decision regarding the acquisition. Therefore, you should identify the matters that might deter them from going ahead with the acquisition or might encourage them to go ahead with the acquisition.

(a)   **Benefits of due diligence to Baltimore Co**

Identification of assets and liabilities

One of the objectives of a due diligence review is for the assets and liabilities of the target company to be identified and valued. Therefore, a benefit of due diligence to Baltimore Co is to gain an understanding of the nature of assets and liabilities which are being acquired, as not all assets and liabilities of Mizzen Co are recognised in its financial statements.

Valuation of assets and liabilities

Mizzen Co has built up several customer databases, which, being internally generated, will not be recognised as assets in its statement of financial position, but these could be valuable assets to Baltimore Co. The due diligence provider will assess the value of these assets as this will influence the purchase price.

Operational, tax and legal issues

The due diligence review should uncover more information about operational issues, which may then help Baltimore Co's management to decide whether to go ahead with the acquisition. For example, only one of Mizzen Co's revenue streams appears to be directly relevant to Baltimore Co's expansion plans, so more information is needed about the other operations of Mizzen Co to determine how they may be of benefit to Baltimore Co.

The due diligence review should cover a wide range of issues, such as reviews of the company's legal and tax positions, which may uncover significant matters.

Expertise

An externally provided due diligence review, as opposed to a review conducted by management of Baltimore Co, is likely to provide information in a time-efficient, impartial manner. Baltimore Co's management has not previously dealt with an acquisition, whereas the audit firm has the financial and business understanding and expertise to provide a quality due diligence review.

Negotiation of purchase price

An externally provided due diligence review will also provide more credibility when negotiating on the purchase price as an independent party will have been involved in valuing the assets and liabilities, therefore is less subject to bias. This puts Baltimore Co in a stronger negotiating position.

Added credibility for obtaining finance

A review report issued by Goleen & Co will add credibility to the planned acquisition, which may help secure the bank loan which is needed to fund the acquisition. The bank may have more confidence in the likelihood of success of the investment which reduces the risk of non-payment of the loan.

Tutorial note

Credit will be awarded for other relevant benefits which are discussed such as assessing the financial position and performance of the target company.

Due diligence conclusion

Due diligence is a specific example of a direct reporting assurance engagement. The form of the report issued in this type of engagement is covered by ISAE 3000 *Assurance Engagements other than Audits or Reviews of Historical Financial Information*, and ISRE 2400 *Engagements to Review Historical Financial Statements* also contains relevant guidance.

The main difference between a review report and an auditor's report is the level of assurance that is given. In a review report a conclusion is expressed in a negative form. The conclusion would start with the wording 'based on our review, nothing has come to our attention...'

This type of conclusion is used because the nature of a due diligence review is that only limited assurance has been obtained over the subject matter. The procedures used in a review engagement are mainly enquiry and analytical review which can only provide limited assurance.

Tutorial note

Credit is equally awarded where answers discuss the due diligence assignment as being based on agreed upon procedures, in which case no assurance is provided.

In comparison, in an audit of historical information, the auditor will use a wide variety of procedures to obtain evidence to give reasonable assurance that the financial statements are free from material misstatement. This means that an opinion expressed in a positive form can be given.

(b) **Matters to focus on in the due diligence review**

Equity owners of Mizzen Co and involvement of BizGrow

The nature of the involvement of the venture capitalist company, BizGrow, is a crucial issue which must be the starting point of the due diligence review. Venture capitalists provide equity when a company is incorporated, and typically look for an exit route within three to seven years. Mizzen Co was incorporated four years ago, so it will be important to determine whether BizGrow retains its original equity holding in Mizzen Co, and if so, whether the acquisition of BizGrow's shares by Baltimore Co would be compatible with the planned exit route.

Key skills and expertise

It appears that the original founders of Mizzen Co, Vic Sandhu and Lou Lien, are crucial to the success of Mizzen Co and it would be in Baltimore Co's interests to keep them involved with the business. However, Vic and Lou may wish to focus on further work involving IT innovation rather than Baltimore Co's planned website and without Vic and Lou's expertise the acquisition may be much less worthwhile. However, there could be other employed personnel with the necessary skills and experience to meet Baltimore Co's needs, or much of the skill and expertise could be provided from freelancers, who will not be part of the acquisition.

Internally generated intangible assets

Mizzen Co is likely to have several important internally generated intangible assets, which will not be recognised in its individual accounts but must be identified and measured as part of the due diligence review. First, Vic and Lou have innovated and developed new website interfaces, and the review must determine the nature of this intellectual property (IP), and whether it belongs to Vic and Lou or to Mizzen Co. The measurement of this asset will be very difficult, and it is likely to form an important part of the acquisition deal if Baltimore Co want to acquire the IP to use in its new website.

There are also several customer databases which need to be measured and included in the list of assets acquired, which again may be difficult to measure in value. It is important for the due diligence review to confirm the relevance of the databases to Baltimore Co's operations, and that the databases contain up-to-date information.

Premises

Mizzen Co currently operates from premises owned by BizGrow and pays a nominal rent for this. Presumably if the acquisition were to go ahead, this arrangement would cease. The due diligence review should consider the need for new premises to be found for Mizzen Co and the associated costs. Possibly there is room for Mizzen Co to operate from Baltimore Co's premises as the operations do not appear to need a large space. The rental agreement may be fixed for a period of time and cancellation may incur a penalty.

Other tangible assets

Mizzen Co appears to own only items such as computer equipment and fixtures and fittings. It needs to be clarified whether these assets are owned or held under lease, and also whether any other tangible assets, such as vehicles, are used in the business. Any commitments for future purchases of tangible assets should be reviewed.

Accounting policy on revenue recognition

Mizzen Co has some fairly complex revenue streams, and the due diligence review should establish that the accounting policies in place are reasonable and in line with IFRS 15 *Revenue from Contracts with Customers*.

The revenue generated from corporate website development should be recognised over time if the website is bespoke and does not have an alternative use i.e. cannot be repurposed for another client.

Revenue generated from maintaining customer websites should be recognised over time as the customer receives the service.

The subscription based provision to technical material should also be recognised over time and the annual fee of $250 should be deferred and recognised over the year.

The customer databases which are made available to companies for marketing purposes should be recognised at a point in time i.e. when the database is made available to Mizzen Co's clients.

There is a risk that revenue is recognised too early, inflating Mizzen Co's profit if for example, revenue in relation to the subscription service or website development is recognised immediately rather than over time.

Sustainability and relevance of revenue streams

The financial statements indicate that revenue has increased each year, and that in the last year it has increased by 23.7%. This is an impressive growth rate and work must be done to analyse the likelihood of revenue streams being maintained and further growth being achieved. For example, the proportion of website development and two-year maintenance contracts which are renewed should be investigated. Not all of Mizzen Co's revenue streams seem very relevant to Baltimore Co's operations, so how these may be managed post-acquisition should be considered.

Operating expenses

The financial extracts indicate a potentially unusual trend in relation to operating expenses. In 20X3 and 20X4, operating expenses represented 60% and 58.3% of revenue respectively. In 20X5, this had reduced to 49.6%. This may be due to economies of scale being achieved as the company grows, or possibly expenses are understated or revenue overstated in 20X5. As freelance web designers have been used in 20X5, operating expenses may have been expected to increase in proportion to revenue. The due diligence review should perform detailed analysis on the operating costs incurred by the company to gain assurance that expenses are complete and accurately recorded.

With the exception of 20X2, the finance cost has remained static at $250,000 per annum. The due diligence review must uncover what this finance cost relates to, and whether it will continue post-acquisition. It may be a bank loan or it could be a payment made to BizGrow, as venture capitalist companies often impose a management charge on companies which they have invested in. Baltimore Co will need to understand the nature of any liability in relation to this finance charge.

Cash position and cash management

Mizzen Co's cash position should be confirmed. Given that the company appears to have limited need for capital (asset) expenditure and working capital, and given the level of profits which has been made in the last three years, it could be expected that the company would be cash-rich. The due diligence review should confirm how the cash generated by the company since incorporation has been used, for example, in dividend payments to BizGrow and to Vic and Lou.

Additional information required

- Contract or legal documentation describing the nature of the investment which BizGrow made when Mizzen Co was incorporated, and detailing the planned exit route.

- A register of shareholders showing all shareholders of Mizzen Co.

- An organisational structure, in order to identify the members of management and key personnel and their roles within Mizzen Co.

- A list of employees and their roles within the company, and their related obligations including salary, holiday entitlements, retirement plans, health insurance and other benefits provided by Mizzen Co, and details of compensation to be paid in the case of redundancy.

- A list of freelance web designers used by Mizzen Co, and a description of the work they perform.

- The key terms of contracts or agreements with freelance web designers.

- A list of all IT innovations which have been created and developed by Mizzen Co, and details of any patent or copyright agreements relating to them.

- Agreements with employees regarding assignment of intellectual property and confidentiality.

- Copies of the customer databases showing contact details of all people or companies included on the list.

- A list of companies which have contracts with Mizzen Co for website development and maintenance.

- A copy of all contracts with customers for review of the period for which maintenance is to be provided.

- A breakdown of the revenue which has been generated from making each database available to other companies, and the dates when they were made available.

- A summary of the controls which are in place to ensure that the database details are regularly updated.

- A copy of the rental agreement with BizGrow, to determine whether any penalty is payable on cancellation.

- Non-current asset register showing descriptions and values of all assets used in the business.

- Copies of any lease agreements, for example, leases of computer equipment, photocopiers, etc.

- Details of any capital (asset) expenditure budgets for previous accounting periods, and any planned expenditure in the future.

- Mizzen Co's stated accounting policy on revenue recognition.

- Systems and controls documentation over the processing of revenue receipts.

- An analysis of expenses included in operating expenses for each year and copies of documentation relating to ongoing expenses, such as salaries and other overheads.

- Copies of management accounts to agree expenses in the audited accounts are in line and to perform more detailed analytical review.

- The full set of financial statements and auditor's reports for each year since the company's incorporation, to:

  - Confirm the assets and liabilities recognised

  - Agree the level of dividends paid each year

  - Review all of the accounting policies used in preparing the financial statements

  - Find the details of any related party transactions that have occurred

  - Review the statement of cash flows for each year.

- Any agreements with banks or other external providers of finance, including finance advanced and relevant finance charges, or confirmation that no such finance has been provided to Mizzen Co.

Tutorial note

Credit will be awarded for other relevant information which would be required as part of the due diligence review.

Examiner's comments

This question focused on due diligence, a topic that has appeared several times previous to this sitting. The scenario described a due diligence assignment to be performed on the target company Mizzen Co, at the request of Baltimore Co. The history and activities of the target company was described in some detail, and some financial information provided for the last four years. For Baltimore Co this would be their first acquisition, and was being considered as a means to diversify the company's operations.

Requirement (a) asked candidates to discuss the benefits to Baltimore Co of a due diligence review being performed on Mizzen Co. While some reasonable answers were given, possibly by candidates who had practiced the past exam question containing a similar requirement, on the whole answers were unsatisfactory. The following factors contributed to inadequate performance in relation to this requirement.

- Writing answers that were much too brief for the marks available.

- At the other extreme, some very lengthy answers were given that usually failed to answer the question requirement and instead either simply wrote in detail on how a due diligence assignment should be performed, or suggested in some detail the operational benefits to Baltimore Co of acquiring Mizzen Co.

The question also required candidates to describe the type of conclusion that would be issued for a due diligence report and to compare this to an auditor's report. This was well answered by most candidates, who compared the type of assurance that could be offered for a due diligence assignment with that given in an auditor's report, and linked this to the type of work that is carried out. Credit was awarded for different types of answers, as some discussed due diligence as being performed as agreed upon procedures rather than a review engagement, either of which is appropriate.

Requirement (b) asked candidates to identify and explain the matters that the due diligence review would focus on, and to recommend the additional information needed. The answers provided to this requirement were extremely mixed in quality. There were some exceptionally sound answers, explaining relevant matters in sufficient depth, and using the financial information provided to come up with reasonable points. These answers also provided relevant requests for additional information. However, the majority of answers were unsatisfactory. Most candidates picked up at least a few marks by identifying some of the matters that the review would focus on, but many candidates let themselves down by failing to explain the matters that they had identified in any real depth. It was common for answers to simply contain a list of bullet points with very little explanation at all, and only a limited amount of marks can be awarded to answers of this type.

Some points were better dealt with, including the following:

- Most answers picked up on the fact that Mizzen Co used premises owned by the venture capitalist company, and the fact that this arrangement would probably cease on the acquisition.

- Many candidates realised that the two founders of Mizzen Co were crucial to the company's success and that without them the acquisition would probably be pointless.

- Many candidates used the financial information to some extent, though sometimes only in a very limited way, but most picked up on the fact that Mizzen Co was paying finance charges, and so information would be needed to understand what those charges relate to.

- Many answers considered that revenue recognition would be a matter to focus on due to the relatively complex nature of the company's revenue streams.

- Some answers performed a little analytical review on the financial information to reveal that expenses were not increasing in line with revenue, and that this would need to be investigated.

The answers that were unsatisfactory, as well as containing inadequately explained points as mentioned above, also tended to focus too much on financial reporting matters, for example giving very lengthy discussions on the calculation of goodwill. While the accounting treatment of some items certainly was relevant to the answer, just focusing on these matters meant that candidates did not provide a broad enough range of comments to score well. Another factor leading to poor marks for this requirement was that many candidates simply failed to recommend any additional information at all that would be needed in the review. Many candidates missed out on marks here, for example for recommending that a statement of financial position, management accounts and cash flow forecasts would be needed. Some candidates supplied a lengthy discussion of matters relating to the acceptance of the due diligence assignment, such as agreeing fees and clarifying deadlines, which was not asked for.

ACCA Marking guide

		Marks
(a)	**Benefit of due diligence** Up to 2 marks for each benefit explained – Identification of assets and liabilities – Valuation of assets and liabilities – Review of operational issues – Added credibility and expertise – Added value for negotiation of purchase price – Other advice can be given, e.g. on obtaining finance **Conclusion on due diligence** Generally 1 mark for each discussion point – Due diligence report to express conclusion of negative assurance – Limited assurance due to nature of work performed – Audit opinion is a positive opinion of reasonable assurance	
	Maximum	8
(b)	**Areas to focus on and additional information** Generally up to 1½ marks for each explanation of area to focus on: – Equity owners of Mizzen Co and involvement of BizGrow – Key skills and expertise – Internally generated intangible assets – Premises – Other intangible assets – Accounting policy on revenue recognition – Sustainability and relevance of revenue streams – Operating expenses – Finance charges – Cash management	

1 mark for each specific additional information recommended:
- Contract or legal documentation dealing with BizGrow's investment
- A register of shareholders showing all shareholders of Mizzen Co
- An organisational structure
- A list of employees and their role within the company, obligations and compensation
- A list of freelance web designers used by Mizzen Co, and a description of the work they perform
- The key terms of contracts or agreements with freelance web designers
- A list of all IT innovations which have been created and developed by Mizzen Co, and details of any patent or copyright agreements relating to them
- Agreements with employees regarding IP and confidentiality
- Copies of the customer databases
- A list of companies which have contracts with Mizzen Co for website development and maintenance
- A copy of all maintenance contracts with customers
- A breakdown of the revenue that has been generated from making each database available to other companies, and the dates when they were made available
- A summary of the controls which are in place to ensure that the database details are regularly updated
- A copy of the premises rental agreement with BizGrow
- Non-current asset register
- Copies of any lease agreements
- Details of any capital (asset) expenditure budgets for previous accounting periods, and any planned expenditure in the future
- Mizzen Co's stated accounting policy on revenue recognition
- Systems and controls documentation over the processing of revenue receipts
- Analysis of expenses included in operating expenses for each year
- Copies of management accounts
- The full set of financial statements and auditor's reports
- Any agreements with banks or other external providers of finance

Maximum | 12

Professional marks
Analysis and evaluation
- Appropriate use of the information to support discussion, draw appropriate conclusions and design appropriate responses
- Effective appraisal of the information to make suitable recommendations for appropriate courses of action

Professional scepticism and judgement
- Effective challenge and critical assessment of the evidence supplied with appropriate conclusions
- Identification of missing information or additional information which would be required
- Appropriate application of professional judgement to draw conclusions and make informed comments

Commercial acumen
- Demonstrate awareness of any wider external factors or implications, in a given scenario

5

Total | 25

52   JACOB *Walk in the footsteps of a top tutor*

Top tutor tips

Part (a)(i) asks for benefits of externally provided due diligence prior to the acquisition of a company. Try and think of reasons why the client might not be able to do the due diligence for themselves.

Part (a)(ii) requires the information you would require for your due diligence review. Think about the information that would help you identify whether there are any financial, operational, tax or legal issues with the company being acquired. Is there anything happening that would deter the client from purchasing the company? Is there anything that would impact the price that they would be prepared to pay for the company?

Part (b) covers the ethical issues arising from a conflict of interest. Explain the ethical issues and actions the firm should take to manage the conflict effectively.

(a) (i) **Benefits of a due diligence review**

Identification of assets and liabilities

One benefit is that by conducting a due diligence review, the assets and liabilities of Locke Co can be identified and a potential value placed on them. Without a due diligence review it will be difficult for management to negotiate a fair price for Locke Co, as the price paid should include consideration of assets and liabilities not necessarily shown in the accounts, for example, any contingent liabilities which may exist in connection with warranties provided to customers of Locke Co.

Gather information on the court case

Locke Co is currently involved in a court case which is attracting media attention. This negative publicity may affect Locke Co's reputation and could have an impact on future revenues which will in turn affect the value of the company. In addition, any liabilities arising as a result of the court case will further impact the value of the company and the price that Jacob Co may be willing to pay. The due diligence review will look at the latest information available on the case which may help Jacob Co decide whether or not they want to take the risk of purchasing a company which is experiencing such problems.

Identification of operational issues

The due diligence review should uncover more information about operational issues, which may then help Jacob Co's directors in deciding whether to go ahead with the acquisition. For example, Locke Co may need to relocate its head office, as it is currently located on the owners' family estate. If this is the case, significant expense could be involved in building or purchasing new premises, or the head office function could be merged with that of Jacob Co. Either way, it is a practical operational issue that will need to be planned for, if the acquisition were to go ahead.

Expertise

Another benefit is that an externally provided due diligence review, as opposed to a review conducted by management of Jacob Co, is likely to provide information in a time-efficient, impartial manner. The audit firm has the financial and business understanding and expertise to provide a quality due diligence review. The management of Jacob Co can focus their attention on operational issues, for example, considering how best to merge the acquired business into existing operations, leaving the detailed due diligence review to be performed by independent experts.

Enhanced credibility

It is not stated how Jacob Co intend to finance the acquisition. If finance is to be obtained externally from a bank or other investor the external due diligence review may provide more assurance than due diligence performed by management who are pursuing the acquisition. Externally provided due diligence will be more objective. The providers of finance may have greater confidence that the investment will be less risky and therefore be more likely to lend money to finance the acquisition.

Liquidity of Locke Co

Locke Co has a significant bank loan and relies on an overdraft for cash flow in winter months. The due diligence review will assess the terms and conditions of these arrangements and assess the potential impact on the future liquidity profile of Lock Co. If Locke Co is unlikely to be able to sustain itself financially Jacob Co may need to inject cash to keep it going. This will make the investment a less attractive proposition and may be a deciding factor in whether to go ahead with the purchase.

(ii) **Further information to be requested**

Directors, and any other key management personnel's contracts of employment – these will be needed to see if there are any contractual settlement terms if the contract of employment is terminated after the acquisition. The family members who founded the company may be looking for an exit route and may not wish to be involved with the company after acquisition, so sizeable amounts could be payable to them on termination of their contracts.

An organisational structure should be obtained, in order to identify the members of management and key personnel and their roles within Locke Co. After acquisition, Jacob Co may wish to retain the services of some members of key management, while others may be made redundant as activities with Jacob Co are streamlined.

Details of any legal arrangement, such as a lease, covering the use of the family owned property by the company. Jacob Co's management may wish to relocate and/or merge Locke Co's head office function. If there is a formal lease arrangement currently in place, there could be early termination penalties to be paid on early termination of the lease.

Purchase documentation regarding the land obtained for the purpose of building a new head office. This will provide information on the location and size of the land. Jacob Co may wish to consider an alternative use for this land, or its sale, or possibly not including the land in the acquisition deal, if it does not wish to go ahead with the construction of the new premises. A copy of planning permission, if any has been sought, regarding the planned construction of a new head office should also be obtained.

Prior-year audited financial statements, and management accounts for this financial year – this information can be used to verify the assertion that Locke Co has enjoyed rapid growth. The financial statements will also provide useful information regarding contingent liabilities, the liquidity position of the company, accounting policies, and the value of assets. Further information should be sought regarding the market value of assets if the financial statements have been prepared using the historical cost convention.

The most recent management accounts for the current year should be analysed. They will reveal any significant change in the company's position or performance since the last audited accounts, for example, if revenue has decreased significantly, or further finance taken out.

Forecasts and budgets for future periods will enable an analysis of the future prospects of the company. Attention should be paid to the cash flow forecast in particular, given that the company has seasonal cash inflows, and uses an overdraft for several months of the year. Expansion in the past should not lead to an assumption that expansion will continue, and the assumptions underpinning the forecasts and budgets should be carefully considered for validity.

The signed loan agreement should be reviewed. Jacob Co will need to know the exact amount and terms of the loan, including the interest rate, any other finance charges, whether the loan is secured on company assets, the repayment terms, and any covenants attached to the loan.

The amount is described as significant, and Jacob Co should be wary of taking on this amount of debt without a clear understanding of its associated risk exposure.

Details should also be obtained regarding the overdraft facility, such as the maximum facility that is extended to the company, the interest rate, when the facility is due for renewal or review, and how many months on average the facility is used in a financial year. If the acquisition were to go ahead, Locke Co could prove to be a cash drain on the group. Jacob Co may plan to alleviate this by an intra-group loan of cash during the winter months, but the seasonality of the cash flows must be clearly understood before an acquisition decision is made.

Legal correspondence pertaining to the court case should be obtained. This should show the amount of damages claimed against the company, and the timescale as to when the case should go to court. The correspondence should also show the amount of legal fees incurred so far, and give an indication as to the future amount of fees likely to be paid. A review of the board minutes of Locke Co may indicate the likelihood of the court case going against the company. Jacob Co will need a detailed understanding of the financial consequences of this legal matter if they are to acquire the company.

Information should also be sought regarding the bad publicity caused by the court case. A copy of any press statements made by company representatives would be useful background information.

It is stated that Locke Co enjoys a 'good reputation'. Information to substantiate this claim should be sought, such as the results of customer satisfaction surveys, or data showing the level of repeat customers. Any exaggeration of the claim regarding the company's reputation could mean that Jacob Co can negotiate a lower purchase price, and will need to consider the impact of Locke Co's reputation on its own operations.

Details of warranties offered to customers should be obtained, including the length of period covered by the warranty, and any limits on the amount that can be claimed under warranty, to consider the level of contingent liability they may represent. If significant potential warranty claims exist, this should be reflected in the price offered to acquire Locke Co.

The contract between Locke Co and Austin Co should be obtained and scrutinised. It is essential to understand exactly what services are performed by the service organisation – which could include bookkeeping, payroll, preparation of management accounts and dealing with tax issues. The cost of the outsourcing should also be considered, as well as the reputation of Austin Co. These are important considerations, as Jacob Co may wish to bring the accounting function back in-house, most likely to streamline Locke Co's accounting systems with that of Jacob Co.

(b) **Conflict of interest**

A potential conflict between the interest of two audit clients arises from our firm offering advice to Jacob Co on the tender being presented to Burke Co. A conflict of interest may create potential threats to objectivity, confidentiality or other threats to compliance with the fundamental ethical principles.

The firm faces the problem of potentially giving advice to one audit client in relation to another audit client, which threatens objectivity. There may also be problems to do with confidentiality of information, as either party could benefit from information obtained from the audit firm about the other party.

In dealing with conflicts of interest, the significance of any threats should be evaluated, and safeguards must be applied when necessary to eliminate the threats or reduce them to an acceptable level. The most important safeguard is disclosure by the audit firm. The audit firm should notify both Jacob Co and Burke Co of the potential conflict of interest and obtain their consent to act.

Other possible safeguards could include:

- The use of separate engagement teams.

- Procedures to prevent access to information (for example, strict physical separation of such teams, confidential and secure data filing).

- Clear guidelines for members of the engagement team on issues of security and confidentiality.

- The use of confidentiality agreements signed by employees and partners of the firm.

- Regular review of the application of safeguards by a senior individual not involved with relevant client engagements.

The firm may decide, having evaluated the threats and available safeguards, that the threats cannot be reduced to an acceptable level, in which case the firm should decline from giving advice to Jacob Co regarding the tender.

Examiner's comments

This question focused on due diligence. The scenario described a potential acquisition being planned by an audit client of your firm.

Requirement (a) (i) required an explanation of the benefits of an externally provided due diligence review to the audit client. This was reasonably well answered, though many answers were not made very specific to the scenario and tended to discuss the benefits of any due diligence review rather than an externally provided one.

Requirement (a) (ii) asked for additional information to be made available for the firm's due diligence review. Answers were satisfactory, and the majority of candidates did not struggle to apply their knowledge to the scenario, usually providing some focused answers dealing well with the specifics of the question scenario. Most answers seemed to use a logical approach – working through the information provided to generate answer points, and this meant that on the whole most of the key issues from the scenario were covered in the answer. A small proportion of answers also included irrelevant discussions of the type of report that would be provided to the client, or a discussion of ethical issues which were not asked for.

Requirement (b) was about a potential conflict of interest between two audit clients and confidentiality of information. The audit firm had been asked to provide advice on a tender for an important contract that one audit client was preparing in relation to a different audit client. Many candidates did correctly determine that a conflict of interest would arise and could recommend appropriate safeguards. However, many answers failed to identify the potential issues surrounding the confidentiality of client information. Some candidates tried to include a comment on every one of the ethical principles – many of which were irrelevant.

ACCA Marking guide			
			Marks
(a)	(i)	**Benefits of due diligence** Up to 2 marks for each benefit explained – Identify and value assets and liabilities to be acquired – Assessment of potential impact of court case – Identify and allow planning for operational issues – Provision by external experts – technically competent and time efficient – Enhanced credibility provided by an independent review – Evaluation of the liquidity position of Locke Co		
		Maximum	6

(ii)	**Information required**		
	Generally ½ mark for identification and up to 1 further mark for explanation (maximum 3 marks for identification):		
	– Service contracts of directors		
	– Organisational structure		
	– Lease/arrangement regarding head office		
	– Details of land purchased		
	– Planning permission for new head office		
	– Prior year accounts and management accounts		
	– Forecasts and budgets		
	– Loan agreement		
	– Overdraft facility details		
	– Legal correspondence		
	– Customer satisfaction surveys		
	– Details of warranty agreements		
	– Outsourcing agreement		
		Maximum	**9**
(b)	**Conflict of interest**		
	– Identify/explain the conflict of interest		
	– Threats to objectivity and confidentiality created		
	– Safeguard of disclosure to both parties		
	– Other safeguards (½ mark each), e.g.		
	• separate teams		
	• confidentiality agreements		
	• review of situation by independent partner		
	– If threats too significant the advice should not be given		
		Maximum	**5**

Professional marks

Analysis and evaluation

– Appropriate use of the information to support discussion, draw appropriate conclusions and design appropriate responses

– Appropriate assessment of the professional issues raised, using examples where relevant to support overall comments

– Effective appraisal of the information to make suitable recommendations for appropriate courses of action

Professional scepticism and judgement

– Effective challenge and critical assessment of the evidence supplied with appropriate conclusions

– Identification of missing information or additional information which would be required

– Appropriate application of professional judgement to draw conclusions and make informed comments

Commercial acumen

– Show insight and perception in understanding the wider implications and impact of implementing relevant recommendations and demonstrate acumen in arriving at suitable conclusions

– Demonstrate awareness of any wider external factors or implications, in a given scenario

	5
Total	**25**

53   MOOSEWOOD HOSPITAL *Walk in the footsteps of a top tutor*

> ### Top tutor tips
>
> *This question covers performance information. In the context of the question produced in this exam kit, the performance information forms part of the integrated report of a private hospital i.e. a company. In the context of an INT variant exam, the hospital in the scenario is likely to be a public sector organisation. You would attempt the question in the same way, irrespective of whether the hospital is private or a public sector organisation.*
>
> *Part (a) deals with ethical and professional issues arising from the client being in breach of laws and regulations. Draw on your knowledge of the relevant auditing standard and explain the auditor's responsibilities when such issues arise.*
>
> *Part (b)(i) requires benefits of an assurance report on KPIs being included in the integrated report. Think of the benefits of assurance and apply them to the scenario.*
>
> *Part (b)(ii) requires procedures to be performed in relation to the KPIs given in the scenario. Think of the documentation that would be produced and kept by the hospital that would help you verify the KPIs. Where you need a better understanding of the KPI an enquiry may be needed to obtain that understanding.*

(a)   **Ethical and professional issues**

Compliance with laws and regulations

It appears that Moosewood Hospital is storing and possibly using medicines which have passed their recommended use by date. This may be illegal, it may breach the terms of agreement with their suppliers and, most significantly, this may lead to patient harm or ineffective treatment.

ISA 250 *Consideration of Law and Regulations in an Audit of Financial Statements* requires that in the event of a suspected non-compliance with law and regulations, the auditor should document the findings and discuss them with management.

The audit team should attempt to obtain more information about the suspected non-compliance, though this will be difficult given the actions of the financial controller, who is denying access to the relevant source of information and the attempt to intimidate the audit team by the finance director.

The audit team should seek appropriate legal advice in relation to the use of out of date medicines. If this is a breach of regulations, then the auditor may have a statutory or public duty to report this incident to the relevant regulator, such as the UK's General Medical Council.

Reporting non-compliance to those charged with governance

If Fern & Co believes that non-compliance with relevant law and regulation is taking place, then according to ISA 250, the matter should be reported to those charged with governance of Moosewood Hospital. This communication should happen without delay given that it appears to be deliberate and owing to the potential seriousness of the use of expired medical inventory.

At present it is unclear whether those charged with governance are aware of these practices. The auditor should request that those charged with governance make any necessary disclosure to the relevant authorities, clearly state the reasons why Moosewood Hospital should make the disclosure and that if the board fails to comply, that Fern & Co will be compelled to make the disclosure themselves.

If the auditor suspects that members of senior management including the board of directors are involved with the non-compliance, then the auditor should report the matter to the next higher level of authority, such as the audit committee.

Confidentiality

Reporting the incident to a regulator would require the auditor to report information about a client to a third party, which is a breach of client confidentiality. In these circumstances, however, legal and regulatory responsibilities, as well as acting in the public interest would be considered to outweigh the confidentiality requirement.

Fern & Co should seek legal advice before they act to minimise the risk of legal dispute with their client or legal action from the regulator due to inaction.

Impact on the financial statements

It is not correct for management to assert that the issue with out of date inventory is not relevant to the audit, because if any of the inventory is obsolete, then it should be written off in the financial statements.

By restricting the audit team's ability to audit inventory, management has imposed a limitation on the scope of the audit. If the auditor is unable to obtain satisfactory evidence relating to inventories, then this may lead to a modification of the audit opinion.

Fern & Co should report this matter to those charged with governance and request that they provide access to the necessary evidence. They should also explain what repercussions this will have on the auditor's report if they fail to comply.

If Moosewood Hospital has failed to comply with any legal, regulatory or contractual requirements, they may incur fines or other financial penalties. The audit approach should now be modified to include additional procedures aimed at investigating the potential implications of the use of out of date medicines and the potential value of fines and penalties.

Intimidation threat

The aggressive actions of the finance director amount to an intimidation threat to objectivity. The finance director has tried to influence the conduct of the audit with threatening behaviour.

Fern & Co should inform those charged with governance, explaining the significance of the matter and that it cannot be tolerated. Fern & Co should explain the reasons for the enquiries made by the audit team and the significance of being allowed to complete these procedures.

Management integrity

While the intentions of management are not clear, it does appear that they are trying to conceal a matter of some significance from the auditor.

The audit team must increase their scepticism of all evidence provided by management, particularly written representations obtained from management as they may be subject to bias and evidence which they could potentially manipulate, such as internal spreadsheets. In particular, if the audit team is given access to the inventory valuation spreadsheet, they must remain vigilant for any indication that this has been subsequently altered.

Withdrawal from engagement

If the audit team believes that management is complicit in any significant illegal activity and/or attempt to manipulate the financial statements, they may reconsider their position as auditor. Fern & Co may wish to resign from the audit engagement to protect their reputation and to protect them from being implicated in any ensuing legal case.

Before taking any action, the matter should be discussed by the senior partners of the audit firm and an appropriate legal adviser.

(b) **(i)** **Benefits of independent assurance**

Obtaining an independent assurance report on the integrated report, and specifically on the key performance indicators (KPIs) contained within the report, is a way to enhance the credibility of the integrated report. Information provided by an organisation without any external assurance being obtained may not be perceived as trustworthy or accurate.

The integrated report is outside the scope of the audit, other than being read as part of 'other information' if it is published alongside the audited financial statements, which is not the case for Moosehead Hospital Co, and therefore without any assurance report being obtained, the contents of the integrated report including the KPIs could be seen as lacking in credibility.

Therefore, for users of the integrated report, a review report by Fern & Co can provide some assurance that the KPIs are relevant, derived from reliable source information and accurate. It is important to note, however, that only a low level of assurance is provided, and that the nature of the assurance will depend on the terms of the engagement between Fern & Co and Moosehead Hospital Co, for example, the engagement may be restricted to certain agreed upon procedures on specific KPIs.

Operating in a regulated industry makes the assurance even more important, as the KPIs may need to be reported to the authorities.

For management, the assurance report will also help in providing some assurance on how the KPIs have been determined, including that the systems and controls are sufficient to produce the necessary information.

Management will presumably be using the KPIs to monitor performance and therefore having assurance on the accuracy of the KPIs should provide comfort to management that appropriate decisions are being made.

(ii)   Procedures

General

- Document the systems which are in place for recording the information relevant to the performance measures, noting the key controls which should operate to ensure the accuracy of the information which is captured, recorded and reported. Evidence of the operating effectiveness of these controls throughout the period should be obtained.

- In particular, the auditor should obtain an understanding of the level of scrutiny of the performance measures by senior management, including: the frequency of their reviews; the level of detail which is provided; and their responses should the reported performance measures differ from their expectations.

- Each of the calculations of the performance measures should be obtained. Using the figures supplied by management, these should be recalculated by the audit team to ensure mathematical accuracy.

- The performance measures should be analytically reviewed against historic performance levels, on a monthly basis if such information is available, to identify any significant fluctuations in reported performance levels. Where fluctuations occur reasons should be sought through management enquiry, which should then be corroborated with evidence wherever possible.

Tutorial note

Other, relevant general procedures will also be awarded credit but will only be awarded credit once, i.e. candidates will not be given credit for repeating the same general procedure for each performance measure.

Patient/nurse ratio

- Obtain copies of the original document in which the basis for calculating the performance measures were agreed. This may be in the form of a strategic document agreed with the National Health Service or it may even be the minutes of the executive board. From this identify whether any specific definition is provided of the term 'average' or whether a specific formula is provided. In particular, it is important to ascertain over what period the average must be calculated.

- From the same document ascertain which patients must be included in the calculation, i.e. should this include emergency patients or just patients admitted for treatment by appointment.

- Confirm the calculation of the number of patients treated through inspection of underlying treatment and appointment records.

- Confirm the calculation of the number of nurses through inspection of underlying staff rotas and records of hours worked supplied to human resources and payroll departments.

Surgical room usage

- Enquire of the manager responsible for planning and co-ordinating surgical operations what the 'normal' period of time (i.e. excluding emergencies) is during which surgical procedures may be performed, i.e. which hours during the day and whether there are any days where scheduled procedures would not be performed.

- Obtain and inspect the hospital plans to identify the total number of surgical rooms available.

- Using the information above, calculate the total number of surgical hours available to the hospital. Compare the figure calculated to the figure used in management's calculation to identify any significant variances.

- Obtain a schedule of the total hours of surgery performed during the year. Confirm a sample of the times recorded to underlying hospital records to confirm the accuracy of the figures used in this calculation.

Admissions for previously treated conditions

- Enquire of management how they define a 'previously treated condition'. For example, does this depend upon the underlying symptoms or the diagnosis of the medical practitioner?

- Obtain a copy of the patient admissions records. Use automated tools and audit techniques to identify patients admitted to the hospital within 28 days of a previous admission. If possible, inspect the underlying patient records to identify whether the patient was treated for either the same or a similar condition. If not, enquire of the medical practitioners responsible for their care during their admission.

- Where the above procedure identifies patients admitted for the same condition, ensure that these patients are recorded in management's calculation of the performance measure to ensure the completeness of the information used in the calculation.

Examiner's comments

This question focused on the audit of a hospital and was generally not well-answered.

Part (a) focused on a potential breach of laws and regulations through the potential use of out-of-date medicines and an intimidating client. Most candidates discussed the implication for inventory valuation reasonably and some suggested highlighting the issues and lack of co-operation from the finance director to those changed with governance and the potential for a limitation on the scope of the audit. Disappointingly only a minority of candidates identified that there was a wider issue that using out-of-date medication could have severe or fatal health consequences and were able to discuss the balance between the auditor's duty of confidentiality to the client compared with their wider ethical duty to notify the appropriate regulators and after seeking legal advice.

Part (b)(i) asked about the benefits of independent assurance provided on key performance indicators for both management and external users. Candidates mostly correctly commented that this would provide greater credibility to the information and so would be relied on more by external users. Fewer candidates identified that this would also provide management with assurance that the systems and controls in place to produce the information was sufficient and operating satisfactorily.

In part (b)(ii) candidates were required to explain how to audit some performance KPIs and although some good points were made a number of candidates stretched their imagination as to how these could be verified and were simply impractical in the nature of their procedures.

ACCA Marking guide	
	Marks
Generally up to 1½ marks for each well explained point and 1 mark for each well explained procedure recommended:	
(a) **Ethical and professional issues**	
– Suspected non-compliance with laws and regulations	
– Attempt to obtain more evidence for discussion with management	
– Reporting non-compliance to those charged with governance	
– Confidentiality threat	
– Report to regulator	
– Limitation on scope of audit	
– Impact on the financial statements	
– Intimidation threat	
– Management integrity	
– Withdrawal from engagement	
Maximum	8
(b) **(i)** **Benefits of an assurance report on the KPIs included in the integrated report**	
– Assurance report enhances credibility of the integrated report generally and specifically the KPIs	
– Integrated report outside scope of audit	
– Important to gain assurance given regulated nature of the industry	
– Management use KPIs to monitor performance so credibility enhances management decision making processes	
Maximum	4
(ii) **Procedures in relation to key performance indicators**	
General:	
– Document systems and test controls	
– Identify level of senior management scrutiny of KPIs	
– Recalculate KPIs to confirm mathematical accuracy	
– Analytical review to historic performance	
Patient/nurse ratio:	
– Obtain definition of 'average' for patient/nurse ratio	
– Identify which patients to include	
– Confirm patient numbers to patient records	
– Confirm staff numbers to HR records	
Surgical rooms:	
– Discuss normal levels of room usage	
– Obtain hospital plans to identify number of surgical rooms	
– Recalculate number of surgical hours available	
– Confirm surgical times to underlying surgery/treatment records	

Admissions for previously treated conditions:		
– Enquire how a previously treated condition is identified		
– Inspect patient admission records to identify readmissions within 28 days		
– Inspect underlying patient records to identify if conditions match		
	Maximum	8

Professional marks

Analysis and evaluation

– Appropriate use of the information to support discussion, draw appropriate conclusions and design appropriate responses

– Appropriate assessment of the professional issues raised, using examples where relevant to support overall comments

– Effective appraisal of the information to make suitable recommendations for appropriate courses of action

– Appropriate use of the information to design appropriate procedures

Professional scepticism and judgement

– Effective challenge and critical assessment of the evidence supplied with appropriate conclusions

– Identification of possible management bias and consideration of the impact on the financial statements and the possible reasons for the management-imposed limitation of scope

– Effective application of technical and ethical guidance to effectively challenge and critically assess how management has responded to the breach of laws and regulations

– Identification of missing information or additional information which would be required

– Appropriate application of professional judgement to draw conclusions and make informed comments

Commercial acumen

– Show insight and perception in understanding the wider implications and impact of implementing relevant recommendations and demonstrate acumen in arriving at suitable conclusions

– Demonstrate awareness of any wider external factors or implications, in a given scenario

– Procedures are practical and plausible in the context of the scenario

		5
Total		25

54   NEWMAN & CO *Walk in the footsteps of a top tutor*

Top tutor tips

This question deals with social, environmental and sustainability reporting.

In part (a) take a methodical approach to the scenario and think of the matters that should be considered before accepting this type of engagement. Remember that the firm should only take on work of an acceptable level of risk. There are several factors mentioned in the scenario that should be considered specific to Eastwood Co.

In part (b), apply your knowledge of audit procedures to this type of engagement.

Part (c) is a common requirement for this topic. This is rote-learned knowledge from the text book which can be applied to the specific KPIs mentioned in the scenario to make it more relevant.

(a)   **Matters that should be considered in making acceptance decision**

Objectivity

The proposed assurance engagement represents a non-audit service. IESBA's *International Code of Ethics for Professional Accountants* does not prohibit the provision of additional assurance services to an audit client, however, the audit firm must carefully consider whether the provision of the additional service creates a threat to objectivity and independence of the firm or members of the audit team.

For example, when the total fees generated by a client represent a large proportion of a firm's total fees, the perceived dependence on the client for fee income creates a self-interest threat. Due to the nature of the proposed engagement, self-review and advocacy threats may also be created, as the Sustainability Report is published with the audited financial statements, and the audit firm could be perceived to be promoting the interests of its client by providing an assurance report on the key performance indicators (KPIs).

Newman & Co should only accept the invitation to provide the assurance engagement after careful consideration of objectivity, and a review as to whether safeguards can reduce any threat to objectivity to an acceptable level. As Eastwood Co is a 'major client', the fee level from providing both the audit and the assurance services could breach the permitted level of recurring fees allowed from one client. The fact that the company is listed means that the assessment of objectivity is particularly important and a second partner review of the objectivity of the situation may be considered necessary.

[**UK syllabus:** FRC Ethical Standard section 5 suggests that the audit engagement partner should assess the significance of any threat to objectivity created by the potential provision of the non-audit service and should consider whether there are safeguards that could be applied and which would be effective to eliminate the threat or reduce it to an acceptable level. If such safeguards can be identified and are applied, the non-audit service may be provided. However, where no such safeguards are applied, the only course is for the audit firm either not to undertake the engagement to provide the non-audit service in question or not to accept (or to withdraw from) the audit engagement.]

The fact that a separate team, with no involvement with the audit, will be working on the KPIs strengthens the objectivity of the assignment.

Eastwood Co's requirements

Assurance engagements can vary in terms of the level of work that is expected, and the level of assurance that is required. This will clearly impact on the scale of the assignment. For example, Eastwood Co may require specific procedures to be performed on certain KPIs to provide a high level of assurance, whereas a lower level of assurance may be acceptable for other KPIs.

Newman & Co should also clarify the expected form and content and expected wording of the assurance report itself, and whether any specific third party will be using the Sustainability Report for a particular purpose, as this may create risk exposure for the firm.

Competence

The audit firm's specialist social and environmental assurance department has only been recently established, and the firm may not have sufficient experienced staff to perform the assurance engagement. The fundamental principle of professional competence and due care requires that members of an engagement team should possess sufficient skill and knowledge to be able to perform the assignment, and be able to apply their skill and knowledge appropriately in the circumstances of the engagement.

Some of Eastwood Co's KPIs appear quite specialised – verification of CO_2 emissions for example, may require specialist knowledge and expertise. Newman & Co could bring in experts to perform this work, if necessary, but this would have cost implications and would reduce the recoverability of the assignment.

Scale of the engagement

The Sustainability Report contains 75 KPIs, and presumably a lot of written content in addition. All of these KPIs will need to be verified, and the written content of the report reviewed for accuracy and consistency, meaning that this is a relatively large engagement.

Newman & Co should consider whether the newly established sustainability reporting assurance team has enough resources to perform the engagement within the required time scale, bearing in mind the time pressure which is further discussed below.

Time pressure

Given that the financial statements are scheduled to be published in four weeks, it is doubtful whether the assurance assignment could be completed, and a report issued, in time for it to be included in the annual report, particularly given the global nature of the assignment.

Newman & Co may wish to clarify with Eastwood Co's management whether they intend to publish the assurance report within the annual report, as they have done previously, or whether a separate report will be issued at a later point in time, which would allow more time for the assurance engagement to be conducted.

Fee level and profitability

Such a potentially large scale assignment should attract a large fee. Costs will have to be carefully managed to ensure the profitability of the engagement, especially considering that overseas travel will be involved, as presumably much of the field work will be performed at Eastwood Co's Sustainability Department in Fartown.

The fee level would need to be negotiated bearing in mind the specialist nature of the work, and the urgency of the assignment, both of which mean that a high fee could be commanded.

Global engagement

The firm's sustainability reporting team is situated in a different country to Eastwood Co's Sustainability Department. Although this does not on its own mean that the assignment should not be taken on, it makes the assignment logistically difficult.

Members of the assurance department must be willing to travel overseas to conduct at least some of their work, as it would be difficult to perform the engagement without visiting the department responsible for providing the KPIs. Other locations may also need to be visited. There are also cost implications of the travel, which will need to be built into the proposed fee for the engagement. Language may also present a barrier to accepting the engagement, depending on the language used in Fartown's location.

Risk

Eastwood Co is a large company with a global presence. It is listed on several stock exchanges, and so it appears to have a high public profile. In addition, pressure groups are keen to see the added credibility of an assurance report issued in relation to the KPIs disclosed. For all of these reasons, there will be scrutiny of the Sustainability Report and the assurance report.

Newman & Co should bear in mind that this creates a risk exposure for the firm. If the assignment were taken, the firm would have to carefully manage this risk exposure through thorough planning of the engagement and applying strong quality measures.

The firm would also need to ensure that the fee is commensurate with the level of risk exposure. Given the inconsistency that has come to light regarding one of the draft KPIs, which appears to overstate charitable donations made by the company, we may need to consider that management are trying to show the company's KPIs in a favourable way, which adds to the risk of the engagement.

Commercial consideration

If Newman & Co does not accept the assurance engagement, the firm risks losing the audit client in future years to another firm that would be willing to provide both services. As Eastwood Co is a prestigious client, this commercial consideration will be important, but should not override any ethical considerations.

(b) **Faster Jets Co**

Procedures to gain assurance on the validity of the performance measures

- Obtain a summary of all amounts donated to charitable causes and agree a sample to the bank ledger account/cash book.

- For large donations above a certain limit (say $10,000) confirm that authorisation for the payment has been made, e.g. by agreeing to minutes of management meetings.

- Review correspondence with charities for confirmation of the amounts paid.

- Review relevant press releases and publicity campaigns, e.g. the free flight scheme and the local education schemes are likely to have been publicised.

- For the $750,000 spent on the local education scheme, obtain a breakdown of the amounts spent and scrutinise to ensure all relate to the scheme, e.g. payments to educators.

- Obtain a sample of classroom registers to confirm attendance of children on certain days.

- For the free flights donated to charity, perform analytical review to confirm that the average value of a flight seems reasonable – the average being $700 ($560,000/800).

- For a sample of the 800 free flights, obtain confirmation that the passenger was a guest of Faster Jets Co, e.g. through correspondence with the passenger and relevant charity.

- Agree a sample of business miles travelled in vehicles to a mileage log, and fuel costs to employee expenses claims forms and the general ledger.

(c) **Difficulties measuring and reporting on social and environmental performance**

It is common for companies to produce a report on corporate social responsibility (CSR), and in some countries this is a requirement. CSR reports contain a wide variety of key performance indicators (KPIs) relating to the social and environmental targets which the company is aiming to achieve. It can be difficult to measure and report on social and environmental KPIs for a number of reasons.

Difficult to define

Measurements of social and environmental performance are not always easy to define. For example, Faster Jets Co aims to develop an education programme, which is vague in terms of measurement. The measurement only becomes precisely defined when a KPI which is capable of being quantified is attached to it, for example, the number of free education days provided in a year. It can also be difficult to identify key stakeholders and the KPIs which each stakeholder group is interested in.

Difficult to quantify

Targets and KPIs may be difficult to quantify in monetary terms. For example, Faster Jets Co's provision of free flights to charitable organisations can be quantified in terms of the number of flights donated, but the actual value of the flights is more questionable as this could be measured at cost price or market value. The monetary value may not even be very relevant to users of the CSR report.

Lack of systems to capture data

In addition, systems and controls are often not established well enough to allow accurate measurement, and the measurement of social and environmental matters may not be based on reliable evidence. However, this is not always the case, for example, the accounting system should be able to determine accurately the amount of cash donated to charity and the amount spent on vehicle fuel.

Difficult to make comparisons

Finally, it is hard to compare these targets and KPIs between companies, as they are not strictly defined, so each company will set its own target. It will also be difficult to make year on year comparisons for the same company, as targets may change in response to business activities.

Examiner's comments

Requirement (a) asked candidates to identify and explain the matters that should be considered in evaluating whether the audit firm should perform an assurance engagement on the client's Sustainability Report. It was clear that most candidates knew the matters that should be considered (ethical constraints, resources, knowledge, timescale, fees etc.), and most candidates took the right approach to the question, by working through the various 'matters' and applying them to the question. The fact that this was not an audit engagement did not seem to faze candidates, and there were many sound answers to this requirement. Some answers evaluated the many ethical problems with taking on the assurance engagement as well as providing the audit for 'a major client', and appreciated that with only four weeks to complete the work, it would probably be impossible to ensure quality work could be performed on a global scale to such a tight deadline by an inexperienced team. Some answers also picked up on the fact that the client's listed status would probably prevent the audit firm from conducting the assurance engagement, and certainly the situation would need to be discussed with, and approved by the audit committee. However, some answers were much too brief for the marks available, amounting to little more than a bullet point list of matters to be considered but with no application to the scenario. Without application it was not possible to pass this requirement. Other common mistakes included:

- Ignoring the fact that the client was already an existing audit client, so discussing the need to contact its auditors for information.

- Not reading the question and thinking that you had been approached to perform the audit.

- Only discussing the potential problems and not identifying the benefits of providing the service (e.g. it would provide experience for the newly established assurance team).

- Ignoring information given in the question (e.g. saying that the firm would need to ask about the use of the assurance report – when the question clearly states that it would be published in the annual report with the financial statements).

In requirement (b) the audit firm had been asked to perform an assurance engagement on Faster Jets Co's corporate social responsibility (CSR) report, and a number of CSR objectives and targets were provided along with the performance indicators to be included in the CSR report. The main weakness in responses was that candidates simply repeated the same procedures for each of the performance measures given, even if they weren't appropriate. For example, one of the performance measures related to free flights that had been donated to charities, and many candidates recommended that this should be agreed to bank statements or bank ledger account/cash book even though it is not a cash transaction. Candidates are encouraged to think about whether the procedures they are recommending are sensible in the context of the scenario. As is often the case when presented with a requirement to detail procedures, many candidates provided procedures that were not well explained, and in many cases weren't procedures at all, e.g. 'review the free flights', 'inspect the education days', 'confirm the vehicle fuel'. This type of comment cannot be given credit as it is too vague and does not answer the question requirement.

Part (c) asked for a discussion of the difficulties in measuring and reporting on social and environmental performance. This short requirement was well attempted by many candidates, with most identifying that it can be difficult to define and quantify CSR measures, that systems are often not in place to capture the relevant information and that comparisons are difficult due to the lack of a regulatory framework.

	ACCA Marking guide		
			Marks

(a) **Acceptance matters**
Up to 2 marks for each matter explained:
– Objectivity (up to 3 marks allowed)
– Client's specific requirements
– Competence
– Large scale engagement
– Fee level and profitability
– Time pressure
– Global engagement
– Risk
– Commercial consideration

Maximum **10**

(b) **Procedures on Faster Jets Co's performance measures**
Generally 1 mark for a well explained procedure:
– Obtain a summary of all amounts donated to charitable causes and agree to bank ledger account/cash book
– For large donation confirm that authorisation for the payment has been made
– Review correspondence with charities
– Review relevant press releases and publicity campaigns
– For the $750,000 spent on the local education scheme, obtain a breakdown of the amounts spent and scrutinise to ensure all relate to the scheme, e.g. payments to educators
– Obtain a sample of registers to confirm attendance of children on certain days
– For the free flights donated to charity, perform analytical review to confirm that the average value of a flight seems reasonable – the average being $700
– For a sample of the 800 free flights, obtain confirmation that the passenger was a guest of Faster Jets Co
– Agree a sample of business miles travelled in vehicles and fuel costs to employee expenses claims forms

Maximum **6**

(c) **Difficulties measuring and reporting on social and environmental performance**
Up to 1½ marks for each point discussed:
– Measures are difficult to define
– Measures are difficult to quantify
– Systems not set up to capture data
– Hard to make comparisons

Maximum **4**

Professional marks
Analysis and evaluation
– Appropriate use of the information to support discussion, draw appropriate conclusions and design appropriate responses
– Appropriate assessment of the professional issues raised, using examples where relevant to support overall comments
– Appropriate use of the information to design appropriate procedures
Professional scepticism and judgement
– Appropriate application of professional judgement to draw conclusions and make informed comments
– Identification of possible management bias and consideration of the impact on the sustainability and CSR reports

Commercial acumen		
– Show insight and perception in understanding the wider implications and impact of implementing relevant recommendations and demonstrate acumen in arriving at suitable conclusions		
– Demonstrate awareness of any wider external factors or implications, in a given scenario		
– Procedures are practical and plausible in the context of the scenario		
Maximum		5
Total		**25**

55 BEYER *Walk in the footsteps of a top tutor*

Top tutor tips

Part (a) requires professional considerations before accepting a forensic investigation. A forensic investigation is a specialist assignment and this must be considered when deciding whether to accept the invitation. General acceptance considerations which are applicable to all types of engagement can also be included such as whether the firm has the resource and competence to perform the work.

Part (b)(i) requires the procedures to be performed to quantify the loss. A common sense approach can be taken here. Also think about the audit procedures which will help quantify the inventory stolen.

In part (b)(ii) consider how the fraud was able to occur, i.e. which controls were missing or ineffective. Explain how, if they had been in place, the fraud could have been prevented. Where controls are missing, these should form the basis of your recommendations to prevent the fraud from occurring again in the future.

(a) Beyer Co

Scope of the investigation

Kaffe & Co should establish the specific work which Beyer Co expects them to perform. It is likely that the quantification of the loss represents an agreed upon procedures engagement and these would need to be confirmed with Beyer Co in advance.

The identification and recommendation on controls issues is more likely to be of a consulting nature and the process and outcomes agreed with the client. The assignment may require specific competencies, such as the use of specialists in the use of automated tools techniques and this should be identified prior to acceptance of the engagement.

Kaffe & Co would also need to establish the time period Beyer Co would like them to investigate. This will all have an impact on the total fee charged.

Establishing how Kaffe & Co's investigation relates to the criminal investigation

If the quantification of the loss were to become a criminal investigation, then the relevant authorities would take the lead. It is not clear whether the authorities would require additional, professional support in their investigation and, if so, what sort of assistance they would require. For example, it is possible that they would gather their own evidence, but they may require the use of an expert witness to verify their findings in court.

It is therefore vital that, before any terms are agreed or engagement contracts are signed, Kaffe & Co speaks to the authorities to ascertain whether there will be any criminal investigation and, if so, what their role might be in the investigation, and how they might interact with any other experts appointed by the authority to assist in the investigation.

Confidentiality

Firms providing professional services must always ensure that information relating to clients is not given to third parties without the permission of the client. In preparing the report for the insurance company, Kaffe & Co will need permission from Beyer Co to disclose the information to the insurance company. In an investigation such as this, it is highly likely that all of the evidence collected will have to be submitted to the authorities to assist with their criminal investigation. It is therefore vital that before Kaffe & Co accepts the assignment, they obtain permission to do so from the board of Beyer Co.

The types of reports and prospective users

The firm must confirm with Beyer Co what types of report they would expect as a result of the engagement and to whom the reports would be distributed. In forensic engagements, the procedures to be performed would normally be agreed and then the results of those procedures would be reported.

It may be that the insurance company expects an opinion to be given on the results of the investigation and if this is the case, then the assurance issued would be limited to negative assurance. Kaffe & Co would usually expressly state that the report is not intended for use by third parties.

In this investigation, it is possible that the relevant authorities would want to use the results of the procedures to compile evidence for their case. It would, if this were the case, be important to establish if additional reports would be required for this.

Management also wants additional reports relating to the deficiencies identified in the control environment and systems recommendations on how to strengthen controls in this area. The form and content of such a report must be agreed upon in advance of accepting the assignment.

Professional competence

Before accepting the role, Kaffe & Co must be certain that they have staff with the requisite competencies to be able to conduct the investigation effectively.

If this were conducted as a criminal investigation, it is also vital that the staff used have sufficient experience in relation to the gathering and safeguarding of evidence. Any failure to follow the relevant protocol may render the evidence useless to the legal case.

Time pressure, deadlines and resource availability

As well as having staff with the requisite competencies to conduct the engagement, it is also vital that those staff are available to be able to conduct the investigation in the time frame suggested. The insurance company is likely to set the time frame for any initial investigation. If the relevant authorities conduct an additional criminal investigation, Kaffe & Co must consider the extent of the possible investigation and whether they are able to commit the necessary resources without adversely affecting their other client commitments.

Client due diligence

As Beyer Co is a new client, Kaffe & Co may be required to perform client identification procedures as part of local anti-money laundering regulations. If this is the case, the firm must explain the need to obtain information about the company and its directors before Beyer Co can be accepted as a client. If Beyer Co is unable, or refuses, to do this, then Kaffe & Co would not be able to take on Beyer Co as a client or proceed with the engagement.

(b) **(i)** **Procedures to be performed to quantify the inventory loss**

- Meet with the audit committee and members of management to understand and document what they know about the fraud and who might be involved.

- Discuss with the company's legal team what is known about the fraud at present and the source of the information.

- If possible, interview the whistle-blower to identify the potential staff involved and the timescales over which the fraud has been perpetrated.

- Obtain the prior year report to management from the auditor and inspect auditor's reports to identify any deficiencies or discrepancies in inventories identified by the auditors.

- Obtain/prepare a reconciliation of all orders placed including cancelled orders to all invoices raised to identify the total of all orders placed but not invoiced to establish the maximum potential value of the theft.

- Arrange to conduct a full inventory count to identify discrepancies between the inventory records and physical inventory.

- Investigate records of inventory written off to identify possible attempts to disguise the missing items.

- Interview sales, warehouse and accounting staff to identify the system in place for creating a sales order and for setting up customers within the sales and inventory systems.

- Use data analytics tools to identify the total of cancelled orders within the inventory records system and any addresses which are associated with large volumes of cancellations.

- Identify which cancelled orders are assigned to the sales representative identified by the whistle-blower.

- Identify which customers those orders are assigned to and verify their existence within the invoicing system and, where possible, their registered business address to ensure they are genuine customers.

- From this, identify fictitious customers and reconcile their cancelled orders to the inventory discrepancies identified.

- Assess if the amounts ordered by the fictitious customers agree to the total discrepancies or if there is a further difference to be investigated.

- Obtain inventory listing to identify the cost of the parts stolen and calculate the cost of the inventory identified as relating to the fictitious customer orders.

- Using data analytics tools, identify any other sales staff with unusual levels of cancelled sales despatches to see if this is a wider issue.

(ii) **Control deficiencies and recommendations**

Lack of segregation of duties and monitoring of order cancellations

There is a lack of internal control over the warehouse team, particularly in relation to authorisation and approval of transactions. The warehouse manager having the ability to create new customers on the system without authorisation has allowed fictitious customers to be created.

The ability of the sales representative to cancel orders and the ability of the warehouse manager to reverse despatches without authorisation gives rise to a lack of segregation of duties. These processes should require authorisation from a senior member of staff, for instance, sales cancellations should be approved by the sales manager and reversed goods despatches by the operations manager.

Additionally, the lack of reconciliation of the sales orders to the amounts invoiced allowed the cancellation of deliveries to avoid detection from any invoicing process. The consistent cancellation of despatches relating to one customer from one sales representative may have drawn attention within the sales system had the transaction made it that far.

The existence of the inventory system in isolation from the invoicing and accounting system allowed for incomplete information to be relayed further up within the business. While this in itself is not an issue, it did mean that any management review of accounting and invoicing reports does not act as a means of review of the inventory management and despatch system.

In many businesses, a system which linked the inventory movements with the accounting and management information system would allow reports to be generated to monitor for unusual levels of returns and cancellations. In the absence of the ability to merge the two systems, it may be possible for additional reporting functions to be added to the inventory system to allow reports of returns and cancellations to be generated for review at a higher level than the warehouse manager to provide oversight of this area.

A proper monitoring system would have flagged that one sales representative in particular had higher than usual cancellation levels which could have been investigated and monitored by management.

It would also be possible to implement a system where all cancelled orders and reversed despatches are processed outside of the sales and warehouse team, for example, by the accounts department.

Lack of segregation of duties in the warehouse counts

The lack of segregation of duties between warehouse staff and inventory count staff allowed the fictitious sales orders to pass unnoticed as the inventory discrepancy which would have flagged the issue was ineffective. An independent inventory count process using an external company or using staff from outside the warehouse to perform counts and reconcile the inventory amounts to inventory records would have identified missing inventory sooner.

Additional implications of the fraud

In addition to the value of the inventory stolen by the warehouse manager and sales representative, the business is not holding accurate records of its inventory, meaning that it may be in breach of the requirement to keep proper records of assets and liabilities and its assets are overstated. This may or may not be a material amount.

There is also a business risk arising from inaccurate inventory in that inventory believed to be on hand to satisfy genuine orders may not exist, causing delays and disruption to the ability of Beyer Co to satisfy customer orders in a timely manner causing customer satisfaction issues and potential loss of customers if the delays become unacceptable.

Recommendations

- Integration of the sales order and invoicing systems into the management information system.

- New customers should be created by the accounts department not the sales/despatch teams.

- Authorisation process for cancelled orders/returns.

- Creation and regular review of exception reports and unusual trends including cancellation reports by higher level management to identify irregular or suspicious patterns.

- Regular inventory counts to be performed by staff independent of the warehouse and sales staff.

Examiner's comments

This question was set in the context of a non-audit assignment for a non-audit client. Candidates were asked to consider acceptance criteria for an investigative forensic appointment in response to a fraud at a manufacturing company. The scenario detailed a fraud where inventory was stolen, and the assignment was to quantify the fraud for an insurance claim. Most candidates demonstrated the ability to apply acceptance criteria with reference to the specific question. A minority of candidates discussed irrelevant considerations that appeared to have been learnt from a previous question set in a similar context. Whilst the criteria for assessment were similar, some of those points were not relevant in this case and candidates wasted time in the exam discussing issues that would only be relevant to an existing audit client.

Part (b)(i) of this question asked candidates to suggest the steps or procedures that could be used to quantify the fraud and answers here tended to be either very good or very poor. Good answers methodically went through the process of identifying the fictitious customer, extracting data on cancelled orders and matching that to missing inventory through an inventory count. Weaker candidates were those who approached this by listing pre-learned procedures or without taking in to account the assignment and scenario. Such candidates often suggested tests that were based on samples as would be relevant to an audit rather than trying to definitively quantify the loss. Other mistakes made here were focusing on sale price rather than cost or trying to trace the stolen inventory with reference to sales invoices despite the goods stolen not being invoiced. There was evidence of candidates listing procedures from a previous forensic investigation question that were not relevant to the scenario described and therefore could not be awarded credit.

Part (b)(ii) required candidates to identify and explain the deficiencies in controls that allowed the fraud to occur and recommend improvements. Candidates were often able to score maximum credit in this area by giving detailed explanations. Weaker candidates tended to identify the deficiency from the scenario but were unable to describe how it resulted in the fraud or made unspecific recommendations e.g. improve segregation of duties or someone should approve cancellations – to obtain full credit more detail was required such as who should approve a process or how duties should be segregated.

ACCA Marking guide		
		Marks
(a) **Acceptance considerations** Up to 2 marks for each issue explained. – Scope of assignment – Interaction with criminal investigation – Form and contents of reports/audience – Confidentiality (max 1 mark) – Competence – Resource availability (including ability to make deadlines) – Customer due diligence requirements/reputational risks (award up to 1 additional mark for specific examples of information required as part of the customer due diligence)		
	Maximum	**8**
(b) **(i)** **Procedures to quantify the loss** 1 mark for each relevant procedure described. – Meet with audit committee/management to understand and document what they know about the fraud and who might be involved – Discuss with the company's legal team what is known about the fraud at present and the source of the information – If possible, interview the whistle-blower to identify the potential staff involved and the timescales over which the fraud has been perpetrated – Obtain the prior year report to management from the auditor and inspect auditor's reports to identify any deficiencies or discrepancies in inventories identified by the auditors – Obtain/prepare a reconciliation of all orders placed including cancelled orders to all invoices raised to identify the total of all orders placed but not invoiced to establish the maximum potential value of the theft – Arrange to conduct a full inventory count to identify discrepancies between the inventory records and physical inventory		

– Investigate records of inventory written off to identify possible attempts to disguise the missing items	
– Interview sales, warehouse, and accounting staff to identify the system in place for creating a sales order and for setting up customers within the sales and inventory systems	
– Use data analytics to identify the total of cancelled orders within the inventory records system and any addresses which are associated with large volumes of cancellations	
– Identify which cancelled orders are assigned to the sales representative identified by the whistle-blower	
– Identify which customers those orders are assigned to and verify their existence within the invoicing system and, where possible, their registered business address to ensure they are genuine customers	
– From this, identify fictitious customers and reconcile their cancelled orders to the inventory discrepancies identified	
– Assess if the amounts ordered by the fictitious customers agree to the total discrepancies or if there is a further difference to be investigated	
– Obtain inventory listing to identify the cost of the parts stolen and calculate the cost of the inventory identified as relating to the fictitious customer orders	
– Using data analytics identify any other sales staff with unusual levels of cancelled sales despatches to see if this is a wider issue	

Maximum	6

(ii) Control deficiencies and contribution to fraud
Up to 2 marks for each point explained with up to 1 mark per recommendation.
- Lack of segregation of duties and monitoring
  - lack of integration of systems
  - lack of monitoring of order cancellations
- Lack of segregation of duties in warehouse counts
- Additional implications
- Recommendations

Maximum	6

Professional marks
Analysis and evaluation
- Appropriate use of the information to support discussions and draw appropriate conclusions
- Appropriate assessment of the ethical and professional issues raised, using examples where relevant, to support overall comments
- Balanced discussion of the issues connected to a non-assurance engagement, resulting in a justified conclusion and proposed course of action

Professional scepticism and professional judgement
- Demonstration of the ability to probe for further information in order to quantify the fraud
- Appropriate recommendations and justification of the procedures to be undertaken in respect of the fraud

Commercial acumen
- Demonstration of commercial awareness by recognising wider issues which may affect the firm or client
- Inclusion of appropriate recommendations of internal controls to prevent such a fraud reoccurring

Maximum	5
Total	25

56 RETRIEVER *Walk in the footsteps of a top tutor*

Top tutor tips

Part (a) requires evaluation of quality management, ethical and other professional matters arising. Typical issues to look out for in such a question are: whether the work has been assigned to the appropriate level of staff, whether sufficient time has been allocated for the audit, whether sufficient appropriate evidence has been obtained (e.g. have the ISAs been followed), whether any ethical threats are apparent (e.g. threats to objectivity or competence).

Part (b) deals with a forensic accounting service to determine the amount to be claimed on insurance for a burglary. A common sense approach can be taken to quantify the extent of the loss.

(a) There are many concerns raised regarding quality management. Audits should be conducted with adherence to ISA 220 (Revised) *Quality Management for an Audit of Financial Statements* and it seems that this has not happened in relation to the audit of the Retriever Group, which is especially concerning, given the Group obtained a stock exchange listing during the year. It would seem that the level of staffing on this assignment is insufficient, and that tasks have been delegated inappropriately to junior members of staff.

Time pressure

The junior's first comment is that the audit was time pressured. All audits should be planned to ensure that adequate time can be spent to obtain sufficient appropriate audit evidence to support the audit opinion.

It seems that the audit is being rushed and the juniors instructed not to perform work properly, and that review procedures are not being conducted appropriately. All of this increases the detection risk of the audit and, ultimately, could lead to an inappropriate opinion being given.

The juniors have been told not to carry out some planned procedures on allegedly low risk areas of the audit because of time pressure. It is not acceptable to cut corners by leaving out audit procedures. Even if the balances are considered to be low risk, they could still contain misstatements.

Directors' emoluments are related party transactions and are material by their nature and so should not be ignored. Any modifications to the planned audit procedures should be discussed with, and approved by, senior members of the audit team and should only occur for genuine reasons.

Method of selecting sample

ISA 530 *Audit Sampling* requires that the auditor shall select items for the sample in such a way that each sampling unit in the population has a chance of selection. The audit manager favours non-statistical sampling as a quick way to select a sample, instead of the firm's usual statistical sampling method. There is a risk that changing the way items are selected for testing will not provide sufficient, reliable audit evidence as the sample selected may no longer be representative of the population as a whole. Or that an insufficient number of items may be selected for testing.

The juniors may not understand how to pick a sample without the use of the audit firm's statistical selection method, and there is a risk that the sample may be biased towards items that appear 'easy to audit'. Again, this instruction from the audit manager is a departure from planned audit procedures, made worse by deviating from the audit firm's standard auditing methods, and likely to increase detection risk.

Audit of going concern

Going concern can be a difficult area to audit, and given the Group's listed status and the fact that losses appear to have been made this year, it seems unwise to delegate such an important area of the audit to an audit junior. The audit of going concern involves many subjective areas, such as evaluating assumptions made by management, analysing profit and cash flow forecasts and forming an overall opinion on the viability of the business.

The going concern audit programme should be performed by a more senior and more experienced member of the audit team. This issue shows that the audit has not been well planned as appropriate delegation of work is a key part of direction and supervision, essential elements of good quality management.

Review of work

The juniors have been asked to review each other's work which is unacceptable. ISA 220 (Revised) requires that the engagement partner shall take responsibility for reviews being performed in accordance with the firm's review policies and procedures. Ideally, work should be reviewed by a person more senior and/or experienced than the person who conducted the work.

Audit juniors reviewing each other's work are unlikely to spot mistakes, errors of judgement and inappropriate conclusions on work performed. The audit manager should be reviewing all of the work of the juniors, with the audit partner taking overall responsibility that all work has been appropriately reviewed.

Deferred tax

It is concerning that the client's financial controller is not able to calculate the deferred tax figure. This could indicate a lack of competence in the preparation of the financial statements, and the audit firm should consider if this impacts the overall assessment of audit risk.

The main issue is that the junior prepared the calculation for the client. Providing an audit client with accounting and bookkeeping services, such as preparing accounting records or financial statements, creates a self-review threat when the firm subsequently audits the financial statements. The significance of the threat depends on the materiality of the balance to the financial statements.

Clients often request technical assistance from the external auditor, and such services do not, generally, create threats to independence provided the firm does not assume a management responsibility for the client. However, the audit junior has gone beyond providing assistance and has calculated a figure to be included in the financial statements.

The Group is listed and the provision of bookkeeping services is not allowed to listed clients. The Code states that in the case of an audit client that is a public interest entity, a firm shall not prepare tax calculations of current and deferred tax liabilities (or assets) for the purpose of preparing accounting entries that are material to the financial statements on which the firm will express an opinion.

The calculation of a deferred tax asset is not mechanical and involves judgements and assumptions in measuring the balance and evaluating its recoverability. The audit junior may be able to perform a calculation, but is unlikely to have sufficient detailed knowledge of the business and its projected future trading profits to be able to competently assess the deferred tax position. The calculation has not been reviewed and poses a high audit risk, as well as creating an ethical issue for the audit firm.

The deferred tax balance calculated by the junior should be assessed for materiality, carefully reviewed or reperformed, and discussed with management. It is unclear why the junior was discussing the Group's tax position with the financial controller, as this is not the type of task that should normally be given to an audit junior.

Tax planning

The audit junior should not be advising the client on tax planning matters. This is an example of a non-audit service, which can create self-review and advocacy threats to independence. As discussed above, the audit junior does not have the appropriate level of skill and knowledge to perform such work.

The junior's work on tax indicates that the audit has not been properly supervised, and that the junior does not seem to understand the ethical implications created. As part of a good quality management system, all members of the audit team should understand the objectives of the work they have been allocated and the limit to their responsibilities.

(b)   Procedures

- Scrutinise the insurance policy to clarify:
  - the exact terms of the insurance, to ensure that both the finished goods and stolen lorry will be included in the claim.
  - The period of the insurance cover, to ensure that the date of the theft is covered.
- Review bank statements and bank ledger account/cash book to confirm that payments to the insurance company are up to date, to ensure the cover has not lapsed.
- Watch the CCTV to form an impression of the quantity of goods stolen, for example, how many boxes were loaded onto the lorry.
- If possible, from the CCTV, determine if the boxes contain either mobile phones or laptop computers.
- Inspect the boxes of goods remaining in the warehouse to determine how many items of finished goods are in each box.

- Agree the cost of an individual mobile phone and laptop computer to accounting records, such as cost cards.

- Perform an inventory count on the boxes of goods remaining in the warehouse and reconcile to the latest inventory movement records.

- Discuss the case with the police to establish if any of the goods have been recovered and if, in the opinion of the police, this is likely to happen.

- Obtain details of the stolen lorry, for example the licence plate, and agree the lorry back to the non-current asset register where its carrying amount should be shown.

Examiner's comments

This question contained two separate requirements in relation to the same client, the Retriever Group. The first requirement was largely based around quality and ethics, the second to do with a forensic investigation. The scenario provided was not long, and candidates did not appear to be time pressured when attempting this question.

Requirement (a) described various matters that had arisen during the performance of the audit as described one of the audit juniors, including time pressure, deviations from the audit plan, and the type of work that had been performed by the audit juniors, some of which was inappropriate. The requirement asked candidates to evaluate the quality, ethical and other professional issues arising in the planning and performance of the audit. Answers on the whole were satisfactory, and candidates seemed comfortable with applying their knowledge of quality management requirements and ethical threats to the scenario. Most answers were well structured, working through each piece of information and discussing the matters in a relevant way. There were a number of scripts where the maximum marks were awarded for this requirement.

The common strengths seen in many answers included:

- Identifying that the audit had not been planned well, as it was time pressured and the allocation of tasks to audit juniors was not commensurate with their knowledge and experience.

- Discussing the problems in the direction and supervision of the audit, including the significant issue of the audit manager instructing the juniors not to follow planned audit procedures.

- Appreciating that review procedures were not being performed in accordance with ISA requirements, and that audit juniors did not know the limit of their responsibilities.

- Explaining the ethical threats caused by the audit junior's inappropriate work on deferred tax and tax planning.

- Describing the lack of competence and integrity of the audit manager in allowing the audit to be performed to such poor quality.

- Recommending that the audit team members receive training on quality and ethical issues, and that the audit files should be subject to a detailed quality review with a view to some areas of the audit possibly being reperformed.

It was especially encouraging to see that most candidates were not just able to identify the problems but could also explain and evaluate them to some extent.

Requirement (b) contained a short scenario describing a burglary that had occurred at the Retriever Group. The Group's audit committee had asked the audit firm's forensic accounting department to provide a forensic accounting service to determine the amount to be claimed on the Group's insurance policy.

The requirement asked for the procedures to be performed. Unfortunately answers to this requirement were overall unsatisfactory indicating that this is not a well understood part of the syllabus.

While some answers gave well described and relevant procedures to quantify the loss, many focused exclusively on determining the volume of goods stolen and said nothing about the value of them. Many suggested discussing the amount to be claimed with the insurance provider and comparing our figure with theirs, clearly not understanding the point of the forensic investigation being to provide the amount to be claimed in the first place. On the plus side, most answers included suggestions that reconciliation should be performed between the latest inventory count records and the amount of goods currently in the warehouse, though these were not often presented as procedures.

On the whole it was clear that many candidates were unprepared for a question requirement of this type, and that again it is apparent that a significant number of candidates rely on rote learnt knowledge and have difficulty to develop relevant answer points for a given scenario. Some candidates barely attempted this requirement, which for scripts achieving a mark that is a marginal fail is obviously a significant issue.

ACCA Marking guide

		Marks
(a)	**Quality, ethical and other professional matters** Up to 2 marks for each matter evaluated (up to a maximum 3 marks for identification only) – Time pressure – Planned procedures ignored on potentially material item – Sampling method changed – increases sampling risk – Inappropriate review by juniors – Inappropriate delegation of tasks – Deferred tax – management not competent – Deferred tax – self-review/management responsibility threat – Tax planning – non-audit service with advocacy threat – Junior lacks experience for this work regardless of ethical issues – Junior not supervised/directed appropriately – Overall conclusion	
	Maximum	**14**
(b)	**Procedures to be performed** 1 mark for each specific procedure recommended – Scrutinise the insurance policy to ensure cover is in place – Review bank statements and bank ledger account/cash book to ensure insurance premiums have been paid – Watch the CCTV – If possible, from the CCTV, determine the type of goods stolen – Determine how many items of finished goods are in each box – Agree the cost of an individual item to accounting records – Perform an inventory count and reconcile to the latest inventory movement records – Discuss the case with the police to establish if any of the goods have been recovered – Obtain details of the stolen lorry and agree to the non-current asset register	
	Maximum	**6**

Professional marks		
Analysis and evaluation		
– Appropriate use of the information to support discussions and draw appropriate conclusions		
– Appropriate assessment of the quality, ethical and professional issues raised, using examples where relevant, to support overall comments		
Professional scepticism and professional judgement		
– Demonstration of the ability to probe for further information in order to quantify the insurance claim		
– Appropriate recommendations and justification of the procedures to be undertaken in respect of the forensic accounting service		
Commercial acumen		
– Demonstration of commercial awareness by recognising wider issues which may affect the firm or client		
– Inclusion of appropriate recommendations regarding the additional actions required by the firm		
	Maximum	5
Total		25

57 LARK & CO *Walk in the footsteps of a top tutor*

Top tutor tips

Part (a) requires the matters to be discussed with the client when planning the fraud investigation. For planning matters, think about what happens at the planning stage for an audit and apply the principles to this engagement.

Part (b) requires knowledge of the auditor's responsibilities when suspicious transactions are identified. Money laundering is a topic regularly examined and this requirement should be quite straightforward.

Part (c) covers professional scepticism and how to apply it. In this scenario the auditor has been given contradictory evidence from the client and the requirement asks for the further actions that should be taken by the auditor. You should think of ways in which to obtain further evidence to reach a conclusion as to which evidence can be relied on.

(a) **Chestnut Co**

- Discuss the purpose, nature and scope of the investigation. In particular, confirm whether evidence gathered will be used in criminal proceedings and in support of an insurance claim.

- Confirm that Chestnut Co's objectives are to identify those involved with the fraud, and to quantify the amount of the fraud. This will help to clarify the terms of the engagement, which will be detailed in an engagement letter.

- Determine the timescale involved, whether Jack Privet needs the investigation to commence as soon as possible and the deadline for completing the investigation. This is necessary to determine the resources needed to perform the investigation, and whether resources need to be diverted from other assignments.

- Enquire as to how many sales representatives have been suspended (i.e. are suspected of involvement in the fraud). This will help the firm to determine the potential scale of the investigation.

- Gain an understanding as to how the fraud came to light (e.g. was it uncovered by internal audit or a member of the sales department) and who reported their suspicions to Jack Privet. This information will indicate how the investigation should commence (e.g. by interviewing the whistleblower).

- Determine whether Chestnut Co will provide resources to help with the investigation, e.g. members of the internal audit team could provide assistance in obtaining evidence.

- Ask for Jack Privet's opinion as to why the fraud had not been prevented or detected by the company's internal controls. In particular, enquire if there has been a breakdown in controls over authorisation of expenses.

- Determine whether recommendations to improve controls are required as an output of the investigative work.

- Discuss the investigative techniques which may be used (e.g. interviewing the alleged fraudsters, detailed review of all expense claims made by sales representatives, analytical review of expenses) and ensure that investigators will have unrestricted access to individuals and documentation.

- Enquire as to whether the police have been informed, and if so, the name and contact details of the person informed. It is likely that a criminal investigation by the police will take place as well as Lark & Co's own investigation.

- Confirm that Chestnut Co grants permission to Lark & Co's investigation team to communicate with third parties such as the police and the company's lawyers regarding the investigation.

(b) **Heron Co**

The circumstances described by the audit senior indicate that Jack Heron may be using his company to carry out money laundering. Money laundering is defined as the process by which criminals attempt to conceal the origin and ownership of the proceeds of their criminal activity, allowing them to maintain control over the proceeds and, ultimately, providing a legitimate cover for the sources of their income. Money laundering activity may range from a single act, such as being in possession of the proceeds of one's own crime, to complex and sophisticated schemes involving multiple parties, and multiple methods of handling and transferring criminal property as well as concealing it and entering into arrangements to assist others to do so.

Heron's business is cash based, making it an ideal environment for cash acquired through illegal activities to be legitimised by adding it to the cash paid genuinely by customers and posting it through the accounts. It appears that $2 million additional cash has been added to the genuine cash receipts from customers. This introduction of cash acquired through illegal activities into the business is known as 'placement'.

The fact that the owner himself posts transactions relating to revenue and cash is strange and therefore raises suspicions as to the legitimacy of the transactions he is posting through the accounts. Suspicions are heightened due to Jack Heron's refusal to explain the nature and reason for the journal entries he is making in the accounts.

The $2 million paid by electronic transfer is the same amount as the additional cash posted through the accounts. This indicates that the cash is being laundered and the transfer is known as the 'layering' stage, which is done to disguise the source and ownership of the funds by creating complex layers of transactions. Money launderers often move cash overseas as quickly as possible in order to distance the cash from its original source, and to make tracing the transaction more difficult.

The 'integration' stage of money laundering occurs when upon successful completion of the layering process, the laundered cash is reintroduced into the financial system, for example, as payment for services rendered.

The secrecy over the reason for the cash transfer and lack of any supporting documentation is another indicator that this is a suspicious transaction. Jack Heron's reaction to being questioned over the source of the cash and the electronic transfer point to the fact that he has something to hide. His behaviour is certainly lacking in integrity, and even if there is a genuine reason for the journals and electronic transfer his unhelpful and aggressive attitude may cast doubts as to whether the audit firm wishes to continue to retain Heron Co as a client.

The audit senior was correct to be alarmed by the situation. However, by questioning Jack Heron about it, the senior may have alerted him to the fact that the audit team is suspicious that money laundering is taking place. There is a potential risk that the senior has tipped off the client, which may prejudice any investigation into the situation.

Tipping off is itself an offence, though this can be defended against if the person did not know or suspect that the disclosure was likely to prejudice any investigation that followed.

The amount involved is clearly highly material to the financial statements and will therefore have an implication for the audit. The whole engagement should be approached as high risk and with a high degree of professional scepticism.

The firm may wish to consider whether it is appropriate to withdraw from the engagement (if this is possible under applicable law and regulation). However, this could result in a tipping off offence being committed, as on withdrawal the reasons should be discussed with those charged with governance.

If Lark & Co continue to act as auditor, the audit opinion must be considered very carefully and the whole audit subject to second partner review, as the firm faces increased liability exposure. Legal advice should be sought.

Nature of reporting

The audit senior should report the situation in an internal report to Lark & Co's Money Laundering Reporting Officer (MLRO). The MLRO is a nominated officer who is responsible for receiving and evaluating reports of suspected money laundering from colleagues within the firm, and making a decision as to whether further enquiries are required and if necessary making reports to the appropriate external body.

Lark & Co will probably have a standard form that should be used to report suspicions of money laundering to the MLRO.

Tutorial note

According to ACCA's Technical Factsheet 145 Anti-Money Laundering Guidance for the Accountancy Sector, there are no external requirements for the format of an internal report and the report can be made verbally or in writing.

The typical content of an internal report on suspected money laundering may include the name of the suspect, the amounts potentially involved, and the reasons for the suspicions with supporting evidence if possible, and the whereabouts of the laundered cash.

The report must be done as soon as possible, as failure to report suspicions of money laundering to the MLRO as soon as practicable can itself be an offence under the money laundering regulations.

The audit senior may wish to discuss their concerns with the audit manager in more detail before making the report, especially if the senior is relatively inexperienced and wants to hear a more senior auditor's view on the matter. However, the senior is responsible for reporting the suspicious circumstances at Heron Co to the MLRO.

Tutorial note

ACCA's Technical Factsheet 145 states that: 'An individual may discuss his suspicion with managers or other colleagues to assure himself of the reasonableness of his conclusions but, other than in group reporting circumstances, the responsibility for reporting to the MLRO remains with him. It cannot be transferred to anyone else, however junior or senior they are.'

(c)   Coot Co

The term professional scepticism is defined in ISA 200 *Overall Objectives of the Independent Auditor and the Conduct of an Audit in Accordance with ISAs* as follows: 'An attitude that includes a questioning mind, being alert to conditions which may indicate possible misstatement due to error or fraud, and a critical assessment of audit evidence'.

Professional scepticism means for example, being alert to contradictory or unreliable audit evidence, and conditions that may indicate the existence of fraud. If professional scepticism is not maintained, the auditor may overlook unusual circumstances, use unsuitable audit procedures, or reach inappropriate conclusions when evaluating the results of audit work. In summary, maintaining an attitude of professional scepticism is important in reducing audit risk.

In the case of the audit of Coot Co, the audit junior has not exercised a sufficient degree of professional scepticism when obtaining audit evidence. Firstly, the reliability of the payroll supervisor's response to the junior's enquiry should be questioned. Additional and corroborating evidence should be sought for the assertion that the new employees are indeed temporary.

The absence of authorisation should also be further investigated. Authorisation is a control that should be in place for any additions to payroll, so it seems unusual that the control would not be in place even for temporary members of staff.

If it is proved correct that no authorisation is required for temporary employees the audit junior should have identified this as a control deficiency to be included in the report to those charged with governance.

The contradictory evidence from comments made by management also should be explored further. ISA 500 *Audit Evidence* states that 'if audit evidence obtained from one source is inconsistent with that obtained from another... the auditor shall determine what modifications or additions to audit procedures are necessary to resolve the matter'.

Additional procedures should therefore be carried out to determine which source of evidence is reliable. Further discussions should be held with management to clarify whether any additional employees have been recruited during the year.

The amendment of payroll could indicate that a fraud ('ghost employee') is being carried out by the payroll supervisor. Additional procedures should be conducted to determine whether the supervisor has made any other amendments to payroll to determine the possible scope of any fraud. Verification should be sought as to the existence of the new employees. The bank accounts into which their salaries are being paid should also be examined, to see if the payments are being made into the same account.

Finally, the audit junior should be made aware that it is not acceptable to just put a note on the file when matters such as the lack of authorisation come to light during the course of the audit. The audit junior should have discussed their findings with the audit senior or manager to seek guidance and proper supervision on whether further testing should be carried out.

Examiner's comments

Requirement (a) asked candidates to explain the matters that should be discussed in a meeting with the client, in terms of planning the forensic investigation. Some answers were very satisfactory, covering a wide range of matters including the timeframe, the required output of the investigation, and access to the client's accounting systems amongst others. Some answers however tended to simply list out the procedures that would be performed in conducting the investigation, or explain to the client's management the controls that should have been in place to stop the fraud in the first place.

Part (b)'s scenario described a cash-based business whose owner-manager was acting suspiciously in relation to the accounting for cash sales. A large sum of cash had been transferred to an overseas bank account and the transaction had no supporting evidence. The requirement was to discuss the implications of these circumstances. This open requirement allowed for discussion of many different implications for the audit firm, included suspected fraud and/or money laundering, a poor control environment, the ethical implications of the owners intimidating behaviour, and problems for the audit firm in obtaining evidence. Most candidates covered a range of points and the majority correctly discussed fraud and/or money laundering. Weaker answers tended to focus on the materiality of the cash transferred to overseas, and seemed not to notice the client's suspicious behaviour.

Candidates are reminded that they will often be expected to identify a key issue in a question scenario and that in a question of this type it is important to stop and think about what is happening in the scenario before rushing to start to write an answer.

This question is a good example of one where a relatively short answer could generate a lot of marks – if the scenario has been properly thought through before writing the answer. The requirement also asked for an explanation of any reporting that should take place by the audit senior. Candidates who had identified money laundering as an issue usually scored well here, describing the need to report to the audit firm's Money Laundering Reporting Officer, and what should be reported to them. Weaker answers discussed the auditor's report or that the fraud/money laundering should be reported to the client's management. This is not good advice given that the owner-manager was the person acting suspiciously and would have resulted in him being tipped off.

Part (c) described a client where unauthorised additions had been made to payroll, and contradictory audit evidence had been obtained. Answers here were reasonably good with most candidates able to identify poor controls leading to a possible fraud involving the payroll supervisor.

ACCA Marking guide		
		Marks
(a) **Chestnut Co: Matters to be discussed**		
Generally 1 mark for each matter explained:		
– Purpose, nature and scope of investigation		
– Confirm objectives of investigation		
– Timescale and deadline		
– Potential scale of the fraud		
– How fraud reported to finance director		
– Possible reasons for fraud not being detected by internal controls		
– Resources to be made available to investigation team		
– Whether matter reported to police		
	Maximum	6
(b) **Heron Co: Money laundering**		
Implications of the audit senior's note		
1 mark for each matter discussed relevant to money laundering:		
– Definition of money laundering		
– Placement – cash-based business		
– Owner posting transactions		
– Layering – electronic transfer to overseas		
– Secrecy and aggressive attitude		
– Audit to be considered very high risk		
– Senior may have tipped off the client		
– Firm may consider withdrawal from audit		
– But this may have tipping off consequences		
Reporting that should take place		
Generally 1 mark for each comment:		
– Report suspicions immediately to MLRO		
– Failure to report is itself an offence		
– Examples of matters to be reported		
– Audit senior may discuss matters with audit manager but senior responsible for the report		
	Maximum	9

(c)	**Coot Co: Professional scepticism**		
	Generally 1 mark for each comment:		
	– Definition of professional scepticism		
	– Coot Co – evidence is unreliable and contradictory		
	– Absence of authorisation is fraud indicator		
	– Additional substantive procedures needed		
	– Management's comments should be corroborated		
	– Control deficiency to be reported to management/those charged with governance		
	– Audit junior needs better supervision/training on how to deal with deficiencies identified		
	Maximum		5

Professional marks

Analysis and evaluation

- Appropriate use of the information to support discussions and draw appropriate conclusions
- Appropriate assessment of the ethical and professional issues raised, using examples where relevant, to support overall comments
- Balanced discussion of the issues connected to a non-assurance engagement, resulting in a justified conclusion and proposed course of action

Professional scepticism and professional judgement

- Demonstration of the ability to probe for further information in respect of the forensic investigation
- Appropriate recommendations and justification of the procedures to be undertaken in respect of the forensic investigation
- Effective application of technical and ethical guidance to effectively challenge and critically assess the audit evidence of Coot Co
- Demonstration of the ability to question contradictory information in relation to Coot Co
- Demonstration of the ability to apply appropriate professional judgement to draw conclusions and make informed decisions about the courses of action appropriate for Coot Co

	Maximum	5
Total		25

58   GANNET & CO *Walk in the footsteps of a top tutor*

Top tutor tips

Part (a) focuses on the review of interim financial information. This is a limited assurance engagement providing negative assurance. In part (i) you are asked for analytical procedures to perform during the review. Be careful to only give analytical procedures as other types of procedure are not relevant and will not score marks. Part (ii) requires matters to be considered in forming a conclusion on the interim financial statements. Even though this is not an audit engagement, the same approach can be taken as for audit completion questions which ask for matters to consider when reviewing the audit and forming a conclusion. Refer to the materiality of the warranty provision made in the previous year, discuss the appropriate accounting treatment and what should be done. In terms of the conclusion, remember that limited assurance will be given so the wording needs to reflect this.

> *Part (b) focuses on the governance and ethics areas of the syllabus. When dealing with ethical threats you must explain the threat. Take the discussion further by considering the significance of the threat. In this case, the situation involves the audit partner which makes the threat more significant. Finish off the discussion by stating any safeguards or actions the firm should implement.*

(a) (i) Interim review analytical procedures

Guidance on reviews of interim financial statements is provided in ISRE 2410 *Review of Interim Financial Information Performed by the Independent Auditor of the Entity*. The standard states that the auditor should plan their work to gather evidence using analytical procedures and enquiry.

The auditor should perform analytical procedures in order to discover unusual trends and relationships, or individual figures in the interim financial information, which may indicate a material misstatement.

Procedures should include the following:

- Comparing the interim financial information with anticipated results, budgets and targets as set by the management of the company.

- Comparing the interim financial information with:

  - comparable information for the immediately preceding interim period

  - the corresponding interim period in the previous year, and

  - the most recent audited financial statements.

- Comparing ratios and indicators for the current interim period with those of entities in the same industry.

- Considering relationships among financial and non-financial information. The auditor also may wish to consider information developed and used by the entity, for example, information in monthly financial reports provided to the senior management or press releases issued by the company relevant to the interim financial information.

- Comparing recorded amounts or ratios developed from recorded amounts, to expectations developed by the auditor. The auditor develops such expectations by identifying and using plausible relationships that are reasonably expected to exist based on the accountant's understanding of the entity and the industry in which the entity operates.

- Comparing disaggregated data, for example, comparing revenue reported by month and by product line or operating segment during the current interim period with that of comparable prior periods.

- Calculate the warranty provision as a percentage of new car sales up to 1 February 20X5 and compare with the year-end ratio to ensure the level of provision is consistent.

- Compare the warranty costs in the 6-month period with the warranty provision and assess whether the warranty provision appears reasonable given the current level of warranty claims.

As with analytical procedures performed in an audit, any unusual relationships, trends or individual amounts discovered which may indicate a material misstatement should be discussed with management. However, unlike an audit, further corroboration using substantive procedures is not necessary in a review engagement.

(ii) **Review of interim financial statements**

Reviews of interim financial statements are governed by ISRE 2410 *Review of Interim Financial Information Performed by the Independent Auditor of the Entity.* Reviews are based on enquiries and analytical procedures, and having determined that Guillemot Co has changed its accounting treatment regarding the warranty provision, management must be asked to explain the reason for the change.

Interim financial statements should be prepared under the same financial reporting framework as annual financial statements, therefore IAS *37 Provisions, Contingent Liabilities and Contingent Assets* should be applied.

It would appear correct that a warranty provision is not recognised for cars sold since 1 February 20X5, as Guillemot Co has no obligation relating to those sales. However, cars sold prior to that date are subject to a three-year warranty, so a warranty provision should continue to be recognised for the obligation arising in respect of those sales. Therefore, Guillemot Co's interim financial statements understate liabilities and overstate profits.

The warranty provision as at 30 November 20X4 represented 5.5% of total assets, therefore material to the financial statements. If the same warranty provision still needs to be recognised at 31 May 20X5, it would represent 5% of total assets, therefore material to the interim financial statements.

ISRE 2410 requires that when a matter comes to the auditor's attention that leads the auditor to question whether a material adjustment should be made to the interim financial information, additional inquiries should be made, or other procedures performed. In this case, the auditor may wish to inspect sales documentation to ensure that warranties are no longer offered on sales after 1 February 20X5. The auditor should also review customer correspondence to ensure that warranties on sales prior to 1 February 20X5 are still in place.

If as a result of performing the necessary procedures, the auditor believes that a material adjustment is needed in the interim financial information, the matter must be communicated to the appropriate level of management, and if management fail to respond appropriately within a reasonable period of time, to those charged with governance. In order to avoid a modification of the conclusion, it is likely that adjustment would be made by management to the interim financial statements.

If the amount remains unadjusted, meaning that the interim financial statements contain a material departure from the applicable financial reporting framework, the report on the review of interim financial information should contain a qualified or adverse conclusion. This is a modification of the conclusion, and the auditor must describe the reason for the modification, which is provided in a paragraph entitled 'Basis for Qualified Conclusion'.

The qualified conclusion would be worded as follows: 'Based on our review, with the exception of the matter described in the preceding paragraph, nothing has come to our attention that causes us to believe that the accompanying interim financial information does not give a true and fair view...'

(b)   (i)   Temporary recruitment of audit partner

Seconding a member of staff to an audit client may create a self-review threat. This would arise if the member of staff returns to the audit firm and considers matters or documentation which is the result of work which they performed while on assignment to the client.

In this situation, it is likely that the individual would be involved in preparing the financial information for the flotation. If this is the case, it would create a significant threat to objectivity. This would be reduced if the role was focused on non-financial matters.

Additionally, the member of staff would work alongside employees of the client on a daily basis. This would overstep the normal professional boundary between auditor and client and may compromise the objectivity of the member of staff due to their familiarity with employees of the client.

In order to reduce this threat, the member of staff seconded to Gull Co should not be a current or future member of the audit team.

An additional risk would be if the seconded member of staff assumed management responsibilities for the client. This is not permitted. Given that Gull Co has specifically requested a partner, it appears as though they require someone senior, indicating that they may need someone to either make or significantly influence decision making.

In order to reduce this risk, the use of a less senior member of staff with relevant experience of the flotation process could be proposed and make it clear in the contract that they are not able to make decisions for Gull Co and that decision making will always remain their responsibility.

Alternatively, it could be recommended that Gull Co recruit the assistance of either the management or transaction advisory services team to assist them with the flotation as a separate engagement, thus circumventing the ethical threats identified.

UK syllabus: FRC Ethical Standard section 2 *Financial, business, employment and personal relationships,* states that an audit firm shall not enter into an agreement with an audited entity to provide a partner or employee to work for a temporary period as if that individual were an employee of the audited entity (a 'loan staff assignment') unless:

- the agreement is for a short period of time and does not involve staff or partners performing non-audit services which would not be permitted under FRC Ethical Standard section 5 *Non-audit/Additional services,* and

- the audited entity agrees that the individual concerned will not hold a management position, and acknowledges its responsibility for directing and supervising the work to be performed, which will not include such matters as making management decisions or exercising discretionary authority to commit the audited entity to a particular position or accounting treatment.

(ii) **Implications of governance and board structure on audit process**

Structure of the board

As a private company with the majority of shares held by the Brenner family, the auditor's report addressed to the shareholders as a body would have been aimed predominantly at the Brenner family. However, the predominance of the Brenner family may undermine the independence of the board. The board may be accustomed to operating in the interests of the family as the majority shareholders. However, once the company is listed, the board will be required to consider the interests of the new shareholders as a group. The executive members of the board are either Brenner family members or long-term employees of the company and potentially loyal to the existing ownership.

With only one non-executive director, the board currently lacks independent oversight and the opinions and decisions of the executive board may not be subject to appropriate levels of challenge and scrutiny.

In addition, non-executive board members are specifically required to scrutinise the performance of management, consider the integrity of the financial statements, determine director remuneration and participate in the appointment and removal of directors. With limited experience outside IT consultancy and limited time, the current non-executive is unlikely to be able to fulfil these roles effectively on their own.

There is no indication that management lacks integrity but the audit firm must remain sceptical of the motivations of the family, particularly leading up to a listing. There will be an incentive to overstate performance and position to inflate the value of the company.

With little effective oversight of the executive board, the audit firm must remain alert for this possibility, particularly when auditing matters involving management judgement in subsequent financial periods.

UK syllabus: As a company listed on the UK stock exchange, the company will be expected to comply with the UK Corporate Governance Code (the Code) or explain any departure from the Code in the annual report. The Code states that the board should include an appropriate combination of executive and non-executive directors (and, in particular, independent non-executive directors) such that no individual or small group of individuals can dominate the board's decision taking. The auditor will be required to review the corporate governance statement produced by Gull plc for any inconsistencies.

Audit committee

The lack of any form of audit committee is a significant departure from corporate governance best practice. The audit committee fulfils a number of significant roles, including monitoring the integrity of the financial statements, reviewing internal financial controls, monitoring the independence of the external auditor and communicating with the external auditor on matters relating to the external audit. The audit committee should have a member with relevant financial expertise and this will become of even more importance once the company is listed.

In the absence of an audit committee, the auditor will have to communicate directly with the board including the requirement to communicate how the auditor has maintained their independence in line with ISA 260 *Communication with Those Charged with Governance*. This may affect the independence of the audit firm, or at least the perception of their independence. It may also reduce the effectiveness of communications between the auditor and the company. The audit committee is responsible for communicating relevant matters, such as deficiencies in internal control, up to the executive board for their consideration. Without an audit committee, matters of significance to the audit may not be given sufficient prominence by the board. Further, the audit committee is responsible for reviewing the integrity of the financial statements and internal controls and currently there is no one at Gull Co capable of carrying out this role. Overall this may make it harder for the auditor to discuss and communicate key findings from the audit including the auditor's qualitative assessment of the company's accounting practices. Also with the lack of an objective audit committee, it may be harder for the auditor to fulfil their responsibilities to communicate any significant difficulties which are encountered during the audit.

Listed status

Further as a listed company, Gull Co will be subject to increased scrutiny and pressure to achieve performance levels, which may motivate the board to manipulate the financial statements to present an improved picture of performance. This increases the level of audit risk and is likely to have a significant impact on the firm's assessment of the risk of fraud and management override.

This is likely to have a significant impact on the firm's approach to auditing areas of the financial statements subject to judgement, such as management estimates and revenue recognition.

As a listed company, Gull Co may be required to produce more detailed financial statements probably in a shorter time frame and as mentioned above, the lack of financial expertise and lack of objective scrutiny by an audit committee may result in errors or omissions. This again increases the level of audit risk and more detailed testing may need to be performed to ensure compliance with appropriate accounting standards and listing rules.

Further, once listed, the auditor's report issued for Gull Co will be available to a much wider audience and will require additional disclosures in line with ISA 701 *Communicating Key Audit Matters in the Independent Auditor's Report*. This will add another level of work and complexity to the audit of Gull Co.

Examiner's comments

Requirement (a)(i) was unsatisfactorily answered by almost all candidates. This asked for the principal analytical procedures that should be used to gather evidence in a review of interim financial information. Candidates are repeatedly reminded that non-audit engagements are part of the syllabus, and likely to feature regularly in the examination. However, few candidates seemed to know the purpose of a review of interim financial information, which meant that their answers lacked clarity. Most answers could only suggest a comparison with the prior period, and hardly any answers mentioned the disaggregation of data, or comparison with budget. Only a handful of candidates seemed aware of the existence of ISRE 2410 *Review of Interim Financial Information Performed by the Independent Auditor of the entity,* on which the requirement is based. Some candidates confused a 'review of interim financial information' with an 'interim audit', despite the short scenario describing a review of interim financial information for the avoidance of any such confusion.

Requirement (a)(ii) was based on a scenario which described a review engagement that was taking place on the interim financial statements of a listed company. An accounting policy in relation to warranty provisions had been changed in the interim financial statements, and based on the information provided, candidates should have appreciated that the accounting treatment was incorrect. Figures were provided to enable materiality to be calculated. The requirement was to assess the matters that should be considered in forming a conclusion on the interim financial statements, and the implications for the review report. Most answers were good at discussing the accounting treatment for the warranty provision, that the non-recognition was not appropriate, and the majority correctly assessed the materiality of the issue. Answers were inadequate in discussing the impact of this on the review report, being mostly unable to say much more than the auditor would need to mention it in the review report. There seemed to be a lack of knowledge on anything other than the standard wording for a review report, with many answers stating that the wording should be 'nothing has come to our attention' followed by a discussion that there actually was something to bring to shareholders' attention but with no recommendation as to how this should be done.

Part (b) had two elements, an ethics part regarding other services which were generally well answered and a second element which required the implications the governance structure and a potential listing may have on the audit process. Many candidates appeared to interpret this as a requirement to comment on how the governance structure of the client fell below best practice and how to improve that structure and did not address the audit implications at all. This is particularly disappointing given the recent examiner's article on the topic and again candidates are reminded to make sure that they read the requirements carefully.

ACCA Marking guide				
				Marks
(a)	(i)	**Interim review analytical procedures**		
		Generally 1 mark per procedure:		
		– Comparisons to anticipated results		
		– Comparison to corresponding interim last year		
		– Comparison to last audited accounts		
		– Comparisons to similar entities		
		– Comparisons to non-financial data/ratios		
		– Develop auditor expectation using understanding of entity		
		– Disaggregation of data		
		– Calculate warranty as a percentage of sales		
		– Compare warranty costs with warranty provision		
		Maximum		**7**

	(ii)	**Interim financial statement review**		

          Up to 1 mark for each matter to be considered in forming conclusion/implication for report:

- Interim financial information should use applicable financial reporting framework
- Identify and explain unrecognised provision
- Correct calculation of materiality
- Communicate adjustment to management/TCWG
- If amount unadjusted, the conclusion will be qualified
- Reason for qualified conclusion to be explained in the report

Maximum	4

(b) (i) Ethical and professional matters

In general up to 1 mark for each well explained point:

Temporary recruitment of audit partner

- Potential self-review threat
- Potential familiarity threat
- Potential management responsibility threat
- Recommendations to reduce the potential threats described (1 mark each to a maximum of 2)

Maximum	4

(ii) Governance structure implications for audit process

In general up to 1 mark for each well explained point:

- Lack of independence and oversight of board
- Ineffective non-executive board
- Need for increased auditor scepticism particularly in light of potential listing
- Increased fraud/manipulation risk which will need to be reflected in audit approach
- No effective audit committee
- Communication in line with ISA 260 harder with no objective audit committee
- Listed company with increased audit risk
- Key audit matters to be included in the report once listed

Maximum	5

Professional marks

Analysis and evaluation

- Appropriate use of the information to support discussions and draw appropriate conclusions
- Appropriate assessment of the ethical and professional issues raised, using examples where relevant, to support overall comments
- Balanced assessment of the information to determine the appropriate review conclusion in the circumstances
- Effective appraisal of the information to make suitable recommendations for appropriate courses of action

Professional scepticism and professional judgement

- Demonstration of the ability to probe for further information
- Appropriate recommendations and justification of the procedures to be undertaken in respect of the review of interim financial statements
- Effective challenge and critical assessment of the assumptions used by management in respect of the warranty provision

Commercial acumen

- Demonstration of commercial awareness by recognising wider issues which may affect the firm or client in a given scenario

Maximum	5
Total	25

PROFESSIONAL AND ETHICAL CONSIDERATIONS, QUALITY MANAGEMENT AND PRACTICE MANAGEMENT

59   FORSYTHIA GROUP *Walk in the footsteps of a top tutor*

Top tutor tips

This question covers quality management and an engagement quality review. Audit quality will be impacted if the audit firm does not comply with professional guidance such as auditing standards, quality management standards and ethical requirements. The question is set in the context of a group audit with quality issues needing to be discussed in respect of several subsidiaries within the group including an evaluation of a component auditor. Consider whether ISAs have been followed and sufficient appropriate evidence has been obtained. Where there are issues, these need to be explained e.g. state what the ISA requires and explain what the auditor has done or not done that means the ISA has not been complied with. Where sufficient appropriate evidence has not been obtained, explain what additional evidence should have been obtained that would meet this criteria.

As the Forsythia Group is a listed entity, it is appropriate that an engagement quality review (EQR) is taking place. This is accordance with *International Standard on Quality Management 1*, which requires an EQR to be performed on the audit of listed entities.

Acquisition of Robin Co

The acquisition of a subsidiary after the financial year end should not be ignored by the audit team. This is an example of a subsequent event which, according to ISA 560 *Subsequent Events*, needs to be considered by the audit team because the event may need to be recognised or disclosed in the Group financial statements. In this case, the acquisition of a subsidiary after the year end is a significant non-adjusting event in respect of which no adjustment is needed to the financial statements, but disclosure should be made in the notes.

The audit engagement partner is therefore incorrect to agree with the chief finance officer's (CFO) assertion that the matter will only be recognised in next year's financial statements. Given that the subsidiary is forecast to increase Group revenue by 20%, it appears that the acquisition is material to the financial statements and audit procedures should be performed to determine and conclude on the disclosures necessary.

The audit engagement partner's statement could indicate a concerning lack of knowledge or could be due to the apparent cost constraints on the audit, encouraging them to cut back on necessary audit work. ISA 220/ISA (UK) 220 (Revised) *Quality Management for an Audit of Financial Statements* includes budgets constraints as one of the key impediments to the exercise of professional scepticism on an engagement. Due to this cost pressure, the audit engagement partner could be failing to apply an appropriate level of professional scepticism by agreeing with the CFO and failing to challenge this assertion.

The leadership team of Magnolia & Co is responsible and accountable for firm-wide audit quality. As it is an audit partner who is at fault here, this suggests potentially wider quality risks within the audit firm, with implications for the quality of other audits performed by this audit partner and possibly other audit partners.

Audit planning should be revisited as the audit progresses. According to ISA 300/ISA (UK) 300 *Planning an Audit of Financial Statements*, the auditor shall update and change the overall audit strategy and the audit plan as necessary during the course of the audit. This may be the case when information comes to the auditor's attention which differs significantly from the information available when the auditor planned the audit procedures. Given the speed at which the acquisition of Robin Co has occurred, it is understandable why this acquisition was not known at the time of planning, but the audit engagement partner should have reacted to the acquisition of Robin Co by modifying the planned audit procedures as necessary. Audit procedures need to be performed as a matter of urgency to ensure that the audit team has sufficient and appropriate audit evidence with regard to the acquisition.

If the Group CFO is planning not to disclose information about the acquisition in this year's financial statements, this could indicate a lack of competence, or a deliberate intention to omit the necessary disclosures which would indicate a lack of integrity. In either case, this increases the level of audit risk, and further audit work may be needed with regard to other areas of the financial statements, for example, more specific procedures to look for significant subsequent events, such as reviewing the minutes of board meetings or correspondence with legal advisers.

If the necessary disclosures are not made in the Group financial statements, a material misstatement would exist, with implications for the auditor's opinion on the Group financial statements. The issue should be discussed with the Group audit committee once relevant audit procedures have been performed to determine the nature and extent of the disclosure to be made in the financial statements.

Delegation of audit work to Camelia Associates

It is not prohibited for audit work to be delegated to other audit firms. However, the evidence obtained should not just be accepted without proper review and the audit work of Camelia Associates cannot simply be relied upon, as suggested by the audit manager. ISA 220/ISA (UK) 220 (Revised) requires that the engagement partner shall determine, through review of audit documentation and discussion with the engagement team, that sufficient, appropriate audit evidence has been obtained to support the conclusions reached and for the auditor's report to be issued. Without review, the audit engagement partner cannot consider whether the evidence obtained has been performed in accordance with the audit plan or whether it is sufficient and appropriate to support the audit opinion.

Delegating the audit of revenue is particularly problematical given that the Group's revenue has increased significantly, by 14.2% this year. Camelia Associates has performed audit work on the revenue of significant subsidiaries, and they may not have appropriate knowledge and understanding of the Group to perform good quality audit work on this significant area of the audit, in particular in relation to the revenue generated by the subsidiary which operates in the agricultural industry. They may also not have sufficient resources to have performed the work to a good quality.

Camelia Associates is a firm of accountants – this does not necessarily mean it is a registered audit firm, and they may not be competent to conduct audit work. It may not have experience of group audits including specialised activities such as agriculture, which increases the level of concern over the quality of audit evidence which has been obtained in respect of the Group's revenue. Further assessment of the competency and qualifications of the staff should be undertaken and to ensure that it is a registered firm of auditors.

Finally, ISA 240/ISA (UK) 240 *The Auditor's Responsibilities Relating to Fraud in an Audit of Financial Statements* requires the auditor to work on the presumption that there are risks of fraud in revenue recognition. Therefore, revenue is usually approached as a high-risk area of the audit, so the delegation of audit work in respect of revenue is likely to be inappropriate.

The work which has been performed by Camelia Associates should be fully reviewed in order to determine whether sufficient and appropriate audit evidence has been obtained in relation to revenue. Further audit procedures, such as analytical procedures on the revenue figures of the subsidiaries, may need to be performed by the audit team if the work of Camelia Associates cannot be relied upon or is insufficient.

Development expenditure

The accounting treatment of the capitalised development costs is also significant as this could indicate deliberate misapplication of the requirements of the relevant financial reporting standards in order to boost the profit reported by the Group during the year, as profit before tax has decreased by nearly 20% on the prior year. The fact that this is the first year in which development costs have been capitalised increases the risk that the accounting treatment is inappropriate.

Insufficient audit evidence has been obtained relating to the capitalised development expenditure. Confirming that a set of management assumptions agrees to the assumptions from another source does not provide evidence on the validity of the assumptions themselves. Further audit procedures need to be performed in order for the auditor to conclude on the appropriateness of the accounting treatment applied, for example, checking that the criteria for classification as development costs set out in IAS 38 *Intangible Assets* have been met.

ISQM 1 requires that individuals are assigned to perform activities within the system of quality management who have appropriate competence and capabilities, including sufficient time, to perform such activities. In this situation, assigning the audit of development expenditure to a junior member of the audit team is not appropriate. This issue should have been dealt with by a more senior member of the audit team, who could have been in a better position to discuss the matter with the Group CFO and would understand that further evidence is necessary before concluding on the appropriateness of the accounting treatment.

Yew Co

Based on the draft financial statements, Yew Co represents 13% of Group assets and 5% of Group revenue and based on the prior year financial statements, Yew Co represented 18% of Group assets and 5.7% of Group revenue in the previous year. ISA 600 Revised *Special Considerations – Audits of Group Financial Statements (Including the Work of Component Auditors)* suggests that when considering which components should be visited for work to be performed, the firm should consider events or conditions that give rise to risks of material misstatement, the size of the component relative to the Group, and components in which significant changes have taken place.

For Yew Co, despite its percentage contribution to the Group this year being less than the prior year, the reduction in the value of its assets of 27.1% is unusual and significant. Additionally, the operations of Yew Co are in the agricultural industry. This is a specialised industry and different from the main operations of the Group. Therefore, in accordance with ISA 600 Revised, it is likely that Yew Co should have been visited for audit work to be performed.

It is concerning that Yew Co was not identified as significant in the previous year, when based on monetary values alone its assets made it significant to the Group. The rationale behind this needs to be investigated and additional audit work may need to be performed on Yew Co, including the engagement of the consultant to provide advice on the specialist aspects of Yew Co's operations. The cost involved should not be regarded as a deterrent.

It is also concerning that the consultant was not engaged due to cost pressure. ISA 220/ISA (UK) 220 (Revised) requires that the audit engagement partner shall take responsibility for consultation on difficult and contentious matters and deciding not to follow the audit strategy for the reason of saving costs is not appropriate. A lack of input and insight from the consultant could mean that audit risks specific to Yew Co have not been identified and that inappropriate and insufficient audit evidence has been obtained, with implications for both the individual financial statements of the company and the consolidated Group financial statements.

ISA 300/ISA (UK) 300 requires that any significant changes to the audit strategy or audit plan, including reasons for the changes, should be fully documented, and it appears that this has not happened. Sections of the audit strategy and audit plan should not be deleted, even if there are valid reasons for changes to them. There could be an integrity issue given that audit working papers have been deleted, perhaps in an attempt to conceal the fact that planned audit procedures have not been performed.

Conclusion

There are many concerns raised regarding the management of engagement quality, at least on the engagement of the Forsythia Group. Audits should be conducted with adherence to ISA 220/ISA (UK) 220, and it seems that this has not happened in relation to the audit of the Group. It appears that due to cost constraints, important elements of the audit plan have not been followed, and the audit has not been appropriately directed, supervised or reviewed. In accordance with ISQM 1, remedial actions in response to the identified deficiencies in audit quality should be designed and implemented.

Further work should be performed as necessary, and these issues resolved prior to the issuance of the auditor's report. The additional procedures to be performed could take some time, and it would be advisable to discuss with the client whether it is possible to extend the deadline for completion of the audit.

Examiner's comments

This was a quality management question with a single requirement to evaluate quality management issues in relation to a group audit. Professional skill marks were available for analysis and evaluation, professional scepticism and judgement and commercial acumen. It is the first quality management question under the new suite of quality management standards and candidates were provided with an article ahead of the session highlighting the main changes. Within the question, topics such as outsourcing of audit work and ethical threats such as intimidation and self-interest were examined.

Answers to this question were mixed. Candidates who answered the question from a practical approach, applying the principles of quality management to the scenario scored well. The majority of answers, however, were generic and unapplied, failing to demonstrate an understanding of how the principles of quality management were potentially breached in the scenario.

The question covered four specific situations which had been identified by the engagement quality reviewer through a review of the audit file. Further information regarding the audit process was obtained through discussion with the audit junior about their experience on the audit.

The first issue related to an acquisition made after the year end. This impacted the time the group chief finance officer (CFO) had available to engage with the audit team during the audit. In addition to the lack of the availability of the CFO, the acquisition had only been determined after the audit planning stage and was, therefore, not included in the audit plan. The audit plan had not been updated as a result of this new information and the CFO had dismissed the acquisition as not being a relevant matter for the current audit. The audit engagement partner agreed with the client position. As this would have formed a material subsequent event requiring disclosure, this was incorrect. Actions that were relevant here, in the pre-issuance stage of the audit cycle, were to obtain the evidence that would be required to support the disclosures before the report is issued. Candidates who then went on to identify that the acceptance of the client's position on this suggesting that the partner is either incompetent or too trusting of the client, were able to obtain professional marks for scepticism and acumen. It was pleasing to see that the majority of candidates were able to identify that the acquisition was relevant to the audit and why this was a significant issue. However, fewer candidates expanded on this conclusion to suggest further appropriate actions or why the situation might have arisen.

The second issue related to the outsourcing of revenue recognition in several subsidiaries to another audit firm, Camellia Associates, without checking the competence and objectivity of the firm beforehand. Most candidates identified that Camelia Associates should be assessed for these criteria and their work reviewed. Fewer candidates questioned the appropriateness of outsourcing such a material risk area, in particular, when one of the subsidiaries operated in a specialist industry. The main motivator for the outsourcing was to keep costs low and candidates were able to obtain professional skills marks for questioning why the costs needed to be minimised and whether there was a self-interest threat at play as a result of quoting an inappropriately low fee.

The third issue was the delegation of audit work on intangible assets to a junior member of the audit team. The majority of candidates were able to say that this was inappropriate due to the complexity of the area, that the junior was likely to lack sufficient knowledge or experience. Fewer candidates explained why the intangible assets contained difficult judgements or why this was higher risk this year (due to this being the first year in which development costs had been capitalised). Additional credit was available for those candidates who questioned whether the junior team member had been intimidated by having to approach the busy CFO for the information, or for assessing that the evidence obtained did not cover all the assertions relating to development costs and was all the evidence was internally generated.

The final issue in the question was centred around a subsidiary operating in the agriculture sector. Several issues arose with respect to this subsidiary and should have been subject to more detailed audit procedures.

Surprisingly few candidates identified the serious breach in quality arising from the deletion of a section of the audit plan to cut costs. Those who did highlight this issue, appropriately questioned the integrity of the person who deleted this and linked this back to the inappropriately low fee and the implication that profits were being prioritised over audit quality. Professional skill marks were available for candidates who demonstrated this professional scepticism.

Candidates were then able to score marks for a conclusion based on their analysis and were awarded professional skills marks for analysing the specific details in the scenario to demonstrate an understanding of the quality issues. This was achieved by explaining **why** there was an issue, not simply that there **was** an issue. Credit was also available for questioning why the issues arose and for recommending actions appropriate to the stage of the audit process, with stronger candidates stating that the auditor's report should not be issued until the issues were resolved and that sufficient appropriate evidence on which to base the audit opinion had been obtained.

ACCA Marking guide	
	Marks
Forsythia Group – evaluation of audit quality 1 mark for each well explained point and ½ mark for relevant trends to a maximum of 2 marks. **General** • Introduction/reason for EQR review as listed (ISQM (UK) 1) • Additional procedures – examples **Robin Co** • Acquisition of Robin Co is a non-adjusting subsequent event • Audit partner ignoring the event indicates lack of knowledge or desire to minimise audit costs • Leadership of Magnolia & Co is responsible and accountable for audit quality, as it is an audit partner who is at fault here, this suggests potentially wider quality issues within the firm • Budget constraints are impediments to professional scepticism • Audit planning should be revisited when new information come to attention of auditor • Lack of competence/deliberate omission of information increases risk of material misstatement • Audit procedures should be performed on this issue as a matter of urgency • Implication for auditor's opinion if necessary, disclosures not made • Discussion with the Group audit committee to discuss the disclosures to be made in the financial statements **Camelia Associates** • Should have been a review of work performed – further audit evidence is required • Camelia Associates may not have sufficient knowledge/understanding of Group • Increase in revenue and unusual activities increase the risk of inappropriate evidence • Revenue contains risk of fraud so problematical to delegate this high-risk area of the audit • The work performed should be subject to urgent review and further procedures may need to be performed **Development expenditure** • Possibility of inappropriate accounting treatment to increase profit • Insufficient audit evidence obtained over assumptions, additional procedures should be performed **Yew Ltd** • Likely to require being visited for audit procedures to be performed (max 3 marks) • Not engaging the consultant to save costs is not appropriate as ISQM 1 requires audit firms to allocate the resources on the engagement to ensure a quality engagement • Possible that some risks have not been identified • Audit strategy and audit plan should not be changed without justification and documentation • Possible issue of integrity due to deleting audit working papers • Overall conclusion on quality of work performed	
Maximum	**20**

Professional marks

Analysis and evaluation

- Appropriate assessment of the issues raised in relation to audit quality, using examples where relevant to support overall comments
- Effective appraisal of the information to make suitable recommendations for courses of action which are appropriate for the stage of the audit process

Professional scepticism and professional judgement

- Effective challenge and critical assessment of how the audit was performed with appropriate conclusions
- Demonstration of the ability to probe into the reasons for quality issues including the identification of missing information or additional information which would be required

Commercial acumen

- Demonstrates commercial awareness regarding the impact of inherent issues on the quality of the engagement

Maximum	5
Total	25

60 JAMES & CO *Walk in the footsteps of a top tutor*

Top tutor tips

This question focuses on a post-issuance audit quality review, therefore falls into the syllabus area of quality management and practice management rather than review of the work during the audit, however, the same approach can be taken when commenting on the quality of the work. Audit quality will be impacted if the audit firm does not comply with professional guidance such as auditing standards, quality management standards and ethical requirements. The question is set in the context of a group audit with quality issues needing to be discussed in respect of several subsidiaries within the group including an evaluation of a component auditor. Consider whether ISAs have been followed and sufficient appropriate evidence has been obtained. Other professional issues include consideration of the auditor's responsibilities in relation to compliance with laws and regulations. Where ethical issues arise, explain how the threat could impair the auditor's judgement and suggest appropriate safeguards.

(a) **Cameron Co**

There are problems indicated by the review in relation to both the audit of Cameron Co's individual financial statements by Carrey Associates, and in the way the Group auditor has dealt with the issue of there being a new component auditor involved in the Group.

Internal audit

First, it is not appropriate that Carrey Associates has relied on the work performed by the internal audit team. A significant self-review threat to the objectivity of Carrey Associates arises from the firm providing both internal and external audit services to Cameron Co. The IESBA International Code of Ethics for Professional Accountants (the Code) suggests that providing an audit client with an internal audit service creates a significant self-review threat because in subsequent audits the audit team will use the internal audit work performed, leading to potential overreliance.

There is therefore a risk that the audit has not been performed with sufficient objectivity and professional scepticism. In addition, it is not clear whether appropriate safeguards are in place to reduce the threats to an acceptable level, for example, by ensuring that the two services were provided by separate teams.

There is a risk that insufficient audit evidence has been obtained over internal controls. This is a breach of ISA 315 (Revised) *Identifying and Assessing the Risk of Material Misstatement*, which requires the auditor to obtain an understanding of the internal controls relevant to the audit, including an evaluation of the design and implementation of the internal controls. It appears that this audit work has not been performed at all, due to overreliance.

There is a further issue with the timing of when the internal controls had been tested, which took place in May 20X4. The financial year ended on 31 January 20X5, so it appears that the controls had not been evaluated for the last eight months of the financial year. ISA 330 *The Auditor's Responses to Assessed Risks* states that if the auditor intends to rely on controls over a period of time, the tests performed must be able to provide audit evidence that the control operated effectively over that period. This exacerbates the risk of overreliance discussed above, as there could have been significant changes in internal controls during that period, which had not been identified by the external audit team.

This raises concerns over the quality of the audit which has been performed by Carrey Associates. Given that Cameron Co is a significant proportion of the Group, any material misstatements which have not been detected by the component auditor could have implications for the Group financial statements, which could also be materially misstated.

In addition to the self-review threat to objectivity, a threat of management responsibility arises, whereby the audit firm, by performing internal audit services, is making decisions and using judgement which is properly the responsibility of management. An audit firm should not assume management responsibility. This raises concern over Carrey Associates' general approach to ethical issues, and whether the ethical threats raised have been properly evaluated by the firm.

Group auditor evaluation of Carrey Associates

The comment made in the Group audit working papers indicates that there has been no understanding obtained by the Group auditor in relation to the scope and extent of the audit evidence obtained by the component auditors. This is a significant quality problem and a breach of ISA 600 *Special Considerations – Audits of Group Financial Statements (Including the Work of Component Auditors)* which requires that the Group audit team obtains an understanding of the component auditor, and be involved with the component auditor's risk assessment to identify risks of material misstatement. This is especially the case, given that Cameron Co is a new component of the Group, and this is James & Co's first experience of working with Carrey Associates.

The fact that an audit partner has left James & Co to work as an audit partner at Carrey Associates has no bearing on whether James & Co should have obtained an appropriate understanding of Carrey Associates. An understanding of whether Carrey Associates follows the same ethical framework as the rest of the Group and an understanding of their competence is required. It appears that the Group audit has been conducted without this necessary understanding being obtained, which is a breach of ISA 600.

In addition, a familiarity threat to objectivity arises because of the connection which the Group audit team will have with the audit partner who is now working for Carrey Associates and who previously worked on the external audit of Cameron Co. The familiarity threat means that the Group audit team may have over-relied on the work of the component auditor, due to this close working connection, and failed to apply appropriate professional scepticism.

Use of local accounting rules

Cameron Co uses local accounting rules in its individual financial statements, which is acceptable. However, for the purpose of consolidation, the same accounting policies must be applied across all Group companies, as required by IFRS 3 *Business Combinations*. The fact that the Group audit partner has concluded that no work is needed in relation to the accounting policies indicates poor quality audit work and insufficient audit evidence has been obtained. Adjustments may have been necessary to Cameron Co's balances and transactions prior to consolidation; with no audit work being performed to assess whether this is the case, there is a risk of material misstatement in the Group financial statements.

The fact that it is the Group audit partner who reached this conclusion indicates a lack of competence and raises concerns over the quality of the audit as a whole.

(b) **Dean Co**

Insufficient audit evidence has been obtained in relation to the financial asset. The audit team should not just have accepted management's valuation of $68,000, which could be based on inappropriate assumptions. An offer of $68,000 may have been received, but this has also not been verified by the audit team. As there is no active market for the shares, fair value should be based on an exit price at the measurement date and should reflect assumptions which market participants would use including risk. Even if the offer was genuinely received, this is not an appropriate basis for the valuation of shares, especially given that the offer was made nine months before the year end. An appropriate level of professional scepticism has not been used in the audit of the financial asset.

Fair values should be determined close to the financial year end, and the $68,000 might reflect out-of-date perceptions of the value of Corden Co. From the information provided, it seems that the financial asset could be impaired and is likely to be overstated in value. Dean Co's 2% shareholding is recognised at $68,000; however, 2% of the net assets of Corden Co at 31 January 20X5 amounts to only $11,000. If the financial asset is overvalued, then any necessary adjustment would have a profit implication and this is not mentioned in the audit working papers.

Using Group materiality in the audit of a subsidiary is not appropriate. The value of the financial asset is less than Group materiality, but it might be material to Dean Co's individual financial statements. It is not clear that the individual audit team determined an appropriate level of materiality as part of their planning of the individual company audit.

The Group audit team should determine component materiality to be used by component auditors in their audit of subsidiary balances and transactions, and component materiality should be lower than materiality for the Group financial statements as a whole. Therefore, it seems likely that the Group audit team has not communicated an appropriate level of component materiality to the team auditing Dean Co.

While the possible adjustments in relation to the financial asset are not material to the Group, they could be material to Dean Co's individual financial statements, and there is a risk that an inappropriate audit opinion has been issued in relation to this subsidiary's individual financial statements.

(c)   Horner Co

There has been a breach of relevant law and regulations. The audit team should have considered the requirements of ISA 250 *Consideration of Laws and Regulations in an Audit of Financial Statements.* ISA 250 states that while it is management's responsibility to ensure that the entity's operations are conducted in accordance with the provisions of laws and regulations, the auditor does have some responsibility in relation to compliance with laws and regulations, especially where a non-compliance has an impact on the financial statements.

The auditor is required by ISA 315 to gain an understanding of the legal and regulatory framework in which the audited entity operates. This will help the auditor to identify non-compliance and to assess the implications of non-compliance. Therefore, the auditor should ensure that a full knowledge and understanding of the relevant data protection laws and regulations is obtained in order to evaluate the implications of non-compliance.

ISA 250 requires that when non-compliance is identified or suspected, the auditor shall obtain an understanding of the nature of the act and the circumstances in which it has occurred, and further information to evaluate the possible effect on the financial statements. Therefore, procedures should have been performed to obtain evidence about the suspected non-compliance, for example, to discuss the breach with management to understand how it happened, whether it was due to deliberate action or an unintentional mistake, and who was responsible.

In addition, the audit team should have performed further procedures, for example, discussion with the company's legal advisers to understand the legal consequences of the breach. From the information provided, it seems that the audit team failed to obtain more information or evidence due to their belief that the situation had little to do with the audit.

The audit has therefore not been performed appropriately, as the requirements of ISA 250 have not been followed. The matter could be immaterial in monetary terms, but without further investigation, it is not possible for the audit team to reach this conclusion. However, in many jurisdictions fines and penalties associated with data protection breaches are often significant. Also, the matter could be material by nature, so regardless of the monetary amounts involved, further work should have been performed.

ISA 250 requires the matter to be discussed with management and, where appropriate, with those charged with governance. It appears that some discussion was held, as the audit manager is aware that the employee has been dismissed. However, the discussions should have been fully documented and raised to the level of Group management, as the matter could impact on the Group and not just on Horner Co.

The audit team should have considered the potential implications for the financial statements. The non-compliance could lead to regulatory authorities imposing fines or penalties on the Group, which may need to be provided for in both the individual and Group financial statements. Audit procedures should have been performed to determine the amount, materiality and probability of payment of any such fine or penalty imposed. The individual and Group financial statements could be materially misstated and given that an unmodified audit opinion has already been issued, this is a significant issue for James & Co to now consider.

In terms of reporting non-compliance to the relevant regulatory authorities, ISA 250 requires the auditor to determine whether they have a responsibility to report the identified or suspected non-compliance to parties outside the entity. In the event that management or those charged with governance of the company or the Group fail to make the necessary disclosures to the regulatory authorities, James & Co should consider whether they should make the disclosure. This will depend on matters including whether there is a legal duty to disclose or whether it is considered to be in the public interest to do so. It seems that this has not been considered so far, but the audit firm can still make any necessary disclosures.

The Code requires auditors to comply with the principle of confidentiality, and if disclosure were to be made by the auditor, it would be advisable to seek legal advice on the matter. Further advice on disclosure in the public interest is given in the Code, which gives examples of situations where disclosure might be appropriate. These examples include references to an entity being involved in bribery and breaches of regulation which might impact adversely on public health and safety.

The Code also clarifies that in exceptional circumstances where the auditor believes there may be an imminent breach of a law or regulation, they may need to disclose the matter immediately to an appropriate authority. The decision to disclose will always be a matter for the auditor's judgement and where the disclosure is made in good faith, it will not constitute a breach of the duty of confidentiality.

Tutorial note

Credit will also be awarded for discussion of relevant ethical threats to objectivity which may arise in relation to the non-compliance, including intimidation and self-interest threats.

Examiner's comments

This question is set at the post-issuance, quality review stage in the audit process and tests several ethical and professional issues which have been identified as part of the review of the Bond Group (the Group) audit. While the context is that of a Group audit, many of the issues in the question are similar to those which would arise in individual company audits.

In this question, candidates are provided with the quality reviewer's findings from the perspective of the performance of the Group audit. Each of these has been given with respect to a subsidiary of the Group and there is detail regarding the audit performed by the component auditor and relevant points regarding the Group auditor's work in this regard.

The points given are those which have caused concern for the quality reviewer. It is therefore not demonstrating a competence in audit to repeat the phrase "this is poor quality" as that is a given in the question – if these points did not reflect poor audit quality then they would not have been highlighted in the scenario. These questions require candidates to evaluate why something demonstrates that a poor quality audit has been performed and what specifically should be done better to address the issues.

This type of question is typically poorly answered by candidates in comparison to questions set at the planning or completion stage. Candidates often appear to lack the skills to apply the rules and principles learned to practical scenarios and often provide unapplied answers as a result. As mentioned, unfortunately many candidates for each issue simply state "audit quality is poor" or "planning was not performed well", which does not demonstrate a candidate's understanding of what should have taken place and why. It is important to remember that the AAA exam is predominantly application and such general comments will not obtain credit as a response to each individual planning or quality failing – often these comments will be restricted to a single concluding mark across the full question and as such candidates cannot obtain additional marks for repeating the same conclusion.

Similarly, recommendations need to be specific and again an answer which simply states "better planning is needed" or "more training is needed" is too generic to score marks at this level.

Another reason many candidates score low marks on these questions arises from a failure to appreciate that these reviews are occurring after the audit has been completed and the auditor's report issued. This means answers which recommend a long list of additional audit procedures, repeatedly saying that something will need to be resolved before issuing the auditor's report, or the firm needs to modify the audit opinion are not appropriate in the circumstances and therefore cannot gain marks.

As with many questions in the AAA exam, candidates will be better prepared to provide relevant responses if they are able to appreciate where in the audit cycle the question is set. Candidates should make sure that they consider this when they are planning their answer.

The following discussion of the question and requirements should be used in conjunction with the model answer and marking guide published with the question.

Cameron Co

Cameron Co was the only subsidiary where the component auditor was not part of the Group audit firm. As such the scenario was testing candidates' appreciation of the relationship between a Group auditor and a component auditor responsible for auditing a subsidiary of a Group. There are three issues in relation to this subsidiary that candidates need to address. First, the ethical threat when an audit firm provides internal and external audit services to an audit client. Second, the responsibility the Group auditor has with respect to determining whether it is appropriate to rely on a component auditor and finally, the issue of a subsidiary of the Group not preparing financial statements using IFRS Accounting Standards.

While an understanding of Group audits was crucial for the second of these issues, candidates could obtain several marks on the first and third issue from a knowledge of ethics and financial reporting and the audit of controls.

Internal audit

This section of the question was often well attempted with candidates being able to identify that there was a self-review threat if a firm provided both internal and external audit services to an audit client and the impact of that self-review threat resulted in a lack of appropriate testing due to this overreliance.

Stronger candidates also mentioned the risk of assuming management responsibilities which arises when an internal audit service is provided by the external auditor. Many were also able to discuss the requirements of ISA 330 *The Auditor's Responses to Assessed Risks*, regarding the periodic testing of controls and the requirement to confirm that no changes of systems and controls had occurred in the intervening period. This was a significant risk in this scenario as Cameron Co had been purchased by the Group during the year and as such it was reasonable to expect that some systems and controls would have changed as a result of the company becoming a subsidiary and being integrated into the Group.

Many candidates were able to identify that proper planning by the Group auditor would have led to a request for safeguards to be put in place to address the self-review threat and that a proper review by the Group auditor prior to the auditor's report being issued should have led to a request that the component auditor perform further procedures. When explained in this detailed context, stating that inadequate planning and inadequate review had occurred could obtain credit.

Weaker candidates were unable to distinguish between component auditors and subsidiary companies and between internal and external audit roles and as such produced unstructured and confused responses. Another area where candidates failed to score marks was through an inability to describe specifically how each ethical threat arose and the specific implication. Candidates are reminded that simply stating a self-review threat exists cannot obtain credit, they must demonstrate how that self-review threat arises – in this case the external auditor is relying on controls to justify a controls based audit approach and has over relied on the internal audit work instead of independently testing those controls. A recent trend has been for candidates to use the phrase "self-review arises because they are reviewing figures for the financial statements they produced" which is not the case in this context and appears to be a rote learnt response for illustrating self-review. Candidates should spend their time trying to identify the specific issues in the scenario as such rote learning results in no marks being awarded as the comments are clearly not relevant to the specific scenario.

Assessment of the component auditor

Candidates were often able to score well in this section for appreciating that the decision to rely on the work of a component auditor should be based on more than a previous relationship with one of the audit partners in the component auditor firm and looking at the firm's website. Generally, candidates knew that the competence and independence of the component auditor was crucial and were able to suggest more detailed aspects over which an understanding was required and where to find that information.

Some candidates demonstrated a lack of understanding of the difference between audit clients and audit firms and gave responses relating to the need to perform client due diligence procedures which was not relevant as the subsidiary had retained their existing auditor or rules relating to audit partners moving to work for audit clients rather than an audit partner moving to another audit firm.

Subsidiary not using IFRS Accounting Standards

Many candidates were able to correctly identify that the subsidiary's financial statements would have to be prepared under the regulations applicable to the country in which the subsidiary operates but that for consolidation purposes adjustments would be required to convert those local financial statements to IFRS Accounting Standards as applied by the rest of the Group. Many candidates were able to discuss that the differences between the two financial reporting frameworks would need to be investigated and evidence of the differences or lack of differences documented on file.

Some candidates appeared to believe that it was illegal for the subsidiary to use local GAAP in their own audited financial statements, which is not true. Financial reporting standards do not override a country's own legislation. The choice to adopt IFRS Accounting Standards or otherwise is down to individual countries to determine. It is quite common for candidates to suggest that financial reporting or auditing standards dictate how businesses are permitted to operate rather than appreciating that financial reporting standards exist to guide the preparation of financial statements and that auditing standards exist to provide guidance on how to conduct a quality audit. It is not uncommon for candidates to suggest that a business cannot change its business processes because IFRS Accounting Standards do not allow it or that auditing standards require businesses to operate in a certain way. This is not the case.

Candidates in this question often stated that the Group audit partner commenting in the file that "local accounting rules were similar to IFRS Accounting Standards so there was no need to perform additional procedures for the consolidation" meant the partner was incompetent and the audit opinion would need to be modified as a result. This demonstrates a lack of understanding of audit risk and audit opinions. It is entirely possible that the Group audit partner was correct and there were no practical differences which would have required adjustment. However, if that is the case, this should have been evidenced on the audit file and work should have been performed to confirm this. In that situation, the auditor's report itself would not have been incorrect. Even if there were differences, without investigation it cannot be determined these would have a material impact on the Group financial statements and therefore have caused the opinion to be incorrect.

Dean Co

In this part of the scenario, there is a subsidiary of the Group, being audited by the Group audit team. When performing the audit of Dean Co, the team appeared to use Group materiality when testing items in the individual financial statements of Dean Co. Dean Co is still required to prepare individual financial statements subject to audit. This should be performed at a suitable materiality level which has been determined to allow the auditor to issue the audit opinion on the individual financial statements of Dean Co. In this situation, the use of the Group materiality level is inappropriate. A significant number of candidates were able to identify and explain this issue.

In this section of the question candidates could also score marks for discussing that the investment was material for the individual company, for identifying that the outdated valuation would not be appropriate, that there was a risk of overstatement of the investment given the net asset value was only $11,000 compared to the director's valuation of $68,000 and for concluding that more audit work should have been performed by the audit team. Many candidates often concluded that the issue was immaterial and gave no further answer. Candidates should make sure that they always check the mark allocation to consider how much depth is required in their answer. The requirement for this subsidiary was worth five marks and as such candidates should have appreciated that there would be more to say than simply the issue is immaterial.

Some candidates inappropriately speculated that the 2% shareholding conveyed control and that Corden Co was a subsidiary or that the investment was significantly undervalued and may exceed the Group materiality level. Due to the requirement in relation to this question and its focus on the quality of the audit which had been performed, long discussions on the financial reporting rules for financial instruments and lists of procedures to audit them were not addressing the requirement. Marks were awarded for stating that more audit work should have been performed to ensure the correct value was in the financial statements. Candidates are again reminded to make sure that they pay close attention to the requirement and answer the question as it is set.

Horner Co

Horner Co was the final part of the question and related to a breach of laws and regulations in a subsidiary company of the Group. This part of the question was well attempted by most candidates. Generally, candidates were able to identify that this was an issue centred around non-compliance with laws and regulations and were able to discuss the potential impacts on the financial statements in terms of the necessary provisions and disclosures. In addition, many candidates were able to discuss the responsibilities of the auditor in this situation with regards to reporting the issue to those charged with governance (TCWG). Stronger candidates were able to go further and discuss the risk in a Group context, identifying the need for TCWG at Group level to be informed rather than just those of Horner Co and to raise the possibility that the Group may be exposed to risks of further breaches if a similar incident could happen in other subsidiary companies.

ACCA Marking guide	
	Marks
Generally, up to 2 marks for each well explained point:	
(a) **Cameron Co**	
– Internal audit – self-review threat and lack of professional scepticism (1 mark)	
– Internal audit – insufficient audit work on internal controls including no understanding or evaluation of year-end controls obtained	
– Internal audit – threat of assuming management responsibility and general risk that ethical code has not been followed by Carrey Associates	
– Timing and reliance on controls testing	
– Group audit firm has not evaluated Carrey Associates or obtained understanding of the firm	
– No audit work performed by Group audit team on Cameron Co's different accounting policies – Group consolidation could be misstated	
– Implications of former partner joining the component audit firm – familiarity and over reliance (1 mark)	
– Possible lack of competence of the Group audit partner (1 mark)	
Maximum	**8**
(b) **Dean Co**	
– Lack of application of professional scepticism regarding valuation of financial asset	
– Asset likely to be overvalued – could have material impact on Dean Co's financial statements	
– Inappropriate application of Group materiality at component level	
Maximum	**5**
(c) **Horner Co**	
– Auditor is incorrect and laws and regulations do impact the audit and financial statements	
– Auditor needs to gain understanding of applicable laws and regulations	
– Further evidence should be obtained and the matter discussed with Group management	
– Provisions for fines and penalties have not been considered	
– Auditor may have a legal duty to disclose, or consider disclosing in the public interest	
– The audit firm may wish to seek legal advice regarding the situation (1 mark)	
Maximum	**7**

Professional marks

Analysis and evaluation

- – Appropriate assessment of the ethical and professional issues raised, using examples where relevant to support overall comments
- – Effective appraisal of the information to make suitable recommendations for appropriate courses of action

Professional scepticism and judgement

- – Effective challenge and critical assessment of the evidence supplied with appropriate conclusions
- – Demonstration of the ability to probe into the reasons for quality issues including the identification of missing information or additional information which would be required
- – Appropriate application of professional judgement to draw conclusions and make informed comments regarding the quality of the work carried out

Commercial acumen

- – Inclusion of appropriate recommendations regarding the additional quality procedures required by the firm
- – Appropriate recognition of the wider implications on the engagement, the audit firm and the company

Maximum	5
Total	25

61 THOMASSON & CO *Walk in the footsteps of a top tutor*

Top tutor tips

Part (a) covers money laundering. Part (i) requires knowledge of money laundering requirements and the policies and procedures an accountancy firm should have in place to comply with the regulations. This is rote-learned knowledge from the text book and should be straightforward. Part (ii) requires application of knowledge to the scenario to evaluate whether there are any indicators of money laundering. Unusual transfers of cash, overly complex arrangements and uncertainty over the source of cash are all indicators of money laundering. You need to justify why you think the issues indicate money laundering. Very limited marks will be awarded for only listing the indicators.

Part (b) covers ethical and professional issues. Identify the type of threat, explain how the threat could influence the audit, discuss whether the threat is significant and finish off by explaining the safeguards the firm should take to reduce the threat to an acceptable level.

(a) **Money laundering**

(i) **Policies and procedures for anti-money laundering programme**

Thomasson & Co should have established an anti-money laundering programme within the firm. As part of this programme, the firm should have appointed a money laundering reporting officer (MLRO) with an appropriate level of experience and seniority.

The audit firm should also have established internal reporting lines which should be followed to report any suspicions. Thomasson & Co will probably have a standard form which should be used to report suspicions of money laundering to the MLRO.

The typical content of an internal report on suspected money laundering may include the name of the suspect, the amounts potentially involved, and the reasons for the suspicions with supporting evidence if possible, and the whereabouts of the laundered cash. The firm's internal policies should have been set up to ensure that all pertinent information is captured in this standardised report.

Any individual in the audit firm who has suspicions of money laundering activities is then required to disclose these suspicions to the MLRO. The report must be done as soon as possible as any non-disclosure or failure to report such suspicions will constitute an offence under the money laundering regulations.

On receipt of the internal report, the MLRO must consider all of the circumstances surrounding the suspicions of money laundering activities, document this process and decide whether to report the suspicions to the appropriate external authorities. The audit firm has a legal duty to report even though this may conflict with the auditor's duty of confidentiality.

Tutorial note

Credit will be awarded for other relevant answer points in relation to a firm's anti-money laundering programme.

(ii) Evaluation of possible indicators of money laundering activities

Money laundering is the process by which criminals attempt to conceal the true origin and ownership of the proceeds of criminal activity, allowing them to maintain control over the proceeds, and ultimately providing a legitimate cover for their sources of income.

In the case of Clean Co, the circumstances which may be indicative of money laundering activities include the following:

Cash-intensive business

Clean Co has a high level of cash-based sales (75%) and a high volume of individual sales reports. The nature of its business therefore creates a significant risk that illicit cash funds are being passed off as legitimate sales.

More specifically Simon Blackers' sale to a business associate for $33,000 may be an example of the placement of illegal funds in order to legitimise them as genuine sales. The size of the transaction in a business selling cleaning products and the round sum amount may be additional grounds for suspicion in relation to this transaction.

International property transactions

The performance of Simon's personal taxation computation has identified a significant number of transactions involving the purchase and sale of properties in international locations. These transactions may be examples of real estate laundering by Simon. It is possible that these properties have been purchased with illegal funds ('placement') and then sold in order to make funds appear legitimate ('integration').

A high volume of such transactions may also be indicative of the 'layering' of transactions in an attempt to make the original source of the funds more difficult to trace.

(b)   Ethical and professional issues

Taxation services

Company tax computation

The performance of the company tax computation creates a self-review threat. A self-review threat arises when an auditor reviews work which they themselves have previously performed – for example, if the external auditor is involved in the process of preparing the financial statements and then audits them. As a result, there is a risk that the auditor will not be sufficiently objective in performing the audit and may fail to identify any shortcomings in their own work. In this case, a self-review threat to auditor independence arises because the tax calculation forms the basis of the tax payable and the tax charge in the financial statements and as such the audit team may be more likely to accept the tax calculations without adequate testing.

There is also a potential advocacy threat. An advocacy threat arises when the auditor is asked to promote or represent their client in some way. In this situation, there is a risk of the auditor being seen to promote the interests of Clean Co with a third party such as the tax authorities and therefore that the auditor will be biased in favour of the client and cannot be fully objective.

Completing tax returns does not generally create a threat of management involvement by the auditor, as completing the tax return may not involve the auditor making any judgements. Provided management takes responsibility for the returns, including any judgements which have been made, the threat to objectivity is not likely to be significant.

Where tax calculations have been prepared by the auditor for the purpose of preparing accounting entries, the IESBA International Code of Ethics for Professional Accountants (the Code) and the FRC Ethical Standard state that this may be acceptable for an unlisted audit client and that the firm should consider implementing safeguards in order to reduce the self-review threat to an acceptable level. In this case, these safeguards might have included, for example, using professionals who are not members of the audit team to prepare the tax computations. The tax services should be reviewed by an independent tax partner, or other senior tax employee.

Therefore, given that Clean Co is an unlisted client, Thomasson & Co should ascertain which members of staff performed the taxation services and should review whether the threat to independence has been adequately assessed before the taxation services were performed and whether adequate safeguards have been applied.

Simon Blackers' personal tax computation

From an ethical perspective, there is no prohibition in the Code or the FRC Ethical Standard on the preparation of personal tax returns for the directors of an audit client such as Clean Co. However, in this case the auditor should consider whether the preparation of Simon's personal tax return may result in the auditor being associated with criminal activities if the suspicions of money laundering activities noted above prove to be well founded.

The auditor should also consider the appropriateness of personal taxation services being billed to the company. Indeed, the preparation of Simon's personal tax return may be a taxable benefit which should be included in the tax return and the fee for this service may need to be reflected in Simon's director's loan account with the company.

Website and online sales system

According to the Code and the FRC Ethical Standard, providing services to an audit client involving the design or implementation of IT systems which form a significant part of the internal control over financial reporting or generate information which is significant to the accounting records or financial statements on which the firm will express an opinion constitutes a self-review threat.

A self-review threat arises when an auditor reviews work which they themselves have previously performed – for example, if the external auditor is involved in the process of preparing the financial statements and then audits them. There is a risk that the auditor will not be sufficiently objective in performing the audit and may fail to identify any shortcomings in their own work.

In this case, the self-review threat arises as the new systems will produce data which will be used directly in the preparation of the financial statements. The audit process will therefore include reviewing and testing of financial data and systems which Thomasson & Co has helped to design and implement. As a result, there is a clear risk that the audit team may too readily place reliance on these systems.

With reference to Clean Co therefore, it is clear that providing assistance with the design and implementation of the website and online sales system will constitute a self-review threat as the auditor will audit sales figures which are generated by the system.

There is also a risk that the firm may assume a management responsibility if they become involved in making management decisions. In the case of revenue, this self-review threat may be heightened further by the auditor's reliance on controls testing and on analytical review of the data summaries generated by the new system.

Tutorial note

UK syllabus: According to the FRC Ethical Standard, providing information technology services can create a management threat to independence. The management threat arises because the design and implementation of information systems is the responsibility of management. If the auditor becomes involved in making management decisions with regard to the website and online sales system, the perception that the auditor is independent of management would be impaired.

It also seems clear that the new online sales system will be significant to the client's financial statements and records. Such a self-review threat may be too significant even for an unlisted client such as Clean Co unless appropriate safeguards are put in place.

Examples of possible safeguards which might assist in managing the self-review threat include the following:

- The client should acknowledge its responsibility for establishing and monitoring the system of internal controls and for the operating system and data it generates

- The respective responsibilities of the audit firm and the client should be clearly defined in a separate engagement letter in order to ensure that the client makes all management decisions in relation to the design and implementation process

- Thomasson & Co should use a separate team made up of non-audit staff to perform the systems design and implementation assignment and the work performed by this team should be subject to independent professional review.

If the self-review threat cannot be reduced to an acceptable level, or the engagement will result in the firm assuming a management responsibility, the service should not be provided.

Examiner's comments

Requirement (a)(i) asked for a discussion of policies and procedures a firm should have in place in relation to an anti-money laundering programme. Most candidates were able to score full marks here. Candidates who did not score well either simply listed points with no discussion or confused the audit firm with the client and discussed controls over cash sales or places where the client could implement policies.

The second requirement (a)(ii) asked candidates to evaluate whether there were indicators of money laundering by the client or its staff. The majority of answers to this requirement were disappointing. Most candidates were able to correctly identify the indicators at the client which might suggest money laundering activities but made no attempt at explaining or evaluating those indicators. Simply stating sales are cash based or there is an off-shore bank account does not demonstrate an understanding of why these things are an indicator. Candidates would do well to add the word because at the end of such sentences to force them to explain why something is a red flag. For example, "the company sales are 75% cash based. This is a potential indicator of money laundering because cash-based sales are harder to trace." An even stronger answer would then relate this back to the stages of money laundering, giving a "So What?" to their answer. "This means that additional cash can be introduced alongside genuine sales. This would represent the placement stage of money laundering". Another mistake candidates often made in this part of the question was to discuss the risk of employee fraud/theft of the cash which was not required.

Part (b) was a requirement to discuss the ethical and professional issues arising at the client. Candidates tended to perform poorly in this requirement. This was partly down to candidates not leaving enough time to properly address the requirement and partly because candidates are still not demonstrating the understanding of ethical issues or how to describe them sufficiently to attain marks. Candidates here also often showed a lack of detailed knowledge of the ethical guidance that would help them to properly analyse the issues in the question. A common mistake made by candidates was to assume that invoicing the company for the tax work done on behalf of the directors was disallowed (rather than identifying that if the company was paying for his tax work, this should be considered director's remuneration and not part of the audit fee for disclosure and possible personal tax reasons).

One of the most concerning points that was made in many answers was to correctly tie in the risk of money laundering at the client and the need to report this to the firm's money laundering reporting officer while avoiding tipping off but then to follow that with the suggestion that the firm resign from the client immediately and inform TCWG of the money laundering – so effectively then tipping off the client.

				Marks
		ACCA Marking guide		
(a)	**Money laundering**			
	(i)	**Reporting duties and procedures**		
		Generally 1 mark per point		
		– Suspicions should be reported to nominated person within audit firm (MLRO); MLRO should possess suitable level of experience/seniority		
		– Audit firm should have established internal reporting lines which should be followed to report any suspicions		
		– Any individual in audit firm who has suspicions of money laundering activities must disclose them to MLRO; non-disclosure/failure to report constitutes an offence		
		– MLRO must consider all circumstances, document the process and decide whether to report to appropriate authorities; legal duty to report even though this may conflict with auditor's duty of confidentiality		
		Maximum		**4**
	(ii)	**Indicators of money laundering**		
		Generally up to 2 marks for each well-explained point of explanation, for example:		
		Cash intensive business		
		– High level of cash sales and high volume of individual sales reports; risk illicit cash funds are being passed off as legitimate sales		
		– Simon Blackers' sale to business associate for $33,000 may be example of placement of illegal funds in order to legitimise them as genuine sales.		
		International property transactions		
		– May be example of real estate laundering by Simon Blackers; may be purchasing international property with illegal funds (placement) and then selling them in order to make funds appear legitimate (integration)		
		– High volume of transactions and off-shore bank accounts in Simon Blackers' name may be indicative of layering of transactions in attempt to make original source of funds difficult to trace		
		Maximum		**6**
(b)	**Ethical and professional issues**			
		Generally 1 mark for each point identified and explained		
		Taxation services		
		– Company tax computation is self-review threat as tax calculation forms basis of tax payable and tax charge in financial statements		
		– Advocacy threat re acting on client's behalf with tax authorities		
		– Completing tax returns does not generally create threat to independence if management takes responsibility for returns including any judgements made		
		– Tax calculations for purpose of preparing accounting entries – may be acceptable for unlisted audit client; firm should consider safeguards, e.g. using professionals not members of audit team or independent senior/partner review		
		– Preparation of Simon Blackers' personal tax return may be taxable benefit which should be included in tax return and fee should be reflected in director's loan account with the company		
		– Preparation of personal tax return may result in auditor being associated with criminal activities (i.e. money laundering as above)		

Website and online sales system
- Self-review threat as auditor will audit sales figures generated by system
- New system appears to be significant to client's financial statements and records
- Risk assume management responsibility relating to design of system and controls
- Threat may be too significant even for unlisted client unless appropriate safeguards put in place
- Examples of possible safeguards include: client acknowledges responsibility for establishing and monitoring system of internal controls; client makes all management decisions re design and implementation process; client is responsible for operating system and data it generates; separate team made up of non-audit staff performs work with independent professional review (max 2 marks for safeguards)

| | Maximum | 10 |

Professional marks
Analysis and evaluation
- Appropriate assessment of the ethical and professional issues raised, using examples where relevant to support overall comments
- Appropriate use of the information to support discussions and draw appropriate conclusions
- Effective appraisal of the information to make suitable recommendations for appropriate courses of action

Professional scepticism and judgement
- Effective challenge and critical assessment of the evidence supplied with appropriate conclusions
- Appropriate application of professional judgement to draw conclusions and make informed comments

Commercial acumen
- Appropriate recognition of the wider implications on the engagement, the audit firm and the company

| | Maximum | 5 |
| Total | | 25 |

62   WESTON & CO *Walk in the footsteps of a top tutor*

Top tutor tips

Part (a) deals with tendering. For the tender document you need to identify ways in which you can sell your firm to the client. Try and match the firm with the prospective client from the information in the scenario. Don't just give rote learnt knowledge without applying it to the scenario.

Part (b) focuses on long association of senior personnel with an audit client. Identify the name of the threat and explain why long association creates an ethical issue. The requirement also asks for discussion of whether the engagement partner can become engagement quality reviewer of the same client in the future. Don't forget to include this in your answer.

(a) (i) **Matters to be included in the audit proposal**

Outline of Weston & Co

A brief outline of the audit firm, including a description of different services offered, and an outline of the firm's international locations. This will be important to Jones Co given that it wishes to expand into overseas markets and will be looking for an audit firm with experience in different countries. The document should also outline the range of services which Weston & Co can provide, and any specialism which the firm has in auditing recruitment companies.

Identify the audit requirements of Jones Co

There should be an outline of the statutory audit requirement in the country in which Jones Co is incorporated, to confirm that the company is now at the size which necessitates a full audit of the financial statements. As this is the first time an audit is required, it will be important to outline the regulatory framework and the duties of auditors and of management in relation to the audit requirement.

Audit approach

A description of the proposed audit approach, outlining the stages of the audit process and the audit methodology used by the firm should be given. The description should state that the audit will be conducted in accordance with ISA requirements. Weston & Co should emphasise the need for thorough testing of opening balances and comparatives given that this is the first year that the financial statements will be audited. The risk-based nature of the audit methodology should be explained, and that it will involve an assessment of accounting systems and internal controls. Controls may not be good given the limited resources of the accounting function, so the audit approach is likely to be substantive in nature.

The audit firm may at this stage wish to explain that while the audit should not be 'disruptive', the audit team will require some input from Jones Co's employees, especially the accountant, and other personnel including Bentley may need to make themselves available to respond to the audit firm's requests for information and to discuss matters relating to the audit.

Communication

The proposal should outline the various communications which will be made with those charged with governance during the audit process, and highlight the value added from such communications, for example, recommendations on any control deficiencies.

Deadlines

The audit firm should clarify the timescale to be used for the audit. Bentley has requested that the audit is completed within four months of the year end. This seems to be reasonable and it should be possible for the audit of a relatively small company with simple transactions and a full-time accountant to be completed within that timeframe.

Ability to provide insight and add value

Given Jones Co's plans for the future and the request for strategic advice, a key selling point to be included in the tender will be the firm's ability to provide insight and add value. Examples from other clients should be included and where appropriate, testimonials from other clients.

Quality management and ethics

Weston & Co should clarify its adherence to the ACCA *Code of Ethics*, and to International Standards on Quality Management. This should provide assurance that the audit firm will provide an unbiased and credible auditor's report. This may be important for the venture capitalists who will wish to gain assurance on the financial information which they are provided with in relation to their investment.

Additional non-audit and assurance services

The audit proposal should describe the various non-audit and assurance related services which Weston & Co would be able to offer Jones Co. These may include, for example, business consultancy and corporate finance advice on overseas expansion and obtaining any necessary additional funding to help the planned overseas expansion.

This discussion should clearly state and emphasise that the provision of such services is subject to meeting ethical requirements and will be completely separate from the audit service.

Tutorial note

Credit will be awarded for discussion of other matters which may be included in the audit proposal, where the matters are relevant to the audit of Jones Co.

(ii) **Matters to be considered in determining the audit fee**

Weston & Co needs to consider a number of matters in determining the audit fee. The commercial need for the firm to make a profit from providing the audit service needs to be considered alongside the client's expectations about the fee level and how it has been arrived at.

Cost of providing the service

First, the audit firm should consider the costs of providing the audit service. This will include primarily the costs of the audit team, so the firm will need to assess the number and seniority of audit team members who will be involved, and the amount of time that they will spend on the audit. There may be the need for auditor's experts to be engaged, and the costs of this should be included if necessary.

Weston & Co will have standard charge out rates which are used when determining an audit fee and these should be used to estimate the total fee. Other costs such as travel costs should also be considered.

Client expectations

Bentley Jones has made some comments in relation to the audit fee which have ethical and other implications. First, he wants the audit fee to be low, and says that he is willing to pay more for other services. One of the problems of a low audit fee is that it can affect audit quality, as the audit firm could be tempted to cut corners and save time in order to minimise the costs of the audit.

Offering an unrealistically low audit fee which is below market rate in order to win or retain an audit client is known as lowballing, and while this practice is not prohibited, the client must not be misled about the amount of work which will be performed and the outputs of the audit. The issue for the client is that an unrealistically low audit fee is unlikely to be sustainable in the long run, leading to unwelcome fee increases in subsequent years.

Tutorial note

UK syllabus: *FRC Ethical Standard section 4 states that the audit engagement partner must be satisfied and able to demonstrate that the audit engagement has assigned to it sufficient partners and staff with appropriate time and skill to perform the audit in accordance with all applicable auditing and ethical standards, irrespective of the audit fee to be charged. This means that the audit fee should be high enough to allow the use of appropriate resources and that a low fee cannot be tolerated if it would impact on audit quality.*

Contingent fee

The second issue is that Bentley Jones has suggested that the audit fee should be linked to the success of the company in expanding overseas, on which he wants the audit firm to provide advice. This would mean that the audit fee is being determined on a contingent fee basis. Contingent fees are fees calculated on a predetermined basis relating to the outcome of a transaction or the result of the services performed by the firm.

A contingent fee charged by a firm in respect of an audit engagement creates a self-interest threat which is so significant that no safeguards could reduce the threat to an acceptable level. Accordingly, a firm shall not enter into any such fee arrangement.

Weston & Co should explain to Bentley Jones that the audit fee will be determined by the level of audit work which needs to be performed, and cannot be in any way linked to the success of Jones Co or advice which may be given to the firm by its auditors. The fee will be determined by the grade of staff that make up the audit team and the time spent by each of them on the audit.

Tutorial note

Credit will be awarded for discussion of other relevant current issues in relation to the setting of audit fees.

(b) **Ethical threats created by long association of senior audit personnel and relevant safeguards**

When a senior auditor acts for an audit client for a long period, several ethical problems can arise. First, the professional scepticism of the auditor can be diminished. This happens because the auditor becomes too accepting of the client's methods and explanations, so stops approaching the audit with a questioning mind.

Familiarity and self-interest threats are created by using the same senior personnel on an audit engagement over a long period of time. The familiarity threat is linked to the issues relating to the loss of professional scepticism discussed above, and is due to the senior auditor forming a close relationship with the client's personnel over a long period of time.

As with any ethical threat, the significance of the threat should be evaluated and safeguards which reduce the threat to an acceptable level put in place. Matters which should be considered in evaluating the significance of the ethical threat could include the seniority of the auditor involved, the length of time they have acted for the client, the nature, frequency and extent of the individual's interactions with the client's management or those charged with governance and whether the client's management team has changed.

Examples of safeguards which can be used include:

- Rotating the senior personnel off the audit team

- Having a professional accountant who was not a member of the audit team review the work of the senior personnel

- Regular independent internal or external quality reviews of the engagement.

Because Ordway Co is a listed company, the audit firm must remove Bobby from the audit team and not allow further contact with the client or the audit process. Bobby may not have any involvement with the audit of Ordway plc for the next five years.

Performing quality reviews forms part of participating in the audit engagement. Therefore, Bobby cannot act as engagement quality reviewer for the audit of Ordway plc, having stepped down as audit engagement partner until the appropriate cooling-off period has been served.

Tutorial note

INT syllabus:

In the case of a public interest company such as Ordway Co, the IESBA International Code of Ethics for Professional Accountants contains a specific requirement that an individual shall not be a key audit partner for more than seven years. After seven years the individual shall not be a member of the engagement team or be a key audit partner for the client for five years. This is known as the cooling off period, and during that period, the auditor shall not participate in the audit of the entity, provide quality reviews for the engagement, consult with the engagement team or the client regarding technical or industry-specific issues, transactions or events or otherwise directly influence the outcome of the engagement.

UK syllabus:

FRC Ethical Standard section 3 states that in the case of listed entities no one shall act as audit engagement partner for more than five years and that anyone who has acted as the audit engagement partner for a particular audited entity for a period of five years shall not subsequently participate in the audit engagement until a further period of five years has elapsed.

Examiner's comments

The first part of the question focused on practice management and client acceptance issues. The scenario described a potential new audit client, Jones Co, a small but rapidly growing company with ambitions to expand internationally. The audit firm had been approached to tender for the audit of Jones Co, and this would be the first year that the company required an audit. The company had previously had limited assurance reviews performed on its financial statements, and had one accountant using an off-the shelf accounting package. Requirement (a)(i) asked candidates to explain the specific matters to be included in the audit proposal document, other than those relating to the audit fee. This was quite well attempted by many, with almost all candidates understanding the main components of an audit proposal document such as a background of the audit firm, discussion of audit methodology, an outline of the firm's resources and timings and deadlines. Where candidates did not score well on this requirement was where the answer provided was very generic and was not made specific to the requirements of Jones Co. For example, some candidates ignored the fact that Jones Co had never previously been audited which would mean that management may have little appreciation of the audit process and as such the audit proposal should explain in some detail the responsibilities of management and the audit firm, and provide a detailed explanation of the audit process including key outputs. Requirement (a)(ii) went on to ask candidates to discuss the issues relating to determining the audit fee to be considered by the audit firm, assuming its appointment as auditor of Jones Co. Unfortunately many answers to this requirement did not identify the relevant matters in the question scenario, including the issue of contingent fees, intimidation on fees and lowballing that were implied by the comments made by the owner-manager of Jones Co. Better candidates were able to make the very valid point that the potential client needed a better understanding of the purpose of an audit and why it needs to be seen to be independent and tied this back to the content of the proposal document. Where these matters were not discussed, answers tended to be generic, and simply focused on the fact that audit fees should be determined by time, resources and charge-out rates. Many of the weaker answers did not focus on the specific nature of the question requirement, and instead discussed matters that had little to do with the audit fee, such as self-review threats and other irrelevant acceptance procedures such as customer due diligence.

Requirement (b) focused on a different audit client – Ordway Co, a listed company. The scenario briefly described that the current audit partner, having acted in that capacity for seven years was to be replaced by another partner, but wanted to stay in contact with the client and act as engagement quality reviewer. Candidates were asked to explain the ethical threats raised by the long association of senior audit personnel with an audit client and the relevant safeguards to be applied. Candidates were also asked to determine whether the partner could in fact act as engagement quality reviewer. This section was well attempted and most candidates correctly identified the familiarity threat and loss of professional scepticism that arises on a long association with an audit client, especially when dealing with senior audit personnel. Most candidates could also explain the relevant safeguards and demonstrated knowledge of the relevant requirements for listed entities. It was pleasing to see this syllabus area well understood by most candidates given its topical nature. The issue of whether the audit partner could remain in contact with the client by acting as engagement quality reviewer was less well understood. While many candidates correctly suggested that this could not happen for ethical reasons, many others thought that it would be appropriate as long as further quality reviews took place. Other candidates misinterpreted the question and thought that the partner was leaving the audit firm to work at the client.

ACCA Marking guide			Marks
(a)	**Jones Co**		
	(i)	**Matters to be included in the audit proposal**	
		Generally up to 2 marks for each matter explained:	
		– Outline of the audit firm	
		– Audit requirement of Jones Co	
		– Audit approach (allow up to 3 marks for well explained points made relevant to scenario)	
		– Deadlines	
		– Ability to provide insight and add value	
		– Quality management and ethics	
		– Additional non-audit and assurance services	
		Maximum	8
	(ii)	**Matters to be considered in determining audit fee**	
		Generally up to 2 marks for each point discussed:	
		– Fee to be based on staffing levels and chargeable hours	
		– Low fees can result in poor quality audit work and increase audit risk	
		– Lowballing and client expectation issues	
		– Contingent fees not allowed for audit services	
		Maximum	6
(b)	**Ordway Co**		
	Long association of senior audit personnel		
	Generally up to 1 mark for each point discussed:		
	– Loss of professional scepticism		
	– Familiarity and self-interest threats to objectivity		
	– Assessing the significance of the threat		
	– Appropriate safeguards (1 mark each where well explained to max of 3 marks)		
	– Cooling-off period required		
	– Conclusion on whether partner can perform EQR role		
		Maximum	6

Professional marks

Analysis and evaluation

– Appropriate use of the information to support discussions and draw appropriate conclusions

– Effective appraisal of the information to make suitable recommendations for appropriate courses of action

– Appropriate assessment of the ethical and professional issues raised, using examples where relevant to support overall comments

Professional scepticism and judgement

– Effective challenge and critical assessment of the evidence supplied with appropriate conclusions

– Appropriate application of professional judgement to draw conclusions and make informed comments

Commercial acumen

– Appropriate recognition of the wider implications on the engagement, the audit firm and the company

– Appropriate recognition of the practical and commercial implications relating to the tender and fee

– Demonstration of the ability to exercise insight and perception when recommending matters to be included in the tender

Maximum	5
Total	25

63 DRAGON GROUP *Walk in the footsteps of a top tutor*

Top tutor tips

Part (a) requires a basic knowledge of the contents of a tender document. You then need to develop this by applying your knowledge to the specific information given.

Part (b) asks you to consider the professional issues you need to consider before accepting a new client. This could include any aspect of audit quality management, ethics or general practice management.

Part (c) requires some basic knowledge and then some common sense suggestions about the difficulty of cross-border audit.

(a) Matters to be included in tender document

Brief outline of Unicorn & Co

This should include a short history of the firm, a description of its organisational structure, the different services offered by the firm (such as audit, tax, corporate finance, etc.), and the locations in which the firm operates.

The document should also state whether it is a member of any international audit firm network. The geographical locations in which Unicorn operates will be important given the multi-national structure of the Dragon Group.

Specialisms of the firm

Unicorn & Co should describe the areas in which the firm has particular experience of relevance to the Dragon Group. It would be advantageous to stress that the firm has an audit department dedicated to the audit of clients in the retail industry, as this emphasises the experience that the firm has relevant to the specific operations of the group.

Identification of the needs of the Dragon Group

The tender document should outline the requirements of the client, in this case, that each subsidiary is required to have an individual audit on its financial statements, and that the consolidated financial statements also need to be audited. Unicorn & Co may choose to include here a brief clarification of the purpose and legal requirements of an audit. The potential provision of non-audit services should be discussed, either here, or in a separate section of the tender document (see below).

Outline of the proposed audit approach

This is likely to be the most detailed part of the tender document. Here the firm will describe how the audit would be conducted, ensuring that the needs of the Dragon Group (as discussed above) have been met. Typically contained in this section would be a description of the audit methodology used by the firm, and an outline of the audit cycle including the key deliverables at each phase of work. For example:

- How the firm would intend to gain business understanding at group and subsidiary level.

- Methods used to assess risk and to plan the audits.

- Procedures used to assess the control environment and accounting systems.

- Techniques used to gather evidence, e.g. the use of audit software.

How the firm would structure the audit of the consolidation of the group financial statements and how they would liaise with subsidiary audit teams.

The firm should clarify its adherence to International Standards on Auditing, ethical guidelines and any other relevant laws and regulations operating in the various jurisdictions relevant to the Dragon Group. The various financial reporting frameworks used within the group should be clarified.

Quality management

Unicorn & Co should emphasise the importance of quality and therefore should explain the procedures that are used within the firm to monitor the quality of the audit services provided. This should include a description of firm-wide quality management policies, and the procedures applied to individual audits. The firm may wish to clarify its adherence to International Standards on Quality Management.

Communication with management

The firm should outline the various reports and other communication that will be made to management as part of the audit process. The purpose and main content of the reports, and the timing of them, should be outlined. Unicorn & Co may provide some 'added value' bi-products of the audit process. For example, the business risks identified as part of the audit planning may be fed back to management in a written report.

Timing

Unicorn & Co should outline the timeframe that would be used. For example, the audits of the subsidiaries' financial statements should be conducted before the audit of the consolidated financial statements. The firm may wish to include an approximate date by which the group audit opinion would be completed, which should fit in, if possible, with the requirements of the group. If Unicorn & Co feel that the deadline requested by the client is unrealistic, a more appropriate deadline should be suggested, with the reasons for this clearly explained.

Key staff and resources

The document should name the key members of staff to be assigned to the audit, in particular the proposed engagement partner. In addition, the firm should clarify the approximate number of staff to be used in the audit team and the relevant experience of the key members of the audit team. If the firm considers that external specialists could be needed, then this should be explained in this section of the document.

Fees

The proposed fee for the audit of the group should be stated, and the calculation of the fee should be explained, i.e. broken down by grade of staff and hourly/daily rates per grade. In addition, invoicing and payment terms should be described, e.g. if the audit fee is payable in instalments, the stages when each instalment will fall due.

Ability to provide insight and add value

Given the Group's plans to grow by 35% in the next four years by acquiring more subsidiaries, a key selling point to be included in the tender will be the firm's ability to provide insight and add value to this process.

Ability to maintain independence and challenge management

Given the listed status of the Group, corporate governance has more emphasis and the need for management to be acting in the best interests of the shareholders. Having an audit firm which maintains independence and effectively challenges management will demonstrate the Group's commitment to good corporate governance.

Additional services

Unicorn & Co should ensure that any non-audit services that it may be able to offer to the Dragon Group are described. For example, subject to ethical safeguards, the firm may be able to offer corporate finance services in relation to the stock exchange listing that the group is seeking, although the provision of this non-audit service would need to be carefully considered in relation to independence issues.

(b) **Acceptance matters to be considered**

Size and location of the group companies

The Dragon Group is a large multi-national group of companies. It is important that Unicorn & Co assesses the availability of resources that can be allocated to the audit team. The assignment would comprise the audit of the financial statements of all 20 current subsidiaries, the audit of the parent company's and the group's financial statements. This is a significant engagement which will demand a great deal of time.

The location of half of the group's subsidiaries in other countries means that the overseas offices of Unicorn & Co would be called upon to perform some or all of the audit of those subsidiaries. In this case, the resource base of the relevant overseas offices should be considered to ensure there is enough staff with appropriate skills and experience available to perform the necessary audit work.

Unicorn & Co must consider if they have offices in all of the countries in which the Dragon Group has a subsidiary.

Depending on the materiality of the overseas subsidiaries to the group financial statements, it is likely that some overseas visits would be required to evaluate the work of the overseas audit teams. Unicorn & Co should consider who will conduct the visits (presumably a senior member of the audit team), and whether that person has the necessary skills and experience in evaluating the work of overseas audit teams.

Planned expansion of the group

In light of the comments above, Unicorn & Co should consider that the planned further significant expansion of the group will mean more audit staff will be needed in future years, and if any subsidiaries are acquired in other countries, the audit is likely to be performed by overseas offices. The firm should therefore consider not only its current resource base in the local and overseas offices, but whether additional staff will be available in the future if the group's expansion goes ahead as planned.

Relevant skills and experience

Unicorn & Co has an audit department specialising in the audit of retail companies, so it should not be a problem to find audit staff with relevant experience in this country.

On consolidation, the financial statements of the subsidiaries will be restated in line with group accounting policies and financial reporting framework, and will also be retranslated into local presentational currency. All of this work will be performed by the management of the Dragon Group. Unicorn & Co must evaluate the availability of staff experienced in the audit of a consolidation including foreign subsidiaries.

Timing

It is important to consider the timeframe when conducting a group audit. The audit of each subsidiary's financial statements should be carried out prior to the audit of the consolidated financial statements. Unicorn & Co should consider the expectation of the Dragon Group in relation to the reporting deadline, and ensure that enough time is allowed for the completion of all audits. The deadline proposed by management of 31 December is only three months after the year end, which may be unrealistic given the size of the group and the multi-national location of the subsidiaries. The first year auditing a new client is likely to take longer, as the audit team will need to familiarise themselves with the business, the accounting systems and controls, etc.

Mermaid Co – prior year modification

If Unicorn & Co accepts the engagement, the firm will take on the audit of Mermaid Co, whose financial statements in the prior year were in breach of financial reporting standards. This adds an element of risk to the engagement. Unicorn & Co should gather as much information as possible about the contingent liability, and the reason why the management of Mermaid Co did not amend the financial statements last year end. This could hint at a lack of integrity on the part of the management of the company.

The firm should also consider whether this matter could be significant to the consolidated financial statements, by assessing the materiality of the contingent liability at group level.

Further discussions should be held with the management of the Dragon Group in order to understand their thoughts on the contingency and whether it should be disclosed in the individual financial statements of Mermaid Co, and at group level. Contacting the incumbent auditors (after seeking relevant permission from the Dragon Group) would also be an important procedure to gather information about the modification.

Minotaur Co – different business activity

The acquisition of Minotaur Co represents a new business activity for the group. The retail business audit department may not currently have much, if any, experience of auditing a distribution company. This should be easily overcome, either by bringing in staff from a different department more experienced in clients with distribution operations, or by ensuring adequate training for staff in the retail business audit department.

Highly regulated/reliance on financial statements and auditor's report

The Group is listed on several stock exchanges, and is therefore subject to a high degree of regulation. This adds an element of risk to the engagement, as the management will be under pressure to publish favourable results. This risk is increased by the fact that a new listing is being sought, meaning that the financial statements and auditor's report of the group will be subject to close scrutiny by the stock exchange regulators.

There may be extra work required by the auditors due to the listings, for example, the group may have to prepare reconciliations of financial data, or additional narrative reports on which the auditors have to express an opinion under the rulings of the stock exchange. The firm must consider the availability of staff skilled in regulatory and reporting listing rules to perform such work.

Previous auditors of Dragon Group

Unicorn & Co should consider the reason why the previous audit firm is not seeking re-appointment, and whether the reason would impact on their acceptance decision. After seeking permission from the Dragon Group, contact should be made with the previous auditors to obtain confirmation of the reason for them vacating office (amongst other matters).

In conclusion, this is a large scale, multi-national group, which carries a fairly high level of risk. Unicorn & Co must be extremely careful to only commit to the group audit if it has the necessary resources, can manage the client's expectation in relation to the reporting deadline, is convinced of the integrity of management, and is confident to take on a potentially high profile client.

Tutorial note

Credit will be awarded in this requirement for discussion of ethical matters which would be considered prior to accepting the appointment as auditor of the Dragon Group. However, as the scenario does not contain any reference to specific ethical matters, marks will be limited to a maximum of 2 for a general discussion of ethical matters on acceptance.

(c) **Discuss how transnational audits may differ from other audits of historical information and how this may contribute to a higher level of audit risk in relation to the audit of Dragon Group.**

A transnational audit means an audit of financial statements which are or may be relied upon outside the audited entity's home jurisdiction for the purpose of significant lending, investment or regulatory decisions.

The Dragon Group is listed on the stock exchange of several countries, and is planning to raise more finance by a further listing, which means that the group is subject to the regulations of all stock exchanges on which it is listed, and so is bound by listing rules outside of its home jurisdiction. The group also contains many foreign subsidiaries, meaning that it operates in a global business and financial environment.

Transnational audit and audit risk

Application of auditing standards

Although many countries of the world have adopted International Standards on Auditing (ISAs), not all have done so, choosing instead to use locally developed auditing regulations. In addition, some countries use modified versions of ISAs. This means that in a transnational audit, some components of the group financial statements will have been audited using a different auditing framework, resulting in inconsistent audit processes within the group, potentially reducing the quality of the audit.

Regulation and oversight of auditors

Similar to the previous comments on the use of ISAs, across the world there are many different ways in which the activities of auditors are regulated and monitored. In some countries the audit profession is self-regulatory, whereas in other countries a more legislative approach is used. This also can impact on the quality of audit work in a transnational situation.

Financial reporting framework

Some countries use International Financial Reporting Standards, whereas some use locally developed accounting standards. Within a transnational group it is likely that adjustments, reconciliations or restatements may be required in order to comply with the requirements of the jurisdictions relevant to the group financial statements (i.e. the jurisdiction of the parent company in most cases). Such reconciliations can be complex and require a high level of technical expertise of the preparer and the auditor.

Corporate governance requirements and consequent control risk

In some countries there are very prescriptive corporate governance requirements, which the auditor must consider as part of the audit process. In this case the auditor may need to carry out extra work over and above local requirements in order to ensure group wide compliance with the requirements of the jurisdictions relevant to the financial statements. However, in some countries there is very little corporate governance regulation at all and controls are likely to be weaker than in other components of the group. Control risk is therefore likely to differ between the various subsidiaries making up the group.

Examiner's comments

The first requirement focused on the audit tendering process, and asked for matters to be included in a tender document to be presented to the Dragon Group. This requirement seemed to polarise candidates. Those candidates who tailored their answer to the question scenario tended to do well, with a significant proportion achieving close to the maximum marks available. However, candidates who provided a list of points to be included in ANY tender, regardless of the information provided about the prospective client, and about your audit firm, scored inadequately. In other words, it is important to apply knowledge to score well, as is true for any scenario-based question.

Sound answers appreciated that the point of the tender document is to sell your audit firm's services to the client, and recommended points to include such as the global positioning of both audit firm and prospective client, the specialism of the audit firm in retail, and the firm's ability to potentially provide services relating to the expansion plans of the group, such as due diligence.

Weak answers simply stated vague comments: 'we should discuss fees', 'we should set a deadline,' etc. Some answers confused a tender document with an engagement letter, and included points more suited to that document, such as a statement of responsibilities or a legal disclaimer. Inadequate answers were those that seemed to confuse the requirements with those of (b). Candidates are reminded that it is important to read ALL of the requirements of a question before beginning their answer, to avoid such confusion. Examples of statements commonly seen in answers to (a) which are more relevant to (b) are:

- 'are we competent to audit the group'

- 'can we audit the goodwill and foreign exchange transactions which are complex'

- 'will any of our audit staff want to go abroad to work'

- 'do any of our partners hold shares in Dragon Group'.

These comments definitely do not belong in a tender document, which should highlight the audit firm's capabilities to service the prospective client, rather than question the firm's competence or ability to take on the assignment. Such comments indicate a failure to read and understand the question requirement, as well as a lack of commercial awareness.

The next requirement asked candidates to evaluate the matters that should be considered before accepting the audit engagement. Answers here were weak, despite this being a regularly examined syllabus area. Most answers were not tailored to the question, and just provided a list of questions or actions, such as 'get permission to contact previous auditor', or 'check the integrity of management', and 'do we have the skill to audit foreign currencies'.

Providing a list of such comments will not generate enough marks to pass the question requirement. Better answers discussed, amongst other points:

- the risk posed by the numerous stock exchange listings of the potential client, and whether the audit fee would be enough to compensate for that risk

- the practical difficulties entailed in co-ordinating an audit of more than 20 companies across many different countries

- the tight deadline imposed by the potential client, especially in light of this being a first year audit, and the learning curve that the audit firm would need to go through.

Some candidates appeared to think that the audit would be too much trouble – a sizeable number of scripts contained comments such as 'auditing a company far from our main office would be tedious and inconvenient'. I would suggest that most audit firms, on being successful in a tender for an audit as significant as this, would consider the inconvenience worthwhile.

The final requirement was the worst answered on the paper. Clearly, very few candidates had studied the issue of transnational audits, and answers displayed a lack of knowledge. Answers appeared to be based mainly on guesswork, with common suggestions being 'language difficulties' and 'communication barriers'. However, some candidates could identify variations in auditing standards and financial reporting frameworks as issues contributing to high risk, but these points were rarely developed to their full potential.

	ACCA Marking guide		
			Marks
(a)	**Contents of tender document**		
	Up to 2 marks per matter described:		
	– Outline of firm		
	– Specialisms		
	– Audit requirement of Dragon Group		
	– Outline audit approach (max 3 marks if detailed)		
	– Quality management		
	– Communication with management		
	– Timing		
	– Key staff/resources		
	– Fees		
	– Additional to provide insight and add value		
	– Ability to maintain independence and challenge management		
	– Additional services		
		Maximum	**8**
(b)	**Acceptance matters to consider**		
	Up to 2 marks per matter described:		
	– Large and expanding group – availability of staff now and in the future		
	– Use of overseas offices		
	– Visits to overseas audit teams		
	– Skills/experience in retail/foreign subsidiaries consolidation		
	– Timing – tight deadline		
	– Mermaid Co – implication of prior year modification		
	– Minotaur Co – implication of different business activity		
	– Highly regulated – risk/additional reporting requirements		
	– Reason for previous auditors leaving office		
		Maximum	**6**
(c)	**Transnational audits**		
	Up to 2 marks per point explained		
	– Definition of transnational audit and application to Dragon Group		
	– Auditing standards		
	– Regulation of auditors		
	– Financial reporting standards		
	– Corporate governance/control risk		
		Maximum	**6**

Professional marks
Analysis and evaluation
– Appropriate use of the information to support discussions and draw appropriate conclusions
– Effective appraisal of the information to make suitable recommendations for appropriate courses of action
– Appropriate assessment of the ethical and professional issues raised, using examples where relevant to support overall comments

Professional scepticism and judgement
– Effective challenge and critical assessment of the evidence supplied with appropriate conclusions
– Appropriate application of professional judgement to draw conclusions and make informed comments

Commercial acumen
- – Appropriate recognition of the wider implications on the engagement, the audit firm and the company
- – Appropriate recognition of the practical and commercial implications relating to the tender
- – Demonstration of the ability to exercise insight and perception when recommending matters to be included in the tender

Maximum	5
Total	25

64 SPANIEL *Walk in the footsteps of a top tutor*

Top tutor tips

Part (a) addresses the issue of auditor liability and whether the audit firm has been negligent due to failure to detect a fraud. Knowledge of the conditions for a negligence claim to succeed and discussion of each of these conditions in turn should help to score the marks available.

Part (b) is a discussion question regarding the difficulties auditing financial instruments and the matters to be considered when planning the audit of forward exchange contracts. For the first part, think about the risks associated with financial instruments. For the planning aspects, think about what the auditor does at the planning stage of an audit and why, and apply this to the specific area of financial instruments.

Part (c) requires a discussion of the risk of fraud in revenue recognition. In this situation, fraud involves manipulating the revenue figure in the financial statements to show a different picture. Therefore, your answer should consider the ways in which management can achieve this.

(a) It is not the auditor's primary responsibility to detect fraud. According to ISA 240 *The Auditor's Responsibilities Relating to Fraud in an Audit of Financial Statements*, management is primarily responsible for preventing and detecting fraud. The auditor is required to obtain reasonable assurance that the financial statements are free from material misstatement whether caused by fraud or error.

The total amount estimated to have been stolen in the payroll fraud represents 5.6% of Spaniel's assets. If the amount has been stolen consistently over a 12-month period, then $3 million (8/12 × 4.5 million) had been stolen prior to the year end of 31 December 20X4. $3 million is material, representing 3.8% of total assets at the year end. Therefore, the fraud was material and it could be reasonably expected that it should have been discovered.

However, material misstatements arising due to fraud can be difficult for the auditor to detect. This is because fraud is deliberately hidden by the perpetrators using sophisticated accounting techniques established to conceal the fraudulent activity. False statements may be made to the auditors and documents may have been forged.

This means that material frauds could go undetected, even if appropriate procedures have been carried out.

ISA 240 requires that an audit is performed with an attitude of professional scepticism. This may not have been the case. Spaniel Co is a long-standing client, and the audit team may have lost their sceptical attitude. Necessary tests of control on payroll were not carried out because in previous years it had been possible to rely on the client's controls.

It seems that ISAs may not have been adhered to during the audit of Spaniel Co. ISA 330 *The Auditor's Responses to Assessed Risks* requires that the auditor shall design and perform tests of controls to obtain sufficient appropriate audit evidence as to the operating effectiveness of relevant controls if the auditor's assessment of risks of material misstatement at the assertion level includes an expectation that the controls are operating effectively.

It can be acceptable for the auditor to use audit evidence from a previous audit about the operating effectiveness of specific controls but only if the auditor confirms that no changes have taken place. The audit partner should explain whether this was the case.

Substantive procedures have not been performed on payroll either. This effectively means that payroll has not been audited.

This leads to a conclusion that the audit firm may have been negligent in conducting the audit. Negligence is a common law concept in which an injured party must prove three things in order to prove that negligence has occurred:

- That the auditor owes a duty of care

- That the duty of care has been breached

- That financial loss has been caused by the negligence.

Looking at these points in turn, Groom & Co owes a duty of care to Spaniel Co, because a contract exists between the two parties. The company represents all the shareholders as a body, and there is an automatic duty of care owed to the shareholders as a body by the auditor.

A breach of duty of care must be proved for a negligence claim against the audit firm to be successful. Duty of care generally means that the audit firm must perform the audit work to a good standard and that relevant legal and professional requirements and principles have been followed. For an audit firm, it is important to be able to demonstrate that ISAs have been adhered to. Unfortunately, it seems that ISAs have been breached and so the audit firm is likely to have been negligent in the audit of payroll.

Tutorial note

Credit will be awarded for references to legal cases as examples of situations where audit firms have been found to have been negligent in performing an audit, such as Re Kingston Cotton Mill.

Finally, a financial loss has been suffered by the audit client, being the amount stolen while the fraud was operating.

In conclusion, Spaniel Co is likely to be able to successfully prove that the audit firm has been negligent in the audit of payroll, and that Groom & Co is liable for some or all of the financial loss suffered.

(b) **The audit of financial instruments**

Complex and difficult to understand

There are many reasons why financial instruments are challenging to audit. The instruments themselves, the transactions to which they relate, and the associated risk exposures can be difficult for both management and auditors to understand.

If the auditor does not fully understand the financial instrument and its impact on the financial statements, it will be difficult to assess the risk of material misstatement and to detect errors in the accounting treatment and associated disclosures. Even relatively simple financial instruments can be complex to account for.

Reliance on experts

The specialist nature of many financial instruments means that the auditor may need to rely on an auditor's expert as a source of evidence. In using an expert, the auditor must ensure the objectivity and competence of that expert, and then must evaluate the adequacy of the expert's work, which can be very difficult to do where the focus of the work is so specialist and difficult to understand.

Lack of evidence

The auditor may also find that there is a lack of evidence in relation to financial instruments, or that evidence tends to come from management. For example, many of the financial reporting requirements in relation to the valuation of financial instruments are based on fair values. Fair values are often based on models which depend on management judgement. Valuations are therefore often subjective and derived from management assumptions which increase the risk of material misstatement.

Professional scepticism

It is imperative that the auditor retains professional scepticism in the audit of financial instruments, but this may be difficult to do when faced with a complex and subjective transaction or balance for which there is little evidence other than management's judgement.

Internal controls

There may also be control issues relating to financial instruments. Often financial instruments are dealt with by a specialist department and it may be a few individuals who exert significant influence over the financial instruments that are entered into. This specialist department may not be fully integrated into the finance function, leading to the accounting treatment being dealt with outside the normal accounting system. Internal controls may be deficient and there may not be the opportunity for much segregation of duty. However, some companies will have established strong internal controls around financial instruments, leading to a lower risk of material misstatement.

Planning implications

Obtain an understanding of the accounting requirements

In planning the audit of Bulldog's financial instruments, the auditor must first gain an understanding of the relevant accounting and disclosure requirements. For example, the applicable financial reporting standards should be clarified, which are likely to be IFRS 9 *Financial Instruments* and IFRS 7 *Financial Instruments: Disclosures.* These standards can be complex to apply, and the auditor should develop a thorough understanding of how they relate to Bulldog's financial instruments.

Obtain an understanding of the financial instruments

The auditor must also obtain an understanding of the instruments in which Bulldog Co has invested or to which it is exposed, including the characteristics of the instruments, and gain an understanding of Bulldog's reasons for entering into the financial instruments and its policy towards them.

Resources

It is important that the resources needed to audit the financial instruments are carefully considered. The competence of members of the audit firm to audit these transactions should be assessed, and it may be that an auditor's expert needs to be engaged. If so, this should be explained to the client. Instructions will have to be drawn up and given to the expert to ensure that the work performed is in line with audit objectives and follows the relevant financial reporting requirements, for example, in relation to valuing the financial instruments.

Consider internal controls

The audit planning should include obtaining an understanding of the internal control relevant to Bulldog's financial instruments, including the involvement, if any, of internal audit. An understanding of how financial instruments are monitored and controlled assists the auditor in determining the nature, timing and extent of audit procedures, for example, whether to perform tests on controls.

Understand management's valuation method

Specific consideration should be given to understanding management's method for valuing financial instruments for recognition in the year-end financial statements. The valuation is likely to involve some form of estimate, and ISA 540 *Auditing Accounting Estimates and Related Disclosures* requires the auditor to obtain an understanding of how management makes accounting estimates and the data on which accounting estimates are based.

Determine materiality

Finally, the materiality of the financial instruments should be determined and the significance of the risk exposure associated with them should be assessed.

(c) **Revenue recognition**

Management under pressure to achieve certain results

One reason is that managers of companies are often under pressure, particularly in listed companies, to achieve certain performance targets. The achievement of those targets often impacts their job security and their compensation. These performance targets often include measures of revenue growth, providing an incentive for management to use earnings management techniques.

In other companies there may be incentives to understate revenues, for example, to reduce reported profits and, therefore, company taxation charges. This may be more relevant to private limited companies where management may not be under such pressure to achieve revenue based targets.

Volume of transactions

There is also usually a high volume of revenue transactions during a financial period. As the volume of transactions increases, the risk of failing to detect fraud and error using traditional, sample based auditing techniques also increases. This means that it is potentially easier for management to successfully manipulate these balances than other balances which are subject to a lower volume of transactions.

Material misstatement through the manipulation of revenue recognition can be readily achieved by recording revenue in an earlier or later accounting period than is proper or by creating fictitious revenues.

Judgemental area

Revenue recognition can also be a judgemental area. Examples include the recognition of revenues on long-term contracts, such as the construction of buildings, and from the provision of services. These require the estimation of the percentage of completion at the period end, increasing the scope for management to manipulate reported results.

Complexity

As well as requiring judgement, revenue recognition can also be a complex issue. For example, some sales have multiple elements, such as the sale of goods and the separate sale of related maintenance contracts and warranties. This added complexity increases the risk of manipulation.

Cash sales

In some companies, for example, those in the retail industry, a high proportion of revenue may be earned through cash sales. This increases the risk of the theft of cash and the consequent manipulation of recorded revenues to conceal this crime.

Accounting fraud

Methods of revenue manipulation have also featured prominently in cases of accounting fraud, such as Enron and Worldcom. The prevalence of these methods in modern accounting frauds and the failure of auditors to detect this in these cases suggests that it is one of the more common methods of earnings management and one which auditors should rightly consider as high risk.

Not always high risk

While revenue recognition in general may be considered a high risk area, it is not always the case. Companies with simple revenue streams or a low volume of transactions may be considered at low risk of fraud through revenue manipulations. Accordingly, ISA 240 *The Auditor's Responsibility Relating to Fraud in an Audit of Financial Statements* permits the rebuttable of the fraud risk presumption for revenue recognition. One example of simple revenue streams would be where a company leases properties for fixed annual amounts over a fixed period of time. If this is the case, the reasons for not treating revenue as a high fraud risk area must be fully documented by the auditor.

Examiner's comments

Requirement (a) provided a scenario which described that an audit firm had given an unmodified audit opinion on Spaniel's financial statements, and that subsequent to the auditor's report being issued a fraud had been discovered that had been operating during the period covered by the auditor's report. The scenario also pointed out that the audit firm had not performed audit procedures in relation to the area in which the fraud was occurring, namely payroll. The requirement asked candidates to explain the matters to be considered in determining the audit firm's liability to Spaniel Co in respect of the fraud. There were some excellent answers to this requirement. The best ones clearly outlined the factors that have to be proven to determine negligence, and applied them methodically to the scenario. The materiality of the fraud was considered, the duty of care owed to the audit client, and the fact that the auditor may not have been exercising professional scepticism during the audit due to the long-standing nature of the audit appointment. It was also appropriate to discuss the responsibilities of management and auditors in relation to fraud, and whether it is appropriate for auditors to rely on the conclusions reached in previous year's audit. Some answers tended to only provide a rote-learnt description of responsibilities in relation to fraud, and usually failed to reach an appropriate conclusion. With little application to the scenario there is limited scope for marks to be awarded.

Requirement (b) described a different audit client, Bulldog Co, which had expanded overseas and set up a treasury management function dealing with forward exchange contracts. The requirement was to discuss why the audit of financial statements is challenging and explain the matters to be considered in planning the audit of the forward exchange contracts. Answers here were extremely mixed in quality. Satisfactory answers focused on why financial instruments generally are difficult to audit, discussing their complex nature, the changing landscape of financial reporting requirements, the potential for both client and auditor to lack appropriate knowledge and skills, and the frequent need to rely on an expert. In terms of planning the audit, adequate answers focused on simple matters such as managing resources, obtaining an understanding of the nature of the contracts and the controls in relation to them, and assessing how management value the financial instruments. Inadequate answers did not include much reference to audit at all, and simply listed out financial reporting rules, with no consideration of audit implications other than saying that financial instruments are complex and subjective. There were very few references to relevant ISA requirements, and little evidence that the audit of complex matters such as financial instruments had been studied at all, even though it is a topical current issue.

The final part required candidates to discuss why auditors should presume that there is a risk of fraud in revenue recognition and this requirement was poorly answered with most candidates setting out lengthy explanations of the respective duties of the auditor and management for the identification and prevention of fraud and thereby not answering the question. Strong answers considered management bias and targets, judgements in complex business and cut-off errors.

	ACCA Marking guide		
			Marks
(a)	**Fraud and auditor's liability**		
	Generally up to 1 mark for each point explained:		
	– Auditor's responsibility in relation to fraud		
	– Materiality calculation of the fraud		
	– Reasons why fraud is hard to detect		
	– Audit firm may not have been sufficiently sceptical		
	– Non-adherence to ISAs on controls assessment and evidence obtained		
	– Discuss whether duty of care owed to client		
	– Discuss breach of duty of care		
	– Identify financial loss suffered and firm likely to have been negligent		
		Maximum	5
(b)	**Audit of financial instruments**		
	Generally up to 1 mark for each point explained:		
	Why is audit of financial instruments challenging?		
	– Financial reporting requirements complex		
	– Transactions themselves difficult to understand		
	– Auditor may need to rely on expert		
	– Lack of evidence and need to rely on management judgement		
	– May be hard to maintain attitude of scepticism		
	– Internal controls may be deficient		
	Planning implications		
	– Obtain understanding of accounting and disclosure requirements		
	– Obtain understanding of client's financial instruments		
	– Determine resources, i.e. skills needed and need for an auditor's expert		
	– Consider internal controls including internal audit		
	– Understand management's method for valuing financial instruments		
	– Determine materiality of financial instruments		
		Maximum	10
(c)	**Fraud and revenue recognition**		
	Generally 1 mark for each point of discussion:		
	– Management targets/incentives		
	– High volume of transactions		
	– Use of judgement		
	– Complexity of accounting		
	– Cash sales		
	– Common in recent accounting frauds		
	– Not always complex/rebuttable permitted		
		Maximum	5
	Professional marks		
	Analysis and evaluation		
	– Appropriate use of the information to support discussions and draw appropriate conclusions and design appropriate responses		
	– Appropriate assessment of the ethical and professional issues raised, using examples where relevant, to support overall comments		
	– Identification of omissions from the analysis or further analysis which could be carried out		

Professional scepticism and professional judgement		
– Effective application of technical and ethical guidance to effectively challenge and critically assess the audit evidence		
– Demonstration of the ability to question contradictory information and probe for further information		
– Demonstration of the ability to apply appropriate professional judgement to draw conclusions and make informed decisions about the courses of action appropriate		
– Effective challenge and critical assessment of the conduct and extent of the audit work and evidence obtained with appropriate conclusions		
– Appropriate application of professional judgement to draw conclusions and make informed decisions about the actions which are appropriate in the context and stage of the engagement		
Maximum		5
Total		25

UK SYLLABUS ONLY

65   ALUCARD *Walk in the footsteps of a top tutor*

Top tutor tips

The first part of this question asks for the key features of the administration process. This is text book knowledge and should therefore be straightforward.

The second part requires application of knowledge of fraudulent and wrongful trading to the scenario to evaluate whether the client is guilty of either offence. Use the information in the scenario and take a logical approach to justify whether there is evidence of fraudulent or wrongful trading.

Key features of the administration process

Alucard Ltd's inability to pay its creditors as they fall due and the net liabilities position shown by the company's management accounts over the last three months indicate that the company is insolvent.

The aim of administration is to save the company, if possible. A licensed insolvency practitioner (IP) is appointed to act as administrator, and effectively takes control of the company in an attempt to rescue it as a going concern. Once the process has been initiated, there is a moratorium on creditors' actions which protects the company while a restructuring plan is prepared. This is important for Alucard Ltd, which is struggling to manage its cash position. In the light of its payment period, some of the creditors' balances may be long overdue and the creditors may already be considering actions to recover the amounts owed.

Administration can commence without a court order. The directors themselves may be able to appoint an administrator, though this depends on the company's articles of association. Alternatively, the company (a majority of shareholders) or qualifying floating charge holders can apply for administration without going through the court. If the directors or the company commence appointing an administrator, notice must be given to any qualifying floating charge holders who are entitled to appoint an administrator. Alternatively, administration proceedings can involve a court order. The company (a majority of shareholders), the directors, one or more creditors or in rare cases, the Justice and Chief Executive of the Magistrates' Court, can apply to the court for an administration order. The court will consider the application and will grant the administration order if it appears that the company is unable to pay its debts.

Whichever method of appointment of an administrator is employed, the advantage for the company is that the moratorium would allow Alucard Ltd some much needed breathing space and time to resolve its cash flow problems. The directors will, however, lose control of the company and all operational decisions will be made by the administrator who also has the power to remove or appoint directors. The administrator will prepare a proposal regarding the future of the company which will be sent to all shareholders and creditors and a creditors' meeting will be held at which the proposal will be accepted or rejected. Administration can normally last for up to 12 months and if at any point the administrator believes that the company cannot be saved, they will recommend that a liquidator should be appointed and the company will be wound up.

Personal liability for the company's debts

The directors of Alucard Ltd may incur personal liability for the company's debts where they have provided personal guarantees or been involved in either fraudulent or wrongful trading. The main difference between the two is intent. Directors who take part in fraudulent trading have a clear intent to deceive and defraud their creditors and customers.

Fraudulent trading

Fraudulent trading is defined by the Insolvency Act 1986 (IA 1986) as carrying on the business of an insolvent company with the intent to defraud the company's creditors. Actions for fraudulent trading can be brought against any person who is knowingly a party to the fraudulent trading.

Fraudulent trading is a criminal offence and as such, the burden of proof in a court action requires the prosecution's evidence to have established its case beyond reasonable doubt. In this regard, it is key to a successful action that the prosecution has established that intent was present in the defendant's actions.

The penalties and liability which may result from a successful action for fraudulent trading are imprisonment for up to 10 years, personal (civil) liability for the debts of company and disqualification from being a company director for up to 15 years.

Wrongful trading

Wrongful trading is defined by IA 1986 as carrying on the business of an insolvent company when it ought to have concluded that there was no reasonable prospect of the company avoiding insolvent liquidation and that the creditors of the company would therefore suffer losses. In contrast to fraudulent trading, it is not necessary to establish intent and wrongful trading is a civil wrong rather than a criminal offence. It is also significant that an action for wrongful trading can only be brought against company directors (including shadow directors).

As a civil wrong, the burden of proof for wrongful trading is the weaker test of the balance of probabilities. The penalties and liability which may result from a successful action for wrongful trading are personal (civil) liability of the directors for the debts of the company and disqualification from being a company director for up to 15 years.

Potential issues for the directors of Alucard Ltd

The contract with Holden Co which represented approximately 45% of the company's total sales revenue was cancelled five months ago. The company's payment period has increased from 45 days to 73 days over this five-month period and the company's cash position has deteriorated to the point where it is unable to pay its creditors as they fall due.

The company's management accounts have shown a negative cash balance in excess of its overdraft facility and a net liabilities position for the last three months. In addition, Alucard Ltd has three months of arrears of unpaid PAYE and NIC and has received penalty notices in relation to its failure to file its last audited financial statements with Companies House. This provides further evidence that the company cannot pay its liabilities as they fall due and that it is failing to make statutory information available to its creditors.

It would appear therefore that there have been clear indicators that the company was potentially insolvent which the directors should have identified and acted upon. Instead of this, however, they have continued to trade at existing operational levels and to make purchases on credit from the company's suppliers. If it can be established that these actions were made with the intention of defrauding creditors, then they will be guilty of fraudulent trading.

Alternatively, if they have carried on the business of the company when they ought to have realised that creditors would suffer losses, then they will have been a party to wrongful trading. In either case, they will incur personal liability to the company's creditors.

ACCA marking guide	
	Marks
Alucard Ltd	
Key features of administration	
Generally up to 1 mark for each point explained:	
– Explanation/definition of administration	
– Key features of administration (up to 2 marks)	
– Explanation of key feature or implication of fraudulent trading:	
• Intent to defraud must be proven	
• Action can be taken against anyone aware of the fraudulent trading	
• Criminal offence, proof must be beyond reasonable doubt	
• Penalties include imprisonment, personal liability for company debts, disqualification as a director	
– Explanation of key feature or implication of wrongful trading:	
• No intent to defraud – the offence is continuing to trade when directors should have known that creditors are likely to suffer losses	
• Action can only be taken against directors	
• Civil offence, a lower level of proof is needed	
• Penalties include personal liability for company debts and disqualification as a director	
– Discussion of indicators from scenario – 1 mark for each valid point	
– Reasoned conclusion on whether Alucard Ltd's directors will incur personal liability	
Total	10

66 KRUPT *Walk in the footsteps of a top tutor*

Top tutor tips

Part (a) asks for the penalties for fraudulent and wrongful trading. This is rote-learned knowledge from the text book and should be easy marks.

Part (b) requires application of knowledge of fraudulent and wrongful trading to the scenario to evaluate whether the client is guilty of either offence. Use the information in the scenario and take a logical approach to justify whether there is evidence of fraudulent or wrongful trading.

(i) Potential liability and penalties as a result of actions for fraudulent and wrongful trading

Fraudulent trading

Fraudulent trading is defined by the Insolvency Act 1986 (IA 1986) as carrying on the business of an insolvent company with the intent to defraud the company's creditors. Actions for fraudulent trading can be brought against any person who is knowingly a party to the fraudulent trading.

Fraudulent trading is a criminal offence and, as such, the burden of proof in a court action requires the prosecution's evidence to have established its case beyond reasonable doubt. In this regard, it is key to a successful action that the prosecution has established that intent was present in the defendant's actions.

The penalties and liability which may result from a successful action for fraudulent trading are imprisonment for up to 10 years, personal (civil) liability for the debts of company and disqualification from being a company director for up to 15 years.

Wrongful trading

Wrongful trading is defined as carrying on the business of an insolvent company when it ought to have been concluded that there was no reasonable prospect of the company avoiding insolvent liquidation and that the creditors of the company would therefore suffer losses. In contrast to fraudulent trading, it is not necessary to establish intent and wrongful trading is a civil wrong rather than a criminal offence. It is also significant that an action for wrongful trading can only be brought against company directors (including shadow directors).

As a civil wrong, the burden of proof for wrongful trading is the weaker test of the balance of probabilities. The penalties and liability which may result from a successful action for wrongful trading are personal (civil) liability of the directors for the debts of the company and disqualification from being a company director for up to 15 years.

(ii)   Implications for Krupt Ltd

Mr and Mrs Krupt appear to have bought a substantial quantity of goods on credit in order to ensure that the bank will have sufficient secured assets to cover its debt without having to call in the personal guarantee on the directors' house. The amounts involved in this transaction may be grounds for additional suspicion that the directors' actions were intended to defraud creditors – the inventory balance is now £1,250,000 (£750,000 + £500,000) which is just enough to cover the bank's secured loan.

The transaction will thereby effectively transfer the losses which the directors would otherwise suffer under their personal guarantees to the bank onto the company's unsecured creditors. If the transaction has been intentionally designed to achieve this outcome, the actions of Mr and Mrs Krupt would constitute fraudulent trading. The key issue in proving this would therefore be whether the evidence establishes this intent beyond reasonable doubt.

If a court were to conclude beyond reasonable doubt that it was intentional, imprisonment for up to 10 years, personal liability for the debts of the company and disqualification from being a company director for up to 15 years will all be possible penalties which the court may impose on Mr and Mrs Krupt.

Alternatively, if there is insufficient evidence of fraudulent trading, it may still be possible for creditors to bring a successful action for wrongful trading as a result of the weaker evidence test of the balance of probabilities and the fact that there is no need to establish intent. Moreover, it seems likely that an action for wrongful trading would succeed against Mr and Mrs Krupt. They are both directors of the company and there appears to be clear evidence based on the audit supervisor's findings that they ought to have realised that the creditors of the company would suffer losses.

As a result of a successful action for wrongful trading, it follows that the liquidator will be able to seize Mr and Mrs Krupt's domestic residence and other assets in order to swell the pool of assets available to distribute to all of the creditors of the company (including the unsecured creditors).

Examiner's comments

For the UK and IRL exams, this requirement was an insolvency question, the first part of which asked for the definitions and implications of fraudulent and wrongful/reckless trading. This section was disappointingly answered with the majority of candidates discussing either the concept of fraud or money laundering.

The second part of the question was the application of those definitions to a client that was clearly wrongful/reckless trading and potentially fraudulent trading. A very small minority appeared to have any knowledge of this part of the syllabus.

	ACCA Marking guide	Marks

(i) **Krupt Ltd**
Generally up to 1 mark for each point explained
Fraudulent trading:
– Definition: carrying on business of insolvent company with intent to defraud creditors
– Can apply to any person knowingly a party to fraudulent trading
– Burden of proof: beyond reasonable doubt (criminal offence)
– Penalties and liability (½ mark each):
• Imprisonment up to 10 years
• Personal (civil) liability for debts of company
• Disqualification as company director for up to 15 years

Wrongful trading:
– Definition: carrying on business of insolvent company when ought to have concluded/realised that no reasonable prospect of avoiding insolvent liquidation (and that creditors would therefore suffer losses)
– Only applies to company directors (including shadow directors)
– Burden of proof: balance of probabilities (civil wrong)
– Penalties and liability (½ mark each):
• Personal (civil) liability for debts of company
• Disqualification as company director for up to 15 years

(ii) **Implications for Krupt Ltd:**
– Mr and Mrs Krupt appear to have bought substantial quantity of goods on credit in order to ensure that bank will have sufficient secured assets to cover its debt without having to call in the personal guarantee on the directors' house; transaction will effectively transfer losses on to unsecured creditors
– Amounts look suspicious in that there is now sufficient inventory to cover the secured loan from the bank, i.e. £750,000 + £500,000 = £1,250,000 compared to a loan of £1,200,000
– If court concludes beyond reasonable doubt that this was intentional, imprisonment/personal liability/disqualification will all be possible penalties
– If court concludes insufficient evidence of fraudulent trading, it seems likely that wrongful trading will apply: Mr and Mrs Krupt are directors of company, clear evidence based on audit supervisor's findings that ought to have realised creditors would suffer losses
– liquidator will be able to seize Mr and Mrs Krupt's house (and other assets) to swell pool of assets available to distribute to all creditors of company (including unsecured)

Total — 10

67 KANDINSKY   *Walk in the footsteps of a top tutor*

Top tutor tips

Part (a) is a straightforward going concern question asking for indicators of problems and audit procedures to be performed. Here you should focus on the company's ability to pay its debts as they fall due.

Part (b) asks for alternatives to a creditor's voluntary liquidation and the implications of these. Make sure you address all parts of the requirement.

(a) Going concern matters

Revenue and profitability

The extract financial statements show that revenue has fallen by 38.2%. Based on the information provided, operating profit was £1,150,000 in 20X4 but is only £340,000 in 20X5. Operating margins have fallen from 29.1% to 13.9% during the year and the fall in revenue and margin has caused the company to become loss-making this year.

These changes are highly significant and most likely due to the economic recession which will impact particularly on the sale of luxury, non-essential products such as those sold by Kandinsky Ltd. The loss-making position does not in itself mean that the company is not a going concern, however, the trend is extremely worrying and if the company does not return to profit in the 20X6 financial year, then this would be a major concern. Few companies can sustain many consecutive loss-making periods.

Bank loan

The bank loan is significant, amounting to 33.7% of total assets this year end, and it has increased by £500,000 during the year. The company appears to be supporting operations using long-term finance, which may be strategically unsound. The loan is secured on the company's properties, so if the company defaults on the payment due in June 20X6, the bank has the right to seize the assets in order to recoup their funds. If this were to happen, Kandinsky Ltd would be left without operational facilities and it is difficult to see how the company could survive. There is also a risk that there is insufficient cash to meet interest payments due on the loan.

Trade payables

The trade payables balance has increased by 38.5%, probably due in part to the change in terms of trade with its major supplier of raw materials. An extension to the payable payment period indicates that the company is struggling to manage its operating cycle, with the cash being generated from sales being insufficient to meet working capital requirements. Relations with suppliers could be damaged if Kandinsky Ltd cannot make payments to them within agreed credit terms, with the result that suppliers could stop supplying the company or withdraw credit which would severely damage the company's operations. There is also a risk that suppliers could bring legal action against the company in an attempt to recover the amounts owed.

Borrowing facility

Kandinsky Ltd has £500,000 available in an undrawn borrowing facility, which does provide a buffer as there is a source of cash which is available, somewhat easing the going concern pressures which the company is facing. However, the availability of the borrowing facility depends on certain covenants being maintained. The calculations below show that the covenants have now been breached, so the bank is within its right to withdraw the facility, leaving Kandinsky Ltd exposed to cash shortages and possibly unable to make payments as they fall due.

	Covenant	20X5	20X4
Interest cover	2	340/520 = 0.65	1,150/500 = 2.3
Borrowings to operating profit	4:1	3,500/340 = 10.3:1	3,000/1,150 = 2.6:1

Contingent liability

The letter of support offered to a supplier of raw materials exposes Kandinsky Ltd to a possible cash outflow of £120,000, the timing of which cannot be predicted. Given the company's precarious trading position and lack of cash, satisfying the terms of the letter would result in the company utilising 80% of their current cash reserve – providing such support seems unwise, though it may have been done for a strategic reason, i.e. to secure the supply of a particular ingredient. If the financial support is called upon, it is not certain that Kandinsky Ltd would have the means to make the cash available to its supplier, which may create going concern issues for that company and would affect the supply of cane sugar to Kandinsky Ltd. There may also be legal implications for Kandinsky Ltd if the cash could not be made available if or when requested by the supplier.

Audit procedures in relation to going concern matters identified

- Obtain and review management accounts for the period after the reporting date and any interim financial accounts which have been prepared. Perform analytical review to ascertain the trends in profitability and cash flows since the year end.

- Read the minutes of the meetings of shareholders, those charged with governance and relevant committees for reference to trading and financing difficulties.

- Discuss with management the strategy which is being developed to halt the trend in declining sales and evaluate the reasonableness of the strategy in light of the economic recession and auditor's knowledge of the business.

- Review the company's current order book and assess the level of future revenue required to break-even/make a profit.

- Analyse and discuss the cash flow, profit and other relevant forecasts with management and review assumptions to ensure they are in line with management's strategy and auditor's knowledge of the business.

- Perform sensitivity analysis on the forecast financial information to evaluate the impact of changes in key variables such as interest rates, predictions of sales patterns and the timing of cash receipts from customers.

- Calculate the average payment period for trade payables and consider whether any increase is due to lack of cash or changes in the terms of trade.

- Obtain the contract in relation to the borrowing facility to confirm the covenant measures and to see if any further covenants are included in the agreement.

- Review correspondence with the bank in relation to the loan and the borrowing facility to gauge the bank's level of support for Kandinsky Ltd and for evidence of deteriorating relationships between the bank and the company's management.

- Obtain the bank loan agreement to confirm the amount of the loan, the interest rate and repayment dates and whether the charge over assets is specific or general in nature.

- Review the bank loan agreement for any clauses or covenants to determine whether there are any breaches.

- Obtain the letter of support in relation to the supplier to confirm the conditions under which Kandinsky Ltd would become liable for payment of the £120,000.

- Discuss with management the reason for the letter of support being given to the supplier to understand the business rationale and its implications, including why the supplier approached Kandinsky Ltd for the letter of support.

- Inspect minutes of management meetings where those charged with governance discussed the letter of support and authorised its issuance.

- Obtain any further documentation available in relation to the letter of support, for example, legal documentation and correspondence with the supplier, to confirm the extent of Kandinsky Ltd's involvement with the supplier and that no further amounts could become payable.

(b) The net liabilities position indicates that Viola Ltd is insolvent, meaning that if the company were to dispose of all of its assets, there would not be sufficient funds to pay off the company's liabilities. In a situation of insolvency coupled with operational difficulties like those being faced by Viola Ltd, if the company wishes to avoid liquidation the best option would be to place the company in administration.

Administration

The aim of administration is to save the company if possible. The directors seek the assistance of experts and the company continues to operate. An insolvency practitioner is appointed to act as administrator, and will effectively take control of the company in an attempt to rescue it as a going concern.

Administration protects the company from the actions of creditors while a restructuring plan is prepared. This is important for Viola Ltd, which is struggling to manage its working capital, meaning that some creditor's balances may be long overdue and the creditors may already be considering actions to recover the amounts owed.

Administration without a court order

Administration can commence without a court order. The directors themselves may be able to appoint an administrator, though this depends on the company's articles of association. Alternatively, the company (a majority of shareholders) or qualifying floating charge holders can apply for administration without going through the court. Given that Viola Ltd's bank loan is secured by a floating charge over the company's assets, the bank could have the right to appoint an administrator, depending on the terms of the floating charge. If the directors or the company commence appointing an administrator, notice must be given to any qualifying floating charge holders who are entitled to appoint an administrator.

Administration with a court order

Alternatively, administration proceedings can involve a court order. The company (a majority of shareholders), the directors, one or more creditors or in rare cases the Justice and Chief Executive of the Magistrates' Court can apply to court for an administration order. The court will consider the application and will grant the administration order if it appears that the company is unable to pay its debts.

Moratorium

Whichever method of appointment of an administrator is employed, the advantage for the company is that a moratorium over the company's debts commences. This means that no creditor can enforce their debt against the company during the period of administration and no security over the company's assets can be enforced. For Viola Ltd this would allow much needed breathing space and time to resolve the working capital problems and lack of cash.

Statement of affairs

The administrator is likely to request that the directors prepare a statement of affairs detailing all of the company's assets and liabilities, information on the company's creditors and any security over assets.

Using the statement of affairs and other information, the administrator will prepare a proposal regarding the future of the company, in which the administrator recommends either a rescue plan to save the company, or states that the company cannot be saved. The proposal must be sent to all shareholders and creditors, and the proposal will be accepted or rejected. Decisions made by the creditors during the insolvency proceedings will be made using the 'deemed consent' process which means that provided the insolvency practitioner does not receive objections from 10% or more of the creditors by value, the proposed decision will be deemed to have been taken. Alternatively, a virtual meeting or electronic communication can be used to obtain creditor consent.

For Viola Ltd, the proposal is likely to focus on the probability of obtaining the new contracts which have been tendered for, and the availability of bank finance which depends on the contracts being secured. If the contracts are secured, then it may be possible to save the company. However, in the event that the contracts are not secured and there is limited demand from other customers, the administrator may well recommend liquidation of the company.

Administration can last for up to 12 months, but the administration period will end sooner if the administration has been successful, or where there is application to court by one or more creditors or by the administrator.

Impact on directors

The impact on the directors is that they will lose control of the company and all operational decisions will be made by the administrator. The administrator has the power to remove or appoint directors.

Impact on employees

The employees will remain employed unless the administrator decides that redundancies are an appropriate measure, and this could be a feature of any proposal to save the company. It must be noted that if the administrator recommends the winding up of Viola Ltd, then the loss of jobs will be inevitable.

Voluntary liquidation

An alternative to administration is a voluntary liquidation, which can be initiated by creditors or by members. Liquidation means that the company will be wound up – the assets will be sold, proceeds used to pay the company's debts in a prescribed order, and any remaining funds would be distributed to the shareholders.

For a member's voluntary liquidation to take place, the shareholders must pass a resolution, which can be an ordinary or a special resolution depending on the articles of association. However, a member's voluntary liquidation can only take place if the directors make a declaration of solvency. This is a statutory declaration that the directors have made full enquiry into the affairs of the company, and their opinion is that it will be able to pay its debts. The declaration must also include a statement of the company's assets and liabilities. According to the information supplied, Viola Ltd is in a position of net liabilities and therefore it does not seem likely that the directors will be able to make this statement. Therefore, a member's voluntary liquidation does not appear feasible.

Conclusion

The recommendation therefore is for the company to be placed into administration, as this will protect the company from the actions of creditors and allow the administrator to consider all relevant facts before making a proposal on the future of the company.

Examiner's comments

This question presented information relating to two different clients. Initially candidates were required to identify indicators in the scenario which gave rise to going concern issues and then to state procedures to audit the going concern status of the company. In general, this was well attempted and candidates scored high marks, however those using a columnar approach tended to lack depth in their explanation of the factors identified in the question and overlooked some of the more encompassing audit procedures that did not arise from a specific scenario point.

The second part of the question was set around alternatives to insolvency for a company in financial distress. Answers to this requirement were mixed. Many candidates provided good answers, showing that they understood this syllabus area and could apply their knowledge to the scenario. Weaker answers were too vague, and some clearly did know this syllabus area well enough to provide any reasonable advice.

	ACCA Marking guide	
		Marks

(a) **Identify and explain going concern matters**
Up to 2½ marks for matter identified and explained, to include 1 mark for relevant calculations:
- Revenue, operating margins and profitability
- Bank loan
- Trade payables
- Borrowing facility
- Contingent liability

Audit procedures in respect of going concern matters
Up to 1 mark for each well explained procedure:
- Review management accounts, perform analytical review
- Read the minutes of the meetings with shareholders
- Discuss with management the strategy which is being developed to halt the trend in declining sales
- Review the company's current order book
- Analyse and discuss the cash flow, profit and other relevant forecasts with management, review assumptions
- Perform sensitivity analysis on forecast
- Calculate the average payment period for trade payables
- Obtain the contract in relation to the borrowing facility to confirm the covenant measures
- Review correspondence with the bank in relation to the loan and the borrowing facility
- Obtain the bank loan agreement to confirm the amount of the loan, the interest rate, repayment dates and charge over assets
- Review the bank loan agreement for any clauses or covenants
- Obtain any further documentation available in relation to the letter of support
- Discuss the reason for the letter of support being given to the supplier
- Inspect minutes of meetings where TCWG discussed the letter of support
- Obtain legal documentation and correspondence with the supplier to determine level of involvement with the supplier

| | **Maximum** | 13 |

(b) **Response to finance director's instructions**
Generally 1½ marks for each point explained
- Identify Viola Ltd as insolvent
- Purpose of administration
- Procedure – commencing administration without court order
- Procedure – commencing administration with a court order
- Moratorium over debts – advantage to the company
- Statement of affairs to be produced
- Administrator proposes rescue plan or liquidation
- Proposals agreed by members and creditors
- Period of administration and cessation of administration
- Impact on directors – lose control of the company
- Impact on employees – depends on recommendation of administrator
- Members' voluntary liquidation is a possibility but depends on declaration of solvency being made
- Conclusion/recommendation

| | **Maximum** | 12 |
| **Total** | | 25 |

68 HUNT & CO *Walk in the footsteps of a top tutor*

Top tutor tips

Part (a) requires knowledge of the difference between fraudulent and wrongful trading. You need to apply your knowledge to the scenario to assess whether the directors are guilty of either offence. The question also asks you to describe the impact of the compulsory liquidation for the employees and creditors. Make sure you identify all aspects of the requirement to avoid missing out on vital marks.

Part (b) (i) asks you to examine the information to determine whether the company is insolvent. This should be relatively straightforward. Consider whether the company has more liabilities than assets.

Part (b) (ii) asks you to set out the options available to the directors for the future of the company. This requires rote learned knowledge from the text book about the key aspects of liquidation and administration. The requirement specifically asks you to provide a recommendation so you must reach a conclusion as to the best way forward for the company.

(a) Personal liability of company directors

Normally, the directors of a company which is placed in liquidation do not have a personal liability for the debts of the company. However, the liquidator who is appointed to wind up the company will investigate the reasons for the insolvency, which includes an assessment of whether fraudulent or wrongful trading has taken place, in which case the directors may become liable to repay all or some of the company's debts.

Wrongful trading is defined under s.214 Insolvency Act 1986, and is the less serious of the two offences. Wrongful trading applies when:

- the company has gone into insolvent liquidation

- at some time before the commencement of the winding up of the company, the directors knew, or ought to have known, that there was no reasonable prospect that the company would avoid going into insolvent liquidation

- the directors did not take sufficient steps to minimise the potential loss to creditors.

In deciding whether or not a director of a company ought to have known or ascertained the company was insolvent, the liquidator will consider the general knowledge, skill and experience which may reasonably be expected of a reasonable diligent person carrying out the same functions as are carried out by that director. If a director has greater than usual skill, they would be judged by reference to their own capacity.

The liquidator needs to apply to the court to proceed with an action against a director for wrongful trading. If found guilty, the director faces a civil liability and can be ordered to make a contribution to the company's assets. A director is not likely to be found guilty if they can demonstrate that they took every step with a view to minimising the potential loss to the company's creditors which they ought to have taken.

Fraudulent trading is the more serious offence. Here, a director faces a criminal charge as well as a civil charge under the Insolvency Act. The definition of fraudulent trading is if in the course of the winding up of a company, it appears that any business of the company has been carried on with intent to defraud creditors of the company, or for any fraudulent purpose. Carrying on a business can include a single transaction.

It is harder to prove fraudulent trading than wrongful trading. Only those directors who took the decision to carry on the business, or played an active role are liable. If found guilty, directors may have to make personal contributions to the company's assets and the court can also impose fines or imprisonment on guilty directors.

In the case of Coxon Ltd's directors, it seems that there was a decision to continue to trade even when there were clear signs of the company's financial distress. The company continued to purchase goods even though the directors were aware of severe cash shortages and difficult trading conditions. Therefore, the liquidator is likely to conclude that there is evidence of at least wrongful trading, especially on the part of the finance director, who should have known that the company was insolvent, and did not take all steps necessary to protect creditors.

Impact of compulsory liquidation for employees and creditors

In a compulsory liquidation the employees are automatically dismissed. The liquidator effectively takes over control of the company, assuming management responsibility. The liquidator can require directors and other staff to assist with matters such as preparing and submitting the statement of affairs.

With regard to creditors, they have no involvement with the actual liquidation process, other than having the right to hold a meeting at which they appoint their choice of insolvency practitioner to act as liquidator.

The main impact of liquidation for both employees and creditors is the allocation of company assets at the end of the winding up. There is a prescribed order of priority for allocating company assets. Employees' salaries in arrears (subject to a maximum amount), pension contributions and holiday pay are all preferential creditors. This means that these amounts will be paid after liquidator's costs and fixed charge holders but before all other creditors.

Unsecured creditors and floating charge holders are paid next, followed by preference shareholders and finally members (equity shareholders). Trade creditors are likely to be unsecured creditors, so rank after employees for payment. They are protected to an extent by the 'prescribed part' which is a proportion of assets which is set aside for unsecured creditors. This means that they may not receive the full amount owed to them, but should receive a percentage of what is owed.

(b) (i) Financial position of Jay Ltd

The company is clearly suffering from a shortage of cash and is reliant on a bank overdraft to manage its working capital. It is unlikely that this situation can be sustained in the long run. However, there is a difference between a company suffering from a cash shortage and a company which is insolvent. Insolvency exists when a company is unable to pay its payables even if it sold all of its assets, in other words the company is in a position of net liabilities.

In order to determine whether Jay Ltd is insolvent it is necessary to look at its net asset or net liability position, using figures from the latest management accounts:

	£000
Property, plant and equipment	12,800
Inventory	500
Trade receivables	400
Cash	0
Long-term borrowings	(12,000)
Trade payables	(1,250)
Bank overdraft	(1,400)
Net liabilities	(950)

Jay Ltd appears to be insolvent, as it is in a position of net liabilities at 31 May 20X4.

Tutorial note

Credit will be awarded where candidates discuss further issues to do with the company being in a position of net liabilities, such as the directors needing to take care to avoid conducting wrongful trading, and the implications of it.

The management accounts show the very different results of 'Jay Sport' (JS) and 'Jay Plus' (JP). JS has clearly been badly affected by the revelation regarding one of its ingredients, with only a small amount of sales being made in the current financial year, and this business segment is loss-making overall. However, there seems to be continued demand for JP, which remains profitable. This indicates that the JP business segment may still be able to make a return for shareholders and creditors.

(ii) **The future of the company – option 1: liquidation**

It may be decided that liquidation or 'winding up' is the best course of action. In this case the company's assets will be sold and a distribution made to its creditors with the proceeds. There is an order of priority for allocating the proceeds raised. Using the information available for Jay Ltd, and ignoring liquidator's costs, the long-term borrowings are secured by a fixed charge over property and rank high in the order of priority and would be paid before the other payables. The employees' wages of £300,000 rank as a preferential creditor and are paid next. Any proceeds remaining would be paid to unsecured creditors, then any residual amount to the shareholders. It is unlikely that the shareholders would receive anything in this case.

The directors cannot themselves begin liquidation proceedings. If they decide that this would be the best course of action for Jay Ltd, they can recommend that a creditor's voluntary winding up should be instigated. In this case a liquidator is appointed by the company's creditors, and a liquidation committee comprising both shareholders and creditors is established, so that the creditors have input to the conduct of the liquidation. A member's voluntary liquidation is not an option, as this form of liquidation can only be used for a solvent company.

If the directors take no action, then a creditor may end up applying to the court for a compulsory winding up order. Any creditor who is owed more than £750 can apply for this action to take place. The directors may wish to avoid the company being placed into compulsory liquidation as this means that employees are automatically dismissed.

In any liquidation the directors will have to stand down to be replaced by the liquidator, unless the liquidator decides to retain them.

The future of the company – option 2: administration

Administration is a very different course of action. It aims to save the company, and an insolvency practitioner is appointed to take control of the company and to attempt to rescue it as a going concern. Administration protects the company from the actions of creditors while a restructuring plan is prepared.

Administration can commence without a court order. The directors themselves may be able to appoint an administrator where a company is unable to pay its debts, though this depends on the company's articles of association.

Alternatively, a majority of shareholders, the directors or one or more creditors can apply for administration through the court. It is likely to be more expensive and time consuming to apply to the court.

The administrator takes on the role of the directors, and within eight weeks of appointment must send a document to the company's shareholders and creditors in which they state their proposals for rescuing the company, or states that the company cannot be saved. In Jay Ltd's case, it is likely that the JS business segment would be discontinued, and further finance may need to be raised to support the JP segment.

Conclusions and recommendation

From the information available, it seems that the JP range is still profitable, and could represent a way for the company to remain a going concern. The damage to the JS range does not seem to have tarnished the JP products, and therefore a rescue plan for the company may be feasible.

However, further information is needed before a definite decision is made. In particular, there may be costs that the company would be committed to continue to pay in relation to JS even if that part of the business were to cease to operate, for example, non-cancellable leases. From the information provided, and assuming that no large commitments are included in the overheads of JS, I would recommend that the directors consider an administration order for the company, which will give some breathing space for an appropriate strategy to be devised.

Administration may also benefit Jay Ltd's shareholders, who will continue to own their shares in what may become a more profitable and solvent business. It may also be preferential for the creditors for the company to continue to trade, as they may be more likely to receive the amounts owed to them through the continued operation of the company compared to a forced sale of its assets.

		ACCA Marking guide	Marks
(a)		**Wrongful and fraudulent trading**	

Up to 1½ marks for each matter explained:
- Liquidator assesses reason for insolvency including director's actions
- Definition of wrongful trading
- Elements which must be proven for wrongful trading (up to 2 marks)
- Matters looked at by court to determine liability – skill and experience
- Implication of being found guilty of wrongful trading
- Definition of fraudulent trading
- Comment on or application of the above to Coxon Ltd's situation
- Employees automatically dismissed but may assist liquidator if required
- Creditors have limited role in liquidation other than ability to appoint liquidator
- Employees rank as preferential creditors
- Creditors can be secured, or unsecured and paid from prescribed part
- Details of any impairment review conducted by management

| | | **Maximum** | **12** |

(b) (i) Examine financial position and determine whether the company is insolvent

Generally 1 mark per comment:
- Calculation of net liabilities position of Jay Ltd
- Determination that Jay Ltd is insolvent
- Explanation of meaning of insolvency
- Discussion of different results of JS and JP business segments

| | | **Maximum** | **4** |

(ii) Evaluate the option available to the directors

Up to 1½ marks per comment:
- Explanation of meaning of liquidation
- Application of order of priority in allocating proceeds of liquidation
- Discussion of means of appointing an administrator
- Benefits of administration over liquidation
- Identify that a definite decision depends on further information
- Overall recommendation

| | | **Maximum** | **9** |
| **Total** | | | **25** |

69   BUTLER (A) *Walk in the footsteps of a top tutor*

Top tutor tips

Part (a) (i) requires analytical procedures to be performed to help identify going concern issues. Be careful not to spend too much time on the calculations to the detriment of talking about the issues.

Part (a) (ii) asks for audit procedures to be performed on the cash flow forecast. Procedures should focus on obtaining evidence to support the assumptions which provide the basis for the forecast. It is important to remember that these events and transactions have not yet happened and therefore cannot be agreed to supporting documentation in the same way as historical figures.

Part (b) requires the procedures involved with placing a company into compulsory liquidation and the consequences to the key stakeholder groups of doing this. This requires rote learned knowledge from the text book.

(a)   (i)   Assessment of draft statement of financial position.

Overdraft

The most obvious issue is that Butler Ltd currently does not have a positive cash balance. The statement of financial position includes an overdraft of £25 million. This lack of cash will make it difficult for the company to manage its operating cycle and make necessary interest payments, unless further cash becomes available.

Net liabilities

Butler Ltd is in a position of net liabilities, as indicated by the negative shareholders' funds figure. The company's retained earnings figure is now negative. Net liabilities and significant losses are both examples of financial conditions listed in ISA (UK) 570 *Going concern,* which may cast doubt about the going concern assumption.

Loss-making

Note 3 indicates that Butler Ltd has been loss-making for several years. Recurring losses are a further indication of going concern problems. Few companies can sustain many consecutive loss-making periods.

Overstatement of assets

There are several items recognised in the statement of financial position, which, if adjusted, would make the net liabilities position worse. For example, a deferred tax asset is recognised at £235 million. This asset should only be recognised if Butler Ltd can demonstrate that future profits will be sufficient to enable the recoverability of the asset. As Butler Ltd has been loss-making for several years, it is arguable that this asset should not be recognised at all.

Additionally, an intangible asset relating to development costs of £120 million is recognised. One of the criteria for the capitalisation of such costs is that adequate resources exist for completion of the development. Given Butler Ltd's lack of cash, this criteria may no longer be applicable. If adjustments were made to write off these assets, the net liabilities would become £580 million.

Fixed charge

Note 2 indicates that fixed charges exist over assets valued at £25 million. If Butler Ltd fails to make repayments to the creditor holding the charge over assets, the assets could be seized, disrupting the operations of Butler Ltd.

Liabilities due for repayment

There are significant short-term borrowings due for repayment – notably a bank loan of £715 million due for repayment in September 20X1. It is hard to see how Butler Ltd will be able to repay this loan given its current lack of cash. The cash flow forecast does not indicate that sufficient cash is likely to be generated post year end to enable this loan to be repaid.

Provisions

Provisions have been classified as non-current liabilities. Given that the provisions relate to customer warranties, it is likely that some of the provisions balance should be classified as a current liability. This potential incorrect presentation impacts on assessment of liquidity, as incorrect classification will impact on the cash flow required to meet the warranties obligation.

Butler Ltd's poor financial position means it is unlikely to be able to raise finance from a third party.

Assessment of cash flow forecast

From an overall point of view, the cash flow forecast indicates that by the end of August, Butler Ltd will still be in a negative cash position. As discussed above, this is particularly concerning given that a loan of £715 million is due to be repaid in September.

Cash receipts from customers

The assumption relating to cash receipts from customers seems optimistic. It is too simplistic to assume that anticipated economic recovery will lead to a sudden improvement in cash collection from customers, even if additional resources are being used for credit control.

Inflows currently being negotiated

£200 million of the cash receipts for this three-month period relate to loans and subsidies which are currently being negotiated and applied for. These cash inflows are not guaranteed, and if not received, the overall cash position at the end of the period will be much worse than currently projected.

Financial assets

The cash inflow for June 20X1 includes the proceeds of a sale of financial assets of £50 million. It is questionable whether this amount of cash will be generated, given the financial assets are recognised on the statement of financial position at £25 million. The assumed sales value of £50 million may be overly optimistic.

Conclusion

In conclusion, the cash flow forecast may not be reliable, in that assumptions are optimistic, and the additional funding is not guaranteed. This means that three months into the next financial year, the company's cash position is likely to have worsened, and loans and trade payables which are due for payment are likely to remain unpaid. This casts significant doubt as to the ability of Butler Ltd to continue operating as a going concern.

Tutorial note

Credit will be awarded for calculation and explanation of appropriate ratios relevant to Butler Ltd's going concern status.

(ii)   Recommended audit procedures:

- Discuss with management the reasons for assuming that cash collection from customers will improve due to 'anticipated improvement in economic conditions'. Consider the validity of the reasons in light of business understanding.

- Enquire as to the nature of the additional resources to be devoted to the credit control function, e.g. details of extra staff recruited.

- For the loan receipt, inspect written documentation relating to the request for finance from Rubery Ltd. Request written confirmation from Rubery Ltd regarding the amount of finance and the date it will be received, as well as any terms and conditions.

- Obtain and review the financial statements of Rubery Ltd, to consider if it has sufficient resources to provide the amount of loan requested.

- For the subsidy, inspect the application made to the subsidy awarding body and confirm the amount of the subsidy.

- Read any correspondence between Butler Ltd and the subsidy awarding body, specifically looking for confirmation that the subsidy will be granted.

- Regarding operating expenses, verify using previous months' management accounts, that operating cash outflows are approximately £200 million per month.

- Enquire as to the reason for the increase in operating cash outflows in August 20X1.

- Verify, using previous months' management accounts, that interest payments of £40 million per month appear reasonable.

- Confirm, using the loan agreement, the amount of the loan being repaid in August 20X1.

- Enquire whether any tax payments are due in the three-month period, such as VAT.

- Agree the opening cash position to bank ledger account/cash book and bank statement/bank reconciliation, and cast the cash flow forecast.

- Ensure that a cash flow forecast for the full financial year is received as three months' forecast is inadequate for the purposes of the audit.

- Enquire if those charged with governance have assessed the going concern assumption for a period of 12 months from the date of approval of the financial statements.

Tutorial note

Marks would also be awarded for the more general procedures required under ISA 570 in relation to audit procedures on a cash flow forecast, such as evaluation of the reliability of underlying data, and requesting a written representation regarding the feasibility of plans for future action.

Conclusion

The review of the draft statement of financial position and cash flow forecast shows that there are many factors indicating that Butler Ltd is experiencing going concern problems. In particular, the lack of cash, and the significant amounts due to be paid within a few months of the year end cast significant doubt over the use of the going concern assumption in the financial statements. The company has requested finance from its parent company, but even if this is forthcoming, cash flow remains a significant problem.

(b) **(i)** A company is usually placed into compulsory liquidation by a payable (creditor), who uses compulsory liquidation as a means to recover monies owed by the company. The payable (creditor) must petition the court and the petition is advertised in the *London Gazette. There* are various grounds for a petition to be made for compulsory liquidation. The most common ground is that the company is unable to pay its debts. In this case the payable (creditor) must show that he or she is owed more than £750 by the company and has served on the company at its registered office a written demand for payment. This is called a statutory demand. If the company fails to pay the statutory demand in 21 days and does not dispute the debt, then the payable (creditor) may present a winding up petition at court.

The application for a winding up order will be granted at a court hearing where it can be proven to the court's satisfaction that the debt is undisputed, attempts to recover have been undertaken and the company has neglected to pay the amount owed.

On a compulsory winding up the court will appoint an Official Receiver, who is an officer of the court. Within a few days of the winding up order being granted by the court, the Official Receiver must inform the company directors of the situation. The court order is also advertised in the *London Gazette.*

The Official Receiver takes over the control of the company and usually begins to close it down. The company's directors are asked to prepare a statement of affairs. The Official Receiver must also investigate the causes of the failure of the company.

The liquidation is deemed to have started at the date of the presentation of the winding up petition.

At the end of the winding up of the company, a final return is filed with the court and the Registrar. At this point the company is dissolved.

Tutorial note

Credit will be awarded to candidates who explain other, less common, means by which a company may face a compulsory liquidation:

A shareholder may serve a petition for compulsory liquidation. The grounds for doing so would normally be based on the fact that that the shareholder is dissatisfied with the management of the company, and that it is therefore just and equitable to wind up the company. This action by the shareholder is only allowed if the company is solvent and if the shareholder has been a shareholder for at least six months prior to the petition.

Very occasionally, if the Crown believes that a company is contravening legislation such as the Trading Standards legislation or is acting against the public or government interest, it is possible for the company to be liquidated compulsorily. This is very serious action to take and is not used very regularly.

(ii)   Payables (creditors) – The role of the Official Receiver (or Insolvency Practitioner, if appointed), is to realise the company's assets, and to distribute the proceeds in a prescribed order. Depending on the amount of cash available for distribution, and whether the debt is secured or unsecured, payables (creditors) may receive some, all, or none of the amount owed to them.

Employees – All employees of the company are automatically dismissed. A prescribed amount of unpaid employee's wages, accrued holiday pay, and contributions to an occupational pension fund rank as preferential debts, and will be paid before payables (creditors) of the company.

Shareholders – Any surplus that remains after the payment of all other amounts owed by the company is distributed to the shareholders. In most liquidations the shareholders receive nothing.

		ACCA Marking guide	
			Marks

(a) **(i)** **Going concern matters**

Up to 1½ marks per matter identified and explained (maximum 3 marks for identification):

- Negative cash position
- Net liabilities position
- Recurring losses
- Possible adjustment to deferred tax and development intangible asset exacerbate net liabilities position (allow 3 marks max)
- Fixed charge over assets
- Significant short term liabilities
- Potential misclassified provisions
- Forecast to remain in negative cash position
- Assumptions re sales optimistic
- Receipt of loan and subsidy not guaranteed
- Assumption of sale value of financial assets could be optimistic

		Maximum	**10**

(ii) **Procedures on cash flow forecast**

1 mark per specific procedure:

- Enquire regarding and consider validity of assumption re cash sales
- Inspect any supporting documentation re additional resources for credit control
- Seek written confirmation from Rubery Ltd re loan
- Review financial statements of Rubery Ltd re adequacy of resources
- Inspect subsidy application
- Seek third-party confirmation that subsidy will be awarded
- Confirm cash outflows for operating expenses and interest appear reasonable
- Enquire about potentially missing cash outflows
- Agree date and amount of short term loan repayment to loan documentation
- Agree opening cash to bank ledger account/cash book and bank statements

		Maximum	**8**

(b) **(i)** **Procedures for compulsory liquidation**

1 mark each point explained:

- Creditors petition court for winding-up order
- Grounds for the petition must be demonstrated – usually an unpaid statutory demand
- Court appoints an Official Receiver
- Official Receiver informs company directors and takes control of company
- Shareholders can apply for compulsory liquidation (rare)
- The Crown can apply for compulsory liquidation (very rare)

		Maximum	**4**

(ii) **Consequences for stakeholders**

1 mark each consequence explained:

- Payables (creditors)
- Employees
- Shareholders

		Maximum	**3**
Total			**25**

INT SYLLABUS ONLY

70   **KANDINSKY** *Walk in the footsteps of a top tutor*

Top tutor tips

Part (a) is a straightforward going concern question asking for indicators of problems and audit procedures to be performed. Here you should focus on the company's ability to pay its debts as they fall due.

Part (b) asks for a discussion of the relevance and measurability of the reported performance information. You need to think about whether the various stakeholder groups would be interested in such information or whether there is other information they would prefer to see (relevance). For measurability, think about whether the information would be readily available to report. Organisations may wish to report on performance matters but if that information is not reliably captured by the information systems the credibility of such information will be called into question.

(a)   (i)   **Going concern matters**

Revenue and profitability

The extract financial statements show that revenue has fallen by 38.2%. Based on the information provided, operating profit was $1,150,000 in 20X4 but is only $340,000 in 20X5. Operating margins have fallen from 29.1% to 13.9% during the year and the fall in revenue and margin has caused the company to become loss-making this year.

These changes are highly significant and most likely due to the economic recession which will impact particularly on the sale of luxury, non-essential products such as those sold by Kandinsky Co. The loss-making position does not in itself mean that the company is not a going concern, however, the trend is extremely worrying and if the company does not return to profit in the 20X6 financial year, then this would be a major concern. Few companies can sustain many consecutive loss-making periods.

Bank loan

The bank loan is significant, amounting to 33.7% of total assets this year end, and it has increased by $500,000 during the year. The company appears to be supporting operations using long-term finance, which may be strategically unsound. The loan is secured on the company's properties, so if the company defaults on the payment due in June 20X6, the bank has the right to seize the assets in order to recoup their funds. If this were to happen, Kandinsky Co would be left without operational facilities and it is difficult to see how the company could survive. There is also a risk that there is insufficient cash to meet interest payments due on the loan.

Trade payables

The trade payables balance has increased by 38.5%, probably due in part to the change in terms of trade with its major supplier of raw materials. An extension to the payable payment period indicates that the company is struggling to manage its operating cycle, with the cash being generated from sales being insufficient to meet working capital requirements. Relations with suppliers could be damaged if Kandinsky Co cannot make payments to them within agreed credit terms, with the result that suppliers could stop supplying the company or withdraw credit which would severely damage the company's operations. There is also a risk that suppliers could bring legal action against the company in an attempt to recover the amounts owed.

Borrowing facility

Kandinsky Co has $500,000 available in an undrawn borrowing facility, which does provide a buffer as there is a source of cash which is available, somewhat easing the going concern pressures which the company is facing. However, the availability of the borrowing facility depends on certain covenants being maintained. The calculations below show that the covenants have now been breached, so the bank is within its right to withdraw the facility, leaving Kandinsky Co exposed to cash shortages and possibly unable to make payments as they fall due.

	Covenant	20X5	20X4
Interest cover	2	340/520 = 0.65	1150/500 = 2.3
Borrowings to operating profit	4:1	3,500/340 = 10.3:1	3,000/1,150 = 2.6:1

Contingent liability

The letter of support offered to a supplier of raw materials exposes Kandinsky Co to a possible cash outflow of $120,000, the timing of which cannot be predicted. Given the company's precarious trading position and lack of cash, satisfying the terms of the letter would result in the company utilising 80% of their current cash reserve. Providing such support seems unwise, though it may have been done for a strategic reason, i.e. to secure the supply of a particular ingredient. If the financial support is called upon, it is not certain that Kandinsky Co would have the means to make the cash available to its supplier, which may create going concern issues for that company and would affect the supply of cane sugar to Kandinsky Co. There may also be legal implications for Kandinsky Co if the cash could not be made available if or when requested by the supplier.

(ii) **Audit procedures in relation to going concern matters identified**

- Obtain and review management accounts for the period after the reporting date and any interim financial accounts which have been prepared. Perform analytical review to ascertain the trends in profitability and cash flows since the year end.

- Read the minutes of the meetings of shareholders, those charged with governance and relevant committees for reference to trading and financing difficulties.

- Discuss with management the strategy which is being developed to halt the trend in declining sales and evaluate the reasonableness of the strategy in light of the economic recession and auditor's knowledge of the business.

- Review the company's current order book and assess the level of future revenue required to breakeven/make a profit.

- Analyse and discuss the cash flow, profit and other relevant forecasts with management and review assumptions to ensure they are in line with management's strategy and auditor's knowledge of the business.

- Perform sensitivity analysis on the forecast financial information to evaluate the impact of changes in key variables such as interest rates, predictions of sales patterns and the timing of cash receipts from customers.

- Calculate the average payment period for trade payables and consider whether any increase is due to lack of cash or changes in the terms of trade.

- Obtain the contract in relation to the borrowing facility to confirm the covenant measures and to see if any further covenants are included in the agreement.

- Review correspondence with the bank in relation to the loan and the borrowing facility to gauge the bank's level of support for Kandinsky Co and for evidence of deteriorating relationships between the bank and the company's management.

- Obtain the bank loan agreement to confirm the amount of the loan, the interest rate and repayment dates and whether the charge over assets is specific or general in nature.

- Review the bank loan agreement for any clauses or covenants to determine whether there are any breaches.

- Obtain the letter of support in relation to the supplier to confirm the conditions under which Kandinsky Co would become liable for payment of the $120,000.

- Discuss with management the reason for the letter of support being given to the supplier to understand the business rationale and its implications, including why the supplier approached Kandinsky Co for the letter of support.

- Inspect minutes of management meetings where those charged with governance discussed the letter of support and authorised its issuance.

- Obtain any further documentation available in relation to the letter of support, for example, legal documentation and correspondence with the supplier, to confirm the extent of Kandinsky Co's involvement with the supplier and that no further amounts could become payable.

(b)   (i)   The relevance and measurability of the reported performance information

Relevance

Performance information should be relevant to the users of that information. In the case of Rothko University, there is likely to be a wide range of interested parties including current and potential students who will be interested in the quality of the teaching provided and the likelihood of securing employment on completion of the university course. Other interested parties will include the government body which provides funding to the University, regulatory bodies which oversee higher education and any organisations which support the University's work, for example, graduate employers.

For current and potential students, performance measures such as the graduation rate and employability rate will be relevant as this will provide information on the success of students in completing their degree programmes and subsequently obtaining a job. This is important because students pay tuition fees to attend Rothko University and they will want to know if the investment in education is likely to result in employment. However, some students may be more interested in further study after graduation, so employability measures would be less relevant to them.

Students will be interested in the proportion of graduates who achieve a distinction as this may lead to better job prospects and a better return on the investment (of time and money) in their education.

Finally, students will find the performance measure on course satisfaction relevant because it indicates that the majority of students rated the quality of the course as high, an important factor in deciding whether to enrol onto a degree programme.

Stakeholders other than current and potential students may find other performance information more relevant to them, for example, potential graduate employers may be interested in the amount of work experience which is provided on the University's degree programme.

The performance measures are most relevant where they can be compared to the measures of other universities. Currently, the University has not provided comparative information and this is likely to make it difficult to assess the performance of the University over time and also makes the current year measures harder to gauge.

Measurability

In terms of measurability, as with many key performance indicators, it is sometimes difficult to precisely define or measure the performance information. Some of the measures are quite subjective, for example, the rating which a student gives to a course is down to personal opinion and it is difficult to substantiate, for example, the difference between a course rating of excellent and very good. Similarly, defining 'graduate level employment' could be subjective. Some measures will be easier to quantify, for example, the degree completion percentage, which will be based on fact rather than opinion.

There may also be problems in how the information is gathered, affecting the validity of the information. For example, only a sample of students may have completed a course evaluation, and possibly the most satisfied students were selected which will improve the measure.

(ii) **Examination procedures**

- Obtain a list detailing all of the University's performance objectives and the basis of measurement for each objective.

- Enquire of the University whether comparative information is available and if this information needs to be verified as part of the disclosure in the current year.

- For the graduation rate, obtain a list of students awarded degrees in 20X5, and a list of all students who registered on the degree programme and use this information to recalculate the %.

- For academic performance, review minutes of meetings where degree results were discussed and approval given for the award of distinction to a number of students.

- For a sample of students awarded a distinction, confirm each student's exam results to supporting documentation, e.g. information in their student files, notices of exam results sent to the student and confirm that the grades achieved qualify for a distinction being awarded.

- Inspect any documentation issued at events such as degree award ceremonies to confirm the number of students being awarded a distinction.

- Obtain supporting documentation from the University for the employability rate and discuss with appropriate personnel, for example, the careers centre, the basis of the determination of the rate.

- For the employability rate, a confirmation could be sent to a sample of students asking for the details of their post-graduation employment.

- If the University supplies references for students seeking employment, inspect the references issued in 20X5 and contact the relevant company to see if the student was offered employment.

- For course satisfaction, inspect the questionnaires or surveys completed by students from which the % was derived, and recalculate.

- Enquire if there is any other supporting documentation on course satisfaction, for example, minutes of student and lecturer meetings about the quality of courses.

Examiner's comments

This question presented information relating to two different clients. Initially candidates were required to identify indicators in the scenario which gave rise to going concern issues and then to state procedures to audit the going concern status of the company. In general, this was well attempted and candidates scored high marks, however those using a columnar approach tended to lack depth in their explanation of the factors identified in the question and overlooked some of the more encompassing audit procedures that did not arise from a specific scenario point.

The second part of the question focused on the audit of performance information and required candidates to discuss the relevance and measurability of key performance indicators (KPIs) in respect of a University and to describe how they might be audited. Well prepared candidates were able to discuss the issues surrounding measuring and determining relevant performance information and were able to draw on the information included in the recent examiner's article on this topic to the scenario. Some candidates did not focus on the question requirement and attempted to describe the theory of public sector KPIs. Many candidates were unprepared and left this requirement out altogether.

ACCA Marking guide				
				Marks
(a)	(i)	**Identify and explain going concern matters** Up to 2½ marks for matter identified and explained, to include 1 mark for relevant calculations: – Revenue, operating margins and profitability – Bank loan – Trade payables – Borrowing facility – Contingent liability		
			Maximum	**9**
	(ii)	**Audit procedures in respect of going concern matters** Up to 1 mark for each well explained procedure: – Review management accounts, perform analytical review – Read the minutes of the meetings with shareholders – Discuss with management the strategy which is being developed to halt the trend in declining sales – Review the company's current order book – Analyse and discuss the cash flow, profit and other relevant forecasts with management, review assumptions – Perform sensitivity analysis on forecast – Calculate the average payment period for trade payables – Obtain the contract in relation to the borrowing facility to confirm the covenant measures – Review correspondence with the bank in relation to the loan and the borrowing facility – Obtain the bank loan agreement to confirm the amount of the loan, the interest rate, repayment dates and charge over assets – Review the bank loan agreement for any clauses or covenants – Obtain any further documentation available in relation to the letter of support – Discuss the reason for the letter of support being given to the supplier – Inspect minutes of meetings where TCWG discussed the letter of support – Obtain legal documentation and correspondence with the supplier to determine level of involvement with the supplier		
			Maximum	**6**

(b) **(i)** **The relevance and measurability of the reported performance information**

Generally up to 1 mark for each point explained:

– 1 mark for explaining why each measure would be relevant to an existing or potential student (4 measures in total, so maximum 4 marks)
– Problems in defining the measures
– Problems in quantifying the measures – some are subjective
– Issues in validity of the reported information
– Lack of comparative information

(ii) **Examination procedures**

Up to 1 mark for well described procedures:

– Obtain a list detailing all of the University's performance objectives and the basis of measurement for each objective
– Discuss with University the availability of comparative information and requirement to include in current year report
– For the graduation rate, obtain a list of students awarded degrees in 20X5, and a list of all students who registered on the degree programme and use this information to recalculate the %
– For academic performance, review minutes of meetings where degree results were discussed and approval given for the award of distinction to a number of students
– Agree a sample of students' exam results to supporting documentation, e.g. information in their student files, notices of exam results sent to the students
– Inspect any documentation issued at events such as degree award ceremonies to confirm the number of students being awarded a distinction
– Obtain supporting documentation from the University for the employability rate and discuss with appropriate personnel, for example, the careers centre, the basis of the determination of the rate
– For the employability rate, a confirmation could be sent to a sample of students asking for the details of their post-graduation employment
– If the University supplies references for students seeking employment, inspect the references issued in 20X5 and contact the relevant company to see if the student was offered employment
– For course satisfaction, inspect the questionnaires or surveys completed by students from which the % was derived, and recalculate
– Enquire if there is any other supporting documentation on course satisfaction, for example, minutes of student and lecturer meetings about the quality of courses

Maximum	10
Total	25

71   PUBLIC SECTOR ORGANISATIONS   *Walk in the footsteps of a top tutor*

Top tutor tips

This question is not taken from a previous exam, but has been added to the exam kit to give you the opportunity to practise requirements relating to the INT syllabus area of public sector performance information.

(a)   **Performance audits** aim to provide management with assurance and advice regarding the effective functioning of its operational activities.

Performance information is information published by public sector bodies regarding their objectives and the achievement of those objectives.

(b)   **Performance targets**

   (i)   **Local police department**

   - Reduce the number of crimes by x%

   - Reduce the number of offenders re-offending by x%

   - Reduce the number of deaths caused by dangerous driving x%

   - Increase public satisfaction to x%

   (ii)   **Local hospital**

   - Reduce emergency department waiting times to a maximum of x hours

   - Reduce the maximum waiting time for an operation to x weeks

   - Reduce the number of infections contracted in the hospital by x%

   - Reduce the number of re-admissions to hospital by x%

   (iii)   **Local council**

   - Increase public satisfaction to x%

   - To build x number of council houses in the next 5 years

   - To spend $x on road maintenance and improvements each year

   - To increase council tax by a maximum of the rate of inflation

Tutorial note

Credit will be awarded for any other relevant examples.

A target does not have to be SMART. Targets are typically more generalised than an objective.

(c) **Stakeholder groups**

(i) **Police department**

Stakeholder	Use
Government e.g. Home Office	To ensure that police departments are achieving the targets set by the government.
	To report to taxpayers on how government money in this area is being used to achieve the stated objectives.
Local residents	Residents may wish to know the level of crime in their area to assess the performance of their local police department.
Prospective residents	Prospective residents may use such information to decide whether to move to a particular town/city. If the crime rate is high they may decide not to move there.

(ii) **Local hospital**

Local residents	To assess the performance of their local hospital as this will be of importance if they were ever to be admitted to hospital.
Patients awaiting treatment	Patients awaiting treatment may have a choice of hospital from which to receive treatment. In this case, patients are likely to choose the option with the lowest infection rates, highest success rates for a particular operation/procedure, or the quickest treatment time.
Government e.g. Department for Health	To ensure that hospitals are achieving the targets set by the government.
	To report to taxpayers on how government money in this area is being used to achieve the stated objectives.

(iii) **Local council**

Local residents	To assess the performance of their local council and how their taxes are being used.
Suppliers/contractors	Suppliers/contractors will be interested to see the plans for the future to assess if there will be additional work being tendered. For example if the council has set a target to build an additional 1000 houses in the coming year, local building firms may be able to bid for the work.
Government e.g. Department for Communities and Local Government	To ensure that councils are achieving the targets set by the government.
	To report to taxpayers on how government money in this area is being used to achieve the stated objectives.

Tutorial note

Credit will be awarded for any other relevant examples e.g. employees to assess whether there is the possibility of redundancies if the target is to reduce costs significantly.

(d) **Difficulties**

All relevant information may not be reported (e.g. number of crimes or number of hospital infections) therefore it may appear as though there has been improvement when problems may not have been recorded completely.

Where information is completely recorded, accuracy of the information may be an issue. The public sector organisation needs to have good internal controls in place in respect of this information in the same way as internal controls would be expected to be in place in respect of financial information.

Definitions of certain targets and measures may be ambiguous resulting in matters going un-recorded due to public sector employees recording the information in a different way. Information may be classified differently by different members of staff unless specific training is given.

Even so, information may not be comparable between different police departments/ hospitals/councils if each interpret the definitions in a different way.

There is also the risk that public sector departments will falsify the figures that have been reported if they are failing to meet the targets set by the government. This may be difficult for the auditor to detect as it is unlikely there will be alternative forms of corroborative evidence to highlight discrepancies.

ACCA Marking guide		Marks

(a) **Definitions**
Up to 1 for each definition
  –   Performance audit
  – Performance information		

	Maximum	2
(b) **Performance targets** 1 mark per performance target. Max of 3 per public sector body.		
	Maximum	9
(c) **Stakeholder groups** ½ mark per stakeholder group and 1 mark per reason for using the performance information.		
	Maximum	9

(d)	**Difficulties** Up to 1½ per point made. – Completeness – Accuracy – Ambiguity of targets – Comparability – Risk of falsification	
	Maximum	5
Total		25

Section 5

SPECIMEN EXAM QUESTIONS

ALL THREE questions are compulsory and MUST be attempted

1   **CRUX GROUP** *Walk in the footsteps of a top tutor*

It is 1 July 20X5. You are a manager in the audit department of Pegasus & Co, a firm of Chartered Certified Accountants. You are assigned to the audit of the Crux Group (the Group), which has a financial year ending 30 September 20X5, and is a listed entity.

Pegasus & Co was appointed auditor to the Group in January 20X5.

The Group operates in the travel industry, offering a selection of worldwide itineraries and has a fleet of 20 cruise ships. The Group operates three brands which provide different types of cruise experience.

The following exhibits provide information relevant to the question:

1   Partner's email – an email which you have received from Norma Star, the Group audit engagement partner.

2   Background information – information and matters relevant to audit planning.

3   Selected financial information – extracts from the Group management accounts.

4   Audit team meeting notes – extracts from meeting notes taken at a recent audit team meeting.

This information should be used to answer the question requirement within your chosen response option(s).

Required: **(50 marks)**

Respond to the instructions in the email from the audit engagement partner.

Note: The split of the mark allocation is shown in Exhibit 1 – Partner's email.   (40 marks)

Professional marks will be awarded for the demonstration of skill in communication, analysis and evaluation, professional scepticism and judgement and commercial acumen in your answer.   (10 marks)

Exhibit 1 – Partner's email

To:	**Audit manager**
From:	**Norma Star, Audit engagement partner**
Subject:	**Audit planning for the Crux Group**
Date:	**1 July 20X5**

Hello

I have provided you with some information which you should use to help you with planning the audit of our new client, the Crux Group (the Group), for the financial year ending 30 September 20X5. Based on the analysis I have done on this industry, it is appropriate for overall materiality to be based on the profitability of the Group as this is a key focus for investors and providers of finance.

I require you to prepare briefing notes for my own use, in which you:

(a) Using the information in all exhibits, evaluate and prioritise the significant audit risks to be considered in planning the Group audit.

Note: You are NOT required to consider audit risks relating to foreign exchange transactions and balances as this will be planned separately. **(25 marks)**

(b) Design the principal audit procedures to be performed on the segmental information relating to the Group's revenue. **(5 marks)**

Using the information in Exhibit 4:

(c) Evaluate the matters to be considered in deciding whether Pegasus & Co should accept the engagement to provide advice on the Group's social and environmental information. **(10 marks)**

Thank you.

Exhibit 2 – Background information

Group operations

The Group operates cruises under three brands which offer passengers a variety of cruise itineraries with a wide choice of destinations. Cruises typically last for two weeks, though some last for up to six weeks.

The brands are internally generated and therefore are not recognised as intangible assets within the Group financial statements.

Information about the three brands operated by the Group is as follows:

Sunseeker Cruises – Cruises which visit beach destinations in the Caribbean, Europe and North America.

Explorer Cruises – Cruises which focus on visiting cities and landmarks around the world.

Pioneer Cruises – Cruises which take in areas of natural beauty including the Antarctic and Alaska.

Business developments in the year

Sunseeker Cruises

In this financial year, the Group will spend $75 million on upgrading and maintenance of the Sunseeker Cruise ships. These luxury ships have to adhere to a very high standard, so the Group regularly incurs high expenditure on their maintenance. As well as refurbishment, several ships have been enhanced by the installation of new entertainment facilities including cinemas and gyms. Equipment in the gyms will need to be replaced on average every three years.

Explorer Cruises

The Explorer Cruise ships, while still luxurious, are the oldest ships in the fleet, and the Group is gradually replacing these with new ships. During this financial year, two new ships with a total cost of $110 million will come into use. The ships took three years to build, and were constructed by Vela Shipbuilders Co, a company which is not owned by the Group. However, the chairman of the Group, Max Draco, is also the chairman of Vela Shipbuilders Co, and his son is the company's chief executive officer. The purchase of the ships was financed through a $110 million loan with a fixed interest rate of 6% per annum. A further three ships are currently under construction by Vela Shipbuilders Co. The Group has taken out a loan of $180 million with a 6.5% fixed interest rate to finance this capital expenditure.

Pioneer Cruises

These cruises are for more adventurous travellers and are growing in popularity. In order to visit certain destinations on these specialist cruises, the Group has to acquire operating licences from the local governments. The cost of licence acquisition is capitalised as an intangible asset.

Exhibit 3 – Selected financial information

	Note	Projected to 30 September 20X5 $ million	Actual to 30 September 20X4 $ million
Group revenue	1	764	670
Operating profit		145	101
Profit before tax		**81**	**65**
Total assets		**1,800**	**1,780**
Included in total assets:			
Intangible assets – operating licences	2	56	57
Property, plant and equipment	3	1,520	1,510

Note 1

Revenue includes passenger ticket sales, which accounts for approximately 85% of revenue. When customers book a cruise, they are required to pay a refundable 20% deposit which is initially recognised as deferred revenue. The balance of 80% is paid at least six weeks before the cruise commences and at that point it is also recognised as deferred revenue. The full amount of the ticket price is transferred to revenue when the cruise starts irrespective of the duration of the cruise.

The remaining 15% of revenue is derived from on-board sales of food, drinks, entertainment and other items to passengers. Management monitor this revenue stream closely as it achieves a high gross profit margin, and staff are encouraged to maximise these sales to customers.

Revenue is presented on a segmental basis in the notes to the financial statements, with segments based on the three brands of the Group:

Revenue per operating segment	Projected to 30 September 20X5 $ million	Actual to 30 September 20X4 $ million
Sunseeker Cruises	320	288
Explorer Cruises	180	190
Pioneer Cruises	264	192
Total	**764**	**670**

Note 2

Operating licences are required for the Pioneer Cruise ships to visit certain destinations. Licences are amortised over the specific period to which each licence relates.

Note 3

Property, plant and equipment is comprised as follows:

Property, plant and equipment	Projected to 30 September 20X5	Actual to 30 September 20X4
	$ million	$ million
Ships in use	2,041	2,010
Ships under construction	83	62
Other property, plant and equipment	180	173
	2,304	2,245
Accumulated depreciation	(784)	(735)
Carrying amount	**1,520**	**1,510**

Exhibit 4 – Audit team meeting notes

A meeting took place yesterday in which the audit engagement partner discussed several issues:

Recent development affecting Pioneer Cruises

Last week, the governments of several countries which form a major part of the Pioneer Cruise itineraries withdrew their operating licences with immediate effect. The governments have stated that this is likely to be a temporary measure being put in place to limit the number of tourists visiting areas of natural beauty, but they will not confirm when the Group can resume operations in these countries.

Cyber-security attack

Last month, the Group suffered a cyber-security attack in which the personal information of 1,400 customers, including their credit card details, were stolen. According to a representative of the Group audit committee, the Group's internal audit team had not properly assessed the risks relating to cyber-security, which is a requirement of recently introduced data protection legislation in the jurisdiction in which the Group operates. The issue which led to the cyber-security attack has now been resolved.

Social and environmental information

The Group audit committee has enquired whether Pegasus & Co can provide an additional service, to advise management on how to measure certain social and environmental information which is to be published on the Group's website and is required by new regulations in the industry and is required to be submitted to regulatory authorities. The social and environmental information relates to matters such as water efficiency, energy consumption, charitable donations and initiatives which support diversity in the workplace. In recognition that this work is quite urgent, as the deadline for submission to the regulatory authorities falls within the next month, the Group audit committee has stated it is willing to pay an 'enhanced fee' for this service.

END OF QUESTION

2   WELFORD & CO   *Walk in the footsteps of a top tutor*

It is 1 July 20X5. You are an audit manager in Welford & Co, a firm of Chartered Certified Accountants. Your role includes performing post-issuance audit quality reviews, and you have been asked to review the audit work performed on Rivers Co for the financial year ended 31 January 20X5.

The following exhibits, available below, provide information relevant to the question:

1   Team and fees – information regarding the audit team composition, the time spent on the audit and fees charged to the client.

2   Going concern – details some matters you have identified during your review of the going concern section of the audit file.

This information should be used to answer the question requirement within the response option provided.

Requirement:

Evaluate the quality of the planning and performance of the audit of Rivers Co, discussing the quality management, ethical and other professional issues raised and recommending appropriate actions to be taken.   **(20 marks)**

Professional marks will be awarded for the demonstration of skill in analysis and evaluation, professional scepticism and judgement and commercial acumen in your answer.   **(5 marks)**

(Total: 25 marks)

Exhibit 1 – Team and fees

Rivers Co is a listed company operating in the construction industry. The company complies with corporate governance regulations and has an audit committee. Rivers Co has been an audit client of Welford & Co for eight years (INT)/six years (UK), and Bob Newbold has been the audit engagement partner during this time.

Rivers Co's auditor's report was signed by Bob Newbold and issued last week. The report contained an unmodified opinion.

Welford & Co requires its staff to record each hour they spend working on each client in the firm's time management system. From reviewing the time records relating to the audit of Rivers Co, you are aware that Bob and the other audit team members recorded the following amount of time on the audit:

Bob Newbold – audit engagement partner	2 hours
Pat Canley – senior audit manager	6 hours
Anesa Kineton – audit manager	35 hours
Six audit assistants	130 hours
	————
Total time spent on audit	**173 hours**
	————

It is apparent from your review that almost all of the detailed review of the audit working papers was completed by Anesa Kineton, who has evidenced her review by stating 'final review' on each page of the audit file. She has recently been promoted to audit manager.

You are also aware that Bob Newbold booked a total of 40 hours to Rivers Co in respect of non-audit work performed. The only information you can find in the documentation is that the non-audit work related to a 'special investigation', and that Bob confirms that it does not create a threat to auditor objectivity.

The total fee charged for the audit was $250,000 and the fee for the 'special investigation' was $890,000.

Exhibit 2 – Going concern

From reviewing the audit working papers, you are aware that going concern was identified as a significant audit risk at the planning stage of the audit due to low profit margins or losses being made on many of the company's construction contracts and increasing economic uncertainty. The company typically has 20 contracts ongoing at any time.

Most of the audit work on going concern was performed by Mary Loxley, an audit assistant who has just taken her last professional exam and is not yet qualified. The majority of the audit work performed on going concern focused on a review of five major contracts to determine their profitability. The management of Rivers Co identified the major contracts for review and provided Mary with forecasts indicating that the contracts would all make a small profit. Mary confirmed that the assumptions used in the forecasts agreed to assumptions used in previous years. Mary also used the firm's data analytics tool to confirm the mathematical accuracy of the forecasts. Following this work, Mary concluded that the contracts which she had reviewed support the going concern status of the company.

Having reviewed these major contracts, Mary completed the conclusion on going concern, stating that there is no significant uncertainty over going concern.

Mary commented that due to the effectiveness of the data analytics tool, she only had to record eight hours in relation to the work she had performed on going concern.

3   MYRON *Walk in the footsteps of a top tutor*

It is 1 July 20X5. You are the manager responsible for the audit of Myron Co, a listed company and you are in the process of completing the audit of the financial statements for the year ended 31 March 20X5. The auditor's report is due to be signed in the next few weeks. The company's principal operating activity is the publication of trade and scientific journals.

The draft financial statements recognise revenue of $108 million (20X4 – $102 million), profit before tax of $9.3 million (20X4 – $8.2 million) and total assets of $150 million (20X4 – $149 million). Materiality has been set at $0.5 million.

The following exhibits, available below, provide information relevant to the question:

1   Completion matters – details regarding issues you have discovered during your review of the audit working papers

2   Chair's statement – management has provided you with an extract from the chair's statement which they intend to publish in the annual report

This information should be used to answer the question requirements within the response option provided.

Requirements:

(a)   **Using the information contained in Exhibit 1:**

(i)   **Comment on the completion matters to be considered in relation to the issue described and recommend the further actions necessary before the auditor's report can be signed; and**

(ii)   **Evaluate the implications for the auditor's report if no adjustments are made to the financial statements.**   **(10 marks)**

(b)   **Using the information contained in Exhibit 2:**

(i)   **Describe the auditor's responsibilities in relation to the other information presented with the audited financial statements and comment on the matters arising from the extract from the chair's statement, and**   **(5 marks)**

(ii)   **Assuming no changes are made to the chair's statement, evaluate the implications for the completion of the audit and the auditor's report.**

(5 marks)

Professional marks will be awarded for the demonstration of skill in analysis and evaluation, and professional scepticism and judgement in your answer.   **(5 marks)**

(Total: 25 marks)

Exhibit 1 – Completion matters

You are in the process of reviewing the audit working papers and have identified the following potential issue:

Sale of division

Myron Co is at the advanced stage of negotiations to sell its scientific publishing division to a competitor. This division contributed revenue of $13 million and profit before tax of $1.4 million during the year to 31 March 20X5. The draft sale agreement which is due to be finalised by 1 August 20X5 shows an agreed sale price after costs of disposal of $42 million. The division is a separate cash generating unit of Myron Co. None of the assets of the division are held under a revaluation policy and depreciation is charged on a straight-line basis over the determined useful life of the assets.

The finance director of Myron Co has not made any disclosures with respect to the upcoming sale in the financial statements for the year ended 31 March 20X5 as he considers it to be part of next year's accounting transactions. However, the division has been written down from its current carrying amount of $45 million to its estimated value in use of $41 million in the financial statements for the year ended 31 March 20X5.

Exhibit 2 – Chair's statement

As part of your review of Myron Co, you have also been presented with an extract from the draft chair's statement which will be published in the annual report alongside the financial statements for the year.

Extract from chair's statement

The company's results for the year are extremely positive. Our year on year revenue growth is 5.9% and our profit growth is even stronger at 13.4%. All our revenue streams have performed well, especially the scientific publishing division, and we are looking forward to exciting and sustained growth levels again next year. As you can see from our auditor's report, the auditors agree that our results are strong and a sound basis for taking the company to an even greater place next year.

We have also made significant progress with our social and environmental aims of reducing our carbon footprint and encouraging re-use and recycling across our divisions. We are proud to announce that we have now moved all our printed products to recycled paper.

To help with your review of the information, you also have the following analysis of the results for the year.

	Year ended 31 March 20X5			Year ended 31 March 20X4		
	Other divisions	Scientific publishing division	Total	Other divisions	Scientific publishing division	Total
	$ million	$ million	$ million	$ million	$ million	$ million
Revenue	95	13	108	93	9	102
Profit before tax	7.9	1.4	9.3	7.5	0.7	8.2

A file note from the audit supervisor states that at least three of the publications Myron Co sells are not prepared on recycled paper.

Section 6

ANSWERS TO SPECIMEN EXAM

1   CRUX GROUP *Walk in the footsteps of a top tutor*

Top tutor tips

Part (a) asks you to evaluate the audit risks to be considered when planning the audit. Audit risk comprises the risk that the financial statements contain material misstatement and detection risk. Risk of material misstatement is usually due to non-compliance with an accounting standard, although it also includes control risk. Think about the requirements of the relevant accounting standards and what the client might be doing incorrectly. Detection risks include auditing a client for the first time or where there is a tight reporting deadline. The requirement specifically instructs you NOT to consider risks relating to foreign exchange transactions, therefore make sure you do not include these.

The email from the partner states that materiality should be based on profit, therefore at the start of your answer you should calculate the range for materiality using that benchmark and justify a figure within that range. If it is a new audit client or a client where there are apparent control risks, materiality should be set at the lower end of the range. If it is an existing client, materiality may be able to be set at the higher end of the range depending on the other risks mentioned in the scenario.

Part (b) asks for audit procedures in respect of the segmental information relating to Group revenue. The procedures should enable the auditor to obtain evidence to determine whether the relevant financial reporting standard has been complied with. Make sure your procedures are clear and provide enough detail that they can be easily followed by the audit team.

Part (c) asks for matters to be considered in deciding to accept a non-audit engagement to provide advice on social and environmental information. It is important to note that the client is a listed entity and therefore there are more restrictions in place which may mean the audit firm cannot provide the additional service. Your answer should explain the ethical threats arising and the actions the firm should take when considering whether to accept.

Professional skills

Professional skills will be awarded for:

Communication – responding to the instructions in the partner's email such as preparing your answers in the form of briefing notes and using the stated benchmark for materiality.

Analysis and evaluation – applying the information from the scenario to answer the question and explaining the issues in sufficient depth.

> *Professional scepticism and judgement – justifying an appropriate materiality level, demonstrating critical thinking and being alert to possible manipulation and management bias.*
>
> *Where relevant, professional marks will be awarded for commercial acumen which requires making practical and plausible recommendations and considering the wider implications of issues to the audit firm.*

Briefing notes

To: **Audit engagement partner**

From: **Audit manager**

Subject: **Crux Group – Audit Planning**

Date: **1 July 20X5**

Introduction

These briefing notes are prepared to assist with planning the audit of the Crux Group (the Group) for the financial year ending 30 September 20X5. The notes contain an evaluation of the audit risks which should be considered in planning the Group audit, which has been structured to prioritise the risks in terms of the likelihood and magnitude of misstatement in relation to each risk. The notes also recommend the audit procedures to be performed on the Group's segmental disclosure of revenue. Finally, there is a discussion of the matters to be considered by Pegasus & Co in relation to a proposed additional engagement to advise management on the Group's social and environmental information.

(a)   Evaluation of audit risk

Materiality

For the purposes of these briefing notes the following overall materiality level will be used to assess the significance of identified risks and as requested this has been based on the profitability of the Group.

Benchmarks

Using profit before tax or operating profit as a suggested benchmark results in a suggested range of $4.05 million (5% × $81 million) to $14.5 million (10% × $145 million).

These benchmarks are only a starting point for determining materiality and professional judgement will need to be applied in determining a final level to be used during the course of the audit. As this is a new client and therefore an initial audit engagement, due to the increased detection risk, materiality should be set at the lower level of the range at $4 million.

New audit client

The Group is a new client, our firm having been appointed six months ago. This gives rise to detection risk, as our firm does not have experience with the client, making it more difficult for us to detect material misstatements.

This risk can be mitigated through rigorous audit planning, including obtaining a thorough understanding of the business of the Group.

In addition, there is a risk that opening balances and comparative information may not be correct. We have no information to indicate that this is a particularly high risk. However, because the prior year figures were not audited by Pegasus & Co, we should plan to audit the opening balances carefully, in accordance with ISA 510 *Initial Audit Engagements – Opening Balances*, to ensure that opening balances and comparative information are both free from material misstatement.

Revenue recognition

An audit risk arises in relation to the timing of revenue recognition. Given the requirement of ISA 240 *The Auditor's Responsibilities Relating to Fraud in an Audit of Financial Statements*, that when assessing audit risks the auditor shall presume there are risks of fraud in relation to revenue recognition this could be a significant area of concern.

It is appropriate that customer deposits are recognised as deferred revenue when they are received. This is in line with IFRS 15 *Revenue from Contracts* with Customers which requires that revenue is recognised when a performance obligation is satisfied, and therefore any amounts paid to the Group by customers before a cruise begins are not revenue and should be deferred.

However, the policy of recognising all the revenue from a ticket sale when the cruise starts may not be in line with the principles of IFRS 15 because the Group is performing its obligations over time, which may be as long as a six-week period for some cruises.

This is a problem of cut-off, meaning that recognition of all revenue at the start of a cruise could result in overstated revenue and understated liabilities.

Upgrade and maintenance costs

The Group incurs high costs in relation to upgrade and maintenance of its fleet of ships. For the Sunseeker ships, $75 million is being spent this year. This amounts to 4.2% of total assets and 92.6% of profit before tax and is therefore material to the financial statements.

There is an audit risk that costs are not appropriately distinguished between capital expenditure and operating expenditure. Upgrade costs, including costs relating to new facilities such as gyms, should be capitalised, but maintenance costs should be expensed.

There is a risk that assets are overstated, and expenses understated, if operating expenses have been inappropriately capitalised.

A further risk relates to depreciation expenses, which will be overstated if capital expenditure is overstated.

Component depreciation

IAS 16 *Property, Plant and Equipment* requires that each part of an item of property, plant, and equipment with a cost that is significant in relation to the total cost of the item must be depreciated separately.

There is a risk that ships in use are not broken down into component parts for the purpose of determining the individual cost, useful life, and residual value of each part. For example, if significant, the gym equipment should be depreciated over three years and therefore requires separate consideration from other assets such as ship exterior, engine, etc.

There is an audit risk that depreciation is not correctly determined on this component basis, meaning that the assets and their associated depreciation expense could be over or understated in value.

This risk is also heightened due to the unusual movement in relation to the accumulated depreciation figure, which has only increased by $49 million in the year. Information is not given on the Group's depreciation policy, however compared to the total cost of PPE at the financial year end of $2,304 million, this equates to only 2.1%, which appears quite low, suggesting understatement.

Cyber-security attack

The recent cyber-security attack could highlight that internal controls are deficient within the Group. Even though this particular problem has now been rectified, if the Group internal audit team had not properly identified or responded to these cyber-security risks, there could be other areas, including controls over financial reporting, which are deficient, leading to control risk.

The situation could also indicate wider weaknesses in the Group's corporate governance arrangements, for example, if the audit committee is not appropriately discharging its responsibilities with regards to internal audit.

Tutorial note

Based on best practice the audit committee should review and approve the annual internal audit plan and monitor and review the effectiveness of internal audit work. The audit committee should ensure that the internal audit plan is aligned to the key risks of the business. Credit will be awarded for discussion of these issues in the context of the cybersecurity attack.

In addition, the cyber-security attack could have resulted in corrupted data or loss of data relating to the sales system, if the customer details were integrated with the accounting system.

There is an audit risk that reported revenue figures are inaccurate, incomplete or invalid. Though the issue could be confined to the sales system, it is possible that other figures could also be affected.

Finally, the cyber-security incident is likely to result in some fines or penalties being levied against the Group as it seems the risk was not properly dealt with, leaving customer information vulnerable to attack.

It may be necessary for the Group to recognise a provision or disclose a contingent liability depending on the likelihood of a cash payment being made, and the materiality of any such payment, in accordance with IAS 37 *Provisions, Contingent Liabilities and Contingent Assets*.

The related audit risk is understated liabilities and understated expenses or incomplete disclosures if any necessary liability is not recognised or disclosure not made in the notes to the financial statements.

Related party transaction

It appears that Vela Shipbuilders Co, which is building new Explorer Cruise ships for the Group, is a related party of the Group. This is because Max Draco is the chairman of both the Group and Vela Shipbuilders Co.

According to IAS 24 *Related Party Disclosures*, a related party relationship exists where a person has control or joint control, significant influence, or is a member of the key management personnel of two reporting entities. The fact that Max Draco's son is the chief executive officer of Vela Shipbuilders Co also indicates a related party relationship between the Group and the company.

IAS 24 requires that where there have been transactions between related parties, there should be disclosure of the nature of the related party relationship as well as information about the transactions and outstanding balances necessary for an understanding of the potential effect of the relationship on the financial statements.

There is an audit risk that the necessary disclosures regarding the Group's purchases of ships from Vela Shipbuilders Co are not made in the Group financial statements.

The related party transactions are material by their nature, but they are also likely to be material by monetary value. The information provided does not specify how much has been paid in cash from the Group to Vela Shipbuilders Co during the year, but the amount could be significant given that the Group has presumably paid any final instalments on the ships which have come into use during the year, as well as initial instalments on the new ships starting construction this year.

Operating licences

The Group's operating licences of $56 million are material to the financial statements, representing 3.1% of Group total assets.

It is appropriate that the licences are recognised as intangible assets and that they are amortised according to their specific useful life. However, an audit risk arises due to the possible impairment of some or all of these licences, which arises from the governments having withdrawn the licenses in some countries where the Group operates their Pioneer cruises.

While the licence withdrawal is apparently temporary in nature, the withdrawal is an indicator of impairment and it is possible that the operating licences are worth nothing, so should be written off in full.

Management should conduct an impairment review in accordance with IAS 36 *Impairment of Assets* to determine the recoverable amount of the licences and if this is less than the carrying amount, recognise an impairment loss accordingly. If this does not take place, the intangible assets are likely to be overstated, and profit overstated.

Tutorial note

Credit will also be awarded for discussion regarding de-recognition of the operating licences as well as their reduction in value, and for considering whether the Pioneer Cruise ships also need to be reviewed for impairment.

Borrowing costs

The ships being constructed fall under the definition of a qualifying asset under IAS 23 *Borrowing Costs*, which defines a qualifying asset as an asset that takes a substantial period of time to get ready for its intended use or sale. This includes property, plant, and equipment during the relevant construction period, which for the ships is three years.

IAS 23 requires that borrowing costs which are directly attributable to the acquisition, construction or production of a qualifying asset should be capitalised.

The audit risk is that interest costs have not been appropriately capitalised and instead have been treated as finance costs, which would understate assets and understate profit for the year.

The amounts involved appear to be material. The information does not state precisely when the loans were taken out and when construction of the ships commenced or when they come into use by the Group on completion, so it is not possible to determine exactly when capitalisation of finance costs should commence and cease. However, looking at the loan of $180 million taken out for the ships currently under construction, the interest for the year would be $11.7 million, which is a material amount.

Revenue and profit trends

Overall group revenue is projected to increase by 14% in the year. The segmental information shows that this overall increase can be analysed as:

- Revenue from Sunseeker Cruises increasing by 11.1%

- Revenue from Explorer Cruises decreasing by 5.3%

- Revenue from Pioneer Cruises increasing by 37.5%.

The different trends for each segment could be explained by business reasons, however there is a potential risk that revenue has been misclassified between the segments, e.g. revenue from Explorer Cruises could be understated while revenue from Pioneer Cruises is overstated.

In particular, the projected revenue for Pioneer Cruises could be impacted by the recent withdrawal of operating licences which affects the operation of these cruise itineraries. Management may not have factored this into their projections, and there is a risk that this segment's revenue is overstated.

Operating profit is projected to increase by 43.6% in the year, and profit before tax is projected to increase by 24.6% in the year. While the increased margins could be due to economies of scale, the increase in profit appears out of line with the increase in revenue and could indicate that expenses are understated or misclassified.

On-board sales

On-board sales of food, drink and entertainment account for approximately 15% of revenue. There is a risk that this is a reportable operating segment, but the projected operating segment information does not disclose this revenue separately.

According to IFRS 8 *Operating Segments*, an operating segment is a component of an entity that engages in business activities from which it may earn revenues and incur expenses, whose operating results are reviewed regularly by the entity's chief operating decision maker and for which discrete financial information is available which seems to be the case in this instance.

A reportable segment exists where the segment's revenue is 10% or more of the combined revenue of all operating segments. There is a risk of incomplete disclosure of revenue by reportable segments if on-board sales meet the definition of an operating segment and it is not disclosed in the notes to the financial statements as such.

(b) **Principal audit procedures to be performed on the segmental information**

- Review the financial reports sent to the highest level of management to confirm the basis of segmental information which is reported internally and confirm that this basis is used in the notes to the published financial statements.

- Review the Group's organisational structure to confirm the identity of the chief operating decision maker.

- Discuss with management the means by which segmental information is reviewed by the chief operating decision maker, e.g. through monthly financial reports and discussion at board meetings.

- Review board minutes to confirm that the segments as disclosed are used as the basis for monitoring financial performance.

- Discuss with management whether the on-board sales should be reported separately given that it appears to constitute a reportable segment contributing more than 10% of total Group sales and is actively monitored.

- Obtain a breakdown of the revenue, e.g. by cruise line or individual ship, to confirm that revenue has been appropriately allocated between the reportable segments.

- Perform analytical procedures to determine trends for each segment and discuss unusual patterns with management.

- Recalculate the revenue totals from the breakdown provided to confirm that they are reportable segments i.e. that they each contribute more than 10% of revenues.

(c) **Additional service to advise management on measurement of social and environmental information**

The Group's request for Pegasus & Co to advise management on its social and environmental reporting creates an ethical threat to objectivity. Providing additional, non-audit services to an audit client can create several threats to the objectivity and independence of the auditor.

The IESBA *International Code of Ethics for Professional Accountants*/FRC Ethical Standard does not specifically discuss this type of additional engagement, so the audit firm should apply the general framework to consider whether it is appropriate to provide the service. This means that the firm should evaluate the significance of the threats to independence, and consider whether safeguards can reduce the threats to an acceptable level.

Perhaps the most significant, is that providing advice to management, which would involve determining how social and environmental information is measured and published could be perceived as taking on management responsibilities, which is prohibited by the *Code*/FRC Ethical Standard.

To avoid taking on management responsibilities, the audit firm must be satisfied that client management makes all judgements and decisions that are the proper responsibility of management. Measures to achieve this could include:

- Ensuring that a member of the Group's management with appropriate skill, knowledge and experience is designated to be responsible for the client's decisions and to oversee the service

- Management oversees the work performed and evaluates the results, and

- Management accepts responsibility for any actions arising as a result of the service provided.

The audit firm should discuss the request with the Group audit committee, who ultimately will need to approve that the firm can perform the service.

A self-review threat could arise if Pegasus & Co provides the service to the Group. Some of the social and environmental information could be related to transactions or balances within the financial statements which will be subject to audit, for example the value of charitable donations.

The self-review threat means that less scrutiny may be used in performing procedures due to over-reliance on work previously performed by the audit firm. This potentially impacts on the level of professional scepticism applied during the audit and the quality of work carried out.

There could be a further self-review threat depending on whether the social and environmental information will form part of the Group's annual report. If this is the case, the audit team is required by ISA 720/ISA (UK) 720 *The Auditor's Responsibilities Relating to Other Information*, to read the other information included in the annual report and to consider whether there is a material inconsistency between the other information and the financial statements and to also consider whether there is a material inconsistency between the other information and the auditor's knowledge obtained in the audit. This requirement creates a self-review threat if members of the audit team have been involved with the additional service to provide advice on measurement of the social and environmental information.

A self-interest threat can be created by the provision of non-audit services where the fee is significant enough to create actual or perceived economic dependence on the audit client. The Group is willing to pay an 'enhanced fee' for this service due to its urgent nature, and while this does not necessarily create fee-dependency there could be a perception that the audit firm has secured a lucrative fee income in addition to the income from providing the audit.

The Group needs the work to be carried out to a tight deadline, which could impact on the scope and extent of the procedures which the firm can carry out, also impacting on the quality of work and the risk of the engagement. This pressure to perform work quickly within the next month could be viewed as intimidation by the client.

All of these threats are heightened by the fact that the Group is a listed entity, therefore a public interest entity in the terminology of the *Code/*FRC Ethical Standard.

Other actions/safeguards

INT syllabus	UK syllabus
Other safeguards could possibly be used to reduce the threats identified to an acceptable level. These may include having a team separate from the audit team, including a separate partner, perform the work on the social and environmental information; and conducting a review of both the audit and additional service by the engagement quality reviewer.	Given that the audit committee has requested this help from the audit firm, it seems unlikely that the audit firm could avoid taking on management responsibility should the service be provided.

The corporate governance code under which the Group operates may restrict or prohibit the provision of non-audit services by the audit firm in the case of listed entities, so the audit committee should consider if any such restrictions exist.	The UK Corporate Governance Code restricts the provision of non-audit services by the audit firm in the case of listed entities, so the audit committee should consider if providing the service would be in breach of this.
Discussions should also be held regarding the new regulatory requirements. The audit firm should be clear on the reliance which will be placed on the report by the regulatory authorities and matters such as whether an assurance report is required, and if so, who will be performing this work. In addition, there may be specific requirements which impact on the scope of the work, for example whether any specific KPIs are required to be published.	It is concerning that the Group audit committee considers it appropriate to request that Pegasus & Co provide this non-audit service as well as the external audit. A provision of the UK Corporate Governance Code states that one of the roles and responsibilities of an audit committee is to develop and implement policy on the engagement of the external auditor to supply non-audit services. This involves ensuring there is prior approval of non-audit services, considering the impact this may have on independence, taking into account the relevant regulations and ethical guidance in this regard. The Group audit committee appears either to not be aware of the ethical issues caused by their requests, or to be ignoring them.

Even if the ethical issues can be overcome, the firm should consider whether it has the skills and competencies to provide the advice to management. This can be quite specialised work and it is not necessarily the case that the firm will have staff with the appropriate skills available to carry out the work, especially if the work is to be carried out to a tight deadline.

In conclusion in terms of providing advice to management on social and environmental information, this will be difficult to do without breaching ethical principles and should be further discussed with the Group audit committee.

Conclusion

These briefing notes highlight a number of significant audit risks, including those relating to property, plant and equipment, revenue recognition and disclosure requirements. A number of audit procedures have been recommended in relation to the audit of segmental information provided in relation to revenue. As mentioned, the provision of the additional service should be further discussed with the Group audit committee.

Examiner's comments

This question was a typical Section A question set at the planning stage, with requirements covering audit risk, audit procedures, ethics, and data analytics for 50 marks. Typically, each session the Section A question is where candidates perform best and there have been progressively better and more focused answers in recent sessions and candidates appear to have taken note of the guidance provided by the examining team in this area.

The Group in this scenario was a new client to the audit firm, operating cruise ship holidays to various markets. Several exhibits were provided to candidates to enable them to develop an understanding of the specific issues facing this client. These were as follows:

- Partner's email – this exhibit typically provides the detailed requirements for the question.

- Background information on the client – includes information the audit partner (examiner) deems relevant to your audit planning.

- Selected financial information – this is the extracts from the management accounts and projections for the year end which will enable candidates to identify risks arising from specific areas in the financial statements.

- Audit team meeting notes – further specific points which are relevant to the audit planning and other requirements in the question.

Unless specified otherwise, all exhibits should be considered when identifying audit risks and candidates should ensure that they carefully read the partner's email for any specific guidance in relation to how the information should be used.

It is recommended that candidates review all the exhibits while planning their answers to the question but as mentioned should ensure they take note of any guidance given by the examining team in terms of which exhibits are relevant to each requirement. Thus, allowing for more detailed analysis and focus on specific information where relevant. It is often the case that there will be interactions between the exhibits which will impact on the analysis performed by candidates. It was quite apparent this session that candidates often approached the question by working through the exhibits and attempting to use each piece of information in isolation which was inefficient and often leads to candidates discussing issues in the wrong context. Candidates using this approach could not identify some risks appropriately and instead spent time trying to create risks where there were none. This will add to the time pressure that candidates experience in the examination as time is spent writing about points which are not relevant. This is discussed further below under requirement (a). Candidates are encouraged to spend adequate time planning and aim to get a holistic view and understanding of the issues present in the question.

An important thing to note for all questions in the AAA examination is the stage of the audit process the scenario relates to. Often candidates do not remain focused on the audit stage and produce answers which are nonsensical in the context. For example, it is common for candidates in planning questions, which are set pre year end, to state that the audit is suffering time pressure because there's only three months left before the year end. The final audit happens after the year end. Planning before the year end is not leaving it too late and is an appropriate response to avoid such time pressure; ensuring that the audit is well planned prior to its commencement.

Requirement (a) required candidates to evaluate audit risks to be considered in planning the Group audit. Candidates were also instructed not to consider audit risks arising from foreign exchange. It is imperative that candidates take note of this guidance as these points have been specifically excluded and therefore no marks will be available.

In this scenario, the client is listed and operates three cruise ship brands. Information on each of those brands is provided in the background information and in the financial information. There is a further issue relating to one of the brands provided in the audit team meeting notes. Candidates are not expected to have detailed industry specific knowledge when answering questions in this examination and the scenario will always have sufficient information to enable sufficient specific risks to be identified and evaluated to achieve full marks.

When attempting the Section A question, candidates will find it useful to break down the information given in the scenario and it is also helpful to consider why specific information has been provided and how it impacts the evaluation of risk in this specific scenario.

Introduction to the question

The important pieces of information here which should impact candidates' planning and answers are:

- The current date is 1 July 20X5 and the client year end is September 20X5 – hence the scenario is set three months prior to the year end in this question so year-end financials are not currently available but will be available when the audit is performed after the year end.

- Crux Group is a listed entity – this piece of information should alert candidates to the possibility that certain disclosures may be required, and also to be alert to the potential for earnings management and that ethical rules will be stricter than those for non-listed entities. At this point, it does not in itself constitute an audit risk and candidates will not receive credit for simple saying that as a listed company there is a risk of management bias. This exam is focused on application of knowledge rather than isolated facts. Similarly, candidates will not be awarded credit for simply stating that listed companies must disclose segmental and earnings per share information. It is a reasonable presumption that unless the entity is newly listed that they will be capable of knowing a disclosure is required and if they failed to make those disclosures in prior years this would have been flagged in the scenario. At this point, candidates should be on the lookout for areas in the scenario where there is a specific risk of manipulating earnings and disclosures.

- The firm was appointed auditor in January 20X5 – therefore this is a new client. It is important to remember in reaching this position, the firm has already performed relevant acceptance procedures, obtained professional clearance from the previous auditor, and determined that the firm has the competence and resources to provide this audit. The audit risks arising from a new client relate to opening balances and heightened detection risk because the firm has less experience with a new client than an existing one. Discussions surrounding whether the firm is competent or assigning more experienced staff to the audit will not obtain credit as the requirement is to evaluate the audit risks not to question whether the firm should have accepted the client or to provide an audit approach to those risks. It is important in reducing time pressure that candidates do not spend time addressing points outside the scope of the requirement.

The rest of the information provides the context for the scenario and gives some idea on the size of the business operations of the client. It describes three brands which suggests that segmental information may be assessed by brand.

Exhibit 1 – Partner's email

In a Section A question the partner's email will always set out the detailed requirements which are to be answered and the mark allocation. It is recommended that candidates refer to the partner's email first to ensure that they understand what they are being asked to do and the best way to allocate their time to each requirement. By reading the requirements first it is easier for candidates to then read through the rest of the information, building that holistic and relevant understanding of the issues pertinent to the question as they go.

Exhibit 2 – Background information

In Exhibit 2 candidates are provided with an overview of the Group. The relevance of each piece of information is described below.

Group operations

- Cruises last 2 – 6 weeks – this signals that the Group has revenue which should be recognised over time.

- The brands are internally generated and therefore are not recognised as intangible assets – indicating that brands are not a risk as they have been treated appropriately and therefore candidates do not need to spend time discussing the possibility that they have been incorrectly treated.

Sunseeker cruises

- $75m was spent on upgrading and maintenance of the ships – this leads to the audit risk arising from the classification of those expenses as revenue or capital in nature.

- Several ships are enhanced with new facilities, some of which need to be replaced after an average of three years – this confirms that some of the $75m spend was capital in nature and also introduces the need to depreciate upgrades over their individual component useful life, hence identifying a second risk in relation to the amounts spent.

In addition to those two risks arising from the information, candidates should be alert to the risk that the classification and useful lives are both areas for potential earnings management through the understatement of expenses.

A common mistake made by candidates here was to say that the gym equipment with the three-year useful life should not be capitalised or that provisions should be made annually with respect to the new equipment the Group might buy three years from now.

Explorer cruises

- The ships for this brand are being gradually replaced – these are the oldest in the fleet – this signals an impairment risk as the value in use of the ships to be replaced may be lower than their carrying amount. It does not mean that the ships should be written off entirely as some are still in use and they are likely to be able to be sold onwards and therefore still have a value.

- The new ships take several years to build – meaning the Group has *assets in the course of construction* which will be recognised on the statement of financial position.

- The ships are being built by a company linked to the Group through the chairman – suggesting that there are related party transactions to disclose.

- The ships were financed via loans – hence the finance costs must be capitalised on the qualifying assets until they are ready for use.

Common errors made by candidates here were to state that old ships must be removed from the financial statements (this would only happen if they were impaired to zero or had been disposed of), stating that the ships being constructed should not be recognised in the statement of financial position and stating that it is a requirement of financial reporting that related party transactions must be on an arms-length basis. Candidates should note that financial reporting rules do not govern legalities of trade they provide rules for presentation.

Pioneer cruises

- The brand has been growing in popularity – this flags that there is an expectation that revenue is growing in this segment.

- Operating licences are required which are capitalised as intangible assets – this is appropriate treatment in line with IAS 38 *Intangible Assets* and therefore at this point this fact does not give rise to an audit risk. Candidates who state that there is an audit risk arising from non-recognition of licences are ignoring the fact that the scenario states appropriate recognition has occurred. Candidates stating that the assets should not be recognised are incorrect. As neither of these gives rise to an audit risk there are no marks for the discussion of the rules for capitalising intangible assets.

Exhibit 3 – Financial Information

This exhibit provides financial information which provides the source for analytical procedures to be performed. Candidates should be aware that unless a ratio, trend or calculation is discussed in the context of a risk then that calculation will not be awarded marks as it is only through this discussion that the calculation becomes relevant. Hence candidates should not spend time calculating lots of figures they will not use.

Key points to take from the financial information are as follows:

- Revenue, profit before tax and total assets – these are the generally accepted benchmarks for materiality. If a candidate calculates materiality on a benchmark other than these, they should justify why that is an appropriate benchmark to obtain materiality credit.

- Total assets are mainly comprised of Property, Plant and Equipment (PPE) which means this could be considered an asset driven business in addition to a profit/revenue driven business when assessing materiality benchmarks.

- By performing a few simple calculations it is apparent that revenue growth is significantly lower than profit growth hence there may be an understatement of expenses – this can be tied back to the risks in other areas where there is a suggestion expenses could be understated, for example the $75m upgrade and maintenance spend in Sunseeker cruises or the risk that the impairment of the old ships in Explorer cruises has not been taken into account.

- Revenue is 85% passenger ticket sales – deposits and final payments received are recognised as deferred income on receipt (hence a liability not as revenue) which is appropriate accounting treatment but then transferred to revenue when the cruise commences – i.e. at a point in time before the performance obligations are fully satisfied and therefore revenue is recognised too early and gives rise to overstated revenue and cut-off issues.

- 15% of revenue is derived from onboard sales and management monitor this closely – therefore this is likely to be a reportable segment as it is a revenue stream over 10% of total revenue, is reviewed regularly by the entity's chief operating decision maker for which discrete financial information exists. This gives rise to the risk that the Group has failed to disclose a reportable segment as the revenue per operating segment information provided only lists the three cruise ship brands. This is an example of a specific risk in relation to listed company disclosures and would therefore be awarded credit.

- The segmental information provided enables candidates to calculate the relative size of each segment to clarify that they are all sufficiently large to be reportable segments and gives the information to be able to analyse the movements in segment revenue year on year. This analysis shows that:

  - Explorer cruises has declining revenue – this is a further indication that there may be an impairment of the assets of this brand, and

  - Pioneer cruises and Sunseeker cruises are both growing.

This section of the financial information also states that the licences held by Pioneer cruises are amortised over the specific period to which the licence relates. Again, this is appropriate accounting treatment and is not judgemental so there is no risk arising from this piece of information. The examining team is communicating that amortisation is not a risk, so candidates do not need to spend time discussing this possibility.

There is then some information which shows how important ships are to the asset value of the business and there is some scope for considering the movements in ships and PPE in the context of risk discussions about capitalisation of expenditure and impairment of assets.

Candidates should note that in the absence of information on additions and disposals, it is not possible to calculate this year's depreciation figures by comparing accumulated depreciation year on year.

Exhibit 4 – Audit team meeting notes

This is an update of information for new issues coming to light which will affect audit planning.

- Temporary withdrawal of licences for Pioneer cruises – this provides information which gives rise to an impairment risk. The licences which were appropriately capitalised and amortised may be impaired as the withdrawal of the licences is an indicator of impairment. It is also possible that due to the restriction on operations, as a result the other assets of the Pioneer brand may be impaired.

- Cyber security attack – this gives rise to several risks as there has been a breach in regulations because of a control weakness. This issue gives rise to an increase in control risk for the audit as well as risks surrounding potential fines and liabilities which may need to be recognised or disclosed in the financial statements.

The remaining information here related to requirement (c).

Candidates should note that audit risks generally arise in areas that are new, complex or judgemental. This means, unless given information to suggest a routine transaction or disclosure is incorrect then these areas are less likely to give rise to a significant audit risk.

For example, in this question, the company has taken out two bank loans. These loans have been taken out to finance the construction of new ships. The ships take three years to build and the first set of ships will come into use this financial year, hence at least one of the loans was in place in the previous financial period. These loans are a simple fixed interest bank loan not complex financial instruments. Hence, they are not likely to create a significant audit risk in relation to the calculation of the finance charge on an amortised cost basis in the same way as a discounted debenture or convertible debenture would. As at least one of these loans was in place last year, the audit partner would have communicated any potential issues with the client's accounting treatment from the review of policies during acceptance.

There is also no information in the question to suggest that these loans are secured on property or are dependent on specific covenants, so discussion about breaches of covenants impacting the going concern presumption would be speculative.

Similarly, where a group structure has not changed and there's no apparent control weakness over the consolidation process, it is unlikely that the Group is unable to eliminate intra group balances or will miss out a subsidiary. As such risks in these areas, not flagged in the question would be deemed speculative and therefore not a significant audit risk for which marks will be available.

Answers to procedure-based requirements are generally handled well by candidates. However, the answers to part (b) were weaker than usual as candidates did not focus on the segmental information and in some cases did not focus on revenue. The requirement was to design procedures to ensure that the segmental information on revenue was appropriate rather than testing revenue recognition and cut-off or proving revenue overall. Here, to remain focused on the requirement, candidates needed to:

- consider the financial reporting requirements surrounding what constitutes a reportable segment to ensure that the auditor can confirm the segments meet the definition of a reportable segment, and
- consider how the Group ensured the right information was recorded for each of those segments.

The suggested solution provides examples of the sort of procedures which are valid, and candidates are encouraged to review these procedures carefully to ensure they understand the source, purpose and relevance of each procedure. Many candidates unfortunately either ignored the segmental reporting aspects of revenue and focused on revenue recognition or in some cases listed procedures for every risk they had identified. These cannot obtain marks for this requirement and candidates should ensure they identify the topic and the assertions they are looking to audit before writing their answer. Candidates should also remember that each procedure is only worth 1 mark hence producing a list of 20 procedures for 5 marks is likely to add unnecessary time pressure in the exam.

Requirement (c) examined the acceptance and ethics area of the syllabus in the context of providing additional services to a listed client.

The additional service requested by the Group was to "advise management on how to measure certain social and environmental information to be published on the Group's website".

Candidates here generally identified the short deadline giving rise to pressure on resources and the need for competence in the area of key performance indicators. Stronger candidates also discussed the need to understand exactly what management were requesting, identified that as a listed client it may be prohibited to provide certain services and were able to identify where a self-review threat may arise and how self-interest could manifest in relation to the offer of an enhanced fee due to the tight deadline.

Weaker candidates simply stated that it is prohibited to provide any non-audit services to an audit client which is not the case and given the requirement was worth 10 marks candidates should realise that the answer is not as simple as a single line.

Some candidates used what appeared to be rote learnt lists of points with no application to the scenario and discussed the need to contact previous auditors, perform client due diligence and also went into detail about who would be receiving the report and appeared to assume this was an assurance engagement despite that not be mentioned in the scenario.

Candidates should also note that listing potential ethical threats without application to the scenario does not attract credit. For example, saying that the service would give rise to an intimidation, self-interest and self-review threat would be awarded no marks as this does not show any understanding of these threats or how they arise.

Candidates are required to describe the threats arising in the context of the scenario. For example, in this context, candidates should identify self-review with reference to the fact that the auditor is required to read the other information issued alongside the financial statements in the annual report or from the requirement to audit the charitable donation in the financial statements. To obtain the full mark candidates must then go on to give the implication of the threat, for example that the audit team may apply less scrutiny or be over-reliant on the work carried out by other members of the firm.

The suggested solution also contains the detailed descriptions of the ethical threats in this question and candidates are encouraged to review this in detail to ensure they understand the level of depth required or these types of requirements.

Some candidates also appeared to lack commercial awareness and stated that the offer of an enhanced fee due to the urgency of the work indicated the client lacked integrity. It would be general business practice in many industries to charge a higher fee if they need to call in more staff from further away or rearrange other staff commitments to make people available at short notice. It may be that the staff assigned would have to work overtime to meet the deadline and be paid more for that. A minority of candidates also seemed to think all fees for work performed by the firm should only be sufficient to cover staff costs and no more.

	ACCA Marking guide	
		Marks

(a)   **Audit risk evaluation**

Up to 3 marks for each audit risk, (unless indicated otherwise). Marks may be awarded for other, relevant audit risks not included in the marking guide.

In addition, ½ mark for relevant trends or calculations which form part of the evaluation of audit risk (max 3 marks).

Appropriate materiality calculations and justified materiality level should be awarded to a maximum of 3 marks.

- New audit client (2 marks)
- Revenue recognition
- Upgrade and maintenance costs
- Component depreciation
- Cyber-security breach (control risk, corporate governance weakness, data corruption, financial statement implications – max 5 marks)
- Related party transaction disclosure
- Operating licences
- Borrowing costs
- Revenue and profit trends
- On-board sales

                                                                              Maximum   **25**

(b)   **Audit procedures on segmental reporting**

Up to 1 mark for each relevant audit procedure. Examples are provided below, and marks will be awarded for other relevant points.

- Review the financial reports sent to the highest level of management to confirm the basis of segmental information which is reported internally
- Review the Group's organisational structure to confirm identify of the chief operating decision maker
- Discuss with management the means by which segmental information is reviewed by the chief operating decision maker
- Review board minutes to see that segmental information is subject to regular review
- Discuss with management whether the on-board sales should be reported separately
- Obtain a breakdown of the revenue to confirm that revenue has been appropriately allocated between the reportable segments
- Perform analytical procedures to determine trends for each segment and discuss unusual patterns with management
- Recalculate the revenue totals from the breakdown provided to confirm that they are reportable segments

                                                                               Maximum   **5**

(c)   **Additional service to provide advice on social and environmental information**

Up to 1 mark for each relevant answer point explained:

- Assuming management responsibility identified and fully explained
- Assuming management responsibility is prohibited
- Self-review threat identified and fully explained
- Self-review threat increased if the social/environmental information included in annual report
- Self-interest threat identified and fully explained
- Pressure to perform work quickly

- Appropriate safeguards recommended (1 mark each to max 3 marks)
- Group audit committee to approve non-audit work
- INT: It may be prohibited in the jurisdiction of the Group
- UK: Audit committee seem not to understand the ethical threats/should not have requested the advice
- Scope of the work, and specific requirements from the regulators
- Level of assurance which may be required and who is going to provide this
- Skill and competence to perform work

Maximum	10

Professional marks

Communication

- Briefing notes format and structure – use of headings/sub-headings and an introduction
- Style, language and clarity – appropriate layout and tone of briefing notes, presentation of materiality and relevant calculations, appropriate use of the CBE tools, easy to follow and understand
- Effectiveness and clarity of communication – answer is relevant and tailored to the scenario
- Adherence to the specific requests made by the audit engagement partner

Analysis and evaluation

- Appropriate use of the information to determine suitable calculations
- Appropriate use of the information to support discussions and draw appropriate conclusions
- Assimilation of all relevant information to ensure that the risk evaluation performed considers the impact of contradictory or unusual movements
- Effective prioritisation of the results of the risk evaluation to demonstrate the likelihood and magnitude of risks and to facilitate the allocation of appropriate responses
- Balanced discussion of the information to objectively make a recommendation or decision

Professional scepticism and judgement

- Effective challenge of information supplied, and techniques carried out to support key facts and/or decisions
- Determination and justification of a suitable materiality level, appropriately and consistently applied
- Appropriate application of professional judgement to draw conclusions and make informed decisions about the courses of action which are appropriate in the context of the audit engagement

Commercial acumen

- Audit procedures are practical and plausible in the context of the scenario
- Use of effective examples and/or calculations from the scenario to illustrate points or recommendations
- Recognition of the appropriate commercial considerations of the audit firm

Maximum	10
Total	50

2   WELFORD & CO *Walk in the footsteps of a top tutor*

Top tutor tips

This question focuses on a post-issuance audit quality review, therefore falls into the syllabus area of quality management and practice management rather than review of the work during the audit, however, the same approach can be taken when commenting on the quality of the work. Typical issues to look out for in such a question are: whether the work has been assigned to the appropriate level of staff, whether sufficient time has been allocated for the audit, whether sufficient appropriate evidence has been obtained (e.g. have the ISAs been followed), whether any ethical threats are apparent (e.g. threats to objectivity or competence).

Rivers Co

A review of the information relating to the audit of Rivers Co indicates many problems with how the audit has been planned and performed which imply that the audit has not been conducted in accordance with ISA 220 (Revised) *Quality Management for an Audit of Financial Statements*, ISQM 1 *Quality Management for Firms that Perform Audits or Reviews of Financial Statements, or other Assurance and Related Services Engagements*, and the IESBA *International Code of Ethics for Professional Accountants* (the *Code*)/FRC Ethical Standard.

Audit partner rotation

Bob Newbold has been acting as audit engagement partner for eight years (INT)/six years (UK). As Rivers Co is a listed company this goes against the requirements of the Code and FRC Ethical Standard which requires that an individual shall not act as the engagement partner for more than seven years (INT)/five years (UK).

The problem is that long association of the engagement partner with the client leads to a self-interest threat to auditor objectivity, whereby the audit firm's judgement is affected by concern over losing the long-standing client.

There may also be a familiarity threat due to close relationships between the audit engagement partner and management of Rivers Co, meaning that the partner ceases to exercise sufficient professional scepticism, impacting on audit quality. This is especially the case given that Bob Newbold is performing additional non-audit services for the client, which will be discussed further below. Bob Newbold should be replaced as soon as possible by another audit engagement partner.

The fact that Bob has been allowed to continue as audit partner for longer than the period allowed by the *Code* indicates that Welford & Co does not have appropriate policies and procedures designed to provide it with reasonable assurance that the firm and its personnel comply with relevant ethical requirements. The firm should review whether its monitoring of the length of time that audit engagement partners act for clients is operating effectively and make any necessary improvements to internal controls to ensure compliance with ISQM 1.

Tutorial note

INT: *The Code does allow a key audit partner to serve an additional year in situations where continuity is especially important to audit quality, as long as the threat to independence can be eliminated or reduced to an acceptable level. Credit will be awarded for appropriate discussion on this issue.*

UK: *The FRC Ethical Standard does allow a key audit partner to serve an additional two years in situations where continuity is especially important to audit quality.*

Supervision and review

Bob Newbold has booked only two hours for audit work performed on Rivers Co. This is not sufficient time for the audit partner to perform their duties adequately. The audit partner is required to take overall responsibility for the supervision and performance of the audit. He should have spent an appropriate amount of time performing a review of the audit working papers in order to be satisfied that sufficient appropriate audit evidence had been obtained. Instead it appears that most of the final review was performed by a newly promoted audit manager who would not have the necessary experience to perform this review. It is possible that there is insufficient evidence to support the audit opinion which has been issued, or that inappropriate evidence has been obtained.

There is also a related issue regarding the delegation of work. Possibly some of the detailed review of the working papers could have been delegated to someone other than the audit partner, in which case the senior audit manager Pat Canley would be the appropriate person to perform this work. However, Pat only recorded six hours of work on the audit. Thus, confirming that too much of the review has been delegated to the junior audit manager, especially given that going concern was identified as a significant audit risk, meaning that the audit partner has even more reason for involvement in the final review of audit work.

There is also an issue around the overall amount of time which has been recorded for the audit work performed on this client. A total of 173 hours does not seem sufficient for the audit of a listed company, suggesting that audit quality could have been impacted by inadequate time spent in planning and performing the audit work.

Special investigation

Bob Newbold's focus appears to have been on the special investigation performed for Rivers Co, to which he booked 40 hours of time.

There is insufficient documentation as to the nature of this non-audit work, and it could relate to the provision of a non-audit service which is not allowed for a public interest entity. Rivers Co is a listed company, and the *Code/FRC Ethical Standard* prohibits the audit firm from providing certain non-audit services, for example certain internal audit services, valuation services and tax services. The lack of documentation means that Welford & Co could have provided a prohibited service and therefore be in breach of the ethical requirements.

The fact that $890,000 was charged for this special investigation indicates that it was a substantial engagement and just the matter of inadequate documentation is a cause for concern. There is also a possibility that in fact no work has been performed, and the firm has accepted this money from the client but provided no service. This would be a very serious issue, could be perceived as a bribe, and it should be investigated with urgency.

However, there are also possible threats to auditor objectivity including a self-interest threat due to the monetary value of the service provided meaning that Bob Newbold's attention seems to have been focussed on the special investigation rather than the audit, leading to the problems of inappropriate delegation of this work as discussed above. His additional involvement with Rivers Co by providing this work compounds the familiarity threat also discussed previously. Depending on the nature of the work performed for the client there may also be other threats to objectivity including self-review and advocacy.

A self-interest threat is created as the value of the services provided is substantial compared to the audit fee. The fact the non-audit fees are so high would create a proportionately bigger intimidation threat because they would form a larger part of the firm's income and the audit firm may not be objective for fear of losing the client.

Welford & Co should ensure that its policies and documentation on engagement acceptance, especially in relation to additional services for existing audit clients, are reviewed and made more robust if necessary.

Tutorial note

UK: *Credit will be awarded for comments in respect of the rule that fees for providing non-audit services to an audited entity which is a public interest entity should be limited to no more than 70% of the average audit fee for the last three years. Depending on the level of fees for the last three years, the firm may be in breach of this rule.*

Engagement Quality Review

As this is a listed audit client, an Engagement Quality Review should have been performed. It is not clear whether this took place or not, but no time has been recorded for this review. If a pre-issuance review was carried out then it should have picked up these problems prior to the audit opinion being issued.

Audit of going concern

The audit work on going concern has been inappropriately delegated to an audit assistant who would not have the necessary skill or experience. This is especially concerning given that going concern was identified as a significant audit risk, and that the work involves using judgement to evaluate information relating to contract performance. The work should have been performed by a more senior member of the team, probably one of the audit managers, who is more able to exercise professional scepticism and to challenge management where necessary on the assumptions underpinning the forecasts. Mary certainly should not have documented the conclusion on going concern, the conclusion should be reached by a more experienced auditor having reviewed all of the evidence obtained.

It is concerning that the audit work appears to have been based on a review of contracts which were selected by management. First, only five contracts were reviewed but the company is typically working on 20 contracts at one time. So it is likely that the coverage of the audit work was insufficient, and more contracts should have been subject to review. Given the risk attached to going concern perhaps all the contracts currently being carried out should have been reviewed, or the sample selected based on the auditor's evaluation of the risk associated with each contract and their materiality.

Second, management may have selected the better performing contracts for Mary to review. This would create a false impression of the performance of the company as a whole, leading to an inappropriate conclusion on going concern being reached. Mary, or one of the more senior members of the audit team, should have challenged management on the selection of these contracts.

Finally, the work performed by Mary on this small selection of contracts appears insufficient and inappropriate. The audit assistant also appears to have placed too much reliance on the firm's data analytics tool and demonstrates a lack of understanding of how the data analytics tools should be used to obtain audit evidence. By simply using the data analytics tool to agree the mathematical accuracy of the forecasts and the assumptions, insufficient testing has been carried out in relation to these key documents. Assumptions should not just be agreed as consistent with the previous year, especially in a situation of increasing economic uncertainty as applies in this case. Assumptions should be challenged and other work performed as required by ISA 570/ISA (UK) 570 *Going Concern*. The data analytics tool could have been used more appropriately, e.g. to perform sensitivity analysis which would have allowed for identification of areas of concern or requiring further investigation.

The lack of further audit procedures means that the audit evidence is not likely to be sufficiently robust in this significant area. This is further demonstrated by the fact that Mary only spent eight hours on this critical area of the audit work and has commented that this was due to the evidence generated by the data analytics tool. This again demonstrates the over-reliance placed on this tool, raising a concern that staff require further training in the use of and interpretation of evidence generated in this way.

Audit committee

It is concerning that the audit committee of Rivers Co does not appear to have raised concerns about the issues discussed, especially the provision of the non-audit service and the length of time which Bob Newbold has served as audit engagement partner. One of the roles of the audit committee is to oversee ethical issues relating to the external auditor and to be involved with the engagement of external providers. Welford & Co should ensure that these matters are discussed with the audit committee so that further ethical issues do not arise in the future.

Conclusion

From the discussion above it can be seen that there are many problems with the audit of Rivers Co. Bob Newbold appears to have ignored his responsibilities as audit engagement partner, and the audit firm needs to discuss this with him, consider further training or possibly taking disciplinary action against him. Welford & Co need to implement procedures to ensure all work is carried out at the appropriate level of personnel with the appropriate experience and that training is given to staff to ensure they understand the client does not pick or specify the audit work to be carried out in any area, it is to be selected by the audit team in accordance with the audit firm's methodology and sampling tools. Training may also need to be provided in the appropriate use of audit data analytics tools as a basis for obtaining audit evidence.

Examiner's comments

Candidates appeared to be familiar with this type of requirement and were able to explain the issues arising from how this audit was performed. Working through the information in a linear way, enabled candidates to discuss each issue in turn. The information was structured around the audit team and fees with some additional information about an undescribed "special investigation" which had been performed for the client as well as some information on the audit of going concern.

In general, candidates were able to identify the familiarity risk arising from long association with the client, discuss the lack of time spent on the audit, particularly in relation to senior members of the team, and the potential ethical and integrity threats arising from the 'special investigation'. Those with practical understanding were able to recognise that while it is normal for audit assistants to have a larger amount of time on the audit than the audit partner, the overall length of time spent on the audit was very low for a listed client in a high-risk industry. The going concern audit issues were well identified by most candidates.

The requirement to recommend actions is one that was more variable in relation to the answers produced. The question did not ask for procedures on going concern and a significant number of candidates confused actions with procedures. Actions in this question included things such as discussion of the ethical threats with the audit committee, investigating what was meant by special investigation and putting into place more robust acceptance procedures for additional services provided to audit clients. Even if a candidate decided that the going concern area was not sufficiently audited, an action would be to perform additional procedures in this area rather than a list of procedures.

The distinction between actions and procedures is one that candidates should ensure they understand – it is very common for candidates to list procedures which are not required or to demonstrate a lack of awareness of the stage of the audit cycle in which the question is set. This has been discussed in many previous examiner's reports. Where detailed audit procedures are required the requirement will ask for procedures or for the evidence you would expect to find.

ACCA Marking guide	
	Marks
Generally, up to 1 mark for each well explained point: **Rivers Co**	
• Long association of audit partner breaches the IESBA Code 7 year/FRC Ethical Standard 5-year maximum period allowed	
• Self-interest threat identified and explained	
• Familiarity threat identified and explained	
• Recommend replace Bob with a new audit partner as soon as possible	
• Firm's monitoring of the length of time partners act for clients seems deficient	
• Audit partner should have spent more time on the audit and in particular on the final review	
• The total amount of time spent on the audit appears low for the audit of a listed company – implications for audit quality	
• Inappropriate delegation of tasks, the junior audit manager lacks experience	
• There may not be sufficient, appropriate evidence to support the audit opinion	
• Welford & Co may have provided a prohibited non-audit service to Rivers Co, a listed company	
• The size of fee for the non-audit service creates a self-interest threat	
• Bob's involvement with the non-audit service creates familiarity threats to audit objectivity	

- Lack of documentation could indicate that no work has been performed – possibly a bribe from the client
- Welford & Co to review policies, procedures and documentation on engagement acceptance
- Apparent lack of Engagement Quality Review being carried out before the audit opinion was issued
- Inappropriate delegation of work on going concern to an inexperienced audit assistant
- Sample of contracts reviewed is too small – insufficient evidence obtained
- Management selection of contracts is likely to be subject to bias – the auditor should select which contracts should be reviewed
- Over-reliance on and misunderstanding of use of data analytics tools
- Insufficient work on going concern – assumptions should be challenged not agreed to prior year
- Data analytics could have been used to carry out specific going concern testing such as sensitivity analysis
- Lack of time spent on going concern testing due to over-reliance on data analytics
- Additional training required
- Client audit committee – should have identified the ethical and audit quality issues
- Overall conclusion relating to the quality of the engagement

Maximum	20

Professional marks

Analysis and evaluation

- Appropriate assessment of the ethical and professional issues raised, using examples where relevant to support overall comments
- Effective appraisal of the information to make suitable recommendations for appropriate courses of action

Professional scepticism and judgement

- Effective challenge and critical assessment of the evidence supplied with appropriate conclusions
- Demonstration of the ability to probe into the reasons for quality issues including the identification of missing information or additional information which would be required
- Appropriate application of professional judgement to draw conclusions and make informed comments regarding the quality of the work carried out

Commercial acumen

- Inclusion of appropriate recommendations regarding the additional quality procedures required by the firm
- Appropriate recognition of the wider implications on the engagement, the audit firm and the company

Maximum	5
Total	25

3   MYRON *Walk in the footsteps of a top tutor*

Top tutor tips

Part (a)(i) requires discussion of an accounting issue. First, consider the materiality of the issue. Next discuss the appropriate accounting treatment and state the material misstatement that has arisen. This requirement also asks for further actions necessary before the auditor's report can be signed. This may be further procedures that need to be performed or discussions that the auditor should have with management and those charged with governance to try and resolve the accounting issue.

For (a)(ii) you need to state the impact to the auditor's report if the client does not amend the financial statements. Consider whether the misstatement is material and pervasive or material but not pervasive. State the impact to both the report and opinion as a result of the issues. Don't waste time stating the reporting implications if the issue is corrected as this is not part of the requirement.

In part (b) you need to give the auditor's responsibilities in relation to the other published information in the annual report. Auditor responsibilities are set out in the auditing standards and therefore this type of question requires knowledge of the relevant ISA.

(a)   Matters, further actions and auditor's report implications

Matters

The company is at an advanced stage of negotiations with a competitor to sell its scientific publishing division. Currently the finance director has not included any reference to the sale in the financial statements for the year ended 31 March 20X5 and there is no appropriate justification for this. The finance director's assessment that the sale only affects next year's financial statements is incorrect.

Materiality

The revenue of the scientific publishing division of $13 million and the profit of the division of $1.4 million are both material. The assets of the division are also material, as they represent 27.3% of the company's total assets, based on their value in use which is recognised in the financial statements.

Discontinued operation and classification of assets held for sale

IFRS 5 *Non-Current Assets Held for Sale and Discontinued Operations* defines a discontinued operation as a component of an entity which either has been disposed of or is classified as held for sale, and:

- represents either a separate major line of business or a geographical area of operations

- is part of a single co-ordinated plan to dispose of a separate major line of business or geographical area of operation.

IFRS 5 requires specific disclosures in relation to assets held for sale and discontinued operations, including that the assets are recognised as current assets and the results of the discontinued operation are presented separately in the statement of profit or loss and the statement of cash flows.

According to IFRS 5, a disposal group of assets should be classified as held for sale where management plans to sell the assets, and the sale is highly probable. Conditions which indicate that a sale is highly probable are:

- management is committed to a plan to sell

- the asset is available for immediate sale

- an active programme to locate a buyer is initiated

- the sale is highly probable, within 12 months of classification as held for sale (subject to limited exceptions)

- the asset is being actively marketed for sale at a sales price reasonable in relation to its fair value

- actions required to complete the plan indicate that it is unlikely that plan will be significantly changed or withdrawn.

In respect of the scientific publishing division, management has decided to sell the division and a buyer has been found. The advanced stage of negotiations would suggest the sale is highly probable.

As a result, important disclosures are currently missing from the financial statements which could mislead users with respect to the future revenue, profits, assets and cash flows of the company. Failing to provide information about the sale of the division could be seen as a significant omission from the financial statements, especially given the materiality of the assets of the division to the company's assets as a whole.

There is therefore a material misstatement as the scientific publishing division has not been classified as held for sale and its profit presented as a discontinued operation and the necessary disclosures have not been made in the financial statements.

Held for sale – valuation

IFRS 5 provides further guidance regarding the valuation of the assets held for sale. Prior to classification as held for sale, the disposal group should be reviewed for impairment in accordance with IAS 36 *Impairment of Assets*. This impairment review would require the asset to be held at the lower of carrying amount and recoverable amount where the recoverable amount is the higher of value in use or fair value less costs of disposal.

In this case the recoverable amount would be $42 million representing the fair value less costs of disposal. Management has valued the disposal group based on its value in use at $41 million which means that assets and profit are currently understated by $1 million. This represents 10.7% of profit before tax and is material to the profit for the year.

After classification as held for sale, non-current assets or disposal groups are measured at the lower of carrying amount and fair value less costs which would continue to be $42 million. Depreciation ceases to be charged when an asset is classified as held for sale.

Further actions

- The auditor should request that management adjusts the financial statements to recognise the discontinued operation and to separately disclose the assets held for sale in accordance with IFRS 5.

- In addition, the client should be requested to amend the carrying amount of the assets to the recoverable amount of $42 million in line with IFRS 5 requirements.

- If management refuses to adjust the financial statements, the auditor should communicate the misstatements to those charged with governance. They should repeat the request and inform them of the modifications which would be made to the auditor's report if the adjustments are not made.

- If management still refuses to amend the financial statements, the auditor should request a written representation from management confirming their intent to proceed without amending the financial statements and that they are aware of the potential repercussions.

Auditor's report implications

If the adjustments are not made then there is a material misstatement in the financial statements. The matter has resulted in an understatement of assets and profits by $1 million which in isolation is unlikely to be pervasive as limited components of the financial statements are affected. This would result in a qualified audit opinion in which the report would state that 'except for' the material misstatement in relation to the valuation of the assets held for sale the financial statements are fairly stated.

However, there are also several important disclosures omitted which would be required for users to understand both the current financial position of the company and its ability to generate future revenue and profits. As such, it would be a matter of judgement as to whether the lack of disclosures in conjunction with the material misstatement mentioned above have a pervasive impact on the financial statements. Depending on the auditor's judgement on this issue, this may give rise to an adverse opinion if the auditor considered the impact of these issues to result in the financial statements being wholly misleading.

Depending on the opinion provided, a basis for qualified or adverse opinion paragraph would be added underneath the opinion paragraph to describe and quantify the effects of the misstatements.

(b) (i) Auditor's responsibility for other information presented with the financial statements

ISA 720/ISA (UK) 720 (Revised) *The Auditor's Responsibilities Relating to Other Information* requires the auditor to read other information, defined as financial or non-financial information (other than financial statements and the auditor's report thereon), included in an entity's annual report.

The purpose of reading the other information is to consider whether there is a material inconsistency between the other information and the financial statements or between the other information and the auditor's knowledge obtained in the audit. If the auditor identifies that a material inconsistency appears to exist, or becomes aware that the other information appears to be materially misstated, the auditor should discuss the matter with management and, if necessary, perform other procedures to conclude whether:

(i)   A material misstatement of the other information exists

(ii) A material misstatement of the financial statements exists, or

(iii) The auditor's understanding of the entity and its environment needs to be updated.

The auditor does not audit the other information and does not express an opinion covering the other information.

Matters identified from the chair's statement

In this case, the chair's statement refers to strong growth in the year, in particular the scientific publishing division and suggests that the growth will continue. In the current year, the scientific publishing division represented 12% of revenue and 15% of profit before tax and is a material component of the company. As the scientific publishing division will be disposed of early in the next financial period, it will not continue to form part of the basis for revenue or growth, and the chair's statement could be considered misleading. Further, as a result of the disposal, on a like for like basis it is more likely that the financial statements for the year ended 31 March 20X6 will include a reduction in revenue rather than growth.

In addition, the remainder of the business has experienced a lower level of growth in revenue and profits in the period than the scientific publishing division. Revenue growth of continuing business is 2% compared to 44% in the scientific publishing division. Profit growth of the ongoing business is 5% compared to 100% for the scientific publishing division.

ISA 720/ISA (UK) 720 states that a misstatement of the other information exists when the other information is incorrectly stated or otherwise misleading, including because it omits or obscures information necessary for a proper understanding of a matter disclosed in the other information. In the case of the chair's statement regarding growth of the company, it could be argued that the way the information is presented obscures the understanding of the growth and profitability of the ongoing business. As mentioned above, this would be considered very misleading.

The chair has also made inappropriate reference to the view of the auditor, implying that the auditor's report validates this assertion. The statement also appears to inappropriately pre-empt that the auditor's report will provide an unmodified opinion which based on the assessment above may not be the case given the material misstatement and lack of disclosures. This is inappropriate and all reference to the auditor's report should be removed.

In addition, there is also an issue arising with respect to the use of recycled paper. The chair's statement in this case is inconsistent with the knowledge obtained during the audit. Whether the auditor considers this to be material would be a matter of judgement, depending on how many publications there are in total and the proportion using non-recycled paper and whether the issue may be material by nature rather than by size. This could be the case if it is perceived that there is a deliberate misrepresentation of facts which may be misleading to the users of the financial statements.

(ii)   **Implications for completion of the audit**

The auditor should discuss with management and the chair the information in the statement which appears inaccurate or inconsistent. In particular, this should focus on a discussion of the misleading growth analysis given that the scientific publishing division will not be contributing to company performance once it is sold.

In the case of the incorrect disclosure relating to the use of recycled paper, the auditor should seek further information to support the file note regarding publications not using recycled paper. The names of those publications should be obtained, and a discussion held with the production manager to confirm the auditor's understanding.

Following these investigations and discussions, the auditor should then request that any information which is inaccurate, inappropriate or inconsistent is removed or amended in the chair's report.

If management refuse to make the changes then the auditor's request should be escalated to those charged with governance. The auditor should also consider the effect of this situation on their assessment of management integrity and whether it affects the reliance which can be placed on written representations from management. If the issue remains unresolved then the auditor should take appropriate action, including:

- Considering the implications for the auditor's report and communicating with those charged with governance about how the auditor plans to address the issues in the auditor's report; or

- Withdrawing from the engagement, where withdrawal is possible under applicable law or regulation.

Implications for the auditor's report

If the other information remains uncorrected the auditor would use the Other Information section of the auditor's report to draw the users' attention to the misstatements in the chair's statement. This paragraph would include:

- A statement that management is responsible for the other information

- A statement that the auditor's opinion does not cover the other information and, accordingly, that the auditor does not express (or will not express) an audit opinion or any form of assurance conclusion thereon

- A description of the auditor's responsibilities relating to reading, considering and reporting on other information as required by this ISA, and

- A statement that describes the uncorrected material misstatement of the other information.

As the inconsistency is in the chair's statement rather than the audited financial statement the audit opinion is not modified as a result.

Examiner's comments

This question was set at the later stages of audit completion, close to the issuance of the auditor's report, when audit evidence has been obtained and is being reviewed and remaining issues are to be resolved with management.

Part (i) of the question is focused on resolving the outstanding potential issue in order to be able to determine the form of the auditor's report which should be issued.

The issue arose from how the directors have treated the scientific publishing division which is in the process of being sold to a competitor. In the audit file it is noted that the company is at the advanced stage in this sale process and is expected to be complete in less than one month. There are two problems arising from the way the directors have treated this in the financial statements. One is that the impairment review on the division has used value in use as recoverable amount and not the higher agreed selling price so there is a material misstatement in relation to the valuation of the assets of the division. The second issue is the lack of disclosure regarding the sale which should have been disclosed as a discontinued operation with the assets classified as held for sale. Information given in the scenario states that the company does not use a revaluation policy. This is intended to allow candidates to note that any impairment loss would be charged to the statement of profit or loss so that they do not lose time discussing the allocation of any impairment write off to revaluation reserves. The company was also a single company rather than a Group therefore candidates did not need to spend time speculating over the value of goodwill.

When approaching a question like this, candidates should assess the appropriateness of the accounting treatments used by the company, justifying any amendments needed to the financial statements as a result. They should also consider the materiality of each of those amendments required, ready to discuss these with management to resolve.

Candidates generally identified that the scientific publishing division met the criteria of an asset held for sale and were able to discuss the impacts of this on the statement of financial position. It was less common for candidates to discuss the fact that this division would therefore be a discontinued operation and the impact on the statement of profit or loss. Candidates also often identified the valuation error and were able to obtain marks in this area.

Having determined the correct accounting treatment and the materiality of the misstatements, candidates needed to recommend further actions necessary before the auditor's report could be signed. These actions would involve requesting changes with management, escalating issues to those charged with governance and where relevant obtaining a written representation from management confirming their intention to proceed without amending the financial statements.

Candidates who remained focused on actions were able to score highly here. Again, many candidates resorted to listing out audit procedures, many of which would already have been performed by this stage of the audit. Many candidates also treated the requirement like a matters and evidence style requirement, listing out evidence which was expected to be on file rather than thinking about the actions which would be needed to finalise the audit. This distinction is important and candidates listing out audit procedures at this stage of completion demonstrate a lack of understanding of the stages of an audit.

Part (ii) of the requirement asks candidates to consider the opinion if the adjustments are not made to the financial statements. Candidates almost universally assess each misstatement in turn rather than in combination which would be the case if none of the adjustments are made. It is extremely hard for a candidate to assess the pervasiveness of a number of misstatements if they do not consider all the misstatements together. Candidates need to note whether the requirement asks for the implication of each issue separately or in aggregate. If separate consideration is needed this will be clearly stated in the requirement.

Candidates seem to struggle with the topic of auditor's reports in general and often use outdated or ambiguous terminology for reporting. Common reasons why candidates do not perform well on this type of question stem from a lack of knowledge of the types of audit opinion available. Many also demonstrate a lack of appreciation as to how material misstatements arise, particularly that a lack of disclosure can also give rise to a material misstatement.

One problem commonly seen when describing the audit opinion is candidates referring to the impact of the misstatements on the audit opinion as a modification but then not specifying which modification is appropriate in the circumstances. Candidates are expected to be able to describe the four types of audit opinion:

- Qualified on the basis of a material misstatement

- Qualified on the basis of an inability to obtain sufficient audit evidence

- Adverse opinion due to misstatements which are material and pervasive

- Disclaimer of opinion due to an inability to obtain sufficient audit evidence, the possible effects of which are material and pervasive

The use of the terms modified or except for are not sufficiently detailed to attract the mark for the type of opinion.

Candidates are also expected to evaluate the opinion which should be issued and should apply knowledge to the scenario in the question. If a candidate simply states that a pervasive misstatement would result in an adverse opinion and a material, but not pervasive misstatement would result in a qualified opinion then they have not applied the requirements of the ISA to the scenario. While true, as the requirement asks for an evaluation of the type of audit opinion, candidates must come to a decision on which is appropriate in the circumstances. Credit is awarded for the discussion of pervasiveness in the context of the specific scenario.

Candidates often seem to struggle with the concept of pervasiveness which is an inherently judgemental area. ISA 705 *Modifications to the Opinion in the Independent Auditor's Report*, describes pervasive as those misstatements which in the auditor's judgement are:

- Not confined to specific elements, accounts or items in the financial statements

- If so confined, represent or could represent a substantial proportion of the financial statements, or

- In relation to disclosures are fundamental to the users' understanding of the financial statements

There appear to be a significant number of candidates who consider the definition of pervasive to be something which would change a profit into a loss. This is not the case in all circumstances – quite often a small change that converts a profit to a loss is due to a single specific element of the financial statements and may not be considered pervasive. When discussing the pervasiveness of an issue candidates should ensure that they clearly convey their rationale as to why an item is pervasive in their answer.

It should also be noted that a lack of disclosure may not only be material but could also be pervasive.

Candidates should also note that an emphasis of matter paragraph is not an alternative to a qualification of the audit opinion. An emphasis of matter can only be used to draw attention to something which is already disclosed in the financial statements.

Requirement (b)(i) was generally well answered with respect to the auditor's responsibility for the other information presented with the financial statements. A minority of candidates suggested that the audit included auditing the other information to ensure it was true and fair. This is not the case, the auditor only provides an opinion on the financial statements but in line with ISA 720 *The Auditor's Responsibilities Relating to Other Information*, is required to read the other information. Most candidates identified that the auditor should look for inconsistencies between the financial statements and the other information, however, fewer appeared to know that the auditor would be looking for areas which are misleading or factually incorrect even if that information was not in the financial statements.

The applied part of this requirement was less well answered. The client is in the process of divesting a large part of its business, yet the chairman's report illustrated the prospect of sustained growth for the company which was being driven by the division to be sold. This meant that the calculated trends quoted by the chairman were correctly calculated in line with the financial statements but were misleading and the growth trends should have been separately mentioned for the retained part of the business.

Candidates were also faced with a misstatement of fact that was not related to any disclosures in the financial statements. Generally, the factual inaccuracy was identified but candidates suggested ensuring the disclosure in the financial statements was correct in this regard. That is not possible for information not in the financial statements.

Requirement (b)(ii) was well answered by most candidates. It was concerning however how few candidates were able to name the section of the auditor's report which should be used to disclose this type of inconsistency. Again, suggesting a lack of knowledge in relation to the reporting ISAs. Candidates should have been referring to the "other information" section yet many candidates suggested the use of the "other matter" or "emphasis of matter" paragraphs which are used in completely different circumstances. Candidates must ensure they know the difference between these sections of the auditor's report.

		ACCA Marking guide	
			Marks

(a) **Matters, further actions and auditor's report implications**

Up to 1 mark for each point unless otherwise stated

Matters

- Assessment of finance director's approach
- Assessment of materiality
- Disclosure rules re held for sale/discontinued operations
- Application to the scenario to conclude asset is held for sale (HFS)
- Material misstatement of classification and disclosure
- Accounting rule on valuation of held for sale assets
- Rule that depreciation should cease when asset meets criteria of HFS
- Application to the scenario to derive correct value
- Materiality of the error in valuation

Further actions

- Request adjustment from management to recognise the discontinued operation and to separately disclose the assets held for sale
- Request management to amend the carrying amount of the assets to the recoverable amount of $42 million
- If management refuse, escalate to Those Charged With Governance (TCWG)
- If still refuse obtain written representation confirming intent to proceed

Reporting implications

- Qualified opinion on basis of material misstatement
- Justification of whether pervasive and possible adverse impact due to lack of significant disclosures
- Basis of opinion paragraph position and content

| | | **Maximum** | **10** |

(b) **(i)** **Auditor's responsibilities in relation to other information presented with the financial statements**

Assessment of ISA requirements including:

- Auditor must read other information for inconsistency with financial statements or understanding of the business
- Consider the source of the inconsistency
  - (i) A material misstatement of the other information exists
  - (ii) A material misstatement of the financial statements exists; or
  - (iii) The auditor's understanding of the entity and its environment needs to be updated.
- Auditor does not give opinion on the other information

Matters arising from chair's statement

- Growth discussion ignores discontinued operation
- Calculations to support the ongoing growth
- Statement obscures actual growth hence misleading/material misstatement in other information
- Inappropriate reference to the content of the auditor's report
- Misstatement of fact regarding recycled paper usage
- Judgement as to whether it is material misstatement of other information

| | | **Maximum** | **5** |

(ii) **Implications for the completion of the audit**
- Seek further information to confirm understanding
- Request management to correct
- Escalate to TCWG
- Impact on assessment of management integrity and written representations
- Notify TCWG effect on auditor's report
- Consider resigning

Implications for the auditor's report arising from the draft Chair's statement
- Addressed in other information paragraph to draw attention to issue covering
  - Statement other information not audited
  - Responsibilities of auditor regarding other information
  - Description of uncorrected misstatements
- Auditor's opinion is not modified

Maximum	5

Professional marks

Analysis and evaluation
- Appropriate use of the information to support discussion, draw appropriate conclusions and design appropriate responses
- Identification of omissions from the analysis or further analysis which could be carried out
- Balanced assessment of the information to determine the appropriate audit opinion in the circumstances

Professional scepticism and judgement
- Effective challenge of information, evidence and assumptions supplied and, techniques carried out to support key facts and/or decisions
- Appropriate application of professional judgement to draw conclusions and make informed decisions about the actions which are appropriate in the context and stage of the engagement

Maximum	5
Total	25

Section 7

REFERENCES

The Board (2022) *IFRS 15 Revenue From Contracts with Customers*. London: IFRS Foundation.

The Board (2022) *IFRS 16 Leases*. London: IFRS Foundation.